Teen Health

Teachers & Students

glencoe.com

New Student Edition Includes

- Content Based on the Latest Health Research
- Guide to Reading and Graphic Organizers
- Spanish Edition
- Student Edition Online
- TIME® health news

Reading Skills and Assessment

- Reading Skills Reinforcement
- Writing Support
- Activating Prior Knowledge Strategies
- Academic Vocabulary
- Comprehensive Reading Tutor
- Standardized Test Practice

Health Online Resources

- Complete Student Edition Online
- Audio Summaries (English and Spanish)
- Study Guides with Interactive Vocabulary
- Education Resources, Conferences, and Grants
- Professional Development Articles
- Correlations to National and State Standards

New Technology Resources

- Teen Health PowerPoint®
- TeacherWorks™ Plus
- StudentWorks™ Plus
- ExamView® Assessment Suite
- Vocabulary PuzzleMaker (English and Spanish)

Improving Active Reading and Study Skills

Dinah Zike's FOLDABLES®

Foldables® are easy-to-make, three-dimensional, interactive graphic organizers that students create out of plain sheets of paper. The Teacher Classroom Resources includes *Dinah Zike's Reading and Study Skills Foldables® for Teen Health.* This booklet provides you with step-by-step instructions for using Foldables® in your classroom. Each Foldable® is designed to be used as a study guide for the main ideas and key points presented in a chapter. Foldables® can also be used for a more in-depth investigation of a concept, idea, opinion, event, or a person or place studied in a chapter. These unique hands-on tools for studying and reviewing were created exclusively for Glencoe by education specialist Dinah Zike.

Why Use Foldables® in Health?

Because they

- organize, display, and arrange information, making it easier for students to grasp health skills concepts, theories, facts, opinions, questions, research, and ideas.

- are student-made study guides that are compiled as students listen for main ideas, read main ideas, or conduct research.

- integrate language arts into the study of health.

- replace teacher-generated writing or photocopied sheets with student-generated print.

- incorporate the use of such skills as problem solving, comparing and contrasting, recognizing cause-and-effect, and finding similarities and differences.

- continue to immerse students in previously learned vocabulary, concepts, information, generalizations, ideas, and theories, providing them with a strong foundation that they can build upon with new concepts and knowledge.

- can be used by students or teachers to easily communicate data through graphs, tables, charts, models, and diagrams, including Venn diagrams.

- can be used as alternative assessment tools by teachers to evaluate student progress or by students to evaluate their own progress.

- provide a sense of student ownership or investiture in the health curriculum.

▼ *Student Edition, p. 477*

FOLDABLES® Study Organizer

As You Read   Make this Foldable® to help you record main ideas about the causes of communicable diseases. Begin with a plain sheet of 11" X 17" paper.

1 Hold the paper like a placemat. Fold the short sides inward so they meet in the middle.

2 Fold the top to the bottom.

3 Open and cut along the inside fold lines. This makes four tabs.

4 Label the tabs as shown.

Pathogens and Disease	Types of Pathogens
How Pathogens Are Spread	Preventing the Spread of Disease

Under the appropriate tab, summarize what you learn about pathogens and how to prevent communicable diseases from spreading.

Teen Health

COURSE 3

Teacher Wraparound Edition

Mary H. Bronson, Ph.D.

Michael J. Cleary, Ed.D., C.H.E.S.

Betty M. Hubbard, Ed.D., C.H.E.S.

Contributing Authors

Dinah Zike, M.Ed.

TIME®

Teacher Manual

Glencoe

Meet the Authors

Mary H. Bronson, Ph.D., recently retired after teaching for 30 years in Texas public schools. Dr. Bronson taught health education in grades K–12, as well as health education methods classes at the undergraduate and graduate levels. As Health Education Specialist for the Dallas School District, Dr. Bronson developed and implemented a district-wide health education program. She has been honored as Texas Health Educator of the Year by the Texas Association for Health, Physical Education, Recreation, and Dance and selected Teacher of the Year twice, by her colleagues. Dr. Bronson has assisted school districts throughout the country in developing local health education programs. She is also the coauthor of the *Glencoe Health* textbook.

Betty M. Hubbard, Ed.D., C.H.E.S., has taught science and health education in grades 6–12, as well as undergraduate- and graduate-level courses. She is a professor at the University of Central Arkansas, where, in addition to teaching, she conducts in-service training for health education teachers in school districts throughout Arkansas. In 1991, Dr. Hubbard received the university's teaching excellence award. Her publications, grants, and presentations focus on research-based, comprehensive health instruction. Dr. Hubbard is a fellow of the American Association for Health Education and serves as the contributing editor for the Teaching Ideas feature of the *American Journal of Health Education.*

Michael J. Cleary, Ed.D., C.H.E.S., is a professor at Slippery Rock University, where he teaches methods courses and supervises field experiences. Dr. Cleary taught health education at Evanston Township High School in Illinois and later served as the Lead Teacher Specialist at the McMillen Center for Health Education in Fort Wayne, Indiana. Dr. Cleary has published widely on curriculum development and assessment in K–12 and college health education. Dr. Cleary is also coauthor of the *Glencoe Health* textbook.

Contributing Authors

Dinah Zike, M.Ed., is an international curriculum consultant and inventor who has designed and developed educational products and three-dimensional, interactive graphic organizers for over thirty years. As president and founder of Dinah-Might Adventures, L.P., Dinah is author of over 100 award-winning educational publications. Dinah has a B.S. and an M.S. in educational curriculum and instruction from Texas A&M University. Dinah Zike's *Foldables®* are an exclusive feature of McGraw-Hill textbooks.

TIME® is the nation's leading news and information magazine. With over 80 years of experience, TIME® provides an authoritative voice in the analysis of the issues of the day, from politics to pop culture, from history-making decisions to healthy living. TIME® Learning Ventures brings the strength of TIME® and TIME® For Kids' editorial and photographic excellence to educational resources for school and home.

 Glencoe

The *McGraw-Hill* Companies

Printed in the United States of America.

Send all inquiries to:
Glencoe/McGraw-Hill
21600 Oxnard Street, Suite 500
Woodland Hills, California 91367

ISBN: 978-0-07-877449-2 (Course 3 Student Edition)
MHID: 0-07-877449-7 (Course 3 Student Edition)
ISBN: 978-0-07-877450-8 (Course 3 Teacher Wraparound Edition)
MHID: 0-07-877450-0 (Course 3 Teacher Wraparound Edition)

3 4 5 6 7 8 9 043/058 12 11 10 09

Health Consultants

Alia Antoon, M.D.
Chief of Pediatrics
Shriners Hospital for Children
Assistant Clinical Professor, Pediatrics
Harvard Medical School
Boston, Massachusetts

Elissa M. Barr, Ph.D., C.H.E.S.
Assistant Professor of Public Health
University of North Florida
Jacksonville, Florida

Beverly Bradley, Ph.D., R.N., C.H.E.S.
School Health Consultant
Retired Assistant Clinical Professor
University of California, San Diego
San Diego, California

Donna Breitestein, Ed.D.
Professor and Coordinator, Health Education
Appalachian State University
Boone, North Carolina

Roberta L. Duyff, M.S., R.D., C.F.C.S.
Food and Nutrition Consultant/President
Duyff Associates
St. Louis, Missouri

Kristin Danielson Fink, M.A.
National Director
Community of Caring
Salt Lake City, Utah

Kathryn J. Gust, M.A.
Instructional Technology Specialist
Freedom High School
Morganton, North Carolina

Christine A. Hayashi, M.A. Ed., J.D.
Attorney at Law, Special Education Law
Adjunct Faculty, Educational Leadership
and Policy Studies Development
California State University, Northridge
Northridge, California

Michael E. Moore, M.A., LCSW
School Psychologist
Speech Education Coordinator
Centerville/Abington Community Schools
Centerville, Indiana

Tinker D. Murray, Ph.D., FACSM
Professor of Health, Physical Education, and Recreation
Texas State University
San Marcos, Texas

Don Rainey, M.S., C.S.C.S.
Director, Physical Fitness and Wellness
Texas State University
San Marcos, Texas

John Rohwer, Ed.D.
Professor of Health Education
Bethel University
St. Paul, Minnesota

Michael Rulon, M.S.
Instructional Coach
Health Instructor
Albuquerque Public Schools
Albuquerque, New Mexico

Robin Scarcella, Ph.D.
Director, Academic English/ESL
University of California, Irvine
Irvine, California

Diane Tanaka, M.D.
Assistant Professor of Clinical Pediatrics
Keck School of Medicine
Attending Physician
Division of Adolescent Medicine
University of Southern California
Los Angeles, California

Robert Wandberg, Ph.D.
Staff Development
St. Paul Public Schools
St. Paul, Minnesota

Peter T. Whelley, M.S., N.C.S.P.
School Psychologist
Moultonborough School District
Adjunct Faculty
Plymouth State University
Plymouth, New Hampshire

David C. Wiley, Ph.D.
Professor of Health Education
Texas State University
San Marcos, Texas

Reviewers

Neile Bennett
Health Educator
Pierce County Middle School
Blackshear, Georgia

Kathy Bowman-Harrow
Supervisor, Health Education
Orange County Public Schools
Orlando, Florida

David Bryant
Health/Physical Education
Athletic Director
Greene County Middle School
Snow Hill, North Carolina

Mary Capaforte
Healthful Living Teacher
Department Chair
Lufkin Road Middle School
Apex, North Carolina

Jason S. Chandler
Physical Education/Health Teacher
Head Certified Athletic Trainer
Prince George County Public Schools
Prince George County, Virginia

Pamela Rizzo Connolly, M.E.
Curriculum Coordinator for Health
and Physical Education
North Catholic High School
Diocese of Pittsburgh
Pittsburgh, Pennsylvania

Audrey Maria Diamond
Science Teacher
Ellis G. Arnall Middle School
Newnan, Georgia

Allison Duckworth, M.A.
Physical Education Teacher
Head Athletic Trainer
Freedom High School
Morganton, North Carolina

Valerie Hernandez, BSN RN, M.S.
Registered Nurse/Health Educator
Escambia County School District
Pensacola, Florida

Andy Keyes
Health/Physical Education Teacher
Hastings Middle School
Upper Arlington, Ohio

April Lane
Health Teacher
Portland Middle School
Portland, Tennessee

Norma H. Lee, M.A.
Wellness Instructor
Jefferson County High School
Dandridge, Tennessee

Cindy Meyer, M.A.T.
Health Educator
South Oldham Middle School
Crestwood, Kentucky

Bobby Jean Moore, M.A.T.
Health Education Specialist
Creekland Middle School
Lawrenceville, Georgia

Dale Mueller
Health/Physical Education Teacher
New Holstein School District
New Holstein, Wisconsin

Tammy Smith
Administrator
Tulsa Public Schools
Tulsa, Oklahoma

Joan Gilger Stear, M.Ed
Health Education Instructor
West Clermont Institute of Performing Arts
Glen Este High School
Cincinnati, Ohio

Stacia K. Tatum
Physical Education Teacher
Westridge Middle School
Orlando, Florida

Jeanne Title
County Coordinator
Office of Safety and Wellness
Napa County Office of Education and Physical
Education
Napa, California

Lisa Ward
Health/Physical Education Teacher
Kernodle Middle School
Greensboro, North Carolina

Robert T. Wieselberg
Health Educator
Westridge Middle School
Orlando, Florida

Teen Health

Table of Contents

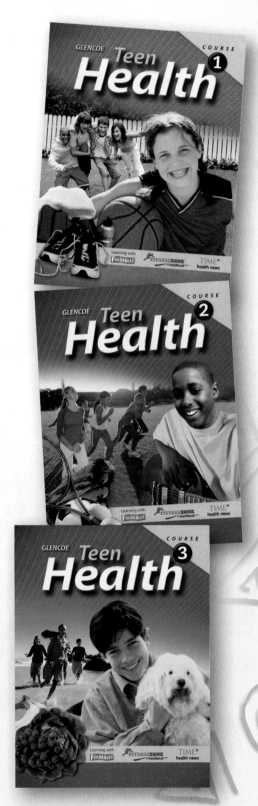

Your Solution for K–12 Health & Fitness

McGraw-Hill, the leader in health education, offers a comprehensive and sequential K–12 health education program designed to assist schools in developing and implementing a coordinated school health education curriculum.

Start with a Healthy Foundation

Macmillan/McGraw-Hill presents *Health & Wellness* for grades K–5. This easy-to-manage program provides integrated curriculum strategies tailored for the elementary classroom. The easy-to-do, student-guided activities are structured for success, which helps lay the foundation for building lifelong health skills.

Promote Healthy Behaviors with *Teen Health*

Teen Health, offered by Glencoe/McGraw-Hill, is a three book series designed specifically for students in grades 6–8. The inviting style, easy-to-read format, and motivating activities engage middle school learners. *Teen Health* combines scientifically accurate, age-appropriate health content with extensive practice and application of skills. Colorful and informative photos, visuals, charts, and diagrams engage student interest and facilitate learning.

> *"Quality physical education and health education programs in all K–12 schools provide the foundation for healthy, active lifestyles that support all learning and help ensure success in future pursuits."*
>
> —American Association for Health, Physical Education, Recreation and Dance, 2005

Foster Lifelong Health and Wellness Behaviors

A comprehensive approach to health and fitness is essential in motivating teens to develop healthy behaviors. For high school students, *Glencoe Health*, *Health & Wellness*, and *Foundations of Personal Fitness* provide flexible formats to improve health and wellness. Real-life application of health skills helps students apply what they learn in health class toward practicing healthy behaviors for a lifetime. Hands-on features are integrated with technology, embedded assessments, and up-to-date health content.

  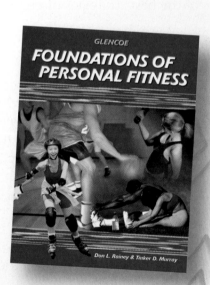

Glencoe's Online Learning Centers: Offering Technology Solutions

At **glencoe.com,** you and your students will find a variety of interactive features and study tools to enhance the print programs.

Physical Activity Benefits All Students

Our new edition of **Teen Health** places a greater emphasis on developing and maintaining personal fitness. By increasing their participation in physical activity, teens not only adopt a more active lifestyle, they reduce their risk of developing certain diseases and illnesses. Evidence shows that low levels of physical activity in adults are associated with increased risk of chronic diseases and premature death. Adolescent obesity and diabetes are increasing at alarming rates in the United States. National programs have responded by emphasizing the importance of physical activity as an important step toward reversing these trends.

Teen Health supports the philosophy that an active lifestyle is one of the best strategies of preventive health care.

The **Fitness Zone Handbook,** located at the front of the Student Edition, provides students with functional knowledge and interactive experiential activities to develop and maintain personal fitness throughout their lifetime. This easy-to-use handbook includes

- the five elements of physical fitness.
- a personal fitness plan.
- proper stretches and toning exercises.
- fun group activities.

In the Teacher Wraparound Edition, we've inserted point-of-use suggestions for integrating the Fitness Zone Handbook into your health curriculum.

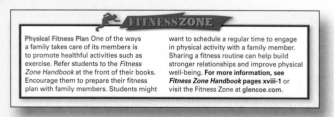

FITNESS ZONE

Physical Fitness Plan One of the ways a family takes care of its members is to promote healthful activities such as exercise. Refer students to the *Fitness Zone Handbook* at the front of their books. Encourage them to prepare their fitness plan with family members. Students might want to schedule a regular time to engage in physical activity with a family member. Sharing a fitness routine can help build stronger relationships and improve physical well-being. **For more information, see** *Fitness Zone Handbook* **pages xviii-1** or visit the Fitness Zone at **glencoe.com.**

 Online

Go Online to visit the virtual Fitness Zone at **glencoe.com.** (See page TM19 for more about Glencoe's online fitness resources.)

Dynamic Instruction Motivates Students

Dynamic Instructional Strategies present a clear, comprehensive coverage of health.

- Engaging lesson introductions include Guide to Reading, Key Terms, Reading Strategy, and Quick Write.
- Hands-on Health, What Teens Think, and TIME® health news provide real-life applications to the study of health concepts and behaviors.
- Chapter Summary and Reading Review offer concise summaries of chapter topics and can be used to preview, review, or summarize chapter content.

A Research-Based Reading Strand encourages active reading and learning for students of all reading levels.

- Foldables® help students organize and process key concepts as they read.
- Analyzing Graphics, Photos, Charts, and Tables questions asks students to interpret and evaluate a visual.
- Reading Checks help students check their reading comprehension.
- Academic Vocabulary words are highlighted and defined.
- The Reading Skills Handbook provides effective strategies to improve reading comprehension skills.

Differentiated Instruction makes *Teen Health* accessible to all students.

- Differentiated Instruction activities and strategies are designed for students of differing abilities and learning challenges.
- How Do I Use My Textbook? teaches students how to approach the text to retain course information and get the most value out of the Student Edition.

Standardized Test Practice gives students the opportunity to practice for state and national exams.

- Chapter assessments and workbooks provide a variety of standardized test practice, including multiple choice, open-ended short response, and open-ended extended response.
- Test-Taking Tips help students learn how to successfully approach test questions.

A Variety of Interdisciplinary Activities and Features are essential for student success and get students excited about health.

- Connect To...Math, Science, and Language Arts integrates core curriculum.
- Developing Good Character emphasizes character traits in teens.
- Media Watch guides students to develop critical media literacy skills.

Teacher Resources provide convenient strategies for new and experienced teachers.

- The Planning Guide in each chapter provides background information to help you prepare for each chapter's key topics.
- *Fast Files* chapter resources contain important reproducible masters.
- Chapter Resources help you organize your daily lessons.

Technology provides time-saving software products to help you creatively engage students and reduce preparation time.

- Health eSpotlight DVD and online videos
- Teen Health PowerPoint® Presentation
- *TeacherWorks™ Plus*
- *StudentWorks™ Plus*
- Go Online at **glencoe.com** for additional study tools and activities.

Energize Your Students...

Teen Health introduces students to vital health concepts and provides opportunities to practice health skills that can lead to health-enhancing behaviors.

Chapter Opener

Engage students at the beginning of every chapter with motivational start-up activities.

Health **eSpotlight** engages students with video presentations available online and on DVD.

HEALTH INVENTORY evaluates teens' healthy behaviors—with additional interactive inventories at **glencoe.com**.

HEALTH QUIZ piques curiosity and quickly assesses prior knowledge.

Working with the Photo visually introduces the chapter and guides students with an engaging question to help them interpret the meaning.

Guide to Reading introduces each lesson's key concepts and builds vocabulary and reading skills.

Building Vocabulary activities enhance vocabulary development.

Focusing on the Main Ideas previews the learning outcome for students.

Reading Strategy and **Foldables®** provide lesson-specific study tools so students can effectively organize content and increase comprehension.

to Make Real-Life Connections

What Teens Think

This feature poses relevant health questions for teens today. Real teens surveyed throughout the United States provide the answers. Use this high-interest feature to jumpstart your classroom discussions.

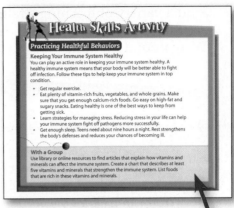

Health Skills Activity

These activities reinforce lesson content and teach valuable health skills at the same time. From goal setting and communication skills to accessing information and analyzing influences, all the essential health skills are addressed.

Building Health Skills

Standards-based health skills features connect skills to real life.

- **Model** presents positive modeling of a skill.

- **Practice** gives students a chance to practice the skill in a realistic situation.

- **Apply** lets students personalize and perform the skill on their own and evaluate performance.

Additional Features

Hands-on Health features in selected chapters present students with another chance to create a product or demonstration to show what they have learned.

Careers for the 21st Century gets students thinking about their future with health career options.

Power Your Classroom...

Find a variety of teaching strategies coded to the student text with Glencoe's easy-to-follow lesson cycle — *Focus, Teach, Assess, Close* — in this Teacher Wraparound Edition.

Activating Prior Knowledge

Foldables® Study Organizers

Quick Write

Highlighted discussion answers

Media Watch gives background information for teachers to make meaningful connections between health and media.

Caption answers

Lesson Resources

Fitness Zone provides connections between lesson content and the Fitness Zone Handbook to support the integration of fitness activities.

Teaching Strategies for all features

Reading Check answers to recall questions, and answers at the end of every main section.

Assessment Resources provided for each lesson, including reproducible masters, technology, and online components.

Teacher to Teacher presents teaching strategies and classroom activities submitted by health educators across the country. These tested and proven ideas can help recharge your lesson plans.

Lesson Reviews Answers

with Flexible, Focused, and Fully Accessible Teaching Strategies

Reading Strategies and Writing Support to aid student comprehension of concepts and skills.

Strategies are coded for differentiated learning throughout the text.

Point-of-use coding matches strategies with student edition content.

U Universal Access

Support for Teaching Reading

Reading Support

Reading Preview

Activating Background Vocabulary Ask students what they think the term *social health* means. Record their responses on the board. Guide students into a discussion about relationships with others and the role of the family in society. Ask students to compare social health with physical health. Is there a relationship between the two?

FOLDABLES *Study Organizer* Dinah Zike's *Reading and Study Skills for Teen Health* provides interactive graphic organizers that help students comprehend and retain health concepts as they read. Use the Foldable® on page 129 or find more Foldables® activities for the chapter on **Promoting Social Health** in the separate booklet, available in the TCR.

Lesson 1 You and Your Relationships

Organizing Information Direct students to scan the lesson and list the main idea of each section on an index card. Discuss that each heading is a main idea and the text beneath the heading holds the details that support the main idea. As students read about social health and building healthy relationships, have them write the supporting details on the back of each main idea index card.

Lesson 2 Getting Along with Your Family

Responding Have students stop at any point while reading and discuss with a partner what they like, do not like, or find interesting or surprising about what they have read so far. Direct students to the sections on responsibilities within the family and coping with family changes. Have students write an independent journal entry, describing their thoughts or feelings about these issues.

Lesson 3 Marriage and Parenthood

Directed Reading/Thinking Activity (DR/TA) Direct students to divide a paper into 4 columns titled: *What I know, What I think I know, What I think I'll learn, and What I know I learned.* Have students skim the lesson's boldface headings and discuss the topics of teen marriage and parenthood. Direct students to fill out the first three sections of the chart based on that discussion. Have students complete the final column of the chart as they read the lesson.

Post Reading

Twin Text Reports In addition to the text, provide students with the opportunity to find fictional reading material about teen relationships, family life, coping with family problems, or teen marriage and pregnancy. After reading, have students demonstrate recognition of the logical, ethical, and emotional appeals in both the fictional and informational materials in a written report, edited for correct spelling, punctuation, and grammar.

Key for Using the Teacher Wraparound Edition

Use this key to help you identify the different types of prompts found in the Teacher Wraparound Edition.

R Reading Strategies activities help you teach reading skills and vocabulary.

C Critical Thinking strategies help students apply and extend what they have learned.

U Universal Access activities provide differentiated instruction for students learning to speak English, along with suggestions for teaching various types of learners.

HS Health Skills Practice activities reinforce Health Skills concepts and help students apply these skills in their everyday lives.

W Writing Support activities provide writing opportunities to help students comprehend the text.

AL Active Learning strategies provide a variety of activities for presenting lesson content, including Quick Demos and engaging classroom projects that get students actively involved.

Key to Ability Levels

Teaching Strategies and activities have been coded for ability level and appropriateness.

AL Activities for students working above grade level
OL Activities for students working on grade level
BL Activities for students working below grade level
EL Activities for English Learners

Symbols

Transparencies
CD-ROM
glencoe.com
Print Resources

128D

Refusal Skills

Negative peer pressure can be very strong. When anyone challenges your beliefs or values, you need to be strong, too. While negative pressure is often easy to recognize, it can be difficult to resist. One way to resist negative pressure is by using refusal skills. **Refusal skills** are *communication strategies that help you say no effectively.* They help you avoid doing things you do not want to do without feeling uncomfortable about your decision. By using refusal skills, you stand up for your values, which builds self-respect. You also show others that you have strength and character. These qualities will win their respect as well.

CHAPTER 5
Lesson 3

U Universal Access

English Learners Discuss with students the terms *negative* and *positive.* Explain that *positive,* in the context of positive peer pressure, means healthful. Have students identify how the word *positive* is used in other subject areas. For example, in math, a *positive* number is a number greater than zero. **EL**

R Reading Strategy

Analyzing a Graphic Have students examine **Figure 5.1** that lists questions that students can use to determine if peer pressure is negative. Have students classify these questions into three categories: those that concern physical health, those that concern social health, and those that concern mental/emotional health. Have volunteers share their classifications. **OL**

Reading Check

Answer Negative peer pressure can take the form of threats, dares, or bribes.

Academic Vocabulary

Manipulate Ask students: How do dares, threats, bribes, teasing, and name-calling manipulate your emotions? How do bribes, teasing, and name-calling manipulate your emotions? Why is it important to recognize that your emotions are being manipulated? You will find academic vocabulary activities in the Student Activities Workbook.

Negative Peer Pressure

Negative peer pressure is pressure to do something that could hurt you or others, or get you into trouble. It often goes against your own wants, needs, or values. For example, the pressure that Stephanie felt to laugh at another girl was negative peer pressure. If Stephanie had gone along with her friends, she would have felt bad about what she had done.

Some teens endanger their health when they let themselves be influenced by negative peer pressure. For example, they might use alcohol, tobacco, or other drugs. Giving into these pressures can negatively affect your performance at school, your health, and your future. That is a good reason to choose friends who share your values, and who won't try to pressure you into doing something you do not want to do.

Negative peer pressure takes many forms. Teens who put negative pressure on you may try to **manipulate** your emotions or find your weaknesses. The pressure may come as a dare or threat. It may come in the form of a bribe, teasing, or name-calling. Recognizing negative peer pressure in all its forms is important. This is a first step toward standing your ground and protecting your beliefs. **Figure 5.1** lists questions you can ask yourself to help you decide if peer pressure is negative.

Reading Check List Name some forms that negative peer pressure can take.

Academic Vocabulary

manipulate (muh NIP yuh leyt) (verb) to change or control for one's own purpose. *It is wrong to use negative peer pressure to manipulate a friend.*

FIGURE 5.1

RECOGNIZING NEGATIVE PEER PRESSURE

When you feel you are being pressured, analyze the possible outcomes and health consequences. What are two questions to ask yourself when you are feeling peer pressure?

Possible Outcomes	Health Consequences
• Is this activity dangerous?	• How will this activity affect my physical health?
• Does it break the law?	• Am I being asked to do something that could bring me physical harm?
• Can it lead to punishment, such as suspension from school, or arrest?	• Is the activity something that can lead to an addiction?
• Will it lead to disapproval or disappointment from parents or guardians?	• What effect will it have on my emotional health?
• Will I feel guilty if I do this activity?	• Will I disappoint myself?
	• Is it something I simply do not feel ready for?
	• How will this decision affect the health of others?
	• Could someone else be hurt?

114 Chapter 5 Relationships: The Teen Years

Refusal Skills

Negative peer pressure can be very strong. When anyone challenges your beliefs or values, you need to be strong, too. While negative pressure is often easy to recognize, it can be difficult to resist. One way to resist negative pressure is by using refusal skills. **Refusal skills** are *communication strategies that help you say no effectively.* They help you avoid doing things you do not want to do without feeling uncomfortable about your decision. By using refusal skills, you stand up for your values, which builds self-respect. You also show others that you have strength and character. These qualities will win their respect as well.

A Strategy for Refusing

Like other skills, refusal skills take practice. One way to make the S.T.O.P. strategy to be an effective way to say no to risky behaviors like using drugs or alcohol or engaging in sexual activity. The letters in S.T.O.P. represent the four steps in the strategy. You can use one or all of the following steps:

• **Say no in a firm voice.** State your feelings firmly but politely. Just say, "No, I don't want to." Make your "no" sound like you really mean it. Use body language to support your words. Make eye contact with the person.

• **Tell why not.** If the other person keeps up the pressure, explain why you feel the way you do. You do not need to use phony excuses or make up reasons. Simply say, "No thanks, I care about my health." Do not apologize. You have done nothing wrong.

• **Offer other ideas.** If the person pressuring you to do something is a friend, you can choose to suggest alternatives. Recommend an activity that is safe and fun.

• **Promptly leave.** If all else fails, just walk away. Make your actions match your words. If you are someplace where you need a ride, phone a parent to come and pick you up.

Reading Check Identify Tell what the letters in the S.T.O.P. strategy stand for.

Styles of Communication

When you use refusal skills, your goal is to say no. You are not trying to start an argument. However, the other person does need to hear you and understand your position. How your words are received is largely a matter of your communication style. There are three basic styles of communication: aggressive, passive, and assertive.

Lesson 3: Peer Pressure and Refusal Skills 115

CHAPTER 5
Lesson 3

Careers for the 21st Century

School Counselor

A school counselor is an important member of your education team. They help students in many areas of their academic, personal, and social lives. They may help you prepare for college or settle an argument between you and a peer. School counselors are important resources for students and help shape their future. If you are interested in becoming a school counselor, you should practice your communication skills.

What other skills does a school counselor need? Go to Career Corner at glencoe.com to find out.

AL Active Learning

Comic Strip Have students work in small groups to create a comic strip that shows a character using refusal skills to avoid negative peer pressure. Provide several examples of comic strips for students to use as models. Remind students that comic strips use art and text to convey an idea. **OL**

U Universal Access

At-Risk Students At-risk students are more likely than other students to exert and/or be influenced by negative peer pressure. Without singling out individual students, stress the importance of practicing refusal skills to help resist negative peer pressure. Have students work in groups to practice the steps of the S.T.O.P. strategy. **OL**

Reading Check

Answer The letters in the S.T.O.P. strategy stand for **Say no, Tell why not, Offer other ideas, and Promptly leave.**

HEALTH LITERACY

Peer Pressure and Sexual Activity Peer pressure affects all aspects of teen life, including sexual activity. Studies have found that approximately one-third of teen boys and one-quarter of teen girls have experienced peer pressure to engage in sexual activity. Teens are also strongly influenced by the perception of what their peers are doing. Studies routinely show that teens overestimate the percentage of their peers who are sexually active. When students read Lesson 4, which discusses abstinence from sexual activity, have students review the importance of resisting negative peer pressure.

114

What Teens Want to Know

How can I avoid negative peer pressure? After students have read the lesson material about peer pressure, have a class discussion about strategies for avoiding negative peer pressure. Invite a school counselor to speak to students about peer pressure and high-risk behavior. Ask the counselor to discuss strategies for avoiding negative peer pressure. Also have the speaker discuss the consequences of giving in to negative peer pressure. Have students prepare written questions to submit to the speaker. **OL**

115

Bottom Column Boxes provide supplemental information related to the lesson.

Strengthen Student Reading and Writing...

Teen Health is designed to enhance students' health literacy while providing tools to improve reading comprehension.

In the Student Edition

Guide to Reading at the beginning of each lesson provides an overview of main ideas, vocabulary building exercise, and reading strategies, often with graphic organizers that work with the lesson.

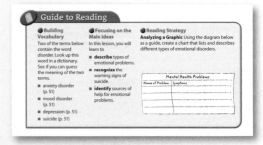

The **Reading Skills Handbook** at the back of the book is a handy resource of tips and strategies to help students get the most out of their reading. Includes tools to help students increase their vocabulary and improve reading comprehension and retention.

**Foldables®
Study Organizers** open each chapter to help students organize and process information as they read through the chapter.

Academic Vocabulary

affect (uh FEKT) *(verb)* causes change or influences. *Julio was deeply affected by the music his son played at the school recital.*

Academic Vocabulary words are highlighted and defined.

Writing Activities at the beginning of each lesson start students thinking about the topic and can be done independently.

Reading Check

Reading Checks at the end of every main section stimulate quick recall and keep students focused on the main ideas.

After You Read

Reading Reviews at the end of each chapter provide students with a quick overview of the material they have just read.

with Active Reading and Study Skills

In the Teacher Edition

- **Support for Reading** sections at the start of every chapter in the Teacher Wraparound Edition provide specific, proven prereading, during reading, and postreading strategies for every lesson.

- **Reading Strategies** at point-of-use provide activities to help teach reading within the health content.

- **Writing Support** strategies found throughout the Teacher Wraparound Edition offer writing opportunities to aid comprehension while developing writing skills.

- **Academic Vocabulary** features provide added information for teachers to explain common words used in textbooks that every successful student should know. These include a description of each word and an exercise to help students grasp the meaning.

- **Teaching Tips** features at the end of each chapter include additional, effective reading techniques.

Reading Support Materials

Reading Tutor is designed to help students strengthen reading skills. This booklet provides essential lesson content in a condensed format. It includes vocabulary terms and definitions and activities to guide students in applying their knowledge of health concepts and skills. This resource is developed for the reluctant reader, and can also help English language learners and students with learning disabilities.

Student Activities Workbook is expanded to include **Building Academic Vocabulary** activities.

Available in the Chapter *FAST FILES*

- Guided Reading and Writing Activities
- Concept Mapping Activities
- Chapter Summaries

Available at the Online Learning Center

- eFlashcards and Crossword Puzzles
- Online Audio Summaries

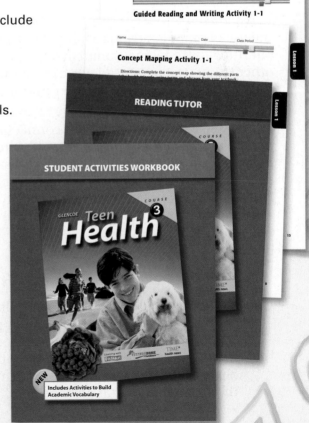

Generate High Achievers...

Teen Health incorporates the most current educational research in health literacy while reinforcing academic skills essential for student success.

No Child Left Behind: Building Academic Skills

The emphasis on student achievement in basic academic skills is an important part of the No Child Left Behind Act. These academic skills are reinforced throughout the *Teen Health* program. Teaching strategies and support give you the tools you need to reinforce academic skills while teaching health content.

- **Activating Prior Knowledge** *Teen Health* encourages students to use their prior knowledge from all subject areas by adding relevance to the material they read in the health text. Students are referred back to other parts of the text or to their own real-life experiences as they are introduced to new content.

- **Using Proven Study Strategies** Through the use of graphic organizers, highlighting, outlining, note-taking, summarizing, and other study strategies, students can monitor their own progress and organize information more effectively.

- **Integrating Academics** Activities connecting health to core curriculum areas are featured in every chapter. Students apply math concepts, examine science principles, develop critical language arts skills, and use technology tools in every chapter as they develop essential skills for lifelong learning.

- **Using Visuals to Communicate, Organize, and Reinforce Learning** High-quality, visually engaging photos, art, and graphics throughout the text communicate concepts more efficiently and reinforce learning, while allowing students to organize and comprehend information.

- **Developing Decoding and Reading Comprehension Strategies** Throughout the text, students are supplied with caption questions, Reading Checks, discussion starters, and other strategies to aid in comprehension.

Research-Based Learning Strategies

The *Teen Health* White Paper outlines the educational strategies on which this program was based. This document provides specific examples from the Student Edition, Teacher Wraparound Edition, ancillary program, and technology resources, highlighting extensive use of educationally sound strategies that help students learn health concepts and practice academic skills. The White Paper is available online in the Teacher Center at **glencoe.com**.

...and Enhance Student Learning

Learning healthy behaviors is a complex process that requires students to bridge the gap between reading the text and mastering the subject matter. Glencoe provides a series of scientifically based reading strategies that enhance students' access to the text, no matter what their reading level. In the Teacher Wraparound Edition, each chapter planning guide includes the following reading support components:

Before You Read

Vocabulary is a key component of reading comprehension, especially in the health area. Many students acquire a superficial understanding of vocabulary terms but fail to grasp the complex associations, applications, or facets of the key concepts they represent. Research reveals that students must have multiple exposures to a word to comprehend its meaning, so Glencoe has provided activities and strategies in each section to guide teachers in helping students unlock vocabulary before they begin to read. By examining new vocabulary through structural analysis, activating prior knowledge, and/or explicit instruction, students will learn more than new words—they will learn strategies for future encounters with difficult vocabulary. Once students develop an understanding of health concepts through word study, they will be introduced to additional strategies during and after reading to fully incorporate the concept described by the word. Instructional techniques such as word webbing, brainstorming, previewing, and setting a purpose for reading will ensure that students are prepared to comprehend the text.

Reading Check

Reading is constructing meaning from text. Teachers can help students construct meaning during reading by providing systematic instructional techniques that increase comprehension as students internalize strategies that hone their cognitive skills. Teachers and students will practice activities that build strong comprehension skills such as identifying cause and effect, making inferences, and drawing conclusions. Students will also learn when and how to use graphic organizers, charts, and notes to summarize, categorize, and clarify. Students will learn to rely on such tools when comprehension breaks down. A combination of individualized activities, cooperative learning, and meaningful dialogue will provide the differentiated instruction necessary to meet the needs of each student.

After You Read

Because reading is an active process, comprehension questions at the end of each chapter are not enough to ensure mastery of the content. Interactive projects in which students work together to gain deeper understanding, written responses that stimulate reflection, and extended learning based on practicing and applying will engage students and encourage them to own the concepts provided in the text.

Academic Integration

How Can I Help My Students Learn Academic Vocabulary?

By Robin Scarcella, Ph.D.

What Is Academic English?

Academic English is the language used by the educated and by leaders in business, academic, and other professional disciplines. It is the type of English used in professional books, including textbooks, and it contains specific linguistic features that are associated with academic disciplines including health. Proficiency in reading and using academic English is especially related to long-term success in all aspects of life.

Academic vocabulary is the basis for academic English. By reinforcing academic vocabulary and academic English, teachers help learners to access authentic, academic texts—not simplified texts that dummy down the content. In this way they can provide information that will help build their students' background knowledge rapidly.

What Is Academic Vocabulary?

By the time children have completed elementary school, they must have acquired the knowledge needed to understand academic vocabulary. How many words should they acquire to be able to access their textbooks? A basic 2,000-word vocabulary of high-frequency words makes up 87 percent of the vocabulary of academic texts. Eight hundred other academic words comprise an additional 8 percent of the words. Three percent of the remaining words are technical words. The remaining two percent are low-frequency words. There may be as many as 123,000 low-frequency words in academic texts.

Why Should Students Learn Academic Vocabulary?

English learners who have mastered a basic 2,000-word vocabulary are ready to acquire the majority of general words found in their academic texts. Knowledge of academic words combined with continued acquisition of general words can significantly boost an English learner's comprehension level of academic texts. English learners who learn and practice these words before they graduate from high school are likely to be able to master academic material with more confidence and speed. They waste less time and effort in guessing words or consulting dictionaries than those who only know the basic 2,000 words that characterize general conversation.

Also consider academic success in terms of measurement and assessment—state standards-based assessments, the SAT, the ACT, and the GRE—with regards to word mastery. All demand an understanding of academic vocabulary.

How Do I Include Academic Vocabulary and Academic English in My Teaching?

Teachers can provide their students with rich samples of academic vocabulary and help students understand and attend to the academic English of their texts.

To develop academic English, learners must have already acquired a large amount of basic proficiency in the grammar of everyday English.

Academic English should not be taught overtly, but rather within contexts that make sense. In terms of instruction, teaching academic English includes providing students with access to core curriculum—in this case in the health classroom.

Academic English arises not only from knowledge of a linguistic code and cognition but also from social practices in which academic English is used to accomplish communicative goals. The acquisition of academic vocabulary and grammar is necessary to advance the development of academic English.

Tips for Teaching Academic Vocabulary:

- **Expose Students to Academic Vocabulary** Do not teach it. You do not need to call attention to words students are learning, because they will acquire them subconsciously.

- **Do Not Correct Students' Mistakes When Using the Vocabulary Words** All vocabulary understanding and spelling errors are developmental and will disappear once the student reads more.

- **Help Students Decode the Words Themselves** Once they learn the alphabet, they should be able to decode words. Decoding each word they don't recognize will help them more than trying to focus on sentence structure. Once they can recognize the words, they can read "authentic" texts.

- **Do Not Ignore the English Learner in This Process** They can learn academic vocabulary before they are completely fluent in oral English.

- **Helping Students Build Academic Vocabulary Leads to Broader Learning** Students who have mastered the basic academic vocabulary are ready to continue acquiring words from the rest of the groups. To help determine which words are in the 2,000-word basic group, refer to *West's General Service List of English Words*, 1953. The list is designed to serve as a guide for teachers and as a checklist and goal list for students. For additional information about the list, visit **glencoe.com** Teacher Tools and Resources.

There are a number of guidelines that teachers can follow when teaching academic English and vocabulary:

Guidelines for Teaching Academic Vocabulary
1. Direct and planned instruction
2. Models—that have increasingly difficult language
3. Attention to form—pointing out linguistic features of words
4. Practice
5. Motivation
6. Instructional feedback
7. Assessment—on a regular basis

Robin Scarcella is a professor and director of the program in Academic English/ESL, University of California at Irvine, Irvine, CA.

Classroom Activity: Writing About Health and the Environment
Advice from Robin Scarcella

Give students an impromptu writing assignment. Ask them to write a short essay about one of the topics listed below in the left column. Have students use as many of the academic vocabulary words in the right column as they can in their essay. Give students a time limit for their writing. When completed, ask student volunteers to share their writing. Note what academic vocabulary words they use.

Topic	Academic Vocabulary
The challenges of reducing waste products in America	recycle
	environment
	conserve
Recent technological advances in health	computers
	technology
	laptop
	desk station
	digital
	transmit

Teen Health comes with an extensive variety of easy-to-use resources and support materials designed for your convenience.

Chapter Resource Masters contain all the materials you need for the chapter, in one convenient booklet, with answer keys and reproducible lesson plans.

Reproducible Student Resources

- Chapter Summary and Activity is a complete overview of the chapter content.
- Performance Assessment Activity provides outcome-based projects to challenge students.
- Building Health Skills Activity
- Concept Mapping Activity helps preview or review lesson.
- Reteaching Activity helps review key concepts.
- Enrichment Activity extends the lesson for those who have mastered the content.
- Guided Reading and Writing guides students to organize and comprehend what they read.
- Chapter Test
- Lesson Quizzes
- Hands-on Health includes Cross-Curriculum Activity, Decision-Making Activity, and Health Lab worksheets.
- Student Activities Workbook is a separate booklet that includes a study guide, a health inventory, and an activity sheet for each chapter. It also has Building Academic Vocabulary Activities.

Teacher Support and Planning

- Parent Letters and Activities
- Universal Access Activities
- Performance Assessments and Rubrics
- Transparency Previews
- Answer Keys
- Reproducible Lesson Plans

Transparencies with Instructor Guide

A booklet with 75 full-color overhead transparencies and teaching strategies for each lesson facilitates classroom discussion of key ideas.

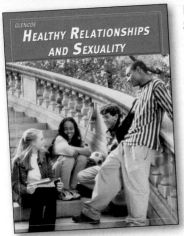

Healthy Relationships and Sexuality This full-color module takes a close look at the choices and decisions students make in their relationships. It provides basic and factual sexuality information that is both relevant and appropriate. All information is presented in a manner consistent with students' needs and emotional maturity.

Violence Prevention Help your students acquire knowledge of violence in schools, guns, and gangs, and the difference between conflict and violence. This module presents strategies to help diffuse a potentially violent situation. There are skill-building articles on personal safety, conflict resolution, peer mediation, and school safety.

Glencoe's Professional Health Series

Planning a Coordinated School Health Program increases awareness of the need for coordinated school health programs throughout the United States.

Dealing with Sensitive Issues provides background information and teaching strategies to guide health educators in presenting sensitive issues to students.

Promoting Character Education outlines the principles of character education and includes activity ideas for the teacher.

Home, School and Community Involvement designed to involve family and community members in students' health education, including service learning projects.

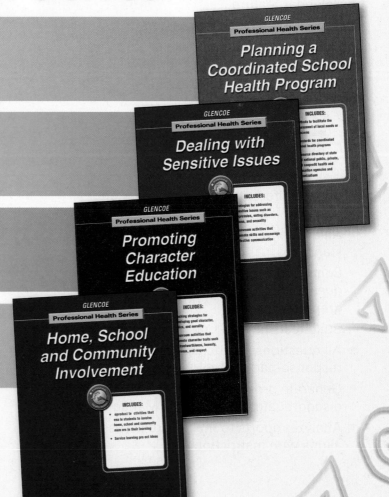

Seize the Possibilities

Teen Health's time-saving digital tools and software give teachers options for organizing materials, presenting concepts and skills, and tracking student progress.

Teacher Works Plus™

This all-in-one teacher resource center helps teachers personalize lesson plans, access resources from the Teacher Wraparound Edition, connect to the Internet, or create a to-do list. Many other features assist in planning and organizing lessons for the health classroom.

Also includes

- Calendar feature
- Access to all blackline masters
- Standards correlations
- Worksheet editor

StudentWorks Plus™

This is the student's backpack solution, bringing together a complete collection of resources in one, convenient digital platform.

Includes

- Complete Student Edition
- Full audio of English and Spanish chapter summaries
- Place for students to record assignments and keep track of grades
- Links to online activities and additional student resources
- Access to all student worksheets

ExamView® Assessment Suite

- Create differentiated tests quickly and easily
- All questions correlated to national standards
- Enhance tests with document-based questions (DBQ) or add your own photos or graphics
- Build tests in both English and Spanish
- All questions can be used with CheckPoint response-pad technology
- Generate progress reports and disaggregate data with Test Manager
- Analyze reports to make sure assessment aligns with instruction

PowerPoint® Presentation

This is a valuable resource for presenting lecture notes, graphs, and assessment questions for each chapter. The *Teen Health* PowerPoint program comes with an overview of content from each lesson, discussion notes, and lesson review questions. All assessment questions are TurningPoint® enabled, making content ready for use with response-pad technology. The report feature allows teachers to record, analyze, and generate performance reports to track individual student progress.

Online Accessibility

Announcing premium online access to the *Teen Health* Student Edition available to students with adoption of the *Teen Health* program.

Student Center

- At **glencoe.com** click on Online Student Edition to access the entire text of *Teen Health*
- Health eSpotlight Video Series
- Student Web Activities
- Building Health Skills
- Interactive Study Guides
- Health Inventories
- Health Podcast Activities
- Online Quizzes
- Lesson Review Activities
- Podcast Audio Chapter Summaries (English/Spanish)
- eFlaschcards
- Career Corner

Teacher Center

- At **glencoe.com** click any of the features below to access both student and teacher-specific resources
- Correlations to National and State Standards
- Lesson Plans
- Professional Development Articles
- Conference/Grant Links
- National Organizations
- Teaching Today
- Inclusion Strategies
- Health Podcast Activities
- Scope and Sequence
- Parent Letters (English/Spanish)
- *ExamView® Assessment Suite* Instructions

Fitness Zone Online is a multimedia resource that helps students find ways to be physically active each day.

The Nutrition and Physical Activity Resources include:

- Clipboard Energizer Activities
- Fitness Zone Videos
- Polar Heart Rate Monitor Activities
- Nutrition, Physical Activity, and Injury Prevention Tips
- Links to Nutrition and Physical Activity Resources
- And More!

STUDY TO GO Study-to-Go lets students download free content to their PDA and gain instant mobile access to online quizzes and eFlashcards directly from the *Teen Health* Web site at **glencoe.com**. Students can study anytime and anywhere – between classes, during work breaks, or while waiting for the bus.

Vocabulary PuzzleMaker

Build vocabulary skills with custom-designed puzzles. Create word searches and crossword puzzles using vocabulary words from each lesson. Includes English and Spanish vocabulary.

Sharpen Your Approach

Throughout the **Teen Health** program, assessment options are provided for teachers to measure students' progress and knowledge of concepts and skills presented in the text.

Student Edition Assessment

- **Lesson Review** Students are asked to recall facts and vocabulary, answer critical thinking questions, and apply health skills they are learning. Answers to each question are provided in the Teacher Wraparound Edition.

- **Health Skills Activities** These skills assessments can be found wherever a key concept is presented. These engaging activities give students a chance to demonstrate their understanding of the lesson content by applying the skills to health concepts.

- **Chapter Assessment** Each chapter is followed by a review page and a two-page assessment. The test includes vocabulary, multiple choice, modified true-false, fill-in-the-blank, and short-answer questions.

- **Standardized Test Practice** At the end of each chapter, health-related questions connected to Language Arts, Math, or Science enable students to test their knowledge while practicing for state and national standardized testing.

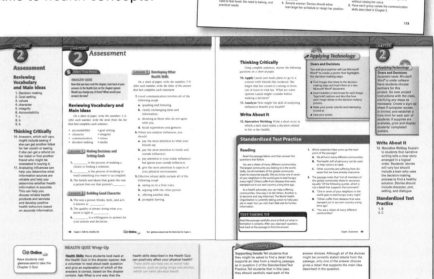

Chapter Fast Files Assessment Resources

- Lesson Quizzes and Chapter Tests
- Performance Assessment

Technology Assessment Options

- Online Quizzes
- *ExamView*® Assessment Suite

Help Students Make Health-Enhancing Choices

Health skills are identified by health educators across the nation as essential for students to make responsible decisions. They are included in the national standards for health education to provide professionals with a framework to help determine the content of health education curricula. These skills can be developed and practiced by your students.

Teen Health presents these skills in a unique way that guides students through the learning process. Each skill is modeled for the student. Then, students have the opportunity to practice the skill. Finally, students apply the skill to their own lives. They can use these skills to promote their own health and the health of others.

Rubrics and teaching tips are provided for each skill in the Teacher Wraparound Edition to help you assess student mastery of the health behavior being taught.

ASSESSMENT SCORING

Student work should meet all criteria to achieve the highest score.

Skills Student work
- identifies three sources of information.
- locates relevant sources.
- evaluates the validity of the sources.
- explains why the sources are accurate.

Concepts Student work
- provides factual and complete information.
- shows relationships among ideas.
- draws accurate conclusions.

ASSESSMENT SCORING

Using a rubric, student work should meet all criteria for the highest score.

Skills Student work:
- identifies influences that affect health practices.
- differentiates internal and external influences.
- addresses the relationship between influences and behaviors.

Concepts Student work:
- draws accurate conclusions about the food item.
- provides accurate and comprehensive information about good nutrition.

Accessing Information
This skill addresses the important steps to take to get valid health information and appropriate health services.

Stress Management
This skill involves the use of techniques that reduce and manage stress.

Conflict Resolution
This skill involves specific strategies to resolve conflicts peacefully.

Analyzing Influences
This skill involves analysis of the dynamic factors of families, media, peers, personal interests, and pressures that affect health decisions.

Communication
This skill is an interactive process between and among individuals to clarify ideas, thoughts, needs, and feelings.

Practicing Healthful Behaviors
This skill is the actual practice of healthful behaviors. It includes the steps and procedures used to promote wellness.

Refusal Skills
This skill involves strategies to refuse involvement in behaviors that may put one's health at risk.

Decision Making
This skill requires speculation into the future based on a particular action.

Goal Setting
This skill is an interactive process for individuals. It requires planning and revision throughout the application of the process.

Advocacy
This skill calls for the use of persuasion to promote positive health choices personally and for others.

Universal Access

Strategies for differentiated learning are provided throughout the Teacher Wraparound Edition to help you adapt your lessons to each student's preferred learning style. Many of these activities will be helpful for a variety of students in your classroom. You will find strategies labeled specifically for

- students with vision impairments.
- students with hearing impairments.
- students with learning impairments.
- students with physical impairments.
- students with speech or language impairments.
- gifted students.
- at-risk students.
- students with behavioral problems.

In addition, each chapters *FAST FILE* booklet contains a variety of Universal Access activity worksheets developed especially for teaching students in the differentiated classroom.

Name _____ Date _____ Class Period _____

Universal Access Activity 1

Your Total Health

What to Do: Draw lines to match each activity with the area of your total health affected by that activity.

Mental/Emotional	Get plenty of rest
	Use positive thinking
	Build relationships with others
Physical	Eat healthy foods
	Get plenty of exercise
	Ask for help when you need it
	Express feelings in positive ways
Social	Avoid harmful drugs and alcohol
	Listen to a friend's problems
	Show respect for others

Chapter 1 Teen Health Course 1 **51**

Differentiated Learning

Glencoe addresses the national concern for access to learning for all students in the differentiated classroom. Students from diverse cultural backgrounds, students with different learning styles, students with special needs, and gifted or advanced students must learn the important concepts and skills to ensure healthful behaviors.

Each of the teaching strategies in the Teacher Wraparound Edition is coded for teaching students at a variety of levels. Look for the following codes following the appropriate materials in every lesson.

AL Activities for students working above grade level

OL Activities for students working on grade level

BL Activities for students working below grade level

EL Activities for English learners

Lesson 1

AL Active Learning
Video Have students work in small groups to write a script for a 5-minute video that would show a student using the H.E.L.P. criteria to evaluate a health decision. Allow groups 15 minutes to write their scripts. Then allow time for practice and filming. After all groups have completed filming, share the videos with the class. Ask students if they feel teen advocates have more influence than parents on this issue. Why? **OL**

U Universal Access

Learning Disabled Help students understand how to make responsible decisions by showing them how to organize the lesson in an outline format. Write the first main head on the board or with an overhead projector and follow with bullet points beneath:
Decisions and Values
- Your decisions show what's important to you
- Choices should be based on values
These bullet points should include the definitions of vocabulary terms as well as one or two other important points. Have students continue the outline as they read through the lesson. **BL**

Modifying Activities for Differentiated Learning

As the number of English language learners (ELL) increases across the United States, it is important for teachers to develop a proficient skill in modifying activities to increase the likelihood that all students will learn important health-related knowledge and skills.

When modifying activities to meet the needs of your ELL students, first ask yourself this question: *What is the language level (proficiency) of my students?* Many school sites, after sufficient assessments, place their ELL students in one of four (or sometimes five) language proficiency levels.

ELL Level 1 (Starting):
These students typically have been in the United States 0 – 3 years.
Level 1 students read at 0 – 1.5 grade level.
Key terms: tell, list, label, underline, state, match

ELL Level 2 (Emerging):
Level 2 students read at 1.6 – 2.5 grade level.
Typically, they are able to
- write short simple paragraphs.
- identify main ideas.
- identify story characters.
Key terms: explain, describe, discuss, locate, draw

ELL Level 3 (Developing):
Level 3 students read at 2.6 – 3.5 grade level and can often write paragraphs and identify "wh" questions. Level 3 students generally have good oral English skills.
Key terms: show, solve, plan, demonstrate, use, apply

ELL Level 4 (Expanding) and Level 5 (Bridging):
Level 4 and 5 students are near proficient.
They read at 4 – 5.5 grade level.
They are fluent in oral English. They often need help with academic and written English.
Key terms: compare, classify, design, predict, decide, rank, summarize, evaluate

Sample Activity: Have students write a research report that explains and prioritizes the risk factors associated with cardiovascular disease.

Once the language proficiency level is determined, a teacher will be better able to modify an activity designed for "on grade level (OL)" students. Prior to any activity modification, the teacher should confirm that all associated vocabulary is clearly understood by all students. In this example activity, the terms "explain," "prioritize," "risk factor," and "cardiovascular" should be clarified in the context of the activity. For each activity it is recommended that a criteria rubric be prepared for the students.

Modification for Level 1 students: In pairs, have students name and correctly spell four risk factors associated with cardiovascular disease.

Modification for Level 2 students: In pairs, have students describe to a partner four risk factors associated with cardiovascular disease.

Modification for Level 3 students: Have each student prepare a four-spoke web that identifies four risk factors associated with cardiovascular disease. Explain to a partner which risk factor you believe is most important and why.

Modification for Level 4/5: In pairs, have students create a poster, newspaper article, skit, report, or brochure that explains and prioritizes two risk factors associated with cardiovascular disease.

La salud de los jóvenes

A complete Spanish translation of the **Teen Health** Student Edition is available for your Spanish-speaking students. The dynamic photo and illustration program, engaging infographics, and fun, hands-on activities will motivate English language learners as they develop health knowledge and skills.

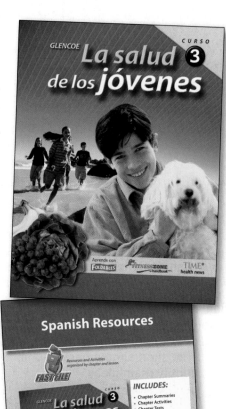

Go Online

Spanish Online Student Edition

Spanish Resources Booklet includes worksheets in Spanish

- Chapter Summaries
- Chapter Activities
- Chapter Tests
- Lesson Quizzes
- Parent Letters
- Answer Keys

Technology Options for the English Language Learner

Spanish Audio Summaries on StudentWorks™ Plus

Chapter and lesson summaries provide the English language learner with additional practice to comprehend the main ideas in each lesson and apply what they have learned. Also available at **glencoe.com**.

ExamView® **Assessment Suite and Vocabulary Puzzlemaker**

Each of these CD-ROM programs include a Spanish version, making assessment components and vocabulary practice accessible to students who are English language learners.

TIME *health news*

TIME health news features health-related topics in the news, developed by TIME magazine to capture the interests of today's middle school students. Teaching Strategies make connections to media, technology, and culture, encouraging students to understand their own culture and the culture of others in the ways that media and technology impact their health.

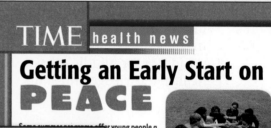

TIME *health news*

Getting an Early Start on PEACE

Some summer programs offer young people a chance to learn about international harmony.

...people to ...gs between ...cult when ...ng. Troubles ...to achieving ...w offering ...nderstanding

...kids a series ...er in Maine. ...vith teens ...dia, Pakistan, ...ther. The ... which they ...a respect and ...attended ...ectives as

Kids learn to trust and respect one another during group activities at Seeds of Peace.

Teens who want a longer experience interacting with young people from other nations can go to the United World College (U.W.C.), which has 10 campuses around the globe. At the U.S. branch in New Mexico, 200 students ages 16 to 18 work toward a two-year diploma. In addition to academics, there are classes in nonviolent conflict resolution. The object, says Philip Geier, president of U.W.C.'s American campus, is "to create a global network of future decision makers." At the school, Israeli students joined Palestinian classmates in a presentation on the history of conflict in their homelands. "We...agreed on some topics and decided we would never agree on others," says Gadi Maayan, 17. Now, however, Maayan better understands other viewpoints.

Such encounters can be life changing for American teens, too. "I can no longer make stereotypical judgments about anyone," says Matt Farwell, a U.W.C. graduate. "I feel responsible for sharing what I learned with as many people as I can."

TIME *health news*

The good news: Few germs actually cause great harm. The bad news: The ones that do can be really dangerous—even deadly. Here's how to stay healthy.

GERM GUIDE

...bacteria, viruses, and fungi. Luckily, ...perform many important tasks, such ...o germs that can cause stomachaches, ...you from those microscopic bad guys.

...cuts with a bandage. Dab on a ...little antibacterial ointment while ...you're at it, or use a bandage that ...has antibiotic ointment built in. This ...will help protect and heal an open ...wound, another place germs can ...enter the body.

...hol-based hand sanitizers ...chool bag. They work faster than ...soap and kill bacteria ...more efficiently, without ...encouraging antibacterial-...resistant germ strains.

...s healthy. Cats and dogs can carry ...t are easily transmitted to humans. ...e your pets' immunizations are

...up-to-date and ...that the animals ...are groomed ...regularly. Wash ...your hands after ...touching pets.

TIME *health news*

Meet Me at the Gym!

Objectives

After completing this activity, students will be able to
- describe ways that working out improves physical health
- identify how working out with friends and family members can improve mental/emotional health and social health

Motivator

Ask volunteers to name a positive result of exercising or working out. Encourage students to think beyond the physical benefits of exercise.

Teaching the Activity

- After students have read the feature, have them make a bulleted list of reasons that teens work out. **BL**
- Have students research various fitness centers in your area. Have students inquire about any special programs offered for teens, and the cost of joining the center. Have students write a short report summarizing their findings. **AL**

TIME *health news*

Whether they're headed to a local health club or another fitness center, growing numbers of teens are saying...

"Meet Me at the GYM!"

Victor Scotti wasn't feeling quite as fit as he wanted to be. So, like more and more fitness-conscious teens, he started going to a gym. Scotti showed up five times a week for circuit-training, which included a cardio workout, push-ups, crunches, and weight training. Now, Scotti says, "I've definitely gotten faster and a lot more limber."

Teens on the Move

Scotti is just one of a rapidly growing group of teens who regularly hit health clubs and gyms. There they lift weights, run on treadmills, and take spinning classes.

It was once thought that weight training could stunt growth by harming young developing bones. However, the American Academy of Pediatrics has determined that workouts, performed correctly, can benefit young people. So, with the number of overweight kids at an all-time high and teens wanting to train for organized team sports, health clubs are becoming popular places for young people to get active.

Be Your Best

There are many reasons why more and more teens are headed to a gym after school. Workouts serve as a way to reduce stress, and they are an option for students who are less interested in school team sports. In addition, growing numbers of teens also use the clubs to improve their strength and agility on the basketball, tennis, and volleyball courts.

Mike DeMaria is director of a sports-performance academy in Mandeville, Louisiana. He oversees daily training for some 200 young people, including six girls' volleyball teams. Other teens organize routines on their own, sometimes even hiring a personal trainer. DeMaria says of the students, "They're very aware now that if they want to be the best they can be at their chosen sport, they have to be strong."

Some teens are discovering that working out can be an easy and enjoyable way to spend time with a parent. Rebecca Sernick asked her dad to teach her how to work out to help fight the weight gain that was affecting her performance on the softball team. Thanks to her dad's guidance, Rebecca lost 40 pounds and met her fitness goals. However, neither Rebecca nor her dad has any plan to stop their weekly workouts. It's just too much fun!

98 Chapter 1: Physical Activity and Fitness

Activity Media, Technology, and Culture

Media Have students perform independent research to learn additional benefits of working out. Then, have students create a public service announcement explaining the benefits of regular workouts. Students should use the ideas in the feature as well as the information they learned through research. Remind students to include the benefits of working out for all three side of the health triangle. Obtain permission for students to present their public service announcement to the school or to other health classes. **OL**

98

The Teen Health Program Meets the National Health Education Standards

The National Health Education Standards were created with the goal of improving educational achievement for students and improving health in the United States through the promotion of health literacy. The health standards for middle school students highlight eight key components of health knowledge and skills.

Standard 1

Students will comprehend concepts related to health promotion and disease prevention to enhance health.

1.8.1 Analyze the relationship between healthy behaviors and personal health.

1.8.2 Describe the inter-relationship of emotional, intellectual, physical, and social health in adolescence.

1.8.3 Analyze how the environment impacts personal health.

1.8.4 Describe how family history can impact personal health.

1.8.5 Describe ways to reduce or prevent injuries and other adolescent health problems.

1.8.6 Explain how appropriate health care can promote personal health.

1.8.7 Describe the benefits of and barriers to practicing healthy behaviors.

1.8.8 Examine the likelihood of injury or illness if engaging in unhealthy behaviors.

1.8.9 Examine the potential seriousness of injury or illness if engaging in unhealthy behaviors.

Standard 2

Students will analyze the influence of family, peers, culture, media, technology, and other factors on health behaviors.

2.8.1 Examine how the family influences the health of adolescents.

2.8.2 Describe the influence of culture on health beliefs, practices, and behaviors.

2.8.3 Describe how peers influence healthy and unhealthy behaviors.

2.8.4 Analyze how the school and community can impact personal health practices and behaviors.

2.8.5 Analyze how messages from media influence health behaviors.

2.8.6 Analyze the influence of technology on personal and family health.

2.8.7 Explain how the perceptions of norms influence healthy and unhealthy behaviors.

2.8.8 Explain the influence of personal values and beliefs on individual health practices and behaviors.

2.8.9 Describe how some health risk behaviors can influence the likelihood of engaging in unhealthy behaviors.

2.8.10 Explain how school and public health policies can influence health promotion and disease prevention.

Standard 3

Students will demonstrate the ability to access valid information and products and services to enhance health.

3.8.1 Analyze the validity of health information, products, and services.

3.8.2 Access valid health information from home, school, and community.

3.8.3 Determine the accessibility of products that enhance health.

3.8.4 Describe situations that may require professional health services.

3.8.5 Locate valid and reliable health products and services.

Standard 4

Students will demonstrate the ability to use interpersonal communication skills to enhance health and avoid or reduce health risks.

4.8.1 Apply effective verbal and nonverbal communication skills to enhance health.

4.8.2 Demonstrate refusal and negotiation skills to avoid or reduce health risks.

4.8.3 Demonstrate effective conflict management or resolution strategies.

4.8.4 Demonstrate how to ask for assistance to enhance the health of self and others.

Standard 5

Students will demonstrate the ability to use decision-making skills to enhance health.

5.8.1 Identify circumstances that can help or hinder healthy decision making.

5.8.2 Determine when health-related situations require the application of a thoughtful decision-making process.

5.8.3 Distinguish when individual or collaborative decision making is appropriate.

5.8.4 Distinguish between healthy and unhealthy alternatives to health-related issues or problems.

5.8.5 Predict the potential short-term impact of each alternative on self and others.

5.8.6 Choose healthy alternatives over unhealthy alternatives when making a decision.

5.8.7 Analyze the outcomes of a health-related decision.

Standard 6

Students will demonstrate the ability to use goal-setting skills to enhance health.

6.8.1 Assess personal health practices.

6.8.2 Develop a goal to adopt, maintain, or improve a personal health practice.

6.8.3 Apply strategies and skills needed to attain a personal health goal.

6.8.4 Describe how personal health goals can vary with changing abilities, priorities, and responsibilities.

Standard 7

Students will demonstrate the ability to practice health-enhancing behaviors and avoid or reduce risks.

7.8.1 Explain the importance of assuming responsibility for personal health behaviors.

7.8.2 Demonstrate healthy practices and behaviors that will maintain or improve the health of self and others.

7.8.3 Demonstrate behaviors to avoid or reduce health risks to self and others.

Standard 8

Students will demonstrate the ability to advocate for personal, family, and community health.

8.8.1 State a health-enhancing position on a topic and support it with accurate information.

8.8.2 Demonstrate how to influence and support others to make positive health choices.

8.8.3 Work cooperatively to advocate for healthy individuals, families, and schools.

8.8.4 Identify ways that health messages and communication techniques can be altered for different audiences.

Cited from pre-publication document of National Health Education Standards, PreK–12, American Cancer Society. December 2005–April 2006.

The Teen Health Program at a Glance

Teen Health, the three-book series for students in grades 6, 7, and 8, provides middle school students with the foundation of concepts and skills necessary for lifelong health. Current health concepts are integrated with nationally recognized, health-based skills.

CHAPTER 6 Promoting Social Health

CHAPTER 8

Violence Prevention

CHAPTER 9

Physical Activity and Fitness

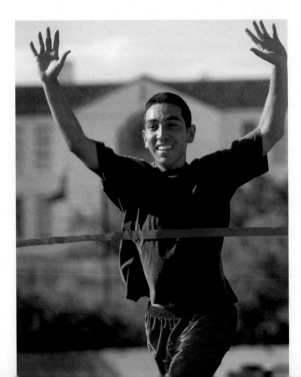

CHAPTER 10

Nutrition for Health

CHAPTER 11

Your Body Image

CHAPTER 12   Alcohol

CHAPTER 13   Tobacco

CHAPTER 18

Common Communicable Diseases

CHAPTER 19

Noncommunicable Diseases

Be Healthy and Active with Teen Health

Physical activity and fitness are important to good health. Use the Fitness Zone Handbook and Glencoe's Online Fitness Zone to develop personal fitness.

Fitness Zone Handbook
The Fitness Zone Handbook on pages xviii – 1 can help you create a personal fitness plan to balance your activities and build your overall fitness level. You'll also learn about the elements of fitness and discover fun group activities.

Physical Fitness Plan

Everyone should have a fitness plan. A personal plan can help you get started in developing your physical fitness. If you are already active or even athletic, a physical fitness plan can help you balance your activities and maintain a healthy level of activity.

Planning a Routine

When you're ready to start a fitness routine, it may be tempting to exercise as hard as you can for as long as you can. However, that approach is likely to leave you discouraged and even injured. Instead, you should plan a fitness routine that will let your body adjust to activity. Work up to your fitness goals slowly. Gradually increase both the length of time you spend exercising and the number of times you exercise each week. For example, you might start by doing a fitness activity for just 5 minutes a day, 3 days a week. Increase the amount of time you exercise, to say 7 minutes the next week and to 10 minutes during the third week of your plan. When you are exercising 20 minutes, 3 days a week, you're ready to add a fourth day to your fitness routine. Eventually, you will be exercising for 20 to 30 minutes, 5 days a week.

Warming Up

There's more to a physical fitness plan than fitness activities. It's important to prepare your body for exercise. Preparation involves warm-up activities that will raise your body temperature and get your muscles ready for your fitness activity. Easy warm-up activities include walking, marching, and jogging, as well as basic calisthenics.

When you're developing your own fitness plan, you should include warm-ups in your schedule. As you increase the time you spend doing a fitness activity, you should also increase the time you spend warming up.

This chart shows how you can plan the time you spend on warm-ups and fitness activities.

Sample Physical Fitness Plan

DAY	Monday		Tuesday		Wednesday		Thursday		Friday	
WEEK	Warm Up	Activity	Warm Up	Activity	Warm Up	Activity	Warm Up	Activity	Warm Up	Activity
1	5 min	5 min	---	---	5 min	5 min	---	---	5 min	5 min
2	5 min	7 min	---	---	5 min	7 min	---	---	5 min	7 min
3	5 min	10 min	---	---	5 min	10 min	---	---	5 min	10 min
4	5 min	12 min	---	---	5 min	12 min	---	---	5 min	12 min
5	7 min	15 min	---	---	7 min	15 min	---	---	7 min	15 min
6	7 min	17 min	---	---	7 min	17 min	---	---	7 min	17 min
7	10 min	20 min	---	---	10 min	20 min	---	---	10 min	20 min
8	10 min	20 min	10 min	20 min	10 min	20 min	---	---	10 min	20 min
9	10 min	20 min	10 min	20 min	10 min	20 min	10 min	20 min	10 min	20 min

xviii Fitness Zone Handbook

Go Online

Get energized with Glencoe's *Fitness Zone Online* at *glencoe.com*

Fitness Zone Online is a multimedia resource that helps students find ways to be physically active each day.

The Nutrition and Physical Activity Resources include:

- Clipboard Energizer Activities
- Fitness Zone Videos
- Polar Heart Rate Monitor Activities
- Tips for Healthy Eating, Staying Active, and Preventing Injuries
- Links to additional Nutrition and Physical Activity Resources

Reading in the health classroom with
Teen Health

Review Key Terms
Complete the Building Vocabulary activity to become familiar with these terms before you read the lesson. Vocabulary terms are highlighted in yellow to make them easy to find.

Do the QuickWrite
This feature will help you start thinking about the information in the lesson.

Look at the Reading Checks
When you see a Reading Check, stop and answer the question to make sure that you understand what you have just read.

Reading Skills Handbook
The Reading Skills Handbook on pages 592–601 offers strategies to help you become a faster, more effective reader. Strong reading skills can help you improve your grades, study skills, and writing skills.

Preview the Lesson
Get a preview of what's coming by reading the lesson objectives in Focusing on the Main Ideas. You can also use this feature to prepare for quizzes and tests.

Strengthen Your Reading Skills
Complete the Reading Strategy activity to help you understand some of the information in the lesson.

Lesson 1

Friendships During Adolescence

Guide to Reading

Building Vocabulary
As you read this lesson, write each new highlighted term and its definition in your notebook.
- relationships (p. 102)
- sympathetic (p. 103)
- clique (p. 105)
- peer pressure (p. 105)

Focusing on the Main Ideas
In this lesson, you will learn to
- **explain** changes that occur in friendships during adolescence.
- **identify** the qualities of a good friend.
- **develop** communication skills to make new friends.

Reading Strategy
Classifying Using the diagram as a guide, create a concept map that shows the qualities of a good friend.

Qualities of a Good Friend

FOLDABLES Study Organizer Use the Foldable® on p. 101 as you read this lesson.

Quick Write
Write a short paragraph that completes this sentence opener with a definition and examples: "A friend is _____."

Friendships

If you ask a group of people what they like most about their closest friend, you will probably get many different answers. One person might respond, "She makes me laugh." Another might say, "We have a great time together."

Unlike other types of relationships, friendships are relationships people choose to have. **Relationships** are connections you have with other people and groups in your life. Friendships form as a result of common interests and shared values. They are an important part of good social health.

Reading Check Define What are relationships?

◄ We tend to make friends with people who share similar interests. **What are some things you and your friends enjoy doing together?**

102

Reading Skills Handbook

▶ Reading: What's in It for You?

What role does reading play in your life? There are many different ways that reading could be part of what you do every day. Are you on a sports team? Perhaps you like to read the latest news about your favorite team or find out about new ways to train for your sport. Are you interested in music or art? You might be looking for information about ways to create songs or about styles of painting. Are you enrolled in an English class, a math class, or a health class? Then your assignments probably require a lot of reading.

Improving or Fine-Tuning Your Reading Skills Will:
- Improve your grades
- Allow you to read faster and more efficiently
- Improve your study skills
- Help you remember more information
- Improve your writing

▶ The Reading Process

Good reading skills build on one another, overlap, and spiral around just like a winding staircase goes around and around while leading you to a higher place. This Reading Guide will help you find and use the tools you'll need before, during, and after reading.

Strategies You Can Use
- Identify, understand, and learn new words
- Understand why you read
- Take a quick look at the whole text
- Try to predict what you are about to read
- Take breaks while you read and ask yourself questions about the text
- Take notes
- Keep thinking about what will come next
- Summarize

▶ Vocabulary Development

Vocabulary skills are the building blocks of the reading and writing processes. By learning to use a number of strategies to build your word skills, you will become a stronger reader.

Use Context to Determine Meaning

The best way to increase your vocabulary is to read widely, listen carefully, and take part in many kinds of discussions. When reading on your own, you can often figure out the meanings of new words by looking at their **context**, the other words and sentences that surround them.

592 Reading Skills Handbook

Physical Fitness Plan

Everyone should have a fitness plan. A personal plan can help you get started in developing your physical fitness. If you are already active or even athletic, a physical fitness plan can help you balance your activities and maintain a healthy level of activity.

Planning a Routine

When you're ready to start a fitness routine, it may be tempting to exercise as hard as you can for as long as you can. However, that approach is likely to leave you discouraged and even injured. Instead, you should plan a fitness routine that will let your body adjust to activity. Work up to your fitness goals slowly. Gradually increase both the length of time you spend exercising and the number of times you exercise each week. For example, you might start by doing a fitness activity for just 5 minutes a day, 3 days a week. Increase the amount of time you exercise, to say 7 minutes the next week and to 10 minutes during the third week of your plan. When you are exercising 20 minutes, 3 days a week, you're ready to add a fourth day to your fitness routine. Eventually, you will be exercising for 20 to 30 minutes, 5 days a week.

Warming Up

There's more to a physical fitness plan than fitness activities. It's important to prepare your body for exercise. Preparation involves warm-up activities that will raise your body temperature and get your muscles ready for your fitness activity. Easy warm-up activities include walking, marching, and jogging, as well as basic calisthenics.

When you're developing your own fitness plan, you should include warm-ups in your schedule. As you increase the time you spend doing a fitness activity, you should also increase the time you spend warming up.

This chart shows how you can plan the time you spend on warm-ups and fitness activities.

Sample Physical Fitness Plan

DAY	Monday		Tuesday		Wednesday		Thursday		Friday	
WEEK	Warm Up	Activity	Warm Up	Activity	Warm Up	Activity	Warm Up	Activity	Warm Up	Activity
1	5 min	5 min	---	---	5 min	5 min	---	---	5 min	5 min
2	5 min	7 min	---	---	5 min	7 min	---	---	5 min	7 min
3	5 min	10 min	---	---	5 min	10 min	---	---	5 min	10 min
4	5 min	12 min	---	---	5 min	12 min	---	---	5 min	12 min
5	7 min	15 min	---	---	7 min	15 min	---	---	7 min	15 min
6	7 min	17 min	---	---	7 min	17 min	---	---	7 min	17 min
7	10 min	20 min	---	---	10 min	20 min	---	---	10 min	20 min
8	10 min	20 min	10 min	20 min	10 min	20 min	---	---	10 min	20 min
9	10 min	20 min	10 min	20 min	10 min	20 min	10 min	20 min	10 min	20 min

Five Elements of Fitness

When you're making a plan for your own fitness program, you should keep the five elements of fitness in mind.

Cardiovascular endurance is the ability of the heart and lungs to function efficiently over time without getting tired. Activities that improve cardiovascular endurance involve non-stop movement of your whole body or of large muscle groups. Familiar examples are jogging, walking, running, bike riding, soccer, basketball, and swimming.

Muscle endurance is the ability of a muscle or a group of muscles to work non-stop without getting tired. Many activities that build cardiovascular endurance also build muscular endurance, such as jogging, walking, and bike riding.

Muscle strength is the ability of the muscle to produce force during an activity. You can make your muscles stronger by working them against some form of resistance, such as weights or gravity. Activities that can help you build muscle strength include push-ups, pull-ups, lifting weights, and running stairs.

Flexibility is the ability to move a body part freely, without pain. You can improve your flexibility by stretching gently before and after exercise.

Body composition is the amount of body fat a person has compared with the amount of lean mass, which is bone, muscle, and fluid. Generally, a healthy body is made up of more lean mass and less body fat. Body composition is a result of diet, exercise, and heredity.

On the next pages, you'll find ten different fitness activities for groups. They can help you develop all five elements of fitness, with an emphasis on cardiovascular endurance. They can also help you add variety and fun to your fitness plan.

Group Fitness Activities

Activity 1: Fitness Day

The exercises on this page should be completed with a teacher or other adult supervising the student. Correct form is important in order to reduce the risk of neck and back injuries.

Fitness Elements Muscle strength and endurance, flexibility

Equipment With a group of other students, make a set of exercise cards. Each card should name and illustrate an exercise. You can include some or all of the exercises shown here.

Formation Stand in two lines facing each other, or stand in a large circle.

Directions Take turns leading the group. The leader picks a card, stands in the center of the formation, and leads the group in the exercise on that card.

Reach for the Sky

Hold for a count of 10, rest, and repeat.

Plank

Hold for a count of 10, rest, and repeat.

Crab

Hold for a count of 10, rest, and repeat.

Open/Closed Pike

Open

Closed

Hold for a count of 10, rest, and repeat.

Flyer (half)

Raise legs. Hold for a count of 10, rest, and repeat.

Pointer

For each side, hold for a count of 10, rest, and repeat.

Single Knee Hug

Hold for a count of 10, rest, and repeat.

Activity 2: Fitness Circuit

Fitness Elements Muscle strength and endurance, flexibility, and cardiovascular endurance

Equipment 2–4 jump ropes, 2–4 aerobic steps, signs or posters naming each station spread throughout the activity area (see diagram.)

Formation Set up stations as shown in the diagram. Form pairs, so that each student has a partner.

Directions With your partner, move through the stations: planks, jump rope, seated toe touches, sit-ups, push-ups, jumps in place, leg raises, jumping jacks, arm circles, step-ups. Each pair can start at any station. If your group is large, two pairs may use the same station. At each station, perform as many repetitions as you can in 30 seconds. After 30 seconds, have a teacher or a student volunteer signal the end of the time. With your partner, move in a clockwise direction to the next station.

FITNESS CIRCUIT

Planks, Step-Ups, Jump Rope, Arm Circles, Seated Toe Touches, Jumping Jacks, Sit-Ups, Leg Raises, Jump In Place, Push-Ups

Activity 3: Multi-Ball Crab Soccer

Fitness Elements Muscle strength and endurance

Equipment 3–6 crab soccer balls or other large balls

Formation Mark a goal line at each end of the playing area, and divide the players into two teams. All the players on both teams get into the crab position and remain in that position throughout the game.

Directions Put the crab soccer balls in the middle of the playing area. Members of both teams kick the balls past the other team's goal line to score. Remember, all players have to stay in the crab position all the time. The game continues until all the balls have been scored.

Activity 4: Crab Relay

Fitness Elements Muscle strength and endurance

Equipment 4–5 flying disks

Formation Mark two lines 15–25 feet apart, depending on the fitness level of group members. One is the starting line, and the other is the turn-around line. Divide the group into four or five single-file lines behind the starting line. The first player in each group is in the crab position with a flying disk resting on his or her abdomen.

Directions Have a teacher or a student volunteer give a signal to start the relay. The first player in each line crab-walks to the turn-around line and back to the starting line. The players have to move in the crab position and must keep the disks on their abdomens. If the disk falls off, the player has to stop, pick the disk up, and place it back on his or her abdomen. When players return to the starting line, they hand their disks to the next player in line. The next player follows the same procedure. Continue playing until all the members of each team have participated. If you want to play again, reorganize the teams by having the first player in each line move to the team on his or her right.

Activity 5: Piranha River

Fitness Elements Cardiovascular endurance and flexibility

Equipment None

Formation Mark a line at each end of the activity area. One is the starting line and the other is the finish line. Mark two more lines, about ten feet apart, between the starting line and the finish line. The space between these two lines is the "river." Let two volunteers stand in the "river." They are the "piranhas." All the other players stand behind the starting line.

Directions Have a teacher or a student volunteer give the signal to begin. The players behind the starting line run down the river. As they run, the "piranhas" try to tag them. Players who reach the finish line without being tagged are safe. Players who are tagged stay in the "river" and become "helper piranhas." "Helper piranhas" must keep their feet in one place but can bend and stretch to tag the players running down the "river."

Activity 6: Partner Walk Tag

Fitness Element Cardiovascular endurance

Equipment None

Formation Form pairs, so that each player has a partner. With your partner, decide which one of you will begin as the tagger and which will begin as the walker.

Directions Have a teacher or a student volunteer give the signal to begin. If you are the tagger, chase and try to tag your partner. If you are the walker, walk to stay away from your partner. You must both walk at all times, not run. Once the tagger tags the walker, change roles with your partner. Continue until the teacher or student volunteer signals the end. You can vary this activity by hopping, skipping, or using another movement instead of walking.

Activity 7: Scarf Tag

Fitness Element Cardiovascular endurance

Equipment Scarves (one for each player)

Formation Each player should tuck one end of a scarf into the back of his or her waistband or into a rear pocket. Then players should scatter over the activity area.

Directions Have a teacher or a student volunteer give the signal to start. Each player moves throughout the activity area, trying to grab and pull out other players' scarves. Students who pull a scarf must say, "I got a scarf," bend down on one knee, and place the new scarf in their waistbands or pockets. They are "safe" while they are doing this. Players who lose their scarves continue playing, trying to capture other scarves. Players may pull only one scarf at a time. They may not hold onto their own scarves, and they may not push, pull, or grab other players. Play continues until the teacher or student volunteer gives the signal to stop.

Activity 8: Alien Invaders

Fitness Element Cardiovascular endurance

Equipment None

Formation Mark a goal line at each end of the playing area, and divide the players into two teams. One team is the "aliens," and the other team is the "soldiers." Form pairs, so that each player has a partner. Throughout the game, partners have to remain together, with their arms locked. All the players on the "aliens" team stand behind one goal line, and all the players on the "soldiers" team stand behind the other.

Directions The "aliens" stand with their backs to the playing area. The "soldiers" walk quietly toward the "aliens." When the "soldiers" are close to the "aliens," a teacher or student volunteer calls out "There are soldiers in your galaxy!" The "aliens" turn around and chase the "soldiers." All the "soldiers" who are tagged, or whose partners are tagged, become "aliens." "Soldiers" who reach their own goal line are safe.

 Activity 9: Par Course

Fitness Elements Cardiovascular endurance, muscle strength and endurance

Equipment 4 jump ropes, 4 cones, signs or posters naming each station on the par course (See diagram.)

Formation: Set up stations as shown in the diagram. Mark each station with a cone and identify it with a sign or poster. Form groups of four.

Directions With the three other members of your group, start at one station on the course. Perform the activity identified there. Then jog to the next station, and perform that activity. Continue around the course until you have completed each activity at least once. If you're participating with a large class, you might work in two shifts, with half the groups completing the full par course and then giving the other groups a turn.

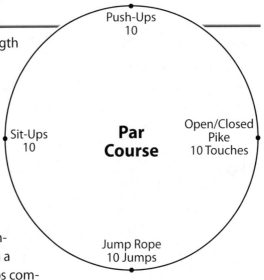

Push-Ups
10

Sit-Ups
10

Par Course

Open/Closed
Pike
10 Touches

Jump Rope
10 Jumps

 Activity 10: Intervals

Fitness Element Cardiovascular endurance

Equipment Whistle, 5-8 cones (optional)

Formation If possible, use a running track for this activity. If no track is available, use cones to mark a large circle on a gym floor or a field. All the players stand around the circle, not too close together, and all facing the same direction.

Directions Have a teacher or a student volunteer serve as the leader. The leader uses a whistle to signal how players should move. One blast on the whistle means walk, two blasts mean jog, and three blasts mean run. The leader varies the whistle commands, paying attention to the players' energy and to the temperature.

CHAPTER 1	Standards		Skills and Activities
	National	State/Local	
CHAPTER 1 *pp. 2–23*	National Health Education Standards 1.8.1, 2.8.1, 2.8.3, 2.8.4, 2.8.5, 2.8.7, 2.8.8, 5.8.2, 6.8.1, 7.8.2		**HEALTH INVENTORY**, *p. 3* **BUILDING HEALTH SKILLS** *Analyzing Influences* Analyzing Influences, *pp. 18–19* **HANDS-ON HEALTH** Your Personal Health, *p. 20*
Lesson 1 **What Is Health and Wellness?** *pp. 4–7*	National Health Education Standards 1.8.1, 1.8.2, 1.8.5, 1.8.6, 1.8.7, 1.8.8, 1.8.9, 3.8.1, 3.8.2, 6.8.1, 6.8.2, 7.8.1, 7.8.2		**Careers for the 21st Century** Registered Nurse, *p. 5*
Lesson 2 **Changes During the Teen Years** *pp. 8–12*	National Health Education Standards 1.8.2, 2.8.1, 2.8.4, 3.8.2, 4.8.2, 4.8.4, 5.8.3, 5.8.4, 5.8.6, 6.8.1, 6.8.4, 7.8.1, 7.8.2, 8.8.1		**What Teens Think** What is one of the greatest challenges for teens today? *p. 9* **DEVELOPING GOOD CHARACTER** Your Growing Responsibility, *p. 9* **HEALTH SKILLS ACTIVITY** *Practicing Healthful Behaviors* Making Health a Habit as You Grow, *p. 11* **Go Online** Turning Peer Pressure Around, *p. 12*
Lesson 3 **Taking Responsibility for Your Health** *pp. 13–17*	National Health Education Standards 1.8.1, 1.8.5, 1.8.6, 1.8.7, 1.8.8, 1.8.9, 2.8.7, 2.8.8, 2.8.9, 3.8.2, 3.8.4, 5.8.2, 5.8.5, 5.8.6, 5.8.7, 6.8.1, 6.8.2, 7.8.1, 7.8.2, 8.8.1		**DEVELOPING GOOD CHARACTER** Self-Discipline, *p. 14*

PACING THE CHAPTER					
Lesson 1	45 min				
Lesson 2	45 min	**Chapter Review**	45 min	**Hands-on Health**	20 min
Lesson 3	45 min	**Building Health Skills**	45 min		

BLOCK SCHEDULING

For block scheduling, assign students Building Health Skills feature *Analyzing Influences*, pages 18–19, and Guided Reading and Writing. 📁

Planning Guide

StudentWorks™ Plus

Glencoe Exclusive!
TeacherWorks™ Plus
All-In-One Planner and Resource Center

Reproducible Resources	Assessment	Media and Technology
Chapter FAST FILE Resources Chapter Summaries and Activities REVIEW Building Health Skills Activity TEACH Performance Assessment Activity EXTEND Universal Access Activities TEACH Parent Letter and Activities 📁 **Student Activities Workbook** TEACH 📁 **Reading Tutor** TEACH	Building Health Skills Activity, *pp. 18–19* Chapter 1 Assessment, *pp. 22–23* **Chapter FAST FILE Resources** Performance Assessment Activity, *p. 4* Chapter 1 Test, *p. 7* 💿 *ExamView® Assessment Suite*	**TeacherWorks™ Plus** includes: • Interactive Teacher Edition • Lesson Planner with Calendar • Access to all blackline masters • Correlations to standards 💿 StudentWorks™ Plus 🖱 Online Student Edition Dinah Zike's Teaching Health with Foldables®
Chapter FAST FILE Resources Concept Mapping Activity 1-1 REVIEW Cross-Curriculum Activity 1-1 EXTEND Enrichment Activity 1-1 EXTEND Lesson Plan 1-1 Guided Reading and Writing 1-1 TEACH Reteaching Activity 1-1 REVIEW	Lesson 1 Review, *p. 7* 🖱 Vocabulary PuzzleMaker 💿 *ExamView® Assessment Suite*	🖱 Vocabulary PuzzleMaker 💿 *ExamView® Assessment Suite* 💿 StudentWorks™ Plus ⬇ Transparency 1-1 **Go Online** glencoe.com
Chapter FAST FILE Resources Concept Mapping Activity 1-2 REVIEW Health Lab 1-2 EXTEND Enrichment Activity 1-2 EXTEND Lesson Plan 1-2 Guided Reading and Writing 1-2 TEACH Reteaching Activity 1-2 REVIEW	Lesson 2 Review, *p. 12* 🖱 Vocabulary PuzzleMaker 💿 *ExamView® Assessment Suite*	🖱 Vocabulary PuzzleMaker 💿 *ExamView® Assessment Suite* 💿 StudentWorks™ Plus ⬇ Transparency 1-2 **Go Online** glencoe.com
Chapter FAST FILE Resources Concept Mapping Activity 1-3 REVIEW Decision-Making Activity 1-3 EXTEND Enrichment Activity 1-3 EXTEND Lesson Plan 1-3 Guided Reading and Writing 1-3 TEACH Reteaching Activity 1-3 REVIEW	Lesson 3 Review, *p. 17* 🖱 Vocabulary PuzzleMaker 💿 *ExamView® Assessment Suite*	🖱 Vocabulary PuzzleMaker 💿 *ExamView® Assessment Suite* 💿 StudentWorks™ Plus ⬇ Transparency 1-3 **Go Online** glencoe.com

Chapter and Lesson Resources

The *Teen Health* resources are designed for differentiated learning abilities. You may want to use the coded items in this way:

REVIEW —activities to review or reinforce content
TEACH —activities to teach basic concepts
EXTEND —activities to extend or enrich lesson content

 OUT OF TIME?

Use Health Skills Activities *Making Health a Habit as You Grow,* page 11, or Developing Good Character, page 9.

Health Care for Adolescents

Preventive health care can have a positive impact on all three sides of a teen's health triangle. The American Medical Association recommends that physicians provide heath counseling about risk behaviors, such as smoking and unplanned pregnancy, as a part of their medical care. However, adolescents visit the doctor the fewest times per year of any age group. A study showed that the average teen visits the doctor less than two times per year.

In addition to medical care for illness and injury, an adolescent should receive one preventive checkup each year. During that visit, the teen's physical health is addressed with screenings for medical problems and administration of recommended vaccines. Dental health and vision are also usually addressed. During the visit, doctors can take the opportunity to counsel teens about risks to physical health, such as sedentary lifestyle, sexual activity, and alcohol, tobacco, or drug use.

During a preventive visit, doctors also have the opportunity to screen for mental/emotional problems, such as eating disorders, difficulties at school, and depression. A doctor may also address social health by asking about relationships with family and friends, dating, and violence in the school.

When teaching students about risk behaviors, prevention, and precautions, be sure to stress the importance of routine medical checkups, even for teens who feel healthy. Work with the school nurse to develop a list of resources for those who are experiencing difficulty in obtaining health care due to financial, language, or transportation barriers.

Common Risk Behaviors

There are many risk behaviors that threaten the health of teens. The Centers for Disease Control and Prevention (CDC) monitor these risk behaviors using the Youth Risk Behavior Surveillance Survey.

Students may not realize that unintentional injury is the leading cause of death for people their age. Risk behaviors that can lead to unintentional injury are one subset of the behaviors monitored by the CDC. For example, the leading cause of unintentional injury in teens is automobile accidents, yet more than 18 percent of teens rarely or never wear a seatbelt. Bicycle accidents are also a major cause of unintentional injuries in teens, but more than 85 percent of teens reported rarely or never wearing a bicycle helmet when riding their bikes.

Homicide is the second leading cause of death among 15–24-year-olds. Behaviors that can lead to homicide, such as carrying a weapon on school property and engaging in a physical fight, are two of the behaviors measured in the Youth Risk Behavior Surveillance Survey.

For ages 10–24, suicide is the third leading cause of death. Suicidal thoughts, having a suicide plan, and attempting suicide are all risk behaviors tracked by the CDC.

When students are learning about risk behaviors, lead discussions in which students connect risk behaviors to their consequences. Have students reflect on risk behaviors in their own lives that could be changed. The CDC and The National Center for Injury Prevention and Control Web sites have resources that can be used when discussing risk behaviors with students.

Support for Teaching Reading

 Reading Support

Reading Preview

Activating Background Vocabulary Ask students what comes to mind when they hear the terms *healthy*, and/or *wellness*. Create a word web on the board, placing these terms in the center. Record students' responses in the surrounding spaces. Guide students in a discussion of what constitutes good health and what things they need to do to keep their bodies, minds, and emotions healthy.

FOLDABLES Study Organizer *Dinah Zike's Reading and Study Skills for Teen Health* provides interactive graphic organizers that help students comprehend and retain health concepts as they read. Use the Foldable® on page 3 or find more Foldables® activities for the chapter on **Understanding Your Health** in the separate booklet, available in the TCR.

Lesson 1 What Is Health and Wellness?

Determining Main Ideas Ask students to identify the main ideas in the lesson. Guide them to the boldface headings and the key terms. Ask students to find the main idea in the first section. Guide them to answer "What is Health?" and to identify details regarding the areas of physical, mental/emotional, and social health that support the main concept of health.

Lesson 2 Changes During the Teen Years

Preview and Predict Show students how to skim the lesson title, headings, and captions to get an overall view of what the lesson is about. Direct students to write one sentence for each subheading, predicting what they will learn when they read that section. After they read, have students work in pairs to review their predictions and revise as necessary.

Lesson 3 Taking Responsibility for Your Health

Review and Remember Encourage students to read at a pace that lets them retain what they have read. Stop students during the reading process and ask them to review the key terms and to remember what they have learned so far. Ask: What are lifestyle factors? Are there consequences to risk behaviors? How can your attitude affect your health? Have students return to the text and reread to clarify remaining questions.

Post Reading

Multimedia Presentations Guide students in a discussion about the health triangle, physical changes for teens, and maintaining a healthy lifestyle. Have students work in pairs to develop an oral presentation for the class that incorporates audiovisual aids and technology and covers one of the areas involved in this lesson. Encourage students to use appropriate volume, stress, and pacing in presenting their information.

Key for Using the Teacher Wraparound Edition

Use this key to help you identify the different types of prompts found in the Teacher Wraparound Edition.

R **Reading Strategies** activities help you teach reading skills and vocabulary.

C **Critical Thinking** strategies help students apply and extend what they have learned.

U **Universal Access** activities provide differentiated instruction for students learning to speak English, along with suggestions for teaching various types of learners.

HS **Health Skills Practice** activities reinforce Health Skills concepts and help students apply these skills in their everyday lives.

W **Writing Support** activities provide writing opportunities to help students comprehend the text.

AL **Active Learning** strategies provide a variety of activities for presenting lesson content, including Quick Demos and engaging classroom projects that get students actively involved.

Key to Ability Levels

Teaching Strategies and activities have been coded for ability level and appropriateness.

AL Activities for students working above grade level

OL Activities for students working on grade level

BL Activities for students working below grade level

EL Activities for English Learners

Symbols

Transparencies

CD-ROM

glencoe.com

Print Resources

Understanding Your Health

Chapter at a Glance

Lesson 1 defines health, identifies the three sides of the health triangle, and explains how health habits affect wellness.

Lesson 2 describes physical changes that occur during the teen years, identifies the mental and emotional changes that hormones cause, explains how relationships may change, and explains how to practice healthful behaviors to improve total health.

Lesson 3 explains the role of lifestyle factors in a person's health, identifies ways to reduce risks, tells how abstinence benefits the three sides of the health triangle, and explains how to evaluate a source of health information.

R Reading Strategy

Interpreting the Photo Have students examine the photo. Ask: How would the activity shown benefit one's mental/emotional health? Sample answer: *Rafting is a type of exercise that raises the heart rate and burns calories. Most physical activity helps improve a person's mental outlook and general sense of wellbeing.* Then have students answer the caption question. OL

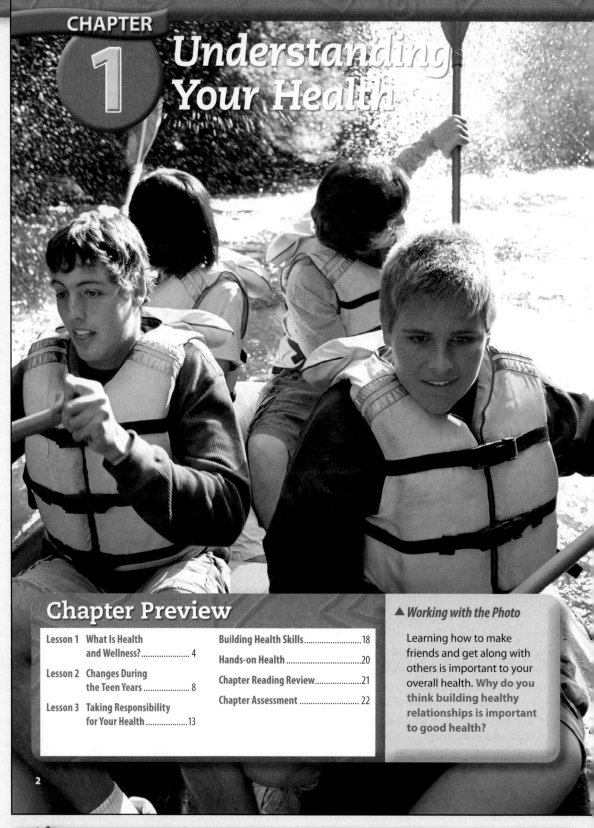

CHAPTER
1
Understanding Your Health

Chapter Preview

2

▲ Working with the Photo

Learning how to make friends and get along with others is important to your overall health. **Why do you think building healthy relationships is important to good health?**

👥 Universal Access

Differentiated Learning Glencoe provides teacher support and student materials for all learners in the health classroom.

- Spanish Glosario and chapter summaries for the English Language Learners.
- *Reading Tutor* and related worksheets support reluctant readers.

- Universal Access strategies throughout the Teacher Wraparound Edition and Fast Files help you present materials for gifted students, at-risk students, physically impaired students, and those with behavior disorders or learning disabilities.

Start-Up Activities

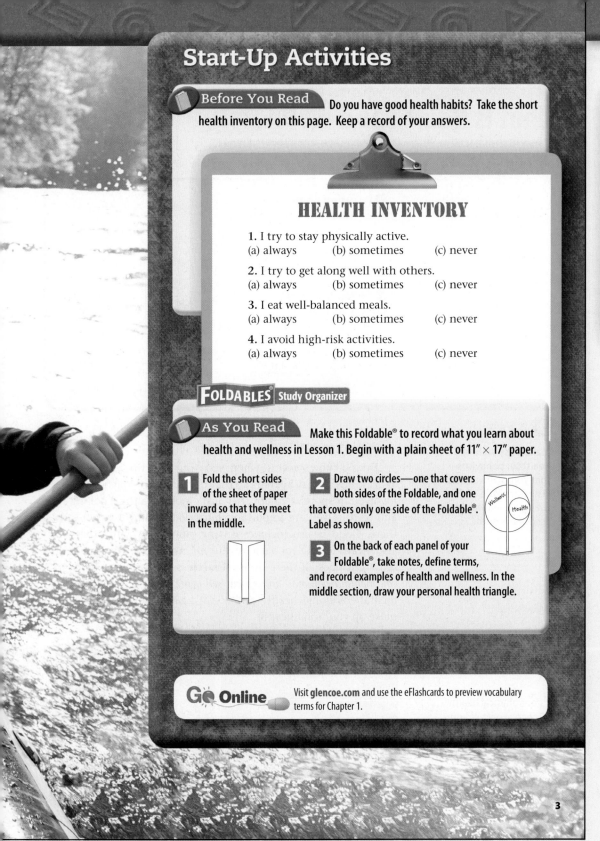

Before You Read Do you have good health habits? Take the short health inventory on this page. Keep a record of your answers.

HEALTH INVENTORY

1. I try to stay physically active.
(a) always   (b) sometimes   (c) never

2. I try to get along well with others.
(a) always   (b) sometimes   (c) never

3. I eat well-balanced meals.
(a) always   (b) sometimes   (c) never

4. I avoid high-risk activities.
(a) always   (b) sometimes   (c) never

FOLDABLES Study Organizer

As You Read Make this Foldable® to record what you learn about health and wellness in Lesson 1. Begin with a plain sheet of 11″ × 17″ paper.

1 Fold the short sides of the sheet of paper inward so that they meet in the middle.

2 Draw two circles—one that covers both sides of the Foldable, and one that covers only one side of the Foldable®. Label as shown.

3 On the back of each panel of your Foldable®, take notes, define terms, and record examples of health and wellness. In the middle section, draw your personal health triangle.

Go Online Visit **glencoe.com** and use the eFlashcards to preview vocabulary terms for Chapter 1.

3

FOCUS

Activating Prior Knowledge

What I Know Ask students to describe what they think of when they hear the word *healthy*. Then challenge students to explain how *health* differs from *wellness*.

 Guide to Reading

Building Vocabulary
- Explain that the word part *-ness* means "the state or condition." Ask students to relate this to the meaning of the term *wellness*.
- Use Vocabulary PuzzleMaker to reinforce vocabulary terms.

Reading Strategy
Classifying Have students make a copy of the health triangle concept map on a piece of paper. Have students fill in their graphic organizer as they read the lesson.

 Have students use their Foldables® as they read Lesson 1.

Quick *Write*

To introduce the Quick Write, have students work as a class to brainstorm a list of healthful behaviors.

Academic Vocabulary

Accurate The text gives an accurate definition of health. Explain that *accurate* means "exact or free from error." Ask students to use the word *accurate* in a spoken sentence .

4

What Is Health and Wellness?

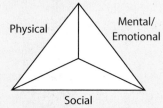 **Guide to Reading**

Building Vocabulary
As you read this lesson, write each new highlighted term and its definition in your notebook.

- health (p. 4)
- wellness (p. 6)

Focusing on the Main Ideas
In this lesson, you will learn to

- **define** *health*.
- **identify** the three sides of the health triangle.
- **explain** how health habits affect wellness.

Reading Strategy
Classifying Using the health triangle to the right as a guide, create a concept map that gives examples of each of the three types of health.

 Use the Foldable® on p. 3 as you read this lesson.

Quick *Write*

Make a list of three healthful behaviors that you can practice. List which side of the triangle each would be associated with.

What Is Health?

Do you know someone whom you would describe as "healthy"? What kinds of healthy traits do they demonstrate? Maybe they are involved in sports. Perhaps they just "look" healthy. Looking fit and feeling well are important, but good health does not stop there. Good health includes getting along well with others. It also means feeling good about yourself. An accurate definition of *health* includes all these traits. **Health** is *a combination of physical, mental/emotional, and social well-being.* Your physical health, mental/emotional health, and social health are all related and make up your total health.

▶ Your physical health is one aspect of your total health. **What are some positive ways of improving your physical health?**

4 Chapter 1: Understanding Your Health

Chapter *FAST FILE* Resources
Guided Reading and Writing 1-1
Concept Mapping Activity 1-1
Cross-Curriculum Activity 1-1
Reteaching Activity 1-1
Enrichment Activity 1-1
Lesson Quiz 1-1

Technology
Transparency 1-1
Audio Summaries
ExamView® Assessment Suite
Vocabulary PuzzleMaker
StudentWorks™ Plus
G⊙ Online

The choices you make and actions you take every day shape your health. Look back at the Health Inventory that opened this chapter on page 3. Your answers provide a first glimpse of your behaviors and decisions. In the pages ahead you will learn how your behaviors influence your health. You will also learn steps for making good decisions and ways of practicing good health habits.

Your Health Triangle

AL Total health is sometimes pictured as a triangle (see **Figure 1.1**). Each side represents a part of your total health. These sides are physical health, mental/emotional health, and social health.

Physical Health

Connie plays on the basketball team. Her sister, Danielle, walks to and from school. Both girls make regular physical activity part of their daily routine. How about you? Do you take part in behaviors that promote good physical health?

Registered Nurse

Registered nurses perform many duties, including treating and educating patients, giving advice and support to patients' family members, and operating medical equipment. There is a great need for registered nurses because people are living longer. The best way to get ready for a career as a registered nurse is to volunteer at a local hospital.

What kinds of facilities hire registered nurses? Go to *Career Corner* at **glencoe.com** to find out.

TEACH

Careers for the 21st Century

Registered Nurse
Have students meet in groups to read and discuss the information about this career. Also have group members work together to visit **glencoe.com** and learn about facilities that hire registered nurses. Then ask one group to find out about volunteer opportunities at local hospitals. Let these students share their findings with the rest of the class.

▶ FIGURE 1.1

THE HEALTH TRIANGLE

R Each picture shows a different side of health. The health triangle has three equally important sides. Which side deals with managing stress?

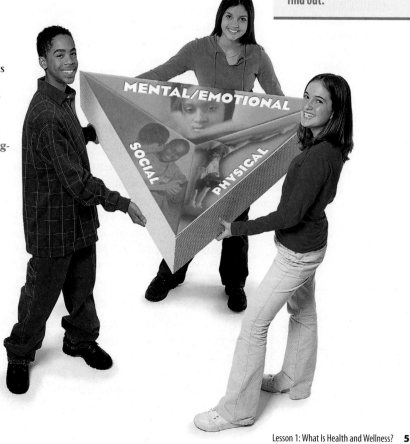

Lesson 1: What Is Health and Wellness? **5**

AL Active Learning

Role-Plays Divide the class into small groups. Have each group prepare and perform a role-play that demonstrates how the three sides of the health triangle are connected. Allow 10 minutes for the groups to write the role-plays, and then allot 5 to 10 minutes for practice. **OL**

R Reading Strategy

Analyzing a Graphic Have students examine **Figure 1.1**, which shows the three sides of health. Have students name other activities that could improve one or more of the three sides of health. **OL**

FITNESS ZONE

Physical Fitness and Your Health Triangle
After students have discussed the three sides of the health triangle, have them turn to the *Fitness Zone Handbook* at the front of their books. Let them read the introductory paragraph aloud, and then ask: Why do you think everyone should have a fitness plan?

How do you think having and following a fitness plan promotes health on all three sides of the health triangle? **For more information, see Fitness Zone Handbook pages xviii-1 or visit the Fitness Zone at glencoe.com.**

Caption Answers
Photo Caption, p. 4
Participate in a variety of physical activities.
Figure Caption, p. 5 mental and emotional health

Writing Support

Expository Writing Explain that having a positive attitude is a part of good mental/emotional health. Ask students to write a paragraph explaining how a positive attitude can also affect social and physical health. Remind students that expository writing is writing that explains or informs. Remind students to proofread their work and make any necessary corrections. **AL**

R Reading Strategy

Analyzing a Graphic Have students examine **Figure 1.2** on the next page. Ask each student to write a short paragraph that identifies his or her place on the health continuum. Have each student reflect on one change that he or she could make to move closer to peak health. Allow students to keep their work confidential. **OL**

Reading Check

Answer Exercising can build physical health, sharing feelings with a friend can improve mental/emotional health, and good communication can improve social health.

▲ Eating healthful foods for breakfast is one extremely important health habit during your growth years. **What are some other important health habits?**

Go Online

Visit **glencoe.com** and complete the Interactive Study Guide for Lesson 1.

You can improve your physical health in different ways. One way is by eating nutritious meals and snacks. Another way is to get regular checkups from a doctor and a dentist. You can also maintain good physical health by avoiding harmful behaviors. This includes avoiding alcohol, tobacco, and other drugs.

Mental/Emotional Health

Do you like and accept yourself? Are you able to handle challenges that come your way? Do you find positive solutions to problems? These actions are part of good mental/emotional health.

Your mental/emotional health also involves how you handle your feelings, thoughts, and the situations you face each day. You can improve your mental/emotional health by expressing yourself in a healthy way. This includes sharing your thoughts and feelings with a friend or with your family, and having a positive attitude.

Social Health

Do you get along well with friends, classmates, and teachers? Do you spend time with your family? Good social health includes supporting the people you care about. It also includes communicating with, respecting, and valuing people. The ability to keep and make friends is another mark of good social health. When you have good relationships with others, you feel cared for and respected.

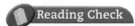 **Reading Check** **List** Name one way you can build good physical health. Do the same for mental/emotional health and social health.

Achieving a Healthy Balance

The three sides of the health triangle are connected. When one side changes, the other two are affected. For example, Sean awoke late for school this morning and did not have time for breakfast. Now it is mid-morning and Sean is having trouble paying attention in class. He also feels hungry and tired. Sean doesn't like feeling this way. His choice to skip breakfast is negatively affecting his mental and physical health. Being healthy means balancing all three sides of your health triangle.

Wellness and Total Health

When your health is in balance, you are more likely to have a high level of wellness. **Wellness** is *a state of well-being, or total health*. It is an indication of your current health habits and behaviors. Any decision you make can affect your wellness. Wellness is sometimes represented by a *continuum,* or scale, such as the one in **Figure 1.2.** It provides a picture of your health

Caption Answer

Photo Caption *Sample answer:* Exercising and good grooming are important health habits for teens.

Teacher to Teacher

Mary Capaforte   **Lufkin Road Middle School, Apex, NC**

Health Triangle
"On a blank sheet of paper, students will create their own personal health triangle. For each component of the triangle, have students write adjectives that describe themselves or activities they participate in that relate to that component."

triangle at any given time. It also lets you know if you are taking good care of your health, or if you need to improve your health habits. The pages ahead will give you ideas and suggestions for maintaining wellness. These ideas will help you achieve good total health now and in the future.

 Reading Check **Define** What is *wellness*?

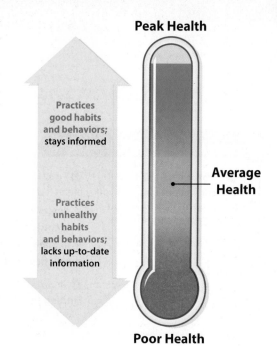

▶ FIGURE 1.2

R THE WELLNESS CONTINUUM

Personal health varies. Where would you place your health currently on the wellness continuum?

Peak Health

Practices good habits and behaviors; stays informed

Average Health

Practices unhealthy habits and behaviors; lacks up-to-date information

Poor Health

 Reading Check

Answer Wellness is a state of well-being, or total health.

ASSESS

Assessment Resources

Lesson Review Quiz
- *ExamView*
- Fast Files Activities
- Online Quizzes and Activities

Reteaching

- Assign Concept Map 1-1 or Reteaching Activity 1-1 in the Fast Files. 📁
- Have students write a sentence identifying three positive health habits and explaining how each affects total wellness.

Enrichment

- Assign Enrichment Activity 1-1 in the Fast Files. 📁
- Have students write a puppet show for younger students about the three sides of the health triangle. Arrange for students to present their puppet shows to other classes.

CLOSE

Call on students to explain the difference between health and wellness.

Lesson 1 Review

 After You Read

Review this lesson for new terms, major headings, and Reading Checks.

What I Learned

1. *Vocabulary* Define *health*.

2. *List* Name the three sides of the health triangle.

3. *Describe* What role do decisions play in wellness? What other factors affect a person's wellness?

Thinking Critically

4. *Evaluate* Kathy spends a lot of time with her friends. They watch movies, listen to CDs, and go shopping. Kathy gets good grades except in her physical education class. Evaluate which part of her total health could be out of balance. What

could Kathy do to improve this area of wellness?

5. *Apply* Masaki rarely catches a cold. Does this mean he has a high level of wellness? Why or why not?

Applying Health Skills

6. *Practicing Healthful Behaviors* Look back at your behaviors over the past week. What behaviors helped you improve your wellness? What behaviors brought down your wellness? What changes can you make to improve your total health? How important is it for you to assume responsibility for your personal health behaviors?

Go Online For more Lesson Review Activities, go to glencoe.com.

Lesson 1: What Is Health and Wellness? **7**

Lesson 1 Review Answers

1. Health is a combination of physical, mental/emotional, and social well-being.
2. The three sides of the health triangle are physical, mental/emotional, and social health.

3. Positive decisions increase your level of wellness. Other factors that affect your level of wellness include health habits and health knowledge.
4. Kathy needs to work on her physical health. She could ask her friends to exercise with her.

5. No, it simply means he has good physical health.
6. Help students brainstorm habits that can improve overall wellness. Students should explain ways that health behaviors influence health.

FOCUS

Activating Prior Knowledge

What I Know Ask volunteers to define and differentiate between the terms *adolescence* and *puberty*.

Guide to Reading

Building Vocabulary
■ Have students write a sentence that explains how two of the vocabulary terms from this lesson are related.
■ Use Vocabulary PuzzleMaker to reinforce vocabulary terms.

Reading Strategy
Finding the Main Idea
Have students write the main idea of the text under each heading using their own words, rather than copying a sentence from the text.

Quick Write

To get students started on the Quick Write, have them discuss ways that relationships can change. Respect student privacy during this activity.

Changes During the Teen Years

Guide to Reading

Building Vocabulary
Write definitions for terms you think you may know. As you read, make any corrections.

■ adolescence (p. 8)
■ puberty (p. 9)
■ hormones (p. 9)
■ peers (p. 12)
■ community service (p. 12)

Focusing on the Main Ideas
In this lesson, you will learn to

■ **describe** physical changes that occur during the teen years.
■ **identify** the mental and emotional changes hormones cause.
■ **explain** how your relationships may change.
■ **practice** healthful behaviors to improve total health.

Reading Strategy
Finding the Main Idea For each of the main headings in this lesson, write one sentence that states the main idea.

Quick Write

Write a paragraph about the ways in which your relationships with family and peers have changed over the past year.

Adolescence: Time of Change and Challenge

Next to infancy, the fastest period of physical growth is during **adolescence.** Also known as the teen years, this is *the stage of life between childhood and adulthood.* It is a time when you begin to form your own beliefs and values. Adolescence is a period of discovery. The object of discovery is *you.* Maybe without realizing it, you begin seeking answers to the question "Who am I?"

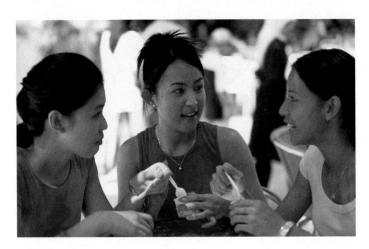

▶ Your teen years connect your childhood with your adult years. **What are some changes that take place during adolescence?**

Caption Answer

Photo Caption Physical growth and more mature behavior are two changes that take place during adolescence.

Lesson 2 Resources

📁 **Chapter *FAST FILE* Resources**
Guided Reading and Writing 1-2
Concept Mapping Activity 1-2
Health Lab 1-2
Reteaching Activity 1-2
Enrichment Activity 1-2
Lesson Quiz 1-2

Technology
🔌 Transparency 1-2
💿 Audio Summaries
💿 *ExamView®* Assessment Suite
💿 Vocabulary PuzzleMaker
💿 StudentWorks™ Plus
G⊙ Online

As a result of this search, you learn more about yourself and your abilities. You meet new people and have new experiences. You gain greater independence and take on new responsibilities.

These changes in life can be very exciting, but they can also be challenging, and even a little scary. The changes you experience during adolescence affect all three sides of your health triangle. You might grow a few inches, make some new friends, discover new interests, and experience mood swings—all within a short period of time. Knowing what to expect can make this a smoother transition.

Physical Changes

Josh couldn't believe his eyes the first day of school. His classmate Adrian had grown much taller over the summer. Growth spurts are a normal part of adolescence. Some, like Adrian's, can be quite dramatic.

In addition to growing taller, some of the changes that occur during adolescence include the growth of body hair and changes to the shape of your body. Boys may also notice that their voices are getting deeper. These and other changes are the result of **puberty** (PYOO·buhr·tee). This is *the time when you start developing physical characteristics of adults of your gender.* For girls, puberty usually begins between ages 8 and 14. For boys, puberty usually begins between ages 11 and 14.

The changes that occur during puberty are all related to the release of **hormones.** These are *chemical substances, produced in glands, that help regulate many body functions.* The changes hormones cause can make some teens feel uncomfortable. This is because the rapid growth during adolescence is sometimes uneven. Your hands and feet sometimes grow first, which may make them feel too big for the rest of your body. It is important to remember that puberty is a normal part of the growth process. You should be respectful of these changes in your peers and your peers should be respectful of these changes in you. If you have concerns, talk with a parent or other trusted adult.

 Reading Check **Explain** How do hormones relate to physical changes during adolescence?

 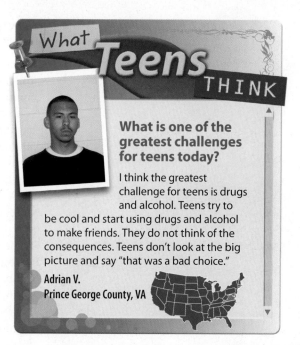

What Teens THINK

What is one of the greatest challenges for teens today?

I think the greatest challenge for teens is drugs and alcohol. Teens try to be cool and start using drugs and alcohol to make friends. They do not think of the consequences. Teens don't look at the big picture and say "that was a bad choice."

Adrian V.
Prince George County, VA

ACTIVITY
DEVELOPING Good Character

Your Growing Responsibility

The responsibilities you take on during adolescence prepare you for your adult years. Your current responsibilities may include helping with household chores, such as washing the dishes or mowing the lawn. You may also be responsible for looking after a younger brother or sister, or for walking the dog.

List responsibilities that you believe lie ahead. What responsibilities are you looking forward to?

TEACH

 What Teens THINK

What is one of the greatest challenges for teens today? Help students review the choices and risks they have read about in this lesson. Then read the *What Teens Think* question and let volunteers share their responses. Finally, have a volunteer read the *What Teens Think* response aloud, and let students share their reactions and opinions.

ACTIVITY
DEVELOPING Good Character

Your Growing Responsibility
Students may currently be responsible for looking after a younger sibling or for walking the dog. Have students list responsibilities they believe lie ahead as they mature. Then have volunteers describe some of the responsibilities they are looking forward to.

 Reading Check

Answer Many of the physical changes of adolescence are caused by hormones.

What Teens Want to Know

Is my growth normal? One of the most noticeable physical changes of puberty is a growth spurt. Teens may feel that their body is not developing normally if they experience their growth spurt before or after their classmates. Explain that, on average, females experience growth spurts two years earlier than males. During a growth spurt, an adolescent can grow at a rate of 4 to 6 inches in a year. Remind students that there is a wide variation in the age at which the growth spurt occurs. Explain that accepting differences in people shows maturity.

▲ Your emotional growth helps you better understand what others are going through. This enables you to become a source of support for them. **How could you help a friend who is feeling sad?**

Mental/Emotional Changes

Another change that occurs during adolescence is in the way you think and reason. You are able to face problems that are more complex. You are able to imagine the possible consequences of your actions. You begin to understand different points of view. You begin realizing that your choices affect others. Many teens also begin developing their own values and beliefs.

Adolescence brings emotional changes as well. Many teens experience mood swings. You may feel happy one minute and sad the next. These sudden emotional changes are caused by the release of hormones. Although mood swings can be confusing and even challenging, they are normal. It is important that you know how to use resources from home, school, and the community to help you deal with these emotional changes. If you are feeling alone, angry, or sad, talking to a friend, family member, or trusted adult can help.

Another emotional development that occurs during adolescence is feelings of attraction toward others. These feelings lead some teens to think about dating. However, not all teens feel ready or are interested in dating. These feelings develop at different times for different people.

An increased awareness in what is important to you is another emotional change experienced during adolescence. You may begin to understand how important your family, friends, and physical activity are to you. You might also realize that setting and achieving goals is important to you. You may also become aware of the importance of assuming responsibility for your personal health behaviors.

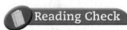 **Reading Check** **Describe** Tell how a teen's thinking is likely to change during adolescence.

Social Changes

Another change that occurs in adolescence is in your *relationships*. These are social connections you have with other people and groups. Healthy relationships are important to good social health. During adolescence you are likely to experience changes in your relationships with family, peers, and the community.

AL

U

Cultural Perspectives

Teen Dating One of the emotional changes of adolescence mentioned in the text is attraction toward others and dating. A teen's family, cultural background, and personal readiness may all affect if and when a teen begins to date. For example, students from certain social or cultural backgrounds may be forbidden to date. Keep in mind these widely varied attitudes toward teen dating when leading class discussions on this topic.

Health Skills Activity

Practicing Healthful Behaviors

Making Health a Habit as You Grow

Changes that occur during your teen years affect all three sides of your health triangle. Therefore, you need to develop good health habits for all three areas of your health. The health habits you develop now will have positive long-term effects on your health and wellness. Here are some examples of good health habits for each side of your health triangle:

PHYSICAL HEALTH
- Make physical activity part of your daily routine.
- Eat well-balanced meals and healthy snacks.
- Get plenty of sleep so you will have enough energy during the day.

MENTAL/EMOTIONAL HEALTH
- Think about possible consequences of your actions and behaviors.
- Talk to a friend or trusted adult when you are feeling sad or overwhelmed.
- Keep a positive attitude.

SOCIAL HEALTH
- Ask family members what you can do to help them instead of waiting to be asked.
- Be a good friend by listening and giving encouragement.
- Help out at a community event.

On Your Own

What are some strategies for improving and maintaining your personal health? What new health habits can you develop to improve your total health? Name at least one example for each side of your health triangle.

Family Relationships

You may no longer depend as much on parents or other family members as you once did. Now you are learning to act independently and to make decisions for yourself. Sometimes this can cause differences between you and your family members. For example, you may disagree with your parents on how late you are allowed to stay up at night. Despite your differences, keeping a positive relationship with your family is important to having good social health. Talking openly with your parents about your needs and feelings can help you maintain a good relationship with them. Spending time with all family members also helps you strengthen those relationships.

Go Online

Visit **glencoe.com** and complete the Interactive Study Guide for Lesson 2.

Health Skills Activity

Practicing Healthful Behaviors

Making Health a Habit as You Grow

Use the following strategies to help students complete the activity.

- Have students work individually to read the introductory paragraph and the bulleted lists of positive health habits. Then, lead a class discussion of other health habits that could be added to the lists.
- Challenge students to complete the On Your Own activity by identifying a new health habit they could develop to improve total health. Give students the following guidelines for selecting health habits to develop: they must choose at least one positive health habit for each side of the health triangle; the health habits they select must be habits that will be new for them; and the health habits must be realistic.

Dealing with Sensitive Issues

Importance of Families Family relationships have an impact on many teen risk behaviors, so it is important to discuss positive, healthful family relationships. Adolescents often have conflicts with their parents or guardians. In fact, a study by the U.S. Department of Health and Human Services found that 32 percent of teens in the United States find it difficult or very difficult to talk to their mothers about things that are bothering them. Point out strategies for managing potential conflicts and resources available to those who are having difficulties.

Caption Answer

Photo Caption, p. 10
Listening and offering encouragement are ways to help when a friend feels sad.

Reading Check

Answer A friend suggesting you study together is a positive influence.

ASSESS

Assessment Resources

Lesson Review Quiz
- *ExamView*
- Fast Files Activities
- Online Quizzes and Activities

Reteaching

- Assign Concept Map 1-2 or Reteaching Activity 1-2 in the Fast Files.
- Give examples of changes that occur during the teen years, classify the changes as physical, social, or mental/emotional, and explain how they are interrelated.

Enrichment

- Assign Enrichment Activity 1-2 in the Fast Files.
- Have students develop a presentation that describes ways to make healthy habits a part of everyday life.

CLOSE

Have students work in small groups to discuss common ways in which relationships change during adolescence.

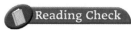
Go Online

Topic: Turning Peer Pressure Around

Visit glencoe.com for Student Web Activities to learn about different kinds of peer pressure and how you can deal with it in a positive way.

Activity: Using the information provided at the link above, come up with a list of at least five responses to negative peer pressure.

Peer Relationships

During adolescence, your friends and peers take on a greater importance. **Peers** are *people in your age group.* You may begin spending more time with your friends. Your opinions and behaviors will often be influenced by your peers. You may feel pressure to think and act like them. Peer pressure can influence healthful choices. Good social health includes learning to benefit from positive peer influence while resisting negative influences. Helping a friend with homework, volunteering with a friend, or simply listening to a friend are examples of positive peer influence.

Relationships with the Community

When you think of the word *community,* you probably think of your neighborhood. However, your community also includes your school and the city you live in. Social growth includes making positive contributions to your community. You might become involved, for example, in a neighborhood cleanup or park project. Many schools have begun sponsoring **community service** programs to get teens involved. These are *volunteer programs whose goal is to improve the community and the life of its residents.* These programs allow teens to help at different community events or help others in need. Many teens find community service to be a rewarding experience.

 Reading Check **Explain** In what ways can peer pressure be a positive influence?

Lesson 2 Review

After You Read

Review this lesson for new terms, major headings, and Reading Checks.

What I Learned
1. *Vocabulary* Define *puberty.*
2. *Identify* What are mood swings? What causes them?
3. *Recall* What are some physical changes that occur during the teen years?

Thinking Critically
4. *Analyze* Regi's cousin told her she is upset about differences she is having

with her parents. What advice would you give this teen if you were in Regi's place?

5. *Apply* What are two ways that you could become involved in your own community?

Applying Health Skills
6. *Analyzing Influences* Give two examples of how peer influence can positively affect a teen's decisions.

Go Online For more Lesson Review Activities, go to **glencoe.com**.

Lesson 2 Review Answers

1. Puberty is the time when the physical characteristics of adults develop.
2. Mood swings are sudden shifts in emotion caused by hormones.
3. These include changes in height and the shape of the body.
4. *Sample answer:* Regi might tell her cousin that it is normal for family relationships to change during adolescence.
5. *Sample answer:* I could help at the senior center or tutor younger students.
6. *Sample answer:* Peer influence can be positive if it encourages teens to participate in physical activity or to study.

Taking Responsibility for Your Health

Guide to Reading

● **Building Vocabulary**
As you read this lesson, write each new highlighted term and its definition in your notebook.

- lifestyle factors (p. 13)
- risk behaviors (p. 14)
- sedentary lifestyle (p. 15)
- cumulative risks (p. 15)
- precautions (p. 15)
- prevention (p. 15)
- abstinence (p. 16)
- attitude (p. 17)

● **Focusing on the Main Ideas**
In this lesson, you will learn to

- **explain** the role of lifestyle factors in a person's health.
- **identify** ways to reduce risks in your life.
- **tell** how abstinence benefits the three sides of your health triangle.
- **describe** ways in which you can take responsibility for your health.

● **Reading Strategy**
Predicting Quickly look at the main headings, figures, and captions before you read this lesson. Write down the sort of information you think this lesson will provide.

Choosing to Live Healthfully

Do you protect your skin from the sun's harmful rays? Do you get enough sleep so you are not tired in class? If a friend approached you with a problem, would you stop to listen? How you answer these questions reflects your personal **lifestyle factors.** These are *behaviors and habits that help determine a person's level of health and wellness.* These factors are related to the cause or prevention of health problems. Positive lifestyle factors promote good health. Negative lifestyle factors promote poor health. **Figure 1.3** on the next page lists some positive lifestyle factors.

▶ Protective gear is one type of safety precaution that can help reduce the risk of injury. **What are some others?**

 uick Write
What does the word *responsibility* mean to you? Write a brief definition. Then list the ways you show that you are responsible.

Lesson 3: Taking Responsibility for Your Health   **13**

TEACH

R Reading Strategy

Analyzing a Graphic After students have examined **Figure 1.3**, have them work in small groups to develop an infographic depicting a different situation that involves cumulative risks. Have students use art, text, and an equation format as shown in **Figure 1.4** to identify how risks add up. Have each group share its infographic with the class. OL

DEVELOPING Good Character

Self-Discipline
Have students write down one healthy habit that involves self-discipline and try to practice that habit during the week.

C Critical Thinking

Categorize After students have read the information about risk behaviors, have them work as a class to develop two lists of risk behaviors—those with immediate consequences and those with consequences that occur later in life. Some risk behaviors may be included on both lists. Have students justify their classifications. OL

Caption Answer
Figure Caption Answers will vary.

R ► **FIGURE 1.3**

POSITIVE LIFESTYLE FACTORS

Lifestyle factors affect your total health. **Which of these lifestyle factors do you currently practice?**

 Eating well-balanced meals, starting with a good breakfast.

 Getting at least 60 minutes of physical activity daily.

 Sleeping at least eight hours every night.

 Doing your best in school and other activities.

 Avoiding tobacco, alcohol, and other drugs.

 Following safety rules and wearing protective gear.

 Relating well to family, friends, and classmates.

Risks and Your Health

"Dangerous intersection. Proceed with caution." "Don't walk." "No lifeguard on duty." You have probably seen these signs or ones like them. They are there to alert you to possible risks or dangers and to ensure your safety.

Risks are an unavoidable part of life. Everyday tasks such as preparing food with a sharp knife or crossing a busy street both carry a degree of risk. Even when there are no signs to warn you, you have some awareness of risks. For example, you know that stairways carry a risk of falls. If you hurry or push through people on stairs, you increase your own and others' risk of getting hurt. Taking responsibility for your personal health behaviors is a part of growing into a responsible adult.

Risk Behaviors

Risk behaviors are *actions or behaviors that might cause injury or harm to yourself or others.* Some of these behaviors are obvious. Not using a crosswalk to cross the street is an example. Other risk behaviors are less obvious because the effects are not immediate. Even though you may not notice any immediate damaging effect, unhealthful lifestyle behaviors like smoking may have a lasting negative impact on your health. When you understand the short-term and long-term consequences of safe, risky, or harmful C

DEVELOPING Good Character

Self-Discipline

Developing a healthy lifestyle takes commitment. For example, you may need to remind yourself to turn off the TV or computer, and participate in activities that build good physical health.

What are some other ways you can show self-discipline?

TECHNOLOGY AND HEALTH

Sedentary Teens Leading a sedentary lifestyle is an increasingly common risk behavior of teens. Studies have found that the average student spends between 4½ and 5½ hours each day watching television, using video games, or using a computer. Have students develop a list of physical activities that could take the place of television viewing, computer use, or video game use. Have each student make a personal health goal to reduce sedentary behavior and increase physical activity. OL behavior, you will probably stop to consider the impact your behavior can have on your health.

Another risk behavior is a **sedentary lifestyle.** This is *a way of life that includes little physical activity.* Sitting in front of the TV or a computer is a sedentary behavior. Either becomes a risk factor when it continually replaces sports or other physical activities.

 Reading Check **Explain** What role do risky behaviors play in life?

Risks and Consequences

All risk behaviors have consequences. Some consequences are **minor** or short-term. For example, eating a candy bar too close to mealtime may prevent you from eating more of the healthy foods your body needs for proper growth.

Other risk behaviors carry serious and sometimes life-threatening consequences. These are long-term consequences. Experimenting with alcohol, tobacco, or other drugs is an example. These types of risk behaviors can seriously damage your health. Using these substances can affect all three sides of your health triangle. They can lead to dangerous *addictions*—physical and mental dependencies. These substances can cloud the user's judgment, increasing the risks he or she takes. Using these substances can also lead to problems with family and friends, and problems at school.

Risks that affect your health are further complicated when they are cumulative. **Cumulative risks** are *related risks that increase in effect with each added risk.* **Figure 1.4** on the next page shows an example of a cumulative risk that could be prevented.

 Reading Check **Define** What are *cumulative risks*?

Reducing Risks

Taking precautions can minimize the possibility of harm. **Precautions** are *planned actions taken before an event to increase the chances of a safe outcome.* You can use positive health behaviors to reduce some risks. Examples include checking the depth of water before diving and wearing a safety helmet when bike riding. Another strategy for reducing risks is **prevention.** This means *taking steps to keep something from happening or getting worse.* Prevention includes getting regular medical and dental checkups. Checkups can detect health or dental problems early, thus preventing the problems from getting worse.

AL

▼ The Internet is a good source for current health information. **How can staying informed help you maintain your health?**

Lesson 3: Taking Responsibility for Your Health **15**

HEALTH LITERACY

R **Reading Strategy**

Analyzing a Graphic Have each student focus on one positive lifestyle factor in **Figure 1.3** on page 14 and create a public service announcement encouraging teens to practice that healthful behavior. **OL**

W **Writing Support**

Focusing on Details After students have read the material under the heading *Choosing Abstinence,* have students write one or two sentences in their own words that state the main ideas of this section. Ask volunteers to share their sentences with the class. Have the class reach a consensus of the main ideas of the section. **BL**

Reading Check

Answer Abstinence maintains your family's trust in you, shows that you are responsible, and shows that you respect yourself and others.

▼ **FIGURE 1.4**

R ## CUMULATIVE RISKS ADD UP

Notice that each added risk brings about a result that is more severe. **What precautions could this person take to avoid a bad outcome?**

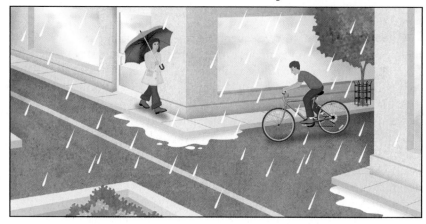

Blind intersection   +   Bad weather   +   Not wearing a helmet   =   **Disaster**

Go Online

Visit **glencoe.com** and complete the Interactive Study Guide for Lesson 3.

Choosing Abstinence

One of the most effective forms of prevention is **abstinence.** This is *the conscious, active choice not to participate in high-risk behaviors.* Often, the word *abstinence* is used in connection with avoiding sexual activity. As a preventive strategy, however, abstinence extends to any high-risk behavior. This includes the use of tobacco, alcohol, and other drugs.

Abstinence benefits all sides of your health triangle. It promotes your physical health by helping you avoid injury and illness. It protects your mental/emotional health by giving you peace of mind. When you avoid taking risks, you also avoid the pressure and worries that go along with these actions. Abstinence is a smart choice because it maintains your family's trust in you. It also benefits your relationships with peers and friends. Practicing abstinence shows that you are assuming responsibility for your personal health behaviors and that you respect yourself and others. **W**

Reading Check **List** Identify three benefits of abstinence.

Caption Answer

Figure Caption *Sample answer:* Wearing a helmet is a precaution that could help this teen avoid a bad outcome.

Cultural Perspectives

The Effect of the Media on Risk Behaviors Television and music are factors in American culture that have been linked to risk behaviors in teens. According to a study in *Pediatrics,* the amount of sexual content a teen views on television has an impact on teen sexual activity. The more time a teen spent viewing television and music videos, the more likely that teen is to start drinking. Discuss media influences that can lead teens to take part in risky behaviors. Have students develop recommendations for managing the influence of the media on health decisions. **OL**

Taking Responsibility for Your Health

Are you eager to take on more responsibility in your life? Many teens are. You can now begin by accepting responsibility for your health. You can choose behaviors that promote good health.

Staying informed is one way of taking responsibility for your health. Learning about developments and breakthroughs in health is an important part of maintaining your own health.

You will also have greater success in taking responsibility for your health if you keep a positive attitude. An **attitude** is *a personal feeling or belief.* Teens who have a positive attitude about their health are more likely to practice good health habits and take responsibility for their health.

Taking responsibility for your health means more than just recognizing healthy choices and risk factors. It means *believing* that good health habits can have a positive effect.

▼ Getting regular medical checkups is one form of prevention.

ASSESS

Assessment Resources

Lesson Review Quiz
- *ExamView*
- Fast Files Activities
- Online Quizzes and Activities

Reteaching

- Assign Concept Map 1-3 or Reteaching Activity 1-3 in the Fast Files.
- Ask volunteers to identify two health risk behaviors and describe ways to avoid those risks.

Enrichment

- Assign Enrichment Activity 1-3 in the Fast Files.
- Have students use presentation software to make a slide show explaining how to access reliable health information.

CLOSE

Ask students to describe how abstinence benefits all sides of the health triangle.

Lesson 3 Review

After You Read

Review this lesson for new terms, major headings, and Reading Checks.

What I Learned

1. *Vocabulary* What are *lifestyle factors*?

2. *List* What are some ways teens can reduce risks related to health problems?

3. *Explain* How does abstinence benefit all sides of your health triangle?

Thinking Critically

4. *Compare* Steve and Michael are brothers who both play on the school basketball team. Before practice, Michael takes a few minutes to stretch and warm up, but Steve does not. Compare and contrast the teens' methods for preventing injuries.

5. *Apply* Give an example of a cumulative risk that affects all three sides of your health triangle. Identify each risk.

Applying Health Skills

6. *Practicing Healthful Behaviors* Identify a positive lifestyle factor you would like to start practicing. Develop a plan for making this behavior a regular part of your life.

Go Online For more Lesson Review Activities, go to glencoe.com.

Lesson 3: Taking Responsibility for Your Health **17**

Lesson 3 Review Answers

1. Lifestyle factors are behaviors that help determine a person's level of health.
2. Eating healthy foods and being physically active are two ways to reduce health risks.
3. *Sample answer:* Abstinence prevents illness, gives you peace of mind, and helps maintain the trust of your family.

4. Michael takes precautions to avoid injury, but Steve does not.
5. *Sample answer:* Drug use affects physical health by causing addiction, mental/emotional health by affecting school performance, and social health by undermining family trust.

6. Help students develop realistic plans for incorporating the behavior into their lives.

Building Health Skills Analyzing Influences

Skill

Analyzing Influences

Activating Prior Knowledge

Ask students to identify some of the factors that influence their decisions.

- **Objective** After completing the activity, students will be able to identify external and internal influences on their decisions.
- **Time** 45 minutes
- **Materials** paper, pencil

Teacher Classroom Resources

📁 Building Health Skills Activity

🕹 Transparency 2-3

Model

- Have students read about the influences on Sebastian's decision. Ask: Why can Sebastian feel confident that he made a good decision? *Sample answer: He took the time to sort out all of the influences on his decision.*

National Health Standards Addressed

2.8.1, 2.8.3, 2.8.4, 2.8.5, 2.8.7, 2.8.8, 5.8.2, 6.8.1, 7.8.2

Building Health Skills

What Does Analyzing Influences Involve?

Analyzing influences involves recognizing the factors that affect your health choices. Theses factors include:

- Family and culture
- Friends and peers
- Messages from the media
- Your likes, dislikes, values, and beliefs

Analyzing Influences

Follow the Model, Practice, and Apply steps to help you master this important health skill.

① Model

Read how Sebastian uses the skill of analyzing influences to decide on a sport.

Sebastian was thinking of trying out for the volleyball team. His older brother said that he should continue a family tradition and try out for track instead. However, Coach Walker felt Sebastian would be a natural at volleyball because of his jumping ability. Sebastian's friends were encouraging him to try out for basketball.

Sebastian made a chart to look at the factors that were influencing him.

Factors That Are Influencing Me

Personal beliefs	I would like to play volleyball.
Friends	My friends want me to play basketball.
Family	Track is a family tradition.
Coach	Coach Walker thinks that I would be good at volleyball.

Sebastian realized that his personal beliefs affected him the most. He decided to try out for volleyball.

18 Chapter 1: Understanding Your Health

Teaching Tips

Being a Good Listener Explain to students that the skill of saying little or nothing (while waiting for the other person to speak) often feels awkward because we often want to dive right in and offer quick solutions to our friends. Sometimes, however, simply allowing the person to express their concerns without interruption is very helpful.

Using Skits Effectively Suggest students work in teams to prepare skits demonstrating how a teen recognizes influences. Be prepared to suggest topics for students to demonstrate this skill.

❷ Practice

Read the passage and then practice the skill of analyzing influences by answering the questions that follow.

Andrew used the skill of analyzing influences to help him plan a training program to prepare for soccer tryouts. He wants to run two miles every day to strengthen his heart and lungs. Andrew lives in a region that gets a lot of snow. This makes running outdoors difficult. He also needs to allow time for another school club. This club meets every Tuesday, after school. Plus, Andrew's father does not want him running after dark.

1. What factors have an influence on Andrew's training program?
2. In your opinion, which influences would affect Andrew the most? Explain.

❸ Apply

Apply what you have learned about analyzing influences by completing the activity below.

What activities do you participate in? Do you belong to any clubs or community groups? Do you take music lessons or play sports? Think about what influences your activities. Make a chart of your own influences and how they influence you. Identify which influence affects you most and tell why. Write one paragraph to explain how your activities affect your health triangle.

Self-Check
■ Did I analyze the influences on my choice of activities?
■ Did I explain how my health triangle is affected?

Building Health Skills

Building Health Skills **19**

Practice

● Divide the class into small groups. Ask students to read and discuss the Practice paragraph with their groups.
● Have each group prepare a chart listing the influences on Andrew's choice to include running as a part of his training program.
● Call on different groups to share influences they identified. Have each group name the influences it felt affected Andrew the most.

Apply/Assess

● Have students work individually to complete the Apply activity.
● Have volunteers share their results with the class.
● Lead a class discussion of the influences that were identified as most affecting students.
● Encourage students to describe how their activities affect the three sides of their health triangle.
● You may wish to distribute the Building Health Skills Activity in the Fast Files. 🗀

ASSESSMENT SCORING

Student work should meet all criteria to achieve the highest score.

Skills Student work:
● identifies influences.
● shows a variety of influences.
● addresses the relationship between influences and behaviors.

Concepts Student work:
● supplies accurate and comprehensive information about the health triangle.
● shows relationships between activities and health.
● makes factual conclusions about health.

HANDS-ON HEALTH

Your Personal Health

Time: 20 minutes
Materials: pencil or pen, paper

Introducing Hands-on Health

- Have students recall the three sides of the health triangle. Have a volunteer explain how each side is important for overall good health.

Teaching the Activity

- Have students make three vertical columns on a piece of paper.
- Assure students that they will be allowed to keep their answers confidential.
- Allow students 10 minutes to respond to the statements.
- After students have completed the inventory, have students score their responses.
- Have students write a short summary of their results identifying areas that need improvement.

HANDS-ON HEALTH

Your Personal Health

The personal health inventory that follows will help you find out if your health triangle is balanced.

What You Will Need

- pencil or pen
- paper

What You Will Do

Make three columns with the name of each side of the health triangle at the top of each column. Number the paper 1–5 for each health area. Think about each of the following statements and respond with a *yes* or *no* answer.

Physical Health

1. I eat well-balanced meals each day.
2. I get at least 60 minutes of physical activity daily.
3. I sleep at least eight hours a night.
4. I avoid the use of tobacco, alcohol, and other drugs.
5. I have good personal hygiene.

Mental/Emotional Health

1. I feel good about who I am.
2. I can name several things that I can do well.
3. I generally keep a positive attitude.
4. I ask for help when I need it.
5. I try to improve myself.

Social Health

1. I relate well to family, friends, and classmates.
2. I try to work out any differences I have with others.
3. I express my feelings in positive ways.
4. I treat others with respect.
5. I can say no to risky behaviors.

Wrapping It Up

Give yourself 1 point for each yes answer. A score of 5 in any area reflects excellent health. A score of 3–4 shows good health. If you score 0–2 in any area, plan to improve that part of your health triangle.

20 Chapter 1: Understanding Your Health

HANDS-ON HEALTH Assessment

Discussion Ask students: Why is it important to assess all three sides of the health triangle? Sample answer: *All three areas are important for good health.*

Why is a parent or trusted adult a good source of information about teen health? Sample answer: *Adults have been through the teen years and have experienced the changes I am now undergoing.*

Reading Review

Visit glencoe.com to download
quizzes and eFlashcards for Chapter 1.

FOLDABLES Study Organizer

Foldables® and Other Study Aids Take out the Foldable® that you created for Lesson 1 and any graphic organizers that you created for Lessons 1–3. Find a partner and quiz each other using these study aids.

Lesson 1 What Is Health and Wellness?

Main Idea The choices you make and the actions you take every day affect your health and wellness.

- The three sides of the health triangle are physical health, mental/emotional health, and social health.
- Health is defined as a combination of physical, mental/emotional, and social well-being.
- The behaviors and decisions you make will affect one or more of the three sides of your health triangle, which will in turn determine your degree of wellness.

Lesson 2 Changes During the Teen Years

Main Idea Adolescence is a period of rapid change and discovery.

- Physical changes that occur during the teen years include growth spurts, changes in body shape, the growth of body hair, and the release of hormones.

- During adolescence you develop a greater ability to solve more complex problems. You are able to recognize the consequences of your actions. You may experience mood swings. Also, you may develop feelings of attraction toward others.
- Relationships with family, peers, and friends may change. Adolescence is a time when you are learning to act more independently.
- Community service can be a rewarding experience for many teens.

Lesson 3 Taking Responsibility for Your Health

Main Idea Taking responsibility for your health means practicing healthful behaviors.

- Positive lifestyle factors promote good health, while negative lifestyle factors promote poor health.
- Sometimes the effects of risk behaviors are not immediate.
- Ways to reduce risks in your life include taking precautions, practicing prevention, and choosing abstinence.
- Abstinence is avoiding participation in high-risk behaviors. Abstinence promotes all sides of the health triangle: physical health by helping you avoid injury and illness; mental/emotional health by giving you peace of mind; and social health by maintaining your family's trust in you.
- Your health is your responsibility.

Chapter 1 Reading Review   **21**

Assessment Resources

- Chapter 1 Summary and Activity
- Audio Summaries
- Reading Tutor
- Performance Assessment
- Chapter 1 Test
- *ExamView*
- Vocabulary PuzzleMaker
- Online Learning Center

Reading Review

Study Aids

- **Using the Dinah Zike Foldable® Study Organizer** Have students use the Foldable® to review total health and wellness. Have them make a Venn diagram to compare and contrast the areas of the health triangle.
- **Online Learning Tools** Have students go to the *Teen Health* Online Learning Center at **glencoe.com** to:
  - Download a **Podcast**.
  - Download free **Study-to-Go** content to their PDAs or cell phones.

Vocabulary Review

- **Word Puzzles** Have students create their own word puzzles that include all of the chapter vocabulary terms and their definitions. Students can exchange puzzles and solve them.

Teaching Tips

Reading in Health Class Before students read each of the lessons, direct their attention to the Main Ideas, found on the lesson opener page. Have students copy each Main Idea onto a piece of paper, leaving space beneath each. Then, as students read the lesson, have them write supporting details and vocabulary terms under the appropriate Main Idea. After students have completed their reading, ask volunteers to share what they have written for each of the Main Ideas.

Reviewing Vocabulary and Main Ideas

1. Health
2. Wellness
3. adolescence
4. peers
5. hormones
6. Puberty
7. b
8. c
9. a
10. b

Thinking Critically

11. By recognizing that health also has mental/emotional and social sides, a person can take action to build all three sides of his or her health triangle. A healthful mental and emotional state is important for your overall health and wellness. Social health contributes to good mental/emotional health.

12. Answers might include the observation that such changes are a normal part of adolescence caused by the release of hormones.

CHAPTER
1
Assessment

After You Read

HEALTH INVENTORY

Now that you have read the chapter, look back at your answers to the Health Inventory on the chapter opener. Is there anything that you should do differently?

Reviewing Vocabulary and Main Ideas

On a sheet of paper, write the numbers 1–6. After each number, write the term from the list that best completes each sentence.

- adolescence
- health
- hormones
- peers
- puberty
- wellness

Lesson 1 What Is Health and Wellness?

1. _____ is a combination of physical, mental/emotional, and social well-being.

2. _____ is a state of well-being, or total health.

Lesson 2 Changes During the Teen Years

3. The stage of life between childhood and adulthood is known as _____.

4. Your _____ are people in your age group.

5. Chemical substances, produced in glands, that help regulate many body functions are called _____.

6. _____ is the time when you start developing physical characteristics of adults of your gender.

Lesson 3 Taking Responsibility for Your Health

On a sheet of paper, write the numbers 7–10. After each number, write the letter of the answer that best completes each statement.

7. A way of life that includes little physical activity is called a(n)
   a. cumulative risk.
   c. attitude.
   b. sedentary lifestyle.
   d. prevention.

8. Behaviors and habits that help determine a person's level of health are known as
   a. cumulative risks.
   b. sedentary lifestyles.
   c. lifestyle factors.
   d. risk behaviors.

9. You can reduce risks in your life by doing all of the following *except*
   a. becoming sedentary.
   b. practicing prevention.
   c. taking precautions.
   d. choosing abstinence.

10. All of the following statements are true of abstinence *except*
    a. It helps you avoid injury and illness.
    b. It applies only to avoiding sexual activity.
    c. It is a preventive strategy.
    d. It helps you maintain your family's trust in you.

Go Online Visit glencoe.com and take the Online Quiz for Chapter 1.

Go Online

Have students visit **glencoe.com** to take the Chapter 1 Quiz.

HEALTH INVENTORY WRAP-UP

Health Habits Ask students to review their answers to the chapter opener Health Inventory. Have students identify the side of the health triangle associated with each habit listed in the Health Inventory. Ask volunteers to use what they learned while reading the chapter to explain how each habit could contribute to overall wellness.

Thinking Critically

Using complete sentences, answer the following questions on a sheet of paper.

11. **Analyze** Why is it important to recognize that health is more than just looking good or feeling fit?

12. **Apply** What advice might you have for a friend who is concerned about mood swings she or he has been experiencing?

Write About It

13. **Personal Writing** Write a private journal entry describing some of the physical, mental/emotional, and social changes you are experiencing.

✦ Applying Technology

Healthy Habits

You and your partner will use Microsoft Word® and iMovie® to create a movie that discusses physical, mental/emotional, and social health.

- Write a five minute script that discusses one side of the health triangle: physical, mental/emotional, or social health. Be sure to discuss how the side you choose affects your total health.
- Make sure that your facts are accurate.
- Videotape your movie and import it into a new iMovie® file.
- Edit your movie for time and clarity.
- Save your project.

✦ Applying Technology

Healthy Habits
Equipment needs: Microsoft Word® and iMovie or similar software
Read and discuss the project instructions with students, and then have students choose partners. If computer time is limited, create a sign-up sheet and establish a time limit for each pair. Schedule time for students to share their completed movies with the rest of the class.

Write About It

13. **Personal Writing**
Students' journal entries will vary but should describe changes experienced during the teen years and express emotions that accompany these changes. Remember to respect student privacy by allowing them to keep journal entries private.

Standardized Test Practice

1. C
2. B

Standardized Test Practice

Math

The Centers for Disease Control and Prevention gathers data on teen risk behaviors. This table shows trends in several risk behaviors over a four-year period. Use the table to answer the questions that follow.

Selected Risk Behaviors Among Teens, 1999–2003			
Risk Behavior	1999	2001	2003
Rarely or never wore safety belts	16.4%	14.1%	18.2%
Rarely or never wore bicycle helmets	85.3%	84.7%	85.9%
Rode with a driver who had been drinking alcohol	33.1%	30.7%	30.2%

TEST-TAKING TIP

Make sure you understand the parts of a table. Read the title of the table. This will help you figure out its subject. Read each column heading and the label of each row.

1. Which risk behavior steadily decreased over the time span shown?
   A. Rarely or never wore safety belts.
   B. Rarely or never wore bicycle helmets.
   C. Rode with a driver who had been drinking alcohol.
   D. None of the above.

2. Which risk behavior is the most common among teens?
   A. Rarely or never wore safety belts.
   B. Rarely or never wore bicycle helmets.
   C. Rode with a driver who had been drinking alcohol.
   D. None of the above.

Test-Taking Tips

Charts and Tables Tell students that some test questions will require reading and interpreting a table, graph, or chart. Have students examine the chart on this page. Ask a volunteer to describe the data contained in the chart. Explain that reading column heads is the first step to using the data to answer the test questions.

CHAPTER 2 pp. 24–49	Standards		Skills and Activities
	National	State/Local	
	National Health Education Standards 2.8.3, 4.8.2, 4.8.3, 5.8.2, 5.8.4, 5.8.6, 6.8.1		**HEALTH QUIZ**, *p. 25* **BUILDING HEALTH SKILLS** *Refusal Skills* Saying No to Unhealthy Choices, *pp. 44–45* **HANDS-ON HEALTH** Sending "I" Messages, *p. 46*
Lesson 1 **Making Decisions and Setting Goals** pp. 26–31	National Health Education Standards 1.8.1, 2.8.1, 2.8.8, 2.8.10, 5.8.2, 5.8.3, 5.8.4, 5.8.5, 5.8.6, 5.8.7, 6.8.1, 6.8.2, 6.8.3, 6.8.4, 7.8.1, 7.8.2, 8.8.1		**DEVELOPING GOOD CHARACTER** *Respect, p. 28* **HEALTH SKILLS ACTIVITY** *Goal Setting* Achieving Group Goals, *p. 31*
Lesson 2 **Building Your Character** pp. 32–37	National Health Education Standards 1.8.1, 1.8.2, 1.8.7, 2.8.1, 2.8.6, 2.8.7, 2.8.8, 3.8.2, 5.8.6, 6.8.1, 7.8.1, 7.8.2		**DEVELOPING GOOD CHARACTER** *Being a "Good Winner," p. 34* **G Online** Making a Difference, *p. 36*
Lesson 3 **Developing Other Health Skills** pp. 38–43	National Health Education Standards 1.8.1, 1.8.2, 1.8.5, 2.8.1, 2.8.2, 2.8.3, 2.8.4, 2.8.5, 2.8.7, 2.8.8, 2.8.9, 2.8.10, 3.8.2, 4.8.1, 4.8.2, 4.8.4, 6.8.1, 6.8.3, 7.8.2, 8.8.1, 8.8.3		**What Teens Think** If you had a disagreement with a classmate, how would you handle it? *p. 40* **Careers for the 21st Century** Physician's Assistant, *p. 41*

PACING THE CHAPTER		
Lesson 1 45 min	**Chapter Review**	45 min
Lesson 2 45 min	**Hands-on Health**	30 min
Lesson 3 45 min	**Building Health Skills**	90 min

BLOCK SCHEDULING

For block scheduling, assign students Building Health Skills feature *Saying No to Unhealthy Choices*, pages 44–45, and Guided Reading and Writing. 📁

Planning Guide

Glencoe Exclusive!
TeacherWorks Plus™
All-In-One Planner and Resource Center

Reproducible Resources	Assessment	Media and Technology
Chapter FAST FILE Resources Chapter Summaries and Activities REVIEW Building Health Skills Activity TEACH Performance Assessment Activity EXTEND Universal Access Activities TEACH Parent Letter and Activities 📁 **Student Activities Workbook** TEACH 📁 **Reading Tutor** TEACH	Building Health Skills Activity, *pp. 44–45* Chapter 2 Assessment, *pp. 48–49* **Chapter FAST FILE Resources** Performance Assessment Activity, *p. 4* Chapter 2 Test, *p. 7* 💿 *ExamView® Assessment Suite*	**TeacherWorks Plus** includes: ● Interactive Teacher Edition ● Lesson Planner with Calendar ● Access to all blackline masters ● Correlations to standards 💿 StudentWorks™ Plus 💿 Online Student Edition Dinah Zike's Teaching Health with Foldables®
Chapter FAST FILE Resources Concept Mapping Activity 2-1 REVIEW Decision-Making Activity 2-1 EXTEND Enrichment Activity 2-1 EXTEND Lesson Plan 2-1 Guided Reading and Writing 2-1 TEACH Reteaching Activity 2-1 REVIEW	Lesson 1 Review, *p. 31* 💿 Vocabulary PuzzleMaker 💿 *ExamView® Assessment Suite*	💿 Vocabulary PuzzleMaker 💿 *ExamView® Assessment Suite* 💿 StudentWorks™ Plus ⚡ Transparency 2-1 **Go Online** glencoe.com
Chapter FAST FILE Resources Concept Mapping Activity 2-2 REVIEW Cross-Curriculum Activity 2-2 EXTEND Enrichment Activity 2-2 EXTEND Lesson Plan 2-2 Guided Reading and Writing 2-2 TEACH Reteaching Activity 2-2 REVIEW	Lesson 2 Review, *p. 37* 💿 Vocabulary PuzzleMaker 💿 *ExamView® Assessment Suite*	💿 Vocabulary PuzzleMaker 💿 *ExamView® Assessment Suite* 💿 StudentWorks™ Plus ⚡ Transparency 2-2 **Go Online** glencoe.com
Chapter FAST FILE Resources Concept Mapping Activity 2-3 REVIEW Health Lab 2-3 EXTEND Enrichment Activity 2-3 EXTEND Lesson Plan 2-3 Guided Reading and Writing 2-3 TEACH Reteaching Activity 2-3 REVIEW	Lesson 3 Review, *p. 43* 💿 Vocabulary PuzzleMaker 💿 *ExamView® Assessment Suite*	💿 Vocabulary PuzzleMaker 💿 *ExamView® Assessment Suite* 💿 StudentWorks™ Plus ⚡ Transparency 2-3 **Go Online** glencoe.com

Chapter and Lesson Resources

The *Teen Health* resources are designed for differentiated learning abilities. You may want to use the coded items in this way:

REVIEW —activities to review or reinforce content

TEACH —activities to teach basic concepts

EXTEND —activities to extend or enrich lesson content

 OUT OF TIME?

Use Health Skills Activities *Achieving Group Goals,* page 31, or Developing Good Character, pages 28 and 34.

Character Education

Character education is a term used to describe methods of teaching about and incorporating traits of good character into the school environment. Character education in schools takes many forms and ideally extends throughout all curriculum areas. In addition, effective character education in schools involves the intentional promotion of good character in student activities outside the classroom, such as sports, the lunchroom, and after-school activities.

The following tips provide some ideas for reinforcing traits of good character in the school environment:

- **Make character education a part of all subject areas.** For example, have students discuss traits of good character displayed by historical figures or characters in books.

- **Provide students with opportunities to serve others in the school environment or in the community.** Opportunities to work as a peer tutor, a big buddy for younger students, or as a community volunteer help students develop traits of good citizenship and caring.

- **Celebrate students who display traits of good character.** Recognize students who show honesty, integrity, and loyalty.

- **Stress cooperation by assigning group projects in the classroom.** Several times throughout the year, have the entire class work together to accomplish an assignment or project. Ask students to reflect on the skills required to work as a team rather than as an individual.

Influences on Teen Decision Making

The skill of decision making has a profound influence on the health of teens. Understanding the influences that affect teens' decisions can help educators prepare teens to make healthy choices when confronted with difficult decisions.

Influences on teens' decisions fall into two broad categories: internal influences, such as goals and values, and external influences, such as the opinions of parents and friends.

According to a study sponsored by SADD (Students Against Destructive Decisions), the relative importance of internal and external influences on decision making changes during the teen years. Younger teens' decisions about drug use and sexual activity are more influenced by external influences, such as peers, than those of older teens. Internal influences gradually become more important in decision making as a teen gets older.

This study found that close friends are the most important external influence cited by teens who have decided to use drugs, drink alcohol, or engage in sexual activity. Incorporating refusal skills and strategies for resisting negative peer pressure into discussions about decision making can help young teens to make healthy choices about these risk behaviors.

It can be difficult and embarrassing for students to discuss their own decision-making experiences. Discuss and provide practice in these skills using hypothetical situations and role-plays rather than asking teens to relate their own experiences or feelings.

Support for Teaching Reading

 Reading Support

Reading Preview

Activating Background Vocabulary Ask students what comes to mind when they hear the terms *values* and *good character*. List responses on the board. Next, ask students what they know about *decision making*. Guide students in a discussion of the connection that decision making has in developing values, life skills, and good character.

FOLDABLES Study Organizer *Dinah Zike's Reading and Study Skills for Teen Health* provides interactive graphic organizers that help students comprehend and retain health concepts as they read. Use the Foldable® on page 25 or find more Foldables® activities for the chapter on **Skills for a Healthy Life** in the separate booklet, available in the TCR.

Lesson 1   Making Decisions and Setting Goals

Identifying Sequence Have students scan the sections on the **Decision-Making Process** and the **Goal-Setting Process** in this lesson. Direct students to look for words that point to time order, steps in a process, or logical order of events. Encourage student pairs to choose one of these processes and practice the steps with one another.

Lesson 2   Building Your Character

Connecting Encourage students to link what they read in the lesson to their own character, their own life, and their own role models. Have students rephrase the bold headings from the lesson into personal questions, such as: What is *my* character? What traits of good character do *I* have? What has shaped *my* character? Who are *my* role models? Direct students to write their responses in a personal journal entry. Allow students to keep journal entries private.

Lesson 3   Developing Other Health Skills

Question-Answer Relationship (QAR) Help students identify the four task demands of questioning: "Right there" questions are text explicit, such as, "What is communication?"; "Think and search" questions are text implicit, such as, "What are the differences between refusal skills and conflict-resolution skills?"; "Author and you" questions require reading the text, such as, "Does the author think you should advocate on behalf of others?"; and "On my own" questions can be answered without reading, such as, "What causes you to feel stress?"

Post Reading

Dramatic Presentations Guide students in a discussion about strategies that can help them say no to others effectively. Reread the steps of the S.T.O.P. method. Have students work in groups to create a presentation for the class that incorporates main ideas from this chapter and includes a scenario demonstrating use of refusal skills in a challenging situation.

Key for Using the Teacher Wraparound Edition

Use this key to help you identify the different types of prompts found in the Teacher Wraparound Edition.

R **Reading Strategies** activities help you teach reading skills and vocabulary.

C **Critical Thinking** strategies help students apply and extend what they have learned.

U **Universal Access** activities provide differentiated instruction for students learning to speak English, along with suggestions for teaching various types of learners.

HS **Health Skills Practice** activities reinforce Health Skills concepts and help students apply these skills in their everyday lives.

W **Writing Support** activities provide writing opportunities to help students comprehend the text.

AL **Active Learning** strategies provide a variety of activities for presenting lesson content, including Quick Demos and engaging classroom projects that get students actively involved.

Key to Ability Levels

Teaching Strategies and activities have been coded for ability level and appropriateness.

AL Activities for students working above grade level
OL Activities for students working on grade level
BL Activities for students working below grade level
EL Activities for English Learners

Symbols

- Transparencies
- CD-ROM
- glencoe.com
- Print Resources

Chapter at a Glance

Lesson 1 describes how decisions affect personal health and the health of others, explains how to develop decision-making skills to make healthful choices, identifies the benefits of goal setting, and explains how to practice the goal-setting process to work toward an accomplishment.

Lesson 2 identifies the traits of good character, explains the role of tolerance in social health, describes qualities found in a good citizen, and explains how to practice the six main traits of good character.

Lesson 3 explains how to find reliable information, identifies influences on health, explains how to develop refusal skills to avoid certain situations, and describes how to practice refusal skills to avoid making unhealthy choices.

R Reading Strategy

Interpreting the Photo Have students examine the photo. Ask: What can you infer about this teen's goals? *His goals might be to run quickly, to win the race, or to beat a personal record.* What steps do you think this teen might have taken to achieve these goals? Sample answer: *joining a running club, running daily* **OL**

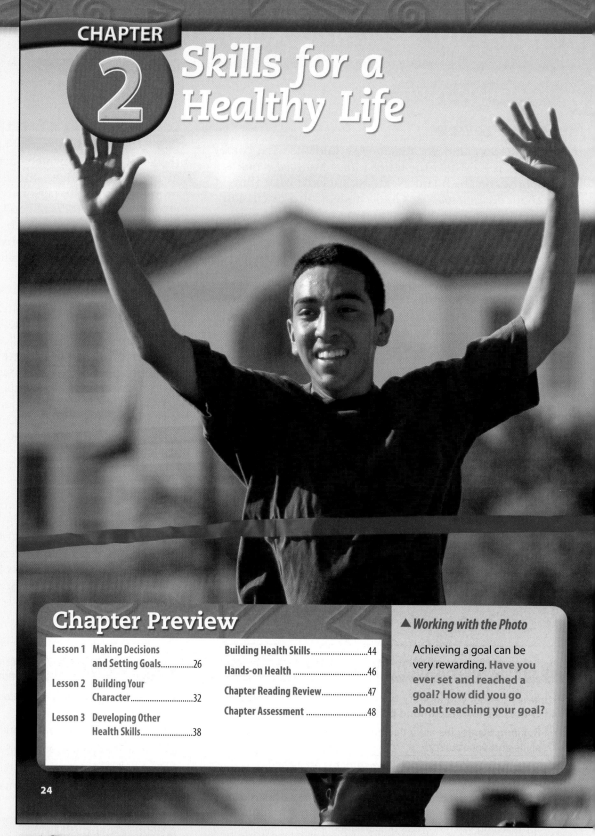

CHAPTER
2 Skills for a Healthy Life

Chapter Preview

24

▲ Working with the Photo

Achieving a goal can be very rewarding. **Have you ever set and reached a goal? How did you go about reaching your goal?**

Universal Access

Differentiated Learning Glencoe provides teacher support and student materials for all learners in the health classroom.

- Spanish *Glosario* and chapter summaries for the English Language Learners.
- *Reading Tutor* and related worksheets support reluctant readers.

- Universal Access strategies throughout the Teacher Wraparound Edition and Fast Files help you present materials for gifted students, at-risk students, physically impaired students, and those with behavior disorders or learning disabilities.

Start-Up Activities

Before You Read

Do you know how to make good decisions? Do you know how to set and reach goals in your life? Take the short quiz on this page. Keep a record of your answers.

HEALTH QUIZ Choose the best answer for each of the following questions:

1. All of the following are steps in making informed decisions *except*
   a. listing your options.
   b. weighing the possible outcomes.
   c. avoiding tough decisions.
   d. evaluating a past decision.

2. Setting goals helps you
   a. identify what you want out of life.
   b. use your time, energy, and other resources wisely.
   c. select goals that are realistic.
   d. all of the above.

3. All of the following are steps to take when setting a goal *except*
   a. set up checkpoints to evaluate your progress.
   b. make excuses for yourself if you do not achieve your goal.
   c. identify a specific goal and write it down.
   d. give yourself a reward once you have achieved your goal.

ANSWERS: 1. c; 2. d; 3. b.

FOLDABLES® Study Organizer

As You Read

Make this Foldable® to help you progress through the six steps of the decision-making process. Begin with a plain sheet of notebook paper.

1 Fold the sheet of paper from side to side, leaving a ½" tab along the side.

2 Turn the paper and fold it into thirds.

3 Unfold and cut the top layer along both folds. Then cut each tab in half to make six tabs.

4 Label the tabs as shown.

Under the appropriate tab, define terms and record information about each step in the decision-making process.

Go Online Visit **glencoe.com** and complete the Chapter 2 crossword puzzle.

HEALTH QUIZ

Health Skills Have students record their responses to the Health Quiz. Ask volunteers to share their answers to each of the questions. Use students' responses to generate a class discussion of the ways in which health skills affect all three sides of the health triangle. Remind students that they will have a chance to review and revise their answers after they have read the chapter.

No Child Left Behind

Technology in the Classroom

Technology can be used in many different ways in the health classroom. Computer research is a way in which students can access up-to-date information on the topics covered in the health curriculum. Discuss ways to access reliable information, for example, by using government and university Web sites. Students are directed to use the prescreened links provided at **glencoe.com** for research. Discuss the technology resources available at your school with the school's media specialist.

FOLDABLES® Study Organizer

Dinah Zike Foldables®

Decision Making Have students use their Foldables® to record the steps of the decision-making process. As students read about decision making, have them record the steps on the front of the Foldable® flaps. Then, have students record details about each step under the flaps. Students should then prepare a second Foldable® with the flaps labeled with the steps of the decision-making process. Have students use their second Foldable® to record details about a decision they have recently made. **BL**

Go Online

Have students visit **glencoe.com** and complete the crossword puzzle for Chapter 2.

FOCUS

Activating Prior Knowledge

What I Know Have students name some of their goals. List their responses on the board. Ask a volunteer to relate how decision-making skills relate to goal setting.

Guide to Reading

Building Vocabulary
■ Have students write a sentence that shows how the three vocabulary terms for this lesson are related.
■ Use Vocabulary PuzzleMaker to reinforce vocabulary terms.

Reading Strategy
Comparing and Contrasting
Check that students' charts show similarities and differences between decision making and goal setting.

 Have students use their Foldables® as they read Lesson 1.

Quick Write

Have them recall the various influences discussed in Chapter 1.

Making Decisions and Setting Goals

Guide to Reading

● Building Vocabulary
As you read this lesson, write each new highlighted term and its definition in your notebook.
■ decision making (p. 27)
■ values (p. 28)
■ goal setting (p. 29)

● Focusing on the Main Ideas
In this lesson, you will learn to
■ **describe** how decisions affect your health and the health of others.
■ **develop** decision-making skills to make healthful choices.
■ **identify** the benefits of setting goals.
■ **practice** the goal-setting process to work toward an accomplishment.

● Reading Strategy
Comparing and Contrasting Create a chart to compare and contrast the steps used in decision making and goal setting.

FOLDABLES Study Organizer Use the Foldable® on p. 25 as you read this lesson.

Quick Write

Identify an important decision you made in the last month. Explain what factors influenced your decision. Were you pleased with the outcome?

Decisions and Goals

Do you have privileges now that you did not have a few years ago? Maybe you are able to stay up—or out—later. Perhaps you make more of your own decisions, such as which clothes to buy. You might even have more say in how you spend your time and who you spend it with. As you grow older, you gain more freedom, but with it comes more responsibility. For example, you will be challenged to make decisions that are sometimes tough. You will need to understand the short-term and long-term consequences of decisions you make. Another responsibility is setting goals for yourself and planning how to reach those goals. Making decisions and setting goals will help give you purpose and direction in your life. These skills will allow you to focus on the future as well as the present.

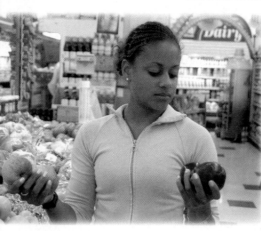

◀ Making good decisions is a skill you can learn. **What are some decisions you have made in the last week?**

Academic Vocabulary

Benefit Guide students in brainstorming synonyms for *benefit* (such as *help, assist, improve*). You will find academic vocabulary activities in the Student Activities Workbook. 📁

Lesson 1 Resources

📁 **Chapter FAST FILE Resources**
Guided Reading and Writing 2-1
Concept Mapping Activity 2-1
Decision-Making Activity 2-1
Reteaching Activity 2-1
Enrichment Activity 2-1
Lesson Quiz 2-1

Technology
🔦 Transparency 2-1
💿 Audio Summaries
⊙ *ExamView® Assessment Suite*
💿 Vocabulary PuzzleMaker
⊙ StudentWorks™ Plus
G⊙ Online

In this lesson, you will learn healthful skills for making decisions and setting goals that will **benefit** you now and in the future.

Making Responsible Decisions

Life is filled with decisions. You make plenty of them every day. Some decisions are small, like what to wear or what to eat for breakfast. Even minor decisions, however, can have major consequences. They could permanently change your life and the lives of others. One example is whether or not to fasten your safety belt before riding in a car. This is a small choice, but the consequences could be great if you were involved in a car accident. Wearing a safety belt is a decision that responsible teens make.

Parents trust responsible teens because responsible teens make healthful decisions. Parents feel comfortable allowing their responsible teens to express their independence. They may let their teens have a later curfew or spend more time alone or with friends. Independence is something that you should never take for granted. Responsible teens never use their independence to engage in risky behaviors.

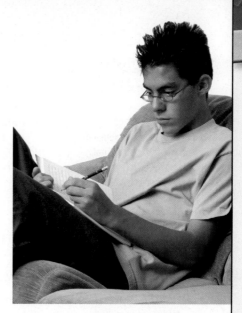

▲ The decision-making process can help you make responsible decisions. **Why is it helpful to write down the steps you take to reach a decision?**

 Reading Check **Give Examples** Give an example of a minor decision that can affect your health.

The Decision-Making Process

When faced with a decision, whether big or small, you want to make the best one you can. **Decision making** is *the process of making a choice or finding a solution.* It involves a series of six steps.

Step 1: State the Situation

The first step in making any decision is to identify the situation. One useful approach is to ask yourself questions. What choice do you need to make? Who else, if anyone, is involved? This first step is important because it sets the stage for making a decision that will affect your health.

Step 2: List the Options

Next, make a list of your options. It may be helpful to ask other people for suggestions. Make sure that your options are safe ones. Risking your health or the health of others is never an option.

Academic Vocabulary

benefit (BEN uh fit) *(noun)* an advantage; something that is good. *One of the benefits of eating healthy foods is having the energy to play your favorite sports with your friends.*

TEACH

AL Active Learning

Small Group Project Divide the class into small groups. Ask students if they are familiar with "play-by-play" sports broadcasting. Explain that this style of announcing a sporting event describes all of the action for those watching the event on television or listening on the radio. Have each group write a script for a "play-by-play" broadcast that describes a student using the six steps of the decision-making process in an everyday situation. Have each group share its broadcast with the class. OL

HS Health Skills Practice

Advocacy Have students create a poster that shows how the steps of decision making can be applied to an everyday situation. Ask each student to present his or her poster to the class. Obtain permission for students to display their posters in the hallways or school cafeteria. OL

Reading Check

Answer A minor decision would be choosing what clothes to wear on a particular day.

HEALTH LITERACY

Teens and Decisions Researchers investigating brain activity during decision making have found differences between the teen brain and the adult brain. The study suggests that the frontal lobes, which are involved in rational decision making, are less developed in teens. The study found that brain activity associated with decision making gradually shifted to the frontal lobes during the late teen and early adult years. This evidence underscores the importance of teaching the decision-making process and providing students with opportunities to practice this skill in class.

Caption Answer

Photo Caption This lets you go back and review your steps.

27

Respect

Have students work in small groups to read the feature. Then have each group make bulleted lists of ways that teens can show respect for themselves and for others. Go around the room and have various groups share entries from each of the lists. Then ask: What do the entries on the two lists have in common? *Sample answer: By avoiding alcohol use, I respect myself and I respect my family by following their rules.* **OL**

U Universal Access

English Learners Divide students into small groups. Have students recall a past event in which they had to make a decision. Each group should pick one situation and create a small role-play and/or dialogue. The role-play/dialogue should demonstrate why the student came to his or her decision and the considerations that the student took into account. **EL**

Respect

Liking and respecting yourself is important to good mental health. However, it is hard to do this when you make a decision that goes against your values. When you are faced with a difficult choice, you want to earn the respect of others, but more importantly, you want to respect yourself. Making healthy decisions shows that you respect yourself and your health.

What are some other ways of showing respect for yourself?

Step 3: Weigh the Possible Outcomes

The third step is to consider the possible outcomes, or consequences, of each option. One possible outcome of riding your bike without a helmet could be serious injury in the event of an accident. When weighing your choices, you might use the *H.E.L.P.* formula:

- **H (Healthful)** Will my choice affect my well-being or the well-being of those around me?
- **E (Ethical)** Will my choice show respect for myself and other people?
- **L (Legal)** Will I be breaking the law? Is it legal for someone my age?
- **P (Parent Approval)** Would my parents approve of my decision?

Step 4: Considering Values

When making a decision, always consider your values. **Values** are *the beliefs and principles that guide the way a person lives.* Kevin wore his safety helmet because he valued his health and safety. Honesty, respect, and trust are all important values. Can you think of some other values? Considering your values will guide you in the right direction as you make decisions.

Step 5: Make a Decision and Act

Once you have weighed your options and considered the risks and consequences, you are ready to take action. Choose the course that seems best and that supports your values. Make sure you are **U** comfortable with your decision and how it may affect others as well as yourself. If you are unsure about your decision, ask a parent or trusted adult for help. Some decisions may take longer to come to than others.

Step 6: Evaluate Your Decision

After you have taken action, you should evaluate the outcome of your decision. Did you expect the outcome to turn out the way it did? How did your decision affect others? Do you think you made the right decision? How did your decision make you feel about yourself? If the outcome was not what you had expected, use the decision-making process and try again. Think about what you could do differently. Talk to a trusted friend or adult if you need a second opinion.

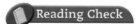 **List** What are the four parts of the *H.E.L.P.* formula?

Reading Check

Answer The four parts of the H.E.L.P. formula are Healthful, Ethical, Legal, and Parent Approval.

TECHNOLOGY AND HEALTH

Ethics and Internet Use When discussing legal and ethical decision making, have a class discussion about illegal downloads. Students may not think downloading copyrighted music or software from the Internet is stealing. Explain to students that copyrighted material is not free for the taking, and copying this material is against the law. Have students use online resources to research illegal downloads. Then have students make posters that can be placed throughout the school reminding others not to download copyrighted material without permission or payment. **OL**

Setting Realistic Goals

A realistic goal is one that you can reach. For example, running a mile in under ten minutes is a realistic goal. An unrealistic goal is one that you cannot reach. For example, no matter how much you try, you will never be able to run a mile in one minute. Achieving a realistic goal can be very rewarding. **Goal setting** is *the process of working toward something that you want to accomplish.* Health-related goals help you improve your physical, mental/emotional, and social health. What health-related goals can you set for yourself?

Types of Goals

There are two basic types of goals—*short-term* and *long-term*. Short-term goals are just that: goals you plan to accomplish in a short period of time. This might be a period of hours, days, or weeks. Short term goals may include doing well on a test or writing an e-mail to a friend. Long-term goals are those you plan to achieve within a period of months or years. These may include learning how to play an instrument or becoming a professional athlete. Often, long- and short-term goals are connected. Many short-term goals are stepping stones to achieving long-term goals.

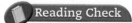 **Reading Check** **Identify** What are the two types of goals? How are they related?

The Goal-Setting Process

Like the skill of decision making, goal setting is a process. This process might be viewed as a road map to your accomplishments. It provides a well-defined plan you can follow. Another benefit of the process is that it helps you focus on achievable goals. Finally, this process helps you to make the best use of your time, energy, and other resources.

Step 1: Identify a Specific Goal and Write It Down

Instead of saying "I want to be a better baseball player," try to make your goal more specific. Chris's goal is to make the school's baseball team.

▶ Chris wants to eventually become a starter on the school's baseball team. **What are some short- and long-term goals of your own?**

W Writing Support

Narrative Writing Have each student write a narrative essay about a realistic goal he or she has set. Remind students that narrative writing tells a real-life story of actual events. Students' writing should include characters and a setting. Remind students to proofread their work before turning it in. To respect students' privacy, do not ask students to share their work with others. **OL**

AL Active Learning

Small Group Learning Have students work in small groups to identify one example of a long-term goal and four short-term goals that could be used as stepping stones to achieving that particular long-term goal. Ask each group to share its results with the class. **OL**

Reading Check

Answer Two types of goals are short-term goals and long-term goals. Short-term goals are stepping stones to achieving long-term goals.

Caption Answers

Photo Caption *Sample answer:* My short-term goal is to do well at the track meet. My long-term goal is to get a college scholarship based on my athletic achievements.

FITNESS ZONE

Physical Fitness Goals After students have discussed realistic goals and the difference between short-term goals and long-term goals, ask them to review the information about making a physical fitness plan in the *Fitness Zone Handbook.* Ask: *Why is it important to set realistic goals when you* *plan your fitness routine? How can short-term fitness goals help you reach your long-term goals?* **For more information, see *Fitness Zone Handbook* pages xviii-1 or visit the Fitness Zone at glencoe.com.**

C Critical Thinking

Interpreting Share the following quote by Dr. Martin Luther King, Jr.: "You don't have to see the whole staircase, just take the first step." Have a large group discussion on the following points: How does this quote relate to what you know about the Civil Rights Movement? How does this quote reflect the difference between short-term and long-term goals? Share a situation where you needed to take the first step without knowing what the whole staircase looked like. **AL**

Health Skills Activity

Goal Setting

Achieving Group Goals

Use these strategies to help students complete the activity on the next page.

- Divide the class into small groups. Have each group read the activity and select a worthy cause. If students are having difficulty, offer suggestions of causes that may interest them.
- Provide each group with six index cards. Have students use one index card for each step of the decision-making process. **OL**

 Reading Check

Answer Two steps in the goal-setting process are identifying a specific goal and listing steps to reach your goal.

Caption Answer
Photo Caption You will feel a sense of accomplishment.

30

▲ Often, just reaching your goal is the best reward of all. **How can reaching a goal be rewarding?**

Step 2: List the Steps You Will Take to Reach Your Goal

Achieving big goals can be easier when you break them down into smaller tasks. To achieve his long-term goal, Chris began by setting a short-term goal to improve his throwing and batting skills. He practices for one hour each weekday.

Step 3: Get Help and Support from Others

Identify people who can help you achieve your goals. Possibilities include your friends, parents, teachers, or other trusted adults. Chris's adult neighbor, Royce, who used to be on the school baseball team, is helping Chris train. Chris also practices with his dad, when he comes home from work.

Step 4: Identify and Overcome Specific Obstacles

Sometimes, you may run into a specific obstacle that prevents you from moving forward. Before continuing, you should identify this obstacle and consider ways to overcome it. If you cannot move past this obstacle, you may have to change your goal. Chris, for example, needs a baseball glove in order to practice his catching skills. He will need to borrow a glove from someone until he can save enough money to buy one.

Step 5: Evaluate Your Progress

Regularly check to see how well you are progressing toward your goal. Chris was able to measure his progress at the plate by keeping a record of his batting average. Evaluating your progress allows you to measure your success and adjust your plan to better reach your goal.

Step 6: Give Yourself a Reward

Celebrate your accomplishments. When you reach a goal, reward yourself. When Chris succeeded in making the baseball team, he rewarded himself by buying a new glove.

Go Online

Visit **glencoe.com** and complete the Interactive Study Guide for Lesson 1.

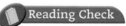 **Reading Check**

List Name two steps in the goal-setting process.

Teacher to Teacher

Patricia A. London   **Bermudian Springs Middle School, York Springs, PA**

Looking Out for One Another

"My eighth grade students create a booklet that includes health skills for new fifth graders to help them be successful and to provide them with a buddy they can turn to during the year. Fifth graders read and write responses to ideas, tips, and hints. Besides the cross-curricular benefits, the eight graders also feel responsible for the younger students and enjoy contributing to their middle school success."

Health Skills Activity

Goal Setting

Achieving Group Goals

Reaching group goals can be challenging. That is because groups are made up of individuals with different personalities, ideas, and skills. Reaching a goal as a group requires effective communication, respect, and teamwork. Imagine that your health class wants to raise money for an important cause. Use the goal-setting process to help you develop a plan to achieve this goal.

- **Identify a specific goal.**
- **List the steps to reach your goal.**
- **Get help from others.**
- **Identify and overcome specific obstacles.**
- **Evaluate your progress.**
- **Reward yourself.**

With a Group

Decide on a worthy cause you might raise funds for. Then, use the six-step process to map out a way of reaching your goal.

ASSESS

Assessment Resources

Lesson Review Quiz
- *ExamView*
- Fast Files Activities
- Online Quizzes and Activities

Reteaching

- Assign Concept Map 2-1 or Reteaching Activity 2-1 in the Fast Files.
- Have students work with a partner to apply the steps of decision making to an everyday situation. Call on several pairs of students to share their work.

Enrichment

- Assign Enrichment Activity 2-1 in the Fast Files.
- Have students write a fictional story about a teen who follows the steps in the goal-setting process to achieve his or her goal.

CLOSE

Have students describe the six steps in the goal-setting process. Then ask students to contrast short- and long-term goals and to explain how these two types of goals are related.

Lesson 1 Review

 After You Read

Review this lesson for new terms, major headings, and Reading Checks.

What I Learned

1. *Vocabulary* Define *values*. Use the word in an original sentence.

2. *Recall* What are the steps of the decision-making process?

3. *Identify* What are the benefits of using the goal-setting process?

Thinking Critically

4. *Analyze* How are the skills of decision making and goal setting related?

5. *Hypothesize* Sometimes goals need to be changed. What are some possible reasons for this?

Applying Health Skills

6. *Decision Making* You have to study for a big test. A friend calls to invite you to a party. Use the decision-making process to help you make a choice. Consider the short-term and long-term consequences of your decision.

Go Online For more Lesson Review Activities, go to glencoe.com.

Lesson 1: Making Decisions and Setting Goals **31**

Lesson 1 Review Answers

1. Values are the beliefs and principles that guide the way a person lives. Sentences will vary.

2. state the situation, list options, weigh possible outcomes, consider values, take action, evaluate your decision

3. The goal-setting process is a road map to your accomplishments. The process helps in setting achievable goals and using resources wisely.

4. Both include identifying a situation or specific goal, and both include evaluating progress.

5. *Sample answer:* Goals need to be changed if they are not realistic or if long-term goals change.

6. Answers should reveal an understanding of the decision-making process, as well as risks and benefits.

FOCUS

Activating Prior Knowledge

What I Know Ask students to describe a person of good character. Have students identify specific traits they expect a person of good character to have. List their responses on the board, and have students add to this list as they read the lesson.

Guide to Reading

Building Vocabulary
- Have students skim the lesson to find the definitions of the vocabulary terms. Then have students write a sentence that contrasts the terms *tolerance* and *prejudice*.
- Use Vocabulary PuzzleMaker to reinforce vocabulary terms.

Reading Strategy
Predicting Have students record their predictions as they preview the chapter. As students read, have them note which of their predictions were correct.

Quick Write

Have volunteers identify one of the good deeds on their list. Then have the class discuss how that trait shows good character.

Building Your Character

Guide to Reading

Building Vocabulary
Define the terms you think you know. As you read, revise your definitions as needed.
- character (p. 32)
- integrity (p. 33)
- tolerance (p. 34)
- prejudice (p. 34)
- accountability (p. 35)
- empathy (p. 36)

Focusing on the Main Ideas
In this lesson, you will learn to
- **identify** the traits of good character.
- **explain** the role of tolerance in social health.
- **describe** qualities found in a good citizen.

Reading Strategy
Predicting Quickly look at the main headings, figures, and captions before you read this lesson. Predict the kinds of information you think this lesson will provide.

Quick Write

Make a list of the good deeds you did this month. Which of these do you think reveal good character?

What Is Character?

How would you describe someone you know? You would probably mention what the person looks like—their physical appearance. You might also mention other qualities, such as what the person says and does. These qualities reveal a person's character. **Character** is *the way in which a person thinks, feels, and acts.*

Character involves understanding, caring about, and acting upon certain values. Most people around the world respect certain ethical values, such as trust, respect, responsibility, and fairness. **Figure 2.1** shows different factors that influence character.

Character in Action

Good character is not something you show only once in a while. It is part of who you are and how you live. By having good character, you promote not only your own mental/emotional health but the health of others. Having good character also builds good social health. It strengthens your relationships with others. For example, if you are honest, people will trust you. You also set a good example for others to follow.

There are six main traits of good character. These are *trustworthiness, respect, responsibility, fairness, caring,* and *citizenship.*

Lesson 2 Resources

 Chapter *Fast File* Resources
Guided Reading and Writing 2-2
Concept Mapping Activity 2-2
Cross-Curriculum Activity 2-2
Reteaching Activity 2-2
Enrichment Activity 2-2
Lesson Quiz 2-2

Technology
- Transparency 2-2
- Audio Summaries
- *ExamView® Assessment Suite*
- Vocabulary PuzzleMaker
- StudentWorks™ Plus

Go Online

▼ FIGURE 2.1

WHAT INFLUENCES CHARACTER?

There are many factors that can influence a person's character. **Can you think of other factors that are not shown here?**

Parents or Guardians	Stories
The earliest influence on your character was likely a parent or guardian. Parents or guardians are our first teachers of character.	Stories have morals. These are lessons that teach about values or character traits.

Life Experiences	Examples Set by Others
Experience is often a great teacher. Think about sports and games that build and reinforce character and values.	Role models inspire us to act or think in a certain way. They set good examples. What people do you look up to for inspiration?

Trustworthiness

At the beginning of this school year, Keith was given a key to his house. His parents explained that, as a teen, he was becoming more independent. They felt he could be *trusted* with this responsibility.

People who are trustworthy are reliable. They follow through with what they promise they will do. Suppose you agree to meet a friend after school to work on a project. If you are trustworthy, you show up at the agreed-upon location—on time. If you cannot make it, you let the other person know.

Trustworthy people are also honest, or truthful. This is a quality that cannot be compromised. You cannot be "a little honest" or "truthful some of the time." Honest people do not lie or give false impressions. They do not steal or cheat.

Trustworthy people have integrity. **Integrity** is *the quality of doing what you know is right.* Imagine seeing a wallet lying on the street outside your school. Would you keep it for yourself or return it to its owner? Even though it may be difficult, a person with integrity would make the second choice. At the very least, he or

Lesson 2: Building Your Character **33**

TEACH

R Reading Strategy

Analyzing a Graphic Have students discuss each of the influences on character that are shown in **Figure 2.1**. Ask: What are some additional influences on your character? *Sample answer: television and movies* Have students note whether each influence they identify is a positive influence or a negative influence. OL

U Universal Access

Reluctant Readers and Writers Prepare an outline that lists each of the six main character traits, with space underneath each. Then read aloud each section to students. Have students write down several key words or phrases that summarize the main idea of each section. BL

AL Active Learning

Lesson for Younger Students Have students make an illustrated picture book for students in grades K–2 that describes character traits of honesty and trustworthiness in a fictional story. Have students display their finished storybooks in the classroom. If possible, have students share their stories with younger students. OL

🏠 Home, School, and Community

In the Community Community service becomes a part of the school curriculum in service-learning programs. These programs, which tie in academic content with volunteer activities, have been shown to increase test scores and student motivation. Service learning can be implemented at any grade level, and many sources of information about service learning are available online. Have a class discussion of a community need that could be met. Have students brainstorm ways that meeting this need could tie in with a topic being studied at school. OL

Caption Answer

Photo Caption *Sample answers:* peers, friends, religious leaders, and political leaders

U Universal Access

At-Risk Students Students who take part in health-risk behaviors often have low self-esteem and frequently do not show respect for themselves, others, or property. Without singling out individual students, lead a class discussion of self-respect and self-esteem. Ask students to brainstorm activities and actions that can increase an individual's self-esteem. Then have students discuss ways that increased self-esteem leads to increased respect of self and others. **OL**

DEVELOPING Good Character

Being a "Good Winner" Have a class discussion of positive ways of behaving as a winner and being fair. Remind students that these skills do not apply only to sporting events. Have students think of other times that being a good winner is important, for example, when being awarded a part in the school play or a solo in the school band. **OL**

Reading Check

Answer Trustworthy people are honest, loyal, truthful, and reliable. Trustworthy people also have integrity.

Caption Answer

Photo Caption *Sample answer:* Yes, I have traveled to cheer for my school's team at "away" games.

34

▶ Loyalty is one quality of a trustworthy person. **Do you show loyalty to your school's teams? Describe an action you have taken that shows your loyalty to your school or community.**

she would take the wallet to the school office or lost-and-found. A trustworthy person is also loyal, or *faithful.* A loyal friend will not allow others to say untrue or mean things about you.

 Reading Check   **List** Name two qualities displayed by trustworthy people.

Respect

What does *respect* mean to you? You might say it means being polite, but respect is much more than that. When you respect people, you consider their feelings. For example, when you disagree with friends or family members, you listen to what they have to say without criticizing them. You also respect their wishes and never ask them to do things that are unhealthy or unsafe.

Showing respect also applies to yourself. When you respect yourself, you avoid dangerous situations and high-risk behaviors. You abstain from sexual activity and from using alcohol, tobacco, or other drugs. Respecting yourself means respecting your body. It means keeping yourself physically active and giving your body the rest it needs.

One element of respect that is especially critical in today's world is **tolerance.** This is *the ability to accept other people as they are.* We live in a society made up of people who come from different cultures and backgrounds. Learning about these groups and their customs can enrich your life. Tolerance can also be a tool for fighting prejudice, or intolerance. **Prejudice** is *an opinion or fear formed without having facts or firsthand knowledge.* Examples include negative opinions formed for no good reason, usually against a different racial, religious, or cultural group.

U

DEVELOPING Good Character

Being a "Good Winner"

It is just as important to be a "good winner" as it is to be a "good loser." Good winners do not taunt or tease their opponents. Instead, they look for ways to show them appreciation and respect.

What are some positive ways of behaving when you win?

Dealing with Sensitive Issues

Promoting Tolerance School populations have become increasingly diverse and include students from different racial, ethnic, and religious groups. Help students find ways to be tolerant of one another in the school setting and elsewhere.

Have students discuss ways in which the character traits of caring, respect, fairness, and citizenship contribute to, and are a result of, tolerance. Have a class discussion of the following quote: "The highest result of education is tolerance." —Helen Keller. **OL**

Responsibility

Think about some of the things you are responsible for now. You may be responsible for helping out with family chores. Maybe you are responsible for watering the plants, setting the table, or doing your own laundry. As you grow older, your responsibilities will increase even more.

With responsibility comes **accountability.** This is *a willingness to answer for your actions and decisions.* When you are accountable, you do not blame others for your mistakes. You accept the consequences for your actions.

 Reading Check **Give Examples** What are some behaviors that demonstrate trustworthiness, respect, and responsibility?

Fairness

Fairness is a character trait learned early in life. You may recall being taught the importance of sharing at an early age. In sports, being fair means obeying a set of rules. It also means including and being supportive of other players no matter their skill level, gender, or ethnic background. If you are fair, you keep an open mind. You are willing to listen to people whose opinions differ from yours.

Another quality shared by fair people is good sportsmanship. Life is filled with contests and competitions. Whenever two people compete, someone loses. A good sport is able to accept defeat gracefully. A fair person is a good sport, on and off the playing field.

▼ Responsibility includes following through with assigned tasks. **In which of these two scenes is the teen acting responsibly?**

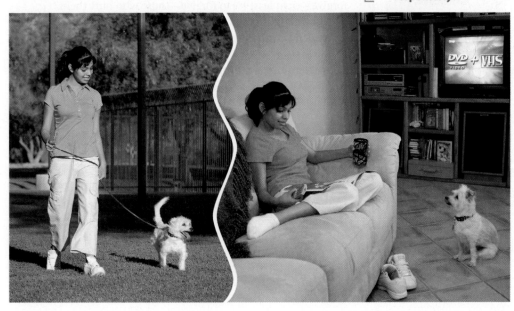

U Universal Access

English Language Learners Write the terms *responsibility* and *accountability* on the board. Explain that these words are nouns. Then, write the terms *responsible* and *accountable* on the board. Tell students that these words are adjectives, and can be used to describe a person. Have students use these terms in spoken sentences. **OL**

C Critical Thinking

Categorizing Have each student make three lists describing responsibilities they had as a young child, responsibilities they have now, and responsibilities they will have in the future. Call on students to name entries from each of their lists. Then ask students to identity positive and negative effects of having increased responsibility. **OL**

Reading Check

Answer Students' answers will vary.

🏠 Home, School, and Community

At Home Ask students to discuss ways in which the character trait of responsibility can be demonstrated at home. Explain to students that responsible behavior at home often increases the trust that parents have in their children. That can lead to parents or guardians trusting teens with more privileges. Remind students that one part of mature, responsible behavior is assuming responsibilities without being asked. Have students work as a class to generate a list of ways to show responsibility in the home. Have each student make a health goal to show the character trait of responsibility at home. **OL**

Caption Answer

Photo Caption The photo of the teen caring for the dog is showing responsibility because she is taking it for a walk.

35

▶ This teen volunteers his time tutoring other students. **What are some ways in which you could demonstrate the spirit of giving?**

Caring

When you care about others, you are kind to them. You consider their feelings by showing **empathy.** This is *the ability to understand and show concern for another person's feelings.*

Caring people do not try to take revenge when they feel mistreated. They do not think about ways to get even. Instead, they forgive—or at least *try* to forgive—those who hurt them.

One quality found in caring people is the spirit of giving. This does not mean giving material objects, such as *gifts*. Rather, it means giving of yourself, by sharing your time and talents. Rochelle helps out at a local homeless shelter on weekends by making sandwiches. Sal shares his knowledge of Spanish by tutoring other students at school.

AL
HS

📖 **Reading Check** **Define** What is the meaning of *empathy*?

Citizenship

Citizenship is the way you conduct yourself as a member of a community. Good citizens look for ways to improve their surroundings. They respect their community and its members. A "community" includes a neighborhood, a school, or a whole city.

As a good citizen, you also have a responsibility to protect your environment. You can do this by keeping your environment clean, conserving natural resources, and recycling. You can also

---

CHAPTER 2
Lesson 2

AL Active Learning

Slogan Have students work in pairs to develop a slogan to promote caring and empathy. Remind students that a slogan should be catchy and should sum up the character trait of caring in a few words or in a short sentence. Have students share their slogans with the class. **OL**

HS Health Skills Practice

Practicing Healthful Behaviors Have students work in small groups to write a short play about a teen who uses a caring response to defuse a potential conflict. After each group has performed its play for the class, lead a discussion of how the character trait of caring is related to the health skill of conflict resolution. **OL**

📖 **Reading Check**

Answer Empathy is the ability to understand and show concern for another person's feelings.

G⊙ Online

Making a Difference Be sure students follow school policies when surveying other teens. Remind them to respect personal privacy and keep information confidential.

Caption Answers

Photo Caption, p. 36 Students should name ways to share their time or talents in a caring way.
Photo Caption, p. 37 Conserving natural resources is a way to show good citizenship.

36

G⊙ Online

Topic: Making a Difference

Visit **glencoe.com** for Student Web Activities to learn about how teens can make a difference by taking action on issues that are important to them.

Activity: Using the information provided at the link above, interview other teens about an issue at your school. Then, post the results where other students can view them (with the permission of school officials).

Cultural Perspectives

Entertainers as Role Models Television, movies, and music are important parts of American culture. When students discuss traits of good character, have them discuss ways in which some professional entertainers demonstrate these traits. Students might also name examples of entertainers who do not demonstrate traits of good character. Have students discuss the relative amount of media attention paid to entertainers who do and those who do not display good character traits. Have each student write a paragraph naming an entertainer and explaining how they display one particular character trait. **OL**

encourage others to do the same. Picking up litter you see on the ground is one way to help.

Good citizens work at making the community a better place, not only for themselves, but also for future generations. One way to achieve this goal is to become active in your community. You can speak out, or look for ways to improve your community.

Visit glencoe.com and complete the Interactive Study Guide for Lesson 2.

ASSESS

Assessment Resources

Lesson Review Quiz
ExamView
Fast Files Activities
Online Quizzes and Activities

Reteaching

● Assign Concept Map 2-2 or Reteaching Activity 2-2 in the Fast Files. 📁
● Ask students to write down one of the traits of good character and describe one way that trait can be demonstrated in everyday life.

Enrichment

● Assign Enrichment Activity 2-2 in the Fast Files. 📁
● Have students create a photo essay about one of the traits of good character. Tell students that the photos or pictures they select should show the chosen character trait in action. The written portion should provide an in-depth discussion of the character trait.

CLOSE

Have students identify one specific trait of good character and describe how a person demonstrating that trait can make a positive impact on his or her home, school, or community.

◀ Showing concern for the environment is one way of demonstrating good citizenship. **What are some other ways of showing this character trait?**

Lesson 2 Review

 After You Read

Review this lesson for new terms, major headings, and Reading Checks.

What I Learned

1. *Vocabulary* What is *character*?

2. *Recall* Name the six traits of good character.

3. *Identify* How is giving related to the character trait of caring?

Thinking Critically

4. *Synthesize* How does intolerance affect others? How would you promote tolerance in your neighborhood?

5. *Apply* Larry sometimes leaves garbage on top of the lunch tables at school and assumes the janitor will pick it up. Does this action show good citizenship? Explain your answer.

Applying Health Skills

6. *Analyzing Influences* Many professional athletes try to be a positive influence on young people. As a group, research one such athlete. Be prepared to discuss your professional athlete's sportsmanship on and, if possible, off the field. What other character traits does this athlete demonstrate?

G℮ Online For more Lesson Review Activities, go to **glencoe.com**.

Lesson 2: Building Your Character **37**

Lesson 2 Review Answers

1. Character is the way in which a person thinks, feels, and acts.
2. trustworthiness, respect, responsibility, fairness, caring, and citizenship
3. Caring people are willing to share their time, talents, and resources with others.

4. *Sample answer:* Intolerance has a negative affect on everyone. It creates fear and negative opinions formed for no good reason. I would organize a block party in my neighborhood to promote tolerance. Everyone could get to know each other.

5. Larry is not showing respect for the custodian or responsibility for the school environment.
6. Students should identify and report on an appropriate athlete to research.

FOCUS

Activating Prior Knowledge

What I Know Ask students to describe how the skills of decision making and goal setting, which were discussed in Lesson 1, can positively influence a person's health. Then have students name other skills that are important for good health.

Guide to Reading

Building Vocabulary
- Have students skim the chapter to find the definition of the terms *communication* and *advocacy.* Then have students write a sentence explaining why good communication skills are important for the health skill of advocacy.
- Use Vocabulary PuzzleMaker to reinforce vocabulary terms.

Reading Strategy
Organizing Information Have students prepare a sheet of paper with two headings before they read the lesson. Then, as students read, they can add to their lists.

Quick Write

To help students get started on their Quick Writes, have them brainstorm a list of skills and talents.

Caption Answer

Photo Caption verbal and nonverbal

Developing Other Health Skills

Guide to Reading

● Building Vocabulary
Some of the terms below may seem familiar. Using a pencil, write the definition of words you think you know.

- communication (p. 39)
- refusal skills (p. 40)
- conflict resolution (p. 40)
- media (p. 41)
- stress (p. 43)
- advocacy (p. 43)

● Focusing on the Main Ideas
In this lesson, you will learn to

- **describe** ten important health skills.
- **explain** how to find reliable information.
- **identify** influences on your health.
- **develop** refusal skills to avoid certain situations.

● Reading Strategy
Organizing Information Arrange the health skills from this lesson in two lists. One list should contain skills that have to do with information and how it is passed along. The other should be a list of skills dealing with managing your health.

Quick Write

Write a paragraph about a skill or talent you have learned. Identify how this skill or talent has benefited you.

Skills for a Healthy Life

In Lesson 1, you learned about two important *health skills:* decision making and goal setting. In this lesson, you will learn about eight others. All ten of these skills appear in **Figure 2.2.** They are sometimes called life skills. That is because they can help you maintain good health now and in the future.

Developing good health skills will help you maintain your physical, mental/emotional, and social health. Health skills will help you develop positive health behaviors to prevent injury, illness, disease, and other health problems. Health skills will also help you communicate effectively and develop healthy relationships.

◀ Good communication is important to healthy relationships. **What are two types of communication?**

Lesson 3 Resources

📁 **Chapter *FAST FILE* Resources**
Guided Reading and Writing 2-3
Concept Mapping Activity 2-3
Health Lab 2-3
Reteaching Activity 2-3
Enrichment Activity 2-3
Lesson Quiz 2-3

Technology
🔦 Transparency 2-3
💿 Audio Summaries
⚙ *ExamView® Assessment Suite*
💿 Vocabulary PuzzleMaker
⚙ StudentWorks™ Plus
Go Online

▼ FIGURE 2.2

THE HEALTH SKILLS

R These ten skills affect your physical, mental/emotional, and social health. These skills can help you, not just during your teen years, but throughout your entire life. **How do refusal skills protect your health?**

Health Skills	What It Means to You
Accessing Information	You know how to find valid and reliable health information and health-promoting products and services.
Practicing Healthful Behaviors	You take action to reduce risks and protect yourself against illness and injury.
Stress Management	You find healthy ways to reduce and manage stress in your life.
Analyzing Influences	You recognize the many factors that influence your health, including culture, media, and technology.
Communication Skills	You express your ideas and feelings and listen when others express theirs.
Refusal Skills	You can say no to risky behaviors.
Conflict-Resolution Skills	You can work out problems with others in healthful ways.
Decision Making	You think through problems and find healthy solutions.
Goal Setting	You plan for the future and work to make your plans come true.
Advocacy	You take a stand for the common good and make a difference in your home, school, and community.

Communication Skills

The idea of communicating may seem obvious to you. You may be saying to yourself "I already know how to communicate." To understand communication skills, consider the difference between *hearing* and *listening*. Imagine that someone is speaking to you while your attention is elsewhere. Maybe you are in the middle of watching a TV show, or perhaps your mind is just wandering. In such cases, you may have *heard* the speaker's words without really listening to what is being said.

AL **Communication** is *the clear exchange of ideas and information*. Verbal communication involves a speaker or writer on one end, and a listener or reader on the other. Good communication involves speaking clearly and carefully. It also involves good listening skills. A speaker's message has meaning only if the listener receives it.

Communication also has nonverbal aspects, such as tone of voice. Often, how you say something is more important than what

Lesson 3: Developing Other Health Skills **39**

TEACH

R Reading Strategy

Analyzing a Graphic Have students examine **Figure 2.2**, which identifies the ten health skills. Have students make a list of the three skills that they feel are most important in their lives right now. Ask: Why do different students identify different skills as most important in their lives right now? Sample answer: *Different students are facing different challenges and have different goals.* Emphasize to students that mastering each of these health skills will have a positive impact on their total health. OL

AL Active Learning

Small Group Presentation Have students work in small groups. Provide each group with a different sentence written on a sheet of paper, each expressing a mood or emotion. Have each group member take a turn saying the assigned sentence, using nonverbal cues to indicate a different mood or emotion. After each group member has said the sentence, have the remainder of the class identify the emotions indicated by the nonverbal cues. When all of the groups have finished their presentations, lead a class discussion of the importance of nonverbal communication in everyday life. OL

Caption Answer

Figure Caption They keep you from engaging in risky behaviors.

Cultural Perspectives

Nonverbal Communication Although students are familiar with different languages, they may not know that there are vast differences in nonverbal communication between cultures. Asian cultures, for example, use fewer facial expressions than most Western cultures. People from some African and Caribbean cultures show respect by avoiding eye contact while speaking, while American speakers and listeners usually maintain eye contact. Have students investigate cultural differences in communication and share their findings with the class. OL

What **Teens** THINK

If you had a disagreement with a classmate, how would you handle it? Have students brainstorm a list of disagreements classmates might have; record their ideas on the board. Then divide the class into groups of four or five, and assign one of the topics of disagreement to each group. Have the members of each group discuss how they would handle that disagreement and then share their ideas with the rest of the class. Finally, have students read and comment on the *What Teens Think* response.

 Writing Support

Persuasive Writing Have students write a paragraph that uses facts to support the opinion that peaceful conflict resolution is an important health skill for teens. Remind students that persuasive writing uses facts to support an opinion. Have students edit and correct their work before turning it in. **OL**

Reading Check

Answer Refusal skills help you say no to an unhealthy or risky situation. Conflict resolution helps you solve a disagreement.

What **Teens** THINK

If you had a disagreement with a classmate, how would you handle it?

If I had a disagreement with a classmate, the way I would solve it is by compromising. I would take part of my idea and part of their idea. That way we will both be satisfied with the outcome. I have used this problem-solving technique before and it has always worked for me.

Jessica J.
Santa Clarita CA

you say. Body language is also a form of communication. Body language includes facial expressions and gestures.

Refusal Skills

Two other related communication skills are *refusal skills* and *conflict-resolution skills*. The first of these, **refusal skills,** are *communication strategies that help you say no to others effectively.* This skill is especially useful during your teen years. There may be occasions when you are asked to do something you do not want to do or that you are unable to do. Maybe you are not interested. Maybe the activity costs money and you are low on cash. Maybe it is an activity that goes against your values—something you feel is wrong or unhealthy. Even though using refusal skills can sometimes be challenging, they can help you stay true to yourself and to your beliefs. Also, other people will respect you for being honest about your needs and wants.

The steps for practicing refusal skills are based on the letters in the word S.T.O.P. This makes it easy to remember.

- **S**ay no in a firm voice.
- **T**ell why not.
- **O**ffer another idea.
- **P**romptly leave.

When you use refusal skills, show that you mean what you say by using strong body language. Strong body language includes eye contact, crossed arms, and a serious expression.

Conflict Resolution

Conflict resolution involves *solving a disagreement in a way that satisfies both sides.* Conflicts, or disagreements with others, are part of life. Learning to deal with them in a healthy way is important. Imagine that your favorite TV show is about to begin when a family member comes along and changes the channel. At such times, conflict-resolution skills can help you find a solution that satisfies everyone involved. Also, by using this positive health behavior, you can prevent conflicts from getting out of hand. Maybe the solution to this conflict is turning off the television and doing something else the family enjoys.

Reading Check **Compare** How do refusal skills differ from conflict-resolution skills?

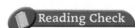 **What Teens Want to Know**

Why should I be involved in after-school activities? After school, a time when many teens are home alone, is a peak period for teens to make unhealthy decisions and to be exposed to negative influences. Studies have shown that teens who are involved in constructive, supervised after-school activities are less likely to use alcohol, drugs, or tobacco. This is also associated with a decrease in delinquency, arrests, and weapon use. Have students make a brochure describing the opportunities for constructive, supervised activities available to students at the school or in the community. **OL**

Accessing Information

Being informed means having correct, up-to-date information. Much of the health information you get comes from the media. The **media** are *the various methods for communicating information.* The media include newspapers, magazines, radio, television, and the Internet. Before you accept a report from any of these sources, you need to find out if the health information you receive is valid. Is the report based on research done by a respected institution? Or is it simply one person's opinion, unsupported by evidence or facts?

When you check the reliability of a source, you might ask your health teacher, school nurse, family doctor, or other trusted adult about the source. Any media source that sells products should be considered with caution.

Analyzing Influences

Analyzing influences involves recognizing factors that affect or influence your health. Some of these factors come from inside you. Others come from outside sources. **Figure 2.3** shows many of these sources.

▼ FIGURE 2.3

INFLUENCES ON YOUR HEALTH

**Several influences can affect your health.
Which of these influences affect you?**

Physician's Assistant

A physician's assistant can treat patients. They can also orders tests and prescribe medicines. There is a great need for physician's assistants because as the population grows, more people will need medical care. If you want to become a physician's assistant, you should take science classes and volunteer at your local hospital or clinic.

What kind of skills does a physician's assistant need? Go to *Career Corner* **at glencoe.com to find out.**

Physician's Assistant Have students read and discuss the information in their texts and at **glencoe.com**. Then ask: What do you think are the advantages of a career as a physician's assistant? What could be the disadvantages?

HS Health Skills Practice

Accessing Information Tell students that their parents or guardians, the school nurse, doctors, pharmacists, and other medical professionals are all excellent sources of information. Have students make a brochure that could be used by other teens, explaining how to obtain accurate answers to questions about health. **OL**

AL Active Learning

Real-World Connection Provide students with examples of health information from reliable sources. Have students evaluate the information. Then have students explain to the class how they can tell that the information is reliable. Ask: How can you verify the accuracy of this information? *Consider the source, look for documentation, or find supporting evidence at another source.* **OL**

TECHNOLOGY AND HEALTH

Health Information on the Internet Studies have found that 65 to 75 percent of teens and young adults have searched for health information on the Internet. For this reason, it is critical that teens know how to discern what information is reliable and what is not. Have students discuss situations in which the advice of a doctor or medical professional cannot be replaced by the Internet; for example, if a teen has symptoms that may indicate a serious problem. Have students write guidelines for finding reliable health information on the Internet that could be distributed by the school nurse. **OL**

Practicing Healthful Behaviors

The skill of *practicing healthful behaviors* can help you balance your health triangle. This skill involves taking care of yourself and avoiding risks. It includes developing health-promoting habits. The checklist in **Figure 2.4** explores some of these habits and behaviors. How many of these are part of *your* personal checklist? How does practicing health-promoting behaviors help you prevent diseases and other health problems?

▶ **FIGURE 2.4**

HEALTH BEHAVIORS CHECKLIST

Habits are things you do regularly and almost without even thinking about them. Establishing good habits are key elements for good health. **Which of these health habits do you practice every day?**

- ✔ I eat well-balanced meals, including breakfast, and choose healthful snacks.
- ✔ I get regular physical activity, and at least 8 hours of sleep each night.
- ✔ I avoid using tobacco, alcohol, and other drugs.
- ✔ I understand the health benefits of brushing and flossing my teeth regularly.
- ✔ I understand the benefit of wearing a safety belt every time I ride in a car.
- ✔ I stay within 5 pounds of my healthy weight.
- ✔ I practice good personal hygiene habits.
- ✔ I get regular, physical checkups.
- ✔ I can name several things I do well.
- ✔ I generally keep a positive attitude.
- ✔ I express my emotions in healthy ways.
- ✔ I ask for help when I need it.
- ✔ I take responsibility for my actions.
- ✔ I take on new challenges to improve myself.
- ✔ I relate well to family, friends, and peers.
- ✔ I have several close friends.
- ✔ I can disagree with others without becoming rude.
- ✔ I treat others with respect.
- ✔ I use refusal skills to avoid risk behaviors.
- ✔ I get along with all kinds of people.

Caption Answer

Figure Caption Answers will vary; students should indicate health behaviors from the checklist.

Stress Management

Do you get nervous just before a big test? How about when you have to speak in front of an audience? Do you get stage fright? These are symptoms of **stress**, which is *your body's response to change*. Stress is a normal part of life.

The health skill of *stress management* can help you develop strategies for managing stress. Some ways of **positively** managing stress include relaxation and exercise. In Chapter 3, You will learn coping techniques and ways to better manage your time.

Advocacy

To advocate for something means "to support it or speak out in favor of it." The health skill of **advocacy** means *informing others about health practices and encouraging healthful behaviors*. Some people choose careers as advocates. Their job is to raise the community's awareness of health issues and concerns. Advocacy includes warning people about possible risks and sharing knowledge of positive health behaviors. As you will discover, health advocacy goes hand in hand with citizenship. Advocating on behalf of others is part of growing into a mature, responsible adult.

 Reading Check **Define** What does *advocacy* mean?

Academic Vocabulary

positively (POZ i tiv lee) *(adverb)* with certainty, absolutely. *Listening to your favorite music is one way to positively manage stress.*

Visit **glencoe.com** and complete the Interactive Study Guide for Lesson 3.

 Lesson 3 Review

 After You Read

Review this lesson for new terms, major headings, and Reading Checks.

What I Learned

1. **Vocabulary** Define *communication* when used as a health skill.

2. **Recall** Give two examples of influences when making health decisions.

3. **Identify** What are two kinds of stress?

Thinking Critically

4. **Explain** Why is it important to practice refusal skills?

5. **Apply** Suppose you discovered that a factory in your community was dumping waste products into a local river. Explain how you could use the skill of advocacy to help put an end to this behavior. How could eliminating this risk factor prevent disease and other health problems?

Applying Health Skills

6. **Advocacy** Identify a problem in your school or city. Write an article for your school newspaper that will raise readers' awareness of this problem.

 Go Online For more Lesson Review Activities, go to **glencoe.com**.

Lesson 3: Developing Other Health Skills **43**

Lesson 3 Review Answers

1. Communication is the clear exchange of ideas and information.

2. *Sample answers:* personal ambitions and fears; peers and family

3. Two types of stress are positive stress and negative stress.

4. Practicing refusal skills gives you confidence when you say no to an unhealthy choice.

5. Students could advocate by writing a letter to the president of the company or writing a letter to the editor of a newspaper. Keeping water supplies free from waste products helps stop the spread of disease.

6. Remind students that an article is a form of expository writing that uses facts to inform others. Provide examples of editorials as models.

 Reading Check

Answer Advocacy means informing others and encouraging healthful behaviors.

ASSESS

 Assessment Resources

Lesson Review Quiz
- *ExamView*
- Fast Files Activities
- Online Quizzes and Activities

Reteaching

- Assign Concept Map 2-3 or Reteaching Activity 2-3 in the Fast Files.
- Ask students to explain each of the steps in the S.T.O.P. strategy. Then, ask volunteers to describe everyday situations in which the S.T.O.P. strategy could help them avoid unhealthy choices.

Enrichment

- Assign Enrichment Activity 2-3 in the Fast Files.
- Have students create a checklist that could be used by others to determine the reliability of a source of health information.

CLOSE

Have students name internal and external health influences.

Saying No to Unhealthy Choices

Skill

Refusal Skills

Activating Prior Knowledge

Have volunteers identify what each letter in the S.T.O.P. strategy stands for.

- **Objective** After completing the activity, students will be able to apply refusal skills to avoid unhealthy choices.
- **Time** 30 minutes
- **Materials** paper, pencil

Teacher Classroom Resources

📁 Building Health Skills Activity

🖱 Transparency

Model

- Have students work individually to read about Sam using refusal skills to avoid making a choice that goes against his values. Ask: Sam offered to go to a game with his friends on the weekend. What are some other alternatives Sam could have offered?

  Sample answer: Sam could have offered to have his friends over after the game to hear about the team's performance, or he could have offered to go to a night game sometime.

National Health Standards Addressed

2.8.3, 4.8.2, 5.8.2, 5.8.4, 5.8.6

Building Health Skills

- Accessing Information
- Practicing Healthful Behaviors
- Stress Management
- Analyzing Influences
- Communication Skills
- **Refusal Skills**
- Conflict Resolution
- Decision Making
- Goal Setting
- Advocacy

What Are Refusal Skills?

Refusal skills are strategies that help you say no effectively. If a peer asks you to engage in risky behavior, like drinking alcohol, remember the S.T.O.P. formula:

- **Say no firmly.** Be direct and clearly state how you feel. Use direct eye contact and keep your statement short.
- **Tell why not.** Use "I" messages to give your reasons.
- **Offer another idea.** Suggest an activity that does not involve the risky behavior.
- **Promptly leave.** If you have to, just walk away.

Saying No to Unhealthy Choices

Follow the Model, Practice, and Apply steps to help you master this important health skill.

① Model

Read how Sam uses refusal skills to help him say no effectively.

James told his friends he had three tickets to a baseball game. Sam saw that the game started at 3:00 P.M. He knew that going would mean cutting class and that would violate his parents' trust in him. Sam uses the S.T.O.P. strategy to help him say no effectively.

JAMES: Listen, Sam. Time is running out. We've gotta get going. Are you coming?

SAM: No. I'll pass. **(Say no in a firm voice)**

LOUIS: What is your problem?

SAM: I don't want to cut class. **(Tell why not)**

JAMES: Would you stop being weird? If we don't leave now, we'll be late.

SAM: Why don't we wait and go to a weekend game. **(Offer another idea)**

LOUIS: You've got to be kidding.

SAM: Later, guys. **(Promptly leave)**

44 Chapter 2: Skills for a Healthy Life

Teaching Tips

Learning New Skills Ask students how it felt to ride a bike, in-line skate, use a new computer program, or skateboard for the first time. (Students will probably say it felt awkward or not natural.) Explain that it is normal not to feel comfortable doing a new skill the first few times. Emphasize that with practice, however, using health skills such as refusal skills begins to feel more natural. Encourage students to stand in front of a mirror or use a tape player at home to practice refusal skills in a strong, confident voice.

❷ Practice

Help Jeff use the S.T.O.P. strategy to refuse negative peer pressure.

Form a group with two or three classmates, and read the situation below. Then write lines of dialogue for each of the boys. Use the S.T.O.P. strategy to show how Jeff refuses to do something wrong.

Jeff is with friends at the park. One of his friends dares him to take a bicycle. Show how Jeff can refuse by using the S.T.O.P. strategy. Write a paragraph to tell how refusing shows Jeff's character.

Your conversation should be guided by the following questions:

1. Does your dialogue follow the S.T.O.P. strategy?

2. Does your dialogue show how to refuse to do something wrong?

3. Do you tell how refusing shows character?

❸ Apply

Use the S.T.O.P. procedure to complete the activity below.

Choose one of the following situations. Working with a partner, write a skit that shows refusal skills in action. Perform your skit for the class and then explain how your refusal shows character in action.

Situation 1: *Someone offers you the answers to a test. The test begins in a few minutes.*

Situation 2: *You get a phone call inviting you to a party at a classmate's home. You are told that there will be beer at the party.*

Self-Check
- Did our skit follow the steps in the S.T.O.P. strategy?
- Did our skit show an effective way to resist pressure to do something wrong?
- Did we explain how our refusal shows character?

Building Health Skills

Building Health Skills **45**

Practice
- Have students work in small groups to complete the Practice activity.
- Call on groups to share how they applied the S.T.O.P strategy to this situation.
- Ask students to evaluate different groups' responses. Have students identify the strategies they feel would be most effective and give an explanation for their choice.
- Have students explain how Jeff's refusal shows his character.

Apply/Assess
- Have students work with a partner to choose a situation and write a skit.
- Have each pair of students perform its skit.
- After each group performs, have audience members identify how each of the steps in the S.T.O.P. strategy was demonstrated in the skit.
- Ask students to explain how their refusal shows character.
- You may wish to distribute the Building Health Skills Activity in the Fast Files.

ASSESSMENT SCORING

Using a rubric, student work should meet all criteria to achieve the highest score.

Skills Student work:
- uses the word "no."
- tells why not.
- offers another idea.
- leaves promptly.

Concepts Student work:
- provides accurate and comprehensive information about character.
- explains the relationship between refusal and character.
- draws factual conclusions about refusal and character.

HANDS-ON HEALTH ACTIVITY

Sending "I" Messages

Time: 30 minutes
Materials: pencil or pen, index cards

Introducing Hands-on Health

● Have students discuss the examples of "I" and "You" messages found in the introductory paragraph. Ask students to identify three reasons why an "I" message is a more effective way to communicate than a "You" message.

Teaching the Activity

● Have students work in pairs. Have each pair of students discuss the sample situations listed in the activity.

● Then have each pair of students identify an everyday situation and write a "You" message and an "I" message for the situation.

● Ask each pair of students to describe the situations and read their "You" and "I" statements.

● Then, as a class, have students discuss the Wrapping It Up Questions.

HANDS-ON HEALTH

Sending "I" Messages

Communicating effectively is especially important when there is a disagreement. When you use "I" messages, you express your feelings. "I" messages are unlike "you" messages, which place blame on the other person. To see the difference, compare these two statements:

■ **"You" message:** You always get your way! You're selfish!

■ **"I" message:** Sometimes I would like to have a say in what we do.

This activity will give you the opportunity to practice sending "I" messages. If you practice this skill, you will become a better communicator.

What You Will Need

■ pencil or pen   ■ paper

ACTIVITY What You Will Do

❶ Working in pairs, imagine an everyday situation in which "you" messages might occur. Think of your own "you" message. Write the situation across the top of the paper. Then write the "you" message below on the left. Change that same message into an "I" message, writing the "I" version on the right.

❷ Here are three sample situations:

■ Your older brother kept you waiting at the mall. He arrived an hour late and had no excuse.

■ A classmate told a lie about you.

■ Your sister borrowed something of yours and returned it in damaged condition.

❸ Read each "you" message to the class. Then read the corresponding "I" message.

Wrapping It Up

Was the "you" message or "I" message most effective? Explain why.

Think of a recent disagreement you had with a family member or friend. How could using "I" messages have helped resolve the conflict? How does practicing positive health behaviors, such as "I" messages, benefit your health?

HANDS-ON HEALTH Assessment

Discussion Ask students: How can "I" statements help to avoid conflicts? Sample answer: *By stating your own needs, rather than making accusations about someone else, you can avoid some disagreements.*

Ask: How can nonverbal communication play a part in making an "I" statement effective? Sample answer: *By using a nice tone of voice and a pleasant facial expression, you can help your listener be receptive to your message.*

Reading Review

 Visit glencoe.com to download quizzes and eFlashcards for Chapter 2.

FOLDABLES Study Organizer

Foldables® and Other Study Aids Take out the Foldable® that you created for Lesson 1 and any graphic organizers that you created for Lessons 1–3. Find a partner and quiz each other using these study aids.

Lesson 1) Making Desicions and Setting Goals

Main Idea Making decisions and setting goals will help give you direction and purpose in your life.

- Making healthy decisions shows that you respect yourself and your health.
- The steps in making healthful decisions include stating the situation, listing the options, weighing the possible outcomes, considering your values, making a decision, taking action, and evaluating your decision.
- Goal-setting skills enable you to have a well-defined plan to follow. It allows you to focus on realistic, achievable goals. It also lets you make the best use of your time, energy, and other resources.

Lesson 2) Building Good Character

Main Idea Character involves having, understanding, caring about, and acting upon certain values.

- Your character can be influenced by your family, life experiences, and examples set by others.
- Traits of good character are trustworthiness, respect, responsibility, fairness, caring, and citizenship.

- Tolerance is important to social health. It helps us accept people who are different from ourselves. Being tolerant helps us get along better with others.
- Good citizens obey the community's rules and laws, respect authority, protect their environment, and work to make the community a better place.

Lesson 3) Developing Other Health Skills

Main Idea Health skills will help you develop positive health behaviors to prevent injury, illness, disease, and other health problems.

- Habits are things that you do without thinking.
- Health skills can help you stay healthy now and in the future. They can improve and maintain your physical, mental/emotional, and social health.
- Ten important health skills are accessing information, practicing healthful behaviors, stress management, analyzing influences, communication skills, refusal skills, conflict resolution, decision making, goal setting, and advocacy.
- The S.T.O.P. strategy can help you say no. The letters in S.T.O.P. stand for: **S**ay no in a firm voice. **T**ell why not. **O**ffer another idea. **P**romptly leave.
- Influences on a person's health include personal likes and dislikes, desires and ambitions, curiosity, fears, family, culture, friends and peers, environment, media, and technology.

Assessment Resources

- 📁 Chapter 2 Summary and Activity
- Audio Summaries
- 📁 Reading Tutor
- 📁 Performance Assessment
- 📁 Chapter 2 Test
- 💿 *ExamView*
- Vocabulary PuzzleMaker
- Online Learning Center

Reading Review

Study Aids

- **Using the Dinah Zike Foldable® Study Organizer** Have students use the Foldable® to review the six steps of the decision-making process.

- **Online Learning Tools** Have students go to the *Teen Health* Online Learning Center at **glencoe.com** to:

  - Download a **Podcast**.

  - Download free **Study-to-Go** content to their PDAs or cell phones.

Vocabulary Review

- **Vocabulary Sentences** Have each student select five vocabulary terms from the chapter. Have the students write five sentences, each correctly using one of their selected chapter vocabulary terms. Then, for each chapter vocabulary term, ask for a volunteer to read his or her sentence.

Teaching Tips

Writing in Health Class Use the writing support strategies found throughout the Teachers' Wraparound Edition to integrate writing into the health curriculum. Various types of writing, including descriptive, expository, narrative, persuasive, and personal writing are suggested throughout the lessons and in the chapter assessments. Remind students that all writing assignments should be edited before they are turned in. Allow time for the writing and editing during the class period. Occasionally have students exchange their work with another student for peer review and feedback.

Assessment

Reviewing Vocabulary and Main Ideas

1. Decision making
2. Goal setting
3. values
4. character
5. integrity
6. Accountability
7. c
8. b
9. b

Thinking Critically

10. Answers, which will vary, might include seeing if she can get another ticket for her cousin or seeing if she can get a refund on her ticket or find another friend who might be interested in buying it.

11. Analyzing influences can help you determine what information sources are reliable and help you determine whether health information is accurate. This can help you choose reliable health products and services and develop positive health behaviors based on accurate information.

After You Read

HEALTH QUIZ

Now that you have read the chapter, look back at your answers to the Health Quiz on the chapter opener. Would you change any of them? What would your answers be now?

Reviewing Vocabulary and Main Ideas

On a sheet of paper, write the numbers 1–6. After each number, write the term from the list that best completes each sentence.

- accountability
- character
- communication
- decision making
- goal setting
- integrity
- values
- media

Lesson 1 Making Decisions and Setting Goals

1. _____ is the process of making a choice or finding a solution.

2. _____ is the process of working toward something you want to accomplish.

3. The beliefs and ideals that guide the way a person lives are that person's _____.

Lesson 2 Building Good Character

4. The way a person thinks, feels, and acts is known as _____.

5. The quality of always doing what you know is right is _____.

6. _____ is a willingness to answer for your actions and decisions.

Lesson 3 Developing Other Health Skills

On a sheet of paper, write the numbers 7–9. After each number, write the letter of the answer that best completes each statement.

7. Good communication involves all of the following *except*
   a. speaking and listening.
   b. clearly exchanging ideas and information.
   c. shouting at those who do not agree with you.
   d. facial expressions and gestures.

8. When you analyze influences, you should
   a. pay the most attention to what your friends say.
   b. pay the most attention to inside and outside influences.
   c. pay attention to your inside influences but ignore your outside influences.
   d. give the most attention to aspects of your physical environment.

9. Effective refusal skills include all of the following *except*
   a. saying no in a firm voice.
   b. arguing with the other person
   c. offering another idea.
   d. promptly leaving.

Go Online Visit **glencoe.com** and take the Online Quiz for Chapter 2.

Go Online

Have students visit **glencoe.com** to take the Chapter 2 Quiz.

HEALTH QUIZ Wrap-Up

Health Skills Have students look back at the Health Quiz in the chapter opener. Ask a volunteer to read aloud each question and give an explanation of which of the answers is correct, based on the chapter content. Ask: What is one way that the health skills described in the Health Quiz can positively affect your physical health? *These skills can help you to avoid risky behavior, such as using drugs and alcohol, which can harm physical health.*

Thinking Critically

Using complete sentences, answer the following questions on a sheet of paper.

10. **Apply** Laurie just made plans to go to a concert with friends this weekend. She forgot that her cousin is coming in from out of town to visit her. What are some options Laurie might consider before making a decision?

11. **Analyze** How might the skill of analyzing influences benefit your health?

Write About It

12. **Narrative Writing** Write a short story in which a teen must make a decision related to his or her health.

➔ Applying Technology

Doers and Decisions

You and your partner will use Microsoft Word® to create a poster that highlights the decision-making steps.

■ Find images that relate to the decision-making steps and insert them in a new Microsoft Word® document.

■ Insert bubbles or text boxes for each image. Type brief captions and describe how each image relates to the decision-making process.

■ Make your poster colorful and interesting to look at.

■ Save your poster.

➔ Applying Technology

Doers and Decisions
Equipment needs: Microsoft Word® or similar software
Have students choose partners for this project. Go over project instructions with the class, clarifying any steps as necessary. Create a sign-up sheet if computer access is limited, and establish a time limit for each pair of students. If supplies are available, print and display students' completed posters.

Write About It

12. **Narrative Writing** Explain to students that narrative writing tells a clear story arranged in a logical order. Students' stories will vary but should include a teen who uses the decision-making process to find a healthy solution. Stories should include character, plot, setting, and dialogue.

Standardized Test Practice

1. B
2. C

Standardized Test Practice

Reading

Read the passage below and then answer the questions that follow.

You are a citizen of many different communities. The largest community you belong to is the world. Sadly, not all members of this global community share its resources equally. Did you know one in seven of your neighbors in the world goes to bed hungry every night? Others suffer from diseases that were stamped out in our own country a long time ago.

As a health advocate, you can help suffering communities. One way is to tell others. Another is to become and stay informed. The World Health Organization is currently taking action to help people in need. You can visit their Web site for further information.

TEST-TAKING TIP

Read the passage carefully once to find out what information it contains. After you read each question, look back at the passage to find the answer.

1. Which statement best sums up the main point of the passage?
   A. We all live in many different communities.
   B. The health skill of advocacy can be used to help nations in need.
   C. Other countries are suffering from diseases that we have already overcome.

2. The passage notes that "not all members of this global community share its resources equally." Of the following quotes, which is *not* a detail that supports that comment?
   A. "One in seven of your neighbors in the world goes to bed hungry every night."
   B. "Others suffer from diseases that were stamped out in our own country a long time ago."
   C. "You are a citizen of many different communities."

Test-Taking Tips

Supporting Details Tell students that they might be asked to find a detail that supports an idea from a reading passage, as in question 2 of the Standardized Test Practice. Tell students that in this case, they should carefully read each of the answer choices. Although all of the choices might be correctly stated details from the passage, only one of the answer choices gives a detail that supports the main idea described in the question.

Mental and Emotional Health

CHAPTER 3 pp. 50–77	Standards		Skills and Activities
	National	State/Local	
	National Health Education Standards 1.8.5, 1.8.7, 2.8.4, 6.8.1, 7.8.2		*Health* eSpotlight, *p. 51* **BUILDING HEALTH SKILLS** *Stress Management* Putting Stress in Its Place, *pp. 72–73* TIME health news Stress Stoppers, *p. 74*
Lesson 1 **Your Mental and Emotional Health** pp. 52–56	National Health Education Standards 1.8.2, 2.8.1, 2.8.8, 3.8.2, 6.8.1, 6.8.2, 8.8.1		**Connect To... SCIENCE** Learning from Mistakes, *p. 54* Go Online Body Image and Self-Esteem, *p. 55*
Lesson 2 **Understanding Your Emotions** pp. 57–62	National Health Education Standards 1.8.5, 3.8.2, 4.8.4, 5.8.6, 6.8.2, 7.8.2		**Careers for the 21st Century** *Social Worker, p. 58* **HEALTH SKILLS ACTIVITY** *Practicing Healthful Behaviors* Anger Management, *p. 60*
Lesson 3 **Managing Stress** pp. 63–68	National Health Education Standards 1.8.1, 1.8.5, 1.8.7, 2.8.1, 2.8.9, 4.8.1, 7.8.2, 8.8.1		**What Teens Think** In your opinion, what causes the most stress for teens, *p. 64* **HEALTH SKILLS ACTIVITY** *Stress Management* Stress Chasers, *p. 66*
Lesson 4 **Coping with Loss** pp. 69–71	National Health Education Standards 1.8.5, 1.8.7, 7.8.2		**DEVELOPING GOOD CHARACTER** *Caring, p. 70*

PACING THE CHAPTER			
Lesson 1 45 min	**Lesson 4** 45 min	**TIME health news** 30 min
Lesson 2 45 min	**Chapter Review** 45 min	
Lesson 3 45 min	**Building Health Skills** 90 min	

BLOCK SCHEDULING

For block scheduling, assign students Building Health Skills feature *Putting Stress in Its Place*, pages 72–73, and Guided Reading and Writing. 📁

Planning Guide

TeacherWorks Plus™
Glencoe Exclusive!
All-In-One Planner and Resource Center

Reproducible Resources	Assessment	Media and Technology
Chapter FAST FILE Resources Chapter Summaries and Activities REVIEW Building Health Skills Activity TEACH Performance Assessment Activity EXTEND Universal Access Activities TEACH Parent Letter and Activities 📁 **Student Activities Workbook** TEACH 📁 **Reading Tutor** TEACH	Building Health Skills Activity, *pp. 72–73* Chapter 3 Assessment, *pp. 76–77* **Chapter FAST FILE Resources** Performance Assessment Activity, *p. 4* Chapter 3 Test, *p. 7* 💿 *ExamView® Assessment Suite*	**TeacherWorks Plus** includes: ● Interactive Teacher Edition ● Lesson Planner with Calendar ● Access to all blackline masters ● Correlations to standards 💿 StudentWorks™ Plus 💿 Online Student Edition Dinah Zike Teaching Health with Foldables®
Chapter FAST FILE Resources Concept Mapping Activity 3-1 REVIEW Cross-Curriculum Activity 3-1 EXTEND Enrichment Activity 3-1 EXTEND Lesson Plan 3-1 Guided Reading and Writing 3-1 TEACH Reteaching Activity 3-1 REVIEW	Lesson 1 Review, *p. 56* 💿 Vocabulary PuzzleMaker 💿 *ExamView® Assessment Suite*	💿 Vocabulary PuzzleMaker 💿 *ExamView® Assessment Suite* 💿 StudentWorks™ Plus 🕹 Transparency 3-1 **Go Online** glencoe.com
Chapter FAST FILE Resources Concept Mapping Activity 3-2 REVIEW Enrichment Activity 3-2 EXTEND Decision-Making Activity 3-2 EXTEND Lesson Plan 3-2 Guided Reading and Writing 3-2 TEACH Reteaching Activity 3-2 REVIEW	Lesson 2 Review, *p. 62* 💿 Vocabulary PuzzleMaker 💿 *ExamView® Assessment Suite*	💿 Vocabulary PuzzleMaker 💿 *ExamView® Assessment Suite* 💿 StudentWorks™ Plus 🕹 Transparency 3-2 **Go Online** glencoe.com
Chapter FAST FILE Resources Concept Mapping Activity 3-3 REVIEW Enrichment Activity 3-3 EXTEND Health Lab 3-3 EXTEND Lesson Plan 3-3 Guided Reading and Writing 3-3 TEACH Reteaching Activity 3-3 REVIEW	Lesson 3 Review, *p. 68* 💿 Vocabulary PuzzleMaker 💿 *ExamView® Assessment Suite*	💿 Vocabulary PuzzleMaker 💿 *ExamView® Assessment Suite* 💿 StudentWorks™ Plus 🕹 Transparency 3-3 **Go Online** glencoe.com
Chapter FAST FILE Resources Concept Mapping Activity 3-4 REVIEW Cross-Curriculum Activity 3-4 EXTEND Enrichment Activity 3-4 EXTEND Lesson Plan 3-4 Guided Reading and Writing 3-4 TEACH Reteaching Activity 3-4 REVIEW	Lesson 4 Review, *p. 71* 💿 Vocabulary PuzzleMaker 💿 *ExamView® Assessment Suite*	💿 Vocabulary PuzzleMaker 💿 *ExamView® Assessment Suite* 💿 StudentWorks™ Plus 🕹 Transparency 3-4 **Go Online** glencoe.com

Chapter and Lesson Resources

The *Teen Health* resources are designed for differentiated learning abilities. You may want to use the coded items in this way:

REVIEW —activities to review or reinforce content

TEACH —activities to teach basic concepts

EXTEND —activities to extend or enrich lesson content

 OUT OF TIME?

Use Health Skills Activities *Anger Management,* page 60, *Stress Chasers*, page 66, or Developing Good Character, page 70.

Maslow's Hierarchy of Needs

In this chapter, students read about and discuss emotional needs. In the 1940s, Abraham Maslow developed a theory that describes the order in which humans meet their needs. This theory, commonly called the hierarchy of needs, is used to explain how people are motivated to reach goals in business, education, and other aspects of life.

The hierarchy of needs starts with the most basic needs of humans at the bottom level. These are the biological needs, such as food and water.

The next level is the need for safety. A safe school environment, free of weapons and violence, helps students meet their need to feel safe. Extensive coverage of war and terrorism in the media has made it difficult for some teens to meet their need to feel safe.

Some of the emotional needs that are discussed in this chapter occupy the next level of the hierarchy of needs. These needs include feeling loved and a sense of belonging. The student text describes healthy ways that students can meet these needs.

The fourth level of the hierarchy is the need for esteem. There are two aspects of esteem—self-esteem and the esteem of others.

At the top of the hierarchy is self-actualization. At this level, people make the best use of their talents and abilities, are able to accept themselves and others, and have a positive outlook on life.

According to Maslow's theory, only when the needs of one level are met can a person move on to meet the needs in the next level. This has important applications in the school environment. For example, a student who comes to school hungry will concentrate on the need for food more than on learning.

When students discuss emotional needs as a part of the chapter, emphasize healthy ways in which these needs can be met. Remind students to use the health skills of decision making and goal setting as they seek to make healthy choices to meet their emotional needs.

Time Management for ADHD Teens

Time management is a health skill that can increase productivity and reduce stress for teens. However, most teens with attention deficit hyperactivity disorder (ADHD) struggle with time management.

ADHD affects the executive functions of the brain. These functions, which include time perception, memory, and organization, directly affect time-management skills.

The sense of time, or time perception, is altered in many individuals with ADHD. Using a watch with an alarm can help mark the passage of time. Electronic devices such as PDAs can also help mark the passage of time with alarms and reminders.

Many individuals with ADHD have difficulty with tasks involving organization. This makes setting up and consistently using a planner a challenge. Remind students that, if they use a notebook for a planner, that should be the only use of that notebook. Tell students to have a specific place for the notebook at school and at home so that it does not get lost. Suggest that students maintain only one planner that contains both school and personal activities, so that information does not need to be transferred between planners.

When discussing planners, point out their advantages to all students. Although there are some specific challenges for individuals with ADHD, the benefits of keeping a planner far outweigh the difficulties.

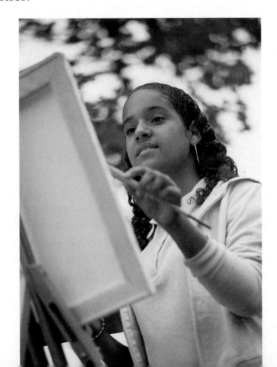

Support for Teaching Reading

 Reading Support

Reading Preview

Activating Background Vocabulary Ask students what comes to mind when they think of the terms mental and emotional health. Guide students to discuss how good mental and emotional health can help people develop a positive outlook on life, deal with challenges that arise, understand their emotions, manage stress, and cope with loss.

FOLDABLES Study Organizer *Dinah Zike's Reading and Study Skills for Teen Health* provides interactive graphic organizers that help students comprehend and retain health concepts as they read. Use the Foldable® on page 51 or find more Foldables® activities for the chapter on **Mental and Emotional Health** in the separate booklet, available in the TCR.

Lesson 1   Your Mental and Emotional Health

Listen-Read-Discuss Give students a brief lecture to provide background information. Next, have students read silently, making a list of questions for clarification. Then, stop students during reading and ask: "What do you understand most from what you have read? What do you understand least? What questions do you still have about self-concept or self-esteem?"

Lesson 2   Understanding Your Emotions

Partner Sharing After students read the section **Mixed Emotions**, ask student pairs to discuss: How do you express anxiety? How do you express fear or anger? What are mixed emotions? Allow student pairs two or three minutes to discuss the questions. Ask some pairs to share their views with the whole class.

Lesson 3   Managing Stress

Visualizing Have students imagine they are ready to give a speech to a large group of people. Ask: What are you feeling? Do you have anxiety? Do you have any physical responses? What is your audience doing? Is there anything you can do to relax? Discuss, and have students describe their images. Encourage students to try this on their own.

Lesson 4   Coping with Loss

Clarifying Text Direct students to read the section on **The Grief Reaction**. Ask students if any concepts remain unclear. Guide students to locate definitions of terms within the context of the lesson, including illustrations, captions, and other textual clues. Encourage student pairs to use their own words to explain concepts to one another.

Post Reading

Informational Presentations Have students use a variety of reference materials, including magazines, newspapers, and computer resources, to gather further information about mental and emotional problems. Instruct students to organize the information into a presentation for the class that reflects understanding and application of the lesson content.

Key for Using the Teacher Wraparound Edition

Use this key to help you identify the different types of prompts found in the Teacher Wraparound Edition.

R **Reading Strategies** activities help you teach reading skills and vocabulary.

C **Critical Thinking** strategies help students apply and extend what they have learned.

U **Universal Access** activities provide differentiated instruction for students learning to speak English, along with suggestions for teaching various types of learners.

HS **Health Skills Practice** activities reinforce Health Skills concepts and help students apply these skills in their everyday lives.

W **Writing Support** activities provide writing opportunities to help students comprehend the text.

AL **Active Learning** strategies provide a variety of activities for presenting lesson content, including Quick Demos and engaging classroom projects that get students actively involved.

Key to Ability Levels

Teaching Strategies and activities have been coded for ability level and appropriateness.

AL Activities for students working above grade level

OL Activities for students working on grade level

BL Activities for students working below grade level

EL Activities for English Learners

Symbols

📖 Transparencies

💿 CD-ROM

🖱 glencoe.com

📁 Print Resources

Chapter at a Glance

Lesson 1 explains traits of good mental and emotional health, explains skills that build self-esteem, and provides practice in communication skills to improve students' mental and emotional health.

Lesson 2 identifies common human emotions, explains how to express emotions in positive and healthy ways, recognizes healthy ways to meet emotional needs, and provides practice in healthful behaviors to manage anger.

Lesson 3 identifies the causes of stress, describes how the body responds to stress, and explains how to develop skills to manage stress.

Lesson 4 identifies stages in the grief reaction, describes strategies for coping with personal loss, and explains how to provide emotional support to someone who is grieving.

R Reading Strategy

Interpreting the Photo Have students examine the photo. Ask: How does playing an instrument manage stress? *It can make the player feel calm. It takes your mind off of your problems.* What kinds of activities help manage your stress? Sample answers: *reading, sports, movies, writing* OL

Chapter Preview

▲ Working with the Photo

Activities such as playing an instrument can help you manage stress in a healthy way. **Why do you think managing stress is important to good mental/emotional health?**

Universal Access

Differentiated Learning Glencoe provides teacher support and student materials for all learners in the health classroom.

- Spanish Glosario and chapter summaries for the English Language Learners.
- *Reading Tutor* and related worksheets support reluctant readers.

- Universal Access strategies throughout the Teacher Wraparound Edition and Fast Files help you present materials for gifted students, at-risk students, physically impaired students, and those with behavior disorders or learning disabilities.

Start-Up Activities

📖 **Before You Read** Do you know how to cope with stress? Answer the Health eSpotlight questions below and then watch the online video. Keep a record of your answers.

Health eSpotlight VIDEO

Coping with Stress

Juggling the demands of school, jobs, and friends can be a difficult task, leading some teens to experience anxiety and, in some cases, depression. How do you cope with stress? What advice would you give to a friend who said he or she was stressed-out?

Go to **glencoe.com** and watch the health video for Chapter 3. Then complete the activity provided with the online video.

FOLDABLES Study Organizer

📖 **As You Read** Make this Foldable® to help you organize the main ideas on mental and emotional health in Lesson 1. Begin with a plain sheet of 8½" × 11" paper.

1 Line up one of the short edges of a sheet of paper with one of the long edges to form a triangle. Fold and cut off the leftover rectangle.

2 Fold the triangle in half, then unfold. The folds will form an X dividing four equal sections.

3 Cut up one fold line, and stop at the middle. This forms two triangular flaps. Draw an X on one tab, and label the other three as shown.

My Personality
My Self-Concept
My Self-Esteem

4 Fold the X flap under the other flap, and glue together to make a three-sided pyramid.

My Self-Concept

Write the main ideas on mental and emotional health on the back of the appropriate side of the pyramid.

G Online Visit **glencoe.com** and complete the Health Inventory for Chapter 3.

Health eSpotlight VIDEO

Coping with Stress Have students write an answer to the questions provided and save their answers for later. Download the video presentation for Chapter 3 from **glencoe.com** or use the DVD to play the video for the class. Use the questions at the end of the video to begin a class discussion on managing stress. Ask students to respond to each question. **OL**

No Child Left Behind

Classroom Management
Help students learn to manage their time and take responsibility for long-term assignments and projects. Explain that monitoring a long-term project involves identifying a series of smaller tasks with a completion date for each. Initially, students should define each step required for the completion of the project. Then have students consider the final due date for the project as they set a completion date for each task. Suggest that students use a written log, spreadsheet, or calendar to monitor their progress toward completion of a project.

FOLDABLES Study Organizer

Dinah Zike Foldables®

Organizing Information As students read Lesson 1, have them record notes, ideas, and vocabulary terms about mental and emotional health on the back of the appropriate sides of their Foldables®. Have students decorate the front sides of their Foldables® with drawings that represent their personalities and favorite activities. Students can use their Foldables® to review the content of Lesson 1 as they prepare for the Chapter Assessment. **BL**

G Online

Have students visit **glencoe.com** and complete the Health Inventory for Chapter 3.

FOCUS

Activating Prior Knowledge

What I Know Write the term *self-esteem* on the board. Ask students to identify ways to build their own self-esteem and the self-esteem of others.

Guide to Reading

Building Vocabulary
- Have students write a sentence that shows how the terms *self-esteem* and *resilience* are related.
- Use Vocabulary PuzzleMaker to reinforce vocabulary terms.

Reading Strategy
Finding the Main Idea Model the Reading Strategy for students by copying the first main heading from the lesson onto the board. Ask a volunteer to summarize the main idea of the first section and record his or her answer under the heading.

 Have students use their Foldables® as they read Lesson 1.

Quick Write

Before students begin their Quick Writes, have them brainstorm a list of descriptive words that could be used to describe a variety of personality traits.

Your Mental and Emotional Health

Guide to Reading

Building Vocabulary
As you read this lesson, write each new highlighted term and its definition in your notebook.
- adapt (p. 52)
- personality (p. 53)
- self-concept (p. 54)
- self-esteem (p. 55)
- resilience (p. 55)

Focusing on the Main Ideas
In this lesson, you will learn to
- **recognize** traits of good mental and emotional health.
- **identify** factors that influence your self-concept.
- **develop** skills to build your self-esteem.
- **practice** communication skills to improve your mental and emotional health.

Reading Strategy
Finding the Main Idea Copy each of the main headings from the lesson into your notebook. For each, write one sentence that states the main idea.

FOLDABLES Study Organizer Use the Foldable® on p. 51 as you read this lesson.

Quick Write

In a short paragraph or poem, describe your personality. Use descriptive words and give examples.

Mental and Emotional Health

Do you have a positive outlook on life? Do you deal effectively with challenges when they arise? If you answered yes to these questions, you probably have good mental and emotional health. People with good mental and emotional health are able to accept themselves and others. They also know how to **adapt,** or *adjust to new situations.*

Other traits of people who are mentally and emotionally healthy appear in **Figure 3.1.** Which of these traits do you have?

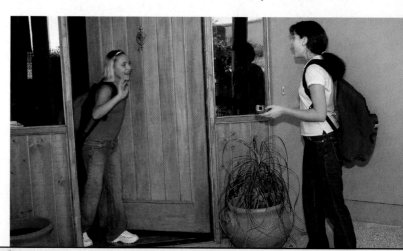

▶ Your mental/emotional health affects every aspect of your life. **What strategies can you use to improve your mental/emotional health?**

52 Chapter 3: Mental and Emotional Health

Lesson 1 Resources

📁 **Chapter** *FAST FILE* **Resources**
Guided Reading and Writing 3-1
Concept Mapping Activity 3-1
Cross-Curriculum Activity 3-1
Reteaching Activity 3-1
Enrichment Activity 3-1
Lesson Quiz 3-1

Technology
🔌 Transparency 3-1
🔊 Audio Summaries
💿 *ExamView*® Assessment Suite
🔊 Vocabulary PuzzleMaker
💿 StudentWorks™ Plus
G⊙ Online

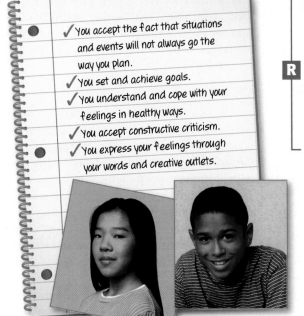

◀ FIGURE 3.1

MENTAL/EMOTIONAL HEALTH CHECKLIST

✓ You accept the fact that situations and events will not always go the way you plan.

✓ You set and achieve goals.

✓ You understand and cope with your feelings in healthy ways.

✓ You accept constructive criticism.

✓ You express your feelings through your words and creative outlets.

R Copy this checklist onto a sheet of paper. Place a check mark next to those traits that currently describe your mental/emotional health. Be as honest as you can. **Can you think of any other traits that describe good mental/emotional health?**

What Makes You Who You Are?

Have you ever thought about what makes you unique? You have a number of qualities that make you who you are. The teen years are a time to develop these qualities and learn more about yourself. You develop your physical and mental abilities. You discover the kinds of people you want to build relationships with and the kinds of activities you enjoy. You also begin to form your own values and to understand the importance of standing behind them. All of these things help shape the unique and special person that you are.

Personality and self-concept also play a big role in shaping who you are. Both of these factors are especially influential during your teen years. Therefore, it is important to develop your personality and self-concept in positive and healthy ways. This can help you develop good mental and emotional health.

Your Personality

Are you outgoing and friendly? Are you shy? Are you someone who takes charge of a situation, or do you wait to be told what to do? These are a few of the many qualities that define your personality. **Personality** is *the unique combination of feelings, thoughts, and behaviors that make you different from everyone else.*

▼ Your personality and self-concept are two factors that determine your mental and emotional health. **How do you view yourself?**

Lesson 1: Your Mental and Emotional Health **53**

Teacher to Teacher

Joan Stear   **West Clermont Institute of Performing Arts, Cincinnati, Ohio**

Defense Mechanisms "Have students use sock puppets to demonstrate defense mechanisms in a scene where a Sock Driver is pulled over by a Sock Police Officer for speeding. Each student can create a sock puppet using a gym sock, and materials like buttons, glitter, pieces of fabric, and fabric glue. The students who don't want to create a puppet can build scenery or props for the scene. "

TEACH

R Reading Strategy

Analyzing a Graphic Have students copy the health behavior checklist shown in **Figure 3.1** onto a piece of paper. Then have students put checkmarks next to those behaviors that currently describe their mental/emotional health. Allow students to keep their answers confidential. Have a class discussion about ways to incorporate each of the health behaviors into everyday life. **OL**

AL Active Learning

Collage Ask each student to make a collage that uses colors, drawings, photos, and other visual media to describe the feelings, thoughts, and behaviors that make up his or her personality. Visually impaired students can prepare sound collages—recordings of song clips and other sounds that describe their personalities. **OL**

Caption Answers

Figure Caption *Sample answer:* You learn from your mistakes.
Photo Caption, this page *Sample answer:* My personality is outgoing and happy.
Photo Caption, p. 52 *Sample answer:* Setting and achieving goals can improve mental and emotional health.

Connect To...
Science

Learning from Mistakes
Help students locate appropriate print or online resources to use for their research. Have students write short summaries of their findings that can be posted in the classroom. **OL**

C **Critical Thinking**

Synthesizing After students read the section on self-concept, have a volunteer read aloud the definition of *resilience* on page 55. Explain that the ability to bounce back is an important part of buiding and maintaining self-esteem. After students have read the section on building self-esteem, ask: What tools can a person call upon to develop and maintain resiliency? *recognizing strengths, learning from experience, being motivated to reach a goal* Then ask the class to brainstorm some assets teens might use to build their resiliency, for example: family support, adult role models, creative activities, sense of purpose. **OL**

 Reading Check

Answer Your self-concept is shaped by your experiences and relationships.

Caption Answer

Photo Caption *Sample answer:* I define myself as an athlete, because I do well at gymnastics.

Connect To...
Science

Learning from Mistakes

What do Thomas Edison, Alexander Graham Bell, and Booker T. Washington have in common? They were all inventors who failed many times before they succeeded in making a discovery. They all learned from their own mistakes and those of others to advance their ideas.

Use outside resources to learn about a person who invented something. List the challenges he or she faced before finally succeeding.

Your personality affects how you handle problems and new situations. How would you feel about moving to a new school, for example? Would you be excited and confident, or scared and nervous? Different people react in different ways to the same situation.

Your Self-Concept

When you see your reflection in the mirror, who do you see looking back at you? How do you believe others see you? Your answers to these questions reveal your **self-concept.** This is *the view you have of yourself.* The environment in which you live affects your personal health. It influences your self-concept.

Self-concept begins to form in early childhood. It grows out of your experiences and relationships with those around you. The earliest influence on self-concept is family. Members of a loving family support and care for each other. Children brought up in this kind of environment are more likely to develop a positive self-concept.

As you grow older and begin school, your peers and teachers influence your self-concept through their words and actions. Praise from a teacher or coach for a job well done promotes a positive self-concept. Being ignored or teased by peers can have the opposite effect.

C When a teen with a positive self-concept makes a mistake, the teen learns from the mistake and moves on. Those with a negative self-concept might feel like one mistake means that everything they do is wrong. This type of attitude can stand in the way of achieving your goals. It is important to remember that everyone makes mistakes. If everyone let a single mistake hold them back, nobody would accomplish anything.

Working toward a positive self-concept is an important part of good mental and emotional health. It can help you form a view of yourself that allows you to work toward and achieve your goals. A positive self-concept will give you confidence and make you feel good about yourself.

Reading Check **Identify** What two factors influence your self-concept?

◀ Part of this teen's self-concept is "musician." **What are some ways that you define yourself? What are some of your skills and talents?**

Cultural Perspectives

Self-Esteem, Body Image, and the Media Body image is an important aspect of self-esteem and self-concept, especially for teens. Teens are bombarded with images of unrealistically perfect bodies in magazines, on television, and in movies. Discuss how these images are digitally manipulated and are not realistic. Teens can develop a poor body image if they compare their bodies to those they see in the media. Have students do additional research and prepare a media presentation countering the messages in these ads. **OL**

Self-Esteem

Your personality and self-concept affect the way you feel about yourself. They affect your **self-esteem.** This is *the way you feel about yourself, and how you value yourself.* When you have high self-esteem, you feel appreciated and valued as a person. You have a high degree of confidence in your abilities, and you meet new challenges with a "can-do" attitude. When things go wrong, you are resilient. **Resilience** is *the ability to bounce back from disappointment.* Resilience is an important personality trait to develop. It enables you to get back on your feet after a disappointment and keep moving forward.

Maria is an example of a resilient teen. Maria spent months practicing to try out for the cheerleading squad. On the day of tryouts, she felt ready, and was sure she would make the team. Maria was disappointed when she was not chosen, but she did not let that stop her. She still practiced cheerleading in her free time because she loved it, and she hoped it would help her make the team next year. She also decided to join the school choir. She wanted to focus on her other strengths as well as get involved in a school activity. She used strategies for improving and maintaining her personal health as a way to develop her self-esteem.

Reading Check **Define** What is *resilience*?

Building Self-Esteem

Whether your self-esteem is high or low, it can always be improved upon. You can develop skills to build your self-esteem and feel good about yourself. These skills can increase your overall level of mental/emotional health. The skills you can practice include:

* **List your strengths.** Identify your talents and abilities. Everyone has special talents and skills. Make a list of them. For example, you may be a loyal friend or a good listener. You may also be a really good basketball player or writer.

▶ Recognizing your talents is one way of building your self-esteem. **How does high self-esteem benefit your health?**

Lesson 1: Your Mental and Emotional Health **55**

Go Online

Topic: Body Image and Self-Esteem

Visit **glencoe.com** for Student Web Activities to learn about how the image you have of your body can affect your self-esteem.

Activity: Using the information provided at the link above, create a questionnaire that tests for self-esteem and body image.

Go Online

Body Image and Self-Esteem
Allow time for students to investigate the Student Web Activities at **glencoe.com.** Then have them work in small groups to prepare questionnaires with 7 to 10 questions on self-esteem and provide tips for each question with ways to improve that area of self-esteem. Have groups trade questionnaires and discuss.

Reading Check

Answer Resilience is the ability to bounce back from disappointment.
Answer, p. 56 Recognize your strengths, remember everyone makes mistakes, and motivate yourself

FITNESS ZONE

Self-Esteem and Physical Fitness Refer students to the *Fitness Zone Handbook* at the front of their books, and let them review the introductory information. Then ask: *What effect can being physically fit have on your self-esteem? How can planning and following a fitness routine affect your self-esteem? What advice would you give a friend about making a physical fitness plan? Why?* **For more information, see *Fitness Zone Handbook* pages xviii-1 or visit the Fitness Zone at glencoe.com.**

Caption Answer

Photo Caption *Sample answer:* A person with high self-esteem has confidence, a positive attitude, and is resilient.

ASSESS

Assessment Resources

Lesson Review Quiz
 ExamView
📁 Fast Files Activities
Online Quizzes and Activities

Reteaching

● Assign Concept Map 3-1 or Reteaching Activity 3-1 in the Fast Files. 📁

● Have pairs of students list and discuss health behaviors that demonstrate good mental and emotional health. Call on several pairs of students to describe one of the behaviors from their list.

Enrichment

● Assign Enrichment Activity 3-1 in the Fast Files. 📁

● Have students write a fictional story about a teen who has to adapt, or adjust, to a new situation. Students' stories should describe how the teen's mental and emotional health are related to the teen's ability to adapt.

CLOSE

Have students list skills that can help to build a person's self-esteem.

● **Remember that everyone makes mistakes.** No one is perfect. Making mistakes is part of being human. When you get something wrong, learn and grow from the experience.

● **Motivate yourself.** Identify your goals and what you need to do to reach them. Make a plan for getting from where you are to where you want to be. Achieving a goal you set for yourself will give you a sense of accomplishment.

Understanding and Managing Your Feelings

An important part of your mental and emotional health is managing your feelings. Like mental and emotional health itself, feelings can be complicated. Sometimes it is difficult to understand why you feel the way you do. In the next lesson, you will examine the subject of feelings more closely. You will also learn skills for managing your feelings.

Visit **glencoe.com** and complete the Interactive Study Guide for Lesson 1.

Reading Check   **Give Examples** What are three ways to build your self-esteem?

Lesson 1 Review

After You Read

Review this lesson for new terms, major headings, and Reading Checks.

What I Learned

1. **Vocabulary** Define *self-esteem*. Use the term in an original sentence.

2. **Recall** What are traits of good mental and emotional health?

3. **Explain** How does your personality affect how you handle problems and new situations?

Thinking Critically

4. **Evaluate** Review the traits of good mental and emotional health described at the beginning of the lesson and in Figure 3.1 on page 53. Which of these traits do you think is the most important, and why?

5. **Hypothesize** Shawn was hoping to make the gymnastics team but was turned down. Now he feels terrible and has vowed never to do gymnastics again. How can Shawn build his self-esteem?

Applying Health Skills

6. **Communication Skills** Like other areas of health, mental and emotional health is better on some days than others. Think about messages that would help you feel better when your mental and emotional health is low. Make a list of these. Remember your list when you are having a low day.

 Go Online   For more Lesson Review Activities, go to **glencoe.com**.

Lesson 1 Review Answers

1. Self-esteem is the way you feel about yourself. Sentences will vary.

2. a positive outlook, deals effectively with challenges, able to accept self and others, adjusts to new situations, sets and achieve goals, accepts constructive criticism

3. Your personality can make you excited and confident or scared and nervous when facing new situations.

4. *Sample answer:* The ability to accept yourself and others is most important; you need to do this every day.

5. *Sample answer:* Shawn should deal with his disappointment in constructive ways. Shawn could continue to practice gymnastics on his own or he could try out for an alternative sports team.

6. Students' lists should include phrases that boost self-esteem and self-concept.

Lesson 2

Understanding Your Emotions

Guide to Reading

● Building Vocabulary
Some of the terms below may seem familiar. Write these terms in your notebook, adding definitions in pencil. As you come across them in your reading, finalize the definitions in pen.

■ emotions (p. 57)
■ anxiety (p. 58)
■ panic (p. 59)
■ emotional needs (p. 61)

● Focusing on the Main Ideas
In this lesson, you will learn to

■ **identify** common emotions.
■ **express** emotions in healthy ways.
■ **recognize** healthy ways to meet emotional needs.
■ **practice** healthful behaviors to manage anger.

● Reading Strategy
Classifying Make a chart that shows some common emotions and healthy ways to express them.

What Are Emotions?

Terri had worked hard over the past several months campaigning to be the student council president. Today, she stood side by side with her opponents on the stage of the school auditorium. The results of the vote were about to be announced.

Have you ever been in a situation like Terri's? Even if you have not, you can probably imagine her emotions at this moment. **Emotions** are *feelings created in response to thoughts, remarks, and events.* Some common emotions are shown in **Figure 3.2.**

Quick Write

Think about times when you have been upset or angry over something. Try to recall how you dealt with these feelings.

◀ It is healthy to express happiness about an achievement. **How do you celebrate your accomplishments?**

Lesson 2: Understanding Your Emotions **57**

Lesson 2 Resources

📁 **Chapter *FAST FILE* Resources**
Guided Reading and Writing 3-2
Concept Mapping Activity 3-2
Decision-Making Activity 3-2
Reteaching Activity 3-2
Enrichment Activity 3-2
Lesson Quiz 3-2

Technology
⚡ Transparency 3-2
💿 Audio Summaries
💻 *ExamView*® Assessment Suite
💿 Vocabulary PuzzleMaker
💻 StudentWorks™ Plus
G🔵 **Online**

FOCUS

Activating Prior Knowledge

What I Know Have students identify the three sides of the health triangle. Record their responses on the board. Circle the phrase *mental/emotional health.* Ask students to list ways to improve or maintain mental/emotional health. Tell students that they can add to the list as they read this lesson.

 Guide to Reading

Building Vocabulary
■ Tell students that *anxiety* is a feeling of uneasiness. Ask: What are some everyday situations in which a teen might experience *anxiety*? Sample answers: *taking a test, trying out for a team*
■ Use Vocabulary PuzzleMaker to reinforce vocabulary terms. 🖊

Reading Strategy
Classifying Remind students to leave room for more than one way to express each of the emotions as they prepare their chart.

Quick Write

After students have completed their Quick Writes, explain that this lesson will help them learn positive ways to manage anger.

TEACH

R Reading Strategy

Analyzing a Graphic Have students discuss each of the common emotions that are listed in **Figure 3.2**. Have students write sentences that describe how any two of the emotions in the chart are related. Have volunteers share their responses with the class. **OL**

AL Active Learning

Illustrated Essay Have the class brainstorm various causes of anxiety. Ask a student to write the suggestions on the chalkboard or a poster board. Then have students cut pictures out of magazines or newspapers that illustrate these situations. Students should select two of their pictures to write about what causes the anxiety and/or nervousness and what they can do to overcome it. **EL**

Careers for the 21st Century

Social Worker After students have read the information in the book, ask: Why do you think there is a high demand for social workers who specialize in substance abuse and in the care of older adults? Which of those social work specialties is more appealing to you? Why? Then have students visit **glencoe.com** and read about the qualities a social worker needs.

▶ **FIGURE 3.2**

SOME COMMON EMOTIONS

R This table lists several emotions that most people experience regularly. Which of these emotions have you experienced?

Emotion	Description
Anger	Strong feeling of displeasure that results from being harmed or hurt
Empathy	Ability to experience the emotions of another person
Fear	An emotion that can help keep you safe from danger
Happiness	A sense of well-being, of feeling good about life in general
Jealousy	Resentment or unhappiness at another's good fortune
Love	A combination of caring and affection that binds one person to another
Sadness	A normal, healthy reaction to an unhappy event or disappointment
Sympathy	Ability to understand and share another's problems or sorrow because you have had similar problems or felt similar sorrow

ACTIVITY

Careers for the 21st Century

Social Worker

Social workers help people live the best way they can in their environment, deal with their relationships, and solve personal and family problems. There is an especially high demand for social workers who specialize in substance abuse or older adult care. If you want to be a social worker, you should take psychology and sociology classes.

What qualities does a social worker need? Go to *Career Corner* at **glencoe.com** to find out.

Expressing Emotions

There are many ways to express how you feel. When you look around you, you can see people expressing emotions in different ways. No emotion is either good or bad by itself. What is important is how you *express* your emotions. The way you express emotions affects your mental/emotional, social, and physical health. Therefore, learning to express emotions in healthy ways is important to maintaining good health. Some basic emotions that you can learn to express in healthy ways include anxiety, fear, and anger.

Expressing Anxiety

Have you ever had "pregame jitters" or waited backstage for your entrance in a performance? At these times, your heart beats faster and your stomach may churn. These physical responses are typical of anxiety. **Anxiety** is *a state of uneasiness, usually associated with a future uncertainty.*

AL Mild anxiety can actually be helpful. It gets your body ready for action and increases your energy levels. This energy can improve your performance. When anxiety builds up, however, it is not helpful. It can interfere with normal and necessary functions like sleeping and eating. To help you deal with feelings of anxiety, you can use resources from your home, school, and community. For example, talking through a problem with a family member, friend, or counselor can help you express your anxiety in a positive way. Sharing your feelings of anxiety with others may give you the reassurance and encouragement you need. When you do overcome anxiety, you build resilience. Another way to manage anxiety is to meet challenges "head on." Escaping from or avoiding situations is

TECHNOLOGY AND HEALTH

Media Coverage of Traumatic Events News is available 24 hours a day on television and the Internet. Constant news coverage of traumatic events, such as war, terrorism, and natural disasters can have an impact on anxiety levels in teens. Increased anxiety may result in sleep disturbances, irritability, or obsession with media coverage of an event. Tell students that strong feelings as a result of a disturbing news story are normal. Remind them that discussing disturbing events and images with parents, teachers, or other trusted adults is a good way to relieve their anxieties. **OL**

not helpful. When you meet a challenge, the anxiety may not be as bad the next time you face a similar challenge.

A heightened state of anxiety produces **panic**, *a feeling of sudden, intense fear.* Symptoms of panic include dizziness and a pounding heart. You will read more about extreme anxiety and panic in the next chapter.

Expressing Fear

 Sometimes, the anxiety you feel is related to fear. Have you ever jumped at a sudden loud noise? This reaction is an expression of fear. Fear is your mind and body's alert system. It prepares you for quick action in case a real threat exists. Therefore, expressing fear can be positive because it can help keep you safe from danger.

However, some fears, such as the fear of failure, may keep you from doing things you want or need to do. Fear stops being a protective force when it becomes a central focus in your life. Being afraid all the time is emotionally and physically draining. A positive way of expressing fear is to talk about it with a family member or friend. Support from family and friends can sometimes help you overcome your fears.

Reading Check **Explain** In what way is fear a helpful emotion?

Expressing Anger

Everyone feels angry sometimes. A younger brother or sister scribbles all over your homework. A friend you were supposed to meet shows up late and has no excuse. Showing anger is not only normal, it is also an important emotional **release**. Keeping this emotion bottled up inside can be physically and emotionally harmful.

Although it is good to express anger, you need to express it in a healthful way. Assuming responsibility for expressing anger in appropriate ways is a positive health behavior. The Health Skills Activity on page 60 gives specific suggestions for expressing anger appropriately. Yelling at the cause of your anger is not a good solution. Neither is using threats, sarcasm, or other negative forms of behavior. These actions will only worsen the problem.

▲ Anxiety is uneasiness, usually over something that is about to occur. **Name a school-related event that has caused you to feel anxious.**

Academic Vocabulary

release (ree LEES) *(noun)* relief, liberation. *Crying and laughing are examples of emotional release.*

C Critical Thinking

Contrasting Ask: What are some situations in which fear is a positive, helpful emotion? *Fear can be positive if it keeps you from taking part in risky behaviors, such as using drugs.* What are some situations in which fear is a negative, unhealthy emotion? *Fear can be unhealthy if it keeps you from trying a sport or club that you've never tried before.* **OL**

AL Active Learning

Comic Strips Have students work in pairs to create a comic strip that shows one friend helping another overcome a fear. Remind students that comic strips use words and illustrations to make a point, and that many comic strips use humor to convey a message. Post the completed comic strips in the classroom. **OL**

Reading Check

Answer Fear is a helpful emotion when it keeps you from danger.

Academic Vocabulary

Release Have volunteers read aloud the definition and the example sentence. Point out that *release* is used as a noun. Ask volunteers to share sentences that use the word release as a verb. *Sample response: I can release my emotions by talking to a friend.*

Caption Answer

Photo Caption Possible response: I feel anxious before competing in track meets.

HEALTH LITERACY

Phobias Although fear is a normal human emotion, sometimes fears are exaggerated or irrational. These extreme fears, called phobias, can affect everyday functioning. Phobias can also lead to more serious problems with emotional health, including depression and social isolation. Tell students that they should talk to a parent or trusted adult if they are struggling with a phobia. Have each student research and share information about one common phobia. **OL**

Health Skills Activity

Practicing Healthful Behaviors

Anger Management

- Have students read the tips for anger management. Ask them to brainstorm any tips they would add to the list.
- Then have students work with a partner to develop a role-play.
- After each pair of students has performed, ask the remainder of the class to identify the specific anger-management skills demonstrated in the role-play. **OL**

W Writing Support

Essay Give students some time to brainstorm about past experiences in which they used defense mechanisms. Ask: What defense mechanisms did you use? Then have students write an essay discussing a defense mechanism and whether it helped them deal with their problem or not. **AL**

Reading Check

Answer Denial is refusing to accept what is real. Displacement is taking your feelings out on someone other than the person who hurt you. Defense mechanisms can keep you from feeling too much pain. They can also hurt other people or keep you from overcoming your problems.

Health Skills Activity

Practicing Healthful Behaviors

Anger Management

When emotions are running high, they can be difficult to control. It is at these times, though, that self-control is most important. The next time you feel angry, try these steps:

1. Take a deep breath. Try to relax.
2. Identify the specific cause of your anger. If necessary, leave the room so that you can collect your thoughts.
3. When you are calm enough to speak, tell the other person how you feel and what action has caused you to feel this way.
4. Write down your thoughts in a journal.
5. Practice the relaxation skills that are described in the next lesson.
6. Do a physical activity. A positive way to manage stress is to keep physically active.
7. Look for opportunities to laugh. Keeping a sense of humor is also a positive skill for managing anger.

With a Group

Role-play a situation in which one or both of you is upset over something. Use anger-management skills to express your anger in a healthy way. Be prepared to perform your role-play for classmates.

Defense Mechanisms

Defense mechanisms are strategies that help people deal with strong emotions. Everyone uses them. Denial and displacement are two defense mechanisms. *Denial is refusing to accept what is real.* For example, Gina's dog just died, but she acts like her dog is still alive. *Displacement is taking your feelings out on someone other than the person who hurt you.* James is angry that he wasn't picked to be on the baseball team. When he goes home, **W** he pushes his little brother. Both Gina and James used defense mechanisms because they didn't want to deal with the stress in their lives.

Some defense mechanisms can be helpful because they can keep you from feeling too much pain. However, they can also keep you from dealing with your problems. Sublimation is a defense mechanism that can help you deal with stress. *Sublimation is taking strong feelings like anger or sadness and using them in a positive way.* You can deal with anger or sadness by talking to a friend, going for a walk, or writing in a journal.

 Reading Check

Analyze Describe two defense mechanisms. How can they be both helpful and harmful?

HEALTH LITERACY

Puberty and Emotions The hormonal changes during puberty can cause changes in the types and intensity of emotions experienced by teens. Most teens have more extreme moods during puberty, and many experience rapidly changing moods. Mixed emotions are also common during puberty. Assure students that emotional changes are typical during puberty. Tell students that even though these changes are normal, any teen who feels extremely sad, angry, or depressed for long periods should talk to a parent, guardian, or trusted adult. **OL**

Recognizing Emotional Needs

Just as everyone has emotions, everyone has emotional needs. These needs can be as important as physical needs such as water, food, and sleep. **Emotional needs** are *needs that affect your feelings and sense of well-being.* It is important to distinguish between a need and a want. A need is something that you must have, like warm clothes in the winter. A want is something you would like to have, like a video game or a CD.

There are three main emotional needs.

- **The need to love and be loved.** Love—caring for others and feeling cared about—is a basic human need. It directs many of the decisions we make and the actions we take. Your need to be loved—to feel special—is met by your family and friends.

- **The need to belong.** You are a member of your family and your class. You may belong to clubs or teams in or outside your school. This sense of belonging is essential. It lets you know there are others who accept and respect you.

- **The need to make a difference.** You need to feel that you are making a contribution, that your life has meaning, and that you are accomplishing something.

Healthy Ways to Meet Emotional Needs

There are healthy and unhealthy ways of meeting emotional needs. How you meet these needs is largely a matter of choice. For example, one healthy way to meet your need for love is to show others that you care about them. Offer to help out at home without being asked. Ask a friend how his or her day went. Encourage others when they feel down. When you show others that you care about them, they are more likely to show you the same caring.

As for your need to belong, think about your favorite hobbies or activities. What do you enjoy doing in your free time? Perhaps there is already a group or club devoted to it. Membership in this type of group will help satisfy your need to belong. It will also promote your social health by putting you in contact with others with similar interests. You may discover it is easier to build a friendship when you share a common interest.

To meet your need to feel you are making a difference, you could try volunteering. Find out some ways that you can help your community. You can offer the gift of your time or talents,

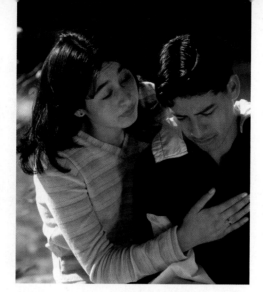

▲ When this teen has a problem, he is comforted by loved ones. **Why do you think it is important to have our emotional needs met?**

61

ASSESS

Assessment Resources

Lesson Review Quiz
* *ExamView*
* Fast Files Activities
* Online Quizzes and Activities

Reteaching

* Assign Concept Map 3-2 or Reteaching Activity 3-2 in the Fast Files.
* Have students make posters that use words, phrases, and art to describe healthy ways to manage and express anger.

Enrichment

* Assign Enrichment Activity 3-2 in the Fast Files.
* Have students analyze a book, movie, or television character who expresses anger. Have each student write a paragraph citing specific examples of healthy or unhealthy ways that this character manages his or her emotions.

CLOSE

Ask students to name the three main emotional needs and identify healthy ways in which these needs can be met.

▶ Joining a group or team can meet your emotional need to belong. **What are some healthy ways to meet your emotional need to make a difference?**

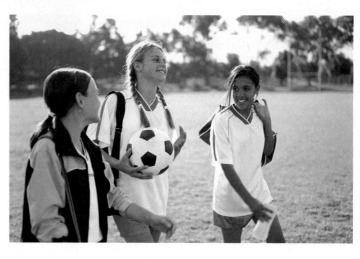

Go Online

Visit glencoe.com and complete the Interactive Study Guide for Lesson 2.

teaching others to do something that you love to do. Having a positive influence on others will give you a sense that you are making a difference.

Reading Check **Identify** Which emotional need can be met by friends and family members?

Lesson 2 Review

After You Read

Review this lesson for new terms, major headings, and Reading Checks.

What I Learned

1. *Vocabulary* Define *panic*. Which emotion does panic grow out of?

2. *Recall* What are mixed emotions?

3. *Explain* What are the basic human emotional needs?

Thinking Critically

4. *Analyze* Rick is annoyed at a teammate whose mistake on the field caused the team to lose the game. What emotions is Rick probably feeling? Explain.

5. *Synthesize* Certain character traits such as caring and respect help meet emotional needs. For example, a person who feels cared for will feel secure and loved. Give another example of a character trait and the emotional need it can meet.

Applying Health Skills

6. *Advocacy* Create a flyer that informs students of volunteer opportunities for teens in your community.

Go Online For more Lesson Review Activities, go to **glencoe.com**.

Lesson 2 Review Answers

1. Panic is a feeling of sudden, intense fear. Panic grows out of anxiety.
2. Mixed emotions are dissimilar feelings that occur at the same time.

3. the need to love and be loved, the need to belong, the need to feel worthwhile
4. He is probably feeling anger at the teammate who made the mistake and sadness over the loss of the game.

5. *Sample answer:* Citizenship makes you feel that your life has meaning and that you accomplished something. It meets the emotional need to make a difference.
6. Students' flyers should accurately describe a volunteer opportunity in the community.

Lesson 3

Managing Stress

Guide to Reading

● **Building Vocabulary**
As you read this lesson, try to identify which terms below are causes of other terms. Which are effects?

- stress (p. 63)
- stressor (p. 64)
- fight-or-flight response (p. 64)
- adrenaline (p. 65)
- time management (p. 67)

● **Focusing on the Main Ideas**
In this lesson, you will learn to

- **identify** the causes of stress.
- **describe** how your body responds to stress.
- **develop** skills to manage stress in your life.

● **Reading Strategy**
Organizing Information Look at Figure 3.4. List each body part in the chart. Tell how each is affected by stress.

What Is Stress?

As Scott waited for the midterm exam to start, his heart raced. His palms sweated, and his stomach felt like it had been tied in knots. What Scott was experiencing was a common form of anxiety called stress. **Stress** is *the body's response to change.* It is a normal reaction to certain situations or events in your life. The long-term physical effects of stress include nervous habits and problems sleeping or eating. Biting or picking your fingernails is an example of a stress-related habit.

Not all stress is bad. In fact, some stress is necessary. Positive stress can motivate you to do your best. For example, a small amount of stress can get you ready for a big game. Stress can also make you more alert and improve your concentration. This type of stress can help you perform to your fullest when faced with a big exam.

 Quick Write

Identify some causes of stress in your life that you have experienced more than once. Choose one, and write about steps you could take to lessen the effects of stress.

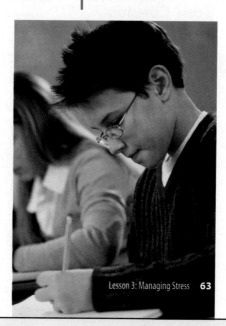

▶ Stress is a normal part of life. **What are some healthy ways of coping with stress?**

Lesson 3: Managing Stress   **63**

Lesson 3 Resources

📁 **Chapter FAST FILE Resources**
Guided Reading and Writing 3-3
Concept Mapping Activity 3-3
Health Lab 3-3
Reteaching Activity 3-3
Enrichment Activity 3-3
Lesson Quiz 3-3

Technology
⬇ Transparency 3-3
◗ Audio Summaries
◉ *ExamView® Assessment Suite*
◗ Vocabulary PuzzleMaker
◉ StudentWorks™ Plus
 Go Online

Lesson 3

FOCUS

Activating Prior Knowledge

What I Know Ask volunteers to describe information about stress and stress management they recall from Chapter 2. Tell students that this lesson will provide more information about healthy ways to manage stress.

Guide to Reading

Building Vocabulary
- Tell students that the word part *-or* means "something that causes a particular condition." Have students use this information to determine the relationship between the terms *stress* and *stressor*.
- Use Vocabulary PuzzleMaker to reinforce vocabulary terms. ◗

Reading Strategy
Organizing Information
Have students use a two-column chart to record the parts of the body and the effect that stress has on each part.

Quick Write

Have students keep their completed Quick Writes and review them after they have read the lesson.

Caption Answer

Photo Caption *Sample answer:* Exercising is a healthy way to cope with stress.

TEACH

What Teens THINK

In your opinion, what causes the most stress for teens? Have students form cooperative groups and, together, read and discuss the stressors listed in **Figure 3.3**. Encourage group members to suggest other stressors that might be included. Ask group members to agree on the "top three" stressors. Then have group members read and discuss the *What Teens Think* question and response.

R Reading Strategy

Analyzing a Graphic Have students examine **Figure 3.3**, which lists some common teen stressors. Ask: Which of these stressors would you consider to be positive stressors? Sample answer: *I would consider getting the lead in the school play to be a positive stressor.* **OL**

Reading Check

Answer, p. 65 a hormone that provides the body with extra energy

Caption Answer

Figure Caption *Sample answer:* I would consider failing at school as the most stressful and getting glasses as the least stressful. Students' responses will vary.

What Teens THINK

In your opinion, what causes the most stress for teens?

The things that cause the most stress for teens are school and peer pressure. We want to do well in school even if we aren't good at something. Peer pressure is also stressful because teens feel pressure to fit in no matter what they have to do.

Lydia F.
Albuquerque, NM

▶ FIGURE 3.3

SOME COMMON TEEN STRESSORS

R Different people respond to stressors differently. **If you were to rank these stressors in terms of most to least stressful, which would come first? Which would you put last?**

Extremely Stressful	Somewhat Stressful
Separation or divorce of parents	Arguing with a sibling or friend
Family member's alcohol or drug problem	Moving to a new home
Getting arrested	Going to a new school
Failing classes	Getting glasses or braces
Being suspended from school	Arguing with a parent
Starting to use alcohol or other drugs	Worrying over height, weight, or acne
Loss or death of a pet	Getting a lead role in the school play
Family member having a serious illness	Being sick or injured

Causes of Stress

Anything that causes stress is called a **stressor.** A stressor ranges from everyday annoyances to serious personal problems. They can be positive or negative. Have you ever been too excited to sleep? Maybe you feel this way the night before your birthday or at the start of a vacation. Positive and negative stress share similar symptoms.

Negative stressors can be minor events or major life-changing events. Some common stressors among teens appear below in **Figure 3.3.** Not all people respond the same way to a given stressor. For example, doing a presentation in front of the entire class may be stressful to one student but not to another. What are some common stressors in your life?

The Body's Response to Stress

Although stress is an emotional reaction to events, your body is also affected. The **fight-or-flight response** is *the process by which the body prepares to deal with a stressor.* Fighting or fleeing is the body's

HEALTH LITERACY

Stress and Depression Stress affects the body and mind in many ways. In some individuals, stress has been shown to lead to depression. Scientists have determined that the form of a particular gene, called 5-HTT, can determine the likelihood of stress turning into depression. Have students research other links between genetics and mental and emotional health. Have students share their findings in a short oral report. **OL**

natural response to threats of harm. Imagine a situation in which you feel afraid. For example, you are walking past a yard when a large dog starts barking at you. Your body undergoes changes that prepare it to act. One is the release of **adrenaline.** This is *a hormone that gives the body extra energy*. In the example of the dog, your response might be to back away. **Figure 3.4** shows how various body parts respond to stress.

 Reading Check **Define** What is *adrenaline*?

Excess Stress

Although some stress can be useful, your body can handle only so much. When stress—positive *or* negative—is **intense**, your health suffers. Excessive stress can affect all sides of your health triangle:

AL
- **Physical Health:** People with too much stress may have headaches, digestive problems, and high blood pressure. Ongoing stress can tire you out physically and reduce your body's ability to fight infection.

Academic Vocabulary

intense (in TENS) *(adjective)* extreme. *Olivia feels intense stress because she is singing a solo in the school play.*

▼ FIGURE 3.4

R THE BODY'S RESPONSES TO STRESS

Many parts of your body respond to stress. How do the lungs respond?

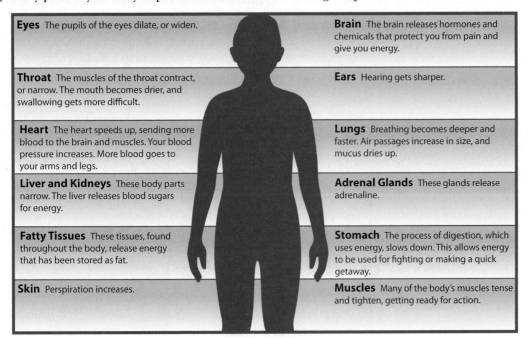

Eyes The pupils of the eyes dilate, or widen.

Brain The brain releases hormones and chemicals that protect you from pain and give you energy.

Throat The muscles of the throat contract, or narrow. The mouth becomes drier, and swallowing gets more difficult.

Ears Hearing gets sharper.

Heart The heart speeds up, sending more blood to the brain and muscles. Your blood pressure increases. More blood goes to your arms and legs.

Lungs Breathing becomes deeper and faster. Air passages increase in size, and mucus dries up.

Liver and Kidneys These body parts narrow. The liver releases blood sugars for energy.

Adrenal Glands These glands release adrenaline.

Fatty Tissues These tissues, found throughout the body, release energy that has been stored as fat.

Stomach The process of digestion, which uses energy, slows down. This allows energy to be used for fighting or making a quick getaway.

Skin Perspiration increases.

Muscles Many of the body's muscles tense and tighten, getting ready for action.

Lesson 3: Managing Stress **65**

AL Active Learning

Real-World Connection Have students reflect on the causes and effects of excess stress in their lives. Then have students prepare a written plan for reducing the stress in their lives to a manageable level. Ask students to include decision making, refusal skills, and communication skills as a part of their plan. In order to maintain student privacy, do not ask students to share their plans with the class. **OL**

R Reading Strategy

Analyzing a Graphic Direct students' attention to **Figure 3.4**, which shows some of the body's responses to stress. Ask: Why does stress sometimes cause an upset stomach? Sample answer: *The process of digestion slows down as a result of stress. This slowdown can cause the stomach to feel uncomfortably full or upset.* **OL**

Academic Vocabulary

Intense After students have read and discussed the definition and example sentence, ask them to suggest synonyms for *intense. Sample responses, in addition to extreme: strong, powerful, deep.* Then have them suggest antonyms. *Sample responses: weak, mild, shallow.*

Caption Answer

Figure Caption Stress causes breathing to become deeper and faster, air passages widen, and mucus dries up.

What Teens Want to Know

Why do I forget things when I'm stressed? Studies have found that stress can cause problems with memory. Cortisol, a hormone released in response to stress, has been shown to negatively impact memory in a temporary and reversible way. However, other studies have shown that stress impairs the ability to solve complex problems but might actually improve performance on simple fact recall. Have students discuss how stress can affect them during test-taking. **OL**

Health Skills Activity

Stress Management

Stress Chasers

Use the following strategies to help students complete the activity:

● Have students rate their current stress levels as described in the feature. Then ask students to practice each of the suggested stress-reducing exercises.

● Have students rate their levels of stress after performing the exercises.

● Have students write short descriptions of each of the exercises on index cards. Have students place the index cards in locations in which they often feel stressed. **OL**

R Reading Strategy

Identifying Cause and Effect Lead a class discussion of the causes and effects of stress and specific skills to manage stress. Then have students work in small groups to create graphic organizers that show causes, effects, and ways to manage stress. Have students further classify each of the effects of stress by identifying which of the three sides of the health triangle they affect. **OL**

Health Skills Activity

Stress Management

Stress Chasers

When you are feeling tense, doing some simple exercises can reduce stress. Practice the exercises below. Remember them for those stressful times when you need them.

- **Shoulder Lift.** Hunch your shoulders up to your ears for a few seconds, then release. Repeat.
- **Elastic Jaw.** Take a few deep, relaxing breaths. Open your mouth, and shift your jaw to the right as far as you can without discomfort. Hold for a count of three. Repeat on the left side.
- **Fist Clench.** Make a fist. Tense the muscles in your hand and forearm, then release. Repeat this with your other hand.

On Your Own

Estimate your current level of body tension or stress. Use a scale of 1 to 5, where 1 is *Totally Calm* and 5 is *Very Stressed*. Then perform one of the exercises listed here. When you are done, write down your estimated level of body tension. Repeat for each of the other exercises. How did each exercise affect your tension level? Compare your results with those of classmates.

- **Mental/Emotional Health:** Excessive stress can make you feel anxious, moody, and irritable. It can interfere with your schoolwork and take away your desire to have fun.

- **Social Health:** Some people under extreme stress will yell at those around them. Others withdraw, or back off, from social contacts.

These reactions are your body's way of telling you that it is overwhelmed. You need to manage your stress.

Skills for Managing Stress

You cannot remove stressors from your life, but you can manage the stress they cause. One way is to practice good health habits. This includes eating well and getting enough rest, especially during the teen years. When your level of wellness is high, you feel **R** good and are better able to handle problems.

Specific skills can also help you deal with stress. These include relaxing, laughing, and maintaining a positive outlook. In addition, staying physically active, managing your time, and socializing with family and friends are great ways to deal with stress.

HEALTH LITERACY

How Stress Affects Diabetics Diabetes is a growing health problem among young people. Stress is a factor that can make existing diabetes more difficult to manage. One of the physical responses to stress is an increase in blood sugar. When people with diabetes experience stress, they need to pay close attention to their blood sugar levels. Many doctors recommend relaxation exercises to their patients with diabetes. These exercises can help diabetics minimize stress and the accompanying increase in blood sugar.

Relaxation

Did you know you have the ability to slow down your heart rate? This ability is part of the stress-management skill known as *relaxation*. Relaxation makes you feel less tense. It helps you sleep better at night, which is an effective stress-reducing tool. Other relaxation skills include taking deep, even breaths and doing exercises that relax your muscles. Even quiet activities, such as reading a book or magazine, can help you relax and reduce stress.

▲ When you are feeling overwhelmed, having a good sense of humor can be a great help. **What are some other actions you could take that would bring a smile to your face?**

 Reading Check **List** What are three specific skills for managing stress?

Laughter and a Positive Outlook

One of the great stress relievers is a good laugh. If you can find a way to laugh when you are tense, you will find that it redirects the energy that stress creates. Think of a funny situation the next time you feel tense, or remind yourself of a good joke.

Even if you cannot laugh, try to maintain a positive outlook. Think positive thoughts. Remind yourself to look at the big picture and keep things in perspective. Ask for help if you need it.

Physical Activity

One of the healthiest ways to manage stress is to do something physical. Run around the block or a track at school. Shoot baskets. Dance to your favorite CD. When you are physically active, your brain releases chemicals that positively affect your mood. You tend to feel happier and more relaxed.

Time Management

One of the biggest causes of stress for teens is scheduling. Do you have trouble finding enough time for activities, chores, and homework? A skill that can help is **time management,** *strategies for using time efficiently.* The key to time management is arranging the hours in your day. One way of doing this is by making a day planner like the one in **Figure 3.5** on page 68. A day planner is an organized list of daily activities. Using a day planner can help you identify priorities and stay organized.

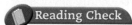 **Reading Check** **Explain** What information goes in a day planner?

Lesson 3: Managing Stress **67**

U **Universal Access**

English Learners Write the terms *positive outlook* and *positive thoughts* on the board. Have students locate these phrases in the student text under the heading "Laughter and a Positive Outlook." Explain that, in this context, *positive* means "happy, healthy, or optimistic." Have students describe any other uses of the word *positive* with which they are familiar (certain, sure, greater than 0) **EL**

R **Reading Strategy**

Analyzing a Graphic Have students examine the planner shown in **Figure 3.5** on page 68. Ask: How are all three sides of this teen's health triangle supported by items shown in the planner? Sample answer: *This teen supports her physical health by exercising at field hockey practice, her mental/emotional health by working on school projects, and her social health by taking time to call friends.* **OL**

 Reading Check

Answer, top sleep, taking deep breaths, and doing stress-reducing exercises **Answer, bottom** *Sample answer:* activities, appointments, and assignments

TECHNOLOGY AND HEALTH

PDAs for Time Management There are several ways in which technology can help with time management. Students may be familiar with electronic organizers, or personal digital assistants (PDAs). These handheld devices can store schedules, addresses, phone numbers, and other information. Many computer programs can also help teens manage their time wisely. Remind students that although technology is one tool for time management, a handwritten schedule can just as effective.

Caption Answer

Photo Caption *Sample answer:* Doing something physical can help me smile when I feel overwhelmed.

ASSESS

Assessment Resources

Lesson Review Quiz
- *ExamView*
- Fast Files Activities
- Online Quizzes and Activities

Reteaching

- Assign Concept Map 3-3 or Reteaching Activity 3-3 in the Fast Files.
- Have students write sentences naming specific ways that stress affects the three sides of the health triangle.

Enrichment

- Assign Enrichment Activity 3-3 in the Fast Files.
- Have students create a booklet describing positive ways that teens can manage stress.

CLOSE

Have students identify three examples of healthy ways to manage stress.

Caption Answer

Figure Caption This teen has scheduled his free time to watch TV and call Frannie, marked in blue.

▼ **FIGURE 3.5**

PLANNER FOR TYPICAL WEEKDAY

Highlighting certain activities can help you identify priorities. On this schedule, school activities are highlighted in yellow. **Which activities are shown in light blue?**

> 12:30 P.M. Lunch
> 1:15 P.M. Math
> 2:00 P.M. Social Studies
> 2:45 P.M. End of school; quick snack
> 3:00 P.M. Field hockey practice
> 4:00 P.M. Cello lesson
> 4:45 P.M. Go home; start homework
> 6:00 P.M. Dinner
> 7:00 P.M. TV
> 8:00 P.M. Finish homework
> 8:30 P.M. Work briefly on poster for group project due next week
> 8:50 P.M. Call Frannie
> 9:00 P.M. Ready for bed

Go Online

Visit glencoe.com and complete the Interactive Study Guide for Lesson 3.

Lesson 3 Review

After You Read

Review this lesson for new terms, major headings, and Reading Checks.

What I Learned

1. *Recall* What causes stress? Give several examples.

2. *Identify* What are three ways that your body responds to stress?

3. *Vocabulary* Define *time management*. Use the term in a sentence that describes how it reduces stress.

Thinking Critically

4. *Evaluate* Which stressor mentioned in the chapter affects you most? Explain why.

5. *Apply* As soon as Lisa came to class, she discovered that a report assigned two weeks earlier was due. Lisa had forgotten about it and was now feeling stress. How could using a planner have helped her?

Applying Health Skills

6. *Practicing Healthful Behaviors* One way to reduce stress is to prepare for it. Make a list of personal health behaviors that will prevent or reduce stress in your life. For example, identify physical activities you enjoy doing. Keep your list handy.

68 Chapter 3: Mental and Emotional Health

Go Online For more Lesson Review Activities, go to glencoe.com.

Lesson 3 Review Answers

1. Stressors cause stress. Some examples are tests at school or a move to a new home.
2. Answers can include any of the physical responses mentioned in **Figure 3.4**, page 65.

3. Time management is a strategy for budgeting your time. Sentences will vary.
4. *Sample answer:* School performance is the stressor that most affects me because I want to get good grades. Answers will vary.

5. Keeping a planner would have reminded Lisa to work on her assignment before the due date.
6. Students' lists will vary but should include healthy ways to prevent or manage stress.

Coping with Loss

Guide to Reading

● **Building Vocabulary**
As you read this lesson, write each new highlighted term and its definition in your notebook.

- grief (p. 69)
- grief reaction (p. 69)
- coping strategies (p. 70)

● **Focusing on the Main Ideas**
In this lesson, you will learn to

- **identify** stages in the grief reaction.
- **recognize** strategies for coping with personal loss.
- **provide** emotional support to someone who is grieving.

● **Reading Strategy**
Predicting Quickly look at the main headings, figures, and captions before reading the lesson. Based on previous knowledge, tell what you think you might learn.

Loss

Loss is unfortunately an unavoidable part of life. Perhaps your team loses a game. Maybe your neighbor loses a bracelet that belonged to her grandmother. Losses can be very painful. Emotional pain can sometimes be more intense than physical pain.

One of the most painful types of loss is when someone close to you dies. This loss can be a relative, a friend, or even a family pet. At such times, it is normal for those who suffer the loss to experience grief. **Grief** is *the sorrow caused by the loss of a loved one.* How long grief lasts after a death depends on the individual.

The Grief Reaction

Any loss or serious disappointment can lead to a grief reaction. A **grief reaction** is *the process of dealing with strong feelings following any loss.* Major stressors in a person's life can cause a grief reaction. The stressor might be the breakup of a friendship following a big argument. It might be disappointment over getting turned down by a club or team. When it comes to grieving, judgments of *right* or *wrong* do not apply. People feel sad for different reasons.

 Quick Write

Write a paragraph describing how you would help a friend who has lost a loved one.

▼ Friends can be a source of comfort when you are grieving. **What are some other ways of coping with loss?**

Lesson 4: Coping with Loss **69**

FOCUS

Activating Prior Knowledge

What I Know Ask students to recall a book or movie in which one of the characters dies. Have students describe the reactions of the other characters. Tell students that in this lesson, they will learn more about the emotions caused by the death of a loved one.

Guide to Reading

Building Vocabulary
- Tell students that a *reaction* is a response to a situation. Ask students to relate this to the term *grief reaction*.
- Use Vocabulary PuzzleMaker to reinforce vocabulary terms.

Reading Strategy
Predicting Have students list three topics they think will be discussed in this lesson. Have each student describe what he or she hopes to learn about that topic.

Quick Write

Ask students to include at least two specific strategies for helping a friend in their Quick Writes.

TEACH

Advocacy Have students work in small groups to create a design for a Web site that could be used to teach other teens about the stages of the grief reaction. Students' designs should include a flowchart or storyboard of the Web site and an outline of the information to be included. Tell students that this activity involves only a design for a Web site, not the actual programming. **OL**

ACTIVITY DEVELOPING Good Character

Caring
Have students work in small groups to identify other situations in which a person might need caring and support. Have each group share its list with the class. Ask volunteers to describe the actions they would take to show caring in one situation.

Reading Check

Answer Grief is the sorrow caused by the loss of a loved one; the grief reaction is the process of dealing with strong feelings after any loss.

Caption Answer

Photo Caption Looking at photographs is one way to remember a loved one.

70

▲ During the acceptance stage of the grief reaction, a person becomes ready to move on. **What are some ways that we remember loved ones whom we have lost?**

ACTIVITY DEVELOPING Good Character

Caring

It can be difficult and awkward to be around people who are grieving. Sometimes you may not know what to say. Yet, your presence can mean a lot to someone who you care about. It shows the person you are there for him or her.

Identify a situation other than a loss where a person might need caring.

The grief reaction usually occurs in five stages. Each stage has a different emotional state. These stages usually happen in the order shown below, but there are no hard and fast rules. Not all people go through all the stages.

Denial. Denial is usually the first stage you go through after a major loss. People who are in denial can't believe that the loss or serious disappointment happened. They may pretend that the loss or disappointment never happened.

Anger. At this stage, you may feel intense bitterness or anger. In the case of a death, the feelings may be toward the person who died. They can even be directed at other family members or friends.

Bargaining. In the bargaining stage, you try to make a deal in order to fix your disappointment or bring back a serious loss. For example, you might think that if you try hard and get good grades on your next report card, your grandfather will be cured of his illness.

Depression. Deep sadness sets in at this stage. The reality of the loss begins to sink in. You begin to acknowledge, maybe for the first time, that the loss is permanent.

Acceptance. This stage, which often comes last, is one where you feel ready to move on with your life. The pain lessens. If the loss was a death, the person now becomes the subject of memories that you can always have with you.

Reading Check

Compare Explain the difference between grief and the grief reaction.

Coping with Grief

As everyone knows, there is no way to undo a loss. Fortunately, there are ways of coping with the grief that loss creates. These **coping strategies** are *ways of dealing with the sense of loss people feel at the death of someone close.* These strategies may help you during a very difficult time.

When you suffer a loss, sadness and crying are normal reactions. Shedding tears is a way that your body deals physically with strong emotions. Instead of keeping your emotions bottled up inside, share them with others. Sometimes just talking about it helps.

HS

Dealing with Sensitive Issues

Students Who Are Grieving Discussions of the grieving process can be painful for students who have recently suffered a loss. Be sensitive to those students who find it too difficult to participate in the activities related to the lesson content. Respect student confidentiality—never ask students to describe their personal reaction to a loss. Without singling out individual students, remind the class that grief is a normal reaction that takes time to work through.

Helping Others Who Are Grieving

When someone close to you, such as a friend, suffers a loss, you can be a great help to that person. It is important, however, to understand the person's needs. Different people have different emotional needs. Here are some suggestions:

- Let the person decide how you can be a source of comfort. Do not insist on talking or giving advice. Sometimes you can be a big source of comfort just by being there. Ask the person what you can do to help.

- Respect the person's feelings. Remember that feeling sad is not wrong or immature. The loss a person feels may not seem important to you, but it may cause great pain to the other person.

- Allow the person to decide how much time he or she need to recover. Some people get over losses faster than others. It is up to each individual to decide how long to grieve.

 Go Online

Visit **glencoe.com** and complete the Interactive Study Guide for Lesson 4.

 Reading Check **Define** What are *coping strategies*?

 Lesson 4 Review

 After You Read

Review this lesson for new terms, major headings, and Reading Checks.

What I Learned

1. *Vocabulary* What is *grief*?

2. *Recall* Name the five stages in the grief reaction.

3. *List* What are three ways of showing emotional support for someone who is grieving?

4. *Explain* What are some coping strategies for dealing with grief?

Thinking Critically

5. *Synthesize* How might coping with a personal loss be said to be both emotional and physical?

6. *Evaluate* Trish just found out her best friend is moving away. Trish is feeling sad and upset. Trish's sister Brittany told her she needs to "get over it." Do you think Brittany's words show emotional support? Explain your answer.

Applying Health Skills

7. *Managing Stress* The death of a loved one can be a very stressful experience. Talk with a grandparent or other older adult about strategies for managing this stress. Share your findings with classmates.

 Go Online For more Lesson Review Activities, go to glencoe.com.

Lesson 4: Coping with Loss **71**

 Reading Check

Answer Coping strategies are ways of dealing with the sense of loss people feel at the death of someone close.

ASSESS

 Assessment Resources

Lesson Review Quiz
 ExamView
 Fast Files Activities
Online Quizzes and Activities

Reteaching

- Assign Concept Map 3-4 or Reteaching Activity 3-4 in the Fast Files. 📁
- For each of the stages of grieving, have students write a summary statement in their own words.

Enrichment

- Assign Enrichment Activity 3-4 in the Fast Files. 📁
- Have students work in pairs to write and perform role-plays that demonstrate one friend helping another who is grieving over the loss of a beloved pet.

CLOSE

Call on students to name a strategy for coping with grief.

 Lesson 4 Review Answers

1. Grief is the sorrow caused by the loss of a loved one.
2. denial, anger, bargaining, depression, and acceptance
3. *Sample answers:* give the person time to recover, ask how to be most helpful, respect his or her feelings

4. Coping strategies include confronting and sharing your feelings, sadness, crying, and participating in religious traditions.
5. A loss is emotional because it involves deep feeling and physical because many expressions of grief, such as crying, are physical.

6. *Sample answer:* No, Brittany needs to give Trish time to feel sad.
7. Remind students to be sensitive when asking older adults about loss and grief.

Building Health Skills Putting Stress in Its Place

Skill

Stress Management

Activating Prior Knowledge

Have students describe tips for time management. Record their responses on the board. Tell students that this activity will show them how to apply time-management skills to reduce stress in their lives.

- **Objective** After completing the activity, students will be able to apply time-management skills to help manage stress.
- **Time** 90 minutes
- **Materials** paper, pencil

Teacher Classroom Resources

📁 Building Health Skills
🖱 Transparency 3-3

Model

- Have students work individually to read about Alexa. Ask: Do you think the problems Alexa was experiencing are common among teens today? Sample answer: *Yes, many teens try to do too much each day.*

National Health Standards Addressed

1.8.5, 1.8.7, 7.8.2

72

Building Health Skills

Accessing Information
Practicing Healthful Behaviors
Stress Management
Analyzing Influences
Communication Skills
Refusal Skills
Conflict Resolution
Decision Making
Goal Setting
Advocacy

What Is Stress Management?

Stress management includes activities and behaviors that help you deal with stress in a healthy way. When you experience stress, do one or more of the following:

- Get plenty of sleep.
- Think positive thoughts.
- Make time to relax.
- Be physically active.
- Talk to someone you trust.
- Manage your time wisely.

Putting Stress in Its Place

Follow the Model, Practice, and Apply steps to help you master this important health skill.

❶ Model

Read how Alexa uses stress-management skills to help her relieve stress.

Alexa has a busy schedule. She works on the school newspaper and plays on two school sports teams. Lately, Alexa has been having trouble sleeping.

Her teacher, Mrs. Grace, explained that Alexa's hectic schedule could be causing her stress. She showed Alexa a strategy for managing her stress.

- **Identify Sources of Stress:** Besides her packed schedule, Alexa was feeling anxious about her upcoming performance in the school play.
- **Set Priorities:** First, she decided which after-school activities were most important to her. She decided to eliminate one after-school sport.
- **Manage Your Time Wisely:** After reducing her activities, Alexa made a day planner to help her stay organized.

The plan worked! Before long, Alexa found herself falling asleep the minute her head hit the pillow.

Teaching Tips

Connecting to Physical Activity Because stress-management skills often involve some form of physical activity, talk with the physical education teacher to find out what is being taught in gym class that month. Connect these activities to healthful stress management. Ask the physical education teacher to mention the stress management benefits of physical activity.

Posting Exemplars Post articles that have attained a rubric score of at least 3. These examples of quality work, or exemplars, will highlight the "real world" assessments from your health classes.

❷ Practice

Use stress-management skills to help Dima resolve his conflict with his sister.

Dima and his sister share a computer at home. Each of them feels the other "hogs" the computer after school. Dima is sometimes up late at night doing his homework as a result of this problem. He is tired at school the next day and finds it hard to concentrate during his classes. Use the three-step stress-management strategy to solve the problem as you think Dima might. Use these questions to guide your work:

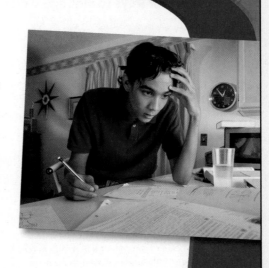

1. What is the source of the stress?
2. What priorities could Dima and his sister set?
3. How could time management apply to this situation?

❸ Apply

Use what you have learned about stress management to complete the activity below.

With a group, write an article for a school newspaper about stress. In your article, explain the effects of stress. Then, choose one source of teen stress. Give examples that show how to set priorities and manage time to reduce this source of stress. Share your article with the rest of the class.

Self-Check
- Did we explain the effects of stress?
- Did we describe a source of stress for teens?
- Did we show how to set priorities and manage time to reduce stress?

Building Health Skills

Practice
- Have students work in small groups to read and discuss the Practice activity.
- Ask each group to prepare a written response to each of the questions in the Practice activity.
- Call on various groups to share how they applied time-management skills to help Dima and his sister develop a plan for sharing the computer.

Apply/Assess
- Have students work in small groups to complete the Apply activity.
- Have each group share its article with the class. Post the completed articles in the classroom, or arrange to have several of the articles published in the school newspaper or Web site.
- You may wish to distribute the Building Health Skills Activity in the Fast Files. 📁

ASSESSMENT SCORING

Student work should meet all criteria to achieve the highest score.

Skills Student work:
- identifies a source of stress.
- demonstrates setting priorities.
- shows how to manage time.

Concepts Student work:
- includes accurate information about stress.
- provides comprehensive information about stress.
- explains the relationship between stress and health.

Stress Stoppers

Objectives

After completing the activity, students will be able to
- Understand how extracurricular activities can be a source of fun
- Identify ways to prevent stressful situations in the classroom
- Describe how breathing exercises can be used to reduce stress

Motivator

Ask: What are some of the main causes of stress for teens? Sample answers: *sports, schoolwork, parents*

Teaching the Activity

- Clarify the difference between stress and stress management with an example of each. Then, have pairs of students take turns telling about an experience in which they felt stress. They should explain how one of the stress-management techniques discussed in the article could have been helpful in combating the stressful event.
- Have students work individually to set a personal health goal to try one of the strategies for stress management in the next week. At the end of the week, ask volunteers to describe their experiences.

TIME *health news*

Looking for ways to manage stress in your life? The tips on this page can help!

STRESS STOPPERS

Whether it's from schoolwork or issues with friends, pressure has a way of popping up all over the place. Keep a handle on the stress in your life by...

HAVING FUN

After-school activities are a great way to blow off steam. Just make sure they make life more fun—not more stressful! Here's how:

1. Follow your heart. Don't think about whether other kids think a club is cool or not. You'll enjoy yourself more if the activity is something that interests you.

2. Don't let extracurriculars run your life. Limit yourself to a few clubs or teams at a time. You can always try a new one next semester.

3. Make it a bonding experience. Sometimes extracurriculars are less about the actual activity and more about the chance to make friends.

GETTING TO KNOW YOUR TEACHER

Prevent stressful situations in the classroom by building a good relationship with your teacher.

1. Figure out what kind of teacher you have. Is your teacher strict or laid back? The answer will tell you how to work in class. Really listen to your teacher about grading and class participation so you know what to expect.

2. Communicate after class. Even if you're just double-checking the details of an assignment, log some one-on-one face time with your teacher. It shows you're taking responsibility for your class performance.

TAKING A BREATH

To get rid of stress, try pausing for five minutes to focus on your breathing.

- Sit down and close your eyes.
- Take slow, deep breaths.
- If your mind wanders to the stress of your day, reign in your thoughts by concentrating on your breathing.
- Inhale slowly and hold the breath in for a few seconds.
- Now exhale, imagining you're exhaling any stress or tension.
- Keep at it for three to five minutes and you'll feel more calm and relaxed.

74 TIME health news: Stress Stoppers

Activity — *Media, Technology, and Culture*

Culture Have students discuss the common tendency of American teens and families to be overscheduled. Ask students to identify positive and negative aspects of being involved in many activities. Then have students prepare pamphlets that explain how stress management and time management can help teens who feel overscheduled. **OL**

CHAPTER 3 Reading Review

Visit **glencoe.com** to download quizzes and eFlashcards for Chapter 3.

FOLDABLES Study Organizer

Foldables® and Other Study Aids Take out the Foldable® that you created for Lesson 1 and any graphic organizers that you created for Lessons 1–4. Find a partner and quiz each other using these study aids.

Lesson 1 Your Mental and Emotional Health

Main Idea Your mental/emotional health affects every aspect of your life.

- To adapt means to adjust to new situations.
- Your personality and self-concept are two factors that determine your mental and emotional health.
- Personality is the unique combination of feelings, thoughts, and behaviors that make you different from everyone else.
- Self-concept is the view you have of yourself.
- Traits of good mental and emotional health include having a healthy outlook on life, dealing effectively with problems, bouncing back from disappointment, and accepting yourself and others.
- Ways to improve your self-esteem include listing your strengths, learning from your mistakes, and motivating yourself.

Lesson 2 Understanding Your Emotions

Main Idea Emotions are feelings created in response to thoughts, remarks, and events.

- No emotion is either good or bad by itself. What is important is how you express them.

- Common human emotions include anxiety, fear, and anger.
- The basic human emotional needs are the need to love and be loved, the need to belong, and the need to make a difference.

Lesson 3 Managing Stress

Main Idea People respond to stress in different ways.

- Stress is the body's response to change.
- Stress is caused by positive or negative stressors.
- Excessive stress can affect your physical, mental/emotional, and social health.
- Positive ways to manage stress include relaxing, laughing, maintaining a positive outlook, staying physically active, and managing your time.

Lesson 4 Coping with Loss

Main Idea Loss is an unfortunate and unavoidable part of life.

- Any loss or serious disappointment can lead to a grief reaction.
- Stages in the grief reaction include denial, anger, bargaining, depression, and acceptance.
- Strategies for coping with personal loss include confronting your feelings, allowing yourself to cry, and letting others know how you feel.

Assessment Resources

- Chapter 3 Summary and Activity
- Audio Summaries
- Reading Tutor
- Performance Assessment
- Chapter 3 Test
- *ExamView*
- Vocabulary PuzzleMaker
- Online Learning Center

Reading Review

Study Aids

- **Using the Dinah Zike Foldable® Study Organizer** Have students use the Foldable® to review verbal and nonverbal communication. Have them make a Venn diagram to compare and contrast the two forms of communication.
- **Online Learning Tools** Have students go to the *Teen Health* Online Learning Center at **glencoe.com** to:
  - Download a **Podcast**.
  - Download free **Study-to-Go** content to their PDAs or cell phones.

Vocabulary Review

- **Newspaper Article** Have students write a newspaper article describing a fictional event that correctly incorporates as many of the chapter vocabulary terms as possible.

Teaching Tips

Reading in Health Class Have students use previewing as a strategy to increase reading comprehension. Before students read each lesson, have them read the Main Ideas and vocabulary terms in the lesson opener. Then have students read the boldface heads in the lesson, and look at the figures and captions. Finally, have students read the questions in the Lesson Review. Tell students that this method will help increase their comprehension of the reading material and will help them locate the main ideas in the lesson content.

Assessment

Reviewing Vocabulary and Main Ideas

1. personality
2. self-concept
3. self-esteem
4. Emotions
5. anxiety
6. emotional needs
7. True
8. False, fight-or-flight response
9. True
10. False, bargaining
11. False, coping

Thinking Critically

12. Kris is feeling overly anxious; he needs to use stress-management techniques to calm himself down. Tom, by contrast, is experiencing a healthy amount of anxiety, which is preparing him for the contest ahead.
13. Felicia is experiencing grief over the loss of a pet. Her brother's gesture is a kind and caring one, but he needs to allow Felicia to determine for herself when she will be ready to move on.
14. Time management strategies might include using a day planner or PDA, identifying priorities, and being organized.

 Go Online

Have students visit **glencoe.com** to take the Chapter 3 quiz.

76

 After You Read

Health eSpotlight **VIDEO**

Now that you have read the chapter, look back at your answers to the Health eSpotlight questions on the chapter opener. What steps do you take to cope with stress and anxiety? What would your answer be now?

Reviewing Vocabulary and Main Ideas

On a sheet of paper, write the numbers 1–6. After each number, write the term from the list that best completes each sentence.

- anxiety
- coping strategies
- emotional needs
- emotions
- personality
- self-concept
- self-esteem
- stress

Lesson 1 Your Mental and Emotional Health

1. Your _____ is the unique combination of feelings, thoughts, and behavior that makes you different from everyone else.
2. The view you have of yourself is your _____.
3. Your _____ is the way you feel about yourself, and how you value yourself.

Lesson 2 Understanding Your Emotions

4. _____ are feelings created in response to thoughts, remarks, and events.

5. A state of uneasiness, that usually relates to being uncertain about something in the future, is called _____.
6. Needs that affect your feelings and sense of well-being are your _____.

*On a sheet of paper, write the numbers 7–11. Write **True** or **False** for each statement below. If the statement is false, change the underlined word or phrase to make it true.*

Lesson 3 Managing Stress

7. <u>Stress</u> is the body's response to change.
8. The process by which the body prepares to deal with a stressor is called <u>adrenaline</u>.
9. Physical activity and <u>laughter</u> are two skills for managing stress.

Lesson 4 Coping with Loss

10. The grief reaction includes denial, anger, <u>time management</u>, depression, and acceptance.
11. One important <u>grief</u> strategy that can help you deal with sorrow over a loss is confronting your feelings head-on.

Thinking Critically

Using complete sentences, answer the following questions on a sheet of paper.

12. **Compare and Contrast** Kris and Tom are both on the hockey team. A big game is coming up. Kris is unable to eat or think about anything else. Tom, meanwhile, cannot wait for the day of the big game. Compare and contrast the teens' levels of anxiety.

Go Online Visit glencoe.com and take the Online Quiz for Chapter 3.

Health eSpotlight **VIDEO** *Wrap-Up*

Coping with Stress Have students reread the Health eSpotlight question at the beginning of the chapter (page 51) and look at their original answer. Ask: Now that you have read the chapter and watched the video presentation, what steps might you suggest to a friend who said he or she was stressed-out? Call on volunteers to give examples of activities they use to relieve or cope with stress.

13. **Analyze** Felicia was very upset by the death of her cat. Her brother offered to get her a new cat, but this made Felicia feel worse. Explain what Felicia is going through. Also, explain her brother's attempt to make her feel better.

14. **Synthesize** What are some time-management strategies a teen could use to reduce stress?

Write About It

15. **Narrative Writing** Write a short story about a teen who is having a stressful day. In your story, identify the cause of the teen's stress. Show how the teen manages stress in healthy ways.

⌁ Applying Technology

Personal Awareness Cube

Using the draw tools in Microsoft Word®, you will create a Personal Awareness Cube, illustrating what makes you who you are.

- Open a new Microsoft Word® document. Use draw tools to form a 3-inch box. Copy and paste the box several more times, making a large square, 4 cubes tall, and 3 cubes wide.
- Write a few sentences for each box that discuss: personality, self-concept, self-esteem, expressing emotions, managing stress, and coping with loss.
- Drop digital images into your squares that demonstrate each of the six aspects of mental/emotional health mentioned above.
- Edit for accuracy of information, punctuation, grammar, clarity, and relevancy to peers.
- Save your project.

Standardized Test Practice

Math

One way of analyzing how you spend your time is by making a time pie chart like the sample chart shown. Use the sample chart to answer the questions that follow.

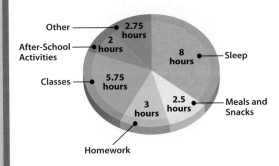

Other — 2.75 hours
After-School Activities — 2 hours
Classes — 5.75 hours
Homework — 3 hours
Meals and Snacks — 2.5 hours
Sleep — 8 hours

TEST TAKING TIP

Make sure you understand the different kinds of graphs and what each shows. Read the title of a graph for added information about what it contains.

1. Based on the number of hours per day this teen spends sleeping, it can be concluded that
   A. the teen gets too little sleep.
   B. the teen sleeps ¼ of the day.
   C. the teen sleeps ⅓ of the day.
   D. the teen spends too much time sleeping.

2. The percentage of the day this teen spends on homework is
   A. 12.5%.
   B. 30%.
   C. 3%.
   D. 8.33%.

⌁ Applying Technology

Personal Awareness Cube
Equipment needs: Microsoft Word® or similar software
Help students review and discuss the project steps, and let students decide whether they want to work independently or with partners. If necessary, draw the cube form on the board and help students understand how the squares will fit together to form a cube. If computer access is limited, create a sign-up sheet and have students agree on a time limit. If possible, have students print and fold their cubes and share their work with classmates.

Write About It

15. **Narrative Writing** Explain to students that narrative writing tells a clear story arranged in a logical order. This type of writing includes interesting characters, plot, setting, and dialogue. Stories will vary but should identify causes of stress and ways to manage it, which may include relaxing, laughing, maintaining a positive outlook, engaging in physical activity, managing time, and socializing with family and friends.

Standardized Test Practice

1. C
2. A

Test-Taking Tips

Interpreting Graphs Tell students that some test questions will require interpreting a graph to find the correct answer. It is important for students to first read the title of the graph, labels, key, and other information that accompanies the graph. Tell students to then read the test question. They can return to the graph to find the information required to answer the question.

CHAPTER 4 pp. 78–99	Standards		Skills and Activities
	National	**State/Local**	
	National Health Education Standards 1.8.7, 2.8.3, 4.8.1, 6.8.1, 7.8.2, 8.8.1, 8.8.2		**HEALTH INVENTORY**, *p. 79* **BUILDING HEALTH SKILLS** *Communication Skills* Listen Up!, *pp. 94–95* **HANDS-ON HEALTH** Interpreting Vocal Stress, *p. 96*
Lesson 1 **Mental and Emotional Disorders** pp. 80–85	National Health Education Standards 1.8.6, 2.8.1, 2.8.9, 3.8.2, 3.8.3, 3.8.4, 4.8.4, 5.8.1		**DEVELOPING GOOD CHARACTER** Compassion, *p. 81* **Go Online** Handling Depression, *p. 84*
Lesson 2 **Suicide Prevention** pp. 86–89	National Health Education Standards 1.8.5, 1.8.6, 2.8.1, 3.8.2, 3.8.4, 4.8.4, 7.8.1, 7.8.2, 7.8.3, 8.8.1, 8.8.2		**What Teens Think** How can you help a friend who is feeling sad? *p. 87* **HEALTH SKILLS ACTIVITY** *Communication Skills* Giving "Emotional First Aid," *p. 88*
Lesson 3 **Help for Mental and Emotional Disorders** pp. 90–93	National Health Education Standards 1.8.1, 1.8.5, 1.8.6, 3.8.2, 3.8.3, 3.8.4, 3.8.5, 4.8.4, 7.8.2, 7.8.3, 8.8.2		**Connect To... SCIENCE** The Brain's Chemical Messengers, *p. 91* **Careers for the 21st Century** Psychiatric Aide, *p. 92*

PACING THE CHAPTER			
Lesson 1	45 min	**Chapter Review**	45 min
Lesson 2	45 min	**Hands-on Health**	20 min
Lesson 3	45 min	**Building Health Skills**	90 min

BLOCK SCHEDULING

For block scheduling, assign students Building Health Skills feature *Listen Up!*, pages 94–95, and Guided Reading and Writing. 📁

StudentWorks Plus

Glencoe Exclusive!
TeacherWorks Plus™
All-In-One Planner and Resource Center

Reproducible Resources	Assessment	Media and Technology
Chapter FAST FILE Resources Chapter Summaries and Activities REVIEW Building Health Skills Activity TEACH Performance Assessment Activity EXTEND Universal Access Activities TEACH Parent Letter and Activities 📁 **Student Activities Workbook** TEACH 📁 **Reading Tutor** TEACH	Building Health Skills Activity, *pp. 94–95* Chapter 4 Assessment, *pp. 98–99* **Chapter FAST FILE Resources** Performance Assessment Activity, *p. 4* Chapter 4 Test, *p. 7* 💿 *ExamView® Assessment Suite*	TeacherWorks Plus includes: ● Interactive Teacher Edition ● Lesson Planner with Calendar ● Access to all blackline masters ● Correlations to standards 💿 StudentWorks™ Plus 🖱 Online Student Edition Dinah Zike's Teaching Health with Foldables®
Chapter FAST FILE Resources Concept Mapping Activity 4-1 REVIEW Cross-Curriculum Activity 4-1 EXTEND Enrichment Activity 4-1 EXTEND Lesson Plan 4-1 Guided Reading and Writing 4-1 TEACH Reteaching Activity 4-1 REVIEW	Lesson 1 Review, *p. 85* 🖱 Vocabulary PuzzleMaker 💿 *ExamView® Assessment Suite*	🖱 Vocabulary PuzzleMaker 💿 *ExamView® Assessment Suite* 💿 StudentWorks™ Plus 🔦 Transparency 4-1 **Go Online** glencoe.com
Chapter FAST FILE Resources Concept Mapping Activity 4-2 REVIEW Decision-Making Activity 4-2 EXTEND Enrichment Activity 4-2 EXTEND Lesson Plan 4-2 Guided Reading and Writing 4-2 TEACH Reteaching Activity 4-2 REVIEW	Lesson 2 Review, *p. 89* 🖱 Vocabulary PuzzleMaker 💿 *ExamView® Assessment Suite*	🖱 Vocabulary PuzzleMaker 💿 *ExamView® Assessment Suite* 💿 StudentWorks™ Plus 🔦 Transparency 4-2 **Go Online** glencoe.com
Chapter FAST FILE Resources Concept Mapping Activity 4-3 REVIEW Health Lab 4-3 EXTEND Enrichment Activity 4-3 EXTEND Lesson Plan 4-3 Guided Reading and Writing 4-3 TEACH Reteaching Activity 4-3 REVIEW	Lesson 3 Review, *p. 93* 🖱 Vocabulary PuzzleMaker 💿 *ExamView® Assessment Suite*	🖱 Vocabulary PuzzleMaker 💿 *ExamView® Assessment Suite* 💿 StudentWorks™ Plus 🔦 Transparency 4-3 **Go Online** glencoe.com

Chapter and Lesson Resources

The *Teen Health* resources are designed for differentiated learning abilities. You may want to use the coded items in this way:

REVIEW —activities to review or reinforce content
TEACH —activities to teach basic concepts
EXTEND —activities to extend or enrich lesson content

 OUT OF TIME?

Use Health Skills Activities *Giving "Emotional First Aid,"* page 88, or Developing Good Character, page 81.

Teens and Antidepressants

Some teens suffering from depression take prescribed antidepressant medications as part of their treatment. Some of these medications have been implicated in negative outcomes for teens, including suicidal tendencies and self-injury. Several well-documented violent incidents have brought this issue to the attention of parents and teachers.

The Food and Drug Administration (FDA) has recently placed a black box warning on antidepressant medications indicating that they might be harmful to teens and children. However, many teens and children tolerate these medications well and have been helped by them.

Currently, the FDA is evaluating the benefits and dangers of antidepressant medications for teens.

One study found that twice as many depressed young people who took an antidepressant tried to harm themselves, as compared to depressed teens who received a placebo. However, it can be difficult to evaluate if suicidal thoughts and self-injury are the result of medication or a natural progression in the course of depression.

Although there appears to be dangers for teens using antidepressants, when used under a doctor's direction these medications can alleviate symptoms of depression in some teens. Recommendations for teens who begin a course of antidepressants include careful observation for symptoms such as aggressive behavior, suicidal thoughts, extreme anger, self-injury, and restlessness. This close observation should take place whenever a teen starts or stops antidepressant medications or has an adjustment in dosage.

Studies are underway to clarify the benefits of different types of antidepressants for teens. The FDA Web site is one resource for updated information about this topic. The school nurse and guidance counselor can also help parents, teachers, and students who have questions about this issue.

Seasonal Affective Disorder

Seasonal affective disorder (SAD) is a form of depression that seems to occur because of the reduced amount of sunlight in the fall and winter.

The symptoms of SAD include episodes of depression that occur primarily in the fall and winter, as well as food cravings, weight gain, irritability, and fatigue. Most people with SAD have very few, if any, episodes of depression in the spring and summer. SAD is more common in regions with short winter days and cold winter weather.

Scientists and doctors are still refining the diagnostic criteria and treatment methods for SAD. Scientists estimate that about 5 percent of the population suffers from this form of depression. A much larger percentage of the population has a mild form of SAD, sometimes called "the winter blues."

Studies show that exposure to light is related to the release of brain chemicals that can affect mood. Treatment with bright lights, called phototherapy, is one method that brings relief from SAD to many patients. Other patients are successfully treated for SAD with antidepressant medications.

Although SAD is more common in adults than in teens, it is a disorder that teens should be aware of. Remind students that they should always discuss any form of depression with a parent, guardian, or trusted adult.

Support for Teaching Reading

 Reading Support

Reading Preview

Activating Background Vocabulary Ask students to write the chapter terms and main concepts on index cards. Encourage students to include terms in addition to the boldface vocabulary terms highlighted in each lesson. Direct students to sort the cards into categories such as: types of mental disorders, types of emotional disorders, suicide prevention terms, and help or treatment for mental disorders.

FOLDABLES Study Organizer *Dinah Zike's Reading and Study Skills for Teen Health* provides interactive graphic organizers that help students comprehend and retain health concepts as they read. Use the Foldable® on page 79 or find more Foldables® activities for the chapter on **Mental and Emotional Problems** in the separate booklet, available in the TCR.

Lesson 1 Mental and Emotional Disorders

SQ3R Guide and direct students to: 1) Survey—scan the title and headings of the lesson. 2) Question—restate each heading or subheading in the form of a question. Reword "**Anxiety Disorders**" to become "What are anxiety disorders?" 3) Read—find out about anxiety disorders by reading about OCD, panic disorder, and phobias. 4) Recite—record information about mental and emotional disorders in a notebook. 5) Review—go over notes and summarize each section with a partner.

Lesson 2 Suicide Prevention

Paraphrasing Have student pairs close their books and take turns using their own words to describe what they have read about the causes and warning signs of suicide. Determine whether students are identifying the main ideas and supporting details of the lesson. If students are unable to explain the information clearly, encourage them to reread the text to clarify the facts.

Lesson 3 Help for Mental and Emotional Disorders

Reciprocal Teaching Direct student pairs to: 1) Summarize—stop after reading the section titled **Kinds of Help** and take turns paraphrasing the content. 2) Clarify—ask each other if they have questions to answer before continuing to read. 3) Question—think about the types of questions a teacher might ask on an exam. 4) Predict—make a guess about what will come next in the lesson.

Post Reading

Multimedia Presentations Guide students in a discussion about mental and emotional problems, including suicide prevention and treatment for mental and emotional disorders. Have student pairs use a variety of reference materials to develop a presentation for the class that incorporates audiovisual aids and technology tools and covers one of the chapter issues.

Key for Using the Teacher Wraparound Edition

Use this key to help you identify the different types of prompts found in the Teacher Wraparound Edition.

R **Reading Strategies** activities help you teach reading skills and vocabulary.

C **Critical Thinking** strategies help students apply and extend what they have learned.

U **Universal Access** activities provide differentiated instruction for students learning to speak English, along with suggestions for teaching various types of learners.

HS **Health Skills Practice** activities reinforce Health Skills concepts and help students apply these skills in their everyday lives.

W **Writing Support** activities provide writing opportunities to help students comprehend the text.

AL **Active Learning** strategies provide a variety of activities for presenting lesson content, including Quick Demos and engaging classroom projects that get students actively involved.

Key to Ability Levels

Teaching Strategies and activities have been coded for ability level and appropriateness.

AL Activities for students working above grade level

OL Activities for students working on grade level

BL Activities for students working below grade level

EL Activities for English Learners

Symbols

Transparencies

CD-ROM

glencoe.com

Print Resources

CHAPTER 4

Mental and Emotional Problems

Mental and Emotional Problems

Chapter at a Glance

Lesson 1 identifies types of anxiety disorders, describes two mood disorders, and identifies signs of major depression.

Lesson 2 identifies warning signs of suicide, and demonstrates ways that effective communication skills can be used to help someone with mental and emotional problems.

Lesson 3 explains how to determine if someone needs professional help, describes the kinds of therapies used to treat mental and emotional disorders, and identifies kinds of professionals who help people with mental health problems.

R Reading Strategy

Interpreting the Photo Have students examine the photo of a teen showing sadness. Why is it important that this teen has someone to listen to her? Sample answer: *Caring and support can help people deal with emotional problems.*

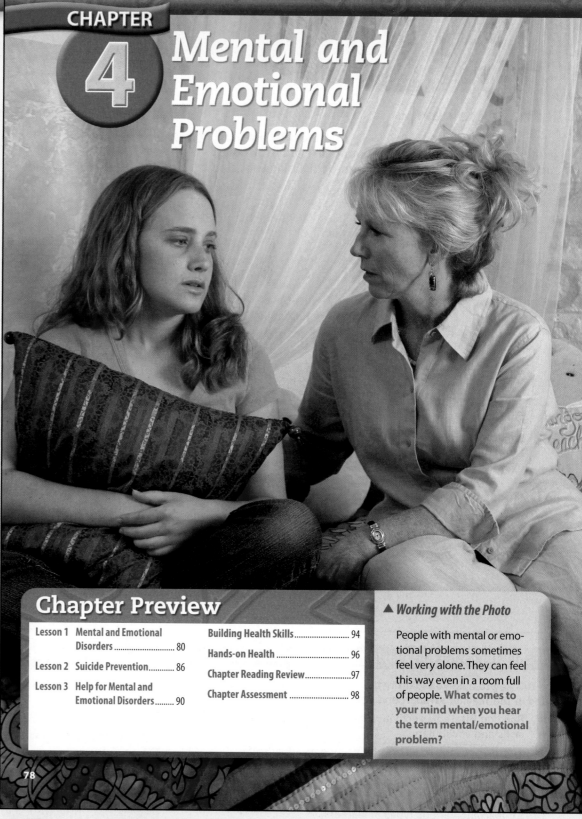

CHAPTER 4

Mental and Emotional Problems

Chapter Preview

78

▲ Working with the Photo

People with mental or emotional problems sometimes feel very alone. They can feel this way even in a room full of people. **What comes to your mind when you hear the term mental/emotional problem?**

 Universal Access

Differentiated Learning Glencoe provides teacher support and student materials for all learners in the health classroom.

- Spanish Glosario and chapter summaries for the English Language Learners.
- *Reading Tutor* and related worksheets support reluctant readers.

- Universal Access strategies throughout the Teacher Wraparound Edition and Fast Files help you present materials for gifted students, at-risk students, physically impaired students, and those with behavior disorders or learning disabilities.

Start-Up Activities

Before You Read Do you handle mental and emotional problems in healthful ways? Find out by taking the short health inventory on this page. Keep a record of your answers.

HEALTH INVENTORY

1. I deal with my problems in healthful ways.
(a) always   (b) sometimes   (c) never

2. I ask for help when a problem arises.
(a) always   (b) sometimes   (c) never

3. I am able to help a friend with an emotional problem.
(a) always   (b) sometimes   (c) never

FOLDABLES Study Organizer

As You Read Make this Foldable® to help you learn about mental and emotional problems. Begin with a plain sheet of 11" × 17" paper.

1 Fold the sheet of paper along the long axis. Leave a 1/2" tab along the side.

2 Turn the paper. Fold in half, then fold again.

3 Unfold and cut the top layer along the three fold lines. This makes four tabs.

4 Turn the paper vertically and label the tabs as shown. Write down the definitions of each type of mental and emotional disorder. Also, list characteristics of each type of mental and emotional disorder under the appropriate tab.

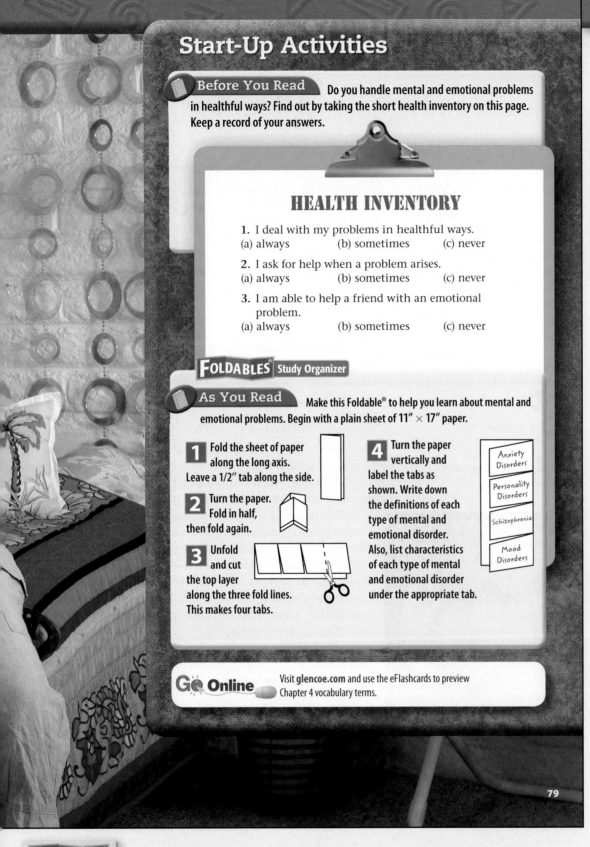

Tabs: Anxiety Disorders / Personality Disorders / Schizophrenia / Mood Disorders

Go Online Visit **glencoe.com** and use the eFlashcards to preview Chapter 4 vocabulary terms.

79

HEALTH INVENTORY

Mental and Emotional Problems Have students record their responses to the Health Inventory. Allow them to keep their responses confidential. Students may review their responses after reading the chapter.

No Child Left Behind

Dealing with Anger
Teachers often find themselves instructing teens who lack skills for coping with anger. Follow these tips to prevent angry outbursts in the classroom.

- Design and distribute a questionnaire about students' anger management skills. Questions should focus on students' behavior the last time they were angry, what they felt like inside, and what helped them calm down. Then lead a class discussion about the questionnaire.
- Create a calm spot in the classroom for students who cannot control their anger. Equip the area with popular magazines as well as paper and pencil. Ask students to write a brief anger log to explain what happened and why.

FOLDABLES Study Organizer
Dinah Zike Foldables®

Recording Main Ideas and Definitions
Model the steps for making the Foldable®. As students read Lesson 1, have them record the definitions of each type of mental and emotional disorder discussed in the text. Have students list characteristics of each type of mental and emotional disorder under each of the labeled tabs. Remind students to use their completed Foldables® to review the content of Lesson 1. **OL**

Go Online

Have students visit **glencoe.com** and use the eFlashcards for Chapter 4 vocabulary.

Lesson 1

FOCUS

Activating Prior Knowledge

What I Know Have students describe the importance of mental/emotional health to total health.

 Guide to Reading

Building Vocabulary

■ Tell students that the word *major* can be used to mean *serious*. Have students use this information to compare *major depression* to *sadness*.

■ Use Vocabulary PuzzleMaker to reinforce vocabulary terms.

Reading Strategy

Comparing and Contrasting Have students prepare compare and contrast diagrams that they can complete while reading the lesson. Have students use their Foldables® as they read Lesson 1.

FOLDABLES
Study Organizer

Quick Write

Have volunteers describe positive strategies they used when they felt upset. Allow students to keep their Quick Writes confidential if they choose.

Caption Answer

Photo Caption Being anxious is a sign of a larger problem when it interferes with normal functioning.

Mental and Emotional Disorders

 Guide to Reading

● Building Vocabulary

As you read this lesson, write each new highlighted term and its definition in your notebook.

■ disorder (p. 80)
■ anxiety disorder (p. 81)
■ phobia (p. 81)
■ personality disorder (p. 82)
■ mood disorder (p. 83)
■ major depression (p. 83)
■ schizophrenia (p. 85)

● Focusing on the Main Ideas

In this lesson, you will learn to

■ **identify** types of anxiety disorders.
■ **describe** two mood disorders.
■ **identify** signs of major depression.

● Reading Strategy

Comparing and Contrasting Create a diagram that shows similarities and differences among mental and emotional health disorders described in the lesson.

FOLDABLES Study Organizer Use the Foldable® on p. 79 as you read this lesson.

Quick Write

Think about a time when you were very sad. Tell what you did to overcome your sadness.

Kinds of Mental and Emotional Disorders

Many myths surround the subject of mental and emotional problems. One myth is that these conditions are not true illnesses, like heart disease or diabetes. Another myth is that people can just "snap out of" these problems if they try hard enough.

The truth is that mental and emotional problems are as real as physical problems. They can affect people of any age. Studies released by the National Mental Health Information Center show that mental disorders affect at least one in five children and adolescents. Like other diseases, mental and emotional disorders can be treated. Treatment can include medication, counseling, or both. Ignoring your problems won't make them go away.

A **disorder** is *a disturbance in the normal function of a part of the body.* In this lesson you will learn about several common mental and emotional disorders.

◀ Some anxiety is normal. **When does being anxious suggest a larger problem?**

80 Chapter 4: Mental and Emotional Problems

Lesson 1 Resources

📁 **Chapter *FAST FILE* Resources**
Guided Reading and Writing 4-1
Concept Mapping Activity 4-1
Cross-Curriculum Activity 4-1
Reteaching Activity 4-1
Enrichment Activity 4-1
Lesson Quiz 4-1

Technology
🔥 Transparency 4-1
Audio Summaries
ExamView® Assessment Suite
Vocabulary PuzzleMaker
StudentWorks™ Plus
Go Online

Anxiety Disorders

Everyone feels anxious at one time or another. For example, you might be worried the night before a big test. Problems at home or at school can also be a source of anxiety. It is normal to feel this way when you are faced with a challenge. Some people, however, become frequently and unreasonably worried. They might have an **anxiety disorder.** This is *a disorder in which intense anxiety or fear keeps a person from functioning normally.* The five types of anxiety disorders and their symptoms are listed in **Figure 4.1.**

One type of anxiety disorder is a **phobia,** or *an exaggerated fear of a specific situation or object.* You have probably heard of certain phobias, such as fear of flying or of spiders. **Figure 4.2** on the next page shows some common phobias. Some fears are not only normal, but necessary. For example, concern over walking down a dark, deserted street in an unsafe neighborhood is an understandable fear. It shows that you have a healthy awareness of risk, not that you have a phobia.

Anxiety disorders may first become **apparent** during the teen years or young adulthood. Treatments are available that can help people with these disorders lead full, productive lives.

Reading Check **Define** What is an *anxiety disorder*?

▼ FIGURE 4.1

TYPES OF ANXIETY DISORDERS

Anxiety disorders are grouped into the five categories shown here. **What are the symptoms of obsessive-compulsive disorder?**

Disorder	Symptoms
Generalized Anxiety Disorder	Restlessness, tiredness, difficulty concentrating, irritability, muscle tension, sleep disturbances
Panic Disorder	Pounding heart, sweating, trembling, shortness of breath, nausea, fear of losing control
Phobia	An intense or exaggerated fear of a specific situation or object
Obsessive-Compulsive Disorder	A need to perform behaviors over and over again, such as handwashing, counting, hoarding, or arranging possessions
Post-Traumatic Stress Disorder	Withdrawal or depression after a distressing experience such as sexual abuse, a natural disaster, an accident, or witnessing violence

DEVELOPING Good Character

Compassion

People with mental and emotional problems need the help and support of those around them. One way of demonstrating support is by showing compassion. This means being sympathetic to the problems others are dealing with. By showing compassion, you let others know that you care about them.

What are some actions you could take to show compassion?

Academic Vocabulary

apparent (uh PAIR uhnt) *(adjective)* clear or easily understood. *Elliot was worried about his dental appointment for no apparent reason.*

TEACH

ACTIVITY DEVELOPING Good Character

Compassion
Have students read the feature. Then ask students to identify actions that show compassion. Record students' responses on the board. Ask students to brainstorm a list of careers that would be well-suited for a person who is good at showing compassion. **OL**

R Reading Strategy

Analyzing a Table Divide the class into small groups. Assign one of the types of anxiety disorders discussed in **Figure 4.1** to each group. Have each group prepare a short lesson to teach the class about its assigned topic. Ask each group to develop and administer a short quiz to assess the other students' understanding of the material. **OL**

Academic Vocabulary

Apparent Explain that the adjective apparent is related to the verb *appear.* Let volunteers explain the meaning of appear. Sample response: *come into sight or show up.* Then ask: How does understanding the word *appear* help you understand *apparent?* 📂

Reading Check

Answer When intense anxiety causes a person to stop functioning normally

---

✚ Promoting Coordinated School Health

School Environment and Anxiety Disorders
Several factors in students' school environments can contribute to the development of mental health problems related to anxiety. The Healthy School Environment component of a Coordinated School Health Plan can be used to reduce or eliminate some of these factors. For example, witnessing or being a victim of violence can contribute to post-traumatic stress disorder. Schools can provide a safe and healthy environment to minimize students' exposure to violence, thereby reducing student anxiety.

▼ **FIGURE 4.2**

R **SOME COMMON PHOBIAS FROM A TO Z**

The table lists several different types of phobias. **What is acrophobia?**

Some Common Phobias from A to Z	
Acrophobia	Fear of heights
Agoraphobia	Fear of crowded places or open areas
Astraphobia	Fear of thunder and lightning
Claustrophobia	Fear of enclosed spaces
Ecophobia	Fear of home
Glossophobia	Fear of public speaking
Hydrophobia	Fear of water
Kenophobia	Fear of empty spaces
Noctiphobia	Fear of night
Socialphobia	Fear of people
Tachophobia	Fear of speed
Zoophobia	Fear of animals

▼ Arachnophobia, a fear of spiders, is a common phobia. **What are some other phobias that you have heard of?**

Personality Disorders

W People have a basic need to belong and be accepted by others. Some people, however, have a lot of trouble relating to others. They may suffer from a personality disorder. A **personality disorder** is *a psychological condition that affects a person's ability to interact normally with others.*

U One example is *passive-aggressive personality disorder.* People with this disorder can have a hard time cooperating with others. They do not like being told what to do, and can become very angry when they feel like they do not have control over a situation. In these cases, they show their anger in unhealthy and inappropriate ways. For example, in a group activity if a passive-aggressive person becomes angry, he or she might respond passively—by not participating at all. He or she may also respond aggressively—by yelling or being mean to others in the group.

Another personality disorder is *borderline personality disorder.* People with this disorder have trouble in close relationships with others. This is because when they are involved in a close relationship with someone, they tend to idealize that person. If they become disappointed in that person, they might lash out in anger or even violence. People with this disorder also tend to engage in high-risk behaviors, have poor self-esteem, and have an intense fear of abandonment.

82 Chapter 4: Mental and Emotional Problems

What Teens Want to Know

Isn't schizophrenia a split personality? A common misconception about schizophrenia is that its symptoms include split, or multiple, personalities. Explain to students that this myth is entirely false. Schizophrenia is a brain disorder, affecting both the structure and the function of the brain. It is more common than many teens realize, affecting about 1 percent of the population at any given time. Have students use online resources to find out more about schizophrenia. Have students discuss their findings in small groups. **OL**

Mood Disorders

People who feel sad over a long period of time and for no explainable reason may have a **mood disorder.** This is *a disorder in which a person undergoes changes in mood that seem inappropriate or extreme.* Being overly happy, giddy, or energetic for no apparent reason can also be a sign of a mood disorder.

One mood disorder, previously known as manic-depressive disorder, is *bipolar disorder.* This illness is known for its mood "cycles." A person with bipolar disorder may experience alternating high and low periods. During the high—or *manic*—periods, the person can have increased energy. In the low—or *depressive*—periods, energy slows down drastically. Sometimes these mood cycles are rapid, but most often they are gradual.

The symptoms that come with the depressive side of bipolar disorder also occur in **major depression.** This is *a very serious mood disorder in which people lose interest in life and can no longer find enjoyment in anything.*

Everyone feels sad from time to time. Having occasional brief periods of sadness does not mean you have a mental or emotional disorder. Sharing your feelings with a parent, trusted adult, or friend can help.

Reading Check   **Define** What is a *mood disorder*?

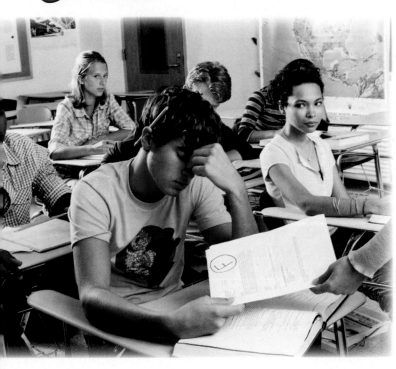

◀ Receiving bad news can make you feel down. **How is this type of sadness different from major depression?**

Lesson 1: Mental and Emotional Disorders   **83**

C Critical Thinking

Synthesizing After students have read the section on mood disorders, review with the class the Mental and Emotional Health Checklist from Chapter 3 (page 53). Ask: Name two factors that can contribute to positive mental/emotional health. *positive attitude, high self-esteem, resilience* Emphasize that while it is normal to experience mood swings and emotional changes, it is important to know how to deal with problems when they arise. OL

HS Health Skills Practice

Advocacy Have students prepare booklets that describe myths about mental disorders and provide facts that might encourage young people to seek help from mental health providers. Have students work with the school nurse or guidance counselor to obtain additional information for their booklets. Post the completed booklets in the classroom, or obtain permission for booklets to be posted in other areas of the school. OL

Reading Check

Answer A mood disorder is when a person has mood changes that seem inappropriate or extreme.

Caption Answer

Photo Caption Feeling down is normal in some situations. Major depression is loss of interest in life and inability to find enjoyment in anything.

FITNESS ZONE

Reaching Out with Physical Fitness Teens with mental and emotional disorders need treatment. However, they also need friendships and social contact with their peers. Have students page through the *Fitness Zone Handbook.* Then ask: How can exercising together help teens develop or maintain friendships? How could the group activities help teens spend positive time together? Why is that important? **For more information, see *Fitness Zone Handbook* pages xviii–1 or visit the Fitness Zone at glencoe.com.**

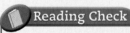

R Reading Strategy

Analyzing a Graphic Direct students' attention to **Figure 4.3.** Explain that many of these symptoms are normal for teens to experience occasionally or for short periods of time. Ask: If you have been experiencing irritability for the past four days, should you worry that you have major depression? Why or why not? *No, this is a typical feeling for teens to have occasionally. It is only a cause for worry if it continues for more than two weeks and is accompanied by other symptoms.* **OL**

Reading Check

Answer See **Figure 4.3.**

Caption Answer

Figure Caption Encourage the person to talk to a parent or other trusted adult.

ACTIVITY

Go Online

Topic: Handling Depression

Visit **glencoe.com** for Student Web Activities to learn about the signs of depression and what can be done to treat it.

Activity: Using the information provided at the link above, create a poster listing the warning signs of depression. Include information on where teens who are concerned about depression can get help.

Depression Among Teens

The teen years can be a difficult time in life. Friendships may suddenly seem more complicated. Your relationship with your parents and other family members are changing. During this time of life, some teens become depressed.

Some studies suggest that as many as 20 percent of teens suffer from major depression. Teens who are depressed may appear moody, angry, hostile, aggressive, and irritable. Depressed teens may turn to alcohol or other drugs. Other common signs of depression are shown in **Figure 4.3.**

When left untreated, depression can become worse. If you know someone who seems depressed, encourage that person to talk to a parent or other trusted adult. If he or she says that talking to someone will not help, you should tell a trusted adult about your concerns.

Reading Check **Explain** How may depressed teens behave?

▼ FIGURE 4.3

R

WARNING SIGNS OF DEPRESSION

A teen showing three or more of these warning signs for more than two weeks may be suffering from depression. **What can you do if you suspect someone you know is depressed?**

1. Irritability, anger, or anxiety
2. Lack of energy; feeling tired all the time
3. Significant change in sleep patterns; an inability to fall asleep, stay asleep, or get up in the morning
4. Inability to concentrate
5. Putting blame on other people for their problems, especially adults
6. Feelings of worthlessness or guilt
7. Indifference to things that used to bring pleasure
8. Pessimism
9. Physical problems, like stomachaches or headaches, that can't be explained
10. Thoughts of death or suicide

HEALTH LITERACY

Hypothyroidism and Depression
Hypothyroidism is a physical problem that can cause depression. This condition occurs when the thyroid gland produces an insufficient amount of hormones. Symptoms include depression, fatigue, hair loss, weakness, and cold intolerance.

Hypothyroidism is diagnosed using a blood test and is treatable with medication. Diabetes is another physical condition associated with an increased risk of depression. Have each student research the link between diabetes and depression and prepare a short written report. **OL**

▶ One characteristic of schizophrenia is a withdrawal from others. **Why might a person who suffers from schizophrenia want to withdraw from interacting with others?**

Schizophrenia

Schizophrenia (skit·zoh·FREE·nee·uh) is *a severe mental disorder in which people lose contact with reality.* They may have hallucinations in which they see or hear things that are not actually there. Schizophrenics are often unable to tell the difference between real events and ones they are imagining. For example, people in this state might think they are historical figures or that they have special powers.

One common aspect of schizophrenia is a withdrawal from others and from society. Schizophrenics tend to function in their own worlds, in which they develop a fear and mistrust of others.

Today, there is medication available to treat schizophrenia. Schizophrenics can lead relatively functional lives if they take these medicines properly.

 Go Online

Visit **glencoe.com** and complete the Interactive Study Guide for Lesson 1.

ASSESS

Assessment Resources

Lesson Review Quiz
* *ExamView*
* Fast Files Activities
* Online Quizzes and Activities

Reteaching

● Assign Concept Map 4-1 or Reteaching Activity 4-1 in the Fast Files.
● Have students work in pairs to review the common signs of depression shown in **Figure 4.3** and explain why symptoms of depression should be taken seriously.

Enrichment

● Assign Enrichment Activity 4-1 in the Fast Files.
● Have students use print and online resources to further research post-traumatic stress disorder. Have students share a short oral report of their findings.

CLOSE

Have students name and describe a disorder that affects mental/emotional health.

Lesson 1 Review

 After You Read

Review this lesson for new terms, major headings, and Reading Checks.

What I Learned

1. *Vocabulary* What is a *disorder*? Use this term in an original sentence.

2. *List* Name two mood disorders, and describe each.

3. *Recall* What are the five types of anxiety disorders?

Thinking Critically

4. *Synthesize* Look back at the myths about mental illness that opened the lesson. What do you think is a negative consequence of spreading these myths?

5. *Evaluate* Carl had worked hard on his entry for the school science fair. He was sad when he did not win an award for his project. Do you think Carl was experiencing major depression? Explain your answer.

Applying Health Skills

6. *Accessing Information* With a group, investigate one of the disorders described in the lesson. Use a variety of reliable sources. Make notes about the kinds of help available.

Go Online For more Lesson Review Activities, go to **glencoe.com**.

Lesson 1: Mental and Emotional Disorders **85**

Caption Answer
Photo Caption fear and mistrust

Lesson 1 Review Answers

1. It is a disturbance in the normal function of a part of the body. Sentences will vary.
2. Bipolar disorder is typified by extreme mood shifts; major depression is a loss of interest in life.
3. Generalized anxiety disorder, obsessive compulsive disorder, panic disorder, post-traumatic stress disorder, and phobia are anxiety disorders.
4. Myths may deter people from seeking the treatment they need.
5. No, sadness is a normal emotion in this circumstance.
6. Students should accurately describe a disorder and correctly identify help that is available for that disorder.

FOCUS

Activating Prior Knowledge

What I Know Ask students to describe symptoms of major depression that they learned about in Lesson 1. Tell students that major depression can lead to suicidal thoughts or actions.

Guide to Reading

Building Vocabulary
- Explain that *suicide* is the intentional taking of one's own life. Have students write a sentence that relates suicide to a mental or emotional problem.
- Use Vocabulary PuzzleMaker to reinforce vocabulary terms.

Reading Strategy
Finding the Main Idea Have students state the main idea of each section in their own words.

uick Write

Encourage students to write about the ways they could talk to a friend and encourage him or her to get help.

Suicide Prevention

Guide to Reading

Building Vocabulary
Find the term below where it appears highlighted in the lesson. Write the term and its definition in your notebook.
- suicide (p. 86)

Focusing on the Main Ideas
In this lesson, you will learn to
- **identify** causes of teen suicide.
- **identify** warning signs of suicide.
- **demonstrate** effective communication skills to help someone with mental and emotional problems.

Reading Strategy
Finding the Main Idea For each of the main headings in this lesson, write one sentence that states the main idea.

uick Write

Write a paragraph describing what you could do to help a friend who is talking about suicide.

Suicide

When depression lasts for weeks or months, the emotional pain can be overwhelming. Life may begin to seem hopeless for some individuals. Some teens may begin having thoughts of **suicide.** This is *the intentional taking of one's own life.* It is important to recognize the warning signs of suicide and seek help if you or someone you know is suffering from severe depression.

Causes of Teen Suicide

During the teen years, you will begin to accept new responsibilities and challenges within your family and at school. Accepting new challenges and responsibilities can cause stress. Life-changing events such as a family breakup or the death of someone close can feel overwhelming. Alcoholism or other drug dependencies within the family can cause a teen to become depressed. So can witnessing domestic violence or being a victim of physical or sexual abuse. In some instances, teens consider suicide because they cannot handle the pressures they face at home or at school. If a teen feels that his or her family is not supportive, he or she may become depressed. Being depressed can lead to thoughts of suicide.

Not all causes of teen suicide involve the home or family. Some teens consider suicide because they feel disconnected from

---

Lesson 2 Resources

 Chapter *FAST FILE* Resources
Guided Reading and Writing 4-2
Concept Mapping Activity 4-2
Decision-Making Activity 4-2
Reteaching Activity 4-2
Enrichment Activity 4-2
Lesson Quiz 4-2

Technology
Transparency 4-2
Audio Summaries
ExamView® Assessment Suite
Vocabulary PuzzleMaker
StudentWorks™ Plus
G⊙ Online

or rejected by peers. Because these teens may have few friends, their sadness can sometimes go unnoticed.

Warning Signs of Suicide

Teens thinking about suicide often share their plans openly. Many drop hints through their words and actions. They may say things like, "I can't take it anymore" or "No one cares if I live or die." Comments like these are warning signs. Never **assume** that a person who makes these kinds of remarks does not really mean it. Talk to a trusted adult immediately about what you heard. You might try suggesting that a person who needs help use resources in home, school, and community that provide valid health information.

Other warning signs of suicide include:

- **A sudden fascination with the topic of death.** The person may talk about different ways of dying. He or she may start reading or writing poems and stories about death.
- **Dramatic changes in the person's appearance.** The person may no longer take an interest in his or her appearance.
- **Self-destructive behavior.** The person may do reckless things. She or he may also suddenly decide to become sexually active or use drugs.

AL - **Withdrawal from friends, family, and regular activities.** Withdrawal is also a symptom of depression, and it shows that the person is letting go of things that were once important. He or she may also begin giving away valued possessions.
- **A sudden change in mood.** After weeks or months of being depressed, the person suddenly appears cheerful. This may look like a positive change, but sometimes it is not. Sometimes it means that the person has made up his or her mind to commit suicide.

Reading Check **List** Name two causes of teen suicide.

What Teens THINK

How can you help a friend who is feeling sad?

I would talk to my friend and find out why she is sad. After that, I would take here somewhere like the movies, mall, or anywhere as long as she won't feel sad anymore. Also, I would hug my friend and cheer her up. I know this would work because friends know how to help each other.

Emmy H.
Albertville, AL

Academic Vocabulary

assume (uh SOOM) *(verb)* to accept without proof, to take for granted. *Pedro didn't go to the dermatologist because he assumed that his acne would clear up on its on.*

TEACH

What Teens THINK

How can you help a friend who is feeling sad? Begin by letting students share their responses to this question: How can you tell that someone else feels sad? Encourage a variety of ideas. Then read the *What Teens Think* question, and let students discuss their own ideas in response. Finally, have students read and discuss the *What Teens Think* response.

AL Active Learning

Presentation Have students work in small groups to prepare a short computer slide presentation about the warning signs of teen suicide and the importance of always taking a threat seriously. Challenge students to present the information in a different way than it is in the text. **OL**

Academic Vocabulary

Assume To provide practice in understanding and using the word *assume,* ask: Why shouldn't you assume that someone who talks about suicide is bluffing? Have students respond in complete sentences using the word *assume.*

Reading Check

Answer Stressors or life-changing events may influence a teen to consider suicide.

Dealing with Sensitive Issues

Crisis Intervention When a student threatens suicide at school, it is traumatic for the students and the staff. Having a crisis intervention plan that every member of the faculty and staff is familiar with will allow for the most effective and efficient intervention possible. Emphasize that teens should always get immediate help from a faculty or staff member if a friend mentions suicide at school. Remind students that they should never promise a friend that they will keep secrets regarding suicidal thoughts or actions.

Health Skills Activity

Communication Skills

Giving "Emotional First Aid"

Use the following strategies to help students complete the activity.

- Have students read the tips for giving "emotional first aid."
- Then have students work in pairs to make a bulleted list of three additional suggestions for helping a friend who is suffering from severe depression.
- Next, have students work with their partners to make the pamphlet as directed in the text. **OL**

Reading Check

Answer *Sample answer:* Listening and showing interest are two ways of providing emotional support for someone who is depressed.

Health Skills Activity

Communication Skills

Giving "Emotional First Aid"

People who are severely depressed have an emotional injury. Eventually, they will need professional treatment for their "wounds." Before they can get that help, they require "emotional first aid." This can come from anyone with good communication skills, including you. Perhaps you can influence the person to make healthful choices. Here are some tips:

- Let the person speak and express his or her negative emotions.
- Don't challenge or dare the person.
- Remind the person of past successes. Recall challenges that she or he overcame.
- Tell the person how important he or she is to you and others. Provide the person with reasons for living.

With a Group

Make a pamphlet with suggestions for helping troubled teens. Pass out copies of your pamphlet.

Providing Support

People who think about or attempt suicide usually do not want to die. Rather, their actions are a plea for help.

You can provide this help and support. If someone you know shows warning signs of suicide, talk to the person. Just showing interest in the person's problem can be a positive first step. It shows the person that he or she is not alone. Do not be afraid to ask whether the individual is planning to harm him- or herself. Urge the person to share her or his feelings and thoughts with a trusted adult. Finally, never promise to keep suicide plans a secret. This is one secret a true friend will never agree to keep.

Reading Check **Explain** What are some ways to give emotional support to someone who is depressed?

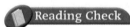

Visit glencoe.com and complete the Interactive Study Guide for Lesson 2.

Dealing with Depression

Depression can feel like a heavy weight. Sometimes, people feel that they cannot get out from under it. This hopelessness is what leads some people to think about taking their own lives. However, you can assume responsibility for your personal health behaviors. If you ever find yourself thinking about suicide, remember:

Caption Answer

Photo Caption, p. 89
Individual counseling and talking with a trusted adult are other ways that depressed teens can get emotional support.

Teacher to Teacher

Robin Pettapiece   **Emmet Belknap Middle School, Lockport, NY**

Question of the Day

"At the start of each lesson, I have a question of the day posted on the board. The question usually relates to what we talked about the previous class and acts as a review of the information. Students can also write their responses in their notebooks. It helps get the class started quickly and gives the students something to do while I take attendance or collect homework."

- Suicide is *never* a solution to depression. Solutions do exist for every problem, but suicide is not one of them.
- Feelings of depression do not go on forever. Spend time with friends and family. This is a healthy defense mechanism that can help get you through a difficult time.
- You are not alone. There are people who love and want to help you. If you are feeling low, talk to someone close.

There are organizations you can contact that help teens deal with suicidal thoughts. One is SPAN USA. The letters in *SPAN* stand for "Suicide Prevention Action Network." Another is the National Youth Violence Prevention Resource Center. Each of these organizations has a Web site and a telephone hot line.

▲ Group counseling is one way a person who is feeling depressed can receive emotional support. **What are some other ways someone who is experiencing depression can receive emotional support?**

ASSESS

Assessment Resources

- Lesson Review Quiz
- *ExamView*
- Fast Files Activities
- Online Quizzes and Activities

Reteaching

- Assign Concept Map 4-2 or Reteaching Activity 4-2 in the Fast Files.
- In small groups, have students discuss what they would do if a friend mentioned thoughts of suicide. Call on several groups to share their responses.

Enrichment

- Assign Enrichment Activity 4-2 in the Fast Files.
- Have students obtain brochures, pamphlets, or other information about suicide-prevention organizations. Have students prepare a display that could be used to share this information with other students.

CLOSE

Ask students to name warning signs of suicide.

Lesson 2 Review

 After You Read

Review this lesson for new terms, major headings, and Reading Checks.

What I Learned

1. **Vocabulary** What is *suicide*? Use this term in an original sentence.

2. **Give Examples** Give two examples of actions or behaviors that suggest that a teen might be thinking about suicide.

3. **Recall** What are some causes of teen suicide?

Thinking Critically

4. **Synthesize** Barbara's parents are getting divorced and selling the home she has lived in all her life. Barbara feels like her life is crumbling. What kind of support can you give Barbara?

5. **Apply** Larry's friend Pete has been very down since his father's death. Lately, Pete seems to be better. However, he has offered Larry his skateboard and his best jacket. Should Larry be concerned about his friend?

Applying Health Skills

6. **Communication Skills** With a partner, perform a role-play about a friend helping another who is feeling down. Use skills from the Health Skills Activity and the lesson as a whole.

Go Online For more Lesson Review Activities, go to **glencoe.com**.

Lesson 2: Suicide Prevention **89**

Lesson 2 Review Answers

1. Suicide is the intentional taking of one's own life. Sentences will vary.
2. Warning signs include fascination with death, a change in appearance, self-destructive behavior, withdrawal from family and friends, giving away possessions.
3. life-changing stressors, domestic violence, abuse, rejection by peers
4. Listen to her thoughts and feelings; encourage her to talk to her parents or another trusted adult.
5. Yes, giving away prized posessions is a warning sign of suicide.
6. Evaluate role-plays based on creativity and use of appropriate and accurate content.

Lesson 3

FOCUS

Activating Prior Knowledge

What I Know Have students describe some symptoms of mental and emotional disorders they learned in Lesson 2.

Guide to Reading

Building Vocabulary
- Tell students that the word part *psych-* means "pertaining to the mind or mental activities." Have students use this information to infer the meaning of the terms *psychologist* and *psychiatrist*.
- Use Vocabulary PuzzleMaker to reinforce vocabulary terms.

Reading Strategy
Comparing and Contrasting Have students prepare charts that they can complete as they read the lesson.

*Q***uick Write**

Have students begin their Quick Writes as directed. Then, as students read the lesson, they can add information to their outlines.

Help for Mental and Emotional Disorders

Guide to Reading

Building Vocabulary
Several of the terms below share a common word part. Look up this word part in a dictionary, and write its meaning.
- therapy (p. 91)
- family therapy (p. 92)
- psychologist (p. 93)
- clinical social worker (CSW) (p. 93)
- psychiatrist (p. 93)

Focusing on the Main Ideas
In this lesson, you will learn to
- **determine** what to do if you or someone you know needs professional help.
- **describe** the kinds of therapies used to treat mental and emotional disorders.
- **identify** kinds of professionals who help people with mental health problems.

Reading Strategy
Comparing and Contrasting Create a chart that lists the different types of mental health professionals and the treatments they provide.

*Q***uick Write**

Create an outline on treatment options for people with emotional problems. Use the terms and headings from the lesson as a guide.

What to Do If You Need Help

It is not always easy to determine whether a mental health problem is serious. However, there are certain symptoms you should be aware of as possible signs of a serious problem. If you have been experiencing any, they should not be ignored. Denying that a problem exists is a defense mechanism that can prevent you from getting help and feeling better.

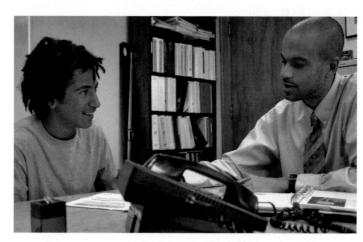

▶ Admitting that help is needed is a first step in dealing with a mental or emotional disorder. **Why do some people avoid seeking the help they need?**

Caption Answer

Photo Caption *Sample answer:* Many people do not want to admit that they have an emotional problem.

Lesson 3 Resources

📁 **Chapter *FAST FILE* Resources**
Guided Reading and Writing 4-3
Concept Mapping Activity 4-3
Health Lab 4-3
Reteaching Activity 4-3
Enrichment Activity 4-3
Lesson Quiz 4-3

Technology
⚡ Transparency 4-3
◗ Audio Summaries
🌐 *ExamView® Assessment Suite*
◗ Vocabulary PuzzleMaker
🌐 StudentWorks™ Plus
 Go Online

If you have been feeling sad or angry for two weeks or longer it is likely an indicator of a problem that will not disappear on its own. Wanting to spend all your time alone is another possible indicator. If your feelings begin to affect your sleep, eating habits, schoolwork, or relationships with family and peers, help is most likely needed. Other factors include feeling "out of control," or feeling worried or nervous all the time.

If you feel that you need help, talk to a parent or guardian, the school nurse, a counselor at school, or other trusted adult. Tell someone what you are feeling and how long you have been experiencing those feelings. They may be able to provide the help you need or point you toward someone who can, such as a mental health professional.

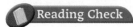 **Reading Check** **Identify** What are some steps to take if you think you need help?

Kinds of Help

Help for mental and emotional problems almost always includes some form of counseling. This is a process of talking through your problems with someone trained to listen. For teens, the first step in this process is talking with a trusted adult. A parent, a guardian, or even an older brother or sister can sometimes be a great source of comfort. So can a teacher or coach to whom you feel close.

Once the problem is out in the open, the emotional healing may begin. For many emotional problems, professional counseling, or therapy, is often needed. **Therapy** is *an approach that teaches you different ways of thinking or behaving.* Therapy gets to the root of your emotional and mental problems and helps you work to find a solution.

◀ When you have a problem, talking to a trusted adult can help. **Who are some people you could talk to if you had a problem?**

91

TEACH

Connect To... **Science**

The Brain's Chemical Messengers
Have students work in small groups to complete the activity. Help students locate appropriate resources for their research on neurotransmitters and endorphins. Then have each group prepare a large poster that uses words and visual images to share its results with the class. **OL**

AL Active Learning

Interview Divide the class into small groups. Have each group interview a guidance counselor or other mental health professional to learn more about the kinds of help available for mental and emotional problems. Have groups prepare interview questions in advance. Have each group prepare a short oral report to share its results with the class. **AL**

Reading Check

Answer If you think you need help, talk to a trusted adult or get a referral to a mental health professional.

Caption Answer

Photo Caption *Sample answer:* My parents or my school guidance counselor would be willing to help me if I had a problem.

HEALTH LITERACY

Cognitive Behavioral Therapy One type of therapy used in older children, teens, and adults is cognitive behavioral therapy. This form of therapy has been found to be useful for many types of mental and emotional problems including anxiety, depression, post-traumatic stress disorder, and some addictions. This type of therapy focuses on two areas: identifying and changing the negative thoughts that feed the emotional problem, and changing behaviors associated with negative feelings to more positive behaviors.

R Reading Skills

Comparing and Contrasting
Ask students: How are group therapy and family therapy similar and different? *Sample answer: In these forms of therapy, there is more than one person meeting with the counselor. In family therapy, a family learns to work better as a unit. In group therapy, each person is dealing with an individual problem.* **OL**

U Universal Access

English Learners Point out the term *imbalances*, which is used to describe drug treatment therapy. In this context, *imbalance* means an unequal amount of brain chemicals. Discuss with students the effects of medicines to balance chemicals in the brain to provide relief for some people. **EL**

Careers for the 21st Century

Psychiatric Aide
Have students meet in groups to read and discuss the information in the book. Ask one member of each group to visit **glencoe.com**, learn about the personal skills a psychiatric aide needs, and share that information with the group.

Caption Answer

Photo Caption *Sample answer:* Family therapy improves family members' communication skills.

▶ Family therapy can help families cope with problems that threaten the health of the family. **How do therapists help?**

Careers for the 21st Century

Psychiatric Aide

Psychiatric aides care for mentally ill patients in hospitals or private care facilities. They help patients bathe, dress, and eat. They also socialize with patients and lead them in recreational activities. The need for psychiatric aides is on the rise because people with severe mental and emotional problems need personal care and attention. If you would like to be a psychiatric aide, you should take psychology classes and volunteer at your local hospital.

What skills does a psychiatric aide need? Go to *Career Corner* at **glencoe.com** to find out.

Therapy Settings

Different settings for therapy are available, depending on the problem and the person's needs. Some possibilities include individual therapy, group therapy, and family therapy.

In *individual therapy*, the individual and therapist meet alone for sessions. This is the setting most often used with people entering therapy for the first time. The privacy of individual therapy allows some patients to open up more freely and talk about their problems.

In *group therapy*, the therapist meets with several people who all have the same or similar problems. Group members are taught to support and show empathy toward one another. It can be reassuring for patients to know they are not alone, and that others share the same difficulties.

A special form of group therapy is **family therapy.** This is *counseling that seeks to improve troubled family relationships.* The therapist does not act as a judge or say who is at fault. Instead, he or she helps the family to help itself. This often includes teaching family members to communicate better.

Drug Treatment Therapy

In the last several decades, effective new medicines for treating emotional disorders have been produced. Many of these work at correcting chemical imbalances in the brain. These medicines can provide relief for depression and other mental disorders.

It is important to be aware that these medicines are not right for everyone. Also, they do not treat every mental and emotional problem. Finally, these medicines are not meant as a replacement for therapy. In fact, they are generally only given to patients who have received, or are currently in, therapy.

Cultural Perspectives

Mental Health Services for Diverse Populations Although mental and emotional disorders are found in people of every race and culture, studies have shown that racial and ethnic minorities are less likely to receive adequate mental health care. Researchers have found that language barriers and cultural attitudes toward mental health care are two reasons for this disparity. Racial and ethnic minorities are also underrepresented as mental health professionals, making it difficult for many of those who seek help to find a provider with whom they can identify.

Mental Health Providers

Different types of mental health professionals provide therapy. All of these professionals have gone through special training to treat people with mental and emotional problems. Often, people with emotional problems will see a **psychologist** (sy·KAH·luh·jist). This is *a mental health professional who is trained and licensed by the state to perform therapy*. Psychologists have a doctoral degree and often specialize in a specific area, such as child psychology.

A **clinical social worker (CSW)** is *a licensed, certified mental health professional with a master's degree in social work*. CSWs can also provide therapy, but they are not usually as specialized as psychologists. Some schools have CSWs on their staff.

A third type of mental health professional is a **psychiatrist** (sy·KY·uh·trist). This is *a medical doctor with a specialty in the treatment of mental health problems*. In most states, a psychiatrist is the only mental health professional who can prescribe medications. Various mental health professionals often work as a team in treating a single patient in order to provide the patient with the best possible care.

 Reading Check **List** Name three types of mental health professionals.

 Go Online

Visit **glencoe.com** and complete the Interactive Study Guide for Lesson 3.

 Reading Check

Answer psychologists, clinical social workers, and psychiatrists

ASSESS

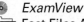 **Assessment Resources**

Lesson Review Quiz
- *ExamView*
- Fast Files Activities
- Online Quizzes and Activities

Reteaching

- Assign Concept Map 4-3 or Reteaching Activity 4-3 in the Fast Files.
- Have students work in pairs to develop three questions and answers about help for mental and emotional disorders. Have each pair of students share one question and answer.

Enrichment

- Assign Enrichment Activity 4-3 in the Fast Files.
- Ask students to research careers in psychiatry or psychology. Have students prepare a short report to share with the class.

CLOSE

Have students identify and describe different types of therapy for mental and emotional disorders.

Lesson 3 Review

 After You Read

Review this lesson for new terms, major headings, and Reading Checks.

What I Learned

1. *Vocabulary* Define *therapy*.

2. *Identify* Name several different types of therapy settings used in treating mental and emotional problems.

3. *Recall* How do current medications work to treat mental and emotional problems?

Thinking Critically

4. *Evaluate* Ernesto has been feeling sad every day for the last two weeks and he doesn't know why. What should he do?

5. *Analyze* What factors might influence which type of mental health provider a person chooses?

Applying Health Skills

6. *Advocacy* With classmates, create posters that address the importance of seeking help for mental and emotional problems. Include some of the possible signs and symptoms that can indicate a serious problem.

Go Online For more Lesson Review Activities, go to **glencoe.com**.

Lesson 3: Help for Mental and Emotional Disorders **93**

Lesson 3 Review Answers

1. Therapy is an approach that offers one different ways of thinking and behaving.

2. Therapy sessions can be in a one-on-one, group, or family setting.

3. Medications correct a chemical imbalance in the brain. As a result, mood improves and thinking becomes clearer.

4. Ernesto should seek help from a parent or trusted adult, or a mental health professional.

5. Factors include the type of problems they are experiencing; whether or not they need medication.

6. Students' posters should include myths and facts about mental and emotional problems.

Building Health Skills Listen Up!

Skill

Communication Skills

Activating Prior Knowledge

Have students brainstorm a list of actions a listener can take to demonstrate that he or she is paying attention to what is being said. Have volunteers share entries from their lists with the class.

- **Objective** After completing the activity, students will be able to use listening skills to help a friend with an emotional problem.
- **Time** 90 minutes
- **Materials** paper, pencil

Teacher Classroom Resources

📁 Building Health Skills Activity

⬇ Transparency 4-2

Model

- Have students read about communication skills that Christa used to help Susan. Ask: Explain the following statement: Being a good listener involves more than listening to spoken language. Sample answer: *Being a good listener involves paying attention to body language, as well as listening to spoken words.*

National Health Standards Addressed

1.8.7, 2.8.3, 6.8.1, 7.8.2, 8.8.1, 8.8.2

94

Building Health Skills

Accessing Information
Practicing Healthful Behaviors
Stress Management
Analyzing Influences
Communication Skills
Refusal Skills
Conflict Resolution
Decision Making
Goal Setting
Advocacy

What Are Communication Skills?

Communication skills involve learning how to effectively express yourself and understand others.

Speaking Skills

- Think before you speak.
- Use "I" messages.
- Be direct, but avoid being rude or insulting.
- Make eye contact, and use appropriate body language.

Listening Skills

- Use conversation encouragers.
- Pay attention.
- Show empathy.
- Avoid interrupting, but ask questions where appropriate.

Listen Up!

Follow the Model, Practice, and Apply steps to help you master this important health skill.

① Model

Read how Christa uses communication skills to help her friend Susan.

Being a good listener is a health skill for life, and one that can improve your social health. Christa noticed that her friend Susan seemed depressed. Christa approached Susan and asked her what was wrong. Susan told Christa she had been feeling sad, but she didn't know why. Christa listened quietly as Susan continued to explain how she had been feeling. While Susan spoke, Christa just looked at Susan reassuringly and listened. She occasionally asked a question or repeated what Susan said to make sure that she understood. When Christa finally spoke, she offered to go with Susan to talk to the school counselor to ask for help.

Teaching Tips

Being a Good Listener Explain to students that the skill of saying little or nothing (while waiting for the other person to speak) often feels awkward because we often want to dive right in and offer quick solutions to our friends. Sometimes, however, simply allowing the person to express their concerns without interruption is very helpful.

Using Skits Effectively The skits suggested here require partners to have a high level of maturity. Be prepared, therefore, to suggest topics for students who are struggling.

❷ Practice

Read how Hailey uses communication skills to help her sister. Then answer the questions below.

Hailey arrived home from school to find her older sister, Jan, sitting in front of the TV. She was obviously in a bad mood. Hailey said, "Jan, you seem angry," and then listened carefully as her sister described the events of an awful day at school. She nodded as Jan spoke and she didn't interrupt her. When Jan told Hailey about a pop quiz in English, Hailey said, "You mean the teacher didn't even tell you that there was going to be a quiz?" After their talk, Jan told Hailey that she felt better and she gave Hailey a hug.

1. What listening skills did Hailey use?

2. How did listening affect Hailey's social health?

❸ Apply

Use what you have learned about communication skills to complete the activity below.

With a partner, brainstorm emotional problems that commonly occur among teens. Choose one of these problems and write a skit that shows the effective use of listening skills to help someone with this problem. When you are finished, perform your skit for your class. Describe the listening skills you used and how listening contributes to good health.

Self-Check
■ Did we choose a common emotional problem for teens?
■ Did our skit show effective listening skills?
■ Did we describe how listening skills improve health?

Building Health Skills

Practice

● Have students work in small groups to read and discuss the Practice activity and questions.
● Call on various groups to share their answers to the questions.
● Have each group brainstorm one other positive way that Hailey could have communicated her willingness to listen to her sister's problems.
● Have each group share its approach with the class.

Apply/Assess

● Have students work in pairs to complete the Apply activity.
● Have each group share its approach with the class.
● Have each pair of students share its skit with the class. Remind students that the remainder of the class will try to identify the problem highlighted in the skit.
● You may wish to distribute the Building Health Skills Activity in the Fast Files.

ASSESSMENT SCORING

Student work should meet all criteria to achieve the highest score.

Skills Student work:
● includes listening without interruption.
● uses body language to show attention.
● demonstrates repetition to confirm.

● provides clarification by asking questions.

Concepts Student work:
● includes a common emotional problem.
● describes the relationship between listening and health.

HANDS-ON HEALTH ACTIVITY

Interpreting Vocal Stress

Time: 20 minutes
Materials: pencil or pen, paper

Introducing Hands-on Health

- Have students listen closely as they speak to one another. Have students note words that are said in a slightly louder voice than the other words in the sentence.

Teaching the Activity

- Divide the class into small groups.
- Have each group create five sentences to use for the activity. Have students note the way in which the meanings of the sentences change when different words are stressed.
- Challenge groups to find as many meanings as possible for their own sentences. Then, when groups exchange sentences, have students see if additional meanings can be found.
- Have students discuss the Wrapping It Up questions with their groups.

HANDS-ON HEALTH

Interpreting Vocal Stress

Sometimes the way in which you say something is more revealing than the words themselves. To better understand this concept, consider this ordinary sentence: "Is he a good catcher?" Read the sentence aloud. Did you notice the sound of your voice rising at the end? This rise in pitch is part of the *intonation pattern* of speech. Different kinds of sentences—statements, questions, and commands—have different intonation patterns.

This activity will give you a chance to work with another aspect of vocal intonation. This time you will be working with *vocal stress*. Also known as "emphasis," vocal stress is saying one word slightly louder than the rest of the words in a sentence. On paper, vocal stress is shown by *italics* or underlining. Changing the word that is stressed in a sentence can change the sentence's meaning.

What You Will Need

- pencil or pen
- paper

What You Will Do

1. Work as part of a small group. Think up and write five ordinary sentences on separate sheets of paper. Try reading each sentence aloud, each time stressing a different word. Notice how the meaning of the sentence changes each time. Consider these examples:

   a. "I told *Ed* to give me the book." (Meaning: I told Ed—not someone else—to give me the book.)

   b. "I told Ed to give me the *book*." (Meaning: I told Ed what to give me—the book, not something else.)

2. Exchange sentences with another group. Try reading each sentence with the stress on different words. See how many different meanings you can come up with.

Wrapping It Up

After each group has exchanged sentences, discuss these questions as a class:

How does changing the vocal stress in a sentence change its meaning? Do you think changes in vocal stress reveal differences in the speaker's feelings? Explain your answer.

HANDS-ON HEALTH Assessment

Discussion Ask students:
- How does listening to intonation patterns relate to being a good listener? Sample answer: *This skill can help you determine the precise meaning of a friend's statement.*

- Ask: How does being aware of vocal stress help you to be an effective speaker? Sample answer: *By using vocal stress, you can accurately convey your thoughts to others.*

Reading Review

 STUDY TO GO
Visit **glencoe.com** to download quizzes and eFlashcards for Chapter 4.

FOLDABLES Study Organizer

Foldables® and Other Study Aids Take out the Foldable® that you created for Lesson 1 and any graphic organizers that you created for Lessons 1–3. Find a partner and quiz each other using these study aids.

Lesson 1 Mental and Emotional Disorders

Main Idea Mental and emotional problems can affect people at any age.

- A disorder is a disturbance in the normal function of a part of the body.
- Types of anxiety disorders include obsessive-compulsive disorder, panic disorder, post-traumatic stress disorder, social phobia disorder, and generalized anxiety disorder.
- Bipolar disorder and major depression are two mood disorders.
- Signs of major depression include irritability, anger, anxiety, lack of energy; significant change in sleep patterns; inability to concentrate; blaming one's problems on other people; feelings of worthlessness or guilt; thoughts of death or suicide.
- Schizophrenia is a severe mental disorder in which people lose contact with reality.

Lesson 2 Suicide Prevention

Main Idea Providing emotional support can aid in suicide prevention.

- If you recognize the warning signs of suicide, seek help.

- Factors in teen suicide include a family breakup or parent's death, alcoholism or drug dependency, witnessing domestic violence, experiencing physical or sexual abuse, and feeling rejected by peers.
- Warning signs of suicide include talking, reading, or writing about death; reckless behavior; impulsively becoming sexually active or using drugs.
- Suicide is never a solution to depression.

Lesson 3 Help for Mental and Emotional Disorders

Main Idea Help for mental and emotional problems usually includes some form of counseling.

- If your feelings begin to affect your sleep, eating habits, schoolwork, or relationships with family or peers, help is most likely needed.
- Medicines can be used to help treat mental and emotional problems. They work to correct chemical imbalances in the brain.
- If you are concerned about your mental health, talk to a trusted adult.
- Therapy settings include individual therapy, group therapy, and family therapy.
- Mental health professionals include psychologists, clinical social workers, and psychiatrists.

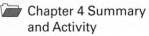
Assessment Resources

- Chapter 4 Summary and Activity
- Audio Summaries
- Reading Tutor
- Performance Assessment
- Chapter 4 Test
- *ExamView*
- Vocabulary PuzzleMaker
- Online Learning Center

Reading Review

Study Aids

- **Using the Dinah Zike Foldable® Study Organizer** Have students use their Foldables® to review information about mental and emotional disorders.

  FOLDABLES Study Organizer

- **Online Learning Tools** Have students go to the *Teen Health* Online Learning Center at **glencoe.com** to:
  - Download a **Podcast**.
  - Download free **Study-to-Go** content to their PDAs or cell phones.

Vocabulary Review

- **Flashcards** Have students use index cards to make flashcards for the lesson vocabulary terms. Have students use their flashcards to review the lesson vocabulary with a partner.

Teaching Tips

Writing in Health Class When students are preparing for a writing assignment, have them organize their information in a graphic organizer. Explain that a graphic organizer can help them to see how different pieces of information are related. Explain that different types of graphic organizers can be used, depending on the focus of the writing assignment. For example, an essay that requires comparing and contrasting two items might be prepared for by using a Venn diagram.

Assessment

Reviewing Vocabulary and Main Ideas

1. phobia
2. personality disorder
3. Suicide
4. self-destructive behaviors
5. c
6. c

Thinking Critically

7. Answers will vary. Some students may observe that teens in periods of emotional lows may mistake these moods as depression. Students should be aware that to be considered major depression, this condition needs to be ongoing.

8. Answers might include helping the friend recognize that he or she was accepting a myth about the nature of mental problems such as depression. Answers might also include mention of recent discoveries into the true nature of mental problems and effective treatments.

Assessment

After You Read

HEALTH INVENTORY

Now that you have read the chapter, look back at your answers to the Health Inventory in the chapter opener. Is there anything that you should do differently?

Reviewing Vocabulary and Main Ideas

On a sheet of paper, write the numbers 1–4. After each number, choose a term from the list that best completes each sentence.

- mood disorder
- personality disorder
- phobia
- self-destructive behaviors
- suicide

Lesson 1 Mental and Emotional Disorders

1. An anxiety disorder characterized by an exaggerated fear of a specific situation or object is a(n) _____.

2. A psychological condition that affects a person's ability to interact normally with others is called a _____.

Lesson 2 Suicide Prevention

3. _____, the intentional taking of one's own life, is a leading cause of death among teens.

4. Doing reckless or impulsive things and other _____ may be warning signs of suicide.

Lesson 3 Help for Mental and Emotional Disorders

On a sheet of paper, write the numbers 5–6. After each number, write the letter of the answer that best completes each statement.

5. All of the following are signs that a person may need help with an emotional problem *except*
   a. feeling sad or angry for no apparent reason.
   b. having aches or pains that cannot be explained.
   c. treating an injury at home with items from the medicine cabinet.
   d. sleeping too much or waking up too early.

6. Which statement is true of therapy?
   a. It uses the same techniques for everyone.
   b. It may be provided only by psychiatrists.
   c. It is an approach that teaches different ways of thinking or behaving.

Thinking Critically

Using complete sentences, answer the following questions on a sheet of paper.

7. **Synthesize** Do mood swings make teens more likely to become depressed? Explain.

8. **Apply** A friend who is depressed considers seeking help a sign of weakness. What do you tell your friend?

Go Online Visit **glencoe.com** and take the Online Quiz for Chapter 4.

Go Online

Have students visit **glencoe.com** to take the Chapter 4 quiz.

HEALTH INVENTORY WRAP-UP

Mental and Emotional Problems Have students look back at their responses to the Health Inventory in the chapter opener. Ask: What is one specific skill that you learned in this chapter that would allow you to help a friend with an emotional problem? Sample answer: *The listening skills discussed in the chapter will allow me to help a friend with an emotional problem.*

Write About It

9. Persuasive Writing Write a paragraph persuading others that people who are mentally ill deserve the same level of respect and care as people who are physically ill.

10. Expository Writing Write an article describing the warning signs of suicide. What are some ways to provide support to someone who may be considering suicide?

11. Narrative Writing Write a short story about a teen who is depressed. Explain how the teen makes a decision to get help and who the teen goes to for help.

Applying Technology

Mental Peace Board Game

You and a partner will use draw tools to create a board game about mental health.

- Using Microsoft Word®, open draw tools, then auto shapes, and then open basic shapes. Select a 2" square, and copy and paste that square 20 times. Make an interesting shape with the squares on 11" × 14"-sized paper.
- On a new Microsoft Word® document, create two columns with 30 lines. One column will contain questions. The other column will contain answers.
- Write 30 questions and 30 answers about mental and emotional problems.
- Edit and save your game.

Applying Technology

Mental Peace Board Game
Equipment needs: Microsoft Word® or similar software
Have students choose partners. Then go over the project instructions with the class. Remind students that they will be using their 2" squares to make a game board, so the squares should be connected to form whatever shape partners choose. Establish a sign-up sheet for computer use if access is limited. Also help students agree on a time limit for computer use. If possible have students print their completed game boards and play the games created by their classmates.

Write About It

9. Persuasive Writing Remind students that persuasive writing takes a stand, states facts and opinions, gives logical reasons, uses examples, and quotes experts.

10. Expository Writing Students' articles will vary but should describe warning signs of suicide, which may include a sudden fascination with the topic of death, dramatic changes in the person's appearance, and self-destructive behavior.

11. Narrative Writing Stories should include the six steps of decision making.

Standardized Test Practice

Reading

Read the passage and then answer the questions.

One of the first people to closely study the human mind was an Austrian doctor, Sigmund Freud. In 1893, Freud published a study on what he called *hysteria*. Freud used this term to mean uncontrollable emotion, such as panic or fear. In the study, he claimed that hysteria was unspent emotional energy connected to forgotten disturbing events.

By 1899, Freud was convinced that dreams were a window to the inner workings of the mind. That year he published *The Interpretation of Dreams*.

Over the next thirty years, Freud revised and added to his theory. Later, many other researchers disagreed with Freud's theory, but few disagreed with his reputation as the "father of modern psychology."

1. Which sentence states an opinion?
- **A.** One of the first people to study the human mind was Sigmund Freud.
- **B.** In 1899, Freud published *The Interpretation of Dreams*.
- **C.** In 1893, Freud published a study on hysteria.
- **D.** Dreams are a window to the inner workings of the mind.

2. What is the theme of the biography?
- **A.** Different people find different topics interesting.
- **B.** Freud's investigations led to the founding of the field of modern psychology.
- **C.** Today, no one disagrees with Freud's ideas.
- **D.** Sigmund Freud was a Austrian doctor.

Chapter 4 Assessment **99**

Test-Taking Tips

Students may be asked to distinguish between facts and opinions in a reading passage. Discuss the difference between a fact and an opinion. Make a variety of statements—some facts and some opinions—and ask students to classify them.

Ask students to find the theme of a passage. Explain that the theme is simply the main idea expressed in the passage. Remind students to look for a general statement that sums up the entire passage when they are asked to find the theme of a reading selection.

Standardized Test Practice

1. D
2. B

Relationships: The Teen Years

	Standards		Skills and Activities
	National	**State/Local**	
CHAPTER 5 pp. 100–127	National Health Education Standards 2.8.3, 4.8.2, 4.8.3, 4.8.4, 5.8.1, 6.8.2, 7.8.2, 8.8.2		**HEALTH QUIZ,** *p. 101* **BUILDING HEALTH SKILLS** *Goal Setting* Setting Limits, *pp. 122–123* TIME health news How to Deal with Tricky Situations, *p. 124*
Lesson 1 **Friendships During Adolescence** pp. 102–107	National Health Education Standards 1.8.1, 2.8.3, 2.8.7, 7.8.2, 8.8.1		**DEVELOPING GOOD CHARACTER** *Friendships and Character, p. 104* **HEALTH SKILLS ACTIVITY** *Communication Skills* "Breaking the Ice," *p. 105*
Lesson 2 **Practicing Communication Skills** pp. 108–111	National Health Education Standards 1.8.7, 2.8.6, 3.8.2, 4.8.1, 6.8.1, 7.8.2		**G⊙ Online** Body Language Basics, *p. 109*
Lesson 3 **Peer Pressure and Refusal Skills** pp. 112–117	National Health Education Standards 1.8.8, 1.8.9, 2.8.3, 2.8.5, 2.8.7, 2.8.8, 2.8.9, 2.8.10, 3.8.2, 4.8.2, 6.8.1, 8.8.1		**What Teens Think** In your opinion, what form of peer pressure is most common among teens?, *p. 113* **Careers for the 21st Century** School Counselor, *p. 115* **HEALTH SKILLS ACTIVITY** *Refusal Skills* Responding to "Lines," *p. 117*
Lesson 4 **Limits and Abstinence** pp. 118–121	National Health Education Standards 1.8.5, 1.8.8, 1.8.9, 2.8.1, 2.8.10, 4.8.2, 4.8.3, 4.8.4, 5.8.2, 5.8.4, 5.8.6, 5.8.7, 6.8.2, 6.8.3, 6.8.4, 8.8.1		**Connect To... MATH** The Cost of Raising a Family, *p. 120*

PACING THE CHAPTER		
Lesson 1 45 min	**Lesson 4** 45 min	**TIME health news** 20 min
Lesson 2 45 min	**Chapter Review** 45 min	
Lesson 3 45 min	**Building Health Skills** 45 min	

BLOCK SCHEDULING

For block scheduling, assign students Building Health Skills feature *Setting Limits*, pages 122–123, and Guided Reading and Writing. 📁

Planning Guide

StudentWorks *Plus*

Glencoe Exclusive!
TeacherWorks™ *Plus*
All-In-One Planner and Resource Center

Reproducible Resources	Assessment	Media and Technology
Chapter FAST FILE Resources Chapter Summaries and Activities REVIEW Building Health Skills Activity TEACH Performance Assessment Activity EXTEND Universal Access Activities TEACH Parent Letter and Activities 📁 **Student Activities Workbook** TEACH 📁 **Reading Tutor** TEACH	Building Health Skills Activity, *pp. 122–123* Chapter 5 Assessment, *pp. 126–127* **Chapter FAST FILE Resources** Performance Assessment Activity, *p. 4* Chapter 5 Test, *p. 7* 💿 *ExamView® Assessment Suite*	TeacherWorks *Plus* includes: ● Interactive Teacher Edition ● Lesson Planner with Calendar ● Access to all blackline masters ● Correlations to standards 💿 StudentWorks™ Plus 🖱 Online Student Edition Dinah Zike's Teaching Health with Foldables®
Chapter FAST FILE Resources Concept Mapping Activity 5-1 REVIEW Decision-Making Activity 5-1 EXTEND Enrichment Activity 5-1 EXTEND Lesson Plan 5-1 Guided Reading and Writing 5-1 TEACH Reteaching Activity 5-1 REVIEW	Lesson 1 Review, *p. 107* 🖱 Vocabulary PuzzleMaker 💿 *ExamView® Assessment Suite*	🖱 Vocabulary PuzzleMaker 💿 *ExamView® Assessment Suite* 💿 StudentWorks™ Plus ⚡ Transparency 5-1 **Go Online** glencoe.com
Chapter FAST FILE Resources Concept Mapping Activity 5-2 REVIEW Health Lab 5-2 EXTEND Enrichment Activity 5-2 EXTEND Lesson Plan 5-2 Guided Reading and Writing 5-2 TEACH Reteaching Activity 5-2 REVIEW	Lesson 2 Review, *p. 111* 🖱 Vocabulary PuzzleMaker 💿 *ExamView® Assessment Suite*	🖱 Vocabulary PuzzleMaker 💿 *ExamView® Assessment Suite* 💿 StudentWorks™ Plus ⚡ Transparency 5-2 **Go Online** glencoe.com
Chapter FAST FILE Resources Concept Mapping Activity 5-3 REVIEW Decision-Making Activity 5-3 EXTEND Enrichment Activity 5-3 EXTEND Lesson Plan 5-3 Guided Reading and Writing 5-3 TEACH Reteaching Activity 5-3 REVIEW	Lesson 3 Review, *p. 117* 🖱 Vocabulary PuzzleMaker 💿 *ExamView® Assessment Suite*	🖱 Vocabulary PuzzleMaker 💿 *ExamView® Assessment Suite* 💿 StudentWorks™ Plus ⚡ Transparency 5-3 **Go Online** glencoe.com
Chapter FAST FILE Resources Concept Mapping Activity 5-4 REVIEW Cross-Curriculum Activity 5-4 EXTEND Enrichment Activity 5-4 EXTEND Lesson Plan 5-4 Guided Reading and Writing 5-4 TEACH Reteaching Activity 5-4 REVIEW	Lesson 4 Review, *p. 121* 🖱 Vocabulary PuzzleMaker 💿 *ExamView® Assessment Suite*	🖱 Vocabulary PuzzleMaker 💿 *ExamView® Assessment Suite* 💿 StudentWorks™ Plus ⚡ Transparency 5-4 **Go Online** glencoe.com

Chapter and Lesson Resources

The *Teen Health* resources are designed for differentiated learning abilities. You may want to use the coded items in this way:

REVIEW —activities to review or reinforce content
TEACH —activities to teach basic concepts
EXTEND —activities to extend or enrich lesson content

 OUT OF TIME?

Use Health Skills Activities *"Breaking the Ice,"* page 105, and *Responding to "Lines,"* page 117, or Developing Good Character, page 104.

Dating Abuse and Violence

This chapter discusses the importance of caring and respect in teen dating relationships. However, studies indicate that physical abuse, sexual abuse, or emotional abuse happen in approximately one third of teen dating relationships. When discussing the section on dating with your students, be sure to discuss behaviors that are unacceptable in a dating relationship, and ways a teen can get help for abuse in a dating relationship. Always encourage students to speak to the school guidance counselor for resources.

Abuse in a dating relationship can take many forms. Emotional abuse includes controlling behavior, extreme jealousy, threats, and insults. Remind students that emotional abuse is just as damaging as other forms of abuse and should not be tolerated.

Physical abuse and violence also occur in teen dating relationships. In fact, one study found that 40 percent of teens know of someone their age who had been beaten by a dating partner. Explain to students that physical violence is never acceptable in a dating relationship.

Sexual abuse in dating relationships includes any forced sexual behavior. Explain to students that they always have the right to refuse any form of sexual activity.

Explain safety guidelines that teens can use to establish healthy relationships when they are ready to begin dating. Suggest double-dating as a safe way of getting to know a potential girlfriend or boyfriend. Remind students to carry a cell phone or money for a pay phone, and to always let someone know where they are going, who they will be with, and when they expect to be back.

The Impact of Becoming a Teen Parent

Unplanned pregnancy is one possible consequence of sexual activity. Pregnancy and parenting can have a negative impact on many aspects of a teen's life, including education and future financial success. Mental/emotional and social health are also at risk for teens taking on this responsibility. Helping students to understand the long-range consequences of unplanned pregnancy on education and earnings is one way to promote the benefits of abstinence for teens.

Several studies have examined the impact of teen pregnancy on education. Data suggest that teen parents get 1 to 3 years less schooling than their nonparenting peers. Teen mothers have a high school graduation rate of approximately 30 percent, while females who are not parenting have high school graduation rates between 80 percent and 90 percent. Although most studies show that the educational impact of early parenting is greater for teen mothers than it is for teen fathers, teen fathers do have a lower graduation rate than other male teens.

The reduced educational levels associated with teen parenting impacts future financial success as well. Studies have shown a direct correlation between the age of a female when she has her first child to the level of her future family income. Studies show that 80 percent of those who become teen mothers use welfare at some point to support themselves and their child. Teen fathers have also been shown to be more likely to have lower-paying jobs due to lower levels of education. Teen fathers earn about 18 percent less than those who did not become teen parents.

Reduced education and financial resources also have a negative impact for the children of teen parents. Children born to teen parents are more likely to have a low birth weight, have learning difficulties, repeat a grade in school, and drop out of high school than children born to older parents. In fact, a child born to an unmarried teen mother who has dropped out of high school has a 78 percent chance of living in poverty.

Support for Teaching Reading

Reading Support

Reading Preview

Activating Background Vocabulary Ask students what the word *friendship* means to them. Discuss and list responses on the board. Then ask students what the word *relationship* means. Guide students in a discussion of the differences between a general relationship and the closer nature of a friendship.

FOLDABLES Study Organizer *Dinah Zike's Reading and Study Skills for Teen Health* provides interactive graphic organizers that help students comprehend and retain health concepts as they read. Use the Foldable® on page 101 or find more Foldables® activities for the chapter on **Relationships: The Teen Years** in the separate booklet, available in the TCR.

Lesson 1   Friendships During Adolescence

Guided Reading 1) Activate prior knowledge—ask students what they know about friendships, cliques, and dating. 2) Introduce new key terms and discuss meanings. 3) Give students a purpose for reading—ask: "What are the qualities of a good friend? Can a clique be harmful?" 4) Have students read silently to find the answers. 5) Discuss.

Lesson 2   Practicing Communication Skills

Choral Reading Read the opening paragraph of Lesson 2 aloud, modeling proper tempo, phrasing, and enunciation. Discuss how volume, stress, pacing, and pronunciation can affect comprehension while reading. Direct half of the class to read the first sentence of **Nonverbal Communication** aloud together. Correct mistakes, then have the other half of the class read the next sentence aloud. Continue to alternate.

Lesson 3   Peer Pressure and Refusal Skills

Identifying Sequences Have students reread the section **A Strategy for Refusing** on page 115. Direct students to look for words that point to time order, steps in a process, or logical order of events. Have students write out the steps of the S.T.O.P. strategy. Encourage student pairs to practice the steps of the process against peer pressure tactics.

Lesson 4   Limits and Abstinence

Learning Logs Stop students during some point in the reading process. Assign this topic: How does abstinence relate to the subject of setting limits for teens? Explain your reasoning. Have students consider their response and write in their learning logs for five minutes. Encourage students to share their responses with others.

Post Reading

Dramatic Presentations Guide student groups to create a role-play of teens using good communication skills to say no to negative peer pressure, recognize qualities of good friendship, and choose abstinence from harmful behaviors. Encourage students to incorporate the main concepts of this lesson while organizing and planning their presentations.

Key for Using the Teacher Wraparound Edition

Use this key to help you identify the different types of prompts found in the Teacher Wraparound Edition.

R **Reading Strategies** activities help you teach reading skills and vocabulary.

C **Critical Thinking** strategies help students apply and extend what they have learned.

U **Universal Access** activities provide differentiated instruction for students learning to speak English, along with suggestions for teaching various types of learners.

HS **Health Skills Practice** activities reinforce Health Skills concepts and help students apply these skills in their everyday lives.

W **Writing Support** activities provide writing opportunities to help students comprehend the text.

AL **Active Learning** strategies provide a variety of activities for presenting lesson content, including Quick Demos and engaging classroom projects that get students actively involved.

Key to Ability Levels

Teaching Strategies and activities have been coded for ability level and appropriateness.

AL Activities for students working above grade level

OL Activities for students working on grade level

BL Activities for students working below grade level

EL Activities for English Learners

Symbols

🖐 Transparencies

💿 CD-ROM

🖱 glencoe.com

📁 Print Resources

Relationships: The Teen Years

Chapter at a Glance

Lesson 1 explains changes that occur in friendships during adolescence, identifies the qualities of a good friend, explains how to develop communication skills to make new friends, and explains the advantages of going out with a group.

Lesson 2 describes types of nonverbal communication, explains how to be an effective speaker, identifies ways of being a good listener, and explains how to communicate effectively with the use of "I" messages.

Lesson 3 explains the differences between positive and negative peer pressure, identifies risks of negative peer pressure, and explains how to develop refusal skills to resist negative peer pressure.

Lesson 4 explains why limits are important, identifies why teens should choose abstinence, and identifies healthful ways to demonstrate care and respect.

R Reading Strategy

Interpreting the Photo Ask students: How can you tell that these teens like spending time together? Sample answer: *These teens are smiling. They look like they are having fun.* Explain that during adolescence, friendships take on a greater importance than they did before. OL

100

Chapter Preview

▲ *Working with the Photo*

Friendships take on a greater importance during the teen years. **What qualities do you look for when you make new friends?**

100

Universal Access

Differentiated Learning Glencoe provides teacher support and student materials for all learners in the health classroom.

● Spanish Glosario and chapter summaries for the English Language Learners.
● *Reading Tutor* and related worksheets support reluctant readers.

● Universal Access strategies throughout the Teacher Wraparound Edition and Fast Files help you present materials for gifted students, at-risk students, physically impaired students, and those with behavior disorders or learning disabilities.

Start-Up Activities

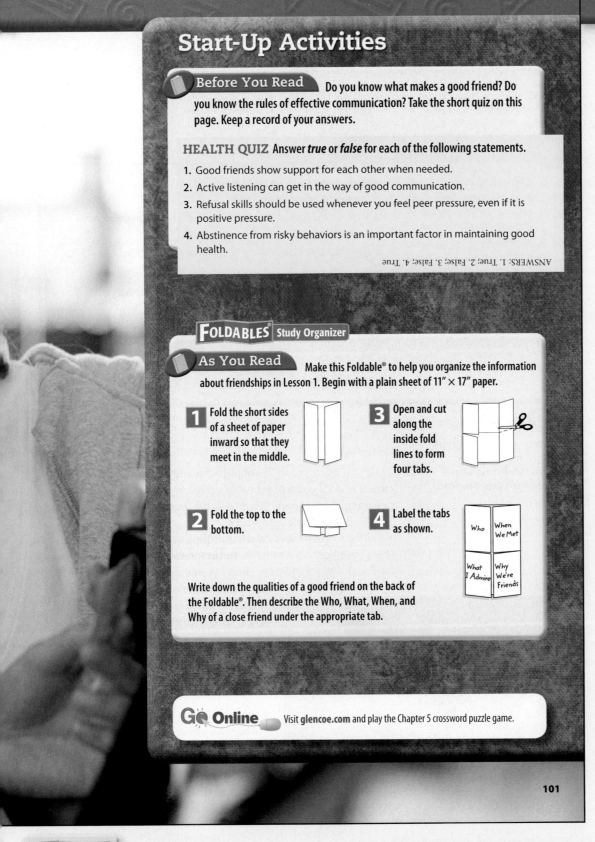

Before You Read Do you know what makes a good friend? Do you know the rules of effective communication? Take the short quiz on this page. Keep a record of your answers.

HEALTH QUIZ Answer *true* or *false* for each of the following statements.

1. Good friends show support for each other when needed.
2. Active listening can get in the way of good communication.
3. Refusal skills should be used whenever you feel peer pressure, even if it is positive pressure.
4. Abstinence from risky behaviors is an important factor in maintaining good health.

ANSWERS: 1. True 2. False 3. False 4. True

FOLDABLES Study Organizer

As You Read Make this Foldable® to help you organize the information about friendships in Lesson 1. Begin with a plain sheet of 11" × 17" paper.

1 Fold the short sides of a sheet of paper inward so that they meet in the middle.

2 Fold the top to the bottom.

3 Open and cut along the inside fold lines to form four tabs.

4 Label the tabs as shown.

Who | When We Met
What I Admire | Why We're Friends

Write down the qualities of a good friend on the back of the Foldable®. Then describe the Who, What, When, and Why of a close friend under the appropriate tab.

Go Online Visit **glencoe.com** and play the Chapter 5 crossword puzzle game.

101

FOLDABLES Study Organizer
Dinah Zike Foldables®

Descriptive Writing Have students use their Foldable® to record information about the qualities of a good friend as they read Lesson 1. Have students write the appropriate information on the back of each tab of their Foldable®. Remind students that these notes can be used to review the content of Lesson 1. **BL**

HEALTH QUIZ

Relationship Skills Have students record their responses to the Health Quiz. Allow students to keep their responses confidential. Remind students that they will have a chance to review their responses after they have read the chapter.

No Child Left Behind

Communicating with Parents

When a project with a grading rubric is assigned, send home a copy of the grading rubric for parents and guardians to refer to. A clearly-worded rubric makes the grading process understandable to parents, and allows them to better monitor their teen's progress. A scoring rubric is provided for each of the Building Health Skills Activities in *Teen Health*. Students may use the Skill Summary and Self Check items to be sure they meet all criteria in the rubric.

Go Online

Have students visit **glencoe.com** and complete the crossword puzzle for Chapter 5.

101

FOCUS

Activating Prior Knowledge

What I Know Ask students to describe strategies for making new friends. Have students compare these strategies with ways they maintain existing friendships.

Guide to Reading

Building Vocabulary

- Tell students that the word part *-ic* means "having the characteristic of." Have students use this information to determine the meaning of the term *sympathetic*.

- Use Vocabulary PuzzleMaker to reinforce vocabulary terms.

Reading Strategy

Classifying Have students copy the diagram in the student text. As students read the lesson, they can fill in the qualities of a good friend.

 Have students use their Foldables® as they read Lesson 1.

*Q*uick Write

Have students recall a friendship they had in elementary school and compare that friendship to one they have now.

Friendships During Adolescence

Guide to Reading

● **Building Vocabulary**

As you read this lesson, write each new highlighted term and its definition in your notebook.

- relationships (p. 102)
- sympathetic (p. 103)
- clique (p. 105)
- peer pressure (p. 105)

● **Focusing on the Main Ideas**

In this lesson, you will learn to

- **explain** changes that occur in friendships during adolescence.
- **identify** the qualities of a good friend.
- **develop** communication skills to make new friends.

● **Reading Strategy**

Classifying Using the diagram as a guide, create a concept map that shows the qualities of a good friend.

 Study Organizer Use the Foldable® on p. 101 as you read this lesson.

*Q*uick Write

Write a short paragraph that describes how your friendships have changed over the years.

Friendships

If you ask a group of people what they like most about their closest friend, you will probably get many different answers. One person might respond, "She makes me laugh." Another might say, "We have a great time together."

Unlike other types of relationships, friendships are relationships people choose to have. **Relationships** are *connections you have with other people and groups in your life.* Friendships form as a result of common interests and shared values. They are an important part of good social health.

 Define What are *relationships*?

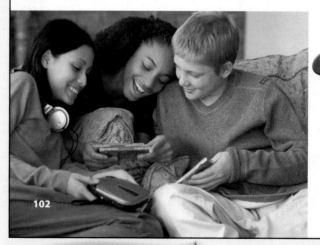

◀ We tend to make friends with people who share similar interests. **What are some things you and your friends enjoy doing together?**

102

Lesson 1 Resources

📁 **Chapter** *FAST FILE* **Resources**
Guided Reading and Writing 5-1
Concept Mapping Activity 5-1
Decision-Making Activity 5-1
Reteaching Activity 5-1
Enrichment Activity 5-1
Lesson Quiz 5-1

Technology
🔦 Transparency 5-1
💿 Audio Summaries
💿 *ExamView® Assessment Suite*
💿 Vocabulary PuzzleMaker
💿 StudentWorks™ Plus
Go Online

Changes in Friendships During Adolescence

Your teen years are a bridge between childhood and adulthood. During these years, friendships take on a greater importance than they once did. They grow and mature, just as you do. You still share good times and have fun with your friends, but you also begin seeking deeper qualities in the people you choose as friends. Such qualities may include loyalty and trust. Your group of friends may also begin to include more members of the opposite gender.

During this **transitional** period, some teens outgrow the friendships they formed when they were younger. New interests in and out of school may cause old friends to drift apart. Differences in growth and emotional maturity also lead some friends in separate directions.

Sometimes, however, a friend may not be ready for a friendship to end. Although it can be painful, saying good-bye to old friends is a normal part of growing up. The healthiest thing you can do when a friend moves on is to do the same. Eventually, you will find another person or people who share your interests, values, and goals.

Qualities of a Good Friend

What makes a friend a *good* friend? Several qualities define strong friendships. One of these is trustworthiness. Trustworthy friends are honest and reliable. You can share private thoughts and feelings with them because they respect you. They also keep their promises to you. You can trust that they mean what they say.

Good friends are **sympathetic** (simp·uh·THET·ik), meaning they are *aware of how you may be feeling at a given moment.* Any friend will be willing to share your happy times. Only a good friend will stand by you during the bad or rough ones. During such times, it is encouraging to have a friend who understands how you feel.

Good friends care about and respect each other. Caring friends value each other's feelings as much as they do their own. They respect each other's decisions, differences, and opinions.

One of the most important qualities of a real friend is forgiveness. True friends understand that neither person in a relationship is perfect. They are willing to forgive mistakes and say "I'm sorry" for their own.

AL

▶ Good friends are loyal. They stay with you through thick and thin. **What are some other qualities of a good friend?**

Academic Vocabulary

transitional (tran ZISH uh nul) *(adjective)* changing. *Pedro's first year of high school was a transitional year because he started a new school and had to make new friends.*

TEACH

AL Active Learning

Photo Essay Have students work in small groups to create a digital photo essay or collage to portray characteristics of a good friend. Have each group share its photo essay with the class and with other students at the same grade level. **OL**

Academic Vocabulary

Transitional Explain, or let volunteers explain, the meaning of *transit*: "the act of moving or carrying something from one place to another." (Students may be most familiar with this word in phrases such as *mass transit*.) Then explain, or have volunteers explain, the meaning of *transition*: "the passage from one place or condition to another." Then have students read the definition of *transitional*, and help them discuss how all three words are related. You will find academic vocabulary activities in the Student Activities Workbook. 🗁

Reading Check

Answer, p. 102 Relationships are connections you have with other people and groups in your life.

Dealing with Sensitive Issues

Dealing with the End of a Friendship It is common for teens to outgrow friendships, and this can sometimes be a painful experience. Discuss some healthful strategies for moving on after a friendship ends. Ending a friendship should not be taken lightly. One should carefully evaluate reasons for ending a friendship. If a student is having trouble accepting that a friend has moved on, suggest focusing on positive memories of the friendship. The school counselor is a valuable resource for those who are struggling with the end of a friendship.

Caption Answer

Photo Caption *Sample answer:* Another quality of a good friend is being a good listener.

Friendships and Character

Have students read the feature. Then ask students to describe the character traits that they share with their friends. Ask students to write a paragraph explaining why these character traits are important to friendships.

AL Active Learning

Pamphlet One of the best ways for students to make new friends is by joining a club, team, or other organization. Have each student make a pamphlet that gives information about a club, activity, or other school group. The pamphlets should encourage other students to try the activity. Have students share their completed pamphlets with others. **OL**

 Reading Check

Answer You can make new friends by joining a club or other group, or by joining a worthwhile effort or cause. You could also become a tutor or find a study partner.

Friendships and Character

You may have noticed that many qualities of good friends happen to be traits of good character. That is no accident. Friendships provide an opportunity to develop and practice good character traits.

Name some character traits that you and your closest friends share.

Making Friends

Life would be much simpler if there were a recipe for making friends. It might begin, "Combine loyalty and caring. Stir in respect." Of course, no such recipe exists. There are, however, suggestions that you can follow to make new friends.

One of the most important things to remember is to be yourself. Do not pretend to be someone you are not. If you do, you will eventually get tired of having to hide your true self. Besides, good friendships are rooted in honesty, and people tend to appreciate others who are genuine and sincere.

One thing you can do to make new friends is make an effort to meet new people. The people around you play an important part in your personal health and well-being. The positive influence of good friendships can impact your physical, mental/emotional, and social health. Think about joining a club or other group, either at school or in your community. What are your interests, talents, and hobbies? There are bound to be others with whom you share common interests.

Another way to make new friends is to join a worthwhile effort or cause. You could volunteer for a community project, such as a park cleanup, or become a tutor at your local elementary school. You could find out if a classmate needs a study partner. Another benefit of participating in these kinds of activities is the sense of accomplishment you will experience. You will feel better about yourself because you will be making a positive contribution to your community.

AL

 Reading Check   **Give Examples** What are some things you could do to meet new people?

▶ Volunteering for a community project or other activity is an opportunity to make a difference. **What character trait does this show?**

Caption Answer

Photo Caption *Sample answer:* Volunteering demonstrates the character trait of caring.

Friends and Physical Fitness After students have discussed friendships, have them review the information in the *Fitness Zone Handbook*. Ask: How can sharing a physical fitness routine help you strengthen your friendships? How can participating in group fitness activities help you make new friends? What other friendship-related benefits do you think a physical fitness plan can offer? **For more information, see *Fitness Zone Handbook* pages xviii–1 or visit the Fitness Zone at glencoe.com.**

Health Skills Activity

Communication Skills

"Breaking the Ice"

Outgoing people often have an easier time making friends than those who are shy. For some people, meeting and getting to know others can be difficult. If this sounds like you, here are some strategies to try:

- Friendships start with a simple conversation. This can be as simple as asking a classmate a question. You can always talk about school. Gradually try to talk about other topics, such as movies or sports. Ask about your classmate's interests.
- Are there others in your class who tend to keep quiet and seem a bit shy? They may also find it hard to meet people. Make an effort to start a conversation with one of them.

On Your Own

Try using one of the above strategies to meet a new person.

Cliques

People tend to feel comfortable around others like themselves. This sometimes leads to the formation of cliques during adolescence. A **clique** is *a group of friends who hang out together and act in similar ways.* Cliques can be a close-knit group of people with a strong common interest or bond. Cliques can satisfy a teen's need to belong and feel accepted. They can also be harmful, especially when members feel negative peer pressure from other members.

Peer pressure is *the influence to go along with the beliefs and actions of other people your age.* Peer pressure is negative when it involves behavior that can damage your health, hurt others, or get someone into trouble. It is positive, however, when peers encourage and support healthy behaviors.

Some cliques are exclusive groups that limit membership to a chosen few. Cliques like this are sometimes hurtful to outsiders. Members may go out of their way to make nonmembers feel bad by teasing or laughing at them. A more positive approach would be to show respect and kindness to others, even those with whom you have nothing in common.

Reading Check **Explain** In what ways can cliques benefit teens?

Health Skills Activity

Communication Skills

"Breaking the Ice"

Use the following strategies to help students complete the activity:

- Have students work in small groups to read the feature.
- Then have each group write a role-play that demonstrates a strategy for breaking the ice when talking to someone new.
- Have each group perform its role-play for the class. Ask students to identify similarities and differences among the strategies shown in the role-plays. **OL**

U Universal Access

English Learners Write the word *clique* on the board. Underline the letters *qu.* Explain that in the word *clique*, the *qu* is pronounced with the *k* sound. Contrast this with the *kw* sound most commonly associated with the letters *qu* in words such as *quite* and *quarter.* **EL**

Reading Check

Answer Cliques can benefit teens by giving them a sense of belonging.

Promoting Coordinated School Health

Cliques Providing a healthy school environment where all students feel valued is a primary goal of a coordinated school health program. Cliques that exclude others and belittle nonmembers are detrimental to a healthy school environment. Counseling services are a component of coordinated school health that can be used to intervene if cliques become a negative influence in the school environment.

C Critical Thinking

Analyzing Ask students for suggestions of famous people or celebrities. As a large group, analyze the personality traits of a few of these people. Then have small groups of students discuss whether or not the chosen famous people would be good to date, based on consideration of good character traits. **AL**

AL Active Learning

Think, Pair, Share Have students read the information under the heading "Spending Time with a Group." Ask: What are some other advantages of spending time with a group instead of individual dating? Tell students to think about an answer to the question. Then have students discuss their thoughts with a partner. Call on several pairs of students to share their ideas with the class. **OL**

Reading Check

Answer Group activities, such as playing volleyball, can keep you physically fit and make conversation easier.

Caption Answers

Photo Caption, this page Cliques can be harmful if they exclude or are hurtful to others.
Photo Caption, p. 107 Sample answer: Teens share many of the same interests and attitudes.

▲ Cliques can help satisfy the emotional need to belong. **What are some ways that cliques can be harmful?**

 Go Online

Visit **glencoe.com** and complete the Interactive Study Guide for Lesson 1.

Dating

During your teen years, you may begin feeling attracted to others. These feelings may take the form of strong emotions. Yesterday, the girl who lives across the street was "just another kid on the block." Today, you find it hard to stop staring at her when she is around. Yesterday, your older brother's best friend was a pest or a bore. Today, you find yourself worrying about your appearance when you know he is coming to your house. These new feelings cause some teens to begin—or at least begin thinking about—dating. Dating is a way to get to know other people better. **C**

There is no specific time when you are supposed to start dating. Some people feel ready to date in their teens, while others do not feel ready until much later.

Spending Time with a Group

An alternative to individual dating is to spend time in a group setting. A mixed group of teens might get together to watch a movie or play a game. Other fun group activities include dancing, skating, and playing volleyball. An added health benefit of these activities is that they keep you physically active. **AL**

There are other advantages to going out with a group as well. One advantage is that it takes the pressure off you to keep the conversation flowing. When there are several teens present, as opposed to only two, you do not have to talk as much. Another benefit is that a group can share the cost of an activity, making the group activity less expensive for each individual.

Reading Check **Explain** Why is spending time in a group setting a good alternative to individual dating?

Individual Dating

At some point, you might feel ready to go out on a date with just one other person. Perhaps your parents will let you know that they feel you are ready for individual dating. Dating is a big step

TECHNOLOGY AND HEALTH

Internet Safety Tips Sometimes teens connect with others through Internet sites and chat rooms. Have students work in small groups to research safety tips for communicating online. Review each group's list to be sure it includes the following tips:

- Never agree to meet an online acquaintance in person.
- Never give any personal information to a person you are chatting with online.
- Discuss your Internet use with parents or guardians.

that should be taken for the right reasons. Some reasons might include having an interest in what another person has to say, and wanting to know that person better. Reacting to peer pressure is not a good reason to begin dating someone.

Think of dating as a special form of friendship. It should involve two people who enjoy each other's company, and who share common interests and values. Like any other friendship, a dating relationship should be based on caring and respect.

▲ Doing group activities is an alternative to individual dating. **Why do you think these teens enjoy each other's company?**

ASSESS

Assessment Resources

Lesson Review Quiz
* *ExamView*
* Fast Files Activities
* Online Quizzes and Activities

Reteaching

● Assign Concept Map 5-1 or Reteaching Activity 5-1 in the Fast Files.
● Have students work in pairs to review the qualities of a good friend. Have each pair of students summarize its discussion by making a list of the qualities of a good friend.

Enrichment

● Assign Enrichment Activity 5-1 in the Fast Files.
● Have students make an illustrated nonfiction book appropriate for students in grades K–3, explaining how to make and keep friends. Provide several books for students in this age group as models.

CLOSE

Go around the room and ask students to identify ways in which friendships change during adolescence.

Lesson 1 Review

 After You Read

Review this lesson for new terms, major headings, and Reading Checks.

What I Learned

1. ***Vocabulary*** Define *peer pressure*. Use it in an original sentence.

2. ***Identify*** Name two qualities of a good friend.

3. ***Recall*** Why do some teens form cliques?

Thinking Critically

4. ***Evaluate*** Milo and Jake have been friends since kindergarten. Recently, they have begun to drift apart. Jake feels rejected and is wondering if Milo is mad at him for some reason. What advice would you give Jake?

5. ***Apply*** Janine, who is new at school, has become part of a clique. Today at lunch, members of the group talked about skipping school to go to the beach. What do you think Janine should do? How could Janine influence her friends to make healthful choices?

Applying Health Skills

6. ***Communication Skills*** With a group, develop a "Friends' Bill of Rights." This document should spell out the things that friends have a right to expect of each other. The bill should contain examples.

Go Online For more Lesson Review Activities, go to **glencoe.com**.

Lesson 1: Friendships During Adolescence **107**

Lesson 1 Review Answers

1. Peer pressure is the influence to go along with beliefs and actions of others your age. Sentences will vary.

2. *Sample answers:* respectful, sympathetic, forgiving, trustworthy

3. Cliques can satisfy a teen's need to belong and feel accepted.

4. *Sample answer:* This is a natural change that occurs during adolescence.

5. *Sample answer:* Janine should recognize that this clique is exerting negative peer pressure, and she might need to seek out new friends. Janine could suggest going to the beach on the weekend.

6. Students' work should include information from the lesson concerning healthy ways that friends interact.

FOCUS

Activating Prior Knowledge

What I Know Have students recall the importance of using "I" messages, introduced in Chapter 2. Have students practice converting "You" messages to "I" messages.

Guide to Reading

Building Vocabulary
- Have students write a sentence that explains how two of the vocabulary terms are related.
- Use Vocabulary PuzzleMaker to reinforce vocabulary terms.

Reading Strategy
Finding the Main Idea Have students state the main idea of each section in their own words. Ask volunteers to share their responses with the class.

Quick Write

Have students share their completed Quick Write with the class. Compile a class list and ask students to identify similarities and differences among these types of communication.

Practicing Communication Skills

Guide to Reading

Building Vocabulary
Make a word diagram that shows the relationship among the terms below. Decide which term is the most general and the one all the others relate to.

- communication (p. 108)
- body language (p. 108)
- mixed message (p. 109)
- "I" message (p. 110)
- active listening (p. 110)

Focusing on the Main Ideas
In this lesson, you will learn to
- **describe** types of nonverbal communication.
- **explain** how to be a more effective speaker.
- **identify** ways of being a good listener.
- **communicate** effectively with the use of "I" messages.

Reading Strategy
Finding the Main Idea For each major heading in this lesson, write one sentence that states the main idea.

Quick Write

Make a list of different ways people communicate, such as speaking, writing letters, instant messaging, and so on. Identify similarities and differences among these methods.

What Is Communication?

An essential skill in building healthy relationships is communication. **Communication** is *the exchange of thoughts, feelings, and beliefs between two or more people.* Good communication is not only about getting a message across successfully. It is also about being able to listen to messages you hear. This means paying attention to and hearing what the other person is saying.

In this lesson, you will take a look at the factors that make up good communication skills. You will learn ways to keep the lines of communication open.

Nonverbal Communication

You have probably noticed that when two people carry on a conversation, they often move their hands around as they talk. Also, the looks on their faces may reveal clues about what they are saying. Gestures and facial expressions are features of *nonverbal communication*—communication without words.

There are two main types of nonverbal communication. One is **body language,** *the use of visual cues to communicate information or feelings.* In addition to gestures and facial expressions, body language includes posture.

Lesson 2 Resources

 Chapter FAST FILE Resources
Guided Reading and Writing 5-2
Concept Mapping Activity 5-2
Health Lab 5-2
Reteaching Activity 5-2
Enrichment Activity 5-2
Lesson Quiz 5-2

Technology
- Transparency 5-2
- Audio Summaries
- *ExamView®* Assessment Suite
- Vocabulary PuzzleMaker
- StudentWorks™ Plus

G⊕ **Online**

The second type of nonverbal communication is *intonation,* or tone of voice. When you speak, the sound of your voice alone can send a message. You may sound angry or unhappy without even realizing it. How you say something can be just as important as what you say.

Mixed Messages

Body language and intonation often occur naturally without any effort. Some people, for example, use hand gestures when speaking. Sometimes, however, verbal and nonverbal messages can send two different messages. For that reason, you should try to become aware of the nonverbal messages you send. Otherwise, you run the risk of sending mixed messages. A **mixed message** occurs *when your words say one thing but your body language and/or intonation say another.* Saying you are sorry while grinning is an example of a mixed message. It tells the person you are apologizing but that you do not really mean it. Can you think of other examples of mixed messages?

▲ Notice that you do not have to hear these teens' words to get a sense of what they are saying or feeling. **What body language tells you that the teen on the right is listening to what the other teen is saying?**

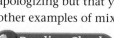 **Reading Check** **Define** What is *intonation?*

Effective Verbal Communication

Communication is a two-way street. In order for it to be effective, two different sets of skills need to be present. The first set is speaking skills. These skills determine how a message is delivered. The second is listening skills, which determine how a message is received. Listening skills are the part of the communication process that is most often overlooked.

Speaking Skills

One rule of effective speaking is to make your message as clear as possible. Consider this message: "You can't do anything right!" These words were spoken by a teen named Josh to his younger brother, Chris. The two had planned to work together on a project. Chris, however, decided to get a head start before Josh got home from school. When Josh came home, he saw that Chris had glued a few parts together incorrectly.

Josh is clearly angry, but his message is not an example of effective speaking. It does nothing more than place blame. Most importantly, it leaves little room for a positive response. Chris will probably feel hurt and may answer back in anger.

 G⊙ Online

Topic: Body Language Basics

Visit glencoe.com for Student Web Activities to learn about how people use body language to communicate.

Activity: Using the information provided at the link above, create a body language game that teaches players how to communicate with their partners using only nonverbal clues.

TEACH

R Reading Strategy

Analyzing a Graphic Have students examine the picture of two teens shown on this page. Ask: How does body language reveal what these teens are thinking and feeling? *The girl with drooping shoulders and a sad expression is using body language to show that she is feeling sad. Her friend is using body language such as leaning forward and looking attentive to show caring and concern.* OL

G⊙ Online

Body Language Basics Have students go to **glencoe.com** to select the student Web Activity for this lesson. Then have students research the online careers section. Ask volunteers to share their completed letters.

Reading Check

Answer Intonation, tone of voice, is one type of nonverbal communication.

Cultural Perspectives

Differences in Body Language Body language is used in different ways in different cultures. For example, in many cultures of Southeast Asia it is not considered appropriate to show facial expressions of sadness or anger. People from these cultures might smile to mask negative feelings or when making a sad or negative statement. Have students work in pairs to research nonverbal communication in a variety of cultures. Have each pair of students give a short oral report explaining its findings. OL

Caption Answer

Photo Caption Leaning forward and looking attentive are two clues that this teen is listening to her friend.

HS Health Skills Practice

Communication Divide the class into four groups. Assign each group one of the suggestions for effective verbal communication. Have each group write a role-play that demonstrates the importance of its assigned tip. Allow each group a short time to rehearse its role-play, and then have each group perform its role-play for the class. **OL**

AL Active Learning

Quick Demo Teach students to recognize good listening skills. At some point during the lesson, ask a volunteer to define one of the lesson vocabulary terms. As the student responds to your question, look through papers or a book. Be sure that you give nonverbal clues to indicate that you are not paying attention to what the student says. Have students explain how they could tell that you were not listening. Use this demonstration to remind students that good listening skills are important for communication. **OL**

Reading Check

Answer "I" messages do not accuse or scold. "I" messages tell how the speaker feels.

Compare that message with this one: "I'm mad because I wanted to work on the project together. I wanted you to wait for me." This is an example of an **"I" message.** This is *a statement that presents a situation from the speaker's personal viewpoint.* "I" messages do not accuse or scold the way "you" messages do. "I" messages tell how the speaker feels. This makes them very powerful communication tools.

"I" messages are a key speaking skill. Here are some other skills for good communication:

HS

- **Stay calm.** Remember, the louder you speak, the less likely you are to be heard. Few arguments are ever settled by screaming or slamming a door.

- **Stick to the point.** Think your ideas through before you begin to speak. Be specific.

- **Choose the right time and place.** Find a time when the other person is not in a hurry or busy with something else. Find a quiet place where there is little chance of interruption.

- **Be aware of your body language and intonation.** Do not send mixed messages. Be sure to maintain eye contact with the other person. Eye contact is a way of showing that you are sincere.

Reading Check

 Identify What are two advantages of "I" messages over "you" messages?

Listening Skills

Have you ever spoken to someone whose attention was on something else—the TV, maybe? It can be a frustrating experience. Good listening skills are just as important to interpersonal communication as speaking skills. A speaker's message has meaning only if the listener receives it.

AL

A good listener is an active listener. **Active listening** is *hearing, thinking about, and responding to the other person's message.* The following suggestions can help you become a more active listener.

◀ An important factor of active listening is appropriate body language. **What are some other skills of active listening?**

Caption Answer

Photo Caption *Sample answer:* Paying careful attention and thinking before speaking are other skills of active listening.

 Teacher to Teacher

Courtney Wolf   **Armstrong Middle School, Flint, MI**

Body Language and Saying No "Model the right way to use body language to say no to someone who is pressuring you (eye contact, speaking clearly, addressing the person by name) and the wrong way (slouched shoulders, looking at the ground, wishy-washy answers, etc.). After I demonstrate I give the students five steps to saying no:
1) Say the person's name.   3) Say 'no.'   5) Walk away."
2) Look them in the eye.   4) Say 'I do not want to do that.'

- **Pay careful attention to all that the speaker has to say.** Do not begin forming your answer while the other person is still speaking. If the two of you are working through a problem, keep an open mind. There are at least two sides to every disagreement. You may end up seeing things in a different way. Also, if you carefully listen to people, others will appreciate it. They will be more likely to carefully listen to you when you speak.

- **Use body language that shows you are listening.** Make eye contact with the speaker. Nod your head from time to time to show that you are paying attention. Back up your body language with comments such as "Really?" or "What happened next?" You can also use body language to show emotion.

- **Think for a moment before speaking.** Take time to collect your thoughts. Decide exactly how you want to respond. Once you do respond, "mirror" the speaker's thoughts and feelings. Repeat what the person said as a way of confirming what you heard.

- **Ask questions.** After the person has finished talking, ask questions or add your own comments or opinions. If you do not understand something, say so.

Go Online

Visit **glencoe.com** and complete the Interactive Study Guide for Lesson 2.

Lesson 2 Review

 After You Read

Review this lesson for new terms, major headings, and Reading Checks.

What I Learned

1. *Vocabulary* What is a *mixed message*?

2. *List* What are the two main types of nonverbal communication?

3. *Identify* Besides active listening, what are some tips for effective listening?

Thinking Critically

4. *Synthesize* Respond to the statement "Actions speak louder than words." Explain the relevance of this expression to the skill of communication.

5. *Apply* Kelly is really upset. A jacket she loaned to a friend came back with a tear in it. How can Kelly express her feelings using an "I" message?

Applying Health Skills

6. *Communication Skills* With a group, develop a booklet on the importance of good communication skills. The booklet should describe and demonstrate techniques such as using "I" messages and active listening.

Go Online For more Lesson Review Activities, go to **glencoe.com**.

Lesson 2: Practicing Communication Skills **111**

ASSESS

 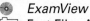

Assessment Resources

Lesson Review Quiz
- *ExamView*
- Fast Files Activities
- Online Quizzes and Activities

Reteaching

- Assign Concept Map 5-2 or Reteaching Activity 5-2 in the Fast Files.
- Have students work in pairs to practice using "I" messages to communicate thoughts and feelings.

Enrichment

- Assign Enrichment Activity 5-2 in the Fast Files.
- Have students watch a video or television broadcast of a speech given by a politician or other public figure. Have students analyze how the speaker uses effective verbal and nonverbal communication skills to convey his or her ideas.

CLOSE

Go around the room and have students identify skills for good communication.

Lesson 2 Review Answers

1. Mixed messages are when your words say one thing but your body language or intonation says another.

2. The two main types of nonverbal communication are body language and intonation.

3. Effective listening skills include paying attention to the speaker, using body language, and thinking before speaking.

4. *Sample answer:* Body language occurs on an unconscious level and often gives a more accurate reading of a person's feelings.

5. *Sample answer:* "I am upset because my jacket is torn. I would like you to sew the tear in my jacket."

6. Students' booklets should include speaking and listening skills described in the lesson.

Lesson 3

FOCUS

Activating Prior Knowledge

What I Know Have students recall a time when they successfully used refusal skills. Challenge students to identify reasons why the strategies they used were successful.

Guide to Reading

Building Vocabulary
- Have students make a graphic organizer that shows how the vocabulary terms are related.
- Use Vocabulary PuzzleMaker to reinforce vocabulary terms.

Reading Strategy
Comparing and Contrasting At the conclusion of the lesson, ask volunteers to share examples from their graphic organizers.

uick Write

When students have completed their Quick Write, ask volunteers to share their responses. Lead a class discussion of ways peer pressure can have a positive impact.

Lesson 3

Peer Pressure and Refusal Skills

Guide to Reading

Building Vocabulary
As you read this lesson, write each new highlighted term and its definition in your notebook.

- refusal skills (p. 115)
- aggressive (p. 116)
- passive (p. 116)
- assertive (p. 116)

Focusing on the Main Ideas
In this lesson, you will learn to
- **explain** the differences between positive and negative peer pressure.
- **identify** risks of negative peer pressure.
- **develop** refusal skills to resist negative peer pressure.

Reading Strategy
Comparing and Contrasting Create a graphic that shows the difference between positive and negative peer pressure. Be sure to include examples of each.

uick Write

Describe a time when you were inspired to do something good because of positive peer pressure.

Peer Pressure

Lately, Stephanie has been spending lunchtime with a new group of girls. She shares some common interests with them, but she does not like the way they gossip and treat some of the girls outside their group. "What is she wearing? That's horrible!" Stacy said, pointing to a girl across from them.

As the girls laughed and pointed, Stephanie stood there feeling bad, wishing they would stop talking about the other girl. "Doesn't she look ridiculous?" Stacy said to Stephanie. Stephanie was not sure what to say. She felt pressured to join in, but she did not want to. "No. She doesn't look ridiculous. She just dresses a little different than us," Stephanie said.

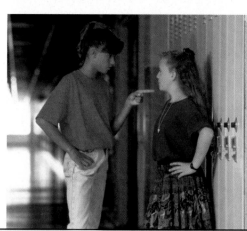

▶ Peer pressure can influence your decisions positively or negatively. **What is peer pressure?**

Caption Answer

Photo Caption Peer pressure is the way that the words and actions of others influence your thoughts and behaviors.

Lesson 3 Resources

📁 **Chapter FAST FILE Resources**
Guided Reading and Writing 5-3
Concept Mapping Activity 5-3
Decision-Making Activity 5-3
Reteaching Activity 5-3
Enrichment Activity 5-3
Lesson Quiz 5-3

Technology
- Transparency 5-3
- Audio Summaries
- *ExamView®* Assessment Suite
- Vocabulary PuzzleMaker
- StudentWorks™ Plus
- **Go Online**

Peer Pressure and Decisions

Peer pressure can be a powerful force during the teen years. Teens look to members of their peer group for acceptance. Pressure to fit in can have an impact, good or bad, on a person's decisions. Peer pressure can influence healthful choices.

Some peer pressure is direct—it takes the form of words or actions directed toward you. Indirect peer pressure is more subtle than direct peer pressure. For example, you may notice many people at school wearing a specific shoe style. Maybe you want to go out and buy those shoes, too, because you think you will fit in with everyone else if you wear them.

Reading Check **Explain** What is the difference between direct and indirect peer pressure?

Positive Peer Pressure

HS In addition to being direct or indirect, peer pressure may also be positive or negative. Positive peer pressure can inspire you to be the best person you can be. When Sally saw a news story about victims of a deadly flood, she decided to take action. The next day, she started collecting money in her neighborhood. Her goal was to send the money to a national organization in charge of the relief effort.

Sally asked her friends and other teens she knew to help raise money, too. Her efforts became a source of direct peer pressure on these teens. Within several days, the teens had raised hundreds of dollars.

Positive peer pressure can benefit your own life, too. You can be positively influenced to do something that improves your own well-being and health. Positive peer pressure can influence you to do better in school or to participate in after-school activities.

What **Teens** THINK

In your opinion, what form of peer pressure is most common among teens?

The most common peer pressure for teens is the pressure to do drugs and alcohol. Teens are always being pressured to do this by friends and boyfriends. They are told that by doing this they will become more popular.

Victoria J.
Portland, TN

▼ Positive peer pressure can encourage healthy habits. **What is an example of positive peer pressure that you have experienced?**

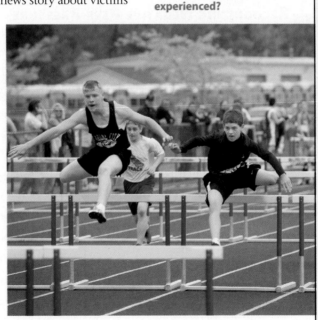

Lesson 3: Peer Pressure and Refusal Skills **113**

CHAPTER 5

Lesson 3

TEACH

What **Teens** THINK

In your opinion, what form of peer pressure is most common among teens? After students have read about direct and indirect peer pressure, help them brainstorm lists of specific things teens do to exert direct and indirect pressure on their peers. Then have students read and discuss the *What Teens Think* question and response.

HS Health Skills Practice

Goal Setting Ask students to read the information about positive peer pressure. Then have students set a goal to be a positive influence on a peer at some time in the next week. Have students write their goal and the steps they will take to achieve their goal on an index card. **OL**

Reading Check

Answer Direct peer pressure takes the form of words or actions directed toward you. Indirect peer pressure is internal.

Caption Answer

Photo Caption *Sample answer:* I experienced positive peer pressure when a friend asked me to come over to study for the math test.

🏠 Home, School, and Community

At School Student groups and clubs are an excellent way for teens to work together to be a positive influence on others. One organization dedicated to this mission is SADD, or Students Against Destructive Decisions. If your school has an active chapter of SADD, have a student representative speak to the class or provide information to distribute to your class. If your school does not have a chapter of SADD, have students research to find out more about starting a chapter at your school. **OL**

Universal Access

English Learners Discuss with students the terms *negative* and *positive*. Explain that *positive*, in the context of positive peer pressure, means healthful. Have students identify how the word *positive* is used in other subject areas. For example, in math, a *positive* number is a number greater than zero. **EL**

R Reading Strategy

Analyzing a Graphic Have students examine **Figure 5.1** that lists questions that students can use to determine if peer pressure is negative. Have students classify these questions into three categories: those that concern physical health, those that concern social health, and those that concern mental/emotional health. Have volunteers share their classifications. **OL**

Reading Check

Answer Negative peer pressure can take the form of threats, dares, or bribes.

Academic Vocabulary

Manipulate Ask students: How do dares, threats, bribes, teasing, and name-calling manipulate your emotions? Why is it important to recognize that your emotions are being manipulated? You will find academic vocabulary activities in the Student Activities Workbook. 📁

114

Negative Peer Pressure

Negative peer pressure is pressure to do something that could hurt you or others, or get you into trouble. It often goes against your own wants, needs, or values. For example, the pressure that Stephanie felt to laugh at another girl was negative peer pressure. If Stephanie had gone along with her friends, she would have felt bad about what she had done.

Some teens endanger their health when they let themselves be influenced by negative peer pressure. For example, they might use alcohol, tobacco, or other drugs. Giving into these pressures can negatively affect your performance at school, your health, and your future. That is a good reason to choose friends who share your values, and who won't try to pressure you into doing something you do not want to do.

Negative peer pressure takes many forms. Teens who put negative pressure on you may try to **manipulate** your emotions or find your weaknesses. The pressure may come as a dare or threat. It may come in the form of a bribe, teasing, or name-calling. Recognizing negative peer pressure in all its forms is important. This is a first step toward standing your ground and protecting your beliefs. **Figure 5.1** lists questions you can ask yourself to help you decide if peer pressure is negative.

Academic Vocabulary

manipulate (muh NIP yuh leyt) *(verb)* to change or control for one's own purpose. *It is wrong to use negative peer pressure to manipulate a friend.*

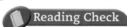 **Reading Check** **List** Name some forms that negative peer pressure can take.

▼ FIGURE 5.1

RECOGNIZING NEGATIVE PEER PRESSURE

When you feel you are being pressured, analyze the possible outcomes and health consequences. **What are two questions to ask yourself when you are feeling peer pressure?**

Possible Outcomes	Health Consequences
• Is this activity dangerous?	• How will this activity affect my physical health?
• Does it break the law?	• Am I being asked to do something that could bring me physical harm?
• Can it lead to punishment, such as suspension from school, or arrest?	• Is the activity something that can lead to an addiction?
• Will it lead to disapproval or disappointment from parents or guardians?	• What effect will it have on my emotional health?
• Will property be destroyed or damaged?	• Will I feel guilty if I do this activity?
	• Will I disappoint myself?
	• Is it something I simply do not feel ready for?
	• How will this decision affect the health of others?
	• Could someone else be hurt?

HEALTH LITERACY

Peer Pressure and Sexual Activity Peer pressure affects all aspects of teen life, including sexual activity. Studies have found that approximately one-third of teen boys and one-quarter of teen girls have experienced peer pressure to engage in sexual activity. Teens are also strongly influenced by the perception of what their peers are doing. Studies routinely show that teens overestimate the percentage of their peers who are sexually active. When students read Lesson 4, which discusses abstinence from sexual activity, have students review the importance of resisting negative peer pressure.

Refusal Skills

Negative peer pressure can be very strong. When anyone challenges your beliefs or values, you need to be strong, too. While negative pressure is often easy to recognize, it can be difficult to resist. One way to resist negative pressure is by using refusal skills. **Refusal skills** are *communication strategies that help you say no effectively.* They help you avoid doing things you do not want to do without feeling uncomfortable about your decision. By using refusal skills, you stand up for your values, which builds self-respect. You also show others that you have strength and character. These qualities will win their respect as well.

A Strategy for Refusing

Like other skills, refusal skills take practice. Many teens find the S.T.O.P. strategy to be an effective way to say no to risky behaviors like using drugs or alcohol or engaging in sexual activity. The letters in S.T.O.P. represent the four steps in the strategy. You can use one or all of the following steps:

- **Say no in a firm voice.** State your feelings firmly but politely. Just say, "No, I don't want to." Make your "no" sound like you really mean it. Use body language to support your words. Make eye contact with the person.

- **Tell why not.** If the other person keeps up the pressure, explain why you feel the way you do. You do not need to use phony excuses or make up reasons. Simply say, "No thanks, I care about my health." Do not apologize. You have done nothing wrong.

- **Offer other ideas.** If the person pressuring you to do something is a friend, you can choose to suggest alternatives. Recommend an activity that is safe and fun.

- **Promptly leave.** If all else fails, just walk away. Make your actions match your words. If you are someplace where you need a ride, phone a parent to come and pick you up.

 Reading Check **Identify** Tell what the letters in the S.T.O.P. strategy stand for.

Styles of Communication

When you use refusal skills, your goal is to say no. You are not trying to start an argument. However, the other person does need to hear you and understand your position. How your words are received is largely a matter of your communication *style*. There are three basic styles of communication: aggressive, passive, and assertive.

CHAPTER 5

Lesson 3

Careers for the 21st Century

School Counselor

A school counselor is an important member of your education team. They help students in many areas of their academic, personal, and social lives. They may help you prepare for college or settle an argument between you and a peer. School counselors are important resources for students and help shape their future. If you are interested in becoming a school counselor, you should practice your communication skills.

What other skills does a school counselor need? Go to *Career Corner* at **glencoe.com** to find out.

Careers for the 21st Century

School Counselor Have students meet in small groups to read and discuss the information in the text and in the Career Corner at **glencoe.com**. Then ask: Why are good communication skills important for school counselors?

AL Active Learning

Comic Strip Have students work in small groups to create a comic strip that shows a character using refusal skills to avoid negative peer pressure. Provide several examples of comic strips for students to use as models. Remind students that comic strips use art and text to convey an idea. **OL**

U Universal Access

At-Risk Students At-risk students are more likely than other students to exert and/or be influenced by negative peer pressure. Without singling out individual students, stress the importance of practicing refusal skills to help resist negative peer pressure. Have students work in groups to practice the steps of the S.T.O.P. strategy. **OL**

What Teens Want to Know

How can I avoid negative peer pressure? After students have read the lesson material about peer pressure, have a class discussion about strategies for avoiding negative peer pressure. Invite a school counselor to speak to students about peer pressure and high-risk behavior. Ask the counselor to discuss strategies for avoiding negative peer pressure. Also have the speaker discuss the consequences of giving in to negative peer pressure. Have students prepare written questions to submit to the speaker. **OL**

Reading Check

Answer The letters in the S.T.O.P. strategy stand for **S**ay no, **T**ell why not, **O**ffer other ideas, and **P**romptly leave.

Health Skills Activity

Refusal Skills

Responding to "Lines"

Use the following strategies to help students complete the activity on page 117:

- Have students work in small groups to read the activity.
- Then have students practice the lines as directed. Have students develop their own responses as well.
- Ask students to explain ways in which they have incorporated effective verbal and nonverbal communication skills in their responses. **OL**

W Writing Support

Persuasive Writing
Emphasize to students that saying no once may not be enough when using refusal skills. Teens should be prepared to repeat their refusals a number of times and to not allow pressure to wear them down. Have students write a conversation using three sentences they may use to effectively express refusal to someone who is not listening. Ask volunteers to share their sentences.

 Reading Check

Answer behaving with confidence and clearly stating your intentions

Caption Answer

Photo Caption The teen is using aggressive communication.

▶ Your communication style can affect how well you communicate. **What style of communication do you think the teen on the left is using?**

Aggressive communication means *speaking in a way that is overly forceful, pushy, hostile, or otherwise attacking in approach.* The speaker may talk in a loud voice, leaning in toward the other person. This approach is not an effective way to communicate and get a message across. People are not likely to listen to what you are saying if they feel like you are being pushy. Aggressive communication can stir up anger in the listener, and can even lead to violence.

W The **passive** style of communication includes *a tendency to give up, give in, or back down without standing up for your rights and needs.* A passive communicator might speak in a very quiet voice and avoid looking directly at the listener. This style of communication suggests that the person might be uncertain and easy to persuade. Speaking in a firm voice and making eye contact are important strategies for refusal.

One effective style of communication is an assertive style. Being **assertive** means *behaving with confidence and clearly stating your intentions.* Speak in a firm but positive voice. Your body language and attitude should back up your words. Hold your head high and make eye contact. When you are assertive you stand up for your own rights while respecting the rights of others.

Go Online

Visit **glencoe.com** and complete the Interactive Study Guide for Lesson 3.

 Reading Check **Recall** What is an assertive communication style?

TECHNOLOGY AND HEALTH

Practicing Communication Skills Use video technology to help students practice and refine their communication skills. Have students work in small groups to make video recordings of one another as they practice using assertive communication skills to refuse negative peer pressure.

Review with students the school's policies on videotaping students before they begin. Remind them to use the video to assess both verbal and nonverbal aspects of communication. Allow students to make a second video after evaluating their first attempt. **OL**

Health Skills Activity

Refusal Skills

Responding to "Lines"

Teens who use negative peer pressure can often be persuasive. They may flatter you or even beg you to do something. They may also use common phrases, or "lines," such as, "Everyone's doing it." It is a good idea to have a response planned for common lines. Here are some possibilities:

"LINE"	POSSIBLE RESPONSES
• Everyone's doing it.	• You're wrong. I'm not doing it.
• A real friend would do it.	• A real friend wouldn't ask.
• Are you afraid?	• No, just smart.

With a Group

Practice these lines. Add some responses of your own. Which responses do you think are most effective, and why?

ASSESS

Assessment Resources

Lesson Review Quiz
 ExamView
 Fast Files Activities
Online Quizzes and Activities

Reteaching

- Assign Concept Map 5-3 or Reteaching Activity 5-3 in the Fast Files.
- Have each student develop a list of three examples each of positive and negative peer pressure. Call on students to share examples.

Enrichment

- Assign Enrichment Activity 5-3 in the Fast Files.
- Have students develop a lesson for teaching others how to use refusal skills and assertive communication. Have students share their lessons with the class.

CLOSE

Have students identify and describe the steps in the S.T.O.P. strategy.

Lesson 3 Review

 After You Read

Review this lesson for new terms, major headings, and Reading Checks.

What I Learned

1. *Vocabulary* What are *refusal skills*?

2. *Give Examples* Give one example of positive peer pressure and one of negative peer pressure.

3. *Identify* Name the three communication styles. Tell which one is the most effective in helping you say no to negative peer pressure.

Thinking Critically

4. *Analyze* Ralph has told Peter twice that he does not want to sneak into the movies. He has even offered to pay for Peter's ticket to the show. Peter insists on sneaking in. What should Ralph do next?

5. *Apply* Zoey is pressuring Alicia to let her copy Alicia's homework assignment. Alicia knows this is wrong. How can she express her feelings to Zoey in an assertive way?

Applying Health Skills

6. *Communication Skills* Act out body language that reflects one of the three communication styles. Challenge classmates to guess which style you are demonstrating.

Go Online For more Lesson Review Activities, go to **glencoe.com**.

Lesson 3 Review Answers

1. Refusal skills are communication strategies that help you say no effectively.
2. *Sample answers:* Encouraging a friend to exercise is positive peer pressure. Encouraging a friend to smoke is negative peer pressure.
3. The three styles are passive, aggressive, and assertive. Assertive communication is the most effective.
4. *Sample answer:* Ralph needs to move to the fourth step of the S.T.O.P. strategy, which is promptly leaving the area.
5. *Sample answer:* "I feel that cheating is wrong. I have to say no."
6. Have each student demonstrate one style of communication for his or her classmates.

FOCUS

Activating Prior Knowledge

What I Know Ask a volunteer to define the term *consequences.* Then have students identify the consequences of breaking a rule at school.

Guide to Reading

Building Vocabulary
- Explain that a *limit* is a boundary or rule. Have students identify how limits relate to consequences.
- Use Vocabulary PuzzleMaker to reinforce vocabulary terms.

Reading Strategy
Predicting Have students share their predictions with the class. After students have completed the lesson, ask students to note whether or not their predictions were correct.

***Q**uick Write*

Have students share their completed sentences with the class.

Limits and Abstinence

Guide to Reading

● Building Vocabulary
As you read this lesson, write each new highlighted term and its definition in your notebook.

- limits (p. 118)
- consequences (p. 119)
- abstinence (p. 119)
- affection (p. 120)

***Q**uick Write*

Identify some limits that are set by the law. Write a sentence explaining why these limits are set.

● Focusing on the Main Ideas
In this lesson, you will learn to

- **explain** why it is important to set limits.
- **identify** reasons why teens should choose abstinence.
- **demonstrate** care and respect for someone in a healthy way.

● Reading Strategy
Predicting Look over the lesson, including the headings and pictures. Then write a sentence predicting what information you think the lesson will provide.

Limits: Invisible Boundaries

Can you imagine playing a sport or game that had no rules? The activity would seem pointless, and would likely be dangerous. Rules bring a sense of order and purpose to games. They serve a similar purpose in daily life, where they sometimes take the form of limits. **Limits** are *invisible boundaries that protect you.* The laws used by a society are an example of limits.

As a teen, you probably have limits set by your parents or guardians. Your limits may include what TV shows you can watch, what Web sites you can visit, and how late you can stay up at night. Like laws, these limits are meant to keep you safe and protect your health. Internet browsing rules, for example, may keep you away from dangerous chat rooms or inappropriate Web sites. Also, having a fixed bedtime ensures that you will get the sleep you need as a growing teen. These are some of the ways to promote good health and prevent illness.

◄ A stop sign is a limit set by law. **What is the purpose of this limit? What are the possible consequences facing people who choose not to obey this limit?**

118　Chapter 5: Relationships: The Teen Years

Caption Answer

Photo Caption This is to protect drivers, passengers, and pedestrians. People who don't follow this limit get a fine or jail time.

Lesson 4 Resources

📁 **Chapter *Fast File* Resources**
Guided Reading and Writing 5-4
Concept Mapping Activity 5-4
Cross-Curriculum Activity 5-4
Reteaching Activity 5-4
Enrichment Activity 5-4
Lesson Quiz 5-4

Technology
🔧 Transparency 5-4
🔊 Audio Summaries
⚙ *ExamView®* Assessment Suite
🔊 Vocabulary PuzzleMaker
⚙ StudentWorks™ Plus

Recognizing Your Own Limits

As you grow older, you will probably spend more and more time outside your home. You will become more independent. Sometimes adults will not be present to enforce limits. Knowing your own limits will become increasingly important for you because where you go and who you spend time with can directly affect your personal safety. You will need to be able to evaluate situations and avoid people who might be bad influences. Growing up means having the freedom to express yourself. But, it is important to recognize your limits and recognize the risks of expressing your independence.

Consider the decision made by a teen named Steve. On Sunday night, Steve spent the night at his friend, Tom's house. Though Tom's parents thought they were sleeping, Tom and Steve stayed up all night watching television, playing video games, and eating pizza. Monday morning, both boys could hardly find the energy to get out of bed for school. Throughout their classes they could hardly keep their eyes open, let alone take a test. These were the negative consequences of their actions. **Consequences** are *outcomes or effects that may occur as a result of a decision or an action.*

One way to establish limits in your own life is to write down goals you wish to achieve. Once you understand what you would like to achieve, you will have a better idea of boundaries you need to set that will help you reach your goal. Chapter 2 describes the goal-setting process in detail.

Reading Check **Give Examples** What are two typical limits for teens?

Choosing Abstinence

One of the most important limits you can set for yourself during adolescence is choosing abstinence. **Abstinence** is *the conscious, active choice not to participate in high-risk behaviors.* When you begin dating, choosing abstinence from sexual activity is the responsible choice. It is a choice more and more teens are making. The Centers for Disease Control and Prevention does a yearly report on high-risk behaviors among teens. One recent report shows that over the past ten years, the percentage of teens choosing abstinence has steadily increased.

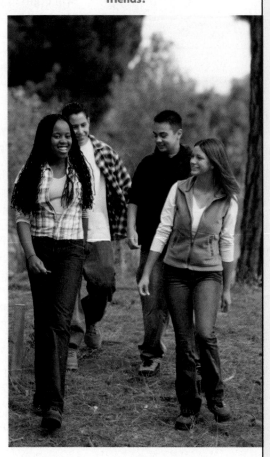

▼ Choosing abstinence allows you to focus on positive activities that will maintain your health. **What are some positive activities you can do with your friends?**

Lesson 4: Limits and Abstinence **119**

TEACH

C Critical Thinking

Analyzing Lead a class discussion of limits that are imposed by society, by family, and by the individual. Ask: Why are each of these types of limits valuable? Sample answer: *Society's limits keep civil order, family limits reinforce family beliefs and values, individual limits help each person manage his or her own behaviors and actions.*

W Writing Support

Descriptive Writing Have students write a short fictional story that describes a teen learning to establish limits in his or her life. Remind students that a story uses descriptive language to describe a plot, a setting, and characters. Have students edit their stories before turning them in. **OL**

Reading Check

Answer Two typical limits for teens are a curfew and limits on television viewing.

HEALTH LITERACY

Factors that Promote Abstinence The percentage of teens who choose to abstain from sexual activity has risen in the past several years. Studies have shown that strong family relationships and parents or guardians who clearly state their disapproval of sexual activity before marriage are factors that promote abstinence in teens. According to the National Institutes of Health, pledges to delay sexual activity until marriage also are an effective method of promoting abstinence in teens.

Caption Answer

Photo Caption Answers will vary but should include health-enhancing behaviors and activities.

**Connect To...
Math**

The Cost of Raising a Family
Provide grocery advertisements or parenting magazines as resources for students to use for this activity. Remind students that diapers and baby food are only two of the expenses involved in parenting. Have students brainstorm a list of other expenses that new parents incur. **OL**

Reading Check

Answer Teens who practice abstinence do not contract STDs or risk unplanned pregnancies.

Caption Answer
Photo Caption Demonstrating that you care is one way to show affection in a friendship.

120

**Connect To...
Math**

The Cost of Raising a Family

Raising a child is a huge responsibility, both emotionally and financially. To get a sense of this responsibility, find out about the costs of diapers and baby food. These are just two of the many expenses related to parenting.

Multiply the price of these items to determine their cost in weeks, months, and years. Share your findings with classmates.

120 Chapter 5: Relationships: The Teen Years

Reasons for Choosing Abstinence

Many teens feel pressure to engage in sexual activity. You are probably bombarded with images on television and in the movies. Maybe you feel pressure from your friends. Know that practicing sexual abstinence until marriage shows respect for yourself. It also shows respect for the physical and emotional well-being of others.

The choice to be sexually abstinent until marriage has other benefits as well. You promote good health and avoid the risks that many sexually active people face. One of these is the risk of being infected with a sexually transmitted disease (STD). STDs can damage the reproductive system, preventing a person from ever having children. Some STDs remain in the body for life—even after they are discovered. Still others—especially HIV/AIDS—can lead to death.

Another risk of sexual activity is unplanned pregnancy, which can change the entire course of a person's life. It can be particularly difficult for teens, who typically do not have the emotional or financial resources to be parents. Over the next few years you will begin to realize what you want out of life. Parenthood at this time will complicate an already complex time in your life. When people wait until adulthood to become parents, they are better able to achieve long-term goals, such as attending college.

Reading Check **List** Give reasons why abstinence is an important choice for teens.

Healthy Ways of Displaying Affection

Finding someone special—someone to care about deeply—is a goal most people share. It is one of the great gifts and joys of life. Showing **affection,** or *feelings of love for another person,* can take many different forms. One of these is sexual intimacy. This expression of caring is best postponed until adulthood and marriage. Becoming sexually active during the teen years, as you have read, carries risks. It also involves an emotional commitment that most teens are not prepared to make.

◀ Showing affection lets someone know that you care. **Why do you think it is important to show someone that you care?**

There are plenty of healthy ways for teens to show their affection. One way is to do something thoughtful for the other person. For example, you might give him or her a card or a small gift. Show the other person that you are a good friend. Make it clear you are willing to listen to his or her thoughts and ideas. Actions such as these deepen the bonds of affection. They also display good character, a sure sign that you are maturing. Holding hands and hugging are physical ways to show affection.

Dealing with Sexual Feelings

Sexual feelings are normal and healthy. You cannot prevent them, but you do have control over how you deal with them. There are ways of managing these feelings during the teen years. Think about talking through your feelings with a trusted adult. A parent, coach, counselor, or teacher will be able to offer useful suggestions. They will be able to answer questions you might have about sexual feelings.

 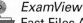 **G Online**

Visit **glencoe.com** and complete the Interactive Study Guide for Lesson 4.

 Reading Check **Define** What is *affection*?

 Lesson 4 Review

Reading Check

Answer Affection is a feeling of love for another person.

ASSESS

Assessment Resources

Lesson Review Quiz
* *ExamView*
* Fast Files Activities
* Online Quizzes and Activities

Reteaching

● Assign Concept Map 5-4 or Reteaching Activity 5-4 in the Fast Files.
● In small groups, have students discuss the benefits of having limits at home, in the school, and in the community.

Enrichment

● Assign Enrichment Activity 5-4 in the Fast Files.
● Have students find out how rules and limits are set and enforced at school. Suggest they interview the principal or other school administrator and share their findings in a written report.

CLOSE

Ask students to name healthy, respectful ways of showing affection.

After You Read

Review this lesson for new terms, major headings, and Reading Checks.

What I Learned

1. *Vocabulary* What are *limits*?

2. *Recall* What are some negative consequences of sexual activity during adolescence?

3. *List* Name two healthy ways for teens to show affection.

Thinking Critically

4. *Apply* Connie is at a party. One of the teens suggests turning out the lights and playing a kissing game. What action can Connie take that shows she understands the importance of limits?

5. *Analyze* Gayle and Eddie have been dating for a while. Eddie recently suggested that he and Gayle explore their affection physically. What would you advise Gayle to tell him?

Applying Health Skills

6. *Goal Setting* Make a contract with yourself in which you set the goal of choosing abstinence. The contract should establish limits that you set for yourself. Sign your contract and keep it in a safe place.

G Online For more Lesson Review Activities, go to **glencoe.com**.

Lesson 4: Limits and Abstinence **121**

Lesson 4 Review Answers

1. Limits are invisible boundaries that protect you.
2. Negative consequences of sexual activity include the risk of STDs and unplanned pregnancy.

3. *Sample answers:* doing something nice for the other person, being a good friend, hugging, and holding hands
4. Connie could suggest an alternate activity.

5. *Sample answers:* Gayle might point out the negative consequences of sexual activity, such as the risk of STDs and unplanned pregnancy.
6. Allow students to keep their contracts confidential.

Building Health Skills Setting Limits

Skill

Goal Setting

Activating Prior Knowledge

Have students recall the refusal skills they used to complete the Health Skills Activity in Lesson 3.

- **Objective** After completing the activity, students will be able to use goal setting and refusal skills to avoid risk behaviors.
- **Time** 45 minutes
- **Materials** index card, pencil or pen

Teacher Classroom Resources

📁 Building Health Skills Activity
🔖 Transparency 2-1

Model

- Have students read about how Ron used goal setting and refusal skills to avoid drugs. Ask: Why is it important to have a plan for avoiding risk behaviors, such as drug use? Sample answer: *Having a plan allows you to rehearse refusal skills for dealing with negative peer pressure and allows you to define your limits in advance so you sound confident when refusing.*

National Health Standards Addressed

2.8.3, 4.8.4, 5.8.1, 6.8.2

122

Building Health Skills

Accessing Information
Practicing Healthful Behaviors
Stress Management
Analyzing Influences
Communication Skills
Refusal Skills
Conflict Resolution
Decision Making
Goal Setting
Advocacy

What Is Goal Setting?

Goal setting is a five-step plan for improving and maintaining your personal health. Some goals are easy to reach while others may be more challenging.

The 5 Steps of the Goal-Setting Plan

Step 1: Choose a realistic goal and write it down.

Step 2: List the steps that you need to take to reach the goal.

Step 3: Find others, like family, friends, and teachers, who can help and support you.

Step 4: Set checkpoints along the way to evaluate your progress.

Step 5: Reward yourself once you have reached your goal.

Setting Limits

122

Follow the Model, Practice, and Apply steps to help you master this important health skill.

① Model

Read how Ron uses goal-setting skills to prepare for negative peer pressure.

Ron's family just moved to a new city. He uses the following steps to help him achieve his goal of avoiding negative peer pressure at his new school.

1. ***Identify a specific goal.*** "I want to avoid negative peer pressure."
2. ***List the steps you will take.*** "I will not go anywhere where tobacco, alcohol, or other drugs are present."
3. ***Get help and support from others.*** "My neighbor John, a student at the same school, feels the same way I do. He can introduce me to his friends."
4. ***Evaluate your progress.*** "I will talk to John about any negative pressure I experience."
5. ***Reward yourself.*** "I will feel good about myself because I am sticking to my goal."

 Teaching Tips

The Goal Setting-Decision Making Connection Ask students "How do goal setting and decision making go hand in hand?" Students' responses should indicate that because goals give us directions, they help us make better decisions. The decisions, in turn, lead us closer to our intended goals. Together, these two health skills provide a road map to success!

Action Plans Monitor action plans to ensure that they include healthful, responsible goals that promote teen health and do not cause harm to others.

② Practice

Use goal setting to help Pavel resist negative peer pressure.

Shortly after Pavel started school, he became friends with Reggie. The two began spending a lot of time together. When the first big social studies test of the semester came up, the boys studied together. As they were studying, Reggie commented that Pavel looked tense. He then said, "I have something you can smoke that can help you calm down." What response could Pavel give that would help him stick to his goal? Use the following questions to help you decide.

1. Where could Pavel get help and support from others?

2. In your opinion, which goal-setting step is most important? Tell why.

③ Apply

Use what you have learned about goal setting to complete the activity below.

Think about your long-term goals and choose one. Develop a plan for achieving this goal. At each step, identify actions you could take to resist negative peer pressure. Explain how yielding to negative peer pressure might interfere with achieving your goal.

Self-Check
- Did I identify a long-term goal I hope to achieve?
- Does my plan show ways of resisting negative peer pressure at each step?
- Did I explain how negative peer pressure might interfere with my goal?

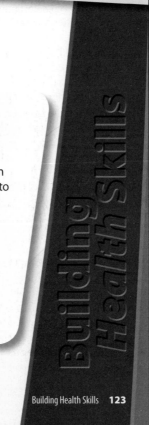

Building Health Skills

Practice
- Have students work in small groups to read and discuss the Practice activity and the questions.
- Have each group prepare an answer to the practice questions.
- Ask each group to state its answer to practice question 2. Explain that there may be more than one correct answer to this question, but that each answer should be well supported.

Apply/Assess
- Have students work individually to complete the Apply activity.
- Ask volunteers to share their plans with the class. To respect students' privacy, do not require students to share their plans with the class.
- You may wish to distribute the Building Health Skills Activity in the Fast Files.

How to Deal with Tricky Situations

Objectives

After completing this activity, students will be able to

- Identify common problems involving friends.
- Describe positive ways to solve problems with friends.
- Develop skills for making new friends.

Motivator

Have students recall and describe situations in books or movies in which a character faces a problem with friends. Ask students to describe strategies the character uses to solve the problem.

Teaching the Activity

- After students have read the feature, divide the class into four groups. Assign each group one of the situations described in the feature. Have each group write and perform a role-play that demonstrates healthy ways to resolve the assigned situation. If the groups are large, help students fairly divide the work of writing and performing the role-play among the group members. **OL**
- Have students work as a class to add to the list of signs that someone might make a good friend. Record students' responses on the board. Use the list of responses to generate a class discussion of the qualities people look for in friends. **OL**

TIME *health news*

How to Deal with TRICKY SITUATIONS

What do you do when friends get pushy or just plain mean?

Friends can make life a blast—but they can also present a problem or two. Here's some *friendly* advice on what to do when things get tricky.

THE SITUATION

You have been snubbed by the popular crowd!

THE FIX

First, feel empowered—you can handle this. Now, try talking one-on-one with individual kids in the group—away from the others. It can be easier to connect with one person rather than many. This will help you determine if the crowd is really for you anyway.

THE SITUATION

Your friends are pushing you to drink or smoke.

THE FIX

Be prepared with smart reasons to just say no. For example, find out how many people die from lung cancer each year and drop that data on the friends urging you to smoke.

THE SITUATION

Your best friend has a new friend, and now they're totally ignoring you.

THE FIX

Have a heart-to-heart with your friend and explain how this hurts your feelings. He or she might start to include you. But sometimes friends drift apart. If you're still feeling left out, it might be time to start forming new friendships.

THE SITUATION

You're clueless about making new friends.

THE FIX

Rehearse icebreakers on safe topics like the big game or cafeteria food. Once someone responds, chat him or her up, but resist the urge to spill your whole life story right away.

> ### SIX SIGNS THAT SOMEONE MIGHT MAKE A GOOD FRIEND
>
> He or she is...
>
> 1. reading your favorite book.
> 2. making comments that are very similar to what you'd say.
> 3. called a "good guy" or "very nice" by his or her friends.
> 4. speaking passionately in class about an issue you care about, too.
> 5. playing on the same team or is in the same club as you.
> 6. giving you a friendly wave or smile.

124   TIME health news: How to Deal with Tricky Situations

Activity   *Media, Technology, and Culture*

Culture Have a class discussion of the factors that determine what group, or clique, a person belongs to. Students will probably state that students form groups based on interests, physical appearance, athletic ability, cultural background, or other factors. Discuss the positive aspects of having a diverse group of friends. Have students prepare a multimedia presentation encouraging teens to look outside their usual group when making new friends. **OL**

Reading Review

 STUDY TO GO Visit glencoe.com to download quizzes and eFlashcards for Chapter 5.

FOLDABLES® Study Organizer

Foldables® and Other Study Aids Take out the Foldable® that you created for Lesson 1 and any graphic organizers that you created for Lessons 1–4. Find a partner and quiz each other using these study aids.

Lesson 1 Friendships During Adolescence

Main Idea During adolescence, friendships take on a greater importance than ever before.

- Friendships are relationships that you choose to have.
- Good friends are trustworthy, sympathetic, caring, and respectful.
- It is easy to make new friends when you remember to be yourself, make an effort to meet new people, and volunteer or do community service.

Lesson 2 Practicing Communication Skills

Main Idea Good communication is about getting your message across successfully and listening to other people's messages.

- Nonverbal messages are important to communication because they give a more reliable reading of a person's feelings than words.
- You can be a more effective speaker by using "I" messages, staying calm, sticking to the point, choosing the right time and place, and being aware of your body language and intonation.

- Active listeners pay careful attention to what the speaker is saying. They use body language that shows that they are listening. They think before they speak, and they ask questions.

Lesson 3 Peer Pressure and Refusal Skills

Main Idea Practicing refusal skills will help you deal with peer pressure.

- Positive peer pressure and negative peer pressure both influence your behavior.
- Negative peer pressure is pressure to do something that goes against your needs, wants, and values.
- An effective strategy for refusing is the S.T.O.P. formula.

Lesson 4 Limits and Abstinence

Main Idea One of the most important limits you can set for yourself during your teen years is choosing abstinence.

- Setting limits is important because it keeps you safe and protects your health.
- Engaging in sexual activity is best postponed until adulthood and marriage.
- Teens who choose abstinence avoid serious health consequences, such as an unplanned pregnancy and infection with an STD.

Chapter 5 Reading Review **125**

Assessment Resources

- Chapter 5 Summary and Activity
- Audio Summaries
- Reading Tutor
- Performance Assessment
- Chapter 5 Test
- *ExamView*
- Vocabulary PuzzleMaker
- Online Learning Center

Reading Review

Study Aids

- **Using the Dinah Zike Foldable® Study Organizer** Have students use their Foldable® to review information about friendships. **FOLDABLES® Study Organizer**
- **Online Learning Tools** Have students go to the *Teen Health* Online Learning Center at **glencoe.com** to:
  - Download a **Podcast**.
  - Download free **Study-to-Go** content to their PDAs or cell phones. **STUDY TO GO**

Vocabulary Review

- **Vocabulary Story** Have students write a fictional story that correctly incorporates at least 10 of the chapter vocabulary terms.

Teaching Tips

Reading in Health Class Start off each reading assignment by writing a question pertaining to the main idea passage on the board. The question should be answerable using only the information in the text. Have students write down the answer when they locate it in the reading. Call on volunteers to share their answers. Have students note the page on which they located the answer and share that information with the class. This activity also works well if the question is distributed on index cards on which students can write the answer.

Reviewing Vocabulary and Main Ideas

1. relationships
2. sympathetic
3. clique
4. mixed message
5. "I" message
6. Active listening
7. True
8. True
9. False, assertive
10. False, limits
11. True
12. False, affection

Thinking Critically

13. Answers might include looking her friend in the eye and saying calmly but firmly that she does not approve of these activities. Her body language should help her communicate the same message.

📖 **After You Read**

HEALTH QUIZ

Now that you have read the chapter, look back at your answers to the Health Quiz on the chapter opener. Would you change any of them? What would your answers be now?

Reviewing Vocabulary and Main Ideas

On a sheet of paper, write the numbers 1–6. After each number, write the term from the list that best completes each sentence.

- active listening
- body language
- clique
- "I" message
- mixed message
- peer pressure
- relationships
- sympathetic

Lesson 1 Friendships During Adolescence

1. Connections you have with other people and groups in your life are known as _____.

2. Good friends are _____, meaning they understand how you may be feeling at a given moment.

3. A(n) _____ is a group of friends who hang out together and act in similar ways.

Lesson 2 Practicing Communication Skills

4. A(n) _____ occurs when your words say one thing but your body language and/or intonation say another.

5. A statement that presents a situation from the speaker's personal viewpoint is known as a(n) _____.

6. _____ is hearing, thinking about, and responding to the other person's message.

*On a sheet of paper, write the numbers 7–12. Write **True** or **False** for each statement below. If the statement is false, change the underlined word or phrase to make it true.*

Lesson 3 Peer Pressure and Refusal Skills

7. <u>Peer pressure</u> may be direct or indirect, positive or negative.

8. One way to resist negative peer pressure is by using <u>refusal skills</u>.

9. When you use a <u>passive</u> style of communication, you show confidence and clearly state your intentions.

Lesson 4 Limits and Abstinence

10. Like laws or rules, <u>consequences</u> are meant to keep you safe and protect your health.

11. When you choose to be sexually <u>abstinent</u>, you avoid the risk of STDs.

12. Showing <u>sympathy</u> toward another person is showing feelings of love for that person.

Go Online Visit **glencoe.com** and take the Online Quiz for Chapter 5.

Have students visit **glencoe.com** to take the Chapter 5 quiz.

HEALTH QUIZ Wrap-Up

Relationship Skills Have students look back at their responses to the Health Quiz in the chapter opener. Ask: Did any of your answers change after reading the chapter? Sample answer: *Yes, I learned that active listening is a part of good communication.*

How can abstinence from sexual activity positively affect your health? Sample answer: *Abstinence from sexual activity protects you from STDs and unplanned pregnancy.*

Thinking Critically

Using complete sentences, answer the following question on a sheet of paper.

13. **Analyze** Della was invited to a get-together at the home of a friend's friend. Della found out the girl's parents would not be home and that there would be drinking and smoking. What would be an assertive way for Della to let her friend know she is no longer interested in going?

Write About It

14. **Persuasive Writing** Take a stand on whether or not you think cliques are a positive or negative influence. Write a paragraph supporting your position.

Applying Technology

Teen Relationships

Using a video camera and iMovie®, your group will create and film a short video about healthy friendships.

- Write a five-minute script about one of the following topics: qualities of good friends; cliques; verbal and nonverbal communication; making friends; or peer pressure.
- Videotape your movie and import it into iMovie®.
- Using the editing tab, add titles over a colored screen that summarize your messages about friendships.
- Edit for time and clarity.
- Save your project.

Standardized Test Practice

Math

Teens who are sexually active run the risk of getting STDs. The most serious of those is HIV/AIDS. Below are some HIV/AIDS statistics. Use the information to answer the questions that follow.

- By 2004, an estimated 40,059 young people, between the ages of 13 and 24, in the United States were found to have AIDS.
- These individuals accounted for 4 percent of all people found to have AIDS in this country.
- Of these young people, an estimated 10,041 died.
- This number accounted for 2 percent of all deaths from AIDS in the United States.

> **TEST-TAKING TIP**
>
> Make sure you understand the relationships between number statements.

1. Based on the statistics shown, which of the following CANNOT be inferred?
   A. Of all the young people found to have AIDS, 28,449 did not die.
   B. Some young people with AIDS became infected by sharing needles.
   C. 96 percent of the people found to have AIDS by 2004 were not young people.
   D. AIDS is a deadly disease.

2. Based on the statistics, the total estimated deaths of young people with AIDS was
   A. under 20,000.
   B. between 21,000 and 100,000.
   C. between 100,000 and 300,000.
   D. over half a million.

Chapter 5 Assessment **127**

Applying Technology

Teen Relationships
Equipment needs: video camera, iMovie® or similar software
Discuss the project requirements with students, and help them choose partners or group members. Create a sign-up sheet if access to video cameras or computers is limited, and establish a time limit for equipment use. If possible, schedule class time for students to view and discuss their classmates' videos.

Write About It

14. **Persuasive Writing** Explain to students that persuasive writing is writing that takes a stand and states a position. This type of writing states facts and opinions, uses supporting evidence giving logical reasons, uses examples, and quotes experts. Student writing will vary, but should take a stand on whether cliques are a positive or negative influence, and clearly support the position taken.

Standardized Test Practice

1. B
2. A

Test-Taking Tips

Using Percentages Some test questions will require students to understand the relationship between a series of statements. In the example in the student text, the student must use numbers and percentages to find the answers to the questions.

Remind students to preview the questions. Then they should read the series of bulleted statements. Finally students must answer each question, carefully referring back to the statements and statistics to find the answers.

127

	Standards		Skills and Activities
	National	**State/Local**	
CHAPTER 6 *pp. 128–151*	National Health Education Standards 1.8.5, 2.8.1, 4.8.1, 5.8.7		*Health* eSpotlight *p. 129* **BUILDING HEALTH SKILLS** *Communication Skills* Sending the Right Message, *pp. 146–147* **HANDS-ON HEALTH** A Taste of Parenthood, *p. 148*
Lesson 1 **You and Your Relationships** *pp. 130–133*	National Health Education Standards 1.8.1, 1.8.2, 1.8.3, 2.8.1, 2.8.2, 2.8.3, 2.8.4, 6.8.1, 6.8.4, 7.8.2, 8.8.1		**DEVELOPING GOOD CHARACTER** *Respect, p. 131* **What Teens Think** What qualities do you look for in a friend?, *p. 132* **HEALTH SKILLS ACTIVITY** *Advocacy* Relating to Your Community, *p. 133*
Lesson 2 **Getting Along with Your Family** *pp. 134–139*	National Health Education Standards 1.8.3, 2.8.1, 2.8.5, 3.8.4, 3.8.5, 4.8.4, 8.8.1		**MEDIA WATCH** *Television Families, p. 135* **G⊛ Online** Coping with Abuse, *p. 139*
Lesson 3 **Marriage and Parenthood** *pp. 140–145*	National Health Education Standards 1.8.3, 1.8.7, 2.8.9, 4.8.3, 5.8.7, 6.8.2, 6.8.3, 6.8.4, 8.8.1		**Careers for the 21st Century** Marriage Counselor, *p. 141* **Connect To... LANGUAGE ARTS** Learning Good Parenting Skills, *p. 143*

PACING THE CHAPTER		
Lesson 1 45 min	**Chapter Review** 45 min	
Lesson 2 45 min	**Hands-on Health** 30 min	
Lesson 3 45 min	**Building Health Skills** 45 min	

BLOCK SCHEDULING

For block scheduling, assign students Building Health Skills feature *Sending the Right Message*, pages 146–147, and Guided Reading and Writing. 📁

Planning Guide

Glencoe Exclusive!
Teacher Works Plus™
All-In-One Planner and Resource Center

Reproducible Resources	Assessment	Media and Technology
Chapter *FAST FILE* **Resources** Chapter Summaries and Activities `REVIEW` Building Health Skills Activity `TEACH` Performance Assessment Activity `EXTEND` Universal Access Activities `TEACH` Parent Letter and Activities 📁 **Student Activities Workbook** `TEACH` 📁 **Reading Tutor** `TEACH`	Building Health Skills Activity, *pp. 146–147* Chapter 6 Assessment, *pp. 150–151* **Chapter** *FAST FILE* **Resources** Performance Assessment Activity, *p. 4* Chapter 6 Test, *p. 7* 💿 *ExamView® Assessment Suite*	TeacherWorks Plus® includes: ● Interactive Teacher Edition ● Lesson Planner with Calendar ● Access to all blackline masters ● Correlations to standards 💿 StudentWorks™ Plus Online Student Edition Dinah Zike's Teaching Health with Foldables®
Chapter *FAST FILE* **Resources** Concept Mapping Activity 6-1 `REVIEW` Cross-Curriculum Activity 6-1 `EXTEND` Enrichment Activity 6-1 `EXTEND` Lesson Plan 6-1 Guided Reading and Writing 6-1 `TEACH` Reteaching Activity 6-1 `REVIEW`	Lesson 1 Review, *p. 133* Vocabulary PuzzleMaker 💿 *ExamView® Assessment Suite*	Vocabulary PuzzleMaker 💿 *ExamView® Assessment Suite* 💿 StudentWorks™ Plus 🔌 Transparency 6-1 **Go Online** glencoe.com
Chapter *FAST FILE* **Resources** Concept Mapping Activity 6-2 `REVIEW` Health Lab 6-2 `EXTEND` Enrichment Activity 6-2 `EXTEND` Lesson Plan 6-2 Guided Reading and Writing 6-2 `TEACH` Reteaching Activity 6-2 `REVIEW`	Lesson 2 Review, *p. 139* Vocabulary PuzzleMaker 💿 *ExamView® Assessment Suite*	Vocabulary PuzzleMaker 💿 *ExamView® Assessment Suite* 💿 StudentWorks™ Plus 🔌 Transparency 6-2 **Go Online** glencoe.com
Chapter *FAST FILE* **Resources** Concept Mapping Activity 6-3 `REVIEW` Decision-Making Activity 6-3 `EXTEND` Enrichment Activity 6-3 `EXTEND` Lesson Plan 6-3 Guided Reading and Writing 6-3 `TEACH` Reteaching Activity 6-3 `REVIEW`	Lesson 3 Review, *p. 145* Vocabulary PuzzleMaker 💿 *ExamView® Assessment Suite*	Vocabulary PuzzleMaker 💿 *ExamView® Assessment Suite* 💿 StudentWorks™ Plus 🔌 Transparency 6-3 **Go Online** glencoe.com

Chapter and Lesson Resources

The *Teen Health* resources are designed for differentiated learning abilities. You may want to use the coded items in this way:

`REVIEW` —activities to review or reinforce content
`TEACH` —activities to teach basic concepts
`EXTEND` —activities to extend or enrich lesson content

 OUT OF TIME?

Use Health Skills Activity *Relating to Your Community*, page 133, or Developing Good Character, page 131.

Emotional Intelligence and Social Health

The concept of emotional intelligence was formally introduced in the 1990s by Daniel Goleman, a psychologist. *Emotional intelligence* is a term that describes a person's social and emotional skills.

Researchers have found that emotional intelligence is one predictor of future success in life. In fact, studies have indicated that emotional intelligence may be more important than IQ in determining an individual's level of professional attainment and financial success.

The set of skills that determines overall emotional intelligence falls into two broad categories—those pertaining to self and those pertaining to others. Emotional intelligence skills in the first category include understanding one's own feelings and mood, being self-motivated, and managing and expressing emotions appropriately. Skills of emotional intelligence pertaining to others include understanding others' feelings and moods and the ability to carry on an appropriate conversation.

These skills can be reinforced and practiced in the classroom throughout the year. Responsibility, respect, tolerance, patience, caring, and trust are character traits mentioned in this chapter. Point out to students how these traits translate into skills that promote social health. Remind students of the role of social health in overall wellness.

Challenges Faced by Blended Families

It is very likely that some of the students in your classes are a part of a blended family. In fact, various studies indicate that between one-third and one-half of American children live in blended families. Although blended families are one of the more common family types in America, misconceptions and unrealistic expectations about blended families are common.

One of the most common misconceptions comes from the myth of the "wicked stepmother." At the opposite extreme is the belief that blended families have no different challenges than typical nuclear families.

It is important to acknowledge that most blended families form after a death or divorce. Students who are a part of a blended family have experienced a loss, and may have deep feelings of sadness or anger associated with that loss. Some teens in blended families also struggle with accepting the authority of a stepparent. The growing sense of autonomy associated with the teen years makes it particularly difficult for some teens to accept a new authority figure in the family.

When the class discusses different types of families, remind students that each type of family faces challenges. As a part of the study of family relationships, discuss school and community resources that are available to students who are struggling with family relationships.

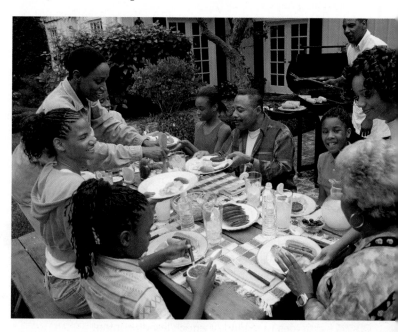

Support for Teaching Reading

Reading Support

Reading Preview

Activating Background Vocabulary Ask students what they think the term *social health* means. Record their responses on the board. Guide students into a discussion about relationships with others and the role of the family in society. Ask students to compare social health with physical health. Is there a relationship between the two?

FOLDABLES | Study Organizer *Dinah Zike's Reading and Study Skills for Teen Health* provides interactive graphic organizers that help students comprehend and retain health concepts as they read. Use the Foldable® on page 129 or find more Foldables® activities for the chapter on **Promoting Social Health** in the separate booklet, available in the TCR.

Lesson 1   You and Your Relationships

Organizing Information Direct students to scan the lesson and list the main idea of each section on an index card. Discuss that each heading is a main idea and the text beneath the heading holds the details that support the main idea. As students read about social health and building healthy relationships, have them write the supporting details on the back of each main idea index card.

Lesson 2   Getting Along with Your Family

Responding Have students stop at any point while reading and discuss with a partner what they like, do not like, or find interesting or surprising about what they have read so far. Direct students to the sections on responsibilities within the family and coping with family changes. Have students write an independent journal entry, describing their thoughts or feelings about these issues.

Lesson 3   Marriage and Parenthood

Directed Reading/Thinking Activity (DR/TA) Direct students to divide a paper into 4 columns titled: *What I know, What I think I know, What I think I'll learn,* and *What I know I learned.* Have students skim the lesson's boldface headings and discuss the topics of teen marriage and parenthood. Direct students to fill out the first three sections of the chart based on that discussion. Have students complete the final column of the chart as they read the lesson.

Post Reading

Twin Text Reports In addition to the text, provide students with the opportunity to find fictional reading material about teen relationships, family life, coping with family problems, or teen marriage and pregnancy. After reading, have students demonstrate recognition of the logical, ethical, and emotional appeals in both the fictional and informational materials in a written report, edited for correct spelling, punctuation, and grammar.

Key for Using the Teacher Wraparound Edition

Use this key to help you identify the different types of prompts found in the Teacher Wraparound Edition.

R **Reading Strategies** activities help you teach reading skills and vocabulary.

C **Critical Thinking** strategies help students apply and extend what they have learned.

U **Universal Access** activities provide differentiated instruction for students learning to speak English, along with suggestions for teaching various types of learners.

HS **Health Skills Practice** activities reinforce Health Skills concepts and help students apply these skills in their everyday lives.

W **Writing Support** activities provide writing opportunities to help students comprehend the text.

AL **Active Learning** strategies provide a variety of activities for presenting lesson content, including Quick Demos and engaging classroom projects that get students actively involved.

Key to Ability Levels

Teaching Strategies and activities have been coded for ability level and appropriateness.

AL Activities for students working above grade level

OL Activities for students working on grade level

BL Activities for students working below grade level

EL Activities for English Learners

Symbols

Transparencies

CD-ROM

glencoe.com

Print Resources

Promoting Social Health

Chapter at a Glance

Lesson 1 explains differences among friendships, identifies needs that relationships satisfy, and explains how to build strong, healthy relationships.

Lesson 2 identifies the types of needs families meet, describes responsibilities within families, explains changes that affect families, and describes healthy ways to deal with changes and problems in the family.

Lesson 3 identifies the factors that affect the success of a marriage, describes the responsibilities involved in being a parent, and identifies the consequences of teen parenthood.

R Reading Strategy

Interpreting the Photo Ask students: How does getting along with your family members improve your social health? Sample answer: *Family relationships are the earliest relationships we have and some of the most important relationships we will ever have. Families have an important influence on the relationships that I have now and those that I will develop later in life.* What needs are met by healthy social relationships? *the need to be loved, the need to belong, the need to make a difference in another's life.* **OL**

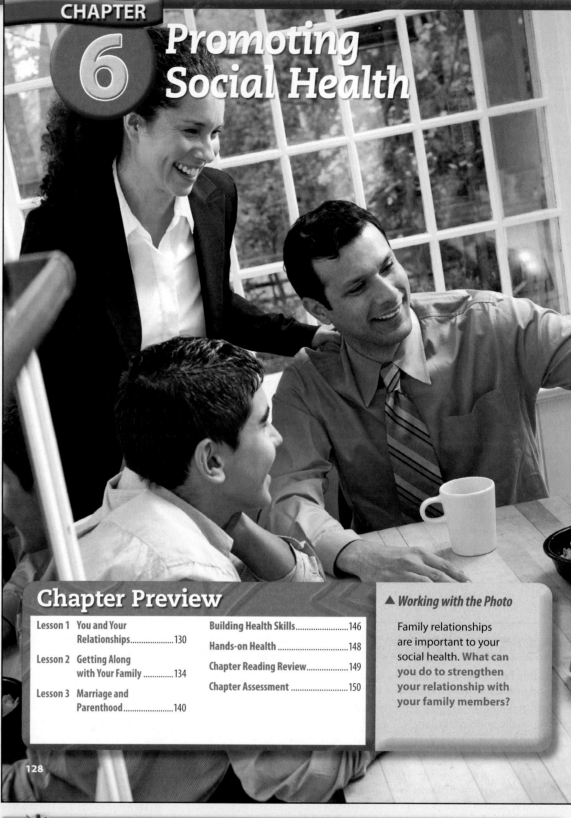

Chapter Preview

▲ *Working with the Photo*

Family relationships are important to your social health. **What can you do to strengthen your relationship with your family members?**

128

👪 Universal Access

Differentiated Learning Glencoe provides teacher support and student materials for all learners in the health classroom.

● Spanish Glosario and chapter summaries for the English Language Learners.
● *Reading Tutor* and related worksheets support reluctant readers.

● Universal Access strategies throughout the Teacher Wraparound Edition and Fast Files help you present materials for gifted students, at-risk students, physically impaired students, and those with behavior disorders or learning disabilities.

Start-Up Activities

Before You Read Do you have good relationships with your peers? Answer the Health eSpotlight question below and then watch the online video. Keep a record of your answer.

Health eSpotlight

VIDEO

Social Health

Respect and trust are two traits that are important to a healthy relationship. What other traits do you think are important in a healthy peer relationship? Explain your answer in detail.

Go to **glencoe.com** and watch the health video for Chapter 6. Then complete the activity provided with the online video.

FOLDABLES Study Organizer

As You Read Make this Foldable® to help you organize what you learn in Lesson 1 about building healthy relationships. Begin with a plain sheet of 11" × 17" paper.

1 Fold the sheet of paper in half along the long axis, then fold in half again. This makes four rows.

2 Open and fold the short side on the left to make a 3" column.

3 Label the chart with the health skills shown.

| Trust |
| Respect |
| Patience |
| Tolerance |

Take notes on the character traits that help build healthy relationships.

Go Online Visit **glencoe.com** and complete the Health Inventory for Chapter 6.

FOCUS

Activating Prior Knowledge

What I Know Ask students to describe ways that healthy relationships benefit the three sides of their health triangle.

Guide to Reading

Building Vocabulary

■ Explain that a *role* is a part you play when you interact with another person. Have students identify some of the roles they play in relationships.

■ Use Vocabulary PuzzleMaker to reinforce vocabulary terms.

Reading Strategy

Classifying Have students prepare a blank chart with space to add information as they read the lesson. After students have completed the lesson, ask volunteers to share some of the entries in their charts with the class.

FOLDABLES Study Organizer

Have students use their Foldables® as they read Lesson 1.

Quick Write

Challenge students to identify specific character traits that contribute to the successful relationship described in their Quick Write.

Caption Answer

Photo Caption friends, peers, family members, teachers

You and Your Relationships

Guide to Reading

● **Building Vocabulary**
As you read this lesson, write each new highlighted term and its definition in your notebook.

■ social health (p. 131)
■ role (p. 131)
■ tolerance (p. 132)

● **Focusing on the Main Ideas**
In this lesson, you will learn to

■ **explain** differences among relationships.
■ **identify** needs that relationships satisfy.
■ **develop** skills to build strong, healthy relationships.

● **Reading Strategy**
Classifying Make a chart of the kinds of relationships described. Identify people in your life that fit each type of relationship.

FOLDABLES Study Organizer Use the Foldable® on p. 129 as you read this lesson.

Quick Write

Write a short paragraph describing a successful relationship you have. Tell what makes the relationship work.

Relationships: The Foundation of Social Health

Josh balances his schoolwork and other responsibilities with the activities he enjoys doing with his family and friends. He likes talking with his friends at soccer practice and meeting new people at his school. He is also looking forward to the family reunion that is coming up. Every summer his extended family gathers for a picnic in the park. It is a time to laugh, share new experiences, and play games together. This year Josh decided to invite a friend from school to the family picnic. What are some activities you enjoy doing with your family and friends?

◀ An important factor of your social health is how you relate to others. **Who are some of the people you interact with every day?**

130 Chapter 6: Promoting Social Health

📁 **Chapter *FAST FILE* Resources**
Guided Reading and Writing 6-1
Concept Mapping Activity 6-1
Cross-Curriculum Activity 6-1
Reteaching Activity 6-1
Enrichment Activity 6-1
Lesson Quiz 6-1

Technology
🖱 Transparency 6-1
💿 Audio Summaries
💿 *ExamView®Assessment Suite*
💿 Vocabulary PuzzleMaker
💿 StudentWorks™ Plus

Go Online

Social health is *your ability to get along with the people around you.* The relationships you form with other people are the foundation of your social health. Relationships are the connections you have with groups and people in your life. In your teen years, your relationships are mainly with family, friends, peers, and teachers. These relationships are part of your environment, and they can impact your health. Healthy relationships are important to good social health.

Differences Among Relationships

Not all relationships are the same. Some relationships are close and familiar, and others are more formal.

Different relationships also meet different needs. Some relationships, such as those with family and friends, meet emotional needs. They satisfy your need to feel that you are loved and that you belong. Other relationships meet more practical needs. Your relationships with teachers, for example, are based on your need to learn.

 Another factor that makes different relationships unique is the role you play. A **role** is *a part you play when you interact with another person.* Everyone plays many different roles. **Figure 6.1** shows some typical teen roles. Each role you play carries responsibilities and expectations. The responsibilities that come with a role may change over time. You will also take on new roles and responsibilities as you get older.

Reading Check **Compare** How are relationships different?

▼ **FIGURE 6.1**

SOME TEEN ROLES

Roles like these carry responsibilities. **Which of these roles describe you? What responsibilities do they carry?**

- Daughter/Son
- Sister/Brother
- Friend
- Granddaughter/Grandson
- Niece/Nephew
- Babysitter
- Student
- Peer tutor
- Teammate
- Club member
- Volunteer

Lesson 1: You and Your Relationships **131**

DEVELOPING Good Character

Respect

Every relationship benefits from respect. One way to show respect for another person is through simple courtesies—for example, holding the door for the person behind you. Using good manners when you are in someone else's home is another sign of respect.

What other ways can you think of to show respect for people in your life?

CHAPTER 6

Lesson 1

TEACH

ACTIVITY
DEVELOPING Good Character

Respect
After students have read the feature, divide the class into small groups. Ask the members of each group to list five ways to show respect to others. Point out that showing respect to others benefits social health. **OL**

Reading Check

Answer Relationships may be formal or close, they meet emotional or practical needs.

AL **Active Learning**

Photo Essay Have students work in small groups to create a photo essay showing the many different roles played by teens. Have each group share its photo essay with the class. **OL**

R **Reading Strategy**

Analyzing a Graphic After students have examined **Figure 6.1**, Ask: What is one additional role you play that is not listed in the chart? Sample answer: *I am an uncle.* **OL**

Caption Answer

Figure Caption *Sample answer:* One of the roles is a student. My responsibilities include completing my schoolwork.

✖ Promoting Coordinated School Health

Family and Community Involvement A coordinated school health program recognizes the positive impact that family and community relationships can have on student health. Review your school's policies to be sure that family involvement and use of community resources are priorities. For example, parents can be represented on school health planning committees, and medical professionals in the community can share their expertise with students. Successfully partnering with families and community members creates relationships that are critical for healthy teens. **OL**

What Teens THINK

What qualities do you look for in a friend? Begin by helping students read about and discuss the traits of good character identified on this page. Ask: How can developing these traits help make you a good friend? Which of these traits do you look for in friends? Why? Then guide students in reading and discussing the What Teens Think question and response.

What Teens THINK

What qualities do you look for in a friend?

The qualities I look for in a friend include someone I can trust and someone who shows loyalty. I like friends who are fun to be with, who look out for me, and who don't care what other people think.

**T'Kaira W.
Atlantic City, NJ**

Health Skills Activity

Advocacy

Relating to Your Community

Use the following to help students complete the activity on the next page.

● To get students thinking of ways to build community involvement, have them identify one specific way to show respect or tolerance in his or her community. Then have each student prepare a poster expressing their ideas.

● Help students identify local community centers or agencies where posters may be displayed.

Go Online

Visit **glencoe.com** and complete the Interactive Study Guide for Lesson 1.

Building Healthy Relationships

Relationships can grow just like other living things. When a plant is neglected, its leaves droop and turn brown. As a living thing, it needs to be watered and cared for. In the same way, relationships need attention if they are to grow and thrive. One way to care for a relationship is to practice traits of good character. These traits include:

● **Trust.** Can your friends confide in you? Can they trust you with their private thoughts and feelings? If you are trustworthy, you are honest and reliable. You mean what you say and you don't make promises you can't keep. For example, when Janet's mom said she was going to pick her up after school, Janet did not wonder if she would actually show up or not. She trusted her mom to be there.

● **Respect.** Showing respect in a relationship means being polite and considerate. It also means knowing and accepting a relationship's "social boundaries"—the appropriate ways of behaving in a relationship. For example, whenever Enrique meets an adult, he addresses the person by the title "Mr." or "Ms." Another way to show respect is to not interrupt people when they are speaking.

● **Patience.** No one is perfect. Everyone has behaviors that can annoy others. Being patient with people is an important trait to develop. Waiting in line requires patience and so does helping a sibling or peer who may be learning something new that you are already familiar with.

● **Tolerance.** Accepting people who are different from you is an example of tolerance. **Tolerance** is *the ability to value other people as they are.* This includes people of different races, cultures, and religions, as well as those who have disabilities or impairments. Building relationships with people from other backgrounds can be enriching. For example, Sergio invited Steve to his house for a Cinco de Mayo dinner. Steve enjoyed the time he spent with Sergio's family because it allowed him to experience some of the Latino customs practiced by Sergio's family.

Reading Check **Define** What is *tolerance*?

Reading Check

Answer Tolerance is accepting those who are different than you.

FITNESS ZONE

Relationships and Physical Fitness Ask students to review the suggestions for making a physical fitness plan in their Fitness Zone Handbook. Then have students write journal entries in response to these questions: Which friends and family members might help you start and maintain a physical fitness routine? What do you think you would do together? How would exercising together affect your relationship? **For more information, see** *Fitness Zone Handbook* **pages xviii-1 or visit the Fitness Zone at glencoe.com.**

Health Skills Activity

Advocacy

Relating to Your Community
Building a healthy relationship with the community includes the following skills:

- **Respect.** Show your respect for your community by taking pride in it. Help keep it clean. Avoid littering or defacing property.
- **Tolerance.** Demonstrate tolerance by getting to know people in your community who are different from you. When you demonstrate tolerance, you encourage others around you to do the same.

With a Group
Create several posters encouraging teens to show respect for their community. Include posters that discuss intolerance and how it affects the community. Your posters should also encourage teens to demonstrate tolerance to others.

Lesson 1 Review

 After You Read

Review this lesson for new terms, major headings, and Reading Checks.

What I Learned

1. *Vocabulary* What is a *role*?
2. *Recall* What are some needs that relationships meet?
3. *Identify* Which character traits are found in strong, healthy relationships?

Thinking Critically

4. *Analyze* Denise was elected to her school's student council but realized that soccer practice would conflict with most student council meetings. In what way is Denise failing to meet the responsibilities of her role as a student council representative? What should she do?

5. *Apply* Suzy often disagrees with her history teacher. Sometimes she interrupts him when he is speaking, and raises her voice when addressing him. How can Suzy disagree with her teacher in a way that shows respect?

Applying Health Skills

6. *Communication Skills* With a group, discuss the role of communication in building strong, healthy relationships. Role-play a situation in which you use communication skills to show respect for a friend.

 For more Lesson Review Activities, go to **glencoe.com**.

Lesson 1: You and Your Relationships **133**

Assessment Resources

Lesson Review Quiz
- *ExamView*
- Fast Files Activities
- Online Quizzes and Activities

Reteaching

- Assign Concept Map 6-1 or Reteaching Activity 6-1 in the Fast Files.
- Have students work in pairs to review character traits that are important for healthy relationships. Have each pair write a paragraph that summarizes its discussion.

Enrichment

- Assign Enrichment Activity 6-1 in the Fast Files.
- Have students analyze a friendship portrayed in a book they have read. Have students note the traits of good character that are demonstrated and how they affect the health of the relationship. Have students share their analysis with the class.

CLOSE

Ask students to describe various roles they play in relationships.

Lesson 1 Review Answers

1. A role is a part you play when you interact with another person.
2. Needs met by relationships include the need to feel loved, the need to belong, and practical needs.
3. Character traits found in healthy relationships include trust, respect, patience, and tolerance.
4. *Sample answer:* Denise should either rearrange her schedule or resign her position.
5. *Sample answer:* Suzy should raise her hand, wait to be called on, and share her opinions without raising her voice.
6. Have each group review the communication skills described in Chapter 5.

FOCUS

Activating Prior Knowledge

What I Know Have students identify healthy ways to meet emotional needs from Chapter 3. Record students' responses on the board. Tell students that this lesson will describe ways that families can meet these needs.

Guide to Reading

Building Vocabulary
■ Have students make graphic organizers showing how the vocabulary terms for this lesson are related.
■ Use Vocabulary PuzzleMaker to reinforce vocabulary terms.

Reading Strategy
Comparing and Contrasting Have students write sentences that compare and contrast different family types as they read the lesson. Ask volunteers to share their sentences with the class.

Quick Write

Explain as students complete their Quick Writes that this activity is for their own information and should be kept private.

Getting Along with Your Family

Guide to Reading

● **Building Vocabulary**
Define each term as best as you can. Then check your definitions as you read the lesson.

■ family (p. 134)
■ extended family (p. 135)
■ single-parent family (p. 135)
■ blended family (p. 137)

● **Focusing on the Main Ideas**
In this lesson, you will learn to

■ **identify** the different types of families.
■ **describe** responsibilities within the family.
■ **explain** changes that affect families.
■ **develop** healthy ways to deal with family changes.

● **Reading Strategy**
Comparing and Contrasting Read about the different family types described in the lesson. Find the similarities and differences among them.

Quick Write

Write a short essay titled "My Family Is _____." Fill in the blank with a word that best describes your family.

The Family Unit

When you look closely at the words *relationship* and *relative*, you discover that they share a common root: *relate*. Your earliest and most important relationships are with family—your relatives. The **family** is *the basic unit of society, and includes two or more people brought together by blood, marriage, adoption, or a desire for mutual support.*

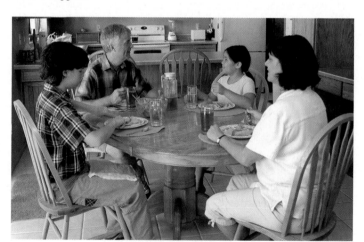

▶ Families have an important influence on the relationships you develop later in life. **What traits do you value and look for in others that were taught to you by your family?**

Caption Answer

Photo Caption *Sample answer:* I value the trait of trustworthiness, a character trait I was taught by my mother.

Lesson 2 Resources

📁 **Chapter *FAST FILE* Resources**
Guided Reading and Writing 6-2
Concept Mapping Activity 6-2
Health Lab 6-2
Reteaching Activity 6-2
Enrichment Activity 6-2
Lesson Quiz 6-2

Technology
🔦 Transparency 6-2
💿 Audio Summaries
💿 *ExamView®* Assessment Suite
💿 Vocabulary PuzzleMaker
💿 StudentWorks™ Plus
Go Online

The way you relate with your family prepares you for all future relationships. It is within your family that you begin developing social skills. Through your family, you form a sense of who you are, and you learn to care for and share with others. Developing a positive relationship with your family helps you keep all three sides of the health triangle in balance.

Types of Families

Shari's family consists of her younger brother, her mother, and herself. Her neighbor Latesha lives with her mother, her father, and her grandfather. These family units are just two of the many types of families that exist.

Latesha lives in an **extended family,** *a family in which one or more parents and children live with other relatives such as grandparents, aunts, uncles, and cousins.* Shari, by contrast, lives in a **single-parent family,** *a family made up of one parent plus a child or children.* **Figure 6.2** shows some other types of family units. Which type describes your family?

 Reading Check **Give Examples** List two different types of families, and identify the members that might belong to each family.

▼ FIGURE 6.2

[R] **FAMILY TYPES**

There are many different types of families. Do you know families who are examples of some of the family types shown?

Family Type	Composition
Couple	Married people with no children
Nuclear family	Two parents and one or more children
Adoptive family	A couple plus one or more adoptive children
Foster family	Adults caring for a child or children born to different parents
Joint-custody family	Two parents living apart, sharing custody of their children
Single-custody family	Two parents living apart, and a child or children living with only one parent
Single-parent family	One parent and children

TEACH

Television Families

Many television programs focus on the daily challenges of family life. These programs often show a variety of different family types. Some have couples with no children and some have nuclear families with a mom, dad, and children. Some programs show more than one type of family in the same program.

Think of several different television "families." What types of families are they? Are the challenges they face similar or are they different? Explain.

Television Families

Divide the class into small groups. Have each group select a family that is portrayed in a television program. Ask each group to prepare a short presentation describing the relationships within this family, character traits demonstrated in these relationships, and how emotional needs are met within this family. OL

[R] Reading Strategy

Analyzing a Graphic Have students examine **Figure 6.2**, which lists types of families. Ask: Although there are many different types of families, what are some characteristics that all families share? Sample answers: *Families meet the needs of their members. Families provide love, support, and caring.* OL

[Reading Check]

Answer *Sample answer:* A nuclear family consists of two parents and their children; a couple consists of married people with no children.

Caption Answer

Figure Caption *Sample answer:* My family is a single-parent family. I know families who are examples of several of the other types listed in the chart.

Cultural Perspectives

Family Roles in Different Cultures The role of the individual in the family unit varies among cultures. American culture has a tradition of individualism, in which family members work for independence, self-reliance, and individual achievement. In some cultures, the individual's role is to promote the success of the family. Achievements and financial success are valued for the benefits they bring to the family, rather than the individual. Have students further explore how family roles are influenced by cultural background. Ask each student to prepare a short oral report summarizing his or her findings. OL

C Critical Thinking

Analyzing Have students read the section on meeting needs. Explain that all family members, not just the adults, are responsible for helping meet the needs of the other family members. Have students work in small groups to identify specific ways that a student their age could help meet the physical, mental/emotional, and social needs of other family members. Have each group share its results. **OL**

Academic Vocabulary

Secure Have students read the definition and the example sentence. Then write security and insecure on the board. Help students discuss how those two words are related, in both structure and meaning, to secure. You will find academic vocabulary activities in the Student Activities Workbook. 📁

AL Universal Access

English Learners In groups of four or five, assign each student a role in the family (brother, mother, etc.). Provide each group with a family situation in which needs need to be met (sister broke her leg, brother is depressed, etc.). The small groups will then act out the situation and show a way in which every family member could help meet the need. **EL**

Caption Answer

Photo Caption *Sample answer:* I wash the dishes and care for my younger sister.

Families Meet Needs

As you learned in Lesson 1, relationships satisfy needs. This includes family relationships. The most important function that a family performs is meeting the physical, mental/emotional, and social needs of its members.

- **Physical needs.** Families provide physical necessities, such as food, clothing, safety, and shelter. They care for family members when they are sick. They protect members from accidents and other threats. Finally, they teach members how to achieve and maintain good health.

- **Mental/emotional needs.** Families teach members love and acceptance and help them feel emotionally **secure**. Having your emotional needs met promotes a positive self-image and high self-esteem. Family members can turn to each other when they feel hurt or discouraged.

- **Social needs.** Families guide members in developing social skills, such as effective communication and good manners. Families also teach children values. The family can share cultural traditions with its members and encourage them to be proud of their heritage.

C

Academic Vocabulary

secure (si KYOOR) *(adjective)* safe, protected. *Teens who feel secure about themselves are not affected by negative peer pressure.*

Responsibilities Within the Family

As with any other group, family members have individual roles, which have their own responsibilities and expectations. Parents or guardians have the most responsibility. They are responsible for financially supporting other family members. Parents are also the emotional anchor of the family. It is their job to establish a loving environment in which children can grow. Parents or guardians are often the first to teach their children values—the difference between right and wrong.

AL

Children may play many roles in a family. For example, you may be responsible for helping prepare meals or other chores. Maybe you look after a younger sibling while adults are at work.

Some teens volunteer for responsibilities in the home that go beyond what their

▼ Different family members have different roles and responsibilities. **What are your responsibilities within your family?**

Dealing with Sensitive Issues

Meeting Needs In this lesson, students learn that the most important function of a family is to meet the social, physical, and mental/emotional needs of its members. However, some teens might be in a situation where it is necessary to reach further to fulfill some basic needs. When discussing the ways that family relationships meet various needs, explain that healthful relationships outside of the family unit can also be a way to meet needs. Trusted adults, school staff, and religious or community leaders can provide healthful relationships that can help students meet their needs.

◀ Families experience many changes. **What change might the family in this picture be going through?**

parents or guardians expect from them. Taking responsibility is one way of showing maturity within the family.

 Reading Check   **Identify** What kinds of responsibilities might children in a household be expected to take on?

Changes in the Family

Families sometimes face changes. When Teresa's older brother graduated from high school and joined the Navy, she became the oldest child living at home. She is now expected to do the chores that her brother used to do. She also receives some of the privileges of being the oldest child at home.

Some changes that occur in a family are unexpected or beyond the family's control. These changes include the end of a marriage or death of a family member. These kinds of changes can create stress for all members of the family.

Changes in Family Structure

The last 50 years have brought about big changes in the structure of the American family. Couples today are having fewer children. More marriages end in divorce. In 1960, 9 percent of children under the age of 18 lived with only one parent. Since then, that percentage has more than tripled.

Many adults who get divorced eventually remarry. This trend has led to an increase in the number of blended families. A **blended family** is *a family that consists of a parent, a stepparent, and the children of one or both parents.* For children, becoming part

Lesson 2: Getting Along with Your Family   **137**

W **Writing Support**

Descriptive Writing Have students write a fictional story about a teen who is experiencing a change in his or her family. Remind students that their story should include a setting, a plot, and characters. Challenge students to use dialogue to identify and describe the emotions experienced by the main characters in the story. **OL**

 Reading Check

Answer *Sample answers:* Responsibilities in a family might include doing dishes, caring for pets, or mowing the grass.

What Teens Want to Know

Why do I have to do chores? Household chores are an important part of family responsibility. According to a study conducted by researchers at Arizona State University, 90 percent of American children have some responsibility for household chores. A study by researchers at the United States Census Bureau found that teens with no responsibility for household chores were more likely to engage in risk behaviors than those with responsibility for a moderate amount of household work.

Caption Answer

Photo Caption *Sample answer:* The family in this picture is experiencing a change because one of the family members is moving.

R Reading Strategy

Identifying Problems and Solutions Have students prepare a two-column chart. Ask students to record changes in families that may cause problems in the left column. In the right column, have students list some of the solutions to these problems that are described in the text. Ask several volunteers to share information they have recorded in their charts. Remind students that there is usually more than one appropriate solution to family problems, and that what is right for one family might not be right for another. **BL**

HS Health Skills Practice

Accessing Information Have students work in pairs to find information about community resources for students who are dealing with family changes. Then have each pair of students make a pamphlet or poster that could be used to share this information with others. Display students' work in the hallways, cafeteria, or guidance office. **OL**

Reading Check

Answer *Sample answer:* Family changes that cause stress can be caused by financial problems, job loss, illness, death, divorce, or a move.

Caption Answer

Photo Caption I could ask a new student to sit with me at lunch.

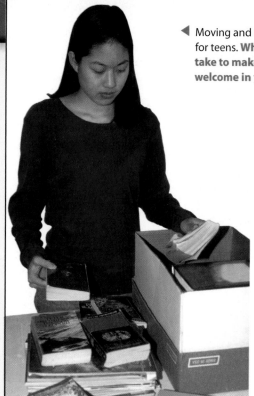

◀ Moving and changing schools can be stressful for teens. **What are some actions you could take to make a recently arrived teen feel welcome in your community?**

of a blended family often involves making adjustments. These changes can sometimes be hard to deal with both emotionally and socially. It is important to talk with parents or other trusted adults about these difficulties.

Changes in Family Circumstances

Changes in a family's circumstances can also result in added stress. For example, families sometimes have to move to a new city or town. For children, moving means not only saying good-bye to old friends, but also having to make new ones.

Financial problems or the loss of a parent's job can also put an emotional strain on a family. Teens in the family may be asked to help out in various ways, such as earning their own spending money.

The serious illness of a family member can also disrupt daily life. Adult family members may be unavailable or unable to perform normal duties and responsibilities. Again, the teens in the family may be called upon to help out.

Reading Check

Describe What are some changes that can be stressful for families?

Coping with Family Changes

Most families are able to work through problems caused by change. One skill that can be especially useful during difficult times is good communication. Talk with a parent or guardian. Explain how you feel. Being scared or uncertain about what lies ahead is a normal reaction. Your parents or guardians may have similar feelings.

In some situations, parents may feel overwhelmed and may even be the source of the problem. If this is the case, talk to a trusted adult outside the family. Your teachers and school counselors are trained to help. Religious leaders may also be able to help.

Some family problems are too big to solve by family members alone. Families who need guidance can find it through counseling or other community resources. Check your local phone directory for numbers you can call.

Visit glencoe.com and complete the Interactive Study Guide for Lesson 2.

Promoting Coordinated School Health

Counseling and Psychological Services Family problems can have a negative impact on students' overall wellness and ability to learn. Services for students who are coping with family problems and changes are an integral part of a coordinated school health plan. Counseling, intervention, and referrals to outside agencies can help students cope with family changes. These services can help students and their families overcome problems.

Abuse

One family problem that always requires outside help is abuse. Abuse can take several different forms, including neglect, physical and sexual abuse, and substance abuse. Neglect occurs when parents do not provide food, clothing, housing, medical care, or emotional support to their children. Children and infants who are neglected may suffer what is called *failure to thrive,* meaning that they don't develop physically, emotionally, and socially. Children who are emotionally neglected may also suffer from low self-esteem.

Physical abuse involves the use of physical force. It can cause injuries such as bruises, cuts, or broken bones. Every year, about 1,500 children die as a result of physical abuse. Another 140,000 are injured. Sexual abuse involves any mistreatment of a child or adult involving sexual activity. Substance abuse involves addiction to alcohol or drugs. Even if only one family member has a substance abuse problem, it affects every family member.

Any teen who is a victim of abuse needs to seek help. Speak with a teacher, school counselor, or other adult you trust. You will learn more about getting help for abuse in Chapter 8.

 Reading Check Identify What are two types of abuse?

 ACTIVITY

 G Online

Topic: Coping with Abuse

Visit **glencoe.com** for Student Web Activities to learn about the different kinds of abuse and what can be done about them.

Activity: Using the information provided at the link above, create a brochure that lists the kinds of abuse, what a teen can do to stop abuse, and the names and numbers of local resources that can help.

Lesson 2 Review

 After You Read

Review this lesson for new terms, major headings, and Reading Checks.

What I Learned

1. *Vocabulary* What is a *blended family*?

2. *Give Examples* Name two physical needs that a family provides.

3. *Identify* What can a teen do to cope with family changes?

Thinking Critically

4. *Evaluate* Which family change described in the lesson do you think would be the hardest to deal with?

5. *Apply* Carla's mother and stepfather recently had a new baby. How might this change affect Carla? What effect might it have on her responsibilities within the family?

Applying Health Skills

6. *Accessing Information* Use the phone book to find names of organizations that provide support to family members of substance abusers. Create a card showing how to contact these places.

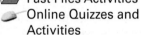 **G Online** For more Lesson Review Activities, go to **glencoe.com**. Lesson 2: Getting Along with Your Family **139**

CHAPTER 6
Lesson 2

 Reading Check

Sample answers: Physical abuse and neglect are two types of abuse.

ASSESS

Assessment Resources

Lesson Review Quiz
- *ExamView*
- Fast Files Activities
- Online Quizzes and Activities

Reteaching

- Assign Concept Map 6-2 or Reteaching Activity 6-2 in the Fast Files.
- Have students work in pairs to write three questions and answers about the ways families meet needs. Check answers for completeness.

Enrichment

- Assign Enrichment Activity 6-2 in the Fast Files.
- Have students research and report on the availability of family counseling services in your community. Students should include information about methods used by family counselors to improve family relationships.

CLOSE

Go around the room and have students identify various types of families.

Lesson 2 Review Answers

1. A blended family consists of a parent, stepparent, and the children of one or both parents.

2. *Sample answers:* food, clothing, shelter, care for those who are sick, protection from accidents, health promotion

3. Teens concerned with family changes can talk to a parent or trusted adult.

4. Answers will vary but should be supported by facts from the text.

5. *Sample answer:* Carla may feel that her parents have less time for her and she may have additional responsibilities.

6. Provide phone books or other resources for students to use to complete this project.

FOCUS

Activating Prior Knowledge

What I Know Have students identify and describe commitments they have made. Then have a volunteer describe how responsibility is related to commitment.

Guide to Reading

Building Vocabulary
- Explain that the word part *un-* means "free from." Ask students to relate this to the meaning of the term *unconditional love*.
- Use Vocabulary PuzzleMaker to reinforce vocabulary terms.

Reading Strategy
Drawing Conclusions Have students use the Reading Strategy to anticipate the content of the lesson. After students have completed the lesson, ask students to write a sentence expanding their response to the Reading Strategy.

Quick Write

After students have completed their Quick Write, lead a class discussion about the challenges of parenting.

Caption Answer

Photo Caption
Sample answer: A commitment is a pledge or promise. It is important because marriage partners pledge to live together and care for one another for the rest of their lives.

140

Lesson 3

Marriage and Parenthood

Guide to Reading

Building Vocabulary
Write what you think each term below means. As you read, make corrections as needed.

- commitment (p. 140)
- divorce (p. 142)
- unconditional love (p. 143)

Focusing on the Main Ideas
In this lesson, you will learn to
- **identify** the factors that affect the success of a marriage.
- **describe** the responsibilities involved in being a parent.
- **identify** the consequences of teen parenthood.

Reading Strategy
Drawing Conclusions Based on this lesson, what assumptions can you make about teen marriage and parenthood?

Quick Write

Write a paragraph describing what you think is one of the challenges of being a parent.

Marriage

The tradition of marriage—a union between two people—is very old. Some people view marriage as something that should happen automatically when you become an adult. Others wait until they are truly ready for a long-term commitment. A **commitment** is *a pledge or promise*.

When two people get married, they make a legal and social commitment to each other. They pledge to live together and care for each other for the rest of their lives. They agree to respect each other's needs and desires. If they have children, they agree to raise and support their children together. They agree to work at all times to make their relationship as strong as possible. The decision to marry is one of the biggest decisions a person can make.

◀ Couples who are ready for marriage need a strong commitment to each other. **What does this mean? Why is a commitment so important?**

140 Chapter 6: Promoting Social Health

Lesson 3 Resources

📁 **Chapter *FAST FILE* Resources**
Guided Reading and Writing 6-3
Concept Mapping Activity 6-3
Decision-Making Activity 6-3
Reteaching Activity 6-3
Enrichment Activity 6-3
Lesson Quiz 6-3

Technology
🔖 Transparency 6-3
💿 Audio Summaries
⚙ *ExamView® Assessment Suite*
💿 Vocabulary PuzzleMaker
⚙ StudentWorks™ Plus

 Online

Factors Affecting Marriage

A successful marriage depends on many factors. Marriage requires emotional and physical maturity. Being emotionally mature means knowing yourself and accepting your strengths and weaknesses. It means knowing what you value. People who are emotionally mature also have life goals and a plan for reaching them. They are able to understand and respect someone else's feelings and needs.

Besides emotional maturity, other factors that lead to a successful marriage are the same as those that build good friendships. These factors include common interests and shared values. In fact, many married couples see each other as best friends. **Figure 6.3** shows some other factors that affect the success of a marriage.

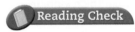 **Reading Check** **Identify** What are some commitments that married couples make to each other?

▼ FIGURE 6.3

FACTORS THAT AFFECT THE SUCCESS

 OF A MARRIAGE

These are some of the factors that can help a marriage last. Why do you think communication is important to a healthy marriage?

Factors that Affect the Health and Strength of a Marriage

☑ Effective communication between partners. This includes the ability to share feelings, needs, and concerns as they arise.

☑ Similar values, goals, outlooks, and spiritual beliefs. When couples share the things that are most important to them, they move forward in their lives together.

☑ Ability to solve problems through compromise and conflict resolution. This requires both partners in a marriage to respect, trust, and care for each other.

☑ Emotional maturity. This involves understanding a partner's needs and wants. Each partner is able to consider what is best for the relationship, not just for himself or herself.

Marriage Counselor

🗣 A marriage counselor is a mental health professional who helps married couples resolve conflicts and improve their marriage. Marriage counselors are in demand because couples can't always solve their problems on their own. If you want to be a marriage counselor, you should practice your communication and conflict-resolution skills.

What kinds of issues does a marriage counselor deal with? Go to *Career Corner* **at glencoe.com to find out.**

Lesson 3: Marriage and Parenthood **141**

CHAPTER 6
Lesson 3

TEACH

Careers for the 21st Century

Marriage Counselor Before students read the career information, ask them to list at least five facts about marriage counselors. Then have students read and discuss the information in the box on this page and in the *Career Corner* at **glencoe.com**. Ask students to revise their lists, adding, removing, and clarifying their facts.

Reading Check

Answer Married people make a commitment to love and care for one another for the rest of their lives.

R Reading Strategy

Analyzing a Graphic Have students examine **Figure 6.3**. Ask: How are these factors similar to factors that lead to successful friendships? *Sample answer: Effective communication is important for both a successful marriage and for a successful friendship.* **OL**

HEALTH LITERACY

Premarital Education and Counseling Studies have shown that premarital education and counseling programs can increase a couple's chances of having a successful marriage. In fact, some states have passed legislation that waives the marriage license fee for couples who have participated in premarital education. Have students research to find out more about the topics addressed in premarital education programs. Have students discuss how each of the topics is related to building a successful marriage. **OL**

Caption Answer

Figure Caption Communication helps in understanding the needs of each partner.

HS Health Skills Practice

Goal Setting Ask students to read the information about teen marriage. Have students work in small groups to discuss ways a teen marriage would affect a young person's long-term goals for higher education or career training. Ask each group to summarize its discussion in a written paragraph. **OL**

W Writing Support

Expository Writing Have students do additional research on the problems associated with teen marriage. Ask each student to prepare a one-page expository essay to share his or her findings with others. Remind students that expository writing is writing that teaches or informs others. **AL**

Reading Check

Answer *Sample answer:* Teen marriages often fail because of lack of experience, teens not being ready to be parents, or financial hardship.

Caption Answer

Photo Caption Before getting married, a person should consider his or her emotional maturity, goals, values, beliefs, and what he or she wants from life.

Marital Problems

Even the best marriages sometimes have problems. Couples may disagree or argue over money, children, or other issues. When the marriage is based on a foundation of trust, respect, and communication, these disagreements can usually be resolved.

Sometimes, married people cannot overcome their differences or solve the problems they face as a couple. In such cases, one or both spouses may seek a **divorce,** *a legal end to a marriage contract.*

Teen Marriage

HS Teens may want to get married for a number of reasons. They may want to leave their parents' home and be independent. They may be afraid of losing their partner, so they want to get married to secure their relationship. No matter what the reason, teen marriage isn't a good idea. More than 60 percent of teenage marriages fail within five years. Why do teen marriages fail so often? One reason is that most people are not ready for marriage during adolescence. They have not had enough experience with relationships to make a long-term commitment to another person.

Many teens get married because of an unplanned pregnancy. Taking care of a baby is often a bigger responsibility than many teen couples can handle. That is why it is important for teens to practice sexual abstinence.

W A lack of money is another factor that can cause marital problems. Teens lack the work experience and education needed to get most high-paying jobs. This can make it difficult to support a family. These responsibilities and pressures can put strain on a teen marriage.

Reading Check **List** What are some reasons teen marriages fail?

▶ Marriage is one of the biggest decisions a person can make. **What are some factors to consider before getting married?**

142 Chapter 6: Promoting Social Health

Cultural Perspectives

Teen Marriage In some cultures, teen marriage is expected and common. For example, there are some cultures in the world where teens may be married by the age of 15 or 16. Students from diverse cultural backgrounds might have differing views on teen marriage. Discuss differences in marriage traditions among cultures with the class, noting that different cultures have different perceptions of teen marriage.

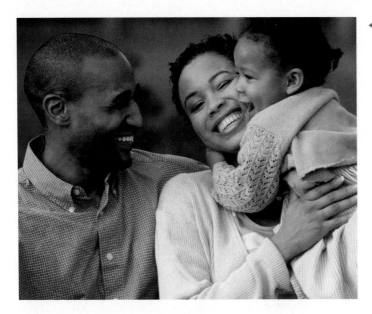

◄ Parenthood can be very rewarding, but it also involves many challenges. **What are some of the challenges of being a responsible parent?**

Parenthood

Parenthood involves making a lifelong commitment to another person. It involves meeting the physical, mental/emotional, and social needs of a child. Parenthood can be a wonderful experience, but it is important to wait until you are ready for the responsibilities that come with parenthood.

The Responsibilities of Becoming a Parent

Parenthood can be very challenging. It requires a person to juggle many responsibilities and fill many roles. Parents are responsible for the health and safety of their children. Additional responsibilities include the following:

C

- **Setting fair limits.** Small children need to know their limits—what they can and cannot do. It is up to parents to set fair rules and then enforce them.

- **Teaching values.** Parents are their children's first teachers. Children learn social skills and values by watching or listening to their parents. Parents need to be good role models for their children and demonstrate fairness, trust, caring, and respect.

- **Providing patience and love.** Raising children can be a difficult and sometimes exhausting job. When it comes to their children, parents must be slow to anger and quick to forgive. They must show their children **unconditional love.** This is *love without limitation or qualification*. Devoted parents support their children through good times and bad.

ACTIVITY
Connect To...
Language Arts

Learning Good Parenting Skills

Developing good parenting skills can help parents raise a happy, responsible child. There are many books available that help parents develop effective parenting skills. Some books teach parents how to care for an infant. Other books help parents learn positive ways to discipline their children.

Research what other resources exist to help parents learn good parenting skills.

C Critical Thinking

Applying Concepts Have students read about the responsibilities of parenthood. Then divide the class into three groups. Assign each group one of the sides of the health triangle (physical health, mental/emotional health, social health). Have each group do additional research about the impact of teen parenthood on its assigned aspect of health. Ask each group to prepare a presentation to share its results with the class. Remind students to include information about teen fathers as well as teen mothers. **OL**

ACTIVITY
Connect To...
Language Arts

Learning Good Parenting Skills

After finding books to research, have students generate a schedule that shows all of their activities on a typical day. On the bottom half of the paper, have students write a paragraph explaining how their schedule and activities would need to change if they were to become a teen parent. **OL**

TECHNOLOGY AND HEALTH

Multimedia Presentations Have advanced students use the Internet to further research the impact of teen parenthood on teen mothers, teen fathers, and children born to teen parents. Remind students to search for reliable sources to use in their research. Have students prepare a computer presentation outlining the facts from their research. Ask each student to share his or her presentation with the class and with other students at the same grade level. **OL**

Caption Answer
Photo Caption lifetime commitment, caring for another person, full-time job

C Critical Thinking

Applying Ideas Remind students of the definition of abstinence introduced in Chapter 5. Ask: How do the risks and consequences of teen parenthood reinforce the idea that abstinence is the responsible, healthful choice for teens? Sample answer: *Teen parenthood has a negative impact on all three sides of the health triangle, and negative consequences for the child as well. Understanding these facts can lead teens to make the healthful choice of abstinence from sexual activity.* **OL**

Reading Check

Answer The babies of teen mothers are at risk for low birth weight and premature delivery.

U Universal Access

English Learners Give each student several minutes to write down or draw a picture of a long-term goal. Encourage students to think big and be creative. Have volunteers share their goals and start a class discussion of ways in which teen parenthood could hinder the accomplishment of these goals. If students agree, post their drawings or writing around the room. **EL**

Caption Answer

Photo Caption set limits, provide support, caring, patience, and love

---

▶ It is a parent's job to establish a loving environment in which a child can grow. **What are some ways a parent can establish a loving environment?**

Risks of Teen Parenthood

The decision to become a parent is one that requires serious thought and planning. Most teens do not have the emotional maturity to plan for parenthood.

Teen pregnancy can also create health risks for both mother and baby. A female teen's body is still developing and may not be ready to support and nourish an unborn child. Babies born to teen mothers are at an increased risk of being born prematurely, or before they are ready to be born. They are more likely to have low birth weights, which can lead to serious health problems. A pregnant teen may not be aware of the things she can do to protect the health of her developing baby. She may not be able to afford proper prenatal care.

C

Online

Visit **glencoe.com** and complete the Interactive Study Guide for Lesson 3.

Reading Check

Describe What are some of the risks associated with teen pregnancy?

HEALTH LITERACY

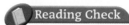

Children of Teen Parents Studies have shown that children of teen parents are more likely to struggle in school and repeat grades. As adolescents, children born to teen parents are more likely than children of older parents to drop out of school, be unemployed, or be incarcerated. In spite of these statistics, some children born to teen parents lead healthy, successful lives. Some of your students may have been born to teen parents, so it is important to present the negative consequences of teen parenting in a sensitive way.

Consequences of Teen Parenthood

Teen parents who are committed to raising their children face many challenges. One of these challenges is meeting the expenses of raising a child. This includes the cost of baby food, diapers, clothes, medical care, and more.

Between school, work, and raising a child, many teen parents find themselves physically and emotionally exhausted. They may begin to envy their peers who are not raising children. Some teen parents may have to put education plans on hold, limiting their career choices. All of these difficulties can put a great deal of stress on a teen parent.

▶ Teen parenthood can be difficult both emotionally and financially. **What are some challenges this teen might face?**

ASSESS

Assessment Resources

Lesson Review Quiz
ExamView
Fast Files Activities
Online Quizzes and Activities

Reteaching

- Assign Concept Map 6-3 or Reteaching Activity 6-3 in the Fast Files.
- Have students discuss some of the risks of teen parenthood with a group. Call on each group to describe one risk it has identified and discussed.

Enrichment

- Assign Enrichment Activity 6-3 in the Fast Files.
- Challenge students to develop survey questions they might pose to parents to learn more about the responsibilities of parenting.

CLOSE

Have students identify and describe some of the responsibilities of becoming a parent.

> ### Caption Answer
> **Photo Caption** conflicts with school and child-care responsibilities

Lesson 3 Review

After You Read

Review this lesson for new terms, major headings, and Reading Checks.

What I Learned

1. *Vocabulary* What is *unconditional love*?

2. *Recall* What are two factors that contribute to the success of a marriage?

3. *Identify* What are some of the responsibilities of parenthood?

Thinking Critically

4. *Evaluate* How might a person's emotional maturity affect his or her marriage?

5. *Synthesize* What have you learned from this lesson that helps you better understand or appreciate your own parent or guardian?

6. *Analyze* Roseanne discovered that her older teen sister was planning to elope with her boyfriend. Roseanne shared with her sister what she learned about teen marriage. Her sister responded, "Maybe that's all true, but Robert and I really love each other." How could Roseanne help her sister make a healthful choice?

Applying Health Skills

7. *Goal Setting* Identify a goal you hope to accomplish in the next five years. Explain how becoming a parent would affect your success in reaching that goal. Be prepared to share your ideas in a class discussion.

Go Online For more Lesson Review Activities, go to glencoe.com.

Lesson 3: Marriage and Parenthood **145**

Lesson 3 Review Answers

1. Unconditional love is love without limitation or qualification.
2. *Sample answers:* emotional maturity, ability to communicate, and similar values
3. meeting child's needs, teaching right from wrong, setting limits, teaching values, love
4. A person with emotional maturity understands a partner's needs and what's best for the relationship.
5. *Sample answer:* I recognize the commitment required for parenting.
6. Roseanne should explain to her sister that love is not enough to sustain a healthy marriage.
7. Students will probably note that becoming a parent will have a negative impact on the ability to achieve goals.

Building Health Skills

Sending the Right Message

Skill

 Communication Skills

Activating Prior Knowledge

Have students recall and describe effective communication skills. Have volunteers give examples of "I" messages.

- **Objective** After completing the activity, students will be able to use communication skills to build and maintain healthy relationships.
- **Time** 45 minutes
- **Materials** paper, pencil or pen

Teacher Classroom Resources

📁 Building Health Skills Activity

 Transparency 6-2

Model

- Have students read about the ways that Gil and his mother used communication skills to discuss a problem in a healthful way.
- Then have students work in small groups to discuss and answer the questions in the text.

National Health Standards Addressed

1.8.5, 4.8.1

Building Health Skills

Accessing Information
Practicing Healthful Behaviors
Stress Management
Analyzing Influences
Communication Skills
Refusal Skills
Conflict Resolution
Decision Making
Goal Setting
Advocacy

What Are Communication Skills?

Communication skills involve learning how to effectively express yourself and understand others.

Speaking Skills

- Think before you speak.
- Use "I" messages.
- Be direct, but avoid being rude or insulting.
- Make eye contact, and use appropriate body language.

Listening Skills

- Use conversation encouragers.
- Pay attention.
- Show empathy.
- Avoid interrupting, but ask questions where appropriate.

Sending the Right Message

Follow the Model, Practice, and Apply steps to help you master this important health skill.

❶ Model

Read how Gil and his mother use communication skills to solve their problem.

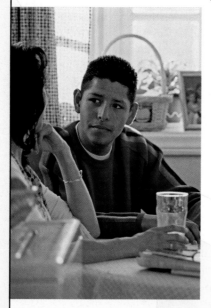

An important ingredient in any healthy relationship is communication. Gil was planning to practice fielding with his teammate Chris. Gil's mother, however, reminded him that he had promised to help clean out the garage.

Gil made eye contact with his mother and said, "Mom, I know I made a promise to you, but I forgot we had a big game coming up. Can I clean out the garage next weekend?"

Gil's mother responded, "I wish I could say yes, but I can't. A local charity is picking up the old clothes and other items on Tuesday."

Gil's mother saw the look of disappointment on his face. "I'll tell you what," she said. "You can ask your brother if he's willing to swap chores with you. If he agrees to clean the garage, will you do some of his chores in exchange?"

"That sounds like a deal, Mom," said Gil.

146

 Teaching Tips

Using Role-Plays and Skits Effectively Role-plays and skits allow students to practice skills in low-risk situations. Here are some tips for using role-plays effectively.

- Keep role-plays short and use props when appropriate.
- Give feedback on positive modeling.

- Involve observers by having them list Communication Skills from the Skill Summary and record when they see these skills demonstrated.
- Check all skits for appropriate content and tone before they are performed.

❷ Practice

Elena and her mother use communication skills to solve their problem. Read the passage below and then practice communication skills by answering the questions that follow.

Elena and her mother used good communication skills when Elena wanted to have a sleepover during the same weekend her grandparents were visiting from out of town. Elena and her mother both used "I" statements. Elena said, "I haven't had my friends over in a long time." Her mother said, "Your grandparents are driving a long way to see us and I miss spending time with them." As Elena's mother spoke, Elena nodded her head to show that she was listening. Elena's mother did the same when Elena spoke. Elena agreed to have the sleepover the weekend after her grandparents' visit.

1. What "I" statements did Elena and her mother use?
2. How did Elena and her mother show that they were listening to each other?
3. Why do you think this conversation had a positive outcome?

❸ Apply

Apply what you have learned about communication skills to complete the activity below.

With a partner, develop a skit that shows a conversation between a fictional couple in a teen marriage. Your dialogue should portray a common problem that occurs in teen marriage. Use at least two speaking skills and two listening skills. Perform your skit for classmates. See if they are able to identify the communication skills used.

Self-Check
- Did we show a problem common to teen marriages?
- Did we use two speaking skills in our conversation?
- Did we use two listening skills?

Building Health Skills (vertical)

Practice

- Let students read the conversation between Elena and her mother. Have them note specific communication skills as they read. Then let them write examples and responses to the questions in the Practice section.

Apply/Assess

- Have students work in pairs to complete the Apply activity.
- At the conclusion of each skit, have students identify the communication skills used in the skit.
- You may wish to distribute the Building Health Skills Activity in the Fast Files.

ASSESSMENT SCORING

Using a rubric, student work should meet all criteria to achieve the highest score.

Skills Student work:
- displays at least two speaking skills.
- demonstrates at least two listening skills.

Concepts Student work:
- includes a common problem in teen marriages.
- provides accurate information about the problem.

A Taste of Parenthood

Time: 20 minutes in class, one evening at home
Materials: pencil or pen, paper

Introducing Hands-on Health

- Ask students to work in pairs to discuss any babysitting experiences they have had. If some students have not had babysitting experience, have them list three responsibilities they think are required when babysitting. *feeding the child, playing with the child, keeping child safe* Have students describe how meeting a baby's or child's needs affected their ability to focus on their own activities.

Teaching the Activity

- Have students read the instructions for the activity.
- Give students some flexibility to choose a night on which they have a light workload to complete this activity.
- Have students write paragraphs for Wrapping It Up, summarizing their experiences. Have a class discussion during which students can compare experiences.

HANDS-ON HEALTH

A Taste of Parenthood

Many teens do not understand how demanding parenthood can be. This brief experiment will give you a glimpse of the responsibilities.

What You Will Need

- Help of a parent, guardian, brother, or sister
- Clock or watch with an alarm feature
- Paper
- Pencil or pen

What You Will Do

1. Select an evening or weekend when you have a light workload. Arrange with a family member to help you with your experiment.

2. Go about your normal activities. These might include watching a favorite TV program or speaking to a friend on the phone.

3. Without warning, your partner is to set off the alarm. He or she should be close enough to where you are so that you can hear the alarm. Stop what you are doing and go to the alarm and turn it off. The alarm interruption represents the attention a baby requires.

4. On your paper, note the time when you heard the alarm, and what you were doing when the alarm went off.

5. Return to your normal activities. Your partner is to set the alarm off a minimum of five times.

Wrapping It Up

Write about this experience and what it has taught you. As you write your thoughts, imagine what it would be like to respond to the alarm every day. How might this be like caring for a child? Share your report with classmates and compare your experience with theirs.

HANDS-ON HEALTH Assessment

Discussion Ask students:
- What emotions did you experience when the alarm sounded? Sample answers: *frustration, annoyance*
- Ask: In what ways is responding to an alarm similar to responding to the needs of a baby? Sample answer: *The alarm went off unpredictably, no matter what I was doing at the time.*
- Ask: In what ways is responding to an alarm different from responding to the needs of a baby? Sample answer: *Turning off an alarm is easier than feeding or comforting a baby.*

Reading Review

 Visit glencoe.com to download quizzes and eFlashcards for Chapter 6.

FOLDABLES Study Organizer

Foldables® and Other Study Aids Take out the Foldable® that you created for Lesson 1 and any graphic organizers that you created for Lessons 1–3. Find a partner and quiz each other using these study aids.

Lesson 1 You and Your Relationships

Main Idea An important part of your social health is how you relate to others.

- Relationships vary in terms of the degree of closeness, the needs they satisfy, and the roles involved.
- In your teen years, your main relationships are with family, friends, peers, and teachers.
- Relationships satisfy emotional needs, such as the need to feel loved and to belong.
- Features found in strong, healthy relationships include trust, respect, patience, tolerance, and caring.

Lesson 2 Getting Along with Your Family

Main Idea Developing a positive relationship with your family keeps all sides of your health triangle in balance.

- Your family has an important influence on the relationships that you will have later in life.
- There are several types of families. They include: a couple, nuclear family, single-custody family, joint-custody family, single-parent family, foster family, and adoptive family.

- Families meet the physical, mental/emotional, and social needs of their members.
- Parents or guardians must provide financial support, create a loving environment, and teach values. A child's responsibilities may include helping with chores and being respectful.
- Changes in a family's structure include divorce and remarriage. Changes to a family's circumstances can include moving to a new city, financial problems, job loss, and illness.

Lesson 3 Marriage and Parenthood

Main Idea Both marriage and parenthood require making a lifelong commitment to another person.

- Marriage is a legal and social commitment between two people. These two people agree to live together and care for each other. If they have children, they promise to care for them. They agree to respect each other's needs and desires. They promise to keep their relationship strong.
- Factors that affect the success of a marriage include good communication skills, sharing similar goals and values, emotional maturity, and the ability to compromise.
- Responsible parents set fair limits and provide safety, support, encouragement, patience, and love.
- Consequences of being a teen parent include financial problems, physical and emotional exhaustion, changed relationships with peers, and stress.

Chapter 6 Reading Review **149**

CHAPTER
6

Assessment Resources

- Chapter 6 Summary and Activity
- Audio Summaries
- Reading Tutor
- Performance Assessment
- Chapter 6 Test
- *ExamView*
- Vocabulary PuzzleMaker
- Online Learning Center

Reading Review

Study Aids

- **Using the Dinah Zike Foldable® Study Organizer** Have students use their Foldables® to review information about character traits.
- **Online Learning Tools** Have students go to the *Teen Health* Online Learning Center at **glencoe.com** to:
  - Download a **Podcast**.
  - Download free **Study-to-Go** content to their PDAs or cell phones.

Vocabulary Review

- **Vocabulary Quiz** Have each student create a 10-question vocabulary quiz that can be used to assess a classmate's understanding of the chapter vocabulary. Each student should prepare an answer key to accompany their quiz.

Teaching Tips

Writing in Health Class After a reading assignment or lecture, ask students to write a paragraph about the topic in their own words. This writing will help students solidify their understanding of the topic. Ask students to share their paragraphs with others in a small group. Move among the groups to assess students' understanding of the topic and to identify any misconceptions students have about the topic.

149

Assessment

Reviewing Vocabulary and Main Ideas

1. social health
2. role
3. tolerance
4. family
5. single-parent family
6. blended families
7. d
8. b
9. a
10. d

Thinking Critically

11. Having support from friends and families strengthens your mental/emotional health and gives you security and confidence. Changes in relationships can cause stress and anxiety.

12. Lists of topics will vary but might include goals, values, spiritual beliefs, plans for future, and communication.

Have students visit **glencoe.com** to take the Chapter 6 quiz.

150

Assessment

After You Read

Health eSpotlight

VIDEO

Now that you have read the chapter, look back at your answer to the Health eSpotlight question on the chapter opener. What traits would you change or add to the list of traits that are important in a healthy relationship?

Reviewing Vocabulary and Main Ideas

On a sheet of paper, write the numbers 1–6. After each number, write the term from the list that best completes each sentence.

- blended families
- family
- role
- single-parent family
- social health
- tolerance

Lesson 1 You and Your Relationships

1. Your ability to get along with the people around you is your _____.

2. A(n) _____ is a part you play when you interact with another person.

3. The ability to accept other people as they are is known as _____.

Lesson 2 Getting Along with Your Family

4. A(n) _____ is the basic unit of society, and includes two or more people.

5. A family made up of one parent plus a child or children is known as a(n) _____.

6. Remarriage among divorced adults has led to an increase in the number of _____.

Lesson 3 Marriage and Parenthood

On a sheet of paper, write the numbers 7–10. After each number, write the letter of the answer that best completes each statement.

7. Being emotionally mature includes all of the following *except*
   a. accepting your strengths and weaknesses.
   b. knowing what is important to you.
   c. putting another person's needs ahead of your own.
   d. marrying a person because you reached a certain age.

8. Which is *not* a commitment of marriage or parenthood?
   a. Pledging to care for each other
   b. Making sure that a child does not become a financial burden
   c. Setting and enforcing fair rules for a child

9. Giving birth to a child prematurely is an example of
   a. a risk facing teen females who become pregnant.
   b. a consequence faced by parents who fail to set limits.
   c. prenatal care.

10. The statement about teen parents that is true is:
    a. They may face serious money problems.
    b. They may find themselves physically and emotionally exhausted.
    c. They may feel added stress.
    d. All of the above.

  Go Online Visit **glencoe.com** and take the Online Quiz for Chapter 6.

Health eSpotlight VIDEO *Wrap-Up*

Social Health Have students reread the Health eSpotlight question at the beginning of the chapter (page 129) and look at their original answer. Ask: Now that you have read the chapter and watched the video presentation, what traits do you feel are essential to a healthy friendship with your peers, friends, and teachers? Have students work in groups to come up with a list of important traits for these relationships.

Thinking Critically

Using complete sentences, answer the following questions on a sheet of paper.

11. Analyze How do your relationships affect your mental/emotional health?

12. Apply Create a list of topics you think a couple should discuss before getting married.

Write About It

13. Narrative Writing Write a short story about a family that is coping with problems brought on by a change in circumstances. How do these changes affect interpersonal communication?

Roles and Relationships

In pairs, you will write and record an audio podcast about relationships using Audacity® or GarageBand™. Choose one of the following relationships: grandparent/grandchild, teen mother/teen father, stepparent/child, or single parent/child.

- Write a five-minute dialogue between your characters. What kind of relationship do they have? What challenges do they face? How has their relationship changed? How do they cope with these changes?
- Record your dialogue.
- Add lead-in music.
- Save your file and share it with iTunes®.

 ↗ *Applying Technology*

Roles and Relationships
Equipment needs: Audacity® or Garageband™ or similar software
Assign partners, and help students review the steps in this project. Emphasize the importance of writing a clear script and practicing that script before beginning to record. If access is limited, use a sign-up sheet to plan computer time. To reduce background noise, you may want to have students use the computer in an isolated corner; limit each pair of students to 8-10 minutes on the computer. Encourage students to download and listen to their classmates' podcasts.

Write About It

13. Narrative Writing Explain to students that narrative writing tells a clear story arranged in a logical order, and presents interesting characters, a plot, a setting, and dialogue. Students should identify the change and demonstrate how the family healthfully manages the situation.

Standardized Test Practice

1. C
2. C

Standardized Test Practice

Reading

Read the passage and then answer the questions.

In Japan, the ancient practice of *arranged marriage* is still common. In this custom, the bride and groom see each other for the first time at an arranged meeting.

When a woman in Japan whose family practices this tradition turns 25, she and her parents assemble an "information kit." The kit contains photos and descriptions of her background, education, hobbies, and interests. The parents then pass out copies of the information kit to friends and neighbors. These people ask around to see if anyone knows of an eligible bachelor. Once an interested male is located, he will prepare an information kit of his own. This is then sent to the woman and her family.

If the two parties are willing, a meeting is arranged. Members of both families go to the meeting, which takes place in a fancy restaurant. Upon meeting, the couple decides if they are interested in dating. A woman might have as many as ten such meetings before she finds a marriage partner.

1. The main idea of this passage is best summed up by which statement?
- **A.** Arranged marriages are the best kind.
- **B.** Every married couple should have an information kit.
- **C.** Marriage customs are different in different places.
- **D.** In an arranged marriage, the couple sees each other only once.

2. What is the next step after a woman assembles an "information kit"?
- **A.** She gets engaged to the first man who responds.
- **B.** The parents meet any interested men before their daughter does.
- **C.** Her parents pass out copies of the "information kit" to friends and neighbors.
- **D.** The woman chooses her husband based on the "information kit" he prepared.

Chapter 6 Assessment **151**

Test-Taking Tips

Steps in a Process Tell students that they may be asked to order the steps of a process during reading. This is made easier by carefully reviewing the passage after reading the question.

Other questions will ask students to find the main idea. Remind students that the main idea summarizes the overall meaning of the reading passage. In the example shown in the Practice Test, point out that the main idea of the passage, *Marriage customs are different in different places,* is not stated directly. Remind students that the main idea might not be stated word-for-word in the passage.

CHAPTER 7 pp. 152–173	Standards		Skills and Activities
	National	**State/Local**	
	National Health Education Standards 2.8.4, 4.8.3, 7.8.2		**HEALTH INVENTORY**, *p. 153* **BUILDING HEALTH SKILLS** *Conflict Resolution* *TALK*ing Out a Problem, *pp. 168–169* TIME health news *Unnecessary Roughness, p. 170*
Lesson 1 **The Nature of Conflict** *pp. 154–158*	National Health Education Standards 1.8.9, 2.8.1, 2.8.3, 2.8.5, 2.8.8, 4.8.1, 4.8.3, 4.8.4, 5.8.2, 5.8.4, 5.8.6, 8.8.1		**Go Online** Handling Conflict at Home, *p. 155* **HEALTH SKILLS ACTIVITY** *Decision Making* You Be the Judge, *p. 156* **What Teens Think** What can a teen do if he or she is being bullied?, *p. 157*
Lesson 2 **Preventing Conflicts** *pp. 159–163*	National Health Education Standards 1.8.5, 1.8.9, 2.8.7, 2.8.9, 4.8.3, 4.8.4, 5.8.4, 5.8.6, 6.8.1, 7.8.2, 8.8.1		**DEVELOPING GOOD CHARACTER** Citizenship, *p. 160* **HEALTH SKILLS ACTIVITY** *Stress Management* Letting Off Steam, *p. 161*
Lesson 3 **Resolving Conflicts** *pp. 164–167*	National Health Education Standards 2.8.3, 4.8.3, 4.8.4, 5.8.6, 8.8.1		**Careers for the 21st Century** Professional Mediator, *p. 165*

PACING THE CHAPTER		
Lesson 1 45 min	**Chapter Review** 45 min	
Lesson 2 45 min	**TIME health news** 30 min	
Lesson 3 45 min	**Building Health Skills** 45 min	

BLOCK SCHEDULING

For block scheduling, assign students Building Health Skills feature *TALKing Out a Problem*, pages 168-169, and Guided Reading and Writing. 📁

Planning Guide

StudentWorks Plus

Glencoe Exclusive!
TeacherWorks Plus™
All-In-One Planner and Resource Center

Reproducible Resources	Assessment	Media and Technology
Chapter *Fast File* Resources Chapter Summaries and Activities REVIEW Building Health Skills Activity TEACH Performance Assessment Activity EXTEND Universal Access Activities TEACH Parent Letter and Activities 📁 **Student Activities Workbook** TEACH 📁 **Reading Tutor** TEACH	Building Health Skills Activity, *pp. 168–169* Chapter 7 Assessment, *pp. 172–173* **Chapter *Fast File* Resources** Performance Assessment Activity, *p. 4* Chapter 7 Test, *p. 7* 💿 *ExamView® Assessment Suite*	TeacherWorks Plus includes: ● Interactive Teacher Edition ● Lesson Planner with Calendar ● Access to all blackline masters ● Correlations to standards 💿 StudentWorks™ Plus 💿 Online Student Edition Dinah Zike's Teaching Health with Foldables®
Chapter *Fast File* Resources Concept Mapping Activity 7-1 REVIEW Decision-Making Activity 7-1 EXTEND Enrichment Activity 7-1 EXTEND Lesson Plan 7-1 Guided Reading and Writing 7-1 TEACH Reteaching Activity 7-1 REVIEW	Lesson 1 Review, *p. 158* 💿 Vocabulary PuzzleMaker 💿 *ExamView® Assessment Suite*	💿 Vocabulary PuzzleMaker 💿 *ExamView® Assessment Suite* 💿 StudentWorks™ Plus 🔦 Transparency 7-1 **Go Online** glencoe.com
Chapter *Fast File* Resources Concept Mapping Activity 7-2 REVIEW Cross-Curriculum Activity 7-2 EXTEND Enrichment Activity 7-2 EXTEND Lesson Plan 7-2 Guided Reading and Writing 7-2 TEACH Reteaching Activity 7-2 REVIEW	Lesson 2 Review, *p. 163* 💿 Vocabulary PuzzleMaker 💿 *ExamView® Assessment Suite*	💿 Vocabulary PuzzleMaker 💿 *ExamView® Assessment Suite* 💿 StudentWorks™ Plus 🔦 Transparency 7-2 **Go Online** glencoe.com
Chapter *Fast File* Resources Concept Mapping Activity 7-3 REVIEW Health Lab 7-3 EXTEND Enrichment Activity 7-3 EXTEND Lesson Plan 7-3 Guided Reading and Writing 7-3 TEACH Reteaching Activity 7-3 REVIEW	Lesson 3 Review, *p. 167* 💿 Vocabulary PuzzleMaker 💿 *ExamView® Assessment Suite*	💿 Vocabulary PuzzleMaker 💿 *ExamView® Assessment Suite* 💿 StudentWorks™ Plus 🔦 Transparency 7-3 **Go Online** glencoe.com

Chapter and Lesson Resources

The *Teen Health* resources are designed for differentiated learning abilities. You may want to use the coded items in this way:

REVIEW —activities to review or reinforce content
TEACH —activities to teach basic concepts
EXTEND —activities to extend or enrich lesson content

 OUT OF TIME?

Use Health Skills Activities *You Be the Judge,* page 156, or Developing Good Character *Citizenship*, page 160.

Constructive Effects of Conflict

Conflicts may have a positive effect when handled effectively and resolved in a healthful manner. Often in middle school conflicts may result in one person forcing the other to give in, or one person withdrawing from the conflict. If the people involved face up to the problem and find ways to deal with it in positive ways, conflict can have constructive effects. When handled effectively, conflict can

- **strengthen relationships**
- **increase social development**
- **improve academic achievement**
- **encourage the practice of ethical reasoning**
- **clarify and identify values**
- **release anger, anxiety, or insecurity**
- **clarify how one might need to change**

You can help students handle conflict effectively by helping them understand that conflict can result in insight, learning, problem solving, and even laughter. Most students see conflict as generating anger, hostility, and even alienation. Counteract these preconceptions by spending as much time as possible discussing what conflict is and meaningful steps in resolving it. Practice the *T.A.L.K.* strategy frequently in role-plays and with advocacy. Also practice methods of reducing anger and stress. Teach students how to communicate their feelings with "I" statements and to be aware of their nonverbal signals. Emphasize win-win solutions and the value of compromise.

Learning how to successfully resolve conflicts will help students throughout their lives. They will

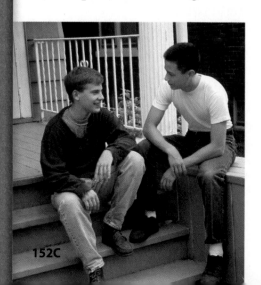

improve their relationships with family, friends, and coworkers. Effective conflict-resolution skills will also help them achieve academic and career success.

Peer Mediation Programs

With the rising incidences of violence, many schools have implemented violence prevention programs. Peer mediation is an effective approach. Schools that have adopted peer mediation programs report a decrease in suspensions due to fighting. Teachers and other staff often find that they have more time for teaching because they spend less time dealing with interpersonal conflicts.

To make a peer mediation program successful, it is critical that the program has the full support of teachers, administration, and support staff. Students who are selected as peer mediators must represent the student body in terms of gender, race, ethnicity, and ability levels. It makes sense to train a large pool of mediators because the mediators themselves gain the most from the experience.

Teens participating in these programs should be trained by an experienced mediator. Many schools use community mediation professionals or trained staff members to provide training for their students. Middle school mediators should receive 12 to 15 hours of training with additional follow-up training throughout the year. If the peer mediation program is new at the school, it is very helpful if the faculty and staff are also trained.

Other issues to consider when setting up a peer mediation program is to identify the types of conflicts that will be settled by mediation and when mediation should be used. A neutral, private location should be selected as the site to hold mediation hearings.

Once a peer mediation program is in place, mediators will need continued training and new students will have to be recruited. Consider devising a method to evaluate the success of the program to determine if it is meeting its goals.

Support for Teaching Reading

Reading Preview

Activating Background Vocabulary Have students think of the word *conflict*. Ask: What is conflict? What are some types of conflict? Have you ever experienced conflict? Explain that conflict is a disagreement between people with opposing viewpoints. Ask: "Can a conflict be within yourself?" Have students record their thoughts in a journal entry.

FOLDABLES Study Organizer *Dinah Zike's Reading and Study Skills for Teen Health* provides interactive graphic organizers that help students comprehend and retain health concepts as they read. Use the Foldable® on page 153 or find more Foldables® activities for the chapter on **Conflict Resolution** in the separate booklet, available in the TCR.

Lesson 1   The Nature of Conflict

List-Describe-Example While reading, have students make a list of the various types of conflict covered in the lesson. Have student pairs define or describe each type of conflict, record it on a simple chart, then give an example of each. To illustrate: type of conflict=interpersonal; definition=conflict between two or more people; example=you and your parents disagree about how late you stay out.

Lesson 2   Preventing Conflicts

Sensory Imagery Have students stop reading and imagine two people involved in a conflict. Ask students to describe what the conflict might look like, sound like, or feel like. Ask: Can you imagine feelings such as fear and anger? Can you imagine yourself using the right words and actions to prevent the conflict from turning violent? Encourage students to continue to independently use this strategy as they finish reading the lesson.

Lesson 3   Resolving Conflicts

Summarizing Direct students to silently read the text. Then have student pairs take turns identifying and describing the main concepts of the lesson, including various conflict-resolution skills and the mediation process. Guide students in a discussion to review and differentiate main ideas and supporting details. Finally, have each student independently write a brief summary of each of the subsections in the lesson.

Post Reading

Dramatic Presentations Have students work in small groups to create a role-play scenario that illustrates the use of good conflict-resolution or peer mediation skills. Encourage students to refer to the main concepts and supporting details of this lesson while organizing and planning their dramatic presentations. Have each group perform before the entire class.

Key for Using the Teacher Wraparound Edition

Use this key to help you identify the different types of prompts found in the Teacher Wraparound Edition.

R **Reading Strategies** activities help you teach reading skills and vocabulary.

C **Critical Thinking** strategies help students apply and extend what they have learned.

U **Universal Access** activities provide differentiated instruction for students learning to speak English, along with suggestions for teaching various types of learners.

HS **Health Skills Practice** activities reinforce Health Skills concepts and help students apply these skills in their everyday lives.

W **Writing Support** activities provide writing opportunities to help students comprehend the text.

AL **Active Learning** strategies provide a variety of activities for presenting lesson content, including Quick Demos and engaging classroom projects that get students actively involved.

Key to Ability Levels

Teaching Strategies and activities have been coded for ability level and appropriateness.

AL Activities for students working above grade level

OL Activities for students working on grade level

BL Activities for students working below grade level

EL Activities for English Learners

Symbols

 Transparencies

 CD-ROM

 glencoe.com

📁 Print Resources

Conflict Resolution

Chapter at a Glance

Lesson 1 identifies different kinds of conflicts, sources of conflict, and effective ways to deal with bullying.

Lesson 2 gives factors that escalate conflicts, recommendations for preventing conflicts from building, and identifies stress-management techniques.

Lesson 3 describes strategies for resolving conflicts, the mediation process, and traits of a good mediator.

R Reading Strategy

Interpreting the Photo Invite students to describe what is happening in the photo and answer the question. Ask: What do you think peer mediation is? Sample answer: *Teens help each other solve differences.* Why might these teens need help solving their problem? Sample answer: *The teens look angry and may not be able to solve their conflict peacefully on their own.* Explain that in this chapter, students will learn what causes conflicts and how to resolve them. **OL**

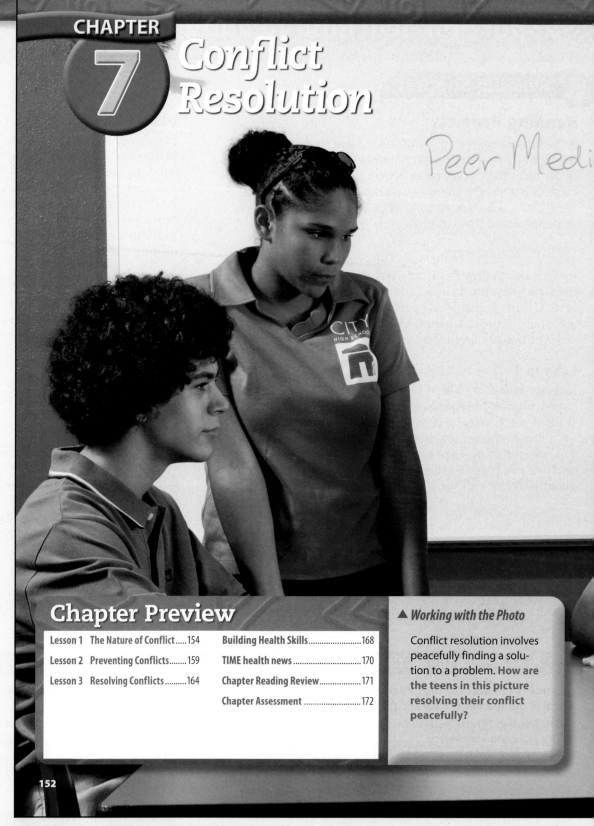

CHAPTER

7 *Conflict Resolution*

Peer Medi...

Chapter Preview

▲ *Working with the Photo*

Conflict resolution involves peacefully finding a solution to a problem. **How are the teens in this picture resolving their conflict peacefully?**

152

 Universal Access

Differentiated Learning Glencoe provides teacher support and student materials for all learners in the health classroom.

● Spanish Glosario and chapter summaries for the English Language Learners.
● *Reading Tutor* and related worksheets support reluctant readers.

● Universal Access strategies throughout the Teacher Wraparound Edition and Fast Files help you present materials for gifted students, at-risk students, physically impaired students, and those with behavior disorders or learning disabilities.

Start-Up Activities

Do you know how to deal with conflicts positively and effectively? Take the short health inventory on this page. Keep a record of your answers.

HEALTH INVENTORY

1. When I am involved in a conflict, I try to listen to what the other person has to say.
   (a) always   (b) sometimes   (c) never

2. I walk away from conflicts that are not worth my time and energy.
   (a) always   (b) sometimes   (c) never

3. I seek help when I cannot resolve a conflict on my own.
   (a) always   (b) sometimes   (c) never

FOLDABLES Study Organizer

As You Read Make this Foldable® to help you organize what you learn in Lesson 1 about the nature of conflict. Begin with a plain sheet of 8½″ × 11″ paper or notebook paper.

1 Fold the sheet of paper from top to bottom, leaving a 2″ tab at the bottom.

3 Unfold the paper once. Cut along the center fold line of the top layer only. This makes two tabs.

2 Fold in half from side to side.

4 Label the tabs as shown.

Under the appropriate tab, record information on some common causes of conflict at home and outside the home.

Go Online Visit **glencoe.com** and use the eFlashcards to preview Chapter 7 vocabulary terms.

153

FOCUS

Activating Prior Knowledge

What I Know Ask students to give reasons why conflicts occur. List their responses on the board. Review this list as you teach the lesson.

Guide to Reading

Building Vocabulary
■ Have students give one example representing each vocabulary term.
■ Use Vocabulary PuzzleMaker to reinforce vocabulary terms.

Reading Strategy

Comparing and Contrasting After students have finished reading the chapter, have them create a Venn diagram to show the similarities and differences between conflicts at home and outside the home. **FOLDABLES** Study Organizer Have students use their Foldables® as they read Lesson 1.

Quick Write

Help students trigger their memories by giving examples of conflicts a teen might have. Allow students to keep their Quick Writes private.

Caption Answer

Photo Caption *Sample answers:* relationships, space, property, power, rewards, or privileges

---

Lesson 1

The Nature of Conflict

Guide to Reading

Building Vocabulary
Choose the term from the list below that is central to the lesson's main idea. Explain the relationship this term has with each of the other terms.
■ conflict (p. 154)
■ bully (p. 157)
■ labeling (p. 158)
■ prejudice (p. 158)

Focusing on the Main Ideas
In this lesson, you will learn to
■ **explain** some reasons why conflicts occur.
■ **describe** different kinds of conflict.
■ **develop** healthy and effective ways to deal with bullying.

Reading Strategy
Comparing and Contrasting As you read the lesson, list similarities and differences between conflicts at home and those outside the home.

FOLDABLES Study Organizer Use the Foldable® on p. 153 as you read this lesson.

Quick Write

List any disagreements you've had in the last month, what they were about, and with whom you disagreed.

▼ Conflicts can start for a variety of reasons. **What kinds of conflicts can occur at school?**

What Is Conflict?

It began as an innocent episode. Tyler was waiting patiently in the cafeteria line when someone accidentally bumped into him from behind. He fell against Frank, a classmate standing in line in front of him. "What's your problem?" Frank asked, shoving Tyler back. Tyler got angry and shoved Frank back. A campus supervisor spotted the boys and took them both to the vice-principal's office. Tyler felt that he had been wrongly accused, but he was as much to blame as Frank was for contributing to the conflict. A **conflict** is *a disagreement between people with opposing viewpoints, ideas, or goals.*

Conflicts can be caused by a difference of opinion over just about anything. They can occur over relationships, space, or property. They can also be about power, rewards, or privileges.

Reading Check **Define** What is *conflict*?

154 Chapter 7: Conflict Resolution

Lesson 1 Resources

📁 **Chapter FAST FILE Resources**
Guided Reading and Writing 7-1
Concept Mapping Activity 7-1
Decision-Making Activity 7-1
Reteaching Activity 7-1
Enrichment Activity 7-1
Lesson Quiz 7-1

Technology
⚓ Transparency 7-1
🔊 Audio Summaries
💿 *ExamView® Assessment Suite*
🔊 Vocabulary PuzzleMaker
💿 StudentWorks™ Plus

 G♦ **Online**

Kinds of Conflict

Conflicts can take many different forms depending on what and who is involved. Some conflicts involve only a simple exchange of words. These conflicts are fairly minor. Others, such as gang confrontations, can be ongoing and severe. When conflicts involve weapons that can lead to injury or death, they are extremely serious.

Many conflicts are interpersonal—between two or more people. Others are internal—they take place inside your own mind. Imagine being asked to judge a talent contest in which your best friend is a contestant. You might be torn between loyalty to a friend and responsibility for choosing the best act.

People have different needs and wants, and conflicts are often unavoidable. Maybe you want to watch a certain TV show, but your sister wants to watch a different one. Maybe two girls have a crush on the same boy. Conflicts are not necessarily negative. They are a part of everyday life. In fact, they can be a good force in people's lives. Resolving conflicts can help people settle their differences, get along peacefully, and move on to positive action.

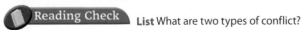 **Reading Check** List What are two types of conflict?

Conflicts at Home

The more time you spend with people, the more chances there are for disagreements to arise. If you spend a large part of your day with family, conflicts with family members may be common. It is important to maintain a positive relationship with your family members because these relationships can affect your overall health.

Conflicts with parents or guardians usually occur over limits, responsibilities, or expectations. You may feel that a rule set by a parent is unfair. Maybe, in your opinion, you should be able to stay up—or out—later. Perhaps you feel that you have been asked to do more chores than other family members. As a maturing teen, you may feel that you have proven yourself ready for more independence. Your parent or guardian, however, may feel differently. When conflicts like these come up, try to remember

Go Online

Topic: Handling Conflict at Home

Visit glencoe.com for Student Web Activities to learn about the different kinds of conflict and what you can do to resolve conflict when it happens at home.

Activity: Using the information provided at the link above, create a "Conflict Tip Sheet" that will remind you of things you can do to resolve conflicts that occur at home.

▼ Conflicts with parents or guardians can be over restrictions, responsibilities, or expectations. **What do you need to remember when you have a conflict with an adult in charge at your home?**

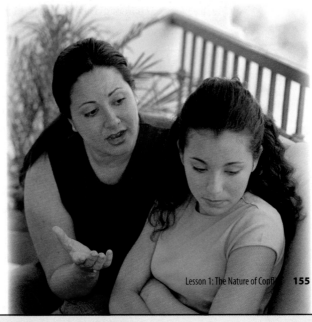

Lesson 1: The Nature of Conflict **155**

TEACH

AL Active Learning

Learning Stations Divide the class into five groups that will rotate through five learning stations. Place index cards at each station that instruct students to write examples of

- the meaning of *conflict*
- minor conflicts
- serious conflicts
- internal conflicts
- interpersonal conflicts

Then lead a class discussion about the topics at each learning station. Have groups share their responses. **OL**

Reading Check

Answer, p. 154 Conflict is a disagreement between people with opposing viewpoints, ideas, or goals. **Answer, this page** interpersonal and internal

W Writing Support

Narrative Instruct students to write a fictional narrative in which they describe a conflict occurring between a teen and his or her parents/guardians or siblings. In their narratives, students should identify the source of the conflict. Remind students to make the characters and setting interesting and to include dialogue. **OL**

What Teens Want to Know

Why does it seem like I'm always arguing with my parents? Remind students that parents have been making decisions for them for years. Teens at this age are developing likes and dislikes that are more similar to their peers. Emphasize that parents make decisions to keep their teens healthy and safe. Tell students to accept the judgment of their parents on some issues, but work toward compromise so that both sides are satisfied. Usually parents are willing to give teens more privileges as they gain confidence in their ability to make good decisions. **OL**

Caption Answer

Photo Caption Parents and guardians have a responsibility to keep you safe and healthy.

Health Skills Activity

Decision Making

You Be the Judge

Use the following strategies to help students complete the activity.

- Before partners role-play the decision-making process, have them write responses for each step. Encourage them to brainstorm a list of options and evaluate the possible outcomes.

- Invite volunteers to role-play their decision-making process for the class. Involve the rest of the class in a discussion about how this decision will help mend this relationship.

AL Active Learning

Real-World Connection Have students find newspaper or magazine articles that describe conflicts between siblings. Consider having some articles on hand for students to use. Have students write a paragraph describing what the conflict is about, the effects of the conflict on the siblings involved, and whether or not the conflict was resolved. Challenge students to write their opinion of how the conflict might have been prevented in the first place. **OL**

 Reading Check

Answer expectations, property, space, and competition

Health Skills Activity

Decision Making

You Be the Judge

Mike and his friends were having a party and needed a CD player. Mike borrowed his brother's without asking. As Mike was riding his bike over to his friend's house, he dropped the CD player on the road, breaking it. When Mike told his brother what happened, his brother was angry. "How could you take my things without asking? I thought I could trust you," his brother said and then walked away.

Mike did not know what to do next. How could he mend his relationship with his brother? Critique how Mike's behavior affected his communication with his brother.

What Would You Do?

Apply the six steps of decision making to Mike's problem. With a partner, role-play a scene in which Mike thinks through his decision, and then acts on it. How would his brother respond to his action?

1. State the situation.
2. List the options.
3. Weigh the possible outcomes.
4. Consider your values.
5. Make a decision and act.
6. Evaluate your decision.

---

that parents set limits to ensure their children's well-being. As parents, they are responsible for keeping you safe and healthy. You, in turn, have a responsibility to respect their authority and to try to keep a positive relationship with them.

AL Conflicts between siblings—sisters or brothers—often involve property or space. Older siblings may be upset by younger siblings who get in their way or who use their possessions without asking first. This often happens when siblings share a room. Also, conflict between siblings often involves competition. One sibling may feel that another is getting more attention from parents or guardians. A younger sibling may resent an older sibling because he or she has more privileges. Although conflicts are a normal part of family life, it is important to behave positively toward family members in order to build strong family relationships.

 Reading Check **Identify** What are conflicts between siblings often about?

Dealing with Sensitive Issues

Students in Conflict It is very common for students in middle school to experience conflict. They might be jockeying for position in various social groups, dealing with bullying, or simply having a misunderstanding with a good friend. The effects of these conflicts can reduce a teen's self-esteem or make it difficult to work with specific students in group work. Pay attention to the behavior of your students in the hallway and during lunch. Watch how students interact with one another to get an idea of the social relationships. When grouping students for an activity, try to avoid putting together students who are in conflict.

Conflicts Outside the Home

At this point in your life, you spend much of your day in school. As a result, many of the conflicts you have outside the home relate to school, friends, and peers.

Conflicts at school may be with teachers or other authority figures. More often, however, they happen between peers or friends. These conflicts can involve an incident, like the one Tyler experienced in the lesson-opening paragraph. Other times differences in personality, beliefs, or opinions are involved.

Sometimes conflicts are one-sided and unprovoked. One person may not take the time to understand another. Sometimes a person seeks power and attention by putting others down. This type of conflict is a form of bullying. The person who is the target of these behaviors usually feels upset and possibly helpless.

Bullying

A **bully** is *someone who picks on individuals who are smaller or weaker.* Bullies can be males or females of any age. Bullies may limit their behavior to teasing and name-calling, or they may become physical. Some bullies try to show how tough they are by taking away the property of others. The best way to deal with bullies is to walk away and share the matter with a trusted adult. Bullies expect victims to react with fear or anger. When you walk away, you take away the bully's power. Bullying can be serious. If you know someone who is a bully or if you are targeted by a bully in your school, talk with a person in authority. Bullying should not be allowed under any circumstances. You can use the resources available to you to improve the safety of your environment inside and outside the home.

Teasing is a form of bullying. The person doing the teasing may think it is harmless. However, teasing can be harmful. When Joel started wearing braces on his teeth, an older student, Max, started teasing him. Max and his friends found the teasing hilarious. Joel found it irritating. At first he tried ignoring it and avoiding Max whenever he could. When that did not work, Joel made his own joke about his braces. That did the trick. If Joel was in on the joke, there was nothing for Max to make fun of. Joel was glad the teasing was over, but if his approach had

What Teens THINK

What can a teen do if he or she is being bullied?

If a teen is being bullied, he should try to help himself or herself out. The teen should tell a trustworthy friend, parent/guardian, or teacher. The teen should try and avoid the bully, and should not try and face the bully alone.

J.T. J.
Blackshear, GA

Lesson 1: The Nature of Conflict **157**

What Teens THINK

What can a teen do if he or she is being bullied? Help students read and discuss the information about bullying (on pages 157–158). Then ask: How do you think teens should react when they are being bullied? How do you think teens should react when friends or classmates are being bullied? When does it make sense to ask an adult for help in handling bullying? After students have shared their own ideas, have then read the question and response in *What Teens Think.*

HS Health Skills Practice

Advocacy One way to prevent bullying is for students to take a stand against it themselves. Have the class work together on a campaign to prevent bullying. Assign different student groups various tasks, such as making posters or performing skits that describe how to deal with a bully and what to do when witnessing bullying. **OL**

AL Active Learning

Think, Pair, Share In the left column of a "T" chart on the board, write down student suggestions of how students are teased. In the right column, students can think of ways to respond to each type of teasing. From this list, students can get into pairs, choose one set of items, and act it out for the class. **EL**

⚜ Promoting Coordinated School Health

Dealing with Bullies Studies show that between 15 to 25 percent of students are bullied. Unfortunately, many adults are unaware of this problem because most bullying occurs when adults are not present. If your school does not have an antibullying program, consider working with the administration and the guidance counselor to start one. Online resources are available from the Substance Abuse and Mental Health Services Administration or Students Against Destructive Decisions.

Reading Check

Answer Talk to the bully or get help from an adult.

ASSESS

Assessment Resources

Lesson Review Quiz
- *ExamView*
- Fast Files Activities
- Online Quizzes and Activities

Reteaching

- Assign Concept Map 7-1 or Reteaching Activity 7-1 in the Fast Files.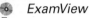
- Have students identify the kinds of conflicts (internal or interpersonal) shown in the photos in this lesson. Then have them write possible causes for each conflict pictured.

Enrichment

- Assign Enrichment Activity 7-1 in the Fast Files.
- Challenge students to write a poem about an imaginary conflict in which they describe the source of the conflict and how it affects the people involved.

CLOSE

Have students explain what a conflict is and describe some sources of conflict at home and outside the home.

---

not worked, he still had the option of confronting Max. He could have explained to Max how the teasing made him feel so that Max would hopefully understand and decide to stop.

Labeling, or *name-calling*, is another form of bullying. Name-calling is hurtful, especially when it is based on **prejudice**—*a negative and unjustly formed opinion, usually against people of a different racial, religious, or cultural group.* A student who is a target of this kind of labeling should attempt to resolve the matter by talking with a school counselor, parent, or other trusted adult. This is a very serious problem that needs action right away.

Being teased, labeled, or bullied can be an emotionally painful experience. It is difficult not to feel hurt by what others say. Remember that words should be used to build others up, not to tear them down.

Go Online

Visit **glencoe.com** and complete the Interactive Study Guide for Lesson 1.

Reading Check

Recall What should a person do if he or she is being bullied?

Lesson 1 Review

After You Read

Review this lesson for new terms, major headings, and Reading Checks.

What I Learned

1. *Vocabulary* What is *prejudice*? Use the term in a sentence.

2. *Give Examples* Give an example of an interpersonal conflict and an internal conflict.

3. *Recall* What kinds of conflicts often occur in the home?

4. *Explain* What are some factors that contribute to bullying? Who can victims of bullying turn to for help?

Thinking Critically

5. *Analyze* Alisa and her mother had an argument over the amount of time Alisa spends watching TV. Alisa is feeling angry with her mother. What do you think Alisa could do to maintain a positive relationship with her mother?

6. *Apply* Ever since Dave got his hair cut in a new style, he has been feeling self-conscious about it. To make matters worse, Ted makes fun of Dave every time he sees him. What type of hurtful behavior is Ted using to target Dave? What should Dave do?

Applying Health Skills

7. *Analyzing Influences* Sometimes negative song lyrics or other media messages encourage negative behaviors. Evaluate song lyrics that promote positive behavior. Write a review of these lyrics to share with classmates.

Go Online
For more Lesson Review Activities, go to **glencoe.com**.

Lesson 1 Review Answers

1. Prejudice is a negative and unjustly formed opinion, usually against people of a different racial, religious, or cultural group. Sentences will vary.

2. Interpersonal—siblings want to watch two different television shows at the same time. Internal—being invited to the movies with friends after volunteering to babysit.

3. Conflicts with parents: limits, responsibilities. Siblings: property, space, and competition.

4. Factors include reacting to a bully with fear or anger. Victims can turn to a trusted adult.

5. *Answers may include:* listen and respect her mother's authority, express her feelings, work together to find an agreeable solution.

6. Ted is teasing Dave. Dave should try to ignore Ted. If that does not work, then Dave should make a joke about the haircut himself. Dave can explain to Ted how the teasing is hurtful.

7. Students should describe why these lyrics are positive.

Lesson 2

Preventing Conflicts

Guide to Reading

● **Building Vocabulary**
As you read this lesson, write the three new highlighted terms in your notebook. Next to each, write its definition.

■ escalate (p. 159)
■ revenge (p. 161)
■ mob mentality (p. 162)

● **Focusing on the Main Ideas**
In this lesson, you will learn to

■ **identify** factors that build conflicts.
■ **prevent** conflicts from becoming serious.
■ **develop** stress-management techniques to release anger.

● **Reading Strategy**
Classifying Using the diagram to the right as a guide, create a concept map that shows why conflicts build.

Why Conflicts Build

Many conflicts do not go beyond an exchange of words. Others **escalate,** or *become more serious.* Fortunately, this can be avoided. You can take steps to prevent conflicts from becoming violent. One step is recognizing signs that a conflict is building. Some well-known signs appear in **Figure 7.1.** Another step toward prevention is identifying the emotions and other factors that fuel conflict. These include anger, jealousy, group pressure, and the use of alcohol and other drugs.

Quick Write

Write a paragraph describing what you typically do when you get angry.

The Warning Signs of Building Conflict	
Physical Signs	*Emotional Signs*
• A knot in the stomach	• Feeling concerned
• Faster heart rate	• Getting defensive
• A lump in the throat	• Wanting to cry
• Balled-up fists	• Not feeling valued
• Cold or sweaty palms	• Wanting to lash out
• A sudden surge of energy	• Wanting to escape

◀ **FIGURE 7.1**

Some warning signs that a conflict is building are physical. Others are emotional. **Can you think of other signs of building conflict?** **R**

Lesson 2

FOCUS

Activating Prior Knowledge

What I Know Ask students: What causes conflicts to grow into a physical fight? List all responses on the board. Edit the list as needed throughout the lesson.

Guide to Reading

Building Vocabulary
■ Have students draw a picture or cartoon to illustrate the meaning of each vocabulary term.
■ Use Vocabulary PuzzleMaker to reinforce vocabulary terms.

Reading Strategy
Classifying As students read the lesson, have them complete the concept map. Encourage them to add details to the concept map to better describe each reason that conflicts build.

Quick Write
To get students started, have them think of examples of things that make them angry. Allow students to keep answers private.

Lesson 2 Resources

 Chapter *FAST FILE* **Resources**
Guided Reading and Writing 7-2
Concept Mapping Activity 7-2
Cross-Curriculum Activity 7-2
Reteaching Activity 7-2
Enrichment Activity 7-2
Lesson Quiz 7-2

Technology
Transparency 7-2
Audio Summaries
ExamView® Assessment Suite
Vocabulary PuzzleMaker
StudentWorks™ Plus

Caption Answer

Figure Caption *Sample answer:* An angry crowd gathering and shouting may signal a building conflict.

TEACH

DEVELOPING Good Character

Citizenship

Review with students the school rules that apply to fights. Remind students where school officials are located and who they can call on for help. Emphasize that students should never intervene in a physical fight. As a class, discuss strategies for helping two people resolve their conflict in a positive way.

R Reading Strategy

Analyzing a Chart Review the warning signs of building conflict in **Figure 7.1** on the previous page. Ask: What are some emotional signs that a conflict is building up? *Accept any answer listed on the chart.* What are physical signs? *Accept any answer from the chart.* What should you do if you have any of these emotional or physical signs? *Realize that a conflict is building and work to prevent the conflict from escalating.* OL

 Reading Check

Answer Express anger in healthy ways; walk away; concentrate on the problem, not the person.

Caption Answer

Photo Caption *Sample answers:* not being picked for a team, not having certain clothes

160

DEVELOPING Good Character

Citizenship

When a fight is developing, you can show good citizenship by encouraging those involved to find a positive way to resolve the conflict. However, if the fight turns violent, do not get involved. Instead, get help from a trusted adult right away.

Who would be an appropriate person at your school to report a fight to?

Anger

Nearly everyone gets angry at some point. Imagine that you and a friend have plans to meet outside a movie theater. Your friend arrives after the film has started, and does not give a reason for why he is late. Or imagine that you arrive at school after being out sick for several days. You discover that your sister failed to tell you about an important test even though you asked her to keep you informed about what you were missing. Anger would be a natural response to these situations. When you get angry, it is important to express your anger in a healthy way. In fact, keeping anger inside can harm you emotionally and physically.

Dealing with anger in an appropriate way can be challenging. Yelling at another person never accomplishes anything positive. This will only hurt or annoy the other person, creating a larger conflict. The best strategy when emotions are running high is to step away from the situation. Be quiet for a few moments and allow yourself to cool down. Share your feelings with a friend or trusted adult who is not directly involved in the situation. Focus your attention on something other than your anger and its source. When you are ready to speak calmly, let the other person know what is bothering you. Be sure to concentrate on the problem, not the person.

 Reading Check **Recall** What should you do when you are angry?

Jealousy

"Why does *she* always get special treatment? It's not fair! I can't believe you got picked and I didn't!"

Have you ever heard statements like these? They are expressions of jealousy, a gateway to other emotions. It leads to feelings of anger and resentment. Jealousy has been known to ruin friendships, especially when the jealous person feels wronged. It is normal to feel jealous sometimes, especially when someone does better than you or gets more attention than you.

◀ Talking about feelings of jealousy with a trusted adult is a better idea than seeking revenge. **What are some situations that might cause a teen to feel jealous of someone else?**

160 Chapter 7: Conflict Resolution

 FITNESS ZONE

Physical Fitness Plan Dealing with stress and anger can be challenging, especially for teens. Many teens find that physical exercise can help them "let off steam," which then gives them an opportunity to identify their emotions and express them appropriately. Have students review the first pages of the *Fitness Zone Handbook* and then discuss how a regular physical fitness program can help them handle their emotions. **For more information, see** *Fitness Zone Handbook* **pages xviii-1 or visit the Fitness Zone at glencoe.com.**

Health Skills Activity

Stress Management

Letting Off Steam

It is not always easy to know how or when to deal with anger. Sometimes you may think it is best to say nothing only to later realize that you are still angry. When you allow anger to build, the emotion becomes like water heating up in a kettle. At such times, you need to let off steam. Here are some suggestions that can help you release built-up anger or frustration:

- Close your eyes and focus on relaxing and breathing.
- Find a way to turn your negative energy into positive energy. Write in your journal or work on a hobby. Look for an opportunity to laugh.
- Do some physical activity. Go for a run, bike ride, or walk.
- Talk to a friend, parent, or trusted adult.

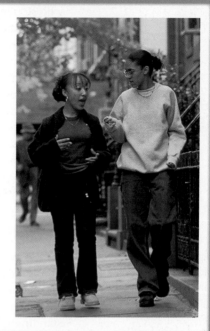

With a Group

Make a list of some of the different techniques each member in your group has used to redirect negative energy. Share your list with other groups in the class.

Just be sure to deal with these feelings in a healthy way. Talk to a friend or trusted adult. You can also write down your feelings in a private journal.

AL When you are jealous of someone, seeking revenge is not a healthy way to deal with your feelings. **Revenge** is *punishment, injury, or insult to the person seen as the cause of the strong emotion.* Revenge is often seen as "payback" or an opportunity to "even the score." Seeking revenge, however, never helps a jealous person get what he or she really wants. It also has a way of turning a minor conflict into a major one. Maybe the person you sought revenge on now wants to seek revenge on you. You could end up hurting someone or getting hurt yourself. Instead, manage your feelings of jealousy by talking about them with someone you trust or writing them down in a private journal.

Lesson 2: Preventing Conflicts **161**

Health Skills Activity

Stress Management

Letting Off Steam

Use the following strategies to help students complete the activity.

- After the class has read the introductory paragraph, lead them all in a deep breathing exercise to help them focus on relaxing.
- Suggest students brainstorm a list of activities that they enjoy. These activities should be both physical activities that make the body tired and mental activities that completely engage their mind.
- Invite students to share other techniques for releasing negative energy. Include these in the classroom resource folder.

AL Active Learning

Public Service Announcement Have small groups of students write and act out for the class a public service announcement (PSA) that describes one of the four factors that cause conflicts to escalate (anger, jealousy, group pressure, and alcohol or drugs). Explain that the focus of the PSA should be on raising awareness about the factor, as well as how to deal with it. You might wish to videotape the PSAs and show them to other classes in the school. **OL**

HEALTH LITERACY

Violence in Relationships By the age of 20, one out of three women will have experienced dating violence. Dating violence arises from conflict and is a symptom of an abusive relationship. Make your students aware of the signs of abusive relationships. Make sure they know that jealousy in a relationship has nothing to do with love. Explain that jealousy is a sign of possessiveness and a lack of trust. Also explain that abuse in a relationship sometimes occurs because one partner does not know how to properly manage his or her feelings. **OL**

Active Learning

Learning Stations As a follow-up to the Learning Stations activity from Lesson 1, divide the class again into five groups and have them rotate through another set of learning stations. Place an index card at each station that has a scenario describing a teen's conflict with family, friends, school, or him- or herself. Then list one factor that could cause the conflict to escalate. Instruct groups to write what could happen if the conflict escalated. Then have them write how to prevent the conflict from escalating. When groups have finished, lead a class discussion about the group responses for each scenario. **OL**

Reading Check

Answer The onlookers of a conflict take sides and "egg on" the people involved in the conflict.
Answer, p. 163 to avoid mob mentality

Caption Answer

Photo Caption Keep conflicts private, show respect, avoid alcohol and drugs.

Group Pressure

Sometimes when people have a disagreement in public, a crowd forms. Usually this begins with one or two curious people who stop to watch. Eventually, others join in as a result of **mob mentality.** This is *acting or behaving in a certain and often negative manner because others are doing it.* The onlookers may "egg on" the people involved in the conflict.

When this type of situation arises, the people in the middle of the conflict can get swept up in the mob mentality themselves. This can cause them to put aside their own thoughts of right and wrong and give in to the crowd. These situations usually have bad outcomes. If you find yourself in such a crowd, you should go get help from an adult right away.

 Reading Check **Explain** How can pressure from a group of peers cause a conflict to escalate?

Alcohol and Other Drugs

Alcohol and conflicts do not mix well. Typically, alcohol only makes matters worse—in some instances, causing the situation to become violent.

Using alcohol affects a person's emotional state and understanding of a problem. The same is true of many other drugs. Teens who use alcohol or other drugs may lose self-control. They may lash out at others in violent ways. In fact, violent crimes committed under the influence of alcohol are a leading cause of teen deaths. The use of alcohol and other drugs can make it difficult to resolve conflicts in a peaceful way. To protect themselves from violence and other harmful effects, teens should avoid using alcohol and other drugs.

▼ Reaching an agreement that puts an end to a conflict is gratifying. **What are some other ways to prevent conflicts from building?**

Preventing Conflicts from Building

Conflicts are a normal part of life. You can usually prevent a conflict from building by dealing with the problem in appropriate ways. The following strategies can help:

• **Learn to understand your feelings.** It is especially important to recognize why you are angry. It is also helpful to understand that some emotions are impulsive, lasting for only a moment. Other emotions are more steady.

AL

Teacher to Teacher

Tyler Champ   **Fox Middle School, Hartford, CT**

Violence, Anger, and Conflict "I like to give my students a chance to be creative. To reinforce what we have studied, they choose a story, rap/poem, song, or poster. The story must be about a teen who is struggling with violence, anger, or conflict-resolution issues, and the rap/ poem, poster, or song has to deal with issues surrounding violence, anger, or conflict. Then I have the students share their projects with the class."

- **Keep your conflicts private.** Find a quiet, out-of-the-way spot to share your differences with another person. Trying to resolve a conflict in public may draw a crowd. This invites mob mentality, which can lessen the chances of resolving the conflict peacefully.

- **Avoid using alcohol or other drugs.** Using alcohol and drugs can affect a person's emotions, judgment, and decision-making ability, making it difficult to resolve conflicts peacefully.

- **Show respect for yourself and for others.** This will help you build healthy relationships, which in turn will help you resolve conflicts when they arise.

- **Learn to accept others.** Accepting people who have different views and customs than you can enrich your life.

- **Try putting yourself in the other person's situation.** If you understand the other person's point of view, you may be more sympathetic, understanding, and willing to resolve the conflict in a positive way.

Reading Check **Explain** Why is it important to keep conflicts private?

Go Online

Visit **glencoe.com** and complete the Interactive Study Guide for Lesson 2.

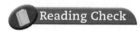

After You Read

Review this lesson for new terms, major headings, and Reading Checks.

What I Learned

1. *Vocabulary* What is *mob mentality*?

2. *Recall* Name two factors that fuel conflicts.

3. *List* Name two ways to prevent conflicts from building.

Thinking Critically

4. *Evaluate* Andy and his best friend, Jake, tried out for the concert band. Jake made it, but Andy did not. Now Andy cannot bring himself to congratulate Jake, but he is not sure why. Tell what Andy may be feeling and what he can do about it.

5. *Synthesize* Jill and Connie were discussing a problem. Connie began to raise her voice out of anger. What strategies should Jill take to resolve the conflict in a positive way? Why are these strategies important?

Applying Health Skills

6. *Practicing Healthful Behaviors* On a sheet of paper, describe your strengths and weaknesses when preventing conflicts from growing. List ways to change your weaknesses to strengths that will help you improve your ability to deal with conflict.

Go Online For more Lesson Review Activities, go to **glencoe.com**.

Lesson 2: Preventing Conflicts **163**

ASSESS

Assessment Resources

Lesson Review Quiz
- *ExamView*
- Fast Files Activities
- Online Quizzes and Activities

Reteaching

- Assign Concept Map 7-2 or Reteaching Activity 7-2 in the Fast Files.
- Have student pairs work together to create a brochure about preventing conflicts. Brochures should include information about what causes conflicts to escalate and how to prevent conflicts from building up.

Enrichment

- Assign Enrichment Activity 7-2 in the Fast Files.
- Have students choose a riot that occurred in American history and learn how and why a mob mentality took over. Challenge students to make inferences about what might have prevented the mob from forming.

CLOSE

Have students explain the importance of preventing conflicts from building.

Lesson 2 Review Answers

1. acting or behaving in a certain and often negative manner because others are doing it

2. *Any two:* anger, jealousy, group pressure, use of alcohol or other drugs

3. *Any two:* understand your feelings, keep conflicts private, avoid alcohol or other drugs, respect yourself and others, accept people different from yourself, put yourself in the other person's situation

4. *Sample answer:* Andy might be feeling jealous. Andy can talk to a trusted adult or write down his thoughts in a journal.

5. *Sample answer:* Jill should try to walk Connie to a quiet, out-of-the-way spot. Then she should listen to Connie and try to put herself in Connie's situation. The strategies could help avoid a mob mentality from occurring.

6. Allow students to keep their lists private.

FOCUS

Activating Prior Knowledge

What I Know Describe a typical conflict that teens might have. Then have students come up with ways to resolve the conflict. Explain that they will learn some skills for resolving conflicts in this lesson.

Guide to Reading

Building Vocabulary
■ Have students make a concept map to show the relationships among the vocabulary terms.
■ Use Vocabulary PuzzleMaker to reinforce vocabulary terms.

Reading Strategy
Sequencing Suggest that students organize the steps in the T.A.L.K. strategy in a sequencing diagram. Make sure they realize that the steps in the process mirror the order of the letters in the acronym.

uick Write

To help students get started with the Quick Write activity, suggest that they recall a time someone caused them to have hurt feelings or made them angry or jealous.

Caption Answer

Photo Caption **T**ake a time-out. **A**llow each person to tell his or her side. **L**et each person ask questions. **K**eep brainstorming.

164

Resolving Conflicts

Guide to Reading

Building Vocabulary
Write what you think each term means. As you come across the word in the lesson, make changes as needed.

■ conflict resolution (p. 164)
■ win-win solution (p. 165)
■ mediation (p. 165)
■ compromise (p. 166)

Focusing on the Main Ideas
In this lesson, you will learn to

■ **demonstrate** effective skills for resolving conflicts.
■ **recall** the steps of the mediation process.
■ **identify** traits of a good mediator.

Reading Strategy
Sequencing Explain the order in which the steps in the T.A.L.K. strategy should be carried out.

uick Write

Write two ways of communicating that could lead to conflict. Next to each, write how the same idea could be expressed in a more positive way.

Finding Constructive Solutions

Sometimes it is easy to find a solution to a conflict. When this task is more difficult, however, you might be tempted to ignore the conflict or set it aside. Yet, conflicts or other differences that remain unsettled or unresolved can damage relationships. Avoiding a conflict is also likely to make it worse. Fortunately, there is a constructive approach to dealing with any conflict—an approach in which the parties involved work together toward a positive, healthy outcome. This approach uses the skill of **conflict resolution,** which involves *solving a disagreement in a way that satisfies both sides.*

◀ There are constructive ways of dealing with conflict. **Can you name the steps in the T.A.L.K. strategy?**

164 Chapter 7: Conflict Resolution

Lesson 3 Resources

📁 **Chapter FAST FILE Resources**
Guided Reading and Writing 7-3
Concept Mapping Activity 7-3
Health Lab 7-3
Reteaching Activity 7-3
Enrichment Activity 7-3
Lesson Quiz 7-3

Technology
🔦 Transparency 7-3
🎵 Audio Summaries
⊙ *ExamView® Assessment Suite*
🎵 Vocabulary PuzzleMaker
⊙ StudentWorks™ Plus

Go Online

Conflict Resolution

The skill of conflict resolution starts with the word *TALK*. Each letter represents one step in the T.A.L.K. strategy. This strategy can effectively end conflicts and improve and maintain your personal and family health. The meaning of the letters is as follows:

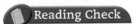

- **Take a time-out.** Wait at least 30 minutes before you discuss the situation with the other person. This will give both of you a chance to calm down and think more clearly.

- **Allow each person to tell his or her side.** Each person should have the chance to explain his or her feelings without interruption.

HS
- **Let each person ask questions.** Each person should have the chance to question the other. Stay calm and respectful.

- **Keep brainstorming.** Be open to trying different solutions that will satisfy both of you. Do not let your emotions prevent you from trying different solutions.

Conflict-resolution skills tie in with other health skills—especially communication skills.

Conflict Resolution: Win-Win Outcomes

People have a natural tendency to think of conflicts in terms of winners and losers. This is not always accurate, however. If one person gets his or her way when a conflict is settled, does that mean that the other person automatically ends up losing? Not necessarily. When the T.A.L.K. strategy is used, a **win-win solution** is possible. This is *an agreement or outcome that gives each party something it wants.* Win-win solutions are more desirable than win-lose solutions. That is because both parties come away with something.

Reading Check **Define** What is a *win-win solution*?

A Need for Mediation

In some instances, you and another person might reach a win-win solution on your own. This will give both of you the satisfaction of knowing that you worked together to achieve a constructive solution.

Suppose that you and the other person are unable to come to an agreement. When this happens, your best bet is to seek outside help. One form of help is **mediation.** This is *a process in which a third person, a mediator, helps those in conflict find a solution.* A mediator can be an adult or a student. With the help of a mediator, most people discover creative ways to solve problems. **Figure 7.2** on the next page details the steps in the mediation process.

Lesson 3: Resolving Conflicts **165**

TEACH

ACTIVITY
Careers for the 21st Century

Professional Mediator Guide students in reading and discussing the information about professional mediators. If your school has a peer-mediation program, let volunteers share what they know about it, and ask: How could participating in our peer-mediation program help you consider a career as a professional mediator? Then have a volunteer read the information about professional mediators at **glencoe.com** and share that information with the rest of the class.

HS Health Skills Practice

Practicing Healthful Behaviors Divide the class into pairs and assign each partner a role in an imaginary conflict. Make the conflicts as silly or completely unrealistic as possible. Then have students use the steps in the T.A.L.K. strategy to resolve their conflict. When pairs have finished, invite them to share their resolutions with the class. **OL**

Reading Check

Answer A win-win solution is an agreement or outcome that gives each party something it wants.

🏠 Home, School, and Community

At Home Students can benefit from practicing health concepts in a safe environment before they are called upon to apply behaviors in a real conflict situation. Suggest that students discuss this lesson with their families and try the T.A.L.K. strategy at home the next time they have a conflict with their parents, guardians, or siblings. Invite volunteers to share how well the strategy worked, without revealing the nature of the conflict. **OL**

165

R Reading Strategy

Analyzing a Chart As you review **Figure 7.2** with students, address each step of the mediation process. Discuss the caption question. Then ask: Why is it important that both parties agree to seek a mediator's help? Sample answer: *Both must participate fully with the mediator in order to resolve the conflict.* Then ask: What role does the mediator play in the conflict? Sample answer: *The mediator serves to prevent the conflict from building, helps each side see the other's point of view, helps evaluate solutions, and helps reach a compromise.* **OL**

Academic Vocabulary

Neutral Have volunteers read aloud the definition and the example sentence. Ask: Why is it important for a mediator to be neutral? How do you think a mediator demonstrates that he or she is neutral? 📁

📖 Reading Check

Answer *Any two:* good communicators, active listening skills, fair and neutral judges, effective problem solvers

Caption Answer

Figure Caption, p. 167
Sample answer: These traits reflect a person who has good communication skills, good problem-solving skills, and an interest in helping people—all of which are useful for solving conflicts.

▶ **FIGURE 7.2**

R A key element to successful mediation is cooperation. Each party must be willing to work with the other and the mediator. **How does a mediator help people in conflict find a solution?**

Steps in the Mediation Process
1. The parties involved in the conflict agree to seek an independent mediator's help.
2. The mediator hears both sides of the dispute.
3. The mediator and the parties work to clarify the wants and needs of each party.
4. The parties and mediator brainstorm possible solutions.
5. The parties and mediator evaluate each possible outcome.
6. The parties choose a solution that works for each of them.

Academic Vocabulary

neutral (NOO truhl) *(adjective)* not supporting a side in an argument. *When two of your friends are fighting, it is best for you to remain neutral.*

Visit glencoe.com and complete the Interactive Study Guide for Lesson 3.

The Mediation Process

The mediation process begins in a private location. The only people present are the mediator and the two parties with the problem. Each party presents his or her side. The mediator, who is **neutral**, listens carefully. The mediator may ask questions to make sure each side understands the other's point of view. Finally, the mediator will steer both sides toward a **compromise.** This is *an arrangement in which each side gives up something to reach a satisfactory solution.*

Effective mediators must be good communicators. They must have good listening skills, enabling them to hear each side of an argument. They must also be fair and neutral judges. Finally, good mediators need to be effective problem solvers. They need to be able to get to the root of the conflict.

Peer Mediation

Do you think you have what it takes to be a good mediator? If you do, you may want to find out if your school has a peer-mediation program. Many schools today do. Teens are often good mediators because they can put problems into words that other students understand. **Figure 7.3** shows some other traits of an effective peer mediator. Which of these traits do you have?

Students who want to be peer mediators need to go through a training program. This is done on the students' own time and is voluntary. Ask your teacher or school counselor if your school has a peer-mediation program.

📖 Reading Check

Identify What are two skills shared by effective mediators?

▶ What Teens Want to Know ◀

How do I know if I need a peer mediator? Sometimes teens find a conflict quickly escalates into a disagreement or physical fight. If your school has a peer mediation program, refer to it often so that students remember to use it. Frequently discuss successes of the program, refer students to the program, and identify mediators in the class. In the absence of such a program, tell students to trust their feelings. Encourage them to talk to someone—a parent, teacher, or guidance counselor—about their conflict before it escalates. **OL**

▼ FIGURE 7.3

TRAITS OF AN EFFECTIVE PEER MEDIATOR

One trait of an effective peer mediator is good listening skills. Why do you think it is important for a peer mediator to have many of these traits?

Problem Solver
Easy to Talk to
Enthusiastic
Responsible

Mature
Effective Listener
Decisive
Interested
Alert
Trustworthy
Open-minded
Reliable

ASSESS

Assessment Resources

Lesson Review Quiz
- *ExamView*
- Fast Files Activities
- Online Quizzes and Activities

Reteaching
- Assign Concept Map 7-3 or Reteaching Activity 7-3 in the Fast Files.
- Have pairs create an informational poster that describes the steps in resolving conflicts using the T.A.L.K. strategy. Display posters throughout the school.

Enrichment
- Assign Enrichment Activity 7-3 in the Fast Files.
- Invite students to undergo peer mediation training. If your school does not have a peer mediation program, challenge students to implement one with help from the student guidance counselor and the school principal.

CLOSE

Have students describe how the T.A.L.K. strategy and peer mediation are two effective ways to resolve conflicts.

Lesson 3 Review

 After You Read

Review this lesson for new terms, major headings, and Reading Checks.

What I Learned

1. *Vocabulary* What is *compromise*? How is it used in conflict resolution?

2. *Recall* What are the four steps in the T.A.L.K. strategy?

3. *Identify* Name a skill or value that an effective mediator has.

Thinking Critically

4. *Apply* Think about an actual conflict you experienced. Then explain how the skill of conflict resolution helped or could have helped you reach a solution.

5. *Evaluate* Can learning peer-mediation skills be useful to teens even if they are not interested in becoming peer mediators? Why or why not?

Applying Health Skills

6. *Communication Skills* Imagine a situation in which younger students are involved in a conflict. With several classmates, role-play how peer mediators might interact with the students involved.

Go Online For more Lesson Review Activities, go to **glencoe.com**.

Lesson 3: Resolving Conflicts **167**

Lesson 3 Review Answers

1. Compromise is an arrangement in which each side gives up something to reach a satisfactory solution. Conflict resolution settles a disagreement in a way that satisfies both sides.

2. **T**ake a time-out; **A**llow each person to tell his or her side; **L**et each person ask questions; **K**eep brainstorming.

3. *Any one:* good communication skills, active listening skills, fair and neutral judges, effective problem solvers

4. Answers should include an application of the T.A.L.K. strategy as well as an understanding of compromise and win-win solutions.

5. Most students will agree that these skills are useful to help resolve any life problem.

6. Role-plays should include each step of the mediation process as described in **Figure 7.2**, on page 166.

Building Health Skills

TALKing Out a Problem

Skill

Conflict Resolution

Activating Prior Knowledge

Invite volunteers to share experiences they have had with successfully resolving a conflict. Have them explain what they did to solve the conflict and whether or not both parties felt like the solution was a good one.

- **Objective** After completing the activity, students will be able to use the T.A.L.K. strategy to resolve a conflict.
- **Time** 30 minutes
- **Materials** paper, pencil

Teacher Classroom Resources

 Building Health Skills Activity

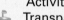 Transparency 7-2

Model

- Ask: How did the conflict between Mary and Ally start? *They disagreed over responsibilities.* Have students identify the steps in the T.A.L.K. strategy. Ask: From talking to each other, what did Mary and Ally learn? *they both wanted to decide how to divide the work* What was their solution? *to do research separately and combine the results*

National Health Standards Addressed

4.8.3, 7.8.2

Building Health Skills

Accessing Information
Practicing Healthful Behaviors
Stress Management
Analyzing Influences
Communication Skills
Refusal Skills
Conflict Resolution
Decision Making
Goal Setting
Advocacy

What Is Conflict Resolution?

Conflict resolution involves finding a positive solution to a disagreement or preventing it from becoming a larger conflict. The T.A.L.K. strategy can help you resolve conflicts in a positive way.

T Take a time-out, at least 30 minutes.

A Allow each person to tell his or her side uninterrupted.

L Let each person ask questions.

K Keep brainstorming to find a good solution.

TALKing Out a Problem

Follow the Model, Practice, and Apply steps to help you master this important health skill.

❶ Model

Read how Mary and Ally use the T.A.L.K. strategy to work on a project together.

Mary and Ally were having trouble working together on a class project.

Mary: Let's take a break for a minute and then try to work out a plan.

T—Take a time-out.

Ally: I feel I don't have any control over how the parts of the project are divided.

A—Allow each person to tell his or her side uninterrupted.

Mary: I'm sorry. How do you think we should divide the project?

L—Let each person ask questions.

Ally: How about if you do the library research and I do research on the Internet at home?

K—Keep brainstorming to find a good solution.

Mary: That sounds good! Then we can both write parts of the paper and combine our work into a finished project.

168

Teaching Tips

To Compromise or Not? Remind students that most successful relationships involve compromise. Brainstorm with students situations when compromise would not be appropriate (health in jeopardy, emergencies, family values, breaking the law).

The Power of Win-Win The best outcome for a conflict is a "win-win" solution. This allows everyone to have their needs met so nobody feels resentful or ignored. Practicing the T.A.L.K. steps can actually improve relationships!

❷ Practice

Sophie uses the T.A.L.K. strategy at home when she has a disagreement with her brother. Read the passage and practice conflict resolution by completing the activity below.

Sophie used the T.A.L.K. strategy at home. Sophie and her brother are having a disagreement over whose turn it is to wash after-dinner dishes. Sophie had taken her brother's turn the week before so that he could make soccer practice. Now it is her brother's turn to do the dishes, but he claims not to recall this agreement.

Write a conversation between Sophie and her brother in which they use the T.A.L.K. strategy. Label each step with a T., A., L., or K. Write an end to the conversation where Sophie and her brother find an agreeable solution.

❸ Apply

Apply what you have learned about conflict resolution by completing the activity below.

Imagine that you are dealing with one of the conflicts listed below. Show how you would resolve this conflict with a healthy win-win solution. Share your strategy with classmates and explain why win-win solutions are the most desirable way to resolve conflicts.

- You and a friend each want to see a different movie. Neither one of you is willing to compromise.
- Your friend is having a sleepover the same night that your cousins are coming into town. You want to go to the sleepover, but your parents want you to stay home and spend time with your cousins.

Self-Check
- Did I use each step in the T.A.L.K. strategy?
- Did I show a win-win solution?
- Did I explain why win-win solutions are desirable?

Building Health Skills

Practice

- After students have read the introductory paragraph, instruct them to work in small groups to discuss possible solutions.
- Address each step in the T.A.L.K. strategy as a class. List all responses on the board. Discuss how the answer to each step leads them to resolve the conflict.

Apply/Assess

- Have students work individually to apply the steps in the T.A.L.K. strategy to their chosen conflict.
- Lead a class discussion for each conflict. Diagram the T.A.L.K. strategy on the board and invite students to share their ideas for each step. Then allow time for students to write their conversations.
- Have the class evaluate each decision and vote for the one they think offers the best win-win solution.
- You may wish to distribute the Building Health Skills Activity in the Fast Files.

ASSESSMENT SCORING

Using a rubric, student work should meet all criteria to achieve the highest score.

Skills Student work:
- includes a time-out from the situation.
- explains both points of view.
- asks questions to clarify the conflict.
- shows brainstorming to find a solution.

Concepts Student work:
- presents a win-win solution.
- demonstrates a health-enhancing solution.
- provides accurate information about win-win solutions.
- includes comprehensive information about win-win solutions.

Unnecessary Roughness

Objectives

After completing this activity, students will be able to:

- Describe trends in fan behavior at sporting events.
- Identify causes of anger and poor sportsmanship displayed by fans at sporting events.
- Form an opinion of the role of popular culture in promoting poor sportsmanship.

Motivator

Ask students to describe poor behavior they have witnessed at sporting events.

Teaching the Activity

- Have students ask a parent or other trusted adult to describe changes in fan behavior they have noted over a period of years. Then have students work as a class to determine the percentage of interviewed adults who felt that fan behavior had become better, the percentage that felt there was no change, and the percentage that felt fan behavior had become worse. **OL**
- Have students watch a sporting event on television. Ask students to record specific instances of good sportsmanship by the fans or the players. Have students share their results with the class. Then have students prepare pamphlets encouraging good sportsmanship at school sporting events. **OL**

Bad behavior is increasing at sporting events—and both fans and players are crying "foul."

UNNECESSARY ROUGHNESS

Nine fans were injured in a fight between National Basketball Association (NBA) players and fans in Auburn Hills, Michigan. In Philadelphia, crowds frustrated by the team's awful playing booed Santa Claus during a half-time show. Behavior at some Philadelphia Eagles' football games got so bad that officials set up a court in the stadium—with a jail—to handle the worst offenders.

WHO'S TO BLAME?

How did fan behavior become so horrible? University of Pennsylvania professor Ken Shropshire thinks the change in the way fans relate to their teams is fueled by everything from close-up TV coverage to video games. "With the realistic, violent sports video games and the pervasiveness of sports on television, fans feel they're actually part of things now," he says. "All the major sports convey that fans are right in the middle. So they feel they should be part of the game."

Games aren't mere athletic contests. They are in-your-face productions. Laser-light-show introductions and scoreboard messages calling for more noise contribute to an atmosphere of confrontation.

"There is no question that the anger in the voice of a small percentage of fans has escalated," says Tom Gamboa, first-base coach for the Kansas City Royals. "I have no idea when this started, but there are some people now, when they pay for a sports event, instead of watching it, they feel like they're entitled to take part in it."

REMEMBER: IT'S JUST A GAME

The bad behavior isn't limited to pro sports, either. Many colleges take pride in their lack of hospitality for visiting teams. Players shooting free throws at basketball games used to be given respectful silence. Now fans attempt to distract them by jeering and waving towels.

At Duke University, a group called the Cameron Crazies specializes in personal taunts that often cross the line. They once dangled chicken nuggets near an overweight visiting player. Many argue that the Crazies are just having fun.

That visiting player might have a different opinion.

© Grant Halverson/AP

Activity   *Media, Technology, and Culture*

Media Analysis Have students discuss ways that popular culture encourages bad sportsmanship, for example, by showing a player's rude behavior on the news, rather than showing an excellent play. Ask students to write an essay giving their opinion of the media's role in promoting bad behavior at sporting events. Have students share their completed essays with the class. **OL**

Reading Review

FOLDABLES Study Organizer

Foldables® and Other Study Aids Take out the Foldable® that you created for Lesson 1 and any graphic organizers that you created for Lessons 1–3. Find a partner and quiz each other using these study aids.

Lesson 1 The Nature of Conflict

Main Idea A conflict can be caused by just about anything.

- Conflicts can be minor or major, interpersonal or internal.
- Conflicts with parents or guardians can be over limits, responsibilities, or expectations. Conflicts between siblings can involve property or space, or can take the form of competition or rivalry.
- You can use the six steps of the decision-making process to resolve a conflict.
- Conflicts at school can be over an incident or differences in personality, beliefs, or opinions.
- The best way to deal with bullies is to walk away from them and share the matter with a trusted adult.

Lesson 2 Preventing Conflicts

Main Idea You can prevent a conflict from building by recognizing both the physical and emotional warning signs.

- The physical signs of conflict include: feeling like there is a knot in your stomach, faster heart rate, a lump in your throat, balled-up fists, cold or sweaty palms, and a sudden surge of energy.

- The emotional signs of conflict include: feeling concerned, getting defensive, wanting to cry, not feeling valued, wanting to lash out, and wanting to escape.
- Factors that cause conflicts to build include anger, jealousy, group pressure, and the use of alcohol and other drugs.
- Ways to prevent conflicts from building include learning to understand your feelings; keeping your conflicts private; avoiding alcohol or other drugs; showing respect for yourself and for others; accepting people who are different from you; and trying to put yourself in another person's situation.

Lesson 3 Resolving Conflicts

Main Idea Conflicts that remain unsettled or unresolved can damage relationships.

- Conflict resolution involves solving a disagreement in a way that satisfies both sides.
- Effective skills for resolving conflicts include the T.A.L.K. strategy. The letters stand for <u>T</u>ime-out, <u>A</u>llow each person to tell his or her side, <u>L</u>et each person ask questions, and <u>K</u>eep brainstorming.
- Compromise is important in conflict resolution because it helps achieve a win-win solution.
- Traits of a good mediator include conflict-resolution skills, good communication skills, fairness, and an ability to help solve problems.
- A win-win solution is a solution to a conflict that satisfies both sides. This is the most desirable solution to a conflict.

Teaching Tips

Integrating Technology Middle school students learn best and retain information longer when they are able to manipulate the concepts that they are learning. One way of doing this is to use teaching strategies that integrate computer programs. Students might use a spreadsheet program to organize or manipulate data. They might use Internet gateway software to research topics and gather or report data. They might even construct and maintain their own Web page.

Assessment Resources

- Chapter 7 Summary and Activity
- Audio Summaries
- Reading Tutor
- Performance Assessment
- Chapter 7 Test
- *ExamView*
- Vocabulary PuzzleMaker
- Online Learning Center

Reading Review

Study Aids

- **Using the Dinah Zike Foldable® Study Organizer** Have students use the Foldable® to review the causes of conflicts at home and outside the home. Ask students to give a definition for the word *conflict*.

  FOLDABLES® Study Organizer

- **Online Learning Tools** Have students go to the *Teen Health* Online Learning Center at **glencoe.com** to:

  - Download a **Podcast**.

  - Download free **Study-to-Go** content to their PDAs or cell phones. **STUDY TO GO**

Vocabulary Review

- **Categorizing** Have students sort all the vocabulary terms in this chapter into specific categories. Then instruct students to switch category titles with a partner and re-sort the terms accordingly.

Reviewing Vocabulary and Main Ideas

1. conflict
2. Prejudice
3. bully
4. escalate
5. Revenge
6. mob mentality
7. False, Take a time-out.
8. False, win-win
9. True
10. False, compromise

Thinking Critically

11. *Sample answer:* Zoey could make her own joke about it. If Kathy still does not stop, Zoey could calmly explain to Kathy in private how the teasing makes her feel. If that does not work, Zoey could talk to a trusted adult.

12. *Sample answer:* finding a compromise that both parties can agree to; people involved in the conflict might think that their sacrifice is greater than the other person's.

 Go Online

Have students visit **glencoe.com** to take the Chapter 7 quiz.

172

CHAPTER

7 Assessment

 After You Read

HEALTH INVENTORY
Now that you have read the chapter, look back at your answers to the Health Inventory on the chapter opener. Is there anything that you should do differently?

Reviewing Vocabulary and Main Ideas

On a sheet of paper, write the numbers 1–6. After each number, write the term from the list that best completes each sentence.

- bully
- conflict
- conflict resolution
- escalate
- labeling
- mob mentality
- prejudice
- revenge

Lesson 1 The Nature of Conflict

1. A(n) _____ is a disagreement between people with opposing viewpoints, ideas, or goals.

2. _____ is a negative and unjustly formed opinion, usually against people of a different racial, religious, or cultural group.

3. A(n) _____ is someone who picks on individuals who are smaller or weaker.

Lesson 2 Preventing Conflicts

4. A conflict that becomes more serious is said to _____.

5. _____ is punishment, injury, or insult to the person seen as the cause of the strong emotion.

6. People who act or behave in a certain and often negative manner because others are doing it have a(n) _____.

Lesson 3 Resolving Conflicts

*On a sheet of paper, write the numbers 7–10. Write **True** or **False** for each statement below. If the statement is false, change the underlined word or phrase to make it true.*

7. The *T* in the T.A.L.K. strategy stands for Tell the other person to cooperate.

8. When a conflict is resolved to the satisfaction of both parties, a win-lose solution has been achieved.

9. Mediation can help two people unable to reach a compromise on their own.

10. An arrangement in which each side gives up something to reach a satisfactory solution is known as a resolution.

Thinking Critically

Using complete sentences, answer the following questions on a sheet of paper.

11. **Synthesize** Zoey recently moved from a different part of the country. She speaks with an accent that is different than that of the students in her new school. Kathy, a girl in class, imitates Zoey's accent, teasing her whenever she speaks. Kathy's teasing really bothers Zoey. What should she do?

172 Chapter 7: Conflict Resolution

 Go Online Visit **glencoe.com** and take the Online Quiz for Chapter 7.

HEALTH INVENTORY WRAP-UP

Dealing with Conflict As students review their answers to the Health Inventory, have them write key ideas, vocabulary terms, or other concepts from the chapter that address the question and lead them to change their answer. Then, for questions that students selected the answers *sometimes* or *never*, have them write what they would do in that situation.

12. **Evaluate** Which step in the peer mediation process do you think would be the most challenging? Explain your answer.

Write About It

13. **Narrative Writing** Think about a difficult decision you have had to make that involved an internal conflict. Explain how you resolved this conflict.

14. **Expository Writing** Write a story about an imaginary conflict between two people. Tell how conflict-resolution skills were used to bring about a win-win solution.

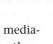 **Applying Technology**

Cleaning Up Conflict Q & A

You and a partner will use PowerPoint® to create a question-and-answer game that covers the various elements of conflict resolution discussed in this chapter.

- Create a list of 20 questions and answers from the chapter content.
- Open a new PowerPoint® project. You will need 42 slides. Each question gets a slide. Each answer gets a slide. The first slide is for the title of your game. The last slide will contain any concluding remarks you want to make about conflict resolution.
- Enter all of your written content into the slides. Edit for clarity. Save your game.
- Exchange your game with another group.

Standardized Test Practice

Reading

The following are observations made by famous people about conflict. Read the quotes, and then answer the questions.

A. Conflict is inevitable, but combat is optional.
—Max Lucado

B. Whenever you're in conflict with someone, there is one factor that can make the difference between damaging your relationship and deepening it. That factor is attitude.
—William James

C. A good manager doesn't try to eliminate conflict; he tries to keep it from wasting the energies of his people.
—Robert Townsend

D. You can't shake hands with a clenched fist.
—Indira Gandhi

E. Don't be afraid of conflict. Remember, a kite rises against, not with, the wind.
—Hamilton Mabie

> **TEST-TAKING TIP**
>
> When reading, make sure you understand all words and phrases. If you are not sure of a meaning, look the word up in a good dictionary.

1. The two quotes that suggest conflict is a fact of life are
   A. A and B.
   B. B and C.
   C. A and C.
   D. D and E.

2. Which two quotes carry the message that "violence never solves a problem"?
   A. The quotes by Max Lucado and Robert Townsend
   B. The quotes by William James and Hamilton Mabie
   C. The quotes by Robert Townsend and Indira Gandhi
   D. The quotes by Max Lucado and Indira Gandhi

Chapter 7 Assessment **173**

 Applying Technology

Cleaning Up Conflict Q & A
Equipment needs: PowerPoint® or similar software
Help students review the project requirements; remind them that they should plan their questions and answers before opening PowerPoint®. Then let students choose their partners. Create a sign-up sheet if computer access is limited, and establish a time limit for each pair's computer use. When students have completed their games, provide time for sharing and playing other partners' games.

Write About It

13. **Narrative Writing** Explain that in narratives, characters, setting, and plot are presented in a clear and logical order. Students should clearly describe an internal conflict and how the conflict was resolved. They should also evaluate the outcome of the solution.

14. **Expository Writing** Tell students that expository writing is meant to inform others. Stories should describe the conflict and the appropriate skills to resolve the issue.

Standardized Test Practice

1. C
2. C

Test-Taking Tips

Preparing Students for Tests Give students many opportunities to practice taking standardized tests. Routinely give them questions written in the same style as typical test questions. Consider using these types of questions for chapter tests and quizzes, or as warm-ups for the daily lesson. When students answer these practice questions, set up an environment that is typical of a standardized test environment. Start students at the same time by having them flip over their papers. Set a time limit. Arrange seating appropriately.

CHAPTER 8 pp. 174–201	Standards		Skills and Activities
	National	State/Local	
	National Health Education Standards 1.8.1, 5.8.2, 5.8.7, 7.8.2, 7.8.3		**HEALTH QUIZ**, *p. 175* **BUILDING HEALTH SKILLS** Standing Up to Harassment, *pp. 196–197* **HANDS-ON HEALTH** A Nonviolent Response to a Threatening Situation, *p. 198*
Lesson 1 **Avoiding and Preventing Violence** *pp. 176–179*	National Health Education Standards 1.8.3, 1.8.5, 1.8.8, 1.8.9, 2.8.4, 2.8.5, 2.8.9, 2.8.10, 6.8.1, 7.8.3		**What Teens Think** What can schools do to protect students from violence?, *p. 177*
Lesson 2 **Dealing with Violence** *pp. 180–183*	National Health Education Standards 1.8.5, 3.8.4, 4.8.4, 7.8.3, 8.8.1, 8.8.3		**DEVELOPING GOOD CHARACTER** Caring, *p. 181*
Lesson 3 **Bullying and Harassment** *pp. 184–187*	National Health Education Standards 2.8.3, 2.8.4, 4.8.1, 4.8.2, 4.8.3, 4.8.4, 7.8.3		**Go Online** Stopping the Bullies, *p. 185* **HEALTH SKILLS ACTIVITY** *Communication Skills* Using "I" Messages, *p. 186*
Lesson 4 **Abuse** *pp. 188–191*	National Health Education Standards 1.8.3, 2.8.1, 3.8.4, 4.8.4, 8.8.3		**Careers for the 21st Century** Family Counselor, *p. 190*
Lesson 5 **Preventing and Coping with Abuse** *pp. 192–195*	National Health Education Standards 1.8.3, 1.8.4, 1.8.5, 2.8.1, 2.8.2, 3.8.2, 3.8.4, 4.8.4, 7.8.2, 7.8.3, 8.8.1		

PACING THE CHAPTER

Lesson 1	45 min	**Lesson 4**	30 min	**Chapter Review**	45 min
Lesson 2	30 min	**Lesson 5**	30 min	**Hands-on Health**	30 min
Lesson 3	45 min	**Building Health Skills**	45 min		

BLOCK SCHEDULING

For block scheduling, assign students Building Health Skills feature *Standing Up to Harassment*, pages 196–197, and Guided Reading and Writing. 📁

Planning Guide

Glencoe Exclusive!
TeacherWorks Plus™
All-In-One Planner and Resource Center

Reproducible Resources	Assessment	Media and Technology
Chapter FAST FILE Resources Chapter Summaries and Activities REVIEW Building Health Skills Activity TEACH Performance Assessment Activity EXTEND Universal Access Activities TEACH Parent Letter and Activities 📁 **Student Activities Workbook** TEACH 📁 **Reading Tutor** TEACH	Building Health Skills Activity, *pp. 196–197* Chapter 8 Assessment, *pp. 200–201* **Chapter FAST FILE Resources** Performance Assessment Activity, *p. 4* Chapter 8 Test, *p. 7* 💿 *ExamView® Assessment Suite*	TeacherWorks Plus includes: ● Interactive Teacher Edition ● Lesson Planner with Calendar ● Access to all blackline masters ● Correlations to standards 💿 StudentWorks™ Plus 🖱 Online Student Edition Dinah Zike's Teaching Health with Foldables®
Chapter FAST FILE Resources Concept Mapping Activity 8-1 REVIEW Health Lab 8-1 EXTEND Enrichment Activity 8-1 EXTEND Lesson Plan 8-1 Guided Reading and Writing 8-1 TEACH Reteaching Activity 8-1 REVIEW	Lesson 1 Review, *p. 179* 🖱 Vocabulary PuzzleMaker 💿 *ExamView® Assessment Suite*	🖱 Vocabulary PuzzleMaker 💿 *ExamView® Assessment Suite* 💿 StudentWorks™ Plus 🔦 Transparency 8-1 **Go Online** glencoe.com
Chapter FAST FILE Resources Concept Mapping Activity 8-2 REVIEW Cross-Curriculum Activity 8-2 EXTEND Enrichment Activity 8-2 EXTEND Lesson Plan 8-2 Guided Reading and Writing 8-2 TEACH Reteaching Activity 8-2 REVIEW	Lesson 2 Review, *p. 183* 🖱 Vocabulary PuzzleMaker 💿 *ExamView® Assessment Suite*	🖱 Vocabulary PuzzleMaker 💿 *ExamView® Assessment Suite* 💿 StudentWorks™ Plus 🔦 Transparency 8-2 **Go Online** glencoe.com
Chapter FAST FILE Resources Concept Mapping Activity 8-3 REVIEW Decision-Making Activity 8-3 EXTEND Enrichment Activity 8-3 EXTEND Lesson Plan 8-3 Guided Reading and Writing 8-3 TEACH Reteaching Activity 8-3 REVIEW	Lesson 3 Review, *p. 187* 🖱 Vocabulary PuzzleMaker 💿 *ExamView® Assessment Suite*	🖱 Vocabulary PuzzleMaker 💿 *ExamView® Assessment Suite* 💿 StudentWorks™ Plus 🔦 Transparency 8-3 **Go Online** glencoe.com
Chapter FAST FILE Resources Concept Mapping Activity 8-4 REVIEW Decision-Making Activity 8-4 EXTEND Enrichment Activity 8-4 EXTEND Lesson Plan 8-4 Guided Reading and Writing 8-4 TEACH Reteaching Activity 8-4 REVIEW	Lesson 4 Review, *p. 191* 🖱 Vocabulary PuzzleMaker 💿 *ExamView® Assessment Suite*	🖱 Vocabulary PuzzleMaker 💿 *ExamView® Assessment Suite* 💿 StudentWorks™ Plus 🔦 Transparency 8-4 **Go Online** glencoe.com
Chapter FAST FILE Resources Concept Mapping Activity 8-5 REVIEW Cross-Curriculum Activity 8-5 EXTEND Enrichment Activity 8-5 EXTEND Lesson Plan 8-5 Guided Reading and Writing 8-5 TEACH Reteaching Activity 8-5 REVIEW	Lesson 5 Review, *p. 195* 🖱 Vocabulary PuzzleMaker 💿 *ExamView® Assessment Suite*	🖱 Vocabulary PuzzleMaker 💿 *ExamView® Assessment Suite* 💿 StudentWorks™ Plus 🔦 Transparency 8-5 **Go Online** glencoe.com

Chapter and Lesson Resources

The *Teen Health* resources are designed for differentiated learning abilities. You may want to use the coded items in this way:

REVIEW —activities to review or reinforce content
TEACH —activities to teach basic concepts
EXTEND —activities to extend or enrich lesson content

 OUT OF TIME?

Use Health Skills Activity *Using "I" Messages*, page 186 or Developing Good Character, page 181.

Bullying in Schools

According to a recent study at the UCLA/Rand Center for Adolescent Health Promotion, more than 20 percent of 12-year-olds are either bullies, victims, or both. Another survey found that 11 percent of students in grades 6 to 10 reported being bullied. In the United States, bullying has traditionally been viewed as a normal part of growing up. In recent years, greater emphasis has been put on ending these abusive behaviors at schools, where bullying is most likely to occur.

Bullying can take many forms. Physical bullying includes hitting and kicking as well as threats of physical harm. Emotional bullying often involves excluding a child from activities, such as isolating a child at lunch in the cafeteria. Verbal bullying often involves taunting, name calling, and laughing at another child. A new form of bullying is cyber bullying—bullying through e-mail, instant messaging, or Internet chat rooms.

As you teach students about bullying, provide them with strategies to deal with this form of abuse.

- **Don't show anger.** Getting angry makes the bully feel powerful.

- **Walk away.** Bullies want to see a reaction from bullying, and if there is no reaction the bully may get bored and stop.

- **Never try to be physical back to the bully.** The bully may relish the fight.

- **Tell an adult.** Parents, teachers, school counselors, principals, and lunchroom personnel can help stop the bully.

- **Talk about the bullying with a friend, a teacher, or a school counselor.**

Youth Violence as a Public Health Problem

The traditional approach to violent youth is to see it as a criminal justice concern. In recent years, though, youth violence has increasingly been addressed as a public health problem. Such an approach allows the teacher, the counselor, and other professionals to consider the environmental, social, and mental health factors that contribute to youth violence. With the public health approach, the emphasis can be on prevention rather than mainly on punishment.

As you teach students about youth violence, emphasize a focus on the causes of violence. If the causes can be understood, then methods to prevent violence can be implemented. This is part of the public health approach to youth violence. It is similar to a public health approach to any other problem, such as the outbreak and spread of a communicable disease. Discovering the cause of the outbreak is the first step in stopping the epidemic.

Schools have a tremendous responsibility in preventing violence among youth. Schools must create an environment in which students feel safe. In schools, any form of aggressive behavior must be seen as unacceptable.

The National Association of School Psychologists (NASP) has worked to identify elements that are common in school programs that focus on violence prevention and intervention. The following are among the characteristics the NASP cites:

- **Effective programs implement specific programs such as peer mediation, conflict resolution, anger management, social skills training, and problem solving.**

- **Effective programs encourage students to recognize potential threats and inform an adult of those threats.**

- **Effective programs minimize both the availability of weapons and their use.**

- **Effective programs create a climate of caring and respect in which every student is valued.**

Support for Teaching Reading

Reading Preview

Activating Background Vocabulary Ask students to write the main terms of the chapter on index cards. Examples of these terms are *violence, homicide, abuse,* etc. Direct students to write their own definitions of the terms on the backs of the cards. While students read the chapter, have them adjust or add to their definitions as necessary.

FOLDABLES Study Organizer *Dinah Zike's Reading and Study Skills for Teen Health* provides interactive graphic organizers that help students comprehend and retain health concepts as they read. Use the Foldable® on page 175 or find more Foldables® activities for the chapter on **Violence Prevention** in the separate booklet, available in the TCR.

Lesson 1   Avoiding and Preventing Violence

Reading with a Purpose Direct students to read the section titled **Factors in Teen Violence** to discover the various factors that cause young people to become involved in violent behavior. After reading the section, have students respond in a brief descriptive paragraph. Continue to give students a purpose for reading each section.

Lesson 2   Dealing with Violence

Monitoring Comprehension Show students how to find answers to their questions when they become aware they do not comprehend the text. For example, ask: "What is my purpose in reading **Effects of Violence on Victims**? My purpose must be to learn the ways a victim may be affected by violence." Have students write the answers to their questions and to reread if necessary.

Lesson 3   Bullying and Harassment

Pairs Reading Have student pairs take turns reading aloud. Name one student as the coach and the other as reader. Have the reader read **Dealing with a Bully** aloud, while the coach listens. After reading, have the coach summarize the main ideas, and have the reader clarify any questions. Direct students to reverse roles and continue reading.

Lesson 4   Abuse

Skim and Scan Show students how to *skim* the lesson to find main ideas by identifying titles and headings, such as: **What Is Abuse?**, **Kinds of Abuse**, and **Effects of Abuse.** Next, ask students to *scan* the lesson to find specific meanings of key words, such as *abuse* or *neglect.* Have students discuss the main ideas and terms with a partner.

Lesson 5   Preventing and Coping with Abuse

Interactive Reading Have students write three questions regarding ways to deal with abuse. The questions must begin with the words *why, when, where,* or *how.* As they read about ways to prevent and cope with abuse, direct students to discuss the answers they find with a classmate.

Post Reading

Informational Report Guide students to gather additional data about violence and abuse using all available library and Internet resources. Have students write an informative report about some aspect of violence prevention, editing for appropriate grammar, spelling, and usage.

Key for Using the Teacher Wraparound Edition

Use this key to help you identify the different types of prompts found in the Teacher Wraparound Edition.

R **Reading Strategies** activities help you teach reading skills and vocabulary.

C **Critical Thinking** strategies help students apply and extend what they have learned.

U **Universal Access** activities provide differentiated instruction for students learning to speak English, along with suggestions for teaching various types of learners.

HS **Health Skills Practice** activities reinforce Health Skills concepts and help students apply these skills in their everyday lives.

W **Writing Support** activities provide writing opportunities to help students comprehend the text.

AL **Active Learning** strategies provide a variety of activities for presenting lesson content, including Quick Demos and engaging classroom projects that get students actively involved.

Key to Ability Levels

Teaching Strategies and activities have been coded for ability level and appropriateness.

AL Activities for students working above grade level

OL Activities for students working on grade level

BL Activities for students working below grade level

EL Activities for English Learners

Symbols

 Transparencies

 CD-ROM

 glencoe.com

📁 Print Resources

Chapter at a Glance

Lesson 1 identifies factors that contribute to teen violence, describes measures taken to prevent violence in schools, and explains ways to be protected from violence.

Lesson 2 describes ways to avoid becoming a victim of violence, identifies actions victims of violence need to take, and advocates for the defeat of violence in America.

Lesson 3 describes ways of dealing with bullies and identifies different forms of harassment.

Lesson 4 explains forms of abuse and describes the effects of abuse on its victims.

Lesson 5 describes the cycle of abuse, develops a plan to stop the cycle of abuse, and identifies where to get help if you are abused.

R Reading Strategy

Interpreting the Photo Have students look at the photo as you introduce the topic of violence prevention. Point out that violence is a problem at many schools and in many communities. Ask each student to make a list of three ways that violence in schools can be prevented. Have volunteers share one entry from their lists with the class. OL

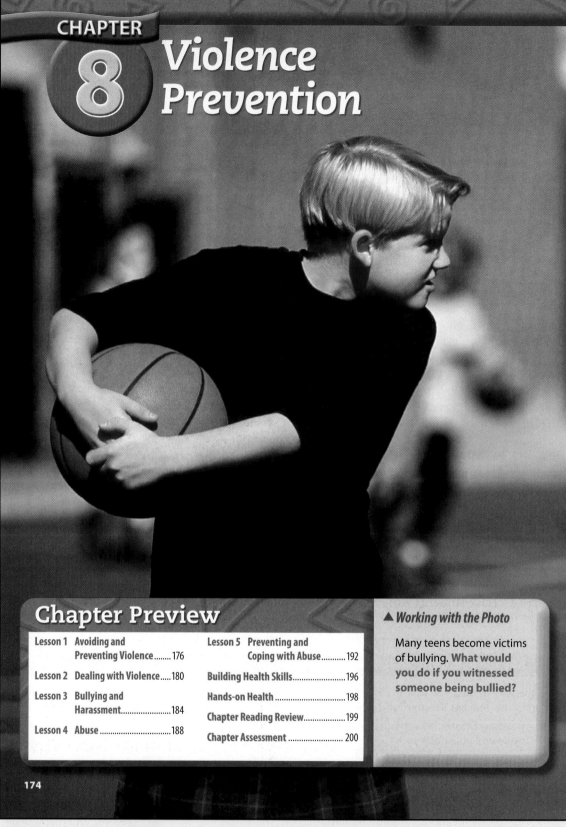

Chapter Preview

174

▲ *Working with the Photo*

Many teens become victims of bullying. **What would you do if you witnessed someone being bullied?**

🏃 Universal Access

Differentiated Learning Glencoe provides teacher support and student materials for all learners in the health classroom.

● Spanish *Glosario* and chapter summaries assist English Language Learners.
● *Reading Tutor* and related worksheets support reluctant readers.

● Universal Access strategies throughout the Teacher Wraparound Edition and Fast Files help you present materials for gifted students, at-risk students, physically impaired students, and those with behavior disorders or learning disabilities.

Start-Up Activities

📖 **Before You Read**   What do you know about violence and abuse?
Take the short quiz on this page. Keep a record of your answers.

HEALTH QUIZ Answer *true* or *false* for each of the following statements:

1. Violent gangs are found only in large cities.
2. Victims of violence can suffer emotional and physical injuries.
3. There are no effective ways to deal with bullies.
4. The term *abuse* refers only to physical violence.
5. When abuse occurs in a family, all members may be affected.

ANSWERS: 1. False; 2. True; 3. False; 4. False; 5. True

FOLDABLES® Study Organizer

📖 **As You Read**   Make this Foldable® to record what you learn about
violence prevention at home and away from home. Begin with a sheet of
11″ × 17″ paper.

1 Fold the short sides of the sheet of paper inward so they meet at the middle.

2 Label the Foldable® with the title "Violence Prevention" in bold letters along the upper edge. On one of the front sides of the Foldable®, write "Home." On the other front side, write "Away from Home."

3 Under the appropriate tabs, list ways you can reduce your risk of becoming a victim of violence both at home and away from home.

> Violence | Prevention
> Home | Away from Home

G⊙ Online — Visit **glencoe.com** and play the Chapter 8 crossword puzzle game.

175

FOCUS

Activating Prior Knowledge

What I Know Ask students to identify reasons why some teens become involved in violent behavior. For each reason identified, ask a volunteer to describe a way to prevent such violence.

Guide to Reading

Building Vocabulary

- Explain to students that the word part *homi-* means "human being" and the word part *-cide* means "to kill." Have students use this information to define *homicide.*
- Use Vocabulary PuzzleMaker to reinforce vocabulary terms.

Reading Strategy

Classifying Demonstrate how to make the chart by drawing a two-column chart on the board, with column heads *Type of Violence* and *Example.* Have students copy the chart on a sheet of paper and complete the chart as they read Lesson 1.

 Have students use their Foldables® as they read Lesson 1.

Quick Write

Instruct students to write about three factors they think are responsible for school violence. Call on volunteers to share one factor with the class.

Avoiding and Preventing Violence

Guide to Reading

● Building Vocabulary
Some of the terms below have word parts that signal meaning. Examples are *-ence* and *-cide.* Learn and use these parts to figure out definitions.

- violence (p. 176)
- homicide (p. 176)
- gang (p. 177)
- drug trafficking (p. 177)
- zero tolerance policy (p. 178)

● Focusing on the Main Ideas
In this lesson, you will learn to

- **identify** factors that contribute to teen violence.
- **analyze** how the media influence teen violence.
- **describe** measures taken to prevent violence in schools.
- **explain** ways to protect yourself from violence.

● Reading Strategy
Classifying Make a chart of the types of violence detailed in the lesson. Identify an example of each.

FOLDABLES | Study Organizer Use the Foldable® on p. 175 as you read this lesson.

Quick Write

Write about what you think is most responsible for school violence and why.

The Many Faces of Violence

On most days, the front page of any major newspaper will carry at least one story involving violence. **Violence** is *any behavior that causes physical or psychological harm to a person or damage to property.* Violence can take the form of words as well as actions. Threatening another person with physical harm is considered violence. So is defacing or destroying public or private property. Homicide is violence at its worst. **Homicide** is *the killing of one human being by another.*

A recent study by the CDC reported that more than 750,000 young people were treated in emergency rooms for injuries related to violence. That same survey revealed that 33 percent of students reported being in a physical fight one or more times in a year. The study also found that of the 5,570 youth homicides reported, 82 percent were killed with firearms.

◀ Cleaning up graffiti is an ongoing challenge in many cities. **What do you think could be done about this problem?**

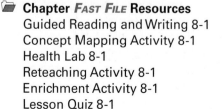

Lesson 1 Resources

📁 **Chapter *FAST FILE* Resources**
Guided Reading and Writing 8-1
Concept Mapping Activity 8-1
Health Lab 8-1
Reteaching Activity 8-1
Enrichment Activity 8-1
Lesson Quiz 8-1

Technology
⚓ Transparency 8-1
💾 Audio Summaries
🌐 *ExamView® Assessment Suite*
💾 Vocabulary PuzzleMaker
🌐 StudentWorks™ Plus
Go Online

Factors in Teen Violence

One factor that appears to have a strong influence on the increase of teen violence is the media. Statistics show that by age 18, a child will have witnessed as many as 200,000 acts of violence on television. Movies and popular music often portray violence as acceptable. Many researchers see a connection between these messages and the rise in teen crime. Other **factors** in teen violence include the influence of gangs, the availability of weapons, and the use of drugs.

Gangs, Weapons, and Drugs: A Vicious Cycle

Gangs

At one time the word *gang* referred to a group of loyal friends. Today, a **gang** is *a group whose members often use violence or take part in criminal activity.* While gangs are most often found in cities, they also form elsewhere.

Gangs contribute to violence on the streets and in schools. Their violence frequently leads to the injury and death of innocent people. Gang members may carry weapons and sell drugs. In fact, gang members are 50 percent more likely to carry guns than any other youth group. Most gangs that have guns buy them illegally, often with money made through **drug trafficking**—*the buying or selling of drugs.* Drug trafficking is a serious crime.

Weapons

In a nationwide survey, 17 percent of students reported carrying a gun, knife, or other weapon. If you carry a gun, you are twice as likely to be injured by gun violence. You also increase your risk of hurting or killing an innocent person.

Drugs

One national survey found that 85 percent of violent teens reported using marijuana. Some 55 percent reported using several illegal drugs. Drugs affect a person's ability to think clearly, show good judgment, and make wise decisions. A person under the influence of a drug is more likely to be involved in violent crime. He or she may commit an act of violence in order to get money to buy drugs.

 Reading Check **Explain** What is the relationship between gangs, weapons, and drugs?

Academic Vocabulary

factor (FAK ter) *(noun)* something that contributes to a result. *Talking about your problems with friends or family is a factor of good mental/emotional and social health.*

What Teens THINK

What can schools do to protect students from violence?

My advice would be to make sure a teacher is in the hallway at all times. Make sure teachers talk to their students, not just about school but about life. Ask new students to sit with you.

Hannah W.
Centerville, IN

Lesson 1: Avoiding and Preventing Violence **177**

What Teens THINK

What can schools do to protect students from violence? Have students read and discuss the section *School Violence* (on page 178). Then ask: What measures has our school taken to protect students from violence? What else do you think should be done here? Follow this discussion by having students read and react to the *What Teens Think* question and response.

Reading Check

Answer Most gangs that have guns buy them illegally. The guns are often bought with money made through drug trafficking.

Academic Vocabulary

Factors On this page, students read that the influence of gangs and the availability of weapons and drugs are *factors* in teen violence. After students have read and discussed the definition of *factor*, help them review other *factors* in teen violence (including movies, music, and television). You will find academic vocabulary activities in the Student Activities Workbook. 📁

Caption Answer

Photo Caption, p. 176
Sample answer: Organize neighborhood graffiti clean-up projects.

What Teens Want to Know

What do I do if I find out someone has a gun at school? Explain to students that the first thing to do if you even suspect another student has a gun is to get away as quickly and as quietly as possible. The best thing to do is simply to walk away. After removing yourself from the area, immediately report what you saw to a trusted adult, such as a teacher, counselor, or school administrator. You should tell the adult exactly what you saw, including what kind of weapon it was. Call 911 and anonymously report the incident. Finally, you should write down everything you saw.

AL **Active Learning**

School Policy Divide the class into small groups, and challenge each group to develop a policy for the middle school that seems both fair and effective in preventing violence at school. Explain that the policy should consist of specific actions the school might take as well as fair discipline for students who violate the policy. Invite groups to present their policies to the class. Compare their policies with actual school policies currently in place. **OL**

R **Reading Strategy**

Identifying Problems and Solutions Provide students with appropriate articles from newspapers and/or magazines that describe acts of violence involving teenagers. Next, using the list in **Figure 8.1**, have students choose one or two protection strategies that could have prevented the violence described by the article. **EL**

Caption Answers

Figure Caption, this page
Sample answer: Choose friends who are not part of a gang, and who do not carry weapons or use drugs.

Photo Caption, p. 179
Sample answer: My school makes me feel safer by limiting entry to the school to one door and keeping all others locked.

School Violence

Most schools are safe places. Every year, however, 3 million young people in the United States become victims of crime at school. Two-thirds of these incidents are violent. Many schools have responded to this problem by adopting a **zero tolerance policy.** This is *a policy that makes no exceptions for anybody for any reason.* In schools with zero tolerance policies, any student who brings a weapon to school is expelled. Students who take part in any violent act are also expelled.

Many schools have taken other measures to improve safety and reduce violence. These actions include limiting entry to a single door, and keeping all others locked. Many schools have also begun performing random searches of lockers and backpacks. Still others have added metal detectors at entrances to prevent students from bringing weapons into their schools.

Protecting Yourself from Violence

You can reduce your risk of becoming a victim of violence by avoiding unsafe situations. Be alert to what is going on around you and trust your instincts. If a situation feels unsafe, it probably is. **Figure 8.1** lists some additional precautions you can take to protect yourself at home and away from home.

▶ **FIGURE 8.1**

PROTECTING YOURSELF FROM
R **VIOLENCE**

These strategies can help you reduce the risk of becoming a victim of violence. **What other strategies could you use to avoid violence, gangs, and weapons?**

At Home
• Lock doors and windows when you are home alone.
• Open the door only to people you know well.
• Do not give personal information over the telephone or computer.
• Never tell a stranger that you are home alone. Say your parents are busy and can't come to the phone.
• Never agree to meet with a person you met online.
• When you come home, have your key ready before you reach the door.
• Never shoot a gun or pick it up, even if it is unloaded.
• If someone comes to the door or window and you feel you are in danger, call 911.

Away from Home
• Walk in pairs or in a group. Stay in familiar neighborhoods.
• Tell your family where you are going and what time you will be home.
• If you think someone is following you, go into a store or other public place.
• Never hitchhike or accept a ride from strangers.
• If a stranger stops his or her car to ask you for help or directions, walk or run the other direction. Do not get close to the car.
• Don't look like an easy target. Stand tall and walk confidently.
• Never carry your wallet, purse, or backpack in a way that is easy for others to grab.
• If someone wants your money or possessions, give them up.
• If someone tries to grab you, scream and run away.

🏃 **FITNESS ZONE**

Avoiding Violence Teens who participate in positive, healthy activities are better able to avoid the risk factors for teen violence, especially gang associations and drug use. Let students review the information in the *Fitness Zone Handbook.* Then ask: How can a fitness plan help you improve all aspects of your health—physical, mental/emotional, and social? How can good health help you avoid violence? **For more information, see *Fitness Zone Handbook* pages xviii-1 or visit the Fitness Zone at glencoe.com.**

▶ Many schools today are stepping up measures to prevent acts of violence. **What steps have officials in your school taken to make you feel safer?**

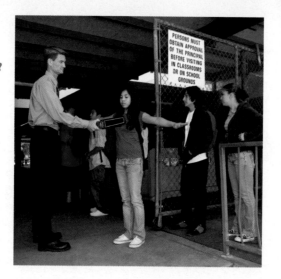

Preventing Violence

You can do your part to help stop the spread of violence. Develop your own personal zero tolerance policy regarding violence. Make a pact with yourself never to fight with or threaten others. Encourage others to resolve conflicts peacefully. Be a role model for nonviolence. Encourage your family to become a member of your Neighborhood Watch program. If you see or hear anything that may lead to violence, talk to a trusted adult right away.

 Reading Check **Recall** What can you do to help stop the spread of violence?

 G⊙ Online

Visit **glencoe.com** and complete the Interactive Study Guide for Lesson 1.

 Reading Check

Sample Answer Be a role model for nonviolence by never fighting with or threatening others.

ASSESS

 Assessment Resources

Lesson Review Quiz
* *ExamView*
* Fast Files Activities
* Online Quizzes and Activities

Reteaching

* Assign Concept Map 8-1 or Reteaching Activity 8-1 in the Fast Files.
* Have students list the factors in teen violence and ways to prevent violence. Then have students compare lists with a partner.

Enrichment

* Assign Enrichment Activity 8-1 in the Fast Files.
* Ask students to write a script for a favorite TV show that shows the characters working to prevent violence in their community.

CLOSE

Ask volunteers to describe how to protect themselves from violence at school and in the community.

Lesson 1 Review

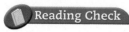 **After You Read**

Review this lesson for new terms, major headings, and Reading Checks.

What I Learned

1. *Vocabulary* What is *violence*? Use the word in an original sentence.

2. *Recall* What steps are schools taking to help prevent the spread of violence?

3. *Identify* If you were approached by a stranger in person, on the phone, or on the Internet, how would you protect yourself?

Thinking Critically

4. *Evaluate* Greg has been studying at a friend's house all day. Now, it is dark outside and he is uncomfortable walking home alone. What could Greg do?

5. *Analyze* Some people feel that school searches violate a person's right to privacy. How might you respond to this argument?

Applying Health Skills

6. *Conflict Resolution* Some violent acts happen because conflicts are allowed to escalate. With a partner, develop a story about two teens in conflict. Show how the teens use the T.A.L.K. strategy (see p. 165) of conflict resolution to peacefully resolve their differences.

 G⊙ Online For more Lesson Review Activities, go to glencoe.com.

Lesson 1: Avoiding and Preventing Violence **179**

Lesson 1 Review Answers

1. Violence is any behavior that causes physical or psychological harm to a person or damage to property. Sentences will vary.

2. Many schools have adopted a zero tolerance policy, expelling any students who bring weapons to school or participate in violent acts. Schools are also performing random searches of lockers and backpacks, and limiting student entry to a single door.

3. Do not let strangers know you are home alone and never agree to meet someone you met online.

4. *Sample answer:* He should ask an adult in his friend's family to take him home, or he should call home to have an adult come to get him.

5. Answers will vary. Students should explain their responses.

6. Stories, which will vary, should demonstrate an understanding of how the T.A.L.K. strategy can be used to resolve differences peacefully.

FOCUS

Activating Prior Knowledge

What I Know Ask students to explain what steps a teen should take if he or she has just been attacked by another student on the way to school.

Guide to Reading

Building Vocabulary
- Tell students that the word *battery* comes from a French word meaning "to beat." Explain that the word *battle* comes from the same French word.
- Use Vocabulary PuzzleMaker to reinforce vocabulary terms.

Reading Strategy
Predicting Give students 5 minutes to look at the main ideas, photos, and captions of Lesson 2. Call on volunteers to predict the kinds of information discussed in the lesson.

Quick Write

Divide students into small groups, and provide each group with a newspaper from a day in the last week. Have students scan the paper for news stories about people victimized by violence. Ask each student to write a summary of one of the stories.

Caption Answer

Photo Caption *Sample answer:* A trusted adult can be a source of help.

Dealing with Violence

Guide to Reading

Building Vocabulary
As you read this lesson, write each new highlighted term and its definition in your notebook.
- victim (p. 180)
- assault (p. 181)
- battery (p. 181)
- rape (p. 181)

Focusing on the Main Ideas
In this lesson, you will learn to
- **identify** several types of violent crimes.
- **describe** actions that victims of violence need to take.
- **advocate** for the prevention of violence in America.

Reading Strategy
Predicting Look at the main headings, figures, and captions before you read this lesson. Predict the kinds of information you think you might learn.

Quick Write

Find and write a summary of a news story about someone victimized by crime or violence.

Effects of Violence on Victims

Did you know teens are twice as likely as adults to be victims of violent crime? A **victim** is *any individual who suffers injury, loss, or death due to violence.* Victims who survive violent attacks are affected in different ways. In addition to the physical injuries that can result from violence, a victim's emotional injuries can be even more painful and long-lasting. Victims of any kind of violence should seek help to deal with the effects. Talking with a trusted adult or a mental health professional can lessen some of the pain. With help, victims of violence can recover.

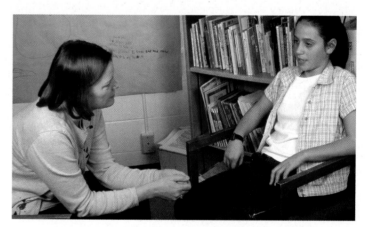

▶ A school counselor can be one source of help for victims of violence. **What are some other sources of help for victims?**

Lesson 2 Resources

📁 **Chapter *FAST FILE* Resources**
Guided Reading and Writing 8-2
Concept Mapping Activity 8-2
Cross-Curriculum Activity 8-2
Reteaching Activity 8-2
Enrichment Activity 8-2
Lesson Quiz 8-2

Technology
🔌 Transparency 8-2
Audio Summaries
ExamView® Assessment Suite
Vocabulary PuzzleMaker
StudentWorks™ Plus
Go Online

Assault and Battery

Two violent crimes that often go hand in hand are assault and battery. **Assault** is *an unlawful threat or attempt to do bodily injury to another person.* Assault can be with a weapon or with bare hands. **Battery** is *the unlawful beating, hitting, or kicking of another person.* Often people who threaten to assault go on to batter, or beat, their victims. Assault and battery can occur anywhere, and anyone can be victimized.

One category of battery victims is people injured by domestic abuse. This crime involves beating or doing other physical harm to a family member. Women and children are the most common targets of domestic abuse. Anyone who is a victim of domestic abuse needs to get outside help right away.

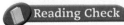 **Reading Check** **Compare** What is the difference between assault and battery?

Rape

Rape is *any kind of sexual intercourse with a person against her or his will.* Most rape victims are female; however, males can also be victims.

In most rape cases involving teens, the attacker and victim know each other. Sometimes the person who commits the rape is a peer whom the victim has dated or is dating. No matter what the circumstances are, rape is always a crime and is *never* the victim's fault.

HS The best way to avoid becoming a rape victim is to avoid situations that might lead to attack. Stay with a group of peers when you go places. Avoid walking alone, especially at night. Avoid going anywhere with a date where there are no other people around. Instead, go on group dates with other couples and stay in public places. Do not let anyone touch you in a way that makes you feel uncomfortable. Remember, it is your right to say no and to have control over your own body. No one should be forced to engage in sexual activity against his or her will.

 Reading Check **Recall** Who can become a victim of rape?

▶ Many communities work together with law enforcement to make their neighborhoods safer. **What is being done in your community?**

Lesson 2: Dealing with Violence **181**

ACTIVITY
DEVELOPING Good Character

Caring

If someone you know has been a victim of violence, you can demonstrate the character trait of caring by showing concern and compassion for that person. Listen if the person wants to talk. Help him or her know when to seek help from a parent or other trusted adult.

What communication skills would be helpful in this type of situation? What are some other ways you could show the person that you care?

TEACH

DEVELOPING Good Character

Caring
Have students make a list of communication skills that would help in talking with a victim of violence. List their ideas on the board, along with other ways to show compassion and concern.

 Reading Check

Answer, top Assault is a threat or attempt to injure another person. Battery means beating, hitting, or kicking another person.
Answer, bottom Both females and males can be rape victims.

HS Health Skills Practice

Practicing Healthful Behaviors Ask students to reread the paragraph about ways to avoid becoming a rape victim. Divide the class into small groups, and challenge each group to develop a list of strategies teens should follow to reduce the risk of being a rape victim. Tell students that they can start with the suggestions in the text, but they should also generate other steps to follow. Have groups share their strategies with the class.

Caption Answer

Photo Caption *Sample answer:* My community has a Neighborhood Watch program.

What Teens Want to Know

How can teens avoid date rape? Explain to students that rape that occurs between two people who know each other is often called date rape, and it usually happens in a social situation. Here are some date-rape prevention tips:

● Meet a date at a public place and stay around others. Avoid secluded places.
● Stay sober. Alcohol use is involved in many date rapes.
● If you go to a party, go with a friend.
● Always have a plan to get home.
● Carry a cell phone, if possible.
● Say no and use refusal skills effectively.

W Writing Support

Expository Writing Ask students to write an informative article about steps a person should take if he or she becomes a victim of assault. Articles should focus on steps the victim should take after the attack. The article should include information from the text and suggest ways the victim can take action to get help. **OL**

U Universal Access

English Learners Draw a T chart and begin by asking students to list various violent crimes in the left-hand column. In the right-hand column, brainstorm ideas of what can be done to combat violent crimes in general. Then, have students draw lines linking each crime with the best course of action. **EL**

Reading Check

Answer get medical attention

▶ One way to help defeat violence is through education. **What can you do to advocate for an end to violence?**

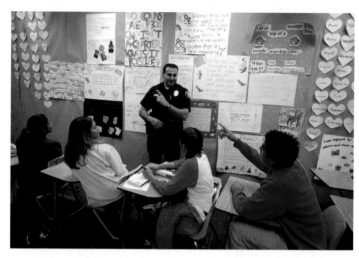

Getting Help

One of the worst things a victim can do after an attack is nothing. Unfortunately, that is exactly what most people do, especially victims of rape. A report by the National Institute of Justice estimates that 95 percent of all rapes go unreported. Perhaps the biggest reason why this number is so high is that many rape victims feel ashamed or embarrassed. They somehow feel that they are partly or totally to blame for the attack.

If you are a victim of violent crime, you need to take three important actions. The first is to get medical attention. Sometimes victims of crime have been injured and are not even aware of it. Many are in a state of shock, which can temporarily block out pain.

The second action you need to take is to report the incident to the police. This is especially important in the event of rape. Making a report can be difficult, but it is a necessary step. Revealing the incident to the police can help them bring the person responsible to justice. It can also be a step toward preventing that person from harming others.

Third, seek out treatment for the emotional effects of what you have been through. Being a victim of violence is a traumatic experience for most people. It has long-term emotional effects that can interfere with normal life. Victims may have flashbacks and nightmares. They may also have trouble forming relationships. Counseling can help most victims recover from the experience and move on with their lives.

Reading Check

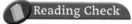

Recall What is the first action that a victim of violence needs to take?

Caption Answer

Photo Caption *Sample answer:* You can encourage two friends who are angry with each other to resolve their conflict peacefully.

Home, School, and Community

In the Community The Youth Outreach for Victim Assistance (YOVA) is a project from the National Center for Victims of Crime, whose goal is to educate adolescents about victimization and to provide resources where teens can turn for help. Sites around the country have been established where teens and adults can work together to design campaigns that address teen victimization through support, advocacy, education, and prevention programs. Ask students to find out whether a YOVA site has been established near their community.

Helping Defeat Violence

Violence has lasting effects on the victims, their families, and society. It is also very expensive. The cost of youth violence exceeds, $158 billion each year.

Both the government and private organizations work to help reduce and prevent youth violence. You can also help stamp out the epidemic of violence. Here are some ways:

- Any time you witness an act of violence, report what you have seen. Talk to a trusted adult first. He or she will take the necessary steps to involve law enforcement.

- Become an advocate for safety and victims' rights. One is the Youth Outreach for Victim Assistance (YOVA) program. Sponsored by the National Center for Victims of Crime, this youth-adult partnership educates teens about what victims go through. It also tells young people where they can go for help if they are victimized.

 Reading Check **Identify** Who does violence affect?

 G Online

Visit **glencoe.com** and complete the Interactive Study Guide for Lesson 2.

Reading Check

Answer Violence affects individuals, families, and society.

ASSESS

Assessment Resources

Lesson Review Quiz
- *ExamView*
- Fast Files Activities
- Online Quizzes and Activities

Reteaching

- Assign Concept Map 8-2 or Reteaching Activity 8-2 in the Fast Files.
- Have students make a bulleted list of ways that victims of violence can get help. Ask volunteers to share one of the entries on their list.

Enrichment

- Assign Enrichment Activity 8-2 in the Fast Files.
- Have students use print and online resources to identify organizations in their community that help and advocate for victims of violence.

CLOSE

Call on students to explain why victims of violence should seek help and describe the kinds of help available.

Lesson 2 Review

 After You Read

Review this lesson for new terms, major headings, and Reading Checks.

What I Learned

1. *Vocabulary* Define the term *assault*.

2. *List* Name two ways a person can avoid becoming a victim of rape.

3. *Identify* What are three actions a victim of violence should take?

4. *Recall* How can you personally help stamp out violence?

Thinking Critically

5. *Explain* Why is it important to tell someone if you are a victim of violence?

6. *Apply* Jacob and Tom are walking home from a movie when some older teens grab and shove them. After the incident has ended, Tom says he wants to forget about it and just go home. As Tom speaks, his voice is shaking. What might you say to your friend if you were in Jacob's place?

Applying Health Skills

7. *Advocacy* Find out about programs in your community that work to prevent violence. How can students get involved? Report your findings in the form of a chart.

G Online For more Lesson Review Activities, go to **glencoe.com**.

Lesson 2: Dealing with Violence **183**

Lesson 2 Review Answers

1. An assault is an unlawful threat or attempt to do bodily injury to another person.
2. *Sample answer:* Don't walk alone at night, and remain alert when walking outdoors.
3. A victim of violence should get medical attention, report the incident to the police, and seek treatment for the emotional effects.

4. Any time you witness an act of violence, report what you have seen. Become an advocate for safety and victims' rights.
5. Telling someone is the first step in getting help. A trusted adult can help report the crime to police.
6. *Sample answer:* One of the worst things a

victim can do after an attack is nothing. He should report the incident to a trusted adult.
7. Tell students that they should find out about at least two programs in the community. The chart students make to report their findings might have three columns, with the column headings *Program, Purpose,* and *Location/Phone.*

FOCUS

Activating Prior Knowledge

What I Know Ask a volunteer to describe what bullying is. Tell students this lesson will explain ways to deal with a bully.

Guide to Reading

Building Vocabulary
- Tell students that the word *harass* comes from a French word meaning "to set a dog upon." Explain that *harass* can be pronounced with either the emphasis on the first syllable or the second. Both pronunciations are correct.
- Use Vocabulary PuzzleMaker to reinforce vocabulary terms.

Reading Strategy
Finding the Main Idea
Give students five minutes to skim the main headings and write their sentences. As students read, suggest that they revise their sentences and add details that support each main idea.

*Q*uick Write

Ask volunteers to share their poems or stories with the class.

Caption Answer

Photo Caption You can walk away and report the incident.

Bullying and Harassment

Guide to Reading

Building Vocabulary
Each of the terms below is an act of wrong-doing. Define each as best you can. Be prepared to change or correct your definitions as you read the lesson.
- intimidation (p. 185)
- harassment (p. 186)
- gender discrimination (p. 186)

Focusing on the Main Ideas
In this lesson, you will learn to
- **describe** ways of dealing with bullies.
- **identify** different forms of harassment.
- **develop** effective communication skills to deal with harassment.

Reading Strategy
Finding the Main Idea For each of the main headings in this lesson, write one sentence that states the main idea.

*Q*uick Write

Write a poem or short story involving a bully. Give your poem or story a positive ending.

Bullying

Vic was waiting patiently in line at school. It was a hot day and he wished the line would move faster. Just then he felt someone push him, almost causing him to fall over. Vic turned and saw Tony and three of his buddies. "Out of the way, loser," Tony said as the four cut in front of Vic. Tony glared at Vic and then grinned at his friends. They all started laughing. Vic felt an immediate urge to push back, but he noticed that a teacher was walking toward him. He was glad that the teacher intervened.

▶ Most students have been bullied at one time or another. **What actions can you take if you are confronted by a bully?**

Lesson 3 Resources

📁 **Chapter *FAST FILE* Resources**
Guided Reading and Writing 8-3
Concept Mapping Activity 8-3
Decision-Making Activity 8-3
Reteaching Activity 8-3
Enrichment Activity 8-3
Lesson Quiz 8-3

Technology
🔋 Transparency 8-3
📀 Audio Summaries
💿 *ExamView® Assessment Suite*
📀 Vocabulary PuzzleMaker
💿 StudentWorks™ Plus
G⊙ Online

Dealing with a Bully

Have you ever been bullied? If so, you are not alone. Three out of every four students have been bullied at one time or another. Bullying is reported to be the most severe in grades 7 through 9. Dealing with bullies can be a source of frustration and fear.

Bullies often taunt people who are shy or stand out in some way. Bullies can be male or female. Male bullies often use threats of physical violence. Female bullies often use verbal put-downs that hurt other people's feelings. Sometimes bullying takes the form of **intimidation.** This is *purposely frightening another person through threatening words, looks, or body language.*

People who are victims of bullying can feel helpless. They may believe there is nothing they can do to change the situation. Their self-esteem may suffer as a result of repeated put-downs. Although the victim is seldom aware of it, bullies have low self-esteem, too. Many bullies have been bullied by peers themselves. They usually pick on others to make themselves feel better. Also, bullies almost always have an audience that supports his or her actions.

If you are being bullied, try to ignore the person and, if possible, just walk away. If the bully refuses to be ignored, walk away anyway. If the bully blocks you, try to remain calm. Be forceful without being physical. Stand up for yourself. Whatever happens, it is important to report the incident to a person in authority. At school, let a teacher, counselor, or other trusted adult know what is going on. No one should have to put up with bullying. All students have a right to learn in a safe environment.

Reading Check **Define** What is *intimidation*? How should a person react if he or she feels intimidated?

◀ Making fun of others is a form of bullying. **How might this behavior affect a person's self-esteem?** W

Lesson 3: Bullying and Harassment **185**

ACTIVITY

Go Online

Topic: Stopping the Bullies

Visit **glencoe.com** for Student Web Activities to learn about bullying and what can be done to stop it.

Activity: Using the information provided at the link above, create a "Bully Bookmark" with tips for what to do if you are bullied on one side, and tips for what to do if you see someone else bullied on the other.

TEACH

W Writing Support

Narrative Writing Ask students to write a story that describes a teen being bullied and how the teen feels as a result. Ask that the story end with the victim taking steps to end the bullying. **OL**

Reading Check

Answer Intimidation is purposely frightening another person through threatening words, looks, or body language. If someone attempts to be intimidating, you should try to ignore the person, just walk away, be forceful without being physical, and report the person to a teacher, counselor, or other trusted adult.

R Reading Strategy

Finding the Main Idea Have students ask a librarian for help in finding *The Bully* by Gregory Clark, *The New Kid on the Block* by Jack Prelutsky, or another work of poetry or fiction that focuses on bullies. Ask that each student write a paragraph that describes the work he or she reads and explains the point of view the author takes toward bullies. **AL**

Caption Answer

Photo Caption Laughing at or joking about another person in a way that hurts the person's feelings can lower a person's self-esteem.

 Promoting Coordinated School Health

Bullying Prevention Programs Many schools around the country have addressed the serious problem of bullying with programs designed for use in elementary, middle, or junior high schools. After training, school staff is mostly responsible for implementing the program. All students participate in most aspects of the program. Students who are identified as bullies or as targets of bullying receive special attention. The program includes the development of schoolwide rules against bullying as well as regular classroom meetings about bullying.

Health Skills Activity

Communication Skills

Using "I" Messages

Use the following strategies to help students complete the activity:

- Ask a volunteer to read the introductory paragraph aloud.
- Call on a volunteer to read the first "You" statement, and call on another volunteer to read the corresponding "I" statement. Continue through all three examples. Ask students to explain why the "I" statements might be a better way to object to a friend's offensive behavior.
- Divide the class into pairs, and have each member change the partner's "You" statements into "I" statements.
- After all pairs have traded papers and changed the statements, call on volunteers to share with the class a "You" statement and how it was changed to an "I" statement.

Health Skills Activity

Communication Skills

Using "I" Messages

Sometimes the person making ethnic jokes or inappropriate remarks may be a friend of yours. He or she may not realize that you find this conduct offensive. When a friend behaves in a way that offends you, you need to let her or him know that you are offended by these actions. At the same time, you may not want to jeopardize the friendship or create a conflict. You can express your feelings in a positive way by using "I" statements instead of "you" statements. Here are a few examples of "you" statements that can be substituted with "I" statements.

Instead of "You" Statements...	...Use "I" Statements
✗ You're being offensive.	✔ I am offended by what you are saying.
✗ You're embarrassing me.	✔ I feel embarrassed.
✗ You aren't being funny.	✔ I don't think that is funny.

With a Partner
Both you and your partner should each write three "you" statements. Trade papers and change the "you" statements to "I" statements.

Harassment

Joking can be fun, not to mention a sign of good mental health. However, a joke is neither funny nor healthy when it disrespects another person. When this kind of disrespectful behavior happens repeatedly, it is considered **harassment** (huh·RAS·muhnt). This is *ongoing conduct that offends another person by criticizing his or her race, color, religion, physical disability, or gender.* Harassment can take many forms. It can be a spoken or written comment, gesture, or unwanted physical contact.

Harassment that involves obscene behavior or remarks of a sexual nature is labeled *sexual harassment.* Sexual harassment includes unwelcome touching and inappropriate or offensive sexual remarks, or jokes. Obscene or inappropriate e-mails, text messages, or voice mails can also be a form of sexual harassment. Lesson 4 contains additional information on sexual harassment.

A type of conduct related to sexual harassment is **gender discrimination**—*singling out or excluding a person based on gender.* Gender discrimination can be directed at a male or a female. Either way, gender discrimination is wrong. You should never judge or presume something about a person based on his or her gender.

HEALTH LITERACY

Sexual Harassment at School According to the U.S. Department of Education, sexual harassment is a serious problem in education at all levels, including in elementary and secondary schools. Sexual harassment has been illegal in schools since passage of Title IX in 1972.

Nevertheless, sexual harassment continues to be a problem for students. According to a national survey of students in eighth through eleventh grades, 83 percent of girls and 79 percent of boys reported having experienced sexual harassment at some time in the past.

Dealing with Harassment

"What's the matter—can't you take a joke? You're just too sensitive." Comments like these are often directed at people who are targets of harassment. These remarks can make the victim feel as though he or she deserves the harassment.

No one, however, has to put up with harassment. If you are a target of harassment, here are some strategies for dealing with the problem:

- Tell the person to stop what he or she is doing. Make it clear that this pattern of behavior is hurtful and unacceptable. Explain that if it continues, you will report the harassment.
- Use an assertive communication style. Speak in a firm but positive voice with your head and shoulders up.
- Look the person in the eye as you speak.
- Let your family know what is happening and seek their advice. Get help if you need it and do not allow the behavior to continue.
- If the harassment continues, tell a trusted adult. Charges can then be filed against the peer. If the harassment takes place at school, tell a teacher or a school administrator.

Go Online

Visit **glencoe.com** and complete the Interactive Study Guide for Lesson 3.

Lesson 3 Review

 After You Read

Review this lesson for new terms, major headings, and Reading Checks.

What I Learned

1. **Vocabulary** What is *gender discrimination*?

2. **List** Name two ways of dealing with bullies.

3. **Recall** What are some forms harassment can take?

Thinking Critically

4. **Analyze** Shelby is being teased repeatedly by Matt. His sexual remarks bother her. She doesn't know what to do. What advice do you have for Shelby?

5. **Apply** Your cousin writes to tell you about a "really funny kid" who just came to his school. He explains that this new person gets a laugh by knocking other students' books out of their hands. How would you explain to your cousin that the action is inappropriate behavior?

Applying Health Skills

6. **Accessing Information** Harassment is considered a hate crime in 46 of the 50 states. Find out what the laws are in your community regarding harassment. Make a poster explaining the penalties for this behavior.

Go Online For more Lesson Review Activities, go to **glencoe.com**.

Lesson 3: Bullying and Harassment **187**

ASSESS

Assessment Resources

Lesson Review Quiz
- *ExamView*
- Fast Files Activities
- Online Quizzes and Activities

Reteaching

- Assign Concept Map 8-3 or Reteaching Activity 8-3 in the Fast Files.
- Have students make posters illustrating how to deal with bullying and harassment.

Enrichment

- Assign Enrichment Activity 8-3 in the Fast Files.
- Have students design a Web site that would inform teens how to deal with bullying, sexual harassment, and gender discrimination.

CLOSE

Have students write a brief description of a bullying incident and describe how a student being bullied could deal with it.

Lesson 3 Review Answers

1. Gender discrimination is singling out or excluding a person based on gender.
2. *Sample answer:* You can try to ignore the person. You can report the person to a teacher, counselor, or other trusted adult.
3. It can be a spoken or written comment, gesture, or unwanted physical contact.
4. *Sample answer:* Matt's behavior is sexual harassment, and it should be reported.
5. *Sample answer:* This behavior probably isn't funny to the students whose books are knocked out of their hands. The new student's behavior is bullying and should be reported to a teacher, counselor, or other trusted adult.
6. Encourage students to research whether harassment is a crime in their state by using library or valid online resources.

FOCUS

Activating Prior Knowledge

What I Know Describe an example of emotional abuse, such as the repeated belittling of a younger brother by an older brother. Ask students how this abuse might affect the younger brother throughout the rest of his life.

Guide to Reading

Building Vocabulary
- Explain to students that *domestic* means "relating to the family or the household." Before students read, have them use this information to determine the definition of *domestic violence*.
- Use Vocabulary PuzzleMaker to reinforce vocabulary terms.

Reading Strategy
Classifying Model the Reading Strategy by making a two-column chart on the board, with the column headings *Type of Abuse* and *Action Victim Can Take*. Have students copy the chart into their notebooks and complete it as they read.

Quick Write

Students might write a paragraph describing problems between friends or between partners in a marriage. Have students reconsider their Quick Writes after reading the lesson.

Abuse

Guide to Reading

Building Vocabulary
As you read this lesson, write each new highlighted term and its definition in your notebook.

- abuse (p. 188)
- domestic violence (p. 189)
- neglect (p. 190)
- sexual abuse (p. 190)
- sexual harassment (p. 191)

Focusing on the Main Ideas
In this lesson, you will learn to
- **explain** the different forms of abuse.
- **describe** the effects of abuse on victims.

Reading Strategy
Classifying Make a chart identifying the four types of abuse. For each type, identify what action a victim of abuse can take.

Quick Write

Write a paragraph describing problems that might affect a relationship. Identify healthy ways of dealing with such problems.

What Is Abuse?

Every close relationship has its ups and downs, its good days and bad days. When the relationship is healthy, the people involved care for and respect each other.

When a relationship is unhealthy or unbalanced, difficulties that arise can become worse. In some cases, abuse may occur.

Abuse is *the physical, emotional, or mental mistreatment of one person by another.*

Abuse is a problem that affects people of all ages, skin colors, and economic groups. Any type of abuse is a crime. It is damaging to everyone involved and is never the victim's fault.

 Reading Check **Define** What is *abuse*?

◀ Abuse can affect the physical, social, and mental/emotional health of the victim. **What are some types of abuse?**

Lesson 4 Resources

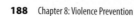

📁 **Chapter FAST FILE Resources**
Guided Reading and Writing 8-4
Concept Mapping Activity 8-4
Decision-Making Activity 8-4
Reteaching Activity 8-4
Enrichment Activity 8-4
Lesson Quiz 8-4

Technology
🔦 Transparency 8-4
Audio Summaries
ExamView® Assessment Suite
Vocabulary PuzzleMaker
StudentWorks™ Plus
 Go Online

Kinds of Abuse

Abuse takes place mostly in close relationships, often between people who are related by blood or marriage. Parents or guardians may abuse their children or each other. Abuse may also occur between siblings or other family members. Many abusers try to make their victims feel as if they deserve to be treated harshly. Abuse is not an acceptable form of discipline. No one ever deserves to be abused.

Physical Abuse

The most common type of abuse is **domestic violence,** *physical abuse that occurs within a family.* The term *domestic* refers to the home or family setting, which is where most abuse occurs. Domestic violence is about power and control. The abuser seeks to establish and maintain authority over the family or a family member. Half of all reported abuse cases involve domestic violence.

Physical abuse ranges from pushing and slapping to punching and choking. Sometimes a household item may be used as a weapon. When the victim is a small child, the abuser often makes up excuses for the child's injuries. For example, the abuser may claim that the child fell down. Adults who are physically abused sometimes make excuses for their own injuries. Victims may also make excuses for the abuser. This type of behavior, which is called *enabling*, establishes a pattern of abuse.

Emotional Abuse

AL While physical abuse can leave visible signs, emotional abuse is harder to spot. The effects, however, can be just as severe and last longer than bruises. Emotional abuse uses words or gestures to mistreat another person. It may include yelling, bullying, teasing, or threats of violence. All share the same intent, which is to make the victim feel stupid, worthless, or helpless.

Neglect

People need basic necessities such as food, clothing, a place to live, and medical care. In addition, they have emotional needs, such as the need for love and nurturing. Children rely on their parents and guardians to meet those needs.

▼ Emotional abuse can make a person feel isolated or unwanted. **How could you reach out to a person who needs help?**

Lesson 4: Abuse **189**

TEACH

 Reading Check

Answer, p. 188 Abuse is the physical, emotional, or mental mistreatment of one person by another.

AL Active Learning

Pantomime Skits Put students in small groups and give each group a card naming and describing a different type of emotional abuse or neglect. The students will prepare a short, silent skit. Have the rest of the class describe what is happening and name the specific type of emotional abuse or neglect. **EL**

Caption Answers

Photo Caption, p. 188 Types of abuse include physical abuse, emotional abuse, neglect, and sexual abuse.
Photo Caption, p. 189 Ask if the person needs to talk to someone.

HEALTH LITERACY

Warning Signs In every state, teachers are by law required to report suspected child abuse. According to the American Psychological Association, these are some of the warning signs of abuse and neglect:
- Cuts and bruises
- Broken bones or internal injuries
- Burns
- Constant hunger or thirst
- Lack of interest in surroundings
- Dirty hair or skin
- Hard-to-believe stories about how accidents occurred

Reporting abuse could save a life.

ACTIVITY
Careers for the 21st Century

Family Counselor
Guide students in reading and discussing the information about careers in family counseling. Let a pair of volunteers visit **glencoe.com** to learn about the training family counselors need; have them share what they learned with the rest of the class.

 Reading Check

Answer children, elderly people, and people with disabilities

R Reading Strategy

Analyzing a Graphic After students have examined **Figure 8.2**, explain that the term *hyper* means "in excess." Ask: What does a "hyperarousal" response by certain areas of the brain mean? *It means that certain parts of the brain responded excessively, or were overactive.* Emphasize the cause-and-effect relationship between child abuse and neglect and the consequences. **OL**

Caption Answer

Figure Caption Mental/emotional effects of child abuse and neglect include depression, panic disorder, post-traumatic stress disorder, alcohol and drug abuse, academic difficulties, and suicide.

ACTIVITY
Careers for the 21st Century

Family Counselor

Sometimes families cannot handle problems on their own. When that happens, a family counselor can help. A family counselor is a health professional who deals with all kinds of issues, like substance abuse, lack of communication, and recovering from a traumatic event. If you want to be a family counselor, you should practice your communication and conflict-resolution skills.

What training does a family counselor need? Go to *Career Corner* at glencoe.com to find out.

▶ **FIGURE 8.2**

CHILD ABUSE AND NEGLECT

R The effects of child abuse and neglect can appear on all three sides of the health triangle. **What are some mental/emotional effects?**

When parents or guardians do not meet their children's basic needs, they are guilty of the crime of neglect. **Neglect** is *the failure to meet a person's basic physical and emotional needs.* Children are the most common targets of neglect, but older adults and people with disabilities may also suffer neglect. More than 2 million cases of child abuse and neglect are reported every year in the United States. Abuse and neglect can have long-lasting effects on a child. **Figure 8.2** lists some of the physical, mental/emotional, and social effects.

 Reading Check **Identify** Who are typical targets of neglect?

Sexual Abuse

Sexual abuse occurs when *a person forces another person to participate in a sexual act against his or her will.* According to one estimate, 150,000 to 200,000 new cases of sexual abuse occur each year. Often the targets of sexual abuse are children, and the abuser is an adult in the household or a relative or friend of the family. People who commit the crime of sexual abuse do not always use physical force. They may use bribes, trickery, or other means to persuade a child to perform sexual acts. All sexual abuse is illegal and damaging.

Long-Term Consequences of Child Abuse and Neglect
Physical Health Consequences
• Impaired brain development
• Impaired physical, mental, and emotional development
• A "hyper-arousal" response by certain areas of the brain, which may result in hyperactivity and sleep disturbances
• Poor physical health, including various illnesses
Mental/Emotional Health Consequences
• Increased risk for emotional problems such as depression, panic disorder, and post-traumatic stress disorder
• Alcohol and drug abuse
• Difficulty with language development and academic achievement
• Suicide
Social Health Consequences
• Difficulty forming secure relationships
• Difficulties during adolescence
• Criminal and/or violent behavior
• Abusive behavior

HEALTH LITERACY

Long-Term Consequences of Abuse The U.S. Department of Health and Human Services estimated that there were 906,000 victims of childhood abuse in a recent year. This abuse can affect emotional development as well as damage to the growing brain. Studies have shown that abused and neglected children are at least 25 percent more likely to experience problems in adolescence, such as delinquency and low academic achievement. Long-term consequences of child abuse include self-destructive behavior, sexual acting out, drug and alcohol abuse, and school failure.

A kind of sexual abuse that may happen at school is **sexual harassment,** which is *uninvited and unwelcome sexual conduct directed at another person.* As mentioned in the previous lesson, sexual harassment includes words, touching, jokes, looks, notes, or gestures with a sexual manner or meaning. This kind of unwelcome and uninvited behavior is illegal and must be reported to school personnel.

 Reading Check **Define** What is *sexual abuse*?

Effects of Abuse

Abuse can leave emotional scars that remain long after physical signs have gone away. Victims often blame themselves for what happened. They may be too afraid or ashamed to get the help they need. Children who suffer abuse often have a number of emotional problems, including low self-esteem. These problems may show up in the form of self-destructive behaviors, including attempts at suicide, alcohol and drug abuse, and eating disorders. Some victims of abuse turn to criminal or violent behavior. Many go on to become abusers themselves.

Help exists for victims of abuse. You will learn about available resources in the next lesson.

 Go Online

Visit **glencoe.com** and complete the Interactive Study Guide for Lesson 4.

Lesson 4 Review

 After You Read

Review this lesson for new terms, major headings, and Reading Checks.

What I Learned

1. *Vocabulary* What is *domestic violence*?

2. *List* Name several forms of abuse.

3. *Identify* What are some ways in which abuse can affect its victims?

Thinking Critically

4. *Evaluate* Respond to the statement "All forms of abuse negatively affect the victim's physical health." Tell whether you agree or disagree, and why.

5. *Analyze* Why do you think it is important for victims of abuse to get help?

Applying Health Skills

6. *Advocacy* With classmates, develop a handbook for identifying and dealing with different types of abuse. In your handbook, define the different types of abuse, and steps to take when dealing with abuse. Also, list trustworthy organizations that can help victims of abuse. Make a copy available to everyone in the class.

 For more Lesson Review Activities, go to **glencoe.com**.

Lesson 4: Abuse **191**

 CHAPTER 8

Lesson 4

 Reading Check

Answer Sexual abuse occurs when a person forces another person to participate in a sexual act against his or her will.

ASSESS

Assessment Resources

Lesson Review Quiz
- *ExamView*
- Fast Files Activities
- Online Quizzes and Activities

Reteaching

- Assign Concept Map 8-4 or Reteaching Activity 8-4 in the Fast Files.
- Have students identify and write a description of each kind of abuse.

Enrichment

- Assign Enrichment Activity 8-4 in the Fast Files.
- Ask students to use print and online resources to investigate the long-term effects of the abuse of children. Have students prepare a brief report of their findings.

CLOSE

Name different kinds of abuse and ask students to describe the effects.

Lesson 4 Review Answers

1. physical abuse that occurs in the family
2. physical abuse, emotional abuse, neglect, sexual abuse
3. *Sample answer:* Abuse can cause physical injuries and emotional problems, which can lead to self-destructive behaviors like suicide, drug and alcohol abuse, or eating disorders.
4. *Sample answer:* I agree with the statement. Physical abuse will probably directly affect the victim's physical health and may result in self-destructive behaviors.
5. *Sample answer:* Victims of abuse should get help to deal with the emotional problems caused by abuse.
6. Have students respond to this question in small groups. Handbooks, which will vary, should identify different kinds of abuse, describe strategies to deal with each kind, and list organizations that can assist victims of abuse.

FOCUS

Activating Prior Knowledge

What I Know Ask students to suggest where a person victimized by domestic abuse could go to find help.

Guide to Reading

Building Vocabulary

■ Explain to students that the word *crisis* comes from a Greek word for "decision." A *crisis* is an important time in which the outcome will make a difference—a decisive moment in a person's life.

■ Use Vocabulary PuzzleMaker to reinforce vocabulary terms.

Reading Strategy

Identifying Cause and Effect Have students write their explanations in a short paragraph. Explain that the cause is the abuse, and the effect is the victim's silence. Ask volunteers to share their explanations with the class.

uick Write

For students who are unfamiliar with the phrase, explain that a vicious cycle is a chain of events in which the solution of one problem creates a new problem of ever-increasing difficulty.

Caption Answer

Photo Caption *Sample answer:* Students can turn to a trusted teacher or to a school counselor.

Preventing and Coping with Abuse

Guide to Reading

● **Building Vocabulary**
As you read this lesson, be on the lookout for the terms below. Write each term and its definition in your notebook.

■ cycle of abuse (p. 193)
■ crisis hot line (p. 193)

● **Focusing on the Main Ideas**
In this lesson, you will learn to

■ **describe** the cycle of abuse.
■ **develop** a plan to stop the cycle of abuse.
■ **identify** where to get help if you are abused.

● **Reading Strategy**
Identifying Cause and Effect Explain why a victim of abuse may be unwilling to say anything.

Quick Write

Identify a phenomenon that might be described as a *vicious cycle*. Write a brief description of this phenomenon.

Those Affected by Abuse

Whenever abuse is present in a family, all family members are affected. The effects of abuse are serious and long-lasting. For this reason, all members of the family need help.

Abused spouses are sometimes enablers in domestic violence. By concealing the true cause of their injuries, they help maintain the cycle of violence. They prevent themselves and their abusers from getting the help they need. In this lesson, you will learn about where victims of abuse can get help.

▶ Help is available in any community for abuse victims and their families. **Who can students in your school turn to if they need to report an abuse problem?**

192 Chapter 8: Violence Prevention

📁 **Chapter *FAST FILE* Resources**
Guided Reading and Writing 8-5
Concept Mapping Activity 8-5
Cross-Curriculum Activity 8-5
Reteaching Activity 8-5
Enrichment Activity 8-5
Lesson Quiz 8-5

Technology
🔦 Transparency 8-5
Audio Summaries
ExamView® Assessment Suite
Vocabulary PuzzleMaker
StudentWorks™ Plus
 Go Online

The Cycle of Abuse

The cycle of violence in abusive relationships goes beyond domestic partners. In fact, mental health experts have found that patterns of abuse often go back many **generations**. Many children who were abused or who witnessed abuse see this behavior as an acceptable model for how to treat people. As adults, they often go on to become abusers themselves. This *pattern of repeating abuse from one generation to the next* is known as the **cycle of abuse.** Breaking this cycle of abuse can be difficult and often requires outside help.

Breaking the Cycle of Abuse

Each of us has the power to break the cycle of abuse. If you suspect that a friend is being abused, it is important to ask your friend about it. If you are still concerned, tell a trusted adult. The first step a victim of abuse should take is to confide in a trusted adult. This can be a parent, another family member, a teacher, a school nurse or counselor, or a doctor. Victims can also call a **crisis hot line,** *a toll-free telephone service where abuse victims can get help and information.* **Figure 8.3** lists some organizations that provide toll-free crisis hot lines for victims of abuse, parents, and other concerned individuals. The people who staff these phone lines have received special training in dealing with abuse problems and helping victims of abuse. The person who calls is not asked to give his or her name. Conversations are kept strictly confidential.

Organization	Whom They Help
Childhelp USA	Child abuse victims, parents, concerned individuals
Youth Crisis Hotline	Individuals reporting child abuse, youth ages 12 to 18
Stop It Now!	Child sexual abuse victims, parents, offenders, concerned individuals
National Domestic Violence Hotline	Children, parents, friends, offenders
Girls and Boys Town	Abused, abandoned, and neglected girls and boys, parents, and family members

NAIC, U.S. Department of Health and Human Services.

Academic Vocabulary

generations (jen uh REY shuhnz) *(noun)* groups of individuals born and living at about the same time. *You, your parents, and your grandparents represent three different generations.*

◀ **FIGURE 8.3**

CRISIS HOT LINES FOR VICTIMS OF ABUSE

These organizations help victims of abuse by providing hot lines, where victims can talk about the abuse and get advice. **Who else do these organizations help?**

R

CHAPTER 8

Lesson 5

TEACH

Academic Vocabulary

Generations To help students recognize different *generations*, guide them in brainstorming a list of relatives who might attend a family reunion. Then help students group the relatives by *generation*, asking questions such as this: Which relatives are in the same *generation* you're in? 📁

AL Active Learning

Student-Led Learning Divide the class into four groups. Assign each group to develop a presentation that illustrates the cycle of abuse as it is defined on this page. Challenge groups to show in their posters ways to break the cycle of abuse by telling someone, confiding in a trusted adult, using a crisis hot line, or contacting another organization. Allow groups to share their presentations. **OL**

R Reading Strategy

Analyzing a Graphic After students have examined **Figure 8.3**, ask: Who does the Youth Crisis Hot Line help? *individuals reporting child abuse, youth ages 12 to 18* Point out that the organizations listed on the chart are national organizations and there may be local organizations that also operate crisis hot lines. **OL**

HEALTH LITERACY

Crisis Hot Lines A crisis hot line can be a way that an abused teen can feel safe in getting help. For example, the Girls and Boys Town National Hot Line has trained counselors ready to talk every day of the year, 24 hours a day. The hot line has an 800 number that allows a teen in trouble to get help free of charge. Spanish-speaking counselors as well as translation services for other languages are available at all times. Emphasize the importance of getting help, even if the victim has been threatened not to tell.

C Critical Thinking

Analyzing After students have read about shelters for abused family members, ask: Why do you think a victim of abuse might need a shelter to stay in for a while? Sample answer: *A victim may not be able to protect herself or himself. People at a shelter can make sure the abuser cannot contact the victim.* **OL**

 Reading Check

Answer Abused people may feel ashamed and do not want to discuss the problem. Also, they may fear what will happen to the abuser or to themselves if they report the problem.

Caption Answers

Figure Caption, p. 193 Organizations provide help for parents, concerned individuals, individuals reporting child abuse, friends, and offenders.

Photo Caption *Sample answer:* You can listen to the teen, comfort the teen with your friendship, encourage the teen to report any problems of abuse, and report problems yourself if the teen will not.

Ending abuse is not easy. Abused people—especially children—may feel ashamed, especially if the abuse was sexual. They may have fears over what will happen if they tell. They may fear that talking about the abuse will lead to the break up of their family. They may also have concerns about getting someone in trouble with the law, particularly if the abuser is a family member. Even though these concerns are understandable, the cycle of abuse will not end until someone reports the problem.

Sometimes victims are reluctant to say anything because they promised the abuser to keep the abuse secret. Sometimes abusers threaten their victims to keep them quiet. If you are the victim of abuse or you know someone who is, you need to be aware that keeping it a secret is never a good idea. The only way an abuser will ever stop is by getting help. It is important for you to know that you are not alone. Others have experienced the same thing, and there are people who are willing to help you.

 Reading Check **Recall** Why is ending abuse not easy?

▲ Some families who are living in abusive homes might go to shelters, where they can be safe and get emotional support. **How can you help another teen in need of emotional support?**

HEALTH LITERACY

Breaking the Cycle When authority figures, parents, and teachers distinguish between proper discipline techniques and abusive behaviors, teens can learn to work productively in society. Following some specific guidelines can instill discipline without damaging a child's self-esteem:

Be consistent so that the child knows what to expect. Remain calm but firm. Distinguish between the misbehavior and the child so the child realizes it's the behavior that is wrong. Praise positive behavior. Give children choices whenever possible.

Help with Abuse Problems

Most people need professional help to overcome the emotional trauma of abuse. For many, help means counseling—talking through their problems with someone trained to listen. Teens who have been abused sometimes find comfort in group counseling sessions. These sessions give teens an opportunity to discuss their situation with others who have experienced similar problems.

In extreme situations or ones where abuse is ongoing, abused family members may be sent to shelters—community-run residences where victims of abuse can feel safe. They can stay at the shelter while getting help putting their lives back together.

If you suspect that a friend is a victim of abuse, share what you have learned. Strongly urge the person to seek help.

 Reading Check **List** Name some sources of help for abuse problems.

 G☺ Online

Visit **glencoe.com** and complete the Interactive Study Guide for Lesson 5.

 Reading Check

Answer community shelters, local support groups, or hot lines

ASSESS

Assessment Resources

Lesson Review Quiz
- *ExamView*
- Fast Files Activities
- Online Quizzes and Activities

Reteaching
- Assign Concept Map 8-5 or Reteaching Activity 8-5 in the Fast Files. 📁
- Ask students to write a paragraph that explains what the cycle of abuse is and how the cycle can be broken.

Enrichment
- Assign Enrichment Activity 8-5 in the Fast Files. 📁
- Have students write stories that describe a cycle of abuse and how a victim is able to break that cycle.

CLOSE

Call on volunteers to describe an example of a cycle of abuse. Call on other volunteers to explain how each victim described could break the cycle.

 ## Lesson 5 Review

After You Read

Review this lesson for new terms, major headings, and Reading Checks.

What I Learned
1. *Vocabulary* What is the *cycle of abuse*?
2. *Identify* What is the first step any abuse victim should take to end the cycle of abuse?
3. *List* What are some crisis hot lines for victims of abuse?

Thinking Critically
4. *Apply* Debbie, a victim of family abuse, says she really wants to report the problem but doesn't know who to turn to. What might you tell Debbie that would encourage her to make a healthful choice to call for help?

5. *Analyze* Why might some victims of abuse be reluctant to report the abuse?
6. *Explain* Why do children who are abused sometimes become abusers themselves?

Applying Health Skills
7. *Accessing Information* With a group, learn about specific resources in your community for abused families. Identify what types of resources they are, such as shelters, counseling, or hot lines. Share your findings with other groups.

G☺ Online For more Lesson Review Activities, go to **glencoe.com**.

Lesson 5: Preventing and Coping with Abuse **195**

Lesson 5 Review Answers

1. the pattern of repeating abuse from one generation to the next
2. Telling someone is the first step.
3. Childhelp USA, Youth Crisis Hot Line, Stop It Now!, National Domestic Violence Hot Line
4. *Sample answer:* The cycle of abuse will not end until someone reports the problem.

Debbie should talk to a trusted adult, such as a teacher, school nurse or counselor, or her doctor. She could also call a crisis hot line.
5. *Sample answer:* Some abuse victims may believe that reporting the abuse will get the abuser or themselves in trouble. They may feel too afraid or ashamed to report the abuse.

6. *Sample answer:* Children who are abused can become abusers themselves as adults because they see this behavior as an acceptable model for how to treat people.
7. Encourage each group to use library and online resources as well as the local telephone book to carry out their research.

Building Health Skills Standing Up to Harassment

Skill

Desicion Making

Activating Prior Knowledge

Ask students to explain what harassment is and describe an approach that could be used to deal with harassment.

- **Objective** After completing the activity, students will be able to use their decision-making skills to deal with a situation that involves harassment.

- **Time** 45 minutes

- **Materials** paper, pencil, markers or crayons

Teacher Classroom Resources

 Building Health Skills Activity

Transparency 2-2

Model

- Have students read about Marcus's experience. Ask: What were the three options Marcus decided he had? *He could talk to the coach, talk directly to Gil, or quit the team.* Why did he reject two of the options? *Talking to Gil might make him angry. And Marcus was not a quitter.*

National Health Standards Addressed

5.8.2, 5.8.7

Building Health Skills

Accessing Information
Practicing Healthful Behaviors
Stress Management
Analyzing Influences
Communication Skills
Refusal Skills
Conflict Resolution
Decision Making
Goal Setting
Advocacy

What Steps Can You Take to Make Healthy Decisions?

The decision-making process can help you make healthy and responsible choices. The six steps of the decision-making process are as follows:

1. State the situation.
2. List the options.
3. Weigh the possible outcomes.
4. Consider your values.
5. Make a decision and act.
6. Evaluate the decision.

Standing Up to Harassment

Follow the Model, Practice, and Apply steps to help you master this important health skill.

❶ Model

Read how Marcus used the decision-making process to solve a problem with a teammate.

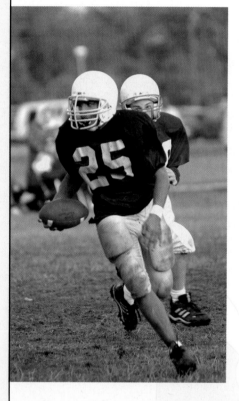

196

Marcus had worked hard to make the football team. Gil, one of his teammates, was continually making fun of him, which really bothered Marcus.

Step 1: State the Situation: I am being harassed by a teammate, and I would like it to end.

Step 2: List the Options: I could talk to the coach or directly to Gil. I could also quit the team.

Step 3: Weigh the Possible Outcomes: Talking to the coach would probably help. If I talk to Gil, he may get angry or tease me even more.

Step 4: Consider Your Values: I am not a quitter. I worked hard to make the team.

Step 5: Make a Decision and Act: I will tell the coach. I know he will be able to help.

Step 6: Evaluate the Decision: The coach talked to both Gil and I, and helped us work out the problem.

Teaching Tips

Time to Think Emphasize that the decision-making skill can help persons such as Marcus calmly think through what they want to do without "flying off the handle" and possibly reacting in an unhealthy way.

Relate to School Policies Bring in the school policy that describes expectations regarding how students are to treat one another at your school. Ask students to read sections of the policy aloud. Ask: How can showing respect to others improve the school's learning environment?

② Practice

Read the passage below and practice the decision-making process by answering the questions that follow.

Carla is being teased by classmates about her clothes. She doesn't wear the same designer labels that all the popular kids wear. Some of Carla's peers pass mean notes to her in class and make fun of her on the playground. A group of girls even follows Carla home from school, making fun of her clothes all the way. As a result, Carla dreads going to school. She wants to make the teasing stop, but she is not sure about what she should do. Imagine that you are Carla. Use the decision-making steps to guide you in making a good decision.

1. What is Carla's situation?
2. What are some of Carla's options?
3. What are the possible outcomes?
4. Consider what Carla's values might be.
5. What decision does Carla make?

③ Apply

Use what you have learned about decision making to complete the activity below.

With a small group, brainstorm some other situations a teen might face that involve harassment. Then write a story about the teen and explain the type of harassment he or she is experiencing. Show how decision making is used to end the harassment.

Self-Check
- Did we use each step in the decision-making process?
- Did we include an explanation of the harassment the teen was experiencing?

Building Health Skills

Practice

- Have students read the introduction in the Practice activity.
- Have students work in small groups to discuss the questions. Ask each small group to write a response to the questions.
- Lead a class discussion of the responses. Ask volunteers to share how they answered each of the questions. As students suggest options that Carla had, make a list of options on the board. Discuss the possible outcome of each.
- Encourage the class to come to a consensus about what Carla's decision should be and how she should act.

Apply/Assess

- Review with each group the situations they brainstormed. Help each group choose one about which to write and illustrate a story.
- Remind each group to review the Skills Summary before writing the story.
- Provide groups with markers or crayons to use in creating the illustrations for their stories.
- Have each group write answers to the Self-Check questions.
- You may wish to distribute the Building Health Skills Activity in the Fast Files.

ASSESSMENT SCORING

Using a rubric, student work should meet all criteria to achieve the highest score.

Skills Student work:
- states the situation.
- lists the options.
- weighs the outcomes.
- considers values.
- makes a decision.
- evaluates the decision.

Concepts Student work:
- describes a health-enhancing decision.
- includes an accurate and complete explanation of the harassment.

HANDS-ON HEALTH
ACTIVITY

A Nonviolent Response to a Threatening Situation

Time: 30 minutes
Materials: poster board, markers or crayons

Introducing Hands-on Health

- Have a class discussion on ways teens can respond to threatening situations in nonviolent ways. Describe specific situations in which a teen is harassed, intimidated, emotionally abused, or bullied. Call on volunteers to describe how the teen can deal with the situation.

Teaching the Activity

- Divide the class into six small groups. Assign each group one of four threatening situations listed.
- Have each group imagine a specific scenario in which a teen is faced with the situation.
- Encourage each group to create a poster that illustrates the situation.
- After all groups have completed the activity, ask each group to present its poster to the class. Then lead a class discussion about the situations illustrated and how the teens in the situations responded in a nonviolent way.
- Have students write a paragraph that answers the question in Wrapping It Up.
OL

HANDS-ON HEALTH

A Nonviolent Response to a Threatening Situation

When faced with a threatening situation, a common reaction is to want to lash out in anger. When people are pushed, either physically or emotionally, they want to push back. This chapter presents a number of different situations that are threatening, which include harassment, intimidation, abuse, and bullying. When you are faced with a threatening situation, be prepared to respond in a nonviolent way. This activity can help you learn some nonviolent responses.

What You Will Need

- Poster board
- Markers or crayons

☀ACTIVITY What You Will Do

1 Your teacher will divide the class into four small groups and assign each group one of the following threatening behaviors: harassment, intimidation, emotional abuse, and bullying.

2 In your group, brainstorm nonviolent ways of responding to your threatening situation. First, imagine an instance in which the threatening behavior takes place. For example, if your group was assigned the behavior of bullying, think of a situation in which someone your age might be bullied. Discuss how this young person might respond in a nonviolent way.

3 Now, create a colorful poster. On one side of the poster write "The Situation" at the top. Below that, describe the situation your group has come up with. On the other side of the poster write "A Nonviolent Response." Below that write a nonviolent way of responding to the situation.

Wrapping It Up

After all the groups have presented their posters, discuss these questions as a class: How can teens help other teens respond to threatening situations in a nonviolent way? Also, discuss the benefits of responding in a nonviolent way.

Display your posters where your classmates can see them. This will help students learn a variety of nonviolent responses.

198 Chapter 8: Violence Prevention

HANDS-ON HEALTH Assessment

Discussion After the class has had time to complete the activity, ask students to:
- Describe a situation in which a teen is faced with a threatening situation.
- Explain how the student in each situation described could respond in a nonviolent way.

Reading Review

STUDY TO GO Visit glencoe.com to download quizzes and eFlashcards for Chapter 8.

FOLDABLES Study Organizer

Foldables® and Other Study Aids Take out the Foldable® that you created for Lesson 1 and any graphic organizers that you created for Lessons 1–5. Find a partner and quiz each other using these study aids.

Lesson 1 Avoiding and Preventing Violence

Main Idea You can take steps to avoid being the victim of violence. You can also take steps to prevent the spread of violence.

- Violence can take the form of words as well as actions.
- Many researchers see a connection between media and teen violence.
- Factors that add to teen violence include the media, gangs, weapons, and drugs.
- Many schools have taken steps to prevent violence on their campus.

Lesson 2 Dealing with Violence

Main Idea Victims need to get help to deal with the effects of violence.

- Victims of violence suffer both physical and mental/emotional injuries.
- Ways to avoid becoming a victim of rape include going out with a group of peers, avoiding going anywhere with a date where you are alone, and refusing to allow someone to touch you in a way that makes you feel uncomfortable.
- You can help defeat violence by reporting any crimes that you witness, and by becoming an advocate for safety and victims' rights.

Lesson 3 Bullying and Harassment

Main Idea Bullies often taunt people who are shy or stick out in some way.

- Forms of harassment include bullying, intimidation, teasing, and sexual harassment.
- You can deal with harassment by being assertive and telling your bully to stop harassing you. If that doesn't work, ask a trusted adult for help.

Lesson 4 Abuse

Main Idea Abuse affects the physical, mental/emotional, and social health of the victim.

- Abuse can take several forms, including physical abuse, emotional abuse, neglect, and sexual abuse.
- Children who have been abused often have low self-esteem and can be self-destructive. If they don't seek help, they can become abusers themselves.

Lesson 5 Preventing and Coping with Abuse

Main Idea Each of us has the power to break the cycle of abuse.

- Many children who were abused or witnessed abuse see this behavior as an acceptable model for how to treat people.
- Victims and abusers need help in order to end the cycle of abuse.
- Ways for abuse victims to get help include talking to a trusted adult, calling a crisis hot line, counseling, and staying in community shelters.

CHAPTER 8

Assessment Resources

- Chapter 8 Summary and Activity
- Audio Summaries
- Reading Tutor
- Performance Assessment
- Chapter 8 Test
- *ExamView*
- Vocabulary PuzzleMaker
- Online Learning Center

Reading Review

Study Aids

- **Using the Dinah Zike Foldable® Study Organizer** Have students use the Foldable® **FOLDABLES** Study Organizer to review the content of Lesson 1. Have students reexamine their answers to the reading strategies to review content in Lessons 2 through 5.
- **Online Learning Tools** Have students go to the *Teen Health* Online Learning Center at **glencoe.com** to:
  - Download a **Podcast**.
  - Download free **Study-to-Go** STUDY TO GO content to their PDAs or cell phones.

Vocabulary Review

- **Vocabulary Concept Map** Have students work in small groups to make a concept map that uses many of the chapter's vocabulary terms.

Teaching Tips

Using the K-W-L Method The ability to read effectively is important to student success. One way you can engage students in reading is to experiment with the K-W-L method—What I **K**now, What I **W**ant to Know, What I've **L**earned. Before students read, have them brainstorm everything they know about a topic (What I Know). Then ask them to make a list of questions about the topic (What I Want to Know). After students have read about the topic, see if they can answer the questions (What I've Learned). Finally, have them explore new ideas related to the topic.

Reviewing Vocabulary and Main Ideas

1. Violence
2. homicide
3. Zero tolerance policy
4. victim
5. assault
6. Rape
7. True
8. False, harassment
9. True
10. False, domestic violence
11. True
12. True
13. False, shelters

Thinking Critically

14. *Sample answer:* He needs to know that becoming a member of a gang increases his risks of becoming a victim of violence and of serving time in jail for possession of drugs or weapons.

Write About It

15. **Expository Writing** Answers, which will vary, should identify how violence in the media can influence teen behavior. Teens can learn to imitate violent acts depicted on television, or be persuaded that violence is an acceptable way to resolve conflict. Media violence rarely shows the negative consequences for the offenders and often portrays violent acts in a glamorous light.

Have students visit **glencoe.com** to take the Chapter 8 quiz.

200

 After You Read

HEALTH QUIZ
Now that you have read the chapter, look back at your answers to the Health Quiz on the chapter opener. Would you change any of them? What would your answers be now?

Reviewing Vocabulary and Main Ideas

On a sheet of paper, write the numbers 1–6. After each number, write the term from the list that best completes each sentence.

- assault
- battery
- gang
- homicide
- rape
- victim
- violence
- zero tolerance policy

Lesson 1 Avoiding and Preventing Violence

1. _____ is any behavior that causes physical or psychological harm to a person or damage to property.

2. The killing of one human being by another is known as _____.

3. _____ is a policy that makes no exceptions for anybody for any reason.

Lesson 2 Dealing with Violence

4. A(n) _____ is any individual who suffers injury, loss, or death due to violence.

5. An unlawful threat or attempt to do bodily injury to another person is known as _____.

6. _____ is any kind of sexual intercourse against a person's will.

*On a sheet of paper, write the numbers 7–13. Write **True** or **False** for each statement below. If the statement is false, change the underlined word or phrase to make it true.*

Lesson 3 Bullying and Harassment

7. <u>Intimidation</u> is purposely frightening another person through threatening words, looks, or body language.

8. A repeating pattern of behavior that includes making fun of someone is called <u>violence</u>.

9. When harassment involves obscene behavior or remarks of a sexual nature, it is called <u>sexual harassment</u>.

Lesson 4 Abuse

10. The most common type of abuse is <u>zero tolerance</u>.

11. Children, <u>older adults</u>, and people with disabilities all may be targets of neglect.

Lesson 5 Preventing and Coping with Abuse

12. The <u>cycle of abuse</u> is a pattern in which children of abuse go on to become abusers.

13. If abuse is ongoing or violent, family members may go to community-run residences known as <u>crisis hot lines</u>.

Go Online Visit **glencoe.com** and take the Online Quiz for Chapter 8.

HEALTH QUIZ Wrap-Up

Violence and Abuse Have students retake the chapter opener Health Quiz. Some students may find that their answers have changed after reading the chapter. Ask: What is a specific idea from the chapter that changed one of your answers on the Health Quiz? Sample answer: *I thought violent gangs were only found in large cities, but now I know that many suburban and rural communities have gangs.*

Thinking Critically

Using complete sentences, answer the following question on a sheet of paper.

14. **Analyze** A teen named Tom lives in a community that has gangs. Tom does not want to join a gang, but he feels that doing so is the only sure way of surviving. What information does Tom need to have that might help him make a healthier decision?

Write About It

15. **Expository Writing** Write a paragraph describing how the media might influence violent behavior.

↗ Applying Technology

Violence Prevention Poster

You will use Comic Life or Microsoft Word® to create a poster that illustrates what you have learned about violence prevention. Follow the directions below to complete this project.

- Locate images or take digital pictures that illustrate the message of your poster.
- Drag these images into a new ComicLife or Microsoft Word® template.
- Insert text boxes to add titles to your images.
- Write a few sentences about each image. Make sure to say how they relate to violence prevention.
- Edit for accuracy, clarity, spelling, and grammar.
- Save your project.

↗ Applying Technology

Violence Prevention Poster
Equipment needs: ComicLife or Microsoft Word® or similar software Guide students in discussing ideas for their posters, and help them review the steps in the project. If computer access is limited, establish a sign-up list and determine a time limit for each student. Ask students to help one another edit their work for accuracy, clarity, spelling, and grammar. If materials are available, print each student's poster, and display the posters in public areas of your school.

Standardized Test Practice

Math

The table below contains data about victims of violence for a 10-year period. Use the data to answer the questions that follow.

Violent Victimization Rates by Age, 1994–2003*

Year	12–15	16–19	20–24
1994	118.6	123.9	100.4
1995	113.1	106.6	85.8
1996	95.0	102.8	74.5
1997	87.9	96.3	68.0
1998	82.5	91.3	67.5
1999	74.4	77.5	68.7
2000	60.1	64.4	49.5
2001	55.1	55.9	44.9
2002	44.4	58.3	47.6
2003	51.6	53.1	43.5

* Violent crime per 1,000 persons in age group

TEST-TAKING TIP

When dealing with tables or charts, read the title and examine the information. Make sure you understand what type of data the table or chart contains.

1. The only year in which 20- to 24-year-olds experienced a higher rate of crime than 12- to 15-year-olds was
   - **A.** 2002
   - **B.** 1996
   - **C.** 1998
   - **D.** 2003

2. For the years 2000 to 2003, the mean victim rate for 12- to 15-year-olds was
   - **A.** 51.6
   - **B.** 55.1
   - **C.** 56.4
   - **D.** 52.8

Standardized Test Practice

1. A
2. D

Test-Taking Tips

Determining the Mean Tell students that some test questions may call for a calculation to determine the answer. Question 2 of the Standardized Test Practice is such a question. In this case, students must determine the mean of a list of numbers. Remind students that the mean of a list of numbers is the numerical average. You calculate the mean by adding all the numbers together and then dividing the sum by how many numbers there are in the list. In this case, students should add the victimization rates for 12- to 15-year-olds in the years 2000, 2001, 2002, and 2003. To find the mean, students should divide the sum by 4.

Physical Activity and Fitness

CHAPTER 9 pp. 202–231	Standards		Skills and Activities
	National	**State/Local**	
	National Health Education Standards 1.8.5, 6.8.2, 6.8.3		*Health* eSpotlight *p. 203* **BUILDING HEALTH SKILLS** *Practicing Healthful Behaviors* Playing It Safe, *pp. 226–227* TIME health news Run for It!, *p. 228*
Lesson 1 **The Benefits of Physical Activity** pp. 204–208	National Health Education Standards 1.8.1, 1.8.2, 1.8.5, 1.8.7, 2.8.5, 5.8.6, 5.8.7, 7.8.2, 8.8.1		**MEDIA WATCH** Fitness in a Bottle, *p. 205* **HEALTH SKILLS ACTIVITY** *Practicing Healthful Behaviors* Activity + Eating + Sleeping = Good Physical Health, *p. 207*
Lesson 2 **Endurance, Strength, and Flexibility** pp. 209–214	National Health Education Standards 1.8.1, 1.8.4, 1.8.5, 1.8.7, 3.8.2, 6.8.2, 7.8.2, 8.8.2		**Careers for the 21st Century** Personal Trainer, *p. 211*
Lesson 3 **Setting Fitness Goals** pp. 215–220	National Health Education Standards 1.8.1, 1.8.5, 1.8.7, 6.8.2, 6.8.3, 7.8.1, 7.8.2		**HEALTH SKILLS ACTIVITY** *Accessing Information* Measuring Your Heart Rate, *p. 218* **Connect To... MATH** Target Heart Rate, *p. 218* **What Teens Think** How can you make physical activity part of your daily routine? *p. 219* **Go Online** Stretching for Fitness, *p. 219*
Lesson 4 **Sports Conditioning and Avoiding Injury** pp. 221–225	National Health Education Standards 1.8.1, 1.8.5, 1.8.8, 1.8.9, 7.8.2, 8.8.3		**DEVELOPING GOOD CHARACTER** Being a Team Player, *p. 222*

PACING THE CHAPTER		
Lesson 1 30 min	**Lesson 4** 30 min	**TIME health news** 30 min
Lesson 2 45 min		**Chapter Review** 45 min
Lesson 3 45 min	**Building Health Skills** 90 min	

BLOCK SCHEDULING

For block scheduling, assign students Building Health Skills feature *Playing It Safe*, pages 226–227, and Guided Reading and Writing. 📁

Reproducible Resources	Assessment	Media and Technology
Chapter FAST FILE Resources Chapter Summaries and Activities REVIEW Building Health Skills Activity TEACH Performance Assessment Activity EXTEND Universal Access Activities TEACH Parent Letter and Activities 📁 **Student Activities Workbook** TEACH 📁 **Reading Tutor** TEACH	Building Health Skills Activity, pp. 226–227 Chapter 9 Assessment, pp. 230–231 **Chapter FAST FILE Resources** Performance Assessment Activity, p. 4 Chapter 9 Test, p. 7 💿 ExamView® Assessment Suite	TeacherWorks Plus includes: ● Interactive Teacher Edition ● Lesson Planner with Calendar ● Access to all blackline masters ● Correlations to standards 💿 StudentWorks™ Plus 💿 Online Student Edition Dinah Zike's Teaching Health with Foldables®
Chapter FAST FILE Resources Concept Mapping Activity 9-1 REVIEW Decision-Making Activity 9-1 EXTEND Enrichment Activity 9-1 EXTEND Lesson Plan 9-1 Guided Reading and Writing 9-1 TEACH Reteaching Activity 9-1 REVIEW	Lesson 1 Review, p. 208 💿 Vocabulary PuzzleMaker 💿 ExamView® Assessment Suite	💿 Vocabulary PuzzleMaker 💿 ExamView® Assessment Suite 💿 StudentWorks™ Plus 📎 Transparency 9-1 Go Online glencoe.com
Chapter FAST FILE Resources Concept Mapping Activity 9-2 REVIEW Health Lab 9-2 EXTEND Enrichment Activity 9-2 EXTEND Lesson Plan 9-2 Guided Reading and Writing 9-2 TEACH Reteaching Activity 9-2 REVIEW	Lesson 2 Review, p. 214 💿 Vocabulary PuzzleMaker 💿 ExamView® Assessment Suite	💿 Vocabulary PuzzleMaker 💿 ExamView® Assessment Suite 💿 StudentWorks™ Plus 📎 Transparency 9-2 Go Online glencoe.com
Chapter FAST FILE Resources Concept Mapping Activity 9-3 REVIEW Cross-Curriculum Activity 9-3 EXTEND Enrichment Activity 9-3 EXTEND Lesson Plan 9-3 Guided Reading and Writing 9-3 TEACH Reteaching Activity 9-3 REVIEW	Lesson 3 Review, p. 220 💿 Vocabulary PuzzleMaker 💿 ExamView® Assessment Suite	💿 Vocabulary PuzzleMaker 💿 ExamView® Assessment Suite 💿 StudentWorks™ Plus 📎 Transparency 9-3 Go Online glencoe.com
Chapter FAST FILE Resources Concept Mapping Activity 9-4 REVIEW Decision-Making Activity 9-4 EXTEND Enrichment Activity 9-4 EXTEND Lesson Plan 9-4 Guided Reading and Writing 9-4 TEACH Reteaching Activity 9-4 REVIEW	Lesson 4 Review, p. 225 💿 Vocabulary PuzzleMaker 💿 ExamView® Assessment Suite	💿 Vocabulary PuzzleMaker 💿 ExamView® Assessment Suite 💿 StudentWorks™ Plus 📎 Transparency 9-4 Go Online glencoe.com

Chapter and Lesson Resources

The *Teen Health* resources are designed for differentiated learning abilities. You may want to use the coded items in this way:

REVIEW —activities to review or reinforce content

TEACH —activities to teach basic concepts

EXTEND —activities to extend or enrich lesson content

 OUT OF TIME?

Use Health Skills Activities *Activity + Eating + Sleeping = Good Physical Health,* page 207, or Developing Good Character, page 222.

Physical Activity in Adolescence

Recent studies show that almost 50 percent of teens fail to meet current recommendations of 60 minutes of moderate-to-vigorous physical activity at least five days per week. Studies also show that the majority of teens become less active throughout adolescence and even more inactive as adults.

A major reason for the drop in physical activity during adolescence is a corresponding increase in sedentary activities, especially watching TV and playing computer games. Teens who spend the most time in these inactive pursuits have the lowest levels of physical activity. On the other hand, teens who participate in daily physical education classes or use community recreation facilities have higher rates of physical activity.

What can you do to help students become more physically active?

- Encourage students to play sports or participate in other physical activities, especially activities that they can continue to enjoy throughout life, such as walking or swimming.

- Urge students to spend less time watching TV and playing computer games. Experts recommend that teens spend no more than two hours per day involved in sedentary activities such as these.

- Become a strong advocate of physical education programs in your school and of recreational facilities in your community.

Sports-Related Brain Injuries

Although the brain is well protected by the skull, brain injuries such as concussions are common in many sports. Brain injuries are also the main cause of sports-related fatalities. Sports with a high risk of brain injuries include football, boxing, soccer, horseback riding, skating, skateboarding, snow skiing, ice hockey, and baseball. In high school football, for example, every year about one in five players receives a brain injury. In horseback riding, brain injuries account for almost 20 percent of all injuries received while participating in the sport.

Evidence suggests that receiving one brain injury makes the brain more susceptible to subsequent injuries. When an athlete suffers from a second or third brain injury, the outcome is likely to be very serious. Repeated mild brain injuries over a long period, such as months or years, can cause permanent brain damage. Repeated mild brain injuries over a shorter time, such as days or weeks, can be fatal. In such cases, death usually is caused by swelling of the brain, which occurs because a previous brain injury did not have time to heal.

Experts recommend that athletes who receive brain injuries, even mild concussions, should not resume playing until healing can occur, generally for at least one week. Athletes who receive repeated brain injuries may be advised to stop playing the sport altogether to prevent risk of permanent brain damage or death from another brain injury.

Reading Support

Reading Preview

Activating Background Vocabulary Ask students what comes to mind when they hear the term *physical fitness*. Create a word web on the board, with this term in the center surrounded by students' responses. Guide students in a discussion of the benefits of physical activity and what students need to do to keep their bodies, minds, and emotions physically fit.

FOLDABLES **Study Organizer** *Dinah Zike's Reading and Study Skills for Teen Health* provides interactive graphic organizers that help students comprehend and retain health concepts as they read. Use the Foldable® on page 203 or find more Foldables® activities for the chapter on **Physical Activity and Fitness** in the separate booklet, available in the TCR.

Lesson 1   The Benefits of Physical Activity

3-2-1 Strategy Ask students to write a brief summary identifying **three** key points they found while reading about an active lifestyle and the importance of physical activity. Next, have students list **two** things in the lesson they thought were interesting. Last, ask students to write **one** question they still have. Have student pairs reread to find the answers.

Lesson 2   Endurance, Strength, and Flexibility

Thinking Aloud 1) Ask students to predict what **Measures of Fitness** will be about. 2) Model the images you form while reading—"I see people taking tests to see what shape they are in." 3) Relate the reading to your own experience—"This reminds me of measuring my heart rate." 4) Note questions—"I don't understand this part…", and model strategies to clarify—"I think I'll read this page again."

Lesson 3   Setting Fitness Goals

Reciprocal Teaching Have student pairs: 1) Summarize—stop after reading **Building Fitness Levels** and paraphrase the content. 2) Clarify—ask each other if they have questions to answer before reading on. 3) Question—think about the types of questions a teacher might ask on an exam. 4) Predict—make a guess about what is next in the lesson.

Lesson 4   Sports Conditioning and Avoiding Injury

Writing to Learn Stop students during reading and discuss ways to prepare oneself before playing sports. Have students reflect on the discussion and write a question they still have. Then have students exchange papers and write for five minutes on the topic, answering the writer's question or giving the writer resources to find the answer.

Post Reading

Multimedia Presentations Guide students in a summative discussion about physical activity, measures of fitness, fitness goals, conditioning, and avoiding injury. Direct students to work in pairs to use classroom and library resources to develop a presentation that incorporates audiovisual aids and technology and covers one of the topics in this chapter.

Key for Using the Teacher Wraparound Edition

Use this key to help you identify the different types of prompts found in the Teacher Wraparound Edition.

R **Reading Strategies** activities help you teach reading skills and vocabulary.

C **Critical Thinking** strategies help students apply and extend what they have learned.

U **Universal Access** activities provide differentiated instruction for students learning to speak English, along with suggestions for teaching various types of learners.

HS **Health Skills Practice** activities reinforce Health Skills concepts and help students apply these skills in their everyday lives.

W **Writing Support** activities provide writing opportunities to help students comprehend the text.

AL **Active Learning** strategies provide a variety of activities for presenting lesson content, including Quick Demos and engaging classroom projects that get students actively involved.

Key to Ability Levels

Teaching Strategies and activities have been coded for ability level and appropriateness.

AL Activities for students working above grade level

OL Activities for students working on grade level

BL Activities for students working below grade level

EL Activities for English Learners

Symbols

🔖 Transparencies

💿 CD-ROM

✏️ glencoe.com

📁 Print Resources

Physical Activity and Fitness

Chapter at a Glance

Lesson 1 describes benefits of physical activity and physical fitness and explains the importance of exercise in an overall fitness plan.

Lesson 2 identifies the five elements of physical fitness and describes exercises to improve them.

Lesson 3 explains how to choose activities to meet fitness goals, apply the F.I.T.T. principle, and warm up and cool down.

Lesson 4 describes sports conditioning, nutrition guidelines for athletes, and ways to minimize and treat sports injuries.

R Reading Strategy

Interpreting the Photo Ask students to look at the photo of a teen being physically active. Call on volunteers to answer the caption question. Sample answer: *When you exercise, you feel good about yourself. You are able to think more clearly. You can handle stress better.* OL

202

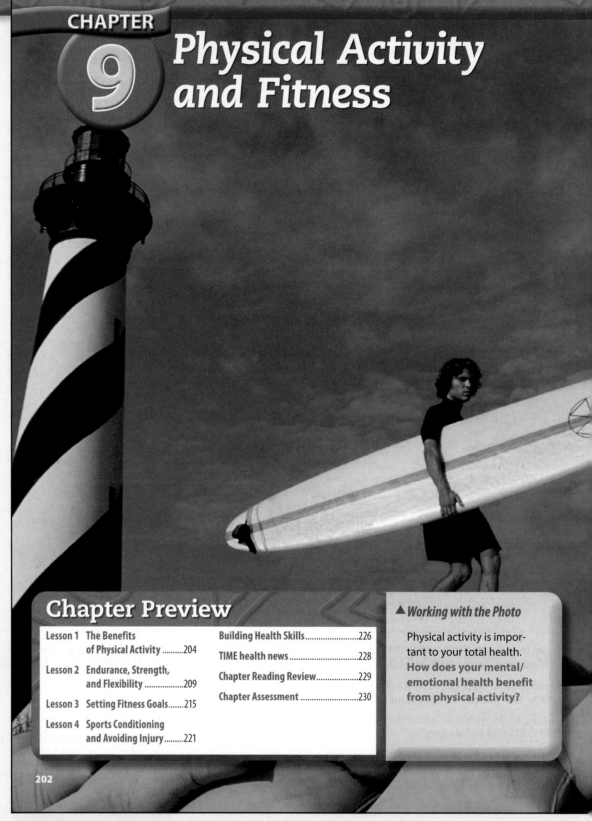

CHAPTER 9 Physical Activity and Fitness

Chapter Preview

▲ **Working with the Photo**

Physical activity is important to your total health. **How does your mental/emotional health benefit from physical activity?**

202

Universal Access

Differentiated Learning Glencoe provides teacher support and student materials for all learners in the health classroom.

● Spanish Glosario and chapter summaries assist English Language Learners.
● *Reading Tutor* and related worksheets support reluctant readers.

● Universal Access strategies throughout the Teacher Wraparound Edition and Fast Files help you present materials for gifted students, at-risk students, physically impaired students, and those with behavior disorders or learning disabilities.

Start-Up Activities

Before You Read
Do you know how to achieve your fitness goals? Answer the Health eSpotlight questions below and then watch the online video. Keep a record of your answers.

Health eSpotlight
VIDEO

Achieving Fitness Goals

Achieving fitness goals often requires careful planning. Some goals, like participating in a race for charity, require a schedule and time in order to be successful. What fitness goals would you like to achieve? What short- and long-term goals are necessary to achieve your plan?

Go to **glencoe.com** and watch the health video for Chapter 9. Then complete the activity provided with the online video.

FOLDABLES Study Organizer

As You Read
Make this Foldable® to help you organize the information on physical activity, exercise, and physical fitness presented in Lesson 1. Begin with a plain sheet of 11" × 17" paper.

1 Fold the sheet of paper in half along the short axis, then fold in half again. This forms four columns.

2 Open the paper and refold it in half along the long axis, then fold in half again. This forms four rows.

3 Unfold and draw lines along the folds.

4 Label the chart as shown.

Chapter 9	Definition	Examples	Impact on my life
Physical Activity			
Exercise			
Physical Fitness			

In the appropriate section of the chart, write down definitions and examples of physical activity, exercise, and physical fitness, as well as the impact each has on your daily life.

Go Online Visit **glencoe.com** and complete the Health Inventory for Chapter 9.

203

FOCUS

Activating Prior Knowledge

What I Know Have students list all the ways that they were physically active on the previous day. Call on a few volunteers to read their lists to the class. Tell students they will learn about the benefits of physical activity in this lesson.

 Guide to Reading

Building Vocabulary

- Ask: How do you think the terms *physical activity* and *physical fitness* are related?
  Sample answers: *Physical activity improves physical fitness. You need to have physical fitness to do some physical activities.* Students can see if they were right when they read the lesson.
- Use Vocabulary PuzzleMaker to reinforce vocabulary terms.

Reading Strategy

Predicting Students may predict that they will learn how to be more active and why physical activity is important.

FOLDABLES Study Organizer Have students use their Foldables® as they read Lesson 1.

uick Write

Remind students to start their paragraph with a topic sentence. Have volunteers read their paragraphs to the class, and then discuss ways to be physically active.

204

The Benefits of Physical Activity

 Guide to Reading

● **Building Vocabulary**
Write each term below in your notebook and add a definition in pencil. As you read the lesson, be prepared to make corrections to your definitions.

- physical activity (p. 204)
- coordination (p. 205)
- balance (p. 205)
- calories (p. 205)
- physical fitness (p. 206)
- exercise (p. 207)
- aerobic exercise (p. 207)
- anaerobic exercise (p. 208)

● **Focusing on the Main Ideas**
In this lesson, you will learn to

- **analyze** the benefits of physical activity.
- **develop** habits to improve your physical health.
- **describe** various types of physical activities.
- **explain** the importance of exercise to overall fitness.

● **Reading Strategy**
Predicting Examine the headings, figures, and captions before you read this lesson. Predict what kinds of information you think you will learn.

FOLDABLES Study Organizer Use the Foldable® on p. 203 as you read this lesson.

uick Write

Write a short paragraph about the kinds of physical activity you do in a typical day.

Choosing an Active Lifestyle

Connor and Marcus are identical twins. Although they look alike, their interests and health habits are different. When they have a choice between playing basketball or a video game, Connor chooses basketball and Marcus chooses the video game. When there is a choice between taking the stairs or an elevator, Connor takes the stairs. Can you guess which choice Marcus makes?

Which brother are you more like? If you are like Connor, you follow an active lifestyle that includes plenty of physical activity. **Physical activity** is *any form of bodily movement that uses up energy*. Health experts advise teens to get 60 minutes of physical activity on most days. This can be done all at once or divided into 10- or 15-minute bursts of activity.

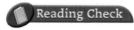 **Reading Check** **Identify** How much physical activity is recommended for teens?

Lesson 1 Resources

📁 **Chapter *FAST FILE* Resources**
Guided Reading and Writing 9-1
Concept Mapping Activity 9-1
Decision-Making Activity 9-1
Reteaching Activity 9-1
Enrichment Activity 9-1
Lesson Quiz 9-1

Technology
🔧 Transparency 9-1
🔊 Audio Summaries
⚙️ *ExamView®* Assessment Suite
🔊 Vocabulary PuzzleMaker
⚙️ StudentWorks™ Plus

Go Online

Why Is Physical Activity Important?

Like a machine, your body is made up of many moving parts. Staying physically active helps keep those parts in good working order. Physical activity benefits each side of the health triangle:

- **Physical Health:** When you choose to make regular physical activity a part of your life, you have more energy to complete your daily activities. Physical activity helps your heart and lungs work more efficiently and strengthens your bones. It improves **coordination,** *the smooth and effective working together of your muscles and bones.* It also improves your **balance,** *the feeling of stability and control over your body.* Physical activity during the day helps you sleep better and more soundly at night. It also helps you maintain a healthy weight by burning **calories.** These are *units of heat that measure the energy available in foods.* Physical activity helps "use up" calories that could lead to unwanted extra pounds. **Figure 9.1** on the next page shows the calories burned doing various activities for one hour.

- **Mental/Emotional Health:** Physically active people are better able to handle the stress and challenges of everyday life. They also tend to have higher self-esteem. Being physically active will help you think more clearly and concentrate better in school.

MediaWatch

Fitness in a Bottle

Have you seen TV or magazine ads that promise to make you physically fit without any effort on your part? The ad may claim that the product will magically tone muscles or take off pounds. If these products sound too good to be true, they probably are. The best way to achieve fitness is to engage in physical activity.

Find an ad for a health product that claims to easily improve physical health. Does the ad seem believable? Where can you find more information on the product?

◀ Some forms of physical activity are done in a group. **What are some social benefits of these kinds of activities? How do they benefit your health triangle?** **R**

TEACH

MediaWatch

Fitness in a Bottle

Describe some ads of this nature in case students have not seen them, such as ads for pills that "melt" body fat. Encourage students to search the Internet for information about whether the claims on the ad they selected are reliable.

R Reading Strategy

Identifying Cause and Effect As students read about the importance of physical activity, have them list the effects of physical activity on each side of the health triangle. This will help them organize the material in the section and give them practice identifying cause and effect when they read. **BL**

Reading Check

Answer, p. 204 Health experts recommend that teens get 60 minutes of physical activity on most days.

Caption Answer

Photo Caption Social benefits include making new friends and having fun with others. They benefit physical health by keeping you active; they benefit mental and emotional health by requiring you to learn new skills.

HEALTH LITERACY

Exercise Benefits Depression A 2005 study found that exercise is an effective way to treat mild to moderate depression. The study was the first to investigate the effects of exercise alone on depression. Researchers found that 30 minutes of aerobic exercise three times a week for 12 weeks reduced symptoms of depression by almost 50 percent. This is about the same effectiveness as antidepressants or cognitive therapy but without the side effects or expense. Given relatively high rates of depression in teens, this is another important reason to promote physical activity in students.

R **Reading Strategy**

Analyzing a Graphic Ask: In **Figure 9.1**, which activities burn more than 400 calories an hour in a 130-pound person? *backpacking, basketball, bicycling, canoeing, football, stair climbing, swimming* Which activities burn less than 200 calories? *bowling, Frisbee, water volleyball, weight lifting* How do the two sets of activities differ? *Sample answer: You move much more in the first group.* **OL**

AL **Active Learning**

Posters Divide students into pairs and have each pair create two posters. One poster should depict a physical benefit of exercise. The other poster should depict a social benefit of exercise. Posters should be colorful and easy to read. Have students share their posters with the rest of the class. If possible, display the finished posters in the gym or schoolyard. **OL**

▼ FIGURE 9.1

CALORIES BURNED IN ONE HOUR FOR VARIOUS PHYSICAL ACTIVITIES

Activities that burn the most calories are shown in green. Those that burn the least amount are shown in red. **How does burning calories affect your physical health?**

ACTIVITY	If You Weigh 130 Lbs	If You Weigh 155 Lbs
Backpacking	413	493
Basketball (game)	472	563
Basketball (shooting baskets)	266	317
Bicycling (average effort)	472	563
Bowling	177	211
Canoeing (moderate effort)	413	493
Dancing (general)	266	317
Football, touch	472	563
Frisbee playing (general)	177	211
Frisbee playing (ultimate)	207	246
Golf (general)	236	281
Horseback riding (general)	236	281
House cleaning (general)	207	246
Mowing lawn	325	387
Stair climbing	472	563
Swimming (general)	590	704
Water volleyball	177	211
Weight lifting (moderate)	177	211

- **Social Health:** Whether you are on a team or working out with a partner, physical activity can benefit your social health. Physical activity can help you meet new people with similar interests but from different backgrounds. It also improves your ability to work with others as a team, and also demonstrates your willingness to join others of diverse culture, ethnicity, and gender.

Physical Activity and Fitness

Physical activity is also a key to **physical fitness,** *the ability to handle the physical demands of everyday life without becoming overly tired.* People who are physically fit have enough energy to do the

Caption Answer

Figure Caption Burning calories affects your physical health by preventing unwanted weight gain.

FITNESS ZONE

Group Fitness Activities After students have read and discussed *The Importance of Exercise*, have them review the Fitness Zone Handbook. Focus their attention on the Group Fitness Activities, and ask: Why is it important to add variety to a physical fitness plan? How can group activities such fitness plan? How can group activities such as these help you keep your activity routine fun and interesting? What other group activities could be part of a fitness plan? **For more information, see *Fitness Zone Handbook* pages xviii-1 or visit the Fitness Zone at glencoe.com.**

Health Skills Activity

Practicing Healthful Behaviors

Activity + Eating + Sleeping = Good Physical Health

In a way, physical health can be viewed as a health triangle within a health triangle. The three sides to physical health—physical activity, good eating habits, and adequate rest—are interrelated. Teens who are active during the day tend to get more restful sleep during the night. When you eat the right foods, you give your body the fuel it needs for physical activity. Taking care of your physical health can help you maintain a healthy weight and lower your risk of developing serious health problems.

On Your Own

Describe your own physical health triangle. If the sides are not balanced, identify which areas need work. Tell what habits you can adopt that will improve your overall physical health. Develop a plan to practice these habits regularly.

things they want to do. They also have a reserve of energy for times when their bodies need it.

People who are physically fit tend to live longer and healthier lives. Later in this chapter, you will learn how to set fitness goals that will help you improve your fitness level.

The Importance of Exercise

Look again at Figure 9.1. Several of the activities shown, including weight lifting and stair climbing, are exercises. **Exercise** is *planned physical activity done regularly to build or maintain one's fitness*. Exercise is an important ingredient in an overall fitness plan. The reason is simple: while every physical activity works various muscles, exercise targets specific muscles.

Exercises fall into two basic categories—aerobic and anaerobic—though many exercises have elements of both. Each of these categories serves an important role in physical fitness. **Aerobic exercise** is *rhythmic, nonstop, moderate to vigorous activity that requires large amounts of oxygen*. Aerobic exercise works a very important muscle in your body—your heart. It also benefits the lungs. Stair climbing, swimming, running, biking, and many forms of dancing are examples of aerobic exercise.

Health Skills Activity

Practicing Healthful Behaviors

Activity + Eating + Sleeping = Good Physical Health

Tell students to draw a triangle to represent their physical health and to label each side with one of the three parts of physical health. Then have them use the triangle to record information about these parts of their own physical health. Students should identify whether their triangles are balanced and list habits to adopt if they are not.

C Critical Thinking

Categorizing Ask: Which type of exercise increases heart and lung endurance: aerobic or anaerobic? *aerobic* Call on volunteers to explain how aerobic exercise increases endurance. (*Sample answer:* by giving the heart and lungs a workout) With the class, brainstorm examples of other aerobic exercises in addition to those listed in the text. OL

Promoting Coordinated School Health

Advocating Physical Education Just as youth obesity is reaching epidemic proportions, schools are being forced by limited funds to drop physical education programs. Become informed about the wide range of benefits of physical education and use the information to advocate physical education programs in your school. Promote physical activity in students by offering extra credit for planned physical activity. Suggest that they form an after-school walking club, participate in a team sport, or join a walk or run for charity.

Caption Answer

Photo Caption, p. 208 swimming is aerobic exercise.

Lesson 1

 Reading Check

Answer planned physical activity done regularly to build or maintain one's fitness

ASSESS

 Assessment Resources

Lesson Review Quiz
- *ExamView*
- Fast Files Activities
- Online Quizzes and Activities

Reteaching

- Assign Concept Map 9-1 or Reteaching Activity 9-1 in the Fast Files.
- Have students make posters illustrating the principle that activity + eating + sleeping = good physical health.

Enrichment

- Assign Enrichment Activity 9-1 in the Fast Files.
- Ask students to create infomercials extolling the benefits of physical activity for all three parts of total health.

CLOSE

Have students write a paragraph correctly using lesson vocabulary terms.

▶ Swimming can be a leisure activity, a sport, or an exercise. **Which kind of exercise is swimming?**

Go Online

Visit **glencoe.com** and complete the Interactive Study Guide for Lesson 1.

Anaerobic exercise is *intense physical activity that requires little oxygen but uses short bursts of energy.* Lifting weights, gymnastics, and football are examples of anaerobic exercises. In the next lesson you will learn more about the benefits of aerobic and anaerobic exercise.

 Reading Check **Define** What is *exercise*?

Lesson 1 Review

 After You Read

Review this lesson for new terms, major headings, and Reading Checks.

What I Learned

1. *Vocabulary* What is *physical activity*?

2. *Explain* What are the physical, mental/emotional, and social health benefits of being physically active?

3. *Identify* What are the two types of exercise? Describe each of them.

Thinking Critically

4. What is the relationship between physical activity, nutrition, sleep, and weight management?

5. *Analyze* Alex would like to become more physically active but only if he can avoid exercising. What advice would you give Alex?

Applying Health Skills

6. *Advocacy* Develop a poster campaign that emphasizes the importance of physical activity. Include ideas for different types of physical activity that would appeal to teens. Get permission to post these in school hallways.

208 Chapter 9: Physical Activity and Fitness

Go Online For more Lesson Review Activities, go to **glencoe.com**.

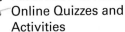 **Lesson 1 Review Answers**

1. Physical activity is any form of bodily movement that uses up energy.

2. *Sample answer:* physical benefits: more energy; social benefits: meeting new people; mental/emotional benefits: higher self-esteem, reduced stress

3. Aerobic exercise is activity that requires large amounts of oxygen. Anaerobic exercise is exercise that requires little oxygen, but uses small bursts of energy.

4. Teens who are active get more restful sleep. Healthful food gives the body fuel for activity. Activity, sleep, and nutrition contribute to maintaining a healthy weight.

5. *Sample answer:* He can be active in other ways, such as mowing the lawn, canoeing, or playing softball.

6. Posters should convey any of the benefits of physical activity covered in the lesson.

Lesson 2

Endurance, Strength, and Flexibility

Guide to Reading

● Building Vocabulary
List each term below in your notebook. As you come across it in your reading, write the definition.

■ heart and lung endurance (p. 210)
■ muscle strength (p. 211)
■ muscle endurance (p. 211)
■ flexibility (p. 212)
■ body composition (p. 213)
■ heredity (p. 214)

● Focusing on the Main Ideas
In this lesson, you will learn to

■ **identify** the five elements of physical fitness.
■ **describe** exercises that improve different areas of physical fitness.
■ **develop** behaviors that will improve your body composition.

● Reading Strategy
Organizing Information
Copy the graphic organizer below onto a sheet of paper. Complete the organizer with information from the lesson.

Measures of Fitness

Measures of Fitness

Before you start any physical fitness progam, you should have your level of physical fitness measured. There are five elements of physical fitness. They are cardiovascular endurance or heart and lung endurance, muscle strength, muscle endurance, flexibility, and body composition. In this lesson, you'll learn how to measure and improve your physical fitness.

Quick Write

Write a paragraph describing why you think flexibility is important. What activities do you think can help improve flexibility?

▶ Types of physical activity that can improve heart and lung endurance include running, walking, and cycling. **Why are activities that involve endurance important to the health of your heart and lungs?**

Lesson 2 Resources

📁 **Chapter *Fast File* Resources**
Guided Reading and Writing 9-2
Concept Mapping Activity 9-2
Health Lab 9-2
Reteaching Activity 9-2
Enrichment Activity 9-2
Lesson Quiz 9-2

Technology
🔦 Transparency 9-2
📑 Audio Summaries
⚙ *ExamView® Assessment Suite*
📑 Vocabulary PuzzleMaker
⚙ StudentWorks™ Plus

G⊙ Online

FOCUS

Activating Prior Knowledge

What I Know Call on students to complete this sentence: "You know you are physically fit if you can [blank]." (*Sample answers:* lift heavy weights, run a mile, climb stairs without getting winded) Tell students this lesson will show them how to tell whether they are physically fit.

Guide to Reading

Building Vocabulary
■ Point out the term *heart and lung endurance.* Ask: Why are the heart and lungs considered together in this term? *because they work together in the body*
■ Use Vocabulary PuzzleMaker to reinforce vocabulary terms. 🖰

Reading Strategy
Organizing Information
Students should fill in the graphic organizer with heart and lung endurance, muscle strength, muscle endurance, flexibility, and body composition.

Quick Write

Have students begin their paragraphs by explaining why flexibility is important. Then they should identify different activities they could perform to improve their own flexibility.

Caption Answer

Photo Caption because the activities improve heart and lung endurance

TEACH

R Reading Strategy

Analyzing a Graphic Divide the class into pairs, and have them follow the steps in **Figure 9.2**. Each pair should have a watch with a second hand or a stopwatch. Instead of a bench, you can use the first step in a flight of stairs. Demonstrate on yourself where to find a pulse in the neck. Tell students that they do not have to share their information but should work on improving their heart and lung endurance if their ratings are low. **OL**

Academic Vocabulary

Indicator Have students read and discuss the definition, the example sentence, and the sentence in the text that uses the word *indicator*. Then write the words *indicate* and *indication* on the board. Ask students how those two words are related, in both structure and meaning, to the word *indicator*. You will find academic vocabulary activities in the Student Activities Workbook. 📁

Reading Check

Answer to play or work for long periods of time without running out of energy

Caption Answer

Figure Caption Low heart and lung endurance

Academic Vocabulary

indicator (IN di kay tor) *(noun)* a sign. *Having a close group of friends is an indicator of good social health.*

Heart and Lung Endurance

Blood pressure is a measure of how well your heart pumps blood through your body. It is an **indicator** of heart health. In a way, the same thing can be said about cardiovascular endurance, or **heart and lung endurance.** This endurance is *a measure of how efficiently your heart and lungs work when you exercise and how quickly they return to normal when you stop.* The word *endure* means "to last." When you have high heart and lung endurance, you can work or play for long periods without running out of "steam." **Figure 9.2** shows a test that measures heart and lung endurance.

If your score is low, do not be discouraged. Heart and lung endurance can be improved. Try doing nonstop moderate to vigorous exercise for at least 20 minutes, three to five times a week. You will notice an improvement after a few weeks.

Activities that build heart and lung endurance include swimming and cycling. Swimming carries the added advantage of providing a total body workout.

Other related exercises that can improve heart and lung endurance are walking, jogging, and running. If you walk, your goal should be 30 minutes at a brisk pace. If you jog or run, aim for at least 20 minutes. If that is difficult, try alternating walking and jogging and slowly work up to 20 minutes of jogging.

Reading Check

Explain Why is it important to build heart and lung endurance?

▼ **FIGURE 9.2**

MEASURING HEART AND LUNG ENDURANCE

R This test will help you determine if you need to improve your heart and lung endurance. You can take this test when you first start working out and again, when you have been working out for a few weeks. **What does a score of 101 or more mean?**

1. Work with a partner, taking turns. Using a sturdy bench about 8 inches high, step up in 2 seconds and down in 2 seconds for 3 minutes.
2. Fully extend each leg as you step. Step up with your right foot, then your left. Step down with your right foot first. Stepping should be continuous.
3. Step at the rate of 24 steps per minute for 3 minutes.
4. Find your pulse on the side of your neck. Count the number of pulses you feel for 1 minute.
5. To rate your heart and lung endurance, find your recovery heart rate on the chart. This term refers to how quickly your heart rate returns to normal right after exercise is stopped.

Scoring (number of heartbeats)	Rating
70-100	Acceptable heart and lung endurance
101 or more	Low heart and lung endurance

Dealing with Sensitive Issues

Physical Fitness Students who are overweight or unfit may be uncomfortable or embarrassed to take part in the tests of physical fitness. Give students other options, such as doing the fitness tests at home with a parent or sibling. Without singling out students, suggest that students take their pulse and then walk around the room and take it again. Point out how much harder their heart has to work during activity. Keep in mind that the overall aim is to motivate students to improve their physical fitness.

Muscle Strength and Endurance

The ability of your muscles to exert a force is called strength. **Muscle strength** is *a measure of the most weight you can lift or the most force you can exert at one time.* **Muscle endurance** is *a measure of a muscle's ability to repeatedly exert a force over a prolonged period of time.* Both measures are important to overall fitness.

Figures 9.3 and **9.4** provide two different tests of muscle strength and endurance. Figure 9.3 tests the strength and endurance of the muscles in your mid-section. These muscles make up what fitness experts refer to as your *core.* Core muscles are important to safe lifting as well as balance. Developing a strong, durable core will lessen the risk of injury to your back.

Figure 9.4 on the next page tests strength and endurance of the muscles in your upper body. These muscles, which include those of the arms, shoulders, and chest, provide power. Players in contact sports, such as basketball, baseball and football, all work their upper bodies.

Like heart and lung endurance, muscle strength and endurance can be improved. The tests in Figures 9.3 and 9.4 are great strengthening exercises. Others include step-ups, which you practiced in Figure 9.2, and push-ups. Push-ups strengthen muscles in your arms and chest. **Figure 9.5** on the next page illustrates a technique for doing push-ups.

Careers for the 21st Century

Personal Trainer

Do you like being physically fit? Do you want to help other people get fit by creating a personal workout for them that is fun, challenging, and motivating? If so, you may want to become a personal trainer. A personal trainer is a certified specialist who helps people achieve physical fitness. The need for personal trainers is high because the fitness industry is growing. If you want to be a personal trainer, you should practice your goal-setting skills and make sure that you get plenty of physical activity every day.

What kinds of clients does a personal trainer have? Go to *Career Corner* at **glencoe.com** to find out.

▼ FIGURE 9.3

R ## MEASURING ABDOMINAL STRENGTH AND ENDURANCE

Abdominal strength helps reduce the risk of injury to your back. **What are some ways to build abdominal strength?**

1. Work with a partner, taking turns. Lie on your back with your knees slightly bent. Your partner should hold your feet.

2. With your arms crossed on your chest, curl your upper body forward. Return to the starting position. Your head should never touch the floor.

3. Continue to do curl-ups at the rate of about 20 per minute, stopping when you can no longer continue, or have completed 60 curl-ups.

4. To rate your abdominal strength and endurance, find your score on the chart. The range shown is acceptable for your age and gender. If you do not score with this range, continue working at this exercise until you do.

Age	Female	Male
12	18–32	18–36
13	18–32	21–40
14	18–32	24–45
15	18–35	24–47

Careers for the 21st Century

Personal Trainer Have students read about personal trainers, and share what they might know about the work of trainers. Ask: Why is it important to practice goal-setting skills if you want to be a personal trainer? Then have students read and discuss the information about trainers' clients at **glencoe.com**.

U ## Universal Access

Gifted Students Have interested students research the history of Pilates, yoga, or another technique. Have them find out about how it is practiced, how it benefits muscle strength and endurance, and where classes are offered in their area. Ask students to make brochures summarizing what they learn. Make copies of the brochures for the rest of the class. **AL**

R ## Reading Strategy

Analyzing a Graphic Have students work with partners and follow the steps in **Figure 9.3**. They should compare their score with the scores given in the table for their age and gender. Tell students that doing curls is a good way to build abdominal strength and endurance if they want to improve their scores. **OL**

Caption Answer
Figure Caption sit-ups (curls), Pilates, and yoga

🏠 Home, School, and Community

At Home Students may think they need to join a fitness club to do strength training. Share these tips for strength training at home with little or no expense.

- Buy a few pieces of inexpensive equipment, such as small dumbbells and resistance bands.

- Instead of buying weights, use household items, such as large plastic water jugs (3.2 kg), large soup cans (0.9 kg), or large tuna fish cans (0.5 kg).

- Do muscle-strengthening exercises that require no equipment at all. Do exercises that strengthen all major muscle groups.

▼ FIGURE 9.4

MEASURING UPPER-BODY STRENGTH AND ENDURANCE

R

You can measure your upper-body strength and endurance by measuring the time you can hang from a bar with your chin above the bar. **What do you think are the benefits of building upper-body strength?**

1. Work with a partner, taking turns. Grasp a horizontal bar with your palms facing toward or away from your body.

2. Raise your body until your chin clears the bar, or you can be lifted into position. Your elbows should be flexed, your chest close to the bar. Your partner should start the stop watch.

3. Hold your position as long as possible. The watch stops when your chin touches or drops below the bar.

4. To rate your upper-body strength and endurance, find your score on the chart. The range of seconds shown is acceptable for your age and gender. If you do not score within this range, continue working at this exercise until you do.

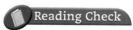

Age	Female	Male
12	7–12	6–13
13–15	8–12	15–20

Another approach to building muscle strength is weight lifting. Also known as *resistance training*, weight lifting can be used to strengthen every muscle group. Just make sure that a fitness instructor or other expert supervises your workout.

Reading Check **Compare** What is the difference between muscle strength and muscle endurance?

▼ FIGURE 9.5

R

DOING A PUSH-UP

1. Lie facedown on the floor. Bend your arms and place your palms flat on the floor beneath your shoulders.

2. Straighten your arms, pushing your entire body upward. Then lower your body to the floor. Repeat.

Flexibility

Are you able to bend and touch your toes? If you can, you probably have good flexibility. **Flexibility** is *the ability of your body's joints to move easily through a full range of motion.* Flexibility permits bending, turning, and stretching. It helps you reduce your risk of muscle injury. Gymnasts and dancers need a high level of flexibility.

AL

You can improve your flexibility through regular stretching, bending, and twisting exercises. Move slowly and gently, holding each stretch. This will gradually improve the flexibility of your muscle groups.

212 Chapter 9: Physical Activity and Fitness

What Teens Want to Know

How can I increase upper body strength if I'm not strong enough to do push-ups? There are other ways to do push-ups and other exercises for upper body strength.

● Do wall push-ups. Stand 2 feet from a wall, place your hands on the wall at shoulder level, and use your arms to lean in and push back from the wall, while keeping your back and neck straight.

● Try bench dips. Sit on the edge of a heavy bench or chair, grip the edge with your hands, slide forward off the chair, and dip down toward the floor. Use your arms to push back up to sitting position. **OL**

Body Composition

The last measure of physical fitness is body composition. **Body composition** is *the ratio of body fat to lean body tissue, such as bone, muscle, and fluid.* Body composition is different than body weight. Your body weight is simply how much you weigh. Your body composition is how much of that weight is body fat, muscle, and other lean body tissue. Too much body fat can lead to serious health problems.

One method for measuring body composition is the skinfold test, which involves pinching a fold of skin at two or three sites on the right side of the body. Each fold is measured with an instrument called a skinfold caliper. To assure accuracy, a trained person should administer the skinfold test using standardized testing procedures and a high quality caliper. Ask your fitness instructor about the skinfold test. Another way to measure body composition is to calculate your body mass index (BMI). Your BMI assesses your body weight relative to your height. It is an indirect measure of body fat for most people. However, people who are physically fit with larger amounts of muscle may have a high BMI score but little body fat. For these people, a skinfold test or other methods of measuring body fat are better. See page 262 in Chapter 11 for instructions on how to calculate your BMI.

One of the keys to improving body composition is to eat healthy foods and increase your physical activity. Teens with too much body fat generally have a weight problem. Taking in fewer calories and burning more calories through exercise will help shed some of the excess weight. Physical activities and exercise build muscle mass while reducing the percentage of body fat. By decreasing the amount of calories you consume and increasing your physical activity, you are choosing positive health behaviors that can protect your health.

Reading Check **Compare** What is the difference between body weight and body composition?

▶ Eating nutritious foods and exercising regularly can improve your body composition. **What are some nutritious foods that you like to eat?**

Lesson 2: Endurance, Strength, and Flexibility **213**

AL Active Learning

Demonstrations Divide the class into groups, and have each group learn how to do three different exercises to improve flexibility. Students can learn about exercises from coaches, dance or yoga instructors, gym teachers, or through online or library research. Allow time for groups to demonstrate their exercises. **OL**

HS Health Skills Practice

Accessing Information Ask students to find out how to convert skinfold or other body measurements to the percentage of body fat. **OL**

U Universal Access

Different Learning Styles Provide students with a box or backpack full of items weighing a total of 10 pounds. Have students pass the box or backpack from student to student. State that a person gaining 10 pounds of excess body fat has to carry that much extra weight around all the time. Discuss how too much body fat might stress joints and strain muscles. **OL**

Reading Check

Answer Body weight is how much you weigh. Body composition is the ratio of body fat to lean body tissue.

Caption Answer

Photo Caption Answers will vary.

Cultural Perspectives

Culture and Body Composition Many teens are overweight or obese, but most desire to be thin. Thinness has been a cultural ideal in the U.S. since the early 1900s, but in earlier centuries plumpness was considered more desirable. For example, nineteenth-century artists often depicted full-figured subjects who were much admired for their beauty and appeal. In some cultures, a plump physique still is the ideal. Take this opportunity to point out the important aspects of maintaining a healthy weight, and remind students how lifestyle behaviors, including cultural norms, influence a person's behaviors and choices.

Reading Check

Answer A positive attitude enables you to set realistic goals for improving your personal fitness level.

ASSESS

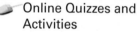

Assessment Resources

Lesson Review Quiz
- *ExamView*
- Fast Files Activities
- Online Quizzes and Activities

Reteaching
- Assign Concept Map 9-2 or Reteaching Activity 9-2 in the Fast Files.
- Have students make a concept map that includes the four measures of physical fitness and two physical activities that improve each measure.

Enrichment
- Assign Enrichment Activity 9-2 in the Fast Files.
- Have students create a 20-minute workout with exercises for endurance, strength, and flexibility.

CLOSE

Call on students to state ways to reduce the ratio of body fat to lean body tissue.

Fitness and a Healthy Attitude

How a person performs on fitness tests depends on a variety of factors. An important one is **heredity,** *the passing of traits from parents to their children.* Speed, for example, is a trait that is often inherited, or passed down, from parents. People who can run fast have more of one type of muscle fiber than another.

Differences likes these don't make one person better—or worse—than another. If you want to improve your level of physical fitness, you will need to set goals for yourself. It is perhaps even more important to keep a positive outlook about what you *can* do. Remember that improvement is possible in every area of fitness and that each improvement you make gives a boost to your physical health. Also remember, however, that everyone has limits. You can make only so much progress in a short period of time. In the next lesson, you will learn how to set up a fitness plan.

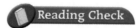

Visit glencoe.com and complete the Interactive Study Guide for Lesson 2.

 Reading Check **Explain** How does attitude affect your fitness level?

Lesson 2 Review

 After You Read

Review this lesson for new terms, major headings, and Reading Checks.

What I Learned

1. **Vocabulary** What is *body composition*?

2. **List** Name the five elements of fitness.

3. **Identify** What are some exercises that will improve muscle strength and endurance? What are some that will improve flexibility?

4. **Describe** What are some ways to improve body composition?

Thinking Critically

5. **Evaluate** Evaluate your current physical fitness level using the methods listed in this chapter or other approved methods. Tell what steps, if any, you need to take to boost your current activity level.

6. **Synthesize** When Don scored low on the test for muscle strength and endurance, he decided that fitness is simply "not for him." What is wrong with Don's attitude? What advice could you give him?

Applying Health Skills

7. **Accessing Information** Research different methods for assessing body composition. Compare and contrast the strengths and weaknesses of each method.

 For more Lesson Review Activities, go to **glencoe.com**.

Lesson 2 Review Answers

1. the ratio of body fat to lean body tissue
2. heart and lung endurance, muscle strength, muscle endurance, flexibility, and body composition
3. *muscle strength and endurance:* curls, chin-ups, step-ups, push-ups, and weight training;

flexibility: stretching, bending, and twisting
4. Eat healthy foods and increase physical activity.
5. Students will measure their level of fitness using the tests described in this lesson or other approved tests. The steps they take to improve their fitness will depend on their

current fitness level.
6. Don's attitude is negative. Students should advise him to exercise to improve his muscle strength and endurance and then take the test again.
7. Remind students to use sources such as government Web sites. Have them compare and contrast different methods.

Setting Fitness Goals

 Guide to Reading

● **Building Vocabulary**
As you read this lesson, write each new highlighted term and its definition in your notebook.

- cross-training (p. 215)
- F.I.T.T. principle (p. 218)
- resting heart rate (p. 219)
- target heart rate (p. 219)
- warm-up (p. 219)
- cooldown (p. 220)

● **Focusing on the Main Ideas**
In this lesson, you will learn to

- **identify** factors to consider when choosing activities and exercises.
- **explain** the parts of the F.I.T.T. principle.
- **develop** warm-up and cooldown techniques for preventing injuries.

● **Reading Strategy**

Sequencing Describe the sequence that should be followed in a workout, along with a short summary of what occurs at each stage.

Identifying Your Fitness Goals

You wouldn't start a long road trip without first mapping out a route. In the same way, reaching a fitness goal requires a plan. A first step in developing such a plan is deciding what your goals are. What do you personally hope to accomplish? Maybe you want to compete in a certain sport or event. If so, your goal will probably focus on a specific fitness measure. Your goals should include strategies that will help you improve and maintain all three sides of your health triangle.

Choosing Activities and Exercises

Once you have identified your goal, you need to select activities and exercises that will help you meet it. **Figure 9.6** on page 216 lists some activities and rates each in terms of its fitness benefits. Your coach or physical education teacher can give you guidance on other activities and exercises. Other factors to consider when selecting activities and exercises include the following:

- **Personal tastes.** Make sure you choose activities that you will enjoy doing. You are more likely to stick with such activities. Another way to keep your interest level high is to vary your routine. *Switching between different activities and exercises on different days* is known as **cross-training.**

 Quick Write

Write a brief description of the type of terrain and weather in your area. Tell what kinds of physical activities would make the most sense in these surroundings.

 Lesson 3 Resources

📁 **Chapter** *FAST FILE* **Resources**
Guided Reading and Writing 9-3
Concept Mapping Activity 9-3
Cross-Curriculum Activity 9-3
Reteaching Activity 9-3
Enrichment Activity 9-3
Lesson Quiz 9-3

Technology
🔖 Transparency 9-3
🎧 Audio Summaries
⚙️ *ExamView® Assessment Suite*
🎧 Vocabulary PuzzleMaker
⚙️ StudentWorks™ Plus

 Go Online

FOCUS

Activating Prior Knowledge

What I Know Ask: What is a fitness goal you would like to reach? Sample answers: *running faster, toning muscles* Tell students they will learn how to set and achieve fitness goals in this lesson.

 Guide to Reading

Building Vocabulary
- Point out that each of the three hyphenated terms consists of a noun or verb and a modifying word. For each term, have students identify the noun or verb and modifying word and predict what the term means.
- Use Vocabulary PuzzleMaker to reinforce vocabulary terms. ✏️

Reading Strategy
Sequencing The correct sequence is warm-up, exercise, cool-down. Students should summarize what occurs at each stage.

Quick Write

Make sure students know that *terrain* means "physical features of land." Students should list activities that are appropriate for their area.

215

TEACH

 Reading Strategy

Analyzing a Graphic Ask: Which activities in **Figure 9.6** promote high fitness in all three measures? *handball and jogging* Which activity in the figure is least effective in improving overall fitness? *softball* Ask students to predict how graphs of other activities, such as karate or canoeing, might look. **OL**

Reading Check

Answer Which activities do you enjoy? Do the activities require any special equipment? Do I need lessons or special instruction to participate? Can I find a partner if I need one for the activity?

Caption Answers

Figure Caption handball, swimming, jogging, bicycling, and brisk walking

Photo Caption Answers will vary but should include specific fitness goals, such as running a mile in 6 minutes or attaining a healthy weight.

▼ **FIGURE 9.6**

SELECTED ACTIVITIES AND THEIR FITNESS BENEFITS

The ratings in this chart show the benefits of activities done for 30 minutes or more. **Which activities have a high rating for heart and lung endurance?**

Activity or Exercise	Low	Midway	High
Handball			
Swimming			
Jogging			
Bicycling			
Tennis			
Brisk walking			
Softball			
Weight Training			

■ Heart and Lung Endurance
■ Muscle Strength and Endurance
■ Flexibility

Working on improving many areas should be a goal of every fitness plan. Your plan, for example, should include at least 20 to 30 minutes of aerobic exercise 3 to 5 times a week.

- **Requirements.** Some activities will require special equipment, such as rackets, balls, gloves, and so on. Many require protective gear, such as helmets or knee pads. Before you start an activity, find out what kind of equipment you will need. Also decide if you will need lessons or special instruction before you start.

Reading Check

Identify What kinds of questions do you need to ask yourself when choosing activities?

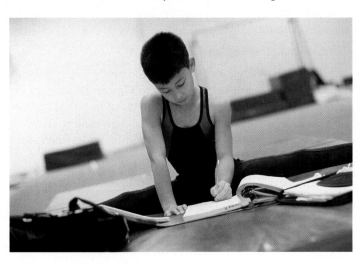

▶ Keeping a fitness log or journal is a good way to identify your fitness goals as well as track your progress. **What are some fitness goals that you might set for yourself? How would you go about working on these goals?**

216 Chapter 9: Physical Activity and Fitness

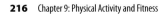

Home, School, and Community

In the Community Have students locate free or inexpensive classes or lessons offered locally. They may include physical activities such as swimming or gymnastics. Possible venues might be a nearby YMCA, a community recreation center, the local department of parks and recreation, and community sports leagues. Ask students to make a brochure describing what is offered, who is eligible to participate, locations, times, and costs. Arrange to have brochures displayed in community locations such as shopping centers and malls. **OL**

Creating a Schedule

Think about the time of day when you will do a particular activity or exercise. Be practical and realistic. If you have a 7:30 A.M. ride to school, it will probably be difficult to fit in an activity before you leave. Another aspect of scheduling has to do with season and climate. Do you live in a region that gets snow? If so, and if one of your exercises is running, you will need an indoor track or a treadmill during the winter months. Most communities have centers that are open to the public, and which offer pools and other exercise facilities.

Be sure to put your plan in writing. A written plan will help you stay on track and stick with your goal. Start by listing all physical activities that are currently part of your routine. For example, most teens have gym class on certain school days. If you are a member of a sports team, include practice sessions and game days. Be sure to count any outside activities that involve physical movement, such as dance lessons. **Figure 9.7** shows one teen's weekly fitness plan.

Reading Check **Recall** What type of information should go into a fitness plan?

▼ FIGURE 9.7

R SAMPLE WEEKLY FITNESS PLAN

A written plan will help you stick with your goals. **Which activities has this teen added to his or her existing schedule? How many hours per day on average is this teen active?**

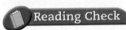

Calendar	Edit	Settings				
Monthly	Weekly	Daily				

Sun	Mon	Tues	Wed	Thurs	Fri	Sat
1 Ride bike (1 hr)	**2** Gym class (30 min)	**3** Basketball after school (40 min)	**4** Gym class (30 min)	**5** Ride bike after school (40 min)	**6** Gym class (30 min)	**7** Soccer game (50 min)
8	**9** Soccer practice (1 hr)	**10** Karate class (1 hr)	**11** Soccer practice (1 hr)	**12** Karate class (1 hr)	**13** Walk home briskly from soccer practice (20 min)	**14** Karate class (1 hr)
15	**16** Walk home briskly from soccer practice (20 min)	**17**	**18**	**19**	**20**	**21**
22	**23**	**24**	**25**	**26**	**27**	**28**

What Teens Want to Know

Do I really need to check with a doctor before I start an exercise program? Unless you are very overweight or have a chronic condition such as asthma, you probably can exercise safely without checking with a doctor. However, just to be sure, you can complete the Physical Activity Readiness Questionnaire (PAR-Q). The questionnaire includes seven questions addressing relevant health issues, such as heart and joint problems. If you answer yes to any of the questions, you should see a doctor before you start an exercise program. The PAR-Q is readily available online. **OL**

R **Reading Strategy**

Analyzing a Graphic Have students examine **Figure 9.7** and then make their own fitness plans based on the sample fitness plan in the figure. After making their plans, have students calculate the amount of time they are active each day. They should add activities to their plans as needed so they are active for about an hour per day on most days. Encourage students to follow their amended plans. **OL**

Reading Check

Answer list of current activities and any team practices; practical and realistic scheduling

Caption Answer

Figure Caption This teen has added bike riding and brisk walking to his or her existing schedule, and is active an average of about 1.5 hours per day.

Health Skills Activity

Accessing Information

Measuring Your Heart Rate

Tell students that the longer they count heart beats, the more accurate the estimate of their heart rate will be. Other reliable methods for measuring heart rate range from counting the pulse at other sites, such as the inside of the wrist, to using a heart rate monitor or ECG (electrocardiogram).

Connect To...
Math

Target Heart Rate

Students can compute the target heart rate range for a 14-year-old teen by substituting 14 for 13 in the calculations. The correct answer is 124 for the low end and 165 for the high end. Ask: In general, how does target heart rate change as you get older? *It decreases.*

HS Health Skills Practice

Practicing Healthful Behaviors Ask students to apply the F.I.T.T. principle to one of the physical activities in which they participate. They should develop a plan for gradually increasing the frequency, intensity, and duration of the activity. Call on volunteers to share their programs with the class. For each program, ask other students to identify how the F.I.T.T. principle was applied. **OL**

Health Skills Activity

Accessing Information

Measuring Your Heart Rate

There are several reliable methods for determining your heart rate, or pulse. One of the easiest is to place two fingers at the base of your neck. Do not use your thumb, which has a pulse of its own. Feel for a throbbing sensation. This sensation is your heart pumping blood through an artery in your neck. Using a clock with a second hand, count the number of throbs in ten seconds. Multiply this number by six to get your heart rate.

On Your Own

Take your current resting heart rate using this method. Investigate other reliable methods for taking this measurement. Share your findings.

Connect To...
Math

Target Heart Rate

The best way to become used to calculating your target heart rate is to practice. Try it right now. If you are 13 years old, for example, your target heart rate will be within this range:

$(220 - 13) \times 0.6 = 124$ low end

$(220 - 13) \times 0.8 = 166$ high end

Compute the range for a 14-year-old.

Building Fitness Levels

Whatever activity you choose to do, remember to start small. If you have never swum laps, you are probably not ready to compete on the school swimming team. Take each activity one day at a time and build up gradually. As you progress, adjust each activity using the **F.I.T.T. principle,** *a method for safely increasing aspects of your workout without injuring yourself.* The letters in the name stand for **F**requency, **I**ntensity, **T**ime, and **T**ype.

Frequency is how often you work different muscle groups. Gradually increase the number of times per week you work a muscle group. You might start by working out two or three times per week. Eventually, you can work out every day.

Intensity refers to how hard you work different muscle groups. If you are lifting weights, you increase intensity by adding more weight. If you are running laps, you increase intensity by increasing your speed.

Time, or *duration,* is a measure of how long you spend per session. Teens should get a total of 60 minutes of activity on most days. If you are just beginning an activity or exercise, you will need to start by doing less than that. You can eventually build up your endurance to a point where you can do the full hour.

HS

HEALTH LITERACY

Monitoring Heart Rate Stopping to take your pulse and calculate your heart rate disrupts your workout. Share these tips with students.

- Count your pulse for just six seconds and then add zero to the number to get your heart rate per minute.

- If you walk for exercise, use the "talk test." If you cannot carry on a conversation as you walk, slow down until you can.
- Use a digital heart rate monitor to measure your heart rate continuously as you work out. Some cost less than $50.

Type refers to the type of activity you choose to do. A complete workout package should feature both aerobic and anaerobic exercises. For some fitness goals, you will want to do more of one type of exercise than another.

It is important that any changes to your workouts be made gradually. Adjust only one F.I.T.T. element at a time. Trying to do too much, too soon, can result in injury.

Monitoring Your Heart Rate

You can monitor the intensity of your workout by checking your heart rate right before, during, and then after your workout. **Resting heart rate** is *the number of times your heart beats per minute when you are relaxing.* Take this measurement at the very beginning of a workout session, before you start any exercise. **Target heart rate** is *the range of numbers between which your heart and lungs receive the most benefit from a workout.* Finding your target heart rate is simple. You start by subtracting your age from 220. Then you multiply the resulting number by 0.6 and again by 0.8. The range of numbers between the two products represents your target heart rate. After you complete your workout, take your recovery heart rate. This measures how quickly your heart returns to normal right after you finish working out. The Health Skills Activity on page 218 gives you instructions on how to measure your heart rate.

Reading Check **Define** What is *target heart rate*?

Warming Up and Cooling Down

Every exercise or activity session should begin with a warm-up and end with a cooldown. A **warm-up** is *a period of low to moderate exercise to prepare your body for more vigorous activity.* Warming up helps prevent injuries to muscles, joints, and connective tissue. Warm-ups should last around ten minutes and should include light aerobic exercise to get your blood flowing. Walking or jogging in place is an excellent choice. Warming up can also include practicing skills related to the activity you will be doing. Complete your warm-up with simple stretches such as those shown in **Figure 9.8.** on the next page. Stretch only the muscles that have been warmed up. Stretching cold muscles could lead to injury.

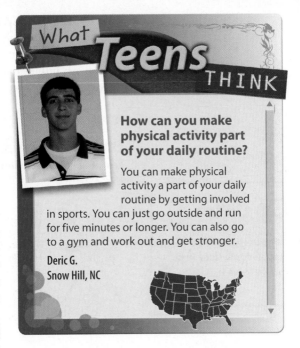

What Teens THINK

How can you make physical activity part of your daily routine?

You can make physical activity a part of your daily routine by getting involved in sports. You can just go outside and run for five minutes or longer. You can also go to a gym and work out and get stronger.

Deric G.
Snow Hill, NC

Go Online

Topic: Stretching for Fitness

Visit **glencoe.com** for Student Web Activities to learn about why stretching is so important, and how you can make stretching part of your overall health plan.

Activity: Using the information provided at the link above, create a personal stretching routine that you can use before and after strenuous exercise.

Lesson 3: Setting Fitness Goals **219**

What Teens THINK

How can you make physical activity part of your daily routine? Help students discuss the *Sample Weekly Fitness Plan* (Figure 9.7). Ask: How can a plan like this help you make fitness activities part of your daily routine? What other steps can you take to include fitness activities in your daily routine? After students have shared their own ideas, guide them in reading and discussing the *What Teens Think* question and response.

U Universal Access

English Learners Create a chart on the board with each student's name and a place for their resting and target heart rates. Have students take their resting heart rate. Record their results on the board. Next, figure the target heart rate for each student. Lastly, students can jog in place, take their heart rate again, and see how it compares to the other figures. **EL**

Reading Check

Answer, the range of numbers between which your heart and lungs receive the most benefit from a workout

Caption Answer
Figure Caption, p. 220 Answers will vary. Students might say in their legs or shoulders.

HEALTH LITERACY

Stretching Stretching may seem simple, but experts disagree on its effectiveness in preventing injury. For example, many people think stretching helps prevent injuries and muscle soreness. However, most experts agree that stretching increases flexibility and that you should stretch

- only to the point of slight discomfort and then ease off a little before holding the stretch for 10 to 30 seconds.
- at least three times a week for 10 to 20 minutes each time.
- all the major muscle groups.
- without bouncing.

219

ASSESS

Reteaching

- Assign Concept Map 9-3 or Reteaching Activity 9-3 in the Fast Files.
- Have students write five true-false questions on lesson content, exchange questions with a partner, and try to answer one another's questions.

Enrichment

- Assign Enrichment Activity 9-3 in the Fast Files.
- Ask students to create a poster showing how to apply the FITT principle to a particular activity.

CLOSE

Have students make a chart with three columns labeled *Warm-Up, Exercise,* and *Cool-Down,* and then add at least two appropriate activities to each column.

A **cooldown** is *a period of low to moderate exercise to prepare your body to end a workout session.* Cooling down helps return blood circulation and body temperature to normal. A cooldown should last around ten minutes and include gentle stretching exercises. You might repeat the same stretches you did during your warm-up.

▼ FIGURE 9.8

BASIC STRETCHES

Learning good stretching techniques can help prevent injury. Try the two techniques illustrated and tell where you feel the "pull."

Visit **glencoe.com** and complete the Interactive Study Guide for Lesson 3.

Lesson 3 Review

 After You Read

Review this lesson for new terms, major headings, and Reading Checks.

What I Learned

1. *Vocabulary* What is the *F.I.T.T. principle?*
2. *Recall* Name two factors that need to be considered when choosing activities or exercises.
3. *Explain* Why are warm-ups and cooldowns important parts of any fitness routine?

Thinking Critically

4. *Synthesize* Rich has made more progress than he expected in the first three weeks of weight lifting. He now plans to increase his load and the length of his sessions. Do you think Rich has made a good decision? What positive health behavior should Rich do to prevent health problems?

5. *Evaluate* Anne has planned out a schedule that includes four hours of activity and exercise each day. Previously she has been sedentary. What do you think are her chances of success with her fitness program?

Applying Health Skills

6. *Goal Setting* Establish a personal physical activity goal. Use the goal-setting steps on page 29 and 30 to develop a plan to achieve your goal. Create a schedule to help you evaluate your progress.

Go Online For more Lesson Review Activities, go to glencoe.com.

Lesson 3 Review Answers

1. a method for safely increasing aspects of your workout without injuring yourself
2. *Any two:* whether you enjoy them; what, if any, special equipment is needed; whether you need lessons or special instruction; and whether a partner is required
3. to prevent injuries to muscles, joints, and connective tissue
4. No; he should increase only one F.I.T.T. element at a time.
5. Anne is likely to fail at her fitness program because it is too ambitious, especially given her previously sedentary lifestyle.
6. Students' goals will vary, but they should use the goal-setting steps mentioned in this lesson.

Sports Conditioning and Avoiding Injury

Guide to Reading

● **Building Vocabulary**
As you read this lesson, write each new highlighted term and its definition in your notebook.

- conditioning (p. 222)
- P.R.I.C.E. formula (p. 224)
- dehydration (p. 225)
- heat exhaustion (p. 225)

● **Focusing on the Main Ideas**
In this lesson, you will learn to

- **describe** the benefits of conditioning.
- **develop** nutrition habits for athletes.
- **identify** ways of minimizing injury risks during sports or activities.
- **show** how to treat sports-related injuries.

● **Reading Strategy**
Identifying Problems and Solutions As you read the lesson, identify injuries described and ways of dealing with each.

Sports Conditioning

Standing behind the center, Evan barked signals. Everyone in the stands sat silently, breathlessly watching. There was one second left on the clock. Time for one last play. North High was down by four points. The game—and season—were on the line.

"Hut! Hut! Hut!" Evan called. He took the snap from the center and moved back in the pocket. Out of the corner of his eye he saw a large linebacker barreling toward him from the right. Evan scrambled left and threw the ball as he skillfully dodged the tackler. Time seemed to stand still as the ball floated downfield. It fell gracefully into the hands of Evan's teammate. "Touchdown!" the official shouted. The North High fans went wild. "Evan!" they cheered. "Evan! Evan! Evan!"

Quick Write

Describe an injury you had while playing a physical game or sport. Tell how this injury was treated.

▶ Proper conditioning will strengthen your muscles so you can play your best when you compete. **What type of conditioning exercises do you think the tennis player in this picture practices?**

Lesson 4: Sports Conditioning and Avoiding Injury **221**

FOCUS
Activating Prior Knowledge

What I Know What physical activities require protective gear to avoid injuries? Sample answers: *football, bicycling, hockey* Tell students they will learn how to prevent injuries during such activities.

Guide to Reading

Building Vocabulary
- On the board, write: *de-* ("opposite"), *hydr-* ("water"), and *-tion* ("condition"). Then ask: What does *dehydration* mean? *condition of no water* Students can check the definition to see if they were right.
- Use Vocabulary PuzzleMaker to reinforce vocabulary terms.

Reading Strategy
Identifying Problems and Solutions Suggest that students make a two-column table, labeling one column *Injury* and the other *Treatment*, and then fill in the table as they read.

Quick Write

Students may not know the medical term for their injury, but they should describe its nature and treatment.

Caption Answer

Photo Caption weight training, exercises such as running for heart and lung endurance, and flexibility exercises such as stretching

---

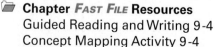
Lesson 4 Resources

📁 **Chapter FAST FILE Resources**
Guided Reading and Writing 9-4
Concept Mapping Activity 9-4
Decision-Making Activity 9-4
Reteaching Activity 9-4
Enrichment Activity 9-4
Lesson Quiz 9-4

Technology
- Transparency 9-4
- Audio Summaries
- *ExamView® Assessment Suite*
- PuzzleMaker
- StudentWorks™ Plus

 Online

TEACH

AL Active Learning

Calendars Divide the class into groups, and have each group create a week-long calendar showing a conditioning schedule for a particular sport. Calendars should include types and durations of relevant physical activities, such as skill drills and exercises to strengthen certain muscles. Display the calendars in the classroom. **OL**

DEVELOPING Good Character

Being a Team Player Students may say that being a team player motivates you to do your best and helps the whole team succeed, whether you play a sport or work with others on a joint project or toward a common goal.

Reading Check

Answer top eat properly and get enough rest
Answer bottom whole-grain products, fruits, and vegetables

▲ Drinking water before and during a game is a good sports nutrition habit. **What is another?**

DEVELOPING Good Character

Being a Team Player

When you play a team sport, you owe it to your team to be your best. Being your best means showing up, and on time, for practice. It means following team rules on and off the playing field. It means being supportive of your teammates, accepting their differences and limitations, and working cooperatively. **In what ways is being a good team player important even if you do not play a sport?**

Playing a sport can seem glamorous, especially when you are a star quarterback. It is also a fun way to make physical activity part of your life. Playing a sport involves much more than showing up for games, however. Athletes devote many hours off the field to physical **conditioning**, *a regular activity and exercise that prepares a person for a sport*. Some conditioning takes place right before a game. Baseball players, for example, practice batting and fielding. Basketball players do passing drills and take practice shots from different spots on the court. Conditioning may also include weight training and other exercises. Additionally, maintaining a healthy diet and getting enough rest are important aspects of conditioning.

AL

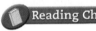 **Reading Check** **Identify** Besides practice and exercise, what are two conditioning practices every athlete should follow?

Sports Nutrition

Everyone needs proper nutrition. The term *nutrition* refers to the nutrients found in food and how they nourish the body. For athletes, good nutrition includes following specific guidelines on and off the field.

One common guideline is to eat carbohydrates before a game or event. Whole grains, fruits, and vegetables are good energy sources. Avoid foods high in simple sugars, such as candy bars. These will provide a burst of energy, but one that lasts only briefly.

Before and during a game, you should drink plenty of water. Your body loses water through perspiration, even outdoors in winter. Drinking water is important for any strenuous workout because it keeps you from getting dehydrated. If you start to feel dizzy, take a break for a few minutes. Sit in the shade and drink more water. Good athletes always take care of their bodies.

Reading Check **Give Examples** Name specific foods that athletes might eat before a game for added energy.

Minimizing Risk

Whether your fitness program includes sports or some other activity, safety should be your first concern. You have already

Caption Answer

Photo Caption *Sample answer:* avoiding foods high in simple sugars, eating carbohydrates before a game or event

 What Teens Want to Know

Should I take nutritional supplements to improve my athletic performance? Most athletes do not require supplements as long as they eat a balanced diet and are not losing weight. A diet based on the MyPyramid food guidance system that includes a variety of foods should ensure that you get all the nutrients you need for peak performance. To get enough energy, add the amount of energy you use in your sport to the amount needed for daily activity based on your size, age, and gender. **OL**

learned some guidelines for minimizing the risk of an activity-related injury. These guidelines include progressing gradually, warming up, and cooling down. Other guidelines include using the right equipment and knowing your limits.

Proper Gear

In sports, proper gear starts with equipment used in your game. For some team sports, you wear cleats. These are shoes with spikes on the bottom that grip the ground and provide traction. Whatever shoes you wear should be suitable to your activity or game. Shoes should also fit properly, feel comfortable, and provide adequate support.

For games played in bright sunlight, a good pair of sunglasses is more than a fashion statement. It is a necessity. Choose shatterproof glasses with lenses that offer UV protection. UV protection will shield your eyes from the same harsh rays that cause sunburns on unprotected skin.

Other protective gear includes athletic supporters, knee pads, elbow pads, and helmets. Specific needs and equipment will depend on your activity or sport. You want to be sure to choose the appropriate gear in order to reduce your risk of injury.

For non-sports activities, wear clothing that is loose-fitting or stretchable. This type of clothing will give you freedom of movement and help you stay cool in warm weather. In cool weather, dress in layers to trap warm air against your body.

Know Your Limits

As Mike stood in his outfield position, his shoulder hurt from where a ball had struck it earlier. The game was important, however, so Mike decided to play through the pain. When Mike learned later that he had separated his shoulder, he felt bad in more than one way. He would be on the bench for the rest of the baseball season.

Do not make the same mistake Mike did. Learn to listen to your body whether you play a sport or exercise. If someone tells you "No pain, no gain," do not believe them. Pain is your body's way of telling you to slow down or stop, if you have been injured. If you experience pain, you should take the appropriate health care measure to protect yourself from further injury.

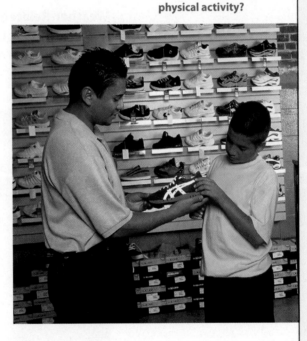

▼ You should remember to use appropriate athletic gear. **What are some features to consider when buying shoes for a sport or physical activity?**

Lesson 4: Sports Conditioning and Avoiding Injury **223**

CHAPTER 9

Lesson 4

TECHNOLOGY AND HEALTH

High-Tech Helmets Each year, about 300,000 sports-related brain injuries occur in the United States. Concern about brain injuries has led to the development of high-tech helmets equipped with tiny sensors that send information to a computer. The helmets have revealed that football players are hit in the head more often and with more force than previously thought. This information may help players avoid recurrent brain injuries, help doctors understand how brain injuries occur, and lead to the development of safer helmets for football and other sports.

223

U Universal Access

Students with Different Learning Styles Bring an ice pack and Ace bandage to class, and work with a student volunteer to demonstrate the five parts of the PRICE formula. Ask other students to identify each part of the formula as you apply it. After the demonstration, discuss when the P.R.I.C.E. formula should be used (e.g., for sprains and strains). **OL**

AL Active Learning

Lessons for Younger Students Divide the class into groups, and have each group create a lesson for younger students on how to prevent either hot- or cold-weather-related injuries during sports or other activities. Lessons should identify the risks, how to avoid them, and what may happen if the risks are not avoided. Arrange for students to present their lessons to younger students. **OL**

Academic Vocabulary

Formula Begin by asking students to recall formulas they may use in math class. For example, ask: What is the formula for finding the area of a rectangle? Then ask: What do formulas tell you. *Sample response: They tell you what steps to follow to find specific information.* Then have students read the definition of *formula* as it is used here. Ask: How is this definition similar to the math-related definition? You will find academic vocabulary activities in the Student Activity Workbook.

Academic Vocabulary

formula (FAWR myuh luh) *(noun)* a way of doing something. *The formula for good health includes eating healthful foods, getting enough physical activity, and getting a good night's sleep.*

Treating Injuries

Sometimes even when you are cautious, injuries can occur, especially when you are playing *contact sports*. This term is used for any sport where physical contact between players is normal. Football, hockey, and boxing are examples of contact sports.

Even if you are not injured through contact, you might experience muscle soreness. For strains, sprains, and muscle soreness, the **P.R.I.C.E. formula** will provide some relief. The letters stand for P*rotect,* R*est,* I*ce,* C*ompress, and* E*levate.* Apply the following **formula** as soon as possible after the game, event, or activity:

- **Protect** the injured part from further injury by keeping it still. Try not to move it too much. Moving it may make the pain worse.
- **Rest** the injured part.
- **Ice** the part using an ice pack.

- **Compress**, or put pressure on, the part using an elastic bandage. This will keep the injury from swelling. It will also help keep that part of your body motionless. Just be careful not to wrap the bandage too tightly. This could cut off the flow of blood.
- **Elevate** the injured part above the level of the heart.

Reading Check **Explain** What do the letters in the P.R.I.C.E. formula stand for?

Weather-Related Injuries

Some sports and activities, such as ice hockey, skiing, and ice skating, are done in cold weather. Other activities tend to be played

▶ Treat an injury such as muscle soreness as soon as possible after it occurs. **Which steps in the P.R.I.C.E. formula is this teen demonstrating?**

HEALTH LITERACY

Hyponatremia A condition called hyponatremia may develop in athletes in ultraendurance events such as triathlons. It is caused by drinking more water than is lost in sweat. The excess water dilutes the sodium in the blood and builds up in tissues of the body and brain. Symptoms of mild hyponatremia include nausea and headache. If the condition worsens, it may lead to coma and even death. Prevention involves ingesting no more water than was lost during the event. Sports drinks containing sodium are also recommended. Tell students about this condition so they can avoid it themselves and recognize it in others.

in hot weather. Temperatures at both extremes pose a health risk to the body. You should follow practices that will reduce your risk of injury.

When the temperature rises in the summer, so does your body's. You perspire more, which is your body's way of cooling you down. If you are not careful to replace this lost water, you risk **dehydration.** This *condition caused by excessive water loss* can lead to other, more serious health problems. One of these is **heat exhaustion**—*an overheating of the body that can result from dehydration.* People with heat exhaustion often feel dizzy and have a headache. Their skin feels clammy when touched. Anyone who shows the symptoms of heat exhaustion needs to be taken to a cool, shady spot. The person should receive plenty of fluids. If the symptoms do not go away, call for help immediately.

Cold weather can bring its own share of problems, including frostbite and hypothermia. Chapter 20 will discuss weather-related risks in further detail.

 AL

 Go Online

Visit **glencoe.com** and complete the Interactive Study Guide for Lesson 4.

Reading Check **Define** What is *dehydration*?

Reading Check

Answer condition caused by excessive water loss

ASSESS

Assessment Resources

- Lesson Review Quiz
- *ExamView*
- Fast Files Activities
- Online Quizzes and Activities

Reteaching

- Assign Concept Map 9-4 or Reteaching Activity 9-4 in the Fast Files.
- Have students write a paragraph describing how they could condition themselves for a particular sport.

Enrichment

- Assign Enrichment Activity 9-4 in the Fast Files.
- Ask students to create a poem or song identifying ways to minimize risks during physical activity.

CLOSE

Have students list three sports-related health problems such as injuries and at least one way each problem could be treated.

Lesson 4 Review

After You Read

Review this lesson for new terms, major headings, and Reading Checks.

What I Learned

1. *Vocabulary* What is *conditioning*? What are some specific practices that are part of conditioning for most sports?

2. *Identify* Name two ways to minimize the risk of injury during sports or activities.

3. *Recall* What type of treatment is used for an exercise-related or sport-related injury such as muscle soreness?

Thinking Critically

4. *Analyze* Brandon has tried on several pairs of cleats. The only pair he thinks look good on him are a size too small. He plans to buy the shoes anyway. How could you help Brandon make a healthful decision if you were the salesperson?

5. *Apply* Keely has one more lap to run around the track to finish her routine for the day. She is feeling light-headed and dizzy. What steps would you take to help Keely if you were there at the track?

Applying Health Skills

6. *Communication Skills* Working with a small group, develop a public service announcement for teens. Your announcement should communicate ways to avoid injury and minimize other risks while being physically active. It should also encourage teens to work cooperatively with peers of different cultures, gender, ethnicities, and skill levels.

Lesson 4 Review Answers

1. regular activity and exercise that prepare a person for a sport; may include weight training, eating properly, rest
2. *Any two:* Progress gradually, warm up, and cool down; use the proper gear; slow down or stop if you have pain.
3. Protect, Rest, Ice, Compress, and Elevate

4. How the shoes fit is more important than how they look. He should buy shoes that are the correct size and provide support.
5. You might assume that Keely has heat exhaustion. You should tell Keely to stop exercising and sit in a cool, shady spot. You should make sure she drinks plenty of

fluids. If the symptoms do not clear up, you should call for help right away.
6. Announcements will vary but should explain concisely and clearly how to avoid injury and other risks during physical activity. It should also encourage teens to work with peers of various cultures, backgrounds, and skill levels.

Building Health Skills — Playing It Safe

Skill

Practicing Healthful Behaviors

Activating Prior Knowledge

Ask: What are some ways to stay safe when you play sports or participate in other physical activities? *Sample answers: Wear a helmet or other protective gear; drink plenty of water; warm up and stretch before vigorous activity.*

- **Objective** After completing the activity, students will be able to exercise safely.
- **Time** 90 minutes
- **Materials** paper, pencil, stapler, colored pencils (optional)

Teacher Classroom Resources

📁 Building Health Skills
📑 Transparency 9-4

Model

- Have students read about Connie and Rebecca in the Model section.
- **Ask:** What possible exercise-related problems did Rebecca help Connie avoid? *heat exhaustion and being hit by a vehicle*

National Health Standards Addressed

1.8.5

226

Building Health Skills

Accessing Information
Practicing Healthful Behaviors
Stress Management
Analyzing Influences
Communication Skills
Refusal Skills
Conflict Resolution
Decision Making
Goal Setting
Advocacy

Why Is It Important to Practice Healthful Behaviors?

When you practice healthful behaviors, you take specific actions to stay healthy and avoid risky behaviors. This will help you prevent injury, illness, disease, and other health problems.

When working out or playing a sport:

- Avoid extreme temperatures.
- Drink water before, during, and after exercise.
- Wear appropriate clothing and protective gear.

Playing It Safe

Follow the Model, Practice, and Apply steps to help you master this important health skill.

❶ Model

Read how Rebecca shows her sister, Connie, how to practice healthful behaviors when preparing to go jogging.

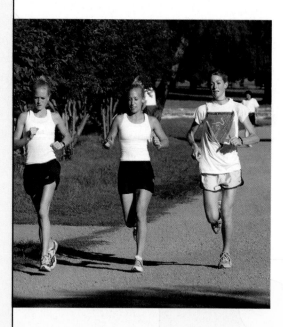

"All set," Connie said. She and Rebecca had decided that they would jog together.

"Wait," Rebecca said. "I just heard that the temperature right now is in the low 90s."

"So?" Connie said. "No pain, no gain!"

"Exercising in the heat can cause heat exhaustion," Rebecca said. "I think we need to wait until it cools down and drink plenty of water."

The girls waited until the late afternoon when the temperature had dropped. Connie went to Rebecca's room. "Now can we go?" she asked.

"Not like that," Rebecca replied. "The clothes you're wearing are dark." "Now that it's starting to get dark out, we need to wear light-colored clothing. That will help drivers see us." She handed her sister a reflective armband. "This will also make us easier to see."

▶ Teaching Tips

Playing Now and Later Introduce this activity by asking students why "playing it safe" today means they will have more opportunities to "play" in the future. (e.g., not as likely to get injured or sick) Ask: What would you think of a soccer player, football player, or race car driver who decided not to wear protective gear? (Students might conclude the person is being foolish, not serious, taking unnecessary risks, or not setting a good example.)

❷ Practice

Anya is going for a bike ride. Read the passage below and answer the questions that follow.

Anya decided to go for a bike ride on a trail that was a few miles outside of town. The countryside surrounding the trail was scenic and peaceful. Anya was looking forward to the bike ride. As Anya was getting ready, she remembered that temperatures sometimes drop quickly during this time of the year. Anya wants to be prepared for the change in weather.

1. What advice would you give Anya about her clothing?

2. What other safety tips would you give Anya before she goes on the bike ride?

❸ Apply

Apply what you have learned about practicing healthful behaviors when completing the activity below.

Working with a partner, develop a pamphlet that would be useful to teens exercising in your community. What weather-related factors or other safety risks exist in your community? How can these dangers be avoided? With your teacher's permission, display your pamphlet in the classroom or school library.

Self-Check
- Did we describe specific safety risks or weather-related factors in our community?
- Did we explain how these dangers can be avoided?

Building Health Skills

Building Health Skills **227**

Practice
- Ask students to read the Practice section, and then call on volunteers to answer the first question. (*Sample answers:* Anya should dress in layers or take a jacket.)
- Have students work in groups to brainstorm answers to the second question. After about 10 minutes, ask groups to share their ideas with the class. (Possible ideas might include taking water, taking a cell phone, telling an adult where she is going, wearing a bike helmet, and checking that her bike is in good working condition.)

Apply/Assess
- Divide the class into pairs to complete the activity. Give partners a chance to work on their pamphlets in class.
- In their pamphlets, students might describe dangers such as cold or heat, heavy traffic, poor air quality, unlighted streets, and potholes in pavement. They should explain at least one way to avoid each of the dangers, such as dressing in layers for the cold, working out with others at night, and wearing helmets and other safety gear.

ASSESSMENT SCORING

Using a rubric, student work should meet all criteria to achieve the highest score.

Skills Student work:
- identifies weather-related or safety risks in the community.
- demonstrates strategies to avoid or manage risks.

Concepts Student work includes:
- includes accurate information about exercise risks.
- provides comprehensive information about exercise risks.
- shows the relationship between exercise and health risks.

Run for It!

Objectives

After completing this activity, students will be able to:

- Identify the benefits of running
- Explain why food, water, warm-ups, and stretches are important to runners
- Describe how to work up to running a 5K race

Motivator

Have students identify the benefits of physical activity to all three sides of the health triangle.

Teaching the Feature

- Have students write paragraphs that explain how the health skill of goal setting can be applied to running in a 5K race. Remind students of the importance of using a series of short-term goals as stepping stones to reaching a long-term goal. **OL**

- Have students work in small groups to research opportunities for teen runners in their school and community. Then have students prepare pamphlets that could be used to share this information with others. **OL**

Looking for an inexpensive activity that will make you feel good?

RUN FOR IT!

Experts agree. Running relaxes you—and doing something physical helps your self-esteem. Follow these basic steps, and you'll be running a 5K (or 3.1 mile) race in no time.

1 GET IN GEAR

Head to your local sporting-goods store and ask the salesperson for a pair of running shoes with good support and cushioning. Mention that you're just starting out, so he or she can recommend the right type of shoe for your needs. When the weather turns cooler, be sure to have warm running gear for the rest of your body.

2 MAKE A GOAL

Check out the Road Runners Club of America's local race schedules. Register for a 5K race for teens that is a few weeks or months away. Then get motivated by imagining yourself crossing the finish line.

3 FUEL UP

Drink at least eight ounces of water up to five minutes before your run, and then again during and after your run. (Avoid caffeinated beverages, which dehydrate you.) You should have a carbohydrate snack about two to three hours before you run. Carbohydrates give you the energy you need to keep going. Perfect pre-run foods include oatmeal or bananas.

4 GET MOVING

After you've warmed up your muscles by stretching, start with a slow-paced jog. If you feel tired, it's okay to walk for a bit and pick up the pace again when you're ready. Once you've finished, you should stretch.

5 TAKE IT UP A NOTCH

Run three to five times a week for eight weeks before a race. Go a little farther each week while gradually picking up your pace. By your third week, you should be up to about 20 minutes (or roughly two miles at an easy 10-minute-per-mile pace). At that rate, you'll be hitting that 5K finish line in about 31 minutes. Then, get ready for your victory lap!

Activity | Activity Media, Technology, and Culture

Technology Have students create a multimedia presentation that shows appropriate warm-ups, exercises, and cooldown stretches for runners. Students can use digital photos, video clips, or information from the Internet as a part of their presentation. Have students share their presentations with the class. If possible, have the physical education teacher share the presentations with other interested students. **OL**

Reading Review

  STUDY TO GO Visit glencoe.com to download quizzes and eFlashcards for Chapter 9.

FOLDABLES Study Organizer

Foldables® and Other Study Aids Take out the Foldable® that you created for Lesson 1 and any graphic organizers that you created for Lessons 1–4. Find a partner and quiz each other using these study aids.

Lesson 1 The Benefits of Physical Activity

Main Idea Physical activity benefits your physical, mental/emotional, and social health.

- Teens should get 60 minutes of physical activity on most days. This can be done all at once or divided into 10- or 15-minute bursts of activity.
- People who are physically active have enough energy to do the things they want to do. They also have a reserve of energy for times when their bodies need it.
- Aerobic exercise works your heart and lungs. It requires large amounts of oxygen.
- Anaerobic exercise requires little oxygen and short bursts of energy.

Lesson 2 Endurance, Strength, and Flexibility

Main Idea The five elements of physical fitness are cardiovascular or heart and lung endurance, muscle strength, muscle endurance, flexibility, and body composition.

- Different exercises improve different areas of physical fitness.
- Heredity is the passing of traits from parents to their children.
- If you want to improve your level of physical fitness, you will need to set goals for yourself and keep a positive outlook.

- Everyone has limits. You can make only so much progress in a short period of time.

Lesson 3 Setting Fitness Goals

Main Idea Whatever activity you choose, remember to start small. Take each activity one day at a time and build up gradually.

- Factors to consider when selecting activities include personal tastes and requirements.
- A written, weekly fitness plan will help you stick to your goals.
- The parts of the F.I.T.T. principle are **F**requency, **I**ntensity, **T**ime, and **T**ype.
- Warming up is important because it prevents injuries to muscles, joints, and connective tissue. Cooling down is important because it helps return blood circulation and body temperature to normal.

Lesson 4 Sports Conditioning and Avoiding Injury

Main Idea Proper conditioning will strengthen your muscles so you can play your best and protect yourself from injury.

- Sports are a fun way to make physical activity part of your life.
- Maintaining a healthy diet and getting enough rest are important aspects of conditioning.
- You can minimize risk by knowing your limits and wearing the proper gear.
- The main treatment for sports-related injuries is the P.R.I.C.E. formula—short for **P**rotect, **R**est, **I**ce, **C**ompress, and **E**levate.

Assessment Resources

- Chapter 9 Summary and Activity
- Audio Summaries
- Reading Tutor
- Performance Assessment
- Chapter 9 Test
- *ExamView*
- Vocabulary PuzzleMaker
- Online Learning Center

Reading Review

Study Aids

- **Using the Dinah Zike Foldable® Study Organizer** Have students use the Foldable® 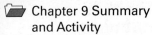 to review the content of Lesson 1. Ask students to reread their answers to the Reading Strategies to review the contents of Lessons 2 through 4.
- **Online Learning Tools** Have students go to the Teen Health Online Learning Center at **glencoe.com** to:
  - Download a **Podcast**.
  - Download free **Study-to-Go** content to their PDAs or cell phones.

Vocabulary Review

- **Quiz Game** Play a game called *Vocabulary Jeopardy,* in which you give vocabulary terms as answers and call on students to give the correct definitions in the form of questions.

Teaching Tips

Prereading Strategy Prereading can help students understand difficult material and become better readers. Copy a reading assignment, cut it into sentences or paragraphs, and give one passage to each student. Ask students to walk around the room reading their passages and listening to the passages of others. Tell them to try to make connections among the passages. After about 15 minutes, ask students to write an anticipatory sentence based on the passages that they have heard and read. Then have students read the entire passage and evaluate the prereading sentences.

Reviewing Vocabulary and Main Ideas

1. physical activity
2. Coordination
3. Balance
4. Heart and lung endurance
5. flexibility
6. Muscle strength
7. True
8. False, target heart rate
9. False, moderate
10. False, conditioning
11. False, carbohydrates
12. True

Thinking Critically

13. *Sample answer:* She should become physically active now so she can enjoy the benefits of physical fitness and become a healthier adult.

 Online

Have students visit **glencoe.com** to take the Chapter 9 quiz.

After You Read

Health eSpotlight **VIDEO**

Now that you have read the chapter, look back at your answer to the Health eSpotlight questions on the chapter opener. Are the short-term goals you created realistic? What other ways can teens keep track of their progress towards a long-term fitness goal?

Reviewing Vocabulary and Main Ideas

On a sheet of paper, write the numbers 1–6. After each number, write the term from the list that best completes each sentence.

- balance
- coordination
- flexibility
- heart and lung endurance
- physical activity
- muscle strength

Lesson 1 | The Benefits of Physical Activity

1. Any form of bodily movement that uses up energy is known as _____.
2. _____ is the smooth and effective working together of your muscles and bones.
3. _____ is the feeling of stability and control over your body.

Lesson 2 | Endurance, Strength, and Flexibility

4. _____ is a measure of how efficiently your heart and lungs work when you exercise and how quickly they return to normal when you stop.
5. The ability of your body's joints to move easily through a full range of motion is known as _____.
6. _____ is a measure of the most weight you can lift or the most force you can exert at one time.

*On a sheet of paper, write the numbers 7–12. Write **True** or **False** for each statement below. If the statement is false, change the underlined word or phrase to make it true.*

Lesson 3 | Setting Fitness Goals

7. Switching between different activities and exercises on different days is known as <u>cross-training</u>.
8. Your <u>resting heart rate</u> is the range of numbers between which your heart and lungs receive the most benefit from a workout.
9. Warm-ups should consist of low to <u>vigorous</u> activity to prepare you for your workout.

Lesson 4 | Sports Conditioning and Avoiding Injury

10. Regular activity and exercise that prepare a person for a sport are known as <u>nutrition</u>.
11. Before a game or event, you should eat foods high in <u>protein</u>.
12. The <u>P.R.I.C.E. formula</u> can provide relief from muscle stiffness or soreness.

 Online Visit **glencoe.com** and take the Online Quiz for Chapter 9.

Health eSpotlight VIDEO Wrap-Up

Achieving Fitness Goals Have students reread the Health eSpotlight question at the beginning of the chapter (page 203) and look at their original answer. Ask: Now that you have read the chapter and watched the video presentation, what are the key steps to achieving a long-term fitness goal? Call on volunteers to give examples of activities or events that require a detailed physical activity plan.

Thinking Critically

Using complete sentences, answer the following questions on a sheet of paper.

13. **Synthesize** Janice understands that physical fitness is important. She says that she plans to start becoming physically active as an adult. How would you encourage Janice to become physically active now as a teen?

Write About It

14. **Persuasive Writing** Write an article for your school paper on the importance of becoming and staying physically active.

↗ *Applying Technology*

Physical Fitness Presentation

In pairs, you will use PowerPoint® to create a physical fitness presentation for younger students.

■ Choose an aspect of physical fitness from this chapter to focus on. Take notes on what information you want to use.

■ Open a new PowerPoint® project with 20 slides. Each slide should have no more than four sentences of information. Turn your notes into complete sentences, making sure to use words that younger children will understand.

■ Add colorful images and illustrations.

■ Save your project. Find an elementary school teacher who will let you show your presentation to his or her class.

↗ *Applying Technology*

Physical Fitness Presentation
Equipment needs: PowerPoint® or similar software
Once students have chosen partners, help them review the steps in this project. Remind students to keep their audience in mind as they work. Establish a sign-up sheet if computer access is limited, and help students agree on a time limit for using the computer. If time permits, have students view one another's presentations, offering constructive feedback, before the presentations are shared with younger students.

Write About It

14. **Persuasive Writing**
Explain that persuasive writing states and supports a position. Articles will vary but should clearly state positive reasons for physical activity and risks of inactivity in teens. Remind students to proofread and make corrections before turning in their work.

Standardized Test Practice

1. C
2. D

Standardized Test Practice

Reading

Read the passage and then answer the questions.

Many teens dream of competing in the Olympic Games. The Olympic spirit of universality, excellence, peace, and friendship is represented in many symbols that date back to early modern Games.

The Olympic motto is one symbol of the Olympic spirit. The Olympic motto is *Citius—Altius—Fortius,* which is Latin for "faster, higher, stronger." The intended meaning is that each athlete should focus on improving his or her own ability, rather than on coming in first.

Another Olympic symbol is the five rings. Each ring is a different color and together they represent the five major continents. (The Americas are treated as one continent.) The rings are interlaced to represent the universality of the Olympics, bringing together athletes from around the world.

The flame is another Olympic symbol, linking the ancient Games to the modern Games. The Olympic flame is lit in Greece and carried by a relay of runners to the site of the Games. There, it is used to light the cauldron that burns until the Closing Ceremony.

TEST-TAKING TIP

Read the passage carefully once to find out what information it contains. After you read each question, look back at the passage to find the answer.

1. The five rings represent
   A. the number of athletes in the first modern Games.
   B. the Olympic motto.
   C. the five major continents in the world.
   D. the five major countries in the world.

2. Which statement best represents the main idea of the passage?
   A. Many teens want to compete in the Olympics.
   B. Athletes from all over the world compete in the Olympics.
   C. There are many Olympic symbols.
   D. Symbols are used to represent the spirit of the Olympics.

Chapter 9 Assessment **231**

Test-Taking Tips

Reading Skills Tell students that answering questions about reading passages is an important skill needed for tests in most subject areas. Advise students to first read or at least skim the entire passage to get an overview of the content. Then they can go back and carefully read the parts of the passage that are relevant to specific questions. When answering multiple choice questions about reading passages, students should try to rule out each of the incorrect answers for a question as a check that the answer they have chosen is correct.

CHAPTER 10 *pp. 232–257*	Standards		Skills and Activities
	National	State/Local	
	National Health Education Standards 1.8.1, 6.8.2, 6.8.3, 7.8.2		**HEALTH INVENTORY**, *p. 233* **BUILDING HEALTH SKILLS** *Goal Setting* Eating for Your Health, *pp. 252–253* **HANDS-ON HEALTH** Jars of Sugar, *p. 254*
Lesson 1 **The Importance of Nutrition** *pp. 234–237*	National Health Education Standards 1.8.1, 1.8.2, 1.8.3, 1.8.5, 1.8.7, 1.8.8, 1.8.9, 2.8.1, 2.8.2, 2.8.3, 2.8.6, 3.8.1, 3.8.2, 5.8.4, 5.8.6, 7.8.2		**Connect To... SCIENCE** Scientific Advancements and Eating Habits, *p. 236*
Lesson 2 **Nutrients for Wellness** *pp. 238–242*	National Health Education Standards 1.8.1, 1.8.5, 1.8.7, 2.8.5, 3.8.2, 7.8.2		**HEALTH SKILLS ACTIVITY** *Practicing Healthful Behaviors* Nutrition from Nature, *p. 239* **Careers for the 21st Century** Dietitian, *p. 240*
Lesson 3 **Following Nutrition Guidelines** *pp. 243–247*	National Health Education Standards 1.8.1, 1.8.5, 1.8.7, 2.8.10, 7.8.2		**Connect To... SCIENCE** Dietary Supplements, *p. 244* **Go Online** MyPyramid, *p. 245*
Lesson 4 **Planning Meals and Snacks** *pp. 248–251*	National Health Education Standards 1.8.1, 1.8.7, 5.8.4, 6.8.1, 7.8.1, 7.8.3		**What Teens Think** Do you think you would be healthier if you ate less fast food?, *p. 249*

PACING THE CHAPTER

Lesson 1 45 min	**Lesson 4** 45 min	
Lesson 2 45 min	**Hands-on health** 30 min	**Chapter Review** 45 min
Lesson 3 45 min	**Building Health Skills** 45 min	

BLOCK SCHEDULING

For block scheduling, assign students Building Health Skills feature *Eating for Your Health*, pages 252–253, and Guided Reading and Writing. 📁

Planning Guide

StudentWorks *Plus*

Glencoe Exclusive!
TeacherWorks™ *Plus*
All-In-One Planner and Resource Center

Reproducible Resources	Assessment	Media and Technology
Chapter *FAST FILE* **Resources** Chapter Summaries and Activities REVIEW Building Health Skills Activity TEACH Performance Assessment Activity EXTEND Universal Access Activities TEACH Parent Letter and Activities 📁 **Student Activities Workbook** TEACH 📁 **Reading Tutor** TEACH	Building Health Skills Activity, *pp. 252–253* Chapter 10 Assessment, *pp. 256–257* **Chapter** *FAST FILE* **Resources** Performance Assessment Activity, *p. 4* Chapter 10 Test, *p. 7* ⊙ *ExamView® Test Generator*	**TeacherWorks** *Plus* includes: ● Interactive Teacher Edition ● Lesson Planner with Calendar ● Access to all blackline masters ● Correlations to standards ⊙ StudentWorks™ Plus ⊙ Online Student Edition Dinah Zike's Teaching Health with Foldables®
Chapter *FAST FILE* **Resources** Concept Mapping Activity 10-1 REVIEW Cross-Curriculum Activity 10-1 EXTEND Enrichment Activity 10-1 EXTEND Lesson Plan 10-1 Guided Reading and Writing 10-1 TEACH Reteaching Activity 10-1 REVIEW	Lesson 1 Review, *p. 237* ⊙ Vocabulary PuzzleMaker ⊙ *ExamView® Test Generator*	⊙ Vocabulary PuzzleMaker ⊙ *ExamView® Test Generator* ⊙ StudentWorks™ Plus 🔋 Transparency 10-1 Go Online glencoe.com
Chapter *FAST FILE* **Resources** Concept Mapping Activity 10-2 REVIEW Cross-Curriculum Activity 10-2 EXTEND Enrichment Activity 10-2 EXTEND Lesson Plan 10-2 Guided Reading and Writing 10-2 TEACH Reteaching Activity 10-2 REVIEW	Lesson 2 Review, *p. 242* ⊙ Vocabulary PuzzleMaker ⊙ *ExamView® Test Generator*	⊙ Vocabulary PuzzleMaker ⊙ *ExamView® Test Generator* ⊙ StudentWorks™ Plus 🔋 Transparency 10-2 Go Online glencoe.com
Chapter *FAST FILE* **Resources** Concept Mapping Activity 10-3 REVIEW Decision-Making Activity 10-3 EXTEND Enrichment Activity 10-3 EXTEND Lesson Plan 10-3 Guided Reading and Writing 10-3 TEACH Reteaching Activity 10-3 REVIEW	Lesson 3 Review, *p. 247* ⊙ Vocabulary PuzzleMaker ⊙ *ExamView® Test Generator*	⊙ Vocabulary PuzzleMaker ⊙ *ExamView® Test Generator* ⊙ StudentWorks™ Plus 🔋 Transparency 10-3 Go Online glencoe.com
Chapter *FAST FILE* **Resources** Concept Mapping Activity 10-4 REVIEW Health Lab 10-4 EXTEND Enrichment Activity 10-4 EXTEND Lesson Plan 10-4 Guided Reading and Writing 10-4 TEACH Reteaching Activity 10-4 REVIEW	Lesson 4 Review, *p. 251* ⊙ Vocabulary PuzzleMaker ⊙ *ExamView® Test Generator*	⊙ Vocabulary PuzzleMaker ⊙ *ExamView® Test Generator* ⊙ StudentWorks™ Plus 🔋 Transparency 10-4 Go Online glencoe.com

Chapter and Lesson Resources

The *Teen Health* resources are designed for differentiated learning abilities. You may want to use the coded items in this way:

REVIEW —activities to review or reinforce content

TEACH —activities to teach basic concepts

EXTEND —activities to extend or enrich lesson content

 OUT OF TIME?

Use Health Skills Activity *Nutrition from Nature*, page 239, and Connect to...Science, page 244.

Healthy Eating on a Budget

Many of the students in your class may have limited food choices due to budget concerns. In fact, 58 percent of students in the United States qualify for free or reduced-price lunches, indicating that their family's income is below the poverty level or that their family participates in one of several federal assistance programs.

Even on a limited budget, healthy eating is possible. Share the following tips with students when discussing meal planning:

- **Buy fruits and vegetables that are in season.**

- **Avoid single-serving packages of foods such as oatmeal, yogurt, and crackers.** Buy large containers and divide the contents at home.

- **Use grocery sale advertisements and coupons to save money on healthful foods.**

- **Use store brand or generic foods in place of name brand foods.**

- **Use beans in place of meats.**

- **Plan a grocery list of healthful food choices before entering the store.**

When students are learning about meal planning, provide them with grocery sale advertisements. Ask students to use the advertisements to plan several healthful meals that incorporate foods that are on sale.

The Importance of Serving Size

When students are learning to use nutrition facts panels to make healthful food choices, emphasize the concept of serving size. Remind students that the calorie count and percentage of daily value figures are based on a measured serving of food. In many cases, the serving size of a food does not match the portion of food a typical teen consumes. In some cases, packages that appear to contain a single serving of food actually contain two or more servings. Use the following activities to help students familiarize themselves with the serving sizes of various foods:

- **Provide measuring cups and boxes of familiar types of breakfast cereal.** Have students compare a measured serving of cereal to the amount they typically consume.

- **Use print restaurant advertisements to point out that restaurant portions of food sometimes contain four or five servings.**

- **Have students research to find everyday items that can be used to represent recommended servings of foods.** For example, a deck of playing cards is sometimes used to represent a single serving of meat. Have students work as a class to develop a display of everyday items labeled with the serving sizes represented by each item.

Support for Teaching Reading

Reading Preview

Activating Background Vocabulary With student input, create a word web on the board around the term *nutrition*. Guide students in a discussion about what constitutes good nutrition. Then ask students the meaning of the word *nutrient*. Make a new category within your word web for vitamins and minerals.

FOLDABLES Study Organizer *Dinah Zike's Reading and Study Skills for Teen Health* provides interactive graphic organizers that help students comprehend and retain health concepts as they read. Use the Foldable® on page 233 or find more Foldables® activities for the chapter on **Nutrition for Health** in the separate booklet, available in the TCR.

Lesson 1   The Importance of Nutrition

Compare and Contrast Create a two-column chart on the board. Ask students to read silently to learn what factors might influence food choices. As they read, have students record facts about appetite on one side of the chart and hunger on the other. Guide students in a discussion of the differences between appetite and hunger.

Lesson 2   Nutrients for Wellness

Jigsaw Divide the class into teams of five and assign each person on the team one topic: carbohydrates, proteins, fats, vitamins and minerals, and water. Have students read their assigned sections carefully, then meet with classmates who have the same topic to share information and take notes. Have students go back to their own teams to teach them about the topic.

Lesson 3   Following Nutrition Guidelines

Active Silent Reading Stop students during the reading process and have them close their books. Ask students what they have read about the MyPyramid food guidance system. Record responses on the board. Then guide students in a discussion about the main concepts. Encourage students to refer back to the text to clarify any remaining questions.

Lesson 4   Planning Meals and Snacks

Review and Record Stop students during reading and ask them to review the key terms. In a class discussion, ask students to describe what they have learned about planning healthy meals. Ask: What is the best way to start the day out right? What does it mean to snack smart? How can you eat right when you eat out? Direct students to record their answers in a journal entry.

Post Reading

Research Presentations Have students locate and organize information for a research presentation on nutrition, nutrients, guidelines for healthy eating, or planning healthy meals. Direct students to gather information from various library and Internet resources, and to edit their final work for correct spelling, punctuation, and sentence structure.

Key for Using the Teacher Wraparound Edition

Use this key to help you identify the different types of prompts found in the Teacher Wraparound Edition.

R **Reading Strategies** activities help you teach reading skills and vocabulary.

C **Critical Thinking** strategies help students apply and extend what they have learned.

U **Universal Access** activities provide differentiated instruction for students learning to speak English, along with suggestions for teaching various types of learners.

HS **Health Skills Practice** activities reinforce Health Skills concepts and help students apply these skills in their everyday lives.

W **Writing Support** activities provide writing opportunities to help students comprehend the text.

AL **Active Learning** strategies provide a variety of activities for presenting lesson content, including Quick Demos and engaging classroom projects that get students actively involved.

Key to Ability Levels

Teaching Strategies and activities have been coded for ability level and appropriateness.

AL Activities for students working above grade level

OL Activities for students working on grade level

BL Activities for students working below grade level

EL Activities for English Learners

Symbols

 Transparencies

 CD-ROM

 glencoe.com

📁 Print Resources

Chapter at a Glance

Lesson 1 explains what nutrients do in the body, identifies factors that influence which foods students choose, and describes how emotions can have an effect on which foods students choose.

Lesson 2 identifies the six major classes of nutrients and explains specific ways the body uses nutrients.

Lesson 3 explains how to use the MyPyramid food guidance system, identifies the names of the five main food groups in MyPyramid, and describes recommendations from the *Dietary Guidelines for Americans*.

Lesson 4 explains why breakfast is important, describes meal planning tips, and identifies healthy ways to snack.

R Reading Strategy

Interpreting the Photo Have students examine the photo. Ask: Teens are often involved in preparing and cooking their own meals. What healthy choices have these teens made? Sample answers: *salad made from fresh vegetables* What are some ways that food choices can impact overall wellness? Sample answer: *Healthful food choices have a positive impact on physical health, energy level, and mood.* **OL**

232

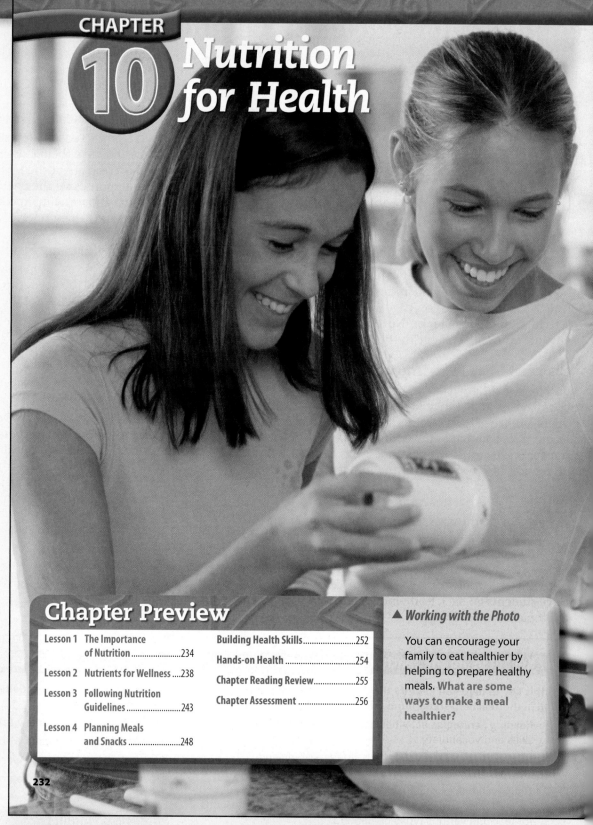

232

Chapter Preview

▲ Working with the Photo

You can encourage your family to eat healthier by helping to prepare healthy meals. **What are some ways to make a meal healthier?**

 Universal Access

Differentiated Learning Glencoe provides teacher support and student materials for all learners in the health classroom.

● Spanish Glosario and chapter summaries assist English Language Learners.
● *Reading Tutor* and related worksheets support reluctant readers.

● Universal Access strategies throughout the Teacher Wraparound Edition and Fast Files help you present materials for gifted students, at-risk students, physically impaired students, and those with behavior disorders or learning disabilities.

Start-Up Activities

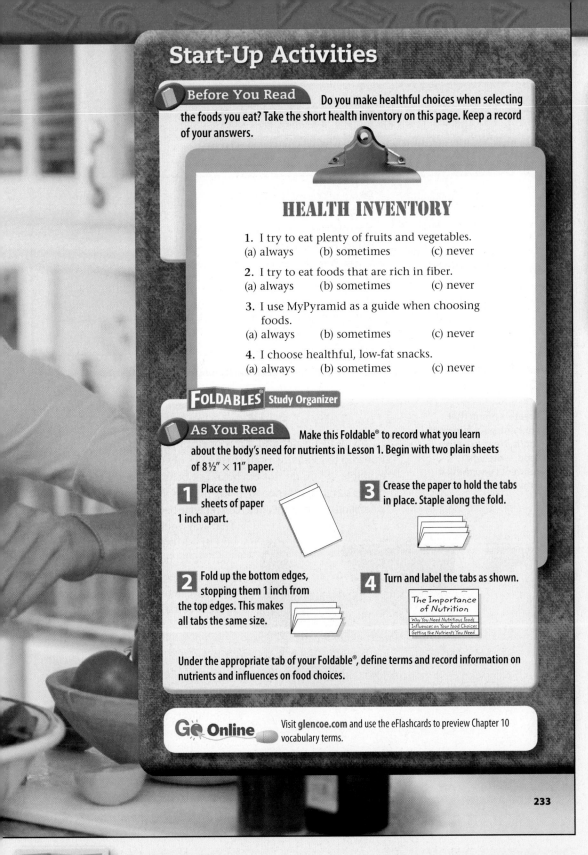

Before You Read Do you make healthful choices when selecting the foods you eat? Take the short health inventory on this page. Keep a record of your answers.

HEALTH INVENTORY

1. I try to eat plenty of fruits and vegetables.
(a) always (b) sometimes (c) never

2. I try to eat foods that are rich in fiber.
(a) always (b) sometimes (c) never

3. I use MyPyramid as a guide when choosing foods.
(a) always (b) sometimes (c) never

4. I choose healthful, low-fat snacks.
(a) always (b) sometimes (c) never

FOLDABLES Study Organizer

As You Read Make this Foldable® to record what you learn about the body's need for nutrients in Lesson 1. Begin with two plain sheets of 8½" × 11" paper.

1 Place the two sheets of paper 1 inch apart.

2 Fold up the bottom edges, stopping them 1 inch from the top edges. This makes all tabs the same size.

3 Crease the paper to hold the tabs in place. Staple along the fold.

4 Turn and label the tabs as shown.

The Importance of Nutrition
Why You Need Nutritious Foods
Influences on Your Food Choices
Getting the Nutrients You Need

Under the appropriate tab of your Foldable®, define terms and record information on nutrients and influences on food choices.

Go Online Visit glencoe.com and use the eFlashcards to preview Chapter 10 vocabulary terms.

233

Lesson 1

FOCUS

Lesson 1

Activating Prior Knowledge

What I Know Have students identify factors that affect their physical health. Record their responses on the board. Circle any answer that pertains to food or nutrition. Explain that this lesson describes how to make healthful food choices.

Guide to Reading

Building Vocabulary

■ Have students skim the lesson to find the meanings of the words *appetite* and *hunger*. Then have students write a sentence that contrasts the meanings of these two words.

■ Use Vocabulary PuzzleMaker to reinforce vocabulary terms.

Reading Strategy
Making Inferences
Have students make a written record of their inferences about the lesson content. After the lesson, have students check to see if their inferences were correct.

FOLDABLES Have students use **Study Organizer** their Foldables® as they read Lesson 1.

Quick Write

Have students share completed Quick Writes with the class. Ask them to reflect on the factors that influence their choices of favorite foods.

The Importance of Nutrition

Guide to Reading

Building Vocabulary
Write the terms you think you know in your notebook. Add a definition in pencil. As you read the lesson, be prepared to correct your definitions.

■ nutrients (p. 235)
■ nutrition (p. 235)
■ appetite (p. 236)
■ hunger (p. 236)

Focusing on the Main Ideas
In this lesson, you will learn to

■ **explain** why the body needs nutrients.
■ **identify** factors that influence which foods you choose.
■ **describe** how your emotions can affect your food choices.

Reading Strategy
Making Inferences Look briefly at the headings, figures, and captions in the lesson. Based on the words and images you see, what do you think you will learn in this lesson?

FOLDABLES Study Organizer Use the Foldable® on p. 233 as you read this lesson.

Quick Write

Create a menu that contains your favorite foods. Next to each food, write what nutrients you think it provides.

The Role of Food

Food, like water and air, is one of life's necessities. Your relationship to food affects all three sides of your health triangle. For example, if you do not eat breakfast before going to school, you might have a hard time focusing in class. Have you ever had days when you could not seem to concentrate because you were hungry?

That was your body's way of telling you that it was running low on fuel. Your body needs food to function properly. Choosing healthy foods is a positive behavior that can help you prevent certain health problems.

◀ Food affects all sides of your health triangle, including your ability to concentrate in school. **Describe other effects food has on your health triangle.**

234 Chapter 10: Nutrition for Health

Lesson 1 Resources

📁 **Chapter *FAST FILE* Resources**
Guided Reading and Writing 10-1
Concept Mapping Activity 10-1
Cross-Curriculum Activity 10-1
Reteaching Activity 10-1
Enrichment Activity 10-1
Lesson Quiz 10-1

Technology
🔋 Transparency 10-1
Audio Summaries
⚙ *ExamView® Assessment Suite*
Vocabulary PuzzleMaker
⚙ StudentWorks™ Plus
G⚙ Online

Food, Nutrients, and Nutrition

Your body depends on nutrients in food to function properly throughout the day. **Nutrients** are *substances in food that your body needs*. They help the body build new tissue, repair damaged cells, and produce energy. The energy from food is measured in units called calories. Each calorie is equal to a certain amount of energy. Chocolate candy, for example, is typically high in calories but provides few nutrients. Fruit, on the other hand, has few calories but has more nutrients the body needs. Calories are further discussed in Lesson 3.

Nutrients nourish the body in two ways: they provide energy and help your body run smoothly. Proteins, carbohydrates, and fats are examples of nutrients that provide energy. Vitamins, minerals, and water are examples of nutrients that help the body run well.

Which nutrients does your body need the most? The best way to answer that question is to learn about **nutrition**—*the study of nutrients and how the body uses them*. Someone who eats plenty of fresh fruits and vegetables has good nutrition. Eating nutrient-rich meals is a good way to **promote** good health and prevent diseases.

 Reading Check **Define** What are *nutrients*?

What Influences Your Food Choices?

Now you know why it is important to eat—but have you ever thought about how people decide *what* to eat?

Yoshi, who grew up in Japan, prefers miso soup and rice for breakfast, while his American friend Carl likes cereal and milk. Both Yoshi's and Carl's tastes in food are influenced by their cultural backgrounds.

Another factor that influences the foods many people choose to eat is availability. Melissa's family enjoys fresh fruits and vegetables from a local market. The meals they prepare depend on which foods are in season. **Figure 10.1** shows several other factors that influence which foods we choose to eat.

Academic Vocabulary

promote (pruh MOHT) (*verb*) to encourage, to further. *Tony and Shana asked their school nurse how they and their classmates can promote good health at school.*

▼ **FIGURE 10.1**

INFLUENCES ON FOOD CHOICES

 Your family and culture influence the foods you eat. **Which factors in this figure play the biggest role in your personal food choices?**

Peer Pressure

Family and Culture

Availability

Advertising

Convenience

Knowledge of Nutrition

Promoting Coordinated School Health

Nutrition Services Nutrition is one of the components of a coordinated school health program. Healthful meals and snacks that reflect the *Dietary Guidelines for Americans* help students to meet their nutritional needs. Have students analyze the food choices available at school. Point out that foods offered in vending machines and snacks available at the cafeteria checkout probably do not meet the same guidelines as the foods available through the school lunch program.

Connect To... Science

Scientific Advancements and Eating Habits

Have students discuss in small groups the food-related advances that affect our food choices today. Go around the room and ask each group to share their ideas. Discuss the benefits these advances have had on healthful eating habits. **OL**

Reading Check

Answer Culture, availability, appetite, and emotions are factors that help determine what a person chooses to eat.

AL Active Learning

Videos Have students work in small groups to plan and produce videos explaining the roles of appetite, hunger, and emotions in making food choices. Have each group share its video with the class. Assess each video based on the accuracy of its health content and the creativity with which the information is presented. **OL**

Caption Answer

Photo Caption, p. 237
Your body needs enough nutrients to provide energy, support growth and body function, and prevent diseases such as anemia.

Connect To... Science

Scientific Advancements and Eating Habits

The microwave oven and frozen foods are examples of advancements in science that have affected the eating habits of many people. Convenience is one benefit of using a microwave oven. Cooking frozen food takes less time than putting together a meal from scratch.

Can you think of other scientific advancements that have influenced eating habits?

Go Online

Visit **glencoe.com** and complete the Interactive Study Guide for Lesson 1.

Appetite and Hunger

Another factor that influences what you choose to eat is **appetite,** or *the psychological desire for food.* The aroma of fresh-baked bread, for example, might make you crave a piece of toast, even if you are not hungry. Psychological desires for food are often connected to memories and feelings. If the smell of fresh-baked bread reminds you of happy times with your family, you might feel like eating some even if your body does not really need fuel at the moment.

People sometimes confuse hunger with appetite. **Hunger** is *the body's physical need for food.* It is important to learn to tell the difference so that you will know why you eat. This will help you make healthful choices when it comes time to satisfy your body's physical need for food. You will learn more about how to make healthful choices later in this chapter.

AL

Food and Emotions

In addition to appetite and hunger, emotions also influence your food choices. Foods bring up feelings connected to past experiences. For example, certain foods may remind you of loved ones or of fun times. If a food is associated with a pleasant or comforting memory, people often crave it even when they are not hungry. The craving can be especially strong when people feel sad, lonely, or discouraged. What they are really craving, however, is not the food, but the pleasant emotions associated with the food. Using food in this way is not a good idea because it can lead to unhealthful eating habits and weight problems. Healthier ways to cope with negative feelings include writing in a journal, listening to music, and talking to a friend.

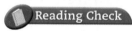
Reading Check

Recall List four factors that influence what a person chooses to eat.

Meeting Nutrient Needs

All bodies need the same nutrients, but the amount a body needs depends upon the person's age, gender, general health, and level of activity. When you do not get enough of a particular nutrient, you could have a *nutrient deficiency,* a shortage of a nutrient.

As a growing teen on the go, your energy demands are greater than those of an older person who is less active. You also need calcium to build strong bones and teeth. A calcium deficiency could affect the strength of your bones as you get older. You also need iron to help your body make enough red blood cells as you grow. A shortage of iron can lead to a blood condition called anemia.

FITNESS ZONE

Nutrition and Fitness Activities Healthy food choices and a regular physical fitness routine are important partners in building good health. Have students review the ideas for establishing a routine in the *Fitness Zone Handbook.* Then ask: Why is it especially important to choose healthful foods when you're physically active? How does physical activity make it easier to choose healthful foods? **For more information, see *Fitness Zone Handbook* pages xviii-1 or visit the Fitness Zone at glencoe.com.**

In general, teens need more of most nutrients to support growth and satisfy energy needs.

Most people in the United States get plenty of food, yet many still do not get the nutrients they need. This is partly because of lifestyles that include too many foods that are high in fat and added sugar. Eating low-nutrient, high-fat foods, along with over-eating, can lead to long-term health problems such as obesity, diabetes, heart disease, and cancer. Developing healthful eating habits, which includes limiting high-fat and high-calorie foods, is your best defense against poor nutrition.

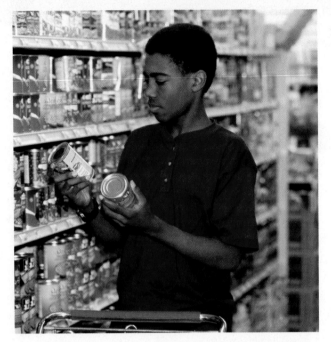

▲ Food labels can tell you which nutrients are in a product, as well as how much fat and calories it has. **Why is it important to provide your body with enough nutrients?**

ASSESS

Assessment Resources

Lesson Review Quiz
ExamView
Fast Files Activities
Online Quizzes and Activities

Reteaching

- Assign Concept Map 10-1 or Reteaching Activity 10-1 in the Fast Files.
- Have students work in pairs to write a short paragraph that explains how appetite, hunger, and emotions affect food choices.

Enrichment

- Assign Enrichment Activity 10-1 in the Fast Files.
- Have students research symptoms that are related to a nutritional deficiency, such as skin problems, brittle nails, or bone loss. Have students prepare a multimedia presentation to share their findings with the class.

CLOSE

Have students explain the two main functions of nutrients.

Lesson 1 Review

After You Read

Review this lesson for new terms, major headings, and Reading Checks.

What I Learned

1. *Vocabulary* Define *appetite*, and explain how it can affect which foods you choose to eat.

2. *Recall* What do nutrients do for your body?

3. *Describe* What role do emotions play in your food choices?

Thinking Critically

4. *Apply* Which factors do you think influence a teen's food choices the most? Explain your answer.

5. *Analyze* How is it possible to have plenty of food and yet be poorly nourished?

Applying Health Skills

6. *Accessing Information* Using online or print resources, locate a country that has famine problems. Research the causes of the famine and what steps are being taken to solve the problem. Share your findings with your classmates.

Go Online For more Lesson Review Activities, go to glencoe.com.

Lesson 1: The Importance of Nutrition **237**

Lesson 1 Review Answers

1. Appetite is the psychological desire for food. It causes people to crave food even when they are not hungry.
2. *Any three:* provide energy for the body, build new tissues, repair damaged cells, ensure body systems run smoothly

3. Emotions can cause us to like or dislike foods because of associations with past experiences.
4. Answers will vary but should reveal an understanding of the factors mentioned in the lesson.

5. Eating too many low-nutrient, high-fat, or high-sugar foods leads to poor nutrition.
6. Help students locate reliable print or online resources to complete their research.

FOCUS

Activating Prior Knowledge

What I Know Have students recall the ways in which nutrients help the body function properly. Explain that this lesson gives more information about specific nutrients and their functions.

 Guide to Reading

Building Vocabulary
- Have students use index cards to create flashcards that can be used to review the Lesson 2 vocabulary terms.
- Use Vocabulary PuzzleMaker to reinforce vocabulary terms.

Reading Strategy
Organizing Information Have students copy the diagram shown in the text. As students read the lesson, they can fill in the diagram. Have volunteers share their completed diagrams with the class.

Quick Write

Use students' Quick Writes to identify misconceptions about the nutrient content of foods.

Nutrients for Wellness

 Guide to Reading

● Building Vocabulary
Write the terms below in your notebook. As you come across each one in your reading, write a definition beside it.
- carbohydrates (p. 238)
- fiber (p. 239)
- proteins (p. 240)
- saturated fats (p. 240)
- unsaturated fats (p. 240)
- vitamins (p. 240)
- minerals (p. 240)

● Focusing on the Main Ideas
In this lesson, you will learn to
- **identify** the six major classes of nutrients.
- **explain** specific ways your body uses nutrients.

● Reading Strategy
Organizing Information Make a diagram similar to the one below. Include a box for each nutrient and foods that are sources of that nutrient.

Carbohydrate	Protein
↓	↓

Food Sources ⟶ | | |

Quick Write

Make a list of foods that you think are high in nutrients. After reading the lesson, check to see if you were right.

Nutrients and Nutrition

Scientists who study the nutrients in food have found more than 40 different kinds. These nutrients are divided into six classes: carbohydrates, proteins, fats, vitamins, minerals, and water. Choosing a variety of healthy foods can help you get enough nutrients from each of these important groups.

Carbohydrates

What does a steaming plate of spaghetti have in common with a ripe peach? Both foods contain carbohydrates, your body's main energy source. **Carbohydrates** are *sugars and starches that occur naturally in foods, mainly in plants*. There are two kinds of carbohydrates: simple and complex.

◄ An apple is a great source of carbohydrates. **What are some other sources of carbohydrates?**

238 Chapter 10: Nutrition for Health

Caption Answer

Photo Caption *Sample answer:* Carrots, peaches, and pasta are all sources of carbohydrates.

 Chapter *FAST FILE* Resources
Guided Reading and Writing 10-2
Concept Mapping Activity 10-2
Cross-Curriculum Activity 10-2
Reteaching Activity 10-2
Enrichment Activity 10-2
Lesson Quiz 10-2

Technology
 Transparency 10-2
Audio Summaries
ExamView® Assessment Suite
Vocabulary PuzzleMaker
StudentWorks™ Plus
G⊙ Online

Health Skills Activity

Practicing Healthful Behaviors

Nutrition from Nature

When carbohydrate-rich foods are processed, they can lose some of their nutrients. The process that turns wheat into refined white flour is a good example of how nutrients can be lost. In this process, the inner and outer parts of the wheat grain are separated, and only one inner portion is used to make the flour. All the nutrients in the grain's outer covering are lost. Cooking, freezing, dehydrating, and canning also remove nutrients from food.

When shopping for carbohydrate-rich foods, try to choose whole grains—such as oats, millet, and brown rice—or foods that contain them, such as whole wheat bread, popcorn, and oatmeal. Try to snack on fresh fruits and vegetables. They are naturally rich in nutrients and haven't been processed.

On Your Own

Make a list of carbohydrate-rich foods that you enjoy eating. Which of these foods contain whole grains? Develop a plan for including more whole grains in your food choices.

TEACH

Health Skills Activity

Practicing Healthful Behaviors

Nutrition from Nature

Use the following strategies to help students complete the activity:

● Have students develop a list of their favorite carbohydrate-rich foods as directed in the feature.

● Provide students with packaging from various carbohydrate-rich foods. Ask students to use the ingredient lists and Nutrition Facts panels to infer the degree of processing the carbohydrates in these foods have undergone. **OL**

All carbohydrates are made of sugar molecules. When these molecules remain separate, they are called *simple carbohydrates*. Foods that contain simple carbohydrates include fruits, many vegetables, milk, and milk products.

Sugar molecules that join together to form long chains are called *starches*, or *complex carbohydrates*. Foods that contain complex carbohydrates include grains such as rice and pasta, dried beans, and starchy vegetables such as potatoes. Nutritionists say that about 45 to 65 percent of your daily energy should come from carbohydrates.

 Reading Check **Identify** What are complex carbohydrates? Name some foods that contain this nutrient.

Fiber

Fiber is *the parts of fruits, vegetables, grains, and beans that your body cannot digest*. It is a special type of complex carbohydrate, found in fruits, vegetables, and especially whole grains. As it passes through the digestive system, fiber pushes other food particles along. Choosing to eat high-fiber foods can help reduce your risk of certain types of cancer and heart disease.

▼ A great way to include fiber in your diet is by eating whole-grain cereals. **Why is it important to get enough fiber?**

U Universal Access

Gifted Students Challenge students to research the structure of carbohydrate, protein, and fat molecules. Have students make a model of one of the molecules using readily available materials. Ask each student to share his or her model with the class. **AL**

Reading Check

Answer Complex carbohydrates are long chains of sugar molecules. Foods that contain complex carbohydrates include whole grains, beans, and starchy vegetables.

Caption Answer

Photo Caption Fiber moves food through the digestive system and reduces the risk of heart disease and some cancers.

Cultural Perspectives

Grains In almost every culture, grains play a prominent role in people's diets. In most North Americans' diets, wheat is the most-used grain. Corn, rice, and oats are also familiar to those who eat a typical North American diet. Rice is the prominent grain in most Asian cultures. Millet is also a staple grain in some Asian diets. Have students work in small groups to research and make a poster showing the nutritional benefits of less-common grains and grain-substitutes, such as amaranth, quinoa, rye, and barley. **OL**

Careers for the 21st Century

Dietitian Ask students: Why do you think classes in chemistry, biology, and psychology are important preparation for a career as a dietitian? How do you think dietitians can affect all three sides of the health triangle for the people they work with?

W Writing Support

Expository Writing Have each student perform additional research and prepare a report about the role of protein in the body. Remind students that expository writing explains information and informs others. Have students edit and correct their reports before they are turned in. **OL**

C Critical Thinking

Nutrition Critique Have students write a list of foods that are a regular part of their diet. Then have students use Nutrition Facts panels or other resources to determine which of the foods on their list are high in saturated fats. Have students circle the foods on their list that are high in saturated fats. Then have students identify a more healthful alternative to each of the circled foods. **OL**

Reading Check

Answer Proteins are nutrients used to build, repair, and maintain cells and tissues.

Careers for the 21st Century

Dietitian

A dietitian is an expert in food and nutrition. They help promote good health through healthful eating. They may also supervise the preparation of food, modify diets, and educate individuals and groups on good nutritional habits. Dietitians will always be an important resource for people who want to learn how to make healthful eating part of their lives. If you would like to become a dietitian, you should study how the body uses food.

What are some other kinds of nutrition workers? Go to *Career Corner* at glencoe.com to find out.

Proteins

Proteins are *nutrients your body uses to build, repair, and maintain cells and tissues*. They are made up of chemical building blocks called *amino acids*. Anyone who has had a stiff muscle get better after a few days of rest has experienced "repair" proteins at work. Proteins also play an important role in fighting disease since parts of your immune system are made of proteins.

Foods that contain protein include beef, pork, veal, fish, poultry, eggs, and most dairy products. Notice that all these foods are animal-based products. These foods have *complete proteins* because they contain all nine of the essential amino acids. Most plant proteins—available from nuts, peas, and dried beans—lack sufficient amounts of one or more essential amino acids.

W

Reading Check   **Define** What are *proteins*?

Fats

Fats are an important part of good nutrition. They promote healthy skin and normal cell growth, and they carry vitamins A, D, E, and K to wherever they are needed in your body.

However, eating a large amount of **saturated fats,** *fats that are solid at room temperature*, is not good for your health. Foods like butter, cheese, and fatty meats are high in saturated fats. Eating too much of these foods can increase your risk of heart disease.

C

Most of the fats in your diet should be **unsaturated fats.** These are *fats that remain liquid at room temperature*. They come mainly from plant-based foods such as olive oil, nuts, and avocados.

Cholesterol

Cholesterol is really two things: a fatlike substance in food and a fatty substance in blood. Cholesterol in food comes only from animal-based foods, such as eggs, meat, poultry, fish, and dairy products. Your body also makes cholesterol. You need some cholesterol, but not too much. Although it can affect blood cholesterol levels, the cholesterol in food doesn't turn into blood cholesterol. However, eating too much saturated fat can raise your blood cholesterol to unhealthy levels. High levels of blood cholesterol can lead to heart disease.

Vitamins and Minerals

Two other kinds of nutrients that the body needs are vitamins and minerals. Though only small quantities of each are needed, they are essential to your body's health. **Vitamins** are *substances that help your body fight infections and use other nutrients, among other jobs*. **Minerals** are *elements that help form healthy bones and teeth, and regulate certain body processes*.

What Teens Want to Know

Should I use protein supplements? Many people believe that protein supplement powders can enhance athletic performance and increase muscle mass. However, extra protein intake has not been proven to have positive effects, and in fact, can have negative consequences for the body. For example, protein digestion and excretion can lead to dehydration and calcium deficiencies. Have students locate scientific studies about the effects of using protein supplements. Have students share their findings with the class. **OL**

There are two kinds of vitamins: water-soluble and fat-soluble. Water-soluble vitamins, which include vitamins C and B complex, dissolve in water. Your body cannot store them, so you need to consume them regularly. Fat-soluble vitamins, including Vitamins A, D, E, and K, are stored in the body's fat until they are needed. **Figure 10.2** lists the functions and food sources of some vitamins and minerals. Most teens do not get enough vitamin E, calcium, or iron. The best way to get vitamins and minerals is to choose nutritious foods.

Go Online

Visit glencoe.com and complete the Interactive Study Guide for Lesson 2.

▼ FIGURE 10.2

VITAMINS AND SELECTED MINERALS: FUNCTIONS AND SOURCES

Vitamins and minerals are essential to your body's health. **What are the benefits of consuming Vitamins A, E, and C, magnesium, calcium, iron, and folic acid?**

	Functions	Food Sources
Vitamins	**Vitamin A** Promotes healthy skin and normal vision	Dark-green leafy vegetables (such as spinach); dairy products; eggs; deep yellow-orange fruits and vegetables
	B Vitamins Needed for a healthy nervous system. Folate, or folic acid, helps produce and maintain new cells.	Poultry; eggs; meat; fish; whole-grain and enriched breads and cereals
	Vitamin C Needed for healthy teeth, gums, and bones; helps heal wounds and fight infection	Citrus fruits (such as oranges and grapefruit); cantaloupe; strawberries; mangoes; tomatoes; cabbage; broccoli and potatoes
	Vitamin D Promotes strong bones and teeth and the absorption of calcium	Fortified milk; fatty fish (such as salmon and mackerel); egg yolks; liver
	Vitamin E An antioxidant that helps protect cells	Fortified cereals; dark-green leafy vegetables (such as spinach); fish; nuts; seeds; vegetable oils
Minerals	**Calcium** Needed to build and maintain strong bones and teeth	Dairy products (such as milk, yogurt, cheese); dark-green leafy vegetables (such as spinach); canned fish with edible bones (such as sardines)
	Fluoride Promotes strong bones and teeth; prevents tooth decay	Fluoridated water; fish with edible bones
	Iron Needed for hemoglobin in red blood cells	Red meat; poultry; dry beans (legumes); fortified breakfast cereal; nuts; eggs; dried fruits; dark-green leafy vegetables
	Magnesium Helps build strong bones; releases energy for muscles	Dark-green leafy vegatables (such as spinach); beans and peas; whole-grain breads and cereals
	Potassium Helps regulate fluid balance in tissues; promotes proper nerve function	Fruits (such as bananas and oranges); dry beans and peas; dried fruits; tomato juice

U Universal Access

Learning Disabled Students with learning disabilities may not be able to retain information about the roles of each of the six types of nutrients in the body. Allow them to focus on the skills of making healthy food choices and planning healthy meals and snacks. Use magazine pictures of various foods to help students visualize healthful meals and snacks. **OL**

R Reading Strategy

Analyzing a Graphic Have students read the information in **Figure 10.2**. Then have students examine various foods' Nutrition Facts panels for information about their vitamin and mineral content. Ask students to work as a class to identify foods that are good sources of each of the listed vitamins and minerals. **OL**

 Reading Check

Answer, p. 242 The body needs plenty of water to prevent dehydration.

Caption Answers

Figure Caption, this page Answers should include information from **Figure 10.2**.

Photo Caption, p. 242 Water helps the body digest food, regulates body temperature and blood circulation, carries nutrients and oxygen to cells, removes toxins, cushions joints, and protects tissues and organs from shock and damage.

HEALTH LITERACY

Vitamin and Mineral Supplements Explain that vitamin and mineral supplements are not a shortcut to good nutrition. In some cases, using a supplement can result in the consumption of an excess of some vitamins and minerals. Excess amounts of water-soluble vitamins are excreted from the body in urine. Excess amounts of fat-soluble vitamins are stored by the body and can lead to health problems. **OL**

ASSESS

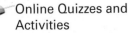

Assessment Resources

Lesson Review Quiz
ExamView
Fast Files Activities
Online Quizzes and Activities

Reteaching

- Assign Concept Map 10-2 or Reteaching Activity 10-2 in the Fast Files.
- Have students work with a partner to develop a six-question quiz about the major classes of nutrients. Call on each pair of students to share some of its quiz questions with the class.

Enrichment

- Assign Enrichment Activity 10-2 in the Fast Files.
- Have students research combinations of foods that can be used by vegetarians to meet their need for essential amino acids. Have each student use his or her findings to create menus for three healthful vegetarian meals.

CLOSE

Ask students to identify the main functions of each of the six major classes of nutrients.

▲ Water is all around us. The water that we drink comes from natural sources like the one in this picture. **What functions does water perform as a nutrient?**

Water

Water plays a role in many of the body's functions. It helps you digest and absorb food, it regulates body temperature and blood circulation, and it carries nutrients and oxygen to cells. It also removes toxins and other wastes, cushions joints, and protects tissues and organs from shock and damage.

Dehydration, or lack of water in the body, can cause problems like fatigue, confusion, and inability to focus. You need to replace the water your body loses by drinking at least six to eight 8-ounce cups of fluid a day. Even more water is needed during vigorous activity or hot weather. Choose water or milk most of the time and limit your intake of juice or soda.

 Reading Check **Explain** Why does the body need plenty of water?

Lesson 2 Review

 After You Read

Review this lesson for new terms, major headings, and Reading Checks.

What I Learned

1. *Vocabulary* What is *fiber*? What function does it have in the body?

2. *List* Name the six major classes of nutrients.

3. *Identify* Name some sources of complete proteins.

Thinking Critically

4. *Apply* Make a list of the foods you have eaten today. Identify which nutrients can be found in each food. Are there any nutrient groups that come up short?

5. *Hypothesize* How can the food you choose to eat today affect your health in the future?

Applying Health Skills

6. *Analyzing Influences* As you learned earlier in this chapter, the media play a role in people's food choices. Find an ad for a food or food product. What methods does the ad use to encourage you to buy the food? Share your findings with those of your classmates.

Go Online For more Lesson Review Activities, go to **glencoe.com**.

Lesson 2 Review Answers

1. Fiber is the part of fruits, vegetables, whole grains, and beans that your body cannot digest. Fiber pushes foods through the digestive system and lowers the risk of certain cancers and heart disease.

2. carbohydrates, proteins, fats, vitamins, minerals, and water

3. *Sample answers:* beef, pork, veal, fish, poultry, eggs, dairy products, soybeans

4. Answers should reflect an understanding of the lesson content.

5. Answers should note the effect of food choices on health and wellness, including the role of foods in the development or prevention of some diseases.

6. Have each student explain why the ad they selected might persuade someone to purchase that food.

Lesson 3

Following Nutrition Guidelines

Guide to Reading

● **Building Vocabulary**
As you read this lesson, write the four new highlighted terms and their definitions in your notebook.

- MyPyramid food guidance system (p. 243)
- calorie (p. 245)
- sodium (p. 246)
- foodborne illness (p. 247)

● **Focusing on the Main Ideas**
In this lesson, you will learn to

- **explain** how to use the MyPyramid food guidance system.
- **identify** the names of the five main food groups in MyPyramid.
- **describe** recommendations from the *Dietary Guidelines for Americans*.

● **Reading Strategy**
Identifying Problems and Solutions Many people, including teens, develop unhealthy eating habits. Can you suggest some solutions to this problem? After reading, come back to this question. See if your answers have changed.

Guidelines for Healthy Eating

Choosing foods that provide the right nutrients can be a challenge. To help you meet this challenge, the United States Department of Agriculture (USDA) has created a tool called the **MyPyramid food guidance system.** This is *a system designed to help Americans make healthful food choices.*

A Closer Look at MyPyramid

MyPyramid includes an illustration (see **Figure 10.3**) on page 244 that shows a pyramid with six colored sections, each representing a different food group. A well-balanced eating plan should contain a variety of foods from the five main food groups. These are grains, vegetables, fruits, milk, and meat and beans. The sixth group, oils and other fats, should only be eaten in very small amounts. MyPyramid can help you develop a personalized eating plan based on your age, gender, and activity level.

Look at Figure 10.3. Notice the figure walking up the steps of the pyramid. The figure is there to remind you to make physical activity a part of your daily routine.

Reading Check   **Identify** What do the colored bands in MyPyramid represent?

 Quick Write

Describe your current eating habits in a short paragraph. Include a list of the foods you eat the most and the kinds of snacks you enjoy.

Lesson 3 Resources

📁 **Chapter *Fast File* Resources**
Guided Reading and Writing 10-3
Concept Mapping Activity 10-3
Decision-Making Activity 10-3
Reteaching Activity 10-3
Enrichment Activity 10-3
Lesson Quiz 10-3

Technology
🔌 Transparency 10-3
💿 Audio Summaries
⊙ *ExamView® Assessment Suite*
💿 Vocabulary PuzzleMaker
⊙ StudentWorks™ Plus

 G⊛ Online

FOCUS

Activating Prior Knowledge

What I Know Have students identify the nutrients that are needed by the body. Tell students that this lesson will explain how they can determine how much of each nutrient they need for good health.

Guide to Reading

Building Vocabulary
- Tell students that the word part *-borne* means "transmitted by." Have students use this information to infer the meaning of the term *foodborne illness*.
- Use Vocabulary PuzzleMaker to reinforce vocabulary terms.

Reading Strategy
Identifying Problems and Solutions Have students make a bulleted list of three suggestions for improving teens' food choices. Challenge students to add to their lists after they have finished reading the lesson.

Quick Write

Have students share their completed Quick Writes to determine the class's five most enjoyed foods. Lead a class discussion about the nutrients found in these foods.

Reading Check

Answer the different food groups

TEACH

R Reading Strategy

Analyzing a Graphic Have students examine **Figure 10.3**. Ask: The sections representing each of the food groups are wider at the base than at the top. What are the characteristics of foods represented by the wider base of each section? *The wide base represents foods in that food group that contain little or no solid fat or added sugar.* **OL**

AL Active Learning

Slogan Divide the class into small groups. Ask students to discuss in their groups the characteristics of slogans with which they are familiar. Have each group choose one recommendation for good nutrition from the lesson. Then have each group devise a slogan that sums up its chosen recommendation. **OL**

Dietary Supplements

Ask students: Does everyone need dietary supplements? *Sample answer: A diet with foods from all the food groups will provide the body with the vitamins and minerals it needs.*

Caption Answer

Figure Caption It reminds you that exercise is just as important as nutrition in developing a healthy lifestyle.

244

▶ **FIGURE 10.3**

MyPyramid

R The goal of MyPyramid is to help you develop a healthy lifestyle. *What does the figure in the illustration remind you to do?*

MyPyramid
STEPS TO A HEALTHIER YOU

| GRAINS Make half your grains whole | VEGETABLES Vary your veggies | FRUITS Focus on fruits | MILK Get your calcium-rich foods | MEAT & BEANS Go lean with protein |

Connect To... Science

Dietary Supplements

Some people take dietary supplements because the foods they eat do not satisfy all of their nutritional needs. However, large doses of vitamins and minerals can be dangerous. It is important to take the recommended daily dose and no more.

Use the Internet to research nutritional supplements. Remember to stick to Web sites that end in *.edu* and *.gov* because they provide the most reliable information. Share your findings with your class.

Other Guidelines for Good Health

MyPyramid reflects science-based advice from the *2005 Dietary Guidelines for Americans*. These guidelines were released by the U.S. Department of Agriculture (USDA) and the U.S. Department of Health and Human Services (HHS). The guidelines help people who are two years of age and older to develop healthful eating habits and increase their level of activity. Doing both improves health and reduces the risk of certain diseases. **AL**

Eat a Variety of Foods

Have you ever heard the expression, "Variety is the spice of life"? That means life is better when things are not always the same. Healthy eating includes choosing a variety of foods so that your body gets all the nutrients it needs. Ask a parent or guardian to help you create some meals and snacks that include a variety of healthy foods.

Eat More Fruits, Vegetables, and Whole Grains

When it comes to eating enough fruits, vegetables, and whole grains, many teens fall short. The guidelines recommend making half the grains you eat each day whole grains. Including leafy greens and colorful vegetables and fruits in your meals will make your food more attractive as well as more nutritious.

Teacher to Teacher

Yvonne Magliocco   **Woodland Middle School, Barrington, NJ**

MyPyramid "Before class, have students record their servings for each food group. Draw a MyPyramid diagram on the board, labeling each group. Pass out index cards with one food type per card. Explain that they should identify where the food (on the index card) belongs on the MyPyramid. Record servings on the board using student responses. Call three students to the board at a time to write their answer in the correct food group."

Balance the Calories You Consume with Physical Activity

Consume only as many calories as your body needs. A **calorie** is *a unit of heat that measures the energy available in food*. It also measures how much energy your body uses. A moderately active teen needs around 2,000 calories a day. If you are involved in regular, strenuous exercise such as running on your school's track team, you may need more. If you eat more calories than your body needs, you could gain more weight than is healthy for your body.

Staying physically active will help you burn some of the calories you take in from food. **Figure 10.4** shows the relationship between calories consumed and calories burned.

Teens should be physically active for at least 60 minutes on most days. In addition to helping you maintain a healthy weight, physical activity builds strength, gives you energy, helps you make new friends, and helps you feel good about yourself.

Reading Check **Explain** Why is physical activity important?

Limit Fats, Sugar, and Salt

Look at the MyPyramid illustration in Figure 10.3 again. Can you see the narrow yellow band? This category represents fats. A healthy choice for good nutrition is to limit your intake of oils, butter, salad dressing, and other high-fat foods. Many processed and prepared foods contain hidden fats. To find out how much fat a single serving of packaged food contains, read the Nutrition

▼ FIGURE 10.4

THE ENERGY "EQUATION"

Physical activity helps you burn calories. The calories out listed below are for a 100-pound person. **What activities are you involved in that help your body burn calories?**

	Calories In		Calories Out Per Hour	
3-Ounce Lean Cooked Hamburger Patty	245		270	**Bicycling (12 mph)**
English Muffin with Egg, Cheese, and Ham	360	**=**	325	**Swimming (50 yds/min)**
Corn Muffin	510		500	**Jumping Rope**
Grilled Chicken Sandwich, Plain Baked Potato, and Bottled Water	640		610	**Jogging (7 mph)**

Source: American Heart Association, 2007.

Topic: MyPyramid

Visit glencoe.com for Student Web Activities that will help you develop a personal eating plan using MyPyramid.

Activity: Using the information from the link above, create a personal eating plan for one week based on your age, gender, and activity level. Include a few meals based on restaurant menu choices.

MyPyramid Direct students to visit **glencoe. com**. Have students form pairs or small groups to share their personal eating plans. Ask each group to compile a list of their food choices for each MyPyramid category. **OL**

AL Active Learning

English Learners Provide pairs of students with the Nutrition Facts panels from several foods. Have each pair of students use the panels to plan out a day's worth of meals. Students should aim for approximately 2000 calories a day. **EL**

Reading Check

Answer Physical activity helps you maintain a healthy weight, builds strength, gives you energy, and enhances your self-esteem.

R Reading Strategy

Analyzing a Graphic Have students examine **Figure 10.4**. Ask them to use print or online resources to find the number of calories burned during other types of physical activity. Have students make charts to show their results. **OL**

🏔️ Home, School, and Community

At Home Many teens do not consume an adequate quantity of whole grains. Use the following tips to help students choose whole-grain foods.

• Use the ingredient lists on several types of bread to demonstrate how to determine if bread contains whole grain.

• Explain that brown rice is the whole-grain alternative to white rice.

• Remind students that oatmeal is a whole-grain food, but to watch for excessive added sugar in some flavored varieties.

Caption Answer

Figure Caption Student answers will vary according to their individual routines.

Health Skills Practice

Refusal Skills Point out that there are two important aspects of making healthful food choices. The first is including more healthful foods in their diet. The second is refusing less healthful choices. Have students work in small groups to practice using refusal skills, including the S.T.O.P. strategy, to turn down unhealthy food choices. **OL**

Reading Check

Answer a nutrient that helps control the amount of fluid in your body

R Reading Strategy

Analyzing a Graphic Have students examine **Figure 10.5**. Ask: What other information should you know before you decide if a snack is a healthy choice? Sample answer: *I would need to know how much sodium the snack food contained.* **OL**

 Go Online

Visit glencoe.com and complete the Interactive Study Guide for Lesson 3.

▶ **FIGURE 10.5**

NUTRITION FACTS LABEL

Food labels provide important nutritional information that can help you make sensible food choices. **How many servings does this product contain? If you ate the whole product, how many calories would you consume?**

Facts label. A typical Nutrition Facts label appears in **Figure 10.5.** Notice that this product contains a total of 12 grams (g) of fat. How much of this fat is saturated fat?

The *Dietary Guidelines* recommend that you limit added sugars and salt. One way to cut back on added sugars is to limit foods such as cookies, cake, candy, and regular soft drinks. Enjoy these sweet treats occasionally, rather than every day. Be aware that added sugars may be present in unexpected foods, such as salad dressings and many breakfast cereals.

Salt contains **sodium,** *a nutrient that helps control the amount of fluid in your body.* Too much sodium can lead to high blood pressure in some people. Once again, you can find out how much sodium a food has by checking the Nutrition Facts panel.

 Reading Check **Define** What is *sodium*?

Nutrition Facts

Serving Size 1 cup (226g)
Servings Per Container 2

Amount Per Serving		
Calories 250		Calories from Fat 110
		% Daily Value*
Total Fat 12g		**18%**
Saturated Fat 3g		**15%**
Trans Fat 3g		
Cholesterol 30g		**10%**
Sodium 470mg		**20%**
Potassium 700mg		**20%**
Total Carbohydrate 31g		**10%**
Dietary Fiber 0g		**0%**
Sugar 10g		
Protein 5g		
Vitamin A		**4%**
Vitamin C		**2%**
Calcium		**20%**
Iron		**4%**

*Percent Daily Values are based on a 2,000 calorie diet. Your Daily Values may be higher or lower depending on your calorie needs.

	Calories	2,000	2,500
Total Fat	Less than	65g	80g
Saturated Fat	Less than	20g	25g
Cholesterol	Less than	300mg	300mg
Sodium	Less than	2,400mg	2,400mg
Total Carbohydrate		300g	375g
Dietary Fiber		25g	30g

Caption Answer

Figure Caption This product contains two servings; 500 calories

HEALTH LITERACY

Hidden Sources of Sodium Besides potato chips and pretzels, there are many hidden sources of sodium that students might not be aware of. For example, canned chicken soup, processed meats and cheeses, some diet sodas, and pickles all contain large amounts of sodium. Many restaurant foods, even some salads and milkshakes, contain a surprising amount of sodium. Have students work as a class to develop a list of foods that contain a large amount of sodium. **OL**

Keep Foods Safe to Eat

Foods must be handled and prepared properly in order to be safe to eat. If foods are improperly handled, they can become contaminated with bacteria that can cause illness. Also known as food poisoning, a **foodborne illness** is *a sickness resulting from eating food that is not safe to eat.* To maintain your health, it is important that you take steps to make sure your food is free from contamination.

The most important thing you can do to protect yourself against foodborne illness is to wash your hands with hot soapy water before handling food. Another way to keep foods safe to eat is by storing and preparing them at the right temperatures. In addition, use a separate cutting board and knife when cutting raw meat to avoid contaminating other foods.

▲ When food shopping, buy perishable foods last. Get them home and into the refrigerator promptly. **What are some other ways to prevent foodborne illness?**

ASSESS

Assessment Resources

Lesson Review Quiz
- *ExamView*
- Fast Files Activities
- Online Quizzes and Activities

Reteaching

- Assign Concept Map 10-3 or Reteaching Activity 10-3 in the Fast Files.
- Have students work with a partner to develop a way to explain the USDA Food Guidance System to younger students.

Enrichment

- Assign Enrichment Activity 10-3 in the Fast Files.
- Have students perform research on one specific foodborne illness. Have each student prepare a poster that can be used to share their findings with the class.

CLOSE

Ask students to identify strategies for limiting the fat, sugar, and salt in their diets.

Caption Answer

Photo Caption *Sample answer:* Wash your hands with hot, soapy water before handling food.

Lesson 3 Review

After You Read

Review this lesson for new terms, major headings, and Reading Checks.

What I Learned

1. *Explain* Who created the MyPyramid food guidance system and what is its purpose?

2. *List* Name the five main food groups in MyPyramid. What does the sixth group represent?

3. *Identify* What are two things you can do to keep your foods safe from harmful bacteria?

Thinking Critically

4. *Synthesize* Explain what MyPyramid is designed to help you know about foods to eat.

5. *Apply* Tom had a peanut butter sandwich and a glass of milk for lunch. Which food groups do these foods represent in MyPyramid? What else could Tom eat to add more food groups to his lunch?

Applying Health Skills

6. *Accessing Information* Check the Nutrition Facts label of several snack foods you enjoy eating. Compare the nutrients in a single label serving of each food and decide which one provides the most nutrients. How do the calories compare?

Go Online For more Lesson Review Activities, go to glencoe.com.

Lesson 3: Following Nutrition Guidelines **247**

Lesson 3 Review Answers

1. The USDA created MyPyramid to help Americans stay healthy, eat right, and stay active.
2. The food groups are grains, vegetables, fruits, dairy products, and meats and beans. The sixth section represents oils.

3. *Sample answer:* Follow guidelines for safe food preparation and storage, and wash your hands before preparing foods.
4. *Sample answer:* MyPyramid's bands represent different groups of foods and the amount of each that should be eaten.

5. His lunch included grains, meat and beans (nuts fall in this category), and dairy. He could add an apple and a green salad.
6. Students' answers should indicate an understanding of how to read Nutrition Facts panels.

FOCUS

Activating Prior Knowledge

What I Know Ask students to explain how the information in MyPyramid can be used to plan healthy meals.

Guide to Reading

Building Vocabulary

■ Explain that *density* is a measure of quantity per unit volume. Have students use this information to determine the meaning of the term *nutrient density*.

■ Use Vocabulary PuzzleMaker to reinforce vocabulary terms.

Reading Strategy
Finding the Main Idea
Model the activity for students by writing the first main heading of the lesson on the board. Have students supply the main idea and record it. Have students continue for the remainder of the lesson.

*Q*uick *Write*

After students have completed the Quick Write, have them discuss whether or not their favorite snack is a healthful addition to their diet.

Lesson 4

Planning Meals and Snacks

Guide to Reading

● **Building Vocabulary**
As you read this lesson, write the two new highlighted terms and their definitions in your notebook.

■ empty-calorie foods (p. 249)
■ nutrient density (p. 250)

● **Focusing on the Main Ideas**
In this lesson, you will learn to

■ **explain** why breakfast is important.
■ **describe** meal-planning tips.
■ **identify** healthy ways to snack.

● **Reading Strategy**
Finding the Main Idea For each of the main sections in this lesson, write one sentence that states the main idea in the section.

*Q*uick *Write*

Write a short description of your favorite snack and when you tend to eat it.

▼ A healthful breakfast gives you energy that lasts throughout the morning. **Why is this important for teens in particular?**

248

Planning Healthy Meals

The advice in MyPyramid can be summed up by the three words *variety*, *moderation*, and *balance*. Variety, as you have seen, can make your meals and snacks more nutritious and interesting. Moderation, which includes eating reasonable portions and limiting fats, sugars, and salt, can lower your risk of developing certain diseases. Balance, which means being careful not to eat more calories than your body can burn, can help you maintain a healthy weight.

In this lesson, you will see how these ideas can be applied to planning healthful meals and snacks. You will learn ways to eat well, both at home and on the go.

Breakfast: Start the Day Out Right

Breakfast has been called the most important meal of the day, and for good reason. After a night of sleep, in which your body rests and renews itself, you need breakfast to aid your body's fuel-producing mechanism. Breakfast gets the body going and provides the fuel you will need later in the morning. This fuel helps you to stay alert so you can

---

Lesson 4 Resources

📁 **Chapter *FAST FILE* Resources**
Guided Reading and Writing 10-4
Concept Mapping Activity 10-4
Health Lab 10-4
Reteaching Activity 10-4
Enrichment Activity 10-4
Lesson Quiz 10-4

Technology
🔦 Transparency 10-4
Audio Summaries
💿 *ExamView® Assessment Suite*
Vocabulary PuzzleMaker
StudentWorks™ Plus
G🔴 Online

concentrate in school. Research suggests that students who make time for breakfast tend to do better academically than teens who do not eat breakfast.

When planning breakfast, round out your meal with a cup of fruit and a glass of low-fat milk. Trail mixes and packaged breakfast bars can also be good as long as the sugar content is low. The ingredient list on the wrapper will tell you if the product contains added sugar. *Honey, sugar, molasses,* and *corn syrup* are a few names for added sugar.

Lunch and Dinner

For many Americans, lunch is a relatively small meal and dinner is large. In other cultures, the opposite is true: the largest meal is consumed at lunchtime. Instead of eating large meals, you can eat four or five small meals spread out over the whole day. Just make sure to watch your total calorie intake. Aim for variety, moderation, and balance in your food choices. Here are some suggestions:

- **Vary your proteins.** You need about five to seven 1-ounce servings of meat and beans daily. Try fish like salmon or a nut butter made from something other than peanuts.

- **Use limited amounts of fats, sugars, and salt.** Eat reduced-fat and nonfat dairy products like cheese, milk, and yogurt. Eat sweets and drink sodas once in a while. They are **empty-calorie foods,** or *foods that offer few, if any, nutrients but do supply calories.* Grab a piece of fruit if you have a taste for something sweet, or try some flavored water that is sweetened with fruit essence. Applesauce is a healthy alternative to baking sugar. You can also avoid excess salt by buying low-sodium or salt-free products. Use spices to flavor your foods.

 Recall How can you prepare food that is low in fat and sugar?

- **Balance your eating plan.** Use a food diary to write down what and how much you eat. This will help you identify which food groups you are eating too little of or too much of. Keeping track of what you eat may also give you an idea of how many calories you are taking in.

Do you think you would be healthier if you ate less fast food?

Yes, I do think I would be healthier if I ate less fast food. Most fast-food restaurants offer you burgers, milk shakes, and fries, etc. Some give you fruits and vegetables, but not a lot. Plus, when you eat out, your parents don't nag you to eat healthy as much as they would at home.

Carolyn D.
Tulsa, OK

TEACH

What Teens THINK

Do you think you would be healthier if you ate less fast food? Guide students in reading and discussing the question and response. Then ask students to name their favorite fast-food meals and snacks; record their ideas on the board. Help students consider each fast-food item on the list: How does this food contribute to your good health? What healthier meal or snack could you substitute for this?

AL Active Learning

Connecting to the Real World Many students are rushed in the morning. Ask students to work in small groups to develop five menus for healthy breakfasts that are quick to prepare and easy to eat on the run. Students may wish to use resources such as cookbooks, parenting magazines, or nutrition Web sites for ideas. Have each group share its menus with the class. If possible, allow students to share their ideas with the school nurse and with other students in the school. **OL**

Reading Check

Answer Use reduced fat or non-fat dairy products and substitute fruit and fruit juice for sugar.

What Teens Want to Know

Should I buy low-fat or low-carb foods? Discuss current diet trends, including low-fat diets and low-carbohydrate diets. Many products in the grocery store are now labeled as low-fat or low-carbohydrate. Remind students that fats and carbohydrates are both necessary nutrients for the body. Explain that some of these products are healthful choices, while others contain a large amount of added sugar and salt. Remind students to use the Nutrition Facts panel to evaluate the healthfulness of food products.

Visit **glencoe.com** and complete the Interactive Study Guide for Lesson 4.

Writing Support

Persuasive Writing Have students write a persuasive paragraph encouraging others to choose nutrient-dense snacks. Remind students that persuasive writing uses facts to support an opinion, so they should specify the benefits of foods with a lot of nutrients compared to those with mostly empty calories.

Reading Check

Answer Nutrient density is a measure of nutrient content relative to the total calories a food provides.

R Reading Strategy

Analyzing a Graphic Have students examine **Figure 10.6**. Ask: What other information should you know before you decide if a snack is a healthy choice? Sample answer: *I would need to know how much sodium the snack food contained.* **OL**

If you are eating more calories than your body can burn during your daily activities, you may want to cut back on calories or increase your exercise. Your eating habits may show you ways you can balance your eating plan to maintain a healthy weight.

Snacking Smart

During adolescence, your body is growing rapidly. Snacking can help you meet your nutritional needs during this period of change, especially if you choose healthful snacks.

When you snack, pay attention to what and how much you are eating. Eating absentmindedly can lead to overeating. Also, avoid snacking just before mealtime so that you will be hungry for your regular meal.

As for *what* to eat, remember to choose healthful foods. Healthful snacks provide important nutrients. Foods that have more nutrients are likely to be nutrient-dense. **Nutrient density** is *the amount of nutrients relative to the number of calories they provide.* The more nutrients a food has in relation to calories, the more nutrient-dense it is. **Figure 10.6** provides some specific ideas for nutrient-dense snacks. You can probably add some snack ideas of your own.

W

Reading Check **Define** What is *nutrient density*?

Eating Out, Eating Right

Choosing nutritious foods and controlling your portion sizes are important strategies for maintaining your health and preventing future health problems. This can often be challenging when eating out. Portions of food tend to be larger at restaurants. Another challenge is not knowing what is in a dish.

▶ **FIGURE 10.6**

SOME SMART SNACKS

 Snacking can help you meet your nutritional needs during the teen years. **What other foods do you enjoy eating that would make healthful snacks?**

Food	Calories from Fat	Food Group Equivalent
Air-popped popcorn, plain, 1 cup	0	1 cup Grains
Applesauce, ½ cup	0	½ cup Fruits
Gelatin with ½ cup sliced banana	0	½ cup Fruits
Graham crackers, 2	2	1 ounce Grains
1½ ounces of low-fat cheese and 4 saltines	52	1 ounce Grains, 1 cup Milk

Caption Answers

Figure Caption *Sample answers:* carrot sticks, yogurt, pretzels, raisins, sliced turkey

Photo Caption, p. 251 *Sample answer:* Boiled or roasted food is usually healthier than fried food.

Dealing with Sensitive Issues

Teens with Limited Food Choices Most middle school students do not have the means to purchase their own food and may have little or no input in the type of groceries purchased by their families. It is important to emphasize the choices that students do have, for example, selecting school lunch foods and choosing a healthy portion of foods that are served in the home. Be sensitive to students who have limited food choices as you discuss this lesson.

When it comes to portion control, try ordering an appetizer as your meal. These are usually smaller servings. Just make sure you choose a dish that is nutrient-dense. If you do decide to order a main course, eat only half and take the other half home for a later meal if the portion is large. Refrigerate your leftovers as soon as you get home so they do not spoil.

Here are some other tips to help you eat healthy in restaurants:

- Check the menu for heart-healthy selections. Many restaurant menus feature dishes approved by the American Heart Association. These items appear with a small red heart next to them.

- Select foods that are grilled, broiled, or roasted instead of fried. These foods usually contain less fat.

- Ask for salad dressing on the side. Use just enough to flavor the greens without smothering them. Do the same with sauces, gravies, and other toppings.

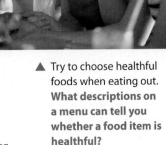

▲ Try to choose healthful foods when eating out. **What descriptions on a menu can tell you whether a food item is healthful?**

ASSESS

Assessment Resources

Lesson Review Quiz
- *ExamView*
- Fast Files Activities
- Online Quizzes and Activities

Reteaching

- Assign Concept Map 10-4 or Reteaching Activity 10-4 in the Fast Files.
- Have students write a bulleted list of tips for planning healthy meals and snacks. Call on students to share one of their tips with the class.

Enrichment

- Assign Enrichment Activity 10-4 in the Fast Files.
- Have students work in small groups to prepare a short skit that gives tips for healthy eating in restaurants. Challenge students to convey the lesson information in a humorous or entertaining way. Have students share their skits with other students at the same grade level.

CLOSE

Ask students to describe the importance of variety, moderation, and balance in a healthy eating plan.

Lesson 4 Review

After You Read

Review this lesson for new terms, major headings, and Reading Checks.

What I Learned

1. *Vocabulary* What makes a food an *empty-calorie food*?

2. *Recall* Why is breakfast important?

3. *Identify* Give three meal-planning tips that allow variety, moderation, and balance to your eating plan.

Thinking Critically

4. *Explain* How can you avoid overeating when you eat at a restaurant?

5. *Apply* You are hungry, but dinner is still an hour away. Can you think of a snack that would help you feel less hungry but still leave you ready to eat dinner? How much of the snack food do you think you should eat?

Applying Health Skills

6. *Practicing Healthful Behaviors* Keep a food log for two days. Record every food you eat and the nutrients that each food contains. Identify ways to improve your eating habits.

Go Online For more Lesson Review Activities, go to **glencoe.com**.

Lesson 4: Planning Meals and Snacks **251**

Lesson 4 Review Answers

1. Empty-calorie foods contain very few nutrients.

2. Breakfast helps you feel alert during the morning.

3. *Sample answer:* Choose a wide range of foods; choose foods that are low in fat, sugar, and salt; and balance physical activity with food intake.

4. *Sample answer:* Avoid all-you-can-eat specials and select a healthful item from the menu.

5. *Sample answer:* I would choose a small piece of fruit or a few whole wheat crackers.

6. Students' food logs should accurately reflect their food intake. Allow students to keep their food logs confidential.

Building Health Skills: Eating for Your Health

Skill

Goal Setting

Activating Prior Knowledge

Have students describe specific goals that could contribute to healthy eating habits.

- **Objective** After completing the activity, students will be able to apply goal-setting skills to improve their eating habits.
- **Time** 45 minutes
- **Materials** paper, pencil

Teacher Classroom Resources

 Building Health Skills Transparency 2-1

Model

- Have students read about how Don applied the health skill of goal setting to include more healthy foods in his diet. Ask: What aspects of Don's plan increased his chances of success? *Sample answers: Don's plan was specific, included a reward, and had the support of his family.*

National Health Standards Addressed

1.8.1, 6.8.2, 6.8.3, 7.8.2

Building Health Skills

Accessing Information
Practicing Healthful Behaviors
Stress Management
Analyzing Influences
Communication Skills
Refusal Skills
Conflict Resolution
Decision Making
Goal Setting
Advocacy

What Is Goal Setting?

Goal setting is a five-step plan for improving and maintaining your personal health. Some goals are easy to reach while others may be more challenging.

The 5 Steps of the Goal-Setting Plan

Step 1 Choose a realistic goal and write it down.

Step 2 List the steps that you need to take to reach the goal.

Step 3 Find others, like family, friends, and teachers, who can help and support you.

Step 4 Set checkpoints along the way to evaluate your progress.

Step 5 Reward yourself once you have reached your goal.

Eating for Your Health

Follow the Model, Practice, and Apply steps to help you master this important health skill.

❶ Model

Read how Don used goal setting to help him change his eating habits and include more foods that are healthful.

Don wanted to change his eating habits to include more healthful foods. He used the goal-setting process to develop a plan for himself.

- **Identify a specific goal.** Don's goal was to improve his eating habits.
- **List the steps to reach your goal.** Don wrote down the following ideas:
  - Choose more fruits and vegetables.
  - Eat smaller portions of food.
  - Limit how many french fries, chips, and other high-fat foods I eat.
- **Get help from others.** Don told his parents about his plan and asked for their support.
- **Evaluate your progress.** Don kept a food log to help him keep track of his food choices.
- **Reward yourself.** After two weeks, Don rewarded himself by buying a new DVD.

252 Chapter 10: Nutrition for Health

Teaching Tips

Healthful Weight Management—In the Long Run Teen girls (and some boys) often fall victim to the pressures of being thin. Fad diets usually promise "quick results" and "amazing weight loss." Emphasize to the class what every reputable nutrition expert knows: *The best way to manage weight is through healthful eating and regular physical activity.* This is the main reason why MyPyramid.gov was created! Following these common sense guidelines throughout one's life will keep students from wasting money on "quick fix" diets and contribute to good physical health.

② Practice

Read the passage below and apply what you have learned about goal setting to help Amy reach her goal of eating breakfast on a regular basis.

Amy decided she wants to change her habit of skipping breakfast. She usually gets up late every morning and does not have time to eat before she leaves for school. Amy knows that eating breakfast is an important part of a healthy eating plan. Use the goal-setting process to help Amy develop a plan to eat breakfast on a regular basis. Show how Amy can use each step in the goal-setting process to help her reach her goal.

③ Apply

Apply what you have learned about goal setting when completing the activity below.

Think about a food habit you would like to change. For example, maybe you tend to snack in front of the TV or maybe you like to eat two helpings of dessert. In a notebook, tell how accomplishing this goal will improve your health. Then, set a goal to change your habit and create a plan to help you reach your goal. Keep track of your progress in your notebook, and bring your results to class.

Self-Check
- Did my plan contain each step in the goal-setting process?
- Did I tell how this goal will improve my health?
- Did I track my progress?

Building Health Skills

Practice
- Have students work in pairs to read the Practice scenario. Have each pair of students complete the Practice exercise.
- Ask each pair of students to share their answers with the class.

Apply/Assess
- Have students work individually to complete the Apply activity.
- Remind students to complete the notebook that shows how they are progressing toward their goals.
- You may wish to distribute the Building Health Skills activity in the Fast Files.

ASSESSMENT SCORING

Using a rubric, student work should meet all criteria to achieve the highest score.

Skills Student work:
- includes a specific goal statement.
- lists steps to achieve the goal.
- identifies sources of help.
- evaluates progress.

- provides a healthy reward.

Concepts Student work:
- identifies a behavior that could be altered to improve an eating plan.
- incorporates accurate information.
- describes connections between eating habits and health.

HANDS-ON HEALTH

Jars of Sugar

Time: 30 minutes
Materials: baby food jars, sugar, measuring spoons

Introducing Hands-on Health

- Write the word *sugar* on the board. Ask students to identify sources of sugar in their diet. Record their responses on the board.

Teaching the Activity

- Divide the class into small groups. Have each group complete the activity as directed.
- Challenge each group to use Nutrition Facts panels to determine the sugar content of some familiar foods.
- Have students use the Wrapping It Up questions to apply and evaluate their findings. **OL**

HANDS-ON HEALTH

Jars of Sugar

According to some estimates, the average American eats about 100 pounds of sugar each year. Some of the sources of this sugar are obvious. For example, it is clear that regular soft drinks contain a lot of sugar. However, some sources of sugar can be hidden. Sugar can also appear in foods under a variety of names. These include *corn sweetener, corn syrup, fructose, sucrose,* and others.

What You Will Need

- Seven empty baby food jars
- A container of sugar
- A set of measuring spoons

What You Will Do

1. The table shown here lists the amount of sugar, in grams, found in several popular foods. Note that 5 grams of sugar is equivalent to 1 level teaspoon of sugar. 1 gram is just under 1/4 teaspoon and 2 grams is a little under 1/2 teaspoon.
2. Calculate how many teaspoons of sugar each product in the list contains.
3. Using the spoons, measure out the amount of sugar in each product and place it in a jar. Label the jar with the name of the product it corresponds to.

Wrapping It Up

Evaluate your findings. Which foods contain the most sugar? Which foods contain other nutrients? What are some ways to reduce your sugar intake?

Food	Grams of Sugar
Cola (12 oz.)	42
Fat-free fruit yogurt (8 oz.)	35
Light popcorn (1 c.)	0
Fruit punch drink (8 oz.)	27
Sweetened breakfast cereal (¾ c.)	15
Three reduced-fat chocolate sandwich cookies	14
Chocolate candy bar (1.55 oz.)	40

HANDS-ON HEALTH Assessment

Discussion Ask students:

- Why is it important to recognize hidden sources of sugar? Sample answer: *Eating a large quantity of sugar is not healthy. By recognizing sources of sugar, I can limit my intake.*

- Ask: Why is sugar considered an empty-calorie food? Sample answer: *Sugar provides calories but few nutrients.*

Reading Review

Visit glencoe.com to download quizzes and eFlashcards for Chapter 10.

FOLDABLES Study Organizer

Foldables® and Other Study Aids Take out the Foldable® that you created for Lesson 1 and any graphic organizers that you created for Lessons 1–4. Find a partner and quiz each other using these study aids.

Lesson 1 The Importance of Nutrition

Main Idea Good nutrition is important because it affects all sides of your health triangle.

- Nutrients in the body do many jobs.
- Emotions can cause you to like or dislike foods because of associations with past experiences.
- You can get the nutrients your body needs by eating a variety of healthful foods.

Lesson 2 Nutrients for Wellness

Main Idea Your body uses nutrients for energy, for building and repairing tissue, and for aiding in body processes such as digestion.

- Scientists have found more than 40 different kinds of nutrients in foods.
- The six types of nutrients are carbohydrates, proteins, fats, vitamins, minerals, and water.
- Your body uses nutrients for energy, for building and repairing tissue, and for aiding in body processes such as digestion.

Lesson 3 Following Nutrition Guidelines

Main Idea MyPyramid is designed to make it easy for you to choose healthful foods, and to encourage you to be physically active.

- The five main food groups in MyPyramid are grains, vegetables, fruits, milk, and meat and beans.
- The sixth food group, oils and other fats, should only be eaten in very small amounts.
- Balancing the calories you take in with the calories you burn off can help you maintain a healthy weight.
- Foods must be prepared and handled properly in order to be safe to eat. If foods are handled improperly, they can become contaminated with bacteria that can cause illness.

Lesson 4 Planning Meals and Snacks

Main Idea Effective meal and snack planning includes variety, moderation, and balance.

- Breakfast is the most important meal of the day.
- Instead of eating large meals, try eating four or five small meals throughout the day.
- Healthy snacking involves being aware of your snack habits and choosing to snack on mostly nutrient-dense foods.
- Try to choose healthful foods when eating out. You can order heart-healthy meals and request salad dressing on the side.

Teaching Tips

Writing in Health Class Teach students to use outlines as a tool for organizing written work. By planning the structure of a written assignment, the main ideas to be presented can be arranged in a logical order. An outline can also help a student to be sure that all required information is included in a written assignment. Prepare and distribute several examples of outlines that students can use as models.

Assessment Resources

- Chapter 10 Summary and Activity
- Audio Summaries
- Reading Tutor
- Performance Assessment
- Chapter 10 Test
- *ExamView*
- Vocabulary PuzzleMaker
- Online Learning Center

Reading Review

Study Aids

- **Using the Dinah Zike Foldable® Study Organizer** Have students use their Foldables® to review information about nutrients.

  FOLDABLES Study Organizer

- **Online Learning Tools** Have students go to the *Teen Health* Online Learning Center at **glencoe.com** to:

  - Download a **Podcast**.

  - Download free **Study-to-Go** content to their PDAs or cell phones.

Vocabulary Review

- **Vocabulary Game Show** Have students prepare game-show-style questions that can be used to review the chapter vocabulary. Have each student use his or her prepared questions to review the chapter vocabulary with a partner.

Assessment

Reviewing Vocabulary and Main Ideas

1. nutrients
2. nutrition
3. Appetite
4. Carbohydrates
5. proteins
6. saturated fat
7. True
8. False, orange
9. False, 60
10. False, breakfast
11. True
12. True

Thinking Critically

13. Calcium-rich foods are an important part of a teen's diet because they build and maintain strong bones and teeth.

14. *Sample answer:* The media influences food choices by associating certain foods with emotions, making people crave food even when they are not hungry.

Have students visit **glencoe.com** to take the Chapter 10 quiz.

CHAPTER

10 Assessment

 After You Read

HEALTH INVENTORY

Now that you have read the chapter, look back at your answers to the Health Inventory in the chapter opener. Is there anything that you should do differently?

Reviewing Vocabulary and Main Ideas

On a sheet of paper, write the numbers 1–6. After each number, write the term from the list that best completes each sentence.

- nutrition
- appetite
- unsaturated **fat**
- carbohydrates
- fiber
- proteins
- nutrients
- saturated **fat**

Lesson 1 The Importance of Nutrition

1. Substances in food that your body needs are called _____.

2. The study of nutrients and how the body uses them is known as _____.

3. _____ is the psychological desire for food.

Lesson 2 Nutrients for Wellness

4. _____ are sugars and starches that naturally occur, mainly in plant sources of food.

5. Nutrients that your body uses to build, repair, and maintain cells and tissues are called _____.

6. Eating large amounts of _____ can increase a person's risk of heart disease.

*On a sheet of paper, write the numbers 7–12. Write **True** or **False** for each statement below. If the statement is false, change the underlined word or phrase to make it true.*

Lesson 3 Following Nutrition Guidelines

7. The MyPyramid food guidance system reflects advice from the <u>Dietary Guidelines for Americans</u>.

8. The <u>yellow</u> band in MyPyramid represents grains.

9. Teens should be physically active at least <u>30</u> minutes per day.

Lesson 4 Planning Meals and Snacks

10. Many health experts think <u>dinner</u> is the most important meal of the day.

11. One way to limit fats, sugars, and salt in your eating plan is to substitute <u>nutrient-dense</u> foods for empty-calorie foods.

12. One way to <u>control portions</u> when you eat out is to eat half of your meal and take the rest home.

Thinking Critically

Using complete sentences, answer the following questions on a sheet of paper.

13. **Explain** Why should calcium-rich foods be an important part of a teen's eating plan?

14. **Evaluate** Explain how the media influence food choices.

Go Online Visit **glencoe.com** and take the Online Quiz for Chapter 10.

HEALTH INVENTORY WRAP-UP

Eating Habits Have students look back at their responses to the Health Inventory in the chapter opener. Ask them to use their responses to the Health Inventory to identify one way that they could improve their eating habits. Have students use the steps of goal setting to make a positive change in their eating habits. Remind the class of the impact that eating habits have on overall wellness.

Write About It

15. **Expository Writing** Write an essay that explains clearly how teens can use MyPyramid to guide their food choices.

16. **Personal Writing** Set a goal to change one of your eating habits. Develop a plan to reach this goal.

Applying Technology

Teen Nutrition Brochure

Use Microsoft Word® to create a brochure that convinces teens to make healthful food choices.

- Open a new Microsoft Word® document with three columns and a landscape view.
- Import digital images that show teens making healthful food choices.
- Add text to your brochure. Write about the benefits of a nutrient-rich diet.
- Save your project

Applying Technology

Teen Nutrition Brochure
Equipment needs: Microsoft Word® or similar software and optional digital camera
Help students discuss the steps in planning and completing their brochures; suggest sources for digital images or instruct students to create their own photos. Establish sign-up sheets and time limits if access to computers and cameras is limited. If materials are available, have students print and share their completed brochures.

Standardized Test Practice

Math

Use the Nutrition Facts label to answer the questions.

Nutrition Facts	
Serving Size 3 pieces (314g)	
Servings Per Container 14	
Amount Per Serving	
Calories 359	Calories from Fat 219
	% Daily Value*
Total Fat 24g	36%
Saturated Fat 12g	60%
Trans Fat 4g	
Cholesterol 60g	20%
Sodium 235mg	10%
Potassium 0mg	0%
Total Carbohydrate 31g	10%
Dietary Fiber 0g	0%
Sugars 10g	
Protein 5g	

1. The total calories in two servings is
   - **A.** 36
   - **B.** 359
   - **C.** 718
   - **D.** None of the above

2. Charlie ate three servings of this product in one day. How much of the Daily Value for sodium did he receive from just this one food?
   - **A.** 10 percent
   - **B.** 30 percent
   - **C.** 100 percent
   - **D.** 235 percent

3. How much saturated fat would you be eating if you ate one piece of this product?
   - **A.** 6 g
   - **B.** 3 g
   - **C.** 12 g
   - **D.** 4 g

Write About It

15. **Expository Writing** Student essays should explain concepts that may be unfamiliar, defining terms as needed. Successful essays will be clear and readable as well as informative.

16. **Personal Writing** Responses will vary but should reflect serious thought and explain strategies for correcting unhealthful eating habits.

Standardized Test Practice

1. C
2. B
3. D

Test-Taking Tips

Interpreting Graphics Explain to students that answering some test questions will require using information found in a graphic. In this review, students are required to find information in a Nutrition Facts panel in order to answer the questions. In all three questions, students are required to find information in the graphic and then multiply or divide to obtain the correct answer. Tell students to be on the lookout for questions that require manipulating information from a graphic.

CHAPTER 11 pp. 258–275	Standards		Skills and Activities
	National	**State/Local**	
	National Health Education Standards 1.8.9, 2.8.5, 2.8.7, 3.8.2		**HEALTH QUIZ,** *p. 259* **BUILDING HEALTH SKILLS** *Accessing Information* Changing Your Weight Safely, *pp. 270–271* TIME health news Pressure to Be Perfect, *p. 272*
Lesson 1 **Maintaining a Healthy Weight** pp. 260–265	National Health Education Standards 1.8.1, 1.8.5, 1.8.6, 1.8.8, 1.8.9, 2.8.5, 2.8.7, 2.8.8, 3.8.4, 6.8.1, 6.8.4, 7.8.1, 7.8.3, 8.8.1		**What Teens Think** How does the media affect a person's body image? *p. 261* **HEALTH SKILLS ACTIVITY** *Accessing Information* Finding Your BMI, *p. 262* Go Online The Lowdown on Diets, *p. 263*
Lesson 2 **Eating Disorders** pp. 266–269	National Health Education Standards 1.8.2, 1.8.8, 1.8.9, 2.8.8, 2.8.9, 3.8.4, 4.8.4, 8.8.2, 8.8.3		**Careers for the 21st Century** Psychologist, *p. 268*

PACING THE CHAPTER

Lesson 1	45 min	**Chapter Review**	45 min
Lesson 2	45 min	**TIME health news**	30 min
		Building Health Skills	45 min

BLOCK SCHEDULING

For block scheduling, assign students Building Health Skills feature *Changing Your Weight Safely*, page 270, and Guided Reading and Writing. 📁

Planning Guide

StudentWorks Plus

Glencoe Exclusive!
TeacherWorks Plus
All-In-One Planner and Resource Center

Reproducible Resources	Assessment	Media and Technology
Chapter FAST FILE Resources Chapter Summaries and Activities REVIEW Building Health Skills Activity TEACH Performance Assessment Activity EXTEND Universal Access Activities TEACH Parent Letter and Activities 📁 **Student Activities Workbook** TEACH 📁 **Reading Tutor** TEACH	Building Health Skills Activity, *pp. 270–271* Chapter 11 Assessment, *pp. 274–275* **Chapter FAST FILE Resources** Performance Assessment Activity, *p. 4* Chapter 11 Test, *p. 7* 💿 *ExamView® Assessment Suite*	TeacherWorks Plus includes: ● Interactive Teacher Edition ● Lesson Planner with Calendar ● Access to all blackline masters ● Correlations to standards 💿 StudentWorks™ Plus Online Student Edition Dinah Zike's Teaching Health with Foldables®
Chapter FAST FILE Resources Concept Mapping Activity 11-1 REVIEW Health Lab 11-1 EXTEND Enrichment Activity 11-1 EXTEND Lesson Plan 11-1 Guided Reading and Writing 11-1 TEACH Reteaching Activity 11-1 REVIEW	Lesson 1 Review, *p. 265* Vocabulary PuzzleMaker 💿 *ExamView® Assessment Suite*	Vocabulary PuzzleMaker 💿 *ExamView® Assessment Suite* 💿 StudentWorks™ Plus Transparency 11-1 **Go Online** glencoe.com
Chapter FAST FILE Resources Concept Mapping Activity 11-2 REVIEW Decision-Making Activity 11-2 EXTEND Enrichment Activity 11-2 EXTEND Lesson Plan 11-2 Guided Reading and Writing 11-2 TEACH Reteaching Activity 11-2 REVIEW	Lesson 2 Review, *p. 269* Vocabulary PuzzleMaker 💿 *ExamView® Assessment Suite*	Vocabulary PuzzleMaker 💿 *ExamView® Assessment Suite* 💿 StudentWorks™ Plus Transparency 11-2 **Go Online** glencoe.com

Chapter and Lesson Resources

The *Teen Health* resources are designed for differentiated learning abilities. You may want to use the coded items in this way:

REVIEW —activities to review or reinforce content
TEACH —activities to teach basic concepts
EXTEND —activities to extend or enrich lesson content

 OUT OF TIME?

Use Health Skills Activity, *Finding Your BMI*, page 262, or Go Online, *The Lowdown on Diets*, page 263.

Healthfully Adjusting to Body Changes During Adolescence

Both young men and women are often surprised as their bodies change during adolescence. It can be very difficult to find clothes that fit properly. Some might come to realize that their new body type no longer allows them to excel at a favorite sport or activity. Others might feel demoralized by the impossibly thin or overly buff bodies of models and celebrities. It is not unusual for adolescent teens to feel like their body has let them down.

As a health teacher, you can help counteract these feelings by helping students realize that these changes are normal and everyone must go through them. Create a climate of total acceptance in your classroom. Focus on taking care of the body with healthful eating and exercise. Teach students to listen to their bodies; eat only when hungry and stop eating when satisfied. Discourage students from comparing themselves to their friends and especially to models and celebrities.

Share these tools with students to help them accept themselves for who they are. This is the best way to cultivate a positive body image and improve self-esteem.

- **Gain self-confidence by trying something that is challenging.** Be proud of what you achieve.

- **Only say nice things about yourself.** If you would not say it to your best friend, then do not think it of yourself.

- **Accept and value every person you meet, whatever their physical appearance.**

- **Identify your strengths and build on them.**

- **Volunteer your time to a good cause.**

- **Have fun.**

Recovery Programs for Eating Disorders

For a person with an eating disorder, no treatment will be successful until the person recognizes that he or she has an eating disorder. Even so, the recovery process can be long, typically taking three to seven years, and can be emotionally challenging with frequent relapses. With treatment, 60 percent of people will completely recover. Unfortunately, 20 percent do not recover at all. Early intervention is critical to success. Eating disorders that are diagnosed early are treated more successfully and in a shorter period of time with less physiological damage to the body.

The most successful treatment programs include psychotherapy with nutrition counseling and medical care. Most treatment programs are outpatient programs. However, people are hospitalized if their physical problems are life-threatening or if their psychological problems become severe.

The primary care physician coordinates the treatment program and attends to any medical issues. Psychological counseling must address both the symptoms of the eating disorder and the underlying issues that caused the disorder. Nutritional counseling provides education about the body's nutritional needs and helps the person learn to make good food choices.

Relapses throughout the recovery process are common and can be frequent. Relapses can be triggered by many different factors, including stress, conflict, and even facing the underlying issues that caused the eating disorder. Planning ahead and learning new coping skills help patients prevent relapses from occurring. So does acceptance and self-love.

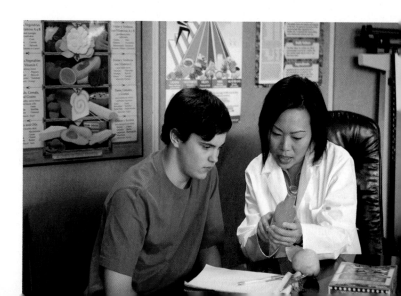

Support for Teaching Reading

Reading Support

Reading Preview

Activating Background Vocabulary Ask students what the term *body image* brings to mind. Guide students in a discussion of their own body images in comparison to famous movie stars or supermodels. Ask students how a poor body image and/or lack of self-esteem might lead someone to develop weight problems or eating disorders.

FOLDABLES® Study Organizer *Dinah Zike's Reading and Study Skills for Teen Health* provides interactive graphic organizers that help students comprehend and retain health concepts as they read. Use the Foldable® on page 259 or find more Foldables® activities for the chapter on **Your Body Image** in the separate booklet, available in the TCR.

Lesson 1   Maintaining a Healthy Weight

Listen-Read-Discuss Present the lesson concepts in a brief lecture to provide background information. Direct students to read the text silently, making a list of questions as they read. Then have students stop reading and ask: "What do you understand most about body image, self-esteem, and/or weight problems? What do you understand least about these issues?" Record student responses on the board. Then ask: "What questions do you still have about reaching or managing a healthy weight?" In a class discussion, seek answers for any remaining questions.

Lesson 2   Eating Disorders

Question-Answer Relationship (QAR) Help students identify the four task demands of questioning: "Right there" questions are text explicit, such as, "What are the types of eating disorders?"; "Think and search" questions are text implicit, such as, "What are the differences between a binge eating disorder and anorexia nervosa?"; "Author and you" questions require reading the text, such as, "Does the author think you can cure someone with an eating disorder without getting professional help?"; "On my own" questions can be answered without reading, such as, "What do you think we could do to help prevent eating disorders?" Direct students to find the answers to each of these different types of questions.

Post Reading

Informational Presentations Have students utilize all available classroom, library, and Internet resources to gather additional information about teen weight problems and eating disorders. Direct students to organize the data and write an informative paper on this subject, editing their work for correct sentence structure, grammar, and punctuation. Encourage student volunteers to present the information in their papers to the class.

Key for Using the Teacher Wraparound Edition

Use this key to help you identify the different types of prompts found in the Teacher Wraparound Edition.

R **Reading Strategies** activities help you teach reading skills and vocabulary.

C **Critical Thinking** strategies help students apply and extend what they have learned.

U **Universal Access** activities provide differentiated instruction for students learning to speak English, along with suggestions for teaching various types of learners.

HS **Health Skills Practice** activities reinforce Health Skills concepts and help students apply these skills in their everyday lives.

W **Writing Support** activities provide writing opportunities to help students comprehend the text.

AL **Active Learning** strategies provide a variety of activities for presenting lesson content, including Quick Demos and engaging classroom projects that get students actively involved.

Key to Ability Levels

Teaching Strategies and activities have been coded for ability level and appropriateness.

AL Activities for students working above grade level

OL Activities for students working on grade level

BL Activities for students working below grade level

EL Activities for English Learners

Symbols

Transparencies

CD-ROM

glencoe.com

Print Resources

Chapter at a Glance

Lesson 1 describes the importance of a healthy body image, the effects of eating and physical activity on weight, and methods to maintain a healthy weight.

Lesson 2 explains the symptoms of various eating disorders, the health risks associated with eating disorders, and the kinds of help available for a person with an eating disorder.

R Reading Strategy

Interpreting the Photo Ask students: What sport do these teens participate in? *soccer* How does playing this sport help maintain a healthy body? Sample answer: *Playing soccer exercises the body.* Besides physical activity, how else can you manage body weight in a healthful way? *by watching what you eat* **OL**

Caption Answer

Photo Caption *Sample answer:* The media portrays an unrealistic and often unhealthy image of the perfect body. It makes some people feel bad about themselves because their bodies don't look "perfect."

258

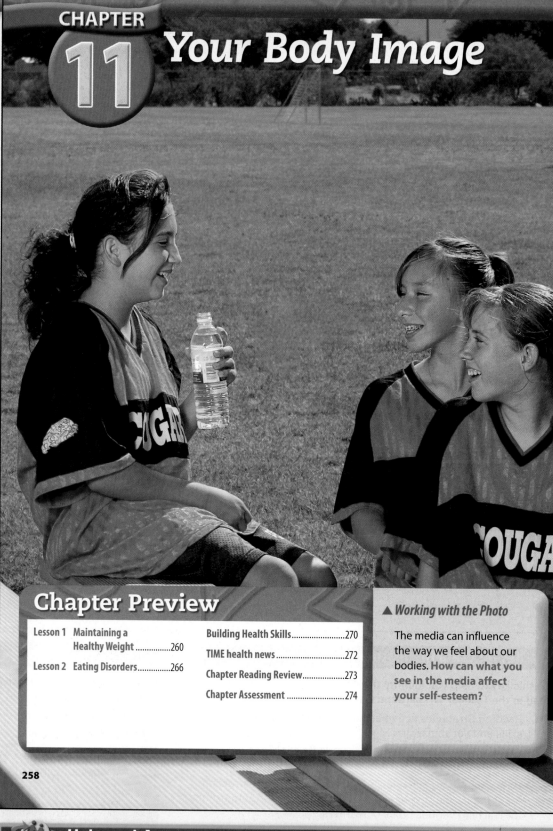

Chapter Preview

▲ *Working with the Photo*

The media can influence the way we feel about our bodies. **How can what you see in the media affect your self-esteem?**

258

👥 Universal Access

Differentiated Learning Glencoe provides teacher support and student materials for all learners in the health classroom.

- Spanish *Glosario* and chapter summaries assist English Language Learners.
- *Reading Tutor* and related worksheets support reluctant readers.

- Universal Access strategies throughout the Teacher Wraparound Edition and Fast Files help you present materials for gifted students, at-risk students, physically impaired students, and those with behavior disorders or learning disabilities.

Start-Up Activities

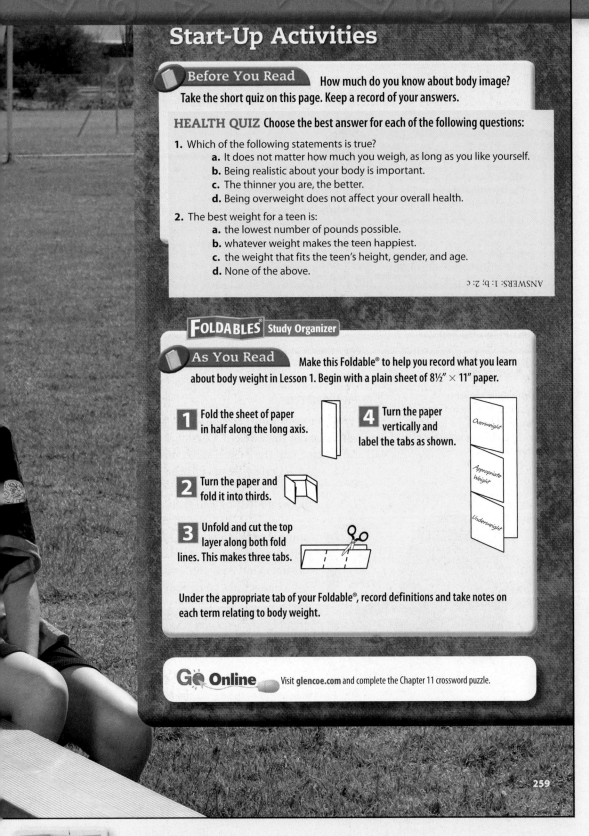

Before You Read How much do you know about body image?
Take the short quiz on this page. Keep a record of your answers.

HEALTH QUIZ Choose the best answer for each of the following questions:

1. Which of the following statements is true?
   a. It does not matter how much you weigh, as long as you like yourself.
   b. Being realistic about your body is important.
   c. The thinner you are, the better.
   d. Being overweight does not affect your overall health.

2. The best weight for a teen is:
   a. the lowest number of pounds possible.
   b. whatever weight makes the teen happiest.
   c. the weight that fits the teen's height, gender, and age.
   d. None of the above.

ANSWERS: 1: b; 2: c

FOLDABLES Study Organizer

As You Read Make this Foldable® to help you record what you learn
about body weight in Lesson 1. Begin with a plain sheet of 8½" × 11" paper.

1 Fold the sheet of paper in half along the long axis.

4 Turn the paper vertically and label the tabs as shown.

Overweight

Appropriate Weight

Underweight

2 Turn the paper and fold it into thirds.

3 Unfold and cut the top layer along both fold lines. This makes three tabs.

Under the appropriate tab of your Foldable®, record definitions and take notes on each term relating to body weight.

Go Online Visit glencoe.com and complete the Chapter 11 crossword puzzle.

FOLDABLES
Study Organizer **Dinah Zike Foldables®**

Formulating Questions Before students read Lesson 1, have them write one question about being overweight, the appropriate weight, and underweight under the appropriate tab of their Foldable®. As students read the lesson, have them use their Foldable® to take notes, record definitions, and answer the questions they asked before reading. **BL**

Go Online

Have students visit **glencoe.com** and complete the crossword puzzle for Chapter 11.

FOCUS

Activating Prior Knowledge

What I Know Ask students to describe how they think most teens feel about the way they look. Explain that in this chapter students will learn how body image affects self-esteem.

Guide to Reading

Building Vocabulary
- Challenge students to develop a graphic organizer that shows the relationships among the vocabulary terms.
- Use Vocabulary PuzzleMaker to reinforce vocabulary terms.

Reading Strategy
Identifying Cause and Effect Suggest that students look for factors that influence how teens feel about their body. The effects will be their feelings, which influences overall health.

FOLDABLES **Study Organizer** Have students use their Foldables® as they read Lesson 1.

Q *uick Write*

Encourage students to describe steps they might take to stay at a healthy weight.

Caption Answers

Photo Caption Teens might think their body is too fat or too thin because it does not look like a "perfect" body.

Maintaining a Healthy Weight

Guide to Reading

Building Vocabulary
Try to define the terms below in your own words. As you read, check and revise your definitions.

- body image (p. 260)
- appropriate weight (p. 261)
- body mass index (BMI) (p. 262)
- overweight (p. 263)
- underweight (p. 263)

Focusing on the Main Ideas
In this lesson, you will learn to
- **identify** the importance of a healthy body image.
- **explain** how eating and physical activity affect weight.
- **describe** ways to maintain a healthy weight.

Reading Strategy
Identifying Cause and Effect As you read, identify factors that can have an effect on your body image.

FOLDABLES **Study Organizer** Use the Foldable® on p. 259 as you read this lesson.

Q *uick Write*

Write a paragraph describing what actions you currently take to try and maintain a healthy body weight.

Body Image

A group of teens were sitting in a circle eating lunch at school and talking about their weight. Crystal, who studies ballet and is tall and slender, said she wished she could lose 10 pounds.

Craig had never been very athletic and was a little thin. "Personally, I'd like to look like a bodybuilder," he said with a laugh.

Have you ever wished you could change something about your body or have you compared yourself to a celebrity or professional athlete? If so, you are not alone. As a teen, your body is going through big changes. As your body changes in your teen years, so do your thoughts and feelings about how you look. *The way you see and feel about your body* is called your **body image.**

◀ Sometimes the media seems to suggest that there is one perfect body type. **How can this cause teens to develop a distorted body image?**

260

 Chapter *FAST FILE* **Resources**
Guided Reading and Writing 11-1
Concept Mapping Activity 11-1
Health Lab 11-1
Reteaching Activity 11-1
Enrichment Activity 11-1
Lesson Quiz 11-1

Technology
- Transparency 11-1
- Audio Summaries
- *ExamView® Assessment Suite*
- Vocabulary PuzzleMaker
- StudentWorks™ Plus

Go Online

Body Image and Self-Esteem

How you feel about your body can affect your self-esteem. Self-esteem refers to what you value about yourself, both inside and out. If you feel uncomfortable about how your body looks, your self-esteem can be negatively affected.

It is important to understand that the changes your body is going through are normal. Though the media tends to portray females as thin and males as muscular, the real world is very different. People come in all shapes and sizes. It is more important for you to be healthy than to try to look like someone else.

The key to a positive body image and high self-esteem is having an optimistic attitude and a healthy lifestyle. Know what makes you happy, set realistic goals, and spend time with people who respect and appreciate you. Eat well, get plenty of rest and exercise, and avoid comparing yourself to people in the media or to those around you. All these things will help you feel good about yourself and your body.

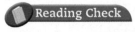 **Reading Check** **List** What are some of the keys to a positive body image and high self-esteem?

Your Appropriate Weight

Many people who have an unhealthy body image complain about their weight. They think they are too fat or too thin. Is there a "right" weight for every person, and if so, how do you find it?

Everyone has an **appropriate weight.** This is *the weight that is best for your body,* and is given as a range. For example, the appropriate weight of a 5-foot, 5-inch female is between 117 and 155 pounds. A range is given because height is not the only factor that affects how much a person should weigh. You also need to consider your **gender**, age, height, and body build or frame. Your frame is the size of your bone structure. Teens must also consider their growth pattern. During adolescence people grow at different rates.

What Teens THINK

How does the media affect a person's body image?

The media promotes that you are only special if you are skinny and beautiful. So when young girls see this, they feel bad about their bodies if they don't look like the stars in the media. But we should not feel pressured because we are all different and unique.

Katie P.
Tucson, AZ

Academic Vocabulary

gender (JEN der) *(noun)* whether a living creature is male or female. *David wanted to know what gender each of Alicia's kittens were before he picked one for his sister.*

FITNESS ZONE

Physical Activity and a Healthy Lifestyle Regular physical activity is an essential part of a healthy lifestyle. That means that regular physical activity is one of the keys to positive body image and high self-esteem. Have students review the suggestions in the *Fitness Zone Handbook*

and help them discuss how a regular fitness routine can help them feel good about themselves. **For more information, see** *Fitness Zone Handbook pages xviii–1* **or visit the Fitness Zone at glencoe.com.**

TEACH

What Teens THINK

How does the media affect a person's body image? Ask students: How would you describe the bodies of models, actors, and performers we see in the media? How can those images affect the way teens see and feel about their own bodies?

AL Active Learning

Think-Pair-Share Ask students to write a sentence that describes the effect of body image on the health triangle. Then invite students to share their responses with the class. OL

Reading Check

Answer Have a positive attitude and a healthy lifestyle; know what makes you happy; set realistic goals; spend time with people who appreciate you; and develop a personal style of your own.

Academic Vocabulary

Gender Encourage students to recall standardized test forms and applications for sports programs that require gender information. Then explain that the word *gender* derives from the Latin word *genus*, which means "kind," as in "What kind of human are you?"

261

Health Skills Activity

Accessing Information

Finding Your BMI

Use the following strategies to help students complete the activity:

- Have students work on their own to calculate their BMI. Allow students to keep their calculations private.

- Provide a scale for students to weigh themselves privately, as well as a tool to measure height.

- Consider having students calculate the BMI of a fictional teen by making up the height, weight, and age.

Reading Check

Answer BMI is a measurement that allows you to assess your body size, taking into account your height and weight. It is limited because it doesn't take a person's frame size into account.

Health Skills Activity

Accessing Information

Finding Your BMI

To determine your BMI, follow these steps:

1. Multiply your weight by 703. If, for example, you weigh 125 pounds, you would get a result of 87,875. Write the result you get on a sheet of paper.

2. Next multiply your height in inches times itself. Write this result down as well.

3. Finally, divide your answer from Step 1 by your answer from Step 2. If you divide 87,875 by 4,225, you get 20.8. This number is your BMI.

4. Find your BMI on the grid for your gender. Remember, however, that this is only an estimate.

On Your Own

Complete the steps above to find your own BMI. Is your weight in the appropriate range for someone your age? The BMI has its limitations. For example, it doesn't take a person's frame size into account. As a result, people with a stockier build may be considered overweight even if they don't have a lot of body fat.

Boys BMI Chart

Girls BMI Chart

Body Mass Index

You can determine if your weight is in an appropriate range for your age by calculating your **body mass index (BMI).** This is *a measurement that allows you to assess your body size, taking your height and weight into account.* The Health Skills Activity above shows how to figure out your BMI.

 Define What is the *body mass index*? How is it limited?

Promoting Coordinated School Health

Managing Weight for Life Students who are not athletic or are uninterested in team sports might be better served by learning life fitness skills as an alternative to traditional physical education classes. Students should also have access to healthful food choices at school. Bring together physical education instructors, the school nutritionist, and school psychologist to evaluate the offerings at your school and make recommendations that work to improve students' body image for life. **OL**

Weight Problems

Many teens who compute their BMI will find that they fall within the range of appropriate weight. Some teens will find that their BMI falls above the appropriate range. This means they may be overweight or at risk of being overweight. **Overweight** means *weighing more than what is appropriate for your gender, height, age, body frame, and growth pattern.* Other teens may find that their BMI falls below the appropriate range, meaning they may be underweight. **Underweight** is *weighing less than what is appropriate for your gender, height, age, body frame, and growth pattern.*

Overweight Teens

The number of young people who are overweight has doubled in the last two to three decades. Currently one child in five is overweight. This increase is in adolescents, of all ages, genders, and ethnicities.

This trend can be traced to lifestyle factors. These include overeating or eating too many empty-calorie foods, and getting too little physical activity. The extra pounds mean added stress on the heart and lungs. They also mean an increased risk of lifestyle-related illnesses. One such illness, type 2 diabetes, has spread rapidly among young people. At one time, type 2 diabetes showed up almost exclusively in adults. Now, adolescents make up 33–45 percent of new type 2 diabetes cases today. Most of these teen patients are significantly overweight. Those who are overweight are also at risk of developing heart disease, cancer, and stroke later on in life.

Underweight Teens

With all the concern about overweight teens, it is easy to overlook the problem of teens who are underweight. Teens who are too thin lack body fat, which insulates the body and is an important source of energy. Underweight teens may also be undernourished. This means their bodies are not getting enough of the nutrients they need to grow and function normally. The absence of some nutrients, including proteins, makes it hard for the body to fight infection. Underweight teens are also at risk of developing anemia. This is a blood condition caused by a lack of iron in the diet. Anemia can make you feel tired and rundown.

 Reading Check

Explain What are two factors that have caused a rise in the number of overweight teens?

▲ Spending too much time in front of a computer can contribute to weight problems. **What are some physical activities you can participate in to maintain a healthy and balanced lifestyle?**

ACTIVITY

Go Online

Topic: The Lowdown on Diets

Visit **glencoe.com** for Student Web Activities to learn about the wide variety of diets on the market and how to tell the difference between the healthy ones and the dangerous ones.

Activity: Using the information provided at the link above, make a flyer entitled "Dieting Do's and Don'ts" that includes important facts about dieting.

The Lowdown on Diets, p. 263
Arrange to have the flyers displayed in the lunch area or cafeteria at your school.

C Critical Thinking

Critiquing Have students bring labels or empty packages from various food products, as well as nutritional information for fresh fruits and vegetables. Have students compare the foods and determine which are better sources of calories. **AL**

U Universal Access

English Learners Based upon the scenarios below, ask students whether these people will gain, lose, or maintain weight over the period of a week.
1) Jessica is a 15 year-old long-distance runner who consumes 1500 calories per day.
2) Darius is a 17 year-old who takes in 3500 calories daily and does little physical activity.
3) Enrique takes in 2800 calories per day, plays baseball three times a week, and is 14 years old. **EL**

Caption Answer

Photo Caption You can keep your energy equation in balance and maintain a healthy weight.

Reaching an Appropriate Weight

The secret to reaching or maintaining a healthful weight is to adjust your "energy equation." This is the balance between "calories in" (from food) and "calories out" (from physical activity and body processes). A pound of weight equals about 3,500 calories. If you are underweight, you need to take in more calories from food than your body burns off. If you are overweight, you need to burn more calories than you take in. If you want to maintain your weight, you should burn as many calories as you take in. Exercise or other physical activities can help you burn some of the calories you take in from food.

The MyPyramid food guidance system recommends that teens get approximately 60 minutes of physical activity on most days. Calorie needs vary by age, gender, and activity level. Females between the ages of 14 and 18 need approximately 1,800 to 2,400 calories each day. Males in the same age group need approximately 2,200 to 3,200.

Reading Check **Explain** How do you balance caloric intake with physical activity if you want to gain, lose, or maintain weight?

Beyond the Energy Equation

Healthy weight management is more than just counting calories. You need to pay attention to the source of the calories you eat. For example, the average chocolate bar provides 250 calories. A turkey breast sandwich on whole wheat bread has the same number of calories. However, the chocolate bar has very few nutrients. The turkey sandwich, by contrast, provides nutrients from at least two different food groups. Make sure that most of the calories you take in provide nutrients your body needs.

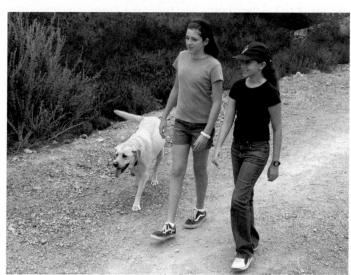

▶ Physical activity can help burn some of the calories you take in from food. **Why is it important to balance the calories you take in with the calories your body burns off?**

What Teens Want to Know

Should I go on a diet? Because many teens are influenced by the body images they see in the media, they often think they are overweight. Teens, however, must be careful about dieting. Because their bodies are growing and changing at a rapid rate, dieting can prevent teens from getting all of the essential nutrients that their bodies require. Dieting can also set up a teen for eating disorders. Teens should always talk to their doctor before deciding to go on a diet. **OL**

The MyPyramid food guidance system, discussed in Chapter 10, can help you develop a personalized eating plan based on your calorie needs.

Managing Weight in a Healthy Way

Both the media and your peers can put pressure on you to look a certain way. This kind of pressure is negative because it is not concerned with what is healthy for you. It is only concerned with achieving an unrealistic ideal, no matter how dangerous. People who need to lose weight should do so gradually by slowly increasing physical activity and eating only as many calories as their bodies need. They should not turn to fad diets, diet pills, smoking, or extreme workout programs that promise fast results. Some of these products may be ineffective and even life threatening.

When it comes to managing your weight in a healthy way, there are no shortcuts. If you need to adjust your weight, talk to your health care provider. He or she can recommend a safe, healthy approach that will help you reach your goal in a reasonable amount of time.

Go Online

Visit **glencoe.com** and complete the Interactive Study Guide for Lesson 1.

ASSESS

Assessment Resources

Lesson Review Quiz
- *ExamView*
- Fast Files Activities
- Online Quizzes and Activities

Reteaching

- Assign Concept Map 11-1 or Reteaching Activity 11-1 in the Fast Files.
- Have student pairs work together to list the effects of a positive body image and a negative body image.

Enrichment

- Assign Enrichment Activity 11-1 in the Fast Files.
- Challenge students to choose a popular diet program and determine reasons it would not be appropriate for a teen to follow. Invite students to share their findings with the class.

CLOSE

Have students explain how to maintain a healthy weight.

Lesson 1 Review

After You Read

Review this lesson for new terms, major headings, and Reading Checks.

What I Learned

1. *Vocabulary* What is the meaning of *appropriate weight*?

2. *Recall* Why is a healthy body image important?

3. *Identify* What are some healthful ways to reach an appropriate weight?

4. *Explain* What are some unhealthful ways to manage weight? Where does the pressure to look a certain way come from?

Thinking Critically

5. *Describe* How can eating and physical activity habits affect weight? What can you do to assure your habits are healthy?

6. *Apply* Imagine that a teen takes in 2,000 calories each day and burns 2,300 calories. Over time, what will happen to the teen's weight? Explain your answer.

Applying Health Skills

7. *Practicing Healthful Behaviors* With a small group, brainstorm good health habits that could affect the energy equation. Make a list of these habits and their impact. Be prepared to share your list with other groups.

Go Online For more Lesson Review Activities, go to **glencoe.com**.

Lesson 1: Maintaining a Healthy Weight **265**

Lesson 1 Review Answers

1. the weight that is best for your body
2. A teen with a healthy body image is more likely to have high self-esteem and interact well with other people.
3. Increase calories if underweight. Reduce calories and/or increase physical activity if overweight. Eat nutritious foods, avoid empty calories, get advice from health care professional.
4. fad diets, diet pills, smoking or extreme workout programs
5. By balancing eating and physical activity, a teen can maintain an appropriate weight.
6. The teen will lose weight because he or she is burning more calories than are being consumed.
7. Student lists should contain habits that affect the energy equation in some way, and include how the habit impacts the energy equation.

Lesson 2

FOCUS

Activating Prior Knowledge

What I Know Have students tell you what they know about eating disorders. Correct any misconceptions they might have. Explain that they will learn about eating disorders in this lesson.

Guide to Reading

Building Vocabulary
- Have students write a short paragraph in which they use all of the vocabulary terms. Each term should be defined within the context of the paragraph.
- Use Vocabulary PuzzleMaker to reinforce vocabulary terms.

Reading Strategy
Comparing and Contrasting Before students read, suggest they look at the headings in the lesson to help them think about how to organize their chart. Consider checking the structure of students' charts before they read.

*Q*uick Write

Have students read the definition of an eating disorder on this page before they begin their Quick Writes.

Reading Check

Answer an extreme and damaging eating behavior that can lead to sickness and even death

---

Lesson 2

Eating Disorders

Guide to Reading

● Building Vocabulary
As you read this lesson, write each new highlighted term and its definition in your notebook.
- eating disorder (p. 266)
- binge eating disorder (p. 267)
- obese (p. 267)
- anorexia nervosa (p. 267)
- bulimia nervosa (p. 268)

● Focusing on the Main Ideas
In this lesson, you will learn to
- **describe** the symptoms of various eating disorders.
- **explain** the health risks associated with an eating disorder.
- **identify** sources of help that are available for a person with an eating disorder.

● Reading Strategy
Comparing and Contrasting Create a chart that shows the similarities and differences among the eating disorders discussed in the lesson.

*Q*uick Write

Write a paragraph explaining why you think some teens develop an eating disorder.

What Are Eating Disorders?

Patricia's parents were worried about her. She had been eating almost nothing at mealtime for several weeks and had lost a lot of weight. When her mother tried to talk to her about how little she was eating, Patricia got angry. "Why do you keep bugging me about eating?" she shouted. "Can't you see how fat I am?" Her mother looked at Patricia in disbelief. The last word anyone would use to describe Patricia was *fat*. If anything, she seemed too thin.

By thinking she was fat and not wanting to eat, Patricia was showing signs of an **eating disorder**—*an extreme and damaging eating behavior that can lead to sickness and even death*. She is one of an estimated 24 million people in this country who have an eating disorder. Many of these people suffer from unrealistic and unhealthy body images.

Eating disorders have little to do with physical hunger. Often, these disorders are brought on by mental/emotional problems, such as depression or low self-esteem. Having an eating disorder places a person at risk for developing severe medical problems. The risk is especially great for teens because their bodies are already undergoing dramatic physical changes.

Reading Check Define What is an *eating disorder*?

Lesson 2 Resources

📁 **Chapter *Fast File* Resources**
Guided Reading and Writing 11-2
Concept Mapping Activity 11-2
Decision-Making Activity 11-2
Reteaching Activity 11-2
Enrichment Activity 11-2
Lesson Quiz 11-2

Technology
🔧 Transparency 11-2
💿 Audio Summaries
💿 *ExamView® Assessment Suite*
💿 Vocabulary PuzzleMaker
💿 StudentWorks™ Plus
 G**⊚** Online

Binge Eating Disorder

A **binge eating disorder,** which is *compulsive overeating,* is the most common eating disorder. A compulsion is something you feel you cannot control. Binge eaters cannot control their desire to eat, so they compulsively overeat. About 25 million Americans suffer from this disorder.

People with this disorder eat even when they are not hungry. They also eat food in amounts large enough to make them physically uncomfortable. They often eat alone so that others do not see the amount of food they eat. They may also hide food for the same reason. Because of the excessive amounts of food they eat, most compulsive eaters have serious weight problems, and many are obese. **Obese** means *weighing more than 20 percent higher than what is appropriate for their height, age, and body frame.*

The guilt and depression that compulsive eaters feel about their problem can contribute to a low self-esteem and poor body image.

Reading Check **Explain** What can a binge eating disorder lead to?

Anorexia Nervosa

Patricia's symptoms described in the lesson opener are typical of **anorexia nervosa.** This is *an eating disorder characterized by self-starvation leading to extreme weight loss.* Anorexia nervosa means "nervous loss of appetite" in Latin.

Anorexia is most common among female teens between the ages of 14 and 18, though the disorder can occur in males as well. People with anorexia often have low self-esteem and a poor body image. In an effort to gain control over their lives and bodies, they begin to change their diet. This usually means eating less and less food in an effort to lose weight. They may also exercise a lot. Even when a person with anorexia is dangerously thin, he or she may still see themselves as being overweight.

When the body is deprived of adequate food, a number of serious problems can develop. The person may become significantly underweight. Without proper nutrients, the body cannot grow and repair itself

▼ An unhealthy body image can lead to an eating disorder. **What are some ways to build a healthy body image?**

Lesson 2: Eating Disorders **267**

TEACH

AL Active Learning

Brochure Have pairs of students create a brochure in which they describe the symptoms and health risks associated with binge eating, anorexia, and bulimia. They should also include information about where people with eating disorders can get help. Consider making these brochures available throughout the school and community. **OL**

Reading Check

Answer Binge eating can lead to serious weight problems and obesity. It can also contribute to a low self-esteem and poor body image.

Caption Answers

Photo Caption *Sample answer:* Set realistic goals, eat healthfully, get enough rest and exercise, and have a positive attitude.
Photo Caption, p. 268 causes dehydration and loss of minerals; hormone imbalance; damage to kidneys, liver, teeth, mouth, and throat

Psychologist Have students meet in cooperative groups to read and discuss the information about psychologists, both in the text and at **glencoe. com**. Ask a member of each group to research the education and training psychologists need and to compare that with the education and training psychiatrists need. If possible, invite a local psychologist to visit the class and discuss his or her career.

Universal Access

Students with Different Learning Styles For visual students, instruct them to make an expanded Venn diagram to compare and contrast the symptoms and health risks of the various eating disorders. For auditory learners, set up small group discussions in which they name the symptoms and health risks for each eating disorder. Have kinesthetic learners create a Web page or poster that describes the symptoms and health risks of each eating disorder. **OL**

Reading Check

Answer, top *Any two:* loss of weight, very thin, sees self as fat, not wanting to eat
Answer, bottom damage to tooth enamel, mouth, and throat; hormone imbalance; damage to kidneys and liver; and loss of minerals

Psychologist

 A psychologist studies the physical, social, and emotional aspects of their patients' behavior. They help their patients with life issues. Psychologists are in demand because there is currently an increased demand for all mental health specialists. If you are interested in becoming a psychologist, you should practice your communication and conflict-resolution skills.

What are the different types of psychologists? Go to *Career Corner* at **glencoe.com** to find out.

▼ People with bulimia often binge on foods high in calories and fat. **How does this type of eating pattern damage the body?**

in normal ways. For example, bones can become thin and brittle from lack of calcium, and body temperature and blood pressure can drop.

If left untreated, a person with anorexia could die from starvation, heart failure, kidney failure, or other medical complications. The depression that often comes with anorexia can sometimes lead to thoughts of suicide.

Reading Check

Identify Name two symptoms of anorexia nervosa.

Bulimia Nervosa

Bulimia nervosa is another eating disorder that primarily affects female teens. However, one in ten people with bulimia is male. **Bulimia nervosa** is *a condition in which a person eats large amounts of food and then secretly purges.* Purging means to get rid of or remove something. People with bulimia purge the food they have eaten by vomiting or taking laxatives. They may also exercise too much in an effort to work off the calories they have eaten.

As with anorexia, people with bulimia are very concerned with losing weight and maintaining strict control of their bodies. They do not usually become extremely thin, however. For this reason it can be hard to tell if a person is suffering from bulimia and needs help. The signs of bulimia are subtle. For example, the person might go into a bathroom immediately after eating a large meal and vomit. He or she may run water to cover the sound of vomiting. Another sign is swollen cheeks caused by vomiting.

Although people with bulimia are not usually at risk of starving to death, the disorder can seriously damage their health in other ways. Stomach acids from frequent vomiting eat away at tooth enamel and injure the mouth and throat. Frequent vomiting can also cause a hormone imbalance, dehydration, damage to the kidneys and liver, and loss of important minerals.

Reading Check

Describe What are some health risks of bulimia nervosa?

Help for People with Eating Disorders

A person with an eating disorder needs help. Treatment can involve working with a counselor, primary care doctor, and nutritionist. These health care providers can help the person rebuild his or her physical and mental/emotional health. When an eating disorder involves serious medical problems or severe depression, a hospital or special treatment facility may be recommended.

What Teens Want to Know

How can I help my friend who has an eating disorder? First, students should talk to their friend privately in a caring and supportive way. They should be honest about their concerns and ask their friend to talk to a parent or medical professional. Students should avoid giving ultimatums or placing shame or blame on their friend. They should also avoid talking about food or monitoring their friend's eating habits and food choices. Students can also model sensible eating, exercise, and self-acceptance. They should discuss their concerns with a trusted adult. **OL**

Getting help is the first step toward recovery. **What are some treatments for people with eating disorders?**

Visit glencoe.com and complete the Interactive Study Guide for Lesson 2.

ASSESS

Assessment Resources

Lesson Review Quiz
ExamView
Fast Files Activities
Online Quizzes and Activities

Reteaching

- Assign Concept Map 11-2 or Reteaching Activity 11-2 in the Fast Files.
- Have students write ten quiz questions about eating disorders and their health risks. Students can exchange quizzes and complete them.

Enrichment

- Assign Enrichment Activity 11-2 in the Fast Files.
- Have students identify treatment facilities in the community for disordered eating. Suggest they learn about the programs these facilities offer and prepare a class resource list.

CLOSE

Ask students to identify three eating disorders and their health risks.

Caption Answer

Photo Caption psychotherapy, hospitalization, and nutritional counseling

Lesson 2 Review

 After You Read

Review this lesson for new terms, major headings, and Reading Checks.

What I Learned

1. *Vocabulary* What is another name for *binge eating disorder*?

2. *List* What are two health risks associated with anorexia nervosa?

3. *Identify* What are two signs of bulimia nervosa?

4. *Describe* What kinds of help are available to a person with an eating disorder?

Thinking Critically

5. *Evaluate* In what ways are the symptoms of anorexia and bulimia similar? In what ways are the two disorders different?

6. *Apply* Shauna suspects that her friend Jenna has an eating disorder. Lately, Jenna hardly eats anything and is getting thin. What could Shauna do to help? Explain your answer.

Applying Health Skills

7. *Advocacy* With a group, create a documentary titled "The Truth Behind Eating Disorders." Reveal facts and statistics you think the average teen may not be aware of. If you have access to a video camera, record your documentary. Otherwise, arrange to perform your documentary live for other classes.

Go Online For more Lesson Review Activities, go to glencoe.com.

Lesson 2: Eating Disorders **269**

Lesson 2 Review Answers

1. compulsive eating
2. *Any two:* extreme weight loss; lack of proper nutrients; drop in blood pressure and body temperature; brittle bones; death caused by starvation, kidney failure, cardiac arrest; or thoughts of suicide
3. Vomiting after meals, swollen cheeks
4. Treatment is handled by a team of specialists including a psychotherapist, primary care doctor, and nutritionist. Treatment takes place at a clinic or in a treatment facility.
5. Both can damage body organs and deprive the body of nutrients. Anorexics have extreme weight loss, while bulimics do not.
6. *Sample answer:* Shauna should tell a trusted adult because eating disorders are often brought on by psychological problems.
7. Documentaries should describe the symptoms, health risks, and incidences of various eating disorders.

Building Health Skills — Changing Your Weight Safely

Skill

Accessing Information

Activating Prior Knowledge

Display the empty containers of a variety of weight-gain and weight-loss products. Invite students to share what they know about these products. Then ask them to explain how they would find out which of these products was healthful.

- **Objective** After completing the activity, students will be able to access and analyze information to make a healthful choice about weight-gain or weight-loss products.

- **Time** 45 minutes

- **Materials** empty containers and advertisements of various weight-loss and weight-gain products, poster board, markers, glue

Teacher Classroom Resources

Building Health Skills
Transparency 11-2

Model

- Ask: How did Allyson find out which product was the most healthful? *She read the product labels and did research.*

270

Building Health Skills

Accessing Information
Practicing Healthful Behaviors
Stress Management
Analyzing Influences
Communication Skills
Refusal Skills
Conflict Resolution
Decision Making
Goal Setting
Advocacy

What Does Accessing Information Involve?

Accessing information involves finding reliable information to make healthy choices. When looking at a source of information, ask yourself these questions:

- Is it scientific?
- Does it give more than one point of view?
- Does it agree with other sources?
- Is it trying to sell something?

Changing Your Weight Safely

270 Chapter 11: Your Body Image

Follow the Model, Practice, and Apply steps to help you master this important health skill.

❶ Model

Read how Allyson used the skill of accessing information to find a nutrient supplement.

At a recent medical checkup, Allyson learned she was underweight. The doctor recommended that she take a nutrient supplement.

Allyson took the following steps to find out which product would be best for her.

- ***Read product labels.*** Allyson looked at the information panel that listed the ingredients.

- ***Consult Internet sources.*** Allyson used Web sites ending in .gov, .org, and .edu to look up information on the different products.

- ***Get advice from an authority.*** Allyson later spoke to a pharmacist who said that the extra fat and sugar in some products were not a good choice for her.

Teaching Tips

Guiding Student Learning

- For the Apply section, you will need to supply several magazines to each group. Whenever possible, these magazines should be ones read by teens.
- Have several Web sites for product information already identified on the board

and ask students to write these down.
- Reinforce the idea that the *best* way to manage weight is through healthful eating and regular physical activity. This is why MyPyramid was developed. Following these guidelines throughout one's life will contribute to overall good health.

② Practice

Read how Amelia uses the skill of accessing information to help her sister make an informed decision about losing weight.

Petra told her younger sister, Amelia, that she wants to try a new diet drink to lose weight. Amelia had just learned how to access valid health information in her health class and recommended that Petra use valid sources to check out the claims made by the diet drink company. Together, they checked out government health agency Web sites (.gov). Amelia also suggested that Petra make an appointment with her doctor before starting any diet.

1. What source of information did Amelia suggest?

2. Why did Amelia suggest Web sites that end in .gov?

③ Apply

Apply what you have learned about accessing information when completing the activity below.

With a small group, find an ad for a weight-loss or weight-gain product. Make a poster showing the front and back label of the product. Circle any claims or information that you believe are questionable. Below the labels, list an online or print resource you found that provides valid information about the product. Share your poster with the other groups and explain why your resource contains valid information.

Self-Check

■ Did we show the front and back labels of our product?

■ Did we circle any claim or piece of information that was questionable?

■ Did we find a valid source of information about this product?

Practice

● After students have read the introductory paragraph, allow them to answer the questions individually.

● Discuss the answers as a class. Solicit from students other sources of independent information that Amelia's sister might consult. (Nutritionists, school nurse, Web sites associated with hospitals or medical clinics)

Apply/Assess

● Have a supply of ads and/or empty containers of weight-loss and weight-gain products.

● If students are unable to find online or print resources that give valid information about the product, encourage them to talk to a pharmacist, nutritionist, or doctor.

● Have groups present their posters to the class. Suggest groups rate their product based on the information they learned about it.

● You may wish to distribute the Building Health Skills Activity in the Fast Files.

ASSESSMENT SCORING

Using a rubric, student work should meet all criteria to achieve the highest score.

Skills Student work:
● identifies a source of information.
● locates a valid source.
● explains why the source contains valid information.

Concepts Student work:
● provides information about a weight control product.
● identifies a questionable claim.

271

TIME *health news*

Pressure to Be Perfect

Objectives

After completing this activity, students will be able to:

- Understand how media portrayal of celebrities affects teens' body image
- Identify the negative results of having unrealistic standards for physical appearance
- Relate a negative body image to eating disorders

Motivator

Ask students to describe ways in which teens are influenced by celebrities. Record their responses on the board. After recording all of the students' responses, circle all of the responses that pertain to physical appearance.

Teaching the Feature

- Have students work in small groups to do further research on anorexia and bulimia. Then have students prepare wallet-sized information cards listing warning signs of eating disorders and instructions for seeking help from an adult if an eating disorder is suspected. Obtain permission for students to distribute their information cards to other students. **OL**

- Have students discuss the actors and actresses who portray teens on television. Ask: Are these teens realistic role models for body size? *Answers will vary depending on the actor being discussed.* **OL**

The heat is on young celebrities to look thinner than ever. Unfortunately, some fans will do almost anything to be just like them.

Pressure to be PERFECT

Surrounded by images of young celebrities who are painfully thin, teens can feel lots of pressure to meet the same standard. Trying hard to look like their idols, some can starve themselves and literally make themselves sick.

"Glamorous teen celebrities seem to have it made," says Dr. Susan Sabin, an expert on body image problems. "It appears that their lives are trouble-free, happy, and constantly entertaining—and the way to get all that is a perfect, skinny body."

STARS IN THEIR EYES

Even young celebrities themselves are not immune from the pressure. "I've been there, trust me," says one young pop star who has appeared in a few movies. "When I was younger, I tried to be skinny. There is so much pressure in today's society to look like the girl on the cover of the magazine. But those photos are airbrushed and have special lighting. The model has gone through two hours of hair and makeup. That just sets expectations really high for girls."

For teens, aspiring to unrealistic standards can lead to self-doubt, depression, extreme dieting—and in some cases, eating disorders. Dr. Sabin notes that many of her patients idolize one young TV star who is extremely thin. Nobody has said the star has an eating disorder, but Dr. Sabin believes that her very thin image is glamorized and admired.

A GROWING PROBLEM

Because many cases go unreported, the statistics vary, but 5 million or more girls and women in America are estimated to suffer from anorexia and other eating disorders. While anorexia is relatively rare—affecting up to 3.7 percent of the female population at some point in their lifetime—it is the most deadly of all mental diseases. About 5 to 10 percent of anorexics die from it or its complications.

LOOK SMART

Here are few ways to keep you—and your friends—on track when it comes to body image.

- Avoid idealizing celebrities whose bodies appear thinner than normal.
- Remember there is no perfect body shape.
- Don't worry about clothing sizes. Just find clothes that fit you best.
- If you're worried that a friend might have an eating disorder, talk to an adult.

272 TIME health news: Pressure to be Perfect

Activity — Media, Technology, and Culture

Culture The size and shape of the "ideal body" has changed over time. Have students research the characteristics of the ideal body type during one era of history. Students can use paintings and sculpture to determine the ideal body type of time periods before movies and television, or research using early television shows and movies. Have students share their results with the class. **OL**

Reading Review

STUDY TO GO Visit glencoe.com to download quizzes and eFlashcards for Chapter 11.

FOLDABLES Study Organizer

Foldables® and Other Study Aids Take out the Foldable® that you created for Lesson 1 and any graphic organizers that you created for Lessons 1–2. Find a partner and quiz each other using these study aids.

Lesson 1 Maintaining a Healthy Weight

Main Idea To maintain a healthy weight, you need to adjust your "energy equation." This means balancing "calories in" from food with "calories out" from physical activity.

- Teens with a healthy body image are more likely to have positive self-esteem. This in turn affects the way they interact with others.

- To build a healthy body image, teens should keep a positive attitude, eat healthy, exercise, get plenty of rest, set realistic goals, and spend time with people who appreciate them.

- You can determine if your weight is in the appropriate range for your age by calculating your body mass index (BMI).

- The rise in overweight teens can be traced to lifestyle factors like overeating, eating too many empty-calorie foods, and not getting enough physical activity.

- Underweight teens lack body fat. They may be undernourished.

- Managing a healthy weight doesn't just mean counting calories. You also need to pay attention to the sources of the calories that you eat.

Lesson 2 Eating Disorders

Main Idea An eating disorder is an extreme and damaging eating behavior that can lead to sickness and even death.

- People with eating disorders suffer from unrealistic and unhealthy body images.

- Symptoms of binge eating disorder include eating when not hungry, eating beyond the point of feeling comfortably full, and depression. Health risks from binge eating disorder include obesity.

- Signs of bulimia nervosa include vomiting after meals and swollen cheeks caused by vomiting. Health risks include loss of tooth enamel and injury to the mouth and throat from stomach acids, dehydration, loss of important minerals, hormone imbalances, and damage to the kidneys and liver.

- Symptoms of anorexia nervosa include extreme weight loss and depression. Health risks include starvation, heart and kidney failure, and other medical complications.

- Help for a person with an eating disorder includes treatment by a team of health care providers. If the symptoms are extreme, the patient may be sent to a hospital or a treatment facility.

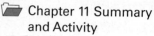

Assessment Resources

- Chapter 11 Summary and Activity
- Audio Summaries
- Reading Tutor
- Performance Assessment
- Chapter 11 Test
- *ExamView*
- Vocabulary PuzzleMaker
- Online Learning Center

Reading Review

Study Aids

- **Using the Dinah Zike Foldable® Study Organizer** Have students use the Foldable® **FOLDABLES Study Organizer** to review the vocabulary terms for Lesson 1. Ask students to identify which weight is a healthy weight.

- **Online Learning Tools** Have students go to the *Teen Health* Online Learning Center at **glencoe.com** to:
  - Download a **Podcast**.
  - Download free **Study-to-Go** content to their PDAs or cell phones.

Vocabulary Review

- **Playing a Game** Have groups of four play a game of "Catch Phrase" using the vocabulary terms from the chapter. Partners guess the terms from phrases given by their partners and pass word cards like a "hot potato" until a timer goes off.

Teaching Tips

Think-Pair-Share This strategy is especially useful for English learners and reluctant readers because it gives time for independent thought before participating in a larger discussion. First, pose the question and give students time to think and write their answer. Students then partner up to discuss their answers. Teach students to ask questions such as "How did you decide that?" or "In other words, you think that. . ." After practicing their answers, invite students to share their answers with the class.

CHAPTER 11

Assessment

Reviewing Vocabulary and Main Ideas

1. body image
2. Appropriate weight
3. body mass index (BMI)
4. Overweight
5. Underweight
6. a
7. b
8. c
9. c
10. d

Thinking Critically

11. *Sample answer:* People like Kim for who she is, not what she looks like, and the party will not be fun without her.

12. Binge eaters may hide food or eat in private. Weight gain is usually slow. People with bulimia may hide the fact that they are vomiting after meals by running water to drown out the sound. Their weight may not change so others might not notice that something is wrong.

Have students visit **glencoe.com** to take the Chapter 11 quiz.

274

CHAPTER 11 Assessment

After You Read

HEALTH QUIZ

Now that you have read the chapter, look back at your answers to the Health Quiz on the chapter opener. Would you change any of them? What would your answers be now?

Reviewing Vocabulary and Main Ideas

On a sheet of paper, write the numbers 1–5. After each number, write the term from the list that best completes each sentence.

- anorexia nervosa
- appropriate weight
- body image
- body mass index (BMI)
- bulimia nervosa
- overweight
- underweight

Lesson 1 Maintaining a Healthy Weight

1. The way you see and feel about your body is your _____.

2. _____ is the weight range that is best for your body.

3. A formula you can use to determine if your weight is appropriate for you is called _____.

4. _____ means weighing more than what is appropriate for gender, height, age, body frame, and growth pattern.

5. _____ is weighing less than what is appropriate for gender, height, age, body frame, and growth pattern.

Lesson 2 Eating Disorders

On a sheet of paper, write the numbers 6–10. After each number, write the letter of the answer that best completes each statement.

6. In this country, anorexia nervosa affects mostly
   a. female teens.　c. male adults.
   b. male teens.　d. female adults.

7. Losing weight to the point of becoming dangerously thin is a sign of
   a. all eating disorders.
   b. anorexia nervosa.
   c. bulimia nervosa.
   d. binge eating disorder.

8. The condition in which a person secretly eats large amounts of food and then tries to purge is called
   a. obesity.
   b. anorexia nervosa.
   c. bulimia nervosa.
   d. compulsive eating.

9. Obesity is a health risk of which of the following conditions?
   a. anorexia　c. compulsive eating
   b. bulimia　d. None of the above

10. Which of the following health care providers usually treats people with eating disorders?
    a. counselor
    b. primary care doctor
    c. nutritionist
    d. All of the above

Go Online Visit **glencoe.com** and take the Online Quiz for Chapter 11.

HEALTH QUIZ Wrap-Up

Body Image Have students review the answers they gave to the Health Quiz at the beginning of the chapter. For each question, have students find the place in the chapter that discusses the answer. Then have them write a sentence that describes the health reasons that support the correct answer.

Thinking Critically

Using complete sentences, answer the following questions on a sheet of paper.

11. **Apply** A number of teens are invited to a swim party. Kim, one of the teens, says she does not want to be seen in a bathing suit. Imagine you are Kim's best friend. What might you tell her?

12. **Explain** Why is it often difficult to tell if a person has an eating disorder?

Write About It

13. **Expository Writing** Using online or print resources, research alternate formulas for computing BMI. Then develop your findings into an article.

⟁ Applying Technology

Body Basics

You and a partner will use GarageBand™ or Audacity® to create an audio podcast about achieving a healthy body image.

- Create a five-minute script with information about body image from this chapter. Make sure that you discuss methods for achieving a healthy body image.
- Open a new podcast project. If you and your partner both have speaking parts, you should have two audio tracks.
- Record your parts.
- Add lead-in music. Edit for clarity, accuracy, and time. Save your project.
- Upload your podcast to iTunes®.

Standardized Test Practice

Reading

Read the passage and then answer the questions.

Dieting is a very popular pastime in America. Everywhere you look you can find advertisements for diets that claim they will help you "Lose Pounds Fast!" Most diets that make this claim focus on helping dieters lose weight by getting rid of excess water rather than fat. Although water is easy to lose, it is also easy to gain. This often leads to what health experts call "seesaw dieting," "weight cycling," or "yo-yo dieting" in which a person gains and loses weight rapidly.

Since part of the weight that many people regain is fat, yo-yo dieting can be unhealthier than being overweight. Any teen who needs to lose weight should do so in a healthy way. This means losing the weight gradually by eating smaller portions and exercising under the supervision of a doctor or other health professional.

> **TEST-TAKING TIP**
>
> Make sure you grasp the main idea of the reading passage as a whole. Make sure that you also understand the main point of each paragraph.

1. Which of the following is *not* a name for "rapid ups and downs in weight"?
   - **A.** seesaw dieting
   - **B.** weight cycling
   - **C.** yo-yo dieting
   - **D.** burning calories

2. Which sentence *best* captures the main point of the second paragraph?
   - **A.** Water is replaced by more body fat.
   - **B.** Yo-yo dieting may be less healthy than being slightly overweight.
   - **C.** Body fat is hard to lose.
   - **D.** Losing weight gets harder the more you diet.

Chapter 11 Assessment **275**

⟁ Applying Technology

Body Basics
Equipment needs: GarageBand™ or Audacity® or similar software
Help students discuss the purpose of their podcasts and the specific steps they should follow. Then have students choose partners for the project. Establish a sign-up sheet if computer time is limited. Also decide on a time limit for each pair of students; emphasize that their scripts should be complete before they begin recording. Encourage students to download and listen to their classmates' podcasts.

Write About It

13. **Expository Writing** Explain that expository writing shares knowledge to help others understand it. Student articles should give clear and concise directions for finding BMI. Articles should also explain the importance of learning to compute BMI.

Standardized Test Practice

1. D
2. B

⟁ Test-Taking Tips

Finding the Main Idea of a Paragraph
Remind students that the main idea of a paragraph is often stated in a topic sentence. Review paragraph structure with students. Show them that some paragraphs begin with the topic sentence, while others end with it. Have students practice writing paragraphs. Then have students exchange paragraphs with a partner and find the paragraph's main idea.

CHAPTER 12 pp. 276–305	Standards		Skills and Activities
	National	**State/Local**	
	National Health Education Standards 1.8.3, 1.8.5, 4.8.2, 5.8.2, 5.8.3, 5.8.4, 5.8.5, 5.8.6, 5.8.7, 8.8.2		*Health* **eSpotlight** *p. 277* **BUILDING HEALTH SKILLS** *Decision Making* Helping Someone Get Help, *pp. 300–301* **HANDS-ON HEALTH** Refusing to Get in a Car with a Driver Who Has Been Drinking, *p. 302*
Lesson 1 Why Alcohol Is Harmful pp. 278–281	National Health Education Standards 1.8.2, 1.8.8, 1.8.9, 2.8.3, 2.8.7, 2.8.9, 4.8.2, 5.8.1, 5.8.5, 5.8.6, 5.8.7, 7.8.3, 8.8.3		**What Teens Think** Why do you think some teens choose to use alcohol?, *p. 279* **HEALTH SKILLS ACTIVITY** *Refusal Skills* Life of the Party, *p. 280*
Lesson 2 Short-Term Effects of Alcohol Use pp. 282–285	National Health Education Standards 1.8.8, 1.8.9, 3.8.1, 4.8.2, 5.8.7		**Connect To... LANGUAGE ARTS** Intoxication, *p. 283*
Lesson 3 Long-Term Effects of Alcohol Use pp. 286–290	National Health Education Standards 1.8.8, 1.8.9, 2.8.4, 5.8.1, 5.8.4, 5.8.6, 5.8.7, 7.8.1, 8.8.1, 8.8.2		
Lesson 4 Alcoholism and Alcohol Abuse pp. 291–295	National Health Education Standards 1.8.8, 1.8.9, 2.8.9, 3.8.2, 5.8.1, 5.8.6, 8.8.1		**Go Online** Speaking Out About Alcohol, *p. 293* **Careers for the 21st Century** Alcohol Abuse Counselor, *p. 294*
Lesson 5 Getting Help for Alcohol Abuse pp. 296–299	National Health Education Standards 1.8.5, 3.8.4, 3.8.5, 4.8.2, 4.8.4, 6.8.2, 6.8.3, 7.8.3, 8.8.2		**HEALTH SKILLS ACTIVITY** *Communication Skills* When Communication Counts Most, *p. 298*

PACING THE CHAPTER		
Lesson 1 30 min	**Lesson 4** 30 min	**Chapter Review** 45 min
Lesson 2 30 min	**Lesson 5** 30 min	**Hands-on Health** 45 min
Lesson 3 30 min	**Building Health Skills** 90 min	

BLOCK SCHEDULING

For block scheduling, assign students Building Health Skills feature *Helping Someone Get Help*, pages 300–301, and Guided Reading and Writing. 📁

Planning Guide

StudentWorks *Plus*

Glencoe Exclusive!
TeacherWorks™ *Plus*
All-In-One Planner and Resource Center

Reproducible Resources	Assessment	Media and Technology
Chapter *FAST FILE* **Resources** Chapter Summaries and Activities `REVIEW` Building Health Skills Activity `TEACH` Performance Assessment Activity `EXTEND` Universal Access Activities `TEACH` Parent Letter and Activities 📁 **Student Activities Workbook** `TEACH` 📁 **Reading Tutor** `TEACH`	Building Health Skills Activity, *pp. 300–301* Chapter 12 Assessment, *pp. 304–305* **Chapter** *FAST FILE* **Resources** Performance Assessment Activity, *p. 4* Chapter 12 Test, *p. 7* ⊙ *ExamView® Assessment Suite*	TeacherWorks *Plus* includes: ● Interactive Teacher Edition ● Lesson Planner with Calendar ● Access to all blackline masters ● Correlations to standards ⊙ StudentWorks™ Plus ⊙ Online Student Edition Dinah Zike's Teaching Health with Foldables®
Chapter *FAST FILE* **Resources** Concept Mapping Activity 12-1 `REVIEW` Cross-Curriculum Activity 12-1 `EXTEND` Enrichment Activity 12-1 `EXTEND` Lesson Plan 12-1 Guided Reading and Writing 12-1 `TEACH` Reteaching Activity 12-1 `REVIEW`	Lesson 1 Review, *p. 281* ⊙ Vocabulary PuzzleMaker ⊙ *ExamView® Assessment Suite*	⊙ Vocabulary PuzzleMaker ⊙ *ExamView® Assessment Suite* ⊙ StudentWorks™ Plus ⊙ Transparency 12-1 **G⊙ Online** glencoe.com
Chapter *FAST FILE* **Resources** Concept Mapping Activity 12-2 `REVIEW` Health Lab 12-2 `EXTEND` Enrichment Activity 12-2 `EXTEND` Lesson Plan 12-2 Guided Reading and Writing 12-2 `TEACH` Reteaching Activity 12-2 `REVIEW`	Lesson 2 Review, *p. 285* ⊙ Vocabulary PuzzleMaker ⊙ *ExamView® Assessment Suite*	⊙ Vocabulary PuzzleMaker ⊙ *ExamView® Assessment Suite* ⊙ StudentWorks™ Plus ⊙ Transparency 12-2 **G⊙ Online** glencoe.com
Chapter *FAST FILE* **Resources** Concept Mapping Activity 12-3 `REVIEW` Decision-Making Activity 12-3 `EXTEND` Enrichment Activity 12-3 `EXTEND` Lesson Plan 12-3 Guided Reading and Writing 12-3 `TEACH` Reteaching Activity 12-3 `REVIEW`	Lesson 3 Review, *p. 290* ⊙ Vocabulary PuzzleMaker ⊙ *ExamView® Assessment Suite*	⊙ Vocabulary PuzzleMaker ⊙ *ExamView® Assessment Suite* ⊙ StudentWorks™ Plus ⊙ Transparency 12-3 **G⊙ Online** glencoe.com
Chapter *FAST FILE* **Resources** Concept Mapping Activity 12-4 `REVIEW` Cross-Curriculum Activity 12-4 `EXTEND` Enrichment Activity 12-4 `EXTEND` Lesson Plan 12-4 Guided Reading and Writing 12-4 `TEACH` Reteaching Activity 12-4 `REVIEW`	Lesson 4 Review, *p. 295* ⊙ Vocabulary PuzzleMaker ⊙ *ExamView® Assessment Suite*	⊙ Vocabulary PuzzleMaker ⊙ *ExamView® Assessment Suite* ⊙ StudentWorks™ Plus ⊙ Transparency 12-4 **G⊙ Online** glencoe.com
Chapter *FAST FILE* **Resources** Concept Mapping Activity 12-5 `REVIEW` Decision-Making Activity 12-5 `EXTEND` Enrichment Activity 12-5 `EXTEND` Lesson Plan 12-5 Guided Reading and Writing 12-5 `TEACH` Reteaching Activity 12-5 `REVIEW`	Lesson 5 Review, *p. 299* ⊙ Vocabulary PuzzleMaker ⊙ *ExamView® Assessment Suite*	⊙ Vocabulary PuzzleMaker ⊙ *ExamView® Assessment Suite* ⊙ StudentWorks™ Plus ⊙ Transparency 12-5 **G⊙ Online** glencoe.com

Chapter and Lesson Resources

The *Teen Health* resources are designed for differentiated learning abilities. You may want to use the coded items in this way:

`REVIEW` —activities to review or reinforce content

`TEACH` —activities to teach basic concepts

`EXTEND` —activities to extend or enrich lesson content

 OUT OF TIME?

Use Health Skills Activities *Life of the Party,* page 280, and *When Communication Counts Most,* page 298.

DUI Laws by State

DUI (driving under the influence) laws vary from state to state, but all 50 states and the District of Columbia have laws prohibiting people 21 and older from driving with a blood alcohol content (BAC) of 0.08% or higher. Almost 40 states also have laws prohibiting people under 21 from driving with a BAC of 0.02% or higher. The remaining states have even stricter BAC limits for drivers under 21, either 0.00% or 0.01%.

Drivers generally have their licenses suspended when they are arrested for DUI offenses. The minimum period of suspension for a first offense ranges from a week (Virginia) to a year (Georgia). In most states, people convicted of DUI offenses can drive during this period only if special ignition locks have been installed on their vehicles. The locks analyze the drivers' breath for alcohol and prevent the vehicles from starting if the drivers test positive.

In addition to loss of driving privileges, DUI convictions are punished with fines in all 50 states and the District of Columbia. Other penalties often are imposed as well, such as jail time, alcohol education programs, or community service. Maximum fines for a first offense range from $250 (Arizona) to $5,000 (Massachusetts and Oregon). Fines and other penalties typically are stiffer for second and subsequent DUI convictions. In 30 states, people with multiple DUI offenses can lose their vehicles.

Binge Drinking and Teen Suicide

Recent studies have found that binge drinking may significantly increase the risk of suicide in teens. For example, a 2004 study of ninth- and tenth-graders found that suicide attempts often followed bouts of binge drinking. An earlier study of eighth graders found that binge drinkers were more than three times as likely to attempt suicide as were nondrinkers.

Binge drinking is defined as having at least five drinks on one occasion, usually in a short period of time. Often the "goal" of binge drinking is "to get drunk." About one in five ninth graders is a binge drinker. Typically, binge-drinking teens increase the severity of their drinking throughout adolescence. Binge drinking is on the rise in teens not only in the United States but also around the world.

The relationship between binge drinking and suicide is complex. Teens who binge drink are more likely to have other serious problems as well, including depression, lack of family support, and high levels of stress. In fact, many binge-drinking teens say that they use alcohol to cope with their problems. All three problems can increase the risk of suicide even in nondrinkers. Adding binge drinking to the mix makes the risk of suicide even greater.

Suicide is already the third-leading cause of death in 14- to 18-year-olds in the United States. Given the rising trend in binge drinking, teaching students about the dangers of alcohol may be a higher priority now than ever before. For the students in your classes, this chapter is a good place to start.

Support for Teaching Reading

Reading Support

Reading Preview

Activating Background Vocabulary Have students write all the chapter vocabulary terms on index cards. Direct students to sort the cards into categories such as facts about alcohol, effects of alcohol, and high-risk behaviors.

FOLDABLES Study Organizer *Dinah Zike's Reading and Study Skills for Teen Health* provides interactive graphic organizers that help students comprehend and retain health concepts as they read. Use the Foldable® on page 277 or find more Foldables® activities for the chapter on **Alcohol** in the separate booklet, available in the TCR.

Lesson 1 Why Alcohol Is Harmful

Text Walk Lead students in examining the text by pointing out the vocabulary terms, pictures, captions, headings, subheadings, and the lesson review. After the preview, have students predict the reasons why alcohol is harmful.

Lesson 2 Short-term Effects of Alcohol Use

Stop and Go During reading, stop students and ask one to summarize what has been read so far regarding the myths of alcohol. Stop the student and ask another student to take over the summarizing. Continue until all main points are covered.

Lesson 3 Long-term Effects of Alcohol Use

Question Maker As they read, have students write their own questions about alcohol use in each of three categories: literal, inferential, and application. Have students exchange papers with a partner and answer each other's questions.

Lesson 4 Alcoholism and Alcohol Abuse

Partner Sharing After students read the section **Binge Drinking**, ask partners to discuss: What are some of the dangers of using alcohol? Allow students a few minutes to discuss, then ask some pairs to share with the whole class.

Lesson 5 Getting Help for Alcohol Abuse

Guided Reading 1) Ask students what they know about alcoholism. 2) Introduce key terms. 3) Give a purpose for reading. Ask: "What are the stages of alcoholism?" 4) Have students read silently to find the answers. 5) Discuss.

Post Reading

Dramatic Presentations Guide students in a discussion about strategies that can help them say no to alcohol use. Have student groups create a presentation for the class demonstrating the harmful effects of teen alcohol use.

Key for Using the Teacher Wraparound Edition

Use this key to help you identify the different types of prompts found in the Teacher Wraparound Edition.

R **Reading Strategies** activities help you teach reading skills and vocabulary.

C **Critical Thinking** strategies help students apply and extend what they have learned.

U **Universal Access** activities provide differentiated instruction for students learning to speak English, along with suggestions for teaching various types of learners.

HS **Health Skills Practice** activities reinforce Health Skills concepts and help students apply these skills in their everyday lives.

W **Writing Support** activities provide writing opportunities to help students comprehend the text.

AL **Active Learning** strategies provide a variety of activities for presenting lesson content, including Quick Demos and engaging classroom projects that get students actively involved.

Key to Ability Levels

Teaching Strategies and activities have been coded for ability level and appropriateness.

AL Activities for students working above grade level

OL Activities for students working on grade level

BL Activities for students working below grade level

EL Activities for English Learners

Symbols

Transparencies

CD-ROM

glencoe.com

Print Resources

Chapter at a Glance

Lesson 1 explains how alcohol causes harm, reasons teens should not drink, and alternatives to drinking.

Lesson 2 identifies myths about alcohol, short-term effects of alcohol use, and factors that determine how alcohol affects different people.

Lesson 3 states long-term effects of alcohol use on the body and on the fetus of a mother who drinks, and describes effects of driving while intoxicated.

Lesson 4 identifies symptoms of alcoholism, stages of alcoholism, and effects of alcoholism on families and society.

Lesson 5 describes symptoms of alcohol withdrawal, steps in recovery from alcoholism, and sources of help for alcoholics and their families.

R Reading Strategy

Interpreting the Photo Have students look at the photo and ask: What is this teen doing? *participating in an anti-alcohol activity* Call on volunteers to answer the caption question. (*Sample answers:* headaches, liver damage, injuries) OL

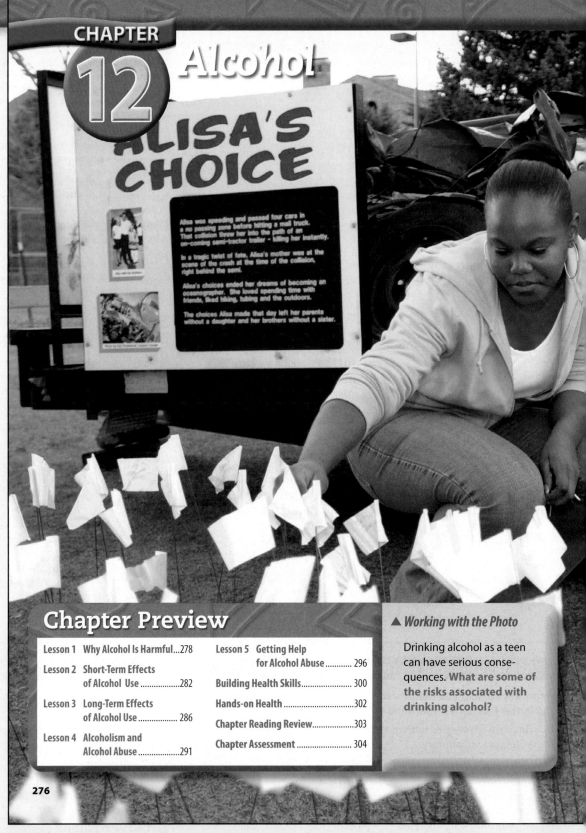

CHAPTER
12 Alcohol

ALISA'S CHOICE

Alisa was speeding and passed four cars in a no passing zone before hitting a mail truck. That collision threw her into the path of an on-coming semi-tractor trailer – killing her instantly.

In a tragic twist of fate, Alisa's mother was at the scene of the crash at the time of the collision, right behind the semi.

Alisa's choices ended her dreams of becoming an oceanographer. She loved spending time with friends, liked hiking, tubing and the outdoors.

The choices Alisa made that day left her parents without a daughter and her brothers without a sister.

Chapter Preview

276

▲ *Working with the Photo*

Drinking alcohol as a teen can have serious consequences. **What are some of the risks associated with drinking alcohol?**

👥 Universal Access

Differentiated Learning Glencoe provides teacher support and student materials for all learners in the health classroom.

● Spanish Glosario and chapter summaries assist English Language Learners.
● *Reading Tutor* and related worksheets support reluctant readers.

● Universal Access strategies throughout the Teacher Wraparound Edition and Fast Files help you present materials for gifted students, at-risk students, physically impaired students, and those with behavior disorders or learning disabilities.

Start-Up Activities

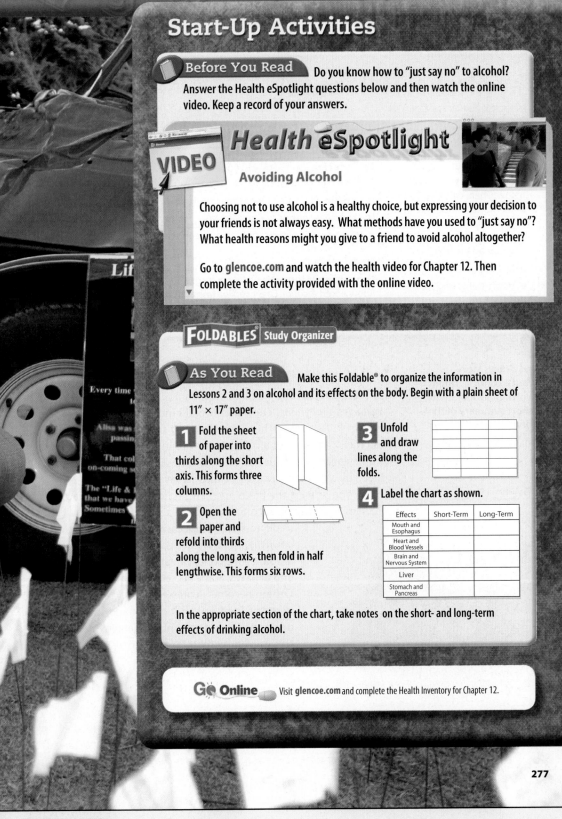

Before You Read Do you know how to "just say no" to alcohol? Answer the Health eSpotlight questions below and then watch the online video. Keep a record of your answers.

Health eSpotlight

VIDEO

Avoiding Alcohol

Choosing not to use alcohol is a healthy choice, but expressing your decision to your friends is not always easy. What methods have you used to "just say no"? What health reasons might you give to a friend to avoid alcohol altogether?

Go to **glencoe.com** and watch the health video for Chapter 12. Then complete the activity provided with the online video.

FOLDABLES Study Organizer

As You Read Make this Foldable® to organize the information in Lessons 2 and 3 on alcohol and its effects on the body. Begin with a plain sheet of 11″ × 17″ paper.

1 Fold the sheet of paper into thirds along the short axis. This forms three columns.

2 Open the paper and refold into thirds along the long axis, then fold in half lengthwise. This forms six rows.

3 Unfold and draw lines along the folds.

4 Label the chart as shown.

Effects	Short-Term	Long-Term
Mouth and Esophagus		
Heart and Blood Vessels		
Brain and Nervous System		
Liver		
Stomach and Pancreas		

In the appropriate section of the chart, take notes on the short- and long-term effects of drinking alcohol.

Go Online Visit **glencoe.com** and complete the Health Inventory for Chapter 12.

277

Lesson 1

FOCUS

Activating Prior Knowledge

What I Know Why is it against the law for teens to consume alcohol? *Sample answer: because alcohol is harmful, especially in young people* Tell students they will learn why alcohol is harmful in this lesson.

 Guide to Reading

Building Vocabulary
■ Ask: How are the terms *alcohol* and *drug* related? *Sample answer: Alcohol is a kind of drug.* Students can see if they were correct when they read the lesson.
■ Use Vocabulary PuzzleMaker to reinforce vocabulary terms.

Reading Strategy
Organizing Information Remind students to include ways alcohol can harm mental/emotional and social health (e.g., by causing memory problems and aggression), not just physical health.

Quick Write

Use completed summaries to motivate a class discussion of problems caused by alcohol use.

Caption Answer

Photo Caption *Sample answer:* It can help prevent harm to your body, brain, and relationships.

278

Lesson 1

Why Alcohol Is Harmful

 Guide to Reading

● **Building Vocabulary**
Read the terms in the list below. Then, write what you think the definitions are in your notebook. Make any corrections that are needed as you read the text.

■ alcohol (p. 278)
■ depressants (p. 278)
■ alternatives (p. 281)

● **Focusing on the Main Ideas**
In this lesson, you will learn to

■ **explain** why some teens drink alcohol.
■ **state** reasons not to drink alcohol.
■ **identify** alternatives to drinking alcohol.

● **Reading Strategy**
Organizing Information Make a diagram titled *What Teens Should Know About Alcohol.* Draw spokes from the heading. Under each, note one of the facts from the lesson.

Quick Write

Find a news story about a traffic accident involving alcohol. Write a short summary of the story.

What Is Alcohol?

Alcohol is *a drug that is produced by a chemical reaction in fruits, vegetables, and grains.* There are several kinds of alcohol. Some are used to kill germs. Others can be found in medicines, cleaners, and fuels. The kind of alcohol we are talking about in this chapter is a beverage. It is called *ethanol* alcohol. Ethanol alcohol is produced by a chemical reaction called *fermentation.*

Alcohol affects the brain and central nervous system, causing changes in behavior. Alcohol belongs to a group of drugs known as depressants. **Depressants** are *drugs that slow down the body's functions and reactions.* Even small amounts of alcohol can affect how a person feels and behaves. Some become relaxed and friendly. Others become depressed and angry. Alcohol makes it hard to think clearly and make good decisions. That is why many people say and do things they regret after they drink.

R

◀ Many teens are making the decision to stay alcohol free. **How can abstaining from alcohol improve your health triangle?**

Lesson 1 Resources

📁 **Chapter *FAST FILE* Resources**
Guided Reading and Writing 12-1
Concept Mapping Activity 12-1
Cross-Curriculum Activity 12-1
Reteaching Activity 12-1
Enrichment Activity 12-1
Lesson Quiz 12-1

Technology
🔦 Transparency 12-1
💿 Audio Summaries
💿 *ExamView® Assessment Suite*
💿 Vocabulary PuzzleMaker
💿 StudentWorks™ Plus
 Go Online

Alcohol Use and Teens

A teen's body and mind are still growing and developing. Research has shown that alcohol use can interfere with long- and short-term growth. Alcohol can harm the brain's ability to learn and its ability to remember. Teens who drink are more likely to fall behind in school. Alcohol also increases the risk of social problems, depression, suicidal thoughts, and violence.

HS It is illegal for anyone under the age of 21 to use alcohol. Teens who drink alcohol risk getting into trouble with the law. If you are caught buying or drinking alcohol, you could be arrested, fined, or sent to a youth detention center.

Finally, alcohol is the cause of hundreds of traffic accidents every year. One-third of all teen traffic deaths are related to alcohol.

Why Some Teens Drink Alcohol

Teens who drink risk damaging their health. Why, then, do some young people drink alcohol? Here are some reasons teens give.

What Teens Think

Why do you think some teens choose to use alcohol?

I personally think that there are many different reasons why teens would drink alcohol. During teenage years, a lot of us think that we need to be cool. In large groups or at parties, drinking can get out of hand and peer pressure easily takes control. Even if you think that peer pressure couldn't overpower you, it could be hard to turn it down in a large crowd. As you get older, most teens want to prove that they can be adult and participate in adult-like activities like drinking.

Kylie N.
Boise, ID

What Teens May Say

- "Drinking will help me forget about my problems."
- "I'll look more grown-up with a drink in my hand."
- "Movies make drinking look cool."
- "My friends keep pressuring me to try alcohol."
- "A drink will help me relax."

What Teens Should Know

- The problems will still be there when the effects of alcohol wear off.
- You won't look mature getting in trouble for underage drinking.
- Movies don't always show the risks associated with drinking alcohol.
- Real friends won't pressure you to do something illegal.
- Alcohol interferes with sleep and performance in school or other activities, creating stress.

Reading Check **Identify** What can happen to a teen who is caught buying or drinking alcohol?

Dealing with Sensitive Issues

Alcohol Abuse in the Family At least six million children in the United States live with a parent who abuses alcohol. It is likely that some of them are in your classroom. These students are likely to find alcohol abuse to be a sensitive issue. They are also at higher risk for a number of problems, including anxiety, depression, their own abuse of alcohol or drugs, and difficulties with learning and school. It is especially important to help these students learn healthy coping strategies.

TEACH

What Teens Think

Why do you think some teens choose to use alcohol? Ask students to name reasons why they think some of their peers use alcohol. Then have students consider each of these reasons and ask them this question: If a friend used one of these reasons as his or her reason for drinking, what would you tell them?

R Reading Strategy

Finding the Main Idea Ask students to find the main idea in the passage about the realities of alcohol. Call on volunteers to read their main ideas to the class. (*Sample answer:* Ads make alcohol use seem very positive, but alcohol is really a harmful drug.) Write a composite of their best ideas on the board. **BL**

HS Health Skills Practice

Accessing Information Ask students to research laws in their state about teens and alcohol, including age limits and penalties. Ask students to summarize what they learn in the form of a chart or other type of graphic organizer. **OL**

 Reading Check

They could be arrested, fined, or sent to a youth detention center.

Health Skills Activity

Refusal Skills

Life of the Party

Remind students to apply the four steps in the S.T.O.P. strategy to Kim's problem. Students might say that Kim should leave the party because drinking alcohol is unhealthy, does not feel right, is illegal, and is not parent-approved.

AL Active Learning

Small Group Learning Divide the class into small groups, and have each group brainstorm alternatives to drinking. After groups have had a chance to think of several alternatives, have them pool their ideas and discuss which ideas might appeal to the most teens. **OL**

C Critical Thinking

Analyzing
Provide each group of students with an article on the effects of alcohol. For example: fetal alcohol syndrome, accidents caused by alcohol, or alcohol poisoning. Challenge each groups to use their assigned articles to make an argument against the use of alcohol. **EL**

Caption Answers

Photo Caption Answers may vary. Students might say that the risk of violence or suicide is also a good reason to stay alcohol free.
Photo Caption, p. 281 Answers will vary but should show healthful activities.

280

Health Skills Activity

Refusal Skills

Life of the Party

Kim has been invited to a party at her friend Terry's house. When she arrives, she finds that Terry's parents are not at home and many teens are drinking beer. Terry tells her that her older brother brought the beer. She urges Kim to try some. Kim knows that it is illegal for teens to drink and has learned about the risks of using alcohol. What do you think Kim should do when her friend laughs at her concerns and continues to offer her a drink?

On Your Own

Apply the S.T.O.P. strategy described below to help Kim say no to using alcohol.

1. **S**ay no in a firm voice.
2. **T**ell why not.
3. **O**ffer other ideas.
4. **P**romptly leave.

Visit glencoe.com and complete the Interactive Study Guide for Lesson 1.

Reasons Not to Drink

Does the phrase, "just say no" sound familiar? Choosing not to use alcohol is a healthy choice. It shows you understand how risky drinking can be and are choosing to stay alcohol free. Some teens may believe that drinking alcohol will help them fit in with their peers.

In reality, most teens are not drinking alcohol. If you choose not to drink alcohol, you will already be fitting in with most of your peers. Many teens realize the negative effects alcohol can have on their health and are saying no to alcohol use.

▶ **C** Alcohol is one of the biggest factors in teen traffic deaths. **Can you think of a better reason to stay alcohol free?**

280 Chapter 12: Alcohol

FITNESS ZONE

Fitness Activities After students have read and discussed *Alternatives to Drinking Alcohol*, have them review the activity ideas in the *Fitness Zone Handbook*. Ask: How can having a fitness routine serve as an alternative to alcohol use? What might make group fitness activities important as part of an alternative to drinking alcohol? **For more information, see *Fitness Zone Handbook* pages xviii-1 or visit the Fitness Zone at glencoe.com.**

There are important reasons why you should join this majority. First, you are risking your health when you drink. Second, using alcohol is against the law for teens. Finally, you want to make decisions that will help you become a strong person. Teens who stay alcohol free are better able to handle the challenges of everyday life.

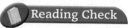 **Reading Check** **Explain** Why is drinking a bad idea for teens?

Alternatives to Drinking Alcohol

Teens who avoid alcohol may want to seek positive alternatives to drinking. But what **alternatives** or *other ways of thinking or acting* are available to teens who choose not to drink? One positive alternative is sports. Learning new skills, discovering a new talent, challenging your body, and being part of a team are all alternatives to drinking alcohol.

Other alternatives include pursuing interests in theater or the arts, volunteering in your community, and advocacy. Becoming an advocate gives you a chance to make a difference in the lives of others. There are many advocacy groups that try to help teens like yourself make smart choices. Some of these include Students Against Destructive Decisions (SADD), Teens Against Tobacco Use (T.A.T.U.), and Youth for Environmental Sanity.

▲ There are much more fun ways to spend time with friends than drinking alcohol. **What activities do you enjoy?**

 Reading Check

Answer Drinking is bad for their health, against the law, and may lead to addiction.

ASSESS

 Assessment Resources

Lesson Review Quiz
ExamView
Fast Files Activities
Online Quizzes and Activities

Reteaching
● Assign Concept Map 12-1 or Reteaching Activity 12-1 in the Fast Files. 📁
● Have students create concept maps summarizing the information on alcohol use by teens.

Enrichment
● Assign Enrichment Activity 12-1 in the Fast Files. 📁
● Ask students to present a panel discussion on reasons for teens to avoid alcohol use.

CLOSE
Go around the class and call on each student in turn to state an alternative to drinking alcohol.

Lesson 1 Review

After You Read

Review this lesson for new terms, major headings, and Reading Checks.

What I Learned

1. *Vocabulary* Define *alcohol,* and use it in a sentence.

2. *State* What are three reasons not to drink alcohol?

3. *Explain* What are two reasons teens give for using alcohol?

Thinking Critically

4. *Evaluate* How can positive alternatives help a teen avoid using alcohol?

5. *Apply* You are at an amusement park with several friends. When it is time to leave, a friend's brother offers to give you a ride. You believe you smell alcohol on his breath. What should you do, and why?

Applying Health Skills

6. *Advocacy* Create a TV ad that encourages teens *not* to drink. Use images and reasons you think will appeal to teens your age. Share your ad with your classmates.

 Go Online For more Lesson Review Activities, go to glencoe.com.

Lesson 1: Why Alcohol Is Harmful **281**

Lesson 1 Review Answers

1. Alcohol is a drug produced by a chemical reaction in fruits, vegetables, and grains. Sentences will vary but should correctly use the term *alcohol.*

2. Alcohol harms health, is against the law for teens, and can lead to addiction.

3. *Any two:* to forget about problems, to look more mature, because movies portray drinking as "cool," peer pressure, to relax

4. *Sample answer:* Positive alternatives like sports encourage behavior that benefits a teen's physical, social, and mental/emotional health.

5. *Sample answer:* I should find another way home, because the brother has been drinking and riding with him would not be safe.

6. Ads will vary but should include teen-appropriate reasons not to drink and pictures to illustrate them.

FOCUS

Activating Prior Knowledge

What I Know Ask: What are some consequences of alcohol use? *addiction, loss of control* Tell students they will learn in this lesson about the effects of alcohol.

Guide to Reading

Building Vocabulary

■ Tell students that the prefix *mal-* means "inadequate, or not enough" and *nutrition* is "the process of taking in and using food." Ask: What do you think *malnutrition* means? *inadequate taking in and using of food*

■ Use Vocabulary PuzzleMaker to reinforce vocabulary terms.

Reading Strategy

Sequencing Students should name the mouth, esophagus, stomach, small intestine, liver, heart, and brain.

 Have students use their Foldables® as they read Lesson 2.

uick Write

Before they begin writing, point out to students that alcohol, like medications, can affect different people in various ways.

Reading Check

Answer the ability of the body to respond quickly and appropriately to situations

282

Short-Term Effects of Alcohol Use

 ## Guide to Reading

● **Building Vocabulary**
As you read this lesson, write each new highlighted term and its definition in your notebook.

■ reaction time (p. 282)
■ intoxication (p. 283)
■ blood alcohol content (BAC) (p. 283)
■ alcohol poisoning (p. 283)
■ malnutrition (p. 285)

● **Focusing on the Main Ideas**
In this lesson, you will learn to

■ **describe** how alcohol travels through the body.
■ **explain** the short-term effects alcohol has on a person.
■ **identify** factors that account for different reactions to alcohol among different people.

● **Reading Strategy**
Sequencing Using Figure 12.1, trace the course alcohol takes after it enters the body. Name the various organs it reaches.

FOLDABLES Study Organizer Use the Foldable® on p. 277 as you read this lesson.

Q *uick Write*

Write a paragraph describing how you think alcohol affects the body.

282 Chapter 12: Alcohol

Alcohol and the Body

Alcohol is a very fast-acting drug. It is quickly absorbed by the bloodstream and reaches the brain within 30 seconds after being swallowed. Alcohol absorption can be delayed if the person who drinks has eaten a heavy meal. Once alcohol reaches the brain, it slows reaction time. **Reaction time** is *the ability of the body to respond quickly and appropriately to situations.* This is what makes drinking and driving so deadly. People with slowed reaction time cannot respond quickly enough to dangers on the road.

Reading Check **Define** What is *reaction time*?

Intoxication

As you can see from the diagram in **Figure 12.1**, the liver's job is to break down alcohol once it enters the bloodstream. The liver breaks down approximately 95 percent of all alcohol consumed. The remaining 5 percent passes

◀ Alcohol consumption can cause delays in reaction time. **How can this make the activity in this picture very dangerous?**

Lesson 2 Resources

📁 **Chapter FAST FILE Resources**
Guided Reading and Writing 12-2
Concept Mapping Activity 12-2
Health Lab 12-2
Reteaching Activity 12-2
Enrichment Activity 12-2
Lesson Quiz 12-2

Technology
🔌 Transparency 12-2
Audio Summaries
ExamView® Assessment Suite
Vocabulary PuzzleMaker
StudentWorks™ Plus
G🌐 **Online**

▼ FIGURE 12.1

R ALCOHOL'S JOURNEY THROUGH THE BODY

Alcohol travels through the body, where it is filtered by the liver. **What effects can alcohol have on the liver?**

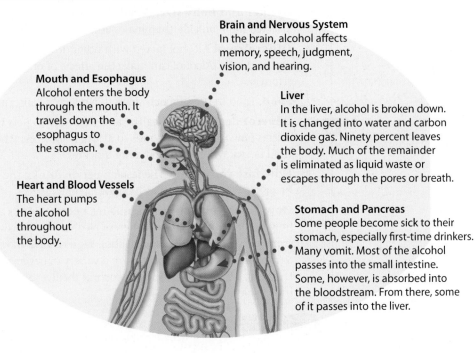

Brain and Nervous System
In the brain, alcohol affects memory, speech, judgment, vision, and hearing.

Mouth and Esophagus
Alcohol enters the body through the mouth. It travels down the esophagus to the stomach.

Liver
In the liver, alcohol is broken down. It is changed into water and carbon dioxide gas. Ninety percent leaves the body. Much of the remainder is eliminated as liquid waste or escapes through the pores or breath.

Heart and Blood Vessels
The heart pumps the alcohol throughout the body.

Stomach and Pancreas
Some people become sick to their stomach, especially first-time drinkers. Many vomit. Most of the alcohol passes into the small intestine. Some, however, is absorbed into the bloodstream. From there, some of it passes into the liver.

out of the body through sweat, urine, and breath. If the amount of alcohol a person drinks is more than what his or her body can tolerate, the person becomes intoxicated. **Intoxication** means *a person's mental and physical abilities have been impaired by alcohol.*

If a person continues to drink, his or her blood alcohol content will continue to rise. **Blood alcohol content (BAC)** is *a measure of the amount of alcohol present in a person's blood.* BAC is expressed as a percentage of the total amount of blood in the body. A BAC of 0.02 percent is enough to make most people feel lightheaded. A BAC of 0.08 percent is enough to make it dangerous for a person to drive a car. If a person has a BAC of 0.08 percent he or she is considered legally intoxicated.

People who are heavily intoxicated are at risk of alcohol poisoning. **Alcohol poisoning** is *a dangerous condition that results when a person drinks excessive amounts of alcohol over a short time period.* And as with any drug overdose, alcohol poisoning can kill you.

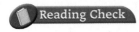 **Identify** What is the BAC of a legally drunk driver?

ACTIVITY
Connect To...
Language Arts

Intoxication

The word *intoxicate* contains the prefix *in-*, meaning "having or toward," and the suffix *–ate*, meaning "the action of." That leaves the root word, *toxic*. Look this root up in the dictionary.

Tell how this root's meaning relates to the terms intoxication and *alcohol poisoning*.

TECHNOLOGY AND HEALTH

High-Tech Alcohol Monitoring Worn as a bracelet, a new device called SCRAM (Secure Continuous Remote Alcohol Monitoring System) measures alcohol vapor in sweat on the skin. It is the first device to use transdermal testing to measure BAC. SCRAM gives reliable BAC readings every half hour, 24 hours a day. The data are stored in a memory chip inside the bracelet and uploaded to a computer via a modem. Available since 2003, SCRAM is used nationwide to monitor repeat DUI offenders and problem drinkers.

TEACH

R Reading Strategy

Analyzing a Graphic Refer students to **Figure 12.1**. Point out that alcohol reaches the brain very quickly because it starts being absorbed into the blood almost as soon as it enters the body. Ask: What organ processes or breaks down alcohol in the blood? *the liver* Explain that this is why many heavy drinkers develop serious liver problems. OL

ACTIVITY
Connect To...
Language Arts

Intoxication
Students will find that *toxic* means "poisonous." They might say that intoxication is a less severe form of alcohol poisoning.

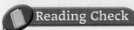 **Reading Check**

Answer 0.08%

Caption Answers

Photo Caption, p. 282
Slow reaction time could prevent the teen from being able to stop soon enough to avoid a collision and serious injury.
Figure Caption, this page
Alcohol can prevent the liver from working normally. Cirrhosis makes it difficult for the liver to remove poisons from the blood, which can damage the brain.

Reading Strategy

Finding the Main Idea Have students identify the main point of the description of how alcohol affects an individual. *There is no way to tell how a person will act.* **OL**

Reading Check

Answer Females and people with low weight are affected more quickly by alcohol.

Critical Thinking

Inferring Remind students that alcohol lowers inhibitions. Ask: How might lowered inhibitions increase the risk of a drinker becoming violent? *by making it harder for the drinker to hold back angry feelings* **OL**

Caption Answer

Figure Caption A 24-oz. beer equals two 5-oz. glasses of wine.

How Alcohol Affects the Individual

One of the greatest dangers of alcohol is that there is no way to tell how a person will act when alcohol is in his or her body. Several things determine the effect alcohol may have:

- **Gender and body size:** Females and smaller people are affected more quickly than males and larger people.

- **Other drugs:** Alcohol mixed with other drugs or medicines can be deadly. Alcohol can make the effects of other drugs stronger.

- **Food:** Food in the stomach slows down alcohol absorption.

- **General health:** How healthy and well rested a person is affects how the body responds to alcohol. Someone who is tired or sick will be affected more quickly.

- **How fast you drink:** The faster a person drinks, the more he or she will be affected by alcohol.

- **How much you drink:** The amount a person drinks affects how his or her body reacts. Different alcoholic beverages contain different amounts of alcohol. **Figure 12.2** shows a comparison of alcohol content in a variety of beverages. Drinking a lot or very quickly overworks the liver and causes intoxication.

Reading Check **Explain** What role does a drinker's weight and gender play in how he or she is affected?

▼ FIGURE 12.2

ALCOHOL CONTENT OF DIFFERENT DRINKS

Alcoholic drinks are only partly alcohol. The rest is water, flavoring, and minerals. Each of the drinks shown contains the same amount of alcohol—0.6 oz. of pure alcohol. **How much beer would a person need to drink to consume the same amount of alcohol in two 5 oz. glasses of wine?**

Beer
12 oz.

Wine
5 oz.

Liquor
1.5 oz.

HEALTH LITERACY

Alcohol and Violence Alcohol use increases the risk of all kinds of violence—homicides, assaults, date rapes, suicides. For example, almost 90 percent of homicides involve offenders who have been drinking. Alcohol's effects on the brain impair judgment and lower inhibitions, making drinkers more likely to misread other people's behaviors and less likely to control their own. Some people may also use alcohol as an excuse for acting out aggressive feelings.

Alcohol Use and Violence

Those who drink are more likely to fight or behave violently. This is because alcohol makes many people aggressive. Alcohol use can cause a great deal of violence both in and outside the home. Two-thirds of all domestic violence cases are related to alcohol abuse. Violence also increases at sporting events where alcohol is served.

Alcohol and Nutrition

Alcohol affects the body's ability to use nutrients. Long-term use of alcohol can lead to **malnutrition,** *a condition in which the body doesn't get the nutrients it needs to grow and function properly.* Because alcohol comes from the breakdown of sugar, it has calories. These calories have almost no nutritional value. When a person drinks alcohol for a long period of time and is not eating enough healthy food, he or she may not be getting enough nutrients. The calories in alcohol can also cause unwanted weight gain, especially when combined with other high-calorie beverages like soda and fruit juice.

Go Online

Visit **glencoe.com** and complete the Interactive Study Guide for Lesson 2.

ASSESS

Assessment Resources

Lesson Review Quiz
* *ExamView*
* Fast Files Activities
* Online Quizzes and Activities

Reteaching

● Assign Concept Map 12-2 or Reteaching Activity 12-2 in the Fast Files.
● Have pairs of students prepare and teach to one another a lesson on the short-term effects of alcohol.

Enrichment

● Assign Enrichment Activity 12-2 in the Fast Files.
● Ask students to research and give brief oral reports on the relationship between alcohol use and violence in teens.

CLOSE

Have students write a paragraph explaining why different people have different reactions to alcohol.

Lesson 2 Review

 After You Read

Review this lesson for new terms, major headings, and Reading Checks.

What I Learned

1. *Vocabulary* What is *blood alcohol content?*

2. *Recall* How long does it take alcohol to reach the brain of a person who has not eaten recently?

3. *Give Examples* List three factors that can influence the effect alcohol has on a person.

Thinking Critically

4. *Apply* Review alcohol's journey through the body in Figure 12.1. Explain why people who have been drinking might smell like alcohol.

5. *Analyze* Allie is at a party at a friend's house. She has had trouble sleeping lately because of worries over a big exam. Someone at the party suggests everyone have a beer. What are at least two good reasons Allie should say no?

Applying Health Skills

6. *Accessing Information* Some teens may believe myths about alcohol. With classmates, research several of these myths. Use your findings to create a poster showing the truths about these concepts.

Go Online For more Lesson Review Activities, go to **glencoe.com**.

Lesson 2: Short-Term Effects of Alcohol Use **285**

Lesson 2 Review Answers

1. Blood alcohol content is an indicator of the amount of alcohol present in a person's blood.
2. less than a minute
3. *Any three:* gender, body size, other drugs, food, health, how fast or how much you drink

4. Alcohol escapes from the body through the pores and breath.
5. Answers will vary but should include that it is illegal for teens, plus at least two negative effects of intoxication, such as interfering with her sleep and making her perform more poorly on the exam.

6. Give students a chance to brainstorm other myths about alcohol. (E.g., drinking alcohol will make you popular; or alcohol is less dangerous than illegal drugs.) Check that students use reliable sources when they research the myths.

FOCUS

Activating Prior Knowledge

What I Know Have students recall from Lesson 2 how alcohol travels through the body. Ask: What organs do you think might be harmed by long-term use of alcohol? *mouth, stomach, liver, brain* Tell students they will learn in this lesson how alcohol harms the body.

Guide to Reading

Building Vocabulary
- Explain that a *syndrome* is a condition defined by a cluster of many symptoms. Have students note the many symptoms of fetal alcohol syndrome as they read.
- Use Vocabulary PuzzleMaker to reinforce vocabulary terms.

Reading Strategy
Identifying Cause and Effect Students should list specific causes; for example, high blood pressure from damage to the heart muscle.

uick Write

Remind students that alcohol abuse endangers social and mental/emotional health as well as physical health. For example, alcohol use can make some teens experience radical mood swings.

Long-Term Effects of Alcohol Use

Guide to Reading

Building Vocabulary
Look at the terms below. Can you see how they might be related? Write down any relationships you see.
- fatty liver (p. 287)
- cirrhosis (p. 287)
- binge drinking (p. 289)
- inhibition (p. 289)
- fetal alcohol syndrome (FAS) (p. 290)

Focusing on the Main Ideas
In this lesson, you will learn to
- **identify** body organs and systems negatively affected by long-term alcohol use.
- **describe** the long-term effects of alcohol use.
- **explain** the risks to a fetus if its mother drinks alcohol.

Reading Strategy
Identifying Cause-and-Effect List the long-term effects caused by alcohol as described in the lesson.

uick Write

Write a short paragraph explaining what you know about the dangers of using alcohol.

Long-Term Physical Effects of Alcohol Use

Alcohol affects all areas of a person's life. Drinking alcohol regularly can lead to a number of serious health problems, including damage to major organs like the stomach, liver, pancreas, and heart. It can also worsen existing health problems. Research has shown that drinking alcohol as a teen can lead to long-lasting learning and memory problems.

Since alcohol is a depressant, it affects a person's emotional health. The more a person drinks, the more problems he or she is likely to have. Many people have mood changes when they drink. Those who are depressed often feel worse with alcohol in their bodies. The combination of alcohol and depression can lead a teen to commit suicide.

For some, alcohol can become addictive. This means that the person needs alcohol both physically and emotionally.

Alcohol and the Mouth

R Alcohol is not digested like other foods. It is absorbed by tissues lining the mouth and stomach, and goes directly into the blood. In some cases, people who drink large amounts of alcohol are more likely to develop mouth or throat cancer than people who don't drink alcohol.

 Chapter *FAST FILE* Resources
Guided Reading and Writing 12-3
Concept Mapping Activity 12-3
Decision-Making Activity 12-3
Reteaching Activity 12-3
Enrichment Activity 12-3
Lesson Quiz 12-3

Technology
Transparency 12-3
Audio Summaries
ExamView® Assessment Suite
Vocabulary PuzzleMaker
StudentWorks™ Plus
Go Online

Alcohol and the Stomach

Alcohol irritates the stomach lining and increases the amount of acid there. Extra acid makes the lining red and swollen, and can produce ulcers. Ulcers are sores that cause bleeding.

Drinking alcohol also weakens the valve that separates the stomach from the esophagus. This valve is like a door that prevents stomach acid from entering the esophagus. When the valve is weak, acid flows back into the esophagus and causes heartburn. Many people who drink regularly have ongoing heartburn.

◄ The picture on the left shows a normal liver. The one on the right shows one damaged by alcohol. **What can happen if your liver stops functioning?**

Alcohol and the Liver

One of the most serious effects of alcohol is damage to the liver. If alcohol is frequently in the blood, liver cells die. When this happens, **fatty liver** can develop. This is *a condition in which fats build up in the liver and cannot be broken down.* The increased amount of fat prevents the liver from working normally and from repairing itself.

A life-threatening problem also associated with heavy alcohol use is **cirrhosis.** This is *a disease characterized by scarring and eventual destruction of the liver.* The scarring from cirrhosis reduces blood flow in the liver. The damaged liver is unable to carry out one of its key functions—removing poisons from the blood. These poisons can eventually reach and damage the brain.

Alcohol and the Brain

Alcohol disrupts the parts of the brain responsible for memory and problem solving. Alcohol also destroys brain cells. Unlike many of the other kinds of cells in your body, brain cells do not grow back. Once you destroy them, they are gone forever. This damage can be serious enough to interfere with everyday functions.

Alcohol can also block messages that are sent to the brain. This can cause problems with movement, vision, and hearing.

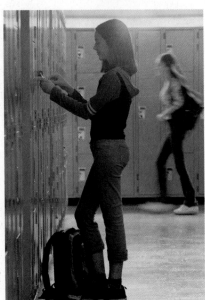

▼ Even simple acts can be difficult when intoxicated. **How might intoxication affect a person's daily activities?**

TEACH

R Reading Strategy

Organizing Information Have students use a variety of types of graphic organizers, such as outlines, concept maps, and spider diagrams, to organize the information about alcohol's effects on the mouth, liver, and stomach. Ask students to compare graphic organizers. Discuss which type of organizer best suits the organization of information in the text. **BL**

AL Active Learning

Posters Ask groups of students to make posters titled "The Brain on Alcohol." Posters should show images (readily available online) of brains of teen users and nonusers of alcohol. Give students a chance to share their posters with the class. They should explain how and why the images are different and how the differences affect brain function. **OL**

Caption Answers

Photo Caption, top Poisons cannot be removed from the blood, and they can eventually reach and damage the brain.
Photo Caption, bottom Alcohol disrupts memory and problem-solving.

HEALTH LITERACY

Alcohol and Medications Many drugs, both prescription and over-the-counter (OTC), interact with alcohol and create health risks, even in moderate drinkers. Alcohol and
- acetaminophen can cause potentially life-threatening liver damage.
- aspirin or ibuprofen can increase the risk of stomach ulcers and bleeding.
- antihistamines can increase sedation and make it dangerous to drive or operate machinery.
- benzodiazepines, including the date rape drug Rohypnol, can increase sedation and impair memory.

287

Reading Strategy

Analyzing a Graphic Ask students to look at the graph in **Figure 12.3**. Tell students that all 50 states and the District of Columbia have so-called *zero-tolerance* laws, prohibiting people under age 21 from driving with a blood alcohol content (BAC) greater than 0.00% to 0.02%. Ask students to use the data in the figure to justify zero-tolerance laws. OL

Reading Check

Answer ulcerations and heartburn

U Universal Access

Gifted Students Have students create a political campaign commercial against drunk driving that includes a creative rap or song, a poster, and data that supports their argument. The commercial should convince the viewers that drunk driving is a danger to everyone. If possible, videotape the commercials and send them to local politicians. AL

Caption Answer

Figure Caption Do not drink; do not ride in a car with a driver who has been drinking.

Alcohol and the Heart

Heavy drinking damages the heart muscle, causing the heart to become weakened and enlarged, and leads to high blood pressure. It increases the risk of congestive heart failure and stroke. Heavy drinking also raises the levels of some fats in the blood.

Reading Check **List** Name two problems of the stomach related to long-term alcohol use.

Driving While Intoxicated

As stated earlier, *a person with a BAC of 0.08 percent* is considered legally intoxicated or drunk. If the person is also driving a car, he or she is said to be driving while intoxicated (DWI).

A devastating long-term consequence of driving while intoxicated is causing your own death or the death of another. On average, someone is killed in a crash involving alcohol every 31 minutes. In 2005, over 16,000 people were killed in alcohol-related crashes. That accounts for 39 percent of all traffic deaths that year. Remember, the driver is not the only person at risk. Passengers, pedestrians, and other drivers are all potential victims of a person who is DWI.

People who are DWI are more likely to die in a fatal crash than sober drivers. **Figure 12.3** shows a numerical link between the amount of alcohol in a driver's blood and the likelihood of a deadly accident occurring.

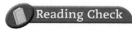 **FIGURE 12.3**

Traffic Deaths and BAC

About three in every ten Americans will be involved in an alcohol-related crash at some time in their lives. **How can you reduce your risk of being involved in an alcohol-related crash?**

Likelihood of Fatal Crash for Drivers Aged 21–34

Source: U.S. Dept. of Transportation, 2000.

Cultural Perspectives

Binge Drinking Binge drinking is increasing among teens in Europe as well as the United States, but there appear to be cultural differences in this trend. Northern Europe has much higher rates of teen binge drinking than southern Europe. For example, about 35 percent of 15- to 24-year-olds in Denmark binge drink three or more times a week, compared with about 7 percent in Italy. Experts think the rates of binge drinking reflect cultural attitudes toward alcohol.

◄ Binge drinking can prevent teens from reaching their long-term goals. **What are some other effects of binge drinking?**

Binge Drinking

Teens who experiment with alcohol also risk becoming binge drinkers. **Binge drinking** is *the consumption of a large quantity of alcohol in a very short period of time.* Although binge drinking is dangerous at any age, it is a special problem for teens.

Binge drinking is harmful because of the potential long-term consequences. Since teens frequently combine high-risk activities with binge drinking, their potential for death or serious injury is very high. Some of the dangers include:

- Death due to falls, drowning, or drunk driving
- Pregnancy or contraction of sexually transmitted diseases due to sexual activity
- Being a victim of violent behavior
- Death from alcohol poisoning

 Reading Check **Define** What is *binge drinking*?

Alcohol Use and Teen Pregnancy

Unplanned pregnancies are sometimes a long-term consequence of alcohol use. Using alcohol can lower a person's inhibitions and affects the ability to make healthy decisions. An **inhibition** is *a conscious or unconscious restraint of a person's own behaviors or actions.* Many inhibitions are normal and healthy because they prevent people from taking dangerous risks.

When using alcohol, people are much more likely to say and do things they normally would not. The things that they say and do could negatively affect their future. Teen pregnancy is a very serious and long-lasting result of lowered inhibitions.

 Go Online

Visit **glencoe.com** and complete the Interactive Study Guide for Lesson 3.

Lesson 3: Long-Term Effects of Alcohol Use **289**

HEALTH LITERACY

Fetal Alcohol Syndrome FAS is the most severe of a group of alcohol-related disorders in infants that together are called fetal alcohol spectrum disorders (FASD). Symptoms of FASD may include brain damage, mental retardation, learning disabilities, hyperactivity, facial deformities, and problems with memory, hearing, vision, and growth. FASD affects about 1 percent of all live births in the United States. Alcohol causes more preventable birth defects and mental retardation than any other factor.

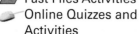
Reading Check

Answer lower birth weight, mental retardation, heart and kidney problems

ASSESS

Assessment Resources

Lesson Review Quiz
⊙ *ExamView*
▢ Fast Files Activities
🖱 Online Quizzes and Activities

Reteaching

● Assign Concept Map 12-3 or Reteaching Activity 12-3 in the Fast Files. ▢
● Have students make posters illustrating long-term effects of alcohol use.

Enrichment

● Assign Enrichment Activity 12-3 in the Fast Files. ▢
● Ask pairs of students to debate whether women who drink during pregnancy should be punished or treated.

CLOSE

Ask students to justify the statement, "Alcohol use can impact all areas of your life."

Caption Answer

Photo Caption to remind people to make healthy choices

1.5L
CONTAINS SULFITES

GOVERNMENT WARNING:
(1) ACCORDING TO THE SURGEON GENERAL, WOMEN SHOULD NOT DRINK ALCOHOLIC BEVERAGES DURING PREGNANCY BECAUSE OF THE RISK OF BIRTH DEFECTS. (2) CONSUMPTION OF ALCOHOLIC BEVERAGES IMPAIRS YOUR ABILITY TO DRIVE A CAR OR OPERATE MACHINERY, AND MAY CAUSE HEALTH PROBLEMS.

▲ Signs like this appear in some restaurants and other locations where alcohol is available. **Why do you think it is important to post these types of warning labels?**

Pregnancy among teens is usually unplanned. One study of female teens with unplanned pregnancies found that one-third had been using alcohol.

An unplanned pregnancy complicates a teen's life. It can disrupt long-term plans and goals, such as going to college. Most teens are not prepared emotionally or financially to be parents. For this reason, pregnancy can be very difficult for teens.

Fetal Alcohol Syndrome

When a female is pregnant, everything she eats and drinks affects her unborn baby. This includes alcohol, which is passed into the baby's blood. A baby's liver is not developed enough to break down alcohol. Therefore, when an unborn baby is exposed to alcohol, it can develop **fetal alcohol syndrome (FAS).** FAS is *a group of alcohol-related birth defects that include both physical and mental problems*. Babies with FAS can have smaller body sizes, lower birth weight, and other problems. Babies with FAS frequently develop problems with their hearts and kidneys as well. Because alcohol limits the supply of oxygen to the baby's brain, learning disabilities and mental retardation can also occur.

Reading Check

List What are some health problems that occur in babies with FAS?

Lesson 3 Review

After You Read

Review this lesson for new terms, major headings, and Reading Checks.

What I Learned

1. *Vocabulary* What is *cirrhosis*? What are the long-term risks associated with this health problem?

2. *Explain* How are three body organs or systems negatively affected by long-term alcohol use?

3. *Recall* What are the risks to the fetus of a pregnant female who uses alcohol?

Thinking Critically

4. *Hypothesize* What are some ways in which experimenting with alcohol can interfere with a teen's future?

5. *Apply* At a party, Cindy sees a pregnant female reach for a beer. What could Cindy say to help the woman understand the health risks of drinking during pregnancy?

Applying Health Skills

6. *Practicing Healthy Behaviors* Some people say that alcohol helps them relax and sleep better. Make a list of things you could do that would help your body relax and sleep better without using alcohol.

Go Online For more Lesson Review Activities, go to glencoe.com.

Lesson 3 Review Answers

1. a disease characterized by scarring and eventual destruction of the liver. The liver will fail and poisons will damage the brain.
2. *Any three:* mouth—greater risk of cancer; stomach—ulcerations, heartburn; liver—fatty liver, cirrhosis; nervous system—brain and CNS damage; circulatory system—heart damage, high blood pressure, greater risk of heart failure or stroke
3. The fetus may develop fetal alcohol syndrome, with symptoms such as low birth weight and mental retardation.
4. It can lead to addiction, cause serious health problems, and increase the risk of violent behavior, injuries, and death.
5. The alcohol the mother drinks ends up in the baby's blood, and the baby's liver cannot break it down.
6. Go for a walk, take deep breaths, read a book.

Lesson 4

Alcoholism and Alcohol Abuse

Guide to Reading

● **Building Vocabulary**
Read the terms below and try to define them. Write your definitions in pencil and make any changes that are needed as you read this lesson.

■ addiction (p. 291)
■ alcoholism (p. 291)
■ tolerance (p. 292)
■ physical dependence (p. 292)
■ enablers (p. 294)
■ alcohol abuse (p. 295)

● **Focusing on the Main Ideas**
In this lesson, you will learn to

■ **identify** symptoms of alcoholism and alcohol abuse.
■ **describe** the stages of alcoholism.
■ **explain** how alcoholism affects families and society.

● **Reading Strategy**
Sequencing As you read the lesson, be aware of the progression of alcoholism. Make notes about what occurs at each stage of the problem.

 Quick Write
Make a list of all the reasons you can think of to avoid alcohol use.

Alcohol's Addictive Power

One of the biggest problems with alcohol is that it is habit-forming. Like other drugs, using alcohol repeatedly can lead to **addiction.** This is *a physical or psychological need for a drug.* Teens 15 and younger are four times more likely to become addicted than older individuals.

An addiction to any drug can change a person's life. It takes the focus off of healthy goals and damages relationships with family and friends. In the following lessons, you will learn more about the dangers of alcohol addiction, and about where people can turn for help.

The Disease of Alcoholism

People who are addicted to alcohol suffer from alcoholism. **Alcoholism** is *a progressive, chronic disease involving a mental and physical need for alcohol.* People with alcoholism are called *alcoholics.* The disease affects all parts of an alcoholic's life—physical, mental, emotional, and social. Currently, an estimated 14 million Americans are alcoholics or have an alcohol abuse problem.

Lesson 4: Alcoholism and Alcohol Abuse **291**

FOCUS

Activating Prior Knowledge

What I Know Ask students to complete the following sentence: "Alcoholics are people who [blank]." Sample answers: *drink too much, can't stop drinking* Tell students they will learn about alcoholism in this lesson.

Guide to Reading

Building Vocabulary
■ Ask students to predict how the terms *alcoholism, physical dependence,* and *alcohol abuse* are related. (Alcoholism includes a physical dependence on alcohol; alcohol abuse does not.) Have students check to see if their predictions were correct when they read the lesson.
■ Use Vocabulary PuzzleMaker to reinforce vocabulary terms.

Reading Strategy
Sequencing Suggest that students create a flow chart of the stages of alcoholism. As they read, they can add notes to the flow chart about what occurs at each stage.

Quick Write
Students may wish to scan the heads in this lesson for ideas for their Quick Writes.

Lesson 4 Resources

📁 **Chapter** *FAST FILE* **Resources**
Guided Reading and Writing 12-4
Concept Mapping Activity 12-4
Cross-Curriculum Activity 12-4
Reteaching Activity 12-4
Enrichment Activity 12-4
Lesson Quiz 12-4

Technology
⚓ Transparency 12-4
💿 Audio Summaries
💿 *ExamView®* Assessment Suite
💿 Vocabulary PuzzleMaker
💿 StudentWorks™ Plus

 Go Online

TEACH

Reading Strategy

Analyzing a Graphic Call on students to describe an example of each symptom in **Figure 12.4**. For example, for making excuses to drink, they might describe using an achievement (winning a game) or disappointment (losing a game) as an excuse to drink. **OL**

Reading Check

Answer Physical dependence is a type of addiction in which the body itself feels a direct need for a drug.

Academic Vocabulary

Displays Have students read and discuss the definition and example sentence. Then ask a volunteer to look up *display* in a thesaurus and read aloud the first five synonyms. Have other volunteers repeat the example sentence, using the synonyms in place of *displays*. You will find academic vocabulary activities in the Student Activities Workbook. 📁

Caption Answer

Figure Caption *Sample answer:* Try to convince the person to get help.

Millions more take part in risky drinking that could lead to mental, emotional, and health problems. People with this disease typically have five major symptoms:

- **Denial.** The person has a hard time believing they have a problem. They are usually the last to admit they need help.
- **Craving.** The person has a strong need, or compulsion, to drink.
- **Loss of control.** The person is unable to limit his or her drinking on any given occasion.
- **Tolerance.** A person who drinks regularly can develop a tolerance. **Tolerance** is *a process in which your body needs more and more of a drug to get the same effect.* For alcoholics, tolerance means needing to drink more and more in order to feel the effects of intoxication.
- **Physical dependence.** This is *a type of addiction in which the body itself feels a direct need for a drug.* If the person stops drinking abruptly, he or she may experience symptoms, such as sweating, shakiness, and anxiety.

Figure 12.4 lists some other symptoms associated with alcoholism. If you know someone who **displays** some of these symptoms, encourage him or her to get help.

Academic Vocabulary

displays (di SPLEYZ) *(verb)* shows. *If someone you know displays signs of depression, talk to a trusted adult immediately.*

Reading Check

Define What is *physical dependence?*

▼ **FIGURE 12.4**

COMMON SYMPTOMS OF ALCOHOLISM

As shown, alcohol affects all areas of life and leads to negative consequences to your physical, mental/emotional, and social health. **What should you do if you think that someone you are close to has an alcohol-related problem?**

- Drinking alone
- Making excuses to drink
- Need for daily or frequent use of alcohol in order to function
- Lack of control over drinking, with inability to stop or reduce the amount of alcohol being consumed

- Episodes of violence associated with drinking
- Secretive behavior to hide alcohol-related behavior
- Hostility when confronted about drinking
- Neglecting to eat regularly

- Neglecting to take care of physical appearance
- Nausea and vomiting
- Shaking in the morning
- Abdominal pain
- Numbness and tingling
- Confusion

Source: National Institutes of Health

HEALTH LITERACY

Alcohol Abuse and the Teen Brain Results of several recent studies suggest that alcohol abuse is much more dangerous for teens than previously thought. The studies reveal that the teen brain still is developing and therefore much more susceptible to damage by alcohol than the adult brain. In teens who binge drink, alcohol interferes with normal development of the part of the brain called the hippocampus and causes permanent problems with verbal abilities, learning, memory, and spatial perception.

Stages of Alcoholism

There are four stages of alcoholism. They develop over a period of time. Each stage can be long or short, depending on the individual and the age at which he or she begins drinking.

Stage One

Most people in the first stage are surprised by how much they can drink. Other symptoms of this first stage include:

- Drinking to relax or get relief from stress and mental fatigue
- Looking for opportunities to drink
- A gradual increase in tolerance

Stage Two

In the second stage, the person has short-term memory loss and blackouts. These are periods of time the alcoholic cannot remember. Other symptoms include:

- Saying or doing hurtful things
- Sneaking extra drinks and feeling guilty
- Making excuses for drinking

Stage Three

In stage three, the alcoholic loses control. He or she cannot predict what will happen. For example, though the alcoholic intends to have only one drink, he or she cannot stop after just one. The alcoholic's body depends on the drug. Other symptoms include:

- Aggressive or resentful behavior
- Making and failing to keep promises
- Losing interest in anything but alcohol
- Avoiding family and friends
- Trouble with money, work, and the law
- Tremors and the start of severe physical problems

Stage Four

The fourth and final stage is chronic, or ongoing. Up until now, the alcoholic may have been able to keep a job. Now, however, he or she lives to drink, and drinking can go on all day. Symptoms include:

- Long periods of being intoxicated all the time
- Strange or unreasonable fears
- Faulty thinking or hallucinations
- Malnutrition caused by not eating properly

Reading Check **Explain** What problems and behaviors occur during stage two of the disease of alcoholism?

▲ Alcoholism is a disease that can shatter a person's entire life and disrupt the lives of those around him or her. **How widespread is this disease in the United States?**

Go Online

Topic: Speaking Out About Alcohol

Visit **glencoe.com** for Student Web Activities to learn about the effects of alcohol and what teens around the country are doing to encourage their peers not to drink.

Activity: Using the information provided at the link above, write a letter to the editor of your local newspaper suggesting ways that underage drinking can be prevented in your community.

U Universal Access

English Learners Provide examples of concept maps and explain how they are used. Include a word bank that helps students organize the different stages of alcoholism. Suggest that students draw their own concept maps to depict their understanding of the stages. **EL**.

W Writing Support

Narrative Writing Ask pairs of students to write a dialogue between an alcoholic and a family member. Make sure all four stages of alcoholism are covered. After the dialogues, ask students to summarize how alcoholism affects the family members of alcoholics. **OL**

Reading Check

Answer saying or doing hurtful things, sneaking extra drinks, feelings of guilt, making excuses for drinking

Go Online

Speaking Out About Alcohol Remind students to proofread and correct their letters. Post completed letters in the classroom or on the school's Web site.

Caption Answer

Photo Caption 14 million Americans suffer from alcoholism.

⚬ What Teens Want to Know ⚬

How can I tell if a friend has a drinking problem? Answer the following four questions. If you answer yes to even one of them, the person may have a drinking problem, and you should notify a parent or other trusted adult.

- Does the person get annoyed if you criticize his or her drinking?
- Does the person ever start drinking first thing in the morning?
- Does the person feel that he or she drinks too much?
- Does the person ever express guilt about drinking? **OL**

Alcohol Abuse Counselor Ask students: Why do alcohol abuse counselors need good speaking skills? Why do they need good listening skills? Have a pair of students go to **glencoe.com**, and read about the skills an alcohol abuse counselor needs.

📖 **Reading Check**

Answer Enabling means making excuses for or lying on behalf of the alcoholic.

AL Active Learning

Small Group Learning Divide the class into small groups, and ask students to brainstorm situations in which family members might enable an alcoholic to keep drinking alcohol. **OL**

C Critical Thinking

Inferring Ask: What are some reasons alcohol abuse costs society so much money? *Sample answers: Alcohol abuse causes higher medical bills, lost wages, higher insurance premiums, and greater police and court costs.* **AL**

Caption Answer

Photo Caption *Sample answer:* It creates an unhealthy cycle of dependency between the alcoholic and the enabler.

ACTIVITY
Careers for the 21st Century

Alcohol Abuse Counselor

An alcohol abuse counselor helps alcoholics recover from their addiction. These professionals give emotional support and show patients how to stay alcohol free. There will always be a demand for alcohol abuse counselors because alcoholics need professional guidance and support to overcome their addiction. If you are interested in becoming an alcohol abuse counselor, you should practice your communication skills. Alcohol abuse counselors need to be good speakers and listeners.

What skills does an alcohol abuse counselor need? Go to *Career Corner* at **glencoe.com** to find out.

▶ Speaking honestly to a family member about an alcohol problem is better than trying to hide the problem. **How** **AL** **can enabling be harmful to both an alcoholic and family members?**

Costs to the Family

Alcoholism affects others apart from the alcoholic. Denial—the biggest symptom of this disease—is a problem for family and friends as well. Often they don't believe the drinker has a problem. They think he or she just needs to stop drinking or cut down. Family members often neglect their own needs to focus on helping the alcoholic. This can have a very negative effect on self-esteem, especially if the alcoholic is abusive to family members.

In some families, members who try to help the alcoholic make the problem worse by becoming enablers. **Enablers** are *persons who create an atmosphere in which the alcoholic can comfortably continue his or her unacceptable behavior.* Enabling includes making excuses for or lying on behalf of the alcoholic. Enablers believe that these actions help, but they do not. An unhealthy cycle of dependency develops between the alcoholic and the enabler. This cycle prevents the alcoholic from getting treatment for his or her disease. **AL**

📖 **Reading Check** **Define** What is *enabling*?

Costs to Society

Alcohol's cost to the national economy is very high. Underage drinking costs society more than 50 billion dollars a year. The total cost of alcohol-related problems is approximately 175.9 billion dollars a year. That's more than the total cost of smoking or other drug-related problems. Alcohol-related problems also cost businesses billions of dollars a year in lost productivity. Productivity is how much work a person does when he or she is on the job. **C**

 Home, School, and Community

In the Community Many community-based programs for teens have been shown to be effective in decreasing alcohol abuse.

● Project Northland, which includes peer leadership and parental involvement.
● All Stars, which promotes development of positive personal characteristics.

● Across Ages, which strengthens bonds between adults and youth.

Find out if your community has such a program. If not, ask students to write letters to editors of local newspapers and to local government leaders urging them to adopt an alcohol-prevention program for teens. **OL**

Alcohol Abuse

Although the terms *alcoholism* and *alcohol abuse* are sometimes used interchangeably, there is a difference. People who abuse alcohol are not physically dependent on the drug. Rather, **alcohol abuse** is *a pattern of drinking that results in one or more well-defined behaviors within a 12-month period.* The four symptoms are:

- Failure to fulfill major work, school, or home responsibilities.
- Drinking in situations that are physically dangerous. For example, driving while intoxicated, or riding in a car driven by someone who is drinking alcohol.
- Having ongoing alcohol-related legal problems. These may include arrests for DWI or physically hurting someone while drunk.
- Continuing to drink even when relationships have been negatively affected by the person's use of alcohol.

 Reading Check **Identify** Name a behavior associated with alcohol abuse.

Go Online
Visit **glencoe.com** and complete the Interactive Study Guide for Lesson 4.

 Reading Check

Answer *Any one:* failure to fulfill responsibilities; drinking in dangerous situations; alcohol-related legal problems; continuing to drink even when relationships have been damaged

ASSESS

Assessment Resources

Lesson Review Quiz
ExamView
Fast Files Activities
Online Quizzes and Activities

Reteaching

- Assign Concept Map 12-4 or Reteaching Activity 12-4 in the Fast Files.
- Have students write a short story about alcohol abuse in which they correctly use vocabulary terms.

Enrichment

- Assign Enrichment Activity 12-4 in the Fast Files.
- Ask students to put on a puppet show that demonstrates enabling of an alcoholic.

CLOSE

Have students chart the stages of alcoholism and include at least two symptoms of each stage.

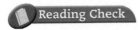
Lesson 4 Review

After You Read

Review this lesson for new terms, major headings, and Reading Checks.

What I Learned

1. *Vocabulary* Define *alcoholism*.

2. *Explain* What is the difference between alcohol abuse and alcoholism?

3. *Describe* Briefly describe the four stages of alcoholism.

Thinking Critically

4. *Analyze* Over the past year, Andrew has secretly been drinking alcohol. He has missed a lot of school and has been in trouble with the law. Would you say Andrew is an alcoholic? Explain your answer.

5. *Synthesize* You are at a friend's house. You overhear your friend's father say,

"I do *not* have a drinking problem." Your friend looks uncomfortable, then says, "He really doesn't have a problem, you know." What kind of behavior is your friend demonstrating?

Applying Health Skills

6. *Stress Management* Some people use alcohol to relieve stress. Make a list of healthy activities a person can do to manage stress without the use of alcohol. As a class, compile the best ideas into a brochure on stress-management techniques. Share copies of your brochure with family and friends.

Go Online For more Lesson Review Activities, go to **glencoe.com**.

Lesson 4: Alcoholism and Alcohol Abuse **295**

Lesson 4 Review Answers

1. a progressive, chronic disease involving a mental and physical need for alcohol
2. People who abuse alcohol are not physically dependent on the drug, as people with alcoholism are.
3. Students should describe each of the four stages of alcoholism listed on page 293.

4. Students might say Andrew is an alcoholic, because drinking alcohol secretly is a symptom of alcoholism.
5. Students are likely to say that the friend is in denial or lying about her father's alcoholism and is enabling his behavior.

6. Students should list stress- and time-management activities, such as exercising, talking to a friend, getting organized, and learning to say no. Give students a chance to compare ideas and select the best ideas for their booklet or Web site.

FOCUS

Activating Prior Knowledge

What I Know Ask: Is the following statement a myth or fact? "Alcoholism can be cured." *myth* Tell students they will learn in this lesson that alcoholism can be treated even though it cannot be cured.

Guide to Reading

Building Vocabulary
- Explain that *intervention* means "coming between in order to hinder." Have students predict what *intervention* means in the context of helping an alcoholic.
- Use Vocabulary PuzzleMaker to reinforce vocabulary terms.

Reading Strategy
Predicting Remind students to read the picture captions before they write their predictions. Predictions might include sources of help for alcoholics and their families and the nature of recovery from alcoholism.

Quick Write

Caution students not to give the names of the people they list. Instead, they can just write *teacher, minister, friend,* and so on. Qualities might include being caring and wanting to help.

Getting Help for Alcohol Abuse

Guide to Reading

● Building Vocabulary
As you read this lesson, write each new highlighted term and its definition in your notebook.
- intervention (p. 296)
- relapse (p. 296)
- recovery (p. 297)
- withdrawal (p. 297)
- detoxification (p. 297)

● Focusing on the Main Ideas
In this lesson, you will learn to
- **explain** what a person experiences during withdrawal from alcohol.
- **describe** the steps in the process of recovery.
- **identify** community resources that can help alcoholics, alcohol abusers, and their families.

● Reading Strategy
Predicting Based on the headings and photos in this lesson, describe what you think you will learn from reading it.

Quick Write

Name a person you turn to when you need help with a problem. Write a brief description of qualities this person has, such as good listening skills.

Help for People with Alcohol Problems

People who are struggling with alcohol use need help. However, many of them may be in denial. Being in denial means refusing to admit a problem with alcohol. To overcome this obstacle, family and friends can hold an intervention. An **intervention** is *a gathering in which family and friends get the problem drinker to agree to seek help.* The drinker is confronted with the facts of his or her problem and strongly urged to stop drinking.

Starting Down the Road to Recovery

Treatment for alcoholism begins with the alcoholic's understanding that he or she has an addiction and must never drink again. If an alcoholic takes even one drink, there is the chance that he or she will have a relapse. A **relapse** is *a return to the use of a drug after attempting to stop.*

◀ Counseling can help a person recover from alcohol abuse. **What are some organizations that provide this type of counseling?**

Lesson 5 Resources

📁 **Chapter FAST FILE Resources**
Guided Reading and Writing 12-5
Concept Mapping Activity 12-5
Decision-Making Activity 12-5
Reteaching Activity 12-5
Enrichment Activity 12-5
Lesson Quiz 12-5

Technology
👆 Transparency 12-5
Audio Summaries
ExamView® Assessment Suite
Vocabulary PuzzleMaker
StudentWorks™ Plus
 G● Online

Recovery starts only after the alcoholic makes the **commitment** never to drink again. **Recovery** is *the process of learning to live an alcohol-free life,* and is usually long and difficult. The alcoholic must cope with the symptoms of withdrawal that occur when he or she stops drinking. **Withdrawal** is *the physical and psychological reactions that occur when someone stops using an addictive substance.* These can be mild to very severe and include headaches, tiredness, strong mood swings, and nausea.

Steps Along the Road

The road to recovery consists of a number of steps. Every person who wants to get better must take all the steps. There are no shortcuts. The steps to recovery are as follows:

- **Admission.** At the start of recovery, the person must admit that he or she has an addiction and ask for help.
- **Counseling.** Alcoholics need outside help from counselors and support groups to recover. Many people find the group Alcoholics Anonymous (AA) helpful. AA is an organization that is made up entirely of recovering alcoholics. They all know from firsthand experience how difficult it can be to break an alcohol addiction.
- **Detoxification.** This is *the physical process of freeing the body of an addictive substance.*
- **Resolution.** Once recovery has begun, the alcoholic resolves or makes the decision to accept responsibility for his or her actions. It is time to move forward, and the person is now referred to as a *recovering alcoholic.* A recovering alcoholic is someone who has an addiction to alcohol but chooses to live without alcohol.

Reading Check **Explain** What makes recovery from alcoholism so difficult?

 Support groups are available to teens with an alcoholic in their family. **What are the benefits of joining such a group?**

Lesson 5: Getting Help for Alcohol Abuse **297**

Academic Vocabulary

commitment (kuh MIT muhnt) *(noun)* a promise. *Julian and Lupe made a commitment to their physical health by running 2 miles, every day.*

TEACH

Academic Vocabulary

Commitment Have volunteers read the definition and the example sentence aloud to the class. Then ask: What is the difference between deciding never to drink again and making a commitment never to drink again? Why is this difference important to beginning recovery? You will find academic vocabulary activities in the Student Activities Workbook. 📁

C Critical Thinking

Justifying Ask students to justify the statement, "Recovery from alcoholism is a lifelong process." Sample answer: *Recovering alcoholics still have the disease, so they can never drink again without risk of relapse.* OL

Reading Check

Answer The alcoholic must cope with withdrawal symptoms.

Caption Answers

Photo Caption, p. 296 Names of organizations are listed on page 298. Answer may also include religious groups, schools, and community services.
Photo Caption, this page It can provide support and information and teach them coping skills.

✴ Promoting Coordinated School Health

Programs to Reduce Alcohol Use Advocate adopting a program in your school to reduce alcohol use in students. Many programs have been shown to work, such as:
- Project Alert: a fourteen-lesson curriculum that teaches resistance skills and negative attitudes toward drugs.

- *Keepin' it REAL:* a ten-lesson, culturally sensitive curriculum that teaches communication and life skills to resist negative peer influences.
- Project Achieve: a set of schoolwide programs to improve staff effectiveness, school safety, and all student development.

Health Skills Activity

Communication Skills

When Communication Counts Most

Use the following to help students complete the activity:

- Partners should brainstorm and then write a dialogue that incorporates the best ideas.
- Remind students to use nonverbal communication, such as eye contact, as well as spoken lines.
- Allow class time for the role-plays.

AL Active Learning

Brochures Have students learn more about Alateen and make brochures conveying the most important information to other teens, including the purpose of the organization and information on local contacts and meetings. Urge students to make their brochures attractive and easy to read. Arrange for them to place their brochures in locations throughout the school. OL

 Reading Check

Answer, p. 299 Avoid parties or other events where alcohol will be served; choose friends who do not drink alcohol and will support your decision to be alcohol free.

Health Skills Activity

Communication Skills

When Communication Counts Most

If a friend or family member has a problem with alcohol, you may be able to help. Here's how.

- **Have an honest talk with the drinker.** Choose a time when the person is sober. Make eye contact and talk honestly about your concerns. Tell him or her about the serious effects alcohol can have on a person's physical, mental, and emotional health.
- **Encourage the person to seek help.** After expressing your concerns, explain why support is needed. Ask the person to get help.
- **Offer information.** Finally, provide useful information about where the person can go for help. Facts and details are important at this stage. Make sure that the person understands what kind of help is available and how to get it.

With a Group

Role-play a conversation in which you use the skills outlined above. Think about specific words that would express your concern and encourage the person to get help.

Help for the Family

AL The families of alcoholics need to recover from the effects of living with alcoholism as well. This is especially true when members of the family have been enablers. There are several organizations that offer help. One well-known example is Al-Anon. This nonprofit group teaches family and friends about alcoholism and helps them understand how they have been affected. It also teaches them skills for coping with the many problems alcoholism creates. Another group that exists within Al-Anon is Alateen. It is specially designed to help teens deal with alcoholic parents. Both groups do community outreach work as well. They educate the public and direct families to counselors, support groups, and mental health facilities.

 Go Online

Visit glencoe.com and complete the Interactive Study Guide for Lesson 5.

Ways to Stay Alcohol Free

You have learned that alcohol use can damage a teen's physical, mental/emotional, and social health. The best way to avoid these risks is to choose to be alcohol free. Avoid situations where

---

Home, School, and Community

In the Community If your community has Alateen or Al-Anon meetings (and most do), encourage any students who are affected by another's drinking problem to attend. Tell students that there are no dues or fees and meetings are always confidential. Members do not have to speak at meetings, just listen and learn. Everyone at the meetings has the same problem—drinking by a family member or friend—and they give each other understanding, help, and support. Have students locate meetings of Alcoholics Anonymous and youth groups in your community.

◀ Staying alcohol free involves knowing how to say no to high-risk situations, like the teen in this picture is doing. **What refusal skills do you use to abstain from high-risk situations?**

alcohol may be present. Choose friends who are alcohol free. They will support your decision not to use alcohol.

If you find yourself in a situation in which you feel pressured to try alcohol, use refusal skills. Practice the S.T.O.P. strategy discussed in Chapter 2. State your decision clearly and assertively. When you speak assertively, you are letting people know you are serious. If the pressure continues, walk away. If needed, get help from a parent or other adult.

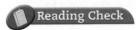 **Reading Check**   **Identify** What are some ways to stay alcohol free?

Lesson 5 Review

 After You Read

Review this lesson for new terms, major headings, and Reading Checks.

What I Learned

1. *Vocabulary* Define *withdrawal*.

2. *List* Name the steps in the recovery process.

3. *Identify* What community organizations are available to help alcoholics and their families?

Thinking Critically

4. *Evaluate* What is the one fact about alcohol addiction you think a problem drinker needs to know most?

5. *Apply* Imagine that a friend admits to having a drinking problem. The way he plans to handle the problem is to gradually cut down on his drinking. Is this a wise plan? Why or why not?

Applying Health Skills

6. *Goal Setting* Think about personal goals you have. Write one or two of these down on a sheet of paper, leaving space under each one. In the spaces, explain how using alcohol could interfere with your goals.

Go Online   For more Lesson Review Activities, go to **glencoe.com**.

Lesson 5: Getting Help for Alcohol Abuse   **299**

Lesson 5 Review Answers

1. the physical and psychological reactions that occur when someone stops using an addictive substance
2. admission, counseling, detoxification, resolution
3. Al-Anon and Alateen

4. *Sample answers:* Alcoholics need help. Alcoholics must never drink again. Alcoholism can be treated.
5. This is not a wise plan, because treatment for alcoholism begins with the alcoholic's understanding that he or she has an addiction and must never drink again.

6. Goals will vary. Alcohol might interfere with goals by getting students in trouble with the law, preventing them from graduating, or causing a car crash.

299

Building Health Skills
Helping Someone Get Help

Skill

Decision Making

Activating Prior Knowledge

Ask: What clues might tell you that a friend has a drinking problem? *Sample answers: The friend is hanging out with other teens who drink, missing a lot of school, or acting guilty about drinking.*

- **Objective** After completing the activity, students will be able to make decisions about helping someone get help for an alcohol problem.
- **Time** 45 minutes
- **Materials** paper, pencil

Teacher Classroom Resources

📁 Building Health Skills
🖲 Transparency 2-3

Model

- Have students read about Darcy and Ellie in the Model section.
- Ask: What values did Darcy consider when she made her decision? *friendship, health*

National Health Standards Addressed

5.8.2, 5.8.3, 5.8.4, 5.8.5, 5.8.6, 5.8.7, 8.8.2

300

Building Health Skills

Accessing Information
Practicing Healthful Behaviors
Stress Management
Analyzing Influences
Communication Skills
Refusal Skills
Conflict Resolution
Decision Making
Goal Setting
Advocacy

What Steps Can You Take to Make Healthy Decisions?

The decision-making process can help you make healthy and responsible choices. The six steps of the decision-making process are as follows:

1. State the situation.
2. List the options.
3. Weigh the possible outcomes.
4. Consider your values.
5. Make a decision and act.
6. Evaluate the decision.

Helping Someone Get Help

Follow the Model, Practice, and Apply steps to help you master this important health skill.

① Model

Read how Darcy uses the decision-making process to decide whether or not she should talk to her friend Ellie about her drinking problem.

Darcy recently realized that her close friend Ellie may have a drinking problem. Darcy used the decision-making process to help her decide what to do.

1. **State the situation:** I'm afraid my friend might have a drinking problem.
2. **List the options:** I could just do nothing. I could try talking to Ellie.
3. **Weigh the possible outcomes:** If I do nothing, Ellie's problem could get worse. If I talk to her about it, she might get mad.
4. **Consider values:** Ellie is my friend. I care about what happens to her.
5. **Make a decision and act:** I will try to talk to Ellie about her problem.
6. **Evaluate the decision:** I spoke to Ellie today after school. She said she knows she has a problem. She asked me go to the school guidance counselor with her to get help.

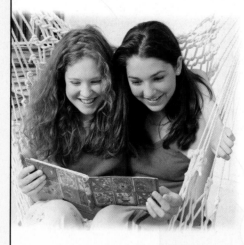

300 Chapter 12: Alcohol

Teaching Tips

Using the Decision-Making Model Remind students that many of their everyday decisions do not need to involve the decision-making steps. Point out, however, that the decision-making model is especially helpful for decisions where friendships are at stake.

Reviewing Student Scenarios For the Apply portion of this activity, carefully check the composition of each group's scenarios for appropriate tone, content, and realism. Do this at the beginning and near the end of the activity. Remind students to use the Self-Check feature to guide their work.

② Practice

Help Stephanie use the decision-making process to convince her cousin that drinking just to be part of a group is wrong.

Stephanie's cousin Stacy told her a secret, after making Stephanie promise not to say anything. "There's this club I want to join," she said. "Before I can be a member, I have to pass a test. I have to drink a beer in two minutes." When Stephanie told Stacy this was a bad idea, Stacy frowned. "I thought you'd understand how important this is to me," she said.

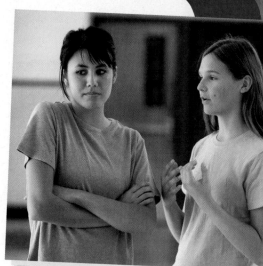

1. What decision is Stephanie faced with?
2. What do you think Stephanie's options are?
3. What are the possible outcomes of these options?
4. What would you do if you were Stephanie?

ACTIVITY

③ Apply

Use what you have learned about decision making to complete the activity below.

In a small group, think of a realistic situation where a decision needs to be made involving a teen and alcohol use. Write your situation down, then trade situations with another group. Each group should write an original story using the situation they have been given. The story should show how the six steps of decision making can be used to make a choice. In your story, explain how avoiding alcohol would affect the teen's health.

Self-Check

- Did our story illustrate the six steps of decision making?
- Did our story show how decision making can be used to make choices involving alcohol?
- Was our story realistic?

Building Health Skills

Practice

- Call on students to state the situation and decision that Stephanie faced in the Practice section. Call on other students to explain how the situation with Stacy compares with the situation with Ellie. (Both involve illegal activity, alcohol, potential danger, and drinking.)
- Divide the class into small groups to discuss possible answers to practice question 3. Give groups a chance to share their decisions and explain how they reached them.

Apply/Assess

- Have students continue working in small groups on the Apply section. Advise groups to think of creative yet realistic situations.
- When groups write their stories, remind them to apply steps 2 through 6 of the decision-making strategy. Also remind them to use only fictitious characters.

ASSESSMENT SCORING

Using a rubric, student work should meet all criteria to achieve the highest score.

Skills Student work:
- states the situation.
- lists the options.
- weighs the outcomes.
- considers values.
- makes a decision.
- evaluates the decision.

Concepts Student work:
- creates a realistic story about alcohol.
- illustrates a health-enhancing decision.
- includes accurate and comprehensive information about avoiding alcohol.

HANDS-ON HEALTH ACTIVITY

Refusing to Get in a Car with a Driver Who Has Been Drinking

Time: 45 minutes
Materials: index card, colored pencils or markers

Introducing Hands-on Health

- Review the refusal skills that were covered in Chapter 2. Call on volunteers to illustrate each refusal skill with a simple example.

Teaching the Activity

- Divide the class into small groups, and give groups time to work on the activity.
- As groups write their skits, remind them to include speaking parts for everyone in the group.
- Display some of the completed index cards in the classroom. Make sure the cards you display represent a diversity of responses.

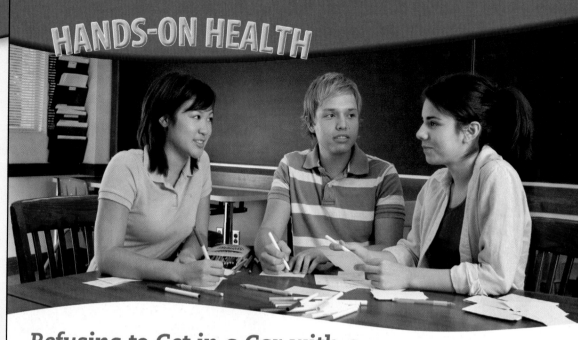

HANDS-ON HEALTH

Refusing to Get in a Car with a Driver Who Has Been Drinking

You have learned that you should not drink and drive. You should also avoid getting into a car with someone who has been drinking. If someone who has been drinking alcohol invites you to ride in a car with him or her, you should know how to refuse that invitation. The following are some suggestions that can help you avoid an unsafe situation.

- Make a decision to never ride with someone who has been drinking, and stick to it.
- Do not make arrangements to go places with a driver who you know will likely drink at an event you are going to.
- Find other ways to get a ride home if you are with a driver who has been drinking.
- Use direct statements: "I am not riding with you. You have been drinking. Don't drive. I'll find us another ride."

What You Will Need

- 1 index card per student
- Colored pencils or markers

Activity — What You Will Do

1. Working with a small group, brainstorm a list of refusal statements a teen can use to avoid riding in a car with a driver who has been drinking.

2. Write a skit that has dialogue showing successful use of refusal skills. Be sure that every group member has a part.

3. Act out your skit for the class.

Wrapping It Up

As a class, discuss the dialogue used in each of the skits. Decide which skit presented the most effective refusal statements. Then, on your own, take your index card and write "Don't Ride with a Drunk Driver" on the card. Then, write at least two statements you can use to refuse such a ride. Use markers or colored pencils to make the card creative and colorful. Display your cards in the classroom.

HANDS-ON HEALTH Assessment

Discussion After the groups have presented their skits, call on students to explain which refusal statements they thought were most effective. Point out that how people say things may be as important as what they say. Let students identify examples of nonverbal communication that were especially effective. Call on volunteers to illustrate the importance of nonverbal communication. Have them repeat the most effective refusal statements, first without and then with appropriate nonverbal cues.

Reading Review

Visit glencoe.com to download quizzes and eFlashcards for Chapter 12.

FOLDABLES Study Organizer

Foldables® and Other Study Aids Take out the Foldable® that you created for Lessons 2 and 3 and any graphic organizers that you created for Lessons 1–5. Find a partner and quiz each other using these study aids.

Lesson 1 Why Alcohol Is Harmful

Main Idea Alcohol is harmful because it can damage a person's physical, mental/emotional, and social health.

- Alcohol is a depressant. It slows down the body's functions and reactions.
- Some of the reasons teens use alcohol include media messages, stress relief, peer pressure, and to look more mature.

Lesson 2 Short-Term Effects of Alcohol Use

Main Idea Alcohol is a very fast-acting drug. It begins to affect the body the moment it enters the mouth.

- Alcohol slows down a person's reaction time. This creates serious safety risks for the drinker and others.
- Factors that influence the effects of alcohol include weight, gender, rate of consumption, amount consumed, amount eaten, other drugs in the system, state of health, and how well rested the person is.

Lesson 3 Long-Term Effects of Alcohol Use

Main Idea Drinking alcohol regularly can lead to a number of health problems. These include damage to major organs like the stomach, liver, brain, pancreas, and heart.

- A devastating long-term consequence of driving while intoxicated is causing your own death or the death of someone else.
- Since teens frequently combine high-risk activities with binge drinking, their potential for death or serious injury is very high.
- Babies born to mothers who use alcohol are more likely to have health problems, learning disabilities, or even mental disorders.

Lesson 4 Alcoholism and Alcohol Abuse

Main Idea Alcoholism is a progressive, chronic disease that involves a mental and physical need for alcohol. Alcohol abuse is a pattern of drinking that results in one or more well-defined behaviors within a 12-month period.

- Symptoms of alcoholism include denial, craving, loss of control, tolerance, and physical dependence.
- There are four stages of alcoholism. Each stage can be long or short, depending on the individual and the age at which he or she started drinking.

Lesson 5 Getting Help for Alcohol Abuse

Main Idea The process of recovery includes admission, detoxification, counseling, and resolution.

- Several organizations offer help for alcoholics and their families.

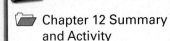

Assessment Resources

- Chapter 12 Summary and Activity
- Audio Summaries
- Reading Tutor
- Performance Assessment
- Chapter 12 Test
- *ExamView*
- Vocabulary PuzzleMaker
- Online Learning Center

Reading Review

Study Aids

- **Using the Dinah Zike Foldable® Study Organizer** Have students use the Foldable® to review the content of Lesson 1. Ask students to use the graphic organizers they made for the Reading Strategies to review the content of Lessons 2 through 5.
- **Online Learning Tools** Have students go to the Teen Health Online Learning Center at **glencoe.com** to:
  - Download a **Podcast**.
  - Download free **Study-to-Go** content to their PDAs or cell phones.

Vocabulary Review

- **Vocabulary Story** Ask students to write a short story about alcohol in which they correctly use at least ten chapter vocabulary terms.

Teaching Tips

Active Learning Students tend to learn more when they are actively involved in their own learning. One way to promote active learning is to have students evaluate the learning process. When you make assignments, ask students to list the learning goals they hope to achieve by completing the assignment. When the assignment is finished, have students evaluate whether they achieved their learning goals. If they did not achieve their goals, encourage them to identify why and what they might have done differently.

Assessment

Reviewing Vocabulary and Main Ideas

1. drug
2. depressant
3. Alternatives
4. Malnutrition
5. reaction time
6. Intoxication
7. False, cirrhosis
8. False, binge drinking
9. False, 0.08%
10. True
11. True
12. True
13. False, Detoxification

Thinking Critically

14. Answers will vary. Students should mention that alcohol is addictive, it is illegal for teens, and has long-term physical effects. Teens also risk fatal crashes if they drive while intoxicated.
15. There is no cure for alcoholism. The recovering alcoholic must continue the fight to stay alcohol free for life. Having even one drink can lead to relapse.
16. Answers will vary, but should include healthful group activities and games that teens enjoy.

G℮ Online

Have students visit glencoe.com to take the Chapter 12 quiz.

Assessment

After You Read

Health eSpotlight VIDEO

Now that you have read the chapter, look back at your answer to the Health eSpotlight questions on the chapter opener. Have you added any important reasons to the list of why you should not drink alcohol? What would your answer be now?

Reviewing Vocabulary and Main Ideas

On a sheet of paper, write the numbers 1–6. After each number, write the term from the list that best completes each sentence.

- alcohol
- alcohol poisoning
- alternatives
- depressant
- drug
- intoxication
- malnutrition
- reaction time

Lesson 1 Why Alcohol Is Harmful

1. A _____ is a substance that changes the structure or function of the body or mind.
2. A(n) _____ is a drug that slows down the body's functions and reactions.
3. _____ to drinking include finding a hidden skill and volunteering.

Lesson 2 Short-Term Effects of Alcohol Use

4. _____ can occur when the body does not receive enough nutrients to function properly.
5. The ability of the body to respond quickly and appropriately to any situation is called _____.

6. _____ means a person is physically and mentally impaired by the use of alcohol.

On a sheet of paper, write the numbers 7–13. Write True or False for each statement below. If the statement is false, change the underlined word or phrase to make it true.

Lesson 3 Long-Term Effects of Alcohol Use

7. A disease characterized by scarring and eventual destruction of the liver is called <u>fatty liver</u>.
8. The consumption of a large quantity of alcohol in a very short period of time is known as <u>inhibition</u>.

Lesson 4 Alcoholism and Alcohol Abuse

9. A person with a blood alcohol content (BAC) of <u>0.80 percent</u> is legally considered to be DWI or driving while intoxicated.
10. An <u>addiction</u> is a physical or psychological need for a drug.

Lesson 5 Getting Help for Alcohol Abuse

11. Loss of control is one symptom of <u>alcoholism</u>.
12. <u>Alcohol abuse</u> is a pattern of drinking that results in one or more well-defined behaviors within a 12-month period.
13. <u>Resolution</u> is a process in which the alcoholic's body adjusts to functioning without the drug.

G℮ Online Visit glencoe.com and take the Online Quiz for Chapter 12.

Health eSpotlight VIDEO **Wrap-Up**

Avoiding Alcohol Have students reread the Health eSpotlight question at the beginning of the chapter (page 277) and look at their original answer. Ask: Now that you have read the chapter and watched the video presentation, what are some creative ways to resist someone who asks you to try alcohol? Call on volunteers to give examples of refusal strategies.

Thinking Critically

Using complete sentences, answer the following questions.

14. **Evaluate** How can alcohol use as a teen cause health problems later in life?

15. **Analyze** Why is an alcoholic always said to be recovering rather than cured?

16. **Apply** Imagine you are planning a birthday party for a friend. What are some fun activities you could choose that do not include the use of alcohol?

Write About It

17. **Persuasive Writing** What reasons might teens use to persuade others to use alcohol? What are some refusal responses to these statements?

✈ Applying Technology

The Dangers of Drinking: A Puppet Show

Using a digital camera and iMovie®, you and a partner will create a puppet show for younger students that teaches them about the dangers of alcohol use.

- Use socks or paper lunch bags to create your puppets. Make them colorful and appealing.

- Write a five-minute script that focuses on one of the topics covered in this chapter. Use language that younger students will understand.

- Use a digital camera to record your puppet show. Export it to your computer. Click, drag, and drop the video from the media files into the iMovie® clipboard.

- Save your puppet show.

✈ Applying Technology

The Dangers of Drinking: A Puppet Show
Equipment needs: digital camera and iMovie® or similar software
Help students discuss the audience for their puppet shows and ask: What are the most important facts younger children should know about alcohol? Assign partners for this project, and establish sign-up sheets if access to cameras and computers is limited. Have students review and discuss their classmates' videos before the shows are shared with younger children.

Standardized Test Practice

Reading

Read the passage and then answer the questions.

A SADD Story

In 1981, a group of students from Wayland, Massachusetts, wanted to make a statement. Having watched peers die in accidents involving drunk driving, the group formed SADD. Back then, the letters in the name stood for "Students Against Driving Drunk." The students' goal was to spread the word that drunk driving kills.

Today, SADD has thousands of chapters in middle schools, high schools, and colleges. In 1997, the letters in SADD were changed to stand for "Students Against Destructive Decisions." The group is now dedicated to preventing all high-risk behaviors among teens. These include underage drinking, substance abuse, violence, and suicide.

1. Which best describes the way in which SADD changed since it was founded?
   A. The founders moved the organization's headquarters to a city out west.
   B. The founders sold the organization to its adult backers.
   C. SADD grew to have thousands of chapters.
   D. The group is no longer dedicated to preventing drunk driving.

2. Sixteen years after SADD was founded, the organization's name was changed to
   A. Students Against Drunk Driving.
   B. Students Against Doing Drugs.
   C. Students Against Dealing Drugs.
   D. Students Against Destructive Decisions.

Chapter 12 Assessment **305**

Write About It

17. **Persuasive Writing**
Responses will vary. Each response should take a clear stand against alcohol use and provide evidence that underage drinking is not healthy. For example, to the come-on line, "You'll have more fun if you drink," students might respond, "I'll have more fun if I don't get sick."

Standardized Test Practice

1. C
2. D

▶ Test-Taking Tips

Reading Skills Remind students that reading skills are important test-taking skills in just about every subject, including health. When students read passages with more than one paragraph, they should try to identify the main idea and supporting details in each paragraph as they read. This will give them an overview of the ideas in the passage as well as the location of specific information. When students answer the questions, they can go back to the relevant paragraph to find the information they need.

CHAPTER 13 pp. 306–331	Standards		Skills and Activities
	National	State/Local	
	National Health Education Standards 1.8.3, 1.8.5, 1.8.8, 1.8.9, 2.8.4, 3.8.1, 4.8.2, 6.8.2		*Health* eSpotlight p. 307 **BUILDING HEALTH SKILLS** *Goal Setting* Saying No to Tobacco, *pp. 326–327* TIME health news *Up in Smoke, p. 328*
Lesson 1 Facts About Tobacco pp. 308–310	National Health Education Standards 1.8.8, 1.8.9, 2.8.3, 2.8.10, 5.8.7, 7.8.3		**DEVELOPING GOOD CHARACTER** *Citizenship, p. 309*
Lesson 2 Health Risks of Tobacco Use pp. 311–314	National Health Education Standards 2.8.7, 3.8.3, 3.8.5, 4.8.4, 8.8.1, 8.8.3		**HEALTH SKILLS ACTIVITY** *Decision Making* Fresh-Air Friend, *p. 314*
Lesson 3 Tobacco Addiction pp. 315–318	National Health Education Standards 4.8.2, 8.8.1		**Go Online** Voices Against Tobacco, *p. 316* **What Teens Think** Why do you think some teens choose to smoke?, *p. 317*
Lesson 4 Tobacco's Costs to Society pp. 319–322	National Health Education Standards 8.8.2, 8.8.3		**Connect To... MATH** Cigarette Taxes, *p. 321*
Lesson 5 Choosing to Be Tobacco Free pp. 323–325	National Health Education Standards 2.8.1, 2.8.4, 2.8.5, 2.8.7, 4.8.2, 8.8.1		**Careers for the 21st Century** Respiratory Therapist, *p. 324*

PACING THE CHAPTER

Lesson 1 30 min	**Lesson 4** 45 min	**Chapter Review** 45 min
Lesson 2 45 min	**Lesson 5** 45 min	**TIME health news** 30 min
Lesson 3 30 min		**Building Health Skills** 45 min

BLOCK SCHEDULING

For block scheduling, assign students Building Health Skills feature *Saying No to Tobacco*, pages 326–327, and Guided Reading and Writing. 📁

Planning Guide

Reproducible Resources	Assessment	Media and Technology
Chapter *FAST FILE* **Resources** Chapter Summaries and Activities REVIEW Building Health Skills Activity TEACH Performance Assessment Activity EXTEND Universal Access Activities TEACH Parent Letter and Activities 📁 **Student Activities Workbook** TEACH 📁 **Reading Tutor** TEACH	Building Health Skills Activity, *pp. 326–327* Chapter 13 Assessment, *pp. 330–331* **Chapter** *FAST FILE* **Resources** Performance Assessment Activity, *p. 4* Chapter 13 Test, *p. 7* 💿 *ExamView® Assessment Suite*	TeacherWorks™ Plus includes: ● Interactive Teacher Edition ● Lesson Planner with Calendar ● Access to all blackline masters ● Correlations to standards 💿 StudentWorks™ Plus 💿 Online Student Edition Dinah Zike's Teaching Health with Foldables®
Chapter *FAST FILE* **Resources** Concept Mapping Activity 13-1 REVIEW Decision-Making Activity 13-1 EXTEND Enrichment Activity 13-1 EXTEND Lesson Plan 13-1 Guided Reading and Writing 13-1 TEACH Reteaching Activity 13-1 REVIEW	Lesson 1 Review, *p. 310* 💿 Vocabulary PuzzleMaker 💿 *ExamView® Assessment Suite*	💿 Vocabulary PuzzleMaker 💿 *ExamView® Assessment Suite* 💿 StudentWorks™ Plus 🔦 Transparency 13-1 **Go Online** glencoe.com
Chapter *FAST FILE* **Resources** Concept Mapping Activity 13-2 REVIEW Health Lab 13-2 EXTEND Enrichment Activity 13-2 EXTEND Lesson Plan 13-2 Guided Reading and Writing 13-2 TEACH Reteaching Activity 13-2 REVIEW	Lesson 2 Review, *p. 314* 💿 Vocabulary PuzzleMaker 💿 *ExamView® Assessment Suite*	💿 Vocabulary PuzzleMaker 💿 *ExamView® Assessment Suite* 💿 StudentWorks™ Plus 🔦 Transparency 13-2 **Go Online** glencoe.com
Chapter *FAST FILE* **Resources** Concept Mapping Activity 13-3 REVIEW Decision-Making Activity 13-3 EXTEND Enrichment Activity 13-3 EXTEND Lesson Plan 13-3 Guided Reading and Writing 13-3 TEACH Reteaching Activity 13-3 REVIEW	Lesson 3 Review, *p. 318* 💿 Vocabulary PuzzleMaker 💿 *ExamView® Assessment Suite*	💿 Vocabulary PuzzleMaker 💿 *ExamView® Assessment Suite* 💿 StudentWorks™ Plus 🔦 Transparency 13-3 **Go Online** glencoe.com
Chapter *FAST FILE* **Resources** Concept Mapping Activity 13-4 REVIEW Cross-Curriculum Activity 13-4 EXTEND Enrichment Activity 13-4 EXTEND Lesson Plan 13-4 Guided Reading and Writing 13-4 TEACH Reteaching Activity 13-4 REVIEW	Lesson 4 Review, *p. 322* 💿 Vocabulary PuzzleMaker 💿 *ExamView® Assessment Suite*	💿 Vocabulary PuzzleMaker 💿 *ExamView® Assessment Suite* 💿 StudentWorks™ Plus 🔦 Transparency 13-4 **Go Online** glencoe.com
Chapter *FAST FILE* **Resources** Concept Mapping Activity 13-5 REVIEW Cross-Curriculum Activity 13-5 EXTEND Enrichment Activity 13-5 EXTEND Lesson Plan 13-5 Guided Reading and Writing 13-5 TEACH Reteaching Activity 13-5 REVIEW	Lesson 5 Review, *p. 325* 💿 Vocabulary PuzzleMaker 💿 *ExamView® Assessment Suite*	💿 Vocabulary PuzzleMaker 💿 *ExamView® Assessment Suite* 💿 StudentWorks™ Plus 🔦 Transparency 13-5 **Go Online** glencoe.com

Chapter and Lesson Resources

The *Teen Health* resources are designed for differentiated learning abilities. You may want to use the coded items in this way:

REVIEW —activities to review or reinforce content

TEACH —activities to teach basic concepts

EXTEND —activities to extend or enrich lesson content

 OUT OF TIME?

Use Health Skills Activities *Fresh-Air Friend,* page 314, or Developing Good Character, page 309.

Emphysema—A Consequence of Smoking

Smoking has many long-term physical effects. These include cardiovascular disease, stomach ulcers, and various kinds of cancers, including lung cancer. Another serious consequence that can be attributed primarily to smoking is emphysema, a condition in which the alveoli in the lungs deteriorate and lose their elasticity. Nearly 3 million Americans have been diagnosed with emphysema, and millions more are undiagnosed but in the early stages of the disease. Chronic obstructive pulmonary disease (COPD) includes emphysema.

When a person inhales, the air moves through the bronchi, into the smaller airways called bronchioles, and finally into the tiny sacs of the lungs called alveoli. In the alveoli, the oxygen in the air moves into tiny blood vessels, and carbon dioxide moves from the blood into the alveoli. When a smoker inhales tobacco smoke, the smoke flows into the alveoli and irritates the tissue. Over time, the smoke eventually destroys the elastic fibers in the alveoli. The alveoli are normally like a balloon—as the air moves out, the tiny balloons deflate. But when the elastic fibers of the alveoli are destroyed, the air becomes trapped inside the alveoli of the lungs.

Because of damage to the alveoli, an emphysema sufferer has great difficulty expelling air from the lungs—trouble breathing out. When emphysema is advanced, the person uses up to 20 percent of his or her energy just in breathing.

Damage to the alveoli is irreversible. At first, a smoker may not have shortness of breath or any other symptoms of the disease, but the damage is being done nevertheless. Eventually, a person with emphysema has difficulty simply taking a walk. Emphysema also requires the heart to work harder to pump blood, because the damaged alveoli block the passage of blood to the lungs. As a result of this strain, the heart may become enlarged. Heart failure is the most common cause of death in people with emphysema.

Quitting Tobacco Use

As students read about the steps in quitting tobacco use, explain that setting a specific date for quitting is an important first step. Choosing a date too far in the future can be a problem. A person should give him- or herself enough time to prepare a plan to quit but not enough time that allows a change of mind. A quit date should be within the month.

Some people can quit "cold turkey"—immediately and completely. Others may plan to cut down a few cigarettes each day in order to quit gradually. Gradual quitting is difficult to accomplish.

Nicotine replacement therapies are helpful in dealing with the physical dependence on nicotine. A person who tries to quit should start nicotine replacement at the beginning of an attempt to quit, not after "cold turkey" has failed. Types of nicotine replacement include nicotine patches, nicotine gum, nicotine nasal spray, nicotine inhalers, nicotine lozenges, and nicotine lollipops and lip balms. Other methods used by some to help in quitting tobacco use include hypnosis and acupuncture, both of which may or may not be useful. Some quitters try filters on cigarettes that reduce tar and nicotine. Studies show that these filters actually cause the smoker to smoke more.

Nicotine replacement therapies work best in combination with support groups and other strategies to address the psychological dependence on nicotine. Online support groups are available for people quitting tobacco use. Many people find success with more traditional support groups in which people meet with one another to discuss their problems. One way to find a local support group is to call the American Cancer Society.

Most smokers usually attempt to quit several times before they are successful. Quitting tobacco use is hard, but the benefits are worth the trouble.

Reading Support

Reading Preview

Activating Background Vocabulary Make a word web on the board with the term *tobacco* in the center. Have students think of all the facts they can remember about types, uses, and/or effects of tobacco. Discuss and record all answers on the board.

FOLDABLES Study Organizer *Dinah Zike's Reading and Study Skills for Teen Health* provides interactive graphic organizers that help students comprehend and retain health concepts as they read. Use the Foldable® on page 307 or find more Foldables® activities for the chapter on **Tobacco** in the separate booklet, available in the TCR.

Lesson 1 Facts About Tobacco

Find and Define Have students write each new term from the lesson on the front of an index card. As the students read, have them find the words in the text and write the definitions in their own words on the back of each index card. Have student pairs review and share each other's definitions.

Lesson 2 Health Risks of Tobacco Use

Top Ten List As they read, direct students to compile a list of the health risks of tobacco use. Have students review their lists and choose the ten most important or dangerous effects of using tobacco. Encourage students to share and discuss their "Top Ten" lists with each other.

Lesson 3 Tobacco Addiction

Paraphrasing Have students close their books and take turns using their own words to describe what they have read about nicotine addiction, dependence, and withdrawal. Determine if students are identifying the main ideas and encourage them to reread the text to clarify the facts.

Lesson 4 Tobacco's Costs to Society

Compare and Contrast Have students create a two-column chart. As they read, have students record facts about the costs to the individual smoker on one side of the chart and the costs to the nonsmoker on the other. Encourage students to compare their charts with a partner.

Lesson 5 Choosing to Be Tobacco Free

Visualizing Have students imagine receiving pressure from a peer to try tobacco. Ask: "How are you feeling? What is your peer saying? What can you say? Do you remember your refusal skills?" Have students write a journal entry, describing their feelings during the visualizations.

Post Reading

Research Presentations Guide student groups to the available classroom, library, and Internet resources. Instruct students to gather additional data about tobacco products, use of tobacco, and ways to say no to tobacco use. Have students present their completed research to the class.

Key for Using the Teacher Wraparound Edition

Use this key to help you identify the **different types of prompts found in the Teacher Wraparound Edition.**

R **Reading Strategies** activities help you teach reading skills and vocabulary.

C **Critical Thinking** strategies help students apply and extend what they have learned.

U **Universal Access** activities provide differentiated instruction for students learning to speak English, along with suggestions for teaching various types of learners.

HS **Health Skills Practice** activities reinforce Health Skills concepts and help students apply these skills in their everyday lives.

W **Writing Support** activities provide writing opportunities to help students comprehend the text.

AL **Active Learning** strategies provide a variety of activities for presenting lesson content, including Quick Demos and engaging classroom projects that get students actively involved.

Key to Ability Levels

Teaching Strategies and activities have been coded for ability level and appropriateness.

AL Activities for students working above grade level

OL Activities for students working on grade level

BL Activities for students working below grade level

EL Activities for English Learners

Symbols

 Transparencies

 CD-ROM

 glencoe.com

 Print Resources

Tobacco

Chapter at a Glance

Lesson 1 identifies the various forms that tobacco takes, identifies some of the harmful substances in tobacco, and describes forms in which tobacco is used.

Lesson 2 explains the short- and long-term damage to the body caused by tobacco use.

Lesson 3 explains tolerance to nicotine, identifies the different types of drug dependence that occur, describes withdrawal from a drug and identifies steps for quitting tobacco use.

Lesson 4 identifies ways tobacco use harms nonsmokers and describes the costs tobacco use has on society.

Lesson 5 identifies ways teens are influenced to try tobacco, explains how to avoid being influenced to try tobacco, and describes the rights of nonsmokers.

R Reading Strategy

Interpreting the Photo Have students look at the photo of teens at an anti-tobacco rally, and ask: How do tobacco companies target teens?
Sample Answer: Answers may include: point-of-sale promotions, TV shows and movies that make smoking look cool, magazine ads that show young adults having a good time while smoking. **OL**

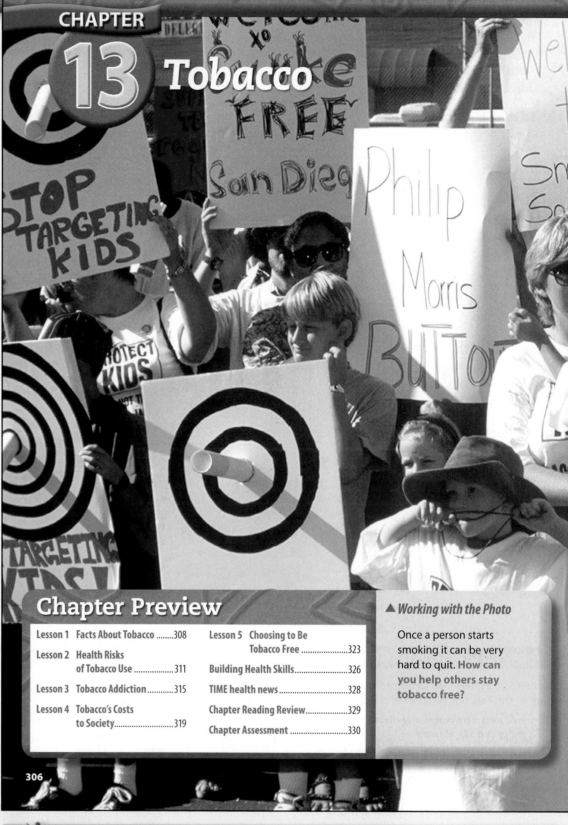

CHAPTER
13 Tobacco

Chapter Preview

▲ *Working with the Photo*

Once a person starts smoking it can be very hard to quit. **How can you help others stay tobacco free?**

306

👥 Universal Access

Differentiated Learning Glencoe provides teacher support and student materials for all learners in the health classroom.

● Spanish Glosario and chapter summaries assist English Language Learners.
● *Reading Tutor* and related worksheets support reluctant readers.

● Universal Access strategies throughout the Teacher Wraparound Edition and Fast Files help you present materials for gifted students, at-risk students, physically impaired students, and those with behavior disorders or learning disabilities.

Start-Up Activities

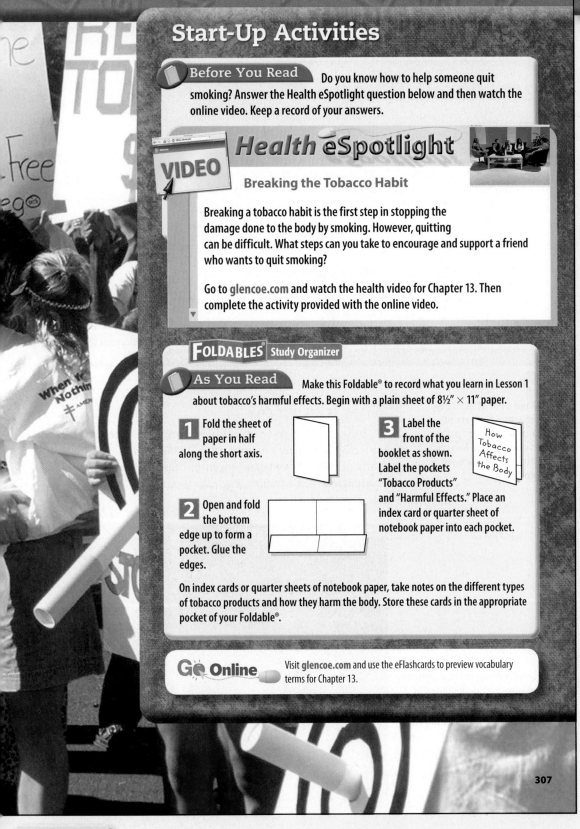

Before You Read

Do you know how to help someone quit smoking? Answer the Health eSpotlight question below and then watch the online video. Keep a record of your answers.

Health eSpotlight

VIDEO

Breaking the Tobacco Habit

Breaking a tobacco habit is the first step in stopping the damage done to the body by smoking. However, quitting can be difficult. What steps can you take to encourage and support a friend who wants to quit smoking?

Go to **glencoe.com** and watch the health video for Chapter 13. Then complete the activity provided with the online video.

FOLDABLES Study Organizer

As You Read

Make this Foldable® to record what you learn in Lesson 1 about tobacco's harmful effects. Begin with a plain sheet of 8½" × 11" paper.

1 Fold the sheet of paper in half along the short axis.

2 Open and fold the bottom edge up to form a pocket. Glue the edges.

3 Label the front of the booklet as shown. Label the pockets "Tobacco Products" and "Harmful Effects." Place an index card or quarter sheet of notebook paper into each pocket.

How Tobacco Affects the Body

On index cards or quarter sheets of notebook paper, take notes on the different types of tobacco products and how they harm the body. Store these cards in the appropriate pocket of your Foldable®.

Go Online Visit **glencoe.com** and use the eFlashcards to preview vocabulary terms for Chapter 13.

Health eSpotlight VIDEO

Breaking the Tobacco Habit Have students write an answer to the question provided and save their answers for later. Download the video presentation for Chapter 13 from **glencoe.com** or use the DVD to play the video for the class. Use the questions at the end of the video to begin a class discussion on strategies to help someone quit smoking. Ask students to respond to each question. **OL**

No Child Left Behind

Assessment Help students familiarize themselves with any standardized tests they will be required to take during the year. Have students review the format of the tests and the types of questions they might encounter. Throughout the year, incorporate questions in your classroom assessments that match the style and format of the standardized test questions required of your students. Use the Standardized Test Practice sections in the *Teen Health* chapter reviews.

Go Online

Have students visit **glencoe.com** and use the eFlashcards for Chapter 13.

FOLDABLES Study Organizer

Dinah Zike Foldables®

Organizing Information About Decision Making Students should use the Foldable® as they read Lesson 1, Facts About Tobacco. If students are having trouble making their Foldables®, demonstrate how to make one for the class. Students can use their Foldables® to store notes about tobacco products and how they harm the body. Suggest that they also add information to their Foldables® as they read the rest of the chapter's lessons.

FOCUS

Activating Prior Knowledge

What I Know Ask volunteers to describe cigarettes and cigars. Then ask students whether they think one is less dangerous to your health than the other.

Guide to Reading

Building Vocabulary
- Explain to students that carbon monoxide is a chemical that is similar to the familiar carbon dioxide. The difference can be inferred from the prefixes *mon-*, which means "one," and *di-*, which means "two." A molecule of carbon monoxide has one oxygen atom, while a molecule of carbon dioxide has two oxygen atoms.
- Use Vocabulary PuzzleMaker to reinforce vocabulary terms.

Reading Strategy
Making Inferences
Give students a few minutes to look briefly at the headings, figures, and captions.

FOLDABLES Have students
Study Organizer use their
Foldables® as they read Lesson 1.

Quick Write

After students have made their lists and described the tobacco products, encourage them to add to and revise their Quick Write as they read.

308

Facts About Tobacco

Guide to Reading

Building Vocabulary
As you read this lesson, write each new highlighted term and its definition in your notebook.
- nicotine (p. 308)
- addictive (p. 309)
- tar (p. 309)
- bronchi (p. 309)
- carbon monoxide (p. 309)
- smokeless tobacco (p. 310)

Focusing on the Main Ideas
In this lesson, you will learn to
- **recognize** the various forms of tobacco.
- **identify** some of the harmful substances in all forms of tobacco.
- **describe** the negative effects tobacco use can have on appearance.

Reading Strategy
Making Inferences Look briefly at the headings, figures, and captions in this lesson. Discuss what kinds of information you think this lesson will provide.

FOLDABLES | Study Organizer Use the Foldable® on p. 307 as you read this lesson.

Quick Write

Make a list of as many tobacco products as you can think of prior to reading this lesson. Briefly describe each product.

What Is Tobacco?

Tobacco is a woody, shrub like plant with large leaves. It is estimated that there are more than 4,000 chemicals in tobacco, many of which have been proven to cause cancer. One of these is **nicotine**—*an addictive drug found in tobacco leaves and in all tobacco products.*

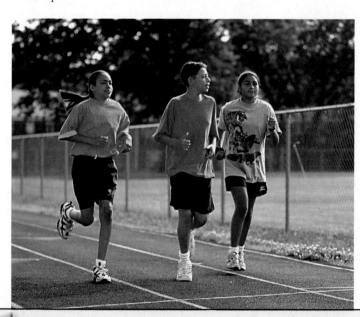

▶ Smoking can make it difficult to breathe during physical activity. **What physical activities do you enjoy that would become much more difficult if you smoked?**

308 Chapter 13: Tobacco

Lesson 1 Resources

📁 **Chapter *FAST FILE* Resources**
Guided Reading and Writing 13-1
Concept Mapping Activity 13-1
Decision-Making Activity 13-1
Reteaching Activity 13-1
Enrichment Activity 13-1
Lesson Quiz 13-1

Technology
🔦 Transparency 13-1
🎧 Audio Summaries
⊙ *ExamView® Assessment Suite*
🎧 Vocabulary PuzzleMaker
⊙ StudentWorks™ Plus

Gɵ Online

C Nicotine is an **addictive** drug, meaning it is *capable of causing a user to develop intense cravings*. Once the drug has been in the body regularly for some time, a person begins to depend on it.

Another dangerous ingredient in tobacco is **tar**, *a thick, oily, dark liquid that forms when tobacco burns*. When smokers inhale, tar deposits form on the **bronchi** (BRONG·ky), which are *passages through which air enters and spreads through the lungs*. If tar builds up, serious diseases such as emphysema and lung cancer can develop. These diseases make it very difficult for a person to breathe.

Carbon monoxide is a third harmful substance that is released when tobacco is burned. **Carbon monoxide** is *a poisonous, colorless, odorless gas*. Carbon monoxide enters the bloodstream through the lungs and reduces the amount of oxygen delivered to the body's organs and tissues. This weakens muscles and blood vessels, which can lead to heart attack and stroke.

Reading Check Define What is *carbon monoxide*?

Different Tobacco Products

There are many different tobacco products on the market today. These include cigarettes, cigars, pipes, specialty cigarettes, and smokeless tobacco.

Cigarettes

Of the many different products that contain tobacco, the most commonly used is cigarettes. Cigarettes put smokers at risk for emphysema and other lung and heart diseases, cancer, infertility, and stroke. Cigarettes and other forms of tobacco can cause bad breath, stain teeth and fingers, and cause the skin to wrinkle prematurely. More than 400,000 cigarette smokers die from smoking-related illnesses every year.

Cigars and Pipes

Cigars contain larger quantities of the same harmful substances as cigarettes. One large cigar can contain as much tobacco as a pack of cigarettes. Cigar smokers have a higher risk of developing cancer of the mouth, larynx, and throat. They are also at greater risk of dying from heart disease.

DEVELOPING
Good Character

Citizenship

Good citizenship includes doing your part to keep your school and community healthy. One way to accomplish this is by spreading the word about the dangers of tobacco use.

What are some ways you could raise awareness in your school and community of the health hazards associated with using or being around tobacco products?

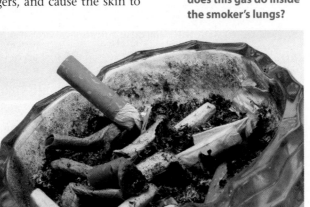

▼ Cigarette smoke releases carbon monoxide. **What does this gas do inside the smoker's lungs?**

TEACH

DEVELOPING
Good Character

Citizenship
Ask a volunteer to read the feature aloud. Then have small groups think of ways to raise awareness in their school and the community, such as with a poster, pamphlet, skit, or a song. Have groups present their projects to this or other classes or in the community.

Reading Check

Answer a poisonous, colorless, odorless gas

C Critical Thinking

Analyzing Ask students: If tobacco contains chemicals that have such terrible effects on the body, why do so many people continue to smoke? *Nicotine in tobacco is an addictive drug. Users develop intense cravings for it.* **BL**

Caption Answers

Photo Caption, p. 308 *Sample answers:* skateboarding, swimming, playing basketball
Photo Caption Carbon monoxide gas reduces the flow of oxygen in blood vessels, which leads to heart attack and stroke.

Teacher to Teacher

Robin Pettapiece   **Emmet Belknap Middle School, Lockport, NY**

Ingredients of Tobacco Smoke "After discussing the harmful and cancer-causing chemicals found in tobacco smoke, use this activity to reinforce the information taught. I use information from the text and from reliable Web sites to teach the information to my students. Have the students develop their own tobacco model using the outline of a cigarette to label the information they find. They can draw or use words to fill in the cigarette with the harmful items."

ASSESS

Reteaching

- Assign Concept Map 13-1 or Reteaching Activity 13-1 in the Fast Files.
- Have pairs of students make a table that lists and describes the forms of tobacco products.

Enrichment

- Assign Enrichment Activity 13-1 in the Fast Files.
- Ask students to research the health consequences of using smokeless tobacco, which some teens may consider relatively harmless. Have students present their findings to the class.

CLOSE

Call on volunteers to name and describe the dangerous ingredients in tobacco.

Some people smoke pipes using loose tobacco. Pipe smokers usually inhale less than cigarette smokers. However, they are still at risk of developing cancer of the lips, mouth, and throat.

Specialty Cigarettes

Two other tobacco products are bidis and kreteks. Bidis (BEE·deez) are flavored, unfiltered cigarettes imported from Southeast Asia. Kreteks (KREE·teks), also called clove cigarettes, are imported from Indonesia. Kreteks typically contain a mixture of tobacco, cloves, and other additives. Both can have higher concentrations of nicotine, tar, and carbon monoxide than regular cigarettes.

Smokeless Tobacco

Smokeless tobacco is *ground tobacco that is chewed or inhaled through the nose*. Nicotine absorbed from smokeless tobacco is three to four times greater than the amount delivered by a cigarette. It can lead to cancers of the mouth, esophagus, larynx, stomach, and pancreas. It also stains the teeth and causes bad breath, tooth decay, and gum disease.

Go Online

Visit **glencoe.com** and complete the Interactive Study Guide for Lesson 1.

Lesson 1 Review

After You Read

Review this lesson for new terms, major headings, and Reading Checks.

What I Learned

1. *Vocabulary* What is *nicotine*?

2. *List* Identify and describe the risks associated with three harmful substances found in all forms of tobacco.

3. *Recall* What is the most common form in which tobacco is used? Name three other tobacco products.

Thinking Critically

4. *Analyze* Julia is at a party where another girl lights a cigarette. When Julia points out that smoking is bad for her health, the other girl shrugs. "I'm a strong person," she says. "I can quit any time I want." How might Julia reply?

5. *Evaluate* Pete chews smokeless tobacco. He uses it when no one else is around so others do not have to watch him spitting tobacco juice. "It's a win-win situation," says Pete. Do you agree with Pete's point of view? Explain your answer.

Applying Health Skills

6. *Analyzing Influences* Some teens start smoking because they see their peers smoking. With a group, brainstorm other reasons teens might start to use tobacco. Make a list of the reasons and compare it with those from other groups.

Go Online For more Lesson Review Activities, go to **glencoe.com**.

Lesson 1 Review Answers

1. Nicotine is an addictive drug found in tobacco.
2. Nicotine causes users to have intense cravings for it. Tar is a thick, oily, dark liquid that forms when tobacco burns and builds up on the linings of the lungs, causing disease. Prolonged exposure to carbon monoxide gas leads to heart attack, stroke, or death.
3. The most common form is the cigarette. Other products include cigars and pipe tobacco, specialty cigarettes, and smokeless tobacco.
4. Tobacco contains nicotine, which is an addictive drug.
5. *Sample answer:* No. Smokeless tobacco contains 15 times more nicotine than cigarettes. It also stains the teeth and causes bad breath, tooth decay, and gum disease.
6. Divide the class into small groups, and have each group generate a list of reasons why teens smoke.

Lesson 2

Health Risks of Tobacco Use

Guide to Reading

● **Building Vocabulary**
Write the terms below in your notebook. Add a definition for each term as you read this lesson.

■ chronic obstructive pulmonary disease (COPD) (p. 313)

■ cardiovascular disease (p. 313)

● **Focusing on the Main Ideas**
In this lesson, you will learn to

■ **describe** how tobacco use affects the body systems.

■ **practice** decision making to protect your health against tobacco smoke.

● **Reading Strategy**
Drawing Conclusions Based on this lesson, list the effects of tobacco use on the body systems.

Tobacco Use Is Hazardous to Your Health

The message that smoking is bad for your health is not new. In 1965, Congress passed a law requiring tobacco manufacturers to print health warnings on cigarette packages. Similar labeling laws have since been passed for other tobacco products.

SURGEON GENERAL'S WARNING: Smoking Causes Lung Cancer, Heart Disease, Emphysema, And May Complicate Pregnancy.

SURGEON GENERAL'S WARNING: Quitting Smoking Now Greatly Reduces Serious Risks to Your Health.

SURGEON GENERAL'S WARNING: Smoking By Pregnant Women May Result in Fetal Injury, Premature Birth, And Low Birth Weight.

SURGEON GENERAL'S WARNING: Cigarette Smoke Contains Carbon Monoxide.

SURGEON GENERAL'S WARNING: Smoking By Pregnant Women May Result in Fetal Injury,

 Quick Write
List two future goals. Then write a short paragraph telling how a tobacco-related illness could affect each of these goals.

◀ Federal law requires that cigarette packages have one of four different warning labels. **Which of these health warnings do you think is most important for teens?**

Lesson 2: Health Risks of Tobacco Use **311**

Lesson 2 Resources

📁 **Chapter** *FAST FILE* **Resources**
Guided Reading and Writing 13-2
Concept Mapping Activity 13-2
Health Lab 13-2
Reteaching Activity 13-2
Enrichment Activity 13-2
Lesson Quiz 13-2

Technology
 Transparency 13-2
Audio Summaries
ExamView® Assessment Suite
Vocabulary PuzzleMaker
StudentWorks™ Plus
G⊙ Online

FOCUS

Activating Prior Knowledge

What I Know Ask volunteers to explain how to tell if a teen they meet is a smoker. Students may mention the smell of the clothes, hair, or breath. Ask if this is socially acceptable.

Guide to Reading

Building Vocabulary
■ Point out that COPD is a chronic disease. Explain that *chronic* means "prolonged or lingering." Contrast this with an acute disease.
■ Use Vocabulary PuzzleMaker to reinforce vocabulary terms.

Reading Strategy
Drawing Conclusions Have students list the effects of tobacco products as they read the lesson. Call on volunteers to help you make a master list on the board.

Quick Write
Give students five minutes to write a short paragraph about how a tobacco-related illness could affect their goals. Then call on volunteers to share their paragraphs with the class.

Caption Answer

Photo Caption *Sample answer:* The warning that quitting smoking now can reduce health risks, because tobacco use by teens impairs physical growth and development.

TEACH

AL Active Learning

Real-World Connection Ask students to observe smokers outside of public buildings or restaurants. Have them think of ways the need to smoke controls the smokers' habits. *forced to take breaks outside* The next day, lead a discussion about what they observed. Caution students against naming or otherwise identifying specific people. **OL**

R Reading Strategy

Analyzing a Graphic After students have examined **Figure 13.1**, ask: What is the difference in physical fitness between a teen who smokes and one who doesn't? *The teen who smokes is less physically fit than the teen who doesn't.* How might poor physical fitness affect the teen who smokes? *Sample answer: The teen might not be able to play school sports. The teen also might not be able to keep up with other teens in activities such as walking or biking.* **OL**

Caption Answer

Figure Caption Short-term effects include changes in brain chemistry, withdrawal symptoms, and increased heart rate and blood pressure. Long-term effects include an increased risk of stroke.

How Tobacco Use Affects the Body

AL The chemicals in tobacco and tobacco smoke can cause damage to most of the body's systems. Tobacco use is particularly damaging to teens because their bodies are still growing and developing. Some of the effects of tobacco use are evident almost immediately. Others become apparent over time. **Figure 13.1** shows both the short-term and the long-term harmful effects of tobacco use on body systems.

▼ FIGURE 13.1

R IMPACT OF SMOKING ON THE BODY SYSTEMS
The negative health effects of smoking begin immediately and grow progressively worse the longer you smoke. **What are the short-term and long-term effects on the nervous system?**

A Nervous System
Short-term effects: Changes take place in brain chemistry. Withdrawal symptoms (nervousness, shakes, headaches) may occur as soon as 30 minutes after the last cigarette. Heart rate and blood pressure increase.
Long-term effects: There is an increased risk of stroke due to decreased flow of oxygen to the brain.

B Circulatory System
Short-term effects: Heart rate is increased. Energy is reduced because less oxygen gets to body tissues.
Long-term effects: Blood vessels are weakened and narrowed. Cholesterol levels increase. Blood vessels are clogged due to fatty buildup. Oxygen flow to the heart is reduced. Risk of heart disease and stroke is greater.

C Respiratory System
Short-term effects: User has shortness of breath, reduced energy, coughing, and more phlegm (mucus). Colds and flus are more frequent. Allergies, asthma, bronchitis, and other serious respiratory illnesses increase.
Long-term effects: Risk of lung cancer, emphysema, and other lung diseases increases.

D Digestive System
Short-term effects: User has upset stomach, dulled taste buds, and tooth decay.
Long-term effects: Risk of cancer of the mouth and throat, gum and tooth disease, stomach ulcers, and bladder cancer increases.

312 Chapter 13: Tobacco

FITNESSZONE

Tobacco and Physical Fitness To help students understand that physical fitness and smoking don't "mix," have them discuss **Figure 13.1**, *Impact of Smoking on the Body Systems*. Then help students review and discuss the *Five Elements of Fitness* in the *Fitness Zone Handbook*. Ask:

Which element of fitness does smoking affect most directly? How do you think smoking affects the other elements of fitness? **For more information, see *Fitness Zone Handbook* pages xviii-1 or visit the Fitness Zone at glencoe.com.**

One long-term physical effect of smoking is a dry, hacking cough. This indicates that the tobacco has done permanent damage to the smoker's body. A dry cough is often a symptom of **chronic obstructive pulmonary disease (COPD),** *a condition in which passages in the lungs become swollen and irritated, eventually losing their elasticity.* This condition includes chronic bronchitis, asthma, and emphysema. In the United States, COPD causes over 100,000 deaths per year. Ninety percent of these deaths are linked to smoking.

Smokers are also at an increased risk of developing lung cancer. **Figure 13.2** gives some important facts about the link between smoking and lung cancer.

Smoking is also a leading cause of **cardiovascular disease,** *a disease of the heart and blood vessels.* Long-term smoking increases cholesterol levels and contributes to arteriosclerosis, a hardening of the arteries. Both conditions reduce oxygen flow to the heart, dramatically increasing a smoker's risk of stroke and heart attack. Other long-term effects of smoking include cancers of the brain, throat, breast, and bladder.

Reading Check Define What do the letters *COPD* stand for?

G Online

Visit **glencoe.com** and complete the Interactive Study Guide for Lesson 2.

▼ FIGURE 13.2

 ## THE FACTS ABOUT LUNG CANCER

Smoking can cause serious damage to the lungs. **What can you do to decrease your chances of getting lung cancer?**

Compare the healthy lung with the cancerous lung. Now think about the following facts:

1. Smoking is the number one cause of lung cancer, causing 87 percent of lung cancer cases.

2. Cigarette smoke contains more than 4,000 different chemicals, many of which are cancer-causing substances.

3. Lung cancer is the leading cancer killer in the United States, causing more deaths than the next three most common cancers combined.

4. Secondhand smoke is also an important cause of lung cancer.

Healthy Lung

Cancerous Lung

Reading Check

Answer chronic obstructive pulmonary disease

R Reading Strategy

Analyzing a Graphic After students have examined **Figure 13.2**, ask: How would you compare the cancerous lung with the healthy lung? Sample answer: *The cancerous lung looks shriveled and discolored.* How often does lung cancer kill Americans compared with other cancers? *Lung cancer causes more deaths than the next three common cancers combined.* What is the number-one cause of lung cancer? *smoking* **OL**

Health Skills Activity

Decision Making

Fresh-Air Friend

Use the following strategies to help students complete the activity on the next page:

- Ask a volunteer to read the paragraph aloud.

- Lead a brief discussion about what students think Mike should do.

- Give students 10 minutes to write a paragraph that applies the decision-making process to Mike's problem. Then call on volunteers to share their plans with the class. Ask students to evaluate each plan according to whether it is realistic.

Caption Answer

Figure Caption avoid smoking tobacco

What Teens Want to Know

Will smoking make a person's skin look older? Smoking cigarettes causes changes in the skin that accelerate aging. In fact, smoking is second only to sun exposure in how much damage it does to the skin. A recent study showed that even when facial wrinkling cannot be seen on the skin of a young smoker, wrinkling is visible under a microscope in smokers as young as 20 years old. In addition, the smokers' skin tends to develop a yellowish or grayish pallor.

ASSESS

Assessment Resources

Lesson Review Quiz
- *ExamView*
- Fast Files Activities
- Online Quizzes and Activities

Reteaching

- Assign Concept Map 13-2 or Reteaching Activity 13-2 in the Fast Files.
- Have pairs of students add to the table of tobacco products they made for the Reteaching strategy at the end of Lesson 1.

Enrichment

- Assign Enrichment Activity 13-2 in the Fast Files.
- Have students further investigate how smoking causes cardiovascular disease. Ask that they sum up their research in a flowchart that shows the steps from smoking tobacco to a heart attack.

CLOSE

Ask students to explain which health risk is most persuasive in causing them to avoid the use of tobacco.

Health Skills Activity

Decision Making

Fresh-Air Friend

Mike gets a ride to school with a girl in his class named Ashley. Mike is concerned about his health because Ashley's mom smokes in the car. Mike hasn't mentioned his concern because he doesn't want to sound rude or ungrateful. He's tried opening a window, but Ashley says it makes her cold. Mike doesn't know what to do or say. Use the decision-making process to help him make a decision.

- State the situation
- List the options
- Weigh the possible outcomes
- Consider your values
- Make a decision and act
- Evaluate the decision

What Would You Do?

Apply the six steps of the decision-making process to Mike's problem. What are Mike's options? Show how Mike makes a healthful decision.

Lesson 2 Review

 After You Read

Review this lesson for new terms, major headings, and Reading Checks.

What I Learned

1. **Vocabulary** What is *cardiovascular disease*? How is this caused by smoking?

2. **List** What are some ways that tobacco use damages the circulatory system?

3. **Describe** What is the relationship between smoking and lung cancer?

Thinking Critically

4. **Analyze** Of the health risks associated with tobacco use, which one do you consider the most serious? Explain your answer.

5. **Explain** Why do you think it is important to put warning labels on cigarette packages?

Applying Health Skills

6. **Advocacy** Make a poster encouraging teens not to smoke. One part of your poster should clearly state the health risks associated with various tobacco products. The other part should try to persuade teens not to use tobacco.

Go Online For more Lesson Review Activities, go to glencoe.com.

Lesson 2 Review Answers

1. Cardiovascular disease is a disease of the heart and blood vessels. Smoking increases cholesterol levels and contributes to hardened arteries, weakens blood vessels, and reduces blood flow to the heart.

2. Answers should include effects shown in **Figure 13.1** on page 312.

3. Smoking causes lung cancer. Tobacco and tobacco smoke contains cancer causing chemicals.

4. *Sample answer:* Getting lung cancer is most serious, because lung cancer claims 150,000 lives in the United States every year.

5. Answers may vary. Labels inform the public of the dangers of smoking and make people think before buying and using cigarettes.

6. Students' posters will vary. An excellent poster will be creative, attractive, and accurate in the information it portrays.

Tobacco Addiction

Guide to Reading

● Building Vocabulary
As you read this lesson, write each new highlighted term and its definition in your notebook.

- tolerance (p. 316)
- physical dependence (p. 316)
- psychological dependence (p. 316)
- withdrawal (p. 317)
- nicotine replacement therapies (NRT) (p. 317)
- relapse (p. 318)

● Focusing on the Main Ideas
In this lesson, you will learn to

- **explain** how a person becomes addicted to tobacco.
- **identify** the different types of dependence that occur as a result of tobacco use.
- **describe** the symptoms of withdrawal.

● Reading Strategy
Sequencing Make a flow diagram that outlines the steps in the addiction process.

Tobacco's Web of Addiction

Nicotine is an extremely powerful and addictive drug. It is just as addictive as heroin or cocaine. When nicotine enters the body, it interacts with receptors in the brain. The brain sends a message to the body to speed up heart and breathing rates. As these feelings go away, they leave the user wanting more. Tobacco use soon becomes a habit, and the user can quickly become addicted. Once addicted, it becomes very difficult to quit smoking.

Q *uick Write*

Make a list of habits you know are hard to break. Choose one you find interesting and write a paragraph describing what you think it would be like to change that habit.

▶ The best way to prevent tobacco addiction is to never start using tobacco. **Why is it difficult to stop smoking once a person has started?**

Lesson 3: Tobacco Addiction **315**

Lesson 3 Resources

Chapter *FAST FILE* Resources
Guided Reading and Writing 13-3
Concept Mapping Activity 13-3
Decision-Making Activity 13-3
Reteaching Activity 13-3
Enrichment Activity 13-3
Lesson Quiz 13-3

Technology
🔊 Transparency 13-3
🗄 Audio Summaries
⊕ *ExamView® Assessment Suite*
🗄 Vocabulary PuzzleMaker
⊕ StudentWorks™ Plus
G⊚ Online

FOCUS
Activating Prior Knowledge

What I Know Call on students to explain what an addict is. Then ask whether users of tobacco can be considered addicts.

Guide to Reading

Building Vocabulary
- Explain that *psychological* in the context of *psychological dependence* means "mental or behavioral." Ask students to contrast psychological dependence with physical dependence.
- Use Vocabulary PuzzleMaker to reinforce vocabulary terms. 🖊

Reading Strategy
Sequencing After students have read about nicotine addiction, lead a discussion about the steps involved in the addiction process.

Q *uick Write*

After students have written their paragraphs, point out that changing a habit is like overcoming a psychological dependence on tobacco.

Caption Answer

Photo Caption Addiction causes the body to crave nicotine.

TEACH

Go Online

Voices Against Tobacco Have students create their advertisements using the resources provided at **glencoe.com.** Encourage students to consider why they believe some nonsmoking ads are better than others before they design their own. **OL**

Academic Vocabulary

Trigger Have volunteers read aloud the definition and example sentence. Then ask students to recall at least one other definition of *trigger*: the small lever on a gun that can be pulled back to fire the gun. Ask: How are these two definitions related? You will find academic vocabulary activities in the Student Activities Workbook.

Reading Check

Answer 90 percent

 ## Reading Strategy

Analyzing a Graphic After students have examined **Figure 13.3**, ask: If you were in a room with ten adult smokers, how many of them likely became regular smokers before they were 18? *8 out of the 10* If a teen starts smoking today, how long will it take for that teen to feel the symptoms of nicotine addiction? *only days or weeks* **OL**

316

 ## Go Online

Topic: Voices Against Tobacco

Visit glencoe.com for Student Web Activities to learn about the effects of smoking and how advertising can be used to speak out against it.

Activity: Locate and analyze an anti-tobacco ad. What does it say about the dangers of tobacco use? Is this ad more effective than the tobacco ads that you have seen? Why, or why not?

Academic Vocabulary

trigger (TRIG er) *(noun)* to cause a reaction or a series of reactions. *Certain foods can trigger headaches in some people.*

Tolerance and Dependence

As the body gets used to nicotine, it develops a tolerance to the drug. **Tolerance** is *a process in which the body needs more and more of a drug to get the same effect.*

Any time the nicotine level drops or is absent, the body experiences a craving. This is a sign that the body has a physical dependence on nicotine. **Physical dependence** is *a type of addiction in which the body itself feels a direct need for a drug.* The cravings that result from a physical dependence can only be satisfied by more nicotine.

Addiction to a drug affects the mind as well as the body. Some people begin to believe they need tobacco to perk up or relax. What these people are experiencing is a psychological dependence on nicotine. A **psychological dependence** is *an addiction in which the mind sends the body a message that it needs more of a drug.* Certain events, situations, and habits **trigger** a desire to use tobacco. For example, some people feel the need to smoke at parties or nightclubs.

Studies have reported that a staggering 90 percent of adult smokers began smoking before the age of 18. Teens are more likely to develop a severe level of addiction than people who begin smoking at a later age. Teens who use tobacco are also much more likely to use drugs such as marijuana, cocaine, and alcohol. **Figure 13.3** provides greater detail on nicotine addiction among teens.

 Reading Check **Identify** What percentage of adult smokers began smoking before the age of 18?

 ▼ **FIGURE 13.3**

THE PATH TO SMOKING ADDICTION

The nicotine in tobacco is very addictive. Based on the facts below, how would you react if a friend said to you, "No way, I won't get addicted"?

The Path to Smoking Addiction
1. Tobacco companies market to young people. Some young people start smoking at 11 or 12 years old.
2. Every day in the United States, more than 6,000 teens and preteens try their first cigarette.
3. Teens can feel symptoms of nicotine addiction only days or weeks after they first start smoking on an occasional basis. Addiction symptoms are felt well before teens begin to smoke daily.
4. The earlier in life smoking is first tried, the higher the chances are of becoming a regular smoker and the lower the chances are of ever being able to quit.

HEALTH LITERACY

Withdrawal from Tobacco A person quitting the use of tobacco will experience temporary symptoms of withdrawal from nicotine. These symptoms sometimes have been called "quitter's flu" because they often are similar to the symptoms of a cold or a mild case of influenza. In addition to the physical symptoms noted in the text, a smoker withdrawing might experience a cough, a sore throat, constipation or stomach pain, dry mouth, postnasal drip, and a sore tongue or mouth.

Breaking the Tobacco Habit

Although some of the damage done by smoking cannot be reversed, it is never too late to quit using tobacco. Here are some steps to do just that:

- **Prepare to stop.** Set a specific date for quitting. Mark that date on a calendar so you won't forget.
- **Get support and encouragement.** Let family and friends know you are quitting and ask them for help and support.
- **Find out about health services.** Doctors, support groups, and certain organizations can help users quit. Explore resources in your community.
- **Change your daily routine.** It helps to avoid smokers and routines that were part of your life as a smoker.
- **Follow a healthy lifestyle.** Eat well, manage stress, and get plenty of physical activity to help you feel good without the use of tobacco.

Withdrawal

Some people choose to quit smoking *cold turkey,* meaning they stop all use of tobacco immediately. When a person stops using tobacco, he or she may experience symptoms of **withdrawal.** These are *physical and psychological reactions that occur when someone stops using an addictive substance.* The physical symptoms of withdrawal include headaches, tiredness, increased hunger, and a jittery, restless feeling. **Nicotine replacement therapies (NRT)** are *products that assist a person in breaking a tobacco habit.* These products reduce the amount of nicotine in the body slowly, reducing the symptoms of withdrawal.

The psychological symptoms of withdrawal can include irritability, sudden cravings for tobacco in certain situations or at certain times, and difficulty concentrating or sleeping. Counseling or support groups can help a user overcome a psychological dependence on tobacco.

 Reading Check **Define** What are *nicotine replacement therapies*?

Why do you think some teens choose to smoke?

In my opinion, some teens choose to smoke because of the influence of their peers. Also, they think it is a way to calm themselves. Another reason is because individuals that influence them the most at that time are also smokers and teens choose to follow them.

Christopher H.
Pensacola, FL

Why do you think some teens choose to smoke? Ask the *What Teens Think* question. Let students share their responses. Conclude by asking: What would you say to a peer who is considering taking up smoking?

W Writing Support

Personal Writing Have students write a letter to a fictitious friend who is addicted to tobacco. The letter should contain accurate information about how to quit smoking. **OL**

AL Active Learning

Role-Play Have the class brainstorm about the negative effects of teen smoking. Then separate the class into groups. Each group will portray one of the effects in a skit. **EL**

 Reading Check

Answer Products that assist a person in breaking a tobacco habit.

Lesson 3: Tobacco Addiction **317**

Cultural Perspectives

Teens and Addiction According to the Centers for Disease Control and Prevention (CDC), children who smoke become addicted to nicotine, just as adults do. Once a teen begins smoking, it takes an average of two to three years for that teen to become a daily smoker. Teens often think that they won't be smoking in the future. Yet once they're addicted to nicotine, they find it just as hard to quit smoking as adults do. In a CDC study, 64 percent of smokers age 12 to 18 had tried to quit and failed. About three-fourths of young people who use tobacco said it is hard to quit.

Caption Answer

Figure Caption, p. 316
Sample answer: More than a third of all teens who ever try one cigarette become regular, daily smokers before leaving high school.

ASSESS

Assessment Resources

Lesson Review Quiz
- *ExamView*
- Fast Files Activities
- Online Quizzes and Activities

Reteaching

- Assign Concept Map 13-3 or Reteaching Activity 13-3 in the Fast Files.
- Have students write a paragraph explaining how withdrawal is related to addiction.

Enrichment

- Assign Enrichment Activity 13-3 in the Fast Files.
- Have students investigate ways to overcome the physical and psychological symptoms of withdrawal from tobacco. Ask that they present their findings to the class.

CLOSE

Call on volunteers to explain the difference between physical dependence and psychological dependence.

Dealing with Relapse

The body undergoes physical changes when a person no longer uses tobacco. Learning to live without tobacco takes time and a lot of willpower.

Sometimes, the symptoms of withdrawal are so bad that a person takes up smoking again. As a result, many people who decide to quit tobacco suffer a relapse within the first three months of quitting. A **relapse** is *a return to the use of a drug after attempting to stop*. Resuming the habit after working hard to quit can be discouraging. Self-esteem often drops and people may feel frustrated and angry.

Most people attempt to quit several times before they succeed. Reviewing what caused a relapse and taking steps to prevent it from happening again can help. For example, if a person is in the habit of smoking after a meal, planning another activity can take the person's mind off smoking.

Go Online

Visit **glencoe.com** and complete the Interactive Study Guide for Lesson 3.

Reading Check **Define** What is a *relapse*?

Lesson 3 Review

After You Read

Review this lesson for new terms, major headings, and Reading Checks.

What I Learned

1. *Vocabulary* Define *tolerance*. How does a tolerance to nicotine form?

2. *Recall* Explain the difference between physical dependence and psychological dependence.

3. *Give Examples* What are the symptoms of nicotine withdrawal?

Thinking Critically

4. *Analyze* What specific dangers does trying tobacco pose for teens?

5. *Synthesize* How do nicotine replacement therapies help a person stop smoking?

6. *Apply* Madison's mother has been trying to quit smoking, but has had several relapses. What can Madison do to help her mother quit smoking?

Applying Health Skills

7. *Refusal Skills* Some teens try tobacco for the first time because of peer pressure. With a small group, brainstorm effective ways to say no when peers offer or suggest that you use tobacco. Make a list of the best ideas and share them with your classmates in a roundtable discussion.

318 Chapter 13: Tobacco

Go Online For more Lesson Review Activities, go to **glencoe.com**.

Lesson 3 Review Answers

1. Tolerance is a process in which the body needs more and more of a drug to get the same effect.
2. Physical dependence is a type of addiction in which the body itself feels a direct need for a drug. With psychological dependence the mind sends the body a message that it needs more of a drug.

3. headaches, tiredness, increased hunger, and a jittery, restless feeling
4. Studies show that teens become more addicted than any other group. Teens who use tobacco are more likely to use other drugs.
5. Nicotine replacement therapies help the body rid itself of nicotine slowly so withdrawal

symptoms are less severe.
6. Madison can give her mother support and tell her about nicotine replacement therapies.
7. Divide the class into small groups, and have each group brainstorm ways to say no to tobacco use. Ask groups to share their lists with the class.

Tobacco's Costs to Society

Guide to Reading

● **Building Vocabulary**
Explain how the terms below are related. Then find each in the lesson and write a definition for each term in your journal.

- secondhand smoke (p. 320)
- sidestream smoke (p. 320)
- mainstream smoke (p. 320)
- passive smoker (p. 320)

● **Focusing on the Main Ideas**
In this lesson, you will learn to

- **identify** ways in which tobacco harms nonsmokers.
- **describe** the costs tobacco use has on society.

● **Reading Strategy**
Identifying Problems and Solutions After reading this lesson, state why secondhand smoke is a problem. Offer your suggestions for dealing with this problem.

uick Write

Make a list of the costs associated with tobacco use. As you read, add costs to your list.

Tobacco's Many Costs

For every dollar spent to spread the word about the dangers of tobacco, tobacco companies spend $23 on marketing. Marketing is a method used by businesses to make the public aware of their product. Each year tobacco companies spend $12.7 billion on advertising alone. Whether or not they smoke, U.S. taxpayers pay around $38 billion each year in federal taxes to treat the many health problems caused by smoking. That averages to about $320 per American household. There are many more costs associated with tobacco use. This lesson takes a look at some of them.

Cost to the Individual

AL

Researchers discovered that the average smoker smokes a pack and a half a day. The average price per pack in most states is up to $5. This means the typical smoker spends $7.50 per day on tobacco. Over the course of a month, that works out to $225. In 10 years' time, the smoker will have spent $27,000 on tobacco.

▶ The average smoker spends $225 a month on cigarettes. **How would you put this money to better use?**

319

CHAPTER 13
Lesson 4

FOCUS

Activating Prior Knowledge

What I Know Ask students if they know how much a pack of cigarettes costs. Then ask students if there are any other costs to the smoker or to society that can be tied to the use of tobacco.

 Guide to Reading

Building Vocabulary
- Explain to students that *passive* means "acted upon by something outside." The word *passive* as used in the term *passive smoker* is often contrasted with the word *active*, which means "characterized by action."
- Use Vocabulary PuzzleMaker to reinforce vocabulary terms.

Reading Strategy
Identifying Problems and Solutions After students read the lesson, ask them to write a paragraph that explains what they have read.

● **uick Write**

Give students a few minutes to make their lists. Call on volunteers to share an item on the list with the class. As students read the lesson, they should add to and revise their lists.

Caption Answer

Photo Caption Save some of the money for college and spend some to buy a camera cell phone.

Lesson 4 Resources

📂 **Chapter *FAST FILE* Resources**
Guided Reading and Writing 13-4
Concept Mapping Activity 13-4
Cross-Curriculum Activity 13-4
Reteaching Activity 13-4
Enrichment Activity 13-4
Lesson Quiz 13-4

Technology
⚖ Transparency 13-4
Audio Summaries
ExamView® Assessment Suite
Vocabulary PuzzleMaker
StudentWorks™ Plus

 Go Online

TEACH

Reading Check

Answer $38 billion

AL Active Learning

Real-World Connection Ask students to find out how much an average pack of cigarettes and an average container of smokeless tobacco costs in their community. They can inquire about prices at a local convenience store, gas station, or grocery store. In class, call on volunteers to share what they have found out about the price of tobacco products. Then ask students to calculate the cost of using tobacco for one day, one week, one month, and one year. **OL**

Academic Vocabulary

Estimated Ask students to explain how and why they find estimated answers to math problems. Then have students read and discuss the definition of *estimated*. Point out how the word is used in the text: "An estimated 40,000 nonsmokers die each year from heart disease." Ask: Why does it make sense to use an estimated number in this sentence? You will find academic vocabulary activities in the Student Activities Workbook. 📂

Caption Answer

Photo Caption *Sample answer:* I can ask a smoker not to smoke inside a building, and I can ask the management to prohibit smoking inside.

Academic Vocabulary

estimated (ES tuh mey ted) *(adjective)* obtained using rough calculations. *Tyra's assignment was to calculate the estimated number of teens who join after-school sports teams.*

▼ Secondhand smoke is particularly hard on small children and people with asthma. **What are some actions that you can take to eliminate secondhand smoke in certain places?**

Buying tobacco products is not the only cost of smoking. Smokers pay higher health insurance rates than nonsmokers. They can also expect to live shorter lives and have more health problems than nonsmokers. This is especially true for females, whose lives are shortened by an average of five years from smoking.

Smoking is costly in two other ways as well. Burning tobacco is a leading cause of forest fires and fires in the home.

Reading Check **Recall** How much does the United States spend each year on health care costs related to tobacco use?

Costs to the Nonsmoker

Smokers are not the only people who pay a price for their habit. The health of those who don't smoke is also affected. Whenever a smoker lights up, smoke is released into the air that everyone breathes. This is referred to as **secondhand smoke,** or *environmental tobacco smoke (ETS)*. ETS is a mixture of two forms of smoke from burning tobacco products. The first is **sidestream smoke,** or *smoke that comes directly from a burning cigarette, pipe, or cigar.* The second type is **mainstream smoke,** or *smoke that is exhaled by a smoker.* Sidestream smoke contains twice as much tar and nicotine as mainstream smoke.

A nonsmoker who breathes in secondhand smoke is said to be a **passive smoker.** Passive smokers develop many of the same health problems as people who actually light and smoke tobacco products. An **estimated** 40,000 nonsmokers die each year from heart disease. About 3,000 additional nonsmokers die of lung cancer.

Secondhand smoke is particularly hard on children younger than 18 months and people with asthma. Each year, between 150,000 and 300,000 infants and toddlers develop pneumonia or bronchitis from secondhand smoke. Of these, some 15,000 need to be hospitalized. Secondhand smoke is also estimated to cause between 200,000 to 1 million asthma attacks each year.

HEALTH LITERACY

The Risks of Secondhand Smoke Environmental tobacco smoke (ETS) contains a mixture of more than 4,000 chemicals. More than 50 of those chemicals are known to be cancer-causing agents, called carcinogens. In addition to the cancers associated with secondhand smoke, ETS also results in chronic coughing, lowered lung function, severe respiratory tract infections in children, eye and nose irritation, and severe and chronic heart disease. Children are particularly susceptible to ETS because their lungs are not fully developed.

Costs to the Unborn Child

Health experts have long recognized that pregnancy and tobacco do not mix. Smoking during pregnancy increases the risk that the baby will be born too soon and have developmental problems. Babies born to smoking mothers also have lower birth weights than those born to nonsmoking mothers. One reason for the lower birth weight is that the developing baby gets too little oxygen. The lack of oxygen is caused by the presence of carbon monoxide gas in the mother's blood.

 Reading Check **Identify** If a pregnant female smokes, how is her baby affected?

Costs of Lost Productivity

Productivity is a measure of how much a person is able to produce based on how much time he or she works. If you finish most of your homework in study hall, you might say study hall is "productive." People who use tobacco have lower productivity levels on the job. They are sick more often than nonsmokers and, therefore, get less done. This reduced or lost productivity is costly to businesses. It is also costly to the nation as a whole. It is estimated that smoking costs the U.S. economy $80 billion per year in lost productivity.

Countering the Costs of Tobacco

According to the Centers for Disease Control and Prevention, the cost of each pack of cigarettes sold in the United States is more than $7 in medical care. Other studies suggest that the cost may be even higher. Some public action groups and Congress have been investigating ways to lower that cost. A ban on the manufacture and sale of tobacco products has been proposed. Many smokers, however, claim that would interfere with their constitutional rights.

Another proposal is to increase the amount of excise tax on cigarettes. This would make it more costly to purchase tobacco products and give the government more money to educate people about the dangers of tobacco use. The graph in **Figure 13.4** on the next page shows the portion of the retail price of cigarettes that goes to excise tax in selected states.

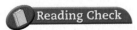 **Reading Check** **Explain** What are two possible solutions to offsetting the costs of tobacco on society?

Connect To... Math

Cigarette Taxes

Research has shown that higher cigarette taxes have been one of the most effective ways to reduce smoking. State and federal taxes can really increase the cost of a pack of cigarettes. For example, in New Jersey the average price of a pack is $6.06. This price includes the following taxes:

$2.40 state excise cigarette tax
.39 federal tax
.34 sales tax

Compute the total tax included in the price of a pack of cigarettes in New Jersey. What percentage of the price is tax? What effect would increasing the state cigarette tax have on the average price?

Connect To... Math

Cigarette Taxes
Ask a volunteer to write the tax amounts on the board. Give students a few minutes to calculate the percentage. *over 51%* Then discuss with students the effect of increasing cigarette taxes. **OL**

Reading Check

Answer, top The baby might be born too soon, weigh less than normal, and have developmental problems.
Answer, bottom a proposed ban on the manufacture and sale of tobacco products; increase sales tax on cigarettes

R Reading Strategy

Analyzing a Graphic After students have examined **Figure 13.4** on page 322, ask: What generalization can you make about the taxes on a pack of cigarettes in the Northeast United States compared to states in the South? *Most southern states have a much lower cigarette tax rate.* What state in this chart has the highest tax rate for a pack of cigarettes? *Rhode Island* In what state is the cigarette tax rate the lowest? *North Carolina* **OL**

 Go Online
Visit **glencoe.com** and complete the Interactive Study Guide for Lesson 4.

Lesson 4: Tobacco's Costs to Society **321**

HEALTH LITERACY

Smoking During Pregnancy Research has shown that a female who smokes during pregnancy increases the risks of premature delivery, stillbirth, low-birth-weight infants, and sudden infant death syndrome. Low birth weight is a leading cause of infant deaths in the United States, resulting in about 300,000 infant deaths per year. When a mother smokes during pregnancy, she reduces her baby's lung function. Studies have also shown that nicotine is found in the breast milk of smoking mothers who nurse their babies.

ASSESS

Reteaching

- Assign Concept Map 13-4 or Reteaching Activity 13-4 in the Fast Files.
- Have students make posters with illustrations and captions that show the costs of tobacco use to individuals and society.

Enrichment

- Assign Enrichment Activity 13-4 in the Fast Files.
- Have students do research using library and online resources on how smoking during pregnancy affects newborn babies.

CLOSE

Call on students to explain how tobacco use costs smokers, nonsmokers, unborn children, and society.

Caption Answer

Figure Caption In Florida, the cigarette tax rate is about 34 cents per pack. The tax rate in New York is $1.50 per pack.

▼ **FIGURE 13.4**

STATE EXCISE TAX RATES ON CIGARETTES

Since January 1, 2002, 41 states have increased their cigarette tax in an effort to reduce smoking. **What is the tax rate for a pack of cigarettes in Florida? In New York?**

State	Tax Rate (¢ per pack)	State	Tax Rate (¢ per pack)
Alaska	160	New York	150
Arizona	118	North Carolina	5
Connecticut	151	Rhode Island	246
Florida	33.9	South Carolina	7
Georgia	37	Vermont	119
Michigan	200	Washington	142.5
Montana	170	Wisconsin	77
New Jersey	240	District of Columbia	100

Source: Compiled by FTA various sources, 2005.

Lesson 4 Review

 After You Read

Review this lesson for new terms, major headings, and Reading Checks.

What I Learned

1. *Vocabulary* What is *secondhand smoke*? How does it affect the nonsmoker?

2. *Identify* How much money do tobacco companies spend each year on advertising?

3. *Vocabulary* What is smoking's cost to the United States in terms of business productivity?

Thinking Critically

4. *Evaluate* Why are pregnant women advised not to smoke?

5. *Analyze* Erin was waiting in line for the movies. When the man in front of Erin lit a cigarette, a woman standing behind the man said it was rude. "Why?" the man asked. "I'm not hurting anyone else, am I?" How would you respond to this question?

Applying Health Skills

6. *Advocacy* With a group, brainstorm ways to lessen the cost of tobacco to society. Once you come up with a plan, share it with those in other groups. Take the best ideas from all plans. Share these with your local government representative in the form of a class letter or e-mail.

Go Online For more Lesson Review Activities, go to **glencoe.com**.

Lesson 4 Review Answers

1. Secondhand smoke is the smoke that is released into the air whenever a smoker lights up. A nonsmoker who breathes in secondhand smoke develops many of the same health problems as smokers.

2. $12.7 billion

3. $80 billion per year

4. Smoking during pregnancy can cause low birth rate, premature birth, and development problems.

5. *Sample answer:* Explain that breathing secondhand smoke causes many of the same health problems as smoking.

6. Divide the class into small groups, and ask each group to develop a plan to lessen the cost of tobacco to the nation. Have groups share their plans with the class. Then have students compose a class letter or e-mail to a local government representative.

Choosing to Be Tobacco Free

Guide to Reading

● **Building Vocabulary**
Write the terms that follow in your notebook. Next to each write the definition that is highlighted in the lesson.

- negative peer pressure (p. 323)
- point-of-sale promotions (p. 324)

● **Focusing on the Main Ideas**
In this lesson, you will learn to

- **identify** ways teens are influenced to try tobacco.
- **explain** how to avoid pressure to use tobacco.
- **describe** the rights of nonsmokers.

● **Reading Strategy**
Predicting Glance at the headings and pictures in this lesson. Predict what this lesson will teach you.

Why Some Teens Start Using Tobacco

With everything you have read in this chapter, you may wonder why any teen would use tobacco. Here, you will find some answers and learn about ways to stay tobacco free.

Pressure from Peers

At some point, most teens will be offered tobacco. Some will not only have it offered to them, but be strongly encouraged to use it as well. This *pressure you feel to go along with harmful behaviors or beliefs of others your age* is called **negative peer pressure.**

▶ Messages like this encourage people to say no to tobacco. **What would you say if someone offered you a cigarette?**

Quick Write

Write a short dialogue between yourself and a peer who wants you to try tobacco. Show how you can politely but firmly refuse.

Smoking Deaths This Year And Counting

American Heart Association · AMERICAN CANCER SOCIETY · American Lung Association · web

Lesson 5: Choosing to Be Tobacco Free **323**

FOCUS

Activating Prior Knowledge

What I Know Call on volunteers to describe reasons why a teen would begin using tobacco when almost all teens know that using tobacco is unhealthy.

Guide to Reading

Building Vocabulary
- Explain to students that *peer* comes from a Latin word meaning "equal." In common usage, a person's peer is someone equal in age and living situation. A teen's peer would be much different, for example, than a professional adult's peer.
- Use Vocabulary PuzzleMaker to reinforce vocabulary terms.

Reading Strategy
Predicting Before students read the lesson, give them a few minutes to glance at the headings and pictures and write a sentence or two about what the lesson will teach.

Quick Write

After students have each written a short dialogue, ask volunteers to share their work with the class.

Caption Answer

Photo Caption *Sample answer:* Use the S.T.O.P strategy

Lesson 5 Resources

📁 **Chapter FAST FILE Resources**
Guided Reading and Writing 13-5
Concept Mapping Activity 13-5
Cross-Curriculum Activity 13-5
Reteaching Activity 13-5
Enrichment Activity 13-5
Lesson Quiz 13-5

Technology
🔦 Transparency 13-5
💿 Audio Summaries
⚙ *ExamView® Assessment Suite*
💿 Vocabulary PuzzleMaker
💿 StudentWorks™ Plus

Go Online

Reading Check

Answer They may be persuaded to use tobacco by seeing others they like or admire smoking.

Respiratory Therapist Have students meet in groups to read and discuss the information about respiratory therapists. Encourage students to share with their groups any experiences they may have had with respiratory therapists. Then have volunteers within each group read more at **glencoe.com** and research your state's requirements for working as a respiratory therapist. Ask these volunteers to share their findings with other group members.

Caption Answer

Figure Caption Most teens appreciate how unhealthy tobacco use can be and choose not to smoke.

Respiratory Therapist

Respiratory therapists evaluate, treat, and care for patients with breathing disorders like asthma or emphysema. Respiratory therapists are in demand because many people have respiratory problems and need help in order to breathe comfortably. If you want to become a respiratory therapist, you should study the respiratory system and learn about environmental factors or personal behaviors that can harm a person's lungs.

What kind of training does a respiratory therapist need? Go to *Career Corner* at **glencoe.com** to find out.

Other Pressures

Some of the pressures to smoke can come from indirect sources, such as the following:

- **Family members.** Teens who live in homes where tobacco is used are more likely to use tobacco themselves.
- **Advertising.** Tobacco companies use strategies such as **point-of-sale promotions,** which are *advertising campaigns in which a product is promoted at a store's checkout counter.* They effectively capture the attention of shoppers as they are waiting to pay.
- **Media.** TV shows and movies often show characters having fun while smoking.

The good news is that fewer and fewer teens are using tobacco every year. **Figure 13.5** shows what teens really think about tobacco.

Reading Check

Describe What are some ways in which teens are pressured to smoke?

▼ **FIGURE 13.5**

TEEN OPINIONS ON SMOKING

Here is what teens across the United States said in response to statements about tobacco use. **How would you respond to these statements?**

All numbers are percentages	Agree	Disagree	No Opinion or Do Not Know
Seeing someone smoke turns me off.	67	22	10
I would only date people who don't smoke.	86	8	6
It is safe to smoke for only a year or two.	7	92	1
Smoking can help you when you're bored.	7	92	1
Smoking helps reduce stress.	21	78	3
Smoking helps keep your weight down.	18	80	2
Chewing tobacco and snuff cause cancer.	95	2	3
I strongly dislike being around smokers.	65	22	13

Source: Centers for Disease Control and Prevention, 2005.

Cultural Perspectives

Smoking in the Media According to the Centers for Disease Control and Prevention (CDC), about two-thirds of films show tobacco use. One study showed that top-billed actors smoked in 59 percent of the movies reviewed. The use of tobacco in films reinforces the misleading perception that smoking is normal behavior and even desirable. One practice that increases tobacco use in films is cigarette companies paying large sums of money for film characters to smoke.

Staying Tobacco Free

You can protect your health now and in the future by making a commitment to stay tobacco free. Ninety percent of adult smokers report having started smoking before age 18. If you avoid using tobacco now as a teen, there is a strong possibility that you won't start smoking as an adult.

There is no question that resisting negative peer pressure can be difficult, but you can do it. Start by choosing friends who do not use tobacco. Also, avoid situations where tobacco is likely to be used. Finally, if you do feel pressure to try tobacco, remember to use the S.T.O.P. strategy to help you say no. The S.T.O.P. strategy is explained in Chapter 5.

Nonsmokers' Rights

You have the right to breathe air that is free of tobacco smoke. Laws have been passed in recent years to protect the rights of nonsmokers. Many local laws forbid smoking in designated areas such as businesses, schools, and public transportation vehicles.

Reading Check **Identify** What action has been taken to protect nonsmokers' rights?

Go Online

Visit glencoe.com and complete the Interactive Study Guide for Lesson 5.

CHAPTER 13
Lesson 5

Reading Check

Answer Local laws forbid smoking in public places.

ASSESS

Assessment Resources

Lesson Review Quiz
- *ExamView*
- Fast Files Activities
- Online Quizzes and Activities

Reteaching

- Assign Concept Map 13-5 or Reteaching Activity 13-5 in the Fast Files.
- Have students write a story about a teen who uses S.T.O.P. to stay free of tobacco.

Enrichment

- Assign Enrichment Activity 13-5 in the Fast Files.
- Ask students to find out about laws limiting smoking in other parts of the country, including in some of the largest cities of the United States. Ask that students prepare a report of their findings.

CLOSE

Call on students to describe the pressures that cause teens to start using tobacco.

Lesson 5 Review

 After You Read

Review this lesson for new terms, major headings, and Reading Checks.

What I Learned

1. *Vocabulary* What is *negative peer pressure*?

2. *Describe* Name ways of avoiding pressure to try tobacco.

3. *Recall* What right is shared by all nonsmokers?

Thinking Critically

4. *Evaluate* Of all the sources that pressure to smoke can come from, which do you find the most persuasive, and why?

5. *Analyze* You are sitting in a nonsmoking area of a restaurant. A person at the next table lights up. When you point to the nonsmoking sign, the person extinguishes the cigarette. She then says, "You know, smokers have rights, too." How do you respond?

Applying Health Skills

6. *Accessing Information* Use the Internet to research government policies and laws related to the sale and use of tobacco products. What laws have been created by your state's government? Analyze the purpose and benefits of these laws.

Go Online For more Lesson Review Activities, go to **glencoe.com**.

Lesson 5: Choosing to Be Tobacco Free **325**

Lesson 5 Review Answers

1. the pressure you feel to go along with harmful behaviors or beliefs of others.
2. Stay away from people who smoke or use other tobacco products. Steer clear of situations where tobacco is likely to be used.
3. You have the right to breathe air that is free of tobacco smoke.

4. *Sample answer:* Seeing people in the entertainment industries is most persuasive because these people are portrayed as heroes.
5. *Sample answer:* Smokers only have the right to smoke when they aren't endangering the

health of another person. Every nonsmoker has the right to breathe air that is free of tobacco smoke.
6. Answers will include your local government's tobacco laws and an analysis of those laws.

Building Health Skills: Saying No to Tobacco

Skill

Goal Setting

Activating Prior Knowledge

Ask students to explain why secondhand smoke is unhealthful for nonsmokers.

- **Objective** After completing the activity, students will be able to use the goal-setting strategy to avoid the use of tobacco during social activities.
- **Time** 35 minutes
- **Materials** paper, pencil

Teacher Classroom Resources

📁 Building Health Skills
🖨 Transparency 2-1

Model

- Review the steps of the goal-setting plan as shown in the Skill Summary. Then have students read about Carrie and Rebecca in the Model section.
- Ask: From whom did Carrie and Rebecca get help to achieve their goal? *Rebecca's fiancé helped by asking the nonsmoking relatives to notify the smokers about the smoke-free reception.* What was the result? *Rebecca had a smoke-free reception.*

National Health Standards Addressed

3.8.1, 4.8.2, 6.8.2

326

Building Health Skills

Accessing Information
Practicing Healthful Behaviors
Stress Management
Analyzing Influences
Communication Skills
Refusal Skills
Conflict Resolution
Decision Making
Goal Setting
Advocacy

What Is Goal Setting?

Goal setting is a five-step plan for improving and maintaining your personal health. Some goals are easy to reach while others may be more challenging.

The Five Steps of the Goal-Setting Plan

Step 1: Choose a realistic goal and write it down.

Step 2: List the steps that you need to take to reach the goal.

Step 3: Find others, like family, friends, and teachers, who can help and support you.

Step 4: Set checkpoints along the way to evaluate your progress.

Step 5: Reward yourself once you have reached your goal.

Saying No to Tobacco

Follow the Model, Practice, and Apply steps to help you master this important health skill.

① Model

Read how Carrie and Rebecca use goal setting to make Rebecca's wedding reception smokefree.

Carrie and Rebecca were discussing plans for Rebecca's wedding reception. Carrie remembered that many of the guests smoke. "What are we going to do?" Carrie asked Rebecca.

Carrie and Rebecca then came up with a plan to make the reception smoke free.

1. ***Identify a specific goal.*** Rebecca wants to have a smoke-free reception.
2. ***List the steps you will take.*** All the smokers will be asked to smoke outside.
3. ***Get help and support from others.*** Rebecca and her fiancé will ask their nonsmoking relatives to notify the smokers about the decision.
4. ***Evaluate your progress.*** Rebecca will make sure that everyone knows that the wedding is a nonsmoking event.
5. ***Reward yourself.*** Rebecca's reward will be a smoke-free reception.

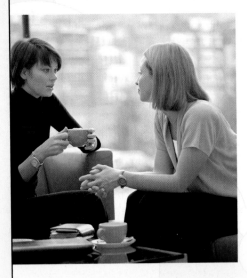

326 Chapter 13: Tobacco

▶ *Teaching Tips*

Reasons to Avoid Secondhand Smoke For this lesson to be most effective, quickly review with students all the dangers of secondhand smoke (e.g., more tar, more nicotine, respiratory illnesses, aggravate allergies and asthma).

Responding to Smokers Emphasize throughout this lesson that smokers are not bad people and should be treated with respect. In addition, remind students of the importance of maintaining good relationships with family members, whether they smoke or not.

❷ Practice

Help Pilar use the goal-setting steps to protect herself from environmental tobacco smoke at a birthday party.

Pilar is on her way to a birthday party with relatives. Her aunt Emily, who smokes, is going to be there. Though Pilar is looking forward to seeing her aunt, she wants to protect her health by avoiding secondhand tobacco smoke.

1. What is Pilar's specific goal?
2. What are some steps she could take?
3. How could she get help and support from others?
4. How can she evaluate her progress?
5. What is Pilar's reward?

ACTIVITY

❸ Apply

Use what you have learned about goal setting to complete the activity below.

Imagine that you are planning to take a vacation with your relatives. Some of your relatives smoke. You know issues will come up about when and where smoking will be allowed. For example, the smokers in the group will want to sit in the smoking section at restaurants. Use your goal-setting skills to help you stay tobacco free. Explain why it is important to stay away from tobacco smoke.

Self-Check

- Did I make a plan for achieving my goal of remaining tobacco free?
- Did I explain why it's important to avoid tobacco smoke?

Building Health Skills

Building Health Skills **327**

Practice

- Have students read about Pilar and her aunt in the Practice section. Have students work in pairs to discuss the questions. Ask each pair of students to write a response to the questions.
- Lead a class discussion of the responses. Ask volunteers to share how they answered each of the questions.

Apply/Assess

- Have students work individually to develop a goal-setting plan for the Apply section. Ask that each student develop a plan by referring to the goal-setting steps. Have each student describe the plan in a paragraph.
- Student plans should explain why it is important to avoid tobacco smoke.
- Call on volunteers to describe their plans to the class. Discuss which plans would be most effective in achieving the goal of staying tobacco free.
- You may wish to distribute Building Health Skills Activity in the Fast Files.

ASSESSMENT SCORING

Using a rubric, student work should meet all criteria to achieve the highest score.

Skills Student work:
- includes a realistic goal statement.
- lists steps to achieve the goal.
- identifies sources of help.
- evaluate your progress.
- provides a healthy reward.

Concepts Student work:
- incorporates accurate and complete information about being tobacco free.
- describes connections between tobacco and health.

TIME *health news*

Up In Smoke

Objectives

After completing this activity, students will be able to:

- Understand how secondhand smoke impacts individuals with heart disease
- Explain why the CDC has issued warnings about exposure to secondhand smoke

Motivator

Have students identify ways in which tobacco smoke is harmful to body systems.

Teaching the Feature

- Have students work in small groups to find out more about the causes and effects of heart attacks. Have each group prepare a short oral report with at least two visual aids to share with the class.
- Provide a summary of local smoking restrictions in your community. Make a list of specific locations such as restaurants or other public places and ask students to create a T chart with columns titled "Smoking Allowed" and "Smoking Not Allowed." Place the names of the locations under the correct sides of the chart. **EL**

UP IN SMOKE

Secondhand smoke might be even more dangerous than experts first thought.

Recently, many people were surprised to hear that the Centers for Disease Control and Prevention (CDC) issued a warning about secondhand smoke. It advised anyone at risk of heart disease to avoid any indoor public spaces where smoking is allowed. According to the CDC, exposure to secondhand smoke for as little as 30 minutes can significantly increase a person's risk of heart attack.

DETECTING A HIDDEN DANGER

The health risks posed by secondhand smoke are well documented, but what triggered the warning was a small study out of Helena, Montana. When the city passed a law banning indoor smoking, Helena's only heart hospital recorded a 40 percent drop in the number of heart attacks. They went from an average of 40 per six months to just 24.

What's more, when a court order lifted the ban half a year later, the heart-attack rate bounced right back. Dr. Robert Shepard, who wrote the Helena study, offers this explanation: "There is laboratory evidence that secondhand smoke makes platelets in the blood stickier.

This causes clots and sends arteries into spasm—both of which can lead to heart attacks." The chemical reaction and the resulting damage occur quickly.

WHAT DOES IT MEAN FOR EVERYONE ELSE?

The study's findings could be very important. The CDC estimates that in the United States, secondhand smoke causes 35,000 deaths a year from heart disease. This figure, some experts believe, will have to be revised upward. Why? Because 60 percent of Americans—both smokers and nonsmokers—show biological effects of tobacco-smoke exposure.

Shepard did offer some reassurance for people who cannot avoid groups of smokers when they walk outside. Exposure for a few seconds probably doesn't do much harm, he says, because the toxins in cigarette smoke are diluted in outside air.

328 TIME health news: Up in Smoke

Activity | *Media, Technology, and Culture*

Media Have students work in small groups to write and produce a short video explaining the dangers of secondhand smoke. Challenge students to develop creative ways to deliver their messages. Ask each group to share its video with the class, and if possible, with other students in the school. **OL**

Reading Review

STUDY TO GO Visit glencoe.com to download quizzes and eFlashcards for Chapter 13.

FOLDABLES Study Organizer

Foldables® and Other Study Aids Take out the Foldable® that you created for Lesson 1 and any graphic organizers that you created for Lessons 1–5. Find a partner and quiz each other using these study aids.

Lesson 1 Facts About Tobacco

Main Idea Tobacco is an addictive and harmful drug.

- Harmful substances in tobacco include nicotine, tar, and carbon monoxide.
- Tobacco products include cigarettes, cigars, pipes, bidis, kreteks, and smokeless tobacco that is chewed or inhaled.

Lesson 2 Health Risks of Tobacco Use

Main Idea The chemicals in tobacco and tobacco smoke can cause damage to most of the body's systems.

- Congress passed a law in 1965 requiring tobacco manufacturers to print health-warning labels on cigarette packages. Other tobacco products have similar labels.
- The long-term effects of tobacco include chronic obstructive pulmonary disease, cardiovascular disease, stomach ulcers, infertility, and cancer.

Lesson 3 Tobacco Addiction

Main Idea Once addicted, it is very hard to quit smoking.

- A tolerance to nicotine forms as the body adjusts to the effects of the drug.
- Physical dependence is a type of addiction in which the body feels a direct need for a drug.

- Psychological dependence is an addiction in which the mind sends the body a message that it needs more of a drug.
- Withdrawal is the physical and psychological reactions that occur when someone stops using an addictive substance.

Lesson 4 Tobacco's Costs to Society

Main Idea There are many costs associated with tobacco use.

- Tobacco products are expensive.
- A nonsmoker who breathes in tobacco smoke is called a passive smoker. They are exposed to secondhand smoke, in the form of sidestream and mainstream smoke.
- Pregnant women who smoke risk having babies born too soon and with developmental problems.
- People who smoke get less work done because they are sick more often than nonsmokers.

Lesson 5 Choosing to Be Tobacco Free

Main Idea You can protect your health now and in the future by making a commitment to stay tobacco free.

- Pressure to use tobacco can come from peers, family members, advertising, and the media.
- Ways to avoid using tobacco include choosing friends who do not use tobacco, avoiding situations where tobacco is likely to be used, and using refusal skills.
- Many local laws forbid smoking at businesses, at schools, and in public transportation vehicles.

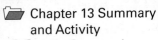

Assessment Resources

- Chapter 13 Summary and Activity
- Audio Summaries
- Reading Tutor
- Performance Assessment
- Chapter 13 Test
- *ExamView*
- Vocabulary PuzzleMaker
- Online Learning Center

Reading Review

Study Aids

- **Using the Dinah Zike Foldable® Study Organizer** Have students use the Foldable® to review the content of Lesson 1. Ask students to reread and revise as necessary their notes about the different kinds of tobacco products in their Foldables®.

- **Online Learning Tools** Have students go to the Teen Health Online Learning Center at **glencoe.com** to:

  - Download a **Podcast**.

  - Download free **Study-to-Go** content to their PDAs or cell phones.

Vocabulary Review

- **Word Game** Students will draw chapter vocabulary terms out of a hat and then flip a coin to determine whether they must define the word (heads) or use the word in a sentence (tails).

Teaching Tips

Reading Question of the Day When given an expository text, struggling readers often require help in order for them to understand what they are reading. One way to provide such help is to focus students on specific information by starting the class with a question of the day. Distribute large index cards to students and have them write the question of the day on the front of the card. Tell students that as they read they should note the page number and location of information on the back of the card.

Assessment

Reviewing Vocabulary and Main Ideas

1. Nicotine
2. carbon monoxide
3. Smokeless tobacco
4. chronic obstructive pulmonary disease (COPD)
5. Cardiovascular disease
6. False, tolerance
7. False, psychological dependence
8. True
9. True
10. False, point-of-sale promotion
11. False, less likely

Thinking Critically

12. *Sample answer:* Nadine can be honest about smelling smoke on Shari's clothes and hair and then mention how important she thinks it is to stay away from using tobacco. Nadine might also offer to talk about anything that might be influencing Shari to use tobacco.
13. Nicotine causes addiction by interacting with receptors in the brain. Physical dependence develops, and the user craves more of the substance.

Go Online

Have students visit glencoe.com to take the Chapter 13 quiz.

330

After You Read

Health éSpotlight   **VIDEO**

Now that you have read the chapter, look back at your answer to the Health eSpotlight question on the chapter opener. What are some additional steps you can recommend to help a friend stop using tobacco products?

Reviewing Vocabulary and Main Ideas

On a sheet of paper, write the numbers 1–5. After each number, write the term from the list that best completes each sentence.

- addictive
- bronchi
- carbon monoxide
- cardiovascular **disease**
- chronic obstructive pulmonary disease (COPD)
- nicotine
- smokeless tobacco
- tar

Lesson 1 Facts About Tobacco

1. _____ is an addictive drug found in tobacco leaves and in all tobacco products.
2. A poisonous, odorless gas found in tobacco smoke is _____.
3. _____ is ground tobacco that is chewed or inhaled through the nose.

Lesson 2 Health Risks of Tobacco Use

4. A condition in which passages in the lungs become swollen and irritated, eventually losing their elasticity, is known as _____.
5. _____ is a disease of the heart and blood vessels.

*On a sheet of paper, write the numbers 6–11. Write **True** or **False** for each statement below. If the statement is false, change the underlined word or phrase to make it true.*

Lesson 3 Tobacco Addiction

6. A process in which your body needs more and more of a drug to get the same effect is called <u>withdrawal</u>.
7. A form of addiction in which the mind sends the body a message that it needs more of a drug is called <u>physical addiction</u>.

Lesson 4 Tobacco's Costs to Society

8. <u>Sidestream smoke</u> is smoke that comes from a lighted cigarette, pipe, or cigar.
9. When people miss work because of a tobacco-related illness, the result is <u>lost productivity</u>.

Lesson 5 Choosing to Be Tobacco Free

10. An advertisement that catches your attention at a checkout counter is an example of <u>negative peer pressure</u>.
11. Teens who avoid smoking are <u>more likely</u> to start smoking as adults.

Go Online   Visit **glencoe.com** and take the Online Quiz for Chapter 13.

Health éSpotlight **VIDEO** *Wrap-Up*

Breaking the Tobacco Habit Have students reread the Health eSpotlight question at the beginning of the chapter (page 307) and look at their original answer. Ask: Now that you have read the chapter and watched the video presentation, has your understanding of how dangerous and difficult nicotine dependence can be changed? Ask volunteers to recommend where teens can turn for support and encouragement to quit smoking.

Thinking Critically

Using complete sentences, answer the following questions on a sheet of paper.

12. **Apply** Nadine smells tobacco on her sister Shari's hair and clothes one afternoon. How could Nadine talk to her sister about the tobacco smell without accusing her of smoking?

13. **Synthesize** Explain how a person becomes addicted to tobacco.

Write About It

14. **Personal Writing** Write a story about a teen faced with a difficult decision. The decision is whether to join a club in which the members smoke. Use the decision-making process to show how the teen makes a healthy choice.

Applying Technology

Targeting Tobacco PSA

You and a partner will use a digital recorder and iMovie® to create a public service announcement (PSA) about the dangers of tobacco use.

- Write a script that is no longer than two minutes with two speaking parts. You can use any information in this chapter as long as it sends the message that tobacco is dangerous.
- Use a digital recorder to record your PSA
- Edit for clarity, accuracy of information, and time. Save your PSA
- Import your PSA into iMovie®.

Applying Technology

Targeting Tobacco PSA
Equipment needs: digital recorder and iMovie® or similar software
Have students choose partners for this project. Then help students discuss the steps in completing the project; emphasize the importance of writing a script and rehearsing the reading before beginning to record. If access to recorders and computers is limited, create a sign-up sheet for each and establish time limits for their use. Have students view and comment on each other's completed announcements.

Write About It

14. **Personal Writing** Stories, which will vary, should demonstrate that remaining tobacco free is absolutely necessary, even if that means not joining the club.

Standardized Test Practice

1. C
2. D

Standardized Test Practice

Math

This chart shows the estimated number of annual smoking-related deaths and their causes. Use this information to answer the questions that follow.

Lung Cancer	123,800
Other Cancers	34,700
Chronic Lung Disease	90,600
Coronary Heart Disease	86,800
Stroke	17,400
Other Diagnoses	84,600

TEST-TAKING TIP

When problems include charts, make sure you understand what type of data it shows.

1. This chart reveals
   A. that lung cancer is not the leading cause of smoking-related deaths.
   B. that more people die of chronic lung disease than lung cancer.
   C. that lung cancer is the leading cause of smoking-related deaths.
   D. that more people die of other cancers and strokes than of lung cancer.

2. Based on this chart, you can assume all of the following *except*
   A. that smoking can cause a person to have a deadly stroke.
   B. that more people die of other cancers than of strokes.
   C. that smoking leads to a number of deadly diseases.
   D. that more people die in car crashes than from smoking.

Chapter 13 Assessment **331**

Test-Taking Tips

Charts Explain that some charts are used to show the differences between the value of two sets of numbers. Values may be shown as whole numbers, percents, or with a decimal point. The chart above provides an estimated number of annual smoking-related deaths and their causes. Students can use the provided data to compare the values and draw their own conclusions regarding smoking-related deaths.

CHAPTER 14 pp. 332–369	Standards		Skills and Activities
	National	**State/Local**	
	National Health Education Standards 1.8.5, 4.8.2, 5.8.2, 5.8.5, 6.8.4, 7.8.1, 7.8.2		**HEALTH QUIZ**, *p. 333* **BUILDING HEALTH SKILLS** *Refusal Skills* Saying No to Drugs, *pp. 364–365* **HANDS-ON HEALTH** Memory Obstacles, *p. 366*
Lesson 1 Drug Misuse and Abuse *pp. 334–337*	National Health Education Standards 1.8.1, 1.8.2, 1.8.5, 1.8.8, 1.8.9, 3.8.2, 3.8.5, 5.8.7, 7.8.2, 8.8.1, 8.8.2		**MEDIA WATCH** Medicine Ads, *p. 335* **HEALTH SKILLS ACTIVITY** *Practicing Healthful Behaviors* Handling Medicine Safely in Your Home, *p. 336*
Lesson 2 Marijuana and Other Illegal Drugs *pp. 338–344*	National Health Education Standards 1.8.2, 1.8.3, 1.8.7, 1.8.8, 1.8.9, 2.8.5, 2.8.7, 2.8.9, 3.8.4, 5.8.1, 5.8.6, 5.8.7, 8.8.3		**Careers for the 21st Century** Pharmacist, *p. 339* **HEALTH SKILLS ACTIVITY** *Accessing Information* Marijuana Myths, *p. 341* **DEVELOPING GOOD CHARACTER** *Citizenship, p. 342* **What Teens Think** How can a teen avoid being pressured to use drugs?, *p. 342*
Lesson 3 Narcotics, Stimulants, and Depressants *pp. 345–351*	National Health Education Standards 1.8.2, 1.8.7, 1.8.8, 1.8.9, 2.8.5, 2.8.9, 5.8.1, 5.8.6, 5.8.7, 6.8.2		**MEDIA WATCH** Antidrug Ads, *p. 348*
Lesson 4 Hallucinogens and Inhalants *pp. 352–355*	National Health Education Standards 1.8.8, 1.8.9, 2.8.9, 5.8.1, 5.8.7, 8.8.2, 8.8.3		**Go Online** Speaking Out Against Drugs, *p. 354*
Lesson 5 Getting Help *pp. 356–359*	National Health Education Standards 1.8.5, 1.8.6, 3.8.4, 4.8.4, 5.8.2, 5.8.3, 5.8.4, 5.8.5, 5.8.6, 6.8.1, 7.8.2, 8.8.2		
Lesson 6 Staying Drug Free *pp. 360–363*	National Health Education Standards 1.8.1, 1.8.2, 1.8.5, 1.8.7, 2.8.7, 2.8.8, 3.8.4, 4.8.2, 4.8.4, 5.8.2, 5.8.4, 5.8.6, 6.8.1, 7.8.2, 8.8.1, 8.8.2		

PACING THE CHAPTER

Lesson 1 30 min	**Lesson 4** 30 min	**Chapter Review** 45 min
Lesson 2 30 min	**Lesson 5** 30 min	**Hands-on Health** 20 min
Lesson 3 30 min	**Lesson 6** 30 min	**Building Health Skills** 30 min

BLOCK SCHEDULING

For block scheduling, assign students Building Health Skills feature *Saying No to Drugs*, pages 364–365, and Guided Reading and Writing. 📁

Planning Guide

Reproducible Resources	Assessment	Media and Technology
Chapter FAST FILE Resources Chapter Summaries and Activities REVIEW Building Health Skills Activity TEACH Performance Assessment Activity EXTEND Universal Access Activities TEACH Parent Letter and Activities 📁 **Student Activities Workbook** TEACH 📁 **Reading Tutor** TEACH	Building Health Skills Activity, *pp. 364–365* Chapter 14 Assessment, *pp. 368–369* **Chapter FAST FILE Resources** Performance Assessment Activity Chapter 14 Test 💿 *ExamView® Assessment Suite*	TeacherWorks^Plus includes: ● Interactive Teacher Edition ● Lesson Planner with Calendar ● Access to all blackline masters ● Correlations to standards 💿 StudentWorks™ Plus 🖱 Online Student Edition Dinah Zike's Teaching Health with Foldables®
Chapter FAST FILE Resources Concept Mapping Activity 14-1 REVIEW Health Lab 14-1 EXTEND Enrichment Activity 14-1 EXTEND Lesson Plan 14-1 Guided Reading and Writing 14-1 TEACH Reteaching Activity 14-1 REVIEW	Lesson 1 Review, *p. 337* 🖱 Vocabulary PuzzleMaker 💿 *ExamView® Assessment Suite*	🖱 Vocabulary PuzzleMaker 💿 *ExamView® Assessment Suite* 💿 StudentWorks™ Plus 🔦 Transparency 14-1 **Go Online** 🖱 glencoe.com
Chapter FAST FILE Resources Concept Mapping Activity 14-2 REVIEW Decision-Making Activity 14-2 EXTEND Enrichment Activity 14-2 EXTEND Lesson Plan 14-2 Guided Reading and Writing 14-2 TEACH Reteaching Activity 14-2 REVIEW	Lesson 2 Review, *p. 344* 🖱 Vocabulary PuzzleMaker 💿 *ExamView® Assessment Suite*	🖱 Vocabulary PuzzleMaker 💿 *ExamView® Assessment Suite* 💿 StudentWorks™ Plus 🔦 Transparency 14-2 **Go Online** 🖱 glencoe.com
Chapter FAST FILE Resources Concept Mapping Activity 14-3 REVIEW Cross-Curriculum Activity 14-3 EXTEND Enrichment Activity 14-3 EXTEND Lesson Plan 14-3 Guided Reading and Writing 14-3 TEACH Reteaching Activity 14-3 REVIEW	Lesson 3 Review, *p. 351* 🖱 Vocabulary PuzzleMaker 💿 *ExamView® Assessment Suite*	🖱 Vocabulary PuzzleMaker 💿 *ExamView® Assessment Suite* 💿 StudentWorks™ Plus 🔦 Transparency 14-3 **Go Online** 🖱 glencoe.com
Chapter FAST FILE Resources Concept Mapping Activity 14-4 REVIEW Decision-Making Activity 14-4 EXTEND Enrichment Activity 14-4 EXTEND Lesson Plan 14-4 Guided Reading and Writing 14-4 TEACH Reteaching Activity 14-4 REVIEW	Lesson 4 Review, *p. 355* 🖱 Vocabulary PuzzleMaker 💿 *ExamView® Assessment Suite*	🖱 Vocabulary PuzzleMaker 💿 *ExamView® Assessment Suite* 💿 StudentWorks™ Plus 🔦 Transparency 14-4 **Go Online** 🖱 glencoe.com
Chapter FAST FILE Resources Concept Mapping Activity 14-5 REVIEW Decision-Making Activity 14-5 EXTEND Enrichment Activity 14-5 EXTEND Lesson Plan 14-5 Guided Reading and Writing 14-5 TEACH Reteaching Activity 14-5 REVIEW	Lesson 5 Review, *p. 359* 🖱 Vocabulary PuzzleMaker 💿 *ExamView® Assessment Suite*	🖱 Vocabulary PuzzleMaker 💿 *ExamView® Assessment Suite* 💿 StudentWorks™ Plus 🔦 Transparency 14-5 **Go Online** 🖱 glencoe.com
Chapter FAST FILE Resources Concept Mapping Activity 14-6 REVIEW Cross-Curriculum Activity 14-6 EXTEND Enrichment Activity 14-6 EXTEND Lesson Plan 14-6 Guided Reading and Writing 14-6 TEACH Reteaching Activity 14-6 REVIEW	Lesson 6 Review, *p. 363* 🖱 Vocabulary PuzzleMaker 💿 *ExamView® Assessment Suite*	🖱 Vocabulary PuzzleMaker 💿 *ExamView® Assessment Suite* 💿 StudentWorks™ Plus 🔦 Transparency 14-6 **Go Online** 🖱 glencoe.com

Chapter and Lesson Resources

The *Teen Health* resources are designed for differentiated learning abilities. You may want to use the coded items in this way:

REVIEW —activities to review or reinforce content

TEACH —activities to teach basic concepts

EXTEND —activities to extend or enrich lesson content

 OUT OF TIME?

Use Health Skills Activity *Handling Medicine Safely in Your Home,* page 336, or Media Watch, page 348.

Methamphetamine

The use of methamphetamine, a highly addictive stimulant, has increased dramatically. Methamphetamine use has devastating effects on the individual user, the family, the community, and the environment.

One factor contributing to the rampant use of methamphetamine is the ease with which it can be manufactured. Cold medications containing pseudoephedrine are the main ingredient used to make methamphetamine. Toxic chemicals, such as battery acid, are also used in the process. These chemicals are released into the atmosphere during the cooking process and are often dumped down the drain or onto the ground after their use. Methamphetamine production is very harmful to the environment.

Methamphetamine has many negative consequences. One physical effect of methamphetamine use is "meth mouth," in which the user's teeth rot away due to the corrosive chemicals used in the manufacturing of methamphetamine. If possible, obtain and display pictures of users who suffer from meth mouth. Teens are sometimes more affected by potential damage to their appearance than they are by other potential effects of drug use.

Methamphetamine use also impacts the community. Crime rates increase as a result of methamphetamine use. Foster care systems in many states have seen an increase in the number of children removed from homes due to methamphetamine use.

Emphasize to students the destructive impact of methamphetamine use on individuals, the environment, and the community. Remind students to always contact a trusted adult if they suspect a friend is using methamphetamine.

Ecstasy

Ecstasy is a dangerous stimulant and hallucinogen that is primarily used at nightclubs and dance parties. Teens may have the misconception that ecstasy is safer than other drugs. When discussing ecstasy and other club drugs with the class, be sure to point out the dangers that these drugs pose to all three sides of the health triangle.

Ecstasy damages physical health in the short term by increasing heart rate and body temperature. Dehydration is a common side effect of ecstasy use, although some users may drink so much water while using ecstasy that they experience life-threatening hyponatremia.

Mental/emotional health is also affected by ecstasy use. Cognitive functions and memory are both impaired in ecstasy users. Depression and confusion are also common side effects of ecstasy use. Remind students that ecstasy, like many other drugs, can damage their ability to do well at school.

Point out to students that it is illegal to buy, sell, or possess ecstasy. An arrest would certainly affect their social and mental/emotional health.

Explain to students that they should immediately leave any location at which ecstasy is being used. Students should contact a trusted adult if they suspect a friend is using ecstasy.

Reading Support

Reading Preview

Activating Background Vocabulary Ask students what comes to mind when they hear the word drugs. Solicit all answers and write them on the board. Ask students to sort the answers into two categories: medicines and illegal drugs.

FOLDABLES Study Organizer *Dinah Zike's Reading and Study Skills for Teen Health* provides interactive graphic organizers that help students comprehend and retain health concepts as they read. Use the Foldable® on page 333 or find more Foldables® activities for the chapter on **Drugs** in the separate booklet, available in the TCR.

Lesson 1 Drug Misuse and Abuse

Interactive Reading Have students write five questions about the use and misuse of drugs. Direct them to use *who, what, why, where, when,* and *how* questions. Have students read the lesson, then discuss their questions with a partner.

Lesson 2 Marijuana and Other Illegal Drugs

Summarizing Have students silently read the text. Then have student pairs identify and describe the main concepts of the lesson, including the effects of marijuana use, safety risks, and addiction. Have each student independently write a brief summary of each of the lesson subsections.

Lesson 3 Narcotics, Stimulants, and Depressants

List-Describe-Example As they read, have students make a list of the types of drugs covered in the lesson. Have students define each type of drug, then give an example of each. To illustrate: type of drug = narcotic; definition = addictive drug made from opium and used to relieve pain; example = heroin.

Lesson 4 Hallucinogens and Inhalants

Reading with a Purpose Direct students to read the section titled **Inhalants** to find the damage inhalants can cause to teens and the warning signs of inhalant abuse. After reading, have students respond in a brief descriptive paragraph. Continue to give students a purpose for reading each section.

Lesson 5 Getting Help

Clarifying the Text Guide students to identify questions they still have about where to get help for drug abuse. Have them go back and slowly reread the section **Getting Help**, looking at illustrations and definitions of terms. Have students discuss any remaining questions with a classmate.

Lesson 6 Staying Drug Free

Responding Direct students to stop at any point during reading and discuss with a partner what they like, do not like, or find interesting about what they have read. Have students write a journal entry, describing their thoughts or feelings about the benefits of choosing to be drug free.

Post Reading

Dramatic Presentations Direct student groups to use audiovisual aids, such as overhead projector slides, a PowerPoint presentation, or a computer-generated show to develop a presentation on the use and misuse of drugs or medication.

Key for Using the Teacher Wraparound Edition

Use this key to help you identify the different types of prompts found in the Teacher Wraparound Edition.

R **Reading Strategies** activities help you teach reading skills and vocabulary.

C **Critical Thinking** strategies help students apply and extend what they have learned.

U **Universal Access** activities provide differentiated instruction for students learning to speak English, along with suggestions for teaching various types of learners.

HS **Health Skills Practice** activities reinforce Health Skills concepts and help students apply these skills in their everyday lives.

W **Writing Support** activities provide writing opportunities to help students comprehend the text.

AL **Active Learning** strategies provide a variety of activities for presenting lesson content, including Quick Demos and engaging classroom projects that get students actively involved.

Key to Ability Levels

Teaching Strategies and activities have been coded for ability level and appropriateness.

AL Activities for students working above grade level

OL Activities for students working on grade level

BL Activities for students working below grade level

EL Activities for English Learners

Symbols

Transparencies

CD-ROM

glencoe.com

Print Resources

Drugs

Chapter at a Glance

Lesson 1 explains the difference between drug misuse and drug abuse, and identifies the ways drug abuse negatively affects all sides of the health triangle.

Lesson 2 describes the effects and risks of marijuana use, club drugs, and anabolic steroids.

Lesson 3 explains the relationship between narcotics abuse and drug tolerance, and identifies specific stimulants and depressants.

Lesson 4 identifies the health risks of hallucinogens and inhalants.

Lesson 5 identifies ways to access reliable information on drug use, and describes different treatment options for drug abuse.

Lesson 6 explains the health benefits of staying drug free, and demonstrates alternative behaviors to drug use.

R Reading Strategy

Interpreting the Photo Have students examine the photo. Ask: What are some effects of drug use that might lead these teens to advocate for being drug free? *Drugs can damage the physical, mental/ emotional, and social health of young people, and in some cases can prevent teens from achieving their goals for adulthood.* **OL**

332

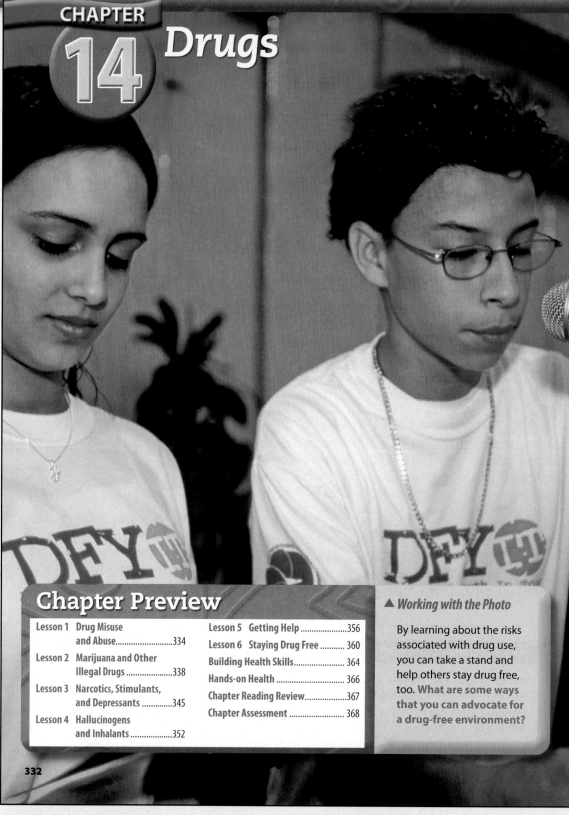

Chapter Preview

332

▲ *Working with the Photo*

By learning about the risks associated with drug use, you can take a stand and help others stay drug free, too. **What are some ways that you can advocate for a drug-free environment?**

Universal Access

Differentiated Learning Glencoe provides teacher support and student materials for all learners in the health classroom.

● Spanish Glosario and chapter summaries assist English Language Learners.
● *Reading Tutor* and related worksheets support reluctant readers.

● Universal Access strategies throughout the Teacher Wraparound Edition and Fast Files help you present materials for gifted students, at-risk students, physically impaired students, and those with behavior disorders or learning disabilities.

Start-Up Activities

Before You Read What do you know about drugs? Take the short quiz on this page. Keep a record of your answers.

HEALTH QUIZ Answer *true* or *false* to each of the following statements:

1. You cannot become addicted to a drug the first time you use it.
2. The abuse of common household products is a serious drug problem in the United States.
3. Marijuana affects all sides of the health triangle.
4. The abuse of anabolic steroids can permanently impair a person's physical growth.

ANSWERS: 1. False; 2. True; 3. True; 4. True

FOLDABLES Study Organizer

As You Read Make this Foldable® to help you organize the information on drugs and medicines in Lesson 1. Begin with a sheet of notebook paper.

1 Fold the sheet of paper along the long axis, leaving a ½" tab along the side.

2 Turn the paper and fold into thirds.

3 Cut the top layer along both folds. Then cut each tab in half to make six tabs.

4 Turn the paper vertically and label the tabs as shown.

1. Drugs
2. Medicines
3. Prescription Medicines
4. OTC Medicines
5. Side Effects
6. Tolerance

Under the appropriate tab, write notes and define terms related to drugs and medicines.

Go Online Visit glencoe.com and complete the Chapter 14 crossword puzzle.

333

FOCUS

Activating Prior Knowledge

What I Know Write the words *drugs* and *medicines* on the board. Have students compare and contrast the meanings of these two terms.

Guide to Reading

Building Vocabulary

- Have students skim the lesson to find the meanings of the terms *drug abuse* and *drug misuse*. Have students contrast the meanings of these two terms.
- Use Vocabulary PuzzleMaker to reinforce vocabulary terms.

Reading Strategy

Drawing Conclusions Ask several students to share one of their conclusions with the class. Follow up after the lesson by asking if the students' conclusions were correct.

 Have students use their Foldables® as they read Lesson 1.

Quick Write

Use student responses to start a brief discussion about the importance of taking personal responsibility for using medications properly.

Caption Answer

Photo Caption Side effects and combining drugs can have dangerous effects.

334

Drug Misuse and Abuse

Guide to Reading

Building Vocabulary
List each new highlighted term and its definition in your notebook.

- drug (p. 334)
- prescription medicines (p. 335)
- over-the-counter (OTC) medicines (p. 335)
- drug misuse (p. 335)
- side effect (p. 335)
- tolerance (p. 335)
- drug abuse (p. 336)

Focusing on the Main Ideas
In this lesson, you will learn to

- **explain** the difference between drug misuse and drug abuse.
- **identify** the risks of drug abuse.
- **develop** strategies for making healthful choices about taking medicines.

Reading Strategy
Drawing Conclusions Based on this lesson, list three different ways drug abuse can affect your health.

FOLDABLES Study Organizer Use the Foldable® on p. 333 as you read this lesson.

Quick Write

Write a sentence explaining why it is important to read the label directions on medicines before taking them.

Drug Use

There is a difference between drugs and medicines. A **drug** is *a substance other than food that changes the structure or function of the body or mind.* A medicine is a drug used to prevent or treat illnesses and disease.

▶ Medicines help treat many kinds of illnesses and diseases. **Why is it important to use medicines only as directed?**

Lesson 1 Resources

📁 **Chapter *FAST FILE* Resources**
Guided Reading and Writing 14-1
Concept Mapping Activity 14-1
Health Lab 14-1
Reteaching Activity 14-1
Enrichment Activity 14-1
Lesson Quiz 14-1

Technology
🔋 Transparency 14-1
💿 Audio Summaries
🌐 *ExamView® Assessment Suite*
💿 Vocabulary PuzzleMaker
💿 StudentWorks™ Plus
G⊙ Online

All medicines are drugs, but not all drugs are medicines. All medicines, including drugs, can be misused and abused.

Types of Medicines

Medicines can be categorized into two general types. The first type, **prescription medicines,** are *medicines that can be sold only with a written order from a physician.* With this type of medicine, a doctor or pharmacist gives specific directions on its use—how much to take, how often, and for how long.

Have you ever taken aspirin for a headache, or used cough syrup for a cold? If so, you have used **over-the-counter (OTC) medicines.** OTC medicines are *medicines that are safe enough to be taken without a written order from a physician.* They are sold in pharmacies and other stores.

▲ Prescription drugs are available only with a written order from a doctor. **What type of directions are provided with prescription drugs?**

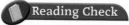
Reading Check **Compare** What is the difference between prescription and over-the-counter medicines?

Drug Misuse

Both prescription medicines and over-the-counter medicines can be misused. **Drug misuse** is *taking or using medicine in a way that is not intended.* A person who does any of the following is misusing drugs:

AL

- Using the drug without following the instructions on the label
- Using a drug not prescribed for you
- Allowing someone else to use a drug prescribed for you
- Taking more of the drug than the doctor prescribed
- Using the drug longer than advised by the doctor

Even when taken correctly, some medicines will cause side effects. A **side effect** is *any effect of a medicine other than the one intended.* Common side effects include stomach upset, drowsiness, sleeplessness, and headache. Side effects should be discussed with your doctor if they occur.

When a physician prescribes a medicine that must be taken for a long period of time, a drug tolerance may develop. **Tolerance** is *a condition in which a person's body becomes used to the effect of a medicine and needs greater and greater amounts of it in order for it to be effective.*

MediaWatch

Medicine Ads

Find several magazine ads for medicines. What information do these ads share?

Use critical thinking skills to interpret the ads' messages. What conclusions can you draw about the legal requirements for medicine ads?

TEACH

AL Active Learning

Advice Column Have students imagine that they are the advice columnist for a school newspaper. Ask students to write a response to a letter asking if the misuse of prescription drugs is harmful or dangerous. Remind students to use facts and statistics from this lesson in their responses. **OL**

MediaWatch

Medicine Ads

Provide appropriate magazines for students to use for this activity. Ask students to compare and contrast advertisements for prescription and over-the-counter medications. Explain that the Food and Drug Administration regulates advertising of prescription drugs. After students have drawn their conclusions about the legal requirements for drug advertisements, have them share their conclusions with the class.

Reading Check

Answer Prescription drugs are sold only with a written order from a physician. Over-the-counter drugs are sold at pharmacies without prescription.

Caption Answers

Photo Caption how much, how often, how long, and side effects

Home, School, and Community

At Home Some teens obtain prescription drugs for misuse at pharming parties, gatherings at which prescription drugs are traded. A portion of the drugs exchanged at these parties are taken from medicine cabinets at home. Discuss with students the health dangers of misusing prescription drugs. If you issue a parent newsletter, describe the importance of properly disposing of unused prescription medications. Remind parents to carefully monitor any prescription medications in their home.

Health Skills Activity

Practicing Healthful Behaviors

Handling Medicine Safely in Your Home

Use the following strategies to help students complete the activity:

- Have students copy the bulleted tips onto a piece of paper or an index card. Ask volunteers to explain the importance of each of the bulleted tips.

- Remind students to review the list with their family and to post the checklist in an appropriate place in their home. To respect student and family privacy, do not require students to share their results.

R Reading Strategy

Analyzing Content Have students read the section which identifies consequences of drug abuse. Ask: Think about the activities you enjoy and the relationships in your life. What is one specific way in which drug abuse could impact your life? Sample answers: *Drug abuse could cause me to be cut from the football team. Drug abuse would cause me to be a poor role model for my younger siblings.* **OL**

Caption Answer

Photo Caption, p. 337
Sample answer: I would feel very lonely.

336

Health Skills Activity

Practicing Healthful Behaviors

Handling Medicine Safely in Your Home
What do you know about medicine safety in the home? Follow these guidelines to store, use, and dispose of medicine safely.

- Know what medicines are in your home and what they are used to treat.
- Store medicines in a cool, dry place.
- Keep medicines safely sealed in childproof containers, and keep them out of the reach of children.
- Never share prescription medicines. They could cause serious harm to someone else.
- Do not use OTC medicines for more than ten days at a time unless you check with your doctor.
- Before taking two or more medicines at the same time, get your doctor's approval. Combining medicines can cause harmful side effects.
- Do not use medicines that have passed their expiration date.
- To safely dispose of outdated or unused liquid or pills, flush them down the toilet.

On Your Own
Create a "Medicine Safety Checklist" suitable for home use. Review the completed checklist with your family. Post the list in an appropriate place in your home.

Drug Abuse

When you hear the term *drug abuse,* what do you think of? **Drug abuse** is *intentionally using drugs in a way that is unhealthy or illegal.* Certainly the person using illegal drugs is abusing drugs. However, using illegal drugs is only one form of drug abuse. Using *legal* drugs for nonmedical reasons or using a medication for something other than its intended use is also drug abuse.

Drug abuse can affect all three sides of your health triangle. The physical effects range from sleeplessness and irritability to heart failure and stroke. Drug abuse interferes with brain function, affecting your mental/emotional health. Some drugs make it difficult to think or concentrate. Other drugs cause depression or anxiety. Your social health is also affected. Teens who abuse drugs may withdraw from family and friends. They may lose interest in school or other activities.

Go Online

Visit glencoe.com and complete the Interactive Study Guide for Lesson 1.

R

FITNESS ZONE

Drugs and Physical Fitness Teens may start misusing or abusing drugs because they feel bored or because they spend time with peers who make unhealthy choices. Physical fitness activities can be an alternative to experimenting with drugs. Have students scan the *Group Fitness Activities* in their *Fitness Zone Handbook.* Ask: How do you think being physically fit can help you avoid using drugs? **For more information, see *Fitness Zone Handbook* pages xviii-1 or visit the Fitness Zone at glencoe.com.**

Addiction

People who abuse drugs risk developing an addiction. An addiction is a physical or psychological need for a drug. When a person uses a drug regularly, he or she will develop a tolerance to the drug. The user needs more and more of the drug to get the same effect. Eventually, the user becomes addicted. There is no telling how many times a person can use a drug before becoming addicted. Once addicted, the user can no longer function without the drug. It becomes the focus of his or her daily life.

Drug addiction, like alcoholism, is a disease. Once a person becomes addicted, it is very difficult to quit using the drug. Treatment options exist that can help drug users overcome their addiction. You will learn more about the different treatment options available to drug users in Lesson 5.

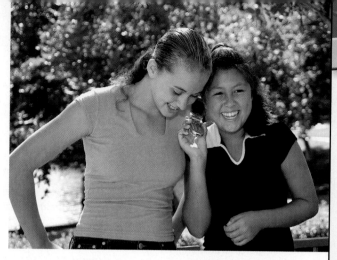

▲ Drug abuse takes you away from your friends and other people in your life whom you love. **Can you imagine what your life would be like without those who are closest to you?**

 Reading Check **Recall** Name two different forms of drug abuse.

 Reading Check

Answer Using illegal drugs or misusing legal drugs

ASSESS

Assessment Resources

Lesson Review Quiz
- *ExamView*
- Fast Files Activities
- Online Quizzes and Activities

Reteaching
- Assign Concept Map 14-1 or Reteaching Activity 14-1 in the Fast Files. 📁
- Call on students to explain ways in which drugs can be misused.

Enrichment
- Assign Enrichment Activity 14-1 in the Fast Files. 📁
- Have students perform research on the changes in brain function that result from drug use. Have students prepare an oral report with visual aids in order to share their findings with the class.

CLOSE

Call on students to explain, in their own words, why drug addiction is considered to be a disease.

Lesson 1 Review

After You Read

Review this lesson for new terms, major headings, and Reading Checks.

What I Learned

1. *Vocabulary* Define *drug*. Use the word in an original sentence.

2. *Identify* Name two side effects that can occur when taking medicine.

3. *Compare* What is the difference between drug misuse and drug abuse?

Thinking Critically

4. *Explain* How does drug addiction occur?

5. *Hypothesize* What might you say to persuade a friend not to take a medicine that has not been prescribed for him or her?

Applying Health Skills

6. *Accessing Information* Use library resources and the Internet to research drug misuse and abuse in the United States. Create a pamphlet to educate others about the dangers.

Go Online For more Lesson Review Activities, go to glencoe.com.

Lesson 1: Drug Misuse and Abuse **337**

Lesson 1 Review Answers

1. A drug is a substance other than food that changes the structure or function of the mind or body. Sentences will vary.

2. Stomach upset, drowsiness, sleeplessness, headache

3. Drug misuse means taking medicines in a way that is not intended; drug abuse means intentionally using drugs in a way that is unhealthy or illegal.

4. Drug addiction is a physical condition in which the user needs more and more of the substance to achieve the same effect.

5. Taking a drug that is not prescribed to you can cause harmful side effects.

6. Help students locate reliable resources to use for their research.

FOCUS

Activating Prior Knowledge

What I Know Ask students to discuss media reports of anabolic steroid use among professional athletes. Challenge students to identify health risks of anabolic steroid use.

Guide to Reading

Building Vocabulary
■ Have students write a sentence that shows how two of the lesson vocabulary terms are related.
■ Use Vocabulary PuzzleMaker to reinforce vocabulary terms.

Reading Strategy
Finding the Main Idea
Have students summarize the main idea of each section in their own words.

*Q*uick Write

Have volunteers share their Quick Writes with the class. Reinforce the fact that this drug damages all three sides of the health triangle.

> **Caption Answer**
> **Photo Caption** Marijuana use impairs coordination and concentration.

Marijuana and Other Illegal Drugs

Guide to Reading

● Building Vocabulary
In your notebook, use each of the new vocabulary terms in an original sentence that illustrates its meaning.

■ marijuana (p. 338)
■ THC (p. 338)
■ amnesia (p. 341)
■ anabolic steroids (p. 343)

● Focusing on the Main Ideas
In this lesson, you will learn to

■ **describe** the effects and risks of marijuana use.
■ **identify** the most commonly used club drugs.
■ **explain** the reasons that teens abuse anabolic steroids.
■ **list** the physical effects of anabolic steroid abuse.

● Reading Strategy
Finding the Main Idea For each major heading in this lesson, write one sentence that states the main idea.

*Q*uick Write

List one physical, mental/emotional, and social risk of using marijuana.

What Is Marijuana?

You may have heard the different names people use when referring to marijuana. **Marijuana** is *dried leaves and flowers of the hemp plant, called Cannabis sativa*. It is also commonly called *pot* or *weed*. Marijuana is an illegal drug that is usually smoked.

What Are Marijuana's Effects?

Marijuana affects the brain of the person using the drug. *The main active chemical in marijuana is* **THC.** THC alters the way the brain processes sensory information.

◀ Marijuana use can cause a lack of interest in the things you once enjoyed. **What are some other reasons to avoid marijuana?**

338 Chapter 14: Drugs

Lesson 2 Resources

📁 **Chapter *FAST FILE* Resources**
Guided Reading and Writing 14-2
Concept Mapping Activity 14-2
Cross-Curriculum Activity 14-2
Decision-Making Activity 14-2
Enrichment Activity 14-2
Lesson Quiz 14-2

Technology
🔋 Transparency 14-2
🎧 Audio Summaries
💿 *ExamView® Assessment Suite*
🎧 Vocabulary PuzzleMaker
🌐 StudentWorks™ Plus

Go Online

Marijuana can cause a variety of reactions. Some people experience a pleasant sensation for a short while. Others may experience unpleasant reactions to the drug. It is also impossible to know what other harmful substances may be mixed in with marijuana.

Short-Term Effects

Marijuana use has many negative effects. It reduces reaction time and coordination, and impairs judgment. It also increases heart rate and appetite. High doses of marijuana can cause anxiety and panic attacks. **Figure 14.1** lists some additional effects of marijuana use.

Long-Term Effects

C

Long-term effects of marijuana use are serious. Since the drug contains many of the same chemicals found in tobacco smoke, users are at risk for the same lung diseases that tobacco users confront, including cancer.

There are over 400 chemicals in the marijuana plant. Research has found that people who abuse marijuana for a long period of time experience changes to the region of the brain that processes information. It has been associated with depression, anxiety, and personality disturbances. Users may fall behind in school or at work.

Marijuana use can also affect a person's social health. The loss of motivation that comes with continued marijuana use can lead to problems with friends or family members.

Reading Check **Explain** How does marijuana affect the user?

Pharmacist

Pharmacists fill prescriptions for patients and show them how to use both prescription and over-the-counter medications. They also discuss types, dosages, and side effects of drugs with doctors. Pharmacists are in demand because everyone takes medication at some point in his or her life, whether it is for a cold or a chronic condition.

What skills does a pharmacist need? Go to *Career Corner* at glencoe.com to find out.

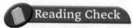

▼ FIGURE 14.1

R

Marijuana Overview

Marijuana affects your ability to think clearly, concentrate on goals, and relate to people in healthful ways. **What are some other effects of marijuana use?**

Marijuana Overview	
Brief Description	The most commonly used illegal drug in the U.S. The main active chemical is THC.
Street Names	Pot, ganja, weed, grass, and many others.
Effects	Short-term effects include memory and learning problems, distorted perception, and difficulty thinking and solving problems.

TEACH

Careers for the 21st Century

Pharmacist
Ask students to describe some of their own interactions with pharmacists. Invite a local pharmacist to visit the class and discuss his or her work.

C Critical Thinking

Analyzing Provide handouts from the CDC or other sources that show recent trends in teen use of marijuana. Have students examine the data about marijuana use. Ask: What trends do you see in this data? What are some factors that might have contributed to this trend? **OL**

R Reading Strategy

Analyzing a Graphic Have students examine **Figure 14.1**. Ask: How could using marijuana affect physical health? *Sample answer: Marijuana use causes changes in brain chemistry.* **OL**

Reading Check

Answer There are long- and short-term effects of marijuana use. Long-term effects include increased risk of lung cancer, damage to the brain, and negative effects on the user's social health. Short-term effects include impaired judgment, reduced reaction time, increased heart rate and appetite.

HEALTH LITERACY

Marijuana's Effects on the Body Marijuana use impacts the entire body. For example, marijuana affects both the male and female reproductive systems. Marijuana use has a negative impact on the immune system. Marijuana use can lead to a decreased ability to fight off infection. Have students further research the effects of marijuana use on the body's systems. Have students work in small groups to prepare multimedia presentations of their results. **OL**

C Critical Thinking

Relating Concepts Ask students to identify health risks of sexual activity. Record students' responses on the board. Then ask students to identify how drug use can lead to risky behaviors. Have students write a short paragraph that explains how drug use and risks of sexual activity are related. **OL**

AL Active Learning

Newspaper Story Have students write a newspaper story describing the harmful effects of marijuana addiction. Remind students to check that their newspaper stories describe the *who, what, where, why, when,* and *how* of the damage caused by club drugs. Provide students with several actual newspaper stories about any topic to use as models. Remind students to edit their work before they turn it in. **OL**

Reading Check

Answer Risks include arrest, harming self or others, and impaired reactions while driving.

Caption Answers

Figure Caption, p. 339
Sample answer: Other consequences of marijuana include anxiety and paranoia.
Photo Caption Marijuana affects judgment, reduces reaction time, and impairs coordination, all of which can affect driving ability.

340

Safety Risks

Using marijuana puts teens at risk in a number of ways. Since it is an illegal substance, users risk getting arrested. Users may also say or do things that could hurt themselves or hurt others. Impaired reaction time and coordination can make driving a car dangerous while under the influence of marijuana.

 Since marijuana can affect judgment, its use can lead to participation in other risky behaviors. These can include using alcohol or other drugs, or engaging in sexual activity. This can increase the risk of sexually transmitted diseases and unplanned pregnancy.

Marijuana and Addiction

Perhaps you have heard someone say, "Marijuana? What's the big deal? It's not like you can get hooked or anything." Not true. Frequent users of marijuana can develop a tolerance to the drug. Developing a tolerance often leads to physical dependency and addiction. Each year, more than 120,000 people seek treatment for addiction to marijuana.

Reading Check **Recall** What are some of the safety risks involved in using marijuana?

▲ Driving under the influence of marijuana can be dangerous.
What are some effects of marijuana use that could impair a person's ability to drive safely?

Home, School, and Community

In the Community Club drugs typically appear at raves, which are large, all-night dance parties that use lighting and music to produce hallucinogenic effects. Signs and flyers promoting raves often mention free water and candy and an alcohol-free environment, leading parents and others in the community to view raves as a safe environment for young teens. If raves are common in your community, prepare a parent education letter explaining the warning signs and dangers of club drug use.

Health Skills Activity

Accessing Information

Marijuana Myths

Marijuana is the most commonly used illegal drug. Because its effects are not as dramatic as some other illegal drugs, it is often mistakenly believed to be a harmless drug. Here are some common myths about marijuana use:

Myth: "Marijuana is not addictive—users can stop whenever they want."

Myth: "Smoking marijuana is safer than using other drugs."

Myth: "Everyone smokes marijuana."

On Your Own

Using this lesson and other reliable print or online resources, find information that shows how these myths may not be true. Develop a fact sheet listing each myth and the truths behind each myth.

What Are Club Drugs?

Club drugs get their name from the dance clubs or raves where they are often used. Some people may falsely believe that club drugs are safe to use. However, research shows that these drugs may produce harmful effects.

Hallucinations, paranoia, and amnesia are among the harmful effects of club drugs. **Amnesia** is *partial or total loss of memory.* When club drugs are mixed with alcohol, which they often are, the effects of both substances are increased. These effects are also unpredictable. People react differently to club drugs. No one can tell ahead of time what their reaction will be. Two forms of club drugs are ecstasy and date rape drugs.

Ecstasy

Ecstasy is a club drug that affects the user in similar ways to hallucinogens and stimulants. It speeds up the central nervous system, making a person feel very alert, or "hyper." The scientific name for ecstasy is MDMA. Unlike marijuana, which comes from a plant, MDMA is a synthetic chemical, created in illegal laboratories. Makers of the drug often add other substances to ecstasy, such as caffeine or amphetamines. As a result, an ecstasy user may not even know what drug is being ingested.

Lesson 2: Marijuana and Other Illegal Drugs **341**

Health Skills Activity

Accessing Information

Marijuana Myths

Use the following strategies to help students complete the activity.

- Direct students to the Student Web Activities at **glencoe.com** to find resources they might use in their research.
- Students may work in pairs to complete their fact sheets.

AL Active Learning

Role-Play Have students read the section on club drugs. Have students work in small groups to write a role-play that shows a teen using refusal skills to turn down a club drug. Challenge students to include some of the information contained in the lesson in their role-play. Ask each group to share its role-play with the class. Have students identify refusal skills that are most likely to be effective in a club environment. **OL**

U Universal Access

English Learners Have students bring in a drawing, illustration from the Internet, or an advertisement that depicts the dangerous effects of club drugs. Have them share the images and findings with the class. **EL**

HEALTH LITERACY

Hyponatremia and Ecstasy Hyponatremia is a potentially devastating condition that can result from excessive water intake by ecstasy users. An increased secretion of antidiuretic hormone decreases urination in ecstasy users. Many ecstasy users drink large quantities of water to combat the increase in body temperature that results from dancing and ecstasy use. The increase in fluid intake and decreased fluid output can combine to cause hyponatremia, a potentially fatal condition.

AL Active Learning

Infomercial Have students make and videotape an infomercial that details the negative effects of ecstasy use. The students must provide a detailed script and an edited video. The video must include statistics and a case study of a victim with impaired brain development due to ecstasy use. **AL**

DEVELOPING Good Character

Citizenship
Ask students to brainstorm school and community groups that educate teens on the dangers of drug use. Ask volunteers to explain why they would be interested in participating in a particular group. **OL**

What Teens THINK

How can a teen avoid being pressured to use drugs?
Read the *What Teens Think* question aloud, and have students' brainstorm a list of specific responses. Record their ideas on the board. Then have each student select the response he or she considers most effective. Have students write persuasive paragraphs, encouraging peers to use their chosen approach to resisting pressure to use drugs.

DEVELOPING Good Character

Citizenship

You can demonstrate good citizenship by encouraging others to stay drug fee. Find out about programs in your school or community that educate teens on the dangers of drug use and tell your classmates about them. Identify what methods they use to reach teens and find out how students can get involved.

What program would you be interested in participating in? Why?

What Teens THINK

How can a teen avoid being pressured to use drugs?

A teen can avoid being pressured to use drugs by hanging around people who do not use drugs. They can also become educated about drugs. Learning about the consequences of drug use can help if you are being pressured.

Allah S.
Blackshear, GA

Ecstasy is usually taken as a pill, tablet, or capsule. When combined with alcohol, the effects can be even more dangerous.

It is hard to predict how ecstasy will affect a user. Some users might feel energized, happy, and relaxed, while others become nervous and agitated. Initial effects start within 30 minutes and can last for three to six hours. However, after effects such as sadness, depression, and memory problems can last for several days or longer. Researchers are currently studying how long-term use of ecstasy may affect the brain.

Other effects include:

- increased heart rate
- nausea and dizziness
- elevated blood pressure
- chills
- sweating
- increased sense of confidence
- loss of appetite

AL

Date Rape Drugs

Rohypnol, commonly called roofies, is a club drug that appeared in the United States in the 1990s. It works by suppressing the central nervous system. Rohypnol is odorless and colorless. In pill form, it can easily be slipped into someone's drink. When a person unknowingly takes rohypnol, he or she is unaware of what is happening and is unable to resist an attack or unwanted sexual advances. The drug also causes amnesia, so the person who has taken it often has no memory of what has occurred.

GHB is another depressant of the central nervous system. Until 1992, GHB was available as an over-the-counter drug used by bodybuilders to increase muscle mass and decrease fat. GHB usually comes in liquid form. Like rohypnol, it has been linked to sexual assault.

Ketamine, sometimes called Special K, is an anesthetic used in medical procedures for humans and animals. Ketamine is usually snorted, or sprinkled over marijuana or tobacco and smoked. Ketamine is so powerful that only a small amount may cause serious health effects, such as hallucinations, memory loss, and even respiratory failure.

TECHNOLOGY AND HEALTH

Teen Brain Development Brain imaging studies of teens performed at the National Institute of Mental Health show that the teen brain differs significantly from an adult brain. The prefrontal cortex, which is responsible for judgment, foreseeing consequences of actions, and impulse control, is not fully developed in teens. It is clear that one factor that causes teen to be vulnerable to trying drugs is their state of brain development.

Anabolic Steroids

Anabolic steroids are *synthetic substances related to the male sex hormones.* Physicians sometimes prescribe these drugs to treat growth problems, lung diseases, and skin conditions. Anabolic steroids are similar to the male hormone testosterone. They help build muscle mass and enhance the development of male characteristics.

Steroids are most often abused by people who want to enhance their athletic abilities by adding muscle mass and increasing their strength and endurance. Abuse of these drugs has become a serious concern in professional sports in the United States. **Figure 14.2** lists some of the harmful effects of using anabolic steroids.

▲ The best way to improve your athletic performance is to practice. **How could using drugs stand in the way of reaching your goals?**

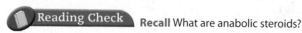

Reading Check   **Recall** What are anabolic steroids?

▼ FIGURE 14.2

THE FACTS ABOUT ANABOLIC STEROIDS

A person caught using steroids can face social consequences, such as being kicked off a team or expelled from school. **Can you think of some consequences of steroid use related to mental/emotional health?**

The Facts About Anabolic Steroids	
Brief Description	Human-made substances related to male sex hormones. Some athletes abuse anabolic steroids to enhance performance. Abuse of anabolic steroids can lead to serious health problems, some of which are irreversible.
Effects	Major side effects can include liver tumors and cancer, jaundice, high blood pressure, kidney tumors, severe acne, and trembling. In males, side effects may include shrinking of the testicles and breast development. In females, side effects may include growth of facial hair, menstrual changes, and deepened voice.
Statistics and Trends	In NIDA's 2004 *Monitoring the Future* study, 3.4% of high school seniors reported using steroids at least once.

Source: NIDA Infofacts: High School and Youth Trends.

Visit **glencoe.com** and complete the Interactive Study Guide for Lesson 2.

Cultural Perspectives

Media, Body Image, and Steroid Use Media is a major part of American teen culture and a major influence on teens' body images. In fact, many female steroid users cite the desire to reduce body fat as the main reason they use steroids. Have students discuss the media's influence on the body image of young people. Remind students that models and actors are not representative of typical teen bodies, and in fact may be dangerously underweight. **OL**

AL Active Learning

Real-World Connection Have students collect media reports of professional athletes who have used anabolic steroids. Ask students to analyze how steroid use has negatively impacted the careers of these athletes. Challenge students to make a list of positive ways in which athletes at all levels can cope with the pressures related to athletic performance (for example, developing a training schedule with a coach, asking a doctor to recommend a healthy diet). **OL**

Reading Check

Answer synthetic substances related to male sex hormones

R Reading Strategy

Analyzing a Graphic Have students examine **Figure 14.2.** Ask students to use the consequences of steroid use, which are listed in the figure, to develop a public service announcement (PSA) that can be used to discourage teens from using steroids. Have each student share his or her PSA with the class. **OL**

Caption Answers

Photo Caption *Sample answer:* I could be suspended from sports, which would interfere with my goal of being a college athlete.

Figure Caption *Sample answer:* Steroid use and its consequences could cause depression.

Reading Check

Answer stunted growth and problems with development

ASSESS

Assessment Resources

Lesson Review Quiz
* *ExamView*
* Fast Files Activities
* Online Quizzes and Activities

Reteaching

* Assign Concept Map 14-2 or Reteaching Activity 14-2 in the Fast Files.
* Have students review the effects of marijuana, club drugs, and anabolic steroids with a partner. Call on random pairs to share some of their results with the class.

Enrichment

* Assign Enrichment Activity 14-2 in the Fast Files.
* Have students perform further research to learn how various types of drugs affect the nervous system. Have students create a multimedia presentation that highlights the adverse effects that drugs have on the nervous system.

CLOSE

Have students identify ways that club drugs can negatively impact all three sides of the health triangle.

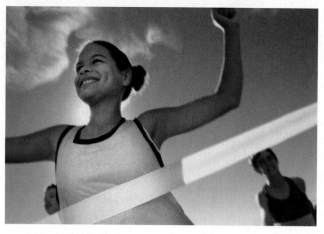

▲ Playing well after hard work and practice can give you a deep sense of pride and accomplishment. **Have you ever felt this way after achieving something that you worked hard for?**

Teens and Steroid Use

Most teens avoid using steroids. Those who do risk damaging their health. They also risk negatively affecting their appearance. Steroids can put acne on your face, make your hair fall out, and stunt your growth. They can also cause a person to become angry or violent, which can result in personal injury or injury to others.

Steroid use can also cause a hormonal imbalance. Hormones are important during the teen years. They are responsible for the physical, mental/emotional, and social changes that all teens go through on their way to adulthood. When hormone levels are not balanced, problems with the development of female and male characteristics can occur. Boys can grow breasts and girls can develop mustaches or beards.

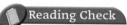 **Reading Check**

Explain How might anabolic steroids affect a teen's health?

Lesson 2 Review

 After You Read

Review this lesson for new terms, major headings, and Reading Checks.

What I Learned

1. *Vocabulary* What is *THC*?

2. *Recall* What are some health risks associated with using anabolic steroids?

3. *Explain* What are two long-term effects of marijuana use?

Thinking Critically

4. *Analyze* Why do you think steroid abuse is a concern in competitive sports?

5. *Hypothesize* What might happen to a person who unknowingly ingests rohypnol while at a club?

Applying Health Skills

6. *Advocacy* Write a script for a public service announcement for radio or television, explaining the short- and long-term effects of marijuana use.

Go Online For more Lesson Review Activities, go to glencoe.com.

Lesson 2 Review Answers

1. THC is the main ingredient in marijuana. It is a powerful chemical that signals the brain to release dopamine.
2. Violent outbursts, mood swings, acne, stunted growth, high blood pressure

3. *Any two:* lung disease, depression, anxiety, personality disturbances, social problems, difficulties at school
4. *Sample answer:* Students may address the character of athletes who may be role models or a concern for the honesty of competition.

5. A person who ingests Rohypnol may be the victim of sexual or physical assault.
6. Students' public service announcements should include information from the lesson about the negative impact of marijuana use.

Narcotics, Stimulants, and Depressants

 Guide to Reading

● **Building Vocabulary**
As you read this lesson, write each new highlighted term and its definition in your notebook.
- narcotics (p. 345)
- opium (p. 345)
- euphoria (p. 346)
- withdrawal symptoms (p. 346)
- stimulants (p. 348)
- amphetamine (p. 348)
- binge (p. 348)
- CNS depressants (p. 350)

● **Focusing on the Main Ideas**
In this lesson, you will learn to
- **name** the most commonly abused narcotics.
- **describe** the effects that narcotics can have on a user's health.
- **identify** specific stimulants and CNS depressants.
- **name** the health risks linked to stimulant and CNS depressant abuse.

● **Reading Strategy**
Identifying Cause and Effect Make a two-column chart. In the first column, write the names of the drugs presented in this lesson. In the second, list the effects of these drugs.

What Are Narcotics?

Narcotics are *specific drugs that are obtainable only by prescription and are used to relieve pain.* Historically, narcotics were made from **opium,** which is *a liquid from the poppy plant containing substances that numb the body.* When used under a doctor's supervision, narcotics are effective in the treatment of extreme pain. However, they are also highly addictive. As a result, their sale and use is controlled by law.

Quick Write
Make a list of reasons why you should avoid using drugs.

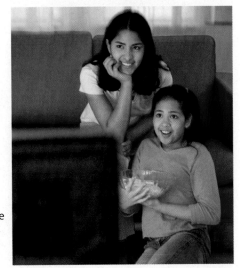

▶ Spending time with your family can help you avoid pressure to use drugs. **What are some healthful activities you can do with your family?**

Lesson 3: Narcotics, Stimulants, and Depressants **345**

FOCUS

Activating Prior Knowledge

What I Know Have students identify types of drugs with which they are familiar. Ask students to identify harmful effects of each type of drug named.

 Guide to Reading

Building Vocabulary
- Tell students that the abbreviation *CNS* stands for *central nervous system*. Explain the role of the central nervous system in controlling the body's functions.
- Use Vocabulary PuzzleMaker to reinforce vocabulary terms.

Reading Strategy
Identifying Cause-and-Effect Have students work in pairs to identify the drugs listed in this lesson and their effects.

Quick Write

Remind students to call upon the information they learned in Lesson 2 as they prepare their Quick Write.

 Chapter *FAST FILE* **Resources**
Guided Reading and Writing 14-3
Concept Mapping Activity 14-3
Cross-Curriculum Activity 14-3
Reteaching Activity 14-3
Enrichment Activity 14-3
Lesson Quiz 14-3

Technology
Transparency 14-3
Audio Summaries
ExamView® Assessment Suite
Vocabulary PuzzleMaker
StudentWorks™ Plus
G⊕ **Online**

Caption Answer

Photo Caption *Sample answer:* shopping, cooking dinner, and camping

TEACH

AL Active Learning

Graphic Organizer Have students read the definition of *narcotics* in their books. Then ask them to define *narcotics* in their own words. Divide students into small groups and provide each group with a piece of poster board or large sheet of paper. Have each group create a simple graphic organizer that lists the different narcotic drugs and their effects as presented on pages 346 and 347. EL

W Writing Support

Persuasive Writing Have students write a persuasive paragraph encouraging others to avoid abusing narcotics such as heroin. Remind students that persuasive writing uses facts to support an opinion. Ask students to proofread their paragraphs before turning them in. OL

Caption Answer

Photo Caption *Sample answer:* Doctors strictly supervise patients who take narcotics in order to prevent health risks due to misuse or abuse.

Narcotics and Addiction

Narcotics affect the body by attaching themselves to certain receptors in the brain to block any painful messages that are being sent. These drugs can also produce **euphoria,** or *a feeling of well-being or elation* because they affect the areas of the brain that perceive pleasure.

When narcotics are abused, the threat of serious health risk increases drastically. Abusing these drugs can result in tolerance, physical and psychological dependence, and addiction. The body becomes accustomed to having the drug, and when it is taken away, the user experiences **withdrawal symptoms.** These are *symptoms that occur after chronic use of a drug is reduced or stopped.* Withdrawal symptoms can be unbearable. They can include pain in the muscles and bones, sleeplessness, diarrhea, agitation, and vomiting. **Figure 14.3** shows some of the effects of narcotic drug abuse.

Heroin

Heroin is an illegal narcotic. It is made from morphine, another narcotic. Black tar heroin is a variety of heroin produced in Mexico. It is the most common type of heroin used in the western United States. Heroin is most often inhaled or injected intravenously, although sometimes users smoke the drug.

Heroin users can become easily addicted. Users can develop a psychological dependence, craving the feelings the drug brings. Regular users build up a tolerance to the drug and then need it in ever-increasing doses. Over time, the user becomes physically addicted and quitting becomes very difficult. If the user tries to quit, he or she may experience painful withdrawal symptoms.

◀ When prescribed by a doctor, narcotics are used to treat extreme pain, such as the pain endured by cancer patients. **Why are patients strictly supervised by doctors when using narcotics?**

What Teens Want to Know

What are the street names of narcotics? When teens are offered drugs by peers or drug dealers, the drug will most often be referred to by a street name. Although students should say no to any drug offered, no matter what it is called, they should still be familiar with the street names of various drugs. For example, students may be offered 40s, 80s, or kicker. Students should know that this is the highly addictive drug OxyContin.

FIGURE 14.3

EFFECTS OF NARCOTIC DRUG ABUSE

R When narcotics are abused, there is a high risk of addiction and other health consequences. **What are some of these consequences?**

Health Effects of Narcotic Drug Abuse

Can cause drowsiness, constipation, and depress breathing.

Taking a large single dose could cause severe respiratory depression or death.

Can cause death if taken with certain medications or alcohol.

Can lead to physical dependence and tolerance. The body becomes used to the substance and higher doses are needed to feel the same initial effect.

Narcotics are highly addictive, often causing uncontrollable drug use in spite of negative consequences.

Withdrawal symptoms occur if use is reduced abruptly. Symptoms can include restlessness, muscle and bone pain, insomnia, diarrhea, vomiting, cold flashes with goose bumps, and involuntary leg movements.

Withdrawal from narcotics usually requires detoxification in a hospital. Although withdrawal is often a painful experience, it is not life-threatening.

OxyContin

OxyContin is a legal narcotic, available through a doctor's prescription. When used in the approved manner, it can control severe pain in patients with cancer, back pain, or arthritis.

However, OxyContin is also abused by users. The long-term effect of OxyContin use is an increased tolerance to the drug, which leads to physical addiction. Withdrawal symptoms when the drug is stopped are similar to those of other narcotics.

Reading Check **Recall** What are some of the effects of narcotic drug abuse?

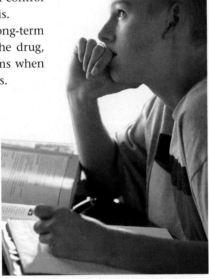

▶ The effects of drug abuse include the loss of ability to concentrate. **How would this affect your performance at school?**

HEALTH LITERACY

Ritalin Abuse Prescription stimulants used to treat ADHD are widely abused. Studies have found that 13 percent of high school students have reported abusing Ritalin. Students who have a prescription for Ritalin may not realize it is illegal for them to share their medication with others. Have students research prescription drugs that are abused by teens. Then have students make a poster describing reasons why teens who use prescription medications should never share their medications with others. **OL**

Antidrug Ads

Have students review various strategies used in advertising, including celebrity endorsements, emotional appeal, testimonials, and catchy slogans. Ask students to identify the strategies used in various antidrug advertisements. Have students write a paragraph evaluating the effectiveness of a selected ad.

Reading Check

Answer, top Stimulants are drugs that speed up activity in the brain and spinal cord.

HS Health Skills Practice

Analyzing Influences Have students study advertising for coffee products and energy drinks. Remind students that although caffeine is legal, in large quantities it can have adverse physical effects. Ask students how the advertisements portray the caffeine-containing products. Ask students to give a presentation that describes the advertising techniques used to make caffeine seem appealing to teens. **OL**

Reading Check

Answer, bottom when the drug is taken repeatedly at increasingly higher doses

348

Antidrug Ads

Research media campaigns that advocate against drug abuse. As a group, develop evaluation criteria for the ads and then evaluate them.

Who is the intended audience? Is the media message suitable for the intended audience? How effective is the message?

What Are Stimulants?

Stimulants are *drugs that speed up activity in the human brain and spinal cord.* They cause the heart to beat faster and blood pressure and metabolism to rise. A person using this type of drug will often move and speak more quickly than usual. The user may feel exhilarated, or excited. Others may become anxious.

Some stimulants are so mild that people may not realize they are ingesting a drug. Caffeine, found in coffee, tea, many soft drinks, and chocolate, is a stimulant. Some stimulants are prescribed by doctors for patients with certain physical or emotional problems. Stimulant abuse, however, can be dangerous. **Figure 14.4** shows several types of stimulants and their harmful effects.

Reading Check **Define** What are *stimulants*?

Amphetamines

An **amphetamine,** also known as speed, is *a drug that stimulates the central nervous system.* Amphetamines are highly addictive. Using large amounts of amphetamines can result in aggressive behavior that is difficult to predict. Other effects include extreme weight loss and loss of physical strength.

Cocaine

Cocaine is an illegal stimulant derived from the coca plant. Usually sold as a fine white powder, cocaine is often mixed with water and injected into the body *intravenously,* or administered into a vein. Cocaine can also be smoked or inhaled. Cocaine is one of the most addictive drugs on the street today.

Cocaine affects the user almost immediately. The effects can last up to a few hours. Taking large amounts of the drug increases these effects, but can also lead to violent and unpredictable behavior. As cocaine use continues, the user develops a tolerance for the drug. Larger and more frequent doses of cocaine are needed. During a cocaine **binge,** *when a drug is taken repeatedly and at increasingly high doses,* the possible consequences are very dangerous.

Reading Check **Identify** What is a cocaine binge?

Cultural Perspectives

Drug Use According to a study in the *American Journal of Public Health,* school performance is the most important factor in determining whether a student uses drugs. Students of all races and ethnicities who perform well at school and feel connected to their school community are less likely to use drugs. Monitor students' performance to identify students who are struggling. Work with other faculty and staff to provide extra help and support to these students.

▼ FIGURE 14.4

R

THE FACTS ABOUT STIMULANTS

The biggest risk associated with stimulant abuse is damage to your heart, sometimes causing heart attacks or death. **What are some other harmful effects of stimulant abuse?**

Substance	Other Names	Forms	Methods of Use	Harmful Effects
Amphetamine	Crystal, ice, glass, crank, speed, uppers	Pills, powder, chunky crystals	Swallowed, snorted up the nose, smoked, injected	Uneven heartbeat, rise in blood pressure, physical collapse, stroke, heart attack, and death
Methamphetamine	Meth, crank, speed, ice	Pills, powder, crystals	Swallowed, snorted up the nose, smoked, injected	Memory loss, damage to heart and nervous system, seizures, and death
Cocaine	Coke, dust, snow, flake, blow, girl	White powder	Snorted up the nose, injected	Damage to nose lining and liver; heart attack, seizures, stroke, and death
Crack	Crack, freebase rocks, rock	Off-white rocks or chunks	Smoked, injected	Damage to lungs if smoked, seizures, heart attack, and death

Crack

When cocaine is heated and processed with baking soda and water, it forms a substance that is smoked. The drug that is created is called *crack*. It gets its name from the cracking sound that occurs when the mixture is smoked. Crack is an extremely addictive and dangerous drug.

Methamphetamine

HS

Methamphetamine is a highly addictive stimulant drug that strongly affects the central nervous system. It is becoming an epidemic in the United States. This drug is produced in illegal laboratories that exist in every state, in both small towns and cities, and are popping up in disturbing numbers.

Methamphetamine, or "meth," as it is commonly known, is taken into the body in a variety of ways. It can be swallowed, snorted, smoked, or injected. Its effects are similar to those of cocaine.

🏠 Home, School, and Community

At School According to the National Center for Educational Statistics, 29 percent of high school students have been given, offered, or sold drugs on school property. Rates of drug availability were similar for schools in urban, suburban, and rural areas. Invite the school principal or a counselor to discuss with the class the penalties for drug trafficking at school. **OL**

U Universal Access

Gifted Students Challenge students to research the effect that methamphetamine use has on neurotransmitters, such as dopamine and serotonin, and the neurons in the brain. Have students share their findings with the class. **AL**

> ### Reading Check
>
> **Answer** They produce a feeling of calm or drowsiness by slowing down brain function.

R Reading Strategy

Analyzing a Graphic Direct students' attention to **Figure 14.5** on page 351, which shows the effects of CNS depressants. Ask: What serious health risks are caused by the misuse of CNS depressants? *Sample answers: coma, reduced heart rate* **OL**

▲ Using or possessing illegal drugs can lead to jail time. **How might this impact other areas of a teen's life?**

Go Online

Visit **glencoe.com** and complete the Interactive Study Guide for Lesson 3.

The Effects of Methamphetamine

Initially, methamphetamine can make users feel confident and full of energy. Because of these feelings, users often binge, sometimes for days without food or sleep. The user's behavior is often unpredictable.

When a methamphetamine user becomes addicted to the drug, it often becomes difficult, if not impossible, to feel any sense of pleasure without the drug. Methamphetamine abuse is so rampant that in 2004, the Drug Enforcement Administration (DEA), a government agency, set aside $151.4 million just to enforce laws and regulations relating to methamphetamine use.

What Are Central Nervous System (CNS) Depressants?

CNS depressants are *substances that slow down normal brain function.* They are sometimes called sedatives or tranquilizers. Physicians can prescribe some CNS depressants for relief of sleeplessness, anxiety, or tension. However, these drugs are sometimes abused. When used for extended periods of time, they can result in drug tolerance and addiction.

CNS depressants produce a feeling of calm or drowsiness in the person taking the drug. Two CNS depressants that are commonly prescribed are:

- **barbiturates** (bar·BI·chur·ruhts), which are prescribed for the treatment of anxiety or tension, or for people with sleep disorders.

- **benzodiazepines,** to treat patients with more serious anxiety and panic attacks.

Like all prescription medicines, CNS depressants should only be taken as prescribed, and under a doctor's supervision. Long-term users can develop a tolerance in which larger doses are needed to achieve the desired effect. **Figure 14.5** shows some of the effects of depressants.

> ### Reading Check
>
> **Explain** How do CNS depressants affect the body?

Caption Answer

Photo Caption *Sample answer:* This would be harmful to one's family and social life.

Promoting Coordinated School Health

Cost Effectiveness of Drug Education According to the National Institute on Drug Abuse, community and school drug education programs are cost effective. Studies have shown that every dollar spent on drug abuse prevention saves between $4.00 and $10.00 in drug enforcement, counseling, and rehabilitation costs. Have interested students research other benefits of drug prevention programs, such as reduced crime rates and increased high school graduation rates. **OL**

▼ **FIGURE 14.5**

THE FACTS ABOUT DEPRESSANTS

R Depressants are sometimes prescribed to treat certain conditions, but when abused, they are dangerous. **What are some harmful effects of depressants?**

Substance	Other Names	Forms	Methods of Use	Harmful Effects
Tranquilizer	Valium, Librium, Xanax	Pills or capsules	Swallowed	Anxiety; reduced coordination and attention span. Withdrawal can cause tremors and lead to coma or death.
Barbiturate	Downers, barbs, yellow jackets, reds	Pills or capsules	Swallowed	Causes mood changes and excessive sleep. Can lead to coma.
Hypnotic	Quaaludes, Ludes, Sopor	Pills or capsules	Swallowed	Impaired coordination and judgment. High doses may cause internal bleeding, coma, or death.

Lesson 3 Review

 After You Read

Review this lesson for new terms, major headings, and Reading Checks.

What I Learned

1. *Vocabulary* Define *narcotics*.

2. *List* Name two commonly abused narcotics.

3. *Give Examples* Give three examples of harmful effects that can result from abusing stimulants.

Thinking Critically

4. *Evaluate* Explain the physical and psychological effects that can cause a person to become addicted to heroin.

5. *Analyze* What are some of the high-risk behaviors that could result from the abuse of narcotics?

Applying Health Skills

6. *Goal Setting* Make a contract with yourself in which you set the goal of remaining drug free. Develop a plan to help you reach this goal. Sign your contract and keep it visible to help you remember your goal.

Go Online For more Lesson Review Activities, go to **glencoe.com**.

Lesson 3: Narcotics, Stimulants, and Depressants **351**

CHAPTER 14

Lesson 3

ASSESS

Assessment Resources

Lesson Review Quiz
ExamView
Fast Files Activities
Online Quizzes and Activities

Reteaching

● Assign Concept Map 14-3 or Reteaching Activity 14-3 in the Fast Files.
● Have students rephrase each of the lesson main ideas to form a question. Then have students work in pairs to ask and answer these questions.

Enrichment

● Assign Enrichment Activity 14-3 in the Fast Files.
● Have students collect articles about drug abuse from newspapers and newsmagazines and make a collage that includes original antidrug slogans.

CLOSE

Ask students to identify one specific drug and describe the effects of that particular drug.

Caption Answer

Figure Caption *Sample answers:* anxiety, mood changes, withdrawal, coma, and death

Lesson 3 Review Answers

1. Narcotics are specific drugs obtainable only by prescription that are used to relieve pain.

2. *Sample answers:* heroin, OxyContin, Vicodin, Dilaudid, codeine

3. *Sample answer:* Stroke, memory loss, and seizures are all harmful effects from stimulant abuse.

4. Regular use of heroin builds up a tolerance, so the user needs more of the drug to get an effect. Withdrawal symptoms lead to further use.

5. *Sample answers:* crime, risky sexual behaviors, impaired driving

6. Remind students to include the health skills of goal setting, decision making, and refusal skills in their contracts.

351

FOCUS

Activating Prior Knowledge

What I Know Have students recall the effects of ecstasy, which were discussed in Lesson 2. Explain that, like ecstasy, several other types of drugs produce hallucinations.

Guide to Reading

Building Vocabulary
- Have students skim the lesson to find the meanings of the vocabulary terms. Then have students write a definition for each term in their own words.
- Use Vocabulary PuzzleMaker to reinforce vocabulary terms.

Reading Strategy
Making an Outline
Remind students to leave space under each of the main headings in their outlines and add details under each main heading as they read.

uick Write

Have volunteers share their completed Quick Write with the class. Use the responses to identify students' misconceptions about inhalants.

Caption Answer

Photo Caption inability to communicate, hallucinations, bizarre or violent behavior

---

Lesson 4

Hallucinogens and Inhalants

 Guide to Reading

● **Building Vocabulary**
In your notebook, write a sentence that describes the meaning of each new term in your own words.
- hallucinogens (p. 352)
- inhalant (p. 354)

● **Focusing on the Main Ideas**
In this lesson, you will learn to
- **define** hallucinogens.
- **explain** how hallucinogens affect the user.
- **identify** the health risks to a person who uses inhalants or hallucinogens.

● **Reading Strategy**
Making an Outline Using the main heads in this lesson, make an outline of the lesson. As you read, fill in your outline with details.

uick Write

Write down three facts you know about inhalants.

▼ Many activities can be very difficult while under the influence of hallucinogens. **What are some other effects of hallucinogens?**

Hallucinogens

Hallucinogens are *drugs that distort moods, thoughts, and senses.* Some of these drugs are made from natural substances in plants, such as cactus and mushrooms. Hallucinogens can also be manufactured.

How Do Hallucinogens Affect the User?

Hallucinogens get their name from the word *hallucinate,* which means to have visions. Hallucinogens affect how a user perceives the passage of time, sees colors, senses motion, or hears sound. These drugs can interfere with a person's thought process and ability to communicate. The user can no longer distinguish between what is real and what is not. This can lead to strange or risky behavior. LSD and PCP are examples of hallucinogens. **Figure 14.6** shows some additional effects of hallucinogens.

Lesson 4 Resources

📁 **Chapter *FAST FILE* Resources**
Guided Reading and Writing 14-4
Concept Mapping Activity 14-4
Decision-Making Activity 14-4
Reteaching Activity 14-4
Enrichment Activity 14-4
Lesson Quiz 14-4

Technology
🔥 Transparency 14-4
Audio Summaries
ExamView® Assessment Suite
Vocabulary PuzzleMaker
StudentWorks™ Plus

 Online

▼ FIGURE 14.6

R EFFECTS OF HALLUCINOGENS

Hallucinogens can cause many harmful effects, including death. **What are two examples of hallucinogens?**

Substance	Other Names	Forms	Methods of Use	Harmful Effects
PCP	Angel dust, supergrass, killer weed, rocket fuel	White powder, liquid	Applied to leafy materials and smoked	Loss of coordination; increased heart rate, blood pressure, and body temperature; convulsions; heart and lung failure; broken blood vessels; bizarre or violent behavior; temporary psychosis; false feeling of having superpowers
LSD	Acid, blotter, microdot, white lightning	Tablets; squares soaked on paper	Eaten or licked	Increased blood pressure, heart rate, and body temperature; chills, nausea, tremors, and sleeplessness; unpredictable behavior; flashbacks; false feeling of having superpowers

LSD

LSD, a drug made from lysergic acid, is one of the strongest and most widely abused hallucinogens. It is sold as tablets, capsules, liquid, or on absorbent paper. A tiny amount produces a powerful effect. The psychological effects of LSD are often very difficult to **predict**. Users may experience hallucinations. They may not know where they are—or even who they are.

Hallucinogens such as LSD can also produce flashbacks. Weeks or even months after taking the drug, a user may relive terrifying thoughts or feelings.

PCP

PCP (phencyclidine) is not a true hallucinogen in its chemical makeup. It is grouped with this category of drugs because its effects are similar to those of LSD. PCP can become addictive, and cause violent and unpredictable behavior. For this reason, PCP users are a threat to others and themselves.

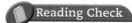

Reading Check **Identify** What are some of the harmful effects of PCP?

Academic Vocabulary

predict (pree DIKT) *(verb)* to indicate or know in advance. *You shouldn't share your prescription medications with friends because you can't predict how your friends will react to them.*

Lesson 4: Hallucinogens and Inhalants **353**

TEACH

R **Reading Strategy**

Analyzing a Graphic Have students examine **Figure 14.6**. Draw a three-column table on the board. Label the columns *physical effects, mental/emotional effects,* and *social effects.* Ask volunteers to add effects of hallucinogens to the correct columns. **OL**

HS **Health Skills Practice**

Advocacy Have students create a pamphlet that discusses the dangers of hallucinogens. Students can use information from the text or perform additional research. Obtain permission for students to share their pamphlets with other students at the same grade level. **OL**

Academic Vocabulary

Predict To help students recognize that some events can be predicted, ask the following question: How do meteorologists predict the weather for coming days? When students recognize that useful predictions are based on evidence, ask: Why do its unpredictable effects make LSD especially dangerous?

Reading Check

Answer PCP can cause violent and unpredictable behavior. It is addictive.

Caption Answer
Figure Caption PCP, LSD

What Teens Want to Know

What is DXM? Many over-the-counter cough medications contain dextromethorphan, or DXM. Powdered DXM is also available online. When used in larger-than-recommended doses, DXM produces hallucinogenic effects. This drug, which is readily available to young teens, can cause a fatal overdose. Help students recognize the dangers of this drug, which is sometimes called skittles, triple-C, dex, or tussin.

Speaking Out Against Drugs Have students use the information at **glencoe.com** to help them develop their slogan. Have each student share his or her slogan with the class.

HS Health Skills Practice

Communication Skills
Remind students that effective communication involves both verbal and nonverbal communication. Ask students to work in small groups to write a skit that shows how communication skills can be applied to discourage a friend from using an inhalant. Have each group share its skit with the class. **OL**

R Reading Strategy

Analyzing a Graphic Ask students to use the information in **Figure 14.7** to write a short paragraph explaining the risks of inhalant use. Obtain permission to post students' completed paragraphs in the school cafeteria or hallways. **OL**

Caption Answers

Figure Caption
unconsciousness, suffocation, choking, seizures

Photo Caption, p. 355
Inhalant abuse can also damage the mouth, brain, heart, and lungs.

Go Online

Topic: Speaking Out Against Drugs

Visit glencoe.com for Student Web Activities to learn more about the effects of drugs and what other teens are saying about using drugs.

Activity: Using the information provided at the link above, create a one-line slogan (for example: Choose to Use and You Lose) that can be made into a bumper sticker, flyer, or poster that states your stand against drugs.

Inhalants

An **inhalant** is *any substance whose fumes are sniffed and inhaled to produce mind-altering sensations.* They can be found in many household products that are readily available.

Toxic, or poisonous, inhalants include paint, vegetable cooking sprays, air freshener, lighter fluid, markers and pens, correction fluid, and hair sprays. Using a product for something other than its intended use is abuse.

Toxic inhalants are not meant to be put into the human body. They can cause serious health effects and even death. **Figure 14.7** lists some of the health effects that can result from abusing inhalants. Hundreds of teens die each year from sniffing or huffing inhalants. However, most teens do not abuse inhalants.

HS

What Damage Do Inhalants Cause?

Abusing inhalants can damage the protective coating that surrounds brain cells, called *myelin*. If myelin is damaged, nerve cells may not be able to send messages to other parts of the body. These results can be permanent and severe. They can affect a person's ability to walk, talk, or think. Inhalant abuse can also kill the user instantly. Even a person experimenting with inhalants for the first time can die from choking, suffocation, or a heart attack.

▼ **FIGURE 14.7**

R **HEALTH EFFECTS OF INHALANTS**

The greatest risk of inhalant use is death, which can occur with a person's first use of the drug. **What are some other health effects of inhalant use?**

Health Effects of Inhalants	
Brief Description	Breathable chemical vapors that users intentionally inhale because of the chemicals' mind-altering effects. The substances inhaled are often common household products that contain harmful solvents or aerosols.
Street Names	Whippets, poppers, snappers
Effects	Most inhalants produce a rapid high that resembles alcohol intoxication. If sufficient amounts are inhaled, nearly all solvents and gases produce anesthesia, a loss of sensation, and even unconsciousness. They can also cause suffocation, choking, seizures, and death.

HEALTH LITERACY

Inhalants Are Deadly According to a survey by the National Institute on Drug Abuse, 17.3 percent of eighth graders have used inhalants. Emphasize to students that inhalant use always carries a risk of death. Death during inhalant use is caused by a variety of mechanisms. Lack of oxygen, due to asphyxiation by vapors or to suffocation by a plastic bag, is a common cause of death. Convulsions, choking, or cardiac arrest, sometimes called sudden sniffing death, also causes inhalant-use fatalities.

◀ One symptom of inhalant abuse is red or runny eyes. **What other parts of the body can inhalant abuse damage?**

 Reading Check

Answer any two symptoms listed on this page

ASSESS

Assessment Resources

Lesson Review Quiz
ExamView
Fast Files Activities
Online Quizzes and Activities

Warning Signs of Inhalant Abuse

Here are some symptoms that may indicate a person is abusing inhalants. If you notice these symptoms in someone you know, speak to a teacher or trusted adult about your concerns.

- Eyes that are red or runny
- Sores or spots near the mouth
- Breath that smells strange or like chemicals
- Holding a marker or pen near the nose

 Go Online

Visit glencoe.com and complete the Interactive Study Guide for Lesson 4.

 Reading Check **Give Examples** What are two symptoms of inhalant abuse?

Reteaching

- Assign Concept Map 14-4 or Reteaching Activity 14-4 in the Fast Files.
- Have students develop a written list of reasons to avoid using hallucinogens and inhalants. Call on several students to share reasons from their lists.

Enrichment

- Assign Enrichment Activity 14-4 in the Fast Files.
- Challenge students to develop an educational pamphlet for parents identifying substances that are commonly used as inhalants, describing the warning signs of inhalant use, and describing the dangers of inhalant use.

Lesson 4 Review

After You Read

Review this lesson for new terms, major headings, and Reading Checks.

What I Learned

1. **Vocabulary** What are *hallucinogens*?

2. **Recall** What are two possible consequences of using hallucinogens?

3. **Identify** List the health risks to a person who uses inhalants.

Thinking Critically

4. **Hypothesize** What might you say to someone you know who is thinking of abusing an inhalant for the first time?

5. **Analyze** Why do you think inhalant abuse might be a serious problem among 12- to 14-year-olds?

Applying Health Skills

6. **Advocacy** Using pictures from magazines, create a poster showing household substances that are abused as inhalants. Add a caption or slogan to let other students know about the dangers of inhalant abuse.

CLOSE

Ask students to define the term *hallucinogen* and explain the ways that hallucinogens affect users.

 Go Online For more Lesson Review Activities, go to **glencoe.com**.

Lesson 4: Hallucinogens and Inhalants **355**

Lesson 4 Review Answers

1. Hallucinogens are drugs that distort moods, thoughts, and senses.
2. *Sample answer:* violent behavior and increased blood pressure
3. Inhalants damage the nervous system and can cause heart attacks, choking, and suffocation.
4. *Sample answer:* I would tell the person about the damaging effects of inhalants.
5. *Sample answer:* Inhalants are usually inexpensive, readily available household products that are accessible to young teens.
6. Provide students with magazines and newspaper circulars to use as they complete their posters.

FOCUS

Activating Prior Knowledge

What I Know Have students discuss the effects of drug addiction on mental/emotional health. Then have them explain why outside help is needed by most people with drug addictions.

Guide to Reading

Building Vocabulary
- Explain that the word part *de-* means "to remove." Ask students to relate this to the meaning of the term *detoxification*.
- Use Vocabulary PuzzleMaker to reinforce vocabulary terms.

Reading Strategy
Predicting Explain that the figures, captions, and bold headings can all be used to predict the lesson content. Have volunteers share their predictions with the class.

Quick Write

After students have completed their Quick Write, ask volunteers to share their responses. Record students' responses on the board. Challenge students to add to the list of sources of help as they read the lesson.

Reading Check

Answer The user must first recognize that he or she has a problem.

Getting Help

Guide to Reading

Building Vocabulary
As you read this lesson, write the new highlighted term in a sentence that illustrates its meaning.
- detoxification (p. 359)

Focusing on the Main Ideas
In this lesson, you will learn to
- **explain** why it is important to get help for drug use.
- **identify** the symptoms of drug abuse.
- **describe** different treatment options for drug abuse.

Reading Strategy
Predicting Look over the lesson, including the headings and pictures. Then write a sentence predicting what information you think the lesson will provide.

Quick Write

List three sources of help for drug use.

▼ Getting help is an important step in kicking a drug habit. Who would you feel comfortable talking to if you needed help?

Getting Help

The first step in getting help for drug abuse is for the user to recognize that he or she has a problem. This can be very difficult for users. It can also be difficult for family members or health care professionals to see that a problem exists. Users may try to hide the problem or deny that one exists.

If you have a drug problem, you need to get help. Talk to a trusted adult. If it is too uncomfortable talking with someone you know, you can turn to organizations that offer counseling and treatment. These sources of help include support groups, alcohol or drug treatment centers, and toll-free hotlines staffed by drug counselors.

Although some effects of drug abuse are permanent, drug addiction is treatable. In this lesson, you will learn about some of the different treatment options available.

Reading Check **Recall** What is the first step in getting help for drug abuse?

Lesson 5 Resources

📁 **Chapter *FAST FILE* Resources**
Guided Reading and Writing 14-5
Concept Mapping Activity 14-5
Decision-Making Activity 14-5
Reteaching Activity 14-5
Enrichment Activity 14-5
Lesson Quiz 14-5

Technology
🔦 Transparency 14-5
🔊 Audio Summaries
💿 *ExamView®Assessment Suite*
🔊 Vocabulary PuzzleMaker
💿 StudentWorks™ Plus
G⊙ **Online**

Recognizing When Someone Needs Help

There are different signs that show that someone may be dealing with a drug abuse problem. Users may lose interest in activities or family and friends. They may also frequently lie to cover up their addiction. **Figure 14.8** lists some of the symptoms of drug abuse. Recognizing these symptoms can help you identify if someone you know has a drug problem.

What should you do if someone you care about has a drug problem? If you think a friend needs help, try talking to him or her about your concerns. If you do not want to talk to the person directly, ask for help from a trusted adult. Encourage him or her to get help.

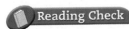 **Reading Check** Give Examples What are some signs that a person may have a drug problem?

▼ FIGURE 14.8

SYMPTOMS OF DRUG ABUSE

Recognizing the symptoms of drug abuse can help you identify if someone needs help. **What should you do if you recognize these signs in someone you know?**

Tolerance	A person will need increasingly larger amounts of drugs to get high.
Craving	A person will feel a strong need, desire, or urge to use drugs, will use a drug despite negative consequences, and will feel anxious and irritable if he or she can't use them. Craving is a primary symptom of addiction.
Loss of control	A person often will take more drugs than he or she meant to, or may use drugs at a time or place he or she had not planned. A person also may try to reduce or stop using drugs many times, but may fail.
Physical dependence or withdrawal symptoms	In some cases when drug use is stopped, a person may experience withdrawal symptoms from a physical need for the substance. Withdrawal symptoms differ depending on the drug, but they may include nausea, sweating, shakiness, and extreme anxiety.

Dealing with Sensitive Issues

Family Members Who Use Drugs Students may feel embarrassed or self-conscious as they read this chapter if a member of their family abuses drugs. Have students work as a class to develop a list of resources, including telephone numbers and Web addresses, for those who are coping with a family member's drug use. After students have completed the list, have students create wallet cards that list the information. Ask the school nurse to distribute the wallet cards. **OL**

TEACH

AL Active Learning

Radio Announcement Have students work in pairs to write a radio announcement that identifies the symptoms of drug abuse and explains why it is important to get help. Have students share their completed radio announcements with the class. **OL**

Reading Check

Answer Loss of interest in activities, withdrawal from family or friends, and lying may indicate that a person has a drug problem.

R Reading Strategy

Analyzing a Graphic Have students examine the symptoms of drug abuse in **Figure 14.8**. Ask: Why is it important to understand the symptoms of drug abuse? *Sample answer: People who abuse drugs might not realize they have a problem. By recognizing the symptoms of drug abuse, you can identify those who might need help.* **OL**

Caption Answers

Photo Caption, p. 356
Sample answer: I would choose to talk to my aunt if I needed help recovering from drug abuse.
Figure Caption, this page
Sample answer: If you recognize these signs of drug abuse, you should point out that the person needs help, and talk to a trusted adult.

U **Universal Access**

Students with Different Learning Styles Invite the school guidance counselor to visit your class to have a question and answer session about drug treatment options. Explain to students that this will be an informal discussion in which they can ask questions in order to learn more about drug treatment. **OL**

R **Reading Strategy**

Analyzing a Graphic Allow students to read about treatment programs. Have students work in small groups to develop lessons about forms of drug treatment. Challenge each group to develop a method to assess students' understanding of its lesson. Have each group share its lesson and assessment with the other students in the class. **OL**

> **Reading Check**
>
> **Answer, p. 359** inpatient and outpatient programs, counseling, and support groups

Drug Treatment Options

Once a person has recognized that he or she has a drug problem, the recovery process can begin. Recovery begins when the person stops using the drug so the body can rid itself of the drug and its effects. If the person is physically and psychologically addicted to the drug, he or she may experience withdrawal. Withdrawal symptoms vary depending on the drug used, but may include headaches, vomiting, chills, and hallucinations.

Drug users need help to recover from a drug addiction. Many communities offer treatment programs, counseling, and support groups to help people recover from drug abuse.

Treatment Programs

Treatment programs include both inpatient and outpatient programs. **Figure 14.9** lists some of the different treatment programs that are available depending on the level of addiction, the type of drug, and the patient. Some hospitals and treatment

▼ **FIGURE 14.9**

R **TREATMENT PROGRAMS FOR SUBSTANCE ABUSE**
There are many options available for those who need help recovering from a drug addiction. **Why do you think different treatment programs work better for some than others?**

- **Inpatient treatment** is provided in special units of hospitals or medical clinics, and offers both detoxification and rehabilitation services.

- **Residential programs** provide a living environment with treatment services. Treatment in these programs lasts from a month to a year or more.

- **Partial hospitalization or day treatment programs** are located in hospitals or freestanding clinics. In these programs, the person attends treatment for 4 to 8 hours per day but lives at home.

- **Outpatient programs** provide treatment at a program site. Many meet in the evenings and on weekends so participants can go to school or work. Some programs meet daily while others meet less frequently.

- **Intensive outpatient treatment programs** require a person to attend 9 to 20 hours of treatment activities per week. These programs last from about 2 months to 1 year.

> **Caption Answer**
>
> **Figure Caption** *Sample answer:* Drug treatment programs vary according to the level of addiction, the type of drug, and the individual patient.

TECHNOLOGY AND HEALTH

Treatment for Heroin Addiction Methadone is a synthetic narcotic that is used to treat heroin addicts. Methadone acts in the brain to block the high provided by heroin. It also stops the cravings associated with heroin withdrawal. Methadone is available only by prescription and is produced by pharmaceutical companies. Have students further research the use of methadone to help those who abuse heroin. Ask each student to write a paragraph summarizing the results of his or her research. **OL**

centers have detoxification units for people going through with-drawal. **Detoxification** is *the physical process of freeing the body of an addictive substance.* Once the physical dependency is overcome, the person can focus on changing his or her thinking and habits that led to their drug use.

Counseling

Some people find the support and help they need to stay drug free through counseling. Counseling provides an opportunity to openly share thoughts and feelings with a trained expert. It can help addicts deal with their psychological dependency on drugs. Counseling may involve only the addict, or it may involve the addict's entire family.

Support Groups

A support group is a group of people who work together to help one another stay drug free. Often, recovering addicts find strength in being surrounded by people who are working toward the same goal. Common support groups for addiction include Narcotics Anonymous and Cocaine Anonymous. Nar-Anon provides help for those who have been affected by someone else's drug use.

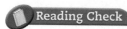 **Reading Check**   **Recall** What are some drug treatment options?

 G. Online

Visit glencoe.com and complete the Interactive Study Guide for Lesson 5.

ASSESS

Assessment Resources

Lesson Review Quiz
- *ExamView*
- Fast Files Activities
- Online Quizzes and Activities

Reteaching
- Assign Concept Map 14-5 or Reteaching Activity 14-5 in the Fast Files.
- Have students write a short paragraph describing sources of help for those who abuse drugs.

Enrichment
- Assign Enrichment Activity 14-5 in the Fast Files.
- Challenge students to use print and online resources, or to interview medical professionals to learn more about drug withdrawal. Have students share their findings with the class in a short oral report.

CLOSE

Ask various students to describe ways to access reliable information about getting help for a drug problem.

Lesson 5 Review

 After You Read

Review this lesson for new terms, major headings, and Reading Checks.

What I Learned

1. *Vocabulary* Define *detoxification*.

2. *Describe* What are some of the ways support groups help people become drug free? Why are they effective?

3. *List* Name three symptoms of drug abuse.

Thinking Critically

4. *Analyze* Why do you think there are so many different drug treatment options available?

5. *Apply* Imagine your friend comes to you and tells you that he has been abusing inhalants and feels that he cannot stop. He begs you not to tell anyone. What would you do?

Applying Health Skills

6. *Decision Making* Imagine that you suspect a friend has a drug problem. Use the decision-making process to help you decide whether to speak to your friend about your concerns or speak to a trusted adult.

G. Online   For more Lesson Review Activities, go to **glencoe.com**.

Lesson 5: Getting Help   **359**

Lesson 5 Review Answers

1. Detoxification is the physical process of freeing the body of an addictive substance.
2. Support groups are effective because they allow recovering drug abusers to find strength with people who are working toward the same goal.

3. *Any three:* tolerance, craving, loss of control, physical dependence or withdrawal symptoms
4. Each person needs to find the best form of treatment for his or her individual problems.

5. *Sample answer:* I would warn him about the dangers of inhalant use and encourage him to get help by speaking with a trusted adult.
6. Answers will vary but should include the six steps of the decision-making process.

FOCUS

Activating Prior Knowledge

What I Know Have students identify choices in their lives that affect the three sides of their health triangle. Explain that the choice to remain drug free has a positive impact on all three sides of their health triangle.

Guide to Reading

Building Vocabulary
■ Have students write a short paragraph that incorporates the lesson vocabulary term.
■ Use Vocabulary PuzzleMaker to reinforce vocabulary terms.

Reading Strategy
Organizing Information Have students create a chart that describes ways that staying drug free will benefit each side of the health triangle. Have students share their ideas with the class.

Quick Write

After students have completed their Quick Write, have students work as a class to make a combined list using all of the students' results. Have students add to the list as they read the lesson.

Caption Answer

Photo Caption *Sample answer:* I will look and feel better and have higher self-esteem.

Lesson 6

Staying Drug Free

Guide to Reading

● **Building Vocabulary**
As you read this lesson, write the new highlighted term and its definition in your notebook.
■ drug free (p. 361)

● **Focusing on the Main Ideas**
In this lesson, you will learn to
■ **explain** the health benefits of staying drug free.
■ **demonstrate** alternative behaviors to drug use.

● **Reading Strategy**
Organizing Information Create a chart that lists the ways staying drug free will benefit each side of your health triangle.

uick Write
Describe how the different sides of your health triangle benefit if you avoid using drugs.

Choosing to Be Drug Free

The choice to refuse drugs is not always an easy one. Negative peer pressure can be a powerful force during the teen years. Yet, however challenging it may be to resist negative peer pressure to experiment with drugs, stopping drug abuse once it has started is much harder. It is also important to be true to yourself and make decisions that will promote a healthy body and mind.

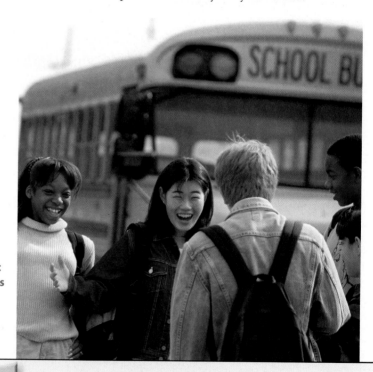

▶ Staying drug free helps you maintain healthy relationships with your family and friends. **What are some other benefits of staying drug free?**

360 Chapter 14: Drugs

📁 **Chapter *Fast File* Resources**
Guided Reading and Writing 14-6
Concept Mapping Activity 14-6
Cross-Curriculum Activity 14-6
Reteaching Activity 14-6
Enrichment Activity 14-6
Lesson Quiz 14-6

Technology
🔦 Transparency 14-6
🖥 Audio Summaries
💿 *ExamView®* Assessment Suite
🖥 Vocabulary PuzzleMaker
🖥 StudentWorks™ Plus
G●**Online**

◀ Staying drug free can help you build a positive self-image. **What are some ways to say no to drug use?**

Choosing to be drug free is one of the most important decisions you can make. **Drug free** is *a characteristic of a person not taking illegal drugs or of a place where no illegal drugs are used.*

Refusing Drugs

Developing skills for refusing drugs is very important. Refusal skills can help you say no to unhealthy behaviors. These skills can help you resist negative peer pressure without feeling guilty or uncomfortable. Saying no in a clear and confident way lets others know you respect yourself and your health. If you feel pressure to experiment with drugs, remember the S.T.O.P. strategy.

- **S**ay no in a firm voice.
- **T**ell why not.
- **O**ffer alternative ideas or activities.
- **P**romptly leave.

Using this strategy is useful when you are **approached** by someone pressuring you to use drugs. However, you can take steps now that will help you to avoid such a situation. Choose friends who are also drug free. Avoid going to places where you know drugs will be present. Finally, always look for healthful ways to deal with problems you are facing. If you feel lonely or depressed, or if you need help solving personal problems, talk to an adult you trust. The people you are with, the places you happen to be, and how you are feeling, all play a role in your ability to be drug free. Your awareness of positive alternatives to drug use and the benefits of staying drug free also play a role.

Academic Vocabulary

approached (ah PROCHED) *(verb)* asked; came near to. *Darren told his little sister what to do if she is ever approached by a stranger.*

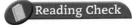 **Reading Check** **Explain** What is a strategy to resist negative peer pressure?

Lesson 6: Staying Drug Free **361**

✖ Promoting Coordinated School Health

Help Students Stay Drug Free Each coordinated school health program has several components that help students stay drug free. For example, classroom health instruction explains the dangers of drug use and teaches refusal skills. Counseling, psychological services, and referrals to community agencies are also components of coordinated school health that can be used to promote the choice to be drug free and to help students who are involved in drug use.

R Reading Strategy

Analyzing a Graphic Have students examine **Figure 14.10** and discuss each of the reasons for remaining drug free identified in the figure. Have students classify each reason as pertaining to physical health, social health, or mental/emotional health. **OL**

R Reading Strategy

Analyzing a Graphic Have students examine **Figure 14.10** and discuss each of the reasons for remaining drug free identified in the figure. Have students classify each reason as pertaining to physical health, social health, or mental/emotional health. **OL**

HS Health Skills Practice

Advocacy Have students develop plans for advocating for a drug-free lifestyle. Challenge students to use one or more of the benefits of choosing to be drug free named in the lesson as a part of their advocacy program. Suggest that students use PSAs, posters, pamphlets, or other means of advocating against drug use. **OL**

 Reading Check

Answer, this page *Sample answer:* trusting relationship with my parents, obeying the law, and self-control

Answer, p. 363 *Sample answer:* sports, reading, practicing a musical instrument

Caption Answer

Figure Caption *Sample answer:* Staying drug free allows me to be a good athlete and a good student.

▼ **FIGURE 14.10**

R REASONS TO BE DRUG FREE

Avoiding drugs will benefit all three sides of your health triangle. **What are your own personal reasons for staying drug free?**

- You will not be breaking the law.
- You will have more natural energy.
- You will have better concentration and memory.
- You will be able to focus on improving your talents and enjoying your interests.
- You will look better because your appearance will not be affected by drugs.
- You will have better control over your feelings and actions.
- You will not regret foolish actions caused by drug-impaired judgment.
- You will not waste money on drugs.
- You will have better relationships with friends and family members.
- You will respect yourself for taking care of your body and mind.

The Benefits of Staying Drug Free

HS Making wise decisions about drugs will have a positive effect on your physical, mental/emotional, and social health. You protect your body against the harmful effects of drugs. You are able to concentrate better and will do better in school. You are able to enjoy other interests with family and friends. **Figure 14.10** lists some additional benefits of being drug free.

 Reading Check

Explain Name at least three benefits of being drug free.

🏠 Home, School, and Community

In the Community According to the Partnership for a Drug-Free America, teens are most likely to abuse drugs between the hours of 3 P.M. and 6 P.M. Compile a list of supervised after-school programs for students. Communicate with parents to be sure that they are aware of these resources.

Remind parents of the importance of after-school supervision for middle-school students. Encourage faculty and staff to offer opportunities for students to participate in adult-supervised after-school activities.

Positive Alternatives to Drug Use

Positive alternatives to drug use are everywhere if you look for them. Positive alternatives allow you to have fun and spend time with family and friends in more healthful ways. Here are some strategies for staying drug free. Can you think of any others?

- Begin a regular physical activity routine.
- Volunteer to help someone in your school or community.
- Join a school club or organize a new one.
- Take part in a drug-free event. Bring a friend.
- Write down your thoughts, or express yourself through art.
- Balance enough physical activity with enough rest.
- Form friendships with people who are drug free.

 Reading Check **Recall** Name three healthy alternatives to drug use.

▶ Staying away from drugs enables you to pursue and achieve your goals. **What steps are you taking to achieve your goals?**

 Go Online

Visit **glencoe.com** and complete the Interactive Study Guide for Lesson 6.

ASSESS

Assessment Resources

Lesson Review Quiz
- *ExamView*
- Fast Files Activities
- Online Quizzes and Activities

Reteaching

- Assign Concept Map 14-6 or Reteaching Activity 14-6 in the Fast Files.
- Have student pairs list alternatives to drug use.

Enrichment

- Assign Enrichment Activity 14-6 in the Fast Files.
- Have students interview a school counselor or law enforcement official about the benefits of staying drug free. Ask students to describe the results of their interviews to the class.

CLOSE

Ask students to explain why choosing to remain drug free is one of the most important decisions a teen can make.

Caption Answer

Photo Caption *Sample answer:* I communicate to others my goal of remaining drug free.

 Lesson 6 Review

After You Read

Review this lesson for new terms, major headings, and Reading Checks.

What I Learned

1. **Vocabulary** Define the term *drug free*.

2. **Recall** What are different strategies for choosing to be drug free?

3. **List** Give five reasons for being drug free.

Thinking Critically

4. **Apply** Imagine talking with a friend who is thinking about experimenting with drugs. What might you say to encourage him or her to stay drug free?

5. **Analyze** Every time someone offers you drugs, you say no. What are some positive alternatives to drug use that you enjoy?

Applying Health Skills

6. **Practicing Healthful Behaviors** Create a poster listing activities that you consider positive alternatives to illegal drug use. With permission from school administrators, hang your poster in a school hallway.

Go Online For more Lesson Review Activities, go to **glencoe.com**.

Lesson 6: Staying Drug Free **363**

Lesson 6 Review Answers

1. A person who is drug free does not abuse or misuse drugs.
2. *Sample answers:* using the S.T.O.P. strategy, choosing friends who do not use drugs, managing feelings in healthful ways
3. Answers will vary but should identify five valid reasons for avoiding drug use.
4. *Sample answer:* Drugs will cause physical harm, ruin your friendships, and cause you to lose your parents' trust.
5. *Sample Answers:* exercising, reading, going to the movies, spending time with family
6. Posters should list positive and practical alternatives to illegal drug use.

Building Health Skills: Saying No to Drugs

Skill

Refusal Skills

Activating Prior Knowledge

Have students recall and describe effective refusal skills. Then ask students to list reasons why it is important to refuse all offers of drugs.

- **Objective** After completing the activity, students will be able to use refusal skills to avoid misusing and abusing drugs.
- **Time** 30 minutes
- **Materials** paper, pencil or pen

Teacher Classroom Resources

📁 Building Health Skills
✋ Transparency 14-6

Model

- Have students work in small groups to discuss the reasons why Jeff's refusal was effective.
- Call on several groups to have students explain why it is important to refuse every offer of drugs, even if the offer comes from a good friend.

National Health Standards Addressed

1.8.5, 4.8.2, 5.8.2, 6.8.4, 7.8.2

Building Health Skills

Accessing Information
Practicing Healthful Behaviors
Stress Management
Analyzing Influences
Communication Skills
Refusal Skills
Conflict Resolution
Decision Making
Goal Setting
Advocacy

What Are Refusal Skills?

Refusal skills are strategies that help you say no effectively. If a peer asks you to engage in risky behavior, like taking drugs, remember the S.T.O.P. strategy:

- **Say no firmly.** Be direct and clearly state how you feel. Use direct eye contact and keep your statement short.
- **Tell why not.** Use "I" messages to give your reasons.
- **Offer another idea.** Suggest an activity that does not involve drugs.
- **Promptly leave.** If you have to, just walk away.

Saying No to Drugs

Follow the Model, Practice, and Apply steps to help you master this important health skill.

❶ Model

Read how Jeff uses refusal skills to say no to drugs.

Jeff and Mark have been friends since grade school, and have always enjoyed the same activities. This year, however, Jeff has noticed some changes in Mark. When Mark's older brother began smoking marijuana, Mark experimented with it, too. On a bike ride one day, Mark stopped behind the neighborhood supermarket and took a joint out of his pocket and looked at Jeff, saying, "Want some?"

Jeff uses the S.T.O.P. strategy to help him say no effectively.

Say no in a firm voice. "No thanks. I'm not interested."

Tell why not. "This ride is already good. I don't need drugs to make it better."

Offer another idea. "Let's get back on the road and get some lunch. I'm starving."

Promptly leave. "If that's what you want to do, I'm out of here."

Teaching Tips

Practice Builds Confidence Explain that it is normal not to feel comfortable or confident doing a new skill the first few times. Practice, however, brings confidence and the greater likelihood of using refusal skills when necessary.

Developing a Drug-Free Reputation Discuss the value of developing a reputation as a "drug-free" teen. Students are less likely to be pressured to try drugs because everyone understands their personal commitment to stay drug free. Ask: How can one develop a drug-free reputation?

❷ Practice

Read the passage below. Then help Brandon use the S.T.O.P. strategy to say no to drugs.

Brandon and Gary are studying for a test that will decide if they qualify for science camp next summer. They know the exam will be hard. After a few hours of intense studying, Gary comes out of his parents' bathroom, holding a prescription bottle. "I bet these pills will help us study," Gary tells Brandon.

In small groups, discuss the ways in which Brandon could refuse the drugs. Use the S.T.O.P. strategy to develop your refusals.

❸ Apply

Take what you have learned about refusal skills and complete the activity below.

Tony sees one of his teammates hanging out with older boys. Tony goes up to say hello and discovers that the guys are talking about using drugs to improve their athletic skills.

Imagine you are Tony. Use the S.T.O.P. strategy to complete the following dialogue. Include reasons why drug use is an unhealthy choice.

Older Boy: "How about a little something to boost your game?"

Tony: _____

Older Boy: "You haven't even tried it."

Tony: _____

Older Boy: "Lots of people get help this way. It's nothing new."

Tony: _____

Older Boy: "You may be passing up a chance to be great!"

Tony: _____

Self-Check
■ Do your responses follow the S.T.O.P. strategy?
■ Did you include reasons why drug use is unhealthy?

Building Health Skills

Building Health Skills **365**

Practice

- Have students continue working in their small groups to complete the Practice.
- Ask each group to plan a refusal strategy for Brandon. Have the students within each group role-play each part.

Apply/Assess

- Have students work individually to create their dialogues and their responses to each of the phrases.
- Have students exchange papers. Ask each student to follow up by identifying one novel way of refusing drugs that they learned during this activity.
- You may wish to distribute the Building Health Skills Activity in the Fast Files.

ASSESSMENT SCORING

Using a rubric, student work should meet all criteria to achieve the highest score.

Skills Student work:
- uses the word *no*.
- tells why not.
- offers another idea.
- promptly leaves.

Concepts Student work:
- provides accurate and complete information about steroids.
- explains consequences of steroid use.
- demonstrates relationships between steroid use and health.

HANDS-ON HEALTH

Memory Obstacles

Time: 20 minutes
Materials: pencil or pen, paper, 2 posters with 25 pictures of everyday items on each, a source of loud music

Introducing Hands-on Health

- Ask students to name tasks in their everyday life that require concentration. Have students imagine how their ability to do these tasks would be affected by drug use.

Teaching the Activity

- Have students form small groups. Have each group select a leader for the activity.
- Ask each group to complete the activity as described in the text. It will be easiest if all of the groups do Step 4 at the same time.
- Have each group evaluate its results by completing the Wrapping It Up questions. Ask several groups to share their answers with the class.

HANDS-ON HEALTH

Memory Obstacles

Many drugs make it difficult to process information. In this activity, loud music and disruptive talk mimics the effects of some drugs. How will these distractions interfere with your ability to recall information?

What You Will Need

- Paper for each member of the group
- Pencil for each member of the group
- 2 posters with 25 pictures of everyday items on each
- A source of loud music

What You Will Do

1. Using pictures from magazines, one person in the group will make 2 posters with 25 everyday items on each one.

2. The leader will hold up the first poster and give the group 30 seconds to look at it. Each student should try to remember as many items as possible.

3. The leader then puts the poster down, and the students write down as many of the items as they can recall.

4. Now loud music is turned on. The leader also asks two people on opposite sides of the room to have a loud conversation with each other.

5. Then the leader holds up the second poster and repeats step 3.

Wrapping It Up

How many people in the group had more trouble remembering items on the second poster than on the first? Why?

Compare what just happened to what can happen to your brain when under the influence of a drug.

HANDS-ON HEALTH Assessment

Discussion Ask students:

- How did loud music and talking affect your memory? Sample answer: *I found it more difficult to remember what was on the poster.*

- Ask: Based on the results of this activity, how would drug use affect your ability to do schoolwork? Sample answer: *I would have a more difficult time doing schoolwork if I was affected by drugs.*

Reading Review

 STUDY TO GO Visit **glencoe.com** to download quizzes and eFlashcards for Chapter 14.

Assessment Resources

📁 Chapter 14 Summary and Activity
💿 Audio Summaries
📁 Reading Tutor
📁 Performance Assessment
📁 Chapter 14 Test
◉ *ExamView*
💿 Vocabulary PuzzleMaker
💿 Online Learning Center

FOLDABLES Study Organizer

Foldables® and Other Study Aids Take out the Foldable® that you created for Lesson 1 and any graphic organizers that you created for Lessons 1–6. Find a partner and quiz each other using these study aids.

Lesson 1 Drug Misuse and Abuse

Main Idea All drugs, including over-the-counter drugs, can be misused.

- Prescription medicines can be sold only with a written order from a doctor. Over-the-counter medicines are safe enough to be taken without a written order from a doctor.
- People who abuse drugs risk developing an addiction.

Lesson 2 Marijuana and Other Illegal Drugs

Main Idea Marijuana and other illegal drugs harm all sides of the health triangle.

- Marijuana affects your ability to think clearly, concentrate on goals, and relate to people in healthful ways.
- Other illegal drugs include ecstasy, rohypnol, ketamine, GHB, and anabolic steroids.

Lesson 3 Narcotics, Stimulants, and Depressants

Main Idea Narcotics, stimulants, and depressants are addictive drugs.

- Stimulants and depressants have opposite effects on the body.

- Heroin is an illegal narcotic. OxyContin is a legal narcotic.
- Stimulants include amphetamines like cocaine, crack, and "meth."
- Depressants include barbiturates and benzodiazepines.

Lesson 4 Hallucinogens and Inhalants

Main Idea Hallucinogens and inhalants interfere with a user's thought process.

- Hallucinogens include LSD and PCP.
- Inhalants are breathable chemical vapors that come from household products.

Lesson 5 Getting Help

Main Idea Treatment for drug abuse includes treatment programs, counseling, and support groups.

- Signs of drug abuse include high drug tolerance, cravings, loss of control, and physical dependence or withdrawal symptoms.
- Treatment for drug abuse includes treatment programs, counseling, and support groups.

Lesson 6 Staying Drug Free

Main Idea There are many physical, mental/emotional, and social benefits of staying drug free.

- If you feel pressure to experiment with drugs, remember the S.T.O.P. strategy.
- Positive alternatives to drug use include physical activity, volunteering in your community, writing, and art.

Reading Review

Study Aids

- **Using the Dinah Zike Foldable® Study Organizer** Have students use their Foldables® to review information about drug use. **FOLDABLES** Study Organizer
- **Online Learning Tools** Have students go to the Online Learning Center at **glencoe.com** to:
  - Download a **Podcast**.
  - Download free **Study-to-Go** content to their PDAs or cell phones.

Vocabulary Review

- **Graphic Organizer** Have students work in small groups to organize the chapter vocabulary terms into a graphic organizer.

> **Teaching Tips**

Reading in Health Class Have students use the following strategy if they encounter an unfamiliar term when they are reading an assignment. First, have students jot down the unfamiliar term on a piece of paper. Then, using context clues, have students develop a possible definition. Then have students use a dictionary, glossary, or other reference tool to check their definition. Finally, have students reread the sentence containing the unfamiliar term.

CHAPTER 14

Assessment

Reviewing Vocabulary and Main Ideas

1. Prescriptions
2. side effect
3. THC
4. Amnesia
5. Barbiturates
6. binge
7. True
8. False, Inhalants
9. True
10. False, different
11. False, Outpatient
12. False, most

Thinking Critically

13. Answers might include peer pressure, feeling overwhelmed by problems, and not understanding the negative effects of drug use.
14. Club drugs interfere with the body's ability to regulate temperature and can cause dehydration as well as lack of judgment in risky situations.

CHAPTER 14 Assessment

  After You Read

> **HEALTH QUIZ**
>
> Now that you have read the chapter, look back at your answers to the Health Quiz on the chapter opener. Would you answer any of the questions differently?

Reviewing Vocabulary and Main Ideas

On a sheet of paper, write the numbers 1–6. After each number, write the term from the list that best completes each sentence.

- amnesia
- barbiturates
- THC
- bing
- side effect
- prescriptions

Lesson 1 Drug Misuse and Abuse

1. _____ are medicines that can be sold only with a written order from a physician.

2. Any effect of a medicine other than the one intended is known as a _____.

Lesson 2 Marijuana and Other Illegal Drugs

3. _____ is a powerful chemical that is the main ingredient in marijuana.

4. _____ is one of the effects of using club drugs.

Lesson 3 Narcotics, Stimulants, and Depressants

5. _____ are examples of CNS depressants.

6. During a _____, a drug is taken repeatedly and at increasingly high doses.

*On a sheet of paper, write the numbers 7–12. Write **True** or **False** for each statement below. If the statement is false, change the underlined word or phrase to make it true.*

Lesson 4 Hallucinogens and Inhalants

7. <u>Hallucinogens</u> are drugs that distort the moods, thoughts, and senses of the user.

8. <u>Depressants</u> are any substance whose fumes are sniffed and inhaled to produce mind-altering sensations.

9. <u>LSD</u>, a drug made from lysergic acid, is one of the strongest and most widely abused hallucinogens.

Lesson 5 Getting Help

10. The physical signs of drug abuse are <u>the same</u> in every person who abuse drugs.

11. <u>Inpatient</u> treatment programs are places where people get treatment for a few hours and then go home.

Lesson 6 Staying Drug Free

12. Staying drug free is one of the <u>least</u> important decisions you can make to be the healthiest person you can be.

Go Online Visit glencoe.com and take the Online Quiz for Chapter 14.

Go Online

Have students visit **glencoe.com** to take the Chapter 14 quiz.

HEALTH QUIZ Wrap-Up

Drugs Have students look back at their responses to the Health Quiz in the chapter opener. Ask students to form small groups. Have students discuss with their groups any answers they would change based on the information in the chapter. Then have the members of each group identify one fact about drug use that they learned while reading the chapter.

Thinking Critically

Using complete sentences, answer the following questions on a sheet of paper.

13. **Hypothesize** What are three reasons someone might begin experimenting with drugs?

14. **Explain** How can taking club drugs put a person's physical health at risk?

Write About It

15. **Personal Writing** Write a journal entry that states your own reasons for making a commitment to be drug free.

16. **Narrative Writing** Write a short story about a teen who is pressured to use a drug and uses refusal skills to say no.

↗ Applying Technology

Drug Discussions

You and a partner will use GarageBand™ or Audacity® to write a three-to-five-minute podcast about the dangers of drugs and how to refuse them.

- Pick one of the drugs discussed in this chapter. Write a dialogue between two people. Make sure they tell what the drug is and its effects on the body.
- Record the dialogue using GarageBand™ or Audacity®.
- Edit for time and clarity.
- Share your podcast with iTunes®.

↗ Applying Technology

Drug Discussions
Equipment needs: GarageBand™ or Audacity® or similar software Let students choose partners, and then help the class review the project instructions. Point out that these podcasts should sound informal but should present information that will help other students avoid drug abuse. If access to computers is limited, prepare a sign-up sheet and establish a time limit for computer use. Encourage students to download and listen to their classmates' podcasts.

Write About It

15. **Personal Writing** Explain to students that personal writing, such as journal writing, uses clear language to express personal thoughts or feelings about an issue. Be sure journal entries are kept private.

16. **Narrative Writing** Explain to students that narrative writing includes a plot, a setting, and characters. Remind students to include refusal strategies as a part of the story.

Standardized Test Practice

Math

The National Institute on Drug Abuse recently conducted its **Monitoring the Future Survey.** The survey found that drug use among eighth graders decreased or stayed the same from 2005 to 2006. Use the information below from the survey to answer the questions that follow.

- Lifetime use of inhalants decreased among eighth graders, from 17.1 percent in 2005 to 16.1 percent in 2006.
- Use of anabolic steroids decreased among eighth graders from 1.1 percent in 2005 to 0.9 percent in 2006.
- There was no change in methamphetamine use among eighth graders from 2005 to 2006. During both years, 1.8 percent of eighth graders used methamphetamine.

1. Based on the statistics shown, which of the following *cannot* be inferred?

   A. In 2005, approximately 98.9 percent of all eighth graders did not abuse steroids.

   B. Fewer eighth graders abused steroids in 2005 than those eighth graders who abused methamphetamine in 2005.

   C. Approximately 82.9 percent of eighth graders did not use inhalants in 2005.

   D. More eighth graders used alcohol in 2006 than those eighth graders who abused steroids in 2006.

2. Based on the statistics, the greatest decrease in one year occurred with which drug?

   A. Marijuana

   B. Inhalants

   C. Anabolic steroids

   D. Methamphetamine

Chapter 14 Assessment **369**

Standardized Test Practice

1. D
2. B

Number Statements Explain that standardized tests often require an understanding of the relationship between number statements. In the example on this page, note that each statement includes several dates, two or more percentages, and a drug type. Each statement also specifies whether the statistics are for lifetime drug use, annual drug use, or 30-day drug use. Model for students how they could use a table to organize the details of these number statements to answer questions.

CHAPTER 15 pp. 370–401	Standards		Skills and Activities
	National	**State/Local**	
	National Health Education Standards 1.8.5, 2.8.4, 3.8.2, 3.8.3, 3.8.5, 5.8.2, 6.8.1, 7.8.1, 7.8.2, 7.8.3, 8.8.3		**HEALTH INVENTORY,** *p. 371* **BUILDING HEALTH SKILLS** *Accessing Information* Finding Reliable Online Information, *pp. 396–397* TIME health news *Danger in the Locker Room, p. 398*
Lesson 1 **Personal Health Care** pp. 372–378	National Health Education Standards 1.8.1, 1.8.5, 1.8.6, 1.8.7, 3.8.1, 3.8.3, 3.8.4, 3.8.5, 5.8.7, 6.8.1, 6.8.2, 7.8.1, 7.8.2, 8.8.1		**MEDIA WATCH** Deodorants, *p. 374*
Lesson 2 **Being a Smart Health Consumer** pp. 379–382	National Health Education Standards 2.8.5, 2.8.7, 2.8.10, 3.8.1, 3.8.2, 3.8.3, 3.8.5, 5.8.2, 7.8.2, 8.8.1		**HEALTH SKILLS ACTIVITY** *Analyzing Influences* Reading Between the Lines, *p. 380* **Connect To... MATH** Unit Price, *p. 381* **What Teens Think** How do companies make their products look appealing to you?, *p. 381*
Lesson 3 **Using Medicines Wisely** pp. 383–387	National Health Education Standards 1.8.1, 1.8.5, 1.8.6, 2.8.10, 3.8.1, 5.8.7, 7.8.1, 7.8.2, 8.8.1		**Careers for the 21st Century** Speech Therapist, *p. 386*
Lesson 4 **Choosing Health Services** pp. 388–391	National Health Education Standards 1.8.3, 2.8.4, 2.8.10, 3.8.4, 3.8.5, 6.8.1, 7.8.1, 8.8.1		
Lesson 5 **Public Health** pp. 392–395	National Health Education Standards 1.8.6, 2.8.4, 2.8.10, 3.8.1, 3.8.2, 3.8.5, 8.8.1, 8.8.3		**HEALTH SKILLS ACTIVITY** *Accessing Information* International Red Cross, *p. 394* Go Online Knowing Community Resources, *p. 394*

PACING THE CHAPTER		
Lesson 1 45 min	**Lesson 4** 30 min	**Chapter Review** 45 min
Lesson 2 30 min	**Lesson 5** 30 min	**TIME health news** 25 min
Lesson 3 45 min	**Building Health Skills** 90 min	

BLOCK SCHEDULING

For block scheduling, assign students Building Health Skills Feature *Finding Reliable Online Information*, pages 396–397, and Guided Reading and Writing. 📁

StudentWorks Plus

Glencoe Exclusive!
TeacherWorks™ Plus
All-In-One Planner and Resource Center

Reproducible Resources	Assessment	Media and Technology
Chapter _Fast File_ Resources Chapter Summaries and Activities REVIEW Building Health Skills Activity TEACH Performance Assessment Activity EXTEND Universal Access Activities TEACH Parent Letter and Activities 📁 **Student Activities Workbook** TEACH 📁 **Reading Tutor** TEACH	Building Health Skills Activity, _pp. 396–397_ Chapter 15 Assessment, _pp. 400–401_ **Chapter _Fast File_ Resources** Performance Assessment Activity, _p. 4_ Chapter 15 Test, _p. 7_ 💿 _ExamView® Assessment Suite_	**TeacherWorks**Plus includes: ● Interactive Teacher Edition ● Lesson Planner with Calendar ● Access to all blackline masters ● Correlations to standards 💿 StudentWorks™ Plus 🖱 Online Student Edition Dinah Zike's Teaching Health with Foldables®
Chapter _Fast File_ Resources Concept Mapping Activity 15-1 REVIEW Decision-Making Activity 15-1 EXTEND Enrichment Activity 15-1 EXTEND Lesson Plan 15-1 Guided Reading and Writing 15-1 TEACH Reteaching Activity 15-1 REVIEW	Lesson 1 Review, _p. 378_ 🖱 Vocabulary PuzzleMaker 💿 _ExamView® Assessment Suite_	🖱 Vocabulary PuzzleMaker 💿 _ExamView® Assessment Suite_ 💿 StudentWorks™ Plus 🔌 Transparency 15-1 **Go Online** glencoe.com
Chapter _Fast File_ Resources Concept Mapping Activity 15-2 REVIEW Health Lab 15-2 EXTEND Enrichment Activity 15-2 EXTEND Lesson Plan 15-2 Guided Reading and Writing 15-2 TEACH Reteaching Activity 15-2 REVIEW	Lesson 2 Review, _p. 382_ 🖱 Vocabulary PuzzleMaker 💿 _ExamView® Assessment Suite_	🖱 Vocabulary PuzzleMaker 💿 _ExamView® Assessment Suite_ 💿 StudentWorks™ Plus 🔌 Transparency 15-2 **Go Online** glencoe.com
Chapter _Fast File_ Resources Concept Mapping Activity 15-3 REVIEW Cross-Curriculum Activity 15-3 EXTEND Enrichment Activity 15-3 EXTEND Lesson Plan 15-3 Guided Reading and Writing 15-3 TEACH Reteaching Activity 15-3 REVIEW	Lesson 3 Review, _p. 387_ 🖱 Vocabulary PuzzleMaker 💿 _ExamView® Assessment Suite_	🖱 Vocabulary PuzzleMaker 💿 _ExamView® Assessment Suite_ 💿 StudentWorks™ Plus 🔌 Transparency 15-3 **Go Online** glencoe.com
Chapter _Fast File_ Resources Concept Mapping Activity 15-4 REVIEW Decision-Making Activity 15-4 EXTEND Enrichment Activity 15-4 EXTEND Lesson Plan 15-4 Guided Reading and Writing 15-4 TEACH Reteaching Activity 15-4 REVIEW	Lesson 4 Review, _p. 391_ 🖱 Vocabulary PuzzleMaker 💿 _ExamView® Assessment Suite_	🖱 Vocabulary PuzzleMaker 💿 _ExamView® Assessment Suite_ 💿 StudentWorks™ Plus 🔌 Transparency 15-4 **Go Online** glencoe.com
Chapter _Fast File_ Resources Concept Mapping Activity 15-5 REVIEW Cross-Curriculum Activity 15-5 EXTEND Enrichment Activity 15-5 EXTEND Lesson Plan 15-5 Guided Reading and Writing 15-5 TEACH Reteaching Activity 15-5 REVIEW	Lesson 5 Review, _p. 395_ 🖱 Vocabulary PuzzleMaker 💿 _ExamView® Assessment Suite_	🖱 Vocabulary PuzzleMaker 💿 _ExamView® Assessment Suite_ 💿 StudentWorks™ Plus 🔌 Transparency 15-5 **Go Online** glencoe.com

Chapter and Lesson Resources

The _Teen Health_ resources are designed for differentiated learning abilities. You may want to use the coded items in this way:

REVIEW —activities to review or reinforce content
TEACH —activities to teach basic concepts
EXTEND —activities to extend or enrich lesson content

 OUT OF TIME?

Use Health Skills Activity _Reading Between the Lines,_ page 380, or Media Watch, page 374.

Hearing Loss in Teens

Evidence suggests that more young people have hearing loss now than just a generation ago. Today, children in their early teens are already starting to experience deafness. The major cause of hearing loss in young people is exposure to loud sounds. Sounds above 85 decibels can damage tiny hair cells in the inner ear that normally transmit sound. The hearing loss is permanent and usually worsens with age.

Loud sounds teens commonly are exposed to include MP3 players, ATVs, lawn mowers, and rock concerts. Damage from these sounds can be prevented with hearing protectors. Convincing teens to protect their ears is an important objective of Lesson 1.

Hearing loss may be gradual, and affected teens may not realize it is happening to them. Have students answer these five true/false questions to see if they might have a hearing problem:

1. You are always being told to turn down your CD player or TV.

2. You often think people are mumbling and ask them to repeat what they said.

3. You often miss too much of a joke to "get" it.

4. You often need to ask others what a teacher said in class or a character said in a movie.

5. You sometimes cannot hear the telephone or doorbell when others can.

If students answer *true* to any of these questions, they should see their family doctor and have their hearing checked.

Take Charge of Your Health Care

With growing specialization in medicine, experts recommend that patients follow these tips to take a proactive role in their own health care:

- **Ask questions when you visit the doctor.** Prepare a list in advance, and make sure you get clear answers to all of them. You should understand what your problem is, as well as what is expected from you as a patient and why.

- **Ask questions when you pick up medicines from the pharmacist.** Make sure you know exactly how to take them, any side effects or risks they may have, and what to do if problems develop.

- **Know your health history.** Learn if you have an elevated risk of diseases such as diabetes or heart disease, and get appropriate tests according to recommended schedules.

The health skills in this chapter and throughout the text will help students take charge of their health care. For example, the ability to access information will help them gain the knowledge they need to understand their health problems and make informed decisions about doctors and treatments. Being able to communicate will help students convey their problems and concerns to health care providers and understand the explanations they receive. Give students ample opportunities to practice these and other health skills.

Reading Support

Reading Preview

Activating Background Vocabulary Ask students what comes to mind when they think about personal care. Guide them in a discussion of the importance of proper skin, hair, and dental care, and how to buy health products, use medicine wisely, and choose an appropriate health service.

FOLDABLES Study Organizer *Dinah Zike's Reading and Study Skills for Teen Health* provides interactive graphic organizers that help students comprehend and retain health concepts as they read. Use the Foldable® on page 371 or find more Foldables® activities for the chapter on **Personal Care and Consumer Choices** in the separate booklet, available in the TCR.

Lesson 1   Personal Health Care

Skim and Scan Show students how to *skim* the lesson to find main ideas by reading titles and headings, such as: **Functions of Skin, Parts of the Skin,** or **Your Hair and Nails.** Next, ask students to *scan* the lesson to find specific meanings of key words, such as *dermis* or *plaque.* Have students discuss their findings with a partner.

Lesson 2   Being a Smart Health Consumer

Sensory Imagery Have students stop reading and imagine what standing in a store aisle looking at health products might look like, smell like, or feel like. Ask: How would you know which products to buy? Can you imagine yourself comparing product labels? Encourage students to use this strategy during independent reading.

Lesson 3   Using Medicines Wisely

Clarifying Text Direct students to read the section on **How Medicines Enter the Body.** Ask students if any of the concepts are still unclear. Model ways to clarify definitions of terms within the context of the lesson, including illustrations, captions, and other textual clues. Have students explain the concepts to each other in their own words.

Lesson 4   Choosing Health Services

Monitoring Comprehension Show students how to ask and answer their own questions during independent reading, such as: "What is my purpose in reading the section **Health Care Providers**? My purpose must be to find out who provides health care." Have students write the answers to their questions (e.g., primary caregiver) and to reread if necessary.

Lesson 5   Public Health

Pairs Reading Direct student pairs to take turns reading aloud to one another. Assign one student the role of coach and the other the reader. After the reader reads the section **What Is Public Health?,** have the coach paraphrase the main ideas. Then have the reader clarify any questions. Have students reverse roles and continue reading.

Post Reading

Multimedia Presentations Guide students in a discussion of personal care and public health issues. Direct student groups to gather additional information from the Internet or library and develop a presentation for the class using various forms of technology, art, and music.

Key for Using the Teacher Wraparound Edition

Use this key to help you identify the different types of prompts found in the Teacher Wraparound Edition.

R **Reading Strategies** activities help you teach reading skills and vocabulary.

C **Critical Thinking** strategies help students apply and extend what they have learned.

U **Universal Access** activities provide differentiated instruction for students learning to speak English, along with suggestions for teaching various types of learners.

HS **Health Skills Practice** activities reinforce Health Skills concepts and help students apply these skills in their everyday lives.

W **Writing Support** activities provide writing opportunities to help students comprehend the text.

AL **Active Learning** strategies provide a variety of activities for presenting lesson content, including Quick Demos and engaging classroom projects that get students actively involved.

Key to Ability Levels

Teaching Strategies and activities have been coded for ability level and appropriateness.

AL Activities for students working above grade level

OL Activities for students working on grade level

BL Activities for students working below grade level

EL Activities for English Learners

Symbols

Transparencies

CD-ROM

glencoe.com

Print Resources

Chapter at a Glance

Lesson 1 describes skin and hair problems, functions of the mouth and teeth, and how to protect the eyes and ears.

Lesson 2 identifies skills of an informed consumer, factors that play a role in comparison shopping, and actions an unhappy consumer can take.

Lesson 3 discusses types of medicines, ways medicines are taken into the body, and factors that determine how medicines affect the body.

Lesson 4 identifies kinds of health care providers, changes in health care settings, and ways people pay for health care.

Lesson 5 explains the role of government and non-government agencies in public health.

R Reading Strategy

Interpreting the Photo Have students examine the photo and ask: What is the teen in this photo doing? *reading labels on personal care products at a store* Then ask students if they comparison shop when selecting health care products. Have them then answer the caption question. *Sample answers: cost, ingredients, product claims.*

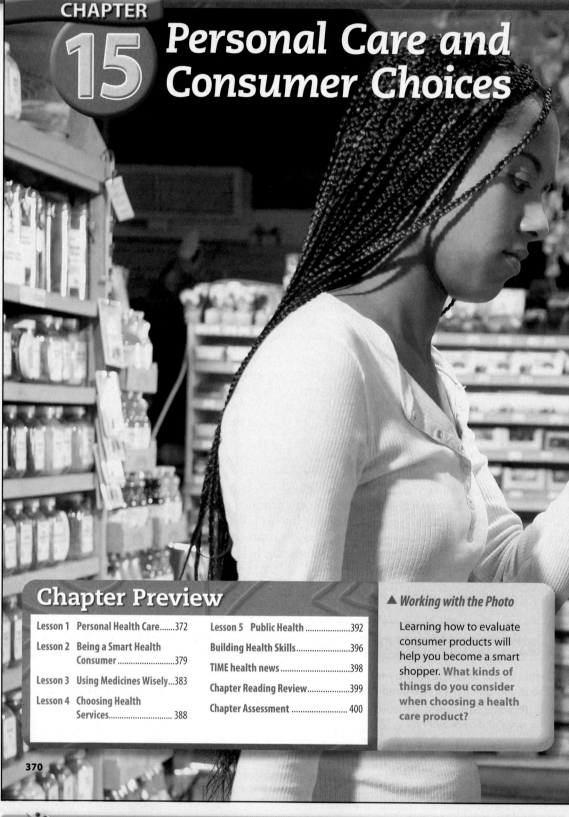

Chapter Preview

370

▲ Working with the Photo

Learning how to evaluate consumer products will help you become a smart shopper. **What kinds of things do you consider when choosing a health care product?**

👥 Universal Access

Differentiated Learning Glencoe provides teacher support and student materials for all learners in the health classroom.

- Spanish Glosario and chapter summaries assist English Language Learners.
- *Reading Tutor* and related worksheets support reluctant readers.

- Universal Access strategies throughout the Teacher Wraparound Edition and Fast Files help you present materials for gifted students, at-risk students, physically impaired students, and those with behavior disorders or learning disabilities.

Start-Up Activities

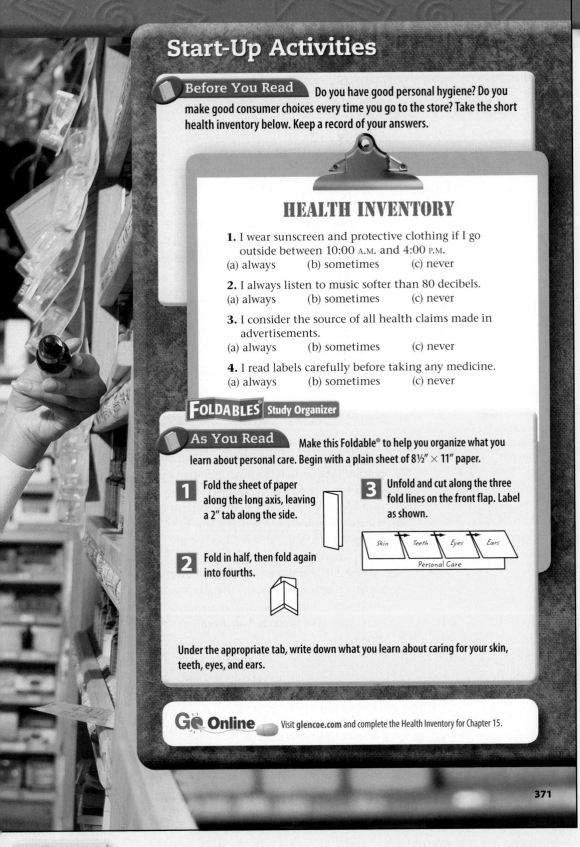

Before You Read Do you have good personal hygiene? Do you make good consumer choices every time you go to the store? Take the short health inventory below. Keep a record of your answers.

HEALTH INVENTORY

1. I wear sunscreen and protective clothing if I go outside between 10:00 A.M. and 4:00 P.M.
(a) always   (b) sometimes   (c) never

2. I always listen to music softer than 80 decibels.
(a) always   (b) sometimes   (c) never

3. I consider the source of all health claims made in advertisements.
(a) always   (b) sometimes   (c) never

4. I read labels carefully before taking any medicine.
(a) always   (b) sometimes   (c) never

FOLDABLES Study Organizer

As You Read Make this Foldable® to help you organize what you learn about personal care. Begin with a plain sheet of 8½" × 11" paper.

1 Fold the sheet of paper along the long axis, leaving a 2" tab along the side.

2 Fold in half, then fold again into fourths.

3 Unfold and cut along the three fold lines on the front flap. Label as shown.

Skin   Teeth   Eyes   Ears

Personal Care

Under the appropriate tab, write down what you learn about caring for your skin, teeth, eyes, and ears.

Go Online Visit glencoe.com and complete the Health Inventory for Chapter 15.

371

FOCUS

Activating Prior Knowledge

What I Know Ask: What are some things that you have heard cause acne? *French fries, chocolate, makeup, bangs, stress, poor hygiene* Tell students they will learn more about acne and other personal health problems in this lesson.

Guide to Reading

Building Vocabulary

■ Define the term *dermis* ("inner layer of skin") and the prefix *epi-* ("outer"). Ask: What does *epidermis* mean? *outer layer of skin*

■ Use Vocabulary PuzzleMaker to reinforce vocabulary terms.

Reading Strategy

Classifying Remind students to add care for each part of the body listed in the chart. For example, under *skin*, they might write, "wash twice daily with mild soap and water."

 Have students use their Foldable® as they read Lesson 1.

Quick Write

Make sure students include practices that keep teeth, hair, and nails clean, not just skin. Call on several volunteers to name one of the hygiene practices they listed and explain how it helps maintain health.

Personal Health Care

Guide to Reading

● **Building Vocabulary**
As you read this lesson, write each new highlighted term and its definition in your notebook.

■ epidermis (p. 373)
■ dermis (p. 373)
■ dandruff (p. 374)
■ plaque (p. 375)
■ tartar (p. 375)
■ decibel (p. 377)

● **Focusing on the Main Ideas**
In this lesson, you will learn to

■ **identify** common skin and hair problems.
■ **explain** functions of the mouth and teeth.
■ **describe** how to protect your eyes and ears.

● **Reading Strategy**
Classifying Make a chart with four columns, one each for skin, mouth, eyes, and ears. Identify ways of caring for each of these.

FOLDABLES Study Organizer Use the Foldable® on p. 371 as you read this lesson.

Quick Write

Write a short description of your daily hygiene routines.

Functions of Skin

The skin is your body's largest organ. Like other organs of the body, it has several important functions. It is a watertight barrier when you swim or take a shower. It also helps control your body temperature. It releases perspiration when you are hot and tells your brain to slow blood circulation when you are cold.

The skin also allows you to feel textures, such as rough and smooth, and alerts you when something is hot, cold, or painful. Your skin also protects you from germs.

▶ Your skin enables you to experience the sense of touch: the roughness of tree bark, the smooth, silky feel of satin, or the softness of a rabbit. **What are some other functions of the skin?**

Lesson 1 Resources

📁 **Chapter *FAST FILE* Resources**
Guided Reading and Writing 15-1
Concept Mapping Activity 15-1
Decision-Making Activity 15-1
Reteaching Activity 15-1
Enrichment Activity 15-1
Lesson Quiz 15-1

Technology
🔦 Transparency 15-1
💿 Audio Summaries
◉ *ExamView® Assessment Suite*
💿 Vocabulary PuzzleMaker
◉ StudentWorks™ Plus

Go Online

Parts of the Skin

The skin is composed of three main layers. The *outermost layer of the skin* is the **epidermis** (e·puh·DER·mis). The *thick inner layer of skin* underneath it is the **dermis.** This is where nerve endings, blood vessels, and oil and sweat glands are found. The innermost layer of skin, the *subcutaneous* (sub·kyoo·TAY·nee·uhs) *layer,* connects your skin to muscle and bone.

 Reading Check **List** Name the three main layers of the skin.

Skin Problems

Oil glands help the skin stay soft. During the teen years, too much oil can cause clogged pores, which leads to acne. Acne sores include whiteheads, blackheads, and pimples.

Minor acne can be treated with over-the-counter products and good hygiene. More serious cases may require visits to a dermatologist (DER·muh·TAHL·uh·jist), a physician who specializes in skin problems.

Other skin problems are caused by sun exposure. Exposure to the sun's ultraviolet (UV) rays increases the risk of developing skin cancer. Sun exposure also damages the skin, causing wrinkles and premature aging.

Viruses can also affect the skin. Cold sores and warts are both caused by viruses. Both can be treated but are contagious. Contagious means the virus can be spread to others. Anyone with a wart or cold sore should avoid skin contact with others, and should wash his or her hands often.

Skin Care

Having clean, healthy skin is part of your overall appearance. During the teen years, you may notice an odor in areas where you sweat heavily. The odor is caused by bacteria. Bathing or showering regularly and using antiperspirants and deodorants can eliminate body odor.

If you have acne, gently wash the affected area with mild soap and warm water. Repeat this twice a day. Never scrub the skin. This can cause even more acne by opening pimples and spreading the bacteria all over your face.

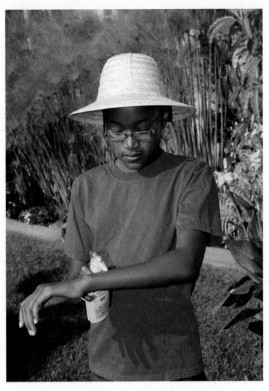

▲ It is healthy to be involved in outdoor activities, but measures must be taken to protect yourself from the sun's harmful rays. **What are some of these protective measures?**

Lesson 1: Personal Health Care **373**

TEACH

Reading Check

Answer epidermis, dermis, subcutaneous layer

AL Active Learning

Surveys Have students search online or develop a list of myths about tanning. (E.g., a tan protects the skin from sunburn; tanning lamps are safer than sunlight; tanning gets rid of acne.) Tell the class to survey other students in their school about whether the myths are true or false. Discuss their survey results in terms of how belief in the myths might lead to unhealthy decisions about tanning. OL

HS Health Skills Practice

Practicing Healthful Behaviors Challenge students to create a plan for daily hygiene that includes all the skin-care tips in the text. Display a few of the most complete and efficient plans. Encourage students to follow their skin-care plans. OL

Caption Answers

Photo Caption, p. 372 providing a watertight barrier, helping control body temperature, protecting from germs

Photo Caption, this page *Sample answer:* wearing protective clothing and sunscreen

---

Dealing with Sensitive Issues

Students with Acne Students who have acne are likely to be self-conscious. In fact, these students may have lower self-esteem because of their acne. When discussing acne in class, avoid calling attention to these students or using language that implies they are responsible for the problem (e.g., "if you pick pimples, you will make them worse"). Make sure students are aware that acne is a very common problem and that serious cases of acne should be treated by a doctor.

Reading Check

Answer, top Body piercings and tattoos expose the skin to germs.
Answer, bottom Your hair and nails are composed of a tough substance called keratin.

MediaWatch

Deodorants

Most students are likely to use deodorants or antiperspirants. Ask students to bring in ads for these kinds of products and identify their product claims.

R Reading Strategy

Identifying Problems and Solutions As students read the material on hair and nails, ask them to make a list of problems and solutions for each body part. Have students compare their lists with the lists of other students around them. If they see any omissions or errors, they should amend their lists. **BL**

MediaWatch

Deodorants

Have you ever seen a deodorant ad that claimed "superior protection" or "extra-long-lasting formulas?" As a health consumer, you need to learn to cut through the media "hype." In Lesson 2, you'll learn how to read product ingredient labels. This will help you compare products to see whether there is really a difference.

Do you use a deodorant or an antiperspirant? Have you seen ads for the product? What claims did the ads make about the product?

Brushing or combing your hair regularly can keep it looking healthy. **What are some other things you can do to take care of your hair?**

Wear sunscreen and protective clothing when you're in the sun between 10:00 A.M. and 4:00 P.M. Make sure you use a sunscreen with at least an SPF (sun protection factor) 15 and UVA/UVB protection. UVA and UVB are harmful sun rays that can damage your skin. Avoid body piercings and tattoos. Even under sterile conditions, the skin is exposed to germs.

Reading Check

Describe Why should you avoid fads like body piercings and tattoos?

Your Hair and Nails

Your hair and nails are composed of a tough substance called keratin. Both grow out of living tissue located in the dermis. Each nail is surrounded by a fold of epidermis called a *cuticle* (KYOO·ti·kuhl).

Hair and Nail Problems

The same oil glands that cause acne can also affect hair, making it look and feel greasy. Another common hair problem is **dandruff,** *a flaking of the outer layer of dead skin cells.* Try using shampoos made for oily hair or flaking scalp.

Head lice is another common hair problem. Lice are tiny insects that live in hair and spread easily. To prevent the spread of lice, avoid sharing combs, brushes, and hats. If you get lice, you can treat it with a medicated shampoo. You will also need to wash all bedding, towels, combs, brushes, and clothing. Your family will need to do the same.

Your nails can have problems as well. A hangnail is a split in the cuticle near the fingernail's edge. You can treat hangnails by carefully trimming the skin. The cuticle should heal in a few days. An ingrown toenail occurs when the toenail pushes too far into the skin along the side of the toe. This can result from trimming the nail on a curve rather than straight across or wearing shoes that are too tight. See a doctor if your toe becomes inflamed and sore as it may be infected.

Reading Check

Identify What substance makes up your hair and nails?

Caption Answer

Photo Caption Answers may include any special ways of taking care of hair, such as using products that give hair more body or shine.

374

Cultural Perspectives

Acne Studies A recent study found that acne may not be the universal problem of adolescence that many Westerners have assumed. In the study, hundreds of teens from the islands of Papua New Guinea and the rain forests of Paraguay were examined for acne, and not a single case was found. According to the researchers, genetic differences alone cannot account for such great population differences. Instead, they think the differences must be due to cultural or environmental factors.

Your Teeth

Like your skin, your teeth are vital to your appearance and health. They chew and grind food, making it easier to digest. They are also necessary for proper speech.

Tooth and Gum Problems

Taking care of your teeth and gums can prevent tooth decay. **Figure 15.1** shows the stages of tooth decay.

The gums serve as anchors for your teeth. Like the teeth, they can also develop problems. One problem is gingivitis (jin·juh·VY·tis). This is a condition in which the gums become inflamed and bleed easily. If left untreated, gingivitis can cause tooth loss.

Tooth and Gum Care

Caring for the teeth and gums is essential. Make it a habit to floss and gently brush the teeth and gums for at least two to three minutes, twice a day. Brushing and flossing clean the teeth and **remove** plaque.

AL

Academic Vocabulary

remove (rih MOOV) *(verb)* to take off; to take away. *Guests are required to remove their shoes before they enter some Asian households.*

▼ **FIGURE 15.1**

R THE PROCESS OF TOOTH DECAY

When teeth are not cared for properly, tooth decay results. **What regular habits can help you prevent tooth decay?**

Stage 1 Food and saliva form **plaque,** *a soft, colorless, sticky film containing bacteria that coats your teeth.* The bacteria combine with sugary foods to form an acid. Plaque that is not removed daily can harden into **tartar,** *a hard, shell-like coating on the teeth that is difficult to remove.*

Stage 2 The acid from the plaque eats a hole, or cavity, in the tooth enamel.

Stage 3 The decay spreads to the dentin. When it reaches the pulp, it exposes a nerve. Air hitting the exposed nerve causes your tooth to hurt.

Lesson 1: Personal Health Care **375**

AL Active Learning

Skits Have students develop skits illustrating the habits of tooth and gum care for younger students. They might use drawings to illustrate each habit, or develop demonstrations. If possible, arrange for students to present skits to elementary classes. **OL**

R Reading Strategy

Analyzing a Graphic Guide students through the process of tooth decay in **Figure 15.1**. Ask: What causes plaque? *food and saliva* What causes cavities? *acid from plaque* When does a cavity first cause pain? *stage 3, when decay reaches the pulp and exposes a nerve* Explain that good hygiene removes plaque and helps prevent cavities, and regular checkups detect cavities in the early stages when they are easier to repair. **OL**

Academic Vocabulary

Remove On this page, students learn that the essential purpose of brushing and flossing is to clean the teeth and to remove plaque. Have a volunteer read aloud the definition of *remove*, and then let other volunteers restate the purpose of brushing and flossing, using other words or phrases in place of *remove*. You will find academic vocabulary activities in the Student Activities Workbook. 📁

Caption Answer

Figure Caption *Sample answer:* Brush and floss after meals, and get regular checkups.

FITNESS ZONE

Personal Health Care and Physical Fitness Healthy skin, hair, nails, teeth, eyes, and ears are all indicators of good health on all three sides of the health triangle. Similarly, physical fitness activities make positive contributions to all three aspects of health. Help students review suggestions for *Planning a Routine* in the *Fitness Zone Handbook,* and ask: How can a physical fitness routine contribute to your good health? **For more information, see *Fitness Zone Handbook* pages xviii-1 or visit the Fitness Zone at glencoe.com.**

HS Health Skills Practice

Advocacy Have students create public service announcements advocating proper care and protection of the eyes. Give students a chance to present their announcements. **OL**

U Universal Access

English Learners Have students create drawings for a poster that shows how the same object would look to a someone who is nearsighted and to someone who is farsighted. Students should include both how the object looks close up and from a distance. **EL**

▲ Your smile is an important part of your appearance. **What steps can you take to keep your smile bright and your teeth healthy?**

Good eating habits also help keep your teeth healthy. Dairy products and other foods high in calcium will help keep teeth strong. You should also limit the number of sugary foods you eat.

You should see a dentist twice a year. The dentist or a dental hygienist will clean and remove hard-to-reach plaque and tartar. The dentist can also treat any cavities and gum problems. If your teeth are growing in crooked, your dentist may recommend that you see an orthodontist. An orthodontist may put braces on your teeth to straighten them.

 Describe Tell how tooth decay occurs.

Your Eyes

Your eyes are your organ of sight. The main parts of the eye are shown in **Figure 15.2.**

Vision Problems

There are several common vision problems. Nearsightedness is when a person can see nearby objects clearly, but distant objects are blurred. With farsightedness, faraway objects are clear, but nearby objects are blur. With astigmatism (ah·STIG·muh·tizm), images appear blurred or distorted due to an irregularly shaped lens or cornea. Most vision problems can be corrected by using eyeglasses, contact lenses, or laser correction surgery. **U**

Eye Care and Protection

HS It is important to protect your eyes from injury, dust, and overexposure to sunlight. Wear sunglasses that have lenses with UV protection. Wear protective goggles when doing any activity that could injure your eyes. Watch television or use a computer in a well-lit room. Avoid rubbing your eyes. This can irritate them and spread bacteria. If you wear contact lenses, always wash your hands before putting in or taking out your lenses. Change your lenses regularly according to your eye doctor's instructions.

Regular vision screenings and eye exams are also important. See an eye doctor for an exam every two years if you don't wear corrective lenses, yearly if you do.

Reading Check **Explain** What is an astigmatism?

 What Teens Want to Know

Are colored contact lenses safe? Colored lenses are safe, as long as you are properly fitted for them by an eye care professional. Never buy colored "cosmetic" lenses that are sometimes sold by street merchants or at flea markets, and never borrow lenses— colored or clear—from another person. There is one problem you may experience with colored lenses that you do not have with clear lenses. The colored portion of a lens may occasionally slide over the pupil and temporarily reduce vision. **OL**

▼ FIGURE 15.2

R **PARTS OF THE EYE**

Each part of the eye has a specific function. **What is the function of the optic nerve?**

A The **cornea** is a clear protective structure that lets in light.

B The **aqueous** (AY·kwee·uhs) **humor** is the watery fluid in between the cornea and lens. It helps maintain pressure in the eye.

C The **iris** is the colored part of the eye. It controls the size of the pupil.

D The **pupil** is a dark opening in the center of the iris. The pupil controls the amount of light that enters the eye.

E The **lens** is a clear flexible structure that focuses light on the retina.

F The **retina** (RE·tin·uh) is a thin layer of nerve cells that absorb light. It covers the interior back of the eye.

G The **optic nerve** is a cord of nerve fibers that carries messages from the retina to the brain.

H The **sclera** (SKLEHR·uh) is the white of the eye. It protects the eyeball and gives it its shape.

Your Ears

Your ears interpret sound. Your ears also enable you to control your balance. Fluid and tiny hair cells inside your ears send messages to your brain when you move or shift positions. The brain interprets the messages and tells your body what adjustments it needs to make. **Figure 15.3** on the next page shows the different parts of the ear.

Hearing Problems

The most common ear problem is hearing loss, caused by middle ear infections and punctured eardrums. Loud noises can also cause hearing loss. Any noise above 80 decibels can be harmful. A **decibel** is *a measure of the loudness of sound.*

Prolonged exposure to loud noise can also lead to *tinnitus* (TIN·uh·tuhs). This is a constant ringing in the ears.

Ear Care and Protection

To protect your ears, never insert anything into the ear. Avoid loud noises. Cover the ears in cold weather to avoid frostbite. Wear earplugs to reduce noise or keep water out. See a doctor for an earache or to treat ringing in the ears.

Go Online

Visit **glencoe.com** and complete the Interactive Study Guide for Lesson 1.

Lesson 1: Personal Health Care **377**

R **Reading Strategy**

Analyzing a Graphic Help students see how the lens focuses an image on the retina by having them trace the path of light through the eye in **Figure 15.2.** You can also use the figure to explain the cause of nearsightedness (image focuses in front of retina) and farsightedness (image focuses behind retina). **OL**

R **Reading Strategy**

Analyzing a Graphic Have students examine **Figure 15.3**, Parts of the Ear, on the next page. Guide students in relating the illustration of parts of the ear to information in the text on hearing problems. Help students identify parts of the middle ear. Ask: What decibel levels are associated with hearing damage? *above 85 decibels* If you have prolonged exposure to sounds as loud as a rock concert, what symptoms might you have? *ringing in your ears, hearing damage* Stress that lower-decibel sounds can also harm hearing if you are exposed to them long enough. **OL**

⌂ **Home, School, and Community**

In the Community Encourage students to become aware of possible damage to their hearing when they are in public places. Lead students in brainstorming places and events that have very loud sounds (e.g., basketball games, rock concerts, construction sites, train stations). Discuss with students ways to avoid permanent damage to their hearing. With the class, list ideas and strategies students can take to protect their ears from loud sounds at public places and events. **OL**

Caption Answer

Figure Caption The optic nerve carries messages from the retina to the brain.

ASSESS

Assessment Resources

Lesson Review Quiz
- *ExamView*
- Fast Files Activities
- Online Quizzes and Activities

Reteaching

- Assign Concept Map 15-1 or Reteaching Activity 15-1 in the Fast Files.
- Have students write a lesson on caring for skin and hair, and teach the lesson to a partner.

Enrichment

- Assign Enrichment Activity 15-1 in the Fast Files.
- Ask students to research the cost and effectiveness of several over-the-counter (OTC) tooth whiteners and make a compare/contrast table to share what they learn.

CLOSE

Call on students to state ways to protect the eyes and ears.

Caption Answer

Figure Caption The ear allows you to hear sound and helps control balance.

▶ **FIGURE 15.3**

PARTS OF THE EAR

R The ear has three main parts: the outer ear, the middle ear, and the inner ear. **What are the functions of the ear?**

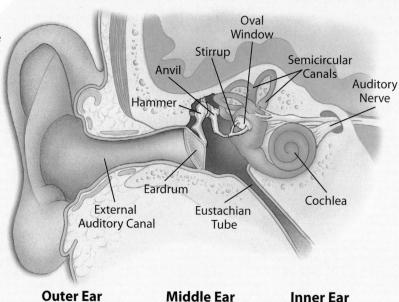

Oval Window
Stirrup
Anvil
Semicircular Canals
Hammer
Auditory Nerve
Eardrum
External Auditory Canal
Eustachian Tube
Cochlea

Outer Ear   **Middle Ear**   **Inner Ear**

Lesson 1 Review

 After You Read

Review this lesson for new terms, major headings, and Reading Checks.

What I Learned

1. ***Identify*** What are the functions of the skin?

2. ***Vocabulary*** What is *plaque*? Why should plaque be removed?

3. ***Recall*** Name two ways of caring for and protecting the ears.

Thinking Critically

4. ***Apply*** A friend of yours is planning to get a pierced lip. What potential risks does this plan involve?

5. ***Analyze*** Tim likes playing handball. However, he doesn't like the way the protective goggles look. What decision does Tim need to make?

Applying Health Skills

6. ***Accessing Information*** Choose one of the body areas discussed in this chapter. Using reliable sources, find out four new facts about the care of this part of the body. Share your findings with classmates.

378 Chapter 15: Personal Care and Consumer Choices

Go Online For more Lesson Review Activities, go to **glencoe.com**.

Lesson 1 Review Answers

1. Answers listed on page 372
2. Plaque is a soft, colorless, sticky film containing bacteria that grows on your teeth. It should be removed because it can harden into tartar.
3. Never insert anything inside your ear, and either avoid or wear earplugs around loud noises.

4. allergic reaction, infection, skin disorder, bleeding
5. *Sample answer:* Tim needs to recognize the risk of eye damage when deciding whether or not he should wear goggles to protect his eyes when playing handball.

6. Answers will vary but should provide four new facts about the care or health of the skin, hair, nails, teeth, gums, eyes, or ears. Check that students have used only reliable sources, and give them time to share their findings with the class.

Lesson 2

Being a Smart Health Consumer

Guide to Reading

● **Building Vocabulary**
Identify the terms you think you know. Define these in your notebook.
- consumer (p. 379)
- consumer skills (p. 379)
- comparison shopping (p. 381)
- warranty (p. 381)
- health fraud (p. 381)

● **Focusing on the Main Ideas**
In this lesson, you will learn to
- **identify** skills of an informed consumer.
- **describe** factors that play a role in comparison shopping.
- **explain** how to resolve problems with purchases.
- **analyze** advertisements for health products or services.

● **Reading Strategy**
Finding the Main Idea For each main heading in this lesson, write one sentence that states the main idea.

Becoming an Informed Consumer

Each day American consumers spend millions of dollars for goods or services. A **consumer** is *anyone who uses products or services.*

As a teen you are making more consumer decisions on your own. As you grow older, you will be responsible for more consumer choices. Learning **consumer skills,** *techniques that enable you to make wise, informed purchases,* will help you become a smart shopper. Smart shoppers know how to compare products in terms of quality, effectiveness, safety, and cost. They also know how to resolve problems with purchases.

Reading Check **Define** What is a *consumer?*

*Q*uick Write

Write a letter to the maker of a product you bought that doesn't work. Explain the problems you had.

▶ Consumer skills help you to make wise, informed purchases. **What are some examples of consumer skills?**

379

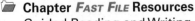
Lesson 2 Resources

📁 **Chapter FAST FILE Resources**
Guided Reading and Writing 15-2
Concept Mapping Activity 15-2
Health Lab 15-2
Reteaching Activity 15-2
Enrichment Activity 15-2
Lesson Quiz 15-2

Technology
🔥 Transparency 15-2
💿 Audio Summaries
⚙ *ExamView® Assessment Suite*
💿 Vocabulary PuzzleMaker
⚙ StudentWorks™ Plus

Go Online

FOCUS
Activating Prior Knowledge

What I Know Ask: What are some things you regularly buy? *beverages, snacks, magazines, CDs, makeup, clothes* Tell students that any time they buy anything or use a service, they are consumers.

Guide to Reading

Building Vocabulary
- Point out the term *comparison shopping*. Ask: What are some things you might compare about different items when you shop? Sample answers: *price, quality, brand, warranty*
- Use Vocabulary PuzzleMaker to reinforce vocabulary terms.

Reading Strategy
Finding the Main Idea Tell students that they may need to skim the text under the main headings to identify the main ideas.

*Q*uick Write

In their letters, students should describe the product and provide details about its flaws.

Reading Check

Answer anyone who uses products or services

TEACH

Health Skills Activity

Analyzing Influences

Reading Between the Lines

Bring to class a variety of print ads. Show students how to analyze ads that use meaningless claims, celebrity endorsements, hidden messages, or testimonials. Then have students find and analyze other ads that use these same techniques. Be sure to talk about the source of the ads and whether or not those sources are credible.

HS Health Skills Practice

Analyzing Influences Ask students to list factors that might influence their decision to buy a certain product, such as a video game (e.g., price, advice of peers, ads). Have students try to prioritize the factors from most to least important. Call on a few volunteers to share their prioritized lists. Use the lists to start a discussion of the types of factors that influence consumer choices. **OL**

Caption Answer

Photo Caption, p. 379 comparison shopping, how to resolve problems with purchases

---

Health Skills Activity

Analyzing Influences

Reading Between the Lines

As a consumer you can use ads to your advantage. This means cutting through what the advertiser wants you to hear or see and getting to the information you need. Here are some ways for doing that:

- **Consider the source.** Where is the information in the ad from? When possible, trace a health claim back to its source. Claims like "nine out of ten doctors recommend" are meaningless. Also, beware of *infomercials*, ads meant to look like impartial TV programs.
- **Consider the approach.** What techniques are being used to attract your attention or appeal to you? Some advertisers use celebrities to promote their products. Admiring a person's talents or looks is not a good reason for choosing a product. Another technique advertisers use is hidden messages. These are often pictures showing seemingly happy, attractive people. The message implies that the product will make you happier and healthier. One last advertising approach is the "testimonial." Ordinary-looking people claim to have gotten great results, but they may be paid actors. Learning to identify these techniques will help you avoid being swayed by them.

On Your Own

Analyze an ad for a health product or service. What technique did the advertiser use? Are the health claims in the ad from a reliable source?

Influences on Your Buying Decisions

Informed consumers are aware of the many factors that play a role in their buying decisions. One factor is personal taste. Many of the products people buy are items they have tried and liked. Another factor is personal need.

HS One of the most important influences on your buying decisions is media messages. Each day you receive hundreds of messages from TV, radio, the Internet, newspapers, and magazines. Advertising is a strong influence. According to one industry source, around 3,000 ads a day are seen by the average American. Informed consumers know how to analyze information in ads. The Health Skills Activity above gives some useful tips for evaluating ads.

HEALTH LITERACY

Teen Consumers Today's teens are the most sought-after age group in the consumer market and the age group most targeted by ads. The number of teens is one reason they are so prized by marketers and advertisers. By 2010, there will be 35 million teens in the United States. The relative wealth of today's teens is another reason. They have more money to spend than any teen cohort in the past. In 2002 alone, teens spent more than 170 billion dollars, and they spend more and more each year.

Comparison Shopping

"Compare and save!" You've probably seen lines like this in ads or on store displays. This advice relates to the consumer skill of **comparison shopping,** or *a method of judging the relative benefits of competing products or services based on quality, effectiveness, safety, and cost.* Suppose you want to purchase a sunscreen that offers maximum protection against the sun's UV rays. You might compare different brands, read the ingredients, and the application instructions. Look for one that has a *sun protection factor (SPF)* of at least 15. This will help protect you against the sun's harmful rays.

How about cost? Some brands may have identical volume and ingredients but vary in cost.

Another factor that may affect your purchase is whether an item carries a **warranty.** This is *a promise to refund your money if the product doesn't work as claimed.* A warranty shows that a company stands behind its product.

Reading Check List What factors are evaluated in comparison shopping?

Managing Consumer Problems

Products usually work as advertised. Unfortunately, some people and businesses sell products or services that don't work. When this is done purposefully to deceive the buyer, the seller has committed *fraud.* This is a crime punishable by law.

One of the most serious kinds of fraud is **health fraud.** This is *the selling of products or services to prevent diseases or cure health problems which have not been scientifically proven safe or effective for such purposes.* Making inaccurate claims about a health product can give false hope to people who are seriously ill. Some products may even pose a risk to your health. If you believe you have been a victim of health fraud, contact the Food and Drug Administration. You will learn more about this agency in the next lesson.

Connect To... Math

Unit Price

Understanding *unit price* is important when comparison shopping. This is cost per unit of weight or volume. To figure out unit price, first find the weight or volume given on a product container. (Make sure that both products are measured in the same type of units.) Next divide the price of the product by its weight or volume. The amount you end up with is the unit price.

An 8 fl. oz. bottle of lotion costs $3.89. What is its unit price?

What Teens THINK

How do companies make their products appealing to you?

In my opinion, what makes a product appealing is how it looks. That says a lot. If it is clothes, it is usually the way they look on and the brand name of the item that counts. If it is a game, it is usually the way the box describes the game. So many things make a product appealing.

Mikel H.
Sandy, UT

Connect To... Math

Unit Price

You can give students real-life practice by providing them with empty product packages that show the size and cost of several different items. Have students find and use the needed information to calculate unit prices of the items. The unit price for the product in the activity is $3.89 ÷ 8 oz. = $0.49 per oz.

Reading Check

Answer cost, quality, effectiveness, and safety

What Teens THINK

How do companies make their products appealing to you? Display three or four different plastic bottles or tubes of shampoo, and let volunteers identify and describe them. Then ask: If you were buying one of these shampoos, which would you choose? Why? Encourage a variety of responses, and help students explore various reasons for their choices. Then have students read the *What Teens Think* question and response and share their reactions.

Teacher to Teacher

Joan Stear   **West Clermont Institute of Performing Arts, Cincinnati, Ohio**

Health Literacy and Technology "Should you trust health information found on the Internet? Have students use the following questions to guide them in researching online health information. Ask: Who is the site's sponsor? Do they have an opinion they are trying to promote? Have your students practice this every time they use the Internet to research important health information."

ASSESS

Reteaching

- Assign Concept Map 15-2 or Reteaching Activity 15-2 in the Fast Files.
- Have students write a paragraph describing how to comparison shop.

Enrichment

- Assign Enrichment Activity 15-2 in the Fast Files.
- Ask students to create and present a skit showing how and why to be an informed consumer.

CLOSE

Have students write an e-mail to an appropriate party about a problem with a product or service of their choice.

AL Active Learning

Comparison Shopping
Ask students to comparison shop for different kinds of items. Each group should gather information on cost, quality, and other relevant factors for several brands.

Problems with Products

In spite of a manufacturer's best efforts, a particular product may be defective. Sometimes, the store where you bought the item will be willing to take it back. For example, you may have bought a bottle of aspirin and opened it to find they were all stuck together. With your receipt, a reputable store will have no problem returning your money. A good consumer habit is to keep your sales receipts until you are certain you are satisfied with the product. You should also ask about the store's return policy before purchasing from a store. In some cases, your only remedy will be to send the product back to its manufacturer.

Online Shopping

Buying over the Internet can be fun, easy, and convenient. However, just like buying in a store, consumers need to be aware and take precautions to prevent problems.

When buying online, know who you are dealing with. Anyone can set up a shop online. Confirm the seller's physical address and phone number in case you need to get in touch with him or her.

Check different Web sites and compare prices of the same item including shipping costs. Find out what their return policies are and whether or not you will have to pay shipping costs to return the item. Always pay by credit card, never send cash. Print and save records or receipts of your online purchases.

Go Online

Visit **glencoe.com** and complete the Interactive Study Guide for Lesson 2.

Lesson 2 Review

After You Read

Review this lesson for new terms, major headings, and Reading Checks.

What I Learned

1. *Vocabulary* What are *consumer skills*?

2. *Recall* Name two factors a comparison shopper evaluates.

3. *Describe* What should you do if a product you purchased is defective?

Thinking Critically

4. *Evaluate* Which factor(s) most influence your shopping decisions—price, quality, effectiveness, or safety? Explain.

5. *Analyze* Why are consumer skills important? Explain your answer.

Applying Health Skills

6. *Analyzing Influences* One influence on teen buying habits is peer pressure. Think about brands of clothing or footwear popular among your peers. Why are these items appealing to teens? Share your thoughts in class.

Go Online For more Lesson Review Activities, go to **glencoe.com**.

Lesson 2 Review Answers

1. techniques that enable you to make wise, informed purchases
2. *Any two:* quality, effectiveness, safety, cost
3. Return the product, keep receipts, ask about return policies, or contact the manufacturer.

4. Answers will vary but should explain why students have identified price, quality, effectiveness, and/or safety as the most influential factor(s) in their shopping decisions.
5. Consumer skills help you to make informed decisions when shopping and allow you to avoid becoming a victim.

6. Students are likely to identify certain brands of clothing or footwear as popular among their peers. They may indicate why teens would be influenced by their peers to buy most if not all of the items.

Using Medicines Wisely

Guide to Reading

● **Building Vocabulary**
Organize the terms into a word web. Decide which term is central to all other terms.

- medicines (p. 383)
- prescription medicines (p. 383)
- over-the-counter (OTC) medicines (p. 384)
- vaccine (p. 384)
- antibiotics (p. 385)
- side effect (p. 386)

● **Focusing on the Main Ideas**
In this lesson, you will learn to

- **identify** types of medicines.
- **explain** ways medicines are taken into the body.
- **describe** factors that determine how medicines affect the body.

● **Reading Strategy**
Classifying Make a chart of the kinds of medicines mentioned in the lesson.

Medicines

When sickness or injury occurs, medicines can often help a person feel and/or get better. **Medicines** are *drugs that are used to treat or prevent diseases and other conditions.* Medicines in the United States are carefully controlled. The Food and Drug Administration (FDA) sets standards for medicine safety and effectiveness. Before a medicine can be manufactured and sold, it must be approved by the FDA.

Prescription and Nonprescription Medicines

One of the FDA's roles is to evaluate a new medicine based on research provided to the agency by the drug manufacturer. The FDA evaluates medicines in two forms:

- **Prescription medicines** are *medicines that can be sold only with a written order from a physician or nurse practitioner.* The FDA requires standard information to appear on the label of any prescription medicine. This information includes instructions on how much medication to take, how often, and how long to continue taking the medicine. A sample label appears in **Figure 15.4** on the next page. As a smart health consumer, you should always read these labels carefully before taking any medicine.

uick Write

Describe a time when you took a medicine. State what the medicine was meant to treat and how you took it.

Lesson 3: Using Medicines Wisely **383**

Lesson 3 Resources

 Chapter *FAST FILE* Resources
Guided Reading and Writing 15-3
Concept Mapping Activity 15-3
Cross-Curriculum Activity 15-3
Reteaching Activity 15-3
Enrichment Activity 15-3
Lesson Quiz 15-3

Technology
Transparency 15-3
Audio Summaries
ExamView® Assessment Suite
Vocabulary PuzzleMaker
StudentWorks™ Plus
Go Online

FOCUS

Activating Prior Knowledge

What I Know Ask: What medicines can you buy without a prescription from a doctor? *pain relievers, laxatives, antacids, cough medicines* Tell students they will learn in this lesson how to use these and other medicines wisely.

Guide to Reading

Building Vocabulary
- Define *anti-* ("opposing") and *biotic* ("relating to life"). Ask: What does *antibiotic* mean? *relating to opposing life* Explain that antibiotics are drugs that kill living things called bacteria but do not affect nonliving causes of disease such as viruses and toxins.
- Use Vocabulary PuzzleMaker to reinforce vocabulary terms.

Reading Strategy
Classifying Charts can include prescription and nonprescription medicines, vaccines, antibiotics, and pain relievers.

*Q*uick Write

Use examples to illustrate types of problems medicines can treat and different ways medicines can be taken. Allow students to keep answers private.

TEACH

R Reading Strategy

Analyzing a Graphic Ask students to look at the medicine label in **Figure 15.4**. Go around the room and ask students to read aloud and identify each item indicated on the label. *Pharmacy name; phone number; doctor name; date of prescription; patient name; refills prescribed; dosage; name of medication; direction lines; warning label.*

U Universal Access

Reluctant Readers and Writers Have students make compare/contrast tables to summarize the similarities and differences between prescription and OTC medicines. Then have them compare their tables with the tables of other students around them. They should correct any omissions or errors they note in their own tables. **BL**

Reading Check

Answer nonprescription medicines

▶ **FIGURE 15.4**

PRESCRIPTION MEDICINE LABEL

R Medicine labels provide important information. How many times can this prescription be refilled?

Lowe's Pharmacy
672 Miller Road
Oakville, TX
(214) 555-6666
Pharmacist: T. NEWHOUSE
Rx 7578034   Dr. FISCHER
06/30/07
MARIA CORA   Refills 0
ONE TEASPOON THREE TIMES DAILY.
PEDIAPRED LIQUID 5MG/5ML
USE THIS MEDICATION EXACTLY AS DIRECTED: DO NOT SKIP DOSES OR DISCONTINUE WITHOUT INSTRUCTIONS FROM YOUR PHYSICIAN.   TAKE WITH MEALS

▼ There are different medicines for many types of illnesses and conditions. What kinds of nonprescription medicines do you have in your house?

- **Nonprescription medicines.** Some medicines are less risky than others. They are sold as nonprescription, or **over-the-counter (OTC) medicines.** These are *medicines that are safe enough to be taken without a written order from a physician.* Even OTC medicines can be harmful if used incorrectly. You should read OTC labels as carefully as you would prescription labels.

U

Reading Check **Identify** What is another name for over-the-counter medicines?

Types of Medicines

Relieving symptoms of a chronic condition is one function of medications. Others include preventing disease, fighting infection, and easing pain.

Medicines to Prevent Diseases

A **vaccine** is *a medicine that prevents a disease from developing.* Vaccines are made from dead or weakened germs that cause the immune system to produce antibodies. *Antibodies* are proteins that attack and kill or disable specific germs that cause disease. Some vaccines provide protection over a number of years. Others, such as the flu vaccine, are given once a year. The chart in **Figure 15.5** shows some common vaccines given today.

384 Chapter 15: Personal Care and Consumer Choices

Caption Answers

Figure Caption No refills are allowed.
Photo Caption Sample answers: aspirin, cold and allergy medicines, anti-acid tablets

---

HEALTH LITERACY

Prescription to OTC Availability Hundreds of formerly prescription-only drugs are now OTC drugs, and many more prescription drugs are likely to become OTC drugs in the future. The FDA is responsible for making the switch from prescription to OTC status, based on drug safety, effectiveness, and risk of being habit-forming. Ask interested students to learn about prescription to OTC availability and argue in favor of or against them in a class debate. Specific issues for the debate might include cost, convenience, and risk of misuse of OTC versus prescription drugs. **AL**

▼ FIGURE 15.5

R

TYPES OF MEDICINES

Different types of medicines treat or prevent different illnesses.
Which of these medicines have you been given?

Type of Medicine	Some Examples	Disease or Problem
Vaccines	• MMR vaccine • Varicella vaccine • HPV vaccine • Pertussis vaccine	• Measles, mumps, and rubella • Chicken pox • Human Papillomavirus • Whooping Cough
Antibiotics	• Penicillin • Cephalosporin • Tetracycline • Macrolides	• Strep throat, pneumonia, STDs • Meningitis, skin rash • Urinary tract infections, Rocky Mountain spotted fever • Given to patients allergic to penicillin
Pain Relievers	• Aspirin, acetaminophen, ibuprofen, codeine	• General pain relief

Medicines to Fight Infection

When a person develops a bacterial infection, his or her doctor may prescribe an antibiotic to treat the infection. **Antibiotics** are *medicines that reduce or kill harmful bacteria in the body.* Several common classes of antibiotics appear in Figure 15.5. Each type of antibiotic fights specific strains of bacteria.

Medicines to Relieve Pain

Have you ever had a sore back, toothache, or headache? If you took medicine to feel better, it was most likely a pain reliever. Some common pain relievers are shown in Figure 15.5. Pain relievers block or lessen pain signals sent through the nervous system. Many pain relievers are available over-the-counter. Some are used to treat more serious pain and are available only with a prescription.

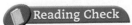 **Reading Check** **List** Name three different types of medicines.

How Medicines Enter the Body

C

There are several common ways medicines enter the body. Swallowing, or ingestion, is the most common way medicines are taken. Pills, tablets, capsules, and liquids are taken this way. The medicine moves through the stomach and small intestine. From

HEALTH LITERACY

New Antibiotics for Superbugs So-called *superbugs*—deadly, highly antibiotic-resistant staph bacteria—first appeared in the United States in the 1960s. In 2005, a new type of antibiotic was developed that uses a unique approach to "disarming" bacteria. It inactivates the enzyme in bacterial cell walls that normally enables the cells to resist antibiotics. Developers of the antibiotic think that this approach opens up a new line of attack on the problem of antibiotic resistance.

ACTIVITY
Careers for the 21st Century

Speech Therapist
Have students read and discuss the information about careers in speech therapy. Ask them to list at least three advantages of a career as a speech therapist. Also have them read about speech therapists at **glencoe.com**. If a speech therapist works at your school, invite him or her to discuss speech therapy with your students.

Reading Check

Answer pills, tablets, capsules, and liquids

HS Health Skills Practice

Accessing Information Divide the class into groups, and give groups package inserts from different prescription medicines. Have each group use its insert to answer the same set of questions: What is the medicine's intended use? How should it be taken? Who should not take it? What are its possible side effects? Are there risks involved with taking other medicines with this? Ask groups to share the information about the medicines, and then lead a class discussion of potential risks of prescription medicines. **OL**

Caption Answer

Photo Caption because medicines can be harmful when not used properly

ACTIVITY
Careers for the 21st Century

Speech Therapist

Speech therapists work with people who have hearing or speech impairments to find possible causes and treatments. There will always be a need for speech therapists because not all people can communicate in the same way. If you would like to become a speech therapist, you should practice your communication skills. You should also study the parts of the body that contribute to hearing and speaking.

What kinds of treatments are available for people with hearing and speaking problems? Go to *Career Corner* at glencoe.com to find out.

there it passes into the bloodstream and circulates throughout the body. Cold medicines and pain relievers are often delivered this way.

Injection, or shot, is another way in which medicines are given. Injected medicines enter the bloodstream and begin to work more quickly.

Medicine can also be inhaled as a mist or fine powder. Inhalation is a relatively new delivery system. People with asthma often use an inhaler. Cold or sinus medication can be breathed in through the nostrils.

Medicines are also given topically, or applied to the skin. Creams and ointments are often applied this way. Skin patches that release medicine over time are a fairly new delivery method.

Reading Check

Describe What types of medicines are swallowed?

Medicine in the Body

How medicines affect the body depends on the type and amount of medicine taken. The individual's chemical makeup, age, gender, and body size also matter. An allergic reaction to a medicine is an unwanted effect that can be deadly.

In general, *any effect of a medicine other than the one intended* is considered a **side effect.** Typical side effects include headache, upset stomach, and drowsiness. Commonly reported side effects of a medicine are listed on or inside the product's packaging. Any reaction that is unexpected or unwanted should be reported to the doctor or pharmacist.

HS

▶ When using medicines, it is important to keep them out of reach of young children. **Why is it important to be responsible when using medicines?**

HEALTH LITERACY

Prescription Drug Abuse by Teens
Prescription drugs, such as pain relievers, are now more commonly abused by teenagers than any illegal drug except marijuana. Their abuse by teens increased 86 percent in just one year from 2004 to 2005. Reasons for the trend include the erroneous belief held by many teens that prescription drugs are safer than illegal drugs. Teens may take pills without regard for dosage or drug interactions and end up in an emergency room or worse. They also risk becoming addicted to some of the drugs.

Risks of Medicines

When a person uses a particular medication for a long period of time, he or she may develop a tolerance. This is a process in which your body needs more and more of a medicine to get the same effect. In some cases, the medicine loses its effectiveness altogether and the doctor will need to prescribe a different medication.

Overuse is another problem. The more an antibiotic is used, the less effective it becomes. Why? Bacteria build up a resistance to antibiotics with frequent exposure. They adapt to—or overcome—the antibiotic. Bacteria can also develop a resistance when antibiotics are not taken as prescribed. For example, if the prescription label says to take the medicine for 14 days and you stop after 7 days, the bacteria may still be present and could make you feel sick again. Medicines should always be used wisely and only as directed.

Finally, taking two or more medicines at once can be dangerous. Always let your doctor and pharmacist know what other medicines you are taking before starting a new medicine.

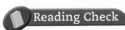 **Reading Check** **Identify** Name two risks of medicines.

Go Online

Visit **glencoe.com** and complete the Interactive Study Guide for Lesson 3.

Lesson 3 Review

 As You Read

Review this lesson for new terms, major headings, and Reading Checks.

What I Learned

1. *Vocabulary* What type of medicine prevents a disease from developing?

2. *List* Name two ways medicines are taken into the body.

3. *Describe* What factors determine a medicine's effect on the body?

Thinking Critically

4. *Analyze* A friend of yours on the football team wants an energy burst before a game. He wants to take a handful of vitamins. When you express concern, he says, "They're over-the-counter vitamins." Respond to this comment.

5. *Hypothesize* Laura's doctor has prescribed a medicine to treat a case of poison ivy. She also regularly takes medicine because she has trouble concentrating. Should Laura tell her doctor what medicine she is already taking? Why or why not?

Applying Health Skills

6. *Accessing Information* The Internet makes it easier than ever to get information about medications. As part of a group, use the Internet to research a popular drug that you have seen advertisements for. What condition does the drug treat? What are its side effects? Share your findings with other groups.

Go Online For more Lesson Review Activities, go to **glencoe.com**.

Lesson 3: Using Medicines Wisely **387**

 Reading Check

Answer *Any two:* tolerance, overuse, combining medicines

ASSESS

Assessment Resources

Lesson Review Quiz
- *ExamView*
- Fast Files Activities
- Online Quizzes and Activities

Reteaching

- Assign Concept Map 15-3 or Reteaching Activity 15-3 in the Fast Files.
- Have students make a concept map of the lesson content.

Enrichment

- Assign Enrichment Activity 15-3 in the Fast Files.
- Ask students to interview a pharmacist or pharmacy technician and report back to the class about how age and weight affect the dosage of medicines.

CLOSE

Have students write a paragraph that starts with the topic sentence, "Medicines have risks."

Lesson 3 Review Answers

1. vaccines

2. *Any two:* swallowing, injection, inhaling, topical application

3. The type and amount of medicine taken and the individual's chemical makeup, age, gender, and body size determine the effect.

4. *Sample answer:* Over-the-counter supplements, such as vitamins, can be harmful if not taken according to directions.

5. Laura should have told her doctor about the other medicine she takes because the two medicines might interact and become ineffective or harmful.

6. Divide the class into groups to work on this question. Students might find out, for example, which drugs are most commonly prescribed and which drugs should not be taken together. Allow class time for groups to share their findings.

FOCUS

Activating Prior Knowledge

What I Know Ask students to name the specialty of each of these types of doctors: pediatrician (children), allergist (allergies), dermatologist (skin), radiologist (X rays). Tell students they will learn in this lesson about doctors and other kinds of health care givers.

Guide to Reading

Building Vocabulary
- Have students review the definitions of vocabulary terms in the text or use the Glossary/ Glosario to look up meanings.
- Use Vocabulary PuzzleMaker to reinforce vocabulary terms.

Reading Strategy
Classifying For health care services not provided locally, students can look for options in the Yellow Pages of a larger community.

Quick Write

Students should not give the names of specific health care givers; instead they should describe their roles (e.g., nurse in my family doctor's office, X-ray technician at the hospital).

Caption Answer

Photo Caption Answers will vary but should state when students were last treated. Allow students to keep answers private.

Choosing Health Services

Guide to Reading

Building Vocabulary
Divide the terms into two lists—one for doctors, one for groups or organizations.
- health care system (p. 388)
- preventive care (p. 388)
- specialist (p. 389)
- allied health professionals (p. 389)
- health insurance (p. 391)
- managed care (p. 391)

Focusing on the Main Ideas
In this lesson, you will learn to
- **identify** different kinds of health care providers.
- **explain** changes in health care settings.
- **describe** ways people pay for health care.

Reading Strategy
Classifying As you read the lesson, list the different health care options. Find examples of each in your own community.

 Quick Write

Write a brief description of your health care team. Name all the doctors and other people who provide health care services to you.

The Role of Health Care

When Rick fell and hurt his leg, his mom took him to the hospital emergency room. There, a nurse wrote down information about Rick's health and medicines he was taking. Rick was taken to another room, where a technician took X rays. A doctor looked at the X ray, examined his leg, and told him it was broken.

The people Rick saw at the hospital are part of our **health care system.** This term refers to *the medical services available to a nation's people and the manner in which these services are paid for.* Different countries have different kinds of health care systems. Originally, health care in America served people who were sick or injured. Today the system also provides preventive care. **Preventive care** is *the steps taken to keep disease or injury from happening or getting worse.*

◄ Health care includes diagnosing illnesses and treating injuries. **When was the last time you were treated by a health care professional?**

Lesson 4 Resources

📁 **Chapter *FAST FILE* Resources**
Guided Reading and Writing 15-4
Concept Mapping Activity 15-4
Decision-Making Activity 15-4
Reteaching Activity 15-4
Enrichment Activity 15-4
Lesson Quiz 15-4

Technology
⚓ Transparency 15-4
🗣 Audio Summaries
💿 *ExamView®* Assessment Suite
🗣 Vocabulary PuzzleMaker
💿 StudentWorks™ Plus
 G**o** Online

Health Care Providers

Rick was treated by a team of health professionals. Your health care is probably also a "team" effort. The leader of your personal health care team is your primary care physician. This is the medical professional who provides physical checkups and general care.

Sometimes a problem will be beyond your primary care physician's specific training or experience. When this happens, she or he will refer you to a **specialist.** This is *a doctor trained to handle particular kinds of patients or medical conditions.* An allergist is one type of specialist. A dermatologist, or skin doctor, is another. **Figure 15.6** lists different kinds of specialists and the conditions they treat.

Still other medical professionals you routinely see may include a dental hygienist. If you wear glasses or contacts, you may have your eyes checked by an ophthalmic (oph·THAL·mik) technician. Professionals like these are known as **allied health professionals.** They are *medical professionals who perform duties which would otherwise have to be performed by doctors or nurses.*

Types of Health Care

Rick's treatment at the hospital was as an *outpatient*. In outpatient care, the person receives treatment and then returns home. *Inpatient* care involves staying at a hospital or other health care facility. Many surgeries are done on an inpatient basis, though some minor surgeries are being done at outpatient surgical centers.

Specialist	Conditions They Treat
Cardiologist	Treats diseases and conditions of the heart.
Psychiatrist	Treats and prescribes medication for patients who have mental, behavioral, or emotional problems.
Osteopath	Treats disorders of the human body, related to bones, muscles, and nerves.
Oncologist	Treats patients with all types of cancer.
Dietitian	Treats nutrition-related diseases, works with patients to develop nutritious eating habits.
Neurologist	Treats diseases of the brain and nervous system.

◀ **FIGURE 15.6**

HEALTH CARE SPECIALISTS

Health care specialists treat specific conditions to provide patients with the best care. **What conditions do oncologists treat?**

TEACH

C Critical Thinking

Categorizing Have students read the definition of the term *preventive care* on the previous page. Then ask: Which type of medicine described in Lesson 3 is an example of preventive care? *vaccine* What are other examples of preventive care? Sample answers: *routine physical checkups, dental X rays, eye exams, medicines to control long-term health problems such as diabetes or depression* **OL**

R Reading Strategy

Analyzing a Graphic Have pairs of students use the information in **Figure 15.6** to make flashcards about health care specialists. They should write a type of health care specialist on one side of each card and the conditions treated by that specialist on the other side of the card. Have partners use the flash cards to quiz each other on the information. **OL**

⬖ Promoting Coordinated School Health

Health Care Knowledge Medical specialties can be confusing to new health care consumers. Empower students with knowledge of medical specialties they are likely to encounter in the health care system.
- Emergency medicine: acute illnesses, injuries
- Family practice: routine health problems
- Internal medicine: chronic illnesses
- Obstetrics-gynecology: female reproductive system, pregnancy, birth
- Surgery: operations
- Pediatrics: children of all ages
- Psychiatry: mental, emotional problems

Caption Answer

Figure Caption
Oncologists treat different types of cancer.

Reading Check

Answer Primary care physician and specialist are two types of health care professionals.

AL Active Learning

Brochures Provide students with brochures from hospitals, clinics, and other places in the local area where surgeries are performed. Ask students to make a brochure that highlights the places where people in their community can go for surgery. **EL**

HS Health Skills Practice

Accessing Information Tell students that most hospices rely on volunteers as well as paid employees. Ask them to go online to learn about hospice services in their community or in a nearby community if their own community does not have a hospice. Call on students to explain what type of training is provided for hospice volunteers. Have students share what they learned. **OL**

Caption Answer

Photo Caption Older adults enter assisted living communities and select the services they need. They live alone as long as they are able.

In these facilities, the person is operated on and released the same day. An example of a surgery done at an outpatient center is the repair of a hernia.

Reading Check

Identify Name two types of health care professionals.

Changes in Health Care Settings

Health care used to be delivered mainly in doctor's offices or hospitals. Over the years, additional types of health care delivery settings have been created.

AL
- **Surgery centers** are facilities that offer outpatient surgical care. For general outpatient care, many people go to clinics. Clinics often have primary care physicians and specialists on staff.

HS
- **Hospice care** provides a place where terminally ill patients can live out the remainder of their lives. Hospice workers are experts at pain management. They are also skilled at giving emotional support to the patient and family. Terminally ill patients can also receive hospice care in their own homes.

- **Assisted living communities** offer older people an alternative to traditional nursing homes. In assisted living communities, older adults are permitted to select the services they need. For example, they may only need help with transportation, remembering to take their medicines, or making meals. As long as they are able, residents live in their own private living quarters. A medical staff is available if and when residents need help.

▶ This teen is visiting a grandparent at an assisted living center. **How do these communities differ from traditional nursing homes?**

TECHNOLOGY AND HEALTH

Robotic-Assisted Surgery The recent increase in outpatient surgery described in the text is partly due to new technologies that make surgery less invasive, so recoveries are quicker and less painful. One of the new technologies uses a robot to perform several different kinds of microsurgeries. The surgeon uses a computer to remotely control the arms of the robot, which are inserted through tiny slits in the patient's body. The doctor views the operation through a tiny high-powered camera.

Covering the Costs of Health Care

Another area of health care that is changing is the way in which costs are covered. Many people have health insurance to help cover costs. **Health insurance** is *a plan in which private companies or government programs pay for part of a person's medical costs.* Traditional health insurance plans may pay up to 80 percent of the cost of outpatient care. They pay an even greater percentage of inpatient care. Many businesses pay a portion of their employees' and their families' health insurance costs.

With recent increases in the cost of health insurance, the insurance industry and care providers have worked to develop lower-cost alternatives, such as **managed care.** This is *a plan that saves money by limiting the choice of doctors to patients who are members.* People pay a monthly fee called a *premium* to the insurance company for health insurance. They are able to save money by seeing doctors and other health care providers who participate in the managed care plan.

Other health insurance alternatives available to some Americans are two government insurance programs, Medicaid and Medicare. The first is designed to assist people with limited income. The second is for adults over the age of 65, and for those with certain disabilities.

 Reading Check Compare Tell how traditional health insurance differs from managed care.

 Go Online

Visit **glencoe.com** and complete the Interactive Study Guide for Lesson 4.

 CHAPTER 15

Lesson 4

 Reading Check

Answer Traditional health insurance pays for medical costs. Managed care programs limit the choice of doctors.

ASSESS

Assessment Resources

Lesson Review Quiz
* *ExamView*
* Fast Files Activities
* Online Quizzes and Activities

Reteaching
● Assign Concept Map 15-4 or Reteaching Activity 15-4 in the Fast Files.
● Have students use the Internet or printed brochures to make posters showing a diversity of health care providers.

Enrichment
● Assign Enrichment Activity 15-4 in the Fast Files.
● Ask students to research and debate the pros and cons of privately owned health insurance and managed care.

CLOSE
Call on students to name and describe new health care delivery settings.

Lesson 4 Review

After You Read
Review this lesson for new terms, major headings, and Reading Checks.

What I Learned

1. *Recall* Name two types of health care providers.

2. *Give Examples* Name two types of health care settings.

3. *List* What are some ways in which people pay for health care?

Thinking Critically

4. *Evaluate* How does managed care help reduce health care costs?

5. *Synthesize* How might an assisted living community affect the health of a senior citizen?

Applying Health Skills

6. *Practicing Healthful Behaviors* One way of reducing health care costs in America is developing positive health behaviors. What are some behaviors that you could do to stay healthy? Make a list of these.

 Go Online For more Lesson Review Activities, go to **glencoe.com**.

Lesson 4: Choosing Health Services **391**

Lesson 4 Review Answers

1. *Any two:* nurse, doctor, nurse practitioner, specialist, dental hygienist, technician

2. surgery centers, hospice care, assisted living communities

3. health insurance, managed care, Medicaid, or Medicare

4. Managed care allows patients to pay one monthly fee for services within the plan.

5. People receive services and medical care when needed in an assisted living community.

6. Students might identify eating a nutritious breakfast, getting more sleep, or getting regular physical activity. Make sure students have allotted adequate time for the behaviors.

FOCUS

Activating Prior Knowledge

What I Know Ask: What health problems can occur in outbreaks that affect many people? Sample answers: *flu, food poisoning, injuries from natural disasters* Explain that protecting the health of the entire population is the role of public health and the topic of this lesson.

Guide to Reading

Building Vocabulary
■ Point out the word *recall*, and have students name some of the many other words that start with the prefix *re-*. (*Sample answers:* return, recycle, react, rewind). Ask students to decide what *re-* means based on the words they named. (again or back)
■ Use Vocabulary PuzzleMaker to reinforce vocabulary terms. 🖱

Reading Strategy
Organizing Information Students might create concept maps or word webs to show the ways public health is protected. They should try to include all the lesson headings in their graphics.

Quick Write

Explain that public health means protecting the health of the population. It is important to keep diseases from spreading.

Lesson 5

Public Health

Guide to Reading

● **Building Vocabulary**
As you read this lesson, write each new highlighted term and its definition in your notebook.
■ public health (p. 392)
■ recall (p. 393)
■ famine (p. 395)

● **Focusing on the Main Ideas**
In this lesson, you will learn to
■ **explain** the role of government agencies in public health.
■ **identify** the health-related jobs done by nongovernment agencies.

● **Reading Strategy**
Organizing Information Using headings from this lesson, create a graphic that shows different ways in which public health is protected.

Quick Write

State what you think the term *public health* means. Then add a short explanation of why public health is important.

What Is Public Health?

Tim had been running nonstop for a half hour. He stopped at a water fountain in the park and took a drink. Tim assumed that the water was safe to drink. Who is responsible for the safety of your drinking water? How about the food you eat or medicines you take?

You can be confident your food, medicine, and water are safe because Americans have systems for public health. **Public health** *involves efforts to monitor and promote the welfare of the population.*

Public health occurs on many levels. Every county in every state has its own public health department. The nation as a whole has agencies to protect the well-being of the American people. The world also has organizations that monitor the health of the "global community."

 Define What is *public health*?

◀ Each community maintains its own safe water supply. This includes the water that comes out of the faucets at your home, school, and from public fountains. **Do you know where the water that comes through your tap originates?**

Lesson 5 Resources

📁 **Chapter** *FAST FILE* **Resources**
Guided Reading and Writing 15-5
Concept Mapping Activity 15-5
Cross-Curriculum Activity 15-5
Reteaching Activity 15-5
Enrichment Activity 15-5
Lesson Quiz 15-5

Technology
🔦 Transparency 15-5
Audio Summaries
ExamView® Assessment Suite
Vocabulary PuzzleMaker
StudentWorks™ Plus

G👁 **Online**

Federal Health Agencies

At the federal level, public health is overseen by the Department of Health and Human Services (HHS). HHS includes more than 300 programs in a variety of health areas. Among these programs are research, disease prevention, and food and drug safety. HHS is also responsible for the Medicare and Medicaid systems, as well as abuse prevention. **Figure 15.7** shows a list of the main agencies of HHS.

The Consumer Product Safety Commission (CPSC) works to reduce risks from unsafe products. If a product is found to cause health problems, or injury, the CPSC will issue a **recall**—*an announcement that informs the public that a product has been determined unsafe.* This is done through media announcements and by direct mail. The recall will list specific model numbers and the addresses where the defective goods should be returned.

▼ FIGURE 15.7

MAIN AGENCIES OF THE DEPARTMENT OF HEALTH AND HUMAN SERVICES

There are several government agencies that work to protect public health. **What is the function of the Centers for Disease Control and Prevention?**

National Institutes of Health (NIH)	World's premier medical research organization. Supports over 38,000 research projects nationwide in diseases.
Food and Drug Administration (FDA)	Assures the safety of foods, cosmetics, medicines, and medical devices.
Centers for Disease Control and Prevention (CDC)	Provides a system of health monitoring to prevent disease outbreaks and maintain national health statistics.
Indian Health Service (IHS)	Provides health services to American Indians and Alaska natives of federally recognized tribes.
Health Resources and Services Administration (HRSA)	Provides access to essential health care services for people who are low-income, uninsured, or live in areas where health care is scarce.
Substance Abuse and Mental Health Services Administration (SAMHSA)	Works to improve the quality and availability of substance abuse prevention, addiction treatment, and mental health services.
Agency for Healthcare Research and Quality (AHRQ)	Supports research on health care systems, health care quality and cost issues, access to health care, and effectiveness of medical treatments.

TEACH

HS Health Skills Practice

Accessing Information Ask students to find recall announcements for items they commonly use, such as scooters or hair dryers. Direct students to conduct their research using the Internet, other media, and library sources. Work with the class to use the results of their searches to develop guidelines for accessing information about recalls. **OL**

R Reading Strategy

Analyzing a Graphic Have students read **Figure 15.7**. Then list several specific health services and ask students to identify the agencies that provide them. For example, list *testing new medicines* (FDA) and *keeping track of flu cases* (CDC). **OL**

Reading Check

Answer, p. 392 Public health involves efforts to monitor and promote the welfare of the population.

Caption Answers

Photo Caption, p. 392 Students may or may not know where their tap water originates. Have volunteers do research and report their findings to the class.
Figure Caption, this page The CDC compiles national health statistics and monitoring to prevent disease outbreaks.

⚡ Promoting Coordinated School Health

Federal School Health Programs Some federal health agencies have divisions focusing on the health of school students. For example, the Centers for Disease Control and Prevention (CDC) has the Division of Adolescent and School Health (DASH), which administers the Coordinated School Health Program (CSHP), among other functions. Information from the CSHP Web site inspired the Promoting Coordinated School Health features in this book. You can visit the CDC Web site to learn more about the CSHP and find other ideas for promoting student health.

Health Skills Activity

Accessing Information

International Red Cross

Allow class time for students to share what they learned about their local chapter of the American Red Cross. You might want to assign interested students to research and report to the class on the founding of the Red Cross or its role in recent major natural disasters, such as hurricanes Katrina and Rita in 2005.

AL Active Learning

Real-World Connection Ask students to visit chapters of the American Heart Association or American Cancer Society. Tell students to talk with employees or volunteers and obtain literature about the organizations' work and how teens can volunteer. Have groups share what they learned in class. **OL**

Go Online

Knowing Community Resources
Have students use the information at **glencoe. com** to help them create their lists. Encourage students to use other reliable Internet resources to find more information about local public health agencies and to share what they have learned with the class. **OL**

Reading Check

Answer They are funded through donations of money and/or time.

Health Skills Activity

Accessing Information

International Red Cross
The Red Cross is an international agency that helps people worldwide during times of war or disaster. The Red Cross was started in Switzerland during the 1800s. Its goal then was to care for wounded soldiers. Today, the Red Cross has chapters in nearly 200 nations.

In times of need, the International Red Cross provides medical treatment, food, clothing, and shelter. It also sponsors classes in first-aid and cardiopulmonary resuscitation (CPR). You may also know the American Red Cross for its blood donation work in the United States. Like the International Red Cross, the agency collects blood from volunteers. After processing, this blood is used for blood transfusions where needed.

On Your Own
Find out what services your local chapter of the American Red Cross provides. Share your findings with the class.

Go Online

Topic: Knowing Community Resources

Visit **glencoe.com** for Student Web Activities to learn about different kinds of public health information and services available.

Activity: Using the information provided at the link above, make a list of public health resources that are available in your community.

Nongovernment Health Organizations

Federal agencies are paid for by tax dollars. Other health organizations exist purely through donations of money and/or time. The American Heart Association and American Cancer Society are two such organizations. Staffed by employees and volunteers, these organizations provide important health information. They help the public to keep informed about research and new developments to treat these diseases. They also help fund research efforts for ways to prevent and cure diseases and respond to sudden illness and injury. Finally, nongovernment health organizations provide programs that teach prevention of disease and respond to health emergencies and disasters. **AL**

Reading Check

Explain How are organizations like the American Heart Association funded differently than government organizations?

Public Health at the International Level

Americans have a vast network of health agencies to rely on. The same is not true for people throughout the world and especially those in developing nations. A lot of diseases that no longer

Cultural Perspectives

Medicines for Those in Need One of the most important efforts of Doctors Without Borders is its Campaign for Access to Essential Medicines. The campaign is on behalf of the 50 percent of people in Africa and Asia who cannot get the medicines they need because the drugs are too expensive, locally unavailable, or no longer produced due to lack of profits. Interested students can learn more at the Doctors Without Borders Web site. **OL**

pose a health threat to Americans are still problems in developing countries. In many places throughout the globe, populations are faced with **famine,** *a widespread shortage of food.* Famine leads to starvation and death.

Fortunately, the international community has made world health a priority. International organizations that head this effort include the World Health Organization (WHO). WHO is an agency of the United Nations with members in 200 countries and territories. Another organization, Doctors Without Borders, is a group of physicians, allied health professionals, and other volunteers. Doctors Without Borders provides care to people in 70 countries who are affected by disasters, medical emergencies, or wars. These groups provide information and aid to struggling communities and nations. Like the nongovernment agencies mentioned earlier, they rely on donations to continue their efforts.

 Reading Check **List** Name an international organization that does public health work in developing countries.

 G Online

Visit **glencoe.com** and complete the Interactive Study Guide for Lesson 5.

Reading Check

Answer World Health Organization or Doctors Without Borders

ASSESS

Assessment Resources

Lesson Review Quiz
● *ExamView*
● Fast Files Activities
● Online Quizzes and Activities

Reteaching

● Assign Concept Map 15-5 or Reteaching Activity 15-5 in the Fast Files.
● Call on students to name public health problems. Call on other students to identify agencies and organizations that help deal with the problems.

Enrichment

● Assign Enrichment Activity 15-5 in the Fast Files.
● Ask students to create and play a quiz game about federal health agencies and their functions.

CLOSE

Have students write a paragraph comparing and contrasting personal health and public health.

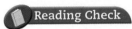 **Lesson 5 Review**

After You Read

Review this lesson for new terms, major headings, and Reading Checks.

What I Learned

1. *Describe* What are some agencies of the Department of Health and Human Services? What kinds of efforts do these groups make in support of public health?

2. *Vocabulary* What is a *recall*? What information is included in a recall?

3. *Recall* Name two nongovernment health organizations. Tell what types of help these organizations offer.

Thinking Critically

4. *Analyze* Look again at Figure 15.7. Tell which of these agencies look after the well-being of less fortunate Americans. Briefly explain your answer.

5. *Synthesize* Imagine that a river floods halfway around the world, destroying farms and homes. Which public health organizations would be most likely to spring into action? What steps might they take to help the people of this region?

Applying Health Skills

6. *Advocacy* Some Americans may not be aware of the role public health agencies play in protecting our health. Working in a group, develop a public service announcement (PSA) that highlights the work of two public health agencies. Share your PSA with other groups.

G Online For more Lesson Review Activities, go to **glencoe.com**.

Lesson 5: Public Health **395**

Lesson 5 Review Answers

1. Students can name any of the agencies in Figure 15.7 and describe their efforts in support of public health.

2. A recall informs the public when a product is unsafe. Recalls include specific model numbers and information about returning the product.

3. *Sample answer:* The American Heart Association and the American Cancer Society offer health information, research funding, prevention programs, and disaster relief.

4. Students are likely to name HRSA, because it gives low-income and uninsured people access to health care services.

5. The World Health Organization, Doctors Without Borders, and International Red Cross would provide medical treatment, food, clothing, and shelter.

6. PSAs should describe the work of two public health agencies, such as a local health department or the CDC

Building Health Skills
Finding Reliable Online Information

Skill

Accessing Information

Activating Prior Knowledge

Ask: How can you tell whether a Web site provides reliable information? *Check that the Web site is up to date and represents a source that can be trusted.*

- **Objective** After completing the activity, students will be able to access reliable online information.
- **Time** 90 minutes
- **Materials** paper, pencil

Teacher Classroom Resources

📁 Building Health Skills
🖨 Transparency 15-3

Model

- Have students read about how Judy used the Internet to find a reliable source.
- Ask: Why are Web sites that end in *.gov* or *.edu* likely to be reliable? *They are Web sites of government agencies or universities.*

National Health Standards Addressed

3.8.2, 3.8.3, 3.8.5, 5.8.2, 7.8.3, 8.8.3

396

Building Health Skills

Accessing Information
Practicing Healthful Behaviors
Stress Management
Analyzing Influences
Communication Skills
Refusal Skills
Conflict Resolution
Decision Making
Goal Setting
Advocacy

What Does Accessing Information Involve?

Accessing information involves finding reliable information to make healthy choices. When looking at a source of information, ask yourself these questions:

- Is it scientific?
- Does it give more than one point of view?
- Does it agree with other sources?
- Is it trying to sell something?

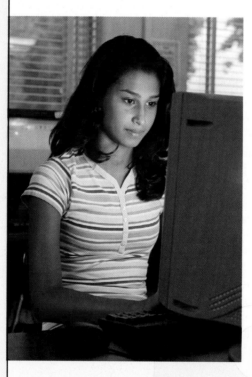

Finding Reliable Online Information

Follow the Model, Practice, and Apply steps to help you master this important health skill.

❶ Model

Read how Judy uses the skill of accessing information to do Internet research for her health class report.

Judy needed to do a report for health class on recent research about vaccines. She knew the Internet would be a good source for finding the latest information.

Judy remembered that government agencies, professional organizations, and universities provide the most valid sources of information. She did a search for vaccines and scanned the pages for links that ended in **.gov, .org,** and **.edu.** Judy clicked on the link that took her to the home page of the Centers for Disease Control and Prevention (CDC). At the CDC Web site, Judy found a listing of current links that gave her everything she needed for her report.

Teaching Tips

Accessing Information If possible, take students to the computer lab and demonstrate how Judy used the search functions to find the information. If a lab is not available, make an overhead transparency of each type of Web site described in the Model, Practice, and

Apply sections and show students where the search engine function is located. Government home pages and related links often change from year to year. Check the links described in this lesson several days in advance to make any last-minute changes in instructions to students.

② Practice

Read how Blair uses the skill of accessing information to do research for her report on bone health.

For her report on bone health, Blair tried the CDC Web site. The site directed her to information that was too technical to understand. What Blair needed was a site designed for teens. She tried typing the word *teen* into the CDC internal search engine. She discovered a whole page with the heading "Health Topic: Adolescents and Teens." She clicked the link to bone health and scrolled down to the bottom of the page.

1. Identify the things Blair did that helped her get reliable information.

2. What problem did Blair encounter? How did she solve the problem?

3. If the CDC site did not provide the information Blair needed, what else could she do?

③ Apply

Use what you have learned about accessing information to complete the activity below.

Work with a small group to prepare a short report on insects, ticks, and disease. Use your textbook to find basic information, then visit a valid Internet site to find four interesting facts about this topic. List the facts you discover and the Web address of the Internet site you visited. Record the date your sources were reviewed. Share your report with the class and explain why your Internet source is a valid source of information.

Self-Check

- Did we provide basic information?
- Did we include four facts?
- Did we use a valid source?
- Was our source current?

Building Health Skills

Practice

- Have students read the Practice section. Call on a volunteer to answer question 1. (She went directly to the same site and searched the site for information she needed.)
- Before students answer question 2, ask: Why did Blair search "bone health" twice at the CDC site? *The first search was of all of CDC, and the result was too technical. The second search was of teen health topics only.*
- Have the class brainstorm answers to question 3. (She could ask her teacher for another reliable health Web site.)

Apply/Assess

- Divide the class into small groups, and ask members of each group to decide on a topic to research. Make sure students select health-related topics that are covered in the text.
- Give each group computer time to find two reliable Web sites on their topic. Remind them to use only recent sources.
- Allow class time for groups to share their reports. Each group should report four facts for their topic. Ask students to justify the reliability of any questionable sources, and point out any sources that are likely to be unreliable.

ASSESSMENT SCORING

Using a rubric, student work should meet all criteria to achieve the highest score.

Skills Student work:
- locates a current and valid source (.gov, .org, or .edu).
- explains why the source is valid.

Concepts Student work:
- provides accurate information.
- includes four facts.
- explains the relationship between insects, ticks, and disease.
- makes factual conclusions.

Danger in the Locker Room

Objectives

After completing this activity, students will be able to:

- Explain how MRSA enters the body and causes illness
- Describe symptoms of MRSA infection
- Explain why MRSA often affects athletes
- Identify ways to prevent MRSA infection

Motivator

Have students identify and describe diseases causes by bacteria. Explain that some bacteria develop a resistance to antibiotics, making treatment difficult.

Teaching the Activity

- Have students develop a bulleted list of three reasons why athletes are one population that is often affected with MRSA. **BL**
- Divide the class into small groups. Have each group use print and online resources to learn more about antibiotic-resistant bacteria.
- Have each group use the results of their research to create a video that explains how antibiotic-resistant bacteria develop, and identifies ways that individuals can help prevent the development and spread of these bacteria. **OL**

DANGER
In the Locker Room

A strain of antibiotic-resistant bacteria is striking athletes at an increased rate.

Twelve-year-old Nicolas Johnson scraped his shoulder during football practice. Infection from the wound spread to his lungs, and Nicolas spent five weeks recovering in a Texas hospital.

What turned this simple scrape into a dangerous illness? The culprit was the bacterium called *methicillin-resistant staphylococcus aureus*—or MRSA for short. It is a highly contagious bug that is resistant to most commonly used antibiotics.

STUDENT OR PRO ATHLETES—THIS BUG DOESN'T CARE

MRSA is infecting the world of sports, from high school wrestling mats and neighborhood health clubs to the locker rooms of colleges and professional teams.

"We're seeing it more and more," says Ron Courson, head athletic trainer at the University of Georgia. "You would be hard-pressed to find a football team at any level that hasn't had to deal with it one way or another."

In some people, the bacteria causes a minor infection. In others, it can lead to more severe illness. When a staphylococcus infection does develop, it's usually treatable with powerful antibiotics.

KEEP IT CLEAN

The Centers for Disease Control and Prevention estimates that roughly 130,000 people are hospitalized with MRSA each year. Why is MRSA difficult to control? Its early symptoms are so tame that people

with the infection often don't seek medical attention until it has begun to spread. Plus, MRSA can be passed easily from one person to another.

For example, scrapes on the skin from artificial turf can provide the entry point into an athlete's body. Then the germ can be passed around in any number of ways—by sharing towels, for instance, or using locker room facilities that aren't completely disinfected.

PREVENTING INFECTION

Some simple steps to keep MRSA from spreading:

- ▶ Wash hands regularly. Soap and water can effectively remove the bacteria before it causes trouble.
- ▶ Cover all wounds, even small ones. This closes off the potential entry points for MRSA.
- ▶ See a doctor at the first sign that a boil or welt seems to be worsening.
- ▶ Don't share towels or other gear, and wipe down heavily used equipment such as weight machines before and after use.

Activity *Media, Technology, and Culture*

Media Have students use online resources and interviews with the school nurse or another medical professional to find out more about MRSA. Then have students prepare posters that explain MRSA and give tips for preventing infection. Obtain permission for students to display their posters in the school gymnasium, locker rooms, and weight rooms. **OL**

Visit glencoe.com to download quizzes and eFlashcards for Chapter 15.

FOLDABLES Study Organizer

Foldables® and Other Study Aids Take out the Foldable® that you created for Lesson 1 and any graphic organizers that you created for Lessons 1–5. Find a partner and quiz each other using these study aids.

Lesson 1 Personal Health Care

Main Idea It is important for you to know how to take care of your personal health.

- Skin problems include acne, sunburn, cold sores, and warts. Hair problems include oily hair, dandruff, and head lice.
- Nail problems include a hangnail or an ingrown toenail.
- Caring for your teeth and gums involves brushing, flossing, and visiting your dentist.
- Protecting your eyes includes wearing sunglasses, avoiding rubbing your eyes, and getting regular eye exams.
- Protecting your ears involves avoiding loud noises and using earplugs.

Lesson 2 Being a Smart Health Consumer

Main Idea Smart shoppers compare products for quality, effectiveness, safety, and cost.

- Factors that influence your buying decisions include personal tastes, need, and media messages.
- When businesses knowingly sell health-related products or services that don't work, they are committing health fraud.

Lesson 3 Using Medicines Wisely

Main Idea Using medicines wisely is a sign of good personal and consumer health.

- Prescription medicines are medicines ordered for you by a health professional.
- Nonprescription medicines (over-the-counter medicines) are medicines that you can buy without your doctor ordering it.
- Factors that determine how medicines affect the body include type and amount of medicine taken and the individual's chemical makeup, age, gender, and body size.
- Types of medicines include vaccines, antibiotics, and pain relievers.

Lesson 4 Choosing Health Services

Main Idea A health care system includes medical services available and the manner in which these services are paid for.

- The steps taken to keep disease or injury from happening or getting worse are known as preventive care.
- Health care providers include primary care physicians, specialists, and allied health professionals.
- Health insurance and managed care are two ways to cover the costs of health care.

Lesson 5 Public Health

Main Idea Public health involves efforts to monitor and promote the welfare of the population.

- A recall informs the public that a product is unsafe.
- Both government and nongovernment agencies work to protect the health and safety of the public.

Chapter 15 Reading Review **399**

Assessment Resources

- Chapter 15 Summary and Activity
- Audio Summaries
- Reading Tutor
- Performance Assessment
- Chapter 15 Test
- *ExamView*
- Vocabulary PuzzleMaker
- Online Learning Center

Reading Review

Study Aids

- **Using the Dinah Zike Foldable® Study Organizer** Have students use the Foldable® to review the content of Lesson 1. Ask students to review their answers to the Reading Strategies to review the contents of Lessons 2 through 5.
- **Online Learning Tools** Have students go to the *Teen Health* Online Learning Center at **glencoe.com** to:
  - Download a **Podcast**.
  - Download free **Study-to-Go** content to their PDAs or cell phones.

Vocabulary Review

- **Crossword Puzzle** Ask students to create crossword puzzles using at least ten terms from the chapter. Have pairs of students exchange and try to solve one another's puzzles.

Teaching Tips

Reading Strategies These strategies can help students understand what they read:

- Stop and talk. Ask students to stop after reading half a passage and discuss what they have read up to that point. You can direct the discussion or let students talk with a partner or small group.

- Rate understanding. After students have read a difficult passage, have them rate their understanding on a scale from 1 (little understanding) to 10 (complete understanding). Ask students to reread the passage as needed.

15 Assessment

Assessment

Reviewing Vocabulary and Main Ideas

1. epidermis
2. Plaque
3. decibel
4. warranty
5. health fraud
6. Consumer skills
7. False, Prescription medicines
8. False, vaccine
9. True
10. True
11. False, Inpatient
12. True
13. False, CPSC
14. True
15. True

Thinking Critically

16. The skill can enable you to identify false claims and make informed purchases. This can play a positive role in your overall health by ensuring that you avoid ineffective or dangerous products.
17. Care of your teeth, hair, and nails helps maintain your physical health, improves your self-esteem, and can contribute positively to your relationships with others.

After You Read

HEALTH INVENTORY

Now that you have read the chapter, look back at your answers to the Health Inventory on the chapter opener. Is there anything that you should do differently?

Reviewing Vocabulary and Main Ideas

On a sheet of paper, write the numbers 1–6. After each number, write the term from the list that best completes each sentence.

- consumer skills
- decibel
- dermis
- epidermis
- health fraud
- lens
- plaque
- warranty

Lesson 1 Personal Health Care

1. The outermost layer of the skin is the _____.
2. _____ is a soft, colorless, sticky film containing bacteria that coats your teeth.
3. A(n) _____ is a measure of the loudness of sound.

Lesson 2 Being a Smart Health Consumer

4. A(n) _____ is a promise to refund your money if the product doesn't work as claimed.
5. The selling of products or services that claim to prevent diseases or cure health problems which have not been scientifically proven safe or effective for such purposes is known as _____.
6. _____ are techniques that enable you to make wise, informed purchases.

On a sheet of paper, write the numbers 7–15. Write **True** or **False** for each statement below. If the statement is false, change the underlined word or phrase to make it true.

Lesson 3 Using Medicines Wisely

7. Over-the-counter (OTC) medicines are medicines that can be sold only with a written order from a physician.
8. A medicine that prevents a disease from developing is called an antibiotic.
9. Medicines applied to the skin are said to be taken topically.

Lesson 4 Choosing Health Services

10. Preventive care is medical care that keeps disease or injury from happening or getting worse.
11. Outpatient care involves a stay at a hospital or some other health care facility.
12. In managed care, the health consumer pays a small fee known as a co-pay.

Lesson 5 Public Health

13. A recall will generally be issued by the HHS.
14. A famine is a widespread shortage of food.
15. The World Health Organization is one international organization that has made world health a priority.

Go Online Visit glencoe.com and take the Online Quiz for Chapter 15.

Have students visit glencoe.com to take the Chapter 15 quiz.

HEALTH INVENTORY WRAP-UP

Personal Care and Consumer Choices Have students retake the Health Inventory found in the Chapter Opener. Ask for volunteers to share ways in which their answers to the questions have changed as a result of reading the chapter.

Thinking Critically

Using complete sentences, answer the following questions on a sheet of paper.

16. Synthesize One skill emphasized in the chapter was learning to analyze advertising claims for health care products. How can this skill benefit you when you are making purchases?

17. Analyze How can taking care of your teeth, hair, skin, and nails affect your total health?

Write About It

18. Persuasive Writing Imagine you are teaching a younger sibling about personal care. Write a dialogue between you and your sibling in which you explain how to care for the eyes, teeth, ears, and skin.

Personal Care Movie

Using iMovie®, you and a partner will make a movie that teaches younger students about personal heath care.

- Pick one of the following topics: skin, ears, teeth, eyes, hair, or nails.
- Write a two to three-minute script that discusses your topic. What is it? Where can it be found on the body? What does it do? How do you care for it?
- Include diagrams and pictures. Make your movie colorful and appealing to younger students.
- Edit for time and clarity. Make sure to use language that the students will understand.
- Arrange to show your movie to a class of younger students.

Personal Care Movie
Equipment needs: digital camera, iMovie® or other video editing program
Help students discuss the steps in this project. Assign partners, and have each pair choose one of the topics. Guide students as necessary to be sure all six topics will be chosen. Emphasize that the audience for these movies will be younger children; remind students to use information, vocabulary, and images appropriate to this audience. Use a sign-up list and a consistent time limit if computer access is limited. If possible, make arrangements with an elementary school to have your students' movies shown there.

Standardized Test Practice

Math

Read the following statistics on hearing loss. Then answer the questions that follow.

- A survey by the National Center for Health Statistics reveals 23.3 million Americans have hearing loss.

- About 1.3 million of these people are 18 years old or younger.

- The National Institutes of Health reports that one-third of all hearing loss results from loud noises. Sources of these noises include power lawn mowers, jet engines, city traffic, loud appliances, and loud music.

TEST-TAKING TIP

Make sure you understand the relationship between integers and percentages in number statements.

1. What percentage of hearing loss cases reported by the National Center for Health Statistics involves teens?
  A. 1.3 percent
  B. 5.6 percent
  C. 23.3 percent
  D. None of the above

2. What approximate percentage of all hearing loss results from loud noises?
  A. 33.3 percent
  B. 25.5 percent
  C. 55 percent
  D. 80.5 percent

Write About It

18. Persuasive Writing Explain that persuasive writing tries to convince the reader with evidence and arguments. The dialogues students write will vary, but their work should be supported by relevant facts and logical reasons about the importance of proper care.

Standardized Test Practice

1. B
2. A

Test-Taking Tips

Math Skills For the questions here, students will need to know how to convert ratios of integers to percentages. Review how to divide integers and move the decimal point in the quotient two places to the right to get the percentage. For example, in the first practice question, divide the number of American teens with hearing loss (1.3 million) by the total number of Americans with hearing loss (23.3. million) to get the integer 0.056. Move the decimal point two places to the right to get the percentage (5.6 percent).

CHAPTER 16 pp. 402–447	National Standards	State/Local	Skills and Activities	
Lesson 1 **Your Skeletal System** pp. 404–408	National Health Education Standards 1.8.5, 1.8.7, 1.8.8, 1.8.9, 7.8.1, 8.8.1		**Connect To... LANGUAGE ARTS** The Achilles Tendon, p. 406 **What Teens Think** How can a person avoid injury when participating in sports or other physical activities?, p. 406	**HEALTH SKILLS ACTIVITY** *Practicing Healthful Behaviors* Got Calcium?, p. 407
Lesson 2 **Your Muscular System** pp. 409–412	National Health Education Standards 1.8.1, 1.8.4, 1.8.7, 7.8.1, 7.8.2, 8.8.1, 8.8.3		**Careers for the 21st Century** Physical Therapist, p. 411	
Lesson 3 **Your Circulatory System** pp. 413–417	National Health Education Standards 1.8.5, 1.8.7, 1.8.8, 1.8.9, 7.8.1, 8.8.1		**Connect To... SCIENCE** Anemia and Teens, p. 415	
Lesson 4 **Your Respiratory System** pp. 418–421	National Health Education Standards 1.8.5, 7.8.1		**Go Online** Breathing for Health, p. 420	
Lesson 5 **Your Nervous System** pp. 422–426	National Health Education Standards 1.8.5, 7.8.1, 8.8.1		**Connect To... SCIENCE** Technology and the Brain, p. 425 **HEALTH SKILLS ACTIVITY** *Practicing Healthful Behaviors* Avoiding Repetitive Motion Injuries, p. 426	
Lesson 6 **Your Digestive and Excretory Systems** pp. 427–432	National Health Education Standards 1.8.1, 1.8.5, 6.8.1, 6.8.3, 7.8.1, 8.8.1		**HEALTH SKILLS ACTIVITY** *Practicing Healthful Behaviors* Adding Sources of Fiber, p. 430	
Lesson 7 **Your Endocrine System** pp. 433–436	National Health Education Standards 1.8.1, 1.8.5, 7.8.1, 7.8.2, 8.8.1, 8.8.3		**Connect To... LANGUAGE ARTS** Chemical Messengers, p. 435	
Lesson 8 **Your Reproductive System** pp. 437–441	National Health Education Standards 1.8.1, 1.8.5, 3.8.1, 7.8.1, 7.8.2, 8.8.1			

Planning Guide

Reproducible Resources	Assessment	Media and Technology
Chapter FAST FILE Resources Concept Mapping Activity 16-1 REVIEW Health Lab 16-1 EXTEND Enrichment Activity 16-1 EXTEND Guided Reading and Writing 16-1 TEACH Reteaching Activity 16-1 REVIEW	Lesson 1 Review, *p. 408* Vocabulary PuzzleMaker *ExamView® Assessment Suite*	**TeacherWorks Plus includes:** ● Interactive Teacher Edition ● Lesson Planner with Calendar ● Access to all blackline masters ● Correlations to standards StudentWorks™ Plus Online Student Edition Dinah Zike's Teaching Health with Foldables®
Chapter FAST FILE Resources Concept Mapping Activity 16-2 REVIEW Cross-Curriculum Activity 16-2 EXTEND Enrichment Activity 16-2 EXTEND Guided Reading and Writing 16-2 TEACH Reteaching Activity 16-2 REVIEW	Lesson 2 Review, *p. 412* Vocabulary PuzzleMaker *ExamView® Assessment Suite*	Vocabulary PuzzleMaker *ExamView® Assessment Suite* StudentWorks™ Plus Transparency 16-2 **Go Online** glencoe.com
Chapter FAST FILE Resources Concept Mapping Activity 16-3 REVIEW Cross-Curriculum Activity 16-3 EXTEND Enrichment Activity 16-3 EXTEND Guided Reading and Writing 16-3 TEACH Reteaching Activity 16-3 REVIEW	Lesson 3 Review, *p. 417* Vocabulary PuzzleMaker *ExamView® Assessment Suite*	Vocabulary PuzzleMaker *ExamView® Assessment Suite* StudentWorks™ Plus Transparency 16-3 **Go Online** glencoe.com
Chapter FAST FILE Resources Concept Mapping Activity 16-4 REVIEW Decision-Making Activity 16-4 EXTEND Enrichment Activity 16-4 EXTEND Guided Reading and Writing 16-4 TEACH Reteaching Activity 16-4 REVIEW	Lesson 4 Review, *p. 421* Vocabulary PuzzleMaker *ExamView® Assessment Suite*	Vocabulary PuzzleMaker *ExamView® Assessment Suite* StudentWorks™ Plus Transparency 16-4 **Go Online** glencoe.com
Chapter FAST FILE Resources Concept Mapping Activity 16-5 REVIEW Decision-Making Activity 16-5 EXTEND Enrichment Activity 16-5 EXTEND Guided Reading and Writing 16-5 TEACH Reteaching Activity 16-5 REVIEW	Lesson 5 Review, *p. 426* Vocabulary PuzzleMaker *ExamView® Assessment Suite*	Vocabulary PuzzleMaker *ExamView® Assessment Suite* StudentWorks™ Plus Transparency 16-5 **Go Online** glencoe.com
Chapter FAST FILE Resources Concept Mapping Activity 16-6 REVIEW Decision-Making Activity 16-6 EXTEND Enrichment Activity 16-6 EXTEND Guided Reading and Writing 16-6 TEACH Reteaching Activity 16-6 REVIEW	Lesson 6 Review, *p. 432* Vocabulary PuzzleMaker *ExamView® Assessment Suite*	Vocabulary PuzzleMaker *ExamView® Assessment Suite* StudentWorks™ Plus Transparency 16-6 **Go Online** glencoe.com
Chapter FAST FILE Resources Concept Mapping Activity 16-7 REVIEW Cross-Curriculum Activity 16-7 EXTEND Enrichment Activity 16-7 EXTEND Guided Reading and Writing 16-7 TEACH Reteaching Activity 16-7 REVIEW	Lesson 7 Review, *p. 436* Vocabulary PuzzleMaker *ExamView® Assessment Suite*	Vocabulary PuzzleMaker *ExamView® Assessment Suite* StudentWorks™ Plus Transparency 16-7 **Go Online** glencoe.com
Chapter FAST FILE Resources Concept Mapping Activity 16-8 REVIEW Decision-Making Activity 16-8 EXTEND Enrichment Activity 16-8 EXTEND Guided Reading and Writing 16-8 TEACH Reteaching Activity 16-8 REVIEW	Lesson 8 Review, *p. 441* Vocabulary PuzzleMaker *ExamView® Assessment Suite*	Vocabulary PuzzleMaker *ExamView® Assessment Suite* StudentWorks™ Plus Transparency 16-8 **Go Online** glencoe.com

Backpack Safety Tips

Carrying a backpack that is too heavy can cause back pain and headaches and injure muscles and joints. Using a backpack correctly helps keep the skeletal and muscular systems healthy. Share these tips with students:

- **Choose a backpack made from lightweight materials that has two wide, padded shoulder straps.** A waist strap pulls the backpack closer to the body and helps distribute the load better. A padded back protects your back from the sharp edges of objects inside it. Consider using a backpack on wheels if the school allows them.

- **When putting on a loaded backpack, bend at the knees when bending down.** Place both shoulders into the shoulder straps and pull the straps snug. The straps should hold the backpack two inches above the waist.

- **Lighten the load as much as possible.** The backpack should not weigh more than 20 percent of your total body weight. While at school, make more frequent trips to your locker. Try to finish homework that requires a heavy textbook at school. Arrange to have a second set of textbooks at home.

- **Strengthen your abdominal and lower back muscles with yoga, weight training, or Pilates.** Stronger torso muscles help support the back and the weight it is carrying.

The Importance of Sleep

Adolescents require 8.5 to 9.25 hours of sleep each night. Only about 15 percent of adolescents report getting that much sleep on a school night. What effect does that have? Plenty.

The body needs sleep. While sleeping, the body repairs itself and grows. Activity in the brain is high as it consolidates all the learning it experienced through the day. Hormones that regulate growth and appetite are released. The immune system powers up to fight off infection. You wake up alert, refreshed, and ready to face the challenges of a new day.

Without sleep, the body wakes up tired and unable to focus. You are grumpy and prone to negative emotions like anger and sadness. Sleepiness has been shown to cause behaviors in students similar to those common in attention-deficit/hyperactivity disorder. Teens who are sleep-deprived are more prone to traffic accidents while driving. They cannot make quick and sound decisions or easily problem solve. Sleep deprivation limits a teen's ability to think creatively, pay attention, and think abstractly. Lack of sleep can cause a teen to overeat or choose foods that are sweet or fatty. It can also contribute to skin problems such as acne.

Over time, teens may turn to stimulants, such as caffeine or nicotine, to help them stay awake and be alert. Teens also tend to oversleep on the weekend. These habits can cause a shift in the sleep phase and poor sleeping habits that they may never overcome.

Recommend that teens allow themselves at least 8 hours of restful sleep every night.

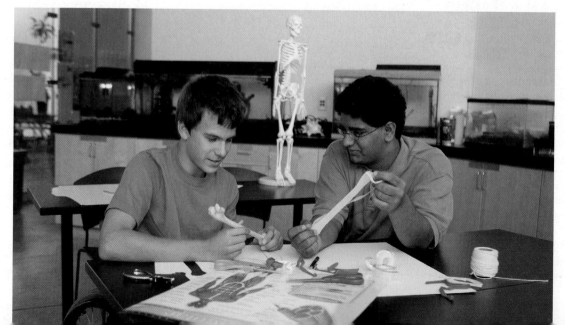

Support for Teaching Reading

 Reading Support

Reading Preview

Activating Background Vocabulary Ask students what they know about the systems of the body: skeletal, muscular, circulatory, and so on. Preview the key terms and have students record the definitions in a vocabulary notebook.

FOLDABLES Study Organizer *Dinah Zike's Reading and Study Skills for Teen Health* provides interactive graphic organizers. Find more Foldables® activities for the chapter on **Your Body Systems** in the separate booklet, available in the TCR.

Lesson 1   Your Skeletal System

Determining Main Ideas Have students identify the main idea in the first section by making the title into a question, such as "What is **Your Body's Framework**?" Have them find supporting details about joints and connective tissues.

Lesson 2   Your Muscular System

Preview/Outline Illustrate an outline graphic, using Roman numerals, capital letters, and sequential numbers. Have students identify the main ideas from the headings, such as **Your Muscles**, and complete the outline as they read.

Lesson 3   Your Circulatory System

3-2-1 Strategy Ask students to write **three** key points they learned while reading about the circulatory system. Next, have them list **two** things that were interesting. Last, ask them to write one question they still have about the lesson.

Lesson 4   Your Respiratory System

Connecting Encourage students to link what they read to events in their own lives by asking: Do I know anyone with asthma? Can I avoid polluted air? Have students respond in a private journal entry.

Lesson 5   Your Nervous System

Adjusted Reading Purpose Have students read the lesson to find general information about the nervous system. Then have students reread the lesson to discover specific details about the central nervous system, brain injury, and so on.

Lesson 6   Your Digestive and Excretory Systems

Writing to Learn Stop students during reading and discuss the parts of the digestive system. Have students write a question they still have. Then have students exchange papers and write for five minutes, answering the writer's question.

Lesson 7   Your Endocrine System

Jigsaw Form teams of four, giving each person one topic: growth, parts/functions, problems, and care. Have students read their section, meet with others who have the same topic to discuss, then return to their own team to teach the topic.

Lesson 8   Your Reproductive System

Review and Record Have students stop reading and think of what they have learned so far. Discuss what they remember about the two reproductive systems. Have them review what they have read and record their responses in a journal entry.

Post Reading

Research Reports Guide students to available classroom, library, and Internet resources. Have them gather data, organize the information logically, and edit their papers for proper sentence structure, word usage, and mechanics.

Key for Using the Teacher Wraparound Edition

Use this key to help you identify the different types of prompts found in the Teacher Wraparound Edition.

R   **Reading Strategies** activities help you teach reading skills and vocabulary.

C   **Critical Thinking** strategies help students apply and extend what they have learned.

U   **Universal Access** activities provide differentiated instruction for students learning to speak English, along with suggestions for teaching various types of learners.

HS   **Health Skills Practice** activities reinforce Health Skills concepts and help students apply these skills in their everyday lives.

W   **Writing Support** activities provide writing opportunities to help students comprehend the text.

AL   **Active Learning** strategies provide a variety of activities for presenting lesson content, including Quick Demos and engaging classroom projects that get students actively involved.

Key to Ability Levels

Teaching Strategies and activities have been coded for ability level and appropriateness.

AL   Activities for students working above grade level

OL   Activities for students working on grade level

BL   Activities for students working below grade level

EL   Activities for English Learners

Symbols

   Transparencies

   CD-ROM

   glencoe.com

   Print Resources

Your Body Systems

Chapter at a Glance

Lesson 1 describes the structures, functions, and care of the skeletal system.

Lesson 2 explains the function and structure of the muscular system.

Lesson 3 describes circulation and discusses health of the circulatory system.

Lesson 4 details how the body uses oxygen, the structures and functions of the respiratory system, and how to keep it healthy.

Lesson 5 explains the structures and functions of the nervous system and how to protect it from injury.

Lesson 6 describes the structures and functions of the digestive and excretory systems.

Lesson 7 describes the endocrine system and the role of hormones.

Lesson 8 describes the menstrual cycle and ways to keep the reproductive systems healthy.

R Reading Strategy

Interpreting the Photo List on the board the nine body systems that students will study in this chapter. As students look at the photo, challenge them to identify what each body system is doing to help the gymnast perform. OL

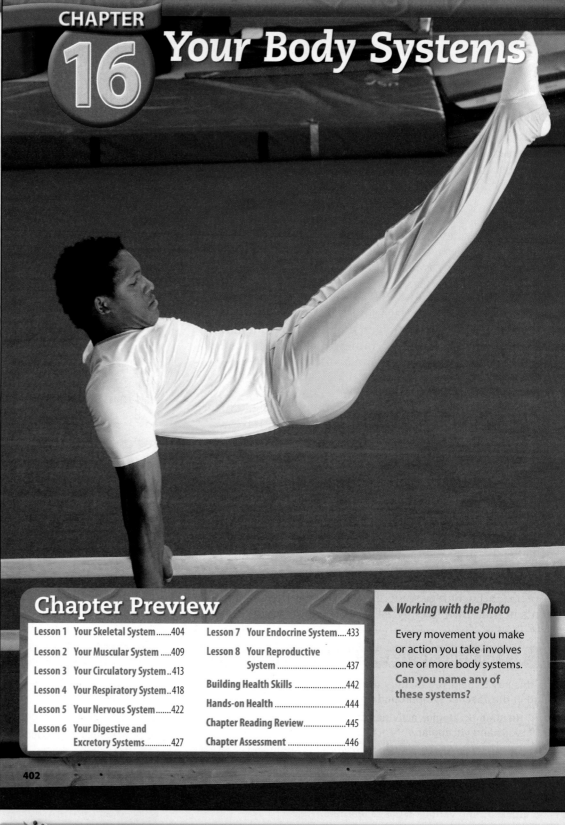

Chapter Preview

▲ *Working with the Photo*

Every movement you make or action you take involves one or more body systems. **Can you name any of these systems?**

402

 Universal Access

Differentiated Learning Glencoe provides teacher support and student materials for all learners in the health classroom.

- Spanish *Glosario* and chapter summaries assist English Language Learners.
- *Reading Tutor* and related worksheets support reluctant readers.

- Universal Access strategies throughout the Teacher Wraparound Edition and Fast Files help you present materials for gifted students, at-risk students, physically impaired students, and those with behavior disorders or learning disabilities.

Start-Up Activities

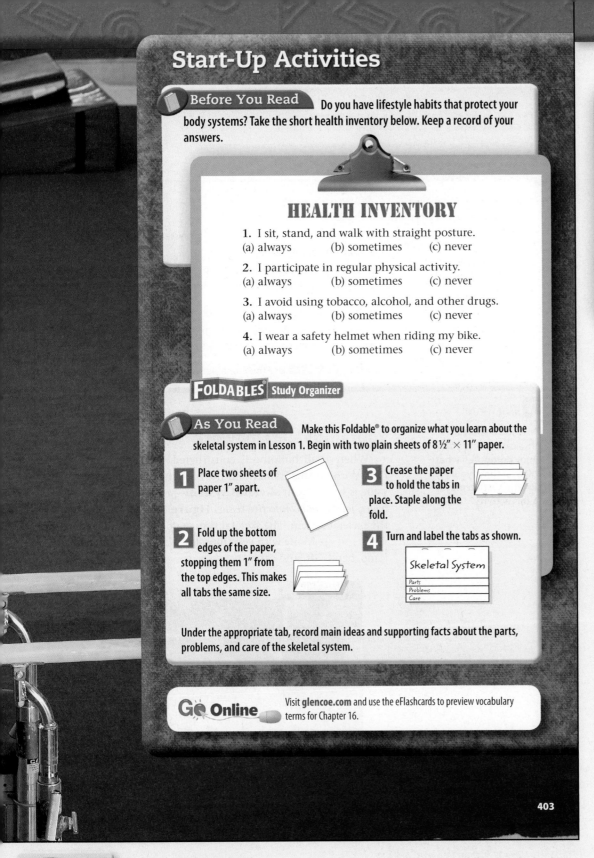

Before You Read

Do you have lifestyle habits that protect your body systems? Take the short health inventory below. Keep a record of your answers.

HEALTH INVENTORY

1. I sit, stand, and walk with straight posture.
(a) always   (b) sometimes   (c) never

2. I participate in regular physical activity.
(a) always   (b) sometimes   (c) never

3. I avoid using tobacco, alcohol, and other drugs.
(a) always   (b) sometimes   (c) never

4. I wear a safety helmet when riding my bike.
(a) always   (b) sometimes   (c) never

FOLDABLES Study Organizer

As You Read

Make this Foldable® to organize what you learn about the skeletal system in Lesson 1. Begin with two plain sheets of 8½" × 11" paper.

1 Place two sheets of paper 1" apart.

2 Fold up the bottom edges of the paper, stopping them 1" from the top edges. This makes all tabs the same size.

3 Crease the paper to hold the tabs in place. Staple along the fold.

4 Turn and label the tabs as shown.

Skeletal System
Parts
Problems
Care

Under the appropriate tab, record main ideas and supporting facts about the parts, problems, and care of the skeletal system.

Go Online Visit **glencoe.com** and use the eFlashcards to preview vocabulary terms for Chapter 16.

403

Lesson 1

FOCUS

Activating Prior Knowledge

What I Know Invite volunteers to share stories about any skeletal injuries they have had, such as broken bones or pulled ligaments. Have students explain how the injury occurred and whether they could have prevented it.

 Guide to Reading

Building Vocabulary
- Have students make a diagram of the skeletal system and use vocabulary terms to label the diagram.
- Use Vocabulary PuzzleMaker to reinforce vocabulary terms.

Reading Strategy
Analyzing a Graphic
Have students make a chart listing the four kinds of joints, examples of each, and how each works.

 Have students use their Foldable® as they read Lesson 1.

Quick Write

For any activity, the skeletal system provides the framework for movement as well as protection for internal organs.

Caption Answer

Photo Caption supports body, protects organs, stores minerals, makes blood cells

---

Lesson 1

Your Skeletal System

 Guide to Reading

● Building Vocabulary
Make a word web using these terms. Decide which term should be the central term.
- skeletal system (p. 404)
- marrow (p. 405)
- joint (p. 406)
- cartilage (p. 406)
- tendons (p. 406)
- ligaments (p. 406)

● Focusing on the Main Ideas
In this lesson, you will learn to
- **explain** the functions of the skeletal system.
- **identify** four types of joints.
- **list** some problems of the skeletal system.
- **practice** healthful behaviors to keep your skeletal system healthy.

● Reading Strategy
Analyzing a Graphic Using Figure 16.1 on page 405, find examples of each kind of joint discussed in the lesson.

FOLDABLES Study Organizer Use the Foldable® on p. 403 as you read this lesson.

Quick Write

Describe a sport or physical activity you enjoy doing. Tell what role you think your skeletal system plays in this activity.

Your Body's Framework

When a tall building is constructed, the steel beams go up first. Without this framework, the building could not stand. The same is true of your **skeletal system**—*a body system made up of bones, joints, and connective tissue.* **Figure 16.1** shows the parts of the skeletal system. The skeletal system does a lot more than help you stand up. Along with your muscles, it allows you to walk, run, jump, bend, lift, and carry.

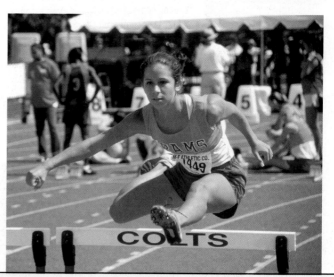

▶ Your skeletal system helps you run and jump. **What are some other functions of the skeletal system?**

404 Chapter 16: Your Body Systems

Lesson 1 Resources

📁 **Chapter *FAST FILE* Resources**
Guided Reading and Writing 16-1
Concept Mapping Activity 16-1
Health Lab 16-1
Reteaching Activity 16-1
Enrichment Activity 16-1
Lesson Quiz 16-1

Technology
🔦 Transparency 16-1
🖊 Audio Summaries
💿 *ExamView® Assessment Suite*
🖊 Vocabulary PuzzleMaker
💿 StudentWorks™ Plus
G⊙ Online

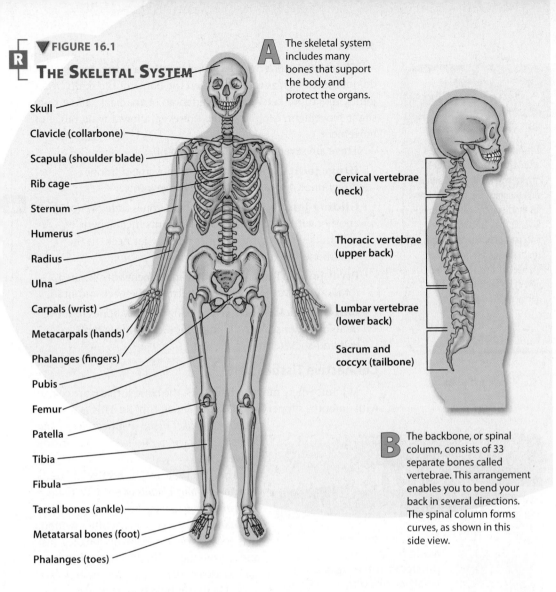

▼ FIGURE 16.1

THE SKELETAL SYSTEM

A The skeletal system includes many bones that support the body and protect the organs.

- Skull
- Clavicle (collarbone)
- Scapula (shoulder blade)
- Rib cage
- Sternum
- Humerus
- Radius
- Ulna
- Carpals (wrist)
- Metacarpals (hands)
- Phalanges (fingers)
- Pubis
- Femur
- Patella
- Tibia
- Fibula
- Tarsal bones (ankle)
- Metatarsal bones (foot)
- Phalanges (toes)

- Cervical vertebrae (neck)
- Thoracic vertebrae (upper back)
- Lumbar vertebrae (lower back)
- Sacrum and coccyx (tailbone)

B The backbone, or spinal column, consists of 33 separate bones called vertebrae. This arrangement enables you to bend your back in several directions. The spinal column forms curves, as shown in this side view.

Functions of Your Skeletal System

The skeletal system has a number of important functions. It provides a strong, stable framework capable of movement. It also supports and protects your delicate internal organs.

The 206 bones that make up your skeleton are living structures that function as storage centers for minerals, such as calcium and phosphorus. They also produce the body's blood cells. Red bone marrow makes millions of blood cells each day. **Marrow** is *a soft tissue in the center of some bones.*

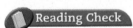 **Explain** What is the function of bone marrow?

TEACH

R Reading Strategy

Analyzing a Graphic Read aloud the names of the bones in the skeleton as shown in **Figure 16.1**. Point out how the rib cage and sternum protect the heart, lungs, liver, and spleen; the skull protects the brain; the vertebrae protect the spinal cord; and the pelvis protects the bladder, intestines, and female reproductive structures. Ask: Why does our body have so many bones in the hands and feet? *The separate bones allow for better movement.* **OL**

Reading Check

Answer Bone marrow makes blood cells.

U Universal Access

English Learners For this chapter, have students make a notebook of all the body systems. For this lesson, have students write each vocabulary term and a definition in both English and their native language. Also help students make a diagram or find one that shows where cartilage, ligaments, and tendons are found in the skeletal system. Require beginning English learners to learn only the terms *skeletal system* and *joints*. Do a similar activity for subsequent lessons. **BL**

What Teens Want to Know

How is calcium related to bones? Without regular exercise and adequate calcium in the teen years (1,300 mg/day), adults could develop osteoporosis. It is calcium that makes bones hard. The body's need for calcium is at its highest between the ages of 9 and 18. This calcium is required for the major growth and rebuilding that bones go through at this time. Calcium is also required because about 50 percent of the calcium in adult bones is deposited during the teen years. **OL**

Connect To... Language Arts

The Achilles Tendon

Read to students the Greek myth about Achilles. Collaborate with the literature teacher on strategies that relate myths to health.

 AL Active Learning

Quick Demo Have students model the movement of each type of joint. Then ask students to identify where nonmoving joints are located in the body. **OL**

Reading Check

Answer Cartilage is a strong flexible, gel-like tissue that cushions the joints.

What Teens THINK

How can a person avoid injury when participating in sports or other physical activities? Ask students to name several sports and physical activities they enjoy. Ask students: How do you protect yourself from getting injured when you participate in this sport or activity? What else do you think you should do to prevent injuries?

Connect To... Language Arts

The Achilles Tendon

The Achilles tendon is named after a character from Greek mythology. Achilles had almost superhuman strength because his mother dipped him in the River Styx as an infant. The only part of him that did not touch the magical water was his heel, so that was the only part of his body that was not immortal.

Do you know any other terms that come from mythology?

What Teens THINK

How can a person avoid injury when participating in sports or other physical activities?

Listen to your leader and do the stretches. Don't do anything you are not ready for. If you doubt your ability in any way, practice more. Stay hydrated and don't be afraid to push yourself, but know your limits.

Katelyn J.
Centerville, IN

Joints

The point at which two bones meet is called a **joint.** Some joints do not move, such as those between the bones of the skull. Other joints, like those between the vertebrae of the back, allow only slight movement. Mobile joints, however, allow a wide range of movement.

There are several types of mobile joints:

- **Hinge joints.** These joints allow movement in one direction. Knees and elbows are hinge joints.

- **Gliding joints.** Gliding joints help bones slide over one another without twisting. Gliding joints include wrists and ankles, and connect bones below your neck, in the collarbone.

- **Pivot joints.** These joints allow movement with limited rotation. A pivot joint is found between the neck and head.

- **Ball-and-socket joints.** These joints allow bones to move in all directions. Your hips and shoulders are examples of ball-and-socket joints.

AL

Connective Tissues

At joints where movement occurs, the bone surfaces are coated with smooth, slippery **cartilage** (KAHR·tuhl·ij). This is *a strong flexible, gel-like tissue that cushions your joints.* Cartilage reduces friction during movement.

Another type of connective tissue is **tendons**—*tough bands of tissue that attach your muscles to bones.* A large tendon that you can easily feel is your Achilles tendon. It is located on the back of your leg just above your heel. Finally, **ligaments** are *cordlike tissues that connect the bones in each joint.* They help hold bones in place.

Reading Check

Define What is *cartilage?*

Problems of the Skeletal System

Bones, joints, and connective tissues are strong and durable. Yet, they can develop problems as a result of injuries, infections,

HEALTH LITERACY

Backpack Injuries In 2003, the U.S. Consumer Product Safety Commission reported about 21,000 backpack-related injuries. While some of these injuries include tripping and falling or getting hit by a backpack, a large number were caused by carrying a backpack that was too heavy.

The weight of a heavy backpack can pull the teen backward. To compensate, the teen will lean forward or arch the back, which causes the vertebrae to press together unnaturally. Over time, this can lead to severe back pain and posture problems. **OL**

Health Skills Activity

Practicing Healthful Behaviors

Got Calcium?

Calcium builds healthy bones and teeth. It also keeps your heartbeat steady and your nerves and muscles in good condition. If the amount of calcium in your blood is too low, your body draws it from your bones. Removing calcium from your bones without replacing it can lead to osteoporosis, a condition where bones become weak and can break easily. To keep your bones strong, exercise and eat plenty of calcium-rich foods. These include low-fat or fat-free dairy products, broccoli, spinach, and calcium-fortified orange juice.

On Your Own

Think of ways to incorporate calcium-rich foods into meals and snacks. For example, throw some spinach leaves into a salad or melt some reduced-fat cheese on top of cooked broccoli. Create a list of your ideas and share them with the class.

Health Skills Activity

Practicing Healthful Behaviors

Got Calcium?

Use the following strategies to help students complete the activity.

- Have students work in small groups to read the activity and then create lists of calcium-rich foods.
- Provide index cards and have groups create Got Calcium? cards with creative calcium-rich snack ideas and recipes to share with family and friends. **OL**

poor posture, and a lack of nutritious foods. Problems of the skeletal system include:

- **Fracture** A break in a bone caused by an injury.
- **Dislocation** This occurs when a bone is pushed out of its joint, usually stretching or tearing a ligament.
- **Sprain** This occurs when the ligaments in a joint are stretched or twisted and causes swelling. This can be treated using the P.R.I.C.E. formula discussed in Chapter 9.
- **Overuse injuries** They happen over time and make up about half of the sports injuries that occur in teens. A shin splint, common among runners and aggressive walkers, is an example of an overuse injury.
- **Scoliosis** A disorder in which the spine curves to one side of the body. It appears to have a slight S- or C-shaped curve. It can cause back pain and difficulty with breathing. In most cases, the cause is not known.
- **Osteoporosis** A condition characterized by brittle and porous bones. It develops because of long-term deficiencies of calcium and certain hormones, insufficient vitamin D, and lack of exercise.

Go Online

Visit **glencoe.com** and complete the Interactive Study Guide for Lesson 1.

Lesson 1: Your Skeletal System **407**

HS Health Skills Practice

Practicing Healthful Behaviors Challenge students to assess how well they care for their skeletal system. Have students consider their nutrition, posture, backpack weight, and use of protective gear for various activities. Have a student volunteer help demonstrate good posture while sitting and standing as well as the correct way to carry a backpack (centered across the back, not slung across one shoulder). Also identify foods that are rich in calcium, vitamin D, and phosphorus. Suggest that students write a plan to describe how they will improve the care of their skeletal system. **OL**

FITNESS ZONE

The Skeletal System and Physical Fitness After students have read and discussed *Caring for Your Skeletal System* (page 408), have them review the information in the *Fitness Zone Handbook*. Then ask: Why are physical fitness activities important in protecting the health of your skeletal system? What can you do to protect your skeletal system when you participate in fitness activities? **For more information, see Fitness Zone Handbook pages xviii–1 or visit the Fitness Zone at glencoe.com.**

Caption Answer

Photo Caption, p. 408
Sample answer: yes; football, baseball, field hockey, soccer

Reading Check

Answer good nutrition, regular exercise, good posture, use of protective gear

ASSESS

Assessment Resources

Lesson Review Quiz
- *ExamView*
- Fast Files Activities
- Online Quizzes and Activities

Reteaching

- Assign Concept Map 16-1 or Reteaching Activity 16-1 in the Fast Files.
- Have students examine each photo in the lesson and explain what the teen in the photo is doing to protect his or her skeletal system.

Enrichment

- Assign Enrichment Activity 16-1 in the Fast Files.
- Have students research skeletal system problems: scoliosis, Osgood-Schlatter disease, or osteomyelitis. Have students present a poster of their findings.

CLOSE

Ask students to describe five functions of the skeletal system.

◄ Wearing protective gear during sports can help prevent injuries to the skeletal system. **Do you play any sports that require protective gear?**

Caring for Your Skeletal System

Now is the time to focus on building healthy bones. Start with good nutrition. Low-fat and fat-free dairy products contain calcium and other nutrients important to good bone health. These include phosphorus, magnesium, and added vitamin D in milk. Regular physical activity increases bone mass, especially weight-bearing exercises such as walking and jogging. Remember to use good posture when you sit, stand, or walk. Good posture keeps your spine healthy.

Sports injuries in the United States are on the rise for teens. If you are injured, take the time to heal completely before you go back to your sport. Use protective gear when playing sports, riding your bike, or in-line skating.

Reading Check

Explain What behaviors help keep the skeletal system healthy?

Lesson 1 Review

After You Read

Review this lesson for new terms, major headings, and Reading Checks.

What I Learned

1. *Vocabulary* What are *joints*? Name four types.

2. *List* Name three functions of the skeletal system.

3. *Identify* What are two problems of the skeletal system?

Thinking Critically

4. *Apply* You and another teen on the gymnastics team are practicing. You see your teammate doing an exercise that the coach said not to do. What risk is your teammate taking?

5. *Synthesize* Jan understands the importance of eating foods rich in calcium. She is allergic to milk, however. What suggestions can you make that might help Jan?

Applying Health Skills

6. *Practicing Healthful Behaviors* During most sports and other physical activities, your body parts are in motion. Name some ways to protect the bones from injury when playing a specific sport.

Go Online For more Lesson Review Activities, go to **glencoe.com**.

Lesson 1 Review Answers

1. the point at which two bones meet; hinge, gliding, pivot, ball-and-socket
2. *Any three:* support body, allow movement, protect internal organs, produce blood cells, store minerals
3. *Any two:* fractures, torn ligaments, overuse injuries, dislocations, back injuries, osteoarthritis, osteoporosis
4. *Sample answer:* The person might risk injuring his or her skeletal system.
5. *Sample answer:* Jan can drink orange juice fortified with calcium, eat vegetables rich in calcium, take a calcium supplement, talk to her doctor.
6. *Sample answer:* Wear protective gear and keep body flexible and strong.

Lesson 2

Your Muscular System

Guide to Reading

● **Building Vocabulary**
As you read this lesson, write each new highlighted term and its definition in your notebook.

■ muscular system (p. 409)
■ skeletal muscles (p. 410)
■ smooth muscles (p. 410)
■ cardiac muscles (p. 410)

● **Focusing on the Main Ideas**
In this lesson, you will learn to

■ **explain** the functions of the muscular system.
■ **identify** how muscle types differ.
■ **describe** ways to keep your muscular system healthy.

● **Reading Strategy**
Comparing and Contrasting Explain similarities and differences among the different muscle types in the lesson.

Your Muscles

Your muscles make it possible for your body to move. They also pump blood throughout your body and move food through your digestive system. Muscles also control the movement of air in and out of your lungs.

Your **muscular system** is *the group of structures that give your body parts the power to move.* **Figure 16.2** on the next page shows some of the different muscles that make up the muscular system. It also tells which tasks each muscle performs.

Quick Write
Write a short journal entry about a time you had a muscle ache or pain. Tell what you did to relieve the symptoms.

 Muscles have a number of important functions. What is one function of the muscular system?

Lesson 2: Your Muscular System **409**

Lesson 2 Resources

 Chapter *Fast File* Resources
Guided Reading and Writing 16-2
Concept Mapping Activity 16-2
Cross-Curriculum Activity 16-2
Reteaching Activity 16-2
Enrichment Activity 16-2
Lesson Quiz 16-2

Technology
Transparency 16-2
Audio Summaries
ExamView® Assessment Suite
Vocabulary PuzzleMaker
StudentWorks™ Plus
 Go Online

FOCUS

Activating Prior Knowledge

What I Know Ask students to describe a time when they have had sore muscles. Challenge them to infer what caused the muscle soreness. Correct any misconceptions as you discuss the lesson.

Guide to Reading

Building Vocabulary
■ Have students make a concept map using the vocabulary terms. Tell them to add examples of each muscle type to the map.
■ Use Vocabulary PuzzleMaker to reinforce vocabulary terms.

Reading Strategy
Comparing and Contrasting Have students make a chart to record the similarities and differences of the different muscle types.

Quick Write

After completing the lesson, have students review their Quick Writes and, if necessary, correct their methods of relieving muscle pain.

Caption Answer

Photo Caption Muscles allow movement, pump blood, and move food and air through the body.

TEACH

R Reading Strategy

Analyzing a Graphic After students have read about functions and types of muscles, review **Figure 16.2**. Point out how the skeleton is wrapped in muscles. Also point out where ligaments hold bones together and tendons hold muscles to bones. Ask: Are the muscles labeled here skeletal, smooth, or cardiac? *skeletal* How do you know? *Organs, blood vessels, and glands are not shown in the diagram, which are made of smooth muscles. The heart, made of cardiac muscle, is also not shown.* **OL**

AL Active Learning

Game Show Have each student write one question about the functions and types of muscles. Create categories of questions, such as muscle function and muscle type, and have students identify the category to which their question belongs. Use the questions to play a game of *Jeopardy!*. You might divide the class into several groups that compete against each other. **OL**

 Reading Check

Answer skeletal, smooth, cardiac

Caption Answer

Figure Caption The trapezius raises the head and shoulders.

▼ **FIGURE 16.2**

R THE MUSCULAR SYSTEM

This figure shows the major skeletal muscles of your body. **What does your trapezius muscle do?**

Extensors straighten your hand at the wrist.

Sternomastoid turns your head.

Trapezius raises your head and shoulders.

Flexors bend your hand at the wrist.

Triceps straighten your arm at the elbow.

Biceps bend your arm at the elbow.

Deltoids raise your upper arm.

Pectoralis major moves your arm across your chest.

Latissimus dorsi muscles lower your upper arm.

Abdominal rectus flexes your torso.

Gluteus maximus extends your thigh and raises your torso from a stooping position.

External obliques assist in breathing.

Abductors move your legs apart.

Quadriceps straighten and raise your leg.

Hamstrings bend your leg at the knee.

Abductors move your legs together.

Sartorius muscle bends your leg at the knee.

Gastrocnemius extends or lowers your foot when you walk or tiptoe.

Achilles tendon attaches your calf muscles to your heel bone.

Anterior tibial muscle flexes your ankle and your foot.

Types of Muscles

Different muscle types carry out different tasks. *The muscles attached to bones that enable you to move* are called **skeletal muscles.** Skeletal muscles are the largest part of the body's muscular system. There are more than 600 skeletal muscles. These muscles are voluntary. You have the power to control their movement.

AL **Smooth muscles** are *the muscles found in organs, blood vessels, and glands.* The mouth, stomach, and lungs are all composed largely of smooth muscles. Smooth muscles are *involuntary* because they operate without your awareness. **Cardiac muscles** are *muscles found only in the walls of your heart.* They are involuntary muscles, working continuously even when you are asleep.

 Reading Check **List** Name the three types of muscles.

What Teens Want to Know

What causes muscle cramps? A muscle cramp occurs when a muscle contracts tightly and does not relax. Cramps are common in the legs and feet. Cramps are caused when the nerves that stimulate muscles are overexcited. This can occur during or after vigorous exercise, while sitting or lying in an awkward position for a long time, after repetitive use, or during periods of dehydration. Low blood levels of sodium, potassium, calcium, and magnesium can also cause muscle cramps. **OL**

How Muscles Work

Muscle movement is triggered by messages or impulses. These impulses are sent to muscle fiber— narrow strands of tissue within the muscle. There are two basic and opposite actions that account for all muscle movement. The first is contraction, the shortening of muscle fibers. The second is extension, the lengthening of muscle fibers. **Figure 16.3** shows these actions at work in two muscles of the arm.

Problems of the Muscular System

Have your muscles ever ached after strenuous exercise or a tough competition? Sore muscles are a temporary condition. Other muscle problems, however, may have a lasting effect on your body. One such problem is muscle strain, which is caused by small tears to a muscle or tendon. Strains usually occur in large muscles that have been overworked. If you feel pain when you exercise, stop what you are doing.

A serious problem that sometimes occurs in teens is muscular dystrophy. This disorder is usually inherited and causes the skeletal muscle tissue to gradually waste away. Eventually, the person can no longer stand or walk.

 Reading Check   **Explain** What causes muscle strain?

Physical Therapist

Physical therapists help people prevent or overcome their physical injuries, using physical activity and movement. They also teach patients to use crutches, artificial limbs, and wheelchairs. Physical therapists are in demand because injured people cannot recover from their injuries on their own. If you are interested in becoming a physical therapist, you should study the bones and muscles of the human body.

What kinds of activities does a physical therapist use to help his or her patients? Go to *Career Corner* at **glencoe.com** to find out.

Physical Therapist Have students read and discuss the information about careers for physical therapists. Then ask a small group of volunteers to learn more about physical therapy as a career. Have them visit the *Career Corner* at **glencoe. com**, as well as other valid web sites, to find out about the movements and equipment used, the possible places of employment, and the educational requirements for physical therapists. Ask the volunteers to share their findings with the rest of the class.

R Reading Strategy

Analyzing a Graphic Have students examine **Figure 16.3**. Instruct them to place their hand on their biceps muscle and straighten and bend their arm. Have them identify when the biceps muscle has shortened. (when the arm is bent) Ask: When does the biceps muscle get longer? *when the arm is straightened* When is the triceps muscle shortened or contracted? *when the arm is straightened*
OL

Reading Check

Answer small tears to a muscle or tendon

Caption Answer

Figure Caption The biceps contract and the triceps extend.

▼ **FIGURE 16.3**

How Muscles Work

R Many of your skeletal muscles work in pairs. When you bend your arm, which muscle contracts and which muscle extends?

1 When you bend your arm, your biceps contract and pull on a bone of your lower arm. At the same time, the triceps extend.

2 When you straighten your arm, your triceps contract and pull on the other bone in your lower arm. At the same time, the biceps extend.

biceps

triceps

biceps

triceps

HEALTH LITERACY

P.R.I.C.E. Formula When muscles are strained, they feel sore because muscle fibers have torn. Following the PRICE formula can help the strained muscle. **P**rotect the strained muscle from further injury—stop the activity. **R**est the strained muscle. Avoid activities that are painful.

Ice the muscle area for 20 minutes every hour while awake to reduce pain and swelling. **C**ompress the muscle with an elastic bandage to provide support and decrease swelling. **E**levate the injured area to decrease swelling.

Reading Check

Answer bend your knees, keeping your back straight

ASSESS

Assessment Resources

Lesson Review Quiz
- *ExamView*
- Fast Files Activities
- Online Quizzes and Activities

Reteaching

- Assign Concept Map 16-2 or Reteaching Activity 16-2 in the Fast Files.
- Have students write several questions about ways to keep the muscular system healthy. Have partners exchange questions and answer them.

Enrichment

- Assign Enrichment Activity 16-2 in the Fast Files.
- Invite students to learn how the structures of smooth, skeletal, and cardiac muscle are different and create a computer presentation of their findings.

CLOSE

Ask students to describe the functions of the muscular system and identify the type of muscle that serves each function.

Care of the Muscular System

You may know the expression "Use it or lose it." This saying is certainly true about muscles. Using muscles helps maintain the natural tension in the fibers. This natural tension is called *muscle tone.* The best way to keep your muscles toned is to stay active and eat well. Remember that the heart is also a muscle, and that regular exercise makes it stronger. A healthy heart pumps more blood and has more time to rest between beats.

Be sure to warm up before exercising or playing sports and to cool down afterward. This will help prevent muscle strain. Using exercise or sports equipment properly can also help prevent muscle injury.

Another way to keep your muscles healthy is to lift properly. Never bend over to lift a heavy object. This puts a lot of strain on your back muscles and can cause injury. Instead, bend your knees, keeping your back straight. Then stand up to lift the load, letting your leg muscles do the work.

Go Online

Visit **glencoe.com** and complete the Interactive Study Guide for Lesson 2.

 Reading Check

Recall What is the proper way to lift a heavy object?

Lesson 2 Review

 After You Read

Review this lesson for new terms, major headings, and Reading Checks.

What I Learned

1. *Vocabulary* What are *skeletal muscles*? Name five of the major skeletal muscles in your body.

2. *Describe* What are the functions of the muscular system?

3. *List* Give two suggestions for keeping the muscular system healthy.

Thinking Critically

4. *Apply* A teen is doing bench presses in the school's weight room. During each repetition, he groans loudly. When you ask if he is in pain, he replies, "Yes—but it's *good* pain." How might you respond?

5. *Evaluate* A teen has been asked to carry some boxes of books to a classroom. He stoops over and pulls a box upward toward his chest. Should he continue lifting this way?

Applying Health Skills

6. *Advocacy* Review the recommendations in the lesson for taking care of your muscular system. Choose one that you think many teens are likely to ignore or be unaware of. Develop a guest editorial for the school paper regarding this habit.

412 Chapter 16: Your Body Systems

Go Online For more Lesson Review Activities, go to **glencoe.com**.

Lesson 2 Review Answers

1. muscles attached to bones that enable you to move; answers will vary, but should include five examples from **Figure 16.2** on page 410

2. allow movement, pump blood through body, move food through digestive system, move air in and out of lungs

3. *Any two:* keep active, eat well, warm up before exercising and cool down afterward, use proper equipment, lift objects correctly

4. *Sample answer:* There is no such thing as "good" pain. If your muscles are sore, you should stop what you are doing so that you do not injure them further.

5. *Sample answer:* No, lifting incorrectly can injure the back.

6. Student work should include facts from the lesson and encourage healthful behaviors.

Lesson 3

Your Circulatory System

Guide to Reading

● **Building Vocabulary**
As you read this lesson, write each new highlighted term and its definition in your notebook.

■ circulatory system (p. 413)
■ cell respiration (p. 414)
■ arteries (p. 415)
■ veins (p. 415)
■ capillaries (p. 415)

● **Focusing on the Main Ideas**
In this lesson, you will learn to

■ **explain** the process of circulation.
■ **identify** the parts of the circulatory system.
■ **describe** ways to keep your circulatory system healthy.

● **Reading Strategy**
Sequencing Using Figure 16.4 on p. 414 as a guide, trace the path of blood flowing to and from the heart.

The Body's Transport System

Even when you are sound asleep, parts of your body are awake. Some of your muscles, for example, never stop working. One of those muscles is your heart. Your heart's job is to pump blood to all parts of your body.

The heart is the main organ of the **circulatory** (SUR·kyuh·luh·tohr·ee) **system.** This system is *a group of organs and tissues that move essential supplies to body cells and remove their waste product*s. This system is also sometimes called the cardiovascular (KAR·dee·oh·VAS·kyoo·lur) system.

Quick Write

Tell in a sentence or two what you know about your own blood. Mention blood type and blood pressure.

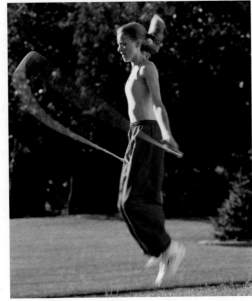

▶ Exercise can help keep your heart healthy. **What are some other ways to care for your heart?**

Lesson 3: Your Circulatory System **413**

FOCUS

Activating Prior Knowledge

What I Know Ask students to explain what they know about blood, how it moves through the body, and what it carries. Explain that they will learn about the circulatory system in this lesson.

Guide to Reading

Building Vocabulary
■ Have students explain the meaning of each vocabulary term to a partner while using Figure 16.4 as a visual aid.
■ Use Vocabulary PuzzleMaker to reinforce vocabulary terms.

Reading Strategy
Sequencing Have students make a flow chart in which they write the names of the four chambers of the heart in the order through which blood flows from the body and back.

Quick Write

If students do not know their blood type or blood pressure, have them describe the different blood types and what blood pressure is.

Caption Answer

Photo Caption *Sample answers:* Eat nutritious foods, avoid tobacco, manage stress

TEACH

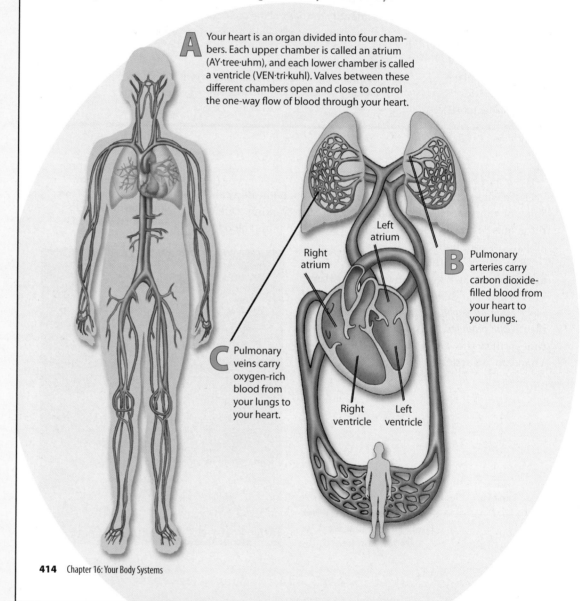 **AL** Active Learning

Creating Graphics Have students make a symbolic map of the circulatory system that depicts how oxygen and carbon dioxide are transported within the system. This map should include the lungs, body cells, heart, veins, and arteries. Students can use symbols such as a car (the blood cells), a road (the veins and arteries), and the stops along the way (the body cells). **EL**

R Reading Strategy

Analyzing a Graphic Have students examine **Figure 16.4.** Ask: Which blood vessels are arteries? *the red vessels* Which blood vessels have blood that has little oxygen? *the veins* In which direction do veins carry blood? *from the body back to the heart* Trace the path of blood through the heart. Name each part of the heart through which the blood travels: body—right atrium—right ventricle—lungs—left atrium—left ventricle—body. **OL**

Caption Answer

Figure Caption Pulmonary veins carry oxygen-rich blood from the lungs to the heart.

Circulation and the Body's Cells

AL Your circulatory system, shown in **Figure 16.4,** is made up of your heart, blood vessels, and blood. Pumped by your heart, blood travels through the blood vessels carrying nutrients and oxygen throughout the body. *The process in which the body's cells are nourished and energized* is called **cell respiration.** As blood

▼ FIGURE 16.4

R THE CIRCULATORY SYSTEM

In this figure, red represents oxygen-rich blood and blue represents blood containing carbon dioxide. **What do the pulmonary veins carry?**

A Your heart is an organ divided into four chambers. Each upper chamber is called an atrium (AY·tree·uhm), and each lower chamber is called a ventricle (VEN·tri·kuhl). Valves between these different chambers open and close to control the one-way flow of blood through your heart.

Left atrium

Right atrium

B Pulmonary arteries carry carbon dioxide-filled blood from your heart to your lungs.

C Pulmonary veins carry oxygen-rich blood from your lungs to your heart.

Right ventricle

Left ventricle

414 Chapter 16: Your Body Systems

HEALTH LITERACY

Sudden Cardiac Arrest Sudden cardiac arrest (SCA) can cause young athletes to die unexpectedly while participating in sports. SCA is usually caused by abnormality in the heart muscle that was present at birth. Unlike a heart attack, a person experiencing SCA collapses and loses consciousness immediately. Breathing stops and blood pressure and pulse are zero. CPR is not an effective treatment for SCA. However, if the heart receives an immediate electric shock (defibrillation), a normal heartbeat can usually be restored.

flows, it picks up nutrients from the digestive system and oxygen from the lungs, which it delivers to the body's cells. The cells use these materials to produce energy for the body. This process creates waste products, which include carbon dioxide gas. The blood picks up these wastes and delivers them to the liver, kidneys, and lungs for removal from the body.

Reading Check **Define** What is *cell respiration*?

Blood

Like the heart, blood plays an important role in circulation. It may surprise you to learn that blood is made up of nearly equal parts of solids and liquids. The liquid part of blood, *plasma* (PLAZ·muh), is about 92 percent water. The solids in blood consist mainly of blood cells. There are three kinds of blood cells. Red blood cells carry oxygen to cells and carry carbon dioxide away from them. White blood cells carry germ fighters from the immune system to areas of the body that need them. Platelets help blood clot at the site of a wound. Clotting seals the wound and prevents excessive blood loss.

Blood Vessels

Look again at Figure 16.4. The thick red lines are **arteries.** These are *blood vessels that carry blood away from the heart to other parts of the body.* The thick blue lines are **veins.** These are *blood vessels that carry blood from the body back to the heart.* The thin red and blue lines branching off from the main ones are **capillaries.** These are *tiny blood vessels that connect the veins and arteries to the body's cells.*

Giving and Receiving Blood

Even though platelets work to stop bleeding, the circulatory system is not designed to handle major wounds. When a serious injury occurs, the body can lose a lot of blood. If too much blood is lost, the person will die unless the lost blood is replaced by means of a *transfusion.*

Before transfusions can be done, however, the doctors need to make sure that the blood type of the injured person matches the blood type of the donated blood. There are four main blood types: A, B, AB, and O. Everyone is born with one of these types. If a person receives blood of the wrong type, their body will reject it. Their immune system will treat the blood as a threat and serious health complications, including death, can result.

Blood safety is a concern since viruses such as HIV can be passed through infected blood. In the United States, the Food and

Connect To...
Science

Anemia and Teens

Anemia is a condition in which the body is not producing enough red blood cells needed to carry oxygen to other cells. Iron-deficiency anemia is the most common type of anemia in teens. You can increase the iron levels in your diet by eating lean meat, eggs, spinach, raisins, dried beans, and iron-fortified cereal.

Research the symptoms of anemia. Find out what the health risks are if left untreated.

Reading Check

Answer the process in which the body's cells are nourished and energized

Connect To...
Science

Anemia and Teens
Students will discover that iron-deficiency anemia results in fatigue, lethargy, and difficulty in concentration. Rapid growth spurts during adolescence sometimes cause anemia in teens. Anemia may also be an indication of other medical conditions. Remind students that a vegetarian diet requires careful planning to include enough iron-rich foods. **OL**

W Writing Support

Expository Writing Have students recall getting a scrape, bleeding, and forming a scab. Explain that the scab forms from blood that has clotted. The scab prevents blood loss and infection. Then have students use their observations to write a paragraph that explains how the body can stop itself from bleeding. Students should include the role of platelets. **OL**

HS Health Skills Practice

Accessing Information Have students gather information from the American Red Cross about donating blood. Suggest they find out who can give blood, who cannot give blood, and why giving blood is important. **OL**

Teacher to Teacher

Patricia A. Lia   **Orange County Public Schools, CA**

The Immune System

"Trying to engage a diverse group of children in complex health concerns is sometimes difficult. Search online for copyright-free or public domain illustrations or photographs and then scan the images to make a PowerPoint® presentation, complete with page-turning animation. The illustrations and presentation format can make a normally dry subject interesting. This is a simple solution to engage all students and encourage classroom participation and retention."

Critical Thinking

Analyzing Explain that blood travels through the body in waves, or pulses. Each pulse represents an opening and closing of valves in the heart. With each new pulse, the blood in a blood vessel is forced against the vessel wall. Between pulses, the vessel relaxes, returning to its normal state. Blood pressure is a measure of the difference between these two. Ask: What happens when artery walls are narrowed by fat buildup? *More force is required to circulate blood through arteries and the heart needs to work harder.* **OL**

> 📖 **Reading Check**

> **Answer** Knowing your blood type is important so that you receive the correct blood type during a transfusion.

▶ Having your blood pressure checked is part of a physical exam. **Why is maintaining a normal blood pressure important?**

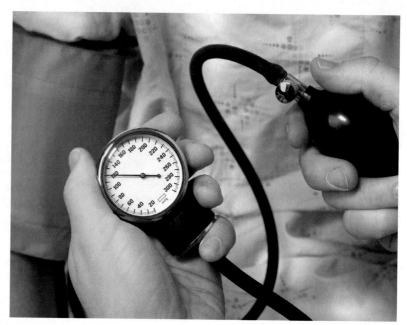

Drug Administration (FDA) is responsible for regulating organizations that collect and distribute donated blood. FDA regulations make it very safe to give and receive blood. All donated blood is tested for HIV and other diseases. Blood that fails any test is discarded.

> 📖 **Reading Check**   **Identify** Why is it important to know your blood type?

Problems of the Circulatory System

Some of the problems of the circulatory system affect the heart and blood vessels. Others affect the blood itself.

- **Hypertension** is also called high blood pressure. It can lead to kidney failure, heart attack, or stroke.
- **Heart attack** is the blockage of blood flow to the heart.
- **Stroke** usually results from blood clots that block vessels in the brain, or from the rupture of a blood vessel.
- **Arteriosclerosis** is a condition in which arteries harden, reducing the amount of blood that can flow through them.
- **Anemia** is an abnormally low level of hemoglobin, a protein that binds to oxygen in red blood cells.
- **Leukemia** is a type of cancer in which large amounts of abnormal white blood cells are produced that interferes with the production of other blood cells.

> **Caption Answer**
>
> **Photo Caption** *Sample answer:* Hypertension can cause kidney failure, heart attack, or stroke.

HEALTH LITERACY

Hypertension in Teens Although only 1 to 3 percent of children in the United States have hypertension, it is still very important for teens to have their blood pressure checked regularly. Teens develop hypertension for several reasons. They may have inherited it from their parents. They might be overweight or do not exercise regularly. Cigarette smoking, drinking alcohol heavily, and taking amphetamines and cocaine can also increase blood pressure. Taking steroids or birth control pills might also increase blood pressure.

Care of the Circulatory System

One way of keeping your heart healthy is to be physically active. Teens should get 60 minutes of physical activity on most days. Regular activity strengthens your heart muscle and allows it to pump more blood with each beat.

Limit the amount of fat in your eating plan. Fats, especially the saturated kind, can cause fat deposits to form on artery walls. These deposits increase blood pressure. As you lower your fat intake, increase your intake of dietary fiber. Whole grains and raw vegetables are a great source of fiber. They also make a filling and satisfying snack.

Another way to keep your heart healthy is to avoid tobacco. Tobacco use can cause lung cancer, emphysema, and other lung diseases. It can also lead to heart disease. Finally, learn to manage the stress in your life. Stress can cause high blood pressure, which puts a strain on the entire cardiovascular system.

 Go Online

Visit **glencoe.com** and complete the Interactive Study Guide for Lesson 3.

Reading Check

List Name two habits that help keep your circulatory system healthy.

 Reading Check

Answer *Any two:* be physically active, limit fat in diet, increase intake of fiber, avoid tobacco, manage stress

Lesson 3 Review

 After You Read

Review this lesson for new terms, major headings, and Reading Checks.

What I Learned

1. **Vocabulary** Define *circulatory system*.

2. **Explain** Tell what happens during cell respiration.

3. **Recall** What are two problems of the circulatory system?

4. **Identify** What are three types of blood vessels? Explain the function of each.

Thinking Critically

5. **Analyze** When a person donates blood, why is it necessary to find out his or her blood type?

6. **Apply** Devin's father recently had a mild heart attack. Devin is concerned about his own heart health. What advice can you give Devin about ways to keep his heart healthy?

Applying Health Skills

7. **Analyzing Influences** In addition to lifestyle, heredity also influences circulatory health. With a group, investigate the role that heredity plays in hypertension and other problems of the circulatory system.

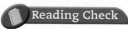 **Go Online** For more Lesson Review Activities, go to **glencoe.com**.

Lesson 3: Your Circulatory System **417**

ASSESS

Assessment Resources

Lesson Review Quiz
* *ExamView*
* Fast Files Activities
* Online Quizzes and Activities

Reteaching

● Assign Concept Map 16-3 or Reteaching Activity 16-3 in the Fast Files.

● Have students use Figure 16.4 to describe to a partner the movement of nutrients, oxygen, and carbon dioxide through the body.

Enrichment

● Assign Enrichment Activity 16-3 in the Fast Files.

● Challenge students to find out about cholesterol and how it relates to circulatory health. Invite them to share their findings with the class.

CLOSE

Ask students to describe the functions and care of the circulatory system and how to keep it healthy.

Lesson 3 Review Answers

1. the group of organs and tissues that move essential supplies to body cells and remove their waste products
2. The body cells are nourished and energized.
3. *Any two:* hypertension, heart attack, stroke, arteriosclerosis, anemia, leukemia

4. Arteries carry blood from the heart, veins carry blood back to the heart, and capillaries connect veins and arteries to cells.
5. If a person receives the wrong blood type, his or her body will reject it. This can lead to serious health complications or even death.

6. Devin should limit fats in his diet, avoid tobacco, and be physically active.
7. Hypertension does run in families. However, just because a parent has hypertension does not mean that the children will have it, too.

FOCUS

Activating Prior Knowledge

What I Know Challenge students to identify ways to keep the respiratory system healthy. List their responses on the board. Review them as you discuss the lesson.

Guide to Reading

Building Vocabulary

- Have students write a short story in which they use each of the vocabulary terms. The meaning of each term should be given within the context of the story.
- Use Vocabulary PuzzleMaker to reinforce vocabulary terms.

Reading Strategy

Organizing Information Have students copy the lesson headings into an outline format. Ask students to add notes to the outline as they read the lesson.

Quick Write

Invite students to share their responses. List on the board the different causes of feeling out of breath. Discuss ways of preventing each type from occurring.

Your Respiratory System

Guide to Reading

● Building Vocabulary
Read each of the words below. If the word is familiar, write down what you think its meaning is. If it's not, guess at its meaning.

- respiratory system (p. 418)
- respiration (p. 418)
- bronchi (p. 420)
- alveoli (p. 420)
- diaphragm (p. 420)
- asthma (p. 420)
- Air Quality Index (AQI) (p. 421)

● Focusing on the Main Ideas
In this lesson, you will learn to

- **explain** how your body uses the air you breathe.
- **identify** the parts and functions of the respiratory system.
- **describe** ways to maintain the health of your respiratory system.
- **analyze** the role of posture on respiratory health.

● Reading Strategy
Organizing Information Create an outline using the major and minor headings in the lesson. As you read, take notes under each heading on your outline.

Quick Write

Write about a time when you felt out of breath. Tell what caused this and what you did to get your breath back to normal.

Breathing

While reading this paragraph you will breathe in and out four or five times. This will happen without you even thinking about it. Breathing is a function of your body's **respiratory system**— *a system that consists of organs that supply the body with constant oxygen and rid the body of carbon dioxide.* Your body needs oxygen to survive. In fact, a person can live only a few minutes without oxygen.

Functions of the Respiratory System

The respiratory system's main job, as its name suggests, is **respiration.** This is *the exchange of gases between your body and the air.* There are two major types of respiration: external and internal.

U

- **External respiration.** This is the exchange of oxygen and carbon dioxide between the blood and the air in the lungs. As you inhale, you breathe oxygen-rich air into your lungs. The oxygen exchanges with carbon dioxide inside your lungs. When you exhale, you release carbon dioxide into the air.

Lesson 4 Resources

📁 **Chapter *FAST FILE* Resources**
Guided Reading and Writing 16-4
Concept Mapping Activity 16-4
Decision-Making Activity 16-4
Reteaching Activity 16-4
Enrichment Activity 16-4
Lesson Quiz 16-4

Technology
🔥 Transparency 16-4
💿 Audio Summaries
💿 *ExamView® Assessment Suite*
💿 Vocabulary PuzzleMaker
💿 StudentWorks™ Plus

G◉ Online

- **Internal respiration.** This is the exchange of gases between the blood and the cells of the body. Oxygen moves from your lungs to your blood where it is carried to all the cells of the body. In the cells, oxygen combines with nutrients to provide energy. This process produces carbon dioxide—a waste gas. Blood carries the carbon dioxide to the lungs where it is released outside the body. Another name for this process, which you already read about in Lesson 3, is *cell respiration*.

 Reading Check **Identify** What is the main function of the respiratory system?

Main Parts of the Respiratory System

The main structures of the respiratory system are shown in **Figure 16.5.** Find the lungs in this diagram. These are the system's main organ. Every day, your lungs take in enough air to fill a large room.

▼**FIGURE 16.5**

R

THE RESPIRATORY SYSTEM

The respiratory system allows the body to take in oxygen and remove carbon dioxide. **Where in the respiratory system does oxygen exchange with carbon dioxide?**

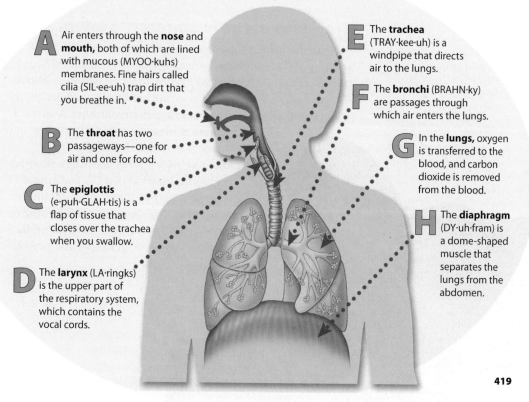

A Air enters through the **nose** and **mouth,** both of which are lined with mucous (MYOO·kuhs) membranes. Fine hairs called cilia (SIL·ee·uh) trap dirt that you breathe in.

B The **throat** has two passageways—one for air and one for food.

C The **epiglottis** (e·puh·GLAH·tis) is a flap of tissue that closes over the trachea when you swallow.

D The **larynx** (LA·ringks) is the upper part of the respiratory system, which contains the vocal cords.

E The **trachea** (TRAY·kee·uh) is a windpipe that directs air to the lungs.

F The **bronchi** (BRAHN·ky) are passages through which air enters the lungs.

G In the **lungs,** oxygen is transferred to the blood, and carbon dioxide is removed from the blood.

H The **diaphragm** (DY·uh·fram) is a dome-shaped muscle that separates the lungs from the abdomen.

419

CHAPTER 16
Lesson 4

TEACH

U **Universal Access**

Learning Disabled Encourage students to take deep breaths in and out. Have them observe how their chest rises when they breathe in and falls when they breathe out. Ask: When does your chest puff out the most? *after taking a deep breath* What are your lungs taking from the air you breathe in? *oxygen* What happens to the oxygen once it is in the lungs? *The oxygen moves into the bloodstream and goes to body cells.* **OL**

Reading Check

Answer The respiratory system supplies the body with oxygen and removes carbon dioxide.

R **Reading Strategy**

Analyzing a Graphic Have students trace the path of air as it moves into the lungs in **Figure 16.5.** Explain that capillaries from the circulatory system surround the alveoli. Ask: What happens in the alveoli? *Oxygen from the air in the lungs moves into the capillaries and the blood stream. Carbon dioxide from blood moves out of the capillaries and into the alveoli.* **OL**

Home, School, and Community

In the Community Invite a paramedic or Red Cross first-aid instructor to the class to demonstrate rescue breathing. Have the instructor explain that rescue breathing helps to move oxygen into the lungs of the person who has stopped breathing. Also have the instructor describe how choking occurs and the role of the epiglottis in keeping food out of the trachea. If possible, have students go through first-aid training and become Red Cross certified. Ask the Red Cross instructor about starting a Red Cross Club at your school. **AL**

Caption Answer

Figure Caption Oxygen and carbon dioxide are exchanged in the lungs.

Go Online

Breathing for Health
Have students research deep breathing techniques using the online resources at **glencoe.com.** Encourage students to explain the benefits of deep breathing in their presentations.

AL Active Learning

Quick Demo Give each student a round balloon. (Students who have respiratory diseases, such as asthma or bronchitis, should not participate.) Suggest that students stretch out the balloon and blow it up a few times to loosen it. Then instruct students to take a deep breath and use it to blow up the balloon. Students should pinch the end shut while a partner measures the circumference of the balloon with a string or measuring tape. **OL**

Reading Check

Answer Its downward motion causes the lungs to fill with air.

Caption Answer

Photo Caption asthma, tuberculosis, pneumonia

Go Online

Topic: Breathing for Health

Visit **glencoe.com** for Student Web Activities to learn how deep breathing techniques can be good for your body and mind.

Activity: Using the information provided at the link above, practice deep breathing for a few days, then prepare a short one- or two-minute presentation about your experience to share with your class.

Each lung is divided into sections called *lobes*. Notice that there are three lobes in the right lung and two in the left. The *main openings through which air enters the lungs* are the **bronchi**. From the bronchi, air moves into smaller tubes called bronchioles. These passages branch into even smaller spaces called **alveoli** (al-VEE·uh·ly). The alveoli are *tiny air sacs in the lungs where carbon dioxide is exchanged with oxygen.*

The Role of the Diaphragm

Have you ever heard of a blacksmith? Blacksmiths use fire to shape metal into tools and other goods. They use devices called bellows to fan the flames of the fire. Human lungs have a lot in common with bellows. Both are responsible for introducing oxygen and both rely on muscle power to accomplish this task. However, while bellows are powered by arm muscles, lungs get their power from the diaphragm. The **diaphragm** is *a dome-shaped muscle that separates the chest from the abdomen.* When you inhale, the diaphragm contracts and flattens. Its downward motion permits the lungs to fill with air. When you exhale, the opposite happens. The diaphragm moves upward, squeezing the lungs and forcing the air out. **AL**

Reading Check

Explain What happens in the lungs when the diaphragm contracts?

Problems of the Respiratory System

One of the most common respiratory diseases suffered by young people is **asthma,** *a serious chronic condition that causes tiny air passages in the respiratory system to become narrow or blocked.* Its symptoms are wheezing, shortness of breath, and coughing. About 6 million Americans under age 18 have asthma. Asthma attacks are often triggered by an allergic reaction to substances in the environment.

Other respiratory problems include bronchitis, pneumonia, tuberculosis (TB), and influenza ("flu"). Symptoms of all three conditions include coughing, wheezing, and difficulty breathing. Fever may be present as well. Tuberculosis and pneumonia are serious problems and may require hospitalization.

◄ One common respiratory illness is the flu. **What are some more serious respiratory illnesses?**

What Teens Want to Know

What happens during an asthma attack? People with asthma have swollen airways that produce mucus. These inflamed airways are overly sensitive to any kind of irritation, such as tobacco smoke, dust, scented perfumes, pet dander, exercise, cold or dry air, or a cold. An asthma attack occurs when the smooth muscles around the airways tighten up and inflamed airways are further irritated. The airways are so narrow that air cannot move freely in and out of the lungs. This causes coughing, wheezing, or tightness in the chest. **OL**

Chronic obstructive pulmonary disease (COPD) is a condition in which the lungs lose their elasticity. It can be caused by asthma that is not controlled properly, as well as tobacco smoke. Emphysema is a form of COPD in which the alveoli are damaged or destroyed and breathing becomes difficult. Lung cancer is a disease in which tissues of the lung are destroyed by the growth of a tumor.

Care of the Respiratory System

Taking care of your respiratory system includes staying physically active, which makes your lungs stronger. It also includes avoiding tobacco smoke and polluted air. Many communities, especially in or near big cities, report local air quality on the news or in the newspaper. An **Air Quality Index (AQI)** is *a measure of ozone, sulfur dioxide, carbon monoxide, and fine particles close to the ground.* On days when the air quality is poor, avoid doing activity outdoors. Knowing your area's AQI can help you maintain your respiratory health.

In addition to exercising regularly, it is important to protect yourself from respiratory infections. When someone in your home is sick with the flu or a cold, wash your hands often with soap and water and avoid touching your nose and mouth.

Go Online

Visit **glencoe.com** and complete the Interactive Study Guide for Lesson 4.

Lesson 4 Review

 After You Read

Review this lesson for new terms, major headings, and Reading Checks.

What I Learned

1. *Vocabulary* What is *asthma*? How can someone who has asthma care for their respiratory system?

2. *Explain* Explain external and internal respiration.

3. *List* Name the main parts of the respiratory system.

Thinking Critically

4. *Apply* A friend calls to ask if you want to ride bikes. Your local news is reporting poor air quality. What choice do you make? What advice do you give your friend?

5. *Evaluate* Marie arrives home from school feeling feverish and coughing. Based on what you have learned, which respiratory illness might Marie possibly have? Are there any illnesses that you can rule out?

Applying Health Skills

6. *Analyzing Influences* Investigate the role of posture on the health of the respiratory system. Share your findings with the class. Use this example to discuss how the health of one body system can affect another body system.

Go Online For more Lesson Review Activities, go to **glencoe.com**.

Lesson 4: Your Respiratory System **421**

ASSESS

Assessment Resources

Lesson Review Quiz
ExamView
Fast Files Activities
Online Quizzes and Activities

Reteaching

- Assign Concept Map 16-4 or Reteaching Activity 16-4 in the Fast Files.
- Ask student pairs to make a list of ways to keep the respiratory system healthy. Make a class list by inviting pairs to share their responses and explain their results.

Enrichment

- Assign Enrichment Activity 16-4 in the Fast Files.
- Have students learn about cystic fibrosis, an inherited respiratory disorder. Students can share their findings with the class.

CLOSE

Have students describe the structures and functions of the respiratory system.

Lesson 4 Review Answers

1. a condition in which the small airways in the lungs narrow, making breathing difficult; stay active, avoid tobacco smoke and pollution, avoid respiratory infections

2. During external respiration, breathing brings oxygen into the lungs and moves carbon dioxide out. During internal respiration, gases are exchanged between the blood and body cells.

3. lungs, bronchi, alveoli, diaphragm

4. *Sample answer:* Choose not to ride bikes because the air quality is poor. Explain to the friend that poor air quality can affect the health of the respiratory system.

5. Marie may have pneumonia, tuberculosis, or influenza. The fever indicates that Marie does not have asthma, allergies, or chronic obstructive pulmonary disease.

6. Students should cite sources they used to research and should include examples.

421

Lesson 5

FOCUS

Activating Prior Knowledge

What I Know Ask students to name parts of the nervous system and their functions. Correct any misconceptions and explain that they will study the nervous system in this lesson.

Guide to Reading

Building Vocabulary
■ Have students give one example for each vocabulary term.
■ Use Vocabulary PuzzleMaker to reinforce vocabulary terms.

Reading Strategy
Predicting After reading the lesson, have students evaluate their predictions. For those predictions that were not correct, instruct students to rewrite them.

Quick Write

When students are finished writing, have them exchange papers with a partner and follow the directions exactly as written. Partners should work together to add steps to the procedure that were missing. When partners have finished, begin a class discussion about what body systems were required to complete the actions.

Caption Answer

Photo Caption *Sample answer:* senses when you are cold, hungry, and tired

---

Lesson 5

Your Nervous System

Guide to Reading

● **Building Vocabulary**
As you read, write each term and its definition in your notebook.

■ nervous system (p. 422)
■ central nervous system (CNS) (p. 423)
■ peripheral nervous system (PNS) (p. 423)
■ neurons (p. 423)
■ somatic system (p. 424)
■ autonomic system (p. 424)
■ traumatic brain injury (TBI) (p. 425)

● **Focusing on the Main Ideas**
In this lesson, you will learn to

■ **explain** the functions of your nervous system.
■ **identify** the different parts of the nervous system.
■ **describe** ways of protecting your nervous system from injury.

● **Reading Strategy**
Predicting Before you read, glance at the main headings, figures, and captions. Predict the kinds of tasks carried out by your nervous system.

Quick Write

Write a detailed step-by-step procedure of a very simple action. An example might be washing your face.

Your Body's Command Center

Computers are amazing machines, capable of doing billions of calculations in a second. Yet, even the fastest computer cannot compose music or write a play. Only the human brain is able to do such work.

Your brain is just one part of your **nervous system.** This is *your body's message and control center.* Your nervous system controls all your body's actions and jobs.

▶ Your nervous system warns you when food is too hot to eat. **What are some other ways that your nervous system helps you to prevent injury?**

Lesson 5 Resources

📁 **Chapter FAST FILE Resources**
Guided Reading and Writing 16-5
Concept Mapping Activity 16-5
Decision-Making Activity 16-5
Reteaching Activity 16-5
Enrichment Activity 16-5
Lesson Quiz 16-5

Technology
🔌 Transparency 16-5
💿 Audio Summaries
⚙ *ExamView® Assessment Suite*
💿 Vocabulary PuzzleMaker
⚙ StudentWorks™ Plus
Go Online

Parts of the Nervous System

The nervous system has two main divisions:

- The **central nervous system (CNS)** includes *the brain and spinal cord.*
- The **peripheral nervous system (PNS)** includes *the nerves that connect the central nervous system to all parts of the body.*

The PNS sends the information it gathers to the CNS. The CNS examines the information, and then sends directions back to the PNS on how to respond. These messages are carried by means of electrical charges called *impulses*. They travel along body pathways at speeds up to 248 miles per hour. The senders and receivers of these transmissions are called neurons. **Neurons** are *specialized nerve cells.*

Reading Check **List** Name two parts of the nervous system.

Central Nervous System

The central nervous system has two parts: the brain and the spinal cord. The brain is the largest, most **complex** part of your entire nervous system. This remarkable structure, which weighs about 3 pounds, contains at least 100 billion neurons. Messages from your brain take the form of thoughts, memories, and commands to carry out actions. Your brain allows you to reason and to direct your muscle movement. It is involved in your emotions and everything you sense. Your brain also controls involuntary processes, such as heartbeat and respiration. **Figure 16.6** on the next page shows the different parts of the brain and their functions.

The spinal cord is a column of nerve tissue about 18 inches long and about as thick as your index finger. This precious cord is protected by *vertebrae,* bones that make up the spine. It is further protected by fluid that surrounds it, acting like a shock absorber. Your spinal cord relays messages to and from the brain and body.

Academic Vocabulary

complex (KOM plecks) *(adjective)* difficult, hard, intricate, elaborate. *Teens can experience a series of complex emotions in a single day.*

 Whether you play a sport or do other activities, protect yourself. **What risks can you avoid by wearing protective gear like the teen in this picture?**

TEACH

AL Active Learning

Role Playing Have student pairs choose an action, such as smelling fire or writing a word. As one partner performs the action, the other partner explains the path of the nerve impulses. Then have partners switch roles and perform and describe a different action. Point out that not all actions begin with the PNS sensing something. When writing a word, the thought originates in the CNS. **OL**

Reading Check

Answer central nervous system and peripheral nervous system

Academic Vocabulary

Complex Have students meet in cooperative groups to read and discuss the definition and example sentence. Let group members work together to list at least four synonyms for *complex* and then at least four antonyms. You will find academic vocabulary activities in the Student Activities Workbook. 📂

What Teens Want to Know

What causes headaches? Between 50 to 75 percent of teens have at least one headache per month. These headaches are most often tension headaches or migraines caused by muscle tension, stress, or changes in certain brain chemicals. Migraines are triggered by stress, lack of sleep, skipping a meal, chocolate, caffeine, weather changes, menstruation, using alcohol, and smoking. If you think you suffer from migraines, see your doctor to learn about prevention techniques and treatment for these types of headaches. **OL**

Caption Answer

Photo Caption injuries to the brain and spinal cord

R Reading Strategy

Analyzing a Graphic Have students examine the parts of the brain in **Figure 16.6**. Ask: Which part of the brain controls involuntary movements, such as heartbeat, breathing, and digestion? *brain stem* Which part of the brain does a gymnast rely on to stay balanced? *cerebellum* Which part of the brain controls the senses, thinking, and speech? *cerebrum* Which part of the nervous system does the brain belong to? *central nervous system* **OL**

U Universal Access

Different Learning Styles
To help students remember the parts of the nervous system, have them make a concept map to show the relationships among the following terms: nervous system, central nervous system, peripheral nervous system, brain, spinal cord, somatic system, and autonomic system. Tell students to include details about the function of each nervous system structure. **OL**

Reading Check

Answer the system that deals with actions you do not control

▼FIGURE 16.6

R **PARTS OF THE BRAIN**

Like a computer, the brain is made up of many distinct parts, each with a different function. **What is the function of the brain stem?**

A The **cerebrum** is the largest portion of the brain. It controls the senses, movement of muscles, thinking, and speech.

B The **cerebellum** controls balance, posture, and coordination.

C The **brain stem** controls some important automatic body functions such as heartbeat, breathing, blood pressure, and digestion.

D The **meninges** are membranes that cover the brain and the spinal cord.

Skull

Midbrain

Pons

Medulla

Spinal Cord

Vertebrae

Peripheral Nervous System

The word *peripheral* means "located away from the center." The peripheral nervous system is made up of nerves that fan out from the CNS. These nerves connect to the muscles, skin, organs, and glands. The PNS carries messages between the CNS and the rest of the body.

Like the CNS and nervous system as a whole, the PNS has two parts. The **somatic** (soh·MA·tik) **system** is *the part of the nervous system that deals with actions that you control*. For example, the nerves to and from your arm muscles are part of the somatic system. The **autonomic** (aw·tuh·NAH·mik) **system** is *a system dealing with actions you do not control*. **U**

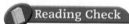

Visit glencoe.com and complete the Interactive Study Guide for Lesson 5.

Reading Check
Identify What is the autonomic system?

Caption Answer

Figure Caption The brain stem controls automatic body functions.

Dealing with Sensitive Issues

Dyslexia Dyslexia is a learning disability characterized by having difficulty with words or numbers. It is an inherited trait that causes the brain to process information differently. Most people with dyslexia actually have average or above-average intelligence. The most common problem in dyslexia is the inability to match a letter with its sound. People with dyslexia will not grow out of it. They find different ways to learn and use these strategies their entire lives.

Problems of the Nervous System

For teens, the most common cause of nervous-system problems is a blow to the head. Head injuries during sports or other activities can cause **traumatic brain injury (TBI)**—*a condition caused by the brain being jarred and striking the inside of the skull.* Traumatic brain injury is the number one cause of death and disability in children and young adults. It can also cause memory loss, loss of one or more senses, and psychological problems.

Spinal-cord injuries from accidents can also lead to serious problems. This includes paralysis, an inability to move body parts. Other problems include nerve inflammation, or "pinched nerve." This condition is very painful. Besides pain medication, the only way to treat nerve inflammation is to rest the affected area.

Not all nervous system problems are caused by injury. Diseases can also affect the nervous system, including the following:

- **Meningitis.** This is a potentially life-threatening infection of the *meninges,* connective membranes in the spine.
- **Brain tumor.** This is an abnormal growth of tissue that kills normal neurons around it. It is also called brain cancer.
- **Epilepsy.** This is an illness in which a small area of the brain is damaged. The result is *seizures,* episodes of uncontrollable muscle activity.
- **Multiple sclerosis (MS).** With this disease, the protective outer coating of the nerves is damaged. They no longer work properly. Multiple sclerosis is a *degenerative* disease, meaning it becomes worse over time.

Care of the Nervous System

Always wear protective head gear during sports or physical activities such as skateboarding and bicycling. Always use your safety belt when riding in a car. In addition, get plenty of rest and avoid alcohol and other drugs. These chemicals can destroy brain cells and interfere with thoughts, emotions, and judgment.

Reading Check **Identify** What are some ways to care for your nervous system?

▶ Helmets can prevent traumatic brain injury. **What are some activities that require a helmet?**

Connect To... Science

Technology and the Brain

Using magnetic resonance imaging (MRI) technology, researchers have learned that the brain develops in stages, generally from back to front. The first part to develop controls the sensory functions such as vision, hearing, and touch. The last part, reaching full development around age 25, controls judgment and decision making.

Research other ways MRI technology is being used in science or health care.

Connect To... Science

Technology and the Brain
Have volunteers research MRI technology. Interested students can prepare a report on magnetic resonance imaging and how this process has advanced brain research, including diagnosis and treatments for a variety of conditions.
AL

Health Skills Activity

Practicing Healthful Behaviors

Avoiding Repetitive Motion Injuries

Use the following to help students complete the activity on page 426.

- Have student groups write a script for a public service announcement (PSA) that describes one specific way to protect the nervous system from repetitive motion injury. Students should explain the recommended steps to prevent this type of injury.

- Have groups act out their PSAs for the class. Encourage them to use props and a suitable backdrop or computer station. You might wish to videotape the groups and show the videotapes to other classes. **OL**

Caption Answer

Photo Caption Bicycling, skateboarding, snowboarding, and football.

HEALTH LITERACY

Concussions A concussion is a bruised brain caused when the head bangs against something or someone and the brain moves around inside the skull. Because there is usually no visible external injury in a concussion, the person who just suffered the injury is likely to ignore any symptoms and return to the activity. Symptoms of a concussion include feeling dazed or light-headed, nausea or vomiting, blurred vision, slurred speech, or memory problems. If symptoms persist longer than 15 minutes, the brain requires about a week to heal.

Reading Check

Answer, p. 425 wear protective head gear, wear safety belts, observe safety rules, avoid repetitive motion injuries, get enough sleep, avoid drugs

ASSESS

Assessment Resources

Lesson Review Quiz
 ExamView
 Fast Files Activities
Online Quizzes and Activities

Reteaching

- Assign Concept Map 16-5 or Reteaching Activity 16-5 in the Fast Files. 📁
- Have students use the photos of teens in this chapter to describe the path of nerve impulses required to carry out the action.

Enrichment

- Assign Enrichment Activity 16-5 in the Fast Files. 📁
- Have students find out how reflexes work and what parts of the nervous system are involved in reflex actions. Students can present their findings to the class.

CLOSE

Ask students to identify the structures of the nervous system and their functions.

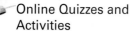

Health Skills Activity

Practicing Healthful Behaviors

Avoiding Repetitive Motion Injuries

Many people use a computer for long periods at a time, either at work or at home. Some of these people may develop a nervous system problem called *repetitive motion injury*. This injury is an inflammation of the nerves in the wrists caused by prolonged, repeated movements. The following strategies can help you prevent this type of injury when using a computer.

1. Keep wrists relaxed and straight. Use only finger movements to strike the keys.
2. Press keys with the least pressure that is necessary.
3. Move your entire hand to press hard-to-reach keys.
4. Take frequent breaks, which is also good for your eyes.

On Your Own

Practice these strategies each time you use a computer.

Lesson 5 Review

 After You Read

Review this lesson for new terms, major headings, and Reading Checks.

What I Learned

1. *Vocabulary* What is the *somatic system*?

2. *Explain* What jobs are done by your brain?

3. *List* Name the two main parts of the nervous system.

Thinking Critically

4. *Apply* You are sitting at home when the telephone rings. Explain the steps that your nervous system takes between the time that the phone rings and the time that you answer it.

5. *Evaluate* Many states now have laws requiring people to wear safety belts in motor vehicles. Tell whether you think this type of law is a good idea. Explain your answer.

Applying Health Skills

6. *Accessing Information* With a group, research current efforts to treat spinal-cord injuries. Determine what makes it so difficult to heal a damaged spinal cord so it works properly again. Share your findings in a brief oral report.

Go Online For more Lesson Review Activities, go to **glencoe.com**.

Lesson 5 Review Answers

1. a system dealing with actions that you control
2. It controls thought, memories, and actions. It permits reasoning and directs muscle movement. It is involved in emotions and senses and adjusts involuntary processes.
3. central nervous system (CNS) and peripheral nervous system (PNS)
4. *Sample answer:* Ear senses sound. Nerves in PNS send a message to the brain about the sound that has been heard. The brain analyzes the sound and sends a message
through the PNS to get up, walk to the phone, and answer it.
5. *Sample answer:* The law is helpful because it helps people avoid injuries to their nervous system.
6. Reports should include recent research on treatment and rehabilitation.

Your Digestive and Excretory Systems

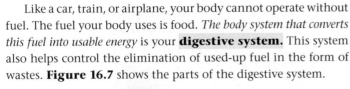

Guide to Reading

● **Building Vocabulary**
Divide a sheet of paper into two columns. In the first column, list the words that relate to the digestive system. In the second column, list the words that relate to the excretory system.

- digestive system (p. 427)
- digestion (p. 428)
- enzymes (p. 428)
- saliva (p. 428)

- small intestine (p. 429)
- excretory system (p. 430)
- excretion (p. 430)
- colon (p. 430)
- kidneys (p. 430)

● **Focusing on the Main Ideas**
In this lesson, you will learn to

- **identify** the parts and functions of the digestive system.

- **explain** the process of excretion.
- **describe** ways to prevent problems to the digestive and excretory systems.
- **practice** healthful behaviors for good excretory health.

● **Reading Strategy**
Sequencing Make a flow chart that traces the path of food through the digestive system. Use Figure 16.7 as a reference.

The Digestive System

Like a car, train, or airplane, your body cannot operate without fuel. The fuel your body uses is food. *The body system that converts this fuel into usable energy* is your **digestive system.** This system also helps control the elimination of used-up fuel in the form of wastes. **Figure 16.7** shows the parts of the digestive system.

 uick Write

Water is important to healthy digestion. Make a list of ways you could increase your water intake.

◀ The digestive system converts the food you eat into active energy. **What are some processes involved in digestion?**

427

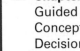 **Chapter FAST FILE Resources**
Guided Reading and Writing 16-6
Concept Mapping Activity 16-6
Decision-Making Activity 16-6
Reteaching Activity 16-6
Enrichment Activity 16-6
Lesson Quiz 16-6

Technology
⚓ Transparency 16-6
Audio Summaries
ExamView® Assessment Suite
Vocabulary PuzzleMaker
StudentWorks™ Plus
Go Online

FOCUS
Activating Prior Knowledge

What I Know Ask students to explain what happens to an apple when they take a bite of it. List their responses on the board and immediately address any misconceptions.

Guide to Reading

Building Vocabulary
- Have students sort the vocabulary terms into categories of their choosing. Then have them trade category names with a partner and re-sort the terms.
- Use Vocabulary PuzzleMaker to reinforce vocabulary terms.

Reading Strategy
Sequencing After students make their flowcharts, have them write a summary that describes what happens when food is digested.

Quick Write

Invite students to share their responses with the class. Challenge students to suggest ways to be sure to drink enough water each day.

Caption Answer

Photo Caption *Sample answers:* tasting, chewing, swallowing, absorbing, breaking down

427

TEACH

Reading Check

Answer fluid made by the salivary glands

U Universal Access

Learning Disabled Give students a piece of apple or a cracker. Instruct them to bite the food and chew it carefully. Have them notice which teeth they used for biting and which they used for chewing. Also have them notice what their tongue does while biting and chewing. Ask them to notice when saliva first started flowing and when it stopped. As students swallow, have them focus on what happens to their throat. **BL**

R Reading Strategy

Analyzing a Graphic Have students use **Figure 16.7** to trace the path of food as it moves through the digestive system. Ask: Where does digestion begin? *in the mouth* What is the purpose of digestion? *to break down food so the body can use it for energy, growth, and repair* How do nutrients move from the digestive system into the body? *Nutrients enter the bloodstream from the small intestine through the villi.* **OL**

Caption Answer

Figure Caption esophagus and then the stomach

The process of changing food into material the body can use is called **digestion** (dy·JES·chuhn). Digestion involves both mechanical and chemical processes. Mechanical processes include chewing and mashing food into smaller pieces. The chemical process involves breaking food down into particles with digestive enzymes. **Enzymes** are *proteins that affect the many body processes.* Digestive enzymes speed up the breakdown of food. Many enzymes are produced in the body.

The Mouth and Teeth

The digestive process starts in the mouth. The teeth tear and grind food into small pieces. When the taste buds on your tongue sense flavor, your mouth produces saliva (suh·LY·vuh). **Saliva** is *a fluid made by the salivary glands* that moistens and softens food, making it easier to swallow. Saliva also contains enzymes that begin breaking down the food.

 Reading Check **Define** What is *saliva?*

▼ FIGURE 16.7

R THE DIGESTIVE SYSTEM

The digestive process begins in the mouth. **Where does partially digested food go when it leaves the mouth?**

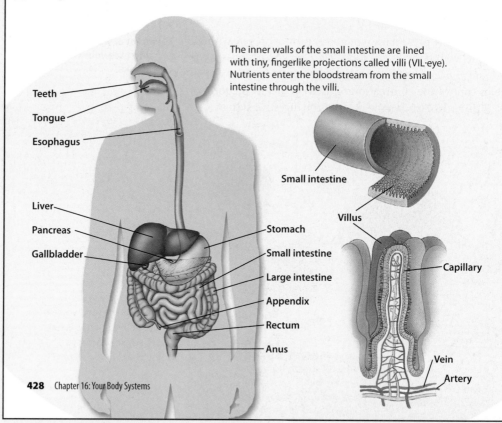

The inner walls of the small intestine are lined with tiny, fingerlike projections called villi (VIL·eye). Nutrients enter the bloodstream from the small intestine through the villi.

Teeth
Tongue
Esophagus
Liver
Pancreas
Gallbladder
Stomach
Small intestine
Large intestine
Appendix
Rectum
Anus
Small intestine
Villus
Capillary
Vein
Artery

428 Chapter 16: Your Body Systems

HEALTH LITERACY

Dangers with Tongue Piercings Risks of tongue piercing include bacterial or viral infections, as well as an increased risk of transmitting hepatitis and HIV. People with tongue piercings have a higher incidence of chipped teeth due to contact with the metal jewelry. Their gum tissue often pulls away from the inside of their lower front teeth. People with tongue piercings often have difficulty speaking clearly, drool frequently, cannot easily chew and swallow food, and often have bad breath. They might also lose their sense of taste and tongue mobility. **OL**

The Stomach and the Small Intestine

As food continues its journey through the digestive system, it passes from the mouth to the esophagus. This is a muscular tube that pushes food down into the stomach in a process called *peristalsis* (pehr·uh·STAHL·sis). Peristalsis is a series of involuntary waves that carry food particles along.

Once it has reached the stomach, food continues to be broken down. Glands in the stomach wall release gastric juices, a blend of hydrochloric acid and enzymes. Hydrochloric acid is strong enough to dissolve metal. A protective stomach lining prevents this powerful acid from digesting the stomach itself. Besides breaking down food, the acid kills most of the bacteria contained in the food.

The stomach also serves as a temporary storage area for food that is not ready for further digestion. Some food remains in your stomach for as long as four hours. The rate at which your stomach empties depends on what you ate.

Most of digestion takes place at the next stage, in the small intestine. The **small intestine** is *a coiled, tubelike organ that is about 20 feet long.* It is here that nutrients are separated from the bulk of the food. The nutrients then enter the bloodstream and travel to body cells where they are used for growth, energy, and repair.

Organs That Aid Digestion

The digestive system is assisted in its work by three important organs through which food does not pass. These are the liver, gallbladder, and pancreas. The liver is the second-largest organ in your body. With more than 500 functions, it is also one of your body's busiest organs. To aid digestion, the liver produces *bile,* a substance that helps break down fats.

The gallbladder stores the bile and releases it into the small intestine as needed. The pancreas makes additional digestive enzymes, which are released directly into the small intestine.

Reading Check
Explain What roles do the liver and pancreas play in the digestion process?

▼ Regular dental checkups will help keep your teeth healthy. **What role in the digestive process do your teeth play?**

AL Active Learning

Game Show Have students write game show questions about the structures and functions of the digestive system. Review the questions beforehand and add questions, if needed, to cover all parts of the digestive system. Divide the class into teams. Team members should sit together but far from other teams so that discussions cannot be overheard. When you ask the question, team members can confer on the answer before writing it down. Set a time limit for answering each question. When the time limit is up, ask teams to show their answers. **OL**

Reading Check

Answer The liver produces bile, which breaks down fats. The pancreas makes digestive enzymes.

TECHNOLOGY AND HEALTH

Examining the Small Intestine Doctors can find abnormalities in the small intestine with a tiny camera inside a pill-like device. The patient swallows the capsule in the same manner as a pill and can go about his or her normal activities—even eating. The capsule contains a color camera, a transmitter, and four tiny lights. The transmitter sends the data to a data recorder worn by the patient around the waist. The data are stored there until the doctor downloads and views them. The capsule is naturally excreted through the digestive system. **OL**

Caption Answer

Photo Caption Teeth tear and grind food into small pieces.

Health Skills Activity

Practicing Healthful Behaviors

Adding Sources of Fiber

Use the following strategies to help students complete the activity:

- Have groups start by reading the introductory paragraph.
- Suggest that groups use the MyPyramid Web site to find foods that are high in fiber.
- Have groups present their completed posters to the class. Consider displaying posters in the lunchroom.
- Encourage students to list the high-fiber foods that they already eat. Then have them list two or three foods they would like to add to their diet.

Health Skills Activity

Practicing Healthful Behaviors

Adding Sources of Fiber

Eating high-fiber foods and drinking plenty of water help move food through the digestive process and protect you against colon cancer, constipation, and diabetes. Fiber also reduces the risk of heart disease. High-fiber foods are also filling, therefore discouraging overeating. To get more fiber from the foods you eat:

- **Start the day with a good breakfast.** If you do not eat breakfast regularly, now is the time to start. Breakfast cereals made with oats or bran are excellent sources of soluble fiber. So are whole-grain muffins.
- **Eat meatless meals several times a week.** Try a bean burrito with cheese at lunch or dinner. The beans will give you a fiber boost.
- **Eat high-fiber snacks.** Popcorn is a great source of fiber, and so are nuts and fruit.

On Your Own

Research additional foods with a high fiber content. Make a list of ways to incorporate these foods into an eating plan.

The Excretory System

Once all the nutrients are extracted from food, all that remains is liquid and solid waste. Body wastes consist of food materials that cannot be digested. Natural plant fiber is one such material. The job of removing this matter from the body falls to the **excretory system**—*your body's waste removal system. The process of removing wastes from the body* is known as **excretion** (ek·SKREE·shuhn).

The Process of Excretion

Food particles that cannot be digested move from the small intestine to *the large intestine,* or **colon** (KOH·luhn). The lining of the colon absorbs much of the liquid contained in this material. Some liquid waste leaves the body through pores in the skin, as perspiration. Other liquid wastes are sent to the **kidneys.** These are *organs that filter water and dissolved wastes from the blood and help maintain proper levels of water and salts in the body.* The waste materials filtered out by the kidneys leave the body as urine. The solid waste products that remain are called *feces* (FEE·seez) and leave the body through the anus (AY·nuhs).

HEALTH LITERACY

Importance of Water Doctors recommend drinking plenty of water each day. Water helps food wastes move through the large intestine more easily. It also helps prevent constipation by making the solid waste softer. Water dissolves minerals, vitamins, and other nutrients so that they are better absorbed into the bloodstream from the small intestine. Besides water, drinking milk, fruit juices, and other beverages also helps meet your daily fluid needs.

Problems of the Digestive and Excretory Systems

Have you ever overeaten or eaten too fast? The discomfort you may have felt afterward was a warning from your digestive system. Indigestion is your body's way of telling you to eat slowly and to control the amount you eat. If you have diarrhea, or watery feces, your food might have been contaminated with bacteria. Diarrhea can also be a symptom of a more serious colon disease.

Heartburn is a common name for a burning sensation in the center of the chest or throat. Despite its name, it has nothing to do with your heart. Heartburn is a result, rather, of stomach acids flowing backward into the esophagus. This problem is sometimes related to diet but can have other causes as well. If you have heartburn that will not go away, tell your doctor.

Ulcers are sores in the stomach or small intestine. They are painful and may cause internal bleeding. Ulcers are usually caused by bacterial infection. Alcohol use, however, can also be a factor. Alcohol use has also been linked to liver disease and colon cancer.

Other problems that can affect the structure of the digestive and excretory systems include the following:

- **Gallstones and kidney stones.** These are both painful blockages caused by mineral crystals. Gallstones affect the gallbladder, while kidney stones affect the kidneys.

- **Appendicitis.** This is the inflammation of the appendix. Appendicitis is a serious condition that requires emergency surgery.

- **Hemorrhoids.** These are masses of swollen veins at the opening of the anus. They may be painful and can bleed.

Reading Check **List** Identify two problems of the digestive and excretory system.

▲ Your body needs plenty of fluids to keep your excretory system working properly. **What are some other ways to keep your excretory system healthy?**

HS Health Skills Practice

Stress Management Explain that some stomach pain is caused by stress. Stress can cause food to speed through the large intestine, but slows down the movement of food out of the stomach. Stress also makes stomach ulcers feel more painful. Teach students this deep breathing exercise to relax: Breathe in deeply, expanding the abdomen, to a count of ten. Hold the breath for a count of five, then slowly release for a count of ten. Repeat several times. **OL**

R Reading Strategy

Creating a Chart Have students make a chart of the causes and effects of different problems of the digestive and excretory systems as presented on this page. You may also choose to create the chart in advance and provide it to students as reinforcement for their reading. **EL**

Reading Check

Answer *Any two:* indigestion, diarrhea, heartburn, ulcers, gallstones, kidney stones, appendicitis, hemorrhoids

TECHNOLOGY AND HEALTH

Kidney Dialysis One in nine adults in the United States suffers from chronic kidney failure. The only treatment is kidney dialysis or a kidney transplant. In one form of dialysis, a patient's blood is filtered through a dialysis machine every three days. The machine removes excess water and wastes from the blood. In the other form of dialysis, a cleansing solution poured into the abdominal area pulls wastes and extra water from the bloodstream. The cleansing solution is drained and refreshed every four hours.

Caption Answer

Photo Caption eat a variety of foods, chew thoroughly, do not rush meals, wash hands regularly

431

Reading Check

Answer to prevent overloading the digestive system

ASSESS

Assessment Resources

Lesson Review Quiz
- *ExamView*
- Fast Files Activities
- Online Quizzes and Activities

Reteaching

- Assign Concept Map 16-6 or Reteaching Activity 16-6 in the Fast Files. 📁
- List on the board the names of the organs in the digestive and excretory systems. Have students copy the list and write the function of each organ.

Enrichment

- Assign Enrichment Activity 16-6 in the Fast Files. 📁
- Have students find out about lactose intolerance, what causes it, how it affects the body, and how to live with it. Students can present their findings to the class.

CLOSE

Ask students to describe the processes of digestion and excretion.

Care of the Digestive and Excretory Systems

The following suggestions will help you maintain the health of your digestive and excretory systems.

- Eat a variety of healthful foods. Choose low-fat and high-fiber foods from all food groups. Include plenty of fruits and vegetables.

- Do not rush your meals. Taking your time to eat will help prevent you from overloading your digestive system. It will also help you avoid overeating.

- Chew your food thoroughly. Do not try to wash large pieces of food down with a beverage.

- Drink plenty of water. Your digestive system needs water to work properly. Drink six to eight 8-ounce glasses each day.

- Wash your hands regularly. Before preparing or eating food, always wash your hands with soap and water. This will help prevent the spread of bacteria that could upset your digestive system.

Go Online

Visit **glencoe.com** and complete the Interactive Study Guide for Lesson 6.

Reading Check **Explain** Why is it important to eat slowly?

Lesson 6 Review

After You Read

Review this lesson for new terms, major headings, and Reading Checks.

What I Learned

1. *Vocabulary* What is *excretion*?

2. *List* Name three organs of the digestive system.

3. *Explain* How does the gallbladder aid digestion?

4. *Identify* Name two habits that will help prevent problems of the digestive and excretory systems.

Thinking Critically

5. *Apply* Explain what happens to an apple from the time you begin eating it to the time that it reaches your colon.

6. *Synthesize* What role does fiber play in the health of the digestive system?

Applying Health Skills

7. *Goal Setting* Identify a behavior that promotes digestive health but which you are not currently practicing. Use the skill of goal setting to help you make this behavior a habit. Share the steps in your action plan with classmates.

Go Online For more Lesson Review Activities, go to **glencoe.com.**

Lesson 6 Review Answers

1. the process of removing wastes from the body
2. See Figure 16.7
3. The gallbladder stores bile and releases it into the small intestine as needed.
4. *Any two:* eat slowly, chew thoroughly, eat fiber-rich foods, drink plenty of water, get regular dental checkups, brush and floss

5. Teeth and saliva break the apple into pieces small enough to swallow. The apple moves down the esophagus to the stomach. Stomach acid and enzymes further digest the apple. It then moves into the small intestine, where the nutrients from the apple are absorbed. Undigested solid and liquid parts of

the apple move into the colon.
6. *Sample answer:* Fiber pushes other materials through the digestive system, keeping the system clean. Fiber also helps prevent digestive system problems.
7. Action plans will vary.

Your Endocrine System

Guide to Reading

● **Building Vocabulary**
As you read this lesson, write each new highlighted term and its definition in your notebook.
- endocrine system (p. 433)
- gland (p. 434)
- pituitary gland (p. 434)

● **Focusing on the Main Ideas**
In this lesson, you will learn to
- **describe** the main function of the endocrine system.
- **explain** the jobs done by different hormones.
- **identify** disorders of the endocrine system.

● **Reading Strategy**
Identifying Cause-and-Effect List several effects caused by glands of the endocrine system.

The Endocrine System and Growth

When you started school this year, were you surprised by how much some classmates had grown? Maybe you underwent a growth spurt that surprised others. Fast growth is common during the teen years. The body system responsible for this and other changes is the **endocrine** (EN·duh·krin) **system.** This is *a chemical communication system that controls many body functions.*

 Quick Write

Write what you already know about hormones and the role they play during adolescence.

◀ Hormones secreted by the glands of the endocrine system are responsible for growth. **What other changes are brought about by these glands?**

Lesson 7 Resources

 Chapter *FAST FILE* **Resources**
Guided Reading and Writing 16-7
Concept Mapping Activity 16-7
Cross-Curriculum Activity 16-7
Reteaching Activity 16-7
Enrichment Activity 16-7
Lesson Quiz 16-7

Technology
Transparency 16-7
Audio Summaries
ExamView® *Assessment Suite*
Vocabulary PuzzleMaker
StudentWorks™ Plus
 G⊙ Online

FOCUS

Activating Prior Knowledge

What I Know Ask students to think of a time when they were scared or excited. What did they feel? Explain that they will learn about the role of the endocrine glands and emotions.

Guide to Reading

Building Vocabulary
- Have students create a concept map for the vocabulary terms. Encourage students to add terms from the lesson as they read.
- Use Vocabulary PuzzleMaker to reinforce vocabulary terms.

Reading Strategy
Identifying Cause-and-Effect Invite students to share their effects with the class. List their responses on the board. Then challenge students to identify what causes the glands to release the hormones.

Quick Write

After students read the lesson, have them return to their Quick Write response and edit it as needed.

Caption Answer

Photo Caption *Sample answer: any change common to puberty*

433

TEACH

 Writing Support

Narrative Writing After reading this section, challenge students to write a narrative in which the main characters are hormones and the setting of the narrative is the endocrine system. Within their narratives, students should describe the function of the endocrine system and the source and function of the hormones they choose to use. **OL**

Reading Check

Answer *Any three:* pituitary, thyroid, parathyroid, adrenals, pancreas, ovaries, testes

R **Reading Strategy**

Analyzing a Table After students read about the glands in **Figure 16.8**, ask: What hormones are produced by the adrenal glands? *corticosteroids, adrenaline* What is the function of corticosteroids? *regulates the balance of salt and water in the body, metabolism, immune system, and the body's response to stress* You might want students to make flashcards with the information from the table to quiz each other or play a game. **OL**

Caption Answer

Figure Caption to regulate the rate at which cells burn fuel from food to produce energy

Parts of the Endocrine System

The endocrine system is made up of glands located throughout your body. A **gland** is *a group of cells or an organ that secretes a substance.* The major glands of the endocrine system include the pituitary, thyroid, parathyroid, adrenals, pineal body, and the reproductive glands. The pancreas is part of the endocrine system because it releases insulin, a hormone that regulates the level of glucose in the blood. The pancreas also produces enzymes that aid in the digestive process.

The endocrine glands work by responding to signals from the brain or from the **pituitary** (pih·TOO·ih·tehr·ee) **gland.** This is **W** *a gland that signals other endocrine glands to produce hormones when needed.* This pea-sized gland is located at the midpoint of the skull, behind the eyes.

Hormones

The chemicals secreted by the endocrine glands are called *hormones.* Hormones travel in the bloodstream to the cells that need them. Some hormones are produced continuously, while others are produced only at certain times. Each hormone has a specific job. **Figure 16.8** lists some of the hormones released by the endocrine system and their functions.

Reading Check

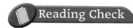 **List** Name three glands of the endocrine system.

▼ FIGURE 16.8

R **SELECTED GLANDS AND SOME OF THE HORMONES THEY PRODUCE**

Glands and hormones are the foundations of the endocrine system. **What is the function of the thyroid gland?**

Gland	Hormone	Function
adrenals	corticosteroids	Regulates salt and water balance, metabolism, the immune system, and the body's response to stress
	adrenaline	Increases heart rate and blood pressure when the body experiences stress
parathyroid	parathyroid	Regulates the level of calcium in the blood
pineal body	melatonin	Regulates the wake-sleep cycle
pituitary	growth	Stimulates the growth of bone and other body tissues
	thyrotropin	Stimulates the thyroid gland to produce thyroid hormones
	corticotropin	Stimulates the adrenal glands to produce certain hormones
thyroid	thyroxine	Regulates the rate at which cells burn fuel from food to produce energy

434 Chapter 16: Your Body Systems

HEALTH LITERACY

Hormones and Mood The interaction with neurons in the brain causes hormones to specifically influence a person's mood. For example, the variation in the hormones produced by the ovaries can affect behavior in females. The amount of hormones produced by the testes can influence males to be more competitive or aggressive. Hormones produced by the thyroid gland affect mood based on changes in metabolism.

The Body's Response to Stress

Can you remember the last time you felt restless or nervous? When your brain recognizes a stressful situation, your adrenal glands release adrenaline, the hormone that allows your body to respond to stress.

Heart rate and blood flow to the brain increase during a stress response. Blood sugar levels and blood pressure rise. Sweat production increases and air passages expand. Digestion and other bodily processes may slow down to conserve energy. After the stressful stimulus has passed, the body returns to its normal state.

Problems of the Endocrine System

The most common problem of the endocrine system is diabetes. Type 1 diabetes occurs when the pancreas cannot produce enough insulin. Type 2 diabetes occurs when the body cannot use the insulin it produces properly. This usually **occurs** in people who are overweight and who do not get enough physical activity. Recently, there has been an increase in the number of teens and children with type 2 diabetes. Maintaining a healthy weight and staying physically active can help prevent type 2 diabetes.

Another common endocrine problem is an overactive or underactive thyroid gland. Symptoms of an overactive thyroid gland include swelling in the front of the neck, nervousness, increased sweating, and weight loss. Symptoms of an underactive thyroid gland include tiredness, depression, weight gain, hair loss, and muscle and joint pain.

Reading Check

Explain What behavioral factors contribute to type 2 diabetes? How can this disease be prevented?

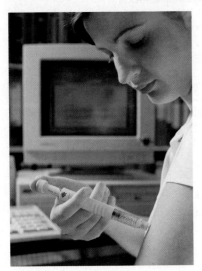

◄ The teen in this picture has diabetes and needs daily shots of insulin. **What can you do to lower your risk of developing diabetes?**

Academic Vocabulary

occur (uh KUR) *(verb)* happen, take place, arise. *Respiratory problems can occur on days when air quality is poor.*

Reading Check

Answer, above Type 1: the pancreas cannot produce enough insulin. Type 2: the body cannot properly use the insulin it produces. **Answer, below** *Any two:* get physical activity, good nutrition, and rest

ASSESS

Assessment Resources

Lesson Review Quiz
- *ExamView*
- Fast Files Activities
- Online Quizzes and Activities

Reteaching
- Assign Concept Map 16-7 or Reteaching Activity 16-7 in the Fast Files.
- Have students describe the function of the different hormones.

Enrichment
- Assign Enrichment Activity 16-7 in the Fast Files.
- Have students draw a diagram of the endocrine system.

CLOSE

Have students describe how to keep the endocrine system healthy.

Endocrine problems can also occur in the pituitary gland. When the pituitary gland releases too much growth hormone, it can result in a very tall person. Too little growth hormone can result in a very small person. Many of these and other problems of the endocrine system can be treated with medicine under a doctor's care.

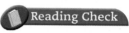 **Reading Check** **Explain** What is the difference between type 1 and type 2 diabetes?

Care of the Endocrine System

The best thing you can do to care for the endocrine system is practice good health habits. Regular physical activity, good nutrition, and adequate rest all contribute to endocrine health. Learn to manage stress in healthful ways. Stress can be harmful if it goes on for too long or occurs too often. Regular medical checkups are also important. Some hormonal disorders have symptoms that are unusual or hard to notice. Your health care professional can perform tests to make sure your hormones are working the way they should.

Reading Check **Identify** What are two habits that are good for the endocrine system?

Go Online

Visit **glencoe.com** and complete the Interactive Study Guide for Lesson 7.

Lesson 7 Review

 After You Read

Review this lesson for new terms, major headings, and Reading Checks.

What I Learned

1. **Vocabulary** What is a *gland*?

2. **Describe** Name the main function of the endocrine system.

3. **Identify** What hormone is released during a stressful situation?

4. **Recall** What are some common problems of the endocrine system?

Thinking Critically

5. **Analyze** Which gland of the endocrine system do you think is most important? Explain your answer.

6. **Synthesize** In what way is the pancreas part of both the endocrine and the digestive systems?

Applying Health Skills

7. **Advocacy** Type 2 diabetes in children and teens is on the rise. With a group, research this trend. Find out what strategies are available to help reduce the risk of developing type 2 diabetes. Use your findings to create a poster or brochure to inform other teens in your school.

Go Online For more Lesson Review Activities, go to **glencoe.com**.

Lesson 7 Review Answers

1. a group of cells or an organ that secretes a substance
2. secrete chemicals that control many body functions
3. adrenaline

4. diabetes, thyroid and pituitary problems
5. *Sample answer:* the pituitary gland, because it regulates other glands
6. The pancreas releases enzymes that aid in digestion and insulin that regulates glucose in the blood.

7. Posters and brochures should outline ways to avoid the risk of developing type 2 diabetes.

Lesson 8

Your Reproductive System

Guide to Reading

● **Building Vocabulary**
As you read this lesson, write each new highlighted term and its definition in your notebook.

- reproductive system (p. 437)
- sperm (p. 437)
- hernia (p. 439)
- fertilization (p. 439)
- ovulation (p. 439)
- menstruation (p. 439)
- menstrual cycle (p. 439)

● **Focusing on the Main Ideas**
In this lesson, you will learn to

- **identify** the parts of the male and female reproductive systems.
- **explain** the three functions of the female reproductive system.
- **identify** problems of the male and female reproductive systems.
- **describe** ways to keep your reproductive system healthy.

● **Reading Strategy**
Comparing and Contrasting Make a list of similarities and differences between the male and female reproductive systems.

 Quick Write

Write what you think is the single most important thing teens can do to care for their reproductive systems.

The Reproductive System

The body systems you have read about so far are the same for both genders. In this lesson, you will learn about the one body system that is different for males and females: the **reproductive system.** This is *the body system containing the organs that make possible the production of offspring.*

The Male Reproductive System

During puberty the testes, the male reproductive glands, produce testosterone, a male hormone. The testes also produce **sperm,** *the male sex cell.* The testes, along with other parts of the male reproductive system, are shown in **Figure 16.9** on page 438.

Sperm are stored in the epididymis, a network of tubes located behind the testes. When sperm leave the epididymis, they pass through the vas deferens (vas·DEF·uh·ruhnz). There, they mix with secretions from the seminal vesicles, the prostate gland, and the Cowper's glands. This mixture of fluids and sperm is called *semen* (SEE·muhn). Semen exits the penis through *ejaculation* (ih·ja·kyuh·LAY·shuhn), a series of forceful muscular contractions.

FOCUS

Activating Prior Knowledge

What I Know Have students call out names of systems they have studied in this chapter. Explain that the reproductive system is a body system and that it develops during puberty.

Guide to Reading

Building Vocabulary
- Have students make a crossword puzzle with the vocabulary terms. Partners can exchange puzzles and solve them.
- Use Vocabulary PuzzleMaker to reinforce vocabulary terms.

Reading Strategy
Comparing and Contrasting After students complete their lists, suggest they make a Venn diagram comparing similarities and differences in the male and female reproductive systems.

Quick Write

Invite students to share their responses. Make a class list of responses. When you have completed the lesson, return to the list and have students reevaluate which is most important.

Lesson 8 Resources

📁 **Chapter *FAST FILE* Resources**
Guided Reading and Writing 16-8
Concept Mapping Activity 16-8
Decision-Making Activity 16-8
Reteaching Activity 16-8
Enrichment Activity 16-8
Lesson Quiz 16-8

Technology
- Transparency 16-8
- Audio Summaries
- *ExamView® Assessment Suite*
- Vocabulary PuzzleMaker
- StudentWorks™ Plus

 Go Online

TEACH

R Reading Strategy

Analyzing a Graphic Have students look over the male reproductive system in **Figure 16.9**. Ask: Where are sperm produced? *in the testes* What do the testes produce besides sperm? *hormones* Remind students that the testes are glands that are also part of the endocrine system. Ask: What job do the seminal vesicles, prostate gland, and Cowper's glands have? *They are glands that secrete fluids that mix with sperm to form semen.* OL

▼ FIGURE 16.9

R MALE REPRODUCTIVE SYSTEM

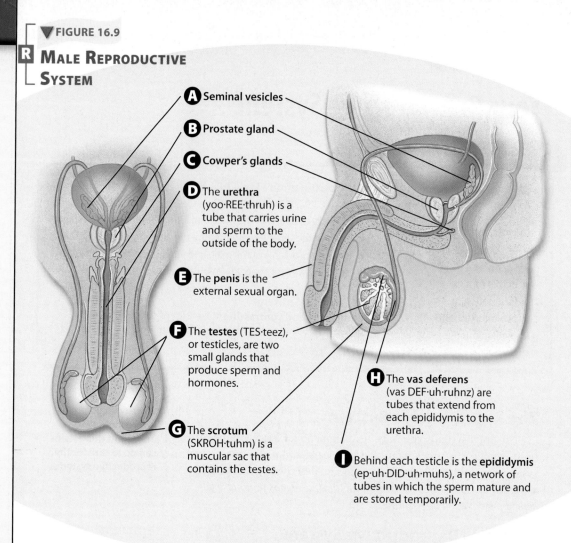

A Seminal vesicles

B Prostate gland

C Cowper's glands

D The **urethra** (yoo·REE·thruh) is a tube that carries urine and sperm to the outside of the body.

E The **penis** is the external sexual organ.

F The **testes** (TES·teez), or testicles, are two small glands that produce sperm and hormones.

G The **scrotum** (SKROH·tuhm) is a muscular sac that contains the testes.

H The **vas deferens** (vas DEF·uh·ruhnz) are tubes that extend from each epididymis to the urethra.

I Behind each testicle is the **epididymis** (ep·uh·DID·uh·muhs), a network of tubes in which the sperm mature and are stored temporarily.

Problems of the Male Reproductive System

For teen males, a common reproductive-system problem is injury to the testes. Wearing appropriate protective gear during sports is one way to avoid this type of injury. A far more serious problem is cancer of the testes, which is one of the most common cancers for males ages 14 to 34. Testicular cancer can spread to other parts of the body. If it is detected and treated early, however, there is an excellent chance of recovering.

✦ Promoting Coordinated School Health

Communicating with Parents Before beginning this lesson, send home the Parent Letter in the Chapter 16 Fast Files to inform them of what you will and will not be teaching. You might also consider having all aspects of the program available for parent review at the beginning of the school year or at a scheduled conference. Encourage parents to engage in a dialogue with their children about reproductive issues. Consider including some conversation starters to help break the ice.

A **hernia** *occurs when an internal organ pushes against or through a surrounding cavity wall.* It appears as a lump or swelling in the groin or lower abdomen. Hernias are caused by muscle weakness and strain. Obesity, coughing or sneezing excessively, or lifting heavy objects are all examples of strains. Inguinal hernias are the most common type of hernia and occur in males when part of the intestine pushes into the scrotum. Hernias can be corrected with surgery.

Testicular torsion occurs when the spermatic cord, the structure that holds the testes together, becomes twisted around a testicle. As a result, blood flow to the testicle is cut off, causing pain and swelling. Immediate treatment is necessary. Other male reproductive problems include contracting sexually transmitted diseases (STDs) and sterility, or not being able to produce offspring.

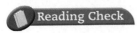 **Reading Check** List Name two reproductive system problems among teen males.

The Female Reproductive System

The female reproductive system shown in **Figure 16.10,** on the next page, has three key functions. The first is to store egg cells. The second function is to create offspring, or babies through the process of fertilization. **Fertilization** (fur·tuhl·lih·ZAY·shuhn) occurs *when a male's sperm cell joins with a female's egg cell.*

The fertilized egg travels from the fallopian tube to the uterus where it attaches to the wall of the uterus and begins to grow. During the first eight weeks, the fertilized egg is called an embryo. After eight weeks, the embryo becomes a fetus. In approximately nine months, the fetus is ready to be born. The third function of the female reproductive system is to give birth to a baby.

The Menstrual Cycle

During puberty, egg cells mature and are released by the ovaries in a process called ovulation. **Ovulation** is *the release of one mature egg cell each month.* Just before one of the ovaries releases an egg cell, the uterus lining thickens. It is getting ready to receive and nourish a fertilized egg. If an egg is not fertilized, the lining breaks down and is shed by the body through menstruation (men·stroo·AY·shuhn). **Menstruation** is *when the lining material, the unfertilized egg, and some blood flow out of the body.* Menstruation, also called a period, usually lasts from 5 to 7 days and happens about every 28 days. This cycle is called the menstrual cycle. The **menstrual** (MEN·stroo·uhl) **cycle** results from *hormonal changes that occur in females from the beginning of one menstruation to the next.*

▲ The woman in this picture just gave birth to a baby. **What part of the female reproductive system nourishes the baby during pregnancy?**

HS Health Skills Practice

Practicing Healthful Behaviors Emphasize the importance of wearing protective sporting equipment to prevent injuries. Then demonstrate proper ways of lifting heavy objects. Invite the class to practice the lifting techniques. Explain that lifting properly helps prevent hernias. **OL**

Reading Check

Answer *Any two:* injury to the testes, cancer of the testes, hernia, STDs

AL Active Learning

Calendar Have student groups create a calendar that shows the stages of a typical menstrual cycle. Emphasize that the length of the actual cycle varies from person to person. Students should include the following stages in their calendars:

● Days 1–13: egg matures in ovary
● Day 14: ovulation occurs; egg released into fallopian tubes
● Days 15–20: egg travels through fallopian tube
● Day 21: egg enters uterus
● Day 28: menstruation begins if egg is not fertilized

Point out that cycles overlap because menstruation usually ends on Day 5 to Day 7 of the next cycle. **OL**

Caption Answer

Photo Caption The uterus shelters and nourishes the fetus.

Dealing with Sensitive Issues

Self-Examinations Performing a monthly self-examination is an important way for teens to care for their bodies. Discussing self-exams, however, is embarrassing. No one should be asked if they do self-exams or know how to do them. Instead, distribute brochures about self-exams. These brochures are readily available from cancer societies, local health departments, and doctors' offices. Have the school nurse or other health professional discuss the brochure in same-gender groups. It helps if the speaker is the same gender as the group. Respect student privacy and school policies. **OL**

Reading Strategy

Analyzing a Graphic Go over the parts of the female reproductive system in **Figure 16.10**. Ask: In what organ are the eggs stored? *ovaries* Remind students that the ovaries produce hormones and are part of the endocrine system. Ask: What is the role of the uterus? *shelters and nourishes the developing fetus* What is the endometrium? *the uterine lining* Explain that this lining thickens each month before ovulation to get ready to receive and nourish the fertilized egg. **OL**

AL Active Learning

Brochure Have student groups prepare a brochure that describes different problems of the female reproductive system and how they might be prevented. Encourage students to be creative when designing their brochures as well as tasteful. **OL**

Reading Check

Answer The uterus lining thickens, an ovary releases an egg, the lining breaks down when the egg is not fertilized, and menstruation begins.

▼ FIGURE 16.10

R FEMALE REPRODUCTIVE SYSTEM

A The **ovaries** contain ova, or eggs, and produce hormones.

B The **fallopian** (fuh·LOH·pee·uhn) **tubes** carry eggs from the ovaries to the uterus.

C The **uterus** shelters and nourishes the fetus.

D The **endometrium** is the lining of the uterus.

E The **cervix** (SER·viks) is the opening of the uterus.

F The **vagina** (vuh·JY·nuh) is a muscular passageway from the uterus to outside the body.

For most girls, menstruation begins anywhere from age 9 to age 16. During the first few years of menstruation, the menstrual cycle may be irregular. It is also normal for females to have cramps before or during their period.

Reading Check

Explain What happens during menstruation?

Problems of the Female Reproductive System

Among the most serious female reproductive problems is cancer. Cancer can occur in the ovaries, uterus, or cervix. Other reproductive problems include:

AL

- **Infertility.** This is the inability to get pregnant. It may be due to blocked fallopian tubes or a failure to produce eggs.

- **Ovarian cysts.** These are growths on the ovary. Symptoms of ovarian cysts include a feeling of heaviness in the abdomen and abdominal pain, swelling, and bloating.

- **Sexually transmitted diseases (STDs).** These diseases are spread through sexual contact.

Dealing with Sensitive Issues

Menstruation Teen girls are especially sensitive to embarrassment during menstruation. They may worry about starting while at school or be concerned with cleanliness. They might feel uncomfortable, headachy, or ill. Work with the school nurse to have a supply of sanitary pads and tampons in the health classroom. Make sure that all girls know where the supplies are and how they can access the supplies with minimal embarrassment. **OL**

Care of the Reproductive System

Both males and females can maintain the health of their reproductive systems by practicing good hygiene. Bathe or shower regularly. Abstaining from sexual activity until marriage will protect you against STDs and unplanned pregnancy.

Males should also avoid wearing tight clothing and check their testes monthly for lumps, swelling, or soreness. Your doctor or other health care professional can show you how to perform a testicular self-exam.

Females should have yearly pelvic exams, beginning at about age 18. The pelvic exam also includes a breast exam. During a pelvic exam, a doctor examines a female's reproductive organs. A female should also keep a record of her menstrual cycle because her doctor may need to know how often her period occurs and how long it lasts. When a woman menstruates, she should change her tampon or sanitary napkin about every four hours. She should see her doctor if she has unusually heavy bleeding or severe cramps.

 Reading Check **Explain** How does abstinence benefit a teen's reproductive health?

 Go Online

Visit **glencoe.com** and complete the Interactive Study Guide for Lesson 8.

Lesson 8 Review

 After You Read

Review this lesson for new terms, major headings, and Reading Checks.

What I Learned

1. *Vocabulary* What is *fertilization*?

2. *List* What are three functions of the female reproductive system?

3. *Describe* Describe two ways to keep your reproductive system healthy.

4. *Identify* What are the male sex cells called?

5. *Recall* Name two female reproductive system problems.

Thinking Critically

6. *Analyze* How are the female and male reproductive systems similar? How are they different?

7. *Apply* Mario will be the catcher this year on his baseball team. What special precautions does Mario need to take to prevent injury to his reproductive system?

Applying Health Skills

8. *Accessing Information* Using print or online resources, research how a testicular or pelvic exam is done. When should these exams be performed? Why are they important?

 Go Online For more Lesson Review Activities, go to **glencoe.com**.

Lesson 8: Your Reproductive System **441**

ASSESS

Assessment Resources

Lesson Review Quiz
- *ExamView*
- Fast Files Activities
- Online Quizzes and Activities

Reteaching

- Assign Concept Map 16-8 or Reteaching Activity 16-8 in the Fast Files.
- Have students make a flow chart that traces an egg cell through the female reproductive system during the menstrual cycle.

Enrichment

- Assign Enrichment Activity 16-8 in the Fast Files.
- Challenge students to choose one of the problems of the male or female reproductive system and research the problem and possible ways to prevent it.

CLOSE

Ask students to identify ways to keep the reproductive system healthy.

Reading Check

Answer Benefits include protection from STDs and unplanned pregnancy.

Lesson 8 Review Answers

1. the joining of a sperm cell and an egg cell
2. store egg cells, create offspring, give birth
3. *Any two:* self-examinations, shower or bathe regularly, practice abstinence; males—avoid wearing tight clothing, wear an athletic protector, avoid steroids; for females—change tampons and pads frequently, record periods

4. sperm cells
5. *Any two:* toxic shock syndrome, cancer, infertility, ovarian cysts, STDs
6. *Sample answer:* Both produce and store reproductive cells. The structures are different in that male structures are external and female structures are internal.

7. Mario should wear a protective cup.
8. Males should perform self-exams monthly to identify problems early. Females should have a yearly pelvic exam.

Building Health Skills — Getting the Facts About Your Body

Skill

Accessing Information

Activating Prior Knowledge

Invite students to share a time when they discovered a new fact on their own. Ask them to describe where they went to find the information they were looking for.

- **Objective** After completing the activity, students will be able to evaluate sources to learn new facts about the body systems.
- **Time** 45 minutes
- **Materials** poster board, markers, paper, pencil

> **Teacher Classroom Resources**
>
> Building Health Skills
> Transparency 16-5

Model

- Ask: Where did Terry look for information about preventing head injuries? *at a government-run Web site aimed at teens that was recommended by his health teacher* Why is this a good source of information? *The Web site was endorsed by his teacher, and it was run by the government.*

Building Health Skills

Accessing Information
Practicing Healthful Behaviors
Stress Management
Analyzing Influences
Communication Skills
Refusal Skills
Conflict Resolution
Decision Making
Goal Setting
Advocacy

What Does Accessing Information Involve?

Accessing information involves finding reliable information to make healthy choices. When looking at a source of information, ask yourself these questions:

- Is it scientific?
- Does it give more than one point of view?
- Does it agree with other sources?
- Is it trying to sell something?

Getting the Facts About Your Body

Follow the Model, Practice, and Apply steps to help you master this important health skill.

① Model

Read how Terry uses the skill of accessing information to find valid information on the Internet about helmets.

Terry needed a new helmet to wear while riding his bike or skateboarding. Terry used the following steps to find valid information about helmets.

1. He went to a Web site his health teacher recommended. It was a government-run site for teens about preventing sports injuries.
2. Terry clicked on a link at the Web site. It took him to another site specializing in information about skateboarding safety. The site provided information on selecting a helmet as well as other tips on skateboard safety.
3. Terry's final stop was the sporting goods store. He brought his older brother, Chuck, with him. Terry knew Chuck might think of questions to ask that wouldn't occur to him.

442

Performance Assessments for Accessing Information

- To ensure fairness, all students should have access to necessary resources. This may involve reserving library or computer lab times, or supplying the materials in the classroom.
- Be prepared to assign groups to a body system so that all nine systems are researched.
- Have several Web sites for the body systems already identified. Briefly review what *.gov, .com, .edu,* and *.org* stand for.

❷ Practice

Help Todd use the skill of accessing information to learn about warming up before participating in sports.

Todd recently began running track. Todd remembers from health class that he should warm up before participating in sports, but he needs details. How should he warm up? How long should he spend warming up?

1. Where can Todd go to find this information?
2. How can Todd choose sources that are accurate?
3. Are there places in the community where Todd can get help?

❸ Apply

Apply what you have learned about accessing information to complete the activity below.

Choose a body system that you want to learn more about. Use valid sources of information from school, the Internet, and home to learn at least three new facts about this system. Develop a fact sheet about your body system that includes a diagram of the system, three new facts, and two sources of valid information. Explain why your sources of information are valid.

Self-Check
■ Did I include a diagram of the body system?
■ Did I provide three new facts?
■ Did I include two valid sources?

Building Health Skills

Practice
● Have students read about Todd and answer the questions.
● Have a class discussion about how Todd will know that the Web site was trustworthy.

Apply/Assess
● Have students work individually to find two facts about caring for the body. Poll each student to make sure that each body system is reviewed.
● Before students begin their research, have them list their resources. After your approval, they may begin researching.
● After their research, organize students into groups based on the body system they researched. Groups can work together to create a poster for the body system. Remind students to include everyone's facts.
● You may wish to distribute the Building Health Skills Activity in the Fast Files.

ASSESSMENT SCORING

Using a rubric, student work should meet all criteria to achieve the highest score.

Skills Student work:
● identifies two valid sources of information.
● explains why the information is valid.

Concepts Student work:
● includes an accurate diagram of the body system.
● demonstrates comprehensive information about the body system.
● incorporates three facts about the body system.

HANDS-ON HEALTH ACTIVITY

How Muscles and Bones Work Together

Time: 30 minutes
Materials: two strips of stiff poster board, hole punch, metal fastener, two long balloons, string

Introducing Hands-on Health

- Invite students to move their arms back and forth. Have them identify the joint in their arm that allows movement. (elbow—hinge joint) Refer students to **Figure 16.3** in Lesson 2 to review how muscles work to move bones.

Teaching the Activity

- Divide the class into groups of two.
- Use **Figure 16.3** to help students visualize what the forearm and upper arm are.
- When students fasten together the two strips of poster board, they should make sure the strips can move easily.
- Have students stretch the balloons several times before slightly inflating them. Caution them against overinflating the balloons. The balloons lose their ability to bend when over-inflated.

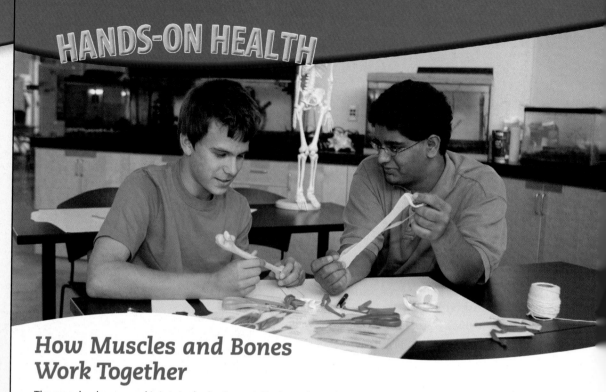

HANDS-ON HEALTH

How Muscles and Bones Work Together

The muscles, bones, and joints in the body work like living levers. They use the same principles used in lifting and moving machines such as cranes. The small movement of one arm of a lever causes a larger movement in the other arm. This activity will show you how to make a model arm. Your finished arm will demonstrate how muscles and bones work together in a system of joints and levers.

What You Will Need

- 2 strips of stiff poster board, 10" × 2"
- Hole punch
- Metal fastener
- 2 long balloons
- String

What You Will Do

1. Round off one end of each strip. Punch holes about 1 inch from both ends of one strip. This strip will represent the upper arm. In the other strip, punch one hole about 1 inch from the rounded end. Punch another hole 4 inches from that same end. This strip will be the forearm.

2. With a fastener, loosely join the rounded ends of the two strips. This represents the elbow joint.

3. Slightly inflate the balloons. Tie knots in both ends of each balloon.

4. Tie the end of one balloon to each end of the upper arm. This balloon represents the triceps muscle on the back of the arm. Tie the second balloon between the top of the upper arm and the second hole in the forearm. This represents the biceps muscle.

5. Experiment with moving the upper arm while the elbow joint rests on a surface. Observe what happens to the balloons and to the forearm.

Wrapping It Up

What happens to the biceps when the forearm is extended? What happens when it is closed? How do the triceps and biceps work together? Observe how far the forearm moves when the upper arm is moved a short distance. Compare these distances.

HANDS-ON HEALTH Assessment

Discussion After pairs have completed the activity and answered the questions, ask:

- Which moves farther, the muscles or the bones? *The muscles in the upper arm move just a little bit to make a big movement in the bones of the forearm.*

- How is your model arm similar to and different from a real arm? Sample answer: *A real arm has more muscles, nerves, tendons, and ligaments. The model arm showed the action of the joint and the paired contracting and relaxing of muscles to move bones.*

Reading Review

 Visit glencoe.com to download quizzes and eFlashcards for Chapter 16.

FOLDABLES Study Organizer

Foldables® and Other Study Aids Take out the Foldable® that you created for Lesson 1 and any graphic organizers that you created for Lessons 1–8. Find a partner and quiz each other using these study aids.

Lesson 1 Your Skeletal System

Main Idea Your skeletal system is your body's framework.

- Functions of the skeletal system include supporting and protecting the internal organs, storing minerals, and making blood cells.

Lesson 2 Your Muscular System

Main Idea Your muscles make it possible for your body to move.

- Functions of the muscular system include pumping blood, moving food through your digestive system, and controlling the movement of air in and out of the lungs.

Lesson 3 Your Circulatory System

Main Idea Your circulatory system moves supplies to cells and removes the cells' waste products.

- There are four main blood types: A, B, AB, and O.

Lesson 4 Your Respiratory System

Main Idea Your respiratory system makes it possible for you to breathe.

- Your respiratory system supplies your body with oxygen and removes carbon dioxide.

- The lungs are the main organ of the respiratory system.

Lesson 5 Your Nervous System

Main Idea Your nervous system is your body's message and control center.

- The nervous system has two parts: the central nervous system and the peripheral nervous system.

Lesson 6 Your Digestive and Excretory Systems

Main Idea Your digestive system converts food into energy. Your excretory system removes waste.

- Eating high-fiber foods and drinking plenty of water help move food through the digestive and excretory processes.

Lesson 7 Your Endocrine System

Main Idea The main function of the endocrine system is to secrete hormones that regulate many body functions.

- Glands are part of the endocrine system and include adrenals, parathyroid, pineal body, pituitary, and thyroid.

Lesson 8 Your Reproductive System

Main Idea Your reproductive system makes it possible to produce offspring.

- Fertilization occurs when a male's sperm cell joins with a female's egg cell.

Teaching Tips

Developing Note-Taking Skills By teaching students organized note-taking skills, you can help them be more effective readers. The traditional outline method is one way to organize note taking. Major and minor heads in the lessons provide a framework for the outline. Another method is a chart with these headings: main ideas, supporting details, key vocabulary, and questions. Model the note-taking method to help students learn the skill. Specifically assign students to take notes, then review their notes and make comments for improvement.

Assessment Resources

- 📁 Chapter 16 Summary and Activity
- 🖱 Audio Summaries
- 📁 Reading Tutor
- 📁 Performance Assessment
- 📁 Chapter 16 Test
- 💿 *ExamView*
- 💾 Vocabulary PuzzleMaker
- 🖱 Online Learning Center

Reading Review

Study Aids

- **Using the Dinah Zike Foldable® Study Organizer** Have students use the Foldable® **FOLDABLES** Study Organizer to review the structures, functions, and problems of the skeletal system. Ask students to name ways to keep the skeletal system healthy.

- **Online Learning Tools** Have students go to the *Teen Health* Online Learning Center at **glencoe.com** to:

  - Download a **Podcast**.

  - Download free **Study-to-Go** content to their PDAs or cell phones.

Vocabulary Review

- **Game Show** Play a game of *Jeopardy!* with the class using the vocabulary terms from the chapter. Divide the *Jeopardy!* board into nine categories, one for each body system.

Assessment

Reviewing Vocabulary and Main Ideas

1. Marrow
2. joint
3. skeletal muscles
4. Cardiac muscles
5. Hypertension
6. True
7. False, diaphragm
8. False, central nervous system (CNS)
9. False, somatic
10. True
11. False, large intestine
12. True
13. False, semen
14. False, ovulation

Thinking Critically

15. *Sample answer:* The digestive system is most helped by positive eating habits such as chewing food slowly and thoroughly before swallowing. Good eating habits help the digestive system work better and keep it healthy.

16. After fertilization, the egg cell travels from the fallopian tube to the uterus and attaches to the thickened lining of the uterus. There it begins to grow into an embryo. In eight weeks the developing embryo is called a fetus.

Go Online

Have students visit **glencoe.com** to take the Chapter 16 quiz.

446

Assessment

After You Read

HEALTH INVENTORY

Now that you have read the chapter, look back at your answers to the Health Inventory on the chapter opener. Is there anything you should do differently?

Reviewing Vocabulary and Main Ideas

On a sheet of paper, write the numbers 1–5. After each number, write the term from the list that best completes each sentence.

- cardiac muscles
- cartilage
- hypertension
- joint
- ligaments
- marrow
- skeletal muscles
- smooth muscles

Lesson 1 Your Skeletal System

1. _____ is a soft tissue in the center of some bones.
2. The point at which two bones meet is called a _____.

Lesson 2 Your Muscular System

3. The muscles attached to bones that enable you to move your body are called _____.
4. _____ are found only in the walls of your heart.

Lesson 3 Your Circulatory System

5. _____, also known as high blood pressure, can lead to kidney failure, heart attack, or stroke.

---

*On a sheet of paper, write the numbers 6–14. Write **True** or **False** for each statement below. If the statement is false, change the underlined word or phrase to make it true.*

Lesson 4 Your Respiratory System

6. <u>Respiration</u> is the exchange of gases between your body and your environment.
7. The <u>bronchi</u> is a muscle that separates the chest from the abdomen.

Lesson 5 Your Nervous System

8. The <u>peripheral nervous system (PNS)</u> includes the brain and spinal cord.
9. The <u>autonomic</u> system deals with actions that you control.

Lesson 6 Your Digestive and Excretory Systems

10. Enzymes are <u>proteins</u> that affect the rate of many body processes.
11. Another name for the colon is <u>small intestine</u>.

Lesson 7 Your Endocrine System

12. The chemicals secreted by the endocrine glands are called <u>hormones</u>.

Lesson 8 Your Reproductive System

13. <u>Sperm</u> is a mixture of fluids including secretions from the seminal vesicles, prostate gland, and Cowper's glands.
14. The release of one egg cell each month is called <u>fertilization</u>.

 Go Online Visit **glencoe.com** and take the Online Quiz for Chapter 16.

HEALTH INVENTORY WRAP-UP

Protecting Your Body Systems Have students review their responses to the Health Inventory. For each question, have students write why each healthful activity helps the body. Students should be specific about which body system is benefited. Then invite students to share their responses with the class. Discuss how these measures protect the body systems.

Thinking Critically

Using complete sentences, answer the following questions on a sheet of paper.

15. Analyze Which body systems do you think benefit most from positive eating habits? Explain your answer.

16. Explain What happens to an egg cell after it is fertilized?

Write About It

17. Expository Writing Choose one of the body systems discussed in the chapter. Write an article for teens on ways they can protect this body system. Include information on the function of this body system and how it can affect other body systems.

➚ Applying Technology

Body Systems Comic Strip

Using Microsoft Word® and Comic Life, you and a partner will create a comic strip about a body system.

- Create a short story about your body system using Microsoft Word®. Your story should have a beginning, a middle, and an end. Discuss the parts, functions, and potential problems of your system.
- Open a new Comic Life document. Decide how many pages and panels you need.
- Copy and paste your story into the panels. Insert speech balloons if appropriate.
- Edit your comic for clarity and accuracy of information.
- Share it with your classmates.

Standardized Test Practice

Reading

Read the passage and then answer the questions.

Have you ever heard that cracking your knuckles is harmful? Some people believe this habit can cause skeletal-system problems such as arthritis. It can't. That is just a myth. The popping noise you hear when you flex your knuckles is gas bubbles escaping inside the joint.

Another urban legend about the skeletal system is that people who can bend their fingers far back are double-jointed. There is actually no such thing as being double-jointed. People who can bend their fingers back have the same number of joints that everyone else does. The real difference is that the ligaments surrounding their joints stretch more than normal.

1. The phrase *urban legend* in the second paragraph seems to mean

   A. city dweller.

   B. knuckle.

   C. joint.

   D. myth.

2. Which statement best captures the main idea of the passage?

   A. Cracking your knuckles is not really harmful.

   B. People who can bend their fingers far back are not really double-jointed.

   C. A number of myths exist about the skeletal system.

   D. Hitting your elbow hurts even if there is no funny bone.

➚ Applying Technology

Body System Comic Strip
Equipment needs: Microsoft Word® or similar software and Comic Life or similar software
Help students review the steps in this project. If appropriate, guide them in brainstorming story ideas. Then have students choose partners; remind partners to begin by agreeing on the body system for their focus. Create a sign-up list if computer access is limited, and establish specific time limits for computer use. Remind students to spend time editing their comics before sharing them with the rest of the class.

Write About It

17. **Expository Writing** Tell students that expository writing shares knowledge to help others understand. Articles should explain detailed methods that the reader can take to maintain the health of the chosen body system.

Standardized Test Practice

1. D
2. C

◢ Test-Taking Tips

Identifying the Meaning of Words Tell students that many tests have questions about the meaning of unusual words to find out how well students use clues in the reading. Help students tackle these questions by first reminding them to read the question carefully to make sure they know what the question is really asking. Remind students to read all the answer choices. Sometimes word meaning is easy to determine based on the answer choices. If not, tell students to return to the reading and look for context clues.

CHAPTER 17 pp. 448–475	Standards		Skills and Activities
	National	State/Local	
	National Health Education Standards 1.8.1, 5.8.6, 7.8.1		**HEALTH QUIZ**, p. 449 **BUILDING HEALTH SKILLS** *Practicing Healthful Behaviors* Coping With the Highs and Lows of Puberty, *pp. 470–471* TIME health news Secrets of a Long Life, *p. 472*
Lesson 1 **The Beginning of Life** pp. 450–454	National Health Education Standards 3.8.1		
Lesson 2 **Heredity and Environment** pp. 455–459	National Health Education Standards 1.8.1, 1.8.3, 1.8.4, 7.8.2, 8.8.1, 8.8.3		**HEALTH SKILLS ACTIVITY** *Accessing Information* Your Family's Health History, *p. 457* **Careers for the 21st Century** Genetic Counselor, *p. 458*
Lesson 3 **From Childhood to Adolescence** pp. 460–465	National Health Education Standards 1.8.2, 2.8.5, 5.8.6, 8.8.1		**What Teens Think** How have your friendships changed from elementary to middle school?, *p. 462* **HEALTH SKILLS ACTIVITY** *Stress Management* Coping with Mood Swings, *p. 464*
Lesson 4 **Adulthood and Aging** pp. 466–469	National Health Education Standards 1.8.1, 1.8.2, 2.8.6, 6.8.2, 6.8.3, 6.8.4, 8.8.1, 8.8.2		**DEVELOPING GOOD CHARACTER** *Respect, p. 467* Go Online Finding Common Ground, *p. 468*

PACING THE CHAPTER		
Lesson 1 45 min	**Lesson 4** 45 min	**Chapter Review** 45 min
Lesson 2 45 min		**TIME health news** 20 min
Lesson 3 45 min	**Building Health Skills** 30 min	

BLOCK SCHEDULING

For block scheduling, assign students Building Health Skills feature *Coping with the Highs and Lows of Puberty*, pages 470–471, and Guided Reading and Writing. 📁

Planning Guide

StudentWorks Plus

Glencoe Exclusive!
TeacherWorks™ Plus
All-In-One Planner and Resource Center

Reproducible Resources	Assessment	Media and Technology
Chapter FAST FILE Resources Chapter Summaries and Activities REVIEW Building Health Skills Activity TEACH Performance Assessment Activity EXTEND Universal Access Activities TEACH Parent Letter and Activities 📁 **Student Activities Workbook** TEACH 📁 **Reading Tutor** TEACH	Building Health Skills Activity, *pp. 470–471* Chapter 17 Assessment, *pp. 474–475* **Chapter FAST FILE Resources** Performance Assessment Activity, *p. 4* Chapter 17 Test, *p. 7* 💿 *ExamView® Assessment Suite*	TeacherWorks Plus includes: ● Interactive Teacher Edition ● Lesson Planner with Calendar ● Access to all blackline masters ● Correlations to standards ● Links to glencoe.com 💿 StudentWorks™ Plus 💿 Online Student Edition Dinah Zike's Teaching Health with Foldables®
Chapter FAST FILE Resources Concept Mapping Activity 17-1 REVIEW Cross-Curriculum Activity 17-1 EXTEND Enrichment Activity 17-1 EXTEND Lesson Plan 17-1 Guided Reading and Writing 17-1 TEACH Reteaching Activity 17-1 REVIEW	Lesson 1 Review, *p. 454* 💿 Vocabulary PuzzleMaker 💿 *ExamView® Assessment Suite*	💿 Vocabulary PuzzleMaker 💿 *ExamView® Assessment Suite* 💿 StudentWorks™ Plus 🕹 Transparency 17-1 **Go Online** glencoe.com
Chapter FAST FILE Resources Concept Mapping Activity 17-2 REVIEW Cross-Curriculum Activity 17-2 EXTEND Enrichment Activity 17-2 EXTEND Lesson Plan 17-2 Guided Reading and Writing 17-2 TEACH Reteaching Activity 17-2 REVIEW	Lesson 2 Review, *p. 459* 💿 Vocabulary PuzzleMaker 💿 *ExamView® Assessment Suite*	💿 Vocabulary PuzzleMaker 💿 *ExamView® Assessment Suite* 💿 StudentWorks™ Plus 🕹 Transparency 17-2 **Go Online** glencoe.com
Chapter FAST FILE Resources Concept Mapping Activity 17-3 REVIEW Health Lab 17-3 EXTEND Enrichment Activity 17-3 EXTEND Lesson Plan 17-3 Guided Reading and Writing 17-3 TEACH Reteaching Activity 17-3 REVIEW	Lesson 3 Review, *p. 465* 💿 Vocabulary PuzzleMaker 💿 *ExamView® Assessment Suite*	💿 Vocabulary PuzzleMaker 💿 *ExamView® Assessment Suite* 💿 StudentWorks™ Plus 🕹 Transparency 17-3 **Go Online** glencoe.com
Chapter FAST FILE Resources Concept Mapping Activity 17-4 REVIEW Decision-Making Activity 17-4 EXTEND Enrichment Activity 17-4 EXTEND Lesson Plan 17-4 Guided Reading and Writing 17-4 TEACH Reteaching Activity 17-4 REVIEW	Lesson 4 Review, *p. 469* 💿 Vocabulary PuzzleMaker 💿 *ExamView® Assessment Suite*	💿 Vocabulary PuzzleMaker 💿 *ExamView® Assessment Suite* 💿 StudentWorks™ Plus 🕹 Transparency 17-4 **Go Online** glencoe.com

Chapter and Lesson Resources

The *Teen Health* resources are designed for differentiated learning abilities. You may want to use the coded items in this way:

REVIEW —activities to review or reinforce content

TEACH —activities to teach basic concepts

EXTEND —activities to extend or enrich lesson content

 OUT OF TIME?

Use Health Skills Activities *Your Family's Health History,* page 457, and *Coping with Mood Swings,* page 464, or *Developing Good Character,* page 467.

Community Service Opportunities for Teens

One of the developmental tasks of adolescence is becoming interested in and caring about the community. By performing community service, teens not only improve their community, they also meet new people, develop their values, experience different roles, and sample a variety of career choices. Studies have shown that volunteering positively affects students' academic achievement and social health. Community service and volunteering are popular activities for students.

Service opportunities for teens take many forms, from one-time events to ongoing commitments. Community-specific resources, available through the local United Way or other service organizations, can provide a starting place for teens who want to serve as community volunteers.

Explain that community service is a chance to further explore areas of interest. For example, a teen who is considering a teaching career might volunteer as a tutor or in the children's section of the library. When you discuss community service with your students, have students consider their interests and abilities. Many online resources are available to help teachers promote community service to their students.

Strategies for Teaching Heredity

More than 2 million children in the United States are adopted. One-half million children in the United States are in foster care. For these students, and for other students who do not live with their biological families, heredity and genetics can be sensitive issues. The following strategies can help teachers to be sensitive to all family types during the study of heredity:

- **Avoid assignments that use a family tree to show how a particular trait is passed from parent to child.**

- **Avoid questions such as "What traits did you inherit from your parents?" or "In what ways do the members of your family look alike?"**

- **Avoid making assumptions about a student's family based on a student's traits—for example, "Your parents must have blue eyes, too."**

- **Use pictures of families from magazines to illustrate the concept of family resemblance.** Never ask students to use their own family photographs for this type of activity.

- **When an assignment calls for family history, such as the family medical history activity in this chapter, make an alternative assignment available to all students.** Do not single out individual students.

- **Point out the ways that families influence our interests and abilities.** Although these are not biological traits, these are characteristics that family members often share.

- **Use inclusive and unbiased language when describing various types of families.**

Reading Support

Reading Preview

Activating Background Vocabulary Ask students what comes to mind when they hear the terms *heredity* and/or *puberty*. Write student responses separately on the board. Guide students in a discussion of each term, including the differences between those characteristics that are family traits and those brought about by hormonal changes.

FOLDABLES Study Organizer *Dinah Zike's Reading and Study Skills for Teen Health* provides interactive graphic organizers that help students comprehend and retain health concepts as they read. Use the Foldable® on page 449 or find more Foldables® activities for the chapter on **Growth and Development** in the separate booklet, available in the TCR.

Lesson 1　The Beginning of Life

Select, Teach, Activate, Review, and Revisit (STARR) Select important vocabulary terms from **The Beginning of Life**, and have students write the terms on note cards. Teach the terms to the students prior to reading. Activate the terms by discussing them in context as students read. Review the terms often. Revisit the terms over the next few weeks.

Lesson 2　Heredity and Environment

Directed Reading/Thinking Activity (DR/TA) Have students divide a paper into four parts, titled *What I know, What I think I know, What I think I'll learn,* and *What I know I learned*. Have students skim the lesson, discuss what they know about the differences between heredity and environment, and fill in the first three columns of the chart. Direct students to finish the chart as they read the lesson.

Lesson 3　From Childhood to Adolescence

SQ3R Guide students to: 1) Survey—scan the title and headings of the lesson. 2) Question—restate each heading in the form of a question. Reword **"Stages of Development"** to "What are the stages of development?" 3) Read—find out about the stages of childhood, adolescence, and adulthood. 4) Recite—record information about the stages of development in a notebook. 5) Review—go over notes and summarize each section.

Lesson 4　Adulthood and Aging

Think Aloud 1) Ask students to predict what **Stages of Adulthood** will be about. 2) Model images you form while reading—"I see people working, getting married, having kids." 3) Link the reading to your experience—"This reminds me of when my grandpa retired from his job." 4) Note questions—"I don't understand this part about measuring age"—and model strategies to clarify—"I think I'll reread this page to clarify this issue."

Post Reading

Nonverbal Presentations Direct students to use movement, placement, gestures, facial expressions, and other nonverbal cues to convey meaning to an audience in a presentation interpreting the stages of life, from the beginning of life, through childhood and adolescence, to the stages of adulthood and aging.

Key for Using the Teacher Wraparound Edition

Use this key to help you identify the different types of prompts found in the Teacher Wraparound Edition.

R **Reading Strategies** activities help you teach reading skills and vocabulary.

C Critical Thinking strategies help students apply and extend what they have learned.

U **Universal Access** activities provide differentiated instruction for students learning to speak English, along with suggestions for teaching various types of learners.

HS **Health Skills Practice** activities reinforce Health Skills concepts and help students apply these skills in their everyday lives.

W **Writing Support** activities provide writing opportunities to help students comprehend the text.

AL **Active Learning** strategies provide a variety of activities for presenting lesson content, including Quick Demos and engaging classroom projects that get students actively involved.

Key to Ability Levels

Teaching Strategies and activities have been coded for ability level and appropriateness.

AL Activities for students working above grade level

OL Activities for students working on grade level

BL Activities for students working below grade level

EL Activities for English Learners

Symbols

 Transparencies

🔘 CD-ROM

 glencoe.com

🗁 Print Resources

CHAPTER 17

Growth and Development

Chapter at a Glance

Lesson 1 identifies the difference between an organ and a system, explains how a single cell develops into a baby, describes the stages of birth, and explains how to access information about the physical and emotional changes a pregnant female experiences.

Lesson 2 explains how characteristics are passed from parent to child, identifies factors that could cause birth defects, and explains the importance of prenatal care.

Lesson 3 explains Erikson's stages of life, identifies some developmental tasks facing adolescents, describes the stages of childhood, and explains the importance of practicing stress management skills to help students cope with mood swings.

Lesson 4 identifies the three stages of adulthood; explains the difference between chronological, biological, and social age; and describes how the health triangle can be maintained during later years.

R Reading Strategy

Interpreting the Photo Have students examine the photo. Ask: What can you learn by interacting with your friends? *Sample answer: I can develop better social skills, learn how to compromise, and learn how to relate to many different people.*

448

CHAPTER 17
Growth and Development

Chapter Preview

▲ *Working with the Photo*

Your teen years are just one of several life stages you will go through. **Can you think of three other stages of life?**

448

🏃 Universal Access

Differentiated Learning Glencoe provides teacher support and student materials for all learners in the health classroom.

● Spanish Glosario and chapter summaries assist English Language Learners.
● *Reading Tutor* and related worksheets support reluctant readers.

● Universal Access strategies throughout the Teacher Wraparound Edition and Fast Files help you present materials for gifted students, at-risk students, physically impaired students, and those with behavior disorders or learning disabilities.

Start-Up Activities

Before You Read

What do you already know about growth and development? Take the short Health Quiz on this page. Keep a record of your answers.

HEALTH QUIZ Answer *true* or *false* to each of the following statements:

1. All human life begins as a single cell.
2. Your eye color is inherited from your parents.
3. Physical changes are not common in adolescence.
4. Late adulthood is the time most people start families.

ANSWERS: 1. true 2. true 3. false 4. false

FOLDABLES Study Organizer

As You Read

Make this Foldable® to help you organize what you learn in Lesson 1 about the beginnings of life. Begin with a plain sheet of 8½" × 11" paper.

1 Fold the sheet of paper along the long axis, leaving a half-inch tab along the side.

2 Turn the paper, fold it in half, and then fold it in half again.

3 Unfold and cut the top layer along the three fold lines. This makes four tabs.

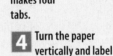

4 Turn the paper vertically and label the tabs as shown.

Cells
Tissues
Organs
Body Systems

Under the appropriate tab, write down major concepts related to cells, tissues, organs, and body systems.

Go Online Visit **glencoe.com** and use the eFlashcards to preview Chapter 17 vocabulary terms.

449

FOCUS

Activating Prior Knowledge

What I Know Ask students to define the term *body system*. Then have students identify human body systems, which were discussed in Chapter 16.

Guide to Reading

Building Vocabulary
- Have students skim the lesson to find the meanings of the terms *embryo* and *fetus*. Have students write a sentence that compares and contrasts these terms.
- Use Vocabulary PuzzleMaker to reinforce vocabulary terms.

Reading Strategy
Analyzing a Graphic Have each student write his or her summary as a series of bullet points. Explain that summarizing and sequencing the steps of a process can help to clarify how the steps are related.

Study Organizer Have students use their Foldables® as they read Lesson 1.

Q *uick Write*

Ask volunteers to share their completed Quick Writes with the class. Use the students' responses to assess their prior knowledge of fertilization and development.

450

The Beginning of Life

Guide to Reading

● Building Vocabulary
Write the terms below in your notebook. As you read the lesson, write down their definitions.

- fertilization (p. 450)
- egg cell (p. 450)
- sperm cell (p. 450)
- uterus (p. 452)
- embryo (p. 452)
- fetus (p. 452)
- placenta (p. 453)
- umbilical cord (p. 453)
- cervix (p. 454)

● Focusing on the Main Ideas
In this lesson, you will learn to
- **identify** the building blocks of life.
- **explain** how a single cell develops into a baby.
- **describe** the stages of birth.
- **access** information on the physical and emotional changes a pregnant female experiences.

● Reading Strategy
Analyzing a Graphic Using Figure 17.2 on page 452, summarize the process that a fetus goes through during the months before its birth.

FOLDABLES | **Study Organizer** Use the Foldable® on p. 449 as you read this lesson.

Q *uick Write*

Write a short paragraph explaining why you think some twins are identical and others are not.

Building Blocks of Life

The cell is the basic unit of life. The human body is composed of trillions of cells, each with its own job to do. Cells that do similar jobs come together to form tissues. Tissues combine to form organs, and organs group together to form body systems. **Figure 17.1** illustrates how cells organize themselves into body systems.

Fertilization

Your body started as a single fertilized cell. **Fertilization** is *the joining together of a male sperm cell and a female egg cell,* to form one cell. *The reproductive cell from the female that joins with a sperm cell to make a new life* is called an **egg cell.** *The cell from the male that enters the egg cell during fertilization* is called a **sperm cell.**

Fertilization takes place in the mother's reproductive system. The egg cell is fertilized in one of her two fallopian tubes. As soon as a sperm cell meets the egg cell, a film is produced around the egg. This prevents any additional sperm cells from entering the egg cell. Once fertilization takes place, a new life begins to grow.

Lesson 1 Resources

📁 **Chapter FAST FILE Resources**
Guided Reading and Writing 17-1
Concept Mapping Activity 17-1
Cross-Curriculum Activity 17-1
Reteaching Activity 17-1
Enrichment Activity 17-1
Lesson Quiz 17-1

Technology
🔲 Transparency 17-1
💿 Audio Summaries
💿 *ExamView® Assessment Suite*
💿 Vocabulary PuzzleMaker
💿 StudentWorks™ Plus

G⊙ Online

FIGURE 17.1

R **FROM CELL TO SYSTEM**

Cells work together in the body to create tissues, organs, and systems.
Can you name some of the body's organs?

1. Cells
- Cells are the basic building blocks of life. There are many different kinds of cells. Some cells come from the stomach where they play a role in digestion. Other kinds of cells in the body include heart, skin, and nerve cells.

AL

2. Tissues
- When cells get together to do similar jobs, tissues are created. There are many kinds of tissues in the body, including muscle tissue and brain tissue.

3. Organ
- When tissues combine to form a structure designed to do a particular job, an organ is created. Examples of organs in your body include the heart, kidneys, lungs, and brain.

U

4. Body System
- When organs work together to do a particular job, they form a body system. For example, the circulatory system shown here is made up of the heart, blood vessels, and blood. These components work together to carry nutrients throughout the body. Other systems in the body, such as the digestive system, have their own jobs. Systems cooperate with one another to keep your body balanced and running smoothly.

Lesson 1: The Beginning of Life **451**

TEACH

R Reading Strategy

Analyzing a Graphic Have students examine **Figure 17.1**. Ask: Name two organs in the human body that contain muscle tissue. Sample answers: *heart, stomach* How are organs related to body systems? *Organs make up body systems.* **OL**

AL Active Learning

Quick Demo Show students a hard-boiled chicken egg. Explain that the egg represents a single cell. Remind students that cells have different sizes and shapes, which are related to the cell's function. **OL**

U Universal Access

Reluctant Readers and Writers Have students work in four groups. Assign each group one of the levels of organization shown in the figure. Challenge students to become experts in their assigned topic. Ask each group to teach the other members of the class about its assigned topic. **BL**

FITNESS ZONE

New Life and Physical Fitness As students discuss fertilization and pregnancy, they should recognize the importance of a mother's good physical health. Refer students to the *Fitness Zone Handbook.* Have them review *Planning a Routine.* Ask: How can a regular fitness routine help prepare a female for a healthy pregnancy? Why does physical fitness make pregnancy and birth easier for the mother? **For more information, see *Fitness Zone Handbook* pages xviii–1 or visit the Fitness Zone at glencoe.com.**

Caption Answer

Photo Caption heart, kidneys, lungs, brain

Growth During Pregnancy

Once an egg cell is fertilized, it travels from the fallopian tube to the uterus. The **uterus** (YOO·tuh·ruhs) is *a pear-shaped organ inside a female's body where the embryo is protected and nourished.* The egg cell begins to divide during a process known as *mitosis.* After three weeks, an embryo is formed. An **embryo** is *the developing organism from fertilization to about the eighth week of its development.* The embryo attaches itself to the wall of the mother's uterus. The cells then continue to divide into cells that do specific jobs.

Over time, cells combine to form tissues. Tissues that do similar jobs combine to form organs, and organs combine to form body systems. By the end of the eighth week, the embryo's organs have started to develop. The embryo is now called a **fetus**—*the developing organism from the end of the eighth week until birth.* The fetus will continue to grow and develop for about nine months. **Figure 17.2** shows how the embryo and fetus develop during those months.

▼ FIGURE 17.2

NINE MONTHS OF DEVELOPMENT

In just nine months, a single cell develops into a full-grown baby. **How big is the fetus at the end of the fifth month?**

End of First Month
The heart, digestive system, backbone, and spinal cord begin to form. The embryo is .25 of an inch long.

End of Second Month
The heart of the fetus begins to beat. The eyes, nose, lips, tongue, ears, and teeth are forming. The fetus is now up to 1 and one-eighth inches long.

End of Third Month
Most of the organs and tissues are developed. Arms, hands, fingers, legs, feet, and toes are fully formed. The heartbeat can be heard. The fetus can weigh up to 1 ounce and can be up to 3 inches in length.

End of Fourth Month
The reflexes are developing. The fetus can suck and swallow. The gender can be determined. The fetus can weigh up to 7 ounces and can be up to 7 inches long.

End of Fifth Month
Hair begins to grow on the head. The mother begins to feel the fetus move. Eyebrows, eyelashes, and eyelids appear. The fetus can weigh up to 1 pound and can be up to 10 inches long.

452

TECHNOLOGY AND HEALTH

Assisted Reproductive Technologies There are many conditions that can cause a couple to be unable to conceive a child, including untreated STDs. Some technologies that are used to overcome infertility, including in vitro fertilization (IVF) and gamete intra-fallopian transfer (GIFT), require both the egg and the sperm to be manipulated in a medical laboratory. In other techniques, such as intrauterine insemination, only the sperm is manipulated in the medical laboratory. In these techniques, fertilization occurs in the female's body.

Growth Inside the Uterus

In order for a fetus to develop, it must get food from its mother. The fetus receives nourishment through the placenta. The **placenta** (plu·SEN·tuh) is *a thick, rich tissue that lines the walls of the uterus during pregnancy and that nourishes the fetus.* The fetus gets food and oxygen through a blood vessel in the **umbilical** (uhm·BIL·i·kuhl) **cord,** *a tube that connects the mother's placenta to the fetus.* The umbilical cord also carries away the wastes produced by the growing fetus.

Substances such as tobacco, alcohol, and other drugs can do harm to a fetus. For that reason, females should avoid using harmful substances when they are pregnant.

Reading Check **Compare** What is the difference between an embryo and a fetus?

Go Online

Visit **glencoe.com** and complete the Interactive Study Guide for Lesson 1.

U **Universal Access**

English Learners Have students use index cards or science glossaries to record definitions for each of the lesson vocabulary terms. Have students work in pairs with English-proficient students to practice pronouncing the lesson vocabulary terms. **EL**

W **Writing Support**

Expository Writing Have students use the information in the text to write expository paragraphs about fetal growth and development. Remind students that expository writing is used to share knowledge or to teach others. Have students review their work to check for proper capitalization, spelling, and grammar. **OL**

Reading Check

Answer *Embryo* is the term used to describe a developing organism from fertilization to eight weeks of development. *Fetus* is the term for the developing organism from the end of eight weeks until birth.
Answer, p. 454 During stage two of birth, the cervix continues to dilate and contractions become very strong.

End of Sixth Month
The fetus can open its eyes for short periods of time. The fetus can weigh up to 2 pounds and can be up to 14 inches long.

End of Seventh Month
The fetus has red and wrinkled skin. The organs are maturing. The fetus can weigh up to 3.5 pounds and can be up to 16 inches long.

End of Eighth Month
The fetus is growing quickly. There is tremendous brain development. Movement is strong enough to be seen from the outside. The fetus can weigh up to 6 pounds and can be up to 18 inches long.

End of Ninth Month
The fetus is now fully developed and can survive outside the mother's body. The fetus changes positions to prepare for birth. The baby weighs at least 7 pounds and at least 19 inches long.

Lesson 1: The Beginning of Life **453**

HEALTH LITERACY

Premature Infants Premature birth can occur for a number of reasons, including alcohol and drug use, infections or medical conditions of the mother, a multiple pregnancy, or abnormalities of the mother's uterus. In the United States, approximately 10 percent of babies are born prematurely. Premature babies are at risk for many health problems related to underdeveloped body systems. However, premature babies who have a birth weight of two pounds or more have a 90 percent chance of survival.

Caption Answer

Photo Caption, page 454 Contractions are strongest in stage two of birth.

ASSESS

Assessment Resources

Lesson Review Quiz
- *ExamView*
- Fast Files Activities
- Online Quizzes and Activities

Reteaching

- Assign Concept Map 17-1 or Reteaching Activity 17-1 in the Fast Files.
- Have students make a graphic organizer that shows how cells, tissues, organs, and body systems are related.

Enrichment

- Assign Enrichment Activity 17-1 in the Fast Files.
- Have students research differentiation, the process by which cells assume different structures to perform different functions in the body. Have each student write a paragraph that explains differentiation.

CLOSE

Ask a volunteer to describe the function of the umbilical cord. Then ask students to explain why it is important for pregnant females to avoid alcohol, tobacco, and drugs.

▲ Nine months after becoming pregnant, a woman gives birth to her baby. **In which stage of birth are contractions the strongest?**

Stages of Birth

After growing and developing for about nine months inside its mother's body, a fetus is ready to be born. Birth occurs in three stages:

- **Stage One.** The muscles in the uterus begin to squeeze and release gently. These muscle movements, called contractions, mean that birth is starting. At this point, *the entry to the uterus,* called the **cervix,** begins to *dilate,* or open.

- **Stage Two.** The cervix continues to dilate, preparing for the baby to pass through. Contractions become very strong, helping to push the baby through the cervix, down the birth canal, and out of the mother's body.

- **Stage Three.** Once the baby is born, the placenta is no longer needed. The muscles of the uterus keep contracting until the placenta is pushed out of the mother's body.

 Recall What happens during stage two of birth?

Lesson 1 Review

After You Read

Review this lesson for new terms, major headings, and Reading Checks.

What I Learned

1. **Vocabulary** Define *fertilization.*

2. **Identify** What structure carries food and oxygen from the mother's body to her developing fetus?

3. **Recall** How is an organ different from a body system?

Thinking Critically

4. **Analyze** How does a woman know that her baby is ready to be born?

5. **Apply** Janice is thinking about having a baby, but she likes to smoke cigarettes. Based on what you learned in this lesson, what advice would you give her?

Applying Health Skills

6. **Accessing Information** A pregnant woman experiences many physical and emotional changes. Use reliable sources to learn more about these changes. Make a list of some of the physical and emotional changes that occur during pregnancy.

 For more Lesson Review Activities, go to **glencoe.com.**

Lesson 1 Review Answers

1. Fertilization is the joining together of two special cells, one from each parent, to form one cell.

2. The umbilical cord carries food and oxygen to a developing fetus.

3. Organs are formed from tissues. Body systems are groups of organs that work together.

4. A pregnant female knows her baby is ready to be born when she has muscle contractions.

5. Janice should stop smoking before she becomes pregnant because tobacco harms the fetus.

6. Help students locate reliable sources to use for their research.

Lesson 2

Heredity and Environment

Guide to Reading

● **Building Vocabulary**
Review the terms below. See if you can determine which terms are related to heredity and which terms are related to environment.

- heredity (p. 455)
- chromosomes (p. 456)
- genes (p. 456)
- genetic disorder (p. 456)
- environment (p. 456)
- prenatal care (p. 457)
- birth defects (p. 458)

● **Focusing on the Main Ideas**
In this lesson, you will learn to

- **explain** how characteristics are passed from parent to child.
- **identify** factors that could cause birth defects.
- **explain** the importance of prenatal care.
- **access** information on your family's health history.

● **Reading Strategy**
Finding the Main Idea Read the main headings in this lesson. For each heading, write one sentence that describes the main idea.

The One and Only You

Each and every person is different. This means that no two people share exactly the same looks, personality, or abilities. Many factors influence the way a person develops. Some factors are related to heredity, and others are environmental factors.

Heredity

Heredity is *the passing of traits from parents to their children.* Traits include characteristics such as eye color, hair color, and body shape. Inherited traits can also include talents and abilities. Children can also inherit a tendency to develop certain diseases and other health problems from their parents.

Quick Write

What steps should a pregnant woman take to care for herself and her developing baby?

▶ The genetic information passed from parent to child can mean that they look a lot alike. **What are some of the physical traits that this parent and child share?**

455

Lesson 2 Resources

📁 **Chapter *FAST FILE* Resources**
Guided Reading and Writing 17-2
Concept Mapping Activity 17-2
Cross-Curriculum Activity 17-2
Reteaching Activity 17-2
Enrichment Activity 17-2
Lesson Quiz 17-2

Technology
🔋 Transparency 17-2
📄 Audio Summaries
💿 *ExamView®* Assessment Suite
📄 Vocabulary PuzzleMaker
💿 StudentWorks™ Plus

FOCUS

Activating Prior Knowledge

What I Know Ask students to explain why medical care is important for all people. Tell students that this lesson includes information on specific medical care for pregnant females and explain why medical care is important in maintaining a healthy environment for developing babies.

Guide to Reading

Building Vocabulary
- Explain that the word part *pre-* means "before" and the word part *-natal* means "birth." Have students relate this to the meaning of the term *prenatal care.*
- Use Vocabulary PuzzleMaker to reinforce vocabulary terms.

Reading Strategy
Finding the Main Idea After students have completed the Reading Strategy activity, have them work in pairs to review the main ideas of the lesson.

Quick Write

Ask students to identify steps named in their answers that would be good health advice for pregnant females.

TEACH

Comparing and Contrasting
Have students compare
and contrast traits that can
be passed from parents to
children with those that are
due to environmental factors.
Ask students to identify traits
from each category, and
record their responses in two
lists on the board. Explain
to students the phrase
nature versus nurture. Have
a class discussion of the
ways in which heredity and
environment affect all of an
individual's characteristics.
OL

Academic Vocabulary

Features Have students
read the definition and the
example sentence. Then
ask students to name facial
features. They might, for
example, mention eyes, nose,
mouth, chin, and forehead.
You will find academic
vocabulary activities in the
Student Activities Workbook.

Reading Check

Answer Genes are the
basic unit of heredity.

Caption Answers

Photo Caption, p. 455 skin
color, hair color, and eyes
are similar
Photo Caption, this page
through the umbilical cord

▲ A fetus needs
nourishment to grow.
**How does a fetus
receive the food and
oxygen it needs?**

Academic Vocabulary

features (FEE churs) *(noun)*
characteristics, traits. *Juan
and his twin sister, Juanita,
have the same physical
features.*

Traits are passed on through chromosomes and genes. **Chromosomes**
are *threadlike structures found within
the nucleus of a cell that carry the codes
for inherited traits.* All but two kinds
of cells in the human body have 46
chromosomes positioned in pairs.
Sperm and egg cells contain only
23 chromosomes. When a sperm and
egg cell combine, the newly formed
cell will have 46 chromosomes—23
from the sperm cell and 23 from the
egg cell.

The tiny bits of information carried
in chromosomes are called **genes**—*the
basic units of heredity.* Genes carry codes
for traits such as eye color and height. Each child inherits different
combinations of chromosomes and genes from his or her parent.
This means that even children with the same parents do not look
exactly the same, or have the same personality.

R

Genetic Disorders

When the genes from one or both parents are abnormal or
changed in some way a baby can be born with a **genetic** (juh·
NE·tik) **disorder.** This is *a disorder caused partly or completely by
a defect in genes.* A defect is a flaw or the absence of something
needed.

Genetic disorders can occur when a fertilized egg has more
or fewer than 46 chromosomes. For example, people with Down
syndrome have an extra chromosome that causes them to have
certain facial **features** and learning disabilities.

Other genetic disorders are caused by abnormal or defective
genes. Sickle-cell anemia is a blood disorder caused by an abnormal gene. People with this disorder have abnormally shaped red
blood cells that can block blood vessels and cause pain in the
bones and joints.

 Reading Check **Explain** What role do genes play in heredity?

Environment

As a fetus develops, its health is affected by its environment.
Environment is *the sum total of a person's surroundings.* A fetus's
environment is its mother's uterus. If the mother is unhealthy or
engages in risky behaviors, the fetus can be affected. A healthy
mother is more likely to have a healthy baby.

HEALTH LITERACY

Mitosis and Meiosis Human body cells are
formed by the process of mitosis, in which
a cell's chromosomes duplicate before the
cell divides. This process results in new
cells with two sets of chromosomes in
each. Egg cells and sperm cells are formed
by the process of meiosis. In this process,
a cell with 46 chromosomes duplicates its
chromosomes, divides, and then divides
again without undergoing chromosome
duplication. In this way, egg cells and
sperm cells that contain 23 chromosomes
are formed.

Health Skills Activity

Accessing Information

Your Family's Health History

Researching your family's health history will let you know if you are at risk for developing certain diseases. It will also help you make healthy decisions that can prevent or lower your risk of disease. One way to learn about the health histories of family members is to create a questionnaire and ask them to fill it out. You will want to know what diseases or other health problems your family members have now or have had in the past.

On Your Own

Brainstorm a list of questions to include on a health history questionnaire. Create the questionnaire and give it to your parents, their siblings, and—if possible—your grandparents. Also ask your grandparents about diseases or other health problems their parents may have had.

Prenatal Care

AL When a female learns that she is pregnant, it is important that she begin prenatal care right away. **Prenatal** (pree·NAY·tuhl) **care** includes *steps taken to provide for the health of a pregnant female and her baby.* Prenatal care includes regular visits to an obstetrician (ahb·stuh·TRI·shuhn). This is a doctor whose specialty is the care of a pregnant female and her unborn child. During a regular visit, the obstetrician may look at the baby using ultrasound. This technology uses sound waves to form a picture of the fetus in its mother's uterus. Doctors use these pictures to check the growth of the fetus and to detect any problems that might exist. A good prenatal program also includes the following positive health behaviors:

- Eating healthful foods
- Participating in moderate exercise
- Getting plenty of rest
- Avoiding alcohol, tobacco, and other drugs
- Talking to a doctor or other health care provider before taking any medicines

 Reading Check **List** Name two health behaviors that are part of a good prenatal program.

Dealing with Sensitive Issues

Students with Genetic Disorders Due to the large number of genetic disorders that affect humans, it is likely that one or more students in your class will have a genetic disorder. When discussing genetic disorders, use sensitive and correct terminology. While some genetic disorders vary in prevalence between cultural or racial groups, it is never appropriate to categorize a particular disease as a problem solely for those of a particular group.

Health Skills Activity

Accessing Information

Your Family's Health History

Use the following strategies to help students complete the activity:

- Help students develop questions that will allow them to discover their family's health history.
- Be sensitive to students who are not in a traditional family, and those who may have no access to their family's medical history. Have an alternative assignment available for any student who cannot complete the survey.
- Caution students to keep personal family information private. The health history questionnaire should be for use at home and not to be turned in to the teacher. **OL**

AL Active Learning

Infomercials Have students work in small groups to make infomercials that describe positive health behaviors that can help mothers have healthy babies. If possible, have each group prepare a video of its infomercial. Ask students to present their infomercials to the class and to other students at the same grade level. **OL**

Reading Check

Answer Good prenatal care includes regular medical checkups, moderate exercise, plenty of rest, eating healthful foods, and avoiding harmful substances.

HS Health Skills Practice

Accessing Information Have students use print or online resources to research the effects of drugs, alcohol, and tobacco on developing fetuses. Remind students of the characteristics of reliable health information found online or in print. Have each student prepare a brief oral report summarizing his or her findings. **OL**

Caption Answers

Photo Caption, this page *Sample answer:* Prenatal care and genetic factors are two factors that determine if a baby will be born healthy.
Photo Caption, p. 459 *Sample answer:* Medicines, alcohol, nutrition, infections, and STDs can all affect the health of an unborn child.

ACTIVITY
Careers for the 21st Century

Genetic Counselor

Genetic counselors help people who are dealing with a genetic disorder. Genetic counselors will always be in demand because people with genetic disorders, and their families, need specialized support that other counselors are not qualified to provide. If you are interested in becoming a genetic counselor, you should study human growth and development, and genetic disorders.

What kind of skills does a genetic counselor need? Go to *Career Corner* at **glencoe.com** to find out.

▼ Using alcohol during pregnancy can result in premature birth and low birth weight. **What factors help determine whether or not a baby will be born healthy?**

Birth Defects

Birth defects are *abnormalities present at birth that cause physical or mental disability or death.* Good prenatal care can help prevent birth defects. Some birth defects, however, are caused by genetic disorders or problems with the fetus's environment. For example, certain infections during pregnancy can cause birth defects.

The following are six kinds of environmental factors that can contribute to a birth defect:

Poor Nutrition

One way a mother can make sure she has a healthy baby is to eat well while she is pregnant. While in the uterus, the fetus relies on its mother for all of its needs. If a mother has an unhealthy diet, her baby could be born prematurely, or too soon. The baby may also have a low birth weight and is at risk of developing physical and mental problems.

Alcohol Use

Everything a pregnant woman drinks is carried in her blood to the fetus. Alcohol makes it difficult for the baby to get the oxygen and nourishment it needs for cell development. If a woman drinks during pregnancy, her baby may develop fetal alcohol syndrome (FAS). Children born with FAS may have physical problems and learning disabilities. Women who are pregnant, or want to become pregnant, should avoid using alcohol.

Medicine and Other Drugs

Medicines and other drugs affect both the mother and her baby. Pregnant women should take only medicines that are approved by a doctor or other health care provider. If a pregnant woman takes certain illegal drugs or prescription drugs, her baby may be born with a drug addiction.

Infections

When a pregnant woman develops an infection, it can sometimes cause serious harm to the fetus. For example, if a woman develops Rubella (German measles) during pregnancy, her baby might be born deaf or suffer from other health problems. To avoid serious problems, women should be vaccinated against certain diseases before they become pregnant.

HS

HEALTH LITERACY

Pregnancy and Secondhand Smoke According to researchers, secondhand smoke exposure causes fetal damage almost identical to the damage caused by maternal smoking. Babies born to mothers who were exposed to secondhand smoke are also more likely to have a low birth weight, which indicates slow fetal growth. Ask students to use this information in a letter to the editor encouraging cities and businesses to provide smoke-free areas for those who wish to avoid secondhand smoke.

▶ Smoking during pregnancy can negatively affect a fetus's health. **What other behaviors during pregnancy affect the health of the unborn child?**

SURGEON GENERAL'S WARNING: Smoking By Pregnant Women May Result in Fetal Injury, Premature Birth, And Low Birth Weight.

Tobacco

When a pregnant woman smokes or spends time around smokers, she risks damaging the health of her unborn child. Tobacco can have a negative effect on a fetus's growth and cause it to be born prematurely. Babies whose mothers smoke while pregnant are also at risk of having a low birth weight.

STDs

Certain sexually transmitted diseases (STDs) can be passed from a mother to her fetus, causing serious health problems. Herpes and syphilis are two examples. A mother infected with herpes or syphilis may not even know it because there may be no visible symptoms. STDs can cause brain damage, blindness, and even death. A pregnant woman who thinks she might have an STD should talk to her doctor immediately.

Go Online

Visit **glencoe.com** and complete the Interactive Study Guide for Lesson 2.

Lesson 2 Review

After You Read

Review this lesson for new terms, major headings, and Reading Checks.

What I Learned

1. *Vocabulary* Define *prenatal care*.

2. *Identify* What are the structures in the nucleus of every cell that carry genetic information?

3. *Give Examples* List two substances that could harm a fetus if its mother uses them while she is pregnant.

Thinking Critically

4. *Analyze* Why should a pregnant female be concerned if she gets sick before she has her baby?

5. *Apply* Cynthia's aunt just learned that she is pregnant. Cynthia knows that her aunt wants to do everything she can to have a healthy baby. What could Cynthia do to help her aunt stay healthy?

Applying Health Skills

6. *Advocacy* Create a brochure that will encourage pregnant women to practice positive health behaviors during their pregnancies. Include actions they can take to stay healthy as well as behaviors they should avoid.

Go Online For more Lesson Review Activities, go to **glencoe.com**.

Lesson 2: Heredity and Environment **459**

ASSESS

Assessment Resources

Lesson Review Quiz
- *ExamView*
- Fast Files Activities
- Online Quizzes and Activities

Reteaching

● Assign Concept Map 17-2 or Reteaching Activity 17-2 in the Fast Files.

● Have students work in pairs to discuss how heredity, chromosomes, and genes are related and how they can impact a person's life. Call on several pairs of students to share their responses.

Enrichment

● Assign Enrichment Activity 17-2 in the Fast Files.

● Have students interview a doctor, nurse, or other medical professional to find out more about good health care for pregnant females. Have students prepare written summaries of their interviews.

CLOSE

Ask volunteers to identify environmental factors that can contribute to birth defects.

Lesson 2 Review Answers

1. Prenatal care includes steps a pregnant female takes to provide for her own health and the health of her baby.

2. Chromosomes are the structures that carry genetic information.

3. *Sample answers:* drugs, tobacco, alcohol, and over-the-counter medicines

4. *Sample answers:* Certain infections can harm the baby.

5. *Sample answers:* offering to exercise with her, helping her to prepare healthy foods, encouraging her to get plenty of rest

6. Have students review the lesson to find information to use in their brochures.

FOCUS

Activating Prior Knowledge

What I Know Ask students to describe physical, social, and mental/emotional characteristics of toddlers and preschoolers.

Guide to Reading

Building Vocabulary
- Point out that a *task* is a duty or a job that needs to be done. Have students relate this to the meaning of the term *developmental tasks*.
- Use Vocabulary PuzzleMaker to reinforce vocabulary terms.

Reading Strategy
Predicting Ask volunteers to share their questions and answers with the class.

Quick Write

After students have completed their lists, ask them to classify the differences as positive or negative. For example, a positive difference might be that an adolescent has more freedom than a child.

Academic Vocabulary

Establish Page 461 states that young adults try to establish close personal relationships. Have a volunteer define the term *establish* for the class. Then have students list synonyms for the word *establish*. (start, institute) **OL**

From Childhood to Adolescence

 Guide to Reading

Building Vocabulary
In your own words, write the definition of each of the following terms. Check to see if you are correct as you read the lesson.
- developmental tasks (p. 460)
- infancy (p. 462)
- toddlers (p. 462)
- preschoolers (p. 462)
- puberty (p. 463)

Focusing on the Main Ideas
In this lesson, you will learn to
- **explain** Erikson's stages of life.
- **identify** some developmental tasks facing adolescents.
- **describe** the stages of childhood.
- **practice** stress management to help you cope with mood swings.

Reading Strategy
Predicting Look over the headings in this lesson. Write a question that you think the lesson will answer. When you are finished reading the lesson, see if your question has been answered.

uick Write

Make a list of all the ways you think adolescence is different from childhood.

Stages of Development

From the day a baby is born, he or she begins to develop in all three areas of the health triangle. The process of developing from a baby to an adult is often explained in stages or steps. According to developmental psychologist Erik Erikson, there are eight stages in the human life cycle. Each stage has its own **developmental tasks.** These are *events that need to happen in order for you to grow toward becoming a healthy, mature adult.* The eight stages of life and their developmental tasks are illustrated in **Figure 17.3.**

When people master the developmental tasks in one stage and move on to the next stage, they improve their emotional and social health. They build confidence and are able to relate to others.

◄ One developmental task of adolescence is to find and express your unique self. **What makes you unique?**

Lesson 3 Resources

📂 **Chapter *FAST FILE* Resources**
Guided Reading and Writing 17-3
Concept Mapping Activity 17-3
Health Lab 17-3
Reteaching Activity 17-3
Enrichment Activity 17-3
Lesson Quiz 17-3

Technology
⚓ Transparency 17-3
🖱 Audio Summaries
⊙ *ExamView® Assessment Suite*
🖱 Vocabulary PuzzleMaker
💿 StudentWorks™ Plus
 Go Online

▼ FIGURE 17.3

R ERIKSON'S STAGES OF LIFE

In each stage, there is a developmental task that involves relating to other people. **What is the developmental task for late childhood?**

❶ Infancy
Birth to 1 year
Characteristic of stage: child must depend on others to meet every need
Developmental task: learn to trust

❷ Early Childhood
1 to 3 years
Characteristic of stage: child is learning to do things on his or her own
Developmental task: to develop the ability to do things for oneself

❸ Middle Childhood
3 to 5 years
Characteristic of stage: child begins to make decisions and to think of and carry out tasks
Developmental task: to develop initiative—the ability to create one's own play

❹ Late Childhood
6 to 12 years
Characteristic of stage: child explores surroundings and masters more difficult skills
Developmental task: to develop interest in performing activities

❺ Adolescence
12 to 18 years
Characteristic of stage: adolescent searches for his or her own identity
Developmental task: to develop a sense of who one is

❻ Early Adulthood (Young Adulthood)
18 to 40 years
Characteristic of stage: young adult tries to establish close personal relationships
Developmental task: to develop intimacy—a strong relationship with another person

❼ Middle Adulthood
40 to 65 years
Characteristic of stage: adult focuses on accomplishment in workplace and is concerned with the well-being of others
Developmental task: to develop the sense of having contributed to society

❽ Late Adulthood (Maturity)
65 years to death
Characteristic of stage: person reflects on and tries to understand meaning of own life
Developmental task: to develop a sense of satisfaction with one's life

HS

Stages of Childhood

The physical and mental/emotional growth that occurs during childhood can be grouped into four stages. These stages are called infancy, early childhood, middle childhood, and late childhood.

Lesson 3: From Childhood to Adolescence **461**

Promoting Coordinated School Health

Counseling and Health Services The school nurse and guidance counselor are excellent resources for students who have questions about their physical, emotional, or social development during adolescence. Invite the school nurse or guidance counselor to speak to the class about the heath services offered at the school. Be certain that students know the procedure for making an appointment with the nurse or guidance counselor if they have questions they would like to discuss.

TEACH

R Reading Strategy

Analyzing a Graphic Ask students to review the contents of **Figure 17.3** in small groups. Have students discuss in their groups how they could help younger family members or neighbors master developmental tasks. Ask: How could a student your age help a child between the ages of 1 and 3 years to develop self-confidence? Sample answer: *I could show patience as the child learns to do things on his or her own.*
OL

HS Health Skills Practice

Goal Setting Ask each student to record some of his or her long-term goals. Ask students to identify the stage of life during which they hope to achieve the identified goals. Then have students write down steps that they could take now in order to achieve their long-term goals.
OL

Caption Answers

Photo Caption, p. 460
Sample answer: Things that make me unique include my ability to sing, my love of movies, and my ability to play basketball well.

Figure Caption, this page
to develop interest in performing activities

U Universal Access

Gifted Students: Enrichment
Have students use print or online resources to research the changes that the human brain undergoes as it grows and changes during childhood. Have students use presentation software to share their findings with the class. **AL**

R Reading Strategy

Organizing Information Have students use index cards to organize the information about the stages of childhood. Have students label a separate index card for each stage. Then have students record three or more bulleted statements on each card, summarizing the information in the text. Students can use their index cards as study aids when they prepare to take the chapter assessment. **OL**

What Teens THINK

How have your friendships changed from elementary to middle school? Read the *What Teens Think* question aloud, and give students five minutes to free-write their personal responses to the question. Assure students that they can keep their responses private if they want. Read aloud the response in the text, and ask volunteers to share their own ideas, based on their free-writes.

What Teens THINK

How have your friendships changed from elementary to middle school?

Your friendships change in many ways. You begin to start new friendships with new people from different schools. You also lose friendships, but in the end you get some benefits and some losses from elementary to middle school.

Cambrielle H.
Monument, CO

Infancy

The first year of life is called **infancy.** During infancy, a child doubles in height and triples in weight. An infant begins to move around, explore, and observe the world. They do this by watching, listening, tasting, and touching. When an infant's needs are met in a loving and consistent way, he or she learns to trust people and feel safe.

Early Childhood

Toddlers are *children between the ages of one and three who are learning to walk and talk.* Toddlers learn to do things on their own like feeding themselves and using the toilet. They can also walk, run, and climb on their own. As children explore and test their abilities, they learn a lot from their failures as well as their successes.

Middle Childhood

Children between the ages of three and five are often called **preschoolers**. This age is a time of curiosity when children ask a lot of questions and use their imaginations. They often enjoy pretending to be adults, so how adults behave around them is important. Preschoolers need lots of encouragement and praise for trying new things. This praise helps them feel good about themselves and builds positive self-esteem. As preschoolers grow, they develop better physical coordination.

Late Childhood

Between the ages of six and eleven, school becomes an important part of most children's lives. At this stage, children become stronger and more coordinated. This is a creative time, and many children put a lot of energy into artistic projects such as drawing and building.

Adolescence

Adolescence is a time when you are no longer a young child, but are not yet an adult. It is the period between the ages of 12 and 18. During adolescence, you will experience many physical, mental/emotional, and social changes. These changes will help prepare you for adulthood.

What Teens Want to Know

What should I know before I babysit an infant? Being familiar with the characteristics and developmental needs of infants can help teens prepare to be good babysitters. Explain that, because infants rely on their caregivers to meet all of their needs, babysitting an infant requires training and a high level of maturity. Provide students with information about Red Cross babysitter-training programs that are available in your community, or work with faculty and staff to develop a babysitter-training program at the school.

Physical Development

The second-fastest period of physical growth is adolescence. These physical changes are the result of puberty. **Puberty** is *the time when you start developing physical characteristics of adults of your gender.* Puberty usually starts between the ages of 8 and 14. Girls typically begin puberty earlier than boys do. However, each individual grows and develops at his or her own rate. So, it is important to respect your peers during this time of change. Many of the physical changes that males and females go through during puberty are listed in **Figure 17.4.** These changes are the result of hormones produced by the body's endocrine system.

▼ FIGURE 17.4

R **PHYSICAL CHANGES DURING PUBERTY**

Males and females go through a variety of changes. **How are they similar and how are they different?**

Female	Both	Male
• Female hormone production increases. • Breasts develop. • Hips get wider. • Uterus and ovaries enlarge. • Ovulation occurs. • Menstruation begins. • Body fat increases.	• Growth spurt occurs. • Acne may appear. • Perspiration increases. • Body hair appears. • Most permanent teeth have come in.	• Male hormone production increases. • Facial hair appears. • The voice gets deeper. • Shoulders broaden. • Muscles develop. • Sperm production begins. • Breasts can become tender and enlarged temporarily. • External genitals enlarge.

Lesson 3: From Childhood to Adolescence   **463**

R **Reading Strategy**

Analyzing a Graphic Have students examine **Figure 17.4**. Ask: The physical changes of puberty happen at different ages in different people. How can differing rates of development cause stress for teens? Sample answer: *A teen who develops much earlier or later than his or her peers might feel embarrassed or stressed.* What is a positive way to deal with stress or questions about physical development? Sample answer: *talk to a parent, guardian, or the school nurse* OL

Cultural Perspectives

Age Variation in the Onset of Puberty In the United States, the age at which females begin the physical changes of puberty has declined over the past few decades. Results of a study published in the journal *Pediatrics* indicate that some American females show physical signs of the early onset of puberty by age 9. Scientists attribute the difference to a combination of genetic and environmental factors, and some consider obesity to be one of the factors.

Caption Answer

Photo Caption *Sample answer:* Males and females both undergo growth spurts; only males develop facial hair.

463

Health Skills Activity

Stress Management

Coping with Mood Swings

Use the following strategies to help students complete the activity:

- Have students discuss in small groups the bulleted suggestions for dealing with mood swings. Challenge students to identify other healthful ways for dealing with mood swings.

- Have each student complete a poster as directed in the text. Ask students to include some of their original tips on their posters.

Reading Check

Answer, p. 465 Approaching life like an adult and establishing a sense of independence are two developmental tasks of adolescence.

U Universal Access

English Learners Ask students to write a journal entry expressing the emotions they have felt over the past week, and what activities helped them manage these emotions. **EL**

Health Skills Activity

Stress Management

Coping with Mood Swings

The mood swings you experience during your teen years can feel like you are on an emotional roller coaster. Below are some tips for dealing with mood swings in healthful ways.

- **Do something nice for yourself.** For example, listen to your favorite music or get together with a friend.
- **Be creative.** Write about what you are feeling or express your emotions through painting or another form of artwork.
- **Get moving.** Physical activities help the body stay in balance. They will also help take your mind off whatever is bothering you.
- **Get some help.** When you are sad or angry it is easy to feel alone. Talk to friends, family, or other trusted adults about what you are feeling.
- **Get some rest.** With all the changes going on in your body, extra rest can really help. Try taking a nap or just relaxing with a book or magazine.
- **Eat well.** Help your body through its many changes by eating nutritious foods.

On Your Own

Create a poster for teens listing healthful ways to cope with mood swings. Include the tips described above and other suggestions you can think of. With permission, hang your posters where other students can see them.

Emotional Development

Emotional changes are a normal part of adolescence. The hormones that control your physical growth and development can also affect your thoughts and feelings. You begin to think and act more independently. You are aware of how your opinions and actions affect others. You might have mood swings, where you are happy one minute and sad the next. Mood swings can be confusing and unpleasant, but they are a normal part of adolescence.

You cannot control your hormones or the emotional changes they cause. You can, however, control your response to these changes. Express your emotions in healthy ways. Talk about your feelings with others. Do activities that help you relax. Listen to music, play sports, take a walk, or spend time with family and friends. Managing your emotions in a healthy way will help you build strong emotional health.

HEALTH LITERACY

Emotions and Adolescence A recent study found that teens read facial expressions differently than adults do. In the study, teens aged 12 to 17 correctly identified faces showing fear only 25 percent of the time (compared with 100 percent for adults). Instead, the teens thought the fearful faces showed anger, confusion, or sadness. MRI scans revealed that the teens used a different part of the brain to process the information than adults normally do. Study authors think that teen brains may not be fully mature and able to process emotions in an adult way until they are in their twenties.

Social Development

As you make the transition from child to adult, you face developmental tasks. These tasks help you develop your self-concept, or the view you have of yourself. They also help you grow socially, by helping you relate to others in a positive way. As you master these developmental tasks, you are preparing for a successful transition to adulthood. Here are some of those tasks:

- Establish independence from your parents and other adults.
- Spend time alone and learn more about yourself.
- Consider what is important to you in life.
- Approach life like an adult, using your intelligence and reason to solve problems.
- Accept your body and its characteristics.
- Form mature relationships with people of both genders.
- Become interested in your community and show that you care about it.

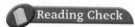 **Reading Check** **Identify** What are two developmental tasks associated with adolescence?

G₀ Online

Visit **glencoe.com** and complete the Interactive Study Guide for Lesson 3.

Lesson 3 Review

 After You Read

Review this lesson for new terms, major headings, and Reading Checks.

What I Learned

1. **Vocabulary** Define *puberty*.

2. **Identify** What are the four main stages of childhood?

3. **Give Examples** List three physical changes that females experience during puberty, and three that males experience.

Thinking Critically

4. **Analyze** Why is it important for adults to support and encourage children?

5. **Apply** Kottiya seems to be on an emotional roller coaster every day. She was cheerful and talkative this morning, but she felt sad and grumpy at lunchtime. All of these emotions leave her feeling confused and worried. What advice would you give Kottiya to help her understand and cope with her mood swings?

Applying Health Skills

6. **Analyzing Influences** Look at several teen magazines. In what ways do the articles, advertisements, and photos try to influence teens? Give an example of a positive influence and an example of a negative influence.

G₀ Online For more Lesson Review Activities, go to **glencoe.com**.

Lesson 3: From Childhood to Adolescence **465**

CHAPTER 17
Lesson 3

ASSESS

Assessment Resources

Lesson Review Quiz
- *ExamView*
- Fast Files Activities
- Online Quizzes and Activities

Reataching

- Assign Concept Map 17-3 or Reteaching Activity 17-3 in the Fast Files.
- Have students work in pairs to write sentences that summarize each of Erikson's eight stages of life.

Enrichment

- Assign Enrichment Activity 17-3 in the Fast Files.
- Have students work in small groups to create video presentations about the stages of childhood. Ask each group to share its video with the class.

CLOSE

Ask students to identify developmental tasks of adolescence. Ask for examples of how teens succeed in this developmental task.

Lesson 3 Review Answers

1. Puberty is the time when teens begin to develop the physical characteristics of adults of their gender.

2. infancy, early childhood, middle childhood, late childhood

3. *Sample answers: females:* menstruation, breast development, ovulation *males:* muscle development, facial hair, sperm production

4. Children need encouragement in order to develop self-esteem.

5. *Sample answer:* Mood swings are a normal part of growing up.

6. Provide teen magazines for students to use for their research.

FOCUS

Activating Prior Knowledge

What I Know Ask students to think about the lives of the adults they know. Then have students identify aspects of being an adult that they are looking forward to.

 Guide to Reading

Building Vocabulary
- Have students make a graphic organizer to show how the lesson vocabulary terms are related.
- Use Vocabulary PuzzleMaker to reinforce vocabulary terms.

Reading Strategy
Organizing Information Have students create a chart with three column headings: *Early Adulthood, Middle Adulthood,* and *Late Adulthood.* Students can add to their charts as they read the lesson.

uick Write

After students have competed their Quick Writes, have them identify reasons why older adults are excellent sources of advice.

Academic Vocabulary

Predictable The text explains that some people move through the stages of adulthood in a predictable sequence. Explain that *predictable* means "able to be known in advance."

466

Lesson 4

Adulthood and Aging

 Guide to Reading

Building Vocabulary
Chrono is the Greek word for "time." Choose the term from the list below that you think describes a person's age by the number of years lived. Write down what you think the definitions are for the other two terms. Check your definitions as you read.
- chronological age (p. 468)
- biological age (p. 468)
- social age (p. 468)

Focusing on the Main Ideas
In this lesson, you will learn to
- **identify** the three stages of adulthood.
- **explain** the difference between chronological, biological, and social age.
- **describe** how to keep your health triangle in balance during your later years.

Reading Strategy
Organizing Information Create a chart that is divided into three parts. Describe one of the stages of adulthood in each of the three parts.

uick Write

Pretend that you are an older person. Write a letter to the person you are now. What kinds of stories or advice would the older you want to share with the younger you?

Stages of Adulthood

Like childhood, adulthood can be divided into stages. These stages are early, middle, and late adulthood. Each stage is marked by certain milestones such as starting a career, raising children, retiring, and so on. While many people go through these stages in a predictable way, some do not. For example, some adults choose to marry later in life or not at all. Some adults retire early, while others continue working as long as they can.

▶ For many people, establishing a career is an important part of early adulthood. **What do you think your goals will be when you reach early adulthood?**

Lesson 4 Resources

📁 **Chapter *FAST FILE* Resources**
Guided Reading and Writing 17-4
Concept Mapping Activity 17-4
Decision-Making Activity 17-4
Reteaching Activity 17-4
Enrichment Activity 17-4
Lesson Quiz 17-4

Technology
⬇ Transparency 17-4
Audio Summaries
ExamView® Assessment Suite
Vocabulary PuzzleMaker
StudentWorks™ Plus
 Online

Early Adulthood

In early adulthood, many people are busy pursuing an education or training for a job or career. They may try several different jobs before they find something they enjoy doing. People form new interests and friendships during this stage. This is also the time when many people choose to get married and start a family. Some people, however, wait until middle adulthood to marry or have children.

Middle Adulthood

At the beginning of this stage, many people are focused on advancing in their jobs. This could mean developing new skills or taking on more responsibility at work. This stage is also a time when many people are raising children. People in middle adulthood are often interested in contributing to their communities. They may volunteer to help young people or raise money for their favorite charity. As people move through middle adulthood, they may begin planning for retirement. Some people may even choose to retire early during this stage.

Late Adulthood

This stage begins around age 65 when many people look forward to retiring from their jobs. When people retire, they often pursue interests they did not have time for while they were working or raising children. Some people continue to work during late adulthood and some pursue new careers. People at this stage may also choose to stay active by doing volunteer work or spending time with their grandchildren. Maintaining good health will help you stay active during late adulthood. Develop good eating and exercise habits now during your teen years. People who develop good habits early are more likely to stick with them later in life.

Reading Check **Compare** What is the difference between early and middle adulthood?

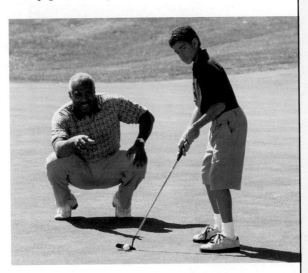

▶ Staying active and being involved with people of all ages is fun for everyone. **Can you think of other sports or activities that older and younger people can enjoy together?**

DEVELOPING
Good Character

Respect

Older adults have a lot of wisdom and experience to share, even though their bodies may not move as fast as yours. You can show respect for older adults by listening and speaking in a polite manner. Make a list of topics you think would be interesting to discuss with older adults.

What are some other ways to show respect to older adults?

TEACH

DEVELOPING
Good Character

Respect
Have students work in small groups to make lists of topics that would be interesting to discuss with older adults. Remind students to consider topics such as changes in technology (an older adult might remember the first televisions, for example), in the local community, and in government. If possible, have students discuss some of these topics with an older adult they know. Have students describe their conversations to the rest of the class. **OL**

Reading Check

Answer During early adulthood, people tend to focus on education, preparing for a career, and on relationships; during middle adulthood, people often focus more on career advancement, contributing to their communities, and on maintaining a family.

Caption Answers
Photo Caption, p. 466
Answers will vary.
Photo Caption, this page
Sample answer: Tennis and board games are two examples.

What Teens Want to Know

How can my health habits affect my adult life? Health habits established during the teen years can have a lasting impact on health. For example, consuming 1,300 milligrams of calcium a day during the teen years can help prevent the development of osteoporosis in late adulthood. Getting enough physical activity as a teen can help prevent cardiovascular disease later in life. Have students set a goal to establish healthy habits that can have a positive impact on their adult years. **OL**

C Critical Thinking

Analyzing After students have read about early adulthood, ask them to recall the developmental tasks of adolescence. Have students discuss the importance of mastering the developmental tasks of adolescence before entering early adulthood. **OL**

Go Online

Finding Common Ground Have students work in small groups to access the resources at **glencoe.com**. Challenge students to identify factors that would contribute to the success of a senior/teen program.

Reading Check

Answer Age measured by lifestyle and connections with others.
Answer, p. 469 Older adults who keep their health triangles balanced make their later years more rewarding and productive.

Caption Answer

Photo Caption *Sample answer:* Establishing good health habits as a teen can help you enjoy good physical, social, and mental/emotional health as an adult.

468

Go Online

Topic: Finding Common Ground

Visit glencoe.com for Student Web Activities to learn more about how communities across the country are bringing seniors and teens together.

Activity: Using the information provided at the link above, create a proposal for a teen-senior program that brings teens and seniors together to benefit your community.

▼ When you stay active, biological age may be younger than chronological age. **How can actions as a teen affect your biological age as you reach late adulthood?**

Measuring Age

Many older people will tell you they feel much younger than their years. As you get older, good health and a positive attitude can help you feel younger than you are. Age can be measured in three different ways:

- **Chronological** (krah·nuh·LAH·ji·kuhl) **age.** You learned earlier that *chrono* is the Greek word for "time." Therefore, your **chronological age** is your *age measured in years.* It is the amount of time you have been living since you were born. You have no control over this number.

- **Biological age.** *Age determined by how well various body parts are working* is your **biological age.** It is affected by diet, exercise, and heredity, among other factors. If you make healthy choices throughout your life, your body will stay healthier longer. However, physical changes will occur naturally as your body ages—no matter how healthy you are.

- **Social age.** *Age measured by your lifestyle and the connections you have with others* is your **social age.** Social age has to do with the activities that society expects you to participate in at certain stages of life. For example, as a young child you were expected to grow, learn, and play. As an adult, you will be expected to work and perhaps contribute to your community. Some adults choose to delay entering the workforce or accepting other responsibilities. These people may have a younger social age than other adults of similar age.

Reading Check
Recall What is social age?

Aging: A Positive Experience

Good health is an important part of the aging process. That is why older people need to pay attention to the health triangle, just as teens do. When adults are careful to keep all sides of their triangle in balance, they help to make their later years rewarding and productive. Here are some tips for keeping your health triangle balanced during late adulthood:

- **Physical health.** Older adults who take care of their physical health usually have a biological age that is younger than their chronological age. They may face fewer illnesses and disabilities that could prevent them from enjoying themselves.

HEALTH LITERACY

Heredity and the Human Lifespan
Researchers at Harvard University and UC Davis have found that a group of genes, called the SIR2 family, influence aging and are thought to impact human lifespan. The genes in the SIR2 family regulate fat,

metabolism, the body's use of energy, and promote the body's defenses. Researchers hope that these discoveries will lead to treatments for diseases and disabilities associated with aging.

► This adult is volunteering to help this child become a skilled reader. **How do they both benefit from this relationship?**

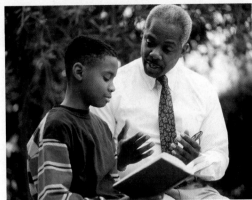

- **Mental and emotional health.** Staying mentally active is just as important as being physically active. Older adults who read, take classes, work, or volunteer are more likely to maintain good mental/emotional health.
- **Social health.** Being involved with other people is important to good social health. When older people stay in contact with family and friends, they are better able to cope with the challenges of aging.

 Reading Check **Identify** Why is it important for older adults to keep their health triangles balanced?

 Go Online
Visit **glencoe.com** and complete the Interactive Study Guide for Lesson 4.

Lesson 4 Review

 After You Read

Review this lesson for new terms, major headings, and Reading Checks.

What I Learned
1. *Vocabulary* Define *social age*.
2. *Compare and Contrast* How is chronological age different from biological age?
3. *Give Examples* List three things that adults are usually focused on during early adulthood.

Thinking Critically
4. *Analyze* How can developing good health habits as a teen affect your adult years?
5. *Apply* Stan thought he would spend all his time working in his garden when he retired. After only a few months, however, he began to feel that gardening was not enough. He missed his friends at work, and he felt lonely. What would you suggest that Stan do to bring his health triangle into balance?

Applying Health Skills
6. *Setting Goals* Choose a goal you would like to accomplish during your adulthood. Using the goal-setting process, develop a plan to achieve your goal. List the steps you can take now as a teen to help you reach this goal.

Go Online For more Lesson Review Activities, go to **glencoe.com**.

Lesson 4: Adulthood and Aging **469**

Lesson 4 Review Answers
1. Social age is age measured by your lifestyle and relationships with others.
2. Chronological age measures age in years; biological age measures physical health.
3. *Sample answers:* education, work, getting married
4. *Sample answer:* Good health habits in the teen years can help you maintain lifelong good health.
5. *Sample answer:* Stan might find a volunteer position or a part-time job.
6. Have students review the steps of goal setting before they complete this activity.

ASSESS

Assessment Resources

Lesson Review Quiz
- *ExamView*
- Fast Files Activities
- Online Quizzes and Activities

Reteaching
- Assign Concept Map 17-4 or Reteaching Activity 17-4 in the Fast Files.
- Ask students to explain, in their own words, the three ways to measure age and how they are different.

Enrichment
- Assign Enrichment Activity 17-4 in the Fast Files.
- Have students research services that are available to older adults in their community. Have students write a report that explains how these services help older adults to meet their needs.

CLOSE
Go around the room and have students identify characteristics of each stage of adulthood.

Caption Answer
Photo Caption The children receive extra attention and guidance, while the adults can feel they are having a positive influence.

Building Health Skills

Coping With the Highs and Lows of Puberty

Skill

Practicing Healthful Behaviors

Activating Prior Knowledge

Ask students to identify emotional changes that are a normal part of adolescence.

- **Objective** After completing the activity, students will be able to use the health skill of goal setting to cope with the emotional changes of puberty.
- **Time** 30 minutes
- **Materials** paper, pencil or pen

Teacher Classroom Resources

📁 Building Health Skills
🖳 Transparency 2-1

Model

- Have students read the Model paragraph.
- Ask volunteers to describe why each of the numbered tips is an effective way to deal with the emotional changes of adolescence.

National Health Standards Addressed

5.8.6, 7.8.1

Building Health Skills

- Accessing Information
- **Practicing Healthful Behaviors**
- Stress Management
- Analyzing Influences
- Communication Skills
- Refusal Skills
- Conflict Resolution
- Decision Making
- Goal Setting
- Advocacy

Why Is It Important to Practice Healthful Behaviors?

When you practice healthful behaviors you take specific actions to stay healthy and avoid risky behaviors. This will help you prevent injury, illness, disease, and other health problems.

One way you can practice healthful behaviors is to learn to deal with the emotional ups and downs during puberty. You can deal with these changes by:

- recognizing what you are feeling and why.
- expressing your feelings in a healthful way.
- finding ways to relax.
- asking for help when you need it.

Coping with the Highs and Lows of Puberty

Follow the Model, Practice, and Apply steps to help you master this important health skill.

❶ Model

Read how Theresa got some practical tips for coping with her changing emotions.

Theresa has been experiencing a lot of highs and lows lately. One morning she woke up in a great mood. At school she felt tired and irritable. By early afternoon, she was feeling happy again. Her good mood lasted until after dinner.

The next day, Theresa talked to the counselor at school. She gave Theresa these practical tips for coping with her changing emotions:

1. Ask yourself what you are feeling and why. For example, I'm feeling irritable because I am sleepy and hungry.
2. Express what you are feeling. Try talking to someone, writing, painting, or dancing.
3. Find a way to relax. Try exercising, listening to music, or deep breathing.
4. Ask for help if you need it. Friends, family, and trusted adults are good resources.

470 Chapter 17: Growth and Development

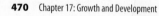 **Teaching Tips**

Handling Emotions Discuss with students the importance of expressing emotions in a positive way. Ask students to share their ideas about this statement: "Emotions are neither good nor bad, right or wrong." Lead a discussion on the ways teens can develop the skill of expressing emotions in healthful ways as students complete the activity. What can make this statement difficult to accept? Why is it important to learn how to deal with different kinds of emotion?

② Practice

Help Shiloh practice healthful behaviors so that she can cope with her emotions.

Shiloh was having another roller-coaster day. She was feeling pretty good until she got to school and discovered that she had gotten a low grade on her English paper. This made her so upset that she ran to the bathroom and cried. She felt like her whole life was a mess.

1. What was Shiloh feeling, and why?
2. What steps can Shiloh take to cope with her changing emotions?
3. What are some healthful ways that Shiloh could express her feelings?
4. Where can Shiloh get help if she needs it?

③ Apply

Apply what you have learned about practicing healthful behaviors when completing the activity below.

Think of a day when your emotions seemed to change. Divide a piece of paper into four parts. Label the parts: morning, afternoon, early evening, and night.

1. Write the emotions you felt and their causes under each part.
2. Tell how you could express each emotion in a positive way.
3. On the back of your paper, list one way that would help you relax.
4. Write the name of someone who can help you when you need it.
5. Explain what mood changes are common during adolescence.

Self-Check

- Did I identify what I was feeling and why?
- Did I tell how to express my emotions in a positive way?
- Did I list one way to relax?
- Did I name someone who can help?
- Did I explain why mood changes are common during adolescence?

Building Health Skills

Building Health Skills 471

Practice

- For the Practice activity, have students work in small groups.
- Ask students to read the Practice section. Have each group prepare written answers to the questions. Remind students to refer to the Model activity as they answer the Practice questions. Ask several groups to share their answers with the class.

Apply/Assess

- Have students work individually to complete the Apply activity as directed in the text.
- Respect student privacy by allowing students to keep their answers confidential.
- You may wish to distribute the Building Health Skills Activity in the Fast Files.

ASSESSMENT SCORING

Using a rubric, student work should meet all criteria to achieve the highest score.

Skills Student work:
- Identify emotions throughout the day.
- Demonstrates strategies to express emotions in healthful ways.

Concepts Student work:
- Includes emotions felt.
- Provides information about coping with emotions.
- Shows healthful ways to express emotions.

Secrets of a Long Life

Objectives

After completing this activity, students will be able to:
- Explain factors that can contribute to longevity
- Identify changes in technology that have occurred during the lifetimes of older Americans

Motivator

Have students identify and describe positive and negative changes that they associate with getting older.

Teaching the Feature

- As students read the feature, have them make a bulleted list of factors that Verona Johnston and her doctors credit for her longevity. Call on students to identify one factor from their lists and explain why that factor contributes to a long life.
- Have students research human population trends in the United States. Have students find out what percentage of the U.S. population is older than 100 years. Then have students create a bar graph that shows the age distribution of the U.S. population.

TIME *health news*

Secrets of a LONG LIFE

Why do some people live long? One woman may have had the answer.

Verona Johnston

What do you eat? Are you a non-smoker? Are you physically active? Do you have a healthy attitude? Do you keep stress under control? How about your genes—have your relatives lived long lives?

Scientists say responses to these questions can indicate how long a person will live. Here is the story of one woman who may have had all the right answers.

A Sharp Mind

Verona Johnston was 114 when she died in December 2004. Until her death, she was the oldest documented person in the United States. TIME spoke with her a few months before she died about her secret of longevity.

"I can remember names pretty well," said Johnston. She lived on her own until age 98 but then moved in with her daughter, Julie Johnston, 81. In fact, Verona Johnston's mind was so sharp until her death, that she solved word jumbles in her head and remembered joke punch lines.

At 114, her vision was nearly gone, and she relied on a cane to take steps, but Johnston could still hear fairly well. Did she dwell on what age had taken away from her? "No. She was never a complainer," says daughter Julie. That attitude may have had much to do with Verona's long life. Not to mention good genes and a whopping dose of good luck.

Small Portions Mean Big Paybacks

Verona had always been big on moderation. At 114, her daily snack consisted of orange juice and exactly one cracker, one cinnamon-drop candy, and one cashew. "That's enough," she insisted.

Johnston never smoked. As for exercise, it was always part of her active lifestyle. Well into her 90s, she climbed up and down seven flights of stairs to her old apartment.

Verona knew how to roll with changes. "Electricity was the most important thing that happened to us," she reflected. The computer was intimidating, but she gave it a whirl. For Verona, every day brought exciting surprises. That curiosity may have been just one more reason for her long and healthy life.

Activity | **Media, Technology, and Culture**

Technology After students have read the feature, have them discuss changes in technology that have occurred in their lifetimes, in the lifetimes of adults such as their parents or guardians, and in the lifetimes of older adults. Have students interview older adults to learn more about the technological changes that have occurred in their lifetimes. Remind students to prepare their interview questions in advance. Have students use presentation software to share their results with the class. **OL**

Reading Review

 Visit glencoe.com to download quizzes and eFlashcards for Chapter 17.

FOLDABLES Study Organizer

Foldables® and Other Study Aids Take out the Foldable® that you created for Lesson 1 and any graphic organizers that you created for Lessons 1–4. Find a partner and quiz each other using these study aids.

Lesson 1 The Beginning of Life

Main Idea The cell is the basic unit of life.

- Cells combine to form tissues, tissues combine to form organs, and organs work together to form body systems.
- Two sex cells, one female and one male, combine to create a fertilized cell that will develop into a baby.
- It takes about nine months for a fetus to develop into a full-grown baby inside the mother's uterus.
- Birth occurs in three stages. Contractions start and grow stronger as the cervix dilates until is large enough for the baby to be pushed out.

Lesson 2 Heredity and Environment

Main Idea Your growth and development are dependent upon heredity and environment.

- Chromosomes and genes carry the information that parents pass on to their children.
- A fetus's environment is its mother's uterus.
- Genetic disorders are problems caused when the genetic material is damaged or changed in some way.
- Birth defects can occur for several reasons, including: poor nutrition, alcohol use, medicines or other drugs, infections, tobacco, and STDs.
- A pregnant female needs to take good care of her body.

Lesson 3 From Childhood to Adolescence

Main Idea Human beings go through stages as they develop from infants to adults.

- There are four stages of childhood: infancy, early childhood, middle childhood, and late childhood.
- The stages of development involve physical, mental/emotional, and social changes.
- Adolescence is a time of transition from child to adult.
- Puberty is the time during adolescence when your body changes to take on the physical characteristics of your gender.

Lesson 4 Adulthood and Aging

Main Idea Adulthood begins at age 18 and ends at death.

- Adulthood can be divided into three stages: early, middle, and late.
- Certain milestones, such as starting a career, raising children, or retiring, mark each stage of adulthood.
- All adults do not age at the same rate or in the same way.
- There are three ways to measure age: chronological, biological, and social.
- Older adults need to focus on all three sides of their health triangle in order to stay healthy and active.

Assessment Resources

- Chapter 17 Summary and Activity
- Audio Summaries
- Reading Tutor
- Performance Assessment
- Chapter 17 Test
- *ExamView Assessment Suite*
- Vocabulary PuzzleMaker
- Online Learning Center

Reading Review

Study Aids

- **Using the Dinah Zike Foldable® Study Organizer** Have students use their Foldables®   to review information about the cells, tissues, organs, and systems in the body.
- **Online Learning Tools** Have students go to the *Teen Health* Online Learning Center at **glencoe.com** to:
  - Download a **Podcast**.
  - Download free **Study-to-Go** content to their PDAs or cell phones.

Vocabulary Review

- **Crossword Puzzle** Have each student create a crossword puzzle that incorporates ten of the chapter vocabulary terms.

Teaching Tips

Reading in Health Class Before students read the lesson, ask volunteers to identify several questions they have about the lesson topic. Write the questions on the board. After students have completed their reading, call on volunteers to answer the questions. Follow up by asking students to identify additional facts they learned about the topic, and to note any questions that were not answered in the reading. Suggest resources for additional research to help students find the answers to their questions.

Reviewing Vocabulary and Main Ideas

1. sperm cell
2. cervix
3. uterus
4. obstetrician
5. chromosomes
6. c
7. a
8. False, different
9. False, Late adulthood
10. False, biological
11. True

Thinking Critically

12. **Interpret** Answers will vary, but should identify that what a mother eats and drinks is carried to the baby via the placenta and umbilical cord. If the mother exposes herself to harmful substances like alcohol, tobacco, or other drugs, the baby could be negatively affected, too.

13. **Analyze** Answers will vary, but could include staying physically active, reading, taking classes, volunteering in the community, and staying in contact with family and friends.

Have students visit **glencoe.com** to take the Chapter 17 quiz.

CHAPTER 17 Assessment

 After You Read

HEALTH QUIZ

Now that you have read the chapter, look back at your answers to the Health Quiz on the chapter opener. Would you change any of them? What would your answers be now?

Reviewing Vocabulary and Concepts

On a sheet of paper, write the numbers 1–5. After each number, write the term from the list that best completes each statement.

- fetus
- sperm cell
- prenatal care
- uterus
- chromosomes
- obstetrician
- placenta
- umbilical cord
- cervix

Lesson 1 The Beginning of Life

1. The _____ must unite with the egg cell in order for fertilization to occur.

2. In order for a baby to be born, the mother's _____ has to widen so the baby can pass through.

3. A baby develops in its mother's _____.

Lesson 2 Heredity and Environment

4. When a woman becomes pregnant, she needs to see an _____ for regular check-ups.

5. Each parent contributes 23 _____ to create an embryo.

Lesson 3 From Childhood to Adolescence

On a sheet of paper, write the numbers 6–7. After each number, write the letter of the answer that best completes each statement.

6. The time when a child doubles in height and triples in weight is _____.
   a. early childhood   c. infancy
   b. adolescence   d. late childhood

7. There are _____ stages of life according to scientist Erik Erikson.
   a. eight   c. three
   b. six   d. ten

Lesson 4 Adulthood and Aging

*On a sheet of paper, write the numbers 8–11. Write **True** or **False** for each statement below. If the statement is false, change the underlined word or phrase to make it true.*

8. All adults age at the <u>same</u> time and in the <u>same</u> way.

9. <u>Middle</u> adulthood is when most people retire from their jobs.

10. The age determined by how well your body parts are working is your <u>chronological</u> age.

11. Volunteering is one way for older adults to build good <u>mental/emotional</u> health.

Go Online Visit **glencoe.com** and take the Online Quiz for Chapter 17.

HEALTH QUIZ Wrap-Up

Stages of Life Have students look back at their responses to the Health Quiz in the chapter opener. Ask students to form small groups. Have students discuss with their groups any answers they would change based on the information in the chapter. Have each group member share one new fact he or she learned while reading the chapter.

Thinking Critically

Using complete sentences, answer the following questions on a sheet of paper.

12. **Interpret** How might the environment inside a mother's uterus affect her baby's health?

13. **Analyze** What are some ways an older adult can keep his or her health triangle balanced?

Write About It

14. **Expository Writing** Find out what organizations in your community pair teens and older adults. Then, write a short letter to the editor of your school paper describing these projects.

Applying Technology

Growing Games

You and a partner will use draw tools to create a game about growth and development.

- Using Microsoft Word®, open draw tools, and select a 2" square. Copy and paste that square 30 times, making a game board.
- Open a new Microsoft Word® document.
- Create two columns with 30 lines each. One column will contain questions. The other column will contain answers.
- Write 30 questions and 30 answers about the various topics discussed in this chapter.
- Edit for accuracy, clarity, and punctuation.

Applying Technology

Growing Games

Equipment needs: Microsoft Word® or similar software
Have students select partners. Go over the steps in this project. Emphasize the importance of editing and rewriting game questions and answers. You may also want to sketch a series of squares on the board as an example of a game board. Create a sign-up list if computer access is limited, and establish a consistent time limit for all student pairs. If time and materials permit, have each pair print their game board and question-and-answer cards, and then let students play one another's games.

Write About It

14. **Expository Writing** Remind students that expository writing is writing that explains or informs. Letters should identify the benefits of teens and older adults interacting. Students should proofread and correct their work before turning it in.

Standardized Test Practice

1. C
2. D

Standardized Test Practice

Reading

Read the passage and then answer the questions.

In addition to physical changes, puberty brings with it many emotional changes. During puberty, young people develop intense friendships, especially with members of the same sex. They care a lot about what other people think, and they want to be liked and accepted by their friends. Sometimes they may want to spend more time with friends and less time with family. This can be a difficult time of adjustment for parents and guardians, who are used to being the center of their child's life.

Many pre-teens feel anxious or self-conscious about the physical changes of puberty. This is especially true when they compare themselves with others. Young people need to be aware that while their friends may grow at different rates, they will eventually catch up with one another. During puberty, many parents also notice their child's moods change quickly and often. Although it can be frustrating, parents need to remember that these mood swings are normal and are probably related to changes in hormone levels in the body.

1. When young people go through puberty, they experience the following emotional changes *except*
   A. They have intense friendships with members of the same sex.
   B. They care deeply about what other people think.
   C. They do not care if they are liked or not.
   D. Sometimes they may want to spend more time with friends and less time with family.

2. During puberty, many parents may notice that their child's moods can
   A. remain steady.
   B. always be positive.
   C. always be negative.
   D. can change quickly and often.

Chapter 17 Assessment **475**

Test-Taking Tips

Reading Questions Carefully Remind students to look for words such as *except* and *not* in test questions. In the first example in the text, students are asked to use the reading passage to determine which of the emotional changes is *not* associated with puberty. Remind students that this type of question asks them to identify which of the answer choices is incorrect or does not fit in a particular category.

CHAPTER 18 pp. 476–505	Standards		Skills and Activities
	National	State/Local	
CHAPTER 18 pp. 476–505	National Health Education Standards 6.8.1, 6.8.2, 6.8.3		*Health* eSpotlight, *p. 477* **BUILDING HEALTH SKILLS** *Goal Setting* Protect Yourself from Pathogens, *pp. 500–501* **HANDS-ON HEALTH** Healthy Habits, *p. 502*
Lesson 1 Preventing the Spread of Disease pp. 478–482	National Health Education Standards 1.8.1, 1.8.5, 1.8.7, 1.8.9, 6.8.1, 7.8.1, 7.8.2, 7.8.3, 8.8.1, 8.8.2		**HEALTH SKILLS ACTIVITY** *Practicing Healthful Behaviors* Keep Your Hands Clean!, *p. 481*
Lesson 2 The Body's Defenses Against Infection pp. 483–487	National Health Education Standards 1.8.1, 1.8.5, 1.8.7, 5.8.4, 5.8.5, 5.8.6, 5.8.7, 6.8.1, 7.8.1, 7.8.2, 8.8.1		**HEALTH SKILLS ACTIVITY** *Practicing Healthful Behaviors* Keeping a Healthy Immune System, *p. 485*
Lesson 3 Common Communicable Diseases pp. 488–491	National Health Education Standards 1.8.1, 1.8.5, 1.8.7, 3.8.3, 5.8.4, 5.8.6, 5.8.7, 7.8.1, 7.8.2, 8.8.1		**Connect To... SOCIAL STUDIES** Fighting Disease, *p. 489*
Lesson 4 Sexually Transmitted Diseases pp. 492–495	National Health Education Standards 1.8.5, 1.8.7, 1.8.8, 1.8.9, 2.8.3, 2.8.8, 3.8.4, 5.8.2, 5.8.6, 5.8.7, 7.8.2, 7.8.3, 8.8.1		**Careers for the 21st Century** Epidemiologist, *p. 493* **What Teens Think** What are some fun activities teens can do with their friends?, *p. 495*
Lesson 5 HIV/AIDS pp. 496–499	National Health Education Standards 1.8.8, 1.8.9, 2.8.9, 3.8.2, 3.8.4, 5.8.7, 6.8.1, 6.8.2, 6.8.3, 6.8.4, 7.8.3		**Go Online** Staying Alive, *p. 497*

PACING THE CHAPTER

Lesson 1	45 min	Lesson 4	45 min	Chapter Review	45 min
Lesson 2	45 min	Lesson 5	45 min	Hands-on Health	30 min
Lesson 3	45 min	Building Health Skills	45 min		

BLOCK SCHEDULING

For block scheduling, assign students Building Health Skills feature *Protect Yourself from Pathogens,* pages 500–501, and Guided Reading and Writing. 📁

Planning Guide

StudentWorks Plus

Glencoe Exclusive!
TeacherWorks Plus
All-In-One Planner and Resource Center

Reproducible Resources	Assessment	Media and Technology
Chapter FAST FILE Resources Chapter Summaries and Activities REVIEW Building Health Skills Activity TEACH Performance Assessment Activity EXTEND Universal Access Activities TEACH Parent Letter and Activities 📁 **Student Activities Workbook** TEACH 📁 **Reading Tutor** TEACH	Building Health Skills Activity, *pp. 500–501* Chapter 18 Assessment, *pp. 504–505* **Chapter FAST FILE Resources** Performance Assessment Activity, *p. 4* Chapter 18 Test, *p. 7* 💿 *ExamView® Assessment Suite*	**TeacherWorks Plus** includes: ● Interactive Teacher Edition ● Lesson Planner with Calendar ● Access to all blackline masters ● Correlations to standards 💿 StudentWorks™ Plus 💿 Online Student Edition Dinah Zike's Teaching Health wih Foldables®
Chapter FAST FILE Resources Concept Mapping Activity 18-1 REVIEW Decision-Making Activity 18-1 EXTEND Enrichment Activity 18-1 EXTEND Lesson Plan 18-1 Guided Reading and Writing 18-1 TEACH Reteaching Activity 18-1 REVIEW	Lesson 1 Review, *p. 482* 💿 Vocabulary PuzzleMaker 💿 *ExamView® Assessment Suite*	💿 Vocabulary PuzzleMaker 💿 *ExamView® Assessment Suite* 💿 StudentWorks™ Plus 🎮 Transparency 18-1 **Go Online** glencoe.com
Chapter FAST FILE Resources Concept Mapping Activity 18-2 REVIEW Cross-Curriculum Activity 18-2 EXTEND Enrichment Activity 18-2 EXTEND Lesson Plan 18-2 Guided Reading and Writing 18-2 TEACH Reteaching Activity 18-2 REVIEW	Lesson 2 Review, *p. 487* 💿 Vocabulary PuzzleMaker 💿 *ExamView® Assessment Suite*	💿 Vocabulary PuzzleMaker 💿 *ExamView® Assessment Suite* 💿 StudentWorks™ Plus 🎮 Transparency 18-2 **Go Online** glencoe.com
Chapter FAST FILE Resources Concept Mapping Activity 18-3 REVIEW Decision-Making Activity 18-3 EXTEND Enrichment Activity 18-3 EXTEND Lesson Plan 18-3 Guided Reading and Writing 18-3 TEACH Reteaching Activity 18-3 REVIEW	Lesson 3 Review, *p. 491* 💿 Vocabulary PuzzleMaker 💿 *ExamView® Assessment Suite*	💿 Vocabulary PuzzleMaker 💿 *ExamView® Assessment Suite* 💿 StudentWorks™ Plus 🎮 Transparency 18-3 **Go Online** glencoe.com
Chapter FAST FILE Resources Concept Mapping Activity 18-4 REVIEW Health Lab 18-4 EXTEND Enrichment Activity 18-4 EXTEND Lesson Plan 18-4 Guided Reading and Writing 18-4 TEACH Reteaching Activity 18-4 REVIEW	Lesson 4 Review, *p. 495* 💿 Vocabulary PuzzleMaker 💿 *ExamView® Assessment Suite*	💿 Vocabulary PuzzleMaker 💿 *ExamView® Assessment Suite* 💿 StudentWorks™ Plus 🎮 Transparency 18-4 **Go Online** glencoe.com
Chapter FAST FILE Resources Concept Mapping Activity 18-5 REVIEW Cross-Curriculum Activity 18-5 EXTEND Enrichment Activity 18-5 EXTEND Lesson Plan 18-5 Guided Reading and Writing 18-5 TEACH Reteaching Activity 18-5 REVIEW	Lesson 5 Review, *p. 499* 💿 Vocabulary PuzzleMaker 💿 *ExamView® Assessment Suite*	💿 Vocabulary PuzzleMaker 💿 *ExamView® Assessment Suite* 💿 StudentWorks™ Plus 🎮 Transparency 18-5 **Go Online** glencoe.com

Chapter and Lesson Resources

The *Teen Health* resources are designed for differentiated learning abilities. You may want to use the coded items in this way:

REVIEW —activities to review or reinforce content

TEACH —activities to teach basic concepts

EXTEND —activities to extend or enrich lesson content

 OUT OF TIME?

Use Health Skills Activity *Keep Your Hands Clean!*, page 481, or Health Skills Activity *Keeping a Healthy Immune System,* page 485.

Bacteria in the School

A recent study of bacteria in schools yielded some surprising results. Scientists collected and analyzed samples on surfaces in elementary schools. They discovered that some surfaces where bacteria were expected to be present in large numbers tested as relatively clean. For example, the scientists found that toilets and door handles—expected to teem with bacteria—were fairly clean. These surfaces, of course, were routinely wiped and disinfected by staff. But other surfaces in the schools were loaded with bacteria. In fact, drinking-water spigots had the highest amount of bacteria on the tested surfaces. Computer keyboards and earphones also tested as very infected. A cafeteria tray had more than 10 times the number of bacteria as a toilet seat. Even a student's hand tested as quite infected with bacterial cells.

With teens at school exposed to so many germs in such unexpected places, routine hand washing becomes even more important. According to the Centers for Disease Control and Prevention (CDC), hand washing is the most important action a person can take to avoid getting sick. The CDC estimates that about 164 million days of school are missed each year because of illness, and half of these days could be prevented by hand washing. The reason hand washing is so effective is that about 80 percent of communicable diseases are spread by hand contact.

In one school, a hand-washing study was carried out. Students were required to wash their hands four times each day. They washed their hands when they first came to school, they washed before lunch, they washed after going to the restroom, and they washed just before leaving school. The result of all this hand washing was that absenteeism decreased sharply.

HPV Infection—Genital Warts

There are more cases of genital warts in the United States than any other type of STD. Genital warts are caused by human papillomavirus (HPV). There are more than 100 types of HPV, most of which cause common warts seen on hands and feet. About 30 types of HPV can cause genital warts.

About 20 million Americans today are infected with HPV. At least 50 percent of people who are sexually active contract the virus during their lives. According to the CDC, about 6.2 million Americans are infected with HPV each year.

HPV infection is usually a "silent" disease—most people who are infected do not know they have HPV. Some HPV infections can cause genital warts. These are soft and moist warts in the genital area that can be flesh colored or white. They usually do not hurt or itch. In females, genital warts can appear on the vulva, in or around the vagina or anus, on the cervix, or on the upper thigh. In males, genital warts can appear on the penis, scrotum, anus, or upper thigh. Some infected people have only one incidence of genital warts, while others may have many occurrences.

People get HPV infections through direct contact of genital areas during sexual activity. People cannot get genital warts by touching warts on the feet or hands. Genital warts are very contagious. An HPV infection can be transmitted both when warts are present and when they are not, though when warts are present there is more chance of spreading the disease. The only completely effective way to prevent getting genital warts is abstinence from sexual activity.

There is no cure for genital warts. In rare cases, genital warts can lead to cervical cancer in females. Most children born to mothers with genital warts are healthy, but very rarely babies exposed to genital warts develop growths in the throat. Most genital warts go away without treatment. In persistent cases, doctors can remove warts.

Support for Teaching Reading

Reading Preview

Activating Background Vocabulary Ask students what they think the word *communicable* means. Then ask what comes to mind when they hear the term *disease*. Guide students in a discussion of what a *communicable disease* might encompass—causes, types, and prevention.

FOLDABLES Study Organizer *Dinah Zike's Reading and Study Skills for Teen Health* provides interactive graphic organizers that help students comprehend and retain health concepts as they read. Use the Foldable® on page 477 or find more Foldables® activities for the chapter on **Communicable Diseases** in the separate booklet, available in the TCR.

Lesson 1   Preventing the Spread of Disease

Guided Reading 1) Activate prior knowledge. Ask students what they know about pathogens. 2) Introduce new key terms. 3) Give students a purpose for reading. Ask: "What are the types of pathogens?" 4) Have students read silently to find the answers. 5) Stop and discuss. 6) Repeat with a new purpose. Ask: "How do pathogens spread?"

Lesson 2   The Body's Defenses Against Infection

Listen-Read-Discuss Present the lesson concepts in a brief lecture. Direct students to read the text silently, making a list of questions as they read. Stop reading and discuss: "What do you understand most about the immune system? What do you understand least? What questions do you still have about the nonspecific immune response or the lymphatic system?"

Lesson 3   Common Communicable Diseases

Restructuring Stop during reading and ask students to think of all the symptoms of communicable diseases they have read about. List all responses on the board. Identify three categories—colds, the flu, and other. Have students state orally why one type of symptom should be in one category or another. Create a new category if necessary.

Lesson 4   Sexually Transmitted Diseases

Active Silent Reading Have students stop reading and close their books. Ask them what they have read about STDs and abstinence. Record responses on the board. Guide students in a discussion about the main concepts. Encourage them to refer back to the text to clarify any remaining questions.

Lesson 5   HIV/AIDS

Summarizing Have students silently read the text. Then have student pairs take turns stating the main ideas of the selection in their own words. In a classroom discussion, clarify any misconceptions students may have about AIDS or HIV. Finally, have each student independently write a brief summary of the selection.

Post Reading

Multimedia Presentations Guide students in the use of multiple media tools such as computers, graphics, animation, and music to enhance communication. Have students work in pairs to develop a presentation for the class that incorporates audiovisual aids and addresses what they learned about pathogens and communicable diseases.

Key for Using the Teacher Wraparound Edition

Use this key to help you identify the different types of prompts found in the Teacher Wraparound Edition.

R **Reading Strategies** activities help you teach reading skills and vocabulary.

C **Critical Thinking** strategies help students apply and extend what they have learned.

U **Universal Access** activities provide differentiated instruction for students learning to speak English, along with suggestions for teaching various types of learners.

HS **Health Skills Practice** activities reinforce Health Skills concepts and help students apply these skills in their everyday lives.

W **Writing Support** activities provide writing opportunities to help students comprehend the text.

AL **Active Learning** strategies provide a variety of activities for presenting lesson content, including Quick Demos and engaging classroom projects that get students actively involved.

Key to Ability Levels

Teaching Strategies and activities have been coded for ability level and appropriateness.

AL Activities for students working above grade level

OL Activities for students working on grade level

BL Activities for students working below grade level

EL Activities for English Learners

Symbols

- Transparencies
- CD-ROM
- glencoe.com
- Print Resources

Communicable Diseases

Chapter at a Glance

Lesson 1 lists some causes of communicable diseases, explains how germs are spread, and describes how to protect yourself against pathogens.

Lesson 2 identifies the main line of defense against pathogens, describes how the immune system functions, and explains how antibodies protect the body.

Lesson 3 explains the causes of colds and their treatments and identifies some common communicable diseases and their symptoms.

Lesson 4 identifies common STDs and the problems they cause, describes how to protect against STDs, and explains why abstinence is the best way to avoid getting an STD.

Lesson 5 explains how people become infected with HIV and develop AIDS and describes how to avoid getting HIV and AIDS.

R Reading Strategy

Interpreting the Photo Have students look at the photo of the scientist studying diseases in her laboratory and ask: What precautions is this scientist taking to protect herself from the disease that she is studying? *Answer: The scientist is wearing glasses to protect her eyes and gloves to protect her hands.*

CHAPTER
18
Communicable Diseases

Chapter Preview

476

▲ Working with the Photo

Preventing the spread of disease is a worldwide concern. Scientists spend many hours studying diseases in labs.
Do you know some ways to prevent the spread of disease?

 Universal Access

Differentiated Learning Glencoe provides teacher support and student materials for all learners in the health classroom.

● Spanish Glosario and chapter summaries assist English Language Learners.

● *Reading Tutor* and related worksheets support reluctant readers.

● Universal Access strategies throughout the Teacher Wraparound Edition and Fast Files help you present materials for gifted students, at-risk students, physically impaired students, and those with behavior disorders or learning disabilities.

Start-Up Activities

Before You Read What do you know about STDs? Answer the Health eSpotlight question below and then watch the online video. Keep a record of your answers.

Health eSpotlight

VIDEO

Thomas Lehman, M.D., F.A.C.P.
Lake Aerie Medical
Barberton, Ohio

The Truth About STDs

Learning the facts about sexually transmitted diseases (STDs) can help you avoid them. What is the best way for teens to avoid getting STDs?

Go to **glencoe.com** and watch the health video for Chapter 18. Then complete the activity provided with the online video.

FOLDABLES Study Organizer

As You Read Make this Foldable® to help you record main ideas about the causes of communicable diseases. Begin with a plain sheet of 11" × 17" paper.

1 Hold the paper like a placemat. Fold the short sides inward so they meet in the middle.

2 Fold the top to the bottom.

3 Open and cut along the inside fold lines. This makes four tabs.

4 Label the tabs as shown.

Pathogens and Disease | Types of Pathogens
How Pathogens Are Spread | Preventing the Spread of Disease

Under the appropriate tab, summarize what you learn about pathogens and how to prevent communicable diseases from spreading.

Go Online Visit **glencoe.com** and complete the Health Inventory for Chapter 18.

477

477

FOCUS

Activating Prior Knowledge

What I Know Call on volunteers to name diseases that can be spread from person to person. Ask students to describe the way each disease is spread.

Guide to Reading

Building Vocabulary
- Explain to students that the word part *patho-* means "disease" and the word part *-gen* means "producer." Ask students to determine the definition of *pathogen* given this information.
- Use Vocabulary PuzzleMaker to reinforce vocabulary terms.

Reading Strategy
Organizing Information
Tell students they should use the table to record information about the spread of diseases and disease prevention as they read the lesson.

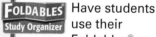 Have students use their Foldables® as they read Lesson

Quick Write

After students have written their explanations, call on volunteers to share their ideas.

Caption Answer

Figure Caption, p. 479
Viruses cause chicken pox.

Preventing the Spread of Disease

Guide to Reading

● Building Vocabulary
Fold a sheet of paper in half, lengthwise. As you read this lesson, write each new term on the left side of the fold and its definition on the other side.

- disease (p. 478)
- communicable disease (p. 478)
- pathogens (p. 478)
- infection (p. 478)
- viruses (p. 479)
- bacteria (p. 479)
- fungi (p. 479)
- protozoa (p. 479)
- vector (p. 480)
- hygiene (p. 480)

● Focusing on the Main Ideas
In this lesson, you will learn to
- **name** some causes of communicable diseases.
- **explain** how germs are spread.
- **describe** how to protect yourself against pathogens.

● Reading Strategy
Organizing Information Create a table like the one shown below. As you read, describe how pathogens spread in the first column. In the second column, describe ways you can prevent spreading pathogens.

Pathogens	
How Pathogens Spread	Preventing the Spread of Pathogens

FOLDABLES Study Organizer Use the Foldable® on p. 477 as you read this lesson.

Quick Write

How do you think people catch colds? Explain your answer.

Common Diseases

You wake up with a runny nose and your eyes itch. Your throat is sore, you sneeze and cough, and your head aches. You have a cold. A cold is one kind of disease. A **disease** is *any condition that interferes with the proper functioning of the body or mind.*

A cold is a **communicable disease,** *a disease that can be passed to a person from another person, animal, or object.* The agents that cause communicable diseases are called pathogens. **Pathogens** are *disease-causing organisms that are so small they can only be seen through a microscope.* Pathogens are also known as germs. When germs enter your body, you can develop an infection. An **infection** is *a condition that occurs when pathogens enter the body, multiply, and cause harm.* **Figure 18.1** shows several kinds of pathogens and the diseases they cause.

Lesson 1 Resources

📁 **Chapter FAST FILE Resources**
Guided Reading and Writing 18-1
Concept Mapping Activity 18-1
Decision-Making Activity 18-1
Reteaching Activity 18-1
Enrichment Activity 18-1
Lesson Quiz 18-1

Technology
⚓ Transparency 18-1
Audio Summaries
ExamView® Assessment Suite
Vocabulary PuzzleMaker
StudentWorks™ Plus
Go Online

▼ FIGURE 18.1

COMMON PATHOGENS AND DISEASES THEY CAUSE

All communicable diseases are caused by pathogens. **What type of pathogen causes chicken pox?**

Pathogens	Diseases
Bacteria	Pink eye, pertussis (whooping cough), strep throat, tuberculosis, Lyme disease, most foodborne illnesses, diphtheria, bacterial pneumonia, cholera
Viruses	Colds, influenza, hepatitis, chicken pox, measles, mumps, mononucleosis, herpes, HIV/AIDS, fever, polio, rabies, viral pneumonia
Fungi	Athlete's foot, ringworm
Protozoa	Dysentery, malaria

Types of Pathogens

Not all pathogens are alike, yet they can all cause diseases. As shown in Figure 18.1, there are four common pathogens:

- **Viruses** (VY·ruh·suhz) are *the smallest pathogens.* Viruses cause common diseases, such as colds and the flu. Most viral infections *cannot* be treated and cured with antibiotics.

- **Bacteria** are *tiny one-celled organisms.* Certain bacteria can be helpful. Bacteria that live in your digestive tract help you digest food. Other bacteria are harmful. They can cause diseases, such as strep throat and pneumonia. Most bacterial infections *can* be treated and cured by antibiotics.

- **Fungi** (FUHN·jy) are *organisms that are more complex than bacteria but cannot make their own food.* They are primitive life-forms that feed on organic materials. They thrive in warm, moist environments. Fungi cause ringworm and athlete's foot.

- **Protozoa** (proh·tuh·ZOH·uh) are *one-celled organisms that are more complex than bacteria.* Malaria is a disease caused by a protozoa that can live in mosquitoes. If an infected mosquito bites a person, the protozoa transfers into the body through the skin.

Reading Check **Compare** How are bacterial infections different from viral infections?

▼ One way in which communicable diseases can be spread is through touch. **What is another way in which communicable diseases are spread from person to person?**

Lesson 1: Preventing the Spread of Disease **479**

TEACH

U Universal Access

English Learners Have students create a health glossary for the vocabulary terms in this lesson. Students should write each term and a short definition in a notebook or on index cards. Encourage students to work in pairs with English-proficient students to review the meaning and pronunciation of each term. Encourage students to expand their health glossaries as they continue to read through the chapter. **EL**

R Reading Strategy

Analyzing a Chart After students have examined **Figure 18.1**, ask: What kind of pathogen causes colds? *viruses* Explain that food-borne illnesses are often called food poisoning. Ask: What kind of pathogen causes foodborne illnesses? *bacteria* **OL**

Reading Check

Answer Most bacterial infections can be treated with antibiotics. Viral infections cannot. Bacterial infections come from bacteria, viral infections from viruses.

Caption Answer

Photo Caption *Sample answer:* Communicable diseases are spread through indirect contact, contact with contaminated food or water, and contact with animals and insects.

🏃 FITNESS ZONE

Communicable Diseases and Physical Fitness As students consider common communicable diseases, such as colds and flu, ask them to think about the effects of these diseases on fitness activities. Have students review the *Sample Physical Fitness Plan* in the *Fitness Zone Handbook*.

Ask: How do you think being ill with flu would affect your fitness routine? What do you think you should do when you feel healthy enough to start fitness activities again? **For more information, see** *Fitness Zone Handbook* **pages xviii–1 or visit the Fitness Zone at glencoe.com.**

Health Skills Practice

Accessing Information Divide the class into small groups, and encourage each group to use print and online resources to find out about drinking water in their community, including the source of fresh water, the local water treatment plant, and the system of pipes that distribute water throughout the community. Ask each group to make a flow diagram that shows water's journey from the source to the school. Invite a representative from the water treatment plant to make a brief presentation to the class. **AL**

Reading Check

Answer direct contact, indirect contact, contaminated food and water, insects and animals

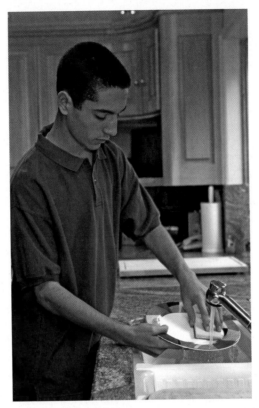

▲ When you immediately wash glasses, plates, or other utensils after using them, you keep bacteria from growing. **Is it important to use warm, soapy water when you wash dishes? Why or why not?**

How Do Pathogens Spread?

Disease can occur when pathogens enter the body. Here are common ways pathogens are spread:

- **Direct contact with others.** Pathogens can spread directly from one person to another. For example, you can pick up a virus or bacteria by shaking hands with or kissing an infected person. Some pathogens are spread through sexual contact.

- **Indirect contact with others.** Pathogens can enter your body by sharing drinking glasses or eating utensils with an infected person. Pathogens can also be spread by contaminated needles used for tattoos, body piercings, and drug injection.

- **Contact with contaminated food and water.** Some pathogens infect people through contaminated food or water. Food that is improperly stored or undercooked provides an environment where pathogens can multiply. Illnesses people get from pathogens in food are called *foodborne illnesses.*

HS

- **Contact with animals or insects.** Animals and insects can spread pathogens. *An organism, such as an insect, that transmits pathogens* is called a **vector.** For example, the bite of a tick can spread the virus that causes Lyme disease. Mosquitoes infected with the West Nile virus can spread that virus to birds, horses, and humans through their saliva.

Reading Check

 Recall What are four ways that pathogens are spread?

How to Keep Pathogens from Spreading

There is no way to completely avoid pathogens. However, you can help protect yourself from them by practicing good personal **hygiene,** or *cleanliness.* Here are some other actions you can take to help prevent the spread of pathogens:

- Eat nutritious foods. Get enough physical activity and rest.

- Avoid close contact with people infected with a communicable disease, especially if they are still contagious.

Caption Answer

Photo Caption *Sample answer:* It is important because warm, soapy water washes away or kills pathogens.

🏠 Home, School, and Community

In the Community The Safe Drinking Water Act is a federal law passed by Congress in 1974 that requires all localities to protect drinking water. These standards require that local water systems test for and cut down on contaminants in the drinking water.

These contaminants include industrial chemicals, pesticides, human wastes, animal wastes, and various naturally occurring substances. Ask students to find out how this law affects the local water supply. **AL**

Health Skills Activity

Practicing Healthful Behaviors

Keep Your Hands Clean!

One of the best ways of stopping pathogens from entering your body or spreading to others is to wash your hands frequently. Practice washing your hands thoroughly using the following steps:

1. Use warm water to wet your hands, and then apply soap.
2. Vigorously rub your hands together, scrubbing your whole hand for 30 seconds or more.
3. Rinse your hands thoroughly. Use a paper towel to turn off the water in public restrooms.
4. Use a clean towel or paper towel to dry your hands. In a public restroom, use a paper towel to open the door when you leave.

With a Group

Create a poster encouraging students to wash their hands regularly. Include the handwashing steps listed above. With permission from school administrators, hang your poster in a school restroom or hallway.

- Never share eating or drinking utensils.
- Do not share toothbrushes or other personal hygiene items.
- Wash your hands thoroughly in warm, soapy water, especially before eating and after using the bathroom, playing with pets, or handling garbage.
- Avoid touching your mouth, nose, and eyes. Do not bite your nails.
- Handle and prepare food safely, especially poultry and fish. Wash vegetables and fruits and cook meat thoroughly.
- Wipe counters thoroughly with a clean sponge or cloth. Wash or replace the sponge or cloth frequently. If these items are dirty or overused, they can actually spread more germs than they remove.
- Keep your environment clean. Empty trash frequently. Keep trash cans clean.

 Reading Check   **Identify** Name five habits you can practice to keep yourself safe from pathogens.

Health Skills Activity

Practicing Healthful Behaviors

Keep Your Hands Clean!

Use the following strategies to help students complete the activity:

- Ask a volunteer to read the introductory paragraph aloud.
- Read aloud to the class the hand-washing tips. Use soap, water, and a basin to demonstrate how to wash your hands thoroughly.
- Divide the class into small groups, and ask students in each group to practice the steps for correct hand washing.
- Set a deadline for the completion of the posters on hand washing. Obtain permission to hang posters.

Reading Check

Answer, this page Any five from the bulleted list on pages 480–481.

Answer, p. 482 If you are ill, stay home from school and other public places. When you sneeze, cover your mouth and nose. If a health care professional prescribes medicine for you, follow the directions exactly.

HEALTH LITERACY

What Washing Does When you wash your hands with soap and water, the rubbing of the hands scrapes off dirt, oils, and other particles, including pathogens. Some soaps contain antibacterial agents designed to kill bacteria, but such chemicals do nothing to eliminate viruses. Studies have shown that a vigorous washing with soap and water washes away many viruses, including cold viruses. The amount of rubbing you do is the key to washing thoroughly, and that is why rubbing the hands for 30 seconds or more is essential.

ASSESS

Assessment Resources

Lesson Review Quiz
- *ExamView*
- Fast Files Activities
- Online Quizzes and Activities

Reteaching

- Assign Concept Map 18-1 or Reteaching Activity 18-1 in the Fast Files.
- Have students expand the table they made for the lesson-opening Reading Strategy by adding to the table the diseases that each kind of pathogen causes.

Enrichment

- Assign Enrichment Activity 18-1 in the Fast Files.
- Ask students to choose one of the diseases listed in **Figure 18.1** and investigate that disease in terms of how it is spread and how to prevent it. Ask that each student prepare a presentation to the class about his or her findings.

CLOSE

Call on volunteers to describe one way to protect yourself from germs and one way to protect others from your germs.

Helping Others Stay Healthy

You may be carrying pathogens and not even know it. When you come in contact with other people, these pathogens can easily spread. You can help protect the people around you from the spread of pathogens. Here are some healthful behaviors to practice:

- If you are ill, stay home from school and other public places. Avoid close contact with others.
- When you sneeze, cover your mouth and nose, and turn your head away from others. Wash your hands immediately.
- Do not share eating utensils, drinking glasses, toothbrushes, or other personal items.
- If a health care professional prescribes medicine for you, follow the directions exactly. Take all medicine that is prescribed.
- Again, prepare and store food safely. Wash vegetables and fruits and cook meat thoroughly. Always wash your hands before handling food.

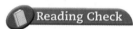

Go Online

Visit **glencoe.com** and complete the Interactive Study Guide for Lesson 1.

Reading Check **Explain** Give three suggestions for protecting others from the pathogens you could spread.

Lesson 1 Review

After You Read

Review this lesson for new terms, major headings, and Reading Checks.

What I Learned

1. *Vocabulary* Define *infection*. Use it in a sentence.

2. *Identify* What is a communicable disease?

3. *Give Examples* What are four types of pathogens? Give an example of a disease caused by each kind.

4. *Describe* What are some ways that pathogens can be spread by indirect contact?

Thinking Critically

5. *Analyze* Why do you think it is important for teens to practice good personal hygiene?

6. *Apply* Brendan is coughing and sneezing at school. What should Brendan do to help prevent the spread of pathogens? Explain your answer.

Applying Health Skills

7. *Practicing Healthful Behaviors* Think of four behaviors that you can practice to help stop the spread of pathogens. Create a plan to practice two of these behaviors during the next week. Follow the plan and write a paragraph describing the results.

Go Online For more Lesson Review Activities, go to **glencoe.com**.

Lesson 1 Review Answers

1. An infection is when pathogens enter the body, multiply, and cause harm. Sentences will vary.
2. A communicable disease is a disease that can be passed to a person from another person, animal, or object.
3. viruses, colds; bacteria, strep throat; fungi, athlete's foot; protozoa, malaria
4. Sharing drinking glasses, eating utensils, and contaminated needles can spread diseases.
5. *Sample answer:* Practicing good personal hygiene helps prevent the spread of diseases.
6. *Sample answer:* Good advice for Brendan would be to cover his nose and mouth when he coughs and sneezes because that prevents the spread of the cold.
7. Plans should include four behaviors that would help stop the spread of pathogens and specific ways to carry out the behaviors.

Lesson 2

The Body's Defenses Against Infection

Guide to Reading

● **Building Vocabulary**
As you read this lesson, write each new term and its definition in a list. Then draw three or four circles. Within each circle, group related terms together.

- immune system (p. 483)
- immunity (p. 483)
- inflammation (p. 484)
- lymphatic system (p. 485)
- lymphocytes (p. 485)
- antigen (p. 486)
- antibodies (p. 486)
- vaccine (p. 486)

● **Focusing on the Main Ideas**
In this lesson, you will learn to

- **name** the body's first line of defense against pathogens.
- **describe** how the immune system functions.
- **explain** how antibodies protect the body.
- **practice** behaviors that keep your immune system healthy.

● **Reading Strategy**
Sequencing Draw a concept map that shows different ways your body works to defend itself from pathogens entering your body. Use Figure 18.2 on p. 484 as a guide.

Body's Defenses

Your Body Defends Itself

Pathogens are everywhere. They are in the air you breathe, the water you drink, and on objects you touch. Most bacteria, viruses, and other pathogens never get the chance to make you sick. Your body has natural barriers between you and pathogens. Your body's five major barriers to pathogens are shown in **Figure 18.2.**

These barriers are your body's first line of defense. If a pathogen gets past them, your body's immune system responds. Your **immune** (i·MYOON) **system** is *a combination of body defenses made up of the cells, tissues, and organs that fight off pathogens and disease.* Your immune system has two main responses—the nonspecific response and the specific response. Together these responses provide **immunity**—*your body's ability to resist the germs that cause a particular disease.*

Reading Check

Explain What is the function of the immune system?

Quick Write

Think about a time you were ill and had a fever. How does a fever help your body fight an infection?

Lesson 2 Resources

📁 **Chapter *Fast File* Resources**
Guided Reading and Writing 18-2
Concept Mapping Activity 18-2
Cross-Curriculum Activity 18-2
Reteaching Activity 18-2
Enrichment Activity 18-2
Lesson Quiz 18-2

Technology
🔖 Transparency 18-2
 Audio Summaries
⦿ *ExamView®* Assessment Suite
 Vocabulary PuzzleMaker
⦿ StudentWorks™ Plus
G⦿ Online

FOCUS

Activating Prior Knowledge

What I Know Remind students that they have learned about several ways by which communicable diseases are spread. Ask volunteers to explain how a body fights a pathogen that gets into the body.

Guide to Reading

Building Vocabulary
■ Have students explain how antibodies are related to antigens.
■ Use Vocabulary PuzzleMaker to reinforce vocabulary terms.

Reading Strategy
Sequencing Encourage students to develop a concept map about the body's defenses as they read Lesson 2. After students have read the lesson, ask volunteers to share their completed concept maps with the class.

Quick Write

Have students write a short paragraph that describes how they felt when they had a fever. Have them conclude the paragraph by explaining how a fever helps the body fight infection.

Reading Check

Answer The immune system functions to fight off pathogens and disease.

TEACH

R Reading Strategy

Analyzing a Graphic After students have examined **Figure 18.2**, ask: How do tears fight off pathogens? *Tears contain chemicals that kill some pathogens.* What other body fluids kill some pathogens? *saliva and stomach acid* What is mucus, and how does it help the body fight off pathogens? *Mucus is a sticky material that coats mucous membranes. Mucus traps pathogens.* **OL**

C Critical Thinking

Analyzing Point out that tattoos and piercings are popular among some teens. Explain that sometimes getting such body ornaments can be dangerous. Ask: Which of the body's five major barriers is broken down when a person gets a tattoo or a piercing? *the skin* If the needle used for tattooing or piercing is not clean, what could get through this barrier to the inside of the body? *pathogens* Explain that there is a risk of infection any time the skin is pierced, and people who do tattoos or piercings may not properly sterilize their instruments. **OL**

Reading Check

Answer The body first responds with inflammation of the affected area.

Caption Answer

Figure Caption Mucous membranes and saliva both protect you from pathogens in your mouth.

484

▼FIGURE 18.2

R THE FIVE MAJOR BARRIERS

Barriers help keep pathogens out of your body. Which barrier protects you from pathogens that might enter your body through your mouth?

- **Tears** cover and protect the eye from dust and pathogens. As they flow, tears carry foreign material away from the eye. Tears contain chemicals that kill pathogens.
- **Mucous Membranes** are the soft skin that lines the nose, mouth, eyes, and other body openings. They are coated in a sticky material called mucus (MYOO·kuhs) that traps pathogens. When you cough, sneeze, or clear your throat, the pathogens trapped in the mucus are expelled.
- **Saliva** washes germs away from your teeth. It contains chemicals that kill pathogens trying to enter through your mouth.
- **Skin** provides a tough, outer protective surface that keeps pathogens from entering your blood. If you get a cut, burn, or scrape, pathogens can get past this barrier.
- **Stomach Acid** is a gastric juice produced by the lining of your stomach. It kills many of the pathogens that make it past the saliva and mucous membranes of your mouth.

Nonspecific Immune Response

C When pathogens enter your body, the immune system reacts with a nonspecific immune response. This response begins with inflammation. **Inflammation** is *the body's response to injury or disease, resulting in a condition of swelling, pain, heat, and redness.* The brain sends signals telling white blood cells to rush to the affected area and destroy the pathogens. Circulation to the area slows down.

With inflammation, the body starts producing a protein called *interferon* (in·ter·FIR·ahn) to stimulate the body's immune system. If pathogens multiply and spread, your body temperature may rise and cause a fever. A higher body temperature makes it harder for pathogens to reproduce. A fever also signals the body to produce more white blood cells to destroy the pathogens.

Reading Check

Explain How does the body first respond to invading pathogens?

HEALTH LITERACY

Stress Affects the Immune System Studies have shown that in a dangerous situation, the body naturally gears up to deal with cuts and scrapes, or even worse. Studies have also shown, though, that long-term, chronic stress suppresses and breaks down the immune system. A person under constant stress becomes less able to fight off the pathogens that cause disease. Handling stress in a healthy way, then, is good for the immune system. Techniques that involve relaxation and positive thinking are ways to meet the challenges of stress.

Health Skills Activity

Practicing Healthful Behaviors

Keeping a Healthy Immune System

Good health habits can keep your immune system healthy. A healthy immune system means your body is better able to fight off infection. Commit to these habits to keep your immune system in top condition!

- Follow a healthful eating plan. Eat plenty of vitamin-rich fruits, vegetables, and whole grains.
- Participate in regular physical activity.
- Learn to manage stress in healthy ways.
- Get plenty of sleep. Rest strengthens your body's defenses.
- Avoid tobacco, alcohol, and other drugs.
- Drink plenty of water.
- Bathe and shower regularly.
- Get regular checkups from a health care professional.

On Your Own

Using print or online resources, research other good health habits that can help you look and feel your best.

Specific Immune Response

Some pathogens can survive the body's nonspecific response. When this happens, the body sets in motion a specific immune response. Each specific response is customized to attack a particular pathogen and its toxins. Our immune system can "recognize" pathogens it has already battled. Once our immune system creates a specific response, cells from that response are ready to attack when the pathogen reappears. As a result, the second response is much quicker than the first.

The Lymphatic System

The **lymphatic** (lim·FA·tik) **system** is *a secondary circulatory system that helps the body fight pathogens and* **maintains** *its fluid balance.* The fluid circulating in the lymphatic system is called *lymph* (LIMF). *The white blood cells in the lymphatic system are called* **lymphocytes** (LIM·fuh·sytes). There are two main kinds of lymphocytes: B cells and T cells. B cells form in the bone marrow. T cells develop in the thymus gland.

Academic Vocabulary

maintains (meyn TEYNS) *(verb)* continues or keeps up. *Simon maintains his health by participating in a variety of physically challenging activities.*

Lesson 2: The Body's Defenses Against Infection **485**

Health Skills Activity

Practicing Healthful Behaviors

Keeping a Healthy Immune System

Use the following strategies to help students complete the activity:

- Read the introductory paragraph, and then call on students to read each item in the bulleted list of habits that keep the immune system in top condition. Lead a discussion about which of these habits students think is most important.

- Divide the class into small groups, and have each group use print and online resources to research good health habits.

- Set a deadline for completion of the research. Invite each group to present its findings to the class.

Academic Vocabulary

Maintains Have students read the definition and example sentence. Let several volunteers restate the example sentence or the sentence in the text, replacing *maintains* with a word or phrase that has the same (or nearly the same) meaning. You will find academic vocabulary activities in the Student Activities Workbook.

HEALTH LITERACY

Exercise and Immunity According to the President's Council on Physical Fitness and Sports, moderate physical activity results in positive changes in the immune system. For example, people who exercise regularly have fewer colds than people who don't exercise regularly. Researchers have found that positive changes actually occur in the immune system during moderate exercise. Recent studies show that near-daily physical activity reduces the number of days with sickness.

▲ Vaccinations protect the body against certain communicable diseases. **How do vaccines help fight pathogens?**

Go Online

Visit **glencoe.com** and complete the Interactive Study Guide for Lesson 2.

Macrophages (MA·kruh·fay·juhz) are also found in the lymph. Their purpose is to attach themselves to invading pathogens and destroy them. Macrophages surround foreign substances and destroy them. Macrophages help the lymphocytes recognize the invader and prepare for future attacks.

Antibodies and Antigens

Lymphocytes react to *antigens*. An **antigen** is *any substance released by invading pathogens.* The immune system responds to these antigens by producing antibodies. **Antibodies** are *proteins that attach to antigens, keeping them from harming the body.* B cells produce a specific antibody for each specific antigen. If the same type of pathogen invades the body again, these antibodies are ready to attack.

T cells either stimulate the production of B cells or attack pathogens directly. There are two main types of T cells: helper cells and killer cells. Helper cells activate the production of B cells. Killer cells attach to invading pathogens and destroy them.

Immunity

Everyone is born with a natural immunity. Even before a baby is born, the mother's antibodies pass from her body to her developing fetus. After a baby is born, antibodies are passed on to the baby through the mother's milk. However, these immunities last for only a few months. Then the baby's immune system becomes active, and produces antibodies on its own to fight pathogens.

Immunity also develops when a vaccine is used. A **vaccine** (vak·SEEN) is *a preparation of dead or weakened pathogens that causes the immune system to produce antibodies.* They help the immune system make antibodies for certain diseases. This process is called immunization.

U

Vaccines have been developed for many diseases, such as polio, measles, and chicken pox. Some vaccinations, such as those for hepatitis B, must be given in a series over a span of a few months. Others, such as the tetanus shot, must be given repeatedly during your lifetime. To keep your body healthy, it is important to keep vaccinations current. **Figure 18.3** provides the vaccination schedule for many common vaccines. Remember that vaccinations protect not only you but also those around you!

Reading Check **Explain** How does your immune system react to a vaccination?

Concerns About Vaccines Fear that vaccinations carry risks has caused some people to refuse to have their children immunized. For example, in recent years some outspoken doctors and parents have charged that the vaccine for measles, mumps, and rubella (MMR) can cause autism in children. As a result of these charges, the Centers for Disease and Prevention (CDC) conducted research and found no evidence of a link between the vaccine and autism. Have interested students investigate this issue. **AL**

▼ **FIGURE 18.3**

R **VACCINATION SCHEDULE**

This table lists common vaccines and the ages at which each vaccine is given. **At what ages is the vaccine for polio given?**

Vaccine	Recommended Ages for Vaccine
Hepatitis B	Birth, 1–2 months, 6–18 months
DTaP: diphtheria, tetanus, pertussis (whooping cough)	2, 3, 4, and 15–18 months, 4–6 years, 11–12 years
HiB (*H. influenzae* type b)	2, 4, and 12–15 months
IPV: Polio	2, 4, and 6–18 months, 4–6 years
MMR: measles, mumps, rubella	12–15 months; 4–6 years
Varicella: chicken pox	12–23 months
Hepatitis A	12–23 months
Human Papillomavirus	(3 doses) 11–12 years (females)

Source: CDC, 2007.

ASSESS

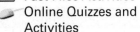
Assessment Resources

Lesson Review Quiz
● *ExamView*
📁 Fast Files Activities
🖱 Online Quizzes and Activities

Reteaching

● Assign Concept Map 18-2 or Reteaching Activity 18-2 in the Fast Files. 📁
● Ask each student to write ten questions using terms and concepts learned in Lesson 2. Then have partners quiz each other with their questions.

Enrichment

● Assign Enrichment Activity 18-2 in the Fast Files. 📁
● Have students create comic strips that show how lymphocytes react to invading pathogens.

CLOSE

Call on students to distinguish between a specific or nonspecific immune response.

> **Caption Answer**
> **Figure Caption** The polio vaccine is given at ages 2, 4, and 6–18 months, and at 4–6 years.

Lesson 2 Review

 After You Read

Review this lesson for new terms, major headings, and Reading Checks.

What I Learned

1. *Vocabulary* Define the term *antigen*. Name two types of white blood cells your immune system produces to fight antigens.

2. *Recall* What is the lymphatic system? How does it protect your body against disease?

3. *Explain* What is the body's first line of defense against pathogens?

Thinking Critically

4. *Analyze* How does fever help fight an infection?

5. *Evaluate* How do vaccines help protect the health of the community?

Applying Health Skills

6. *Decision Making* A teen wakes up with a cold yet wants to go to school to take final exams. Use the decision-making process to help the teen make a healthy decision.

G⊙ Online For more Lesson Review Activities, go to glencoe.com.

Lesson 2: The Body's Defenses Against Infection **487**

Lesson 2 Review Answers

1. An antigen is any substance released by invading pathogens. B cells and T cells.
2. a secondary circulatory system that fights pathogens and maintains fluid balance
3. Circulation to the area slows down. The body produces a protein called interferon that stimulates the immune system. Body temperature may rise, making it harder for pathogens to reproduce.
4. Pathogens reproduce at the body's normal temperature. When your body temperature rises even a little, it is harder for pathogens to reproduce. A fever also signals the body to produce more white blood cells.
5. Vaccines help protect individuals from getting certain communicable diseases, thereby reducing the spread of disease to the greater community.
6. Students should use six steps of decision making and demonstrate an understanding of how diseases spread.

FOCUS

Activating Prior Knowledge

What I Know Ask students to define the flu and explain how it is spread and treated.

 Guide to Reading

Building Vocabulary
- Explain that *contagious* means "spreading or tending to spread from one to another." Have students use that information to determine the meaning of *contagious period*.
- Use Vocabulary PuzzleMaker to reinforce vocabulary terms.

Reading Strategy
Predicting Give students a few minutes to scan the lesson's headings. Then call on volunteers to predict what they will learn in Lesson 3.

 Quick Write

Have students list the symptoms of a cold or flu and then describe in a brief paragraph the actions they would take to prevent contagion. After students have read about these diseases, have them explain whether their ideas have changed.

 Reading Check

Answer A cold is most contagious during the first 24 hours.

Caption Answer

Photo Caption Minimize contact with others.

Common Communicable Diseases

 Guide to Reading

Building Vocabulary
As you read, write each term on one side of an index card and its definition on the other. Use the cards to quiz yourself on the definitions.
- contagious period (p. 489)
- mononucleosis (p. 489)
- hepatitis (p. 490)
- tuberculosis (p. 491)
- pneumonia (p. 491)
- strep throat (p. 491)

Focusing on the Main Ideas
In this lesson, you will learn to
- **explain** what causes colds and how they can be treated.
- **identify** some common communicable diseases.
- **describe** the symptoms of some common communicable diseases.

Reading Strategy
Predicting Look at the main headings, figures, and captions in the lesson. Predict what kind of information you think you might learn.

 Quick Write

List your symptoms if you had a cold or the flu. What actions could you take to prevent others from catching your disease?

Colds

The common cold occurs more frequently than any other communicable disease. Colds are caused by hundreds of different viruses, and can be spread by direct or indirect contact.

You can help treat a cold by getting plenty of rest and drinking lots of fluids. Some over-the-counter (OTC) medicines can help relieve your symptoms. You should stay at home for at least 24 hours after your cold symptoms appear. This is when your cold is most contagious, meaning it is easily spread to others. Anyone who comes in contact with cold viruses can become infected. That is why it is so important to take an active role in preventing the common cold.

Reading Check **Recall** Why is it important to stay home at least the first 24 hours after becoming infected with a cold virus?

◀ Cold germs spread quickly and easily. **How can you help stop the spread of cold viruses to others?**

Lesson 3 Resources

Chapter FAST FILE Resources
Guided Reading and Writing 18-3
Concept Mapping Activity 18-3
Decision-Making Activity 18-3
Reteaching Activity 18-3
Enrichment Activity 18-3
Lesson Quiz 18-3

Technology
Transparency 18-3
Audio Summaries
ExamView® Assessment Suite
Vocabulary PuzzleMaker
StudentWorks™ Plus

Go Online

The Flu

Influenza, or "the flu," is another common communicable disease. Flu symptoms include fever, chills, fatigue, headache, muscle aches, and respiratory problems. Like the cold, the flu can be spread through both direct and indirect contact.

The flu is caused by one of three main types of influenza viruses, each with several different strains. Every year, certain strains of the flu virus spread more quickly than others. Scientists try to anticipate which strains will spread fastest so that they create enough flu vaccines for the following year. Most strains of the flu are relatively harmless, but some can be serious.

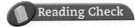 **Reading Check** Compare How are the flu and the common cold similar?

Other Common Communicable Diseases

Every communicable disease has a contagious period. The **contagious period** is *the length of time that a particular disease can be spread from person to person.* Quite often, the contagious period includes a length of time before the infected person starts to show symptoms. Chicken pox, measles, and mumps all have specific contagious periods. Several communicable diseases and their contagious periods are listed in **Figure 18.4.** on the next page. Other common communicable diseases are described below.

Mononucleosis

Mononucleosis (MAH·noh·nook·klee·OH·sis), or "mono," is *a viral disease characterized by a severe sore throat and swelling of the lymph glands in the neck and around the throat area.* Mono most commonly infects teens and young adults. Known as "the kissing disease," it is spread through contact with the saliva of an infected person. Mono is also spread through sharing contaminated eating utensils and drinking glasses.

 Reading Check Define What is a *contagious period*?

▲ Eating healthy foods can help your body fight off communicable diseases such as the flu. **What other choices can you make that will help keep you healthy?**

Connect To...
Social Studies

Fighting Disease

Diseases have shaped the lives of many famous athletes and historical leaders throughout the world. For example, United States President Franklin D. Roosevelt continued to lead our nation after contracting polio.

Research the life of a famous person who had to fight disease. Write a brief report. Tell about the disease and how this person prevailed.

Lesson 3: Common Communicable Diseases **489**

TEACH

 Reading Check

Answer, top Both diseases are caused by viruses and can be spread by direct and indirect contact. Each year a flu vaccine helps mitigate its impact, whereas there is no vaccine for a cold. **Answer, bottom** The contagious period is the time during which a disease can be spread to others.

ACTIVITY
Connect To...
Social Studies

Fighting Disease

Explain that polio is a crippling communicable disease caused by a virus that has largely been eliminated in the United States because of polio immunization. Roosevelt contracted polio as a young man and could not walk without help for the rest of his life. Then call on volunteers to suggest famous athletes or historical figures who have had to fight disease.

HEALTH LITERACY

The Threat of Bird Flu Since 1997, there have been numerous cases of a flu infection found in Asian birds spreading to people in China, Vietnam, and other Asian countries. This bird flu virus is extremely deadly in birds, and it has also caused death in humans. Scientists are worried that a small change in the virus might allow it to spread easily throughout a human population. That might result in a flu pandemic that could kill 100 million people or more.

Caption Answer

Photo Caption get enough rest, stay away from others who may be infected

R Reading Strategy

Analyzing a Chart After students have examined **Figure 18.4**, ask: What are the symptoms of measles? *fever, runny nose, cough, rash* If a child you know first had a measles rash on a Friday, when was that child first contagious for measles? *three to four days before the rash appeared, or on the Monday or Tuesday before* When will the child's contagious period end? *four days after the rash appears, or on the next Tuesday* **OL**

Caption Answers

Photo Caption, p. 491
severe sore throat and swelling of the lymph glands in the neck and around the throat area
Figure Caption, this page
Sample answers: All of these diseases share the presence of a fever as a symptom. Chicken pox, Rubella, and Measles share a rash as a symptom.

▼ **FIGURE 18.4**

R

COMMON COMMUNICABLE DISEASES

This figure shows the symptoms, contagious periods, and vaccines for several communicable diseases. **Which diseases have similar symptoms? What are those symptoms?**

Disease	Symptoms	Contagious Period	Vaccine
Chicken pox	Itchy rash, fever, muscle aches	One to five days before symptoms appear to when spots crust over	Yes
Pneumonia	High fever, chest pain, cough	Varies	For some types
Rubella	Swollen lymph nodes, rash, fever	Seven days before rash starts to five days after	Yes
Measles	Fever, runny nose, cough, rash	Three to four days before rash starts to four days after	Yes
Mumps	Fever, headache, swollen areas in neck and under jaw	Seven days before symptoms to nine days after	Yes
Whooping cough	Fever, runny nose, dry cough (with a whooping sound)	From inflammation of mucous membranes to four weeks after	Yes
Tuberculosis	Fever, fatigue, weight loss, coughing blood	Varies	Yes

Hepatitis

Hepatitis (hep·uh·TY·tis) is *a viral disease of the liver characterized by yellowing of the skin and the whites of the eyes.* Other symptoms might include loss of appetite, weakness, lack of energy, fever, headaches, and a sore throat. Hepatitis A, B, and C are three different virus types.

Hepatitis A is common in areas with poor sanitation. It is spread through food or water that has been contaminated by human waste. People can also become infected if the virus enters the body through an open wound.

Hepatitis B and C are most commonly spread through contact with contaminated blood or other body fluids. Vaccines can protect people from contracting hepatitis A and B. Medications can help treat people infected with hepatitis C.

HEALTH LITERACY

Contagious Periods Some infections that involve pathogens are not contagious. For example, in most cases a type of pneumonia caused by a virus is not contagious. Here are the contagious periods of common diseases not listed in the chart in the text:

- Colds are contagious from the onset of a runny nose until the fever is gone.
- The flu is contagious from the onset of any symptoms until the fever is gone.
- Strep throat is contagious from the onset of a sore throat until 24 hours after first use of an antibiotic.

Tuberculosis

Tuberculosis (too·ber·kyuh·LOH·sis), or TB, is *a bacterial disease that usually affects the lungs.* Since TB can spread easily through the air, people are tested periodically to see if they have the disease. Sometimes people who test positive for TB show no symptoms. Even without symptoms, they can still spread the disease to others.

Pneumonia

Pneumonia is *a serious inflammation of the lungs.* Symptoms include fever, chills, and difficulty breathing. People infected with other diseases are especially vulnerable to pneumonia. This infection can be spread though direct or indirect contact. A virus or bacteria can cause pneumonia. Pneumonia caused by a bacteria can be treated with antibiotics.

Strep Throat

Strep throat is *a sore throat caused by streptococcal bacteria.* Strep throat produces a red and painful throat, fever, and swollen lymph nodes in the neck. It might also cause headaches, nausea, and vomiting. It is spread through direct or indirect contact with an infected person. Left untreated, strep infections can spread to other areas of the body. Fortunately, strep throat is caused by a bacteria and can be treated with antibiotics.

▲ Getting a blood test will determine if a person has mononucleosis. **What are the symptoms of mono?**

Go Online

Visit **glencoe.com** and complete the Interactive Study Guide for Lesson 3.

Lesson 3 Review

After You Read

Review this lesson for new terms, major headings, and Reading Checks.

What I Learned

1. **Vocabulary** Define *mononucleosis.*

2. **Give Examples** What are two examples of how someone might become infected with hepatitis A?

3. **List** Name two symptoms of strep throat.

Thinking Critically

4. **Analyze** Why are hospital patients often at risk for developing pneumonia?

5. **Evaluate** If someone has symptoms such as a fever and fatigue, how will that person know when to seek help from a health care professional?

Applying Health Skills

6. **Practicing Healthful Behaviors** Write a short article describing healthful behaviors teens can use to control the spread of disease. Include a list of some common communicable diseases and how they are spread.

Go Online For more Lesson Review Activities, go to **glencoe.com**.

Lesson 3 Review Answers

1. Mononucleosis is a viral disease characterized by a severe sore throat and swelling of the lymph glands in the neck and around the throat area.

2. by eating or drinking contaminated food or water and by being exposed to contaminated blood or body fluids

3. *Any two:* painful throat, swollen lymph nodes, headaches, nausea, vomiting

4. People who are sick with other illnesses are especially vulnerable to pneumonia.

5. *Sample answer:* Someone should seek help if the symptoms are long lasting or get worse over time.

6. Articles will vary. A good article should include descriptions of prevention methods such as washing hands and covering the mouth and nose when sneezing or coughing. Students should explain why each method described is effective in preventing the spread of disease.

Assessment Resources

Lesson Review Quiz
ExamView
Fast Files Activities
Online Quizzes and Activities

Reteaching

● Assign Concept Map 18-3 or Reteaching Activity 18-3 in the Fast Files.
● Have students work in small groups to write brief dictionary definitions of each of the diseases discussed in Lesson 3.

Enrichment

● Assign Enrichment Activity 18-3 in the Fast Files.
● Have students choose one of the communicable diseases discussed in Lesson 3 to research using print and online resources. Ask students to prepare a short report of what they found.

CLOSE

Call on volunteers to describe the symptoms, the treatment, and how to prevent the spread of a disease discussed in this lesson.

FOCUS

Activating Prior Knowledge

What I Know Ask students to name sexually transmitted diseases. For each STD named, ask volunteers to explain how it is treated.

Guide to Reading

Building Vocabulary

- Have students read the definition of STDs in the first paragraph. Ask for volunteers to name an STD they may have learned about in another health class.
- Use Vocabulary PuzzleMaker to reinforce vocabulary terms.

Reading Strategy

Organizing Information Have students create a three-column chart. List each STD described in the lesson in the left column. Have students describe the symptoms of the STD in the middle column and the treatments in the right column.

Quick Write

Before reading the lesson, have students write a brief paragraph about why it is important for teens to avoid sexual activity. After reading the lesson, call on volunteers to explain how they would change their paragraphs.

Sexually Transmitted Diseases

Guide to Reading

Building Vocabulary
As you read this lesson, write the term below and its definition in your notebook.

- sexually transmitted diseases (STDs) (p. 492)

Focusing on the Main Ideas
In this lesson, you will learn to

- **identify** common STDs and the problems they cause.
- **state** how to protect yourself from STDs.
- **explain** why abstinence until marriage is the best way to avoid getting an STD.

Reading Strategy
Organizing Information Create a chart listing each STD described in this lesson, its symptoms, and treatment.

Quick Write

Write a paragraph about why it is important for teens to avoid sexual activity.

What Are STDs?

Sexually transmitted diseases (STDs) are *infections that are spread from person to person through sexual contact.* They are sometimes called sexually transmitted infections (STIs). In the United States, STDs are a major health problem for teens. Each year, one-quarter of all new cases of STDs appear among 15- to 19-year-olds. One in four sexually active teens has an STD, although many do not even know it. However, STDs are completely preventable. This lesson will help you learn more about STDs, their causes, and how to avoid them. **Figure 18.5** lists some important facts about STDs.

Common STDs

STDs can cause serious health problems if left untreated. Anyone who suspects he or she may have an STD should see a doctor right away. Some common STDs are described below:

- **Chlamydia** (kluh·MI·dee·uh) is a bacterial STD that may affect the reproductive organs, urethra, and anus. Chlamydia can be treated with antibiotics. It is a "silent" disease because in many cases there are no symptoms. Symptoms can include genital discharge and pain when urinating. If left untreated, chlamydia can seriously damage the reproductive organs in both males and females, leading to infertility.

Lesson 4 Resources

📁 **Chapter FAST FILE Resources**
Guided Reading and Writing 18-4
Concept Mapping Activity 18-4
Health Lab 18-4
Reteaching Activity 18-4
Enrichment Activity 18-4
Lesson Quiz 18-4

Technology
🔌 Transparency 18-4
Audio Summaries
💿 *ExamView® Assessment Suite*
Vocabulary PuzzleMaker
StudentWorks™ Plus
Go Online

▼ FIGURE 18.5

R **WHAT YOU SHOULD KNOW ABOUT STDs**

Learning the facts about STDs can help you avoid them. **What is the best way for teens to avoid getting STDs?**

• Most STDs are spread only through sexual contact.
• You cannot tell if someone has an STD by his or her appearance.
• Most STDs have either very mild or no symptoms.
• Many STDs can be treated and cured, but early diagnosis is important.
• Because treatments for STDs vary, they must be accurately identified.
• STDs can recur because the body does not build up an immunity to them.
• STDs can cause sterility, blindness, deafness, and birth defects.

- **Genital herpes** (HER·peez) is a viral STD that produces painful blisters on the genital area. This STD is transmitted by skin-to-skin contact that can occur without having sexual intercourse. It results in periodic outbreaks of painful blisters or sores on the genitals. Herpes can be passed on to another person even when the blisters are not present. Although there is no cure, medicines are available to lessen the outbreaks.

U
- **Genital warts** are growths or bumps in the genital area caused by certain types of the human papillomavirus (HPV). This STD is also transmitted by skin-to-skin contact. Genital warts can be treated, but there is no cure for HPV infection. These infections are the most common type of STD in the United States. Like genital herpes and chlamydia, HPV is often a silent disease. Some strains of HPV are linked to the cause of cervical and skin cancers. A vaccine has recently been developed to protect females against these strains of the HPV virus.

- **Trichomoniasis** (TREE·koh·moh·NI·ah·sis) is an STD caused by the protozoan *Trichomonas vaginalis*. Trichomoniasis can be treated and cured with medications. The disease may be silent, but symptoms can include discomfort during urination, genital discharge, and irritation or itching in the genital area.

Careers for the 21st Century

Epidemiologist

Epidemiologists are medical detectives. They study what causes diseases and how to prevent diseases from spreading. Some epidemiologists work in hospitals and labs. Epidemiologists will always be in demand because diseases are a reality, all over the world. If you are interested in becoming an epidemiologist, you should study communicable diseases, how they affect the body, and how the diseases are spread.

What kind of skills does an epidemiologist need? Go to *Career Corner* at **glencoe.com** to find out.

Lesson 4: Sexually Transmitted Diseases **493**

TEACH

R **Reading Strategy**

Analyzing a Graphic After students have examined **Figure 18.5**, ask: How can you tell by a person's appearance whether that person has an STD? *You cannot tell if someone has an STD by his or her appearance.* If someone thinks he or she has an STD, why must the specific STD be accurately identified by a medical professional? *because treatments for STDs vary* Why can a person have the same STD over and over again? *The body does not build up an immunity to STDs.* **OL**

U **Universal Access**

English Learners Have students make a chart listing the names and symptoms of common STDs. **EL**

Careers for the 21st Century

Epidemiologist Ask students: How are epidemiologists like detectives? Have students read the information about skills an epidemiologist might need at **glencoe.com**. Ask several volunteers to read on-line articles about the work of epidemiologists and to summarize those articles for the rest of the class.

Caption Answers

Figure Caption by avoiding sexual contact

HEALTH LITERACY

Herpes Some people believe that there is a "good" herpes virus and a "bad" herpes virus, but research shows this is not true. There are two viruses that cause herpes, HSV-1 and HSV-2. The virus called HSV-1 generally causes fever blisters on the mouth, lips, and nose. The virus called HSV-2 generally causes sores on the vagina, buttocks, penis, and elsewhere. In reality, both HSV-1 and HSV-2 can cause either genital or oral infections. Both viruses can be spread when there are no symptoms.

HS Health Skills Practice

Good Communication Divide the class into small groups, and ask each group to create a role-play that demonstrates effective refusal skills when a date is pressuring you to engage in sexual activity. Have each group perform its role-play for the class. After all groups have performed, lead a class discussion about which communication strategies would likely prove most effective on a real date. **OL**

Reading Check

Answer examples include chlamydia, gonorrhea, and syphilis

Caption Answer

Photo Caption, this page
Sample answers: play basketball, go to the movies, shop at the mall

What Teens THINK

What are some fun activities teens can do with their friends? Have students read and discuss the question and their responses. Divide students into cooperative groups, and have the members of each group list at least ten activities that are both fun and healthful for groups of teens.

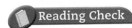

Go Online

Visit **glencoe.com** and complete the Interactive Study Guide for Lesson 4.

- **Gonorrhea** (gah·nuh·REE·uh) is a bacterial STD that affects the mucous membranes of the body, particularly in the genital area. Symptoms include a thick yellowish discharge from the genitals and a burning sensation when urinating. The infection can be treated with antibiotics. Untreated, it can infect other parts of the body, such as the heart, and cause fertility problems for both women and men.

- **Syphilis** (SIH·fuh·luhs) is a bacterial STD that can affect many parts of the body. It can damage body organs, such as the brain. During the advanced stage, the disease can cause mental disorders, blindness, heart problems, paralysis, and even death. If diagnosed early, syphilis can be treated and cured with antibiotics.

- **Pelvic inflammatory disease (PID)** is a general infection of the female reproductive organs. Most females become infected with PID as a result of contracting another STD, such as chlamydia or gonorrhea. When PID is untreated, the infection may worsen over time and cause sterility.

- **HIV/AIDS** is a serious STD covered in the next lesson.

Reading Check

Give Examples Name three STDs that are caused by bacteria.

Practicing Abstinence

The best way to avoid getting an STD is to abstain from sexual activity until marriage. As a teen, deciding to say no to sexual activity is one of the most important health choices that you can make.

▼ Group activities can help you avoid situations where you may feel pressure to engage in sexual activity. **What activities do you and your friends like to do together?**

494

Teacher to Teacher

Ivy Kurland   **Everglades School, Florida**

STD Presentations "I divide students into groups of four and have them create oral presentations on a specific STD, including the disease's symptoms and treatments. The students learn from each other and enjoy doing the work together. This instills collaboration and as teacher, I can work closely with my students."

HS Make a commitment to practice abstinence and demonstrate your commitment through words and actions. Choose friends who share your values and support your decisions.

Avoid being alone on a date. By participating in group activities, you can avoid the pressures of sexual activity. If you do go on a one-on-one date, communicate your limits to your date before you go out. Practice how to respond to a date who tries to pressure you into sexual activity. For example, if your date says, "If you really care for me, you would have sex with me," you can say, "If you really care for me, you would respect my decision."

 Reading Check

Describe What are some ways to avoid being pressured to engage in sexual activity?

What **Teens** THINK

What are some fun activities teens can do with their friends?

My friends and I like to see movies or walk to the park. We also like to go the beach together and just relax. However, I think that it matters most who you're with rather than what you do. The whole point is to have a good time.

Emma D.
Thousand Oaks, CA

Reading Check

Answer Participate in group activities, communicate your limits to your date before going out, and choose friends who support your decision to practice abstinence.

ASSESS

 Assessment Resources

Lesson Review Quiz
ExamView
Fast Files Activities
Online Quizzes and Activities

Reteaching

● Assign Concept Map 18-4 or Reteaching Activity 18-4 in the Fast Files.
● Have students write a brief description of each of the common STDs, including symptoms and treatment.

Enrichment

● Assign Enrichment Activity 18-4 in the Fast Files.
● Ask students to write a script for a favorite TV show that shows teens struggling with abstinence when faced with peer pressure that promotes sexual activity.

CLOSE

Call on students to describe a misconception that they had about STDs before reading Lesson 4 and to explain what changed their thinking.

Lesson 4 Review

After You Read

Review this lesson for new terms, major headings, and Reading Checks.

What I Learned

1. *Vocabulary* Define *sexually transmitted disease*.

2. *Give Examples* What are three examples of STDs that are considered "silent diseases"?

3. *List* Name three consequences of untreated chlamydia.

Thinking Critically

4. *Apply* Why is abstinence until marriage the best choice for teens?

5. *Evaluate* Why is it important to immediately seek help from a health care professional if you suspect you have an STD?

Applying Health Skills

6. *Advocacy* Create a booklet that tells teens about the dangers of STDs. It should highlight the most common STDs, how they are spread, and their symptoms. Also include how teens can avoid getting STDs.

Go Online For more Lesson Review Activities, go to glencoe.com.   Lesson 4: Sexually Transmitted Diseases **495**

Lesson 4 Review Answers

1. A sexually transmitted disease is an infection that is spread from person to person through sexual contact.

2. *Sample answer:* chlamydia, genital herpes, genital warts

3. genital discharge, pain when urinating, infertility

4. Practicing abstinence is the best way to protect yourself from exposure to STDs.

5. If left untreated, STDs can cause a number of serious health problems.

6. You may want to have pairs of students or students in small groups work together to create a booklet. Booklets will vary. A good booklet should be attractive and well written, with accurate information about the most common STDs. It should also discuss the benefits of abstinence.

FOCUS

Activating Prior Knowledge

What I Know Ask for a volunteer to describe the difference between HIV and AIDS. Tell them they will learn what causes AIDS and how the disease is spread.

 ### Guide to Reading

Building Vocabulary
- Explain to students that an acronym is a word formed from the first letters of a name. Ask students whether either AIDS or HIV or both are acronyms.
- Use Vocabulary PuzzleMaker to reinforce vocabulary terms.

Reading Strategy
Identify Problems and Solutions After students have read the lesson, call on volunteers to identify ways that HIV is not spread.

Quick Write

Have each student make a list of myths and facts about HIV and AIDS. After students have read the lesson, call on volunteers to share items from their lists that they would revise with the information they have learned.

HIV/AIDS

 ## Guide to Reading

● **Building Vocabulary**
Write down each term and what you think it means. As you find the terms in this lesson, make any necessary corrections.
- HIV (human immunodeficiency virus) (p. 496)
- AIDS (acquired immunodeficiency syndrome) (p. 496)
- opportunistic infection (p. 496)
- carrier (p. 496)

● **Focusing on the Main Ideas**
In this lesson, you will learn to
- **define** HIV and AIDS.
- **explain** how people become infected with HIV and develop AIDS.
- **describe** how to avoid getting HIV and AIDS.

● **Reading Strategy**
Identifying Problems and Solutions After reading this lesson, identify ways that HIV is transmitted. Then, identify ways to prevent the spread of HIV.

Quick Write

List what you have heard about HIV or AIDS. Are they myths or facts?

What Is HIV? What Is AIDS?

HIV (human immunodeficiency virus) is *the virus that causes AIDS.* **AIDS (acquired immunodeficiency syndrome)** is *a deadly disease that interferes with the body's natural ability to fight infection.* HIV attacks the body's T cells. As mentioned in Lesson 2, T cells are a type of lymphocyte that help the body fight off pathogens. When the HIV virus attacks a T cell, it replaces the cell's genetic information with its own and then multiplies. As more T cells are taken over, the immune system becomes weaker.

Eventually, the body can no longer fight the pathogens that a healthy immune system would destroy. When this happens, AIDS develops. One symptom that signals the onset of AIDS is the presence of opportunistic infections. An **opportunistic infection** is *an infection that rarely occurs in a healthy person.* For example, many AIDS patients develop a type of pneumonia that can cause death.

A person can be a carrier of HIV, without having AIDS. A **carrier** is *a person who appears healthy but is infected with HIV and can pass it to others.* A person may be infected with HIV for ten years or more before starting to show symptoms of AIDS. A blood test is the only way of knowing if a person is infected with HIV. AIDS can affect men, women, and children of all ages. **Figure 18.6** shows the number of new AIDS cases diagnosed by age group in

Lesson 5 Resources

📁 **Chapter *FAST FILE* Resources**
Guided Reading and Writing 18-5
Concept Mapping Activity 18-5
Cross-Curriculum Activity 18-5
Reteaching Activity 18-5
Enrichment Activity 18-5
Lesson Quiz 18-5

Technology
🔦 Transparency 18-5
💿 Audio Summaries
💿 *ExamView®* Assessment Suite
💿 Vocabulary PuzzleMaker
💿 StudentWorks™ Plus
G🔵 **Online**

2005. The table also shows how many total AIDS cases have been diagnosed by age group through the end of 2005. How do you think this information is used to help reduce the spread of HIV?

How Does HIV Spread?

HIV is spread from person to person through contact with specific body fluids. These fluids are sperm, fluid from the vagina, blood, and breast milk.

One of the ways HIV spreads is through sexual contact with an infected person. Just one incident of sexual activity with an infected person can spread the virus. People who have more than one sex partner are at greatest risk.

Another way HIV is spread is through sharing needles. Many injection drug users have contracted HIV. Tattoos and body piercings can also spread HIV if performed with contaminated needles.

HIV can also be spread from mother to child. This can occur either before or after delivery, or through breast-feeding. In recent years, new drug therapies have reduced the rate of transmission of HIV to the fetus during pregnancy.

ACTIVITY

Go Online

Topic: Staying Alive

Visit glencoe.com for Student Web Activities to learn more about HIV/AIDS, and what teens are doing to help stop the spread of HIV.

Activity: Using the information provided at the link above, create a FAQ sheet about HIV and AIDS that can be made available to teens throughout your community.

▼ FIGURE 18.6

U.S. AIDS CASES AT AGE OF DIAGNOSIS, 2005

R AIDS can develop months or even years after infection with HIV. Why would this long span of time make the spread of the disease harder to control?

Age	Estimated # of AIDS Cases in 2005	Cumulative Estimated # of AIDS Cases, Through 2005
Under 13	58	9,089
Ages 13 to 14	66	1,015
Ages 15 to 24	2,480	40,296
Ages 25 to 34	9,374	309,048
Ages 35 to 44	16,792	374,707
Ages 45 to 54	11,230	160,662
Ages 55 to 64	3,308	47,242
Ages 65 to older	899	14,606

Source: CDC—Division of HIV/AIDS Prevention.

TEACH

ACTIVITY

Go Online

Staying Alive
Encourage students to work in teams or small groups to research facts about stopping the spread of HIV/AIDS. Have groups create their FAQs, and allow time for each group to share their results.

R Reading Strategy

Analyzing a Graphic After students have examined **Figure 18.6**, ask: Why do you think there were many more AIDS cases through 2005 for children under 13 than there were for teens ages 13 to 14? *The cases of children under 13 include all babies who had HIV transferred to them during pregnancy.* Which age group had the most AIDS cases, both in 2005 and cumulatively? *ages 35 to 44* Is that surprising to you? Sample answer: *Yes. Most people think that younger people are more likely to contract AIDS.* **OL**

Caption Answer

Figure Caption People will continue to have sexual contact and spread the disease without knowing that they have the disease themselves.

TECHNOLOGY AND HEALTH

AIDS Treatment When the first people were diagnosed with AIDS in the United States, there was no effective treatment. Since then, researchers have developed many medicines to treat AIDS infections. These drugs have changed the disease from one that carried a death sentence to one that can be managed over many years. HIV is a virus that can become resistant to the drugs used against it. As a result, most people infected with HIV and people that have AIDS are treated with a combination of drugs. The multiple drugs people take daily have sometimes been called an "AIDS cocktail."

▲ When people visit an AIDS patient in the hospital, they need to take precautions to protect the patient from infection. **Why is it necessary for these actions to be taken?**

Academic Vocabulary

reluctant (ri LUHK tehnt) *(adjective)* holding back or unwilling. *Just because you feel fine doesn't mean that you should be reluctant to see your doctor for your yearly checkup.*

At one time, HIV was spread through donated blood. Since 1985, all donated blood in the United States is tested for HIV. As a result, the risk of getting HIV from a blood transfusion is extremely low.

How HIV Is NOT Spread

False ideas and myths about how HIV is spread have circulated for many years. They have even made people **reluctant** to donate blood. It is important to be aware of these myths and to learn the facts. HIV is spread only through contact with specific body fluids. It is not spread through casual touching or any of the following ways:

- Breathing the air
- Being bitten by a mosquito
- Swimming in a pool
- Sharing utensils
- Donating blood
- Hugging or shaking hands
- Using the same shower, bathtub, or toilet as an infected person

 Reading Check **Recall** What are four ways that HIV is not spread?

Fighting AIDS

Scientists continue to work on improved medical treatments for people with HIV and AIDS. Currently, there is no cure for HIV or AIDS. However, drugs are available that slow down the progress of HIV infection. Unfortunately, many of these drugs are costly and can have serious side effects. Scientists are also working on a vaccine for HIV, but this will probably take many more years. The best weapons in the fight against HIV and AIDS are knowledge and abstinence until marriage.

 Reading Check **Identify** What treatment is available for people with HIV infection?

What Teens Want to Know

Can I get AIDS by kissing someone infected with HIV? Remind students that saliva is one of the body's five major barriers to pathogens. Saliva contains proteins that reduce the ability of HIV to infect a person. According to the Centers for Disease Control and Prevention (CDC), there is no risk of transmission for a close-mouthed kiss. Because HIV can spread by contact with blood, there is a very low risk of transmission through a prolonged kiss when the infected person has mouth sores.

▶ Practicing abstinence until marriage allows you to enjoy healthful activities with your friends. **How can friends help you practice abstinence?**

Preventing HIV/AIDS

HIV infection and AIDS can be prevented. There are three main ways to avoid these diseases:

- **Practice abstinence.** Abstinence is the conscious, active choice not to participate in high-risk behaviors. This includes avoiding sexual activity until marriage.
- **Avoid drugs and alcohol.** Using drugs and alcohol can impair your ability to make healthful decisions. This can lead to participation in other risky behaviors, such as sexual activity.
- **Avoid sharing needles.** Needles can carry HIV into your bloodstream. This includes needles that are used for tattoos or body piercings.

 Go Online

Visit **glencoe.com** and complete the Interactive Study Guide for Lesson 5.

Lesson 5 Review

 After You Read

Review this lesson for new terms, major headings, and Reading Checks.

What I Learned

1. *Vocabulary* Define *HIV* and *carrier*.

2. *Give Examples* What are two ways teens can get infected with HIV?

3. *Recall* How does HIV weaken the body's immune system?

Thinking Critically

4. *Analyze* Why is HIV an extremely dangerous virus?

5. *Apply* Jasmine doesn't want to share tennis rackets with Mei, who has HIV.

Jasmine is afraid of getting infected with HIV. What could you tell Jasmine?

Applying Health Skills

6. *Goal Setting* Think of how you want to avoid exposure to HIV infection, AIDS, or other STDs. Set a goal to protect yourself from these diseases. Develop a plan to help you reach your goal. Be clear and specific about the steps you will take to reach your goal.

Go Online For more Lesson Review Activities, go to **glencoe.com**.

Lesson 5: HIV/AIDS   **499**

ASSESS

Assessment Resources

Lesson Review Quiz
- *ExamView*
- Fast Files Activities
- Online Quizzes and Activities

Reteaching

- Assign Concept Map 18-5 or Reteaching Activity 18-5 in the Fast Files.
- Have students write five true/false questions that focus on ways that HIV spreads and does not spread, and exchange questions with a partner.

Enrichment

- Assign Enrichment Activity 18-5 in the Fast Files.
- Ask students to identify organizations that provide support for people with HIV/AIDS.

CLOSE

Ask volunteers to explain how their understanding of HIV/AIDS has changed after reading Lesson 5.

Lesson 5 Review Answers

1. HIV is the virus that causes AIDS. A carrier is a person who appears healthy but is infected with HIV and can pass it to others.

2. *Sample answer:* by having sexual contact with an infected person or by using a contaminated needle

3. It attacks and kills T cells so that the immune system cannot attack HIV or any other infection.

4. *Sample answer:* There is no vaccine to prevent infection with HIV. There is no cure for AIDS. AIDS can eventually cause death.

5. *Sample answer:* HIV cannot be spread by casual contact, and so sharing a tennis racket with Mei will not spread the disease to Jasmine.

6. Goals will vary. A goal for most students will be to practice abstinence. Students should be specific about their goals and how they will implement those goals.

Building Health Skills — Protect Yourself From Pathogens

Skill

> Goal Setting

Activating Prior Knowledge

Have students review the material in Lesson 1 about how to keep pathogens from spreading, including the lists of how to protect yourself from germs and how to protect others from pathogens.

- **Objective** After completing the activity, students will be able to set and achieve a personal health goal.
- **Time** 45 minutes
- **Materials** pencil, paper

Teacher Classroom Resources

📁 Building Health Skills
🖨 Transparency 18-1

Model

- Call on volunteers to read aloud the introductory paragraphs in the Model section and the five steps of Jennifer's plan to meet her goal.
- Ask: How did Jennifer's parents help her? *They gave her advice on the best way to clean.*

National Health Standards Addressed
- - - - - - - - - - - - - - - -
6.8.1, 6.8.2, 6.8.3

500

Building Health Skills

Accessing Information
Practicing Healthful Behaviors
Stress Management
Analyzing Influences
Communication Skills
Refusal Skills
Conflict Resolution
Decision Making
> Goal Setting
Advocacy

What Is Goal Setting?

Goal setting is a five-step plan for improving and maintaining your personal health. Some goals are easy to reach while others may be more challenging.

The 5 Steps of the Goal-Setting Plan

Step 1: Choose a realistic goal and write it down.

Step 2: List the steps that you need to take to reach the goal.

Step 3: Find others, like family, friends, and teachers who can help and support you.

Step 4: Set checkpoints along the way to evaluate your progress.

Step 5: Reward yourself once you have reached your goal.

Protect Yourself from Pathogens

Follow the Model, Practice, and Apply steps to help you master this important health skill.

❶ Model

Read how Jennifer uses the skill of goal setting to improve her health.

Jennifer noticed that she was sick a lot during the school year. She thought that it had to do with her messy room. Jennifer used the skill of goal setting to clean her room and get healthy.

1. Jennifer wanted to keep her room clean for a month. (Identify a specific goal.)

2. Jennifer put her dirty clothes in the hamper. She threw out her trash and took her dirty plates to the kitchen. She vacuumed and dusted her furniture. (List the steps you will take.)

3. Jennifer asked her mom and dad for advice on the best way to clean. (Ask for help and support from others.)

4. After two weeks, Jennifer felt better and her room looked good. (Evaluate your progress.)

5. At the end of the month, Jennifer bought a new CD. (Reward yourself.)

Teaching Tips

Planning for Obstacles In the practice section, point out that unexpected obstacles can interfere with achieving one's goals. This is why all steps of the goal-setting process must be used.

Reviewing Students' Health Goals Check each student's health goal for appropriateness at the beginning of the Apply section. Be ready with specific suggestions (proper hand washing, not sharing utensils, seeking medical care, etc.). Near the end of this activity, identify exemplary papers and have students read these aloud.

❷ Practice

Help Paul use goal setting to achieve his goal of reducing the number of colds he gets each year.

Paul likes having a clean, uncluttered room. He also likes how achieving a goal builds his self-confidence. Now Paul wants to reduce the number of colds he gets every school year. He believes that he could achieve this if he washed his hands more frequently.

1. What is Paul's goal?
2. What steps can help Paul reach his goal?
3. Who can Paul get to help him?
4. How can Paul evaluate his progress?
5. How can he reward himself for following his plan?

❸ Apply

Use what you have learned about goal setting to complete the activity below.

Think of how you can better protect yourself from disease. How would you accomplish this goal? Take a piece of paper and make a reminder to post in your room. On your reminder include a plan that will help you reach your goal. Use art to illustrate how achieving your goal will improve your physical, mental/emotional, and social health.

Self-Check

■ Does my reminder contain the steps for achieving my goal?
■ Did I show how my goal will improve my health?

Building Health Skills

Building Health Skills **501**

Practice

- Have students work in pairs to discuss the questions. Ask each pair of students to write a response to the questions.
- Lead a class discussion of the responses. Ask volunteers to share how they answered each of the questions.

Apply/Assess

- Have students work individually to formulate a goal to protect themselves from disease. Have them write down the specific steps to meet that goal.
- Call on volunteers to share their goal-setting plan with the class. Set a date in the future for students to report whether they were able to meet their goals.
- You may wish to distribute Building Health Skills Activity in the Fast Files.

ASSESSMENT SCORING

Using a rubric, student work should meet all criteria to achieve the highest score.

Skills Student work:
- includes a specific goal statement.
- lists steps to achieve the goal.
- identifies sources of help.
- evaluates progress.

- provides a healthy reward.

Concepts Student work:
- identifies a goal.
- provides accurate information.
- shows the relationship between disease prevention/control and health.
- draws conclusions.

Healthy Habits

Time: 30 minutes
Materials: pencil and paper

Introducing Hands-on Health

- Have a class discussion about healthy habits, with a focus on what students have learned about how to keep pathogens from spreading. Ask: Is anything wrong if students playing soccer drink water from the same water bottle? Sample answer: *Water-bottle sharing can spread pathogens and should be avoided.* Have students respond to similar questions about common actions that may or may not be healthy.

Teaching the Activity

- Have students respond *yes* or *no* to each statement.
- Lead a class discussion about the students' responses. Read each question aloud, then ask volunteers to share their responses.
- Ask students to suggest other healthy habits that every person should adopt to prevent the spread of pathogens.

HANDS-ON HEALTH

Healthy Habits

How healthy are your habits? This activity will help you find out.

What You Will Need

- pencil and paper

 What You Will Do

Write *yes* or *no* for each statement.

1. I avoid sharing eating utensils or drinking glasses with others.
2. I avoid drinking water from streams and lakes.
3. I cover my nose and mouth when I cough or sneeze.
4. I make sure leftover food is properly stored.
5. I wash my hands after using the bathroom and before preparing or serving food.
6. When I am sick, I get medical care.
7. When I am sick, I avoid others during the contagious period.
8. I avoid sharing combs, brushes, and towels with others.
9. I avoid contact with people who have a cold or other communicable diseases.
10. I have received all the recommended vaccinations.

Wrapping It Up

Give yourself 1 point for each yes. A score of 8–10 is very good. A score of 6–7 is good. A score of 4–5 is fair. If you score below 4, you need to work on improving your health behaviors.

HANDS-ON HEALTH Assessment

Discussion After students have completed the inventory and reviewed their answers, open a discussion about effective ways to prevent the spread of pathogens. Have students share their suggestions for healthy habits and record suggestions on the board. Ask for a show of hands to determine which habit students think should rank first in importance in their daily routines.

Reading Review

 STUDY TO GO Visit glencoe.com to download quizzes and eFlashcards for Chapter 18.

FOLDABLES Study Organizer

Foldables® and Other Study Aids Get out the Foldable® you created for Lesson 1 and any graphic organizers that you made for Lessons 1–5. Find a partner and quiz one another using these study aids.

Lesson 1 Preventing the Spread of Disease

Main Idea You can help protect yourself and others from pathogens by practicing good hygiene.

- A communicable disease is a disease that can be passed to a person from another person, animal, or object.
- The four common pathogens are viruses, bacteria, fungi, and protozoa.

Lesson 2 The Body's Defenses Against Infection

Main Idea The five major barriers that protect you from infection are tears, mucous membranes, saliva, skin, and stomach acid.

- Your immune system responds when a pathogen gets past the five major barriers of protection.
- The immune system has two main responses: the nonspecific response and the specific response.
- Vaccines help the immune system make antibodies for certain diseases.

Lesson 3 Common Communicable Diseases

Main Idea Common communicable diseases include colds, the flu, mononucleosis, hepatitis, tuberculosis, pneumonia, and strep throat.

- The contagious period is the length of time that a particular disease can be spread from person to person.

Lesson 4 Sexually Transmitted Diseases

Main Idea Chlamydia, genital warts, genital herpes, trichomoniasis, gonorrhea, syphilis, and hepatitis B are common STDs.

- STDs are diseases that are spread from person to person through sexual contact.
- The best way to avoid getting an STD is to abstain from sexual activity until marriage.

Lesson 5 HIV/AIDS

Main Idea HIV is the virus that causes AIDS.

- HIV is spread through contact with sperm, vaginal fluid, blood, or breast milk.
- HIV is not spread through casual touching, breathing the air, mosquito bites, swimming in a pool, sharing utensils, donating blood, hugging or shaking hands, or using the same shower, bathtub, or toilet as an infected person.
- Abstinence until marriage is the only sure way to protect yourself against HIV infection, AIDS, and other STDs.

Chapter 18 Reading Review **503**

 Assessment Resources

- Chapter 18 Summary and Activity
- Audio Summaries
- Reading Tutor
- Performance Assessment
- Chapter 18 Test
- *ExamView®* Assessment Suite
- Vocabulary PuzzleMaker
- Online Learning Center

Reading Review

Study Aids

- **Using the Dinah Zike Foldable® Study Organizer** Have students use the Foldable® **FOLDABLES Study Organizer** to review the content of Lesson 1. Call on volunteers to identify types of pathogens, which diseases are caused by which kinds of pathogens, and how the spread of disease can be prevented.
- **Online Learning Tools** Have students go to the *Teen Health* Online Learning Center at **glencoe.com** to:
  - Download a **Podcast**.
  - Download free **Study-to-Go** content to their PDAs or cell phones.

Vocabulary Review

- **Vocabulary Notebook** Have students define the chapter's vocabulary terms in their own words.

Teaching Tips

Preview Strategies for Reading The ability to read is important to the success of any student. Yet many students experience difficulty in mastering this necessary skill. To improve students' comprehension and retention, have them preview required reading selections. Before students begin reading, make sure they read any introductions. Another good idea is to have them organize all the headings and subheadings in an outline form, leaving spaces for supporting details as they read through the selection.

Reviewing Vocabulary and Main Ideas

1. disease
2. infection
3. Viruses
4. Inflammation
5. immune system
6. Antibodies
7. Influenza
8. contagious period
9. Tuberculosis
10. False, sexual
11. True
12. True
13. True
14. False, cannot
15. False, help manage

Thinking Critically

16. *Sample answer:* AIDS interferes with the body's immune system and its ability to fight infections. As a result, a serious infection can cause death.

17. *Sample answer:* Some vaccinations must be given repeatedly during a person's lifetime because a vaccination may protect the person for only several years.

Go Online

Have students visit **glencoe.com** to take the Chapter 18 quiz.

After You Read

Health eSpotlight   VIDEO

Now that you have read the chapter, look back at your answer to the Health eSpotlight question on the chapter opener. What are some common STDs, and what health problems are associated with these infections?

Reviewing Vocabulary and Main Ideas

On a sheet of paper, write the numbers 1–9. After each number, write the term from the list that best completes each statement.

- disease
- immune system
- infection
- viruses
- antibodies
- vaccine
- influenza
- contagious period
- tuberculosis
- inflammation

Lesson 1 Preventing the Spread of Disease

1. A(n) _____ is any condition that interferes with the proper functioning of the body or mind.

2. A(n) _____ is a condition that occurs when pathogens enter the body, multiply, and cause harm.

3. _____ are the smallest kinds of pathogens.

Lesson 2 The Body's Defenses Against Infection

4. _____ is the body's response to injury or disease, resulting in a condition of swelling, pain, heat, and redness.

5. The _____ is a combination of body defenses made up of the cells, tissues, and organs that fight pathogens in the body.

6. _____ are proteins made by B cells that bind to specific antigens.

Lesson 3 Common Communicable Diseases

7. _____ is a communicable disease characterized by fever, chills, fatigue, headache, muscle aches, and respiratory symptoms.

8. The _____ is the length of time that a particular disease can be spread from person to person.

9. _____ is a bacterial disease that usually affects the lungs.

*On a sheet of paper, write the numbers 10–15. Write **True** or **False** for each statement below. If the statement is false, change the underlined word or phrase to make it true.*

Lesson 4 Sexually Transmitted Diseases

10. Sexually transmitted diseases are infections that spread from person to person through <u>casual</u> contact.

11. Syphilis is a bacterial STD that can affect <u>many parts of the body</u>.

12. Genital herpes <u>can</u> be transmitted when symptoms are not present.

Lesson 5 HIV/AIDS

13. HIV is the virus that causes <u>AIDS</u>.

14. You <u>can</u> become infected with HIV by shaking hands with an infected person.

Go Online Visit **glencoe.com** and take the Online Quiz for Chapter 18.

Health eSpotlight   VIDEO *Wrap-Up*

The Truth About STDs Have students reread the Health eSpotlight question at the beginning of the chapter (page 477) and look at their original answer. Ask: Now that you have read the chapter and watched the video presentation, what role can abstinence play in reducing the new cases of STDs in teens?

15. Scientists have developed powerful new drugs to <u>cure</u> HIV infections.

Thinking Critically

Using complete sentences, answer the following questions on a sheet of paper.

16. **Explain** Why do people who have AIDS actually die from other diseases?

17. **Interpret** Sometimes after you get a vaccination, years later you have to get more of the same vaccine. Why do you think you might need this "booster shot"?

Write About It

18. **Personal Writing** Write a journal entry describing what factors can influence a teen's attitude toward sexual activity. Are these influences positive or negative?

Applying Technology

Communicate Choices, Not Diseases

You and a partner will use Microsoft Word® and Clip Art to create a brochure that reflects your understanding of communicable diseases.

- Open a new Microsoft Word® project with a portrait view and three columns.
- Using information from one of the lessons in this chapter, select five facts and write about them.
- Use Clip Art to locate images, or take digital photos that relate to your topic.
- Add the images and text to your brochure. Make it visually appealing.
- Edit and print your brochure.
- With your principal's permission, pass the brochure out to students.

Applying Technology

Communication Choices, Not Diseases
Equipment needs: Microsoft Word® or similar software and clip art
Help students review and discuss the steps in creating these brochures. Remind students of the importance of editing the brochures carefully so they will be clear and appealing to other students. Assign project partners. Create a sign-up list if access to computers is limited, and help students agree on a time limit for computer use.

Standardized Test Practice

Reading

Read the passage and then answer the questions.

During the Middle Ages, hundreds of people were killed by the bubonic plague in a very short time. The pathogen for the bubonic plague is a bacterium called *Yersinia pestis*. It lived inside fleas, which lived on rats. The rats became infected when the fleas bit them. Even uninfected fleas that bit infected rats could become infected. When the fleas jumped from rat to rat, the plague spread quickly. As the disease moved through the cities' rat populations, the rats died off. As the number of rats decreased, more and more infected fleas started living on and biting humans. People became hosts for the bacterium. During 1347 to 1350, the bubonic plague killed one-third of Europe's population.

TEST-TAKING TIP

When a question asks for the main point of the passage, reread the first and last sentences. This is where the authors often place the most important information.

1. The main point of this passage is to explain how
   A. fleas can live on rats and humans.
   B. the plague killed so many people so quickly.
   C. to prevent the plague from killing humans.
   D. Europe's population became so low.

2. Read this sentence from the passage. The pathogen for the bubonic plague is a bacterium called *Yersinia pestis*. What does *pathogen* mean?
   A. path   C. name
   B. antigen   D. germ

Write About It

18. **Personal Writing**
Students' journal entries, which will vary, should describe factors that can influence a teen's attitudes about sexual activity. For example, a student might describe a family's value of not having sexual contact before marriage as influencing a teen. Ask teens to identify which influences are positive and which are negative.

Standardized Test Practice

1. B
2. D

Test-Taking Tips

The Main Idea Explain to students that paragraphs in textbook writing often follow a pattern of topic, support, and conclusion. The first sentence of the paragraph is often a topic sentence, which clearly states the topic or main idea of the paragraph. The sentences that follow contain details or arguments that support the topic sentence. The paragraph often ends with a concluding sentence, which sums up and often restates the main idea. Explain that this pattern is not always used, but students should keep this common pattern in mind when looking for the main idea of a paragraph.

CHAPTER 19 pp. 506–537	Standards		Skills and Activities
	National	State/Local	
	National Health Education Standards 2.8.1, 2.8.4, 6.8.2		**HEALTH INVENTORY**, *p. 507* **BUILDING HEALTH SKILLS** *Goal Setting* Lifelong Good Health Habits, *pp. 532–533* TIME health news The Road to a Cure, *p. 534*
Lesson 1 **Causes of Noncommunicable Diseases** pp. 508–510	National Health Education Standard 1.8.1, 1.8.3, 1.8.4, 1.8.5, 8.8.1		
Lesson 2 **Cancer** pp. 511–516	National Health Education Standards 1.8.1, 1.8.5, 1.8.6, 1.8.8, 1.8.9, 3.8.4, 8.8.1, 8.8.3		**MEDIA WATCH** Celebrity Cancer Stories, *p. 512* **HEALTH SKILLS ACTIVITY** *Advocacy* Reducing the Risk of Cancer, *p. 516*
Lesson 3 **Heart and Circulatory Problems** pp. 517–521	National Health Education Standards 1.8.1, 1.8.5, 1.8.6, 1.8.8, 1.8.9, 3.8.4, 6.8.3, 7.8.1		**G**⊙ **Online** Taking Positive Action, *p. 519* **HEALTH SKILLS ACTIVITY** *Analyzing Influences* Heart-Healthy Ads, *p. 520*
Lesson 4 **Diabetes and Arthritis** pp. 522–526	National Health Education Standards 1.81, 1.8.5, 2.8.6, 3.8.4, 7.8.1, 8.8.1, 8.8.2		**What Teens Think** If you had to give advice to someone on how to stay healthy, what would you tell them?, *p. 523* **Connect To... SCIENCE** Monitoring Glucose Levels, *p. 523* **Careers for the 21st Century** Family Practice Physicians, *p. 525*
Lesson 5 **Allergies and Asthma** pp. 527–531	National Health Education Standards 1.8.3, 1.8.5, 3.8.1, 3.8.3, 3.8.4, 4.8.4, 8.8.1		

PACING THE CHAPTER

Lesson 1	45 min	Lesson 4	45 min	Chapter Review	45 min
Lesson 2	45 min	Lesson 5	45 min	TIME health news	30 min
Lesson 3	45 min	Building Health Skills	45 min		

BLOCK SCHEDULING

For block scheduling, assign students Building Health Skills feature *Lifelong Good Health Habits*, pages 532–533, and Guided Reading and Writing. 📁

Planning Guide

StudentWorks Plus

Glencoe Exclusive!
TeacherWorks Plus
All-In-One Planner and Resource Center

Reproducible Resources	Assessment	Media and Technology
Chapter FAST FILE Resources Chapter Summaries and Activities `REVIEW` Building Health Skills Activity `TEACH` Performance Assessment Activity `EXTEND` Universal Access Activities `TEACH` Parent Letter and Activities 📁 **Student Activities Workbook** `TEACH` 📁 **Reading Tutor** `TEACH`	Building Health Skills Activity, *pp. 532–533* Chapter 19 Assessment, *pp. 536–537* **Chapter FAST FILE Resources** Performance Assessment Activity Chapter 19 Test ⊙ *ExamView® Assessment Suite*	**TeacherWorks Plus** includes: ● Interactive Teacher Edition ● Lesson Planner with Calendar ● Access to all blackline masters ● Correlations to standards ● Links to glencoe.com ⊙ StudentWorks™ Plus 🖱 Online Student Edition Dinah Zike's Teaching Health with Foldables®
Chapter FAST FILE Resources Concept Mapping Activity 19-1 `REVIEW` Decision-Making Activity 19-1 `EXTEND` Enrichment Activity 19-1 `EXTEND` Lesson Plan 19-1 Guided Reading and Writing 19-1 `TEACH` Reteaching Activity 19-1 `REVIEW`	Lesson 1 Review, *p. 510* 🖱 Vocabulary PuzzleMaker ⊙ *ExamView® Assessment Suite*	🖱 Vocabulary PuzzleMaker ⊙ *ExamView® Assessment Suite* ⊙ StudentWorks™ Plus 🔌 Transparency 19-1 **Go Online 🖱 glencoe.com**
Chapter FAST FILE Resources Concept Mapping Activity 19-2 `REVIEW` Cross-Curriculum Activity 19-2 `EXTEND` Enrichment Activity 19-2 `EXTEND` Lesson Plan 19-2 Guided Reading and Writing 19-2 `TEACH` Reteaching Activity 19-2 `REVIEW`	Lesson 2 Review, *p. 516* 🖱 Vocabulary PuzzleMaker ⊙ *ExamView® Assessment Suite*	🖱 Vocabulary PuzzleMaker ⊙ *ExamView® Assessment Suite* ⊙ StudentWorks™ Plus 🔌 Transparency 19-2 **Go Online 🖱 glencoe.com**
Chapter FAST FILE Resources Concept Mapping Activity 19-3 `REVIEW` Cross-Curriculum Activity 19-3 `EXTEND` Enrichment Activity 19-3 `EXTEND` Lesson Plan 19-3 Guided Reading and Writing 19-3 `TEACH` Reteaching Activity 19-3 `REVIEW`	Lesson 3 Review, *p. 521* 🖱 Vocabulary PuzzleMaker ⊙ *ExamView® Assessment Suite*	🖱 Vocabulary PuzzleMaker ⊙ *ExamView® Assessment Suite* ⊙ StudentWorks™ Plus 🔌 Transparency 19-3 **Go Online 🖱 glencoe.com**
Chapter FAST FILE Resources Concept Mapping Activity 19-4 `REVIEW` Cross-Curriculum Activity 19-4 `EXTEND` Enrichment Activity 19-4 `EXTEND` Lesson Plan 19-4 Guided Reading and Writing 19-4 `TEACH` Reteaching Activity 19-4 `REVIEW`	Lesson 4 Review, *p. 526* 🖱 Vocabulary PuzzleMaker ⊙ *ExamView® Assessment Suite*	🖱 Vocabulary PuzzleMaker ⊙ *ExamView® Assessment Suite* ⊙ StudentWorks™ Plus 🔌 Transparency 19-4 **Go Online 🖱 glencoe.com**
Chapter FAST FILE Resources Concept Mapping Activity 19-5 `REVIEW` Health Lab 19-5 `EXTEND` Enrichment Activity 19-5 `EXTEND` Lesson Plan 19-5 Guided Reading and Writing 19-5 `TEACH` Reteaching Activity 19-5 `REVIEW`	Lesson 5 Review, *p. 531* 🖱 Vocabulary PuzzleMaker ⊙ *ExamView® Assessment Suite*	🖱 Vocabulary PuzzleMaker ⊙ *ExamView® Assessment Suite* ⊙ StudentWorks™ Plus 🔌 Transparency 19-5 **Go Online 🖱 glencoe.com**

Chapter and Lesson Resources

The *Teen Health* resources are designed for differentiated learning abilities. You may want to use the coded items in this way:

`REVIEW` —activities to review or reinforce content
`TEACH` —activities to teach basic concepts
`EXTEND` —activities to extend or enrich lesson content

 OUT OF TIME?

Use Health Skills Activities *Reducing the Risk of Cancer*, page 516, or *Heart-Healthy Ads*, page 520.

A Heart-Healthy Diet

One way to lower the risk of heart disease is by eating healthful foods. A good diet can keep the body's arteries from being clogged and reduce the risk of heart disease and stroke. The U.S. Food and Drug Administration (FDA) sums up a heart-healthy diet with these four tips: eat less fat, eat less sodium (as in salt), eat fewer calories, and eat more fiber. Adopting such a diet can reduce cholesterol, lower blood pressure, lower blood sugar, and reduce body weight.

The American Heart Association asserts that a good diet limits foods that are high in saturated fats and trans fats. The main sources of saturated fats are foods from animals, such as whole milk, butter, cheeses, and meats. The sources of trans fats include cookies, crackers, French fries, and donuts. Instead of these fats, a good diet includes unsaturated fats such as the fats in nuts, seeds, soy, and olive oil.

Here are some strategies in developing a heart-healthy diet:

- **Choose lean cuts of meat, and eat skinless chicken and turkey instead of beef.**

- **Eat more fish. Fish is a good source of protein and also contains beneficial fats.**

- **Eat a variety of vegetables, fruits, and beans (legumes).**

- **Eat a variety of grain products, including whole grains such as brown rice.**

- **Eat foods with complete carbohydrates, such as sweet potatoes and whole-wheat pizza, instead of eating foods with simple carbohydrates, such as sweets and soft drinks.**

- **Choose low-fat dairy products, such as skim milk, low-fat cheese, and low-fat yogurt.**

- **Bake, broil, grill, or steam foods. Eat less fried foods.**

- **Choose low-fat snacks that have been baked instead of fried.**

- **Drink low-calorie beverages, such as diet soda and unsweetened tea.**

Autoimmune Diseases

Type 1 diabetes and rheumatoid arthritis, which are both discussed in Chapter 19, are examples of autoimmune diseases. An autoimmune disease is a noncommunicable disease in which the immune system mistakes healthy tissues for invaders and mounts an inappropriate attack. Although most autoimmune diseases are relatively uncommon, together they affect some 50 million Americans, or about 20 percent of the population. Women are more likely to develop an autoimmune disease than men.

Autoimmune diseases can affect different parts of the body. In multiple sclerosis (MS), the immune disorder is directed at the brain. Type 1 diabetes primarily affects the pancreas. Other autoimmune diseases affect more than one part of the body. Systemic lupus erythematosus—SLE, or lupus—and rheumatoid arthritis are systemic diseases. Other autoimmune diseases include psoriasis, Graves' disease, Crohn's disease, and pernicious anemia.

No one knows what causes autoimmune diseases. There seems to be a genetic factor. That is, a person may inherit the tendency to get a disease from his or her parents. But having the gene does not mean the disease will definitely develop. Scientists think there must also be some kind of agent to begin the destructive immune response. These may include various infections, some drugs, certain chemicals, or the sun.

Autoimmune diseases are generally chronic diseases that require lifelong care and treatment. None of these diseases can be cured in the way that a bacterial infection, for example, can be cured. Treatment often targets the relief of symptoms. For example, an anti-inflammatory medicine can relieve the symptoms of rheumatoid arthritis. Treatment also aims at preserving organ function. For example, drugs are used in the treatment of lupus to control an inflamed kidney. Treatment may also include drugs that target the immune system itself.

Support for Teaching Reading

Reading Preview

Activating Background Vocabulary Ask students to think about what they learned in the last chapter regarding communicable disease. Ask students what they think the differences might be between communicable and noncommunicable diseases. Record responses on the board and discuss.

FOLDABLES Study Organizer *Dinah Zike's Reading and Study Skills for Teen Health* provides interactive graphic organizers that help students comprehend and retain health concepts as they read. Use the Foldable® on page 507 or find more Foldables® activities for the chapter on **Noncommunicable Diseases** in the separate booklet, available in the TCR.

Lesson 1   Causes of Noncommunicable Diseases

Previewing Content Ask students to read the four main headings for this lesson and examine the photos and captions. Then have them write a sentence describing what they think each section will include.

Lesson 2   Cancer

Question Maker As they read, have students write their own questions about cancer, types of cancer, treating cancer, or reducing the risk of cancer in each of three categories: literal, inferential, and application. Give examples of questions for each category. Have students exchange papers with a partner and answer each other's questions.

Lesson 3   Heart and Circulatory Problems

Find and Define Have students write each new vocabulary term on the front of an index card. As the students read about arteriosclerosis, hypertension, and so on, have them find the words in the text and write the definitions in their own words on the back of each index card. Have students work in pairs to review and share each other's definitions.

Lesson 4   Diabetes and Arthritis

Learning Logs Ask: Which of the ways to manage diabetes do you think is the most effective? Explain your reasoning. Have students consider their response and write in their learning logs for five minutes. Encourage students to share their responses with others.

Lesson 5   Allergies and Asthma

Stop and Go Stop students during silent reading. Ask one student to summarize what he or she has read so far about noncommunicable diseases. Stop the student and ask another to continue summarizing what he or she has read about allergies. Continue until all main points are covered.

Post Reading

Twin Text Reports Provide students with the opportunity to find fictional reading material about families who have experienced the effects of noncommunicable disease in their lives. After reading, have students express their ideas in a written report, incorporating the factual information from the text with a response to the fictional material.

Key for Using the Teacher Wraparound Edition

Use this key to help you identify the different types of prompts found in the Teacher Wraparound Edition.

R **Reading Strategies** activities help you teach reading skills and vocabulary.

C **Critical Thinking** strategies help students apply and extend what they have learned.

U **Universal Access** activities provide differentiated instruction for students learning to speak English, along with suggestions for teaching various types of learners.

HS **Health Skills Practice** activities reinforce Health Skills concepts and help students apply these skills in their everyday lives.

W **Writing Support** activities provide writing opportunities to help students comprehend the text.

AL **Active Learning** strategies provide a variety of activities for presenting lesson content, including Quick Demos and engaging classroom projects that get students actively involved.

Key to Ability Levels

Teaching Strategies and activities have been coded for ability level and appropriateness.

AL Activities for students working above grade level

OL Activities for students working on grade level

BL Activities for students working below grade level

EL Activities for English Learners

Symbols

 Transparencies

 CD-ROM

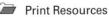 glencoe.com

📁 Print Resources

Chapter at a Glance

Lesson 1 identifies various types of noncommunicable diseases and how lifestyle choices affect diseases.

Lesson 2 identifies common types of cancers and some causes of cancer, explains how cancer can be treated, and describes how to reduce the risk of developing cancer.

Lesson 3 identifies and describes different types of heart disease, describes how to treat heart disease, and explains ways to reduce the risk of heart disease.

Lesson 4 describes the different types of diabetes, explains how to manage diabetes, and explains how to manage arthritis.

Lesson 5 describes how to manage an allergic reaction and identifies ways to manage asthma.

R Reading Strategy

Interpreting the Photo Have students look at the photo. Explain that the teen pictured is living with a noncommunicable disease that cannot be spread from person to person, and that such diseases are the focus of this chapter.

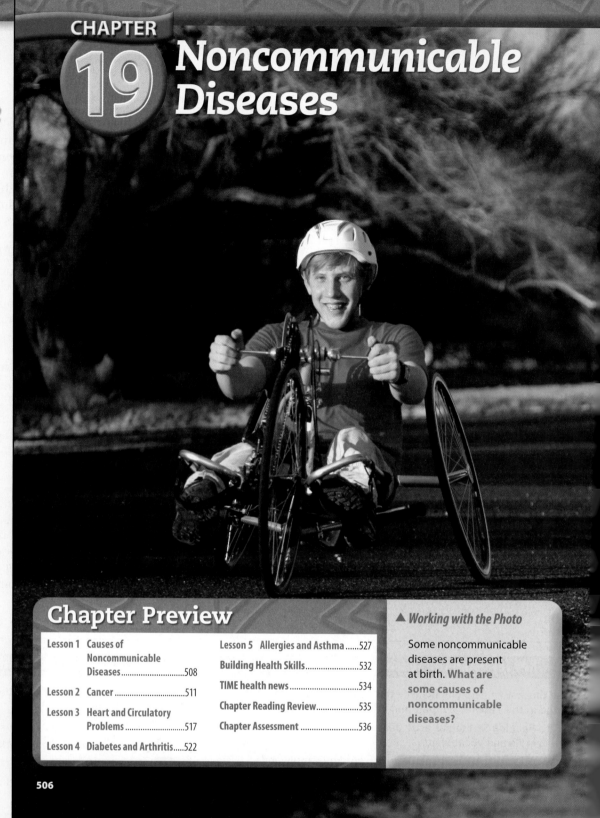

CHAPTER

19 Noncommunicable Diseases

Chapter Preview

▲ *Working with the Photo*

Some noncommunicable diseases are present at birth. **What are some causes of noncommunicable diseases?**

Universal Access

Differentiated Learning Glencoe provides teacher support and student materials for all learners in the health classroom.

- Spanish Glosario and chapter summaries assist English Language Learners.
- *Reading Tutor* and related worksheets support reluctant readers.

- Universal Access strategies throughout the Teacher Wraparound Edition and Fast Files help you present materials for gifted students, at-risk students, physically impaired students, and those with behavior disorders or learning disabilities.

Start-Up Activities

Before You Read Do you practice healthy lifestyle behaviors that help to prevent noncommunicable diseases? Take the Health Inventory below. Keep a record of your answers.

HEALTH INVENTORY

1. I limit foods that are high in salt and fat.
   (a) always   (b) sometimes   (c) never

2. I am physically active each day.
   (a) always   (b) sometimes   (c) never

3. I manage stress in healthful ways.
   (a) always   (b) sometimes   (c) never

4. I apply sunscreen before I go outside.
   (a) always   (b) sometimes   (c) never

FOLDABLES Study Organizer

As You Read Make this Foldable® to record and collect information on the causes of noncommunicable diseases presented in Lesson 1. Begin with a plain sheet of 11" × 17" paper.

1 Fold the sheet of paper into thirds along the short axis.

2 Open and fold the bottom edge up to form a pocket. Glue the edges.

3 Label each pocket as shown.

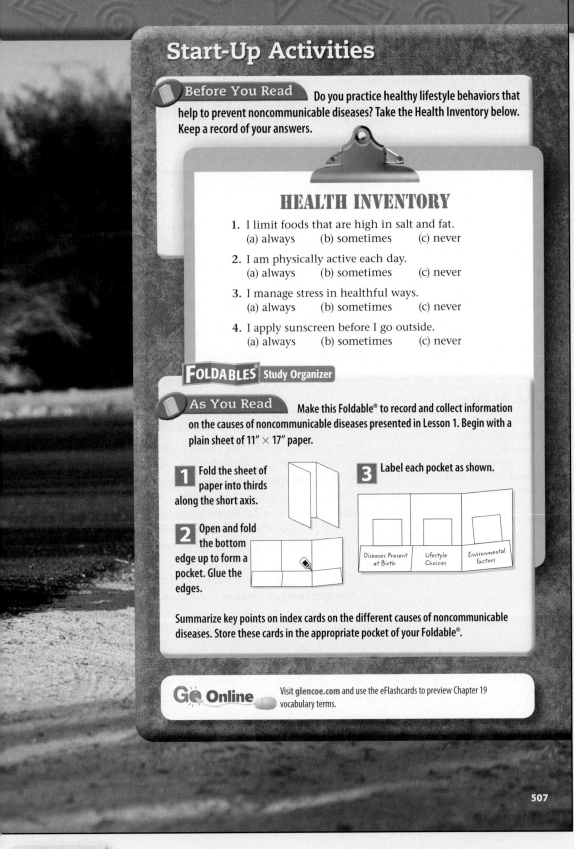

Diseases Present at Birth   *Lifestyle Choices*   *Environmental Factors*

Summarize key points on index cards on the different causes of noncommunicable diseases. Store these cards in the appropriate pocket of your Foldable®.

 Online Visit **glencoe.com** and use the eFlashcards to preview Chapter 19 vocabulary terms.

507

HEALTH INVENTORY

After they record their answers, have students choose one of the Health Inventory statements as the basis for a health goal to reduce their chances of developing a noncommunicable disease. Remind students to periodically record their progress toward achieving their goal.

No Child Left Behind

Working with Different Types of Families Students come from a variety of different family types: blended families, immigrant families, single-parent families, families with grandparents as parents, and so on. The following tips can help you work with diverse family structures:

- Use newsletters, conferences, e-mail, notes, and telephone calls to reach out to all types of families.
- Use literature, social studies, or current events to incorporate discussions of different family structures into classroom activities.

 Online

Have students visit **glencoe.com** and use the eFlashcards for Chapter 19.

FOLDABLES
Study Organizer **Dinah Zike Foldables®**

Organizing Data Students should use the Foldable® as they read Lesson 1. If students are having difficulty making the Foldable®, model the steps for the class. Have students use their Foldable® to take notes about the causes of noncommunicable diseases. Students might add to the treatment column by doing research at the library or online. Have students use their completed Foldables® as a study guide to review information about these diseases.

FOCUS

Activating Prior Knowledge

What I Know Have students discuss what they learned about communicable diseases. Explain that this lesson is about noncommunicable diseases.

Guide to Reading

Building Vocabulary
- Explain to students that the prefix *non-* means "not." Ask students to recall the definition of communicable disease and then explain what a noncommunicable disease is.
- Use Vocabulary PuzzleMaker to reinforce vocabulary terms.

Reading Strategy
Skimming Give students five minutes to skim the headings and write down three main ideas. Call on volunteers to share their ideas with the class.

 Have students use their Foldables® as they read Lesson 1.

Quick Write

Have students write a short list of factors and review their lists after completing the lesson.

Caption Answer

Photo Caption, p. 509 If scientists know the cause of a disease, they can develop a treatment that specifically addresses that cause.

Causes of Noncommunicable Diseases

 Guide to Reading

Building Vocabulary
As you read the lesson, write each term and its definition in your notebook.
- noncommunicable diseases (p. 508)
- chronic diseases (p. 508)
- degenerative disease (p. 508)
- congenital disorder (p. 508)
- heredity (p. 509)

Focusing on the Main Ideas
In this lesson, you will learn to
- **identify** various types of noncommunicable diseases.
- **explain** some causes of noncommunicable diseases.
- **describe** some lifestyle behaviors that can prevent diseases.

Reading Strategy
Skimming Glance at the headings of this lesson. By looking over the major and minor headings, you will have an idea of what the lesson is about. Write three main ideas after skimming the lesson.

FOLDABLES Study Organizer Use the Foldable® on p. 507 as you read this lesson.

 Quick Write

Make a list of as many factors as you can think of that can cause noncommunicable diseases.

What Is a Noncommunicable Disease?

As you learned in Chapter 18, you can get communicable diseases from other people. Some diseases, however, are noncommunicable. **Noncommunicable diseases** are *diseases that cannot be spread from person to person.* For example, you cannot catch diabetes from someone who has this disease. Some noncommunicable diseases are chronic. **Chronic diseases** are *present either continuously or on and off over a long period of time.* Asthma is a chronic disease.

Other noncommunicable diseases are considered degenerative. A **degenerative disease** is *a disease that causes a breakdown of the body cells, tissues, and organs as it progresses.* Multiple sclerosis is an example of a degenerative disease.

Diseases Present at Birth

Some babies are born with physical or mental disabilities caused by birth defects or genetic disorders. The causes of many birth defects are unknown. *All disorders that are present when the baby is born* are called **congenital disorders.** Examples of congenital disorders include cystic fibrosis and sickle-cell anemia. These two diseases are caused by hereditary factors.

Lesson 1 Resources

📁 **Chapter *Fast File* Resources**
Guided Reading and Writing 19-1
Concept Mapping Activity 19-1
Decision-Making Activity 19-1
Reteaching Activity 19-1
Enrichment Activity 19-1
Lesson Quiz 19-1

Technology
- Transparency 19-1
- Audio Summaries
- *ExamView® Assessment Suite*
- Vocabulary PuzzleMaker
- StudentWorks™ Plus

Go Online

Heredity is *the passing of traits from parents to their children.* Some birth defects are caused by the mother's choice of lifestyle. For example, a pregnant woman who drinks alcohol may give birth to a child with fetal alcohol syndrome (FAS).

> **Reading Check** **Recall** List three types of noncommunicable diseases.

Lifestyle Choices and Disease

While it is hard to determine who will develop a particular disease, researchers have found that certain risk factors increase a person's chance of developing a disease. Heredity, age, gender, and ethnic group are factors over which people have no control.

People can, however, control one major group of risk factors—their lifestyle choices. When people make unhealthy choices, they increase their risk of disease. Drinking too much alcohol, for example, can cause cirrhosis of the liver. Smoking tobacco can cause lung cancer and other respiratory diseases. Heart disease can result from eating too many foods that are high in saturated fat, and from a lack of physical activity. To decrease your risk of disease, practice the following healthy lifestyle behaviors:

HS

- **Eat healthful foods.** Eat plenty of whole grains, fruits, and vegetables. Go easy on foods high in fat, sugar, or salt.

- **Stay physically active.** Teens should be physically active at least 60 minutes on most days. Regular physical activity strengthens the heart and lungs, and helps the body systems work better.

- **Maintain a healthy weight.** Keep your weight within the recommended range for your gender, age, height, and body frame.

- **Get enough sleep.** Teens need at least eight hours of sleep a night.

- **Manage stress.** Use time management and other healthful strategies to reduce stress.

- **Avoid tobacco, alcohol, and other drugs.** These substances harm many parts of the body.

▲ Multiple sclerosis (MS) is a degenerative disorder of the brain and spinal cord that causes problems with the use of limbs. **How might discovering the cause of MS help scientists find a cure or treatment?**

Lesson 1: Causes of Noncommunicable Diseases **509**

Cultural Perspectives

Congenital Disorders Cystic fibrosis is a congenital disorder that affects more than 30,000 American children and young adults. An inherited gene makes a child with the disorder vulnerable to lung infections. Most sufferers are diagnosed before the age of three. This serious disorder affects different ethnic groups differently. Other congenital disorders similarly affect some ethnic groups more than others. For example, sickle cell disease is more common among people of African descent.

TEACH

U Universal Access

Reluctant Readers and Writers After students have been introduced to noncommunicable diseases, ask pairs of students to make a Venn diagram that compares and contrasts communicable and noncommunicable diseases. To help students begin, make a Venn diagram on the board that includes only the labels *Communicable Diseases* and *Noncommunicable Diseases.* Students should write similarities in the overlapping section of the two circles and differences in the parts of the circles that do not overlap. **OL**

> **Reading Check**
>
> **Answer** chronic, degenerative, congenital, or hereditary

HS Health Skills Practice

Cause and Effect Collect and display magazine pictures from articles and advertisements that suggest lifestyle choices. For example, display a picture of healthy looking teens playing a sport, of young adults practicing yoga, and of a group of young people relaxing on a cruise ship. Have students analyze each picture and explain how the lifestyle choice increases the risk of disease. For example: How might this lifestyle choice increase or decrease the risk of disease? *It would decrease the risk of disease, because physical activity promotes a healthy respiratory system and circulatory system.* **OL**

ASSESS

Assessment Resources

Lesson Review Quiz
- *ExamView*
- Fast Files Activities
- Online Quizzes and Activities

Reteaching

- Assign Concept Map 19-1 or Reteaching Activity 19-1 in the Fast Files.
- Have students create a 5-question quiz about noncommunicable diseases and factors that cause them.

Enrichment

- Assign Enrichment Activity 19-1 in the Fast Files.
- Encourage students to develop a schoolwide advocacy campaign to keep the environment free from toxins. Let students create flyers and stickers to promote their ideas.

CLOSE

Ask volunteers to name types of noncommunicable diseases.

Caption Answer

Photo Caption landfill fumes or carbon monoxide gas

◀ Smog is one environmental factor that can cause respiratory diseases. **What are other environmental factors that can cause disease?**

Environmental Factors and Disease

Your environment affects your personal health. Many substances in the environment can cause serious health problems. When houses are built near landfills, for example, they can become contaminated by fumes from the chemical waste buried in the landfills. Illness can result years after initial exposure.

Carbon monoxide—a colorless, odorless gas—is another harmful environmental substance. Fumes from car exhaust and some furnaces and fireplaces emit carbon monoxide when used. High levels of carbon monoxide gas can be dangerous and cause serious illness or even death.

Smog is another environmental factor that can cause disease. Smog is a yellow-brown haze that forms when sunlight reacts with air pollution. Breathing smog can cause respiratory diseases in some people. When smog is especially heavy, people with respiratory diseases may need to limit their outdoor activities.

Go Online

Visit **glencoe.com** and complete the Interactive Study Guide for Lesson 1.

Lesson 1 Review

After You Read

Review this lesson for new terms, major headings, and Reading Checks.

What I Learned

1. *Vocabulary* Define *chronic diseases*. Give an example of one.

2. *Identify* What are three risk factors that can cause noncommunicable diseases?

3. *Describe* What are two environmental factors that can cause disease?

Thinking Critically

4. *Synthesize* How can lifestyle choices affect a person's health?

5. *Evaluate* How can communities lower the risk of diseases caused by the environment?

Applying Health Skills

6. *Accessing Information* Using print or online resources, research some common noncommunicable diseases. Choose one and create a fact sheet describing what causes the disease and how it affects the body. Include information on how this disease is treated or managed. Share your findings with the class.

Go Online For more Lesson Review Activities, go to **glencoe.com**.

Lesson 1 Review Answers

1. diseases that cannot be spread from person to person; examples will vary
2. heredity, lifestyle choices, and environment
3. Carbon monoxide gas fumes and smog are environmental substances that can cause disease.

4. Eating healthfully, being physically active, and avoiding tobacco, alcohol, and drugs can decrease the risk of disease.
5. Communities can make laws concerning landfill construction and regulate sources of smog and other substances that harm the environment.

6. Fact sheets should contain accurate and complete information and cite reliable sources.

Cancer

Guide to Reading

● **Building Vocabulary**
Write each term below and its definition on separate index cards. Mix up the cards and try to match each term to its definition.

- cancer (p. 511)
- tumor (p. 511)
- benign (p. 512)
- malignant (p. 512)
- risk factors (p. 513)
- carcinogens (p. 513)
- biopsy (p. 513)
- radiation therapy (p. 514)

- chemotherapy (p. 514)
- remission (p. 515)
- recurrence (p. 515)

● **Focusing on the Main Ideas**
In this lesson, you will learn to

- **identify** common types of cancer.
- **recognize** some causes of cancer.
- **explain** ways that cancer can be treated.
- **describe** how to reduce the risk of developing cancer.

● **Reading Strategy**
Organizing Information Create a chart that shows the different types and treatments of cancers.

What Is Cancer?

Cancer is *a disease characterized by the rapid and uncontrolled growth of abnormal cells.* It can affect people of any age. Although many cancers can be treated, cancer is the second leading cause of death in the United States.

How does cancer develop? More than 50 trillion cells make up the adult human body. Most of the cells are normal, but some are abnormal cells. Usually, your body's immune system destroys abnormal cells. When these cells survive, however, they begin to divide. As they divide, some of them grow into tumors. A **tumor** is *a mass of abnormal cells.*

▶ Before you go outdoors, apply sunscreen with an SPF of 15 or higher. **What other precautions can you take to protect your skin from the sun's ultraviolet rays?**

 Quick Write

Write a couple of sentences that explain why people need to wear sunscreen when they go outdoors.

Lesson 2: Cancer **511**

 Lesson 2 Resources

📁 **Chapter *Fast File* Resources**
Guided Reading and Writing 19-2
Concept Mapping Activity 19-2
Cross-Curriculum Activity 19-2
Reteaching Activity 19-2
Enrichment Activity 19-2
Lesson Quiz 19-2

Technology
🕹 Transparency 19-2
Audio Summaries
ExamView® Assessment Suite
Vocabulary PuzzleMaker
StudentWorks™ Plus
 Go Online

FOCUS
Activating Prior Knowledge

What I Know Call on volunteers to name different kinds of cancer. Then ask what characteristics all cancers have in common.

Guide to Reading

Building Vocabulary
- After students have learned what a benign tumor is, explain that *benign* generally means "favorable or gentle" and is used in many other contexts. Have them describe a benign climate.
- Use Vocabulary PuzzleMaker to reinforce vocabulary terms.

Reading Strategy
Organizing Information Have students make a chart with two column headings: *Type/Treatment* and *Description*. Have them include symptoms in the description of each type of cancer. Students can add to their charts as they read the lesson.

Quick Write

Call on volunteers to share their written explanations with the class. After they read about skin cancer, students may revise their sentences.

Caption Answer
Photo Caption Wear protective clothing.

511

TEACH

Celebrity Cancer Stories

Call on volunteers to answer the questions. Explain that some celebrities publicize their cancer to let others with cancer know that they are not alone in fighting the disease. The benefits include inspiring others to stay positive.

R Reading Strategy

Analyzing a Chart After students have examined **Figure 19.1**, ask: What is the major cause of skin cancer? *exposure to direct sunlight* What can you do to reduce your exposure to direct sunlight? Sample answer: *You can stay out of the sun as much as possible, apply sunscreen when you need to be in the sun, and wear a hat when you're in the sun.* OL

U Universal Access

Gifted Students Have students needing an extra challenge choose one of the common types of cancers listed in **Figure 19.1** to research. Ask them to investigate more about the cancer's cause, symptoms, and treatment. Have students present their findings in a written report. AL

Caption Answer

Figure Caption exposure to direct sunlight

MediaWatch

Celebrity Cancer Stories

The media often feature stories about prominent political, entertainment, and sports figures who have cancer.

Why do you think some public figures choose to publicize their cancer? What are the possible benefits of doing so?

Tumors can be either benign or malignant. **Benign** tumors are *not cancerous* and do not spread to other parts of the body. **Malignant** tumors are *cancerous*. They can spread to other parts of the body.

Types of Cancer

Cancer can develop in many parts of the body. Some types of cancer are more common than others. See **Figure 19.1** for some common types of cancer. Skin cancer is the most common type. Fortunately, if skin cancer is discovered early enough, it can be successfully treated.

Lung cancer is the leading cause of cancer deaths. In 2005, almost one out of every three people who died from cancer had lung cancer. There is good news, however. In recent years, the number of lung cancer deaths has fallen because fewer people are smoking. Smoking is the leading cause of lung cancer.

▼ FIGURE 19.1

R COMMON TYPES OF CANCER

This chart lists some common types of cancer. **What is the leading cause of skin cancer?**

Type of Cancer	Important Facts
Skin cancer	is the most common kind of cancer. Excessive exposure to direct sunlight is the major cause of skin cancer.
Breast cancer	most often occurs in women over 50. It can occur in younger women and occasionally in men.
Reproductive organ cancer	can occur in the testicles and prostate gland in men. It can occur in the ovaries, cervix, and uterus in women.
Lung cancer	is the leading cause of cancer deaths in the United States. Smoking is the biggest risk factor for both males and females.
Colon and rectal cancer	develop in the digestive tract. Early detection and better screening have greatly reduced the number of cases of colon and rectal cancers.
Leukemia	is a cancer of the white blood cells that starts in the bone marrow. An increase in cancerous white blood cells interferes with the healthy white blood cells' immune response.
Lymphoma	is a cancer that starts in the lymphatic system. It weakens the immune system and increases the risk of developing infections.

U

What Teens Want to Know

What cancers are teens at risk for? Cancer is not common among teens. The cancers that teens do get often occur when cells develop abnormally. For most of these cancers, there is no known cause. Leukemia, which is a cancer of the blood cells, is one of the most common childhood cancers. Teens also contract lymphomas, which are cancers of the lymphatic system. Hodgkin's disease, one kind of lymphoma, usually occurs in adolescents and young adults. Other cancers that teens get include osteosarcoma (a bone cancer), Ewing's sarcoma, brain cancer, and testicular cancer.

Risk Factors and Causes of Cancer

Although the causes of some types of cancers are unknown, scientists have identified certain risk factors. **Risk factors** are *characteristics or behaviors that increase the likelihood of developing a medical disorder or disease.* Heredity, age, lifestyle choices, and environmental factors are some of the risk factors that can increase a person's risk of cancer. For example, someone whose diet is high in saturated fats and low in fiber is at an increased risk for colon and rectal cancers.

R Some types of cancer are caused by exposure to carcinogens (kar·SI·nuh·juhnz). **Carcinogens** are *substances that cause cancer.* For example, asbestos is a carcinogen. This material was used in construction and manufacturing until it was discovered to contain cancerous substances. Other common carcinogens are the chemicals in tobacco, which are linked to lung and mouth cancers. Not all carcinogens are chemicals. For instance, ultraviolet light from the sun can cause skin cancer. Radiation, including X-rays, can also cause cancer in large doses.

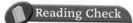

Recall Name two carcinogens and the types of cancers they cause.

Diagnosing Cancer

Health care professionals have many ways to begin checking for cancer. They can identify a group of abnormal cells when looking at the skin. They might feel a lump where the tissue should be soft. X-rays and other scanning equipment can also locate abnormal cell formations. If a suspicious lump or formation is discovered, a biopsy is usually done on the tissue. A **biopsy** is *the removal of a sample of tissue from a person for examination.* To diagnose cancer, the physician will examine tissue samples under a microscope to see if the cells are cancerous. If the cells are found to be cancerous, the patient will begin treatment. In order to diagnose cancer early, it is important to watch for warning signs. **Figure 19.2** on page 514 shows some of the warning signs of cancer. A person who shows a warning sign of cancer should be examined by a physician as soon as possible.

▲ Most cells in your body divide at a controlled rate. Cancer cells divide at an uncontrolled rate. **How are the normal cells in the top picture different from the cancer cells in the bottom picture?**

R **Reading Strategy**

Identifying Cause and Effect Help students understand that many risk factors of cancer are the result of behaviors. Ask: What is a major risk factor for developing colon and rectal cancers? *eating a high saturated fat, low-fiber diet* What is a major cause of lung cancer? *smoking tobacco* What is a major cause of skin cancer? *exposure to ultraviolet light from the sun* What do all these risk factors have in common? Sample answer: *They all are habits or behaviors of people that can be changed to prevent developing cancer.* **OL**

Reading Check

Answer *Sample answer:* Asbestos is a carcinogen that causes lung cancer. Ultraviolet light from the sun is a carcinogen that causes skin cancer.

FITNESS ZONE

Physical Fitness Routines Regular physical activity is one of the essential lifestyle choices teens can make to reduce the risk of developing diseases. Have students turn to the *Fitness Zone Handbook* and review the introductory information there. Ask: Why is it important to establish and follow a fitness routine? How does regular physical activity protect your physical health? How does it affect your mental/ emotional and social health? **For more information, see *Fitness Zone Handbook* pages xviii–1 or visit the Fitness Zone at glencoe.com.**

Caption Answer

Photo Caption The top cells are smooth and symmetrical, the bottom cells are irregular.

Analyzing a Graphic After students have examined **Figure 19.2**, point out that there are several kinds of skin cancer, the most dangerous of which is called melanoma. Ask: What should you regularly examine to check for warning signs of melanoma? *moles and warts* What does it mean to say that a mole is not asymmetrical? *One half of the mole doesn't match the other half.* **OL**

HS **Health Skills Practice**

Advocacy Have students use the seven warning signs of cancer to make a poster showing actions a person should take to reduce the risks of developing cancer. Students could use text as well as pictures cut from magazines, drawings, or cartoons to illustrate the different ways of reducing cancer risks. With permission, display the completed posters in the school hallways. **OL**

U **Universal Access**

English Learners Separate the class into three groups, and assign each group a different cancer treatment to discuss. Have the students present their treatment in the form of a brochure. **EL**

FIGURE 19.2

R **THE WARNING SIGNS OF CANCER**

These tools will help you recognize the warning signs of cancer. What does the "U" in CAUTION stand for?

C **Change in bowel or bladder habits** Bleeding from the rectum is a warning sign of colorectal cancer. Reduced urine output could indicate prostate cancer.

A **A sore that does not heal** or that bleeds easily may indicate skin cancer or oral cancer if the sore is in the mouth or on the tongue.

U **Unusual bleeding or discharge** from the vagina may indicate uterine cancer. Blood in the urine could signal bladder or kidney cancer.

T **Thickening or lump in the breast or elsewhere** may indicate nonmalignant disease or cancer. All lumps should be checked.

I **Indigestion or difficulty in swallowing** could be a sign of cancer of the esophagus or stomach.

O **Obvious change in mole or wart** See the ABCDs of melanoma.

N **Nagging cough or hoarseness** may be a sign of lung cancer.

A **Asymmetry** One half doesn't match the other half.

B **Border** The border is irregular—edges are ragged or blurred.

C **Color** The color is not uniform and may contain shades of brown or black and possibly patches of red, white, or blue.

D **Diameter** The diameter is larger than the size of a pencil eraser (6 mm) or is getting bigger.

Treating Cancer

The best way to treat cancer depends on many factors. These include the type of cancer, the stage of the disease, and the age and general health of the patient. The following are the most common cancer treatments:

- **Surgery** removes cancer cells from the body. It is used for treating breast, skin, lung, and colon cancer, among others.
- **Radiation therapy** is *a treatment that uses X-rays or other forms of radiation to kill cancer cells.* The high-energy rays from radioactive substances destroy or shrink the cancer cells.
- **Chemotherapy** is *the use of powerful medicines to destroy cancer cells.* It is often used to fight cancers that have spread throughout the body, such as leukemia.

All treatments have side effects. For example, the side effects of radiation therapy and chemotherapy include nausea, fatigue,

---

Caption Answer

Figure Caption The "U" stands for unusual bleeding or discharge

---

TECHNOLOGY AND HEALTH

Radiation Therapy Radiation therapy uses high-energy X rays to kill cancer cells. The radiation works by damaging the DNA of cancer cells so that the cancer cells cannot divide and grow. The radiation has more effect on cancer cells than normal cells because cells that are growing and dividing rapidly are more sensitive to the effects of radiation. A treatment usually lasts only a few minutes. Radiation treatment does not cause pain. The skin in the treated area may become red and sensitive. Radiation may also cause hair loss. These side effects are usually temporary.

◄ Health care professionals can often detect signs of cancer in several ways. **Why is early detection of some types of cancer so important?**

and temporary hair loss. When cancer treatment is successful, the cancer is in remission. **Remission** is *when cancer signs and symptoms disappear.* Cancer that is in remission can sometimes return. *The return of cancer after a remission* is called a **recurrence.**

 Reading Check **Recall** What is remission?

Reducing the Risk of Cancer

You can take an active role in promoting good health and reducing cancer risks. Here are some tips:

- **Avoid tobacco and alcohol.** Cigarette smoking is the single major cause of cancer deaths in the United States. Excessive alcohol use increases the risk of several types of cancer.

- **Limit sun exposure.** One way to protect yourself from UV rays is to limit your time in the sun. You should also apply a sunscreen with an SPF of at least 15 before you go outdoors. Wearing a hat that shades your neck, your face, and the tops of your ears is also a way to limit sun exposure.

- **Be physically active.** Be at least moderately active for 60 minutes or more on most days.

- **Perform self-examinations.** Females should perform monthly self-exams of their breasts. Males should perform a testicular self-exam once a month. Ask your health care provider for information on how to conduct both of these exams. In addition, check your skin regularly for moles and other skin growths. If you notice any changes in them, see a health care provider right away.

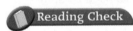 **Reading Check** **Explain** What is meant by the ABCDs of checking moles?

Go Online

Visit **glencoe.com** and complete the Interactive Study Guide for Lesson 2.

HEALTH LITERACY

The Importance of Early Detection It is easier to treat and cure many cancers if there is early detection. The American Cancer Society (ACS) recommends early detection and examinations for these cancers: breast, colon, rectal, cervical, testicular, oral cavity (mouth), and skin. Some cancers, such as breast cancer and testicular cancer, can be detected by self-examination. Other cancers require professional examination or laboratory tests. According to the ACS, if all Americans had early detection testing for the recommended cancers, the five-year survival rate for those cancers would be about 95 percent.

ASSESS

Assessment Resources

Lesson Review Quiz
⊚ *ExamView*
📁 Fast Files Activities
🖱 Online Quizzes and Activities

Reteaching

● Assign Concept Map 19-2 or Reteaching Activity 19-2 in the Fast Files. 📁
● Have pairs of students use the charts they made for the Reading Strategy to quiz each other about types and treatments of cancers.

Enrichment

● Assign Enrichment Activity 19-2 in the Fast Files. 📁
● Have students design a Web site that could inform teens about cancers and the actions they could take to reduce the risk of getting cancer.

CLOSE

Call on students to name a type of cancer. For each type named, ask students to describe the symptoms and suggest what a treatment for that cancer might entail.

Health Skills Activity

Advocacy

Reducing the Risk of Cancer

You can make healthy choices that will reduce your risk of getting certain cancers. Create a resource for your school. Collect information on some preventable cancers. Create a booklet on what teens can do to reduce their risk of getting some types of cancer. Start with this information:

● Lung and mouth cancer: avoid chewing and smoking tobacco.
● Skin cancer: limit exposure to the sun, and wear sunscreen with an SPF of at least 15 when outdoors.
● Liver cancer: avoid excessive use of alcohol.

In a Group

Design a booklet or computer presentation on healthy behaviors to prevent cancer. Think of a creative title for your booklet. Include a slogan and logo. Give your presentation or present your booklet to the class.

Lesson 2 Review

After You Read

Review this lesson for new terms, major headings, and Reading Checks.

What I Learned

1. **Vocabulary** Define *cancer.*

2. **Identify** What are four common types of cancer?

3. **Describe** Describe ways that cancer can be treated.

4. **Give Examples** What are three ways to reduce the risk of cancer?

Thinking Critically

5. **Synthesize** Why is it important to diagnose cancer as early as possible?

6. **Apply** Why do people with outdoor jobs have a higher risk of skin cancer than people who work indoors?

Applying Health Skills

7. **Advocacy** Amina noticed that a lot of the kids at the community pool don't wear sunscreen. She wants to create a pamphlet that talks about skin cancer and how it can be prevented. Create a similar pamphlet and hand it out to anyone who enjoys outdoor activities.

G⊙ Online For more Lesson Review Activities, go to **glencoe.com.**

Lesson 2 Review Answers

1. Cancer is a disease characterized by the rapid and uncontrolled growth of abnormal cells.
2. *Any four:* skin cancer, breast cancer, reproductive organ cancers, lung cancer, colon and rectal cancers, leukemia, lymphoma

3. Surgery removes cancer cells from the body. Radiation therapy is a treatment that uses X rays or other forms of radiation to kill cancer cells. Chemotherapy is the use of powerful medicines to destroy cancer cells.
4. Stay tobacco free. Limit sun exposure. Perform self-examinations.

5. Early diagnosis may stop the spread of cancer.
6. Exposure to the ultraviolet light of the sun is a carcinogen that causes skin cancer.
7. After researching, students should create a pamphlet for anyone who enjoys outdoor activities.

Heart and Circulatory Problems

Guide to Reading

Building Vocabulary
To help you learn each vocabulary term, divide it into syllables. The smaller parts make the longer terms easier to pronounce and understand.

- arteriosclerosis (p. 518)
- atherosclerosis (p. 518)
- hypertension (p. 519)
- stroke (p. 519)
- heart attack (p. 519)
- angioplasty (p. 519)
- Body Mass Index (BMI) (p. 521)

Focus on the Main Ideas
In this lesson, you will learn to

- **identify** and describe different types of heart disease.
- **describe** how to treat heart disease.
- **explain** ways to reduce the risk of heart disease.

Reading Strategy
Identifying Cause-and-Effect List three lifestyle behaviors that can cause heart disease.

What Is Heart Disease?

The term *heart disease* describes any condition that weakens the heart and blood vessels and makes them less functional. More adults in the United States die from heart disease than from any other cause. In fact, in 2004, about 79,400,000 people were diagnosed with one or more forms of cardiovascular disease. That same year, 871,500 people died of the disease. The risk of heart disease depends partly on age and heredity. However, most heart disease is the result of lifestyle behaviors, such as smoking, eating too many foods high in

▶ Eating nutritious foods can help you maintain a healthy heart. **What other factors contribute to the health of your heart?**

Quick Write
What are three ways to keep your heart healthy?

FOCUS
Activating Prior Knowledge

What I Know Ask what causes a heart attack. Ask if there is anything a person can do to reduce the risk of having a heart attack in the future.

Guide to Reading

Building Vocabulary
- Explain to students that the word part *hyper-* means "above or excessive" and the word part *-tension* means "the condition of being stretched to stiffness." Have students use this information to infer the meaning of *hypertension*.
- Use Vocabulary PuzzleMaker to reinforce vocabulary terms.

Reading Strategy
Identifying Cause-and-Effect Have students make their lists before reading and then revise them after reading about the causes of heart disease.

Quick Write
Have students list three ways to keep their hearts healthy before reading and then have them revise their lists after reading the lesson.

Caption Answer
Photo Caption age, heredity, smoking, and physical activity

Lesson 3 Resources

📁 **Chapter *Fast File* Resources**
Guided Reading and Writing 19-3
Concept Mapping Activity 19-3
Cross-Curriculum Activity 19-3
Reteaching Activity 19-3
Enrichment Activity 19-3
Lesson Quiz 19-3

Technology
- Transparency 19-3
- Audio Summaries
- *ExamView*® Assessment Suite
- Vocabulary PuzzleMaker
- StudentWorks™ Plus

G⊙ Online

TEACH

saturated fat, and not getting enough regular physical activity. Teens who make healthy lifestyle choices are less likely to develop heart disease as adults.

Types of Heart Disease

Body cells must have a constant supply of fresh oxygen to survive. The body's tissues and organs depend on the flow of blood through the arteries to deliver oxygen to the cells. When the arteries are clear and healthy, the blood flows through them freely. When the arteries are damaged or blocked, the blood does not flow as well.

Two disorders can result from problems with the blood flow through the arteries. **Arteriosclerosis** is *a group of disorders in which arteries harden and become more rigid.* When the arteries become rigid, less blood is able to flow through them. **AL** **Atherosclerosis** *occurs when fatty substances in the blood build up on the walls of the arteries.* This buildup shrinks the space through which blood can travel. **Figure 19.3** shows how arteries can become blocked. If the space in the coronary arteries narrows, the heart may not get enough oxygen.

 Reading Check   **Explain** What factors contribute to heart disease?

▼ FIGURE 19.3

HOW ARTERIES BECOME BLOCKED

R The heart's muscle tissue gets blood from the coronary arteries. When arteries become blocked, the heart is prevented from getting the blood it needs. **What do you think might happen when the heart does not get enough blood?**

Healthy Artery
Blood is able to flow freely.

Blood Flow

Partially Blocked Artery
A buildup of plaque slows the flow of blood.

Plaque

Blood Flow

HEALTH LITERACY

Atherosclerosis In the process called atherosclerosis, fatty material, cholesterol, cellular waste products, calcium, and other substances build-up on the inner walls of arteries. This build-up is called plaque.

Plaque can grow so large that it can block the flow of blood through an artery. A blood clot can break off and travel through an artery to the heart, brain, or lungs. This is a common cause of stroke and heart attack.

Other Cardiovascular Problems

As your heart beats, it pushes blood through your body's blood vessels, creating pressure on the blood vessels' walls. This force is called blood pressure. When a person's blood pressure is higher than normal, he or she has high blood pressure, or hypertension. **Hypertension** is *a condition in which the pressure of the blood on the walls of the blood vessels stays at a level that is higher than normal.* High blood pressure can lead to a heart attack or a stroke. A **stroke** is *a serious condition that occurs when an artery of the brain breaks or becomes blocked.* Brain cells die from lack of oxygen, affecting the part of the body controlled by those cells.

Have your blood pressure checked regularly by a health care professional. Most hypertension can be treated with a healthful eating plan, physical activity, stress management, and medication.

Heart Attack

A **heart attack** is *a condition in which blood flow to a part of the heart is greatly reduced or blocked.* If the blood is cut off for more than a few minutes, the heart muscle cells are damaged and die. Heart attacks usually cause pain, tightness, or pressure in the chest, or pain spreading in the arms, jaw, back, or abdomen. Other symptoms may include cold skin, shortness of breath, sweating, fainting, nausea, and lightheadedness.

AL

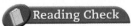

Reading Check **Compare** What do heart attacks and strokes have in common?

Treating Heart Disease

To help people with heart disease, health care professionals use some of the following treatments:

- **Angioplasty** (AN·je·uh·plas·tee) is *a surgical procedure in which an instrument with a tiny balloon, drill bit, or laser attached is inserted into a blocked artery to clear a blockage.* These devices either flatten, cut, or burn away the blockage.

- **Medications** can dissolve blood clots that block arteries. Sometimes aspirin is prescribed to prevent platelets from clumping together to form blood clots.

Go Online

Topic: Taking Positive Action

Visit **glencoe.com** for Student Web Activities to learn more about how young people are taking action to help find cures for noncommunicable diseases like cancer, diabetes, and heart disease.

Activity: Using the information provided at the link above, create your own plan to help find a cure for one of the diseases mentioned in this lesson.

▼ Medication is one way to treat heart disease. **What are some other ways?**

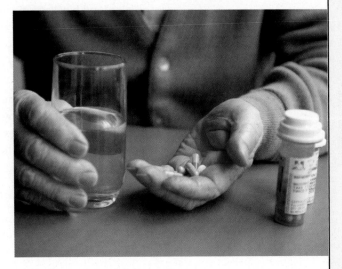

Lesson 3: Heart and Circulatory Problems **519**

Go Online

Taking Positive Action Have each student write a brief report about what he or she learned by following the links at **glencoe.com**. Ask students to end their reports with a plan for raising funds to find a cure for one type of diabetes or arthritis.

AL Active Learning

Interviewing Have each student conduct a brief interview about heart disease with a familiar older adult. Have students ask about symptoms and treatments, as well as about any behaviors or habits that the adult may think could be a risk factor for heart disease. Prepare students for this activity by discussing boundaries for interview questions and the importance of preparing questions in advance. Have each student prepare a written summary of the interview. **OL**

Reading Check

Answer Both occur when blood flow is prevented from supplying oxygen to a part of the body.

HEALTH LITERACY

Heart Disease Risk Factors One recent study found that about two-thirds of adolescents studied had at least one risk factor for heart disease. For example, obesity is a risk factor, and 20 to 30 percent of adolescents can be classified as obese. To decrease risk factors for heart disease, the American Heart Association has issued guidelines for children that include limiting high-fat foods, limiting sedentary time (such as watching TV) to less than 2 hours per day, and being physically active for at least 60 minutes per day.

Caption Answer
Photo Caption angioplasty, pacemakers, bypass surgery, heart transplants

Health Skills Activity

Analyzing Influences

Heart-Healthy Ads

Use the following strategies to help students complete the activity:

● Ask a volunteer to read the introductory paragraph aloud.

● Divide the class into small groups, and provide each group with popular magazines that contain advertisements for foods. Ask each group to find an ad for a food high in saturated fat and an ad for a heart-healthy food. Have groups present these ads to the class.

● Ask each group to create an advertisement for a heart-healthy meal. Students should use print and online resources to find which foods are heart-healthy and which are not.

● Post each group's advertisements around the classroom.

W Writing Support

Expository Writing Show students issues of a popular teen magazine so that they can see the kinds of articles that such a magazine publishes. Then ask students to write an article for the magazine that informs teens about ways they can prevent developing heart disease in their future. Remind students that expository writing shares knowledge to help others understand. OL

Health Skills Activity

Analyzing Influences

Heart-Healthy Ads

Teens are surrounded by food ads in magazines, television, radio, newspapers, billboards, and other media. With heart disease receiving so much attention in the media, food makers have begun advertising many foods as "heart-healthy." Find two advertisements in print, on the radio, or on television that advertise heart-healthy foods. Study the ads. How do the ads promote the foods? What language do they use? How do you think the ad writers want you to feel about eating the food? Do the ads contain any facts? Are these facts reliable? How can you tell?

In a Group

Create an advertisement for a delicious, heart-healthy meal. Include creative lettering, clipped magazine or newspaper pictures, and information about the food. Make your ad inviting, so teens are persuaded to try your heart-healthy meal.

● **Pacemakers** are electronic devices implanted into the chest to help the heart beat regularly. The pacemaker creates electrical signals that control the heartbeat.

● **Bypass surgery** creates new pathways for blood to flow around blockages. Surgeons can take a healthy blood vessel from another part of the body, such as the leg, and make a detour around the blocked part of the coronary artery.

● **Heart valve surgery** is when a faulty valve can be replaced with an artifical one made of metal or plastic.

● **Heart transplants** completely replace a person's damaged heart with the healthy heart of someone who recently died. Heart transplants are extremely complicated, so they are done only when the heart is severely damaged and no other treatment will work.

How to Prevent Heart Disease

W Although symptoms of heart disease usually do not appear until adulthood, heart disease can begin developing in childhood. Making healthy choices today can decrease your risk of

TECHNOLOGY AND HEALTH

Pacemakers The heart's "natural pacemaker" is called the sinus node, which consists of a mass of specialized cells that send out electrical impulses. These electrical impulses cause the heart to beat at a regular rate. When the natural pacemaker becomes defective, an artificial pacemaker can be used to do the same job. An artificial pacemaker is a small, battery-operated device that sends electrical impulses through a wire to the heart wall.

developing heart disease when you are older. Here are some **strategies** for keeping your heart healthy:

- **Eat healthful foods.** Eat a variety of fresh fruits and vegetables, whole-grain cereals, and lean sources of protein.

- **Participate in regular physical activity.** Regular physical activity strengthens the muscle tissue in your heart. Being active also helps you manage stress and maintain a healthy body weight.

W - **Maintain a healthy BMI. Body Mass Index (BMI)** is *a formula you can use to determine if your weight is appropriate for you.* Your heart works best if your BMI is within a healthy range. Ask a health care provider to help you find the right range for you.

- **Manage stress.** Constant stress can lead to high blood pressure. Learn how to relax and reduce stress.

- **Stay tobacco free.** The chemicals in tobacco can lead to heart disease, heart attacks, hypertension, and even strokes.

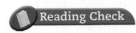 **Recall** What kinds of foods reduce your risk of heart disease?

Academic Vocabulary

strategies (STRAT i jees) *(noun)* plans, methods, or a series of maneuvers. *Carmen and her doctor came up with a few strategies to help Carmen lose weight.*

 Go Online

Visit glencoe.com and complete the Interactive Study Guide for Lesson 3.

Lesson 3 Review

 After You Read

Review this lesson for new terms, major headings, and Reading Checks.

What I Learned

1. *Vocabulary* Define *hypertension.*

2. *Identify* Name two types of heart disease. How are they similar? How are they different?

3. *Explain* What are some ways to reduce the risk of heart disease?

4. *Give Examples* What are three medical procedures that help people with heart disease?

Thinking Critically

5. *Analyze* Why is it a good idea to have your blood pressure checked regularly by a health care professional?

6. *Apply* What questions would you ask a health care provider if you want the provider to help you set up a plan to reduce your risk of heart disease?

Applying Health Skills

7. *Practicing Healthful Behaviors* Both of Tyler's grandfathers died of heart disease. Tyler wants to reduce his own risk of heart disease. Make a list of positive health behaviors Tyler can do to reduce his risk of heart disease.

 Go Online For more Lesson Review Activities, go to **glencoe.com**.

Lesson 3: Heart and Circulatory Problems **521**

Academic Vocabulary

Strategies On this page, students learn about strategies for keeping their hearts healthy. Emphasize that these strategies can begin as carefully planned actions that develop into habits. 📁

Reading Check

Answer fruits, vegetables, whole-grain cereals, and lean protein

ASSESS

Assessment Resources

Lesson Review Quiz
💿 *ExamView*
📁 Fast Files Activities
💊 Online Quizzes and Activities

Enrichment

- Assign Enrichment Activity 19-3 in the Fast Files. 📁
- Ask students to learn more about hypertension and its causes. Have them present their findings to the class.

CLOSE

Call on students to describe how they could decrease their risk of heart disease.

Lesson 3 Review Answers

1. Hypertension is a condition in which the pressure of the blood on the walls of the blood vessels stays at a level that is higher than normal.

2. Arteriosclerosis and atherosclerosis. Both restrict blood flow; the first causes hardening of the arteries, the other causes plaque build-up.

3. Eat healthful foods, participate in regular physical activity, maintain a healthy BMI, manage stress, and stay tobacco-free.

4. angioplasty, medications, bypass surgery

5. Regular blood pressure checks can help determine whether you need to be treated for hypertension.

6. *Sample answer:* How much exercise should I do every day? Which foods should I eat? How often should I get checkups?

7. He can stop snacking on foods high in saturated fat and eat more healthful foods, such as plenty of fruits and vegetables, whole-grain cereals, and protein.

Lesson 4

FOCUS

Activating Prior Knowledge

What I Know Have students describe how arthritis might affect activities teens enjoy.

 Guide to Reading

Building Vocabulary

■ Explain to students that the word part *osteo-* used in *osteoarthritis* comes from a Greek word meaning "bone." An *osteocyte* is a bone cell, and an *osteologist* is a bone doctor.

■ Use Vocabulary PuzzleMaker to reinforce vocabulary terms.

Reading Strategy

Organizing Information Have students complete the table as they read the lesson.

uick Write

Have students write down two facts they know before reading. After students read the lesson, call on volunteers to explain whether new information caused them to rethink what they thought they knew.

Diabetes and Arthritis

Guide to Reading

● Building Vocabulary

Fold a sheet of paper in half to form two columns. Write each term on the left side of the fold and its definition on the other side. Fold the sheet in half again. Look at each term and quiz yourself on its definition. Flip over the paper and check the definition.

- diabetes (p. 522)
- insulin (p. 522)
- type 1 diabetes (p. 523)
- type 2 diabetes (p. 523)
- arthritis (p. 524)
- osteoarthritis (p. 524)
- rheumatoid arthritis (p. 525)

● Focusing on the Main Ideas

In this lesson, you will learn to

- **describe** the different types of diabetes.
- **identify** the different types of arthritis.
- **explain** how to manage diabetes and arthritis.

● Reading Strategy

Organizing Information Using the diagram below as a guide, create a table that helps you sort the information about diabetes and arthritis that appears in this lesson.

Diabetes	Arthritis
Types	Types
Ways to Manage	Ways to Manage

Quick Write

Write two facts that you already know about diabetes.

What Is Diabetes?

Diabetes (dy·uh·BEE·teez) is *a disease that prevents the body from converting food into energy.* People with diabetes are referred to as *diabetics.* Their bodies do not produce or properly use insulin. **Insulin** (IN·suh·lin) is *a protein made in the pancreas that regulates the level of glucose in the blood.* The body uses insulin to convert the food you eat into the energy that your body's cells need.

How does it work? Your body breaks down the food you eat into glucose, a simple sugar. The pancreas, sensing that you have eaten, releases insulin. The insulin allows glucose from the blood to enter the cells throughout the body. Diabetics either do not produce enough natural insulin, or cannot properly use their insulin to move the glucose into their cells. Instead, the glucose stays in the bloodstream and can cause many health problems. If not treated properly, diabetes can cause kidney problems, blindness, and heart disease.

Lesson 4 Resources

📁 **Chapter *FAST FILE* Resources**
Guided Reading and Writing 19-4
Concept Mapping Activity 19-4
Cross-Curriculum Activity 19-4
Reteaching Activity 19-4
Enrichment Activity 19-4
Lesson Quiz 19-4

Technology
🔦 Transparency 19-4
 Audio Summaries
⚙ *ExamView®* Assessment Suite
Vocabulary PuzzleMaker
StudentWorks™ Plus
G⊛ Online

Types of Diabetes

There are two main types of diabetes: type 1 and type 2. **Type 1 diabetes** is *a condition in which the immune system attacks insulin-producing cells in the pancreas*. When the cells that produce insulin are killed, the body cannot control how much glucose is in the bloodstream. Type 1 diabetes often starts in childhood, but it may also begin in adulthood. Somewhere between 5 and 10 percent of diabetics have type 1 diabetes.

Type 2 diabetes is *a condition in which the body cannot effectively use the insulin it produces*. In type 2 diabetes, the cells in the pancreas still make insulin, but the body does not use it well. Between 90 and 95 percent of diabetics have type 2 diabetes, which usually begins in adulthood. Obese people and physically inactive people are especially at risk. Type 2 diabetes is also becoming more and more common among children and teens.

 Reading Check **Recall** How does the body use insulin?

Managing Diabetes

Although there is no cure for diabetes, people with the disease can keep it under control and lead normal lives. Type 1 diabetics usually need to regularly inject insulin into their bodies. Or, they may receive insulin from a pump attached to their bodies. Even children with type 1 diabetes can learn to manage their condition. Type 2 diabetics may also need insulin or other medications. People with either type of diabetes can help control their disease by making healthy food choices, managing their weight, and being physically active. **Figure 19.4** on the next page shows ways people manage this condition.

Reading Check **Describe** How can diabetes be managed?

What **Teens** THINK

If you had to give advice to someone on how to stay healthy, what would you tell them?

If I had to give advice to someone on how to stay healthy, I would tell them to stick to healthy foods and only eat unhealthy foods in moderation. Also, go out and try new sports untill you find one that you enjoy. If you don't like exercising then you won't do it, so make it fun.

Davis D.
Greensboro, NC

Connect To... Science

Monitoring Glucose Levels

Today's technology provides portable blood glucose monitors that can be used anywhere. Several models give voice instructions—in a choice of languages—to guide the user through the test procedure. The machine then announces the test results.

Who might benefit most from one of these "talking" blood glucose monitors?

What **Teens** THINK

If you had to give advice to someone on how to stay healthy, what you would tell them? After students have read about the risk factors for Type 2 diabetes, encourage them to generalize this information to overall physical health. Pose the *What Teens Think* question, and let volunteers share their responses.

Reading Check

Answer Insulin converts food into energy.

Connect To... Science

Monitoring Glucose Levels Ask a volunteer to read the feature aloud to the class. Then ask volunteers to answer the question. (Diabetics who cannnot read or are visually impaired would be among those who would benefit.)

Reading Check

Answer Diabetics with type 1 diabetes usually require regular doses of insulin via injection or pump. Those with type 2 diabetes also may need insulin or other medications. Both diseases can be controlled through healthful food choices, weight management, and physical activity.

HEALTH LITERACY

A Diabetes Diet A proper diet is very important in managing both types of diabetes. To keep blood sugar within a healthy range, a person with diabetes needs to be consistent in the timing and the amount of food eaten each day. Most people with diabetes seek the advice of a dietician or a nutritionist to help in determining which foods to eat and how many calories need to be consumed each day. The main influence on blood glucose level is the amount of carbohydrates a person eats. Carbohydrates should make up about 50 percent of the diet.

R Reading Strategy

Analyzing a Chart After students have examined **Figure 19.4**, ask: What is the goal in creating a food plan for a person with diabetes? *to help keep blood glucose levels within a healthy range* Explain that another term for blood glucose is *blood sugar*. Eating foods high in carbohydrates raises the blood glucose level. Ask: What do many diabetics inject to help regulate blood glucose levels? *insulin* **OL**

C Critical Thinking

Comparing and Contrasting After students have read about both osteoarthritis and rheumatoid arthritis, ask: What is similar about the two types of arthritis? *Sample answer: Both are diseases that affect the joints of the body. Symptoms of both include joint pain, swelling, and stiffness.* What is different about the two types? *Sample answer: Osteoarthritis is the result of the breakdown in cartilage in joints, while rheumatoid arthritis develops when the immune system attacks healthy joint tissue. Osteoarthritis most often affects the knees and hips, while rheumatoid arthritis can affect any joint in the body.* **OL**

Caption Answer

Figure Caption Eat well at every meal, exercise or be physically active before and after work or school, and get regular checkups from a health care professional.

▼ **FIGURE 19.4**

R MANAGING DIABETES

People with diabetes can successfully learn to manage their condition. **What are some ways that people can use the following strategies in their daily lives?**

Healthful Food Plan	Medical professionals can help people with diabetes create a food plan that helps keep blood glucose levels within a healthy range.
Weight Management	To maintain a healthy weight, people with diabetes should engage in regular physical activity.
Insulin Injections	People with type 1 diabetes and some with type 2 diabetes usually inject insulin through a syringe or pump.
Medical Care	Diabetics should be under the care of a health care professional. He or she can monitor the diabetic's health and watch for problems.

What Is Arthritis?

Arthritis (ar·THRY·tus) is *a disease of the joints marked by painful swelling and stiffness.* More than 40 million people in the United States have arthritis. This disease is usually linked to older adults, but even children can get arthritis. The two most common types of arthritis are osteoarthritis and rheumatoid arthritis.

Osteoarthritis

C **Osteoarthritis** (ahs·tee·oh·ahr·THRY·tuhs) is *a chronic disease that results from a breakdown in cartilage in the joints.* Cartilage cushions the place where bones meet in a joint. Osteoarthritis most often affects the knees and hips. When cartilage wears down, the bones in the joints rub against each other. This rubbing creates pain in the joint, swelling, and stiffness. Risk factors for osteoarthritis include age, heredity, and excess weight.

TECHNOLOGY AND HEALTH

Replacing Arthritic Joints When joints become too stiff and painful for an arthritis sufferer, the best option may be joint replacement. The most common reason for replacement is osteoarthritis. When a hip is replaced, a surgeon cuts away the diseased "ball and socket" of the hip joint and replaces the joint with a metal ball at the end of the leg bone (femur) and a plastic-cup socket in the hip. The cup is cemented into place or has tiny holes that allow bone to grow into the cup, holding it in place.

This teen has juvenile rheumatoid arthritis (JRA), which causes joint pain and can limit movement. **What types of challenges might a teen with arthritis face?**

Rheumatoid Arthritis

Rheumatoid (ROO·muh·toyd) **arthritis** is *a chronic disease characterized by pain, inflammation, swelling, and stiffness of the joints.* This type of arthritis is more serious than osteoarthritis. People can develop rheumatoid arthritis when their immune system attacks healthy joint tissue, leading to painful swelling. Rheumatoid arthritis can affect any joint in the body, including joints in the shoulders, elbows, hands, hips, and feet. The joints affected by rheumatoid arthritis often become deformed and no longer function normally. Symptoms include soreness, joint pain and stiffness, body aches, and fatigue.

HS

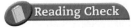 **Reading Check** **Name** What are two common types of arthritis?

Managing Arthritis

Unfortunately, there is no cure for arthritis. However, people with this disease can develop a plan to reduce their symptoms and improve their personal health. Many plans involve a combination of the following healthy behaviors:

- **Physical activity and rest.** A key to managing arthritis is to develop a good balance between low-impact physical activity (such as walking and swimming) and rest. Physical activity can reduce swelling and help increase flexibility

Family Practice Physicians

 A family practice physician is a doctor who provides basic care for people of all ages. If a patient has a specific problem that requires specialized care, the family practice physician will refer the patient to a doctor who specializes in a particular illness or injury. There will always be a need for family practice physicians because people are living longer. If you would like to become a family practice physician, you should study the growth and development of humans, as well as the diseases and injuries than can affect them.

What kind of skills does a family practice physician need? Go to *Career Corner* at **glencoe.com** to find out.

HS Health Skills Practice

Accessing Information Divide the class into small groups. Ask each group to use print and online resources to find out about the challenges that children with juvenile rheumatoid arthritis (JRA) face. Have group members work together to make a brief report of their findings. Remind students that they should list the sources of information in their report. **OL**

Reading Check

Answer osteoarthritis and rheumatoid arthritis

Family Practice Physicians Let a volunteer read aloud the paragraph about family practice physicians, and ask students to share their ideas about this career. Ask another volunteer to read aloud the entry about necessary skills at **glencoe.com**, and help students discuss why these skills are important. If possible, invite a local family practice physician to visit the class and discuss his or her work with students.

Dealing with Sensitive Issues

Students with Diabetes and JRA There may be students in your class that have diabetes or juvenile rheumatoid arthritis. You may need to schedule times during the day when students with diabetes can eat, test blood glucose levels, or give themselves injections. You also might let a diabetic student leave class to use the bathroom or see the nurse without asking special permission. For students with JRA, you should be especially sensitive for symptom flare-ups, including pain and limited mobility of some joints.

Caption Answer

Photo Caption A teen with arthritis might have to deal with swollen and painful joints, rashes, high fevers, and deformed joints.

Reading Check

Answer any four from the list above

ASSESS

 Assessment Resources

Lesson Review Quiz
 ExamView
Fast Files Activities
Online Quizzes and Activities

Reteaching

- Assign Concept Map 19-4 or Reteaching Activity 19-4 in the Fast Files.
- Have students work in small groups to compare and revise the tables they made for the Reading Strategy that contains information about diabetes and arthritis.

Enrichment

- Assign Enrichment Activity 19-4 in the Fast Files.
- Ask students to investigate how an insulin pump works and use what they learn to make a labeled diagram of an insulin pump.

CLOSE

Call on students to explain the differences between type 1 diabetes and type 2 diabetes and the differences between osteoarthritis and rheumatoid arthritis.

---

in the joints. When people with arthritis get enough rest, it helps them cope with the fatigue they often experience.

- **A balanced eating plan.** Eating healthy foods helps maintain overall health and keeps weight under control.
- **Joint protection.** Braces and splints can sometimes be used to help support the joints.
- **Heat and cold treatments.** Hot baths can ease the pain of some kinds of arthritis. Cold treatments can help decrease the swelling.
- **Medication.** Some people who have arthritis take medicine to help ease the pain and swelling and to slow the inflammatory process.
- **Massage.** When given by a properly trained massage therapist, a very mild massage can help relax the joints and increase blood flow to sore areas.
- **Surgery and joint replacement.** Sometimes in extreme cases, surgeons can operate to repair or realign a joint. A joint may even be replaced with an artificial one.

 Go Online

Visit **glencoe.com** and complete the Interactive Study Guide for Lesson 4.

Reading Check **Give Examples** What are four ways to manage arthritis?

Lesson 4 Review

 After You Read

Review this lesson for new terms, major headings, and Reading Checks.

What I Learned

1. *Vocabulary* What is *arthritis*?
2. *Describe* Describe the two different types of diabetes.
3. *Explain* What often happens to a joint affected by rheumatoid arthritis?

Thinking Critically

4. *Analysis* What do type 1 diabetes and rheumatoid arthritis have in common?
5. *Evaluation* Based on what you know about arthritis, how can you help someone with arthritis manage the disease?

Applying Health Skills

6. *Practicing Healthful Behaviors* Participating in regular physical activity can help reduce your risk of developing type 2 diabetes. If you enjoy what you do, you are more likely to participate in the activity on a regular basis. List ten physical activities you enjoy or might enjoy doing. Make a check mark beside three activities you will participate in during the next month. Make a commitment to do each of these activities at least once a week.

526 Chapter 19: Noncommunicable Diseases

 Go Online For more Lesson Review Activities, go to **glencoe.com**.

Lesson 4 Review Answers

1. Arthritis is a disease of the joints marked by painful swelling and stiffness.
2. Students should describe the symptoms of both type 1 diabetes and type 2 diabetes.
3. The joint often becomes deformed and no longer functions normally.
4. In both diseases, the immune system attacks parts of the body.
5. *Sample answer:* Develop a good balance between low-impact physical activity and rest. Have a balanced eating plan.
6. Activities might include dancing, biking, playing soccer, walking, running, swimming, playing basketball, skating, gardening, and hiking.

Allergies and Asthma

Guide to Reading

● **Building Vocabulary**
As you read this lesson, write each term below and its definition in your notebook.
- allergy (p. 527)
- allergens (p. 527)
- pollen (p. 527)
- histamines (p. 528)
- hives (p. 528)
- antihistamines (p. 529)
- asthma (p. 530)
- bronchodilators (p. 531)

● **Focusing on the Main Ideas**
In this lesson, you will learn to
- **describe** how to manage an allergic reaction.
- **explain** what happens during an asthma attack.
- **identify** ways to manage asthma.

● **Reading Strategy**
Comparing and Contrasting Identify the similarities and differences between the symptoms and treatments of allergies and asthma.

Quick Write
List three allergy symptoms. How can they be managed?

What Are Allergies?

Your immune system reacts to foreign substances in your body by trying to weaken or eliminate them. As it reacts, it releases antibodies that fight the foreign substances. Sometimes, your immune system reacts to a fairly harmless substance. This reaction is known as an allergic response. An **allergy** is *an extreme sensitivity to a substance.*

A person can be allergic to a number of different substances in the environment. *Substances that cause allergic responses* are called **allergens.** Allergens are very small. **Figure 19.5** on the next page illustrates some common allergens. When an allergen enters or comes in contact with a person's body, the immune system reacts as though it were harmful. When people are allergic to cats, for example, their allergic response is usually caused by dander on the cat's skin or fur. When people are allergic to ragweed, it is the tiny pollen grains from the plant that cause the allergic reaction, not the plant as a whole. **Pollen** is *a powdery substance released by the flowers of some plants.* It is lightweight, so it can be carried long distances and easily inhaled. When pollen comes into contact with a person who is allergic to it, the pollen causes an allergic reaction.

Lesson 5: Allergies and Asthma **527**

FOCUS
Activating Prior Knowledge

What I Know Ask for volunteers to describe allergies they have heard about and then try to explain what causes allergies.

Guide to Reading

Building Vocabulary
- Let students preview definitions of terms. Have volunteers use each of the vocabulary terms in a sentence.
- Use Vocabulary PuzzleMaker to reinforce vocabulary terms.

Reading Strategy
Comparing and Contrasting
Have students create a two-column chart and fill in symptoms and treatments for allergies and asthma as they read.

Quick Write
Students may need to skim the lesson to get ideas to complete their Quick Writes.

Lesson 5 Resources

Chapter *Fast File* Resources
Guided Reading and Writing 19-5
Concept Mapping Activity 19-5
Health Lab 19-5
Reteaching Activity 19-5
Enrichment Activity 19-5
Lesson Quiz 19-5

Technology
Transparency 19-5
Audio Summaries
ExamView® Assessment Suite
Vocabulary PuzzleMaker
StudentWorks™ Plus
Go Online

527

Academic Vocabulary

Contact Ask volunteers to read aloud the definition and example sentence. Explain that, in this case, *contact* is used as a noun; it can also be used as a verb meaning "to get in touch with." Let students say several sentences using *contact*, either as a noun or as a verb. You will find academic vocabulary activities in the Student Activities Workbook. 📁

AL Active Learning

Active Learning As a class, brainstorm on the board a list of allergens and a list of allergic reactions. Ask students to create a skit in small groups, depicting a situation in which someone has an allergic reaction. **EL**

Reading Check

Answer Students should mention responses described in **Figure 19.6**.

▼ FIGURE 19.5

COMMON ALLERGENS

Some allergens are easier to avoid than others. **What kind of difficulties do people who suffer from allergies face?**

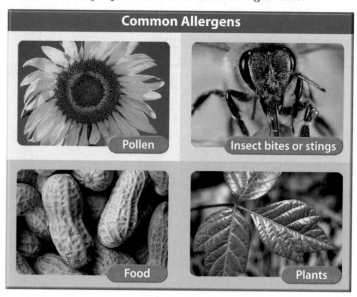

Common Allergens

Pollen · Insect bites or stings · Food · Plants

Allergic Reactions

Academic Vocabulary

contact (KON takt) *(noun)* the act of touching. *When Estella comes into contact with cats, she has an allergic reaction.*

When someone comes into **contact** with an allergen, their body's immune system believes that this substance is harmful to the body. In order to protect the body, the immune system produces chemicals called **histamines** (HIS·tuh·meenz) and releases them into the bloodstream. Histamines are *the chemicals in the body that cause the symptoms of the allergic reaction.* **Figure 19.6** shows some of the symptoms a person may experience during an allergic reaction. Allergic reactions can range from minor irritations to severe problems. For example, some people get hives as a reaction to an allergen. **Hives** are *raised bumps on the skin that are very itchy.* Most allergic reactions happen within seconds or minutes of the time the allergen enters the body. **AL**

Some people are at risk for severe allergic reactions, including throat swelling or extreme difficulty breathing. Because they might die if they are not treated immediately, these people may need to carry medicine called *epinephrine.* Epinephrine slows down or stops the allergic reaction by preventing the body from releasing histamines.

Reading Check

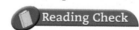 **List** What are five ways that the body responds to allergens?

Caption Answer

Figure Caption *Sample answer:* hives, itching, and redness around the eyes and nose

---

🏠 Home, School, and Community

In the Community The Air Quality Index (AQI) helps people plan outdoor activities based on the level of air pollution each day. The amount of pollution in the air can affect outdoor activity for certain people, including children, older adults, and people with asthma and other lung diseases. The U.S. Environmental Protection Agency (EPA) and other government agencies work together to report the AQI for more than 300 cities across the United States. AQI levels are published in many newspapers on the weather page as well as on television, radio, and Web sites.

How to Manage Allergies

Although there is no cure for allergies, there are three basic ways to manage them.

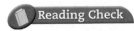

- **Avoid the allergen.** If you have a food allergy, learn to read ingredient labels. Ask about the ingredients of foods in restaurants. Avoid plants or animals that you are allergic to.

- **Take medication.** People with allergies often take medicines that help reduce allergy symptoms. **Antihistamines** are *medicines that help control the effects triggered by histamines.* For example, antihistamines may relieve itching and redness around the eyes and nose.

- **Get injections.** In severe cases, a long-term series of injections is needed. The injections contain a tiny amount of the allergen to help the body build up immunity.

Reading Check **Describe** What are three methods that people can use to manage allergies?

▼ FIGURE 19.6

THE BODY'S RESPONSES TO ALLERGENS

Allergic reactions vary depending on the allergen. Different people react differently to the same allergen. Which allergic reaction do you think has the most dangerous health consequences?

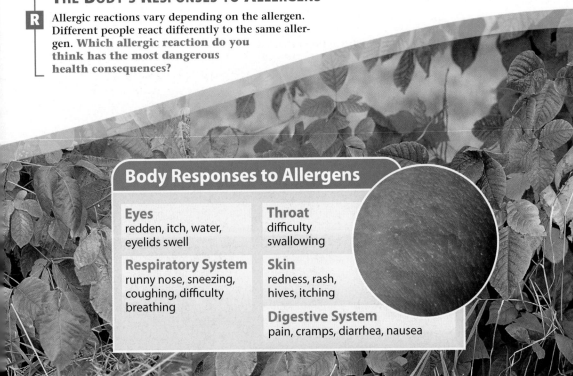

Body Responses to Allergens

Eyes
redden, itch, water, eyelids swell

Throat
difficulty swallowing

Respiratory System
runny nose, sneezing, coughing, difficulty breathing

Skin
redness, rash, hives, itching

Digestive System
pain, cramps, diarrhea, nausea

Lesson 5: Allergies and Asthma **529**

What Teens Want to Know

What is hay fever? Hay fever, which is more properly called allergic rhinitis, is an allergic reaction to various substances in the environment. The symptoms include sneezing, nasal congestion, and itchy eyes. Despite the common name, it does not cause fever, and hay is usually not the allergen. About one out of every five Americans suffers from hay fever. The allergens involved are usually pollens released by grasses, weeds, and trees. Some people are sensitive to indoor allergens, including mold, pet dander, and dust mites.

R Reading Strategy

Analyzing a Graphic After students have examined **Figure 19.7**, remind them that the bronchial tubes connect the trachea to the lungs. Ask: What swells during an asthma attack? *the inner linings of the bronchial tubes* How does that swelling make breathing difficult? *Air cannot pass easily through the bronchial tubes to get to the air sacs in the lungs.* **OL**

Reading Check

Answer Asthma is a serious chronic condition triggered by tobacco smoke, pollution, cold air, emotions, or strenuous activity.

HS Health Skills Practice

Practicing Healthful Behaviors Have students work in pairs to design an asthma health card that an asthma sufferer could carry. After students have completed the cards, call on pairs to share their instructions with the class. Lead a discussion about which card or cards would be most useful for a friend with asthma to carry. **OL**

Caption Answers

Photo Caption Change bedding regularly, bathe pets often, and vacuum and clean rugs, carpets, and floors frequently.
Figure Caption wheezing, coughing, gagging or choking feelings, shortness of breath, tightness or congestion in the chest

▲ Many people with asthma carry inhalers that contain bronchodilators. **What are some other ways to manage asthma?**

What Is Asthma?

Asthma is *a condition in which the small airways in the lungs narrow, making breathing difficult.* More than 20 million people in the United States have asthma. About 6 million of these people are under 18 years old. Some people outgrow their asthma, while others develop this disease in adulthood.

Asthma attacks can be triggered by many substances and conditions. A substance that triggers an attack in one person may have no effect on someone else. Common triggers include tobacco smoke, air pollution, and animal dander. Cold air, strenuous physical activity, strong emotions, and stress can also trigger an asthma attack. **Figure 19.7** explains what happens during an asthma attack. **HS**

Reading Check

Recall What are some common triggers of asthma attacks?

▼ **FIGURE 19.7**

R ASTHMA ATTACK

During an asthma attack, air passages become constricted and clogged with mucus. **What are some symptoms of an asthma attack?**

A Healthy bronchial tubes are clear and open. Air passes easily through them to fill tiny air sacs in the lungs.

B During an asthma attack, muscles around the bronchial tubes tighten. The tubes narrow and their inner lining swells. Excess mucus clogs airways, making breathing difficult.

Swelling

Mucus

Normal, clear airways

Tightened airways

530 Chapter 19: Noncommunicable Diseases

HEALTH LITERACY

Asthma Asthma is one of the most common childhood diseases. About 6.3 million American children have the disease, including almost 1 of every 13 school-aged children. In a recent year, asthma accounted for more than 14 million missed school days in the United States. The causes of asthma are complex, though there seems to be a genetic component. Although asthma cannot be cured, it can almost always be controlled through medical treatment and management of the environment to reduce triggers.

How to Manage Asthma

Since there is no cure for asthma, most people with the disease learn to manage it and lead active lives. Managing asthma is often a team effort. Parents or trusted guardians, health care professionals, and friends can help people with asthma stay healthy. Here are some strategies that people with asthma can use to help avoid asthma attacks:

- **Manage the environment.** Avoid triggers that can cause asthma attacks.

- **Manage stress.** Stress is a major cause of asthma attacks. Learn to manage stress in healthful ways.

- **Take medication.** Relievers and controllers are two kinds of asthma medicines. **Bronchodilators** are *reliever medications used to relax the muscles around the air passages.* They help reduce symptoms during an asthma attack. Controller medications are often taken daily and help prevent asthma attacks from occuring.

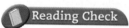 **Reading Check**

Describe How can a teen with asthma reduce triggers in the surrounding environment?

 Go Online

Visit **glencoe.com** and complete the Interactive Study Guide for Lesson 5.

 Reading Check

Answer monitor the condition, manage the environment, manage stress, take medicines

ASSESS

Assessment Resources

Lesson Review Quiz
- *ExamView*
- Fast Files Activities
- Online Quizzes and Activities

Reteaching

- Assign Concept Map 19-5 or Reteaching Activity 19-5 in the Fast Files.
- Have student write lists of the symptoms of allergies and asthma and ways to manage each condition. Then have them compare lists with a partner and add anything they overlooked.

Enrichment

- Assign Enrichment Activity 19-5 in the Fast Files.
- Ask students to investigate why the asthma rate is rising among American schoolchildren. Have them report their findings.

CLOSE

Call on volunteers to describe ways to manage allergies and asthma.

Lesson 5 Review

 After You Read

Review this lesson for new terms, major headings, and Reading Checks.

What I Learned

1. *Vocabulary* Define *allergy* and *asthma.*

2. *Give Examples* What are three ways to manage an asthma attack?

3. *Describe* What are some common symptoms of an allergic reaction?

4. *Identify* Name four common types of allergens.

Thinking Critically

5. *Synthesize* If your friend is having an asthma attack, what are two ways you could help?

6. *Hypothesize* If someone has a food allergy, why do you think it is important for that person to be careful when eating in restaurants?

Applying Health Skills

7. *Communication Skills* Alisha tried out for the cheerleading team and made it! She has asthma, however, and is too embarrassed to tell anyone about it. Write a short letter to Alisha and tell her why you think she should tell her coach and teammates that she has asthma. How can she manage her asthma during practice and games?

Go Online For more Lesson Review Activities, go to **glencoe.com**.

Lesson 5: Allergies and Asthma **531**

Lesson 5 Review Answers

1. An allergy is an extreme sensitivity to a substance. Asthma is a serious chronic condition that causes air passages in the respiratory system to become narrow or blocked.

2. Manage the environment, manage stress, and take medication.

3. itchy eyes, runny nose, difficulty swallowing or breathing, skin rash, hives

4. pollen, insect bites or stings, food, plants

5. *Sample answer:* Calmly alert a trusted adult about the attack. Offer to quickly get the inhaler for the person.

6. *Sample answer:* People may be allergic to unknown ingredients in restaurant food.

7. Letters, which will vary, should focus on Alisha's needing to tell her coach and teammates so that if she has an attack while cheerleading someone knows what to do.

Lifelong Good Health Habits

Skill

Goal Setting

Activating Prior Knowledge

Ask students to review the information they learned in Lesson 4 about how to manage diabetes. Ask: What are three ways that people with either type of diabetes can control their disease? *by making healthful food choices, managing their weight, and being physically active*

- **Objective** After completing the activity, students will be able to use a goal-setting plan to set a goal related to a lifelong health habit.
- **Time** 45 minutes
- **Materials** paper, pencil

Teacher Classroom Resources

📁 Building Health Skills
🖱 Transparency 2-1

Model

- Have students read the paragraph. Ask: How does Sasha use a calendar to help her prepare for the race? *She uses the calendar to schedule her workouts and evaluate her progress* What is Sasha's reward for completing the race? *Her reward is a new pair of shoes.*

National Health Standards Addressed

6.8.2

Building Health Skills

Accessing Information
Practicing Healthful Behaviors
Stress Management
Analyzing Influences
Communication Skills
Refusal Skills
Conflict Resolution
Decision Making
Goal Setting
Advocacy

What Is Goal Setting?

Goal setting is a five-step plan for improving and maintaining your personal health. Some goals are easy to reach while others may be more challenging.

The 5 Steps of the Goal-Setting Plan

Step 1: Choose a realistic goal and write it down.

Step 2: List the steps that you need to take to reach the goal.

Step 3: Find others, like family, friends, and teachers, who can help and support you.

Step 4: Set checkpoints along the way to evaluate your progress.

Step 5: Reward yourself once you have reached your goal.

Lifelong Good Health Habits

Follow the Model, Practice, and Apply steps to help you master this important health skill.

❶ Model

Read how Sasha uses goal setting to prepare for her first 10-mile race.

Sasha is excited about the upcoming 10-mile race. The race is a fundraiser for diabetes research. Sasha has diabetes and wants to support the event. She is physically fit but has never jogged 10 miles.

Sasha decides to set a goal of participating in the race. First, she writes down her goal—jogging in the race. Next, she outlines a program that she can follow to prepare for the 10-mile run. Sasha uses a calendar to schedule her workouts and evaluate her progress. She also decides that she will reward herself with a new pair of running shoes when she reaches her goal. She follows the steps, raises $350 through sponsorships, and ends up having a lot of fun.

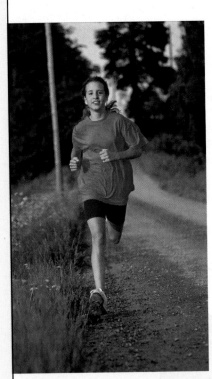

532 Chapter 19: Noncommunicable Diseases

▶ Teaching Tips

Brainstorming Obstacles to Fitness
Brainstorming allows students to generate several ideas quickly. Encourage students to brainstorm all the obstacles a teen might encounter in pursuing his or her fitness goals (weather, family vacations, homework, household chores).

- Have students call out their ideas without comment or discussion.
- List all ideas on the board or flip chart.
- Ask students how they could deal with each obstacle mentioned. Indicate that household chores and other family obligations still have to be met.

❷ Practice

Read how Sanjay uses goal setting to learn how to manage his asthma and prepare for his trip to Los Angeles, CA.

Sanjay is excited to go on his family trip to Los Angeles. However, he has been diagnosed with asthma. Sanjay would like to learn how to manage his asthma well enough so that he can go on the trip and have a good time.

1. What is Sanjay's goal?
2. What are the steps Sanjay needs to take to reach his goal?
3. Whom can Sanjay go to for help?
4. How can Sanjay evaluate his progress?
5. What is Sanjay's reward?

❸ Apply

Use what you have learned about goal setting to complete the activity below.

Think of a physical activity that you want to try, such as in-line skating or bicycling. Choose an activity that will reduce your risk of heart disease. Set a goal to do this activity. Use the goal-setting process to show how you will achieve this goal. Explain how achieving your goal will keep your heart healthy.

Self-Check
- Did I use all of the steps for goal setting?
- Did I explain how attaining this goal will protect my heart?

Building Health Skills

Practice
- Have students read the introduction in the Practice activity about how Sanjay can learn to manage his asthma so that he can go on his family trip.
- Have students work in pairs to discuss the questions. Then ask each individual student to write a response to the questions.

Apply/Assess
- Lead a class discussion of the responses. Ask volunteers to share how they answered each of the questions.
- Have students work individually to choose a physical activity and set a goal to do the activity. Remind students that in setting a goal they should follow the five steps of the goal-setting plan.
- Discuss with each student how he or she might be able to obtain any special equipment needed to do the chosen activity.
- Ask volunteers to share with the class their long-term goals, the steps they set to help reach the long-term goal, and the reward they chose for reaching the goal.
- You may wish to distribute the Building Health Skills Reproducible Master in the Fast Files. 📂

ASSESSMENT SCORING

Using a rubric, student work should meet all criteria to achieve the highest score.

Skills Student work:
- includes a specific goal statement.
- lists steps to achieve the goal.
- identifies sources of help.
- evaluates progress.
- provides a healthy reward.

Concepts Student work:
- identifies a physical activity goal.
- explains the relationship between the activity and heart health.
- incorporates accurate and complete information.

The Road to a Cure

Objectives

After completing this activity, students will be able to
- Understand the global impact of asthma
- Explain the ways in which asthma can affect an individual's day-to-day life

Motivator

Have students describe ways that families can work together to practice the health skill of advocacy.

Teaching the Activity

- After students have read the feature, ask: In what ways did the Eber family members improve their own health by bicycling? Sample answer: *They improved their muscle strength and cardiovascular health.* Ask: In what ways did they have a positive impact on the health of others during their trip? Sample answer: *They raised awareness and money for the fight against asthma.* **OL**

TIME *health news*

The Eber family bikes around the world to help fight asthma.

The Road to A CURE

The Ebers in Germany

Recently, the four members of the Eber family rode their bikes to the U.S. Capitol in Washington, D.C. It was no lazy Saturday-morning outing. It was the last leg of a 16-month bike trip around the world. Paula, Lorenz, Anya, and Yvonne Eber pedaled more than 9,300 miles and visited 24 countries. Their mission: to raise awareness of—and money for—asthma.

"Asthma is a big problem," Anya, 15, said. The disease makes it hard for as many as 150 million people

The Ebers in Holland

throughout the world to breathe. The Ebers hope to collect donations for World Bike for Breath, the organization that they began. The money will be spent on asthma research and programs for kids who have the illness.

Paula, 45, knows how hard having asthma can be. As a child, her severe case forced her to spend months in bed. Medications that enabled her to participate in sports weren't available until she was a teenager. "A lot of kids [with asthma] today still don't get to live an active life," Paula explains.

The Ebers have taken many bike trips, but nothing like this one! Highlights included eating a Christmas dinner of Chinese duck in Hong Kong and celebrating Yvonne's 12th birthday with coconut-and-mango cake in Tonga, which is located in the Pacific Ocean. On most of the journey, the family slept in tents. The hardest part, Yvonne says, was braving the heat, wind, rain, and bugs.

While on the road to help find a cure, the Ebers furthered their love of nature. Returning to life at their home in Bainbridge Island, Washington, wasn't easy. "I've had school outdoors for months," Anya says. "It will be so weird to sit at a desk!"

ASTHMA BY THE NUMBERS

With today's treatments, experts say most kids with asthma shouldn't experience too many symptoms. However, according to the latest information...

- Nine million U.S. children under the age of 18 have been diagnosed with asthma.
- Asthma accounts for 12.8 million absences from school each year.
- Asthma is the third most common cause of hospitalizations for children under 15 years old.

534 TIME health news: The Road to a Cure

Activity | Media, Technology, and Culture

Media There are many professional athletes who have asthma. These athletes serve as advocates and role models for children and teens who have asthma. Have students research a professional athlete with asthma. Challenge students to find out how that athlete deals with his or her asthma while participating in sports. Have students create a storyboard for a Web page to share their findings with the class. **OL**

Reading Review

STUDY TO GO Visit glencoe.com to download quizzes and eFlashcards for Chapter 19.

FOLDABLES Study Organizer

Foldables® and Other Study Aids Take out the Foldable® you created for Lesson 1 and any graphic organizers that you created for Lessons 1–5. Find a partner and quiz each other using these study aids.

Lesson 1 | Causes of Noncommunicable Diseases

Main Idea Noncommunicable diseases are diseases that cannot be spread from person to person.

- Some noncommunicable diseases are chronic, while others are degenerative.
- Congenital disorders are noncommunicable diseases that are present at birth.
- Risk factors include heredity, lifestyle choices, and environmental factors.

Lesson 2 | Cancer

Main Idea Cancer is characterized by the rapid, uncontrolled growth of abnormal cells.

- Types of cancer include: skin, breast, reproductive organ, lung, colon, rectal, leukemia, and lymphoma.
- Use C.A.U.T.I.O.N. and the ABCDs to remember the warning signs of cancer.
- Three common cancer treatments are radiation therapy, chemotherapy, and surgery.
- To reduce cancer risks, avoid tobacco and alcohol, limit sun exposure, be physically active, and perform self-examinations.

Lesson 3 | Heart and Circulatory Problems

Main Idea Heart disease is any condition that weakens the heart or impairs the way it functions.

- Cardiovascular problems include hypertension, stroke, arteriosclerosis, atherosclerosis, and heart attack.
- Eating healthful foods, exercising, maintaining a healthy BMI, managing stress, and staying tobacco and drug free keep your heart healthy.

Lesson 4 | Diabetes and Arthritis

Main Idea Type 1 diabetes and juvenile rheumatoid arthritis often begin in childhood.

- Diabetes is a disease that prevents the body from converting food into energy.
- There are two types of diabetes: type 1 and type 2.
- Arthritis is a joint disease marked by painful swelling and stiffness.
- Osteoarthritis and rheumatoid arthritis are the two common types of arthritis.

Lesson 5 | Allergies and Asthma

Main Idea Allergies and asthma can be managed with medicine, and by avoiding allergens.

- An allergy is an extreme sensitivity to a substance or allergen.
- Common allergens include pollen, insect bites or stings, food, and plants.
- Asthma occurs when the airways in the lungs narrow, making it difficult to breathe.

Chapter 19 Reading Review **535**

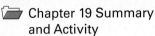
Assessment Resources

- Chapter 19 Summary and Activity
- Audio Summaries
- Reading Tutor
- Performance Assessment
- Chapter 19 Test
- *ExamView*
- Vocabulary PuzzleMaker
- Online Learning Center

Reading Review

Study Aids

- **Using the Dinah Zike Foldable® Study Organizer** Have students use the Foldable® to review the content of Lesson 5. Call on volunteers to identify causes, effects, and treatments of asthma.

  FOLDABLES® Study Organizer

- **Online Learning Tools** Have students go to the *Teen Health* Online Learning Center at **glencoe.com** to:

  - Download a **Podcast**.

  - Download free **Study-to-Go** content to their PDAs or cell phones.

Vocabulary Review

- **Vocabulary Matching** Write this chapter's vocabulary words on a stack of index cards. Write the definition on another stack. Divide your students into groups and have them match the words with their definitions.

Teaching Tips

Narrowing Essay Topics Writing assignments often play a part in student investigations into health-related subject matter. Generally, it is a good idea to give students a list of essay topics to choose from rather than open-ended assignments. Some students would prefer to choose their own topic, and for above level students this may be an option. Most students, though, benefit from a focused teacher-approved list. A list of topics that you are familiar with will also make it easier for you to spot plagiarism.

Reviewing Vocabulary and Main Ideas

1. Chronic
2. heredity
3. tumor
4. malignant
5. Risk factors
6. Arteriosclerosis
7. heart attack
8. stroke
9. True
10. False, Type 2
11. True
12. False, pollens
13. False, histamines
14. True

Thinking Critically

15. *Sample answer:* Swimming is a good physical activity that strengthens the body's muscles but does not put stress on the hip joints.
16. *Sample answer:* During the winter, plants do not have flowers that produce pollen, and pollen is one of the common allergens.

> **After You Read**
>
> **HEALTH INVENTORY**
>
> Now that you have read the chapter, look back at your answers to the Health Inventory in the chapter opener. Is there anything you should do differently?

Reviewing Vocabulary and Main Ideas

On a sheet of paper, write the numbers 1–8. After each number, write the term from the list that best completes each statement.

- chronic
- heart attack
- degenerative
- arteriosclerosis
- heredity
- risk factors
- tumor
- benign
- malignant
- stroke

Lesson 1) Causes of Noncommunicable Diseases

1. _____ disease symptoms are present continuously or off and on over a long period of time.
2. Some noncommunicable diseases can be the result of _____.

Lesson 2) Cancer

3. A group of abnormal cells in the body is called a(n) _____.
4. When tumors are cancerous, they are called _____.
5. _____ are characteristics or behaviors that increase the likelihood of developing a medical disorder or disease.

Lesson 3) Heart and Circulatory Problems

6. _____ is a group of disorders in which arteries harden and become more rigid.
7. When the blood supply to the heart slows or stops and the heart muscle is damaged, a(n) _____ can happen.
8. When an artery of the brain breaks or becomes blocked, the person may have a(n) _____.

*On a sheet of paper, write the numbers 9–14. Write **True** or **False** for each statement below. If the statement is false, change the underlined word or phrase to make it true.*

Lesson 4) Diabetes and Arthritis

9. <u>Arthritis</u> is a disease of the joints marked by painful swelling and stiffness.
10. <u>Type 1</u> diabetes is the most common form of the disease.
11. Keeping <u>physically active</u> helps manage diabetes.

Lesson 5) Allergies and Asthma

12. <u>Hives</u> are a powdery substance released by the flowers of some plants.
13. Chemicals in the body that cause the symptoms of an allergic reaction are called <u>allergens</u>.
14. A serious chronic condition that causes air passages in the respiratory system to become narrow or blocked is <u>asthma</u>.

Go Online Visit **glencoe.com** and take the Online Quiz for Chapter 19.

Go Online

Have students visit **glencoe.com** to take the Chapter 19 quiz.

HEALTH INVENTORY WRAP-UP

Ask students to review their responses to the Health Inventory. Ask volunteers to explain whether they would change any of their answers after reading the chapter about noncommunicable diseases. Then ask volunteers to name a health goal they have developed based on their responses to the Health Inventory and the content of the chapter.

Thinking Critically

Using complete sentences, answer the following questions on a sheet of paper.

15. **Apply** If someone has arthritis, why might swimming be helpful?

16. **Hypothesize** Why might people who are allergic to flower pollen experience fewer symptoms in places with cold winters?

Write About It

17. **Informative Writing** Interview someone you know who is a diabetic. Write a paragraph describing how diabetes has affected this person's life. Include the healthy ways he or she manages the disease.

⌁ Applying Technology

Noncommunicable Diseases Q & A

You and a partner will use PowerPoint® to create a question and answer game that covers the various elements of noncommunicable diseases discussed in this chapter.

■ Create a list of 20 questions and 20 answers from the chapter content.

■ Open a new PowerPoint® project. You will need 42 slides. Each question gets a slide. Each answer gets a slide. The first slide is for the title of your game. The last slide will contain any concluding remarks you want to make about noncommunicable diseases.

■ Enter all of your written content into the slides. Edit for clarity. Save your game.

■ Exchange your game with another group's game.

⌁ Applying Technology

Noncommunicable Diseases Q & A
Equipment needs: PowerPoint® or similar software
Assign project partners, and review the sequence of project steps with the class. Remind students to plan their games so they include a range of information in their questions and answers. If computer access is limited, create a sign-up list and establish a time limit for each pair of students. If possible, provide class time during which students can play their classmates' games.

Write About It

17. **Informative Writing** Paragraphs, which will vary, should include accurate information about the disease and descriptions of how the disease has affected the life of the interviewee.

Standardized Test Practice

1. B
2. B

Standardized Test Practice

Math

Acute lymphoblastic leukemia (A.L.L.) is a serious disease that affects the white blood cells in the body. This table shows the survival rates of patients with A.L.L.

Use the table to answer the questions.

Survival Rates for A.L.L. Patients	
	% of Patients Surviving at Least 5 Years
Adults	40%
Children	80%

TEST-TAKING TIP

When you are trying to find trends by studying the data from a chart, it often helps to sketch a line graph of the data.

1. Which is a *false* statement about the desease, according to the table?
   A. Sixty percent of adults don't survive.
   B. More adults survive than children.
   C. More children survive than adults.
   D. Twenty percent of children don't survive.

2. By reading this chart, you can determine:
   A. the survival rate for adults in ten years.
   B. that most children who have this disease survive for at least five years.
   C. the survival rate for children in ten years.
   D. the survival rate for African American children after five years.

Chapter 19 Assessment **537**

Test-Taking Tips

Trends in Tables Explain to students that answering some test questions will require using information found in tables or graphs. In the Standardized Test Practice, students must compare data from two different age groups.

By comparing the data, students will be able to understand and answer questions about the survival rate of adults and children with A.L.L.

CHAPTER 20 pp. 538–573	Standards		Skills and Activities
	National	State/Local	
	National Health Education Standards 1.8.5, 2.8.1, 3.8.1, 6.8.1, 6.8.2		*Health* eSpotlight, *p. 539* **BUILDING HEALTH SKILLS** *Practicing Healthful Behaviors* Complete a House Inspection, *pp. 568–569* **HANDS-ON HEALTH** A Home Emergency Kit, *p. 570*
Lesson 1 **Safety in the Home and at School** pp. 540–544	National Health Education Standards 1.8.3, 1.8.5, 1.8.8, 1.8.9, 2.8.10, 7.8.1, 7.8.2, 7.8.3, 8.8.1, 8.8.2		**Connect To... SCIENCE** Ergonomics, *p. 541* **Connect To... SCIENCE** Grease Fires, *p. 543*
Lesson 2 **Safety on the Road and Outdoors** pp. 545–549	National Health Education Standards 1.8.3, 1.8.5, 1.8.7, 2.8.10, 3.8.1, 5.8.6, 6.8.1, 7.8.1, 7.8.2		**Careers for the 21st Century** Emergency Medical Technician, *p. 547*
Lesson 3 **Safety in Weather Emergencies** pp. 550–553	National Health Education Standards 1.8.3, 1.8.5, 2.8.4, 2.8.10, 3.8.2, 5.8.2, 6.8.1, 7.8.1, 7.8.2, 7.8.3, 8.8.1, 8.8.2		**MEDIA WATCH** Storm Tracking, *p. 551* **Go Online** Be Prepared!, *p. 552* **HEALTH SKILLS ACTIVITY** *Practicing Healthful Behaviors* Preparing for Weather Emergencies, *p. 553*
Lesson 4 **Basic First Aid** pp. 554–557.	National Health Education Standards 1.8.3, 1.8.5, 3.8.2, 3.8.3, 3.8.4, 3.8.5, 4.8.4, 6.8.1, 6.8.2, 6.8.3, 6.8.4, 7.8.1, 7.8.2, 7.8.3, 8.8.1		**DEVELOPING GOOD CHARACTER** *Citizenship, p. 555* **What Teens Think** What are some ways to stay safe when you are home alone?, *p. 556*
Lesson 5 **First Aid for Common Emergencies** pp. 558–562	National Health Education Standards 1.8.1, 1.8.5, 3.8.4, 3.8.5, 4.8.4, 5.8.2, 7.8.2, 8.8.1		
Lesson 6 **Life-Threatening Emergencies** pp. 563–567	National Health Education Standards 1.8.3, 1.8.5, 3.8.4, 4.8.1, 7.8.1, 7.8.2, 7.8.3, 8.8.1		

PACING THE CHAPTER

Lesson 1	45 min	**Lesson 4**	45 min	**Chapter Review**	45 min
Lesson 2	45 min	**Lesson 5**	45 min	**Hands-on Health**	30 min
Lesson 3	45 min	**Lesson 6**	45 min	**Building Health Skills**	45 min

BLOCK SCHEDULING

For block scheduling, assign students Building Health Skills feature *Complete a House Inspection*, pages 568–569, and Guided Reading and Writing.

Planning Guide

StudentWorks Plus

Glencoe Exclusive!
TeacherWorks Plus
All-In-One Planner and Resource Center

Reproducible Resources	Assessment	Media and Technology
Chapter FAST FILE Resources Chapter Summaries and Activities REVIEW Building Health Skills Activity TEACH Performance Assessment Activity EXTEND Universal Access Activities TEACH Parent Letter and Activities 📁 **Student Activities Workbook** TEACH 📁 **Reading Tutor** TEACH	Building Health Skills Activity, pp. 568–569 Chapter 20 Assessment, pp. 572–573 **Chapter FAST FILE Resources** Performance Assessment Activity Chapter 20 Test 💿 ExamView® Assessment Suite	**TeacherWorks Plus** includes: ● Interactive Teacher Edition ● Lesson Planner with Calendar ● Access to all blackline masters ● Correlations to standards 💿 StudentWorks™ Plus 🖱 Online Student Edition Dinah Zike's Teaching Health with Foldables®
Chapter FAST FILE Resources Concept Mapping Activity 20-1 REVIEW Decision-Making Activity 20-1 EXTEND Enrichment Activity 20-1 EXTEND Lesson Plan 20-1 Guided Reading and Writing 20-1 TEACH Reteaching Activity 20-1 REVIEW	Lesson 1 Review, p. 544 🖱 Vocabulary PuzzleMaker 💿 ExamView® Assessment Suite	🖱 Vocabulary PuzzleMaker 💿 ExamView® Assessment Suite 💿 StudentWorks™ Plus 🖳 Transparency 20-1 **Go Online** glencoe.com
Chapter FAST FILE Resources Concept Mapping Activity 20-2 REVIEW Decision-Making Activity 20-2 EXTEND Enrichment Activity 20-2 EXTEND Lesson Plan 20-2 Guided Reading and Writing 20-2 TEACH Reteaching Activity 20-2 REVIEW	Lesson 2 Review, p. 549 🖱 Vocabulary PuzzleMaker 💿 ExamView® Assessment Suite	🖱 Vocabulary PuzzleMaker 💿 ExamView® Assessment Suite 💿 StudentWorks™ Plus 🖳 Transparency 20-2 **Go Online** glencoe.com
Chapter FAST FILE Resources Concept Mapping Activity 20-3 REVIEW Cross-Curriculum Activity 20-3 EXTEND Enrichment Activity 20-3 EXTEND Lesson Plan 20-3 Guided Reading and Writing 20-3 TEACH Reteaching Activity 20-3 REVIEW	Lesson 3 Review, p. 553 🖱 Vocabulary PuzzleMaker 💿 ExamView® Assessment Suite	🖱 Vocabulary PuzzleMaker 💿 ExamView® Assessment Suite 💿 StudentWorks™ Plus 🖳 Transparency 20-3 **Go Online** glencoe.com
Chapter FAST FILE Resources Concept Mapping Activity 20-4 REVIEW Decision-Making Activity 20-4 EXTEND Enrichment Activity 20-4 EXTEND Lesson Plan 20-4 Guided Reading and Writing 20-4 TEACH Reteaching Activity 20-4 REVIEW	Lesson 4 Review, p. 557 🖱 Vocabulary PuzzleMaker 💿 ExamView® Assessment Suite	🖱 Vocabulary PuzzleMaker 💿 ExamView® Assessment Suite 💿 StudentWorks™ Plus 🖳 Transparency 20-4 **Go Online** glencoe.com
Chapter FAST FILE Resources Concept Mapping Activity 20-5 REVIEW Health Lab 20-5 EXTEND Enrichment Activity 20-5 EXTEND Lesson Plan 20-5 Guided Reading and Writing 20-5 TEACH Reteaching Activity 20-5 REVIEW	Lesson 5 Review, p. 562 🖱 Vocabulary PuzzleMaker 💿 ExamView® Assessment Suite	🖱 Vocabulary PuzzleMaker 💿 ExamView® Assessment Suite 💿 StudentWorks™ Plus 🖳 Transparency 20-5 **Go Online** glencoe.com
Chapter FAST FILE Resources Concept Mapping Activity 20-6 REVIEW Cross-Curriculum Activity 20-6 EXTEND Enrichment Activity 20-6 EXTEND Lesson Plan 20-6 Guided Reading and Writing 20-6 TEACH Reteaching Activity 20-6 REVIEW	Lesson 6 Review, p. 567 🖱 Vocabulary PuzzleMaker 💿 ExamView® Assessment Suite	🖱 Vocabulary PuzzleMaker 💿 ExamView® Assessment Suite 💿 StudentWorks™ Plus 🖳 Transparency 20-6 **Go Online** glencoe.com

Chapter and Lesson Resources

The *Teen Health* resources are designed for differentiated learning abilities. You may want to use the coded items in this way:

REVIEW —activities to review or reinforce content
TEACH —activities to teach basic concepts
EXTEND —activities to extend or enrich lesson content

 OUT OF TIME?

Use Health Skills Activities feature *Preparing for Weather Emergencies,* page 553, or Developing Good Character, page 555.

Automated External Defibrillators

Defibrillators are devices that use an electrical shock to restore the heart rhythm of a person who is in cardiac arrest. Although defibrillators were once used only by doctors and emergency medical personnel, new technology has made defibrillators less difficult to use. Devices called automated external defibrillators (AEDs) require just several hours of training for safe and effective use.

Public access AEDs are located in places such as airports, office buildings, and sports arenas. Using computer technology, an AED can check a patient's heart rhythm to determine if an electrical shock is required. If a shock is required, the AED guides the user with voice or text prompts. The electrical shock delivered by an AED can restart the heart rhythm of a patient who is in cardiac arrest.

AEDs can be purchased only with a doctor's prescription and are regulated by guidelines from the Food and Drug Administration. Although AEDs are placed in public locations, it is not recommended that those without training use the devices. The American Heart Association offers a combined AED/CPR class for those who may be in a position to use an AED to assist a person who is in cardiac arrest. While a trained operator uses the AED to help the victim, other bystanders should immediately call 911 or the local emergency phone number.

Preventing Heat-Related Illness During School Sports

Heat-related illnesses can be a hazard for teen athletes during outdoor practice in the hottest months. Football, in particular, is a sport associated with heat-related illnesses, in part because of the heavy padding, uniform, and helmet required for participation. Heatstroke caused the death of approximately 20 to 25 student athletes between the years of 1995 and 2001. A schoolwide effort to educate students, coaches, faculty, and staff about the hazards of heat-related illnesses can reduce the risk to student athletes.

Heat illnesses vary in severity and symptoms. Heat cramps, for example, are painful muscle cramps caused by sweating. Heat cramps can be effectively treated with rest and rehydration. Heat exhaustion is a more serious heat-related illness characterized by faintness, nausea, and rapid heartbeat. An athlete with heat exhaustion needs to be monitored closely while he or she cools down and is rehydrated to be sure that heatstroke does not develop. Heatstroke is a life-threatening heat illness that requires immediate medical attention. Heatstroke is characterized by a lack of sweating and a high body temperature.

Teens can be particularly vulnerable to heat-related illnesses if they experience peer pressure to continue playing or practicing even when they feel ill. Some teens pressure themselves to continue for fear of being cut from a team. Students should be instructed to monitor themselves and their teammates for signs of heat-related illness. Coaches and trainers should have policies in place that allow student athletes to take frequent breaks for rehydration and cooling.

Support for Teaching Reading

Reading Preview

Activating Background Vocabulary Ask students what comes to mind when they hear the words *accident* and *emergency*. Discuss that these are situations not intended to happen. Encourage students to look for ways to prevent accidents and prepare for emergencies as they read the text.

FOLDABLES | **Study Organizer** *Dinah Zike's Reading and Study Skills for Teen Health* provides interactive graphic organizers that help students comprehend and retain health concepts as they read. Use the Foldable® on page 539 or find more Foldables® activities for the chapter on **Safety and Emergencies** in the separate booklet, available in the TCR.

Lesson 1   Safety in the Home and at School

Text Walk Lead students in examining the text by pointing out the vocabulary terms, pictures, captions, headings, subheadings, and the lesson review. After the preview, have students predict the reasons why it is important to develop safety habits at home and at school.

Lesson 2   Safety on the Road and Outdoors

Sum It Up Have students identify the main points of the lesson. Have them imagine they are placing an ad in a magazine urging other students to practice safety on the road. Tell them each word costs ten cents and each student has five dollars to spend on the ad.

Lesson 3   Safety in Weather Emergencies

Top Ten List As they read, direct students to make a list of the ways to reduce risk during a weather emergency or a natural disaster. Have students review their lists and choose the ten most important safety tips. Encourage students to share and discuss their "Top Ten" lists with each other.

Lesson 4   Basic First Aid

Partner Sharing After students read the section **The First Steps**, ask student pairs to discuss: "What are the signs of an emergency? How would you call for help? What would you do to provide care until help arrives?" Allow student pairs two or three minutes to discuss the questions, then share.

Lesson 5   First Aid for Common Emergencies

Visualizing Stop reading and have students imagine a friend falling and spraining her ankle. Ask: "What should you do first? Do you remember your first-aid skills? Should you call a doctor for help?" Have students write a journal entry, describing their feelings during the visualizations.

Lesson 6   Life-Threatening Emergencies

Drawing Conclusions Direct students to stop during reading and discuss the serious nature of choking, shock, and severe bleeding. In a class discussion, guide students to the conclusion that they could save someone's life if they stay calm, call for help, and provide appropriate first aid.

Post Reading

Informational Presentations Guide student groups to library and Internet resources. Have each group choose a topic from the chapter involving safety practices or first aid. Direct each group to gather data about their topic and develop a short informational presentation for the class.

Key for Using the Teacher Wraparound Edition

Use this key to help you identify the different types of prompts found in the Teacher Wraparound Edition.

R **Reading Strategies** activities help you teach reading skills and vocabulary.

C **Critical Thinking** strategies help students apply and extend what they have learned.

U **Universal Access** activities provide differentiated instruction for students learning to speak English, along with suggestions for teaching various types of learners.

HS **Health Skills Practice** activities reinforce Health Skills concepts and help students apply these skills in their everyday lives.

W **Writing Support** activities provide writing opportunities to help students comprehend the text.

AL **Active Learning** strategies provide a variety of activities for presenting lesson content, including Quick Demos and engaging classroom projects that get students actively involved.

Key to Ability Levels

Teaching Strategies and activities have been coded for ability level and appropriateness.

AL Activities for students working above grade level

OL Activities for students working on grade level

BL Activities for students working below grade level

EL Activities for English Learners

Symbols

Transparencies

CD-ROM

glencoe.com

Print Resources

Safety and Emergencies

Chapter at a Glance

Lesson 1 explains how to stay safe in the home and at school, identifies the parts of an accident chain, and describes how students can avoid injuries.

Lesson 2 describes ways to avoid injuries in the water and outdoors; identifies do's and don'ts of pedestrian safety; and names safety rules for bicycles, skates, skateboards, and scooters.

Lesson 3 explains how to stay safe during severe weather, describes how to protect yourself during a flood or an earthquake, and identifies various kinds of severe weather.

Lesson 4 explains universal precautions, identifies emergencies, and explains how to assemble a first-aid kit.

Lesson 5 describes the different types of common emergencies and explains first-aid treatments for them.

Lesson 6 describes how to provide CPR, identifies the symptoms of shock, and explains how to help someone who is choking.

R Reading Strategy

Interpreting the Photo Ask students: How are these teens getting prepared for an emergency? *Sample answer: These teens are collecting bottled drinking water so that if there is an emergency, they will have a few days' supply of water to keep them hydrated.*

538

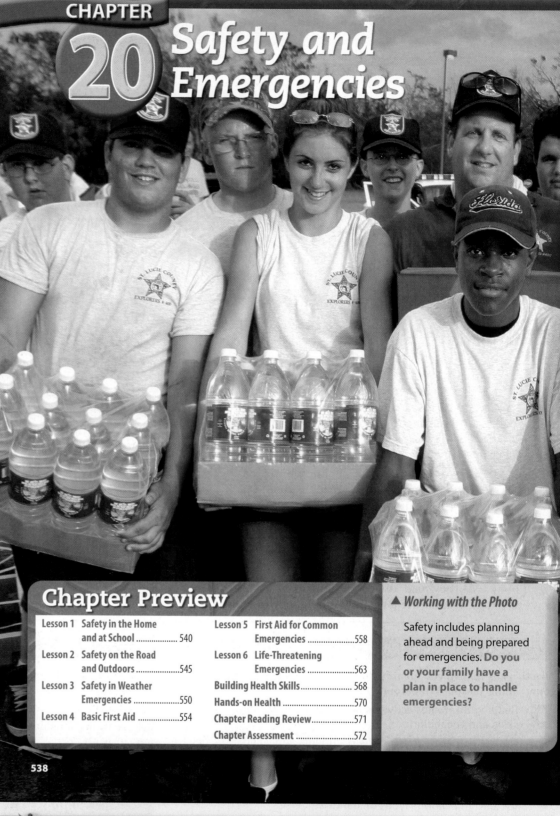

CHAPTER 20 Safety and Emergencies

Chapter Preview

538

▲ *Working with the Photo*

Safety includes planning ahead and being prepared for emergencies. **Do you or your family have a plan in place to handle emergencies?**

Universal Access

Differentiated Learning Glencoe provides teacher support and student materials for all learners in the health classroom.

- Spanish Glosario and chapter summaries assist English Language Learners.
- *Reading Tutor* and related worksheets support reluctant readers.

- Universal Access strategies throughout the Teacher Wraparound Edition and Fast Files help you present materials for gifted students, at-risk students, physically impaired students, and those with behavior disorders or learning disabilities.

Start-Up Activities

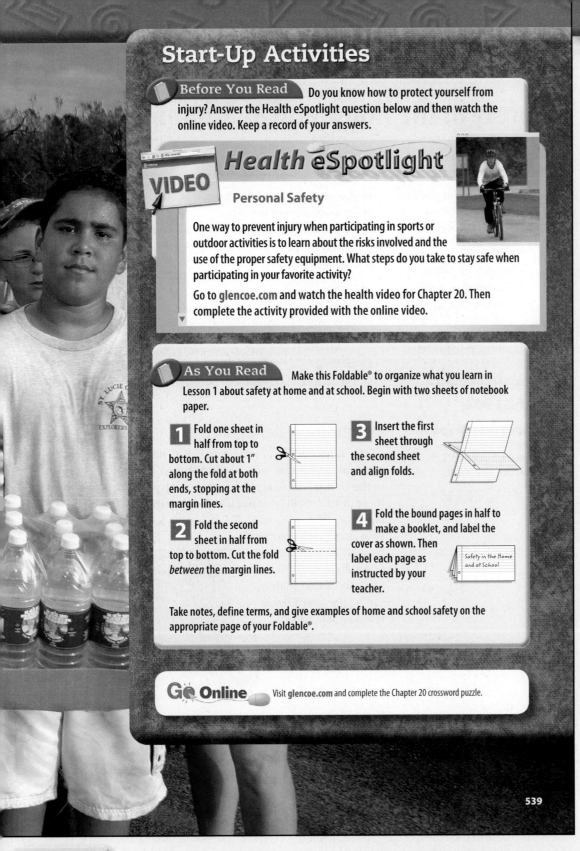

Before You Read Do you know how to protect yourself from injury? Answer the Health eSpotlight question below and then watch the online video. Keep a record of your answers.

Health eSpotlight

VIDEO

Personal Safety

One way to prevent injury when participating in sports or outdoor activities is to learn about the risks involved and the use of the proper safety equipment. What steps do you take to stay safe when participating in your favorite activity?

Go to glencoe.com and watch the health video for Chapter 20. Then complete the activity provided with the online video.

As You Read Make this Foldable® to organize what you learn in Lesson 1 about safety at home and at school. Begin with two sheets of notebook paper.

1 Fold one sheet in half from top to bottom. Cut about 1" along the fold at both ends, stopping at the margin lines.

2 Fold the second sheet in half from top to bottom. Cut the fold *between* the margin lines.

3 Insert the first sheet through the second sheet and align folds.

4 Fold the bound pages in half to make a booklet, and label the cover as shown. Then label each page as instructed by your teacher.

Safety in the Home and at School

Take notes, define terms, and give examples of home and school safety on the appropriate page of your Foldable®.

Go Online Visit glencoe.com and complete the Chapter 20 crossword puzzle.

539

Health eSpotlight VIDEO

Personal Safety Have students write an answer to the question provided and save their answers for later. Download the video presentation for Chapter 20 from **glencoe.com** or use the DVD to play the video for the class. Use the questions at the end of the video to begin a class discussion on personal safety. Ask students to respond to each question. **OL**

No Child Left Behind

Using Technology Effectively

Presentation software is useful for preparing teaching materials and is an excellent way for students to share information with others. These tips can help you and your students make the most of presentation software:

- To save time, use presentation design templates whenever possible.
- Import tables, text, and graphs from suitable software programs.
- Use the *Teen Health* PowerPoint® Presentation for lecture outlines and discussion notes.

Go Online

Have students visit **glencoe.com** and complete the crossword puzzle for Chapter 20.

FOCUS

Activating Prior Knowledge

What I Know Ask students to identify common types of accidents. Then have them describe how such accidents could be prevented.

 Guide to Reading

Building Vocabulary
- Have students create a graphic organizer that shows how the vocabulary terms for this lesson are related.
- Use Vocabulary PuzzleMaker to reinforce vocabulary terms.

Reading Strategy
Predicting Remind students that previewing the boldface headings in a lesson is an effective way to anticipate the lesson content. Ask volunteers to share their sentences with the class.

 Have students use their Foldables® as they read Lesson 1.

Quick Write
After students have completed their writing, follow up by asking them to identify how safe habits can benefit all three sides of the health triangle.

Caption Answer
Photo Caption Resist negative peer pressure that can influence you to participate in unsafe behaviors.

540

Lesson 1

Safety in the Home and at School

 Guide to Reading

● Building Vocabulary
As you read this lesson, write each new highlighted term and its definition in your notebook.
- accident (p. 540)
- accidental injuries (p. 540)
- accident chain (p. 541)

● Focusing on the Main Ideas
In this lesson, you will learn to
- **explain** how to stay safe in the home and at school.
- **identify** the parts of an accident chain.
- **develop** safe habits.

● Reading Strategy
Predicting Quickly look over the headings in this lesson. For each heading, write a sentence describing what information you think will be covered in that section.

FOLDABLES Study Organizer Use the Foldable® on p. 539 as you read this lesson.

Quick Write
Write a short paragraph that completes this sentence opener: "I practice safe habits when I _____."

Developing Safe Habits

An **accident** is *any event that was not intended to happen.* Accidents kill at least one person between the ages of 10 and 19 in the United States every hour of every day. About 60 percent of those deaths result from **accidental injuries,** which are *injuries that result from an accident.* Falling on an icy sidewalk in front of your home and injuring yourself is an example of an accidental injury. Most accidental injuries can be prevented by developing safe habits.

▶ When engaging in physical activity, stay safe by sticking to your level of skill. **What are some other safety precautions you should take?**

Lesson 1 Resources

 Chapter *FAST FILE* Resources
Guided Reading and Writing 20-1
Concept Mapping Activity 20-1
Decision-Making Activity 20-1
Reteaching Activity 20-1
Enrichment Activity 20-1
Lesson Quiz 20-1

Technology
- Transparency 20-1
- Audio Summaries
- *ExamView® Assessment Suite*
- Vocabulary PuzzleMaker
- StudentWorks™ Plus

Go Online

Injuries often occur as a result of an **accident chain.** This is *a series of events that include a situation, an unsafe habit, and an unsafe action.* Understanding accident chains, such as the one illustrated in **Figure 20.1,** can help you avoid injuries. Here are some guidelines:

TEACH

Connect To...
Science

 AL

- **Concentrate on your actions.** Be extra careful when you are tired, excited, upset, sad, or in a hurry.
- **Recognize your limits.** For example, do not mountain bike down a steep hill if you are just learning how to ride a mountain bike.
- **Think ahead.** Plan ahead by thinking of possible risks before it is too late.

Safety in the Home

The most common type of home injury involves falls. Other injuries result from poisonings, electrical shocks, and guns. Fires are the third leading cause of unintentional injury and death in the home. Many home injuries and deaths can be prevented.

Connect To... Science

Ergonomics

The science of ergonomics involves making equipment use, such as computers, less stressful on the body. Making your environment ergonomically correct can help prevent health-related injuries, such as repetitive stress injuries.

Research computer-related repetitive stress injuries. How can ergonomics help prevent these types of injuries? Create a brochure that offers guidelines for making your computer environment ergonomic.

Ergonomics Point out that another way to define *ergonomics* is: the science of making things fit people instead of trying to make people fit things.

AL Active Learning

In groups, have students create an "accident chain" and a corresponding "safety chain" with blank spaces for alternate safe actions that could have been done instead. Have the groups exchange their chains and fill in the blanks in the safety chain. EL

R Reading Strategy

Analyzing a Graphic Ask students to examine **Figure 20.1,** which shows the steps in the accident chain. Have each student make a list of strategies that could have prevented the accident illustrated in the figure. Call on volunteers to share their strategies with the class. Ask: How does personal responsibility play a role in accident prevention? *Sample answer: Taking responsibility for my actions, such as picking up my possessions, could help prevent accidents.* OL

▼ FIGURE 20.1

R **THE ACCIDENT CHAIN**

Many injuries can be prevented by breaking the accident chain. **What strategies could Margo have used to prevent the accidental injury shown here?**

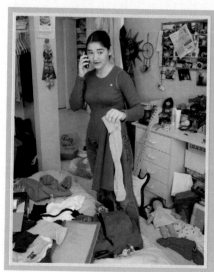

The Situation

1. Margo arrives home from school and rushes to answer the phone.

The Unsafe Habit

2. Margo often leaves her things scattered on the floor of her room.

The Unsafe Action

3. After talking on the phone, Margo goes to get ready for her soccer game and trips over a pile of belongings on the floor.

The Accident and the Injury

4. Margo falls and hurts her ankle. Now she can't go to her soccer game.

Lesson 1: Safety in the Home and at School **541**

Caption Answer

Photo Caption If Margo kept her room clean and organized, she could have prevented the accident.

FITNESS ZONE

Safety and Physical Fitness Safe habits are especially important during physical activity. After students have read and discussed the guidelines for avoiding injuries, refer them to the *Fitness Zone Handbook* at the front of their texts. Ask: How can you apply these guidelines to your own physical activities? How can following these guidelines help you stay safe while exercising? **For more information, see** *Fitness Zone Handbook* **pages xviii–1 or visit the Fitness Zone at glencoe.com.**

W Writing Support

Descriptive Writing Have students write a paragraph that describes a fictional accident such as a fall. Remind students to describe each step in the accident chain that leads up to the fictional accident. Challenge students to include a clear topic sentence and descriptive details in their paragraphs. **OL**

AL Active Learning

Videos Have students work in small groups to write and produce videos about preventing a specific type of accident. Students may need to perform additional research to gather information to use in their videos. Ask each group to share its video with the class. **OL**

AL Active Learning

Bumper Stickers Provide each student with paper in the size and shape of a typical bumper sticker. After students have read the information about fire safety in the text, ask them to create a bumper sticker that communicates one fire safety tip in an original way. **OL**

▲ Keep young children safe from poisonous products by storing them where they cannot be reached. **Do you know who to call if a poisoning does occur?**

Preventing Falls

Most injuries from falling occur in the kitchen, the bathroom, and on stairs. To help prevent falls, wipe up spills right away. Use nonskid rugs, or place a rubber pad under loose rugs. Keep stairways well lit and free of clutter. **W**

Preventing Poisonings

Poisoning can happen by ingestion (swallowing), absorption (through the skin), injection (from a syringe), or inhalation (breathing). Store cleaning products, insecticides, and other potential poisons out of reach of young children.

Preventing Electrical Shocks

Electrical items found in the home can cause serious injury or death if they are misused. Unplug any appliance that is not working properly. Replace broken or frayed electrical cords, and avoid running cords under rugs. Never use electrical appliances near water.

AL

Preventing Gun Accidents

The best way to prevent a gun accident in the home is to not have guns in the home. If a gun must be kept in the home, use the following safety precautions:

- Guns should have trigger locks and be stored unloaded in a locked cabinet.
- Ammunition should be stored in a separate locked cabinet.
- Anyone who handles a gun should be trained in gun safety.
- All guns should be handled as if they are loaded.
- Guns should *never* be pointed at anyone.

Fire Safety

A fire needs three elements to start—fuel, heat, and air. A cigarette, match, or electrical wire are sources of heat. If these sources come in contact with household chemicals, rags, wood, or newspapers, a fire can result.

Here are some safety guidelines to help you prevent fires in the home:

AL

- Keep stoves and ovens clean to prevent pieces of food or grease from catching fire.
- Keep flammable objects at least three feet away from portable heaters.
- Remind adults who smoke never to smoke in bed or on overstuffed furniture.

Caption Answer

Photo Caption If a poisoning occurs, the nearest poison control center should be called. (See Lesson 5, p. 560)

Dealing with Sensitive Issues

Guns in the Home Having a gun in the home is a risk factor for intentional and unintentional injury to teens. In fact, injuries from firearms are the third-leading cause of death among 10- to 14-year-olds. Most teens have little or no control over the presence of a gun in their home. Therefore, it is important to stress the guidelines for gun safety that are explained in the student text. Have students research to find out more about preventing firearm injuries. Ask students to present a short report of their findings. **OL**

- Regularly inspect electrical wires, outlets, and appliances to make sure they are in proper working order.

- Discard old newspapers, oily rags, and other materials that burn easily.

- Use and store matches and lighters properly. Keep them out of reach of young children. Don't leave candles burning unattended.

- Install smoke alarms on each level of the home, including the basement. They should be located in hallways outside bedrooms. Remember to check the batteries regularly.

Reducing Risk of Injury in a Fire

Knowing what to do if there is a fire in your home can reduce your risk of injury. Follow these guidelines:

- Leave the house immediately if possible. Call the fire department from a nearby house or a cellular phone.

- While you are in the house, stay as close to the floor as you can below the smoke. Try to keep your mouth and nose covered to avoid breathing in smoke.

- Before you open a closed door, feel it. If it is hot, find another way to leave the room.

- If your clothing catches fire, *stop, drop,* and *roll.* Stop. Don't run. Drop to the ground and roll to put out the fire.

 Reading Check **Give Examples** What are three ways to prevent fires in the home?

▲ Prevent electrical shock by using the proper number of cords per outlet. **Why might an overloaded electrical outlet cause a problem?**

Connect To... Science

Grease Fires

If a grease fire starts in a pan on the stove, do not throw water on it. If you do, the flames may actually spread because oil and grease float on water. Your best bet is to carefully slide a lid over the pan and turn off the burner. You can also smother the flames with baking soda. Let the pan cool completely before moving it or taking off the lid.

Research what types of fires can be put out with water and what types cannot. Use your findings to create a brochure that will help others be prepared in case of fire.

 G Online

Visit **glencoe.com** and complete the Interactive Study Guide for Lesson 1.

Connect To... Science

Grease Fires

Have students read the feature. Then have students make a poster to teach this information to others. Ask students to take their completed posters home to share with their families.

U Universal Access

Physically Impaired Explain the following modified stop, drop, and roll technique to physically impaired students who use a wheelchair (check first with the school nurse about individual students' capabilities):

- Lock (engage the brake or lock on the wheelchair)
- Drop (slide to the floor and cover the face with the arms if possible)
- Roll (roll on the floor or ground) OL

Reading Check

Answer any three from the list on pages 542–543

Caption Answers

Photo Caption Overloaded electrical outlets carry too much electricity, generating heat that can ignite a fire.
Photo Caption, p. 544 Notify an adult immediately.

TECHNOLOGY AND HEALTH

Smoke Alarms Smoke alarms are an inexpensive, easy-to-use technology that are proven effective in saving lives. According to the Centers for Disease Control and Prevention (CDC), the risk of dying in a residential fire is reduced by 40 to 50 percent when there is a working smoke alarm in the home. Building codes require smoke alarms in new homes. Have students do research to find out more about the installation and maintenance of smoke alarms. Have students make a pamphlet that can be used to inform others of the importance of smoke alarms. OL

543

Reading Check

Answer Follow rules, report weapons or unsafe activities, wear safety gear.

ASSESS

 Assessment Resources

Lesson Review Quiz
 ExamView
 Fast Files Activities
Online Quizzes and Activities

Reteaching

- Assign Concept Map 20-1 or Reteaching Activity 20-1 in the Fast Files.
- Have students work in pairs to describe how safe habits can help prevent accidents. Call on pairs of students to share their responses.

Enrichment

- Assign Enrichment Activity 20-1 in the Fast Files.
- Have students conduct a phone interview with a firefighter to learn more about fire safety. Have each student prepare a written report that summarizes his or her interview.

CLOSE

Ask students to identify tips for staying safe at school.

▲ Some schools have security guards patrolling campus to help keep students safe. **What should you do if you suspect that someone is planning to bring a weapon to school?**

Safety at School

Your school probably has rules in place to keep students and teachers safe. Many accidental injuries at school can be avoided. Follow these strategies to protect the health and safety of students and teachers.

- **Play by the rules.** Rules are made to protect you and others. The cafeteria, classrooms, halls, gym, and auditorium may all have important safety rules to follow.

- **Report weapons or unsafe activities.** It's essential to follow rules prohibiting weapon possession at school. If you think that someone has brought a gun or other weapon to school, report it immediately to a teacher or principal.

- **Wear necessary safety gear.** Working in a science lab or playing sports are two places where appropriate gear will help keep you safe.

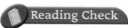 **Reading Check**

Recall What strategies can you and your peers use to stay safe at school?

Lesson 1 Review

 After You Read

Review this lesson for new terms, major headings, and Reading Checks.

What I Learned

1. **Vocabulary** Define *accident*. Use the word in an original sentence.

2. **Identify** Name the sequence of events in an accident chain.

3. **Recall** What are two strategies for preventing falls at home?

Thinking Critically

4. **Apply** Molly's older sister was frying food on their stove last night. Some of the oil she was using spilled onto the stovetop. This morning Molly noticed that the oil was still there. What advice would you give Molly?

5. **Evaluate** What is your family's fire safety plan? How could it be improved?

Applying Health Skills

6. **Advocacy** Kyle is babysitting for a family that has just moved into town. Both of the children are under age 5 and cannot read yet. Kyle notices several bottles of cleaning products, including ammonia, under the kitchen sink. None of the bottles have childproof caps. What can Kyle do to advocate for the safety of the children?

Go Online For more Lesson Review Activities, go to **glencoe.com.**

Lesson 1 Review Answers

1. An accident is any event that was not intended to happen. Sentences will vary.
2. The situation, the unsafe habit, the unsafe act
3. *Sample answers:* wipe up spills, use nonskid rugs, keep stairways well lit and free of clutter

4. *Sample answer:* Molly should clean the stove and tell her family that oil on the stovetop is a fire risk.
5. *Sample answer:* My family has a plan for leaving the house and meeting at a designated area. Answers will vary.

6. *Sample answers:* move the bottles, suggest a childproof lock for the cabinet

Safety on the Road and Outdoors

Guide to Reading

● Building Vocabulary
Write the highlighted word and its definition in your notebook.

■ defensive driving (p. 546)

● Focusing on the Main Ideas
In this lesson, you will learn to

■ **describe** ways to avoid injuries in the water and outdoors.
■ **explain** how to stay safe as a pedestrian.
■ **identify** do's and don'ts of pedestrian safety.
■ **name** safety and traffic rules for bicycles, skates, skateboards, and scooters.

● Reading Strategy
Finding the Main Idea For each major heading in this lesson, write one sentence that states the main idea.

Traffic Safety

The behavior of the passengers riding in a car can be just as important as the driver's behavior. Using good decision-making skills while you are a passenger in a car will reduce your risk of injury. Here are some safety factors to follow:

• Follow the rules of the road.
• Always buckle your safety belt.
• Never get in a car with a driver who has been drinking alcohol or using drugs.
• Don't distract the driver.

Safety on Wheels and Motorized Vehicles

Riding bicycles and using skates, skateboards, scooters, and motorized vehicles are activities many teens enjoy. One way to prevent injury while participating in these activities is to learn about the risks and then follow rules to avoid them.

Quick Write

Make a list of five basic safety rules you should follow while riding a bicycle, skateboard, or scooter.

▶ Buckling up every time you ride in a car is a simple action that could save your life. **What are some other precautions you could take to ensure your safety on the road?**

Lesson 2: Safety on the Road and Outdoors **545**

Lesson 2 Resources

📁 **Chapter FAST FILE Resources**
Guided Reading and Writing 20-2
Concept Mapping Activity 20-2
Decision-Making Activity 20-2
Reteaching Activity 20-2
Enrichment Activity 20-2
Lesson Quiz 20-2

Technology
👆 Transparency 20-2
Audio Summaries
ExamView® Assessment Suite
Vocabulary PuzzleMaker
StudentWorks™ Plus

FOCUS

Activating Prior Knowledge

What I Know Have students think about different ways that students get to and from school and then make a list of safety tips for getting to and from school safely.

Guide to Reading

Building Vocabulary

■ Have a volunteer explain the meaning of the word *defense*. Then have students apply that information to determine the meaning of the term *defensive driving*.
■ Use Vocabulary PuzzleMaker to reinforce vocabulary terms.

Reading Strategy
Finding the Main Idea Challenge students to write an original sentence that summarizes the contents of each section. Have volunteers share their sentences with the class.

Quick Write

After students have completed their Quick Writes, ask volunteers to share their safety tips with the class.

Caption Answer
Photo Caption *Sample answers:* follow the rules of the road, never ride with an impaired driver, don't distract the driver

TEACH

 Active Learning

Puppet Show Have students work in small groups to prepare puppet shows that teach bicycle safety to younger students. Ask students to include at least three tips for bicycle safety in their puppet show. Arrange for students to perform their puppet shows for younger students. **OL**

 Reading Strategy

Organizing Information Have students use index cards to organize the information in the text about traffic safety, bicycle safety, and skateboard safety. Have students use a separate index card for each topic. Suggest that students use bulleted statements to summarize the information about each topic on their cards. **BL**

Reading Check

Answer *Sample answers:* use a helmet, follow the rules of the road, use a light, and wear reflective clothing at night.

Caption Answers

Photo Caption *Sample answers:* use a helmet, use a light, and wear reflective clothing at night
Photo Caption, p. 547 As a pedestrian you should obey all traffic signals and walk on the sidewalk.

Bicycle Safety

The number-one way to stay safe while riding a bicycle is to always wear a bike helmet. Head injuries cause 70 to 80 percent of the deaths from bicycle accidents. Wearing a helmet every time you get on your bike can reduce your risk of head injury by 85 percent.

It is also important for bicycle riders to obey traffic signs and signals. Bicyclists and drivers must practice **defensive driving,** which means *watching out for other people on the road and anticipating unsafe acts.* To stay safe, do not ride at night or in bad weather.

Skates, Skateboards, and Scooters

Skates, skateboards, and scooters can be a lot of fun, but only when they are used safely. Here are some guidelines for having fun while staying injury free.

- Wear protective gear, including a hard-shell helmet, wrist guards, gloves, elbow pads, and knee pads.
- Do not let your speed get out of control.
- Do not skate or ride in parking lots, streets, and other areas with traffic.
- Before you head downhill, practice a safe way to fall on a soft surface.

 Reading Check **Analyze** What are some ways to stay safe when riding a bike?

▶ Bicycle riders need to obey the same traffic rules as drivers. **What else should bicycle riders do to stay safe?**

HEALTH LITERACY

Bicycle Helmets Bicycle helmets are the best way to prevent head and brain injury during a cycling accident. However, the CDC's Youth Risk Behavior Survey for 2003 indicates that between 80 and 90 percent of teens rarely or never use a helmet when bicycling. Explain to students that studies show bicycle helmets could prevent more than 85 percent of the brain injuries incurred in bicycle accidents. Have students develop a PSA encouraging teens to wear bicycle helmets. **OL**

◀ Even if a traffic signal tells you that it's okay to cross, don't forget to look both ways beforehand. **What other safety precautions should you take as a pedestrian?**

Pedestrian Safety

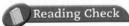

Each year thousands of pedestrians are injured or killed in traffic accidents. A pedestrian is a person traveling on foot. The following guidelines will help you reduce your risk of injury while walking or running.

- Cross streets only at crosswalks. Don't jaywalk, or cross the street in the middle of the block.
- Obey all traffic signals.
- During the day, wear bright clothing. At night, wear reflective gear and carry a flashlight.
- Walk on the sidewalk if there is one. If there is no sidewalk, walk facing oncoming traffic, staying to the left side of the road.

Reading Check **Name** What are two safety guidelines for pedestrians?

Recreational Safety

There are a lot of risks associated with outdoor activities. If you know these risks ahead of time, you can take preventive actions to stay safe. When enjoying an outdoor activity, use common sense and follow these two rules:

- **Be attentive to the weather.** A major risk present during outdoor activities is an electrical storm. If you are caught outdoors during an electrical storm, try to find shelter in a building or car. On a hot day, drink plenty of water, stay in the shade if possible, and do not do any strenuous exercise. On a very cold day, dress in warm layers and stay dry.

Careers for the 21st Century

Emergency Medical Technician

An emergency medical technician (EMT) provides on-the-spot emergency medical care to victims of accidents, injuries, or serious illnesses. EMTs can work in paid positions or as volunteers. Employment for EMTs is growing as paid positions replace many volunteer positions. You can prepare for a career as an EMT by taking biology or anatomy classes that help you learn about the body.

What skills does an EMT need? Go to *Career Corner* **at glencoe.com to find out.**

Lesson 2: Safety on the Road and Outdoors **547**

Home, School, and Community

In the Community Pedestrian safety is an important aspect of community safety. Pedestrian injury is the second-leading cause of unintentional injury to children between the ages of 10 and 14. Pedestrian safety education is one of the strategies suggested by the CDC and the National Highway Traffic Safety Administration for reducing teen pedestrian injuries. Have students work as a class to develop pedestrian safety materials that could be used as a part of a schoolwide pedestrian safety education campaign. OL

547

Academic Vocabulary

technique (tek NEEK) *(noun)* a method used to accomplish a task. *In science class, the students were required to use a certain technique to conduct a lab experiment.*

- **Use the buddy system.** Agree to stay with at least one other person. With a buddy, you can help each other avoid or cope with a potentially dangerous situation.

Water Safety

Thousands of Americans die each year from drowning, including many children. You can protect yourself and others by following these water safety rules:

- Learn to swim if you don't know how.
- Never swim alone.
- Always use a life jacket when boating or waterskiing. If you fall in cold water, use the survival **techniques** shown in **Figure 20.2.**
- If you get caught in a strong current, swim parallel to the shore. When the current lessens, swim to shore.
- Never dive into water unless you know it is at least 9 feet deep and free of obstacles.

Hiking and Camping Safety

Preparation is the first step in a safe and enjoyable hike or camping trip. First, check the weather forecast, and take the necessary clothing and equipment. Always let an adult know where you will be and when you plan to return. Some additional safety guidelines are provided on the next page.

▼FIGURE 20.2

SURVIVAL IN COLD WATER

Hypothermia is a dangerous drop in body temperature which can be life threatening to people in cold water. Use these techniques to help you survive until help arrives. **Why should you always wear a life jacket while boating?**

Reduce heat loss by drawing your knees up to your chest and keeping your upper arms close to the sides of your body. About 50 percent of heat loss is from your head, so try to keep it out of the water.

If you are with other people, huddle close together in a circle to preserve body heat. A child or smaller person who loses heat faster should be placed in the center of the circle.

HEALTH LITERACY

Water Safety The importance of knowing how to swim cannot be overstated. According to the CDC, drowning is the second-leading cause of injury-related death in children aged 1 to 14 years. Provide information to your students about opportunities for swimming lessons in the community. In many communities, the American Red Cross sponsors swimming classes. The school physical education department or the school nurse might also have information about opportunities for swimming lessons in the community.

- **Wear protective clothing.** Dress in layers and wear long pants to protect yourself against ticks.

- **Bring equipment and supplies.** You should have a map, compass, first aid kit, flashlight, extra batteries, and an adequate supply of drinking water.

- **Follow fire safety rules.** Light campfires only where allowed. To put out your campfire, drown it with water or bury it with dirt that is free of debris.

- **Be able to identify poisonous plants and animals.** Learn first aid to treat reactions to poisonous plants, insects, and snakebites.

- **Stay with a buddy.**

Outdoor Sports

Whether you like summer or winter sports, you should always wear appropriate safety gear and stay within your ability level. In the summer, you need to protect yourself against sunburn and heatstroke. Wear sunscreen with a sun protection factor (SPF) of at least 15, sunglasses, a hat, and appropriate clothing. Avoid direct sunlight during the hottest times of the day (10 A.M. to 4 P.M.), if possible, and drink plenty of water. Also, pay attention to your body's signals. If you feel tired or overheated, take a break.

In the winter, protect yourself against cold weather by wearing layers of clothing, a hat, mittens or gloves, and proper footwear.

 Go Online

Visit **glencoe.com** and complete the Interactive Study Guide for Lesson 2.

Lesson 2 Review

 After You Read

Review this lesson for new terms, major headings, and Reading Checks.

What I Learned

1. *Vocabulary* What is *defensive driving*? Use it in an original sentence.

2. *Analyze* What are some safety factors that can reduce your risk of traffic injuries?

3. *Identify* Name three ways to stay safe while in the water.

Thinking Critically

4. *Analyze* How does practicing the buddy system help keep you safe outdoors?

5. *Explain* Why is it important to learn how to fall when skating or riding a bike?

Applying Health Skills

6. *Accessing Information* Think about an outdoor sport or activity you would like to try. Using reliable print or online sources, research how you could get hurt, what safety equipment you would need, and what safety rules you should follow.

Go Online For more Lesson Review Activities, go to **glencoe.com**.

ASSESS

Assessment Resources

Lesson Review Quiz
ExamView
Fast Files Activities
Online Quizzes and Activities

Reteaching

- Assign Concept Map 20-2 or Reteaching Activity 20-2 in the Fast Files.
- Have students work in pairs to make a poster that illustrates tips for pedestrian safety.

Enrichment

- Assign Enrichment Activity 20-2 in the Fast Files.
- Have students research to learn more about choosing a bicycle helmet. Have students prepare a pamphlet they can use to share this information with others.

CLOSE

Go around the room and call on students to describe water safety tips.

Lesson 2 Review Answers

1. Defensive driving means watching out for other people on the road and anticipating unsafe acts. Sentences will vary.

2. *Sample answers:* follow the rules of the road, always buckle your safety belt, never ride with an impaired driver, don't distract the driver

3. *Sample answers:* learn to swim, never swim alone, swim parallel to shore in strong currents, never dive in shallow water, avoid drugs and alcohol

4. If you are injured, your buddy can find someone to help.

5. *Sample answer:* You can reduce your risk of injury by practicing how to fall safely.

6. Answers will vary but should include tips from the lesson.

FOCUS

Activating Prior Knowledge

What I Know Ask students to describe weather emergencies they have experienced or have seen on television. Then have them describe ways to stay safe during such emergencies.

Guide to Reading

Building Vocabulary
- Have students skim the lesson to find the meanings of the vocabulary terms. Then have them make vocabulary flashcards using index cards.
- Use Vocabulary PuzzleMaker to reinforce vocabulary terms.

Reading Strategy
Comparing and Contrasting Have students skim the lesson to find the information. After they have completed the lesson, ask if they would like to add to their answers.

*Q*uick Write

Have students work in pairs to compare their completed Quick Writes. Ask several pairs of students to share their responses with the class.

Caption Answer

Photo Caption because they are so destructive

Safety in Weather Emergencies

Guide to Reading

Building Vocabulary
As you read this lesson, write each new highlighted term and its definition in your notebook.

- tornado (p. 551)
- hurricane (p. 551)
- blizzard (p. 551)
- earthquake (p. 552)

Focusing on the Main Ideas
In this lesson, you will learn to

- **explain** how to stay safe during severe weather.
- **identify** various kinds of weather emergencies and natural disasters.
- **access** information to prepare for weather emergencies.

Reading Strategy
Comparing and Contrasting Both tornadoes and hurricanes are storms with high winds. Explain how you would react to warnings from the National Weather Service for each of these events.

*Q*uick Write

List several weather emergencies that might occur where you live. Write two emergency preparations for each.

Hazardous Weather and Natural Disasters

You have been learning about ways to prevent emergencies. There are some emergencies, however, that even the most careful planning and best safety habits cannot prevent. These include weather emergencies and natural disasters. Perhaps you live in an area where tornadoes, hurricanes, earthquakes, or blizzards occur. Tornadoes are often found in the central states. Hurricanes commonly turn up along the Atlantic Coast and the Gulf of Mexico. Earthquakes typically occur on the West Coast and in southern Alaska. These emergencies can cause serious health problems.

▶ Knowing what to do when a tornado strikes is the key to staying safe. **Why are tornadoes so dangerous?**

550 Chapter 20: Safety and Emergencies

Lesson 3 Resources

📁 **Chapter *Fast File* Resources**
Guided Reading and Writing 20-3
Concept Mapping Activity 20-3
Cross-Curriculum Activity 20-3
Reteaching Activity 20-3
Enrichment Activity 20-3
Lesson Quiz 20-3

Technology
- Transparency 20-3
- Audio Summaries
- *ExamView®* Assessment Suite
- Vocabulary PuzzleMaker
- StudentWorks™ Plus
- **G⊙ Online**

Tornadoes

A **tornado** is *a whirling, funnel-shaped windstorm that may drop from the sky to the ground.* Tornadoes are extremely dangerous storms, often destroying everything in their path. If a tornado is headed your way, take the following steps to help reduce your risk of injury:

- **Stay clear of windows.** Go to an inner hallway or any central, windowless room such as a bathroom or closet.
- **Take cover.** A basement or cellar that has no windows is the safest place to wait out a tornado.
- **Get low.** Lie down in a ditch if you are outside or other low-lying area.

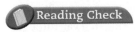 **Reading Check** **Explain** What are some precautions to take in the event of a tornado?

Hurricanes

A **hurricane** is *a strong windstorm with driving rain that originates at sea.* The storm clouds of a hurricane can extend over hundreds of miles and revolve around a calm center called an eye. Hurricanes occur most often in late summer and early fall.

The National Weather Service tracks tornadoes and hurricanes. **Figure 20.3** shows one hurricane's path. To prepare for a hurricane, secure your home by boarding up windows. Close storm shutters before the winds start blowing. Then, leave the area and head inland, away from the hurricane.

Blizzards

A **blizzard** is *a very heavy snowstorm with winds up to 45 miles per hour.* Visibility usually is reduced to less than 500 feet, making it easy to get lost or disoriented. You can protect yourself during blizzards and winter storms by following these precautions:

- **Stay indoors.** The safest place during a blizzard is inside.
- **Bundle up.** If you must go out, wear layers of loose-fitting lightweight clothing under layers of outerwear that is both wind- and waterproof. Add a scarf, hat, gloves, and boots.
- **Don't wander.** Use landmarks to avoid getting lost, or stay put until help arrives.

Storm Tracking

Satellite images and computers help forecasters gather information on the directions in which storms are headed. The newest weather satellites are the GOES series, or Geostationary Operational Environmental Satellite.

Use the Internet to find out where you can get up-to-date hurricane forecast information.

▼ FIGURE 20.3

TRACKING A HURRICANE

R Weather experts track the path of a hurricane by recording the coordinates of its location at regular intervals. **How might hurricane tracking help people who live in coastal areas?**

Frances 2004

Lesson 3: Safety in Weather Emergencies **551**

TEACH

Storm Tracking

Up-to-date hurricane forecasts are available from television news and weather stations, the Emergency Alert System, and reliable Internet sites.

Reading Check

Answer stay clear of windows, take cover under furniture, stay low in a ditch if you are outside

R Reading Strategy

Analyzing a Graphic Have students examine **Figure 20.3**, which shows the path of a hurricane. Explain that the energy of hurricanes comes from the energy contained in warm water. Ask: Why do hurricanes lose strength when they move over land? *because they can no longer draw energy from warm ocean water* OL

Academic Vocabulary

Majority Page 552 mentions that flash floods are responsible for the *majority* of flood fatalities. Tell students that *majority* means "the largest number." OL

Teacher to Teacher

Robin Pettapiece   Emmet Belknap Middle School, Lockport, NY

Weather Safety

"Have your students create colorful, engaging posters promoting weather safety. They will need to find seven safety tips for their poster. Have students search Web sites for ideas: The Weather Channel, NOAA Weather Service, and the Yahooligans Weather Safety. Then have students display posters throughout your school."

Caption Answer

Figure Caption Hurricane tracking allows those in coastal areas to prepare and evacuate before a storm hits the coast.

Health Skills Activity

Practicing Healthful Behaviors

Preparing for Weather Emergencies

Use the following strategies to help students complete the activity on the facing page:

- Have students work in small groups to prepare their information sheets.

- Ask students to make a list of actions that teens can take to help their families prepare for emergencies. Record their responses on the board. Challenge students to carry out as many of those actions as possible. **OL**

Go Online

Be Prepared!
Assign small groups to work together to gather research on natural disasters. Have them outline their script and brainstorm creative ways to present the information. Allow time for groups to present their scripts.

Reading Check

Answer Stay indoors, bundle up, and do not wander.

Caption Answer

Photo Caption *Sample answer:* Yes, my school has tornado safety drills.

552

► Schools have drills to prepare for weather emergencies. **Does your school have drills to practice safety strategies?**

Go Online

Topic: Be Prepared!

Visit **glencoe.com** for Student Web Activities to learn about the various kinds of natural disasters and how to prepare for them.

Activity: With a group, use the information provided at the link above to write a script for a public radio announcement that educates listeners about how to prepare for one of the disasters at school, at home, or in your community.

Go Online

Visit **glencoe.com** and complete the Interactive Study Guide for Lesson 3.

Floods

In the event of a flood, head to high ground and stay away from the water. Never swim, walk, bike, or ride in a car through floodwaters. Drowning and electrocution from downed power lines pose a serious risk.

Flash floods are responsible for the majority of flood fatalities. Water can rise so fast and move so swiftly that people, cars, and even homes can be swept away. During a flood, pay attention to bulletins from the National Weather Service and follow their advice.

Earthquakes

An **earthquake** is *a violent shaking movement of the earth's surface.* Earthquakes can occur anywhere in the United States, but happen most often west of the Rocky Mountains. Collapsing walls and falling debris are responsible for causing most injuries in an earthquake. To reduce your risk of injury, follow these precautions:

- **Stay indoors.** Crouch under a sturdy piece of furniture, against an interior wall, or in a strongly supported doorway. Stay away from objects that might fall, shatter, or cave in. Use your arms or a pillow to cover your head.

- **Get in the open if outdoors.** Avoid buildings, trees, telephone and electric lines, streetlights, and overpasses. Drivers should stop their cars and both the driver and passengers should stay inside the car.

- **Be careful afterward.** After the shaking stops, stay out of damaged buildings. Electrical and gas lines could be damaged and may be hazardous. Small quakes called aftershocks often occur after the main earthquake.

Reading Check

Recall What are three ways to stay safe during a blizzard?

TECHNOLOGY AND HEALTH

Earthquake Prediction Earthquakes are natural disasters that often occur with no warning. Technologies allowing accurate prediction of earthquakes could save many lives. However, scientists have not yet devised a method for accurately forecasting earthquakes. Today's technologies allow scientists to use geological information and statistical models to predict the likelihood of a major earthquake in a region within a certain number of years. But techniques have not yet been developed that can predict earthquakes within days or hours of their occurrence. **OL**

Health Skills Activity

Practicing Healthful Behaviors

Preparing for Weather Emergencies

Follow these tips to plan ahead for weather emergencies:

- Identify which weather emergencies are likely to affect your area.
- Check with a reliable source about precautions to take during these types of weather emergencies.
- Develop and maintain a personal and family emergency plan.
- Prepare and maintain an emergency supplies kit that includes a battery-operated radio and flashlight, extra batteries, canned and ready-to-eat foods, a can opener, water (one gallon per person per day), a first-aid kit, and blankets.
- Identify emergency evacuation routes in your local area.

With a Group

In small groups, choose a weather emergency that occurs in your area. Prepare information sheets on preparing for and staying safe during this type of emergency. Post these at home, with your parents' permission.

ASSESS

Assessment Resources

Lesson Review Quiz
- *ExamView*
- Fast Files Activities
- Online Quizzes and Activities

Reteaching

- Assign Concept Map 20-3 or Reteaching Activity 20-3 in the Fast Files.
- Have students list tips for tornado safety. Have students work in pairs to review and add to their lists.

Enrichment

- Assign Enrichment Activity 20-3 in the Fast Files.
- Have students research technology that is used to make buildings and bridges earthquake safe. Have students create a multimedia presentation to share their findings with the class.

CLOSE

Randomly call on students to describe ways to stay safe during weather emergencies.

Lesson 3 Review

 After You Read

Review this lesson for new terms, major headings, and Reading Checks.

What I Learned

1. *Vocabulary* Define *hurricane*, and use it in a sentence.

2. *Describe* Describe how to protect yourself during a flood.

3. *Identify* What are four kinds of weather emergencies?

Thinking Critically

4. *Analyze* Why is it dangerous to be outside during a blizzard?

5. *Synthesize* After a major earthquake, your friend wants you go with him or her to inspect a damaged building. How would you respond? Explain your answer.

Applying Health Skills

6. *Communication Skills* With a partner, choose a weather emergency from this lesson. Write and perform a skit to demonstrate strategies for staying safe during that event.

Go Online For more Lesson Review Activities, go to glencoe.com.

Lesson 3: Safety in Weather Emergencies **553**

Lesson 3 Review Answers

1. A hurricane is a strong windstorm with driving rain that originates at sea. Sentences will vary.

2. In the event of a flood, you should head to high ground, stay away from the water, and follow the advice of the National Weather Service.

3. *Any four:* tornadoes, hurricanes, earthquakes, floods, blizzards

4. The swirling winds and heavy snow could cause you to become disoriented and lost.

5. Aftershocks are common after an earthquake and damaged buildings may collapse.

6. Students' skits should include weather safety information from the lesson.

FOCUS

Activating Prior Knowledge

What I Know Ask students to brainstorm a list of situations that would require first aid.

Guide to Reading

Building Vocabulary
- Tell students that *universal* means "including all." Have students apply this information to help them infer the meaning of the term *universal precautions*.
- Use Vocabulary PuzzleMaker to reinforce vocabulary terms.

Reading Strategy
Predicting After students have finished reading the lesson, have them indicate by show of hands whether or not their predictions were correct.

Quick Write

Have students share their completed Quick Writes with the class. Use the completed Quick Writes to assess students' misconceptions about first aid.

Caption Answer

Caption *Sample answer:* Family members, police, and poison control should be on an emergency phone list.

Basic First Aid

Guide to Reading

Building Vocabulary
As you read this lesson, write each new highlighted term and its definition in your notebook.

- first aid (p. 554)
- universal precautions (p. 555)

Focusing on the Main Ideas
In this lesson, you will learn to
- **explain** universal precautions.
- **identify** the steps to take in an emergency.
- **assemble** your own first-aid kit.

Reading Strategy
Predicting Look over the lesson, including the headings and pictures. Then write a sentence predicting what information you think the lesson will provide.

Quick Write

Imagine that you and a friend are skating and your friend falls and injures his or her leg. Write a paragraph describing what you would do to help your friend.

First Aid

First aid is *the immediate temporary care given to an injured or ill person until he or she can get professional help.* You can prevent further injury and may even speed recovery if you know what to do in an emergency. Knowing what *not* to do is equally important. Administering the proper first aid sometimes means the difference between life and death. Staying calm allows you to better help the victim. In this lesson you will learn what supplies are needed for a basic first-aid kit. You will also learn how to respond in an emergency and how to protect yourself when providing first aid.

Emergency Phone # List

Emergency Medical Services	911
Family Doctor	444-211-0000
Poison Control Center	1-800-222-1222
Police	444-211-0001
Fire Dept.	444-211-0002
Parent's Work #	444-211-0003
Mom's Cell	444-211-0004
Dad's Cell	444-211-0005
Uncle Jimmy	444-211-0006
Our neighbors the Smiths	444-211-0007

◄ Keeping an emergency phone list handy can save time during an emergency. **What numbers should be on an emergency phone list?**

Lesson 4 Resources

📁 Chapter *FAST FILE* Resources
Guided Reading and Writing 20-4
Concept Mapping Activity 20-4
Decision-Making Activity 20-4
Reteaching Activity 20-4
Enrichment Activity 20-4
Lesson Quiz 20-4

Technology
- Transparency 20-4
- Audio Summaries
- *ExamView®* Assessment Suite
- Vocabulary PuzzleMaker
- StudentWorks™ Plus

Go Online

Being Prepared

Without warning, at any time or place, you might find yourself in a position where you need to give first aid. Learning basic skills will help you handle most common emergencies. Keeping a list of emergency numbers near all phones is one simple way to be prepared. Another way is to keep a first-aid kit at home and in the car. First-aid kits come pre-packaged, or you can assemble your own. **Figure 20.4** lists some basic first-aid supplies. You may need to add specific medicines if someone in your family has a medical condition.

Taking Universal Precautions

Viruses such as HIV and hepatitis B and C can be spread through contact with an infected person's blood. As a result, steps should be taken to minimize contact with another person's blood. To protect yourself when giving first aid, follow **universal precautions.** These are *actions taken to prevent the spread of disease by treating all blood as if it were contaminated.* Wear protective gloves while treating a victim. If possible, use a face mask or shield, when giving first aid for breathing emergencies. Cover any open wounds on your body with sterile dressings. Avoid touching any object that was in contact with the victim's blood. Always wash hands thoroughly after giving first aid.

ACTIVITY

DEVELOPING

Good Character

Citizenship

A good neighbor and citizen is prepared to report accidents, fires, serious illnesses, injuries, and crimes. Familiarize yourself with emergency phone numbers to call in your community. **Make a list to keep handy by the telephone.**

▼ **FIGURE 20.4**

R

First-Aid Supplies

Keeping a first-aid kit in your home will help your family be prepared for emergencies. *What other supplies might you add to this kit?*

Instruments:	Equipment:	Medications:	Dressings:	Miscellaneous:
tweezers, scissors	thermometer, cotton swabs, blanket, cold pack	antiseptic ointment, sterile eyewash, activated charcoal, syrup of ipecac	gauze pads, adhesive tape, adhesive bandages, triangular bandage	small flashlight, tissues, hand cleanser, disposable gloves, face mask, plastic bags

TEACH

R Reading Strategy

Analyzing a Graphic Have students examine **Figure 20.4**. Ask: Why is it important to have a stocked first-aid kit? *because you never know when an accident that requires first aid will happen* Why is it important to periodically review the supplies in your first-aid kit? *to be sure that there is a good supply of each item and that none of the items has reached its expiration date* **OL**

ACTIVITY

DEVELOPING

Good Character

Citizenship
Remind students that most police departments have a nonemergency phone number that should be used for situations that do not require an emergency response. Have students research the nonemergency numbers for the local police department and poison control center, and help students develop a list of emergency and nonemergency situations. **OL**

🏠 Home, School, and Community

In the Community After students have read the information in the text about the first steps to take in an emergency, have them research more about a career as an emergency medical technician. Invite an emergency medical technician to speak to the class to discuss the first four steps of emergency response. Also ask the speaker to describe the training required to become an emergency medical technician. Have students prepare questions in advance for the speaker. **OL**

Caption Answer

Figure Caption *Sample answer:* medicines taken by family members, aspirin or ibuprofen, bottled water

What Teens THINK

What are some ways to stay safe when you are home alone? Help students brainstorm a list of steps they take to stay safe when they are home alone. Record their ideas on the board. Ask students to consider which of those steps they *always* take, and ask: What changes do you think you could make to be sure you're safe when no one else is home? Encourage students to think about that question, and let volunteers who are willing to share discuss their responses. Then have students read and discuss the *What Teens Think* response.

Caption Answer

Photo Caption, p. 557 You should avoid moving an injured person to prevent further pain or injury.

What Teens THINK

What are some ways to stay safe when you are home alone?

When someone calls and you don't know who they are, don't tell them you are alone. Lock the doors, even if it is daylight. Stay indoors if it is dark outside. Of course, don't answer the door to strangers, and don't let people into the house unless you know them.

**Alberto T.
Albuquerque, NM**

Academic Vocabulary

evaluate (ee VAL yoo wayt) *(verb)* determining value or importance. *Cameron wanted to evaluate several different computers before deciding which one to buy.*

The First Steps

Although every emergency situation is unique, there are four steps to take for most emergencies. Recognize the signs of an emergency, take action, call for help, and provide care until help arrives.

Identifying the Signs of an Emergency

Often something you see, hear, or smell will alert you to an emergency. Is someone calling out in trouble? Have you heard glass shattering? Do you smell smoke or anything unusual that makes your eyes sting or causes you to cough or have difficulty breathing? These sensations can signal a chemical spill or toxic gas release.

Taking Action

Before deciding what action to take, **evaluate** the situation. Consider your strengths and limitations. Do not dive into a lake to rescue someone who's drowning unless you are trained in lifesaving. Instead, you might throw a life preserver or something else that floats. Protect your own safety first. Putting yourself in danger can harm both you and the person who needs help. One action that never hurts is calling for help. Getting help can save a life and is sometimes the best and only action for you to take.

Calling for Help

Dial 911 for all emergencies in most of the United States. In some small towns, dialing zero (for operator) is an option. When making a call for help, stay calm. Describe the emergency to the operator and give a street address or describe the location by using landmarks. The operator will notify the police, fire, or emergency medical service departments. Stay on the phone until the operator tells you to hang up.

Providing Care Until Help Arrives

After you have called for help, stay with the victim until help arrives. Carefully loosen any tight clothing on the victim. Use a coat or blanket to keep the person warm or provide shade if the weather is warm. This will help the person maintain a normal body temperature.

TECHNOLOGY AND HEALTH

Calling for Help Prepare students for making 911 calls. When 911 is called from a landline phone, the 911 operator has immediate access to the address from which the call is originating. This allows the operator to send help even if the caller is unable to speak. Cellular phones with enhanced 911 technology also help emergency services locate the caller, but with less precision than a call from a landline phone. Explain to students that they can call 911 from a pay phone without depositing any money.

◄ While you wait for medical help to arrive, help the victim stay calm by providing comfort and reassurance. **Why should you avoid moving an injured person?**

Avoid moving the victim to prevent further pain or injury. Only move the victim if he or she is in danger, such as in the path of traffic.

Cardiopulmonary resuscitation (CPR) may be necessary if the victim is unconscious and unresponsive. This lifesaving technique is described in Lesson 6 of this chapter.

 Reading Check   **Explain** What are some signs of an emergency?

Go Online

Visit **glencoe.com** and complete the Interactive Study Guide for Lesson 4.

 Reading Check

Answer someone calling out for help, glass shattering, smoke or other unusual smells that make you cough

ASSESS

 Assessment Resources

Lesson Review Quiz
- *ExamView*
- Fast Files Activities
- Online Quizzes and Activities

Reteaching
- Assign Concept Map 20-4 or Reteaching Activity 20-4 in the Fast Files.
- Have students write a paragraph that summarizes the content of Lesson 4.

Enrichment
- Assign Enrichment Activity 20-4 in the Fast Files.
- Have students research community organizations that offer first-aid training classes. The American Red Cross is a good place to begin. Have students provide information to the class about first-aid training available in their community.

CLOSE

Call on students to identify items that should be contained in a first-aid kit.

Lesson 4 Review

 After You Read

Review this lesson for new terms, major headings, and Reading Checks.

What I Learned

1. *Vocabulary* Define *first aid*. Use the term in a sentence.

2. *Recall* Name four universal precautions to take when administering first aid.

3. *List* Give two examples of ways you can help an injured person until professional help arrives.

Thinking Critically

4. *Analyze* Why is it important to know basic first-aid strategies?

5. *Apply* If you come upon an injured person on a hiking trail, should you try to move the person off the trail? Why or why not?

Applying Health Skills

6. *Accessing Information* Investigate how to report emergency or dangerous situations to appropriate authorities in your area. Prepare a report of your findings. Keep this information with your emergency phone list at home.

Go Online For more Lesson Review Activities, go to **glencoe.com**.

Lesson 4: Basic First Aid **557**

Lesson 4 Review Answers

1. First aid is immediate, temporary care given to an injured or ill person. Sentences will vary.
2. *Any four:* Wear gloves, use a face mask or shield, cover open wounds on your body, avoid touching objects that have had contact with blood, wash hands after giving first aid.
3. Reassure the victim that help is coming and cover him or her with a coat or blanket.
4. Knowing first-aid strategies will allow you to act quickly and calmly in an emergency.
5. No, an injured person should not be moved unless he or she is in danger.
6. Encourage each student to make a written record of how to report emergency or dangerous situations to the appropriate authorities.

FOCUS

Activating Prior Knowledge

What I Know Have students describe common emergencies. Then ask students to describe appropriate first aid for these emergencies.

Guide to Reading

Building Vocabulary
- Have students skim the lesson to find the meanings of the vocabulary terms. Then have students write a sentence that differentiates the terms *heatstroke* and *heat exhaustion.*
- Use Vocabulary PuzzleMaker to reinforce vocabulary terms.

Reading Strategy
Organizing Information Before students read, suggest they look at the headings in the lesson to help them think about how to organize their charts.

Quick Write

Ask volunteers to share their responses with the class. Have students add to their lists after reading the lesson.

First Aid for Common Emergencies

Guide to Reading

Building Vocabulary
As you read this lesson, write each new highlighted term and its definition in your notebook.

- sprain (p. 559)
- fracture (p. 559)
- heat cramps (p. 562)
- heat exhaustion (p. 562)
- heatstroke (p. 562)

Focusing on the Main Ideas
In this lesson, you will learn to

- **describe** the different types of common emergencies.
- **explain** first-aid treatments for common emergencies.
- **identify** when it is time to call for medical assistance.

Reading Strategy
Organizing Information Create a chart listing the common emergencies discussed in this lesson and the first-aid techniques used to treat them.

Quick Write

Make a list of common emergencies in which you feel capable of providing help.

Common Emergencies

Common emergencies include insect and animal bites, burns, poisoning, foreign objects in the eye, nosebleeds, and fainting. Others include heat cramps and heatstroke as well as sprains, bruises, and broken bones. In this chapter you will learn how to treat these minor conditions and recognize more serious conditions that need professional medical assistance.

▶ Treating a sprained ankle can include elevating it above the level of the heart. **How does this help the injury?**

Caption Answer

Photo Caption Elevating the ankle to the level of the heart reduces swelling by reducing the blood flow to the area.

Lesson 5 Resources

 Chapter FAST FILE Resources
Guided Reading and Writing 20-5
Concept Mapping Activity 20-5
Health Lab Activity 20-5
Reteaching Activity 20-5
Enrichment Activity 20-5
Lesson Quiz 20-5

Technology
- Transparency 20-5
- Audio Summaries
- *ExamView®* Assessment Suite
- Vocabulary PuzzleMaker
- StudentWorks™ Plus

 Go Online

Sprains

A **sprain** is *a condition in which the ligaments that hold the joints in position are stretched or torn.* The most commonly sprained joints are ankles and knees. Symptoms of sprains include swelling and bruising. While a doctor should evaluate serious sprains, minor sprains can be treated using the P.R.I.C.E. method:

- **Protect** the injured part by keeping it still. Moving it could cause further injury.
- **Rest** the affected joint for 24 to 48 hours.
- **Ice** the injured part to reduce swelling and pain. A cloth between the skin and ice bag will reduce discomfort.
- **Compress** the injured area by wrapping it in an elastic bandage.
- **Elevate** the injured part above the level of the heart to reduce swelling.

Broken Bones

A **fracture** is *a break in the bone.* An open fracture is a complete break with one or both sides of the bone piercing the skin. A closed fracture does not break the skin and may be difficult to identify. Pain, swelling and a misshapen appearance are typical symptoms of a closed fracture. However, not all broken bones cause immediate pain. An X ray is the only way to be sure if a bone is broken.

Insect and Animal Bites

Insect bites and stings can be serious for people with certain allergies. Call for help if a person shows signs of an allergic reaction, like difficulty breathing, nausea, or confusion.

To treat insect bites and stings, wash the area with soap and water. Remove an insect's stinger by scraping it off with a firm, straight-edged object. Apply ice or a cold pack to the site for ten minutes to reduce pain and swelling. Alternate ten minutes on and ten minutes off.

For minor animal bites, wash the bite with soap and water and apply pressure to stop the bleeding. Apply antibiotic ointment and a sterile bandage.

Burns

First-aid techniques for treating burns vary depending on the location and the severity of the burn. Third-degree and some second-degree burns are very serious and require immediate medical help. **Figure 20.5** on the next page explains how to recognize and treat three classifications of burns.

▼ If you have a fracture, your doctor will look at an X ray of your bone to determine where the fracture is located. **What are the two different types of fractures?**

Lesson 5: First Aid for Common Emergencies   **559**

TEACH

U Universal Access

Students with Different Learning Styles Have students work in small groups to write a chant, rap, or song that summarizes the steps of the P.R.I.C.E. method of treating sprains. Ask each group to demonstrate its chant, rap, or song for the class. OL

AL Active Learning

Game Show Have students work in small groups to prepare ten game-show style questions about the emergencies described in this lesson. Have each group quiz the class using its questions. Allow students to form teams and keep score. OL

Academic Vocabulary

Vary On pages 559–560, students learn that treatments for burns vary. Explain that *vary* means "to differ in some respect." Ask students to identify other things that vary. OL

Caption Answer

Photo Caption An open fracture occurs when one or both sides of the bone pierce the skin; a closed fracture does not break the skin.

What Teens Want to Know

What common substances cause poisoning? Many everyday items found in the home can cause poisoning. Medicines and vitamins are a common cause of poisonings. In fact, the greatest proportion of poisoning deaths of young children is caused by ingestion of vitamins with iron.

Alcoholic beverages and mouthwashes with alcohol are also common causes of poisonings, as are cleansers, disinfectants, and bleach. Have students evaluate potential poisons in their homes. Ask students to consider safe ways to store these items at home. OL

R Reading Strategy

Analyzing a Table Direct students' attention to **Figure 20.5**, which describes the three classifications of burns. Ask: Which burns require treatment by a medical professional? *All third-degree burns require help from a medical professional; second-degree burns that are larger than 2 inches in diameter, or are on the hands, feet, face, groin, buttocks, or a major joint also require help from a medical professional.* **OL**

AL Active Learning

Pamphlet Ask students to select one of the emergencies described on these pages. Then have students make a pamphlet to teach others how to recognize and properly treat the selected emergency. Have students display their completed pamphlets in the classroom. **OL**

▼ FIGURE 20.5

R THREE DEGREES OF BURNS

Treatment for burns depends on the severity of the burn. **Which type of burns require immediate medical help?**

Three Degrees of Burns		
Type of Burn	**Description**	**Treatment**
First-Degree (superficial burn)	Affects only the outer layer of the skin. The skin is usually red, but the outer layer has not been burned through. There may be swelling and pain.	Flush the burned area with cold water for at least 20 minutes. Do not use ice. Loosely wrap the burn with a sterile bandage.
Second-Degree (partial-thickness burn)	Burns through the first layer of skin and burns the second layer of skin. Blisters develop, and the skin looks red and splotchy. Usually there is severe pain and swelling.	A burn no longer than 2 to 3 inches in diameter can be treated as a first-degree burn. If the burn is larger, or is on the hands, feet, face, groin, buttocks, or a major joint, get medical help immediately.
Third-Degree (full-thickness burn)	Involves all layers of skin and may affect fat, muscle, and bone. The burned area may be charred black or appear dry and white. There may be little or no pain felt at this stage. If the burn is deeper than the skin, then it is called fourth degree.	Call for medical help. While you are waiting, treat the victim for shock as described in Lesson 6. Do not remove burned clothing. Apply cold water to the burn, then cover with a sterile bandage or clean cloth. Keep the victim still and help him or her to sip fluids.

Poisoning

A poison is a substance that causes harm when swallowed, inhaled, absorbed by the skin, or injected into the body. Medicines and household products play a role in about half of all poisonings. All poisonings require immediate treatment. In the event of a poisoning, call the nearest poison control center, a 24-hour hot line providing medical information about treating poisoning victims. Be ready to provide information about the victim and the suspected poison. The poison control center will advise you about how to proceed. The victim might need to drink water or milk to dilute the poison, or a dose of syrup of ipecac, a medication that causes vomiting.

AL If a poisonous chemical such as a pesticide or household cleaning agent has made contact with someone's skin, first remove all clothing that has touched the chemical and rinse the skin with water for 15 minutes. Then wash gently with soap and water. Call the poison control center while the skin is being washed.

560 Chapter 20: Safety and Emergencies

Caption Answer

Figure Caption Some second-degree and all third-degree burns require immediate medical treatment.

HEALTH LITERACY

Emergency Contacts Remind students of the importance of carrying emergency contact information. Explain that hospital and emergency personnel suggest that emergency contact information should be carried in an easy-to-find location, such as a purse or wallet. In addition, people are encouraged to enter the term *ICE* in case of emergency in the directory of their cellular phone with the phone number of their emergency contact. Have students create wallet-sized cards that contain their emergency contact information. **OL**

Foreign Object in the Eye

Do not rub your eye if there is a foreign object in it. Use clean water to flush the object out. Hold the rim of a small, clean glass filled with water against the base of your eye socket. Gently pour the water into the open eye. Repeat the process until the object washes out, or get assistance if you cannot clear your eye.

If someone else has a foreign object in the eye, locate the object by gently pulling the lower lid downward while the person looks up and then holding the upper lid open while the person looks down. If it is floating on the surface of the eye, lightly touch the object with a moistened cotton swab or corner of a clean cloth. Call for medical assistance if you cannot remove the object.

Nosebleed

An injury or even a cold can cause a nosebleed. It can also be caused by being in a very dry place. To stop a nosebleed, pinch the nostrils shut with the thumb and index finger and breathe through your mouth for 5 to 10 minutes. If the bleeding is heavy and it continues for more than 15 minutes, get medical help.

Fainting

Fainting is a brief loss of consciousness that occurs when the blood supply to the brain is cut off for a short amount of time. If you feel faint you should lie or sit down, placing your head between your knees. If someone else faints, here's how to help:

- Leave the person lying down and check the airway. Raise the legs above the level of the head if the person is breathing.

- Loosen any tight clothing.

- Call for help if the person does not regain consciousness in a minute or so. Call for help and start CPR if the person is not breathing. CPR is discussed in Lesson 6.

- Losing consciousness as a result of a head injury is not fainting. If this occurs, call for help immediately. Begin CPR if the person is not breathing.

▲ If you feel faint, sit down and put your head between your knees. This will let blood flow into your head. **What should you do if you are with someone who faints?**

Lesson 5: First Aid for Common Emergencies **561**

HS Health Skills Practice

Accessing Information Have students access reliable online information about treating common emergencies such as eye injuries or nosebleeds. Ask each student to note and share with the class three additional facts he or she learned about common emergencies. Remind students of the characteristics of reliable Internet health resources. OL

📖 Reading Check

Answer, p. 562 Have the person lie down in a cool place, with his or her feet elevated. Loosen the victim's clothing, offer cool (but not iced) water to drink, and fan the person while spraying cool water. Watch the victim carefully for signs of heatstroke.

Caption Answer

Photo Caption If you are with someone who faints, you should establish an airway, raise the legs above the level of the head, loosen any tight clothing, and call for help if the person does not regain consciousness in a minute or so.

Dealing with Sensitive Issues

Intentional Fainting Fainting is a brief loss of consciousness that occurs when the blood supply to the brain is cut off. A dangerous trend among teens is the intentional cutting off of the blood supply to the brain in order to induce a high. Teens either cut off the blood flow to their own brains using belts, shoelaces, or other items or have a friend choke them or press them up against a wall. This is often referred to as "fainting each other," and can lead to permanent brain injury or death. Explain that teens must talk to a trusted adult if they know of others who engage in this potentially deadly behavior.

ASSESS

Assessment Resources

Lesson Review Quiz
- *ExamView*
- Fast Files Activities
- Online Quizzes and Activities

Reteaching

- Assign Concept Map 20-5 or Reteaching Activity 20-5 in the Fast Files.
- Have students work with partners to describe appropriate responses to various types of emergencies.

Enrichment

- Assign Enrichment Activity 20-5 in the Fast Files.
- Have students research the process of healing that a bone undergoes after a fracture. Ask students to create an illustrated report to share their findings with the class.

CLOSE

Have students identify the steps in the P.R.I.C.E. method.

Heat-Related Illnesses

Heat cramps, heat exhaustion and heatstroke are heat-related illnesses. **Heat cramps** are *painful, involuntary muscle spasms that usually occur during strenuous exercise in hot weather.* Resting, cooling down, and drinking water or a sports drink containing electrolytes should help to relieve heat cramps. Gentle stretching exercises and massage also may help.

Heat exhaustion is *characterized by faintness, nausea, rapid heartbeat and hot, red, dry, or sweaty skin.* Anyone with these symptoms needs to lie down in a shady or air-conditioned place and elevate his or her feet. Loosen the victim's clothing and offer cold, but not iced, water to drink. Fan the person while spraying them with cool water. Watch the victim carefully. Heat exhaustion can quickly become heatstroke, the most serious of heat illnesses.

Heatstroke is *the most serious form of heat illness.* A heatstroke occurs because the body has stopped sweating. Sweating is the body's way of releasing heat. Heatstroke can be life-threatening. The primary symptoms are a significant increase in body temperature—generally higher than 104° F—and rapid heartbeat and shallow breathing. Call immediately for medical assistance while treating the victim for heat exhaustion as described above.

Go Online

Visit **glencoe.com** and complete the Interactive Study Guide for Lesson 5.

Reading Check **Explain** How do you treat a person with heat exhaustion?

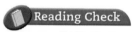

Lesson 5 Review

After You Read

Review this lesson for new terms, major headings, and Reading Checks.

What I Learned

1. **Vocabulary** Define *sprain* and *fracture*. Use both terms in a sentence that demonstrates their meanings.

2. **Name** What are the different types of common emergencies?

3. **List** Name two symptoms of heatstroke.

Thinking Critically

4. **Compare and Contrast** How does the treatment for insect bites differ from that for animal bites?

5. **Analyze** How would you respond to this accidental injury: a burn on the elbow of about 1½ inches in diameter that has burned through the first and second layer of skin.

Applying Health Skills

6. **Practicing Healthful Behaviors** With a partner, write a scenario for dealing with a common emergency. Demonstrate strategies for responding to accidental injury by acting out your scenario for the class.

Go Online For more Lesson Review Activities, go to **glencoe.com**.

Lesson 5 Review Answers

1. A sprain is a torn or stretched ligament. A fracture is a broken bone. Sentences will vary.
2. Insect bites, burns, poisoning, nosebleeds, fainting, heatstroke, sprains, bruises, fractures
3. Heatstroke symptoms include elevated body temperature and shallow, fast breathing.
4. Both bites need to be washed with soap and water. Pressure and antibiotic ointment should be applied to a minor animal bite.
5. This burn can be treated by cooling it with water and covering it with a sterile bandage.
6. Follow up after students have performed their scenarios for the class by asking students to describe responses to emergencies that were not the subject of a role-play.

Lesson 6

Life-Threatening Emergencies

Guide to Reading

● **Building Vocabulary**
Make a word diagram that shows the relationship among the terms below. Decide which term is the one the others relate to.

- abdominal thrusts (p. 564)
- cardiopulmonary resuscitation (CPR) (p. 566)
- shock (p. 567)

● **Focusing on the Main Ideas**
In this lesson, you will learn to

- **explain** different kinds of life-threatening emergencies.
- **describe** how to perform rescue breathing.
- **identify** the symptoms of shock.
- **explain** how to help someone who is choking.

● **Reading Strategy**
Finding the Main Idea For each major heading in this lesson, write one sentence that states the main idea.

When Emergency Strikes

Unless the proper treatment is given, a person may have only minutes to live in a life-threatening emergency. You could help save someone's life if you stay calm, call for help, and provide appropriate first aid.

Choking

Choking kills more than 3,000 people every year in the United States. When a piece of food or some other object blocks a person's airway, oxygen cannot reach the lungs. If a person is clutching his or her throat, that is the universal sign for choking. Other symptoms include gasping or wheezing, a reddish-purple coloration, bulging eyes, and an inability to speak. If a person can speak or cough, it is not a choking emergency.

Quick Write

Make a list of life-threatening emergencies in which you feel capable of helping and write what actions you'd take.

▶ This teen is demonstrating the universal sign for choking—grabbing the throat with thumbs and fingers extended. **How would you respond to someone showing this sign?**

Lesson 6 Resources

📁 **Chapter FAST FILE Resources**
Guided Reading and Writing 20-6
Concept Mapping Activity 20-6
Cross-Curriculum Activity 20-6
Reteaching Activity 20-6
Enrichment Activity 20-6
Lesson Quiz 20-6

Technology
🕹 Transparency 20-6
🔊 Audio Summaries
⚙ *ExamView® Assessment Suite*
🔊 Vocabulary PuzzleMaker
⚙ StudentWorks™ Plus

FOCUS

Activating Prior Knowledge

What I Know Ask volunteers to give a verbal description of the steps of first aid for choking.

Guide to Reading

Building Vocabulary
- Tell students that the word part *cardio-* means "heart" and that the word part *-pulmonary* means "lungs." Ask students to use that information to infer the meaning of the term *cardiopulmonary resuscitation*.
- Use Vocabulary PuzzleMaker to reinforce vocabulary terms. 🔊

Reading Strategy
Finding the Main Idea
Challenge students to write the main idea of each section in their own words.

Quick Write

Have students work in small groups to share their completed Quick Writes. Have students meet with their groups after reading the lesson to discuss how their answers have changed.

Caption Answer

Photo Caption *Sample answer:* I would check to see if he or she could talk or cough; if not, I would call for help and start abdominal thrusts.

563

TEACH

Reading Check

Answer, p. 565 Signs of choking include the person clutching at his or her throat, gasping or wheezing, being unable to speak, and having a reddish-purple coloration and bulging eyes.

R Reading Strategy

Analyzing a Graphic Have students examine **Figure 20.6**, which shows the proper method for using abdominal thrusts to clear an obstruction from a person's airway. Ask: When a person is choking, how can you determine if you should use abdominal thrusts to clear his or her airway? *If a person cannot speak or cough, you should immediately proceed with abdominal thrusts.* **OL**

Academic Vocabulary

Technique describes techniques for giving yourself abdominal thrusts. Ask students to use the word *technique* in a written sentence. Have volunteers share their sentences with the class. **OL**

Caption Answer

Figure Caption If a person can speak, his or her airway is not completely blocked.

A choking person could die if the object is not removed quickly. If an adult or child is choking, give the person five blows to the back. To perform back blows, stand slightly behind the person who is choking. Place one of your arms diagonally across the person's chest and lean him or her forward. Strike the person between the shoulder blades five times. If this does not dislodge the object, give five abdominal thrusts. The **abdominal thrusts** maneuver *involves quick upward pulls into the diaphragm to force out an obstruction blocking the airway.* The proper technique for performing abdominal thrusts is shown in **Figure 20.6.**

If you are alone and choking, there are two ways to give yourself an abdominal thrust. First, make a fist and position it slightly above your navel. With your other hand, grasp your fist and thrust inward and upward into your abdomen until the object dislodges. Another technique is to lean over the back of a chair, or any firm object, pressing your abdomen into it.

▼ FIGURE 20.6

FIRST AID FOR A CHOKING ADULT
R OR CHILD

Before you perform abdominal thrusts, ask the person if he or she is choking. **How can asking this question help you determine if a person is choking?**

A Stand behind the person who is choking. Wrap your arms around the person's waist and tip the person slightly forward. Make a fist. Place the fist just above the person's navel but below the breastbone. Position the fist so the thumb side is against the victim's abdomen. Grab your fist with your other hand.

B Quickly, thrust inward and upward. The motion is similar to one you would use if you were trying to lift the person off the ground. Perform five back blows and then five abdominal thrusts. Repeat this cycle until the food or object is dislodged. If the person becomes unresponsive, call for medical help and begin CPR.

HEALTH LITERACY

Shock Due to the everyday use of the word *shock* to mean a surprise or slight scare, students may not have an understanding of the seriousness of shock as a medical condition. During shock, the major organs of the body do not receive enough oxygenated blood. This can damage organs, including the brain. Shock results from a wide range of illnesses and injuries. Examples include anaphylactic shock, which is brought on by an allergic response, and toxic shock syndrome, which is shock caused by an infection.

Infants who are choking require a different first-aid procedure. If an infant is choking, hold the infant face down along your forearm, using your thigh for support. Give the infant five back blows between the shoulder blades. If this does not dislodge the object, turn the infant over and perform five chest thrusts with your fingers. Chest thrusts are quick presses into the middle of the breastbone to force an object out of the airway. **Figure 20.7** shows the steps to use to provide first aid to an infant who is choking.

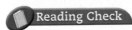 **Reading Check** **Recall** What are some signs that a person may be choking?

Severe Bleeding

Severe bleeding can be a life-threatening emergency because the organs and tissues in the body are not getting enough blood or oxygen to function properly. When providing first aid to a person who is bleeding severely, follow universal precautions. Avoid touching the victim's blood or wear gloves, if possible. Always wash your hands when you are finished. Call 911 or other local emergency number before beginning first aid. Then begin by washing the wound with mild soap and water to remove dirt and debris. Use the following steps to help control the bleeding:

- Raise the wounded body part above the level of the heart, if possible.
- Cover the wound with sterile gauze or a clean cloth. Press the palm of your hand firmly against the gauze and apply continuous pressure for five minutes, or until help arrives.
- If blood soaks through the gauze or cloth, do not remove it. Add another cloth or gauze pad on top of the first and continue to apply pressure.
- Once the bleeding slows down or stops, secure the pad or cloth with a bandage or other material. The pad should be snug, but not too tight.
- Stay with the person until help arrives.

 Reading Check **Explain** What universal precautions should you take when providing first aid to a person who is bleeding severely?

Follow these steps to help an infant who is choking. **How many back blows and chest thrusts should you perform?**

1 **For infants**
Hold the infant facedown on your forearm. Support the child's head and neck with your hand. Point the head downward so that it is lower than the chest. With the heel of your free hand, give the child five blows between the shoulder blades. If the child doesn't cough up the object, move on to chest thrusts (step 2).

2 Turn the infant over onto his or her back. Support the head with one hand. With two or three fingers, press into the middle of the child's breastbone—directly between and just below the nipples—five times. Repeat chest thrusts until the object comes out or the infant begins to breathe, cry, or cough. Make sure a health care professional checks the infant. If the infant becomes unconscious, call 911.

W **Writing Support**

Persuasive Writing Have students write a persuasive paragraph that encourages others to learn first aid and emergency response for severe bleeding and other situations that would require them to help someone. Encourage students to support their opinions with facts, statistics, or data. Students may need to do additional research to complete their paragraphs. Ask students to proofread their work before turning it in. **OL**

Reading Check

Answer You should avoid touching the victim's blood, wear gloves, and wash your hands.

Promoting Coordinated School Health

Dealing with Emergencies and Disasters
Having a disaster-response plan in place can help teachers, staff, and administrators cope with a disaster that occurs during school hours. Because parents are an important part of coordinated school health, be certain to consult parents while preparing a disaster plan

that is appropriate for your area and student population. An important consideration is a procedure for early dismissal that has been established in advance. Having a detailed plan in place will allow the school's staff to concentrate on meeting the students' needs in the event of an emergency.

Caption Answer

Figure Caption Five of each, repeating this cycle until the infant is breating, crying, or coughing

CPR

Imagine being in an emergency situation when someone loses consciousness. The person does not respond when gently shaken and when asked, "Are you okay?" If this happens, a trained person should begin administering **cardiopulmonary resuscitation (CPR)**—*a first-aid procedure that combines rescue breathing with chest compressions to restore breathing and circulation.* The process for combining rescue breaths with chest compressions is illustrated in **Figure 20.8.** For adults and children 12 years and older, alternate two rescue breaths with 30 chest compressions. A first-aid manual will explain the ways in which to administer CPR to younger children and infants.

▼ FIGURE 20.8

THE STEPS OF CPR

R The first steps of CPR involve checking for breathing and rescue breaths. If you have an available breathing mask, follow the directions that come with the mask. **In what type of situation should you use CPR?**

1. Look inside the victim's mouth. If you see anything blocking the airway, remove it. Lay the person flat on a firm surface. Gently tilt the head back with one hand and lift the chin with the other. If you suspect head or neck injuries, do not move the victim's head. Open the airway by lifting the jaw instead.

2. Look, listen, and feel to find out if the victim is breathing. Look for chest movement. Listen at the victim's mouth for breathing sounds. Feel for exhaled air on your cheek. If the victim is not breathing, begin rescue breathing. Pinch the person's nostrils shut, take a normal breath and place your mouth over the victim's, forming a seal. Give two breaths, each about one second long. The victim's chest should rise and fall with each breath.

3. Begin chest compressions. Kneel next to the victim's chest and place one hand on the center of the chest. Place the other hand on top of the first hand and interlock your fingers. Press straight down quickly and firmly at a rate of about 100 compressions per minute. Allow the victim's chest to spring back between compressions. After every 30 compressions, give two rescue breaths.

🏠 Home, School, and Community

In the Community Ask the school nurse, or another person certified in CPR, to discuss this procedure with the class. The American Red Cross may be able to send a trainer to discuss CPR with your students. Ask students to prepare for the speaker by reading the information in the text and developing questions for the speaker. If possible, have the speaker bring a CPR mannequin to class so students can observe a demonstration. Remind students that practicing CPR on a healthy person can result in death. **OL**

Shock

Shock is *a life-threatening condition in which the circulatory system fails to deliver enough blood to vital tissues and organs.* Injury, burns, and severe infection can cause a person to go into shock, as can heat, poisoning, blood loss, and heart attack. Always look for the signs of shock when providing first aid because it can result from a medical emergency.

Signs to watch for include cool, clammy, pale, or gray skin; weak and rapid pulse; and slow, shallow breathing. The eyes may have a dull look with the pupils dilated. The victim, if conscious, may feel faint, weak, confused, and anxious.

If you think someone is in shock or about to go into shock, call for medical help and take these precautions:

- Help the person to lie down quietly on his or her back with feet raised slightly higher than the head. Try to keep the person as still as possible.
- Loosen tight clothing.
- Use a blanket, coat, or any available cover to help keep the person warm.
- Do not give the person anything to drink.
- Roll the person onto his or her side to help prevent choking in the event of vomiting or bleeding from the mouth.

Go Online

Visit **glencoe.com** and complete the Interactive Study Guide for Lesson 6.

ASSESS

Assessment Resources

Lesson Review Quiz
- *ExamView Assessment Suite*
- Fast Files Activities
- Online Quizzes and Activities

Reteaching

- Assign Concept Map 20-6 or Reteaching Activity 20-6 in the Fast Files.
- Have students work in pairs to write a short description of how to perform CPR.

Enrichment

- Assign Enrichment Activity 20-6 in the Fast Files.
- Have students research to find out what food and nonfood items are common causes of choking in young children. Have students make pamphlets that can be used to educate others about common choking hazards.

CLOSE

Go around the room and have students identify steps for treating shock.

Lesson 6 Review

 After You Read

Review this lesson for new terms, major headings, and Reading Checks.

What I Learned

1. *Vocabulary* Define *shock*. Use the term in a sentence.
2. *Recall* What is the universal sign for choking? What is the first thing you should do if an adult is choking?
3. *List* Name two symptoms of shock.

Thinking Critically

4. *Compare and Contrast* How does the treatment for choking for adults differ from the treatment for infants?

5. *Apply* A friend has fallen while hiking. His leg is bleeding severely. You have brought a first-aid kit with you. What will you do?

Applying Health Skills

6. *Advocacy* Research where CPR is taught in your community. Develop a flyer encouraging teens to complete a CPR training class. Include information on the cost, location, requirements, and certifications issued after completion of the course.

Go Online For more Lesson Review Activities, go to **glencoe.com**.   Lesson 6: Life-Threatening Emergencies   **567**

Lesson 6 Review Answers

1. Shock is a condition in which the organs do not get enough blood. Sentences will vary.
2. Clutching the throat is the universal sign for choking. The first thing you should do is ask the person if he or she is choking. Abdominal thrusts are used to treat choking.
3. *Sample answers:* cool, clammy, pale, or gray skin; weak, rapid pulse; slow breathing; dilated pupils; weakness
4. If an adult is choking, you should give him or her abdominal thrusts. If an infant is choking, you should give him or her back blows and chest thrusts.
5. Have your friend lie down. Elevate the leg. Use protective gloves and a clean cloth to apply pressure to the wound.
6. Flyers should be directed to a teen audience and contain facts from the lesson as well as information on CPR classes.

Complete a House Inspection

Skill

Practicing Healthful Behaviors

Activating Prior Knowledge

Have students list tips for fire safety, which were discussed in Lesson 1.

- **Objective** After completing the activity, students will be able to apply the skill of practicing healthful behaviors to reduce fire dangers in their home.
- **Time** 30 minutes in class, 20 minutes at home
- **Materials** paper, pencil

Teacher Classroom Resources

📁 Building Health Skills
⬇ Transparency 20-1

Model

- Have students work individually to read the Model paragraphs. Ask: How is Aaron advocating for the health of others?

  Sample answer: *By helping his family to practice healthful behaviors, he is practicing advocacy.*

Building Health Skills

Accessing Information
Practicing Healthful Behaviors
Stress Management
Analyzing Influences
Communication Skills
Refusal Skills
Conflict Resolution
Decision Making
Goal Setting
Advocacy

Why Is it Important to Practice Healthful Behaviors?

When you practice healthful behaviors you take specific actions to stay healthy and avoid risky behaviors. This will help you prevent injury, illness, disease, and other health problems. The following behaviors will help you practice fire safety at home.

- Change smoke alarm batteries twice a year. Check smoke alarms regularly to make sure they are working properly.
- Make sure all kitchen appliances are in good working order.
- Keep matches out of reach of young children. Never leave candles burning unattended.

Complete a House Inspection

① Model

Read how Aaron practices healthful behaviors to protect his home against potential fire hazards.

Many fires in the home can be prevented. One effective way to keep your family safe is to regularly inspect your home for possible fire dangers.

Aaron decided to complete a home inspection for fire dangers after a fire-fighter came to his school and spoke about the importance of fire prevention. As Aaron went through each room in his home, he made notes of possible fire hazards. Some risks, like *piles of old newspapers,* needed to be removed. Others, like an *appliance with a frayed cord,* needed to be repaired. Aaron showed the list to his parents. The family made a plan to address each fire hazard Aaron identified.

Teaching Tips

Real-World Connection If possible, gather several newspaper articles describing local house fires and their causes (e.g., frayed wiring, smoking in bed). Articles can be accessed online by typing the word *fire* and the name of a newspaper into any search engine. Place these in plastic sleeves and distribute in class prior to this activity. Have students read several of these articles aloud. Ask: What were the four steps of the accident chain that led to this event?

❷ Practice

Practice healthful behaviors by reading the paragraph below and answering the questions that follow.

Below is a list of possible hazards to check for in your home. Use the list to create a Home Inspection Check-Off List that you can use to inspect your home for potential fire hazards.

- Are all kitchen appliances in good working order?
- Is the stove clean?
- Are all electrical wires and outlets working properly?
- Have you thrown out all piles of newspapers or other materials that burn easily?
- Are all flammable objects at least 3 feet away from portable heaters?
- Is there a smoke alarm on each level of your home?
- Does each smoke alarm have working batteries?
- Are matches and cigarette lighters stored out of reach of young children?

❸ Apply

Apply what you have learned about safety by completing the activity below.

Using the Home Inspection Check-Off List you created, complete an inspection of your home. Write down any items on the list that indicate a possible fire danger. Then write down what steps you can take to eliminate each possible fire danger. Be prepared to share your findings with the class.

Self-Check

- Did I identify any possible fire dangers in my home?
- Did I list the steps I need to take to eliminate each possible danger?

Building Health Skills

Practice

- Have students copy the Home Inspection Check-Off List. Ask students if they have any questions about how to complete this activity. Ask each student to complete the Home Inspection Check-Off List at home.
- Respect student and family privacy by keeping students' Home Inspection Check-Off Lists confidential.

Apply/Assess

- Ask students to follow up by working with their family to correct any fire hazards that they noted during their inspection.
- Again, respect student and family confidentiality by keeping students' responses confidential.
- You may wish to distribute Building Health Skills in the Fast Files. 🗁

ASSESSMENT SCORING

Using a rubric, student work should meet all criteria to achieve the highest score.

Skills Student work:
- identifies hazards that may contribute to a fall, poisoning, electric shock, gun accident, or fire.
- indicates steps to eliminate each hazard.

Concepts Student work:
- includes accurate information about causes of injuries in the home.
- shows the relationship between common hazards and steps for prevention.

A Home Emergency Kit

Time: 30 minutes
Materials: poster board, marker, paper, pencil

Introducing Hands-on Health

● Ask students to describe weather emergencies and natural disasters that occur in their area. Ask students to discuss ways they could prepare for these emergencies.

Teaching the Activity

● Have students work in a small group to complete the activity as described.
● Have students review the chapter for ideas if they are unsure of what should be included in their kits.
● Remind students to think of items they use daily as they prepare their lists.

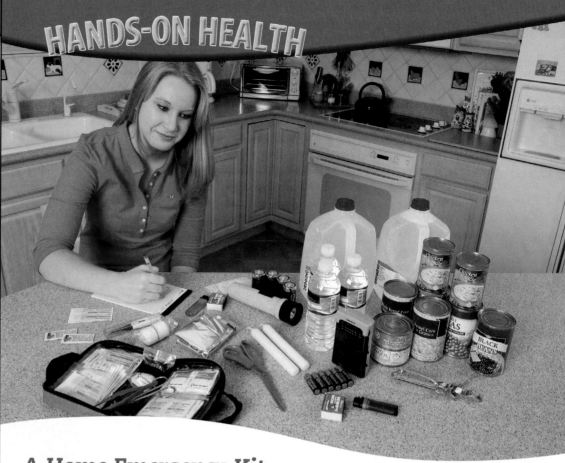

HANDS-ON HEALTH

A Home Emergency Kit

Weather emergencies and natural disasters are situations that no one can prevent. You can, however, be prepared. Creating a home emergency kit for your family can help keep you safe and secure until the emergency is over.

What You Will Need

■ one piece of poster board
■ marker
■ paper
■ pencil or pen

What You Will Do

① Working in a small group, brainstorm all of the supplies you would include in a home emergency kit. Your kit should include enough items to last for three days.

② Have one member of the group write all the items on the poster board.

③ Discuss why you feel certain items should or should not be included.

④ Make your list final. Then, compare your list with other groups in the class. Are your lists similar? How are they different?

Wrapping It Up

Write down the final list on a piece of paper. At home, discuss creating a home emergency kit with your family using the list you created.

HANDS-ON HEALTH Assessment

Discussion Ask students:
● Why might the emergency kits of two different families include different items? Sample answer: *Families vary in size, medical needs, and the ages of their members.*

● Ask: How might the home emergency kit of a family with young children differ from the home emergency kit of a family with teens? Sample answer: *A family with young children might need diapers and baby food in its kit; a family with teens would need greater quantities of food.*

Reading Review

 Visit glencoe.com to download quizzes and eFlashcards for Chapter 20.

Assessment Resources

- 📁 Chapter 20 Summary and Activity
- 🎧 Audio Summaries
- 📁 Reading Tutor
- 📁 Performance Assessment
- 📁 Chapter 20 Test
- 💿 *ExamView Assessment Suite*
- 🖱 Vocabulary PuzzleMaker
- 🖱 Online Learning Center

FOLDABLES Study Organizer

Foldables® and Other Study Aids Take out the Foldable® that you created for Lesson 1 and any other study aids you created for Lessons 1–6. Find a partner and quiz each other using these study aids.

Lesson 1 Safety in the Home and at School

Main Idea Developing safe habits at home and at school can help you prevent accidental injuries.
- Accident chains include a situation, an unsafe habit, an unsafe action, and the resulting injury.

Lesson 2 Safety on the Road and Outdoors

Main Idea Following safety rules can help you prevent injury on the road and outdoors.
- Always wear a helmet when riding a bike or using skates, a skateboard, or a scooter.
- Two important behaviors to keep you safe during outdoor activities are being prepared and using the buddy system.

Lesson 3 Safety in Weather Emergencies

Main Idea Being prepared will help you stay safe during weather emergencies or natural disasters.
- Weather emergencies and natural disasters include tornadoes, hurricanes, floods, blizzards, and earthquakes.

Lesson 4 Basic First Aid

Main Idea Knowing how to administer basic first aid can save a person's life in an emergency.
- There are four steps to take for most emergencies: recognize the signs, take action, call for help, and provide care until help arrives.
- Following universal precautions involves taking action to minimize contact with another person's blood.

Lesson 5 First Aid for Common Emergencies

Main Idea Common emergencies include insect and animal bites, burns, poisoning, nosebleed, fainting, heat-related illnesses, sprains, bruises, and broken bones.
- Sprains require the P.R.I.C.E. method to treat them: Protect, Rest, Ice, Compress, and Elevate.

Lesson 6 Life-Threatening Emergencies

Main Idea During a life-threatening emergency, staying calm, calling for help, and providing first aid can save a person's life.
- Life-threatening emergencies include choking, severe bleeding, loss of consciousness, and shock.
- The process for administering CPR to adults and children 12 years and older involves alternating two rescue breaths with 30 chest compressions.

Chapter 20 Reading Review **571**

Reading Review

Use of Study Aids

- **Using the Dinah Zike Foldable® Study Organizer** Have students use their Foldable® to review ways to stay safe at home, at school, on the road, and in emergencies.
- **Online Learning Tools** Have students go to the *Teen Health* Online Learning Center at **glencoe.com** to:
  - Download a **Podcast**.
  - Download free **Study-to-Go** content to their PDAs or cell phones.

Vocabulary Review

- **Glossary** Have students make a glossary that lists each of the chapter vocabulary terms and a short definition for each. Encourage students to write the definition in their own words rather than copy definitions from the chapter.

Teaching Tips

Reading in Health Class Remind students that the boldface heads divide the reading into sections based on topic. Have students use the following strategies to make long reading assignments manageable:
- Read the material under one boldface head.

- Use the caption questions and reading checks to assess your understanding of the material.
- Work in small groups to discuss the section.
- After completing this strategy for one section of text, move on to the next section.

Assessment

Reviewing Vocabulary and Main Ideas

1. accident
2. poisonings
3. Defensive driving
4. helmet
5. earthquake
6. blizzards
7. True
8. False, Identifying the signs of an emergency
9. False, fracture
10. False, heatstroke
11. False, choking
12. False, Clutching your throat

Thinking Critically

13. If the person loses consciousness and is not breathing, I would begin CPR.
14. Understanding the accident chain helps you change a situation or behavior before an accident results.

Assessment

After You Read

Health eSpotlight VIDEO

Now that you have read the chapter, look back at your answer to the Health eSpotlight question on the chapter opener. What other safety precautions could you take to avoid injury?

Reviewing Vocabulary and Main Ideas

On a sheet of paper, write the numbers 1–6. After each number, write the term from the list that best completes each sentence.

- poisonings
- blizzards
- helmet
- accident
- defensive driving
- earthquake

Lesson 1 Safety in the Home and at School

1. A(n) _____ is any event that was not intended to happen.
2. Cleaning products and medicines are the most common causes of _____ among children.

Lesson 2 Safety on the Road and Outdoors

3. _____ involves watching out for other people on the road and anticipating unsafe acts.
4. Cyclists can reduce the risk of head injury by wearing a(n) _____.

Lesson 3 Safety in Weather Emergencies

5. If you are indoors when a(n) _____ starts, crouch under sturdy furniture.
6. People can easily become disoriented and lost during _____.

*On a sheet of paper, write the numbers 7–12. Write **True** or **False** for each statement below. If the statement is false, change the underlined word or phrase to make it true.*

Lesson 4 Basic First Aid

7. Universal <u>precautions</u> are steps taken to prevent disease by treating all blood as if it was contaminated.
8. <u>Taking action</u> is your first step in any emergency situation.

Lesson 5 First Aid for Common Emergencies

9. A <u>sprain</u> is an invisible break in a bone.
10. A marked increase in body temperature is a main symptom of <u>heat exhaustion</u>.

Lesson 6 Life-Threatening Emergencies

11. The abdominal thrusts maneuver is used to help a victim of <u>shock</u>.
12. <u>Gasping</u> is the universal sign for choking.

Go Online Visit **glencoe.com** and take the Online Quiz for Chapter 20.

Go Online

Have students visit **glencoe.com** to take the Chapter 20 quiz.

Health eSpotlight VIDEO Wrap-Up

Personal Safety Have students reread the Health eSpotlight question at the beginning of the chapter (page 539) and look at their original answer. Ask: Now that you have read the chapter and watched the video presentation, what other steps would you take to stay safe when participating in your favorite physical activity? Ask volunteers to share their steps with the rest of the class.

Thinking Critically

Using complete sentences, answer the following questions on a sheet of paper.

13. Evaluate How would you assess whether a victim needed CPR?

14. Analyze How does an understanding of accident chains help prevent injuries?

Write About It

15. Narrative Writing Write a short story about a teen involved in a situation that leads to an accident. Describe the situation and the events that make up the accident chain. Then, write an alternate ending describing how the teen used strategies to prevent the accident from happening.

↗ Applying Technology

Emergency Plans

Use Comic Life or Microsoft Word® to create an emergency safety poster with digital images and text explaining the need to plan ahead and be prepared for emergencies.

- Working in pairs or triads, create a new Comic Life or Microsoft Word® poster.
- Locate clip art images or take digital photos that reflect planning ahead and being prepared for emergencies.
- Click, drag, and drop digital images from the media files on the right side into the palette of Comic Life or Word®.
- Using the Editing tab, add titles or captions over images highlighting safety procedures.
- Plan and write 1–2 sentences that tell how being prepared prevents injuries.
- Make sure the information is accurate and relevant to your peers.

↗ Applying Technology

Emergency Plans
Equipment needs: Comic Life or Microsoft Word® or similar software and optional digital cameras
Help students discuss the steps in planning and completing their posters. Suggest sources for digital images or instruct students to take their own photos. Establish sign-up sheets and time limits if access to computers and cameras is limited. Have students choose partners or group members. Once students have created and edited their posters, have them share their work with classmates.

Write About It

15. Narrative Writing Remind students that narrative writing includes characters, a setting, and a plot. Students should describe a situation leading up to the accident chain and ways to break links in the chain to avoid injury.

Standardized Test Practice

1. A
2. B

Standardized Test Practice

Reading and Writing

Read the passage and then answer the questions.

A severe lightning storm hit Baltimore yesterday evening, causing a power outage in the northern section of town. One bolt struck a tree branch that fell and injured a Mini Mart employee. The lightning struck when the Mart was crowded with customers. Power was out for more than two hours after the storm.

When the lightning hit, Mini Mart owner Mike Wojer told customers and employees to stay inside and away from the doors and windows. He turned off the lights and appliances and asked customers to not make any phone calls.

"Thankfully, no one in the store was injured by lightning," said Wojer.

The injured employee, however, was outside the store when lightning struck. He was hit by a tree branch that had been struck by lighting, witnesses said. Thankfully, he is now in good condition at the hospital.

1. What is this news article about?
  A. The events of lightning striking near a store
  B. The store owner's bravery
  C. The damage lightning can cause
  D. The injuries caused by lightning

2. A reader can conclude that
  A. lightning is not dangerous.
  B. it's safer to be indoors when lightning strikes.
  C. lightning strikes only trees.
  D. all thunderstorms have lightning.

Chapter 20 Assessment **573**

Test-Taking Tips

Previewing Questions Remind students that it is helpful to preview the questions that are based on a reading passage. Previewing allows the students to focus on the portions of the reading that are relevant to the questions. If students are allowed, they should mark or underline information in the passage that is relevant to the questions. After reading the passage, have students reread the questions and look back in the passage to find the answers. Having relevant portions of the passage marked can help students quickly find the information they need.

CHAPTER 21 pp. 574–591	Standards		Skills and Activities
	National	**State/Local**	
	National Health Education Standards 1.8.1, 1.8.5, 2.8.1, 2.8.4, 6.8.1, 6.8.2, 7.8.2, 8.8.2, 8.8.3		**HEALTH QUIZ,** *p. 575* **BUILDING HEALTH SKILLS** *Advocacy* Make the Most of It, *pp. 586–587* TIME health news Pitch In for the Planet, *p. 588*
Lesson 1 Pollution and Health pp. 576–580	National Health Education Standards 1.8.1, 1.8.5, 1.8.8, 1.8.9, 2.8.10, 3.8.1, 3.8.2, 7.8.2, 7.8.3		**What Teens Think** Do you think global warming is a problem? Why or why not?, *p. 577* **Careers for the 21st Century** Ecologist, *p. 578* **Go Online** Caring for the Environment, *p. 579*
Lesson 2 Preventing and Reducing Pollution pp. 581–585	National Health Education Standards 1.8.1, 1.8.5, 2.8.4, 2.8.7, 2.8.10, 3.8.1, 5.8.6, 6.8.1, 6.8.3, 7.8.2, 7.8.3, 8.8.2, 8.8.3		**HEALTH SKILLS ACTIVITY** *Practicing Healthful Behaviors* Environment-Friendly Shopping, *p. 585*

PACING THE CHAPTER

Lesson 1	30 min	**Chapter Review**	45 min	**TIME health news**	30 min
Lesson 2	30 min	**Building Health Skills**	45 min		

BLOCK SCHEDULING

For block scheduling, assign students Building Health Skills feature *Make the Most of It*, page 586, and Guided Reading and Writing. 📂

StudentWorks Plus

Glencoe Exclusive!
TeacherWorks Plus
All-In-One Planner and Resource Center

Reproducible Resources	Assessment	Media and Technology
Chapter FAST FILE Resources Chapter Summaries and Activities REVIEW Building Health Skills Activity TEACH Performance Assessment Activity EXTEND Universal Access Activities TEACH Parent Letter and Activities 📁 **Student Activities Workbook** TEACH 📁 **Reading Tutor** TEACH	Building Health Skills Activity, pp. 586–587 Chapter 21 Assessment, pp. 590–591 **Chapter FAST FILE Resources** Performance Assessment Activity, p. 4 Chapter 21 Test, p. 7 💿 ExamView® Assessment Suite	**TeacherWorks Plus** includes: ● Interactive Teacher Edition ● Lesson Planner with Calendar ● Access to all blackline masters ● Correlations to standards 💿 StudentWorks™ Plus 💿 Online Student Edition Dinah Zike's Teaching Health with Foldables®
Chapter FAST FILE Resources Concept Mapping Activity 21-1 REVIEW Health Lab Activity 21-1 EXTEND Enrichment Activity 21-1 EXTEND Lesson Plan 21-1 Guided Reading and Writing 21-1 TEACH Reteaching Activity 21-1 REVIEW	Lesson 1 Review, p. 580 💿 Vocabulary PuzzleMaker 💿 ExamView® Assessment Suite	💿 Vocabulary PuzzleMaker 💿 ExamView® Assessment Suite 💿 StudentWorks™ Plus 🔦 Transparency 21-1 **Go Online** glencoe.com
Chapter FAST FILE Resources Concept Mapping Activity 21-2 REVIEW Cross-Curriculum Activity 21-2 EXTEND Enrichment Activity 21-2 EXTEND Lesson Plan 21-2 Guided Reading and Writing 21-2 TEACH Reteaching Activity 21-2 REVIEW	Lesson 2 Review, p. 585 💿 Vocabulary PuzzleMaker 💿 ExamView® Assessment Suite	💿 Vocabulary PuzzleMaker 💿 ExamView® Assessment Suite 💿 StudentWorks™ Plus 🔦 Transparency 21-2 **Go Online** glencoe.com

Chapter and Lesson Resources

The *Teen Health* resources are designed for differentiated learning abilities. You may want to use the coded items in this way:

REVIEW —activities to review or reinforce content
TEACH —activities to teach basic concepts
EXTEND —activities to extend or enrich lesson content

 OUT OF TIME?

Use Health Skills Activity *Environment-Friendly Shopping,* page 585, or Building Health Skills *Make the Most of It,* page 586.

Health Effects of Air Pollution

Air pollution consists of ground-level ozone and small particles suspended in the air. These particles can be chemicals, metals, dust, soil, pollen, and mold. The smallest particles are the ones that do the most damage to the lungs. Inhaling them can cause shortness of breath and even chest pain. Larger particles often do not make it into the lungs but do irritate the eyes, nose, and throat and cause coughing, sneezing, and watery eyes.

Ground-level ozone, or smog, also irritates the respiratory system. When inhaled, smog can cause coughing, throat irritation, and a burning sensation in the airways. It can also trigger asthma attacks and cause wheezing or shortness of breath. Ozone might even reduce the ability of the immune system to fight off bacterial infections in the respiratory system.

People at greatest risk to smog and particle pollution are people with chronic respiratory diseases such as asthma, people with heart disease, children, and adults who are active outdoors. Children are especially susceptible because their lungs are still developing, they spend a lot of active time outdoors, and they are more likely to have asthma or other respiratory illnesses.

Short-term exposure to air pollution has no lasting effects on healthy people. However, long-term exposure can permanently injure the lungs.

To protect respiratory health, people can monitor the air quality index and ozone levels by watching weather reports on television or by going to the EPA Web site. When weather quality is poor, people should limit their outdoor activities.

Uses for Recycled Materials

What happens to the items in the recycling bin? Plastics, aluminum, steel, glass, and paper are sorted and sent to different processing plants to prepare them for their next use. Plastics are shredded before they are melted. The molten plastic might be molded to make floor tiles, pipes, patio blocks, park benches, fencing, garden hoses, bike racks, signage, or various office products. Some recycled plastics are made into fibers, which are then used to make carpeting and clothing.

Glass is broken into small pieces, melted, and reused to make new glass. Aluminum and steel are melted down and reformed into sheets. The sheets are formed into new products or containers. Paper is shredded and mixed with water to form pulp. The pulp is used to make new paper products.

Some recycled products are made from a combination of recycled materials. Decking materials and landscaping timbers are composed of recycled plastic and wood. Many home-building products are made from recycled paper, plastics, and wood fibers. Cement and concrete contain wastes produced from burning coal to make electricity. Rubber is reused in floor tiles, patio blocks, garden hoses, and playground surfacing materials.

As more consumers and businesses purchase products made from recycled materials, the number of products available will increase. The EPA has taken an active role in promoting the purchase of products made from recycled materials. Their Web site offers detailed information about products made from various recycled materials and their manufacturers.

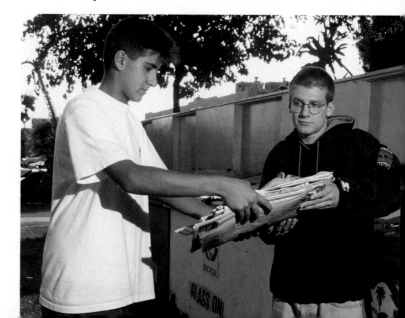

Support for Teaching Reading

Reading Preview

Activating Background Vocabulary Ask students if they have ever recycled an aluminum can. Ask: "What does the term *recycle* mean?" Record answers on the board. Then ask students what comes to mind when they hear the term *pollution*. Guide students in a discussion of the connections between recycling, pollution, and a healthy environment.

FOLDABLES® Study Organizer *Dinah Zike's Reading and Study Skills for Teen Health* provides interactive graphic organizers that help students comprehend and retain health concepts as they read. Use the Foldable® on page 575 or find more Foldables® activities for the chapter on **Environmental Health** in the separate booklet, available in the TCR.

Lesson 1   Pollution and Health

Select, Teach, Activate, Review, and Revisit (STARR) Select important vocabulary terms from **Pollution and Health**, and have students write the terms on note cards. Teach the terms to the students prior to reading. Activate the vocabulary by directing students to identify the terms in the text and discussing the vocabulary in context as students read. Review the terms often. After reading, ask students to use the vocabulary as they summarize the lesson. Revisit the terms over the next few weeks.

Lesson 2   Preventing and Reducing Pollution

Reciprocal Teaching Direct student pairs to: 1) Summarize the lesson—stop after reading **Reduce**, **Reuse**, **Recycle** and take turns paraphrasing the content. 2) Clarify the text—ask each other if they have questions they need to answer before reading on. 3) Question—think about and make a list of the types of questions a teacher might ask on an exam. 4) Predict—make a guess about what is next in the lesson. 5) Read the next section and repeat.

Post Reading

Multimedia Presentation Have students work together using a variety of media, such as computers, video, music, and art, to develop a presentation on environmental health issues for the class. Encourage students to organize data in a logical order and to practice effective speaking skills prior to the presentation.

Key for Using the Teacher Wraparound Edition

Use this key to help you identify the **different types of prompts found in the Teacher Wraparound Edition.**

R **Reading Strategies** activities help you teach reading skills and vocabulary.

C **Critical Thinking** strategies help students apply and extend what they have learned.

U **Universal Access** activities provide differentiated instruction for students learning to speak English, along with suggestions for teaching various types of learners.

HS **Health Skills Practice** activities reinforce Health Skills concepts and help students apply these skills in their everyday lives.

W **Writing Support** activities provide writing opportunities to help students comprehend the text.

AL **Active Learning** strategies provide a variety of activities for presenting lesson content, including Quick Demos and engaging classroom projects that get students actively involved.

Key to Ability Levels

Teaching Strategies and activities have been coded for ability level and appropriateness.

AL Activities for students working above grade level

OL Activities for students working on grade level

BL Activities for students working below grade level

EL Activities for English Learners

Symbols

- Transparencies
- CD-ROM
- glencoe.com
- Print Resources

Environmental Health

Chapter at a Glance

Lesson 1 identifies factors that cause air, water, and soil pollution; strategies to reduce pollution; and effects of pollution on the environment.

Lesson 2 describes actions that individuals can take to protect the environment and conserve nonrenewable resources.

R Reading Strategy

Interpreting the Photo Invite students to describe what is happening in the photo. Explain that conservation groups work to improve the environment. Ask: How does planting trees help the environment? *Sample answers: prevents soil erosion, provides places for animals to live, renews resources* Challenge students to suggest other ways that conservation groups help the environment. *educate about conservation, set up recycling centers, monitor air and water quality* **OL**

Caption Answer

Photo Caption *Sample answers: recycle, buy products with less packaging, join or support a conservation organization*

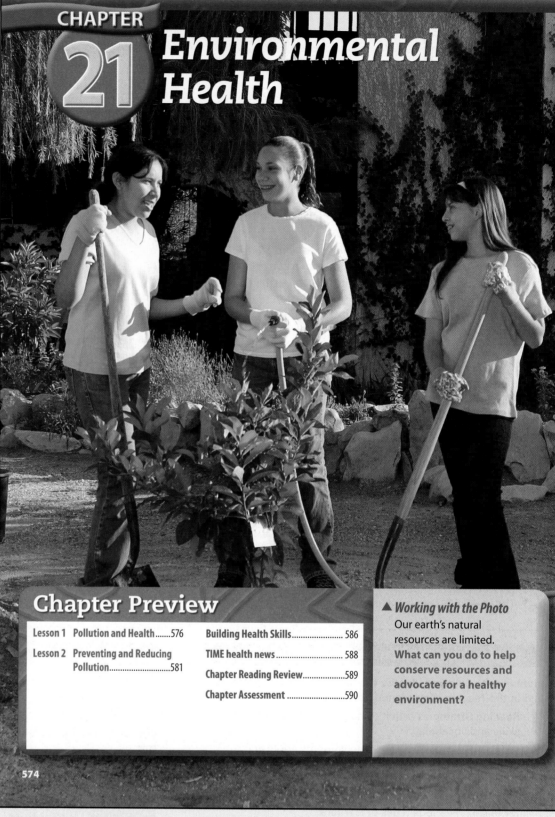

Environmental Health

Chapter Preview

▲ *Working with the Photo*
Our earth's natural resources are limited. **What can you do to help conserve resources and advocate for a healthy environment?**

574

Universal Access

Differentiated Learning Glencoe provides teacher support and student materials for all learners in the health classroom.

- Spanish Glosario and chapter summaries assist English Language Learners.
- *Reading Tutor* and related worksheets support reluctant readers.

- Universal Access strategies throughout the Teacher Wraparound Edition and Fast Files help you present materials for gifted students, at-risk students, physically impaired students, and those with behavior disorders or learning disabilities.

Start-Up Activities

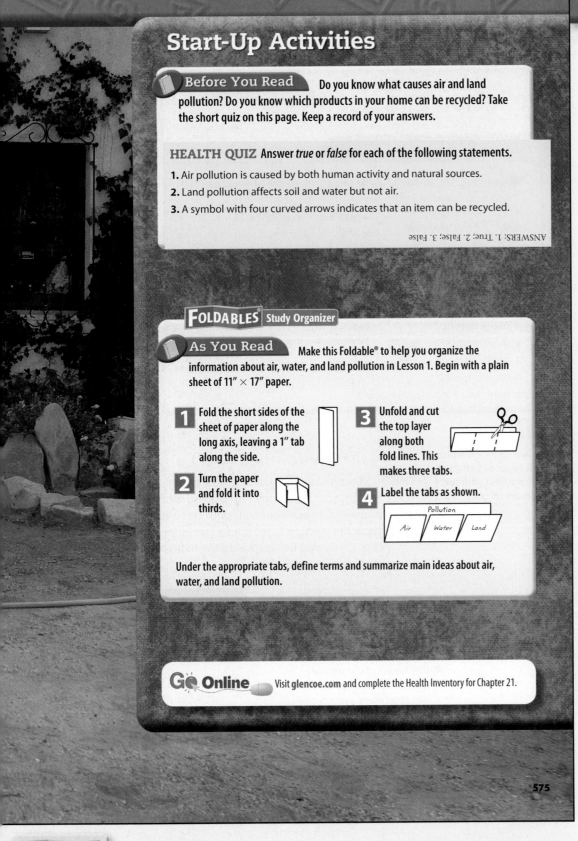

Before You Read Do you know what causes air and land pollution? Do you know which products in your home can be recycled? Take the short quiz on this page. Keep a record of your answers.

HEALTH QUIZ Answer *true* or *false* for each of the following statements.

1. Air pollution is caused by both human activity and natural sources.
2. Land pollution affects soil and water but not air.
3. A symbol with four curved arrows indicates that an item can be recycled.

ANSWERS: 1. True; 2. False; 3. False

FOLDABLES Study Organizer

As You Read Make this Foldable® to help you organize the information about air, water, and land pollution in Lesson 1. Begin with a plain sheet of 11″ × 17″ paper.

1 Fold the short sides of the sheet of paper along the long axis, leaving a 1″ tab along the side.

2 Turn the paper and fold it into thirds.

3 Unfold and cut the top layer along both fold lines. This makes three tabs.

4 Label the tabs as shown.

Pollution
Air | Water | Land

Under the appropriate tabs, define terms and summarize main ideas about air, water, and land pollution.

Go Online Visit glencoe.com and complete the Health Inventory for Chapter 21.

575

HEALTH QUIZ

Air and Land Pollution
Have students complete the Health Quiz. Ask for volunteers to share their answers to each question. Allow for class discussion of each question. Tell students that they will take the quiz again after they have read the chapter.

No Child Left Behind

Working with Parents
Parental support and guidance can help students be successful in school. You can take an active role in soliciting parental involvement by initiating contact with parents during the first weeks of school. Let parents know how they can help their child succeed. Maintain contact with short e-mail or telephone messages or notes sent home. Send home a monthly classroom newsletter that describes what students are learning and how parents can become involved.

Go Online
Have students visit **glencoe.com** and complete the Health Inventory for Chapter 21.

FOLDABLES Study Organizer
Dinah Zike Foldables®

Organizing Information and Summary Writing As students read and discuss the materials presented in Lesson 1, have them take notes on the different types of pollution. They should define key terms and summarize the main ideas on air, water, and land pollution under the appropriate tab of their Foldable®. After students have completed the lesson, instruct them to write a brief summary on the back of their Foldable® that describes how pollution affects the environment. **BL**

FOCUS

Activating Prior Knowledge

What I Know Invite students to tell what they know about air, water, and land pollution. Correct any misconceptions they might have. Explain that in this lesson they will learn what causes pollution and how it affects the environment.

Guide to Reading

Building Vocabulary
- Have students sort the vocabulary terms into different categories of their own choosing.
- Use Vocabulary PuzzleMaker to reinforce vocabulary terms.

Reading Strategy
Skimming After students read the lesson, have them review their sentences. Tell them to revise sentences as needed to better reflect the content of the section.

 Have students use their Foldables® as they read Lesson 1.

Quick Write

To help students get started, suggest that they think of one factor that contributes to the pollution of each of the following: air, water, and land.

Caption Answer

Photo Caption *Sample answer:* pick up litter

Lesson 1

Pollution and Health

Guide to Reading

Building Vocabulary
As you read this lesson, write each new highlighted term and its definition in your notebook.
- pollution (p. 577)
- pesticides (p. 577)
- acid rain (p. 577)
- smog (p. 578)
- ozone layer (p. 578)
- greenhouse effect (p. 578)
- global warming (p. 578)
- landfills (p. 579)
- hazardous wastes (p. 580)

Focusing on the Main Ideas
In this lesson, you will learn to
- **explain** what pollution is.
- **identify** what contributes to air, water, and land pollution.
- **develop** strategies to reduce the ways you contribute to pollution.
- **recognize** how pollution affects the environment.

Reading Strategy
Skimming Quickly look over the headings in this lesson. For each heading, write a sentence describing what information you think will be covered in that section.

FOLDABLES Study Organizer Use the Foldable® on p. 575 as you read this lesson.

Quick Write

Give three examples of types of pollution that affect your local community.

Your Environment

Everything surrounding you makes up your environment. Locally, your environment includes your home, school, and community. Your environment, however, is also the air you breathe, the water you drink, the plants and animals that live nearby, and the climate you live in. It is all the living and nonliving elements that make up your world.

▶ The health of our natural environment has an effect on many aspects of life. **What steps can you take to preserve the beauty and health of your surroundings?**

DANGER
SEWAGE CONTAMINATED BEACH AND WATER
AVOID SHELLFISH HARVESTING, SWIMMING, BEACH COMBING, OR OTHER CONTACT ACTIVITIES

Lesson 1 Resources

📁 **Chapter FAST FILE Resources**
Guided Reading and Writing 21-1
Concept Mapping Activity 21-1
Health Lab 21-1
Reteaching Activity 21-1
Enrichment Activity 21-1
Lesson Quiz 21-1

Technology
🔦 Transparency 21-1
🎧 Audio Summaries
⚙ *ExamView® Assessment Suite*
🎧 Vocabulary PuzzleMaker
⚙ StudentWorks™ Plus
Go Online

Air, water, and land make life on earth possible. However, people pollute these resources. **Pollution** includes *any dirty or harmful substance in the environment.* It **affects** everything in your environment, including the decisions you make. For example, on days when air pollution is heavy, you may have to limit the time you spend outside. Everyone's health depends upon the environment.

Air Pollution

Most air pollution is caused by humans. The major sources of air pollution are described below:

- **Burning fossil fuels.** Burning oil, coal, and natural gas provides the energy that people depend on to carry out their daily tasks. Burning these fossil fuels also releases toxic gases into the atmosphere. These include carbon monoxide, sulfur dioxide, and nitrogen oxides.

- **Chemicals.** Many chemicals also pollute the air. Among them are **pesticides,** which are *products used on crops to control insects and other pests.* Chlorofluorocarbons (CFCs) have damaged the layer of the earth's atmosphere that shields us from solar radiation.

- **Other sources.** Natural sources, such as forest fires, release gases into the atmosphere. Natural sources add to man-made pollution, increasing the overall amount of air pollution.

 Reading Check **Evaluate** What personal behaviors contribute to air pollution?

Effects of Air Pollution

The environment is suffering because of air pollution. Some of the effects are described below:

- **Acid rain.** *Rain that is far more acidic than normal* is known as **acid rain.** Sulfur dioxides and nitrogen oxides—gases that mix with water vapor to form weak acids—are produced when fossil fuels are burned. The acid in the rain can hurt everything from trees to sea life.

Do you think global warming is a problem? Why or why not?

In my opinion, global warming is a major problem and our earth is calling out for help. Our climate and atmosphere are experiencing abnormal temperatures, hurricanes, and other natural disasters. We as a society have to take action immediately to help save our environment so our generation and future generations can experience the beauty of this world.

Darian H.
Pensacola, FL

Academic Vocabulary

affects (a FEKTZ) *(verb)* to influence; to make an impression on. *How often you practice the guitar affects what kind of player you'll become.*

TEACH

U Universal Access

Learning Disabled Give students concrete examples of pollution. Display pictures or take students outside and show them examples of pollution in your community. Relate ozone action days to air pollution. Describe the restrictions on ozone action days and explain how they work to reduce emissions caused by burning fuel. **BL**

Reading Check

Answer using fossil fuels and chemicals

What Teens THINK

Do you think global warming is a problem? Why or why not? Have students work together to create a two-column chart with these headings: *Signs That Global Warming Is a Problem* and *Signs That Global Warming Is Not a Problem.* Then have group members discuss what their charts show.

Academic Vocabulary

Affects Write the words *affect* and *effect* on the board, and have students compare the two words. Explain that *effect* means "a result." Have students work with partners to write health-related sentences using *affect* and *effect.* 📁

FITNESS ZONE

Air Pollution and Physical Fitness The effects of air pollution can be most keenly felt during outdoor physical activities. Have students skim the *Group Fitness Activities* in the *Fitness Zone Handbook.* Ask: How do you think bad air pollution would affect your ability to participate in these activities? Which activities do you think should be limited during periods of serious air pollution? **For more information, see *Fitness Zone Handbook* pages xviii–1 or visit the Fitness Zone at glencoe.com.**

Ecologist Ask students to read the information about ecologists at glencoe.com. Then have them work in groups to list at least five aspects that make the career appealing.

R Reading Strategy

Analyzing a Graphic Walk students through the process of the greenhouse effect shown in **Figure 21.1**. Ask: Where does the heat that is trapped in the atmosphere come from? *the sun* What gases are trapping the heat and intensifying the greenhouse effect? *carbon dioxide and other gases* Explain that these gases come from burning fossil fuels. **OL**

W Writing Support

Writing Support Have students research factors contributing to air pollution and how it affects the environment. Ask students to write a letter to a newspaper, addressing this problem and providing recommendations to the community for solving this problem. In their letters, ask that students take a stand, give facts and opinions, give logical reasons, use examples, and quote experts. **AL**

Caption Answer

Figure Caption *Sample answer:* reduce the amount of carbon dioxide released into the air

Ecologist

Ecologists explore the relationships between humans, animals, and plants. They also study the effects of environmental change. Ecologists will always be in demand because the environment is constantly changing and professionals are needed to monitor and study those changes. If you are interested in becoming an ecologist, you should study environmental issues.

What skills does an ecologist need? Go to *Career Corner* **at glencoe.com to find out.**

- **Smog.** *A yellow-brown haze that forms when sunlight reacts with air pollution* is known as **smog.** When smog levels are high, people with respiratory problems should stay indoors.

- **Destruction of the ozone layer.** The **ozone layer,** located miles above the earth's surface, acts as *a shield that protects living things from ultraviolet (UV) radiation.* Air pollution causes the deterioration of the ozone layer, allowing excessive UV radiation to reach the earth's surface. Too much UV radiation can cause skin cancer.

- **Global warming.** *The trapping of heat by carbon dioxide and other gases in the air* is known as the **greenhouse effect** (see **Figure 21.1**). The earth would be too cold to support life if there were no greenhouse effect. However, air pollution intensifies the greenhouse effect and may be causing increased **global warming**—*a rise in the earth's temperatures.* This could affect weather patterns as well as ocean water levels.

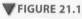

▼ FIGURE 21.1

R THE GREENHOUSE EFFECT

The heating of the earth by gases in our atmosphere is similar to how a greenhouse warms. **What can be done to stop the greenhouse effect from causing an overall rise in temperatures?**

1 Light energy from the sun reaches the earth's lower atmosphere and is converted to heat.

2 A layer of carbon dioxide and other gases surrounding the earth traps the heat.

3 The surface of the earth and the lower atmosphere become warmer because of the trapped heat.

578

► What Teens Want to Know ◄

Is this water safe to drink? Public water utilities filter the water, test it, and disinfect it to remove sediments, chemicals, bacteria, and viruses. However, lead pipes in older homes can leach lead into the water coming out of the faucets. People with private wells might have contaminated groundwater and not know it. They should have their water tested yearly. Bottled water is not necessarily safer to drink. Some bottled water is treated more than tap water, while some is treated less or not at all. **OL**

▶ Litter is one cause of land pollution. What happens to all the trash that is produced?

Water Pollution

Water is vital to all forms of life. However, various kinds of wastes, chemicals, and other harmful substances pollute the earth's water. One type of pollution is sewage—garbage, detergents, and other household wastes washed down drains. Sewage in the United States is treated, but many countries lack the education, money, and facilities needed to properly treat water. Industrial chemicals also contribute to water pollution. Some enter the water from factories. Agriculture also contributes pesticides, herbicides, and fertilizers that run off the land and into the water supply.

Oil spills from large tanker ships have far-reaching effects, killing plants and animals and ravaging delicate habitats. When spilled on land, oil runs off into nearby lakes, rivers, and wetlands.

Water polluted with sewage can spread horrible diseases such as typhoid fever and cholera. Eating shellfish from polluted water can cause hepatitis, a disease of the liver. Drinking water contaminated by heavy metals such as lead or mercury can damage the liver, the kidneys, and the brain. It can also cause birth defects.

AL

Reading Check **Describe** How does water pollution affect your health?

Land Pollution

Land pollution results from littering and the careless disposal of household and industrial garbage. This affects not only the soil but also the water and air. Two forms of land pollution are solid waste and hazardous wastes.

Solid Waste

AL

The average U.S. citizen produces about 4.4 pounds of trash, or solid waste, daily. The solid waste produced by households and businesses usually ends up in **landfills**—*huge pits where wastes are dumped and buried*. Landfills are lined with a protective barrier that prevents wastes from seeping into the surrounding soil and into groundwater.

Go Online

Topic: Caring for the Environment

Visit glencoe.com for Student Web Activities to learn about a variety of environmental groups that teens can take part in.

Activity: Using the information provided at the link above, choose an environmental issue that appeals to you. Then, create a flyer that tells other teens about the issue and what they can do to help.

Lesson 1: Pollution and Health **579**

AL Active Learning

Learning Stations Direct six groups to rotate through six learning stations. At three stations, place an index card that instructs groups to list the causes and effects of air, water, and land pollution. At the other stations, have groups think of ways to reduce air, water, and land pollution. Lead a class discussion about the causes and effects of pollution and ways to reduce pollution. Challenge students to choose one idea to implement in their daily lives. **OL**

Go Online

Caring for the Environment Have students research environmental groups. Ask students to create a flyer detailing the environmental issue a group is concerned about. What efforts are being made by the group to improve this issue? How can teens get involved?

🏠 Home, School, and Community

In the Community Invite a representative from a local waste disposal service, health department, or environmental agency to come to your class to describe how landfills and incinerators work, their pros and cons, and which is used in your community.

Suggest that the speaker trace the path of a candy bar wrapper and a soft drink can beginning from the point when they are thrown away. Ask the speaker to detail the effects of landfills and incinerators on the environment and on human health. **OL**

Caption Answers

Photo Caption, this page buried in landfills, incinerated, recycled
Photo Caption, p. 580 contact your local health department, environmental agency, or waste removal service

Reading Check

Answer solid waste and hazardous wastes

ASSESS

Assessment Resources

Lesson Review Quiz
- ExamView
- Fast Files Activities
- Online Quizzes and Activities

Reteaching

- Assign Concept Map 21-1 or Reteaching Activity 21-1 in the Fast Files.
- Have students examine the photographs in this lesson and write a sentence for each that relates the image to a cause or an effect of pollution.

Enrichment

- Assign Enrichment Activity 21-1 in the Fast Files.
- Challenge students to look for a source of pollution in their community and its effect on the environment and human health. Invite students to present their findings to the class.

CLOSE

Ask students to explain how air, water, and land pollution affect the environment and their health.

◀ The household products shown in this picture are all hazardous materials and need to be disposed of safely. **How do you safely dispose of hazardous wastes in your community?**

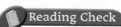

Go Online

Visit **glencoe.com** and complete the Interactive Study Guide for Lesson 1.

Hazardous Wastes

With each new industry and each new product, there is the potential of a new waste problem. **Hazardous wastes** are *human-made liquid or solid wastes that may endanger human health or the environment*. When hazardous wastes pollute the soil, water, or air, they can cause injury, illness, and even death. All hazardous wastes require careful handling and special disposal.

Many products we use daily—and discard—contain hazardous materials: batteries, bleach, insecticides, motor oil, antifreeze, paint, and certain cleaning fluids. These materials should not be discarded in your regular trash can. Your local health department or environmental agency can advise you about how to dispose of them safely and legally.

Reading Check   **Recall** What are two forms of land pollution?

Lesson 1 Review

After You Read

Review this lesson for new terms, major headings, and Reading Checks.

What I Learned

1. *Vocabulary* Define *pollution*. Use the word in an original sentence.

2. *Identify* Name five common products that contain hazardous materials that contribute to pollution.

3. *Recall* Name two sources of air pollution and two sources of water pollution.

Thinking Critically

4. *Explain* How do fossil fuels contribute to global warming?

5. *Evaluate* Why do hazardous wastes pose a greater problem today than they did a century ago?

Applying Health Skills

6. *Accessing Information* Use reliable sources to research the dangers of exposure to lead paint and explain how to avoid this potentially harmful substance. Report your findings to the class.

Go Online   For more Lesson Review Activities, go to **glencoe.com**.

Lesson 1 Review Answers

1. Any dirty or harmful substance in the environment; sentences will vary.
2. *Any five:* batteries, bleach, insecticides, motor oil, antifreeze, certain cleaning fluids
3. *Sample answers:* air: burning fossil fuels and chlorofluorocarbons (CFCs) released into the air from air conditioners or refrigerators; water: sewage, oil spills, fertilizer or pesticide run-off
4. When fossil fuels are burned, gases are released into the air. These gases intensify the greenhouse effect, which may contribute to global warming.
5. New industries and new products bring with them the potential for new disposal problems.
6. Reports should describe the health effects of lead paint exposure, as well as how to prevent exposure to lead paint.

Preventing and Reducing Pollution

Guide to Reading

● **Building Vocabulary**
Make a word diagram that shows the relationship among the terms below. Decide which term is the most general and the one all the others relate to.

- Environmental Protection Agency (EPA) (p. 581)
- biodegradable (p. 582)
- nonrenewable resources (p. 582)
- conservation (p. 582)
- precycling (p. 584)

● **Focusing on the Main Ideas**
In this lesson, you will learn to

- **describe** the three Rs: reduce, reuse, and recycle.
- **explain** actions individuals can take to protect the environment.
- **identify** nonrenewable resources.
- **communicate** your concerns about the environment.

● **Reading Strategy**
Finding the Main Idea For each major heading in this lesson, write one sentence that states the main idea.

Reduce, Reuse, Recycle

Governments around the world are committed to reducing and preventing pollution. Here, in the United States, the **Environmental Protection Agency (EPA)** is *the governmental agency that is committed to protecting the environment.* In addition, many states and countries maintain air and water quality by applying waste management strategies and controlling emissions (the gases, including exhaust, that vehicles release into the air). Waste management involves efforts to dispose of wastes in a way that protects the health of the environment and the people.

▶ Some communities provide bins for collecting different kinds of recyclable materials. **What does your community do to encourage recycling?**

Quick Write
Make a list of actions you already take to protect the environment.

Lesson 2: Preventing and Reducing Pollution **581**

FOCUS

FOCUS

Activating Prior Knowledge

What I Know Ask students to explain what it means to reduce, reuse, and recycle. Explain that they will learn how to reduce pollution.

Guide to Reading

Building Vocabulary
- Challenge students to draw a picture that includes all the vocabulary terms. Terms can be used as labels, in a caption, or embedded in the illustration on signs or package labels.
- Use Vocabulary PuzzleMaker to reinforce vocabulary terms.

Reading Strategy
Finding the Main Idea
Have students review their sentences after reading the lesson and adjust them as they see fit. Ask them to write a main idea sentence for each subheading.

Quick Write
To get students started, share some actions you have taken to protect the environment. Encourage them to brainstorm other environmental protection strategies.

Caption Answer
Photo Caption Answers will vary.

Lesson 2 Resources

 Chapter FAST FILE Resources
Guided Reading and Writing 21-2
Concept Mapping Activity 21-2
Cross-Curriculum Activity 21-2
Reteaching Activity 21-2
Enrichment Activity 21-2
Lesson Quiz 21-2

Technology
- Transparency 21-2
- Audio Summaries
- *ExamView*® Assessment Suite
- Vocabulary PuzzleMaker
- StudentWorks™ Plus

Go Online

TEACH

AL You can help protect the environment by practicing the three Rs: reduce, reuse, and recycle. *Reduce* your consumption of energy and other resources. *Reuse* items by repairing, selling, or donating them. *Recycle* materials so they can be used again.

Many communities have introduced collection programs that make recycling convenient for people. These programs are only effective if citizens participate.

Protecting the Air and Water

Any time you use an electrical appliance, ride in a car, or run a power lawn mower, you are burning fossil fuels to produce energy. You are also contributing to air pollution. If you want cleaner air, try these strategies:

- **Walk or ride your bike instead of having someone drive you.** You can help cut down on air pollution while getting the benefit of some physical activity.
- **Use public transportation or carpool.** Carpooling, or taking a bus, train, or subway, cuts down on the number of cars producing exhaust fumes.
- **Don't burn trash, leaves, and brush.** Let the local waste management facility dispose of your trash.

To keep from polluting the water, use detergents that are **biodegradable**—*broken down easily in the environment.* Discard all waste materials properly and legally. Take hazardous waste materials to the appropriate collection sites.

Conservation

Fossil fuels are natural materials known as **nonrenewable resources**—*substances that cannot be replaced once they are used.* A barrel of oil burned is a barrel of oil gone forever.

Conservation is *the saving of resources.* Using less of a resource is the best way to conserve it. Your own home offers lots of opportunities for you to save energy. When you save energy, you are also saving fossil fuels. **Figure 21.2** shows some ways to reduce your energy and water use at home.

Recycling and Precycling

When you change an item in some way in order to use it again, that is recycling. Recycling conserves energy and natural resources while it helps reduce solid waste. Paper, aluminum, glass, plastics, and yard waste are the most commonly collected recycling materials.

U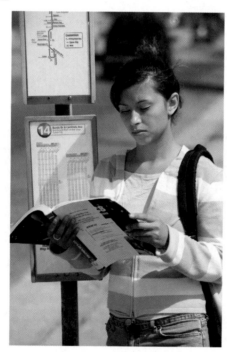

▼ There are many alternate forms of transportation available that can help reduce air pollution. **What can you do to promote cleaner air?**

TECHNOLOGY AND HEALTH

Sources of Renewable Resources
Renewable energy resources include water, wind, solar, and geothermal energy. About 10 percent of the electricity generated in the United States comes from renewable energy resources. Hydroelectric dams use the energy from moving water to produce most of this electricity. Wind turbines generate electricity from moving air. Solar power heats water and powers calculators and yard lights. Geothermal energy is available in areas with underground pockets of hot water, steam, or hot rocks.

▼ FIGURE 21.2

CONSERVATION IN THE HOUSE

The best way to conserve a resource is to use less of it. **What are some ways to save energy and water at home?**

Heating and Cooling

• Seal air leaks around doors, windows, and electric sockets to prevent heat from escaping.

• Keep doors and windows closed during the air-conditioning season, and keep air-conditioning at about 78°F.

• Buy an energy-efficient heating/cooling system that features a thermostat with a timer.

Lighting and Appliances

• Turn off lights when you are not using them.

• Replace traditional lightbulbs with compact fluorescent bulbs. They use less energy and last longer.

• Turn off televisions, computers, fans, and other electric appliances when you are not using them.

Water

• Never let water run unnecessarily.

• Wash clothes in warm or cold water, which uses less energy than hot water.

• Run the washing machine or dishwasher only when you have a full load, and use the short cycle when appropriate.

• If you have an older toilet, place a 1 liter bottle filled with water inside your toilet tank. This will reduce the amount of water used for flushing. Another option is to replace an older toilet with a newer model that requires less water per flush.

Cooking

• Don't preheat a conventional oven for longer than necessary.

• Avoid opening the oven while cooking. Instead, use a timer and the oven door window to check if food is done.

• Heat small quantities of food in a microwave, toaster oven, or slow cooker.

To understand how recycling conserves energy and natural resources, think about aluminum soda cans. It takes energy to mine the ore used to make the aluminum, to **process** the ore, and to manufacture the cans. When aluminum cans are recycled, they are changed back into sheets of aluminum that can be used to make new cans or other products. When less ore is taken from the ground, less energy is needed.

A symbol with three curved arrows appears on many kinds of products. It indicates that an item can be recycled, or that it is made of recycled materials. A number appears in the center of the symbol on plastic items. This is a code identifying the specific type of material. Plastic objects are sorted according to number at recycling facilities.

More and more people are becoming involved in recycling through drop-off centers and curbside programs. However, plastics have not kept pace with other recycling efforts (**Figure 21.3**). Most recycling programs accept plastics but not necessarily all types of plastics.

Academic Vocabulary

process (PROS es) *(noun)* a series of actions that lead to a conclusion; how something is done. *If you want to get a part in the school play, you'll have to go through the audition process.*

Academic Vocabulary

Process Students learn that energy is needed to process aluminum ore. Ask a pair of volunteers to do online research to find out the basic steps in that process and to explain the steps to the rest of the class. You will find academic vocabulary activities in the Student Activities Workbook. 📂

U Universal Access

Learning Disabled Have a variety of items that would be thrown away, including clean empty packages, bottles, cans, and newspapers. Help students identify which plastics can and cannot be recycled. Then have them sort through the materials and identify which are recyclable and which are not. **BL**

HS Health Skills Practice

Advocacy Have small groups develop a plan to advocate ways to reduce pollution. Groups might choose to create posters, brochures, presentations using software, letters to the editor, public service announcements, or magazine advertisements. Have groups present their final product to the class. **OL**

HEALTH LITERACY

Choosing Less Packaging One way to reduce waste is to choose products with less packaging. Try these tips:

● Purchase fresh vegetables that are not prepackaged

● Buy items used frequently in bulk

● Avoid purchasing single-serving food packages

● Use reusable containers instead of disposable ones

● Take a string or mesh bag to the grocery store or reuse grocery bags

Caption Answer

Figure Caption Accept any answers listed in the graphic.

R Reading Strategy

Analyzing a Graph Have students examine the graph in **Figure 21.3**. Ask: How many tons of plastics were discarded in 2000? *22.4 metric tons* What percentage of plastics were recycled in 2000? *5%* Which items are recycled the most? *yard trimmings and paper/paperboard* **OL**

Health Skills Activity

Practicing Healthful Behaviors

Environment-Friendly Shopping

Use the following strategies to help students complete the activity.

● Instruct small groups to start by reading the tips for environment-friendly shopping.

● Before groups begin brainstorming, have them choose one person to list the group's ideas. Remind students that during brainstorming, ideas are expressed without evaluating them. Encourage them to list as many ideas as they can.

● When all groups have made their lists, invite them to share their ideas. Make a class list to post on a bulletin board.

Caption Answer

Figure Caption *Sample answer:* People should reduce the amount of plastic they purchase and discard.

584

▼ **FIGURE 21.3**

R RESULTS OF RECYCLING EFFORTS

As awareness of environmental health grows, people take a more active role in recycling. What else can you infer from this graph?

Material	Amount Discarded (in metric tons)	Amount Recycled	Percentage Recycled
Aluminum	3.1	0.9	28%
Steel	12.4	4.3	35%
Glass	12.5	3.2	25%
Plastics	22.4	1.2	5%
Yard Trimmings	27.7	12.6	45%
Paper/Paperboard	84.1	35.0	45%

Source: U.S. Environmental Protection Agency, 2000.

Precycling—*reducing waste before it occurs*—is another way to put the brakes on consumption of resources. Below are some basic guidelines for precycling:

● Buy products in packages made of glass, metal, or paper (all materials that can be reused or recycled).

● Look for products in refillable containers.

● Carry store-bought purchases home in your own reusable cloth sack or plastic bags.

Protecting the Environment

Everyone needs to play a part in protecting the environment. Here are some suggestions:

● **Lead your family's recycling effort.** Find out which recyclables are collected in your community and set up a system that your family can follow.

● **Practice environmental awareness.** Evaluate advertising, labels, contents, and packaging to determine their environmental friendliness. **HS**

● **Support a conservation organization.** Request information about current environmental issues, attend meetings, and help to make a difference.

Go Online

Visit **glencoe.com** and complete the Interactive Study Guide for Lesson 2.

584 Chapter 21: Environmental Health

Teacher to Teacher

John Lifsey   **Martin Middle School, Martin, TN**

Recycling Project "I have my classes compete in collecting aluminum can tabs for a local senior citizens' home. I promise a reward for the winning class (a movie, a party, etc.). The students bring in garbage bags full of small tabs. It's amazing how many parents say, "I've got some tabs at home for you." The students learn to volunteer, recycle, and involve the whole family. The senior home recycles the tabs and donates the money to a local hospital."

Health Skills Activity

Practicing Healthful Behaviors

Environment-Friendly Shopping

You have an opportunity to help the environment every time you shop. Below are some tips on how to be an environment-friendly consumer.

- **Plan.** Make a shopping list and buy only what you need.
- **Buy in bulk.** Select larger packages of foods such as cereals and snacks. Buying in larger quantities cuts down on the amount of packaging that you'll ultimately discard.
- **Be aware of packaging.** Choose products packaged in materials that easily break down or are recyclable. For example, buy beverages in glass or aluminum containers.
- **Read labels carefully.** Some common household products such as oven cleaners and paint thinners contain substances harmful to humans. Look for safer commercial products or research alternatives.

In a Group
List all the ways you can think of to save energy, packaging, and waste. Combine the ideas on one list and post it on a bulletin board.

Lesson 2 Review

 After You Read

Review this lesson for new terms, major headings, and Reading Checks.

What I Learned

1. *Vocabulary* What is a *nonrenewable resource*?

2. *List* What are three ways that you can conserve energy and water at home?

3. *Identify* Name the three Rs and tell how they are related to your health.

Thinking Critically

4. *Synthesize* Explain why recycling and precycling are keys to a cleaner environment.

5. *Apply* Briefly describe how each of the following strategies helps protect the environment: emission control, monitoring water quality, and waste management.

Applying Health Skills

6. *Goal Setting* Working with family members, evaluate your current approach to the three Rs and set specific goals to improve your household record for reducing, reusing, and recycling.

Go Online For more Lesson Review Activities, go to glencoe.com.

Lesson 2: Preventing and Reducing Pollution **585**

Lesson 2 Review Answers

1. A substance that cannot be replaced once it is used
2. Accept any answers from **Figure 21.2**.
3. *Sample answer:* By reducing, reusing, and recycling wastes, air and water will stay cleaner, which helps protect people's health.
4. *Sample answer:* Recycling conserves energy and natural resources, as well as reduces the amount of waste buried in landfills. Precycling reduces waste before it occurs.
5. *Sample answer:* Emission control reduces air pollution. Monitoring water quality helps keep water clean. Waste management reduces land pollution from solid and hazardous wastes.
6. Students should use the goal-setting steps discussed in Chapter 2 to help make a plan with their family.

Building Health Skills

Make the Most of It

Skill

Advocacy

Activating Prior Knowledge

Invite students to give ideas about ways to reduce waste. Then ask them to explain why reducing waste is a healthful behavior.

- **Objective** After completing the activity, students will be able to identify ways to practice the three Rs (reduce, reuse, and recycle) in their daily lives.
- **Time** 45 minutes
- **Materials** paper, pencil

Teacher Classroom Resources
📁 Building Health Skills
🖨 Transparency 21-1

Model

- Have students work individually to read the Model paragraph. Ask: How is Oliver being an effective advocate? *Oliver takes a stand, persuades his father, and is convincing.*

586

Building Health Skills

Accessing Information
Practicing Healthful Behaviors
Stress Management
Analyzing Influences
Communication Skills
Refusal Skills
Conflict Resolution
Decision Making
Goal Setting
Advocacy

What Is Advocacy?

Advocacy is working to bring about a change by taking a stand for the common good. If you are an environmental advocate, you are taking a stand for the environment in your home, school, and community.

In order to be a good advocate, you should:

- Take a clear stand on an issue.
- Persuade others to make healthy choices.
- Be convincing.

Make the Most of It

Follow the Model, Practice, and Apply steps to help you master this important health skill.

❶ Model

Read how Oliver uses advocacy skills to combat global warming.

Oliver is studying the effects of global warming in his health class at school. He decides that he wants to take action and talks to his dad about how his family can make the earth a healthier place.

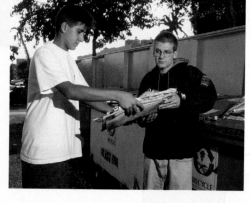

Oliver: We've been studying ways to combat global warming in health class. I'd like our family to do our part. **(Take a clear stand on an issue.)** By making small changes, we can make the earth a healthier place. It's really important and will help keep our family healthy! **(Persuade others to make healthy choices.)**

Dad: What are some of these "small changes"?

Oliver: We need to get more serious about recycling. Also, if we replace regular lightbulbs with compact fluorescent bulbs, we'll use two-thirds less energy. These are small changes, but they help. **(Be convincing.)**

Teaching Tips

Using Props Before beginning this lesson, bring in packaging materials from various products (e.g., gum wrappers, milk cartons, foam plastic peanuts, plastic bags, foam trays, etc.). Before students read the Model section, display the packaging materials.

Ask students what impact these particular materials might have on the environment.

Brainstorming Prior to the Practice section, allot a brief period (about 2 minutes) for students to brainstorm all the ways they could reuse items normally thrown away.

❷ Practice

Use the skill of advocacy to help improve your school's recycling program.

In small groups, evaluate your school's recycling habits. Check the availability and location of recycling bins for paper and other items. For example, are the bins available to every classroom? Are they located in the cafeteria? Are the bins clearly labeled for paper, plastic, and glass?

1. Develop a report on the school's recycling habits. In your report, include at least three suggestions for improving recycling in the school.

2. Share your report with other groups in your class. How is your report similar to or different from theirs?

❸ Apply

Apply what you have learned about advocacy by completing the activity below.

Develop a 30-second public service announcement to persuade other teens to take action to reduce global warming. In your announcement, explain why global warming is harmful. Describe at least three actions students should take to ensure a healthier world.

Self-Check

- Did I explain why global warming is harmful?
- Did I describe three actions students should take?
- Is my announcement persuasive and convincing to teens?

Building Health Skills

Practice

- Instruct small groups to focus on the school's recycling habits for all materials. Have groups develop suggestions for improving recycling all materials at your school.
- Make a class list of your school's current recycling habits and of students' suggestions for improving recycling at your school. Lead a discussion about the differences between the groups' suggestions.

Apply/Assess

- Have students create their own public service announcements.
- Suggest that students think about what they have learned in this chapter and in science classes about why global warming is harmful.
- Invite students to share their public service announcements with the class. Use a computer or tape recorder to record students' public service announcements.

ASSESSMENT SCORING

Using a rubric, student work should meet all criteria to achieve the highest score.

Skills Student work:
- takes a clear stand.
- shows audience awareness.
- encourages others to make healthy choices.

- is convincing.

Concepts Student work:
- explains why global warming is harmful.
- provides three actions to reduce global warming.
- shows a relationship between global warming and environmental health.

Pitch In for the Planet

Objectives

After completing this activity, students will be able to:

- Explain how Earth Day got its start
- Identify ways that individuals can have a positive impact on the environment
- Understand how the health skill of advocacy can be used to help the environment

Motivator

Have students brainstorm a list of ways that individuals can have a positive impact on the environment.

Teaching the Activity

- Have students research to find out the proper procedure for disposing of batteries in their community. Then have students make posters or pamphlets to share this information with others. **OL**
- Have students work in small groups to make a written plan for a clean-up event in their community. Plans should identify a specific site that needs to be cleaned up. Have each group present its plan to the class. If possible, have students carry out their plans and report back to the class. **OL**

TIME *health news*

Pitch In for the PLANET

Five ways for you to be an Earth Day hero.

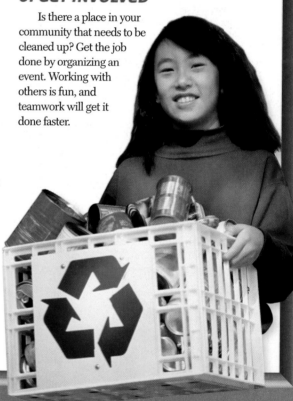

When then Wisconsin senator Gaylord Nelson developed the idea for the first Earth Day in 1970, little did he know how that idea would take root and bloom. Earth Day was meant to draw attention to environmental problems. America's enthusiasm for Earth Day helped persuade lawmakers to pass the 1970 Clean Air Act and to create the Environmental Protection Agency.

More than 30 years after the first Earth Day, people around the world gather to show that they care about our planet. Earth Day is celebrated on April 22, but you can celebrate Earth Day every day. Here are some easy things you can do to protect the air, water, and soil:

1. RECYCLE BATTERIES

The batteries used in toys, cell phones, and other devices can be harmful to the environment. If your batteries contain cadmium, nickel, lead, or mercury, don't throw them in the garbage. Take used batteries to a recycling or collection center in your community.

2. CUT DOWN ON GARBAGE

Prevention is the best way to fight pollution! If you don't create garbage, then no one has to clean it up. Buy products that don't have a lot of packaging. Reuse containers instead of throwing them out. Try to make Earth Day a garbage-free day.

3. AVOID CHEMICALS

Plant marigolds, mint, garlic, or onions in a garden instead of spraying pesticides. Insects don't like these plants and will stay away. Use natural ingredients like vinegar, baking soda, and salt to make cleaners in place of store-bought chemical cleansers.

4. DON'T WASTE ENERGY

Just think how much electricity you could save if you always turned off lights and appliances when not using them. Remind your parents and friends to conserve energy.

Is the heat in your classroom on high with the window open? Do you let the faucet or shower run longer than needed? It takes energy to make hot water. Use less and you'll save precious resources.

5. GET INVOLVED

Is there a place in your community that needs to be cleaned up? Get the job done by organizing an event. Working with others is fun, and teamwork will get it done faster.

588 Chapter 21: Environmental Health

Activity — Media, Technology, and Culture

Technology Have students develop a spreadsheet that can be used to record the mass of the packaging material of common items. For example, students might bring in the packaging from groceries, household products, or small electronic devices. Have students use a balance to measure the mass of the packaging and record the mass in the spreadsheet. Then have students use the spreadsheet to compare the amount of packaging on comparable items. **OL**

Reading Review

STUDY TO GO Visit glencoe.com to download quizzes and eFlashcards for Chapter 21.

FOLDABLES Study Organizer

Foldables® and Other Study Aids Take out the Foldable® that you created for Lesson 1 and any other study guide you created. Find a partner and quiz each other using these study aids.

Lesson 1 Pollution and Health

Main Idea Pollution can have negative health effects on all living things.

- Your environment is all the living and nonliving things that make up your world. It is also the air you breathe, the climate, the animals nearby, and the water you drink.
- Pollution affects your environment as well as the decisions you make.
- Air pollution is caused by burning fossil fuels, chemicals, and natural sources, like forest fires.
- Air pollution causes acid rain, smog, destruction of the ozone layer, and global warming.
- The greenhouse effect is the trapping of heat by carbon dioxide and other gases in the air.
- Global warming is a rise in the earth's temperatures.
- Sewage and oil spills are two examples of water pollution.
- Land pollution comes from littering and improper disposal of household and industrial garbage.
- Hazardous wastes pollute the soil, water, and air. They require careful handling and special disposal.

Lesson 2 Preventing and Reducing Pollution

Main Idea You have the power to prevent and reduce pollution.

- The Environmental Protection Agency is a government agency committed to protecting the environment.
- Waste management involves efforts to dispose of wastes in a way that protects the health of the environment and the people.
- You can protect the air and water by walking or riding your bike to nearby places. You can also use public transportation or carpool. Do not burn trash, leaves, or brush.
- Nonrenewable resources are substances that can't be replaced once they are used.
- Conservation is the saving of resources.
- Recycling conserves energy and natural resources. It also reduces solid waste.
- Precycling is reducing waste before it is used. You can precycle by buying products in recyclable packaging, looking for products in refillable containers, and reusing grocery bags.

Assessment Resources

- Chapter 21 Summary and Activity
- Audio Summaries
- Reading Tutor
- Performance Assessment
- Chapter 21 Test
- *ExamView*
- Vocabulary PuzzleMaker
- Online Learning Center

Reading Review

Study Aids

- **Using the Dinah Zike Foldable® Study Organizer** Have students use the Foldable® 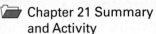 to review the causes and effects of air, water, and land pollution. Ask students to name ways they can help reduce pollution.
- **Online Learning Tools** Have students go to the *Teen Health* Online Learning Center at **glencoe.com** to:
  - Download a **Podcast**.
  - Download free **Study-to-Go** content to their PDAs or cell phones.

Vocabulary Review

- **Short Story** Have students write a short story in which they use all the vocabulary terms from this chapter.

Teaching Tips

Developing Listening Skills Middle school students receive much of their information by listening. You can do some simple things to help students develop their listening skills. Vary your speaking voice to emphasize key ideas. Talk more loudly or softly to attract students' attention. Speak slowly when presenting complex ideas or instructions. You can also group together speaking times and listening times. Speak for only as long as students can listen attentively, then engage students in an activity that reinforces the concepts they just heard.

Reviewing Vocabulary and Main Ideas

1. greenhouse effect
2. Smog
3. fossil fuels
4. Pollution
5. Global warming
6. biodegradable
7. precycling
8. hazardous wastes
9. Nonrenewable resources
10. conservation

Thinking Critically

11. *Sample answer:* Turn out the lights when I leave a room. Take the bus, walk, or ride my bike to go places.
12. *Sample answer:* If they are not disposed of properly, hazardous wastes can cause pollution and harm the health of all living things.
13. *Sample answer:* Everyone's health depends on people taking action now to protect the environment. Ignoring environmental problems can lead to disease, global warming, and the permanent loss of fossil fuels.

Have students visit **glencoe.com** to take the Chapter 21 quiz.

590

After You Read

HEALTH QUIZ

Now that you have read the chapter, look back at your answers to the Health Quiz on the chapter opener. Would you change any of them? What would your answers be now?

Reviewing Vocabulary and Main Ideas

On a sheet of paper, write the numbers 1–10. After each number, write the term from the list that best completes each sentence.

- precycling
- fossil fuels
- greenhouse effect
- hazardous wastes
- biodegradable
- smog
- pollution
- conservation
- nonrenewable resources
- global warming

Lesson 1 Pollution and Health

1. The _____ is the trapping of heat near the earth's surface.
2. _____ is a yellow-brown haze formed when sunlight reacts with air pollution.
3. The burning of _____ contributes greatly to air pollution.
4. _____ is any dirty or harmful substance in the environment.
5. _____ is a rise in the earth's temperatures.

Lesson 2 Preventing and Reducing Pollution

6. You can help keep the water clean by using detergents that are _____.
7. The practice of reducing waste before it occurs is called _____.
8. Advances in science and technology have led to the problem of _____, or waste products that can cause illness, injury, or death.
9. _____ are substances that cannot be replaced once they are used.
10. The saving of resources is _____.

Thinking Critically

Using complete sentences, answer the following questions on a sheet of paper.

11. **Apply** What changes could you make in your life to conserve energy and reduce air pollution?
12. **Analyze** Why is the disposal of hazardous wastes more of a challenge than the disposal of other solid wastes?
13. **Evaluate** Why is it important for people to become actively involved in protecting the environment? What might happen if people ignore environmental problems?

Go Online Visit **glencoe.com** and take the Online Quiz for Chapter 21.

HEALTH QUIZ Wrap-Up

Air and Land Pollution Have students review their answers. Some students may find that their answers have changed after reading the chapter. Ask students to reconsider their answers in light of the information they have learned while reading the chapter. Have volunteers share with the class how their answers have changed.

Write About It

14. Expository Writing Imagine that you are writing an article for a newsletter of the Environmental Protection Agency (EPA). In your article, define and discuss the different forms of pollution. Tell what factors contribute to each form of pollution. Explain how pollution affects the health of our environment.

15. Persuasive Writing Write a public service announcement (PSA) that encourages teens to recycle and conserve resources. In your PSA, state facts about the need to recycle and conserve, and opinions about the benefits of taking these actions. Give examples that show how teens can recycle and conserve resources and how they, too, can advocate for environmental health.

⚡ Applying Technology

Your Community Environment PSA

You and a partner will use Microsoft Word® and iMovie® to create a public service announcement about your community's environment.

- Open a new Microsoft Word® document. Using one of the many topics discussed in this chapter, write a five-minute script about your community's environment. Make sure to use and define relevant vocabulary terms and include local agencies that deal with environmental protection.

- Open a new iMovie® project. Record and save your PSA.

- Edit for time, clarity, and accuracy of information.

- Save your project.

⚡ Applying Technology

Your Community Environment PSA
Equipment needs: Microsoft Word® or similar software and iMovie® or similar software
After students have chosen partners, help them review and discuss the steps in this project. Emphasize the importance of planning at the beginning of the project and editing at the end. If possible, have students share their public service announcements with their classmates.

Standardized Test Practice

Reading and Writing

Read the passage and then answer the questions.

Air, water, and land pollution affect your health and that of your environment. Air pollution can worsen symptoms in people with respiratory problems. Water pollution can contaminate the water we drink, swim, and fish in, causing health problems and negatively affecting aquatic life. When discarded improperly, hazardous substances in common products such as batteries can leak into the surrounding soil. These facts make it clear that it is worth your while to work to reduce pollution.

There are, however, ways to reduce pollution. Use mass transit when it's available and properly dispose of household products, such as bleach and motor oil.

1. Which sentence from the passage represents the author's opinion?

A. Air, water, and land pollution affect your health and that of your environment.

B. Air pollution can worsen symptoms in people with respiratory problems.

C. These facts make it clear that it is worth your while to work to reduce pollution.

D. Water pollution can contaminate the water we drink, swim, and fish in, making us ill and killing aquatic life.

2. The author probably wrote the editorial

A. to explain why pollution occurs.

B. to criticize people who litter.

C. to describe the steps he or she takes to reduce pollution.

D. to persuade readers to take steps to reduce pollution.

Chapter 21 Assessment **591**

Write About It

14. Expository Writing Tell students that expository writing shares knowledge to help others understand. Articles should describe air, water, and land pollution and factors that cause each type of pollution. Articles should also explain how pollution affects the health of the environment and people.

15. Persuasive Writing Explain that persuasive writing states a position and gives facts and opinions to support it. PSAs should explain why recycling and conserving resources is important and give examples of how to do so.

Standardized Test Practice

1. C
2. D

◤ Test-Taking Tips

Fact vs. Opinion Use question 1 in the Standardized Test Practice as an example to explain the difference between fact and opinion. Remind students that a fact is something that is based on a truth or reality. An opinion is a feeling or belief about something. Have students identify the statements in question 1 that are facts and those that are opinions. Point out that by doing so, they can quickly eliminate incorrect answers.

Reading Skills Handbook

▶ Reading: What's in It for You?

What role does reading play in your life? There are many different ways that reading could be part of what you do every day. Are you on a sports team? Perhaps you like to read the latest news about your favorite team or find out about new ways to train for your sport. Are you interested in music or art? You might be looking for information about ways to create songs or about styles of painting. Are you enrolled in an English class, a math class, or a health class? Then your assignments probably require a lot of reading.

> **Improving or Fine-Tuning Your Reading Skills Will:**
>
> ◆ Improve your grades
> ◆ Allow you to read faster and more efficiently
> ◆ Improve your study skills
> ◆ Help you remember more information
> ◆ Improve your writing

▶ The Reading Process

Good reading skills build on one another, overlap, and spiral around just like a winding staircase goes around and around while leading you to a higher place. This Reading Guide will help you find and use the tools you'll need before, during, and after reading.

> **Strategies You Can Use**
>
> ◆ Identify, understand, and learn new words
> ◆ Understand why you read
> ◆ Take a quick look at the whole text
> ◆ Try to predict what you are about to read
> ◆ Take breaks while you read and ask yourself questions about the text
> ◆ Take notes
> ◆ Keep thinking about what will come next
> ◆ Summarize

▶ Vocabulary Development

Vocabulary skills are the building blocks of the reading and writing processes. By learning to use a number of strategies to build your word skills, you will become a stronger reader.

Use Context to Determine Meaning

The best way to increase your vocabulary is to read widely, listen carefully, and take part in many kinds of discussions. When reading on your own, you can often figure out the meanings of new words by looking at their **context**, the other words and sentences that surround them.

Tips for Using Context

Look for clues such as:

A synonym or an explanation of the unknown word in the sentence:
*Elise's shop specialized in **millinery**, or **hats for women**.*

A reference to what the word is or is not like:
*An **archaeologist**, like a historian, deals with the past.*

A general topic associated with the word:
*The **cooking** teacher discussed the best way to braise meat.*

A description or action associated with the word:
*He used the **shovel** to **dig up** the garden.*

Predict a Possible Meaning

Another way to determine the meaning of a word is to take the word apart. If you understand the meaning of the **base,** or **root,** part of a word, and also know the meanings of key syllables added either to the beginning or end of the base word, you can usually figure out what the word means.

Word Origins Since Latin, Greek, and Anglo-Saxon roots are the basis for much of our English vocabulary, having some background in languages can be a useful vocabulary tool. For example, *astronomy* comes from the Greek root *astro*, which means "relating to the stars." *Stellar* also has a meaning referring to stars, but it's from Latin. Knowing root words in other languages can help you figure out meanings, word sources, and spellings in English.

Prefixes and Suffixes A prefix is a word part that can be added to the beginning of a word. For example, the prefix *semi* means "half" or "partial," so *semicircle* means "half a circle." A suffix is a word part that can be added to the end of a word. Adding a suffix often changes a word from one part of speech to another.

Using Dictionaries A dictionary gives the meaning or meanings of a word. Look at the example on the next page to see what else a dictionary can offer.

Thesauruses and Specialized Reference Books A thesaurus gives synonyms and sometimes antonyms. It is a useful tool to expand your vocabulary. Remember to check the exact meaning of words in a dictionary before you use a thesaurus. Specialized dictionaries such as *The New American Medical Dictionary* and *Health Manual* list terms that are not always included in a general dictionary. You can also use online dictionaries.

Glossaries Many textbooks have a condensed dictionary. This kind of dictionary offers an alphabetical listing of vocabulary words used in the text along with definitions.

Dictionary Entry

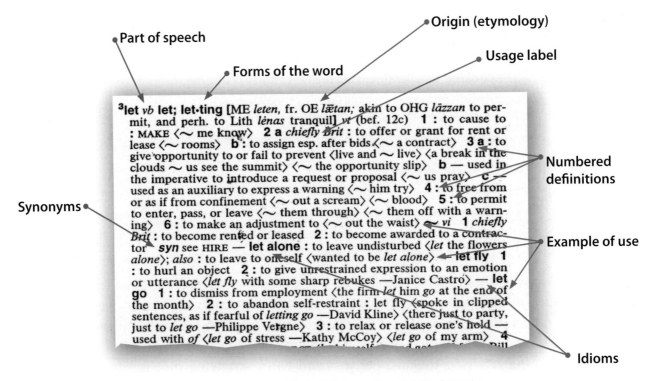

Part of speech

Forms of the word

Origin (etymology)

Usage label

Numbered definitions

Synonyms

Example of use

Idioms

By permission. From *Merriam-Webster's Collegiate® Dictionary, Eleventh Edition*© 2005 by Merriam-Webster, Incorporated (www.merriam-webster.com)

Recognize Word Meanings Across Subjects Have you learned a new word in one class and then noticed it in your reading for other subjects? The word might not mean exactly the same thing in each class, but you can use the meaning you already know to help you understand what it means in another subject area. For example:

Math After you multiply the two numbers, explain how you arrived at the **product.**

Science One **product** of photosynthesis is oxygen.

Health The **product** of a balanced diet and regular exercise is a healthy body.

▶ Understanding What You Read

Reading comprehension means understanding or gaining meaning from what you have read. Using a variety of strategies can help you improve your comprehension and make reading more interesting and more fun.

Read for a Reason

To get the greatest value from what you read, you should **establish a purpose for reading.** In school, you have many reasons for reading. Some of them are to:

- Learn and understand new information
- Find specific information
- Review before a test
- Finish an assignment
- Prepare to write

As your reading skills improve, you will notice that you use different strategies to fit the different reasons for reading. If you are reading for fun, you might read quickly, but if you read to gather information or follow directions, you might read more slowly. You might also take notes, develop a graphic organizer, or reread parts of the text.

Draw on Personal Background

Drawing on your own background is also called activating prior knowledge. Before you start reading a text, ask yourself questions like these:

- What have I heard or read about this topic?
- Do I have any personal experiences that might connect to this topic?

Using a KWL Chart A KWL chart is a good device for organizing information you gather before, during, and after reading. In the first column, list what you already **know,** then list what you **want** to know in the middle column. Use the third column when you review and assess what you **learned.** You can also add more columns to record places where you found information and places where you can look for more information.

K (What I already know)	W (What I want to know)	L (What I have learned)

Adjust Your Reading Speed Your reading speed is an important factor in how well you understand what you are reading. You will need to change your speed depending on the reason you are reading.

Scanning means running your eyes quickly over the material to look for words or phrases. Scan when you need specific information.

Skimming means reading a section of text quickly to find its main idea. Skim when you want to determine what the reading is about.

Reading for detail involves careful reading while paying attention to the structure of the text and to your own understanding. Read for detail when you are learning about new ideas or when you are following directions. It is also important when you are getting ready to analyze a text.

▶ Techniques to Understand and Remember What You Read

Preview

Before beginning a selection, it is helpful to **preview** what you are about to read.

> **Previewing Strategies**
>
> Read the title, headings, and subheadings of the selection.
> Look at the illustrations and notice how the text is set up.
> Skim the reading: Take a quick look at the whole thing.
> Decide what the main idea might be.
> Predict what the reading will be about.

Predict

Have you ever read a mystery, decided who was the criminal, and then changed your mind as more clues were offered? You were changing your predictions based on the information you had available. Did you smile when you found out you guessed the criminal? You were checking your predictions.

As you read, take educated guesses about story events and outcomes; that is, **make predictions** before and during reading. This will help you focus your attention on the text, and it will improve your understanding.

Determine the Main Idea

When you look for the **main idea,** you are looking for the most important sentences in a text. Depending on what kind of text you are reading, the main idea can be found at the very beginning (news stories in a newspaper or magazine) or at the end (scientific research document). Ask yourself:

- What is each sentence about?
- Is there one sentence that is more important than all the others?
- What idea do details support or point out?

Taking Notes

Cornell Note-Taking System There are many methods for note taking. The **Cornell Note-Taking System** is a well-known method that can help you organize what you read. To the right is a note-taking activity based on the Cornell Note-Taking System.

Graphic organizers Using a graphic organizer will help you remember and hold on to new information. You might make a **chart** or **diagram** that helps you organize what you have read. Here are some ways to make graphic organizers:

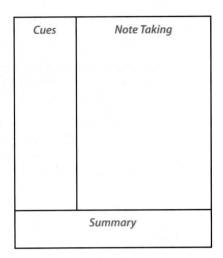

Venn diagrams When mapping out a comparison-and-contrast text structure, you can use a Venn diagram. The outer parts of the circles will show how two characters, ideas, or items contrast, or are different. The overlapping part in the middle will compare two things, or show how they are alike.

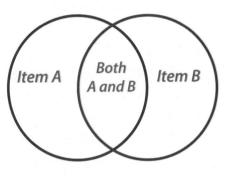

Flow charts To help you track the order of events, or cause and effect, use a flow chart. Arrange ideas or events in their logical, step-by-step order. Then draw arrows between your ideas to show how one idea or event flows into another.

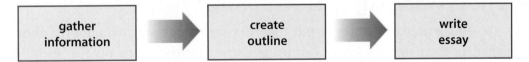

Visualize

Try to form a picture in your mind of scenes, characters, and events as you read. Use the details and descriptions the author gives you. If you can picture, or visualize, what you read, it will be more interesting and you will remember it better.

Question

Ask yourself questions about the text while you read. Ask yourself about the importance of the sentences, how they relate to one another, if you understand what you just read, and what you think is going to come next.

Clarify

If you feel you do not understand the meaning of what you read (through questioning), try these ideas:

> **What to Do When You Do Not Understand**
>
> ◆ Reread confusing parts of the text.
> ◆ Make diagrams that show how pieces of text, ideas, and sentences connect to each other.
> ◆ Look up new words.
> ◆ Talk about the text to yourself.
> ◆ Read the text over again.

Review

Take time to stop and review what you have read. Use your note-taking tools (graphic organizers or Cornell notes charts). Also, think about what you've written in your KWL chart.

Monitor Your Comprehension

Continue to check your understanding by using the following two strategies:

Summarize Pause and tell yourself the main ideas of the text and the key supporting details. Try to answer the following questions: Who? What? When? Where? Why? How?

Paraphrase Pause, close the book, and try to retell what you have just read in your own words. It might help to pretend you are explaining the text to someone who has not read it and does not know the material.

▶ Understanding Text Structure

Good writers do not just put together sentences and paragraphs; they organize their writing with a certain purpose in mind. That organization is called text structure. When you understand and follow the way a text is set up, it is easier to remember what you are reading. There are many ways text may be structured. Watch for **signal words.** They will help you follow the text's organization (also, remember to use these ideas when you write).

Compare and Contrast

This structure shows similarities and differences between people, things, and ideas. This is often used to show that things that seem alike are really different, or vice versa.

Signal words: similarly, more, less, on the one hand / on the other hand, in contrast, but, however

Cause and Effect

Writers use the cause and effect structure to show why something takes place and to look at what happens because of certain actions.

Signal words: so, because, as a result, therefore, for the following reasons

Problem and Solution

Sometimes writers organize text around the question "how?" To do this, they state a problem and then present answers for the reader to think about.

Signal words: how, help, problem, obstruction, overcome, difficulty, need, attempt, have to, must

Sequence

Sequencing tells you in which order to think about ideas or facts. Examples of sequencing are:

Chronological order tells you the order in which events take place.
Signal words: first, next, then, finally

Spatial order describes the way things are arranged in space (to describe a room, for example).
Signal words: above, below, behind, next to

Order of importance lists things or thoughts from the most important to the least important (or the other way around).
Signal words: principal, central, main, important, fundamental

▶ Reading for Meaning

It is important to think about what you are reading to get the most information out of the text and to gain an understanding of what the text is saying. This will also help you to remember the key points and will guide you to form your own thoughts about what you've read.

Interpret

Interpreting is asking yourself, "What is the writer really saying?" and then using what you already know to answer that question.

Infer

Writers do not always say exactly everything they want you to understand. By providing clues and details, they sometimes imply certain concepts. An inference involves using your reason and background to develop ideas on your own. These ideas are based on what an author implies or suggests. What is most important when making inferences is to be sure that you have correctly based your guesses on details from the reading. If you cannot point to a place in the text to help back up your inference, you may need to go back and think about your guess again.

Draw Conclusions

A conclusion is a general statement you can make and explain with reasoning, or with details from a text. If you read a story describing a sport where five players bounce a ball and throw it through a high hoop, you may conclude that the sport is basketball.

Analyze

Persuasive nonfiction is a text that presents facts and opinions that lead to a conclusion. To understand this kind of text, you need to look at statements and examples to see if they connect to the key ideas. An informational text, like a textbook, gives information instead of opinions. To understand this kind of text, you need to notice how ideas are put together to find the key points.

Hint: Use your graphic organizers and notes charts.

Distinguish Facts and Opinions

This is one of the most important reading skills you can learn. A fact is a statement that can be shown to be true. An opinion is what the writer believes. A writer may support opinions with facts, but an opinion cannot be proven. For example:

Fact: California produces fruit and other agricultural products.

Opinion: California produces the best fruit and other agricultural products.

Evaluate

Would you take seriously an article on nuclear fission if you knew a comedy actor wrote it? If you need true and correct information, you need to find out who wrote what you are reading and why. Where did the writer get the information? Is the information one-sided? Can you show that the information is true?

▶ Reading for Research

You will need to think about what you are reading while you read in order to research a subject. You also may need to develop an interesting and fitting **question** that you can study on your own. Be sure to find the right kind of information from many different sources, including print material, and nonprint material. Then you will need to determine key ideas so that you can **organize** the information in a way that fits your readers. Finally, you should **draw conclusions** that connect to your research question. This may lead you to other areas for study.

Locate Appropriate Print and Nonprint Information

In your research, try to use many different sources. This will help you see information in different ways, and will help your project to be interesting and fairly presented.

Literature and Textbooks These texts include any book used for learning or gathering information.

Book Indices A book index, or a bibliography, is an alphabetical listing of books. Some book indices list books on certain subjects; others are more general. Other indices have an array of topics or resources.

Periodicals Magazines and journals are issued regularly, such as weekly or monthly. One way to find information in magazines is to use the *Readers' Guide to Periodical Literature*. This guide can be found in print form in most libraries.

Technical Manuals A manual is a guide or handbook intended to give instruction on how to do a task or operate something. A vehicle owner's manual might give information on how to use and take care of a car.

Reference Books Reference books include encyclopedias and almanacs, and are used to find specific pieces of information.

Electronic Encyclopedias, Databases, and the Internet There are many ways to find information using your computer. Infotrac, for instance, acts as an online reader's guide. The Internet or encyclopedias on CD-ROM can easily provide information on most subjects.

Organize and Convert Information

As you gather information from different sources, taking careful notes, you will need to think about how to **synthesize** the information. This means you will have to join the pieces of information together to make a whole text. You will also need to change it to a form that will fit your audience and will meet the requirements of the assignment.

1. First, ask yourself what you want your readers to know.

2. Then, think about a pattern of organization, a structure that will best show your key ideas. You might ask yourself the following questions:

- When comparing items or ideas, what graphic aids can I use?

- When showing the reasons something happened and the results of certain actions, what text structure would be best?

- How can I briefly and clearly show important information to my readers?

- Would an illustration or even a cartoon help to make a certain point?

The Glossary contains all the important terms used throughout the text. It includes the **boldfaced** terms in the "Building Vocabulary" lists at the beginning of each lesson, which also appear in the text and illustrations.

The Glossary lists the term, the pronunciation (in the case of difficult terms), the definition, and the page on which the term is defined. The pronunciations here and in the text follow the system outlined below. The column headed "Sound" shows the spelling used in this book to represent the appropriate sound.

Pronunciation Key

Symbol	As In	Sound	Example
ă	hat, map	a	abscess (AB·ses)
ā	age, face	ay	atrium (AY·tree·uhm)
a	care, their	eh	capillaries (KAP·uh·lehr·eez)
ä, ŏ	father, hot	ah	biopsy (BY·ahp·See)
ar	far	ar	cardiac (KAR·dee·ak)
ch	child, much	ch	barbiturate (bar·BI·chuh·ruht)
ĕ	let, best	e	vessel (VE·suhl)
ē	beat, See, city	ee	acne (AK·nee)
er	term, stir, purr	er	nuclear (NOO·klee·er)
g	grow	g	malignant (muh·LIG·nuhnt)
ĭ	it, hymn	i	bacteria (bak·TIR·ee·uh)
ī	ice, five	y	benign (bi·NYN)
		eye	iris (EYE·ris)
j	page, fungi	j	cartilage (KAR·tuhl·ij)
k	coat, look, chorus	k	defect (DEE·fekt)
ō	open, coat, grow	oh	aerobic (ehr·OH·bik)
ô	order	or	organ (OR·guhn)
ò	flaw, all	aw	palsy (PAWL·zee)
oi	voice	oy	goiter (GOY·ter)
ou	out	ow	fountain (FOWN·tuhn)
s	say, rice	s	dermis (DER·mis)
sh	she, attention	sh	conservation (kahn·ser·VAY·shuhn)
ŭ	cup, flood	uh	bunion (BUHN·yuhn)
u	put, wood, could	u	pulmonary (PUL·muh·nehr·ee)
ü	rule, move, you	oo	attitudes (AT·i·toodz)
w	win	w	warranty (WAWR·uhn·tee)
y	your	yu	urethra (yu·REE·thruh)
z	says	z	hormones (HOR·mohnz)
zh	pleasure	zh	transfusion (trans·FYOO·zhuhn)
ə	about, collide	uh	addiction (uh·DIK·shuhn)

A

Abdominal thrusts Quick, upward pulls into the diaphragm to force out an obstruction blocking the airway. (page 564)

Abstinence The conscious, active choice not to participate in high-risk behaviors. (pages 16 and 119)

Abuse The physical, emotional, or mental mistreatment of one person by another. (page 188)

Accident Any event that was not intended to happen. (page 540)

Accident chain A series of events that include a situation, an unsafe habit, and an unsafe action. (page 541)

Accidental injuries Injuries resulting from an accident. (page 540)

Accountability A willingness to answer for your actions and decisions. (page 35)

Acid rain Rain that is far more acidic than normal. (page 577)

Active listening Hearing, thinking about, and responding to another person's message. (page 110)

Adapt To adjust to new situations. (page 52)

Addiction A physical or psychological need for a drug. (page 291)

Addictive Capable of causing a user to develop intense cravings. (page 309)

Adolescence The stage of life between childhood and adulthood. (page 8)

Adrenaline A hormone that gives the body extra energy. (page 65)

Advocacy Informing others about health practices and encouraging healthful behaviors. (page 43)

Aerobic exercise Rhythmic, nonstop, moderate to vigorous activity that requires large amounts of oxygen. (page 207)

Affection Feelings of love for another person. (page 120)

Aggressive Overly forceful, pushy, hostile, or otherwise attacking in approach. (page 116)

AIDS (Acquired Immunodeficiency Syndrome) A deadly disease that interferes with the body's natural ability to fight infection. (page 496)

Air Quality Index (AQI) A measure of ozone, sulfur dioxide, carbon monoxide, and fine particles close to the ground. (page 421)

Alcohol A drug that is produced by a chemical reaction in fruits, vegetables, and grains. (page 278)

Alcohol abuse A pattern of drinking that results in one or more well-defined behaviors within a twelve-month period. (page 295)

Alcohol poisoning A dangerous condition that results when a person drinks excessive amounts of alcohol over a short time period. (page 283)

Alcoholism A progressive, chronic disease involving a mental and physical need for alcohol. (page 291)

Allergen (AL·er·juhn) A substance that causes an allergic reaction. (page 527)

Allergy An extreme sensitivity to a substance. (page 527)

Allied health professionals Medical professionals who perform duties which would otherwise have to be performed by doctors or nurses. (page 389)

Alternatives Other ways of thinking or acting. (page 281)

Alveoli (al·VEE·uh·ly) Tiny air sacs in the lungs where carbon dioxide is exchanged with oxygen. (page 420)

Amino acids Small units that make up protein. (page 240)

Amnesia Partial or total loss of memory. (page 341)

Amphetamine (am·FE·tuh·meen) A drug that stimulates the central nervous system. (page 348)

Anabolic steroids A synthetic substance related to the male sex hormones. (page 343)

Anaerobic exercise Intense physical activity that requires little oxygen but uses short bursts of energy. (page 208)

Angioplasty A surgical procedure in which an instrument with a tiny balloon, drill bit, or laser attached is inserted into a blocked artery to clear a blockage. (page 519)

Anorexia nervosa An eating disorder characterized by self-starvation leading to extreme weight loss. (page 267)

Antibiotics (an·ti·by·AH·tiks) Medicines that reduce or kill harmful bacteria in the body. (page 385)

Antibodies Proteins that attach to antigens, keeping them from harming the body. (page 486)

Antigen Substances released by invading pathogens. (page 486)

Antihistamines Medicines that help control the effects triggered by histamines. (page 529)

Anxiety A state of uneasiness, usually associated with a future uncertainty. (page 58)

Anxiety disorder A disorder in which intense anxiety or fear keeps a person from functioning normally. (page 81)

Appetite The psychological desire for food. (page 236)

Appropriate weight The weight that is best for your body. (page 261)

Arteries Blood vessels that carry blood away from the heart to other parts of the body. (page 415)

Arteriosclerosis (ar·tir·ee·oh·skluh·ROH·sis) A group of disorders in which arteries harden and become more rigid. (page 518)

Arthritis (ar·THRY·tuhs) A disease of the joints marked by pain and swelling in body joints. (page 524)

Assault An unlawful threat or attempt to do bodily injury to another person. (page 181)

Assertive Behaving with confidence and clearly stating your intentions. (page 116)

Asthma (AZ·muh) A condition in which the small airways in the lungs narrow, making breathing difficult. (pages 420 and 530)

Atherosclerosis (a·thuh·roh·skluh·ROH·sis) A form of arteriosclerosis in which fatty substances in the blood build up on the walls of the arteries. (page 518)

Attitude A personal feeling or belief. (page 17)

Autonomic (aw·tuh·NAH·mik) **system** The part of the nervous system that deals with actions you do not usually control. (page 424)

Bacteria Tiny one-celled organisms that live nearly everywhere. (page 479)

Balance A feeling of stability and control over your body. (page 205)

Battery The unlawful beating, hitting, or kicking of another person. (page 181)

Benign (bi·NYN) Not cancerous. (page 512)

Binge When a drug is taken repeatedly and at increasingly high doses. (page 348)

Binge drinking The consumption of a large quantity of alcohol in a very short period of time. (page 289)

Binge eating disorder Compulsive overeating. (page 267)

Biodegradable Broken down easily in the environment. (page 582)

Biological age Age determined by how well various body parts are working. (page 468)

Biopsy The removal of a tissue sample from a person for examination. (page 513)

Birth defects Abnormalities present at birth that causes physical or mental disability or death. (page 458)

Blended family A family that consists of a parent, a stepparent, and the children of one or both parents. (page 137)

Blizzard A very heavy snowstorm with winds up to 45 miles per hour. (page 551)

Blood alcohol content (BAC) A measure of the amount of alcohol present in a person's blood. (page 283)

Body composition The ratio of body fat to lean body tissue, such as bone, muscle, and fluid. (page 213)

Body image The way you see and feel about your body. (page 260)

Body language The use of visual cues to communicate a message. (page 108)

Body mass index (BMI) A formula you can use to determine if your weight is appropriate for you. (pages 262 and 521)

Bronchi (BRONG·ky) Passages through which air enters and spreads through the lungs. (pages 309 and 420)

Bronchodilators (brahn·ko·DY·lay·terz) Medicines used to relax the muscles that have tightened around the airways. (page 531)

Bulimia nervosa A condition in which a person eats large amounts of food and then secretly purges. (page 268)

Bully Someone who picks on individuals who are smaller or weaker. (page 157)

Calorie A unit of heat that measures the energy available in food. (pages 205 and 245)

Cancer A disease characterized by the rapid and uncontrolled growth of abnormal cells. (page 511)

Capillaries Tiny blood vessels that connect the veins and arteries to the body's cells. (page 415)

Carbohydrates The sugars and starches that occur naturally in foods, mainly in plants. (page 238)

Carbon monoxide A colorless, odorless, poisonous gas. (page 309)

Carcinogens (kar·SIN·uh·juhn) Substances that cause cancer. (page 513)

Cardiac muscles Muscles found in the walls of your heart. (page 410)

Cardiopulmonary resuscitation (CPR) A first aid procedure that combines rescue breathing with chest compressions to restore breathing and circulation. (page 566)

Cardiovascular disease A disease of the heart and blood vessels. (page 313)

Cardiovascular (KAR·dee·oh·VAS·kyoo·ler) **system** Organs and tissues that transport essential materials to body cells and remove their waste products. (page 413)

Carrier A person who is infected with a virus and who can pass it on to others. (page 496)

Cartilage (KAHR·tuhl·ij) Strong, flexible tissue that provides cushioning at the joints. (page 406)

Cell respiration Process in which the body's cells are nourished and energized. (page 414)

Central nervous system (CNS) The brain and spinal cord. (page 423)

Cervix The entrance of the uterus. (page 454)

Character The way in which a person thinks, feels, and acts. (page 32)

Character trait A quality that demonstrates how a person thinks, feels, and acts. (page 32)

Chemotherapy The use of powerful medicines to destroy cancer cells. (page 514)

Chlamydia (kluh·MI·dee·uh) A bacterial STD that may affect the reproductive organs, urethra, and anus. (page 492)

Chromosomes (KROH·muh·sohmz) The threadlike structures found within the nucleus of a cell that carry the codes for inherited traits. (page 456)

Chronic diseases Diseases that are present either continuously or off and on over a long time. (page 508)

Chronic obstructive pulmonary disease (COPD) A condition in which passages in the lungs become swollen and irritated, eventually losing their elasticity. (page 313)

Chronological (krah·nuh·LAH·ji·kuhl) **age** Age measured in years. (page 468)

Circulatory (SER·kyuh·luh·tohr·ee) **system** Organs and tissues that transport essential materials to body cells and remove their waste products. (page 413)

Cirrhosis (suh·ROH·sis) A disease characterized by scarring and eventual destruction of the liver. (page 287)

Citizenship The way you conduct yourself as a member of a community. (page 36)

Clinical social worker (CSW) A licensed, certified mental health professional with a master's degree in social work. (page 93)

Clique A group of friends who hang out together and act in similar ways. (page 105)

CNS depressants Substances that slow down normal brain function. (page 350)

Cold turkey Term used to describe quitting a habit, such as smoking, all at once. (page 317)

Colon (KOH·luhn) The large intestine. (page 430)

Commitment A pledge or a promise. (page 140)

Communicable (kuh·MYOO·ni·kuh·buhl) **disease** A disease that can be passed to a person from another person, animal, or object. (page 478)

Communication The exchange of thoughts, feelings, and beliefs between two or more people. (pages 39 and 108)

Community service Volunteer programs whose goal is to improve the community and the life of its residents. (page 12)

Comparison shopping A method of judging the benefits of different products and services by measuring and comparing several factors, such as quality, effectiveness, safety, and cost. (page 381)

Compromise An arrangement in which each side gives up something to reach a satisfactory solution. (page 166)

Conditioning Regular activity and exercise that prepare a person for a sport. (page 222)

Conflict A disagreement between people with opposing viewpoints, ideas, or goals. (page 154)

Conflict resolution Solving a disagreement in a way that satisfies both sides. (pages 40 and 164)

Congenital disorders All disorders that are present when the baby is born. (page 508)

Consequences Outcomes or effects that may occur as a result of a decision or an action. (page 119)

Conservation The saving of resources. (page 582)

Consumer Anyone who purchases products or services. (page 379)

Consumer skills Techniques that enable you to make wise, informed purchases. (page 379)

Contagious period The length of time that a disease can spread from person to person. (page 489)

Cooldown A period of low to moderate exercise to prepare your body to end a workout session. (page 220)

Coordination The smooth and effective working together of your muscles and bones. (page 205)

Coping strategies Ways of dealing with the sense of loss people feel when someone close to them dies. (page 70)

Cornea A clear protective structure of the eye that lets in light. (page 377)

Crisis hot line A toll-free telephone service where abuse victims can get help and information. (page 193)

Cross-training Switching between different forms of physical exercise on different days. (page 215)

Cumulative risks Related risks that increase in effect with each added risk. (page 15)

Cuticle (KYOO·ti·kuhl) A fold of epidermis around the fingernails and toenails. (page 374)

Cycle of abuse Pattern of repeating abuse from one generation to the next. (page 193)

Dandruff A flaking of the outer layer of dead skin cells. (page 374)

Decibel A measure of the loudness of sound. (page 377)

Decision making The process of making a choice or finding a solution. (page 27)

Defensive driving Watching out for other people on the road and anticipating unsafe acts. (page 546)

Degenerative diseases Diseases that cause further breakdown in body cells, tissues, and organs as they progress. (page 508)

Dehydration Condition caused by excessive water loss. (page 225)

Depressants Substances that slow down body functions and reactions. (page 278)

Dermatologist (DER·muh·TAHL·uh·jist) A physician who treats skin disorders. (page 373)

Dermis (DER·mis) The thick inner layer of skin. (page 373)

Detoxification (dee·tahk·si·fi·KAY·shuhn) The physical process of freeing the body of an addictive substance. (pages 297 and 359)

Developmental tasks Events that need to happen in order for you to continue growing toward becoming a healthy, mature adult. (page 460)

Diabetes A disease that prevents the body from converting food into energy. (page 522)

Diaphragm (DY·uh·fram) A dome-shaped muscle that separates the chest from the abdomen. (page 420)

Digestion (dy·JES·chuhn) The changing of food you eat into substances your body can use. (page 428)

Digestive system The body system that converts food to a form useful to the body. (page 427)

Disease Any condition that interferes with the proper functioning of the body or mind. (page 478)

Disorder A disturbance in the normal function of a part of the body. (page 80)

Divorce A legal end to a marriage contract. (page 142)

Domestic violence Physical abuse that occurs within a family. (page 189)

Driving while intoxicated (DWI) A driver with a blood alcohol concentration (BAC) of 0.08% or greater. (page 288)

Drug A substance other than food that changes the structure or function of the body or mind. (page 334)

Drug abuse The intentional use of drugs in a way that is unhealthy or illegal. (page 336)

Drug free A characteristic of a person not taking illegal drugs or of a place where no illegal drugs are used. (page 361)

Drug misuse Taking or using medicine in a way that is not intended. (page 335)

Drug trafficking The buying or selling of drugs. (page 177)

Earthquake A violent, shaking movement of the earth's surface. (page 552)

Eating disorder Extreme and damaging eating behavior that can lead to sickness and even death. (page 266)

Egg cell The reproductive cell from the female that joins with a sperm cell to make a new life. (page 450)

Embryo A developing organism from the time of fertilization to about the eighth week of development. (page 452)

Emotional needs Needs that affect a person's feelings and sense of well-being. (page 61)

Emotions Feelings that arise in response to thoughts, remarks, and events. (page 57)

Empathy The ability to understand and show concern for another person's feelings. (page 36)

Empty-calorie foods Foods that offer few, if any, nutrients but do supply calories. (page 249)

Enablers Persons who create an atmosphere in which the alcoholic can comfortably continue his or her unacceptable behavior. (page 294)

Endocrine (EN·duh·krin) **system** The body's chemical communication system that regulates many functions. (page 433)

Environment The sum total of a person's surroundings. (page 456)

Environmental Protection Agency (EPA) The agency of the United States government that is committed to protecting the environment. (page 581)

Enzymes Proteins that affect the many body processes. (page 428)

Epidermis (e·puh·DER·mis) The outermost layer of the skin. (page 373)

Epiglottis (e·puh·GLAH·tis) A flap of tissue that closes over the trachea when you swallow. (page 419)

Escalate To become more serious. (page 159)

Euphoria A feeling of well-being or elation. (page 346)

Excretion (ek·SKREE·shuhn) The process of removing wastes from the body. (page 430)

Excretory system The body system that removes wastes from the body. (page 430)

Exercise Planned physical activity done regularly to build or maintain one's fitness. (page 207)

Extended family A person's immediate family plus other relatives such as grandparents, aunts, uncles, and cousins. (page 135)

F

Family The basic unit of society. Can include two or more people brought together by blood, marriage, adoption, or a desire for mutual support. (page 134)

Family therapy Counseling that seeks to improve troubled family relationships. (page 92)

Famine A widespread shortage of food. (page 395)

Fatty liver A condition in which fats build up in the liver and cannot be broken down. (page 287)

Fertilization The joining together of a male sperm cell and a female egg cell. (pages 439 and 450)

Fetal alcohol syndrome (FAS) A group of alcohol-related birth defects that include both physical and mental problems. (page 290)

Fetus A developing organism from the end of the eighth week of the mother's pregnancy until birth. (page 452)

Fiber The part of fruits, vegetables, grains, and beans that your body cannot digest. (page 239)

Fight-or-flight response The process by which the body prepares to deal with a stressor. (page 64)

First aid The immediate temporary care given to an injured or ill person until professional help is available. (page 554)

F.I.T.T. principle A method for safely increasing aspects of your workout without injuring yourself. (page 218)

Flexibility The ability of your body's joints to move easily through a full range of motion. (page 212)

Foodborne illness Sickness that results from eating food that is not safe to eat. (page 247)

Fracture A break in a bone. (page 559)

Fraud Deliberate deceit or trickery. (page 381)

Fungi (FUHN·jy) Organisms that are more complex than bacteria, but cannot make their own food. (page 479)

G

Gallbladder A small, saclike organ that stores bile. (page 429)

Gang A group of people whose members often use violence or take part in criminal activity. (page 177)

Gender discrimination Singling out or excluding a person based on gender. (page 186)

Genes The basic units of heredity. (page 456)

Genetic (juh·NE·tik) **disorder** A disorder that is caused partly or completely by a defect in genes. (page 456)

Genital herpes (HER·peez) A viral STD that produces painful blisters on the genital area. (page 493)

Genital warts Growths or bumps in the genital area caused by certain types of the human papillomavirus (HPV). (page 493)

Germs Organisms that cause disease and that are so small they can only be seen through a microscope. (page 478)

Gingivitis (jin·juh·VY·tis) A common disorder in which the gums are red and sore and bleed easily. (page 375)

Gland A group of cells, or an organ, that secretes a chemical substance. (page 434)

Global warming A rise in the earth's temperatures. (page 578)

Goal setting The process of working toward something you want to accomplish. (page 29)

Gonorrhea (gah·nuh·REE·uh) A bacterial STD that affects the mucous membranes of the body, particularly in the genital area. (page 494)

Greenhouse effect The trapping of heat by carbon dioxide and other gases in the air. (page 578)

Grief The sorrow caused by loss of a loved one. (page 69)

Grief reaction The process of dealing with strong feelings following any loss. (page 69)

Hallucinogens (huh·LOO·suhn·uh·jenz) Drugs that distort moods, thoughts, and senses. (page 352)

Hangnail A split in the cuticle along the edge of a fingernail. (page 374)

Harassment (huh-RAS-muhnt) Ongoing conduct that offends another person by criticizing his or her race, color, religion, physical disability, or gender. (page 186)

Hazardous wastes Human-made liquid or solid wastes that may endanger human health or the environment. (page 580)

Health A combination of physical, mental/emotional, and social well-being. (page 4)

Health care system All the medical care available to a nation's people, the way they receive the care, and the way the care is paid for. (page 388)

Health fraud The selling of products or services to prevent diseases or cure health problems which have not been scientifically proven safe or effective for such purposes. (page 381)

Health insurance A contract between an insurance company and a person which requires the person to pay a monthly fee. (page 391)

Heart and lung endurance A measure of how efficiently your heart and lungs work when you exercise and how quickly they return to normal when you stop. (page 210)

Heart attack A condition in which blood flow to a part of the heart is greatly reduced or blocked. (page 519)

Heat cramps Painful, involuntary muscle spasms that may occur during strenuous exercise in hot weather. (page 562)

Heat exhaustion An overheating of the body that can result from dehydration. (pages 225 and 562)

Heatstroke A serious form of heat illness in which the body's normal processes for dealing with heat close down. (page 562)

Hepatitis (hep·uh·TYT·uhs) A viral disease of the liver characterized by yellowing of the skin and the whites of the eyes. (page 490)

Heredity The passing of traits from parents to their children. (pages 214, 455, and 509)

Hernia An internal organ pushing against or through a surrounding cavity wall. (page 439)

High blood pressure A condition in which a person's blood pressure stays at a level that is higher than normal. (page 519)

Histamines Chemicals in the body that cause the symptoms of an allergic reaction. (page 528)

HIV (human immunodeficiency virus) The virus that causes AIDS. (page 496)

Hives Raised bumps on the skin that are very itchy. (page 528)

Homicide The killing of one human being by another. (page 176)

Hormones Chemical substances, produced in glands, that help to regulate many body functions. (page 9)

Hospice care Care provided to the terminally ill that focuses on comfort, not cure. (page 390)

Hunger The physical need for food. (page 236)

Hurricane A strong windstorm with driving rain that originates at sea. (page 551)

Hygiene Cleanliness. (page 480)

Hypertension A condition in which the pressure of the blood on the walls of the blood vessels stays at a level that is higher than normal. (page 519)

"I" message A statement that presents a situation from the speaker's personal viewpoint. (page 110)

Immune system A combination of body defenses made up of cells, tissues, and organs that fight off pathogens and disease. (page 483)

Immunity Your body's ability to resist the pathogens that cause a particular disease. (page 483)

Infancy The first year of life. (page 462)

Infection A condition that occurs when pathogens get inside the body, multiply, and damage body cells. (page 478)

Inflammation The body's response to injury or disease, resulting in a condition of swelling, pain, heat, and redness. (page 484)

Ingrown toenail A condition in which the nail pushes into the skin on the side of the toe. (page 374)

Inhalant Any substance whose fumes are sniffed and inhaled to produce mind-altering sensations. (page 354)

Inhibition A conscious or unconscious restraint on his or her behaviors or actions. (page 289)

Insulin (IN·suh·lin) A protein made in the pancreas that regulates the level of glucose in the blood. (page 522)

Integrity The quality of doing what you know is right. (page 33)

Intervention A gathering in which family and friends get the problem drinker to agree to seek help. (page 296)

Intimidation Purposely frightening another person through threatening words, looks, or body language. (page 185)

Intoxication Physically and mentally impaired by the use of alcohol. (page 283)

Iris The colored part of the eye. (page 377)

Joint The point at which two bones meet. (page 406)

Kidneys Organs that filter water and dissolved wastes from the blood and help maintain proper levels of water and salts in the body. (page 430)

Labeling Name-calling. (page 158)

Landfills Huge pits where wastes are dumped and buried. (page 579)

Larynx (LA·ringks) The upper part of the respiratory system, which contains the vocal cords. (page 419)

Lens A clear flexible structure of the eye that focuses light on the retina. (page 377)

Lifestyle factors Behaviors and habits that help determine a person's level of health and wellness. (page 13)

Ligaments (LI·guh·ments) Strong cords of tissue that connect the bones in each joint. (page 406)

Limits Invisible boundaries that protect you. (page 118)

Liver A large gland that has many digestive functions. (page 429)

Lymphatic (lim·FA·tik) **system** A secondary circulatory system that helps the body fight pathogens and maintain its fluid balance. (page 485)

Lymphocytes (LIM·fuh·sytes) White blood cells in the lymphatic system. (page 485)

Mainstream smoke Smoke that is exhaled by a smoker. (page 320)

Major depression A very serious mood disorder in which people lose interest in life and can no longer find enjoyment in anything. (page 83)

Malignant (muh·LIG·nuhnt) Cancerous. (page 512)

Malnutrition A condition in which the body doesn't get the nutrients it needs to grow and function properly. (page 285)

Managed care An arrangement that saves money by limiting the choice of doctors to patients who are members. (page 391)

Marijuana Dried leaves and flowers of the hemp plant, called *Cannabis sativa*. (page 338)

Marrow A soft tissue in the center of some bones. (page 405)

Media Various methods for communicating information. (page 41)

Mediation A process in which a third person, a mediator, helps those in conflict find a solution. (page 165)

Medicines Drugs that are used to treat or prevent diseases and other conditions. (page 383)

Menstrual (MEN·stroo·uhl) **cycle** Hormonal changes that occur in females from the beginning of one menstruation to the next. (page 439)

Menstruation (men·stroo·AY·shuhn) Lining material, the unfertilized egg, and some blood flow out of the body. (page 439)

Mental and emotional health The ability to accept oneself and others, adapt to and cope with emotions, and deal with the problems and challenges one meets in life. (page 6)

Methamphetamine A stimulant similar to amphetamine. (page 349)

Minerals Elements needed in small quantities for forming healthy bones and teeth, and for regulating certain body processes. (page 240)

Mixed message A situation in which your words say one thing but your body language says another. (page 109)

Mob mentality Acting or behaving in a certain and often negative manner because others are doing it. (page 162)

Mononucleosis (mahn·oh·noo·klee·OH·sis) A viral disease characterized by a severe sore throat and swelling of the lymph glands in the neck and around the throat area. (page 489)

Mood disorder A disorder in which a person undergoes changes in mood that seem inappropriate or extreme. (page 83)

Muscle endurance The measure of a muscle's ability to repeatedly exert a force over a prolonged period of time. (page 211)

Muscle strength The most weight you can lift or the most force you can exert at one time. (page 211)

Muscular system The group of structures that make your body parts move. (page 409)

MyPyramid food guidance system A system designed to help Americans make healthful food choices. (page 243)

Narcotics Specific drugs that are obtainable only by prescription and are used to relieve pain. (page 345)

Negative peer pressure Pressure you feel to go along with harmful behaviors or beliefs of others your age. (page 323)

Neglect The failure to meet a person's basic physical and emotional needs. (page 190)

Nervous system The body's message and control center. (page 422)

Neurons (NOO·rahnz) Specialized nerve cells. (page 423)

Nicotine An addictive drug found in tobacco leaves and in all tobacco products. (page 308)

Nicotine replacement therapies (NRT) Products that assist a person in breaking a tobacco habit. (page 317)

Noncommunicable diseases Diseases that are not spread from person to person. (page 508)

Nonrenewable resources Substances that cannot be replaced once they are used. (page 582)

Nutrient deficiency A shortage of a nutrient. (page 236)

Nutrient density The amount of nutrients relative to the number of calories they provide. (page 250)

Nutrients Substances in food that your body needs. (page 235)

Nutrition The study of nutrients and how the body uses them. (page 235)

Obese Weighing more than 20 percent higher than what is appropriate for their height, age, and body frame. (page 267)

Obstetrician (ahb·stuh·TRI·shuhn) Doctor who specializes in the care of a pregnant female and her developing fetus, and who is present at the birth of the baby. (page 457)

Opium A liquid from the poppy plant containing substances that numb the body. (page 345)

Opportunistic infection An infection that rarely occurs in a healthy person. (page 496)

Organ Body part that performs a particular function. (page 451)

Orthodontist (or·thuh·DAHN·tist) A dentist who prevents or corrects problems with the alignment or spacing of teeth. (page 376)

Osteoarthritis (ahs·tee·oh·ahr·THRY·tuhs) A chronic disease that is characterized by the breakdown of the cartilage in joints. (page 524)

Over-the-counter (OTC) medicines Medicines that are safe enough to be taken without a written order from a physician. (pages 335 and 384)

Overweight More than the appropriate weight for gender, height, age, body frame, and growth pattern. (page 263)

Ovulation The release of one mature egg cell each month. (page 439)

Ozone layer A shield above the earth's surface that protects living things from ultraviolet (UV) radiation. (page 578)

Pacemaker A small device that sends steady electrical impulses to the heart to make it beat regularly. (page 520)

Pancreas An organ that produces enzymes that assist in digestion. (page 429)

Panic A feeling of sudden, intense fear. (page 59)

Passive A tendency to give up, give in, or back down without standing up for your rights and needs. (page 116)

Passive smoker A nonsmoker who breathes in secondhand smoke. (page 320)

Pathogens Disease-causing organisms that are so small they can only be seen through a microscope. (page 478)

Peers People in the same age group. (page 12)

Peer pressure The influence to go along with the beliefs and actions of other people of your age. (page 105)

Peripheral nervous system (PNS) The nerves that connect the central nervous system to all parts of the body. (page 423)

Personality The unique combination of feelings, thoughts, and behavior that makes one person different from everyone else. (page 53)

Personality disorder A psychological condition that affects a person's ability to interact normally with others. (page 82)

Pesticides Products used on crops to control insects and other pests. (page 577)

Phobia Intense and exaggerated fear of a specific situation or object. (page 81)

Physical activity Any kind of movement that uses up energy. (page 204)

Physical dependence A type of addiction in which the body feels a direct need for a drug. (pages 292 and 316)

Physical fitness The ability to handle the physical demands of everyday life without becoming overly tired. (page 206)

Pituitary gland A gland that signals other endocrine glands to produce hormones when needed. (page 434)

Placenta (pluh·SEN·tuh) A thick, rich tissue that lines the walls of the uterus during pregnancy and that nourishes the fetus. (page 453)

Plaque (PLAK) A soft, colorless, sticky film containing bacteria that forms on teeth. (page 375)

Pneumonia A serious inflammation of the lungs. (page 491)

Point-of-sale promotion Advertising campaigns in which a product is promoted at a store's checkout counter. (page 324)

Pollen A powdery substance released by the flowers of some plants. (page 527)

Pollution Any dirty or harmful substance in the environment. (page 577)

Precautions Planned actions taken before an event to increase the chances of a safe outcome. (page 15)

Precycling Reducing waste before it occurs. (page 584)

Prejudice An opinion or fear formed without having facts or firsthand knowledge. (pages 34 and 158)

Prenatal (pree·NAY·tuhl) **care** Steps taken to provide for the health of a pregnant female and her baby. (page 457)

Preschoolers Children between the ages of three and five. (page 462)

Prescription medicines Medicines that can be sold only with a written order from a physician. (pages 335 and 383)

Prevention Taking steps to keep something from happening or getting worse. (page 15)

Preventive care Steps taken to keep disease or injury from happening or getting worse. (page 388)

P.R.I.C.E. formula Protect, rest, ice, compress, and elevate. (page 224)

Proteins Nutrients your body uses to build, repair, and maintain cells and tissues. (page 240)

Protozoa (proh·tuh·ZOH·uh) Single-celled organisms that are more complex than bacteria. (page 479)

Psychiatrist (sy·KY·uh·trist) A medical doctor who treats mental health problems. (page 93)

Psychological dependence An addiction in which the mind sends the body a message that it needs more of a drug. (page 316)

Psychologist (sy·KAH·luh·jist) A mental health professional who is trained and licensed by the state to perform therapy. (page 93)

Puberty The time when you start developing physical characteristics of adults of your gender. (pages 9 and 463)

Public health Involves efforts to monitor and promote the welfare of the population. (page 392)

Pupil The dark opening in the center of the iris. (page 377)

Radiation therapy A treatment that uses X rays or other forms of radiation to kill cancer cells. (page 514)

Rape Any kind of sexual intercourse against a person's will. (page 181)

Reaction time The ability of the body to respond quickly and appropriately to situations. (page 282)

Recall An announcement that informs the public that a product has been determined unsafe. (page 393)

Recovery The process of learning to live an alcohol-free life. (page 297)

Recurrence The return of cancer after a remission. (page 515)

Refusal skills Communication strategies that help you say no effectively. (pages 40 and 115)

Relapse A return to the use of a drug after attempting to stop. (pages 296 and 318)

Relationships The connections you have with other people and groups in your life. (page 102)

Remission A period during which cancer signs and symptoms disappear. (page 515)

Reproductive (ree·pruh·DUHK·tiv) **system** The organs that make possible the production of offspring. (page 437)

Resilience The ability to bounce back from disappointment. (page 55)

Respiration The exchange of gases between your body and the air. (page 418)

Respiratory system The organs that provide the body with a continuous supply of oxygen and rid the body of carbon dioxide. (page 418)

Resting heart rate The number of times your heart beats per minute when you are relaxing. (page 219)

Retina (RE·tin·uh) A thin layer of nerve cells in the eye that absorb light. (page 377)

Revenge Punishment, injury, or insult to the person seen as the cause of the strong emotion. (page 161)

Rheumatoid (ROO·muh·toyd) **arthritis** A chronic disease characterized by pain, inflammation, swelling, and stiffness of the joints. (page 525)

Risk behaviors Actions or behaviors that might cause injury or harm to yourself or others. (page 14)

Risk factors Characteristics or behaviors that increase a person's chances of developing a disease. (page 513)

Role A part you play when you interact with another person. (page 131)

Saliva (suh·LY·vuh) Fluid produced by the salivary glands. (page 428)

Saturated fats Fats that are solid at room temperature. (page 240)

Schizophrenia (skit·zoh·FREE·nee·uh) A severe mental disorder in which a person loses contact with reality. (page 85)

Secondhand smoke Environmental tobacco smoke (ETS). (page 320)

Sedentary lifestyle A way of life that includes little physical activity. (page 15)

Self-concept The view you have of yourself. (page 54)

Self-esteem The way you feel about yourself, and how you value yourself. (page 55)

Sexual abuse When a person forces another person to participate in a sexual act against his or her will. (page 190)

Sexual harassment Uninvited and unwelcome sexual conduct directed at another person. (page 191)

Sexually transmitted diseases (STDs) Infections spread from person to person through sexual contact. (page 492)

Shock A life-threatening condition in which the circulatory system fails to deliver enough blood to vital tissues and organs. (page 567)

Side effect Any effect of a medicine other than the one intended. (pages 335 and 386)

Sidestream smoke Smoke given off by the burning end of a cigarette, cigar, or pipe. (page 320)

Single-parent family A family made up of one parent plus a child or children. (page 135)

Skeletal muscles Muscle attached to bones that enables you to move your body. (page 410)

Skeletal system An internal body system made up of bones, joints, and connective tissue. (page 404)

Small intestine A coiled, tubelike digestive organ that is about 20 feet long. (page 429)

Smog A yellow-brown haze that forms when sunlight reacts with air pollution. (page 578)

Smokeless tobacco Ground tobacco that is chewed or inhaled through the nose. (page 310)

Smooth muscles The muscles found in organs, blood vessels, and glands. (page 410)

Social age Age measured by your lifestyle and the connections you have with others. (page 468)

Social health Your ability to get along with the people around you. (page 131)

Sodium A nutrient that helps control the amount of fluid in your body. (page 246)

Somatic (soh·MA·tik) **system** The part of the nervous system that deals with actions that you control. (page 424)

Specialist Doctor trained to handle particular kinds of patients or medical conditions. (page 389)

Sperm Male sex cells. (page 437)

Sperm cell The cell from the male that enters the egg cell during fertilization. (page 450)

Sprain A condition in which the ligaments that hold the joints in position are stretched or torn. (page 559)

Stimulants (STIM·yuh·luhnts) Drugs that speed up activity in the human brain and spinal cord. (page 348)

Strep throat A sore throat caused by streptococcal bacteria. (page 491)

Stress Your body's response to change. (pages 43 and 63)

Stressor Anything that causes stress. (page 64)

Stroke A condition in which a blood vessel bringing oxygen to the brain bursts or is blocked. (page 519)

Subcutaneous (suhb·kyoo·TAY·nee·uhs) **layer** The innermost layer of skin. (page 373)

Suicide The intentional taking of one's own life. (page 86)

Sympathetic (simp·uh·THET·ik) Aware of how you may be feeling at a given moment. (page 103)

Syphilis (SIH·fuh·luhs) A bacterial STD that can affect many parts of the body. It is a very serious STD. (page 494)

T

Tar A dark, thick, oily liquid that forms when tobacco burns. (page 309)

Target heart rate The range of numbers between which your heart and lungs receive the most benefit from a workout. (page 219)

Tartar A hard coating on the teeth that is difficult to remove. (page 375)

Tendons Tough bands of tissue that attach muscles to bones. (page 406)

THC The main active chemical in marijuana. (page 338)

Therapy An approach that teaches you different ways of thinking or behaving. (page 91)

Time management Strategies for using time efficiently. (page 67)

Tissues Groups of similar cells that perform a specific function. (page 451)

Toddlers Children between the ages of one and three who are learning to walk and talk. (page 462)

Tolerance The ability to accept other people as they are. (pages 34 and 132)

Tolerance A condition in which a person's body becomes used to the effect of a medicine or drug, and needs greater amounts of it in order for it to be effective. (pages 292, 316, and 335)

Tornado A whirling, funnel-shaped windstorm that may drop from the sky to the ground. (page 551)

Trachea (TRAY·kee·uh) Windpipe that directs air to the lungs. (page 419)

Traumatic brain injury (TBI) A condition caused by the brain being jarred and striking the inside of the skull. (page 425)

Trichomoniasis (TREE·koh·moh·NI·ah·sis) An STD caused by the protozoan *Trichomonas vaginalis*. (page 493)

Tuberculosis (too·ber·kyuh·LOH·sis) **(TB)** A bacterial disease that usually affects the lungs. (page 491)

Tumor A mass of abnormal cells. (page 511)

Type 1 diabetes A condition in which the immune system attacks insulin-producing cells in the pancreas. (page 523)

Type 2 diabetes A condition in which the body cannot effectively use the insulin it produces. (page 523)

 U

Umbilical (uhm·BIL·i·kuhl) **cord** A tube that connects the fetus and the mother's placenta. (page 453)

Unconditional love Love without limitation or qualification. (page 143)

Underweight Less than the appropriate weight for gender, height, age, body frame, and growth pattern. (page 263)

Universal precautions Actions taken to prevent the spread of disease by treating all blood as if it were contaminated. (page 555)

Unsaturated fats Fats that remain liquid at room temperature. (page 240)

Uterus (YOO·tuh·ruhs) A pear-shaped organ inside a female's body where a fetus is protected and nourished. (page 452)

 V

Vaccine A preparation of dead or weakened germs that causes the immune system to produce antibodies. (pages 384 and 486)

Values The beliefs and principles that guide the way a person lives. (page 28)

Vector An organism, such as an insect, that transmits a pathogen. (page 480)

Veins Blood vessels that carry blood from the body back to the heart. (page 415)

Victim Any individual who suffers injury, loss, or death due to violence. (page 180)

Violence Any act that causes physical or psychological harm to a person or damage to property. (page 176)

Viruses The smallest pathogens. (page 479)

Vitamins Substances that help your body fight infections and use other nutrients, among other jobs. (page 240)

Warm-up A period of low to moderate exercise to prepare your body for more vigorous activity. (page 219)

Warranty A written promise to refund your money if a product fails to work as claimed. (page 381)

Wellness A state of well-being, or total health. (page 6)

Win-win solution An agreement that gives each party something they want. (page 165)

Withdrawal The physical and psychological reactions that occur when someone stops using an addictive substance. (pages 297 and 317)

Withdrawal symptoms Symptoms that occur after chronic use of a drug is reduced or stopped. (page 346)

Zero tolerance policy A policy that makes no exceptions for anybody for any reason. (page 178)

Glosario

A

Abdominal thrusts/presiones abdominales
Presiones rápidas y hacia arriba que se hacen sobre el diafragma para forzar la salida de algo que esté bloqueando la vía respiratoria.

Abstinence/abstinencia Opción activa y consciente de no participar in comportamientos de alto riesgo.

Abuse/abuso Maltrato físico, emocional o mental de una persona a otra.

Accident/accidente Suceso que ocurre de manera no intencional.

Accident chain/accidente en cadena Serie de sucesos que incluye una situación, un hábito peligroso y un acto peligroso.

Accidental injuries/lesiones accidentales Lesiones que resultan de un accidente.

Accountability/responsabilidad Voluntad de responder de tus acciones y decisiones.

Acid rain/lluvia ácida Lluvia que es mucho más ácida de lo normal.

Acquired immunodeficiency syndrome (AIDS)/ síndrome de inmunodeficiencia adquirida (SIDA) Enfermedad mortal que interfiere con la habilidad natural del cuerpo de combatir infecciones.

Active listening/audición activa Oír el mensaje de otra persona, pensar en el mensaje y responder.

Adapt/adaptar Acostumbrarse a nuevas situaciones.

Addiction/adicción Necesidad física o psicológica de una droga.

Addictive/adictivo Capaz de ocasionar que el consumidor desarrolle una necesidad repentina intensa.

Adolescence/adolescencia Etapa de la vida entre la niñez y la edad adulta.

Adrenaline/adrenalina Hormona que proporciona energía adicional al cuerpo.

Advocacy/promoción Informa a otros sobre prácticas de salud y anima a comportamientos saludables.

Aerobic exercise/ejercicio aeróbico Actividad rítmica ininterrumpida de intensidad moderada a vigorosa que requiere grandes cantidades de oxígeno y hace que el corazón trabaje.

Affection/afecto Sentimiento de amor hacia otra persona.

Aggressive/agresivo(a) Excesivamente forzoso, hostil o de otra manera, que ataca durante el acercamiento.

Air Quality Index (AQI)/índice de calidad del aire Medida de ozono, dióxido de sulfuro, monoxido de carbono y finas partículas que hay cerca de a la tierra.

Alcohol/alcohol Droga producida por una reacción química en frutas, verduras y granos.

Alcohol abuse/abuso de alcohol Forma de consumo de alcohol que resulta en uno o más episodios en un periodo de doce meses.

Alcohol poisoning/intoxicación con alcohol Condición peligrosa que ocurre cuando una persona consume cantidades de alcohol excesivas en un corto periodo de tiempo.

Alcoholism/alcoholismo Enfermedad progresiva y crónica caracterizada por una necesidad mental y física de consumir alcohol.

Allergen/alergeno Sustancia que causa una reacción alérgica.

Allergy/alergia Sensibilidad extrema hacia una sustancia.

Allied health professionals/profesionales médicos aliados Profesionales médicos que desarrollan deberes que de otra manera serian desarrollados por doctores o enfermeras.

Alternatives/alternativas Diferentes maneras de pensar o actuar.

Alveoli/alvéolos Pequeños sacos de aire de los pulmones donde el dióxido de carbono es intercambiado por oxigeno.

Amino acids/aminoácidos Unidades pequeñas que forman las proteínas.

Amnesia/amnesia Pérdida total o parcial de la memoria.

Amphetamine/anfetamina Droga que estimula el sistema nervioso central.

Anabolic steroids/esteroides anabólicos Sustancia sintética relacionada con las hormonas sexuales masculinas.

Anaerobic exercise/ejercicio anaeróbico Actividad física intensa que requiere poco oxígeno pero exige breves brotes de energía.

Angioplasty/angioplastia Procedimiento quirúrgico en el cual un instrumento con un globo pequeño, un pequeño taladro, o láser es insertado en una arteria bloqueada para limpiar el bloqueo.

Anorexia nervosa/anorexia nerviosa Trastorno de la alimentación que se caracteriza por autoinanición conducente a una pérdida de peso extrema.

Antibiotics/antibióticos Medicinas que disminuyen o matan bacterias dañinas en el cuerpo.

Antibodies/anticuerpos Proteínas que se adhieren a los antígenos para prevenir que dañen al cuerpo.

Antigens/antígenos Sustancias que liberan los agentes patógenos.

Antihistamines/antihistamínicos Medicinas que ayudan a controlar los efectos que provocan las histaminas.

Anxiety/ansiedad Estado de intranquilidad, usualmente asociado con una incertidumbre futura.

Anxiety disorder/trastorno de ansiedad Trastorno en el cual la ansiedad intensa o el miedo impiden que una persona funcione de manera normal

Appetite/apetito Deseo psicológico de alimentarse.

Appropriate weight/peso apropiado Peso adecuado para tu cuerpo.

Arteries/arterias Vasos sanguíneos que llevan sangre desde el corazón a otras partes del cuerpo.

Arteriosclerosis/arteriosclerosis Conjunto de trastornos por el cual las arterias se endurecen y se tornan rígidas.

Arthritis/artritis Enfermedad de las articulaciones identificada con hinchazón dolorosa y rigidez.

Assault/asalto Amenaza ilegal o intento de lesión corporal hacia otra persona.

Assertive/firme Comportarte con seguridad y declarar claramente tus intenciones.

Asthma/asma Condición en la cual los pequeños pasajes de aire en los pulmones se encogen y dificultan la respiración.

Atherosclerosis/aterosclerosis Un tipo de arteriosclerosis por el cual sustancias grasas en la sangre se acumulan en las paredes de las arterias.

Attitude/actitud Sentimientos y creencias.

Autonomic system/sistema autonómico Sistema que envuelve las acciones que no controlas.

Bacteria/bacterias Organismos diminutos unicelulares que viven en casi todas partes.

Balance/equilibrio Sentimiento de estabilidad y control.

Battery/asalto Paliza, golpiza, o pateadura contra una persona ilegalmente.

Benign/benigno No es canceroso.

Binge/consumo compulsivo de drogas Cuando una droga es usada repetitivamente y en altas dosis que se incrementan.

Binge drinking/borrachera Consumo de cantidades grandes de alcohol en un período de tiempo muy corto.

Binge eating disorder/trastorno de la alimentación compulsiva Sentirse impulsado a comer demasiado.

Biodegradable/biodegradable Que se descompone fácilmente en el medio ambiente.

Biological age/edad biológica Medida de la edad, determinada según el funcionamiento de varias partes del cuerpo.

Biopsy/biopsia Extirpación de una muestra de tejido de una persona para ser examinado.

Birth defects/defecto de nacimiento Anormalidad presente al momento del nacimiento que causa incapacidad física o mental o la muerte.

Blended family/familia mezclada Familia que consiste en padre o madre, padrastro o madrastra y los hijos de uno o ambos padres.

Blizzard/ventisca Tormenta de nieve fuerte, con vientos que llegan a 45 millas por hora.

Blood alcohol content (BAC)/ concentración de alcohol en la sangre Cantidad de alcohol presente en el torrente sanguíneo de una persona.

Body composition/composición del cuerpo Proporción entre la grasa del cuerpo y los tejidos magros, tales como huesos, músculos y líquidos.

Body image/autoimagen La manera en que te ves a ti mismo.

Body language/lenguaje corporal Uso de movimientos corporales y gestos para comunicar un mensaje.

Body mass index (BMI)/índice de masa corporal Fórmula que puede ser utilizada para determinar si tu peso es el apropiado.

Bronchi/bronquios Pasajes a través de los cuales entra el aire en los pulmones.

Bronchodilators/broncodilatadores Medicinas que se usan para relajar los músculos que se han tensado alrededor de las vías respiratorias.

Bulimia nervosa/bulimia Condición en la cual una persona come grandes cantidades de comida y se purga secretamente.

Bully/intimidar Alguien que molesta a individuos que son más pequeños o más débiles.

Calorie/caloría Unidad de calor que mide la energía disponible en los alimentos.

Cancer/cáncer Enfermedad que se caracteriza por el desarrollo rápido e incontrolable de células anormales.

Capillaries/vasos capilares Conductos minúsculos que llevan sangre desde las arterias a las células del cuerpo y de regreso a las venas.

Carbohydrates/hidratos de carbono Azúcares y almidones que le proporcionan a tu cuerpo la mayor parte de su energía.

Carbon monoxide/monóxido de carbono Gas incoloro, inodoro y tóxico que se produce al quemarse el tabaco.

Carcinogens/carcinógenos Sustancias que causan el cáncer.

Cardiac muscle/músculo cardiaco Músculo de las paredes del corazón.

Cardiopulmonary resuscitation (CPR)/ resucitación cardiopulmonar Procedimiento de primeros auxilios que combina la respiración de rescate y compresiones sobre el pecho para restaurar la respiración y la circulación.

Cardiovascular disease/enfermedad cardiovascular Enfermedad del corazón y de los vasos sanguíneos.

Cardiovascular system/sistema cardiovascular Órganos y tejidos que transportan materia esencial a las células del cuerpo y eliminan los desechos.

Carrier/portador Persona que parece saludable pero está infectada con el VIH y puede transmitirlo a otros.

Cartilage/cartílago Tejido fuerte y flexible que amortigua las articulaciones.

Cell respiration/respiración celular Proceso en el cual las células del cuerpo se nutren y energizan.

Central nervous system (CNS)/sistema nervioso central Cerebro y médula espinal.

Cervix/cuello del útero Entrada del útero o matriz.

Character/carácter Manera en la que una persona piensa, siente y actúa.

Character trait/rasgo del carácter Cualidad que demuestra la manera en que una persona piensa, siente y actúa.

Chemotherapy/quimioterapia Uso de medicinas poderosas para destruir células cancerosas.

Chlamydia/clamidia Enfermedad bacteriana trasmitida sexualmente que afecta los órganos reproductivos, uretra y ano.

Chromosomes/cromosomas Estructuras filiformes dentro del núcleo de las células que contienen los códigos de las características hereditarias.

Chronic diseases/enfermedades crónicas
Enfermedades que están siempre presentes o reaparecen repetidamente durante un largo período de tiempo.

Chronic obstructive pulmonary disease (COPD)/inflamación pulmonar crónica
Condición en la cual los pasajes de los pulmones se hinchan e irritan, y eventualmente pierden su elasticidad.

Chronological age/edad cronológica Edad medida en años.

Circulatory system/aparato circulatorio
Órganos y tejidos que transportan materias esenciales a las células del cuerpo y se llevan sus desechos.

Cirrhosis/cirrosis Enfermedad caracterizada por la cicatrización y eventualmente la destrucción del hígado.

Citizenship/civilidad Forma en que te comportas como miembro de una comunidad.

Clinical social worker (CSW)/trabajador social clínico Profesional en salud mental licenciado y certificado en trabajo social.

Clique/camarilla Grupo de amigos que salen juntos y que se comportan de manera similar.

CNS depressants/depresores del SNC
Sustancias que hacen que las funciones corporales sean más lentas, incluyendo el corazón y la respiración.

Cold turkey/parar en seco Expresión que se usa para describir la acción de abandonar un vicio de una vez, por ejemplo, el fumar.

Colon/colon Intestino grueso.

Commitment/compromiso Promesa o voto.

Communicable disease/enfermedad contagiosa Enfermedad que se puede propagar de una persona a otra persona, un animal o un objeto.

Communication/comunicación Intercambio de ideas, sentimientos y creencias entre dos o más personas.

Community service/servicio comunitario
Programas voluntarios desarrollados con la meta de mejorar la comunidad y la vida de los residentes.

Comparison shopping/comparación de productos Método de evaluar los beneficios de diferentes productos y servicios al medir y comparar varios factores, tales como la calidad, las características y el precio.

Compromise/compromiso Acuerdo en el cual los dos lados renuncian a algo para alcanzar una solución satisfactoria.

Conditioning/acondicionamiento Actividad regular y ejercicios que preparan a una persona para algún deporte.

Conflict/conflicto Desacuerdo entre personas con puntos de vista, ideas o metas opuestos.

Conflict resolution/habilidades de solución de conflictos Habilidad que implica el hecho de resolver un desacuerdo satisfaciendo a los dos lados.

Congenital disorders/desordenes congénitos
Todos los desórdenes que se presentan cuando el bebé nace.

Consequences/consecuencias Resultados o efectos que pueden ocurrir como resultado de una decisión o un acto.

Conservation/conservación Ahorro de recursos.

Consumer/consumidor Persona que compra bienes o servicios.

Consumer skills/habilidades del consumidor
Técnicas que te permiten hacer compras inteligentes e informadas.

Contagious period/periodo de contagio Período de tiempo en que una enfermedad se puede propagar de una persona a otra.

Cooldown/recuperación Período en el que se realizan ejercicios de intensidad baja a moderada a fin de preparar al cuerpo para terminar una serie de ejercicios vigorosos.

Coordination/coordinación Funcionamiento conjunto de los músculos y los huesos de manera eficiente y sin complicaciones.

Coping strategies/estrategias de superación
Formas de tratar con el sentido de pérdida que las personas sienten cuando alguien cercano fallece.

Cornea/córnea Tejido transparenle del ojo que dirige la luz.

Crisis hot line/línea de reporte de crisis Servicio telefónico sin pago en cual las víctimas de abusos pueden recibir ayuda e información.

Cross-training/entrenamiento variado Cambiar de un ejercicio físico a otro.

Cumulative risks/riesgos acumulativos Riesgos relacionados cuyos efectos aumentan con cada uno que se añade.

Cuticle/cutícula Doblez de epidermis alrededor de las uñas de los pies y las manos.

Cycle of abuse/ciclo de abuso Patrón de repetición del abuso de una generación a la siguiente.

Dandruff/caspa Escamas de piel muerta en la superficie del cuero cabelludo.

Decibel/decibel Medida del volumen del sonido.

Decision making/toma de decisiones Proceso de hacer una selección o de hallar una solución.

Defensive driving/conducir de manera defensiva Estar atento a las otras personas en la carretera y anticipar acciones peligrosas.

Degenerative diseases/enfermedades degenerativas Enfermedades que causan la destrucción progresiva de las células, tejidos y órganos del cuerpo a medida que avanzan.

Dehydration/deshidratación Condición causada por pérdida excesiva de agua.

Depressants/sedantes Drogas que hacen que las funciones corporales y las reacciones sean lentas.

Dermatologist/dermatólogo Médico que trata trastornos de la piel.

Dermis/dermis Capa gruesa e interna de la piel.

Detoxification/desintoxicación Proceso físico de liberar al cuerpo de una sustancia adictiva.

Developmental tasks/tareas requeridas para el desarrollo Sucesos que deben ocurrir para que continúes desarrollándote hasta llegar a convertirte en un adulto saludable y maduro.

Diabetes/diabetes Enfermedad que impide que el cuerpo convierta los alimentos en energía.

Diaphragm/diafragma Músculo en forma de domo que separa los pulmones del abdomen.

Digestion/digestión Proceso de convertir los alimentos que comes en sustancias que tu cuerpo pueda usar.

Digestive system/aparato digestivo Sistema de órganos que convierten los alimentos en una forma útil para el cuerpo.

Disease/enfermedad Cualquier condición que interfiere con el funcionamiento propio del cuerpo o la mente.

Disorder/desorden Desequilibrio en el funcionamiento normal de una parte del cuerpo.

Divorce/divorcio Fin legal de un contrato matrimonial.

Domestic violence/violencia doméstica Abuso físico que ocurre dentro de una familia.

Driving while intoxicated (DWI)/manejar en estado de ebriedad Persona que maneja un auto con una concentración de alcohol en la sangre de 0/08% o mayor.

Drug/drogas Sustancias, que no sean alimentos, que cambian la estructura o el funcionamiento del cuerpo o la mente.

Drug abuse/abuso de drogas Uso intencional de drogas en forma no saludable o ilegal.

Drug free/libre de drogas Características de una persona que no consume drogas ilícitas, o establecimiento donde no se consumen drogas.

Drug misuse/mal empleo de drogas Tomar o usar medicinas en una forma diferente a la indicada.

Drug trafficking/tráfico de drogas Compra o venta de drogas.

Earthquake/terremoto Sacudimiento violento de la superficie de la tierra.

Eating disorder/trastorno de la alimentación Costumbre en la alimentación por la cual una persona come de manera extrema y nociva y que puede causar enfermedades y aun la muerte.

Egg cell/óvulo Célula reproductora femenina que se une con el espermatozoide para crear una nueva vida.

Embryo/embrión Organismo en desarrollo desde la fecundación hasta aproximadamente la octava semana del desarrollo.

Emotional needs/necesidades emocionales
Necesidades que afectan los sentimientos y el
bienestar de una persona.

Emotions/emociones Sentimientos que surgen
en respuesta a pensamientos, comentarios y
sucesos.

Empathy/empatía Habilidad de entender y
compartir los sentimientos de otra persona.

Empty-calorie foods/comidas sin valor calórico
Comidas que ofrecen pocos nutrientes pero sí
contienen calorías.

Enablers/habilitadores Personas que crean
una atmósfera en la cual el alcohólico puede
continuar su comportamiento inaceptable de
una forma cómoda.

Endocrine system/sistema endocrino Sistema
químico de comunicaciones del cuerpo que
regula varias funciones.

Environment/medio Suma total de lo que rodea
a una persona.

**Environmental Protection Agency (EPA)/
Agencia de Protección Ambiental** Agencia
del gobierno de Estados Unidos a cargo de la
protección del medio ambiente.

Enzymes/enzimas Proteínas que afectan varios
procesos corporales.

Epidermis/epidermis Capa visible y más externa
de la piel.

Epiglottis/epiglotis Pliegue de tejido que cubre
la tráquea cuando tragas.

Escalate/intensificar Llegar a ser más grave.

Euphoria/euforia Sentimiento de bienestar
o regocijo.

Excretion/excreción Proceso de eliminar
desechos del cuerpo.

Excretory system/sistema excretor Sistema del
cuerpo que elimina desechos del cuerpo.

Exercise/ejercicio Actividad física planeada
hecha para mantener el estado físico.

Extended family/familia extensa Familia
nuclear y otros parientes tales como abuelos,
tías, tíos y primos.

Family/familia Unidad básica de la sociedad,
incluye 2 o más personas relacionadas por
sangre, matrimonio, adopción o deseo de
apoyo mutuo.

Family therapy/terapia familiar Asesoramiento
cuyo propósito es mejorar relaciones
problemáticas entre familiares.

Famine/hambre Falta general de alimentos.

Fatty liver/hígado adiposo Condición en la
cual la grasa se forma en el hígado y no puede
ser deshecha.

Fertilization/fertilización Unión de un
espermatozoide y un óvulo.

**Fetal alcohol syndrome (FAS)/síndrome de
alcoholismo fetal** Conjunto de defectos
de nacimiento causados por el alcohol que
incluyen problemas físicos y mentales.

Fetus/feto Organismo en desarrollo desde el
final de la octava semana del embarazo hasta
el momento del nacimiento.

Fiber/fibra Parte de las frutas, verduras, granos y
frijoles que tu cuerpo no puede dirigir.

**Fight-or-flight response/respuesta de lucha o
huída** Proceso mediante el cual el cuerpo se
prepara a enfrentarse con un factor estresante.

First aid/primeros auxilios Cuidado inmediato y
temporal que se le proporciona a una persona
herida o enferma hasta que reciba ayuda
profesional.

F.I.T.T. principle/principio FITT Método
mediante el cual es posible incrementar con
seguridad aspectos del ejercicio sin hacerte
daño a ti mismo.

Flexibility/flexibilidad Habilidad de mover las
articulaciones del cuerpo con facilidad a través
del arco completo de movimiento.

**Foodborne illness/enfermedad producida por
un alimento** Enfermedad que proviene de
haber comido un alimento no sano.

Fracture/fractura Rotura de un hueso.

Fraud/fraude Engaño o deliberado.

Fungi/hongos Organismos que son más complejos
que las bacterias pero no pueden hacer su
propio alimento.

G

Gallbladder/vesícula biliar Pequeño órgano en forma de bolsa que almacena bilis.

Gang/pandilla Grupo en el cual los miembros usan violencia para ser parte de actividades criminales.

Gender discrimination/discriminación sexual Distinguir o excluir a personas de acuerdo con su sexo.

Genes/genes Unidades básicas de la herencia.

Genetic disorder/trastorno genético Trastorno causado parcial o totalmente por defectos en los genes.

Genital herpes/herpes genital Enfermedad viral de transmisión sexual que produce dolorosas heridas en el área genital.

Genital warts/verrugas genitales Crecimiento o hinchazón in el área genital causada por algún tipo de papilomavirus (HPV).

Germs/gérmenes Organismos que causan enfermedades y que son tan pequeños que sólo pueden ser vistos a través de microscopios.

Gingivitis/gingivitis Trastorno común que se caracteriza por el enrojecimiento y dolor de las encías que sangran con facilidad.

Gland/glándula Grupo de células, o un órgano que secreta una sustancia química.

Global warming/calentamiento del planeta Aumento en las temperaturas de la Tierra.

Goal setting/establecer metas Proceso de esforzarte para lograr algo que quieres.

Gonorrhea/gonorrea Enfermedad bacteriana transmitida sexualmente que afecta la membrana mucosa del cuerpo, particularmente el área genital.

Greenhouse effect/efecto invernadero Retención del calor por la presencia de dióxido de carbono y otros gases en el aire.

Grief/pena Pesar provocado por la muerte de un ser querido.

Grief reaction/reacción a la desgracia Proceso de tratar con sentimientos fuertes que se ocasionan por alguna pérdida.

H

Hallucinogens/alucinógenos Drogas que alteran el estado de ánimo, los pensamientos y los sentidos.

Hangnail/padrastro Grieta en la cutícula al lado del borde de la uña.

Harassment/acoso Conducta frecuente que ofende a otra persona con críticas sobre su raza, color, religión, incapacidad física o sexo.

Hazardous wastes/desechos peligrosos Desechos líquidos o sólidos generados por los seres humanos, que pueden perjudicar la salud de las personas o el medio ambiente.

Health/salud Una combinación de bienestar físico, mental/emocional y social.

Health care system/sistema de cuidado de la salud Servicios médicos disponibles para la gente de una nación y las formas en las cuales éstos son pagados.

Health fraud/fraude médico Venta de productos o servicios para prevenir enfermedades o curar problemas de salud que no han sido aprobados científicamente o hechos efectivos para ese uso.

Health insurance/seguro médico Plan en el que las compañías privadas o los programas del gobierno pagan una parte de los gastos médicos de una persona.

Heart and lung endurance/resistencia del corazón y los pulmones Medida de qué tan eficientemente trabajan tu corazón y tus pulmones cuando haces ejercicios y qué tan rápido regresan a lo normal cuando paras.

Heart attack/ataque cardiaco Afección en la cual el flujo de sangre a una parte del corazón está considerablemente reducido u obstruido

Heat cramps/calambres debido al calor Dolorosos espasmos involuntarios de los músculos que pueden ocurrir al realizar ejercicio vigoroso cuando hace mucho calor.

Heat exhaustion/agotamiento por calor Recalentamiento del cuerpo que puede dar como resultado una deshidratación.

Heatstroke/insolación Tipo de enfermedad debido al calor grave en que los procesos normales del cuerpo que controlan los efectos del calor dejan de funcionar.

Hepatitis/hepatitis Enfermedad viral del hígado que se caracteriza por el color amarillo de la piel y del blanco de los ojos.

Heredity/herencia Transferencia de características de los padres a sus hijos.

Hernia/hernia Órgano interno que está empujando contra o a través de la pared de una cavidad.

High blood pressure/presión arterial alta Afección en la que la presión arterial de una persona se mantiene a un nivel más alto de lo normal.

Histamines/histaminas Sustancias químicas del cuerpo que provocan los síntomas de una reacción alérgica.

HIV (Human Immunodeficiency Virus)/virus de inmunodeficiencia humana (VIH) Virus que causa el sida.

Hives/urticaria Granos en la piel que pican mucho.

Homicide/homicidio Acto en que una persona mata a otra.

Hormones/hormonas Sustancias químicas, producidas por glándulas que ayudan a regular varias funciones del cuerpo.

Hospice care/asistencia para enfermos desahuciados Asistencia para personas con enfermedades incurables que apunta a brindar comodidad, no a la cura.

Hunger/hambre Necesidad física de alimentos.

Hurricane/huracán Tormenta de vientos y lluvia torrencial que se origina en alta mar.

Hygiene/higiene Limpieza.

Hypertension/hipertensión Condición en la cual la presión de la sangre en las paredes de los vasos sanguíneos se mantiene a un nivel mas alto de lo normal.

"I" message Declaración que presenta una situación desde el punto de vista personal del que habla.

Immune system/sistema inmunológico Combinación de las defensas del cuerpo, compuesta de células, tejidos y órganos que combaten gérmenes patógenos y enfermedades.

Immunity/inmunidad Habilidad del cuerpo para resistir los agentes patógenos que causan enfermedades particulares.

Infancy/infancia Primer año de vida.

Infection/infección Afección que se produce cuando agentes patógenos invaden el cuerpo, se multiplican y dañan las células del cuerpo.

Inflammation/inflamación Reacción del cuerpo cuando ocurre un daño o enfermedad, resultando en hinchazón, dolor, calentamiento y enrojecimiento.

Ingrown toenail/uña encarnada Afección en la cual la uña se introduce en la piel al lado del dedo del pie.

Inhalant/inhalante Toda sustancia cuyos gases se aspiran para producir sensaciones alucinantes.

Inhibition/inhibición Reprimir comportamientos o acciones consciente o inconscientemente.

Insulin/insulina Proteína que es producida en el páncreas y que regula el nivel de glucosa en el cuerpo.

Integrity/integridad Cualidad de hacer lo que sabes que es correcto.

Intervention/intervención Reunión en la cual familia y amigos hacen que la persona con problemas alcohólicos busque ayuda.

Intimidation/intimidación Asustar a otra persona a propósito con palabras amenazantes, miradas o lenguaje corporal.

Intoxication/intoxicado Física y mentalmente afectado por el consumo de alcohol.

Iris/iris La parte coloreada del ojo.

Joint/articulación Lugares en donde se unen los huesos.

K

Kidneys/riñones Órganos que filtran el agua y los desechos disueltos de la sangre y contribuyen a mantener los niveles adecuados de agua y sales en el cuerpo.

L

Labeling/marcar Dar nombre.

Landfills/terraplenes sanitarios Pozos enormes donde se tiran y se entierran desechos.

Larynx/laringe Parte superior del aparato respiratorio que contiene las cuerdas vocales.

Lens/cristalino Estructura transparente y flexible del ojo que enfoca la luz en la retina.

Lifestyle factors/factores del estilo de vida Conductas y hábitos que ayudan a determinar el nivel de salud de una persona.

Ligaments/ligamentos Tejidos que parecen cables que conectan los huesos con cada articulación.

Limits/límites Barreras invisibles que te protegen.

Liver/hígado Glándula grande que tiene varias funciones digestivas.

Lymphatic system/sistema linfático Aparato circulatorio secundario que le ayuda al cuerpo a combatir los agentes patógenos y a mantener el equilibrio de los líquidos.

Lymphocytes/linfocitos Células blancas del sistema linfático.

M

Mainstream smoke/humo directo Humo que es inhalado por el fumador.

Major depression/depresión mayor Serio desorden del estado de ánimo en el cual las personas pierden interés en su vida y no encuentran placer en nada.

Malignant/maligno Tumor canceroso.

Malnutrition/desnutrición Afección en la que el cuerpo no recibe los nutrientes que necesita para crecer y funcionar de forma adecuada.

Managed care/cuidado controlado Arreglo que ahorra dinero limitando las opciones de los doctores a pacientes que son miembros.

Marijuana/mariguana Hojas y flores secas de la planta de cáñamo, llamada cannabis sativa.

Marrow/médula Tejido en el centro de algunos huesos.

Media/medios de difusión Diversos métodos de comunicar información.

Mediation/mediación Proceso en el cual una tercera persona, un mediador, ayuda a otros a encontrar una solución al conflicto entre ellos.

Medicines/medicinas Drogas que se usan para curar o prevenir enfermedades u otras afecciones.

Menstrual cycle/ciclo menstrual Cambio hormonal que ocurre en las mujeres desde el comienzo de una menstruación hasta el siguiente.

Menstruation/menstruación Material del recubrimiento uterino, óvulos no fertilizados y sangre que fluyen fuera del cuerpo.

Mental and emotional health/salud mental y emocional Capacidad de aceptarse a sí mismo y a otros, de adaptarse a las emociones y sobrellevarlas y de superar los problemas y retos de la vida.

Methamphetamine/metanfetamina Estimulantes parecidos a las anfetaminas.

Minerals/minerales Elementos que se necesitan en cantidades pequeñas para la formación de dientes y huesos saludables y para regular determinados procesos corporales.

Mixed message/mensaje contradictorio Situación en que tus palabras expresan algo pero tu lenguaje corporal lo contradice.

Mob mentality/mentalidad de movimiento Actuar o comportarse de cierta manera, normalmente maneras negativas, sólo porque otros lo están haciendo.

Mononucleosis/mononucleosis Enfermedad viral cuyos síntomas incluyen hinchazón y dolor en áreas del cuello y dolor de garganta.

Mood disorder/trastorno del ánimo humor Trastorno en que la persona cambía de humor de manera aparentemente inapropiada o extrema.

Muscle endurance/resistencia muscular Capacidad que tiene un músculo de ejercer una fuerza repetidamente durante un largo período de tiempo.

Muscle strength/fuerza muscular Medida del peso máximo que puedes cargar o fuerza máxima que puedes emplear a un mismo tiempo.

Muscular system/sistema muscular Grupo de estructuras que permiten el movimiento de las partes de tu cuerpo.

MyPyramid food guidance system/pirámide alimenticia Ayuda visual diseñada para ayudar a los americanos a tomar decisiones alimenticias saludables.

Narcotics/narcóticos Ciertas drogas específicas que se pueden obtener únicamente con receta médica y que se usan para aliviar el dolor.

Negative peer pressure/presión negativa de compañeros Presión que sientes de seguir comportamientos malos o creencias de otras personas de tu misma edad.

Neglect/abandono No satisfacer las necesidades básicas físicas y emocionales de una persona.

Nervous system/sistema nervioso Centro de mensajes y control del cuerpo.

Neurons/neuronas Células especializadas que componen el sistema nervioso.

Nicotine/nicotina Droga adictiva que se encuentra en las hojas del tabaco y en todos los productos del tabaco.

Nicotine replacement therapies (NRT)/terapias para remplazar la nicotina Productos que ayudan a las personas a romper el hábito del tabaco.

Noncommunicable diseases/enfermedades no contagiosas Enfermedades que no pueden ser pasadas de una persona a la otra.

Nonrenewable resources/recursos no renovables Sustancias que no se pueden reemplazar una vez que se han usado.

Nutrient deficiency/deficiencia nutricional Escasez de un nutriente.

Nutrient density/densidad de los nutrientes Cantidad de nutrientes comparados con las calorías que proporcionan.

Nutrients/nutrientes Sustancias de los alimentos que tu cuerpo necesita.

Nutrition/nutrición Ciencia que estudia las sustancias presentes en los alimentos y el modo en que el cuerpo las utilice.

Obese/obeso(a) Más del 20 por ciento del peso que es adecuado para tu estatura, edad y tipo de cuerpo.

Obstetrician/obstetra Médico especialista en el cuidado de la mujer embarazada y el feto en desarrollo y que está presente durante el nacimiento del bebé.

Opium/opio Líquido extraído de la planta de amapola que contiene sustancias que adormecen el cuerpo.

Opportunistic infection/infección oportunista Infección que ocurre raramente en personas saludables.

Organs/órganos Partes del cuerpo que cumplen funciones determinadas.

Orthodontist/ortodoncista Dentista que previene o corrige problemas del alineamiento o del espacio entre los dientes.

Osteoarthritis/osteoartritis Enfermedad que se caracteriza por el deterioro del cartílago de las articulaciones.

Over-the-counter (OTC) medicines/medicinas sin receta Medicinas inofensivas que se pueden consumir sin receta médica.

Overweight/sobrepeso Más del peso apropiado de acuerdo al sexo, estatura, edad, estructura corporal y ritmo de crecimiento.

Ovulation/ovulación Desprendimiento de un óvulo maduro cada mes.

Ozone layer/capa de ozono Capa protectora sobre la superficie de la Tierra que protege a los seres vivos de la radiación ultravioleta.

Pacemaker/marcapasos Pequeño aparato que envía pulsaciones eléctricas constantes al corazón para que los latidos sean regulares.

Pancreas/páncreas Órgano que produce enzimas que ayudan en la digestión.

Panic/pánico Sentimiento repentino de miedo intenso.

Passive/pasivo Tendencia a renunciar, dejar de lado, o hacerse atrás sin reclamar derechos o necesidades.

Passive smoker/fumador pasivo Persona no fumadora que respira el humo de segunda mano.

Pathogens/agentes patógenos Organismos microscópicos que causan enfermedades contagiosas.

Peers/compañeros Personas en grupos de la misma edad.

Peer pressure/presión de pares Influencia que personas de tu misma edad tienen sobre ti para que adoptes sus creeencias y forma de actuar.

Peripheral nervous system (PNS)/sistema nervioso periférico Nervios que conectan al sistema nervioso central con todas partes del cuerpo.

Personality/personalidad Combinación singular de sentimientos, pensamientos y conducta que hacen a una persona diferente de todas las demás.

Personality disorder/desorden de personalidad Condición sicológica que afecta la habilidad de una persona de actuar normalmente con otras.

Pesticides/pesticida Producto que se usa en las cosechas para matar insectos y otras plagas.

Phobia/fobia Miedo exagerado hacia una situación o objeto específico.

Physical activity/actividad física Todo movimiento que usa energía.

Physical dependence/dependencia física Adicción en que el cuerpo siente una necesidad directa de una droga.

Physical fitness/buen estado físico Capacidad de cumplir con las exigencias físicas de la vida diaria sin cansarse demasiado.

Pituitary gland/hipófisis Glándula que indica a otras glándulas endocrinas la necesidad de producir hormonas.

Placenta/placenta Tejido espeso y rico que cubre las paredes del útero o matriz durante el embarazo y que nutre al feto.

Plaque/placa bacteriana Película blanda, incolora y pegajosa que contiene bacterias y que se acumula en los dientes.

Pneumonia/neumonía Inflamación seria de los pulmones.

Point-of-sale promotion/punto de promoción de venta Campañas de publicidad en las cuales un producto puede adquirirse en la caja .

Pollen/polen Sustancia en polvo descargada por flores y otras plantas.

Pollution/contaminación Toda sustancia sucia o nociva en el medio ambiente.

Precautions/precauciones Acciones planeadas que son tomadas antes de un evento para incrementar seguridad.

Precycling/preciclaje Proceso de reducir los desechos antes de que se produzcan.

Prejudice/prejuicio Opinión negativa e injusta, generalmente en contra de personas de otro grupo racial, religioso o cultural.

Prenatal care/cuidado prenatal Medidas que se toman para cuidar de la salud de una mujer embarazada y su feto.

Preschoolers/niño en edad preescolar Niños de entre tres y cinco años de edad.

Prescription medicines/medicinas bajo receta Medicinas que sólo se pueden vender con receta de un médico.

Prevention/prevención Tomar acción para hacer que algo no pase o sea peor.

Preventive care/cuidado preventivo Medidas que se toman para evitar que ocurran enfermedades o daños o que empeoren.

P.R.I.C.E. Protege, descansa, hiela, comprime, y eleva.

Proteins/proteínas Nutrientes que el cuerpo usa para crear, reparar y mantener células y tejidos.

Protozoa/protozarios Organismos de una célula que son más complejos que las bacterias.

Psychiatrist/psiquiatra Médico que trata trastornos de la salud mental.

Psychological dependence/dependencia psicológica Adicción por la cual la mente envía un mensaje al cuerpo indicando que necesita mayor cantidad de una droga.

Psychologist/psicólogo Profesional de la salud mental que está licenciado por el estado para hacer terapias.

Puberty/pubertad Tiempo en el cual empiezas a desarrollar características físicas de adultos de tu mismo sexo.

Public health/salud pública Esfuerzos para comprobar y promover el bienestar de la población.

Pupil/pupila Abertura oscura en el centro del iris.

Radiation therapy/terapia de radiación Tratamiento que usa rayos X u otra forma de radiación para matar células cancerosas.

Rape/violación Todo tipo de relación sexual contra la voluntad de la persona.

Reaction time/tiempo de reacción Habilidad del cuerpo de responder rápidamente y apropiadamente a diferentes situaciones.

Recall/retirar del mercado Solicitud pública de un fabricante de devolver todos los productos que puedan tener defectos o estén contaminados.

Recovery/recuperación Proceso de aprender a vivir una vida libre de alcohol.

Recurrence/reaparición Regreso de cáncer después de una remisión.

Refusal skills/habilidades de rechazo Estrategias de la comunicación para ayudarte a decir que no de manera eficaz.

Relapse/recaída Regresar al uso de la droga después de haber intentado dejarla.

Relationships/relaciones Conexiones que tienes con otras personas o grupos en tu vida.

Remission/remisión Período durante el cual desaparecen las señales y síntomas del cáncer.

Reproductive system/aparato reproductor Órganos que posibilitan la producción de hijos.

Resilience/capacidad de recuperación Habilidad para adaptarse y recuperarse después de una decepción, dificultad o crisis.

Respiration/respiración Intercambio de gases entre el cuerpo y el aire.

Respiratory system/aparato respiratorio Órganos que proporcionan oxígeno continuamente al cuerpo y que eliminan el bióxido de carbono.

Resting heart rate/ritmo cardiaco de descanso Número de veces que el corazón late por minuto cuando estás relajado.

Retina/retina Capa delgada de neuronas en el ojo que absorben la luz.

Revenge/venganza Castigo, daño o insulto hacia una persona por causa de una emoción fuerte.

Rheumatoid arthritis/artritis reumatoide Enfermedad crónica que se caracteriza por dolor, inflamación, hinchazón y anquilosamiento de las articulaciones.

Risk behavior/conducta arriesgada Acto o conducta que puede causarte daño o perjudicarte a ti o a otros.

Risk factors/factores de riesgo Características o comportamientos que incrementan la posibilidad de desarrollar un desorden médico o enfermedad.

Role/papel Parte que tú desempeñas cuando actúas con otra persona.

Saliva/saliva Líquido producido por las glándulas salivales de la boca.

Saturated fats/grasas saturadas Grasas que son sólidas a la temperatura ambiente.

Schizophrenia/esquizofrenia Trastorno mental grave por el cual una persona pierde contacto con la realidad.

Secondhand smoke/humo secundario Humo de tabaco en el ambiente.

Sedentary lifestyle/estilo de vida sedentario Forma de vida que incluye poca actividad física.

Self-concept/autoconcepto Manera en que te ves a ti mismo.

Self-esteem/autoestima Opinión que tienes de ti mismo y cuánto te valoras.

Sexual abuse/abuso sexual Persona que fuerza a otra a participar en actos sexuales en contra de su voluntad.

Sexual harassment/acoso sexual Conducta sexual no solicitada y fuera de lugar dirigida a otra persona.

Sexually transmitted diseases (STDs)/enfermedades de transmisión sexual (ETS) Enfermedades que se propagan de una persona a otra a través del contacto sexual.

Shock/choque Afección que puede causar la muerte en la cual el aparato circulatorio no lleva la suficiente cantidad de sangre a los tejidos y órganos vitales.

Side effect/efecto secundario Todo efecto o reacción inesperada de una medicina.

Sidestream smoke/humo indirecto El humo producido por la colilla encendida de un cigarrillo, puro o pipa.

Single-parent family/familia de un solo padre Una familia constituida por sólo uno de los padres y un niño o más.

Skeletal muscles/músculo del sistema osteoarticular Músculo ligado a huesos que te permite mover el cuerpo.

Skeletal system/sistema osteoarticular Sistema corporal interno compuesto de huesos, articulaciones y tejidos conjuntivos.

Small intestine/intestino delgado Órgano digestivo enrollado y semejante a un tubo que mide unos 20 pies de largo.

Smog/smog Neblina de color amarillo-café que se forma cuando la luz solar reacciona con la contaminación del aire.

Smokeless tobacco/rapé Tabaco molido que es masticado o inhalado a través de la nariz.

Smooth muscles/músculo liso Tipo de músculo que se encuentra en los órganos, los vasos sanguíneos y las glándulas.

Social age/edad social Edad calculada de acuerdo con tu estilo de vida y las conexiones que tienes con los demás.

Social health/salud social Habilidad para llevarte bien con las personas que te rodean.

Sodium/sodio Nutriente que ayuda a controlar la cantidad de fluidos en el cuerpo.

Somatic system/sistema somático Parte del sistema nervioso relacionada con las acciones que tú controlas.

Specialist/especialista Médico que está capacitado para tratar determinada clase de pacientes o problemas de salud.

Sperm/espermatozoides Células reproductoras masculinas.

Sperm cell/espermatozoides Célula del padre que entra en el óvulo durante la fertilización.

Sprain/torcedura Afección en que los ligamentos que mantienen las articulaciones en su lugar están distendidos o quebrados.

Stimulants/estimulantes Drogas que aceleran la actividad en el cerebro humano y la médula espinal.

Strep throat/amigdalitis estreptocócica Dolor de garganta causado por estreptococos.

Stress/estrés Reacción de tu cuerpo a cambios.

Stressor/factor estresante Todo lo que provoca estrés.

Stroke/apoplejía Afección que ocurre cuando un vaso sanguíneo que lleva oxígeno al cerebro estalla o se obstruye.

Subcutaneous layer/capa subcutánea Capa de grasa debajo de la piel.

Suicide/suicidio Quitarse la vida intencionalmente.

Sympathetic/solidario Estar consciente de cómo te puedes estar sintiendo en un momento determinado.

Syphilis/sífilis Enfermedad bacteriana transmitida sexualmente que puede afectar varias partes del cuerpo. Es una enfermedad transmitida sexualmente muy seria.

T

Tar/alquitrán Líquido espeso, oscuro y pegajoso que se forma al quemarse el tabaco.

Target heart rate/ritmo cardiaco meta Distancia de números entre los cuales tu corazón y los pulmones reciben el mayor beneficio por el ejercicio.

Tartar/sarro Placa endurecida que se forma en la superficie de los dientes y que es difícil de quitar.

Tendons/tendones Bandas de tejidos fuertes que unen los músculos y los huesos.

THC Principio activo de la mariguana.

Therapy/terapia Enfoque que enseña una manera diferente de pensar o de comportarse.

Time management/organización del tiempo Estrategias para usar el tiempo eficazmente.

Tissues/tejidos Masa de células similares que desempeñan una función específica.

Toddlers/niño que empieza a andar Niño de entre uno y tres años de edad que está aprendiendo a caminar y a hablar.

Tolerance/tolerancia Habilidad de aceptar a otras personas de la forma que son.

Tolerance/tolerancia Afección por la cual el cuerpo de una persona se acostumbra a los efectos de una medicina y necesita mayor cantidad para que ésta sea eficaz.

Tornado/tornado Tormenta de viento en torbellino, con forma de embudo, que gira en grandes círculos y que puede caer del cielo a la tierra.

Trachea/tráquea Vía respiratoria que dirige el aire a los pulmones.

Traumatic brain injury (TBI)/daño cerebral traumático Condición causada por irritación de cerebro y es notable en el interior del cráneo.

Trichomoniasis/tricomoniasis Enfermedad transmitida sexualmente causada por tricomonas vaginalis.

Tuberculosis/tuberculosis (TB) Enfermedad bacteriana que normalmente afecta los pulmones.

Tumor/tumor Masa de células anormales.

Type 1 diabetes/diabetes tipo 1 Afección por la cual el sistema inmunológico ataca las células productoras de insulina en el páncreas.

Type 2 diabetes/diabetes tipo 2 Afección que se caracteriza por la inhabilidad del cuerpo para usar de manera eficaz la insulina que produce.

U

Umbilical cord/cordón umbilical Conducto que conecta el feto con la placenta de la madre.

Unconditional love/amor incondicional Amor sin restricciones ni reservas.

Underweight/de peso insuficiente Por debajo del peso apropiado de acuerdo con el sexo, estatura, edad, estructura corporal y ritmo de crecimiento.

Universal precautions/precauciones universales Medidas para prevenir la propagación de enfermedades al tratar toda la sangre como si estuviera contaminada.

Unsaturated fats/grasas no saturadas Grasas que permanecen líquidas a la temperatura ambiente.

Uterus/útero Matriz, órgano en forma de pera que se encuentra dentro del cuerpo de una mujer donde el embrión es protegido y alimentado.

V

Vaccine/vacuna Preparado de gérmenes muertos o debilitados que se inyecta en el cuerpo para hacer que el sistema immunólogico produzca anticuerpos.

Values/valores Creencias y principios que guían la vida de las personas.

Vector/vector Organismo, por ejemplo un insecto, que transmite un agente patógeno.

Veins/venas Vasos sanguíneos que llevan la sangre desde el cuerpo de regreso al corazón.

Victim/víctima Cualquier individuo que sufre algún daño, pérdida o muerte debido a la violencia.

Violence/violencia Cualquier comportamiento que cause daño físico o psicológico a una persona o daño a la propiedad.

Virus/virus El organismo más pequeño causante de enfermedades.

Vitamins/vitaminas Sustancias que ayudan al cuerpo a combatir infecciones y aportan otros nutrientes entre otras funciones.

Warm-up/precalentamiento Período de ejercicio suave que se hace para preparar al cuerpo para actividad más vigorosa.

Warranty/garantía Promesa de rembolsar el dinero pagado si es que el producto no funciona como lo anunciado.

Wellness/bienestar Estado de bienestar total.

Win-win solution/solución de ganancia doble Un acuerdo o resultado que da algo de lo que quieren a cada lado.

Withdrawal/abstinencia Reacciones físicas y psicológicas que ocurren cuando una persona deja de usar una sustancia adictiva.

Withdrawal symptoms/síndrome de abstinencia Síntomas que ocurren después que el uso crónico de una droga es reducido o suprimido.

Zero tolerance policy/normativa de tolerancia nula Normativa en que no hay excepciones para nadie por ninguna razón.

Index

Relapse, 296, 318
Relationships, 102–121. *See also*
    Social health
  and abstinence, 119–121
  abuse in, 188–191
  accepting individual
    differences in, 132
  alcohol and, 291
  changes during adolescence,
    10–12
  character as foundation for,
    132
  and cliques, 105
  dating, 106–107
  definition, 102
  differences among, 131
  effect of child abuse/neglect
    on, 190
  family, 134–135
  with family, 134–139
  with friends, 102–104
  and group activities, 106
  healthy, 131–133
  influences on individual/
    community health, 12
  and peer pressure, 112–117
  and social health, 130–133
  strengthening, 131–133
Relaxation, 60, 66–67
Reliability, 33, 41, 103, 396–397
Remarriage, 137
Remission of cancer, 514
Repetitive motion injuries, 426
Reproductive systems, 437–441,
  512
Rescue breaths, 566, *566*
Resistance training (weight
  training), *206*, 208, 212,
  216
Resolving conflict. *See* Conflict
  resolution
Respect
  abstinence for showing, 16
  and character, *28*, 34, *131*
  for feelings of grieving
    person, 71
  in friendships, 103
  for individual differences,
    132
  for older adults, *467*
  in relationships, 132
  for self and others, 163
  self-respect, 16, 120
  and sexual abstinence, 120

for strengthening
  relationships, 132
as trait of dating partner, 107
Respiration, 418–420, *419*
Respiratory system, *312*,
  418–421, *529*
Responsibility
  and character, 9, 35
  in families, 136
  for lifestyle choices, 13–14
  for one's own health, 13–17
  of parenthood, 142–143
  for personal health, 17
  in relationships, 131, 132
  and risk behaviors, 14–16
  for tooth health, 376
Restaurants, eating in, 250–251
Resting heart rate, 219
Reusing items, 582
Ringworm, 479, *479*
Risk(s)
  cumulative, 16
  of disease. *See specific diseases*
  and eating disorders, 266
  marijuana and, 340
  of medicines, 387
  and sports, 222–225
  of teen parenthood, 144
  as unavoidable, 14
Risk behaviors, 14–16, 84, 119,
  352
Risk factor(s), 14–15, 509, 513,
  520–521, 524
Rohypnol, 342
Role models, 33, 324
  and character, 33
  and tobacco use, 324
Roofies, 342
Rubella, 458, *490*
Rules, understanding and
  following, 544
Running, 210

S

Sadness, *58*
Safety, 540–552. *See also* First
  aid
  and accident chain, *541*, 541
  bicycle safety, 546
  fire safety, 542–543
  food safety, 247
  gun safety, 542
  habits for, 541
  and healthy lifestyle, 14

hiking/camping safety,
  548–549
in the home, 541–542
on the Internet, 544
of medicine development,
  383
in medicine use, 336
and nervous system health,
  425
in outdoor activities,
  545–549
for pedestrians, 547
at school, 544
with skates/skateboards/
  scooters, 546
in sports, 222–225
traffic safety, 545
from violence, 178
water safety, 548
in weather emergencies,
  550–553
in workouts, 219
Salad dressings, 245, 246
Sales promotions, 324
Saliva, 375, 428, 484
Salt, 246, 249
SAMHSA (Substance Abuse and
  Mental Health Services
  Administration), 393
Saturated fats, 240, *246*
Scalp problems, 374
Schedule management, 67
Schizophrenia, 85
School(s), 157–158, *178*, 185,
  187, 544
School Counselor, 115
Science connections
  anemia, *415*
  the brain's chemical
    messengers, *91*
  dietary supplements, 244
  ergonomics, 541
  fast-twitch/slow-twitch
    fibers, *411*
  glucose levels, *523*
  grease fires, *543*
  microwaves and frozen
    foods, *236*
  pesticides, 577
  premature infants, 458
  self-esteem (learning from
    mistakes), *54*
  technology and the brain,
    425